The American
Steam Locomotive
in the Twentieth Century

The American
Steam Locomotive
in the Twentieth Century

TOM MORRISON

McFarland & Company, Inc., Publishers

Jefferson, North Carolina

The present work is a reprint of the illustrated case bound edition of The American Steam Locomotive in the Twentieth Century, first published in 2018 by McFarland.

LIBRARY OF CONGRESS CATALOGUING-IN-PUBLICATION DATA

Names: Morrison, Tom (Tom A.), author.
Title: The American steam locomotive in the twentieth century / Tom Morrison.
Description: Jefferson, North Carolina : McFarland & Company, Inc.,
Publishers, 2019 | Includes bibliographical references and index.
Identifiers: LCCN 2018005681 | ISBN 9781476679006
(paperback : acid free paper) ∞
Subjects: LCSH: Steam locomotives—United States—History—20th century. |
Steam locomotives—United States—Design and construction—History—
20th century. | Locomotives—United States—History—20th century. |
Locomotives—United States—Design and construction—20th century.
Classification: LCC TJ603.2 .M675 2018 | DDC 625.26/1097309041—dc23
LC record available at https://lccn.loc.gov/2018005681

BRITISH LIBRARY CATALOGUING DATA ARE AVAILABLE

ISBN (print) 978-1-4766-7900-6
ISBN (ebook) 978-1-4766-2793-9

Front cover: two Virginian USRA 2-8-8-2 heavy Mallet locomotives,
class USE, No. 739, and class USA No. 710
(Denver Public Library, Otto C. Perry Collection, OP-19652)

Printed in the United States of America

McFarland & Company, Inc., Publishers
Box 611, Jefferson, North Carolina 28640
www.mcfarlandpub.com

To my friends on the
Ffestiniog and Welsh Highland Railways
who inspired this book.

Table of Contents

Preface • 1

Introduction • 3

Chapter 4. Locomotive Construction, 1895–1905 • 133

Chapter 5. Traction Other Than Steam, 1895–1905 • 186

Part Three: Transformation, 1905–1920

Chapter 6. General Steam Locomotive Development, 1905–1920 • 190

Chapter 7. Locomotive Engineering, 1905–1920 • 200

Chapter 8. Locomotive Construction, 1905–1920 • 254

Chapter 9. Traction Other Than Steam, 1905–1920 • 340

PART FOUR: SUPERPOWER, 1920–1930

Chapter 10. General Steam Locomotive Development, 1920–1930 • 346

Chapter 11. Locomotive Engineering, 1920–1930 • 359

Chapter 12. Locomotive Construction, 1920–1930 • 394

Chapter 13. Traction Other Than Steam, 1920–1930 • 432

13.1 Electric Traction • 432

13.2 Internal Combustion Traction • 433

PART FIVE: FINEST AND FINAL, 1930–1950

Chapter 14. General Steam Locomotive Development, 1930–1950 • 438

Chapter 15. Locomotive Engineering, 1930–1950 • 454

Chapter 16. Locomotive Construction, 1930–1950 • 491

Chapter 17. Traction Other Than Steam, 1930–1950 • 543

17.1 Internal Combustion Traction • 543

17.2 Gas-Turbine Locomotives • 550

17.3 Electric Traction • 552

Conclusion • 553

Appendix A: Thermodynamics and Dimensions • 555

Preface

My first acquaintance with a steam locomotive was in England in the early 1950s, when I was four or five years old. It was standing in a London terminus, making an enormous and terrifying hissing. The enginemen invited me onto the footplate, but I was shy and frightened and asked to be taken away. This unpromising introduction sowed the seed of a lifelong fascination with steam engines, for which I was teased as a child and which I concealed in later life.

Steam power disappeared from British Railways in the 1960s; my interest in steam engines lapsed with adolescence. It seemed that the steam locomotive was to be only a fond memory, preserved in photographs but otherwise gone forever. This was not true.

In 1998, I took a break from my career as a mining engineer in Canada and had the chance to qualify as a fireman on the Welsh Highland Railway, a steam-hauled tourist railroad in the United Kingdom. I discovered that anything to do with steam locomotives is hot, noisy, filthy and hard work but, at the same time, fascinating and deeply satisfying. Plenty of people want to "drive a steam engine" but few have the commitment to learn the inwardness of this strange machine. And strange it is—apparently simple, but functioning according to a weird, subtle internal logic, operated by sound, feel and experience more like a musical instrument than a machine, almost devoid of instrumentation, all its systems purely mechanical and powered only by the steam that it generates within itself, devoid of electric, electronic or hydraulic systems, temperamental and inherently dangerous.

One lunchtime, as I wolfed my sandwich, tea and potato chips before going back to watch the fire on the engine, I was keeping my ears and eyes open and my mouth shut, as befits the fireman's station in life. The conversation between the engineer, conductor and ticket seller turned to the giant American steam locomotives of the twentieth century; some of them had fireboxes bigger than the lunchroom in which we sat. My curiosity twitched. Since childhood I had known that these monsters existed—I still have a drawing that I did at age 7, recognizably depicting a 2-6-6-2 Mallet, complete with Walschaert valve gear, an Elesco feed water heater and a centipede tender—but, when I returned to Canada to resume my career, I was surprised to find that no one had ever published a comprehensive history of them—at least nothing that satisfied my curiosity; I wondered if I could fill this gap.

I wanted a real, thorough-going, grimy, gritty history of those gigantic locomotives, the people that built and operated them and the industry in which they flourished and became extinct. Some books claimed to be that, but really were not. Either the author was too close to the subject and could not see the wood for the trees or he had not done enough research, filling out the covers of his book with pictures, generalities and sentiment. In particular, no one had taken on the sheer toil of reading through the back issues of the industry trade journals; this was something with which I was familiar from technical histories that I had published previously. In particular, I

was no stranger to two or three years gathering information, followed by seven years or more, sifting through notes and photocopies and writing the book.

John H. White, in *American Locomotives: An Engineering History, 1830–1880* (Baltimore, MD: Johns Hopkins University Press, 1968, 1997), complains of a lack of archive information from the nineteenth century. The student of the twentieth-century American steam locomotive faces the opposite problem. The amount of archive material on U.S. railroads in general and steam locomotives in particular is so vast and so widely scattered that it would be impossible to research it exhaustively within any reasonable expenditure of time and money, or with any hope of producing a readable book within publishers' size restrictions.

Most industries have at least one trade journal of long standing, whose back issues form a record of the industry. These trade journals are primary sources, recording the events and concerns of the day without hindsight. Their disadvantage is that they do not trace matters after they cease to be news. Their staffs depend on the goodwill of management for access to information, with the result that mistakes and failures tend to go unreported—unless they are so serious that they are news in themselves.

For American railroading, this source is a weekly periodical, dating to 1856, variously titled the *Railroad Gazette* (1856–1908), *Railroad Age Gazette* (1908–18) and *Railway Age* (1919 to the present). For most of the period 1890 to 1940 it ran to two thousand or three thousand large, densely printed pages each year, covering every imaginable aspect of the American railroad industry in exhaustive detail—from the state of the industry and its political and economic environment to the design of passenger car spittoons. Steam locomotives figure largely in these pages. The journal was at its most voluminous during the period that I wanted to study.

Those thousands of pages of dense, fine print tell the story of the American steam locomotive in the twentieth century. Here are the original writings, comments and opinions of the most eminent engineers and executives of the American steam locomotive industry, with abundant graphs, drawings and statistics. The story is told from the viewpoint of management and engineering. In American parlance an unfortunate ambiguity exists between an "engineer" that operates a locomotive ("driver" in British parlance) and an "engineer" that designs or tests it, like using the same word for a pilot and an aeronautical engineer. In this book I try to use a qualifier, e.g., "mechanical engineer," "design engineer" or "test engineer," for the man with the slide rule, using the single word "engineer" for the man with his hand on the throttle. Be that as it may, the story is told by those who made locomotive history happen as they wrestled with the problems of their workaday lives. It is the story of their struggles and triumphs, and often of their frustration and bafflement with this strange machine that they and their predecessors had created, but whose inner workings were hard to understand and whose ultimate truths seemed always to elude them. This material, augmented by reference to monographs, memoirs and other published work, is the basis of this book.

The critic may fairly point out that this book relies on one source, the *Railroad Gazette/Railroad Age Gazette/Railway Age*. The material in that journal, however, originated with a wide range of primary sources in the form of technical papers written by railroad mechanical engineers and managers, test reports and research bulletins, letters, company annual reports, proceedings of trade association annual conventions and transactions of area technical groups, reproduced in full or in condensed form. Only a minority originated with staff writers. It is unlikely that any significant development relating to the twentieth-century American steam locomotive has gone unrecorded in its pages. Without this digest, it is difficult to see how this book could have been written.

A downturn in Canadian mining and construction left me unemployed for more than a year in 2000–01, giving me the opportunity to research this book. The University of British Columbia library in Vancouver kindly allowed me to access their bound volumes of *Railroad Gazette/Railroad Age Gazette/Railway Age* from 1919 onward and, when I had exhausted these, the staff borrowed microfilm for me from elsewhere.

I owe a debt of gratitude to George H. Drury for his compendious *Guide to North American Steam Locomotives* (Waukesha, WI: Kalmbach, 1993) and to the Railroad and Locomotive Historical Society for their journal, which provides many valuable insights; both sources cross-reference many of the locomotives mentioned in these pages.

Most of the photographs come from the Otto C. Perry collection at Denver Public Library. Perry (1894–1970) lived in Denver and worked for the U.S. Post Office. His hobby was photographing locomotives—steam, diesel, electric, gas turbine, all were grist to his mill—which he did with extraordinary persistence for forty years. Wars and financial disasters came and went, but Perry went on photographing locomotives, ranging far and wide all over the United States and Canada. The result was a collection of more than nineteen thousand high-quality photographs, representing a significant fraction of the entire steam locomotive fleet of the United States. Perry's photographs are particularly valuable to this book because they provide complete images of locomotives as they were in service, more alive than manufacturers' photographs but more informative than other photographs that may have greater artistic merit. In particular, they are identified by railroad, locomotive number and date, allowing rebuilds and retrofits to be detected. In some cases, the same locomotive can be seen after successive rebuilds.

I would also like to express appreciation for the photographic work of Robert W. Richardson, also housed in Denver Public Library, who reminds us that behind the major railroads and their leading-edge steam power lay an industry of bucolic and decrepit branch lines where time stood still from when they were built and equipped in the 1880s to when they fell into disuse after 1950.

Hardly less than the efforts of Perry himself have been the labors of the staff at Denver Public Library who digitized the Perry, Richardson and other collections, cataloged them and made them available on the internet. To them, too, go my heartfelt thanks.

Great, too, have been the labors of the curators of the California State Railroad Museum photographic archive, said to contain more than a million photographs. The library of the Railroad Museum of Pennsylvania hosts another seventy thousand photographs of locomotives.

A substantial number of people have helped me to assemble the photographs for this book and have supported it financially by offering generous discounts against reproduction and permissions fees. To them go my sincere thanks: Coi Gehrig, Denver Public Library Photosales, Denver, Colorado; Kathryn Santos and Cara Randall, California State Railroad Museum Library, Sacramento; Melissa Nerino, Railroad Museum of Pennsylvania, Strasburg; Diane Laska-Swanke, Classic Trains, Kalmbach Publishing, Waukesha, Wisconsin; Cathy English, Revelstoke Museum and Archives, Revelstoke, British Columbia, Canada; Frances Christman, Richard Bernier, Neal Harmayer, Bindu Komalavelly and Richard Bol, Purdue University Libraries, West Lafayette, Indiana; Heidi Stover, Smithsonian Institution Archives, Washington, D.C.; Melissa Van Otterloo, Stephen H. Hart Library and Research Center, Denver, Colorado; Ellen Jaquette and Jenny McElroy, Gale Family Library, Minnesota Historical Society, St. Paul; Jennifer McDaid, Norfolk Southern Corporation.

The number of photographs of steam locomotives dating from the period 1890 to 1950 must run into the millions. Considering that the American steam locomotive fleet peaked at somewhere about 75,000—even allowing for multiple photographs of the same locomotive—the photographic archive must cover most of the locomotives ever built and certainly all that are noteworthy.

I hardly dared hope that I might write the sequel to John H. White's monumental work, but it became clear that this was the book that I really had in mind. This book is offered to the reader in all humility because, the more I study the steam locomotive, the more I realize how little I know about it.

Introduction

Between 1900 and 1950 the Americans built the biggest and most powerful steam locomotives on the face of the earth and ran them to the limits of their power. The biggest of them were four times the size of their European equivalents—even though running on the same track gauge. The last to be built, in the 1940s, were five times as big and eight times as powerful as their predecessors fifty years earlier. Some of those monsters weighed 500 tons and developed 7,000 horsepower. At this distance in time it is difficult to believe that such machines existed, but they did. Their existence, moreover, was neither fortuitous nor inevitable. The American giant steam locomotive was made possible by advances in engineering and technology but its development was driven by national and even global economics and politics. This book is about how and why this development took place.

The steam locomotive came into being between 1800 and 1830 when two predecessor technologies converged, each with a long history. Steam locomotives are still being built and operated in small numbers at the time of writing; some of their most basic characteristics can be traced to that distant past.

Road builders and haulers knew from time immemorial that a wheeled vehicle moved more easily on a hard, smooth surface than on a soft, rough one. The narrower the running surface, the easier it was to build, but this left the problem of how to keep narrow wheels on narrow running surfaces. Troughed or L-shaped running surfaces soon filled with dirt. Iron wheels with flanges that followed the inner edges of iron rails were the best solution of many that were tried and still provide less rolling resistance than rubber tires on a paved road. Many methods were devised to hold the rails to gauge. The best method was to fix the rails to timber cross ties which served also to spread and cushion the load.

This photograph typifies the old-time American railroad industry as it was at the start of the twentieth century. Note the small locomotive and the brakeman standing on top of a boxcar. Time had stood still on the Sheffield & Tionesta, merged from predecessors built in the 1880s; this photograph was taken near Sheffield, Pennsylvania, on November 10, 1941. The locomotive was probably built before 1900 (Denver Public Library, Robert W. Richardson collection, RR-1460).

This is the result of the fifty years of American steam locomotive development described in this book, biggest of them all, the Union Pacific 4-8-8-4 Big Boy. This is class 4884-1, No. 4001, built by Alco in 1941, photographed near Hermosa, Wyoming, on May 9, 1954. The freight train on the drawbar is probably a mile long (Denver Public Library, Otto C. Perry collection, OP-18452).

A gauge of 4 feet 8½ inches became the international standard for mainline railroads, although many other gauges have been used. Although the American mainline railroads standardized on this gauge, railroads built to narrower gauges were at one time quite extensive, even outside their traditional territory in the Rocky Mountains. They are fully described in *American Narrow-Gauge Railroads,* by G. W. Hilton (Stanford, CA: Stanford University Press, 1990). Why 4 feet 8½ inches? Various people have traced the dimension back to the width of a cart pulled by a single horse; Angus Sinclair's addition to this idea has the ring of truth.[1]

In 1840 there were 33 separate railways in the British Isles with 1,552 miles of track and they had five different gauges, ranging from 4 feet 8½ inches to 7 feet—the narrowest gauge having more mileage than all the others. That was George Stephenson's gauge, and it was established in a curious way. The gateways of the first coal railway, operated by Stephenson's engines, had openings just sufficiently wide to permit wheels to pass extending 5 feet.

More likely, the gateways themselves were not 5 feet wide but the wagon, plus overhang, plus clearance had to fit existing gateways in stone walls.

At that time the flange of the wheel was outside the rail. When the Stockton & Darlington Railway was built Stephenson put the flanges inside. The width of the rail head was about 2 inches, so the inside gauge was 4 feet 8 inches. When the Liverpool & Manchester Railway was under construction, the engineers concluded that it was better to give the wheels plenty of side play to make fast running easy, so they widened the gauge half an inch, making it 4 feet 8½ inches.

The success of the Liverpool & Manchester Railway and of the locomotive "Rocket" made George Stephenson a great man, whose example

was worthy of imitation, so his track gauge was adopted by most of the British railway companies. His son Robert had locomotive building works which supplied many of our early railroads with engines, and the track gauge was frequently established to fit the wheels of the locomotives imported.

European miners built the first "railroads" for moving coal and ore in mines to hoisting shafts as early as the 1500s. The British built the first extensive surface "railroads" or "railways" in the 1700s for hauling coal from mines to seaports; horses or the force of gravity moved the wagons. These lines were private for moving their owners' produce. Problems of traffic control, allocation of space and vehicle design made toll railroads impractical until recently. The common-carrier railroad, with the railroad company owning and operating the structures and rolling stock and charging a fee to carry passengers or freight, was a commercial innovation of the early nineteenth century.

Attempts to use steam power began in Europe in the late 1600s. The prehistory of the steam locomotive is not obvious; we should mention some essential steps because their traces will appear later in our narrative.[2] The first commercial application of steam power was to stationary engines for pumping groundwater out of mines. Thomas Newcomen built the first of these at a coal mine in England in 1712. The first steam engine in America was a Newcomen type imported from England in 1753 and erected on a copper mine at North Arlington, New Jersey.[3]

In Newcomen's engine a piston worked up and down in a vertical cylinder. At rest, the piston was at the top of its stroke, drawn there by a counterweight at the opposite end of a walking beam. The engineman opened a valve to admit steam into the cylinder; he then closed the steam valve and opened a water valve, allowing water to spray into the steam space, condensing the steam and causing a vacuum. The pressure of the atmosphere on the top side of the piston made the power stroke. The counterweight made the return stroke, returning the engine to its at-rest position. A valve gear to automate this tedious and repetitive action was one of the earliest forms of industrial automation. This type of engine was not a true steam engine and was called an "atmospheric" engine.

In 1769 the French engineer Nicholas Cugnot produced a steam-powered artillery tractor using high-pressure steam. The vehicle had two cylinders; the power stroke in one drove the return stroke in the other, as well as driving the vehicle forward. Ratchets converted the reciprocating motion of the pistons into the rotary motion of the driving wheel. Cugnot's invention failed for the lack of proper running surfaces, design deficiencies and manufacturing problems more than for any failure of the concept itself. Seen in this light, Cugnot's vehicle was a true ancestor of the steam locomotive.

In 1775–6 Matthew Boulton and James Watt separated the condenser from the cylinder, allowing the cylinder to be kept constantly hot, the condenser constantly cold, resulting in much greater fuel efficiency.

In 1780–1 Boulton and Watt brought out an engine with a crank and a flywheel, converting the reciprocating piston thrust into a rotary motion for driving mine hoists and factory machinery. At the same time they developed an engine which applied high-pressure steam to both sides of the piston, producing two power strokes in each cycle.

In the main years of his career, between 1770 and 1790, James Watt probably did more to advance the steam engine than any other one person. In 1782 he developed the figure of 33,000 foot-pounds per minute as equaling one horsepower (33,000 pounds lifted one foot in one minute by one horse), a system of calculation and measurement that is still used today. In the late 1700s the manufacturing firm of Boulton & Watt was an extraordinary powerhouse of steam engine development.

Soon after 1800 Richard Trevithick used steam pressure as high as 145 pounds per square inch to produce an engine with enough power in relation to its bulk to power a vehicle. In 1804 he built what was undeniably a steam locomotive and put it into service at the Penydarren ironworks in South Wales. His was the idea of using high-pressure steam, exhausting to atmosphere with no condenser, using the exhaust to draw the fire.

Between 1800 and 1830 these two lines of development—the railroad and the steam engine—came together. The result was the steam-hauled, common carrier railroad, a technological and commercial breakthrough with far-reaching economic and social consequences. The first such railroad was the Stockton and Darlington in England, opened in 1825.

To their surprise, the first locomotive builders discovered that a smooth wheel would exert a useful grip on a smooth rail. If tire and rail were both infinitely hard, smooth and inelastic, this would not be so. At the microscopic scale, however, tire and rail crush into each other under axle load and their microscopic roughness engages like the teeth of cogwheels for both traction and braking. The connection is fragile; its rupture is sudden and is accompanied by a sudden loss of friction. Excessive torque applied to a driving wheel results in slipping and loss of traction. Excessive braking force applied to a rolling wheel results in skidding. Both of these cause rapid abrasion of wheel and rail and can have dangerous consequences. The grip between wheel and rail can be reduced by water, grease, snow, leaves and the like, or increased by sand at the expense of accelerated wear. For these reasons, the practical limit of gradients on conventional railroads is 2.0 to 2.5%. Railroads have operated with steeper grades but the loads that can be hauled uphill and the difficulty of controlling trains downhill have been unacceptable in the long run.

Locomotive builders also discovered empirically that, if the locomotive's pulling force, applied to the rails through the driving wheels, exceeded 25% of the weight on the driving wheel axles, slipping would result. Rails, track bed and axle bearings were limited in the weight that each axle could support. This limited the pulling power of a locomotive with only one pair of driving wheels. Locomotives were therefore built with increasing numbers of driving wheels, with free-running carrier wheels to guide and support the ends of the locomotive. Various ways were used to describe their arrangement.

The standard classification in the English-speaking world is the Whyte system, first proposed by F. M. Whyte, mechanical engineer to the New York Central Railroad at the 1901 convention of the American Railroad Master Mechanics' Association.[4] The first number is the number of free wheels in the leading truck, if any; the second number is the number of driving wheels; the third number is number of free wheels in the trailing truck, if any. Some of the first steam locomotives, for example, had a 2-2-2 wheel arrangement—a leading support axle, a single driven axle and a trailing support axle, three in total (six wheels). A common arrangement, the 2-8-0, had a 2-wheel leading truck, 8 driving wheels (4 axles) and no trailing truck. Tender wheels are not counted. Other classifications existed before the Whyte system, some of them bizarre.[5] Space does not permit their description here.

Wheel arrangements were also named: 4-4-0 American, Eight-wheeler; 2-4-2 Columbia; 4-4-2 Atlantic, North Western, Chautauqua; 0-6-0 Six-wheel switcher; 2-6-0 Mogul; 2-6-2 Prairie; 4-6-0 Ten-Wheeler; 4-6-2 Pacific; 4-6-4 Hudson, Shore Line, Milwaukee, Baltic; 0-8-0 Eight-wheel switcher; 2-8-0 Consolidation; 2-8-2 Calumet, Mikado, Macarthur; 2-8-4 Berkshire; 4-8-0 Twelve-wheeler, Mastodon; 4-8-2 Mountain, Mohawk; 4-8-4 Northern, Confederation, Dixie, Wyoming, Pocono, Niagara, Empire Builder, Greenbrier; 4-10-2 Overland; 2-10-0 Decapod; 2-10-2 Santa Fe; 2-10-4 Texas, Selkirk; 4-12-2 Union Pacific; 4-6-6-4 Challenger; 2-6-6-6 Alleghany; 2-8-8-4 Yellowstone; 4-8-8-4 Big Boy.

Steam locomotive development was limited by several barriers that were never overcome.

Each piston drove a main driving wheel through a main rod; connecting rods transmitted its force to secondary driving wheels. For this reason, the wheels had to be mounted rigidly in relation to each other. The length of the rigid wheelbase limited the curvature of the track and *vice versa*. If the curve was too tight, the wheels would spread the track, bind or derail. Designers spent much thought on overcoming this problem, but with limited success. Devices allowing slight lateral movement of the endmost driving wheels, or wheels with flangeless tires ("blind flanges"), alleviated but never solved this problem. In the 1920s the Union Pacific bought a class of 4-12-2 locomotives; a few 12-drivered engines were built in Europe and the Russians built an unsuccessful 4-14-4 but, otherwise, five driving axles in a rigid wheelbase remained the maximum.

A different approach to this limitation was an articulated locomotive with two (and in rare instances more) sets of cylinders and driving wheels, one or both power units being capable of swiveling in relation to the boiler. Such a locomotive cost more to build and was more difficult and costly to maintain than one with a single rigid frame. Many different types of articulation were invented, mostly in Europe.[6] The Americans accepted the French Mallet system with great enthusiasm; its use and development forms a significant part of American locomotive history.[7] No other articulation system gained acceptance in North America.

Next came the problem of generating enough power to drive a large number of driving wheels at a high rate of speed from a single, rigid, cylindrical boiler with practical restrictions as to size and steam

A Mallet articulated locomotive. The front set of cylinders and driving wheels swing from a hinge pin under the boiler. This is also a compound locomotive; after being used once in the back cylinders, the steam is used a second time in the bigger-diameter front cylinders before exhausting through the stack. This monster is a Norfolk & Western 2-8-8-2, class Y-4a, No. 2097, built in the company's shops at Roanoke, 1930–2, photographed at Elliston, Virginia, on August 3, 1936 (Denver Public Library, Otto C. Perry collection, OP-13819).

pressure. This problem placed a limit on the steam locomotive's power density (the ratio between power output and engine size or weight) that was never overcome.

Stability concerns limited the amount by which a locomotive could overhang the outside of the track and the height of its center of gravity above the rails. Several factors limited its practical length. Its size therefore had definite limits. Even without these limits, tunnels, overbridges and trackside structures constrained height and width, while the strength of track and underbridges restricted locomotive weight.

At maximum 15½ feet height × 10½ feet width (although variable between railroads), American locomotives benefited from a 40% greater available cross-section area than the British loading gauge of 13¼ feet high × 8¾ feet wide. The American railroads built and rebuilt their track and sub-structures to an extent that the British either could not or would not; British locomotives were therefore restricted to axle loadings of 50,000 pounds, compared to the 73,000-pound axle loadings ultimately permissible on major American railroads. Size and weight go far to explain why American locomotives developed three times the tractive effort and power output of their British counterparts.

The steam locomotive was usually the beneficiary, rather than the originator, of advances in steam technology. It began as an offshoot from stationary engines which, having none of the constraints in size and layout of the locomotive, led the way in steam technology. A boiler at a power station, for example, could be a huge, complicated affair standing 120 feet high and generating 500,000 pounds of steam per hour at 1,400 pounds per square inch and 1,000°F, dimensions that were obviously unattainable in a locomotive. Stationary and marine plant could be set up to run at constant power output for long

periods of time. By contrast, a steam locomotive faced continual changes in power demand while subjected to incessant bending, twisting and vibration.

In Europe, the period 1830 to 1890 was one of great ferment in locomotive design as each country came up with new designs aimed at meeting its particular needs, as described by Gustav Reder in *The World of Steam Locomotives* (New York: Putnam, 1974). Although the Americans built their share of strange machines, they settled on the simple, rugged 4-4-0 as early as the 1840s and filled their motive power needs by increasing its size and weight; they began to build locomotives with six and eight driving wheels to deal with local heavy loads and gradients in the 1850s. Angus Sinclair wrote a comprehensive history of American locomotives in the nineteenth century, and the men who built and ran them, publishing it in 1907 as *Development of the Locomotive Engine* (New York: Angus Sinclair, 1907, now available in electronic form through Google Books). John H. White adds his own researches in *American Locomotives: An Engineering History 1830–1880* (Baltimore: Johns Hopkins University Press, 1968, 1997).

From the 1890s onward, the American railroads' demand for power became insatiable. It might be supposed that the need for greater power was inherent in any railroad industry with the passage of time. This was not so. The British were still building locomotives of modest power in the 1950s. Although such engines had to fit the strength and clearance dimensions of infrastructure dating back to the 1860s and earlier, they sufficed for existing traffic. American railroads with similar operating conditions and traffic patterns, such as the Central of New Jersey, likewise went on buying small engines.

In 1905, the British built a 2-8-0 heavy freight engine, weighing 153,000 pounds and developing 37,000 pounds of tractive effort.

Not only were such engines still in service, substantially unaltered, fifty years later; the biggest British engines built in the 1950s were only slightly bigger—194,000-pound 2-10-0s developing 40,000 pounds of tractive effort. German 2-10-0 *Kriegsloks,* built in the 1940s, weighed 185,000 pounds and developed 49,000 pounds of tractive effort; they remained in service in eastern Europe into the 1990s.

American steam locomotives, by contrast, began to diverge in size and power from their European contemporaries as early as 1900. In 1898, the Great Northern bought a 4-8-0 weighing 213,000 pounds with 51,000 pounds of tractive effort, while the Union Pacific's legendary 4-8-8-4s, built in the 1940s, weighed 772,000 pounds and produced 131,000 pounds of tractive effort. The definition of tractive effort and other dimensions used in this book will be found in Appendix A.

As well as increasing in size, American steam locomotives made remarkable advances in power output and efficiency at the same time, due in large part to innovations that were invisible from outside the locomotive.[8]

Year	Type	Maximum Power (i.h.p.)*	Speed of max. power (m.p.h.)	Steaming rate (lb./hr.)	Steam consumption (lb./i.h.p.-hr.)
1900	4-4-0	1,000	?	25,000	25.0
1910	4-6-2	1,870	50	45,000	24.1
1925	4-6-2	3,040	54	65,000	21.4
1927	4-6-4	4,073	65	74,000	18.2
1937	4-6-4	4,700	75	84,000	17.9
1942	4-4-4-4	6,550	86	106,000	16.0

*The abbreviation i.h.p. stands for "indicated horsepower." See Appendix A.

The half century of steam locomotive development covered by this book may be divided into four periods with not only technical, but also political and economic boundaries:

1895–1905, Compounds and Mastodons: A severe economic depression in the mid–1890s, followed by explosive economic growth, marked the closing of the American frontier and the emergence of America as a major industrial power. At the same time, a political tide turned against the railroads; in 1903–5 hostile legislation began to bite.

The rigid-frame, compound locomotive—re-using steam in a succession of cylinders—reached the height of its popularity in America, where it was vigorously promoted but ultimately unsuccessful. This period also saw the first quantity production of engines that were significantly bigger, either than existing American types or than their European counterparts, exemplified by the 4-8-0, or "Mastodon" wheel arrangement. This period also ended the dominance of the 4-4-0 American-type locomotive.

1905–1920, Transformation: During the fifteen years from 1905 to 1920, the railroads fought a losing battle against government regulation that culminated in the take-over by the U.S. Railroad Administration in 1918, followed by a return to corporate operation in 1920.

In 1903, the Baltimore & Ohio ordered a compound, articulated locomotive of unprecedented size from Alco, designed according to the European Mallet system. The same year, the Santa Fe introduced both the 2-8-2 and 2-10-2 types in quantity. These three developments heralded a new era in American freight power. The Mallet was an immediate success, setting off a craze for locomotives of this type and resulting in fantastic designs and dimensions. Especially after 1910, the hitherto conservative American railroads accepted a wide range of innovations, especially superheating, power stokers and power reversing gear. The U.S. Railroad Administration produced twelve classes of new locomotives that exemplified the transforma-tion of the American steam locomotive that had taken place over the previous fifteen years.

1920–1930, Superpower: In 1920, the government returned the railroads to corporate operation, but under new and more pervasive regulations. Even so, the railroads found ways to share in the national prosperity by moving more traffic faster than ever before and upgrading all aspects of their operations. These developments came to a halt with the financial crash of 1929 and the ensuing depression.

Railroad economics of the 1920s, and the lessons of World War I, brought about a demand for high power at high speed, answered by brilliant engineering from the Lima Locomotive Works, a late-comer to mainline locomotive construction. The resulting "Superpower" locomotives rivaled the Mallets in their impact on railroad economics. With the onset of the depression, locomotive construction ceased.

1930–1945, Finest and Final: The depression years brought a new paradigm shift for the railroads as government measures still further distorted their commercial basis. After an apparently never-ending depression, rail traffic began to recover in the late 1930s, intensified by World War II.

Even if locomotive construction ceased in the depression, development did not. The years between 1930 and 1945 produced the ultimate developments of American steam power. On the other hand, the steam locomotive's defects were large, numerous and incurable. Meanwhile, the diesel-electric locomotive developed apace, limited only by its low power. New technology, placing multiple diesel engines under the control of a single throttle, solved this problem; the steam locomotive was finished. The railroads dieselized as fast as they could; forty thousand steam locomotives went for scrap. The period from 1930 to 1945 was the finale of the American steam locomotive.

Between 1901 and 1952, U.S. and Canadian Class I (i.e. major) railroads bought 67,609 steam locomotives, divided as follows.[9]

Builder	Number of Locomotives	Percent
Alco	28,504	42.2
Rogers (1901–4)	1,074	1.6
Baldwin	23,099	34.1
Lima	3,281	4.8
Montreal	1,966	2.9
Canadian Locomotive Co.	1,613	2.4
Miscellaneous & indeterminate (9 companies, some foreign)	396	0.6
Railroad shops (34 railroads)	7,676	11.4
Total	67,609	100.0

The Pennsylvania's own shops built 3,820 locomotives, 42% of the total built by railroad companies. Excluded from these figures are the large numbers of locomotives built for smaller railroads, mines, logging sites, docks, civil engineering contractors and other industrial uses. These included many sizeable engines, such as the 2-8-0s, 2-8-2s and 4-6-0s built for railroads in Nevada in the early 1900s. Orders placed in 1910 exemplify the size and diversity of the market; in that year, U.S. and Canadian builders received orders for 3,787 locomotives from 273 customers, including fifty-four Class I railroads.[10]

Alfred W. Bruce[11] estimates that U.S. manufacturers produced 71,250 steam locomotives before 1901 and a further 105,500 between 1901 and 1952, indicating that in this latter period 41,470 locomotives went to Class II, III and other railroads and to export. These numbers exclude Canadian production.

Bruce summarizes American locomotive construction by type as follows. Numbers include export orders; some types that were obsolete before 1895 are not shown here.

Type	Years Built	Quantity (approx.)	Type	Years Built	Quantity (approx.)
0-4-0	1870–1890	1,500	2-10-10-2	1918	10
0-6-0	?–1946	15,000	Triplex Mallet	1914–1915	4
0-8-0	1850–1951	3,200	2-6-6-4	1935–1950	63
0-10-0	1905–1925	50–60	2-6-6-6	1941–1945	68
4-4-0	1840–1905	25,600	2-8-8-4	1928–1943	213
2-6-0	1860–1910	10,900	4-6-6-4	1936–1944	215
4-6-0	1850–1920	17,100	4-8-8-4	1941–1944	25
2-8-0	1866–1916	33,400	Duplex	1934–1945	81
2-10-0	1870–1926	4,100*	Geared	1831–1950	3,800
4-8-0	1870–1933	600	Tank engines, miscellaneous	1831–1950	24,370
4-2-2	1840–1895	?			
2-4-2	1890–1900	121			
4-4-2	1896–1916	1,900			
2-6-2	1901–1910	1,700			
4-6-2	1902–1930	6,800			
2-8-2	1905–1930	14,100			
4-8-2	1911–1948	2,400			
0-10-2	1936	? (few)			
2-10-2	1902–1920**	2,200			
4-10-2	1925–1926	60			
4-12-2	1926–1930	90			
4-4-4	1915–1935	? (few)			
4-6-4	1927–1948	500			
2-8-4	1925–1949	750			
4-8-4	1927–1946	950			
2-10-4	1925–1944	450			
0-6-6-0	1903–1913	80			
2-6-6-0	1909	10+			
0-8-8-0	1907–1920	150			
2-8-8-0	1916–1925	201			
2-6-6-2	1906–1949	1,315			
2-8-8-2	1909–1950	710			

* The 1926 end date is suspect. The quantity is reconcilable with other sources only if 2,200 built for the USSR in World War 2 are included.

** Probably a misprint for 1930. George H. Drury (*Guide to North American Steam Locomotives*, Waukesha, WI: Kalmbach, 1993) records total procurement at 2,295 between 1902 and 1931.

Over the years, the Americans exported 37,000 steam locomotives (21% of total U.S. construction). Except for locomotives supplied to Russia during both world wars and a flurry of orders for European reconstruction immediately after World War II, relatively few American locomotives went to Europe, but the growing industrial capability of the U.S. competed successfully with European builders in supplying locomotives to other parts of the world.[12] A big American builder, such as Baldwin, could perform such prodigies as delivering nine locomotives within fourteen days of receiving an order, which gave them a strong position competing with the Germans and the British, who were the other suppliers of locomotives to worldwide customers.

Steam locomotive building in the U.S. and Canada reached an all-time peak of about 7,000 a year in 1906–7, of which 700 to 800 were for export. Baldwin, alone, employed 15,000 men on two 10-hour

The Louisville & Nashville built this 2-8-2 in its own shops in 1915–17, Class J-1, No. 1443, photographed at Cincinnati, Ohio, on June 28, 1950 (Denver Public Library, Otto C. Perry collection, OP-12528).

The smaller railroads bought locomotives of conventional design in ones and twos, like this 2-6-0 on the Rockdale, Sandow & Southern. Slide valves, inside valve gear and boiler diameter suggest a construction date around 1900–05, yet it was still going strong when it was photographed at Sandow, Texas, on October 28, 1946 (Denver Public Library, Robert W. Richardson collection, RR-1414).

shifts at that time.[13] Additionally, several railroad shops had varying capacity for new construction; other machine works and foundries built small locomotives for local customers.

Most railroads bought locomotives from specialized locomotive manufacturers (88% of production in the list above). Customer participation in the design varied from almost total to practically none. Some major companies favored either Baldwin or Alco; others spread their orders between Baldwin, Alco and—later—Lima. A few railroads, most notably the Pennsylvania, built their own locomotives to their own designs (11% of production in the list above), contracting out when their capacity was insufficient. At the bottom end of the corporate size range, small railroads bought whatever off-the-shelf designs met their needs, or bought used equipment from other railroads, dealers and brokers. At the end of the chain were the dealers in scrap metal.

The greatest number of steam locomotives in service on mainline railroads at any one time was 69,000 in 1923. In 1940 about 40,000 remained; in 1950 the steam locomotive fleets were scrap steel for the Korean War. By the mid–1950s only a few remained in main-line service. The steam locomotives retreated to branch lines, themselves in decay.

The last steam locomotive on an American common carrier railroad was an antique 2-6-0 on the Mobile & Gulf Railroad, replaced by diesel power in September 1970.[14] Steam locomotives also became a part of the tourist industry and preservation movement, so that it is difficult to point to any single date when steam haulage ceased; in fact it never did.

In spite of temporary concerns about supply and cost of imported diesel oil, the steam locomotive never made a comeback. The Norfolk and Western was the last major railroad in America to retain steam, due to the ready availability of coal and to the railroad's own capability in steam locomotive design, construction and maintenance. Similar considerations resulted in the retention of steam traction elsewhere in the world, in such countries as Britain, Germany, Poland, Turkey, India, Rhodesia and South Africa. Most notable is China, which retained the last factories in the world, capable of building steam locomotives in quantity. The last steam locomotives in mainline service, Chinese 2-8-2s and 2-10-2s, were the technical equivalents of the rigid-frame USRA engines of 1919. American-type Mallets and superpower locomotives appeared overseas only in small numbers.

At the time of writing, about 180 standard-gauge steam locomotives remain in operating condition in the United States and Canada. The greatest concentrations of preserved steam locomotives (operating and static) are in California and Pennsylvania. The former workhorse is now kept as a pet; the working steam locomotives of today are better cared for than they were in the hard service for which they were built so long ago.

PART ONE

Background to Locomotive Development

1

The American Railroad Industry

When Socrates, the Greek philosopher, called man to the study of himself by the memorable precept "Know thyself," he gave him the hardest task possible at that time, but the steam railroad had not been thought of then. (Quoted by Burt, J. C. *The Savor of Old-Time Southern Railroading,* Railway & Locomotive Historical SocietyBulletin #84, October 1951, 36)

The American railroad industry was the habitat—technical, political and economic—in which the American steam locomotive grew, flourished and became extinct. We need to look at this habitat before we can understand why and how the locomotive developed as it did.

Section 1.1 Political and Economic Environment

1.1.1 Early Years of the Industry

The American railroad industry began at Baltimore on July 4, 1828, with the start of construction on the Baltimore & Ohio Railroad.

Charles Carroll, the last man still living of those who signed the Declaration of Independence, placed the cornerstone amid scenes of festivity. Apart from the fact that a railroad did not need a cornerstone, the track was inadequate for all but the lightest traffic; no one knew what the motive power would be, or what the railroad would cost to build and operate. Nevertheless, the construction gangs set off for the Ohio River, 600 miles away beyond forested hills rising to 3,000 feet above sea level, intersected by deep, narrow, sinuous and flood-prone valleys and only sparsely settled. The first appearance of the steam locomotive was tentative; many doubted its capability.

Twenty years later, American railroad construction exceeded 1,000 miles in one year for the first time. The year 1869 saw the completion of the first transcontinental rail link, but also George Westinghouse's invention of the compressed-air train brake which would vitally impact railroad technology. Construction reached an all-time peak of 12,878 miles in 1887; the same year, the federal government set up the Interstate Commerce Commission (ICC) to regulate a chaotic system of railroad freight haulage pricing.

Setting the scene: a huge, grimy steam locomotive hauls a freight train on America's first railroad, the Baltimore & Ohio. This photograph, taken in 1940 somewhere in Ohio, shows a Class EL-5 2-8-8-0, No. 7161, built by Baldwin in 1919–20 (Denver Public Library, Robert W. Richardson collection, RR-1165).

American railroadmen overcame vast distances and extremes of climate and terrain, often in the face of every imaginable human and natural obstruction, in a larger-than-life saga that outran the most lurid fiction. Successful entrepreneurs made colossal fortunes; the railroads pervaded American life.

> Young men, among the flower of the nation, abandoned other occupations to engage in railroading. The then known hazards of the occupation did not deter them…. It had then and still has, a fascination that combines thrills of excitement and responsibility with all the other extraordinary tests of skill, courage and endurance so essential in strong and active manhood.[1]

The railroads were major employers, major consumers of goods and services and were symbiotic with mining, logging, agriculture and the production of iron and steel. Some railroad presidents were better known than some presidents of the United States.

1.1.2 Depression and New Expansion

The year 1893 dawned on an optimistic America. Twenty-seven million people visited the World's Fair in Chicago to see the products of American industry; fifty-two steam locomotives from twelve manufacturers were among the wonders of modern science.

On February 23, 1893, the Philadelphia & Reading Railroad went bankrupt, helping to trigger a worldwide financial panic that developed that summer. The railroads laid off one hundred thousand men from an 1893 workforce of about 874,000. By April 1894, 210 railroads, operating one-fifth of the U.S. total route mileage, were bankrupt. Most were small companies operating less than 500 route miles, but they included the Northern Pacific and the long-troubled Union Pacific; the Baltimore & Ohio failed in 1896.[2]

The depression was bitterly felt and bitterly remembered, but a recovery was already apparent in 1895 and, by 1896–7, railroad activity was back to 1893 levels. The years from 1897 to 1914 were a time of optimism and unprecedented growth in the American economy, as the Civil War receded into history and the horrors and perplexities of the twentieth century were hidden in the future. European settlement already stretched from coast to coast but population density increased with the widespread development of agriculture, mining, logging and manufacturing. No means of land transport competed with the railroads for speed, capacity or convenience. The steam locomotive was the sole form of railroad motive power.

The depression of the 1890s had permanent effects on railroad operation. Decreased earnings enforced economies previously thought unnecessary or even undesirable. Railroadmen demanded that any expenditure yield a useful return.[3]

The Paris Exposition of 1900 surprised both the Americans and the Europeans.[4] Schooled in tough conditions, American engineers suddenly realized that they rivaled their European counterparts. Perhaps their products possessed more strength than beauty, but they were every bit as good and often cheaper, more effective and delivered faster.

By 1900, 45% of world railroad mileage was in North America. Transportation demand was insatiable; not only was the U.S. population growing, but the haulage demand *per capita* was also increasing.[5] In a single year, 1898–9, U.S. freight traffic increased 30% while the population increased only 2%. Between 1894 and 1899, the ton-miles[6] hauled by an average freight engine in a year increased 50%; average freight train loads increased 36% from 180 to 244 tons.[7] Between 1895 and 1901, U.S. freight traffic increased 52%, hauled by only 8% more cars and 4% more locomotives.

The ICC broadened its role when the federal government entrusted it with enforcing the 1893 law requiring MCB couplers[8] on cars and locomotives in interstate commerce. The railroads felt its growing power and by 1898[9]:

"Vast distances and extremes of climate and terrain." The Denver & Rio Grande Western, especially its narrow-gauge lines, ran through some of the toughest country in North America. This Class K-36 2-8-2, No. 482, built by Baldwin in 1925, was photographed near Maysville, Colorado, in 1955, crossing a dilapidated timber trestle (Denver Public Library, Robert W. Richardson collection, RR-2146).

"Vast distance and extremes of climate and terrain." Some of the difficulties of operating in the winter mountains are evident in this photograph, taken on the Colorado & Southern at Georgetown, Colorado, on February 25, 1939, showing narrow-gauge 2-8-0 No. 68 taking water (Denver Public Library, Otto C. Perry collection, OP-6091).

"Vast distances and extremes of climate and terrain." A Colorado & Southern narrow-gauge line clings to the wall of a canyon near Climax, Colorado. The brakemen worked along the insecure catwalk on top of the cars, day, night and all weathers in the smoke and hot cinders from the locomotive. Even in the 1940s, these are still old-style boxcars with brakes operated by the handwheels projecting above the car roofs. It takes two locomotives, Colorado & Southern 2-8-0s, Nos. 74 and 76, to haul this train on June 16, 1943 (Denver Public Library, Otto C. Perry collection, OP-6361).

"The steam locomotive was the sole form of railroad motive power." This was the ubiquitous American-type locomotive of the 19th century. No. 11 on the Sheffield & Tionesta Railway, probably built before 1900, was still in service in 1939, photographed at Sheffield, Pennsylvania, on September 11, 1939 (Denver Public Library, Robert W. Richardson collection, RR-1453).

"More strength than beauty." A typical freight locomotive of the 1890s, Colorado & Southern 2-8-0, No. 427, photographed at Denver, Colorado, in 1917. Note the pile of ash on the left, the disposal of which was one of the abiding problems of the coal-burning steam locomotive (Denver Public Library, Otto C. Perry collection, OP-6563).

The power for which the Commission reaches out is of the most unlimited and far-reaching character.

It is everywhere recognized that administrative tribunals are ambitious for power. They use all they have and ask for more. The Interstate Commerce Commission is no exception to this rule.[10]

Competition forced rates down, even before the ICC and state railroad commissions did so. Revenue per freight ton-mile dropped 48% between 1870 and 1880 and a further 50% between 1880 and 1894. Rising operating costs forced the railroads to scrutinize motive power, train resistance and the optimum length, tonnage and speed of trains as never before. In 1896, J. H. McConnell, Superintendent of Motive Power for the Union Pacific, stated[11]: "An engine in freight service should haul every ton of freight it is capable of doing *regardless of cost for repairs and fuel.*" (Author's italics.)

The rapidity of economic growth after the depression took everyone by surprise. From the viewpoint of 1901:

Had the directors of a Pittsburgh railroad been told, along in 1897, that within four years there would come a time when double the track (miles of which was then useless), when double the cars (hundreds of which were then idle), when double the locomotives (hundreds of which were then dead in roundhouses) would be all inadequate to handle the business that would offer, the informant would have been regarded as crazy. Yet this is exactly what has happened in the last two months.[12]

1.1.3 The New Political Climate

The late 1800s and early 1900s were the years of unrestrained American capitalism. Companies employing tens of thousands of people controlled state legislatures and influenced the economies of whole regions. Names like Vanderbilt, Rockefeller, Carnegie, Astor, Guggenheim and Weyerhauser are evocative to this day. A public reaction burst out with astonishing vehemence between 1903 and 1905. Railroads were among the biggest companies in the U.S.; their high-handedness, callousness, corruption and an appalling accident rate were a ready target for public protest and abuse.[13]

Judging by route mileage in receivership, the industry was healthiest in 1905, the year before hostile legislation took effect, with only 796 miles in receivership, the lowest ever recorded, but the political climate was changing quickly. The ICC and state railroad commissions obtained the authority to set haulage rates, encroaching on the railroads' commercial freedom. In 1903, for example, the International & Great Northern pointed out to the Railroad Commissioners of Texas that, in the preceding five years, wages had increased 15%, materials prices 53%, locomotive prices 56% and car prices 26%, while the freight rates that the railroad was allowed to charge had decreased 22%.[14]

In 1904–5, President Roosevelt put his authority behind legislation on railroad traffic signals, the working hours of train crews and increased rate-setting powers for the ICC. It was significant that the President of the United States should exert his authority on these matters.[15]

ICC Commissioners acquired a pervasive authority, conducting hearings all over the country.[16]

An investigation of some fifteen railroads was begun on August 14 (1906) by the Interstate Commerce Commission in Toledo, through Judson C. Clements, a member of the Commission, regarding the interstate transportation of ice to and from that city. The first day's proceedings developed the fact

that a former purchasing agent of the Ann Arbor Railroad, now under sentence of imprisonment for acts done as the general manager of the Toledo Ice & Coal Co., while in the service of the road had sold ice for the ice company. He also testified that both the former president and general manager of the Ann Arbor were directors of the ice company and that practically all the stock in the company was owned by railroad men. It was also charged that railroad real estate was used by the ice company without compensation and that laborers were transported for its account by the road without paying fare.

Commissioner Knapp even opined that railroads were a public utility; nationalization became a threat overhanging the industry for decades.[17]

Railroad managers looked back with nostalgia to easier times when they were masters of their own house. They knew, too, that much depended on the loyalty of their workforces, but the character and attitudes of the workforce were changing, with alienation and deteriorating morale. In 1907[18]:

A lack of zeal and fidelity among railroad employees seems to be growing. Perhaps it is in part due to the prevailing prosperity, which unsettles the minds of many otherwise contented men; perhaps it is partly due to the open encouragement by those in high governmental authority, of the trade unions and the increasing development of the most vicious elements of the trade union idea.

From the vantage point of 1909, one frustrated trainmaster commented:

There are 243 laws, state, municipal and federal that have to do with my duties directly and indirectly, to say nothing of the laws of the organizations, some of which have assumed the proportions of "Compiled Statutes." I bump into I.C.C. inspectors, dodge those of the Agricultural Department, and am interviewed by representatives of the Department of Justice. Men representing the state railway commissions are becoming more common, and the pure food inspectors, marshals, sheriffs and smaller fry are everywhere aroused to the necessity of regulating the railways.

In 1900, 76 million people lived in the U.S., using 1,860 ton-miles of freight haulage and 211 passenger seat-miles *per capita*. By 1907, 15% more people used 45% more freight ton-miles and 50% more passenger seat-miles *per capita*. With increasing rate regulation, the railroads benefited little from increasing demand, but scrambled to keep

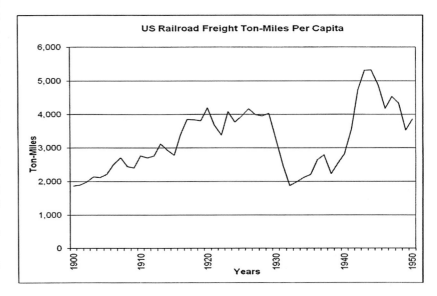

U.S. railroad freight ton-miles per head of population, 1900–1950. Note rapid expansion after 1900, recessions in 1907, 1914 and 1921, the 1930s depression, economic recovery in the late 1930s and effects of war in 1915–18 and 1940–5.

pace by buying 28,000 locomotives, 16,000 passenger cars and 900,000 freight cars between 1902 and 1907.[19]

The financial panic of October 1907, and the recession that followed, was a turning point in the fortunes of the industry. The federal government and the increasingly numerous and powerful state railroad commissions legislated against the railroads as never before, cutting rates, imposing labor laws and specifying the service the railroads were to provide. Erosion of profits made it more difficult to finance increased capacity to meet increasing demand.[20] Equity financing was the first to fail, leading to an unhealthy accumulation of debt. Freight demand dropped 8% in 1907–8, and stagnated until 1910. The railroads laid off a quarter of a million men; twenty-four railroads, operating 8,000 route miles of track, went bankrupt, the highest annual rate since the mid–1890s.

Severe winter weather always caused difficulties, sometimes on a national scale. The abnormally cold winter of 1909–10 raised fuel costs and caused crewing and maintenance problems.[21] Another cold winter in 1911–12 hit the railroads hard; with the 16-Hour Law in effect, crews abandoned their trains when their permitted working hours ran out, leaving locomotives to freeze solid.[22]

National prosperity returned in 1910–11, but not for the railroads; the 1910 ICC rate hearings were a major defeat. Citing "excessive earnings," the ICC cut rates by 20% to 50% on six western railroads; stock prices of the affected railroads collapsed.[23] Railroad taxation was increasing at an 8% compound annual rate and, in Michigan, brought railroad construction to a halt. The number of new locomotives ordered in 1911 was the lowest in ten years.[24] The ICC and others told the railroads that they would have to earn increased profits from improved efficiency and not from rate increases. Bigger locomotives hauling longer trains were

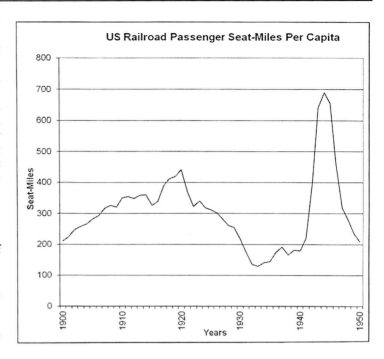

U.S. railroad passenger seat-miles per head of population, 1900–1950. Note effects of war in 1915–18 and 1940–5, competing transportation in the 1920s, the depression of the 1930s and economic recovery in the late 1930s.

one way to do this, offering great economies in fuel and labor costs. It took two men to run a steam locomotive, whether it developed 500 horsepower or 5,000. The accompanying graph shows how U.S. freight train tonnage grew over the years.

"Severe winter weather always caused difficulties," as this photograph shows, taken on the Denver & Rio Grande Western at Cumbres, Colorado, on January 21, 1949 (Denver Public Library, Robert W. Richardson collection, RR-1824).

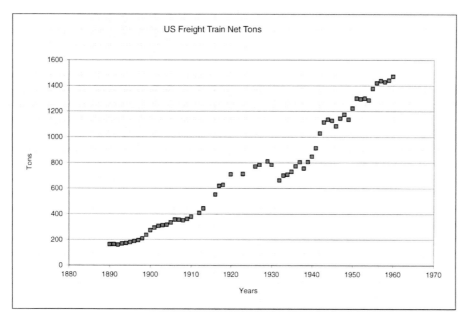

US Freight Train Net Tons

Average U.S. freight train net tons, 1890–1960. Note continuous increase, accelerated by wartime demands 1915–18 and 1940–5, interrupted by 1930s depression.

heating, power stokers and other innovations came on the scene but were some time gaining acceptance.

Some states legislated maximum train lengths, allegedly for safety, actually to force the railroads to employ more men, striking at their ability to increase efficiency.[25] By 1913, twenty states had laws prescribing the size of train crews.[26] Next for scrutiny were the means used by the railroads in their diminishingly successful efforts to finance improvements. The 1912 Hadley Commission brought railroad financing under ICC regulation[27]; in 1914 President Wilson remarked[28]:

> The country is ready to accept and accept with relief as well as approval, a law which will confer upon the Interstate Commerce Commission the power to superintend and regulate the financial operations by which the railroads are henceforth to be supplied with the money they need.

The railroads would not have agreed. Gradually, their entire commercial basis was becoming distorted; this was only the beginning.

The accident rate was so bad that it provoked a movement to nationalize the railroads, taking them out of the hands of callous and inept management.[29] Regulation intruded increasingly into operations.[30] In 1911, Congress legislated federal boiler inspection—assign-

From 1902 to 1907, the average tractive effort of American locomotives increased 30% from 20,500 pounds to 26,500. Average freight train payloads increased 22% from 296 tons to 363 tons in the same period. Mallet articulated compound locomotives, first introduced in America in 1904, revolutionized freight power. Super-

"Bigger locomotives hauling longer trains." The unspectacular but numerous 2-8-0s were powerful machines. This Denver & Rio Grande Western Class C-48 2-8-0, No. 1185, built by Alco in 1906, was still hauling long freight trains when it was photographed near Alamosa, Colorado, on a cold, windy day in January, 1952. Strong side winds, as here, forced the wheel flanges against the downwind rail, materially increasing train resistance (Denver Public Library, Robert W. Richardson collection, RR-2031).

"Mallet articulated compound locomotives ... revolutionized freight power." This Chicago, Burlington & Quincy class T-2 2-6-6-2, No. 4105, was built by Baldwin in 1910 and photographed near Edgemont, South Dakota, on June 20, 1936. Differing cylinder sizes show that this locomotive is still in its as-built compound configuration, when many other compounds had been converted to single expansion or scrapped (Denver Public Library, Otto C. Perry collection, OP-4334).

"The accident rate was so bad that it provoked a movement to nationalize the railroads." In spite of improvements in railroad safety over the years, this accident followed a run-away on the Chicago, Rock Island & Pacific, near Colorado Springs, Colorado, on May 9, 1938 (Denver Public Library, Otto C. Perry collection, OP-5969).

ing inspection to the ICC. The railroads argued that their own inspections sufficed but, under government inspection, the accident rate resulting from boiler defects dropped 40% in three years, 1912–14; related fatalities dropped 77% in the same period, injuries 43%.[31] Congress extended ICC safety jurisdiction to the whole locomotive in 1915; accidents caused by failures of parts of the locomotive dropped 60% between 1912 and 1919.[32]

From 1902 to 1912, 43% more employees hauled 68% more traffic over 31% more route miles, using 48% more locomotives, 42% more freight cars and 37% more passenger cars. However, operating expenses rose by 76%, wages by 87% and taxes by 107%, leaving an increase in dividends of only 33%.[33] Renewed economic growth in 1912 brought car shortages and traffic congestion, but the railroads could not finance the facilities needed to meet demand.[34] Even the ICC predicted that, by 1915, facilities would be inadequate for projected demand—and that prediction never foresaw the effects of World War I.

So vulnerable was the debt-loaded industry that a slackening of trade put sixty-four railroads, operating 37,000 route miles, into bankruptcy between 1912 and 1915. The ICC granted rate increases in 1914–15—small and late.[35] Construction in 1914 was 1,532 miles, half that of 1913 and the lowest since the depression year, 1895. In 1915, construction fell below 1,000 miles for the first time since 1865 and eighty-two railroads, operating 42,000 route miles, were in receivership, the highest figure ever.

Cheap freight rates did much for American industry but the railroads' $4.5 billion investment in improvements between 1907 and 1914 increased their annual net income by only $8.5 million; investment dried up.[36] Recruitment of young talent began to fail. The labor unions exerted ever more authority, both externally and over their own membership.[37] Morale remained good on some railroads; on others, labor relations deteriorated into trivial, bitter, destructive, even murderous conflict.

The railroads laid off a quarter of a million men between 1913 and 1915, although the wages of those still working continued to rise. Train crews were paid partly for distance run and partly for hours worked in a system distorted by special conditions, providing a fertile breeding ground for disputes.[38] In 1913, passenger train engineers were earning up to $3,725 a year (about the same as a state governor), ranging down to $1,890 for freight train firemen. By contrast, the average wage of all railroad employees in 1915 was only $825 a year, and that was up 46% since 1900.[39] The men capable of running huge railroad companies were highly paid; by 1917, presidents, vice-presidents and general managers were earning $20,000 to $30,000 a year and in that year the President of the Pennsylvania received $75,460, more than the President of the United States.

Public abuse targeted the railroads' alleged

inefficiency; in fact, financial stringency, more powerful locomotives, bigger freight cars, civil engineering programs and more rigorous operating controls had remarkable effects. Between 1894 and 1914, American railroads increased annual freight ton-miles by 259% for only 42% more train-miles. The average train load of thirty-five major railroads was 504 tons, up from 180 tons in 1894. They could never have hauled the traffic of 1914 with the facilities of 1894. These improvements were ill rewarded by profit[40]; railroad officials became cynical and pessimistic[41]:

it did not pay to make any improvements of any kind because a commission of some sort or an extra crew law would rise up and take away the profits as soon as they were earned.

Many projects which would have shown a profit a few years ago, will not pay under the present revision downward of freight and passenger rates by railroad commissions.

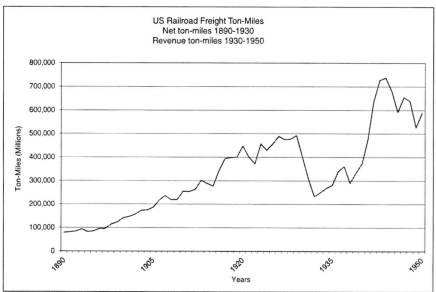

The development of U.S. rail traffic: U.S. railroad freight ton-miles, 1890–1950.

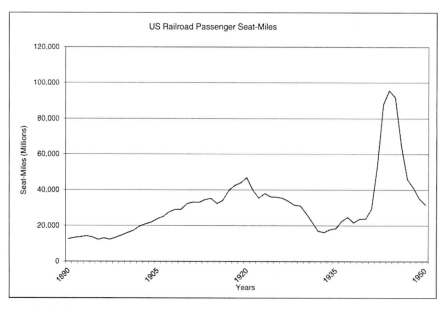

The development of U.S. rail traffic: U.S. railroad passenger seat-miles, 1890–1950.

1.1.4 War and Government Administration

War broke out in Europe in 1914; Britain, France and Russia were soon buying war materials from the U.S., bringing industry out of its recession, but increased demand for freight haulage fell on a sick industry. Car shortages and traffic congestion provoked an ICC inquiry in November 1916. Eastbound traffic blocked the yards with cars that could not be unloaded. Low temperatures and heavy snowfall in the winter of 1916–17 struck the northeast, where traffic problems were worst. One large railroad found its motive power crippled when ICC inspectors shut down many of its engines[42]; the commission set up to ensure fairness in interstate haulage rates was now mandating the power of locomotive headlights and the permissible limits of driving wheel lateral motion.[43]

Railroading had been one of the great industries of America but, under the new rules, its future was bleak[44]:

> This is the first year since the first railroad in the United States was built, in 1831, that there has been any considerable mileage of road voluntarily abandoned by its owners or taken up and sold as junk…. It is startling to find that more railroad mileage was abandoned or about to be abandoned than was built in 1917–1,300 miles.

In December 1917, the ICC recommended to Congress that a national railroad system be created, while rejecting the railroads' plea for rate increases as a solution to their problems.[45] The government acted quickly; the U.S. Railroad Administration took over the operation of the railroads on January 1, 1918.

This coincided with two months of blizzards, burying the railroads of the northeast and midwest, already clogged with traffic, in several feet of snow and adding enormously to their costs and difficulties. Trains were buried in snow or frozen solid; locomotives broke down trying to move them. Locomotive frames broke from running over trackbeds frozen like concrete. Shopmen were out shoveling snow instead of maintaining engines. Ashpans caked with ice increased turnaround times to hours that should have been minutes. Water plugs froze, or splashing water coated their surroundings with ice. In the appalling winter conditions, labor turnover soared; skill levels plummeted.[46] The extreme demand for motive power revealed that many locomotive terminals were obsolete; congestion at roundhouses contributed to congestion of traffic.[47]

The USRA found that improving railroad efficiency was not as easy as the ICC had supposed. As soon as the government took control, it became important that the railroads should not be a drain on the public purse. In May 1918, the USRA increased freight rates by 25%, passenger rates by 50%; the ICC had blocked rate increases of 5% when the railroads asked for them. The USRA also awarded large wage increases to an enlarged workforce; the wage bill increased 49% in a single year, 1917–18.[48]

For all its intentions of improving the railroads' contribution to the American war effort, the USRA displayed all the bureaucratic propensities of the ICC, and more.

> Use of varnish is a subject on which Director General McAdoo desires information. He has addressed the railroads a questionnaire asking information concerning the use of varnish on cars and locomotives during the calendar year 1917. Reports must show the brand, vendor, manufacturer, amount used for various purposes, total cost and price per gallon.[49]

The railroads' difficulties over recent years now bore bitter fruit. Enormous locomotives had been bought with insufficient thought as to their maintenance. Insufficient shop space led to repairs being done outside in freezing weather. Locomotives were being sent for repair to shops with adequate facilities 2,000 miles from their oper-

This New York, New Haven & Hartford 4-6-2, class I-2, No. 1320, built by Baldwin in 1913, struggles with winter conditions at Pittsfield, Massachusetts, on February 22, 1947 (Denver Public Library, Robert W. Richardson collection, RR-1389).

ating territory. One commentator opined in 1918: "The motive power of the country, taken as a whole, is perhaps in worse condition than it has ever been before."[50]

Under USRA operation many employees supported nationalization but higher fares and freight rates caused the wider population, previously in favor of government operation or undecided, to come down against it.[51] Large increases in wages and employment did not result in greater efficiency. In 1924, E. M. Herr, formerly with the Northern Pacific and by then President of Westinghouse Electric, described government administration of the railroads with one word: "disastrous."[52] The railroads never forgot the events of 1917–19.[53]

The USRA did, however, create a landmark in American locomotive design: the USRA standard locomotives.

1.1.5 The 1920s

The Transportation Act of 1920 returned the railroads to corporate operation, but under more pervasive controls than before. Economic and political turbulence continued for several years after the end of the war; only in 1923–4 did the nation's affairs return to normality, indeed, prosperity. Even as rate restrictions and rising costs for taxes, labor and materials suppressed profit margins, the sheer volume of traffic forced the railroads to move freight through their systems faster than before. George Basford, President of the Locomotive Feed Water Heater Co., commented in 1920[54]: "If the railroads are to stay out of the hands of the government, a lot of people have got to wake up." They did.

Traffic boomed in 1920; traffic, earnings, expenses and taxes were the highest on record, but net income was the lowest since ICC statistics began in 1888.[55] The boom was short-lived; 1921 was a year of worldwide slump. Freight ton-miles dropped 23% from 1920 to 1921

in "the worst year in railway history," even worse than the 15% decline between 1893 and 1894. Passenger seat-miles dropped 19% both times.[56] Vagrancy and violent strikes accompanied the slump, spreading and escalating in 1922 into widespread riots, shootings, arson, sabotage and bombings.[57] Locomotive construction in 1921 fell back to the level of 1919, these two years seeing the fewest locomotive orders since 1897.[58]

The railroads faced a zealous, swollen and newly powerful officialdom. Frank McManamy, ICC Commissioner and former USRA Director of Operations, made a speech in 1924, containing the most alarming implications[59]:

> Transportation is a public necessity, therefore a public function, and under the present policy of the American people is to be conducted under a system of adequate governmental regulation. Railroads are primarily public highways and only incidentally common carriers—an important distinction too frequently overlooked....
>
> "Few realize that the greater part of the legislation has been to help transportation, I am speaking now of the transportation machine as distinguished from the corporation which operates it. We must bear in mind that it is the duty of the government to see that adequate transportation is provided just as much as to construct and maintain public highways, and that it has only delegated the duty of furnishing transportation to private corporations.

From its beginnings in 1887 with eleven employees and an annual budget of $113,000, by 1919 the ICC had grown to 2,206 employees with a budget of $5.8 million and wide-ranging powers over freight and passenger rates, safety, mergers and acquisitions, accounting practices, new construction, abandonment and the issuance of shares, even decisions that were properly the function of operating management. In 1921, the Pennsylvania had to answer to the ICC why it had

The light Mikado was the most numerous of the USRA locomotives. The Chicago Great Western classified theirs as class L-3. No. 758 was photographed taking on coal at Des Moines, Iowa, on September 27, 1929. The crewman is attending to lubrication, an essential routine at every stop (Denver Public Library, Otto C. Perry collection, OP-4899).

sent 200 locomotives to Baldwin for repair the previous year "in disregard of efficient and economical management."[60] In 1926, the chairman and president of the St. Louis & O'Fallon were called before the ICC to account for what they did to earn their salaries and how they spent their time.[61]

The Transportation Act made it a criminal offense to extend a railroad without permission from the ICC but, at the same time, failing companies had to petition federal and state governments for permission to cease operations.[62] Between 1916 and 1922 nearly 4,000 miles of railroads were abandoned.[63] Railroads as extensive as the Missouri, Kansas & Texas[64] or as small as the Louisiana & North West,[65] weakened by rate restrictions, obsolete equipment and lack of investment, were pushed into bankruptcy by reduced traffic or some related event. Some were reconstructed in bankruptcy and returned to more or less profitable operation.

The disruptions of 1918–19 and the slump of 1921 gave way to a boom that persisted until 1929. The mid–1920s brought a new cooperation between railroads, unions, customers, government officials and the general public.[66] Some companies did well; the Chesapeake & Ohio carried 35 million tons of coal and coke in 1923, 24% up from the preceding year, and 12.6 million tons of other freight, up 38%.[67] Although hit by a 10% rate reduction, the C&O increased its net income by 38% over 1922 and paid $3.4 million in dividends from gross revenues of $102 million.

Into this arena came the super-power steam locomotives, first produced by Lima and at once imitated by Alco and Baldwin, offering large gains in speed, power and efficiency. These locomotives had more effect on railroad operations and economics in a shorter space of time than any previous improvement in locomotive design.

Although passenger numbers were falling, the railroads shared in the general prosperity, recording their best year ever in 1926 with record freight tonnage and earnings and increased dividends.[68] The Pennsylvania's 1926 annual report drove the company's stock price to the highest level since 1912; even if the 1926 return on invested capital was only 4.8%, earnings per share—the highest since 1902— supported a 6½% dividend. Pennsylvania employees—close to 200,000—outnumbered the company's 141,000 shareholders.[69] Even so, returns on investment never reached the 5¾% that the government considered permissible; federal valuation of the railroads—to find out what their investment was—dragged on for years at great cost and to no effect.

The 1920s brought a new problem for the railroads: rival transportation. By 1924, there were 15 million private automobiles in the U.S., one for every two families.[70] Bus and truck lines began to offer speed, convenience and flexibility that the railroads could not.

Railroad executives greeted 1927 with optimism; twenty-seven railroads budgeted $750 million to $900 million of capital expenditure. Even new construction was up, 1,005 miles of new line being built in 1926, plus double tracking, the highest figure since 1916. Passenger traffic dropped 27% between 1920 and 1927; passenger service was more trouble than it was worth.[71] Users demanded ever faster speeds and ever more luxurious accommodation which translated into weight, bulk and cost. A 1920s dining car could weigh 170,000 pounds, more than some locomotives not long before.[72]

The railroads responded to the conditions of the 1920s with an obsessive analysis of every aspect of steam locomotive operation and maintenance. Locomotives of increasing size and power spent less time in yards and shops and more time hauling heavier trains faster than ever before. Executives and engineers realized that success, indeed survival, depended on the amount of freight that they could

Railroad bankruptcies: The Pittsburgh, Shawmut & Northern operated in receivership from 1905 to 1947, the longest receivership in U.S. railroad history. Boiler diameter and slide valves suggest this 2-8-0, No. 71, was built around 1905, photographed at West Eldred, Pennsylvania, on July 19, 1947 (Denver Public Library, Robert W. Richardson collection, RR-1405).

"Into this arena came the super-power steam locomotives." An early superpower 2-8-4 hauling ninety-four cars. This is Illinois Central No. 7003, built by Lima in 1926, photographed near Ferber, Illinois, on August 15, 1940 (Denver Public Library, Otto C. Perry collection, OP-12355).

move each hour. In the short space of seven years from 1920 to 1927, nation-wide ton-miles per train hour increased by one third.[73]

The railroads benefited little from their gains in efficiency; the 1928 fuel bill was $354 million, 47.5% less than in 1920; the tax bill was $390 million, 43% more.[74]

Freight traffic surged to new heights in 1929.[75] The railroads even figured in the President's annual report to Congress:

> As a whole, the railroads never were in such good physical and financial condition, and the country has never been so well served by them. The greatest volume of freight traffic ever tendered is being carried at a speed never before attained and with satisfaction to the shippers. Efficiencies and new methods have resulted in reduction in the cost of providing freight transportation, and freight rates show a continuous descending line from the level enforced by the World War.

In November 1929, however[76]:

> There is naturally widespread concern regarding the effect upon business that will be produced by the recent great decline in the market prices of stocks.

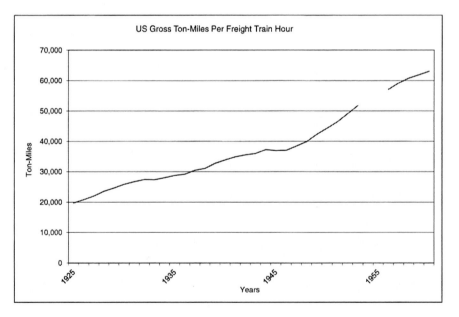

U.S. railroad gross ton-miles per freight train hour, 1925–1960. Note the steady increase 1925–45, regardless of economic conditions, followed by further acceleration with dieselization.

1.1.6 The Depression Years

The magnitude of the economic disaster became apparent with a continued shrinkage in trade.[77] Freight traffic in the spring of 1931 was 30% down from a year before; passenger traffic continued an ongoing decline that brought it down to the level of 1906.[78] In spite of these conditions, the railroads pressed on with efficiency measures, improvements to passenger service and capital investments; capital expenditures totaled $705 million in 1930—$119 million for locomotive purchases and upgrades.[79]

Traffic faded in 1932 to only one-half the volume of 1929.[80] By the

Depression-era traffic: This Colorado & Southern 2-8-0, Class B-4p, No 452, built at Rhode Island in 1900, is running on light track laid cheaply on the prairie with minimal formation construction or ballast, photographed near Denver, Colorado, on February 1, 1931 (Denver Public Library, Otto C. Perry collection, OP-6939).

fall of 1933, the railroads realized that they were 3½ years into a depression that refused to go away.[81]

Employment was down from 1.68 million people in 1929 to 972,000 in 1933. Although the depression bottomed out in 1932, the economy continued weak for many years. By the end of 1934 one-third of American rolling stock stood idle; freight traffic did not recover to 1929 levels until 1941 with U.S. involvement in the biggest war in history.

Most Americans that lived through the depression never forgot it. The economic disaster spawned a new regulatory environment which so much further distorted the free-market operation of the railroads that the question was again raised: "Are we drifting toward government ownership?"[82] By the end of 1936, Public Works Administration and Reconstruction Finance Corporation loans to the railroads totaled $717 million.[83]

The year 1935 was a nadir in the railroads' torment and frustration; a slight (4%) increase in traffic was accompanied by increased taxation and other legislation, actual and proposed, that adversely affected them. The ICC granted an increase in freight rates, but only temporarily and on certain commodities, while investigating passenger fares with a view to yet further reductions.[84] Sixteen companies, operating 29,000 miles, went bankrupt that year, making a total of eighty-nine companies and 72,000 miles in receivership by year-end.[85] Without loans on favorable terms from the Reconstruction Finance Corporation, the bankruptcy rate would have been higher.

Over twenty years the balance of political power diverted railroad income from shareholders to employees and the government. In 1911, the industry paid $397 million in dividends and $99 million in taxes; in 1932, it paid $92 million in (deferred) dividends and $275 million

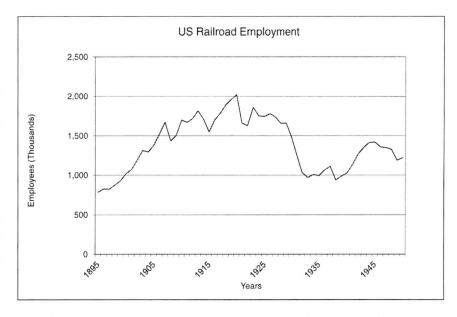

U.S. railroad employment, 1895–1950. Note the rapid increase beginning in 1897, recessions in 1907 and 1914, the all-time high under the USRA, recession in 1921, and the depression years. Major gains in efficiency between 1920 and 1940 allowed fewer people to move more traffic in World War II than in World War I.

in taxes.[86] Taxes exceeded $400 million in a single year for the first time in 1940.[87]

Railroads could not abandon routes and services made unprofitable by loss of traffic or rate controls without going through ICC hearings where vested interests—sometimes including the unions[88]—tried to force them to continue. Between 1920 and 1935, the ICC received 1,020 applications to abandon 18,700 miles; 900 were granted, resulting in the abandonment of 14,600 miles, leaving the operators forced to maintain unprofitable services on the other 4,100 miles.[89]

The railroads faced new competition from air, highway and waterway traffic using federally subsidized infrastructure.[90] By 1936, twenty-one airlines were operating in the U.S., flying 40 million passenger seat-miles and threatening railroad passenger and mail traffic. Air travel would not compete seriously with the railroads until the late 1940s, although they watched the explosive growth of this industry with alarm; the airlines flew a billion seat-miles for the first time in 1940.[91] Legislation prevented the railroads from providing bus, truck or airline services.

Signs of economic recovery appeared in 1936; freight revenue ton-miles increased 18% over 1935, exceeding any year since 1930.[92] Revenues rose, but with materials costs in hot pursuit. The railroads responded with optimism: at the beginning of 1937 more locomotives were on order than the total production of 1932–5. Construction of new locomotives was abetted by a massive effort to rebuild old ones.

Remarkable in the 1930s was the return of passenger traffic. Even in the boom times of 1928, passenger traffic was less than in any year since 1909, leaving the railroads supporting train services,—seven hundred trains a day through the Pennsylvania station in New York—rolling stock and other facilities for a market that lost a third of its volume in eight years.[93] The depression worsened this decline. By the beginning of 1934, passenger service was "…a picture of utter and complete discouragement…."[94] Far from abandoning this traffic, the railroads made extraordinary efforts to regain it by improving speed and comfort. Immense and costly efforts went into passenger car decoration, lighting, furnishing and temperature control. Air-conditioning became practical with the invention of Freon in 1932, although efforts in this direction dated back to 1910; in 1932–7 the industry invested $45 million to air-condition 8,000 cars.[95]

Riding around on trains in the middle part of the country in summer time, with the temperature outside at 110 degrees (and 10 degrees hotter

inside)—and getting my sweaty face and clothes covered with a coating of fine cinders—may have been romantic, but it didn't seem so to me at the time.[96]

Seen in this light, the combination of diesel haulage, air-conditioning and faster speeds was a major breakthrough in passenger service, to which the public responded.

Old-time railroadmen would have turned in their graves[97]:

The consultation of artists in the selection of architectural and decorative features of passenger-car interiors, and to some extent of exteriors as well, continues. Not only does this prevent violations of good taste to which multitudes of railway patrons are sensitive, but monotony is also avoided and interest enlivened by the bold effects which the trained artist may safely employ.

The first of the new trains appeared on the Union Pacific and the Burlington in 1934; public response was "rather astonishing." Thirteen other major railroads followed suit over the next two years, with fifty-four high-speed trains in service by 1938.[98] Suddenly:

The passenger-traffic outlook, which for 12 years from 1920 grew steadily more hopeless, suddenly changed from faintly hopeful to a volume which has placed an embarrassing demand on available rolling stock for the holiday peaks.

Fare reductions enforced by the ICC further increased this "embarrassing demand."

Even greater efforts went into freight haulage.[99] Besides accelerating freight trains to passenger train speeds, the railroads invested heavily in terminals, truck pick-up and delivery services and the more efficient handling of an infinite variety of freight. By 1940, twenty-six major railroads offered overnight freight service between cities up to 500 miles apart. For the first time in history, an average U.S.

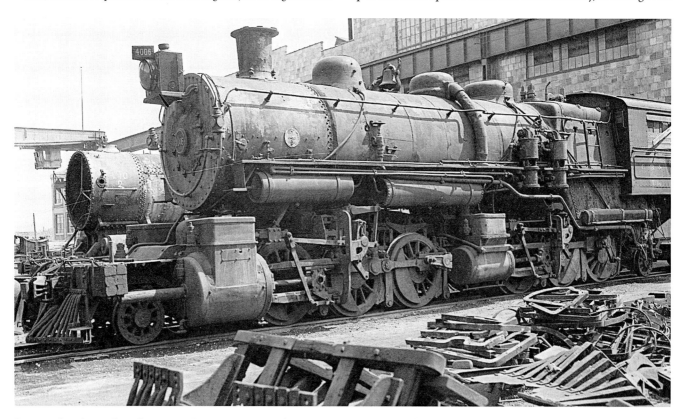

Scrap and replace: This Chicago, Burlington & Quincy class T-1 2-6-6-2, No. 4006, built by Baldwin in 1908–9, is already being scrapped at Denver, Colorado, in 1926. This was one of the early Mallets, with slide valves on both cylinder pairs. Note also the piston rod extension on the low-pressure cylinder and the large, acetylene headlamp (Denver Public Library, Otto C. Perry Collection, OP-3822).

"The 4-8-4 became an all-purpose locomotive." This Union Pacific class FEF-2 4-8-4, No. 831, was built by Alco in 1939 and photographed at Denver, Colorado, on February 19, 1950 (Denver Public Library, Otto C. Perry collection, OP-16552).

freight train traveled more than 400 miles in a day, up 62% from 1920. All through the depression, gross ton-miles per freight train hour continued to increase, from 25,800 in 1930 to 33,900 in 1940.[100] Few as they were, the new steam locomotives combined high power at high speed as never before; the 4-8-4 became an all-purpose locomotive as the distinction between passenger and freight locomotives vanished.

For years there was no point spending money repairing locomotives and cars when there was nothing for them to haul. By 1935, 10,000 locomotives and 280,000 freight cars were parked all over America, awaiting repair; another 4,000 locomotives were stored serviceable. Suddenly, "heroic efforts" were needed to rebuild the rolling stock fleet to meet anticipated 1937 freight demand.[101] Between 1930 and 1936, 16,000 locomotives were scrapped, compared to only 3,700 new installations, most of which were rebuilds. By 1937, sixty percent of the locomotive inventory was more than twenty-one years old. Costs of labor and materials rose, the price of new locomotives with them.

Increased traffic continued into 1937, accompanied by rising costs and cancellation of the ICC's emergency rate support.[102] Materials costs peaked in early 1937, more than 40% up on 1933 levels. Traffic then faded in the last half of the year, leaving the railroads worse off than before. Wages—also under government control—rose 28% between 1933 and 1938. Freight traffic in 1938 was down 20% on 1937; passenger traffic dropped by 12%.[103] These violently unstable conditions, and rising taxation, threatened the ability of the railroads to carry on in corporate ownership.[104]

The depression seemed to have become permanent.[105] Even in 1940, with the economy picking up, one businessman wrote: "We used to assume progress. Now we assume unending depression." Although they had prospered during the 1920s, the railroads were financially weak; the long-continued depression was devastating. Bankruptcies rose all through the 1930s; by 1938, 109 railroads, running 77,000 miles, were in receivership.

1.1.7 War and Aftermath

War broke out in Europe again in September 1939, causing a sudden surge in demand; traffic for the year was up 15% on 1938.[106] The railroads faced the possible demands of war with some confidence; in the summer of 1939, 1,886 freight locomotives and 146,600 freight cars stood on sidings in serviceable condition; this reserve could be returned to service quite quickly.[107] Behind this reserve stood 6,250 freight locomotives and 228,500 freight cars stored unserviceable; some of this stock could be repaired; some was not worth repairing—deteriorated beyond repair or obsolete.

World War II lifted the American economy out of the depression.[108] Businessmen acknowledged that "Except for the war, we would now be in a deep 'recession.'" Freight traffic in 1941 increased 26% over 1940.[109] Orders for new equipment by the railroads reached $1.2 billion. The attack on Pearl Harbor at the end of 1941 brought America into the war; the railroads, in common with the rest of American industry, went into high gear.

In the wartime political arena, the railroads were batted between the ICC, the unions, the War Production Board, the Office of Defense Transportation, the Office of Price Administration and state railroad commissions. The power of the ICC continued to expand; when the Commission expressed disappointment that even quite minor recommendations were not complied with, they were soon forced through as law.[110] In spite of the political situation, labor and management worked together to provide transportation in 1942–5 believed impossible in 1941.[111]

America's first year at war—1942—saw freight and passenger traffic at an all-time high; freight traffic was 41% higher than the previous record in 1929 and nearly double that of 1939, while passenger traffic was 134% higher than in 1939.[112] This was achieved by the utmost utilization of existing equipment—a measure of the slack capacity left over from the depression. In July 1942, the railroads asked the War Production Board for 900 new locomotives, 80,000 new freight cars and 2 million tons of rail; the Board awarded them 386 locomotives, 20,000 freight cars and 480,000 tons of rail. The railroads combed out their scrap lines, scrapping and repairing, so that the total locomotive fleet shrank by 1,272 between 1939 and 1942, but the number of serviceable locomotives increased by 4,459 at the same time. The same process produced 149,000 additional freight cars. The new defense plants took more than 8,000 miles of new track in

These two Atchison, Topeka & Santa Fe 2-10-2s, 900 class, No. 915 (rear), built by Baldwin in 1903–4, and 3800 class, No. 3815 (front), built by Baldwin in 1919–27, are handling wartime traffic near Sedalia, Colorado, on January 21, 1940. No. 915 was one of the first 2-10-2s ever built (Denver Public Library, Otto C. Perry collection, OP-1978).

1942 alone[113]; the same year, 2,516 route miles were abandoned and the track torn up to reuse the rail. Nothing was sacred; the already bypassed track at Promontory Point, Utah, scene of the golden spike ceremony in 1869, was torn up and sent 14,000 tons of rail to Navy plants on the Pacific coast.

Traffic increased again in 1943 but WPB restrictions dropped equipment purchases in 1943 to only two-thirds of their 1941 peak.[114] At the end of 1943, only 488 locomotives remained in storage in the entire U.S., with another 3,519 under repair or awaiting repair. Locomotives—steam, and now diesel-electric—less than ten years old bore a disproportionately large share of the traffic. WPB permitting and the gearing-up of manufacturing capacity resulted in the production of 3,430 locomotives in 1940–3 inclusive.[115]

The railroads surprised both the public and themselves with what they achieved. In 1942, they handled 57% more freight ton-miles and 25% more passenger-miles than in 1918 with 34% fewer locomotives and 25% fewer freight and passenger cars. Heavier track, more stone ballast, improved track drainage, better signaling systems, boiler water treatment, more powerful locomotives with bigger tenders, longer engine runs, long-distance scheduled freight trains run at passenger-train speeds, power tools for track maintenance and shopwork and improved accounting systems all played their part.

The industry wrung out the last of its stored equipment in 1944, with only 875 locomotives in storage at the end of the year; this was not a problem as traffic sagged at the end of the war.[116] With slackening demand, any locomotive built before 1915 was for scrap; that included nearly half the fleet.[117]

More than 90% of all wartime movements of troops and supplies went by rail; the war "revitalized the American railroads."[118] The same was true of American industry in general; though 1946 freight traffic was 20% off the wartime peak of 1944, it was still 30% up from 1929.[119]

Passenger traffic, inflated during the war by massive troop movements, crashed to barely half that of 1944 as travelers took to the air and highways. In 1946, the airlines hauled a sharply rising 10% of all passenger traffic.[120] The railroads placed eighteen new streamlined passenger trains in service in 1947, but to no avail.[121]

The war effort merged surprisingly smoothly into an era of unprecedented prosperity. The steam locomotive was part of a past that no one wanted to remember; locomotive orders in 1947 told the tale: seventy-nine steam, 2,075 diesel.[122] The steam locomotive fleet ran steady at 39,000 during the war; the electric and diesel fleet nearly doubled, from 2,056 in 1941 to 3,730 in 1945. As soon as the war ended, the railroads began scrapping obsolete steam locomotives while diesels continued to proliferate.

The American railroads dieselized between 1945 and 1955. The fascination and frustration of the steam locomotive were gone; a locomotive was a mere thing, bought off the shelf from General Motors, like a car or a washing machine. Sophisticated and aggressive unions, multifarious taxation and hostile legislation absorbed the energies of railroad management. Cars, trucks, buses, ships, planes and pipelines gnawed at the traffic that had been the railroads' monopoly fifty years before. The railroad industry struggled on, but the steam locomotive had no part in it.

Section 1.2 Size and Extent of the Railroad and Locomotive Building Industries

1.2.1 The Railroad Industry

In 1890, the American common carrier railroad system comprised 158,000 route miles.[123]

Some 1,800 to 1,900 corporations worked this system.[124] Because many corporations were subsidiaries of others, these represented only 700 independent operating companies. Ninety companies operated 85% of the route miles. These major companies themselves resulted from mergers and acquisitions; the Wabash, for example, formed in 1889, incorporated fifty predecessors, some dating back to 1838.[125]

These companies operated 35,000 locomotives and 1.3 million freight and passenger cars.

The railroads employed 1.4% of the entire population of the U.S.—874,000 people out of 63 million. As the Pennsylvania alone employed 55,000, hundreds of companies can have employed only a few dozen, exemplified by[126]:

> 8th (February, 1897), on Whippany River Railroad, near Morristown, N.J., a locomotive was derailed by the breaking of an axle and fell down a bank; engineman and fireman slightly injured. It is said that the wrecked engine, which was 40 years old, was the only one owned by the company.

Some of these minor railroads were gorgeously titled and marvelously obscure. Most people know of the Union Pacific, the Pennsylvania and the Atchison, Topeka & Santa Fe; mid-tier railroads, such as the Chicago & North Western, the Lehigh Valley or the Louisville & Nashville are also widely known. By contrast, the Winthrop & Rocky Comfort, the Marinette, Tomahawk & Western, the Ebensburg & Black Lick, or the Rio Grande, Sierra Madre & Pacific are known to few outside their localities. The Ohio River & Charleston reached neither of those destinations, but operated a few miles of track near Johnson City, Tennessee, and became the nucleus of the Clinchfield. The Atlantic & Pacific started at the town of Atlantic, North Carolina, and never went anywhere near the Pacific Ocean.

By 1900, the frontier was no more but European settlement was thickening fast. Without a railroad, the only means of hauling the products of farms, factories, mines and logging sites to market was by horse and cart over bad roads. Before 1910, railroad construction was feasible, profitable and necessary in ways that are hard to imagine today. These hundreds of small railroads were a ready market for the Eight-wheelers, Ten-wheelers, Moguls and Consolidations cast off by the Class I railroads, although they, too, bought new engines from Baldwin and Alco in ones and twos.

The tiny Class III railroads included such enterprises as the Quanah, Acme & Pacific. In 1909[127]:

> An officer writes that this company is the successor to the Acme, Red River & Northern. The line is in operation from Acme, Texas, east via Quanah for about 9 miles, and an extension is being built from Acme southwesterly.

These efforts bore fruit and, in 1913:

> This company has completed work on the extension from Paducah, Texas, west to Roaring Springs, 42 miles and has been authorized by the State Railroad Commission of Texas to issue $300,000 of bonds on the extension. Surveys are now being made, it is said, for the extension west across the Panhandle of Texas to Roswell, New Mexico. It is understood that the line will eventually be extended from Roswell, southwest to El Paso, Texas.[128]

Over the years the small railroads were absorbed by other railroads or went bankrupt and were dismantled, although some survived into the 1950s and 1960s.

> Being a mining railroad operation, the Ludlow & Southern (in Nevada) never was given meticulous consideration. Originally the tracks had been laid in a gully with the expectation that they would be washed out every year, consequently no one was surprised when this happened. About 1932 a particularly heavy cloudburst took out virtually a mile of

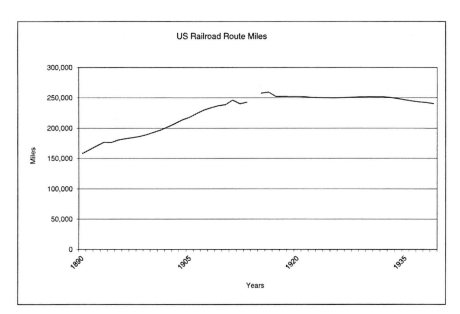

U.S. railroad route miles, 1890–1940.

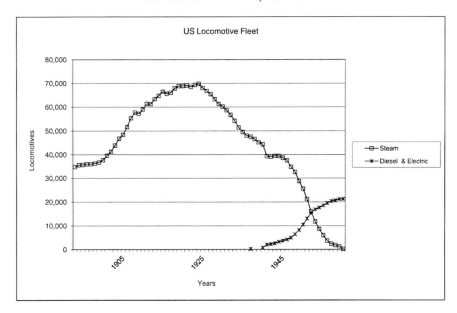

U.S. locomotive fleet, 1895–1960. Note how 20,000 diesel and electric locomotives in the 1950s hauled more freight than 70,000 steam locomotives in the 1920s.

The Quanah, Acme & Pacific exemplifies the many forgotten short lines that survived into the 1940s and 1950s. This 4-6-0, No. 723, was photographed at Roaring Springs, Texas, on July 17, 1946. The 4-6-0 wheel arrangement, small boiler, outside valve gear and piston valves suggest a construction date around 1910 (Denver Public Library, Robert W. Richardson collection, RR-1410).

track and no one bothered to repair it. The railroad remained idle over the years. In the summer of 1935 Botsford & Smith of San Francisco took up the rails; it is believed they were sent to a sugar plantation in the Philippines.

In 1937 the locomotives were cut up for junk, although the tenders remained intact for another twenty years. The old passenger coach, sitting on the ground about a mile north of the mine, was consumed by fire in the fall of 1939. In such fashion the Ludlow & Southern quietly passed out of the picture, no one being able, specifically, to attach a date to its demise."[129]

Whatever the romantic, comic or historic appeal of these forgotten railroads, twentieth-century American locomotive development resulted from the demands of twenty-one major railroads. Eight covered the industrial heartland of the northeastern U.S.: the Pennsylvania, the New York Central, the Baltimore & Ohio, the Erie, the New York, New Haven & Hartford, the Delaware, Lackawanna & Western, the Philadelphia & Reading and the small, but innovative Delaware & Hudson. Three were the Appalachian coal haulers: the Norfolk & Western, the Chesapeake & Ohio and the Virginian. Five radiated from Chicago: the Chicago, Burlington & Quincy, the Chicago & North Western, the Illinois Central, the Chicago, Milwaukee & St. Paul and the Chicago, Rock Island & Pacific. Five sprawled across the western mountains and deserts: the Northern Pacific, the Great Northern, the Union Pacific, the Southern Pacific and the Atchison, Topeka & Santa Fe. These railroads appear in our narrative again and again; few others appear at all.

The ICC classified railroads with revenues more than $1 million per year as Class I. In the early 1890s, ten U.S. railroads earned more than $20 million in annual gross revenues each.[130] Of these, only the Southern Pacific and Northern Pacific were west of the Mississippi. The others were all in New York, Pennsylvania or Illinois.[131] Route mileage did not convert into either revenue or profit; the lines across the empty West were costly and difficult to maintain and generated little local traffic.

Vigorous expansion continued until 1910, when the U.S. had more miles of railroad than the whole of Europe. After the United States,

the country with the greatest mileage was Canada, and that only 40,000 miles. Construction tapered off in the hostile political climate after 1910. Although the network stopped expanding, it handled great increases in traffic. Between 1905 and 1920 the average freight train payload increased from 322 tons to more than 600. Bulk freight trains greatly exceeded this figure; in 1906, during the grain season, the New York Central was hauling 2,000-ton trains and some of the coal carriers exceeded this.[132] Passengers per train increased from 48 to nearly 70, a surprisingly low number, although on some heavily used routes a train could carry as many as 500 passengers.[133]

The big American railroads were gigantic enterprises on a scale never seen before or elsewhere in the world. In 1905, the Santa Fe, with 8,300 route miles, sprawled from Chicago to California and into Texas and New Mexico, hauling 2.5% of total U.S. rail freight.[134] The same year, the Pennsylvania, with 11,000 route miles spread over a much smaller area, hauled 16% of U.S. rail freight and 13% of passenger seat-miles.[135] That year the Pennsylvania put $38 million—more than the gross revenue of most railroads—into new locomotives and cars, coaling and watering facilities, expanded or new freight yards and other construction.

On January 1, 1906, the New York Central, assembled by the Vanderbilts, combined fifty-four railroads into a single management structure.[136] In 1908 the new company bought 18% of the entire locomotive output of the U.S.; in 1909, it operated 3,780 route miles, 2,305 locomotives, 65,840 freight cars, 2,455 passenger cars and 3,670 cars on work trains.

The Santa Fe's annual reports for 1905 and 1918 highlight this growth in capacity.[137] By 1918, the Santa Fe had grown through construction and acquisitions to 11,456 route miles. Freight ton-miles hauled had increased 128%. Total operating revenues were $188 million, up 174% from 1905; net earnings increased only 93% to $44.2 million in 1918. The company's average freight train load in 1918 was 511 tons, with an average of twenty-six loaded cars per train. That year the system employed 53,100 people. Large increases in motive power accompanied and enabled this growth. Not only did the company increase its locomotive fleet from 962 in 1896 to 1,433 in 1904

End of the road for the Utley Valley & Stewart, Utley, Ohio, August 25, 1940 (Denver Public Library, Robert W. Richardson collection, RR-1539).

and 2,150 in 1914, but average tractive effort increased from 26,000 pounds in 1904 to 33,000 pounds in 1914.

The composition of a railroad's traffic depended on size and location. Santa Fe 1914 gross revenues were 66% from freight and 34% from passenger service; two-thirds freight, one-third passenger was typical. The freight comprised 20% agricultural produce, 37% ores and coal, 18% manufactured products and the balance forestry and miscellaneous products. This balance was heavily skewed on the Appalachian coal haulers. In 1915, the Norfolk & Western derived 85% of its revenue from freight, 71% of which was coal.[138]

The last major successful railroad developments after 1900 were the Clinchfield, the Western Maryland and the Virginian, responding to the development of the Appalachian coalfields.[139] Some of the last new lines were built on the optimism of a lost era; great feats of engineering did not alter the fact that they were economically unsound. The Denver, Northwestern & Pacific, built in 1903–05 (reorganized as the Denver & Salt Lake in 1912), following the most direct possible route between Denver and Salt Lake City, crossed the continental divide at 11,300 feet elevation by means of endless curves and steep gradients.[140] Until the Moffat tunnel was built in 1928, the difficulties and high cost of winter operation and the small loads that could be moved by each locomotive and train crew meant that the railroad could never pay.

The San Diego & Arizona connected San Diego with the Southern Pacific at El Centro, California, with 148 miles of line through hostile desert terrain, including seventeen tunnels in 11 miles. With some of the line passing through Mexico, construction began in 1907 and was not completed until 1919.[141] This line, too, never paid.

The American railroad industry reached its greatest extent in 1916, with 259,000 route miles, 64,000 locomotives, 2.3 million freight cars and 55,000 passenger cars. At the time, 181 Class I railroads operated 89% of the route miles and generated 97% of the industry's revenues. Two hundred sixty-three Class II railroads operated a further 7% of route miles and 3% of the locomotives, 410 Class III railroads operated the balance and 1% of the locomotives.[142]

Although route expansion ceased, traffic continued to intensify. In 1923, the New York Central generated $365 million in revenues

from 5,700 route miles, carrying 133 million tons of freight and 55 million passengers.[143] By 1925, the Burlington operated 9,400 route miles, resulting from the absorption of 204 predecessor companies.[144] The Norfolk & Western generated $95 million in annual revenues from 2,240 route miles. While the Santa Fe's revenues were more than twice those of the Norfolk & Western, at $235 million, its trackage sprawled over nearly 12,000 route miles; the Union Pacific was hardly less extensive, with 9,500 route miles and $200 million in revenues.[145] Biggest of them all was the Pennsylvania, comprising eighty companies, operating nearly 11,000 route miles in 1926 and generating revenues of $710 million.[146] The Pennsylvania hauled 11% of the freight ton-miles in the country, 18% of the passengers, operated 11% of the national railroad equipment and employed 199,000 people—12% of the railroad workers in the country. In 1927, the Pennsylvania bought 17 million tons of coal, 3.5% of total U.S. production.[147]

The American steam locomotive fleet peaked at about 70,000 in 1923–5.[148] This figure probably included only the common carrier railroads and excluded an unknown number of steam locomotives at mines, quarries, factories, docks and logging sites. Numbers on the Class I railroads declined to 55,000 in 1930, 46,000 in 1935 and 40,000 in 1940 as smaller, older engines were scrapped and replaced by fewer, more powerful ones. Class II and III railroads added 4,000 to 5,000 locomotives to this total.[149]

Construction almost ceased in the 1930s and abandonments came apace, totaling 9,800 miles between 1932 and 1937, compared to only 550 miles of new construction. Route mileage shrank to 234,000 miles by the end of the decade. The steam era ended on a railroad system of about 225,000 miles.[150]

1.2.2 Locomotive Building

The American railroads of the 1890s bought their locomotives from a dozen manufacturers, all of them in the eastern half of the U.S. Biggest was the Baldwin Locomotive Works at Philadelphia. Some of the bigger railroads, totaling thirty-four over the years, built their own locomotives.

News started to leak in May 1901[151] of a great combination of loco-

Some railroads should never have been built. The Denver & Salt Lake was known for its direct routing but at the expense of steep grades. Here the crew lost control of 2-6-6-0 No. 215 near Rollinsville, Colorado, on November 6, 1935. The crew could ride the train or jump off it; their chances were not good either way (Denver Public Library, Otto C. Perry collection, OP-11390).

motive builders. Eight firms merged to form the American Locomotive Company (Alco) to compete more effectively with Baldwin. The International Power Co., owners of the Rhode Island Locomotive Works, already owned the Cooke Locomotive & Machine Works, Paterson, New Jersey. The other companies in the merger were the Brooks Locomotive Works, Dunkirk, New York, the Manchester Locomotive Works, Manchester, New Hampshire, the Pittsburgh Locomotive & Car Works, Pittsburgh, the Richmond Locomotive Works, Richmond, Virginia, the Dickson Locomotive Works, Scranton, Pennsylvania, and, ultimately the most important, the Schenectady Locomotive Works, Schenectady, New York. In 1904, Alco acquired the Locomotive & Machine Co., Montreal, Canada.[152]

The new company had an immediate 44% market share. Staying out of the merger were Climax Manufacturing, Corry, Pennsylvania, the Rogers Locomotive Works, Paterson, New Jersey, (Rogers joined in 1905), and Stearns Manufacturing, Erie, Pennsylvania. The H. K. Porter Co., Pittsburgh, also stayed out and dominated the market for small locomotives. Another builder staying out was the Lima Locomotive & Machine Works, a small shop at Lima, Ohio, which built Shay locomotives for the mining and logging industries.

Schenectady was the biggest of the new partners and continued building steam locomotives until the late 1940s.[153] Brooks built steam locomotives until 1929, when Alco turned it to other products. The Cooke plant was downgraded over the years to building smaller locomotives, locomotive production ending in 1928. Dickson specialized in small locomotives; production ceased in 1909. Manchester had only limited facilities, served the New England market and ceased locomotive production in 1913. Rhode Island closed down in 1907. Rogers remained active until 1913, Pittsburgh until 1919, Richmond until 1927. After

1929, all Alco production came from Schenectady, with the exception of the Montreal Locomotive Works which continued to build steam locomotives even after Schenectady had stopped doing so.

The productive capacity of this industry was about 2,000 locomotives a year in the 1890s, closely tracking economic conditions and reaching an all-time peak of about 7,000 locomotives a year in the early 1900s, as shown in the following graphs.[154] At that time, the Baldwin works at Philadelphia and the Pennsylvania's Altoona shops each employed 10,000 to 15,000 men.

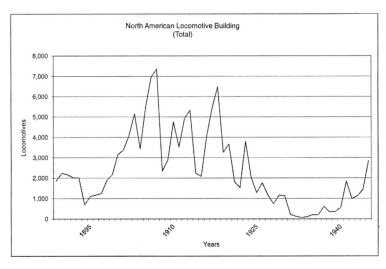

North American locomotive building, total domestic and export, 1889–1945. Includes Canadian production from 1905 onward (typically less than 100 locomotives a year), Canadian and railroad shop production from 1912 onward. 1942–4 figures exclude unknown production for U.S. government and lend-lease. Includes diesel-electric and electric locomotives: 50% of total 1936–45.

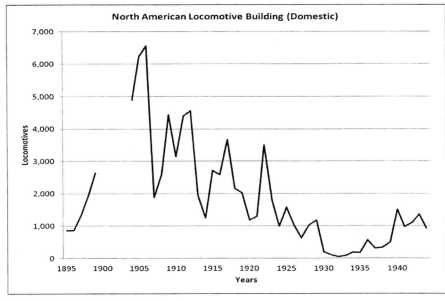

North American locomotive building for domestic service, 1896–1945. Data missing 1901–4.

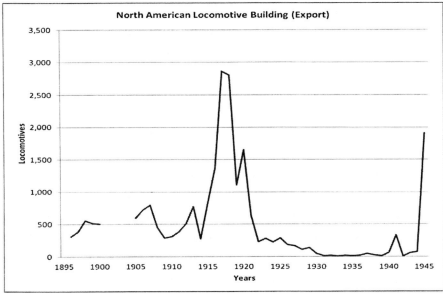

North American locomotive building for export, 1896–1945. Information missing, 1901–4. Available information includes U.S. government orders in World War I, excludes them in World War II. The large total in 1945 was for European reconstruction.

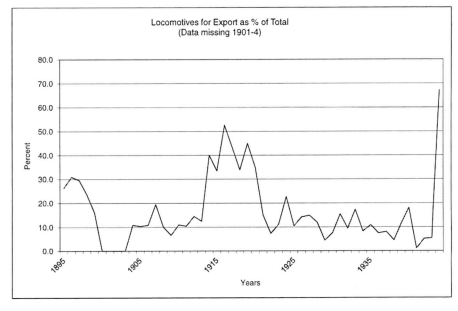

North American locomotives built for export as percentage of total, 1896–1945. Information missing, 1901–4. Available information includes U.S. government orders in World War I, excludes them in World War II. The large total in 1945 is for European reconstruction.

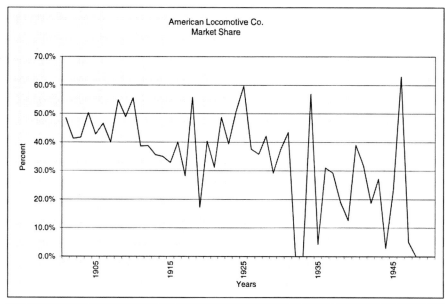

Market share of locomotive orders: American Locomotive Co., 1900–1950.

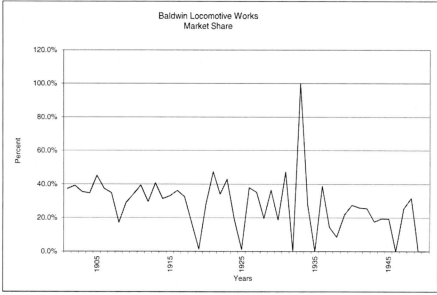

Market share of locomotive orders: Baldwin Locomotive Works, 1900–1950.

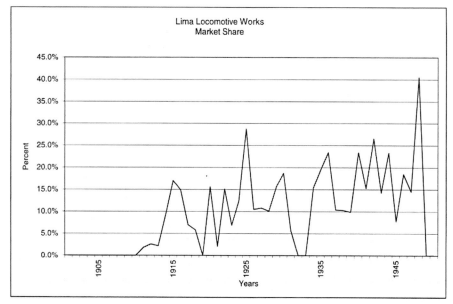

Market share of locomotive orders: Lima Locomotive Works, 1900–1950.

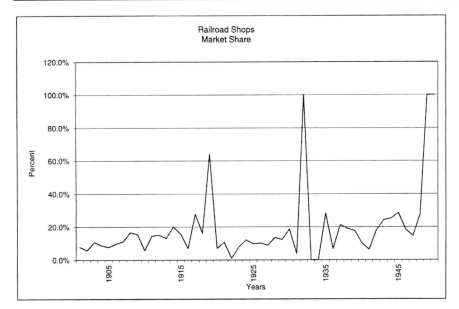

Market share of locomotive orders: railroad shops, 1900–1950.

Of the big three, Baldwin was probably the most innovative and the most willing to indulge the most bizarre wishes of its clients, such as the Santa Fe; Alco was the more strait-laced; Lima combined innovation with high quality.

Section 1.3 Railroad Engineering

In 1895, 36,000 steam locomotives on U.S. railroads hauled 85 billion freight ton-miles and 12 billion passenger seat-miles. In 1945, 39,000 steam locomotives hauled eight times the volume of freight and nearly eight times the passenger volume, using the same basic locomotive technology. What happened? This increase in locomotive power could never have been applied effectually without advances in the broader field of railroad engineering.

1.3.1 Management Science and the Ton-Mile Statistic

Management science, rooted in the belief that industrial management could be numerically measured and analyzed, was an American concept. Originating in Henry R. Towne's paper, *The Engineer as an Economist*,[155] in 1886, the concept was developed further by Towne, F. W. Taylor and F. and L. Gilbreth.[156] Some practitioners took the idea to extremes with fantastic statistical ratios that baffled even their inventors. Sometimes the method was more important than the objective, but it produced interesting results and gained ground in the 1890s. It was still new in 1899 when an exasperated railroad official wrote[157]:

> Way up in the loft of some city office, at the crossroads country station, in the grime and smoke of the store clerk's shack, overhead in the Division Superintendent's office, at the shop clerk's desk and in the Maintenance of Way Department,—everybody is making statistics! We have spent one dollar and we spend two dollars more of the stock-holders' money just to explain to them where the first dollar went…. A cadaverous, pale-faced race has come among us to parcel out our doings by arithmetic.

This maligned activity played a vital part in American steam locomotive development.

The basic unit of railroad output was the freight ton-mile (one ton of freight hauled for one mile); freight provided at least two-thirds of most American railroad revenues. The passenger seat-mile was a more difficult statistic to deal with because of the independent, self-willed nature of the payload. The civil engineers who built the early railroads often managed them in operation. Having been intimately involved with the cost of construction, they paid close attention to profit and loss on operations. The freight ton-mile was the product of much thought in America as early as the 1860s.[158] British railroads, by contrast, compiled ton-mile statistics in their early years, but gave up using them in about 1860, considering that the cost of gathering them exceeded their value as a management tool. As late as 1942, the British had no means of evaluating the effect of locomotive improvements as coal consumption was recorded by the mile run, with no consideration of speed or tonnage hauled.[159]

Ton-miles were calculated in several ways.[160] Gross ton-miles included the weight of engine, tender, cars and payload; the percentage of total train weight taken up by the engine ranged from 8% to 10% in flat country up to 20% to 35% in mountainous terrain. Net ton-miles excluded the engine, but included the weight of cars, whether full or empty, and non-revenue tonnage, such as work trains. Revenue ton-miles comprised the weight of revenue-producing freight and the cars in which it was carried, but could also be calculated from payload only. Unfortunately, the sources consulted are often unclear as to these distinctions.

Whatever the method, the major railroads knew their cost and revenue per ton-mile; almost any aspect of railroad operation could be reduced to these figures or to the ability to produce ton-miles. Comparing revenues and costs per ton-mile—whether for a single company or the U.S. railroad industry—provided a simple and direct measure of its financial health. In particular, American railroad engineers and executives saw plainly that the sole function of a locomotive was to produce ton-miles or passenger-miles at an acceptable unit cost. In the early 1900s, the dominant statistic was ton-miles per train-mile—in other words, tons per train.

Rising wages and legislation on working hours increased the time-based costs of keeping a train on the road; from 1920 onward the governing statistic was the ton-mile per hour, rather than the ton-mile. Every aspect of locomotive design, construction and operation influenced this figure and, after 1920, was influenced by it. Between 1906 and 1916, the U.S. national average increased by 42%, a further 57% between 1916 and 1926,[161] and yet further by 78% between 1926 and 1946. To achieve this as a national average was a prodigious feat in every aspect of railroading.

1.3.2 Locomotive and Train Operating Costs

Typical American locomotive operating costs in the 1890s were[162]:

Item	Cost per mile (cents)	Percentage
Fuel	7.42 (46.2 miles per ton)	42.7
Crew wages	5.39	31.0
Repairs	2.40	13.8
Cleaning	1.25	7.2
Oil	0.32 (15.3 miles per pint)	1.8
Water	0.49	2.8
Miscellaneous	0.10	0.6
Total	17.37	100.0

Even before 1900, managers knew that fuel and crew wages made up three-quarters of total operating costs per locomotive mile with fuel as the biggest single item. Fuel economy and efficiency in the use of crew wages became obsessions in the economic and political climate of the twentieth century.

Robert Quayle, Superintendent of Motive Power and Machinery for the Chicago & North Western, pointed out that, although an engine worked most economically at 25% to 33% cut-off, it hauled substantially more tonnage in full gear, resulting in better use of crew wages.[163]

> The motive power official must consider the locomotive as a tool, representing a large investment of capital and costing annually a considerable sum for its operation, and must be mostly concerned in making it give the largest possible return to the company. If to attain this end he must violate, in the construction or operation of the engine, principles which he knows tend towards economy of water and fuel, it is his business to do it. And I have no hesitation in saying that to the carrying out of this business-like policy are due some features of locomotive practice that are sometimes condemned by those who look upon the subject entirely from the standpoint of economy in fuel.

By 1914 train operating costs on the St. Louis & San Francisco were as follows[164]:

Item	Cents Per mile	Engine Percent	Train Percent
Repairs, renewals, depreciation	9.8	22.4	12.1
Enginehousemen's wages	2.2	5.0	2.7
Enginemen's wages	11.7	26.7	14.4
Fuel	18.2	41.6	22.4

Item	Cents Per mile	Engine Percent	Train Percent
Oil & cotton waste	0.2	0.5	0.2
Water	1.4	3.2	1.7
Locomotive supplies	0.3	0.7	0.4
Sub-total locomotive	43.8	100.0	53.9
Trainmen's wages	14.6		18.0
Train supplies	2.2		2.7
Freight car repairs	20.6		25.4
Total cost per train-mile	81.1		100.0

The increase since the 1890s was due to inflation, bigger engines and, possibly, more sophisticated accounting; fuel and wages remained the biggest items.

Freight train cost curves bottomed out at 15 miles per hour with the engine loaded to its maximum capacity and helper service for local adverse grades. In 1896, the standard freight train on the New York Central & Hudson River was fifty 60,000-pound capacity cars, a trailing load of 2,250 tons.[165] These trains, 2,000 feet long, traveled 150 miles in 6 to 8 hours.[166] Railroads responded to increasing demand by putting more than one locomotive on a train, either double-heading over a whole division or providing helper engines for short adverse grades.[167] This was so inefficient that railroads ordered batches of locomotives to eliminate double-heading or helper service over a few miles of route. Even so, in times of heavy demand, railroads would put as many as three to five locomotives on a train on some steeply graded routes. This was the real benefit of the diesel-electric locomotive—multiple locomotives under the control of a single throttle.

Helper service: The Atchison, Topeka & Santa Fe put three locomotives on the head end of this train over the Raton Pass, New Mexico, on December 29, 1940, as the European war gathered pace. The road engine was 3765 class 4-8-4, No. 3768, built by Baldwin in 1938. The two 3800 class 2-10-2s, Nos. 3814 and 3822, built by Baldwin in 1919–27, were put on as helpers (Denver Public Library, Otto C. Perry collection, OP-1974).

Pusher service was no favorite of the crews.[168]

that is about the last job I'd take. To begin with, running a pusher engine is an extremely dirty job. Not only do you sit on the rear of the train amid all the dust the movement kicks up, you are also subjected to all the coal dust blowing off the hopper cars. Going west out of Williamsport pushing a loaded coal drag, the I1's don't pound you too bad when they are working hard, but running one of them light for sixty-five miles coming back from Sned to Williamsport is enough to shake your gizzard loose, especially if you do it day in and day out. Then, if you get the hill job pushing out of Ralston, at the end of the day you have to run in reverse for thirty-five miles. That isn't a pleasurable trip, either. It's hard to see around the tender and all the dirt on the tender blows back in into your face, plus you're on the wrong side to see the signals. One of the really nasty things about running backward occurs when it's about twenty degrees below zero and the only protection you have is the canvas drop curtain in back of the cab to keep the cold out. The crews almost freeze from this exposure to the elements.

Soaring demand at the end of the nineteenth century set the trend for gigantic locomotives moving immense trains at low speeds. In 1904, the first American Mallet gave a whole new meaning to this trend.

With huge capital expenditures at stake and revenues eroded by legislation, competition and taxation, the pressures on railroad management were extreme; these pressures were the backdrop to the development of the American steam locomotive. Even in the prosperous conditions of 1900:

> Closer profit margins are rapidly forcing railroad administration to a science. Results are severely scrutinized by comparative and statistical methods as never before. Railroad officials rise and fall by results accomplished. The key in a large measure to the operating efficiency of a road to-day is the tonnage hauled for each potential unit of power furnished.

The force driving the management of American railroads at this time—and its effects—was well summarized in 1914[169]:

> The rising ratio of fixed operating costs to gross earnings has been the American railroad manager's nightmare for the past ten years, and particularly, since 1908. In the decade expenses over which a railroad has only limited control and which are, in a degree, non-elastic, have expanded swifter than in any other similar period in railroad history. To meet this situation American ingenuity and efficiency have developed various counteractants, all summarized in the increased freight train load. In ten years the Mallet and mikado engine has passed from an experimental stage into general use; 90-lb. and 100-lb. rails have replaced previous 70 to 85-lb. standards and only a few wooden bridge structures are left standing on main lines. In the period from 1903 to 1912 the train load of American railroads has gone from 391 tons to 509 tons, or 30 per cent, the tractive effort of engines has increased from 22,796 pounds to 30,501 pounds, or 34 per cent, and the average capacity of freight cars has risen to 39½ tons, whereas it was 30.9 tons in 1903.

Demand for good-quality labor put the unions in a strong position which they exploited with increasing militancy and sophistication from about 1910 onward. The effects of legislation continued their upward pressure on operating costs and downward pressure on revenue.

Reducing unit costs meant bigger equipment. A survey of nineteen railroads all over the U.S., made in 1918, showed that the coal burned per revenue ton-mile declined from 0.7 pounds for a 300-net ton train to 0.4 pounds for a train with 600 tons of payload. The average payload of an American freight train increased from 176 tons in 1888 to 357 tons in 1907 and 620 tons in 1917. Even though the cost of coal doubled between 1907 and 1917, the cost per ton-mile hauled stayed the same. This was largely due to the increasing use of very large locomotives.

1.3.3 The Trend to Bigger Equipment

The economics of the late 1890s and early 1900s, analyzed by management science, accelerated a trend to big equipment on American railroads that began soon after the Civil War.[170] After 1895, in particular, everything pointed to bigger freight cars, heavier rail, stronger substructures and bigger engines.

American railroads were less constricted by clearance limits dating from the past than those in Europe; there were no national standard dimensions. Typical dimensions were 15½ feet high and 10½ feet wide. Some lines were more constricted; height limits on the Texas Central and the Pittsburgh, Shawmut & Northern, for example, were as low as 11 feet.[171]

The Americans discovered early on that a freight car running on two four-wheel trucks had a higher capacity and lower rolling resistance than one running on rigidly mounted axles, and was less likely to derail on uneven track.[172] The American railroads discarded their last rigid-axle, four-wheel cars in 1888.[173]

The dead weight and rolling resistance of a freight car did not increase in proportion to its payload.[174] Freight car construction went from wood with metal fittings to steel frame, metal fittings and wood structure to all-steel construction, in response to cheaper steel and improved fabrication processes.[175] All-steel freight cars appeared on the American railroads in increasing quantities from 1897 onward. A steel car cost more to buy, but less to maintain than a wooden one.

In 1870, the average boxcar carried 20,000 pounds. In the 1880s, the New York, Chicago & St. Louis was the first railroad to introduce a high-capacity boxcar carrying 40,000 pounds.[176] By 1895, railroads were using 60,000-pound capacity boxcars, with 80,000-pound cars just entering service. The Pennsylvania bought its first steel-framed boxcars in 1901 with a capacity of 100,000 pounds.[177] Passenger cars grew from 20,000 pounds all-up weight to 100,000 pounds, much of this five-fold increase resulting from steel construction urged on by safety considerations.

Bigger cars, more heavily loaded, demanded greater total tractive effort but the tractive effort per ton of payload decreased. A 100,000-pound freight car took 24% less tractive effort per pound of payload than a 60,000-pound car.[178] The cost of switching a car was constant, regardless of its size, so bigger cars reduced the switching cost per ton of payload. The heavier the train, the smaller the proportion of total train resistance contributed by the locomotive. Fuel consumption did not increase in direct proportion to load. Even though thermal efficiency peaked at less than maximum power output, and then declined as power increased, the total cost per ton-mile continued to decrease.

Longer trains added to the stress on couplers and draft gear. Serious and frequent accidents resulted from trains breaking in two, with the part that had broken away colliding with the part that remained attached to the engine, colliding with other trains or derailing.

3rd (February, 1897) 4 a.m. on Baltimore & Ohio, near Branchville, Maryland, a freight train broke in two, 5 cars being stopped at Muirkirk. The forward part of the train ran on some distance, when several other cars broke away from it and stopped. The engineman then went forward to a side track and leaving what cars he had, started back for the cars at Muirkirk, not knowing that a second break had occurred. The engine collided with the cars that had stopped midway, and the tender and one car were badly wrecked. The engineman, fireman and one brakeman were injured. A blinding snow was falling at the time.[179]

Numerous accidents of this type occurred every month. By 1905, they were on the increase; the old, wooden, 60,000-pound cars were not only uneconomic, they were a safety hazard.[180] Hump yards and relentless demands for freight haulage led to rougher handling of freight cars and rising repair costs. All-steel cars, roughly handled by powerful locomotives, accelerated wear and tear on the older cars when mixed together in a train, and hastened their disappearance.

The federal government mandated the Janney or Master Car Builders' (MCB) automatic coupler in 1893, against the objections of the railroads, to replace the dangerous link-and-pin coupler. Adoption of the MCB coupler reduced the accident rate; to their surprise, railroad officials found that the new couplers increased the efficiency of yard switching.[181] Conversion of 1¼ million cars and 35,000 locomotives was almost complete by 1900.[182] Although the MCB coupler was forced on the railroads for safety reasons, it is difficult to imagine how the enormous freight trains of the 1900s could have functioned without this innovation.

In the early days, brakemen set the brakes by hand, car by car, in response to whistle signals from the engine. A train crew consisted typically of the engineer, fireman and one brakeman on the engine and the conductor and two brakemen in the caboose. On freight trains the brakemen had to move along the tops of the cars in all weathers amid the smoke and hot cinders from the locomotive; their work was always hazardous, especially at night or in bad weather. The brakemen set switches in front of and behind the train and, if the train were forced to stop, went out as flagmen to warn oncoming or following traffic.

Angus Sinclair describes the nineteenth-century development of train brakes in *Development of the Locomotive Engine,* in particular, the work of George Westinghouse. In 1869, Westinghouse patented a compressed-air brake, powered by a steam-driven compressor mounted on the locomotive, with compressed-air-powered brakes on each car and hose connections between cars.[183] If the train line ruptured or the compressor failed, the system failed. In 1872, he solved this problem by installing an air tank on each car, charged from the compressor on the engine and capable of applying the brakes on the car. If the air pressure in the supply line was reduced, whether by the engineer opening his brake valve or by a rupture of the train line, the compressed air in the tank applied the brakes. The system was fail-safe, although accidents occurred because its functioning was too violent.[184]

Air brakes had no positive release mechanism. One engineer remarked[185]:

> Several trains pulled so hard that I simply closed the throttle and let them stop without applying the air brake, after which I went back and found car after car with hot brake shoes.

Starting trains roughly to jar the brakes loose damaged cars and sometimes cargo. The amount of coal burned, driving locomotive air compressors against air leaks and trains against dragging brakes was substantial.

With air brakes, the usual train crew of engineer, fireman, three brakemen and conductor handled longer and longer trains; the wage cost did not increase in proportion to train length. The longer the train, the lower the wage cost per ton-mile, assuming similar speeds. If a whole train could be eliminated by distributing its tonnage among fewer, longer trains, a significant saving resulted.

In spite of the gains in safety and efficiency that continuous air brakes made possible, they were forced on the railroads as part of the

The brakeman's view. Note the old-style wooden boxcars, with catwalk and hand brake wheel, still in use in 1945. This photograph, taken on the Denver & Rio Grande Western in the Black Canyon of the Gunnison, Colorado, on October 14, 1945, illustrates the hazards of the brakeman's job, even in daylight and fair weather (Denver Public Library, Robert W. Richardson collection, RR-2210).

These two Virginian USRA 2-8-8-2 heavy Mallets, class USE, No. 739, and class USA No. 710, passing Page, West Virginia, epitomize the concept of the maximum-tonnage, slow-moving freight train. Virginian class USA was built at Alco Richmond; the USE was built at Alco Schenectady, both classes in 1919. The Virginian bought a third batch, class USB, from Alco in 1923. These two locomotives were still at work in their as-built compound configuration, when photographed on July 9, 1953 (Denver Public Library, Otto C. Perry Collection, OP-19652).

1893 Coupler Bill; full implementation took until 1913.[186] The railroads' cynical, reactionary attitude was[187]:

> There has been no debate on the merits of this bill, but it has been treated as an *ad captandum* measure, having in it great possibilities as a vote getter, and, of course, the politicians of both parties have "tumbled over each other," as the saying is, to get for themselves whatever political advantage was to be had from the passage of the bill. It is a melancholy but not altogether unexpected result.

The Automatic Straight Air Brake, developed between 1910 and 1918, was more economical in its use of compressed air, as well as providing smoother stops and graduated or quick release. Automatic couplers and air brakes may not have been essential in the early 1890s; the 100-car freight trains of the twentieth century would have been unmanageable without them.[188]

A 100-car train contained 100 feet of slack. Controlling slack required consummate skill on the part of the engineer; failure to control it could break a train in two or cause a derailment.[189] To stop a train, the engineer needed either to close the throttle, allowing the slack to bunch, or to apply the brakes before closing the throttle to keep the slack stretched, depending on the make-up of the train and the grade and curvature where he intended to stop. Pressurizing a train took as long as twenty minutes, with another five minutes to release the brakes. If the engineer moved off before the brakes at the back of the train had released, it caused flat spots on the car wheels or pulled the train apart.

In 1913, the Norfolk & Western started buying 180,000-pound gondola cars with a dead weight of 65,200 pounds,[190] followed by even bigger hopper cars in 1918, on six-wheel bogies, with a capacity of 200,000 pounds and a dead weight of only 60,000 pounds.[191] In 1919, the Pennsylvania introduced a 240,000-pound capacity hopper car weighing 83,600 pounds empty.[192]

In 1920, the Virginian took this tendency to new extremes with a 240,000-pound gondola car, more than twice the payload of its existing coal cars, supported on two six-wheel trucks.[193]

1.3.4 The Trend to Higher Speeds

At the end of the nineteenth century, speed was a vital concern in passenger service, especially in the northeastern U.S. where several lines competed for a dense traffic. Although speed was not a concern in freight service at that time, as early as 1894 C. H. Quereau, Engineer of Tests on the Burlington, expressed the opinion[194]:

> The weight and hauling capacity of locomotives have been increased in the past few years to such proportions that it is doubtful whether their size and number of parts can be still further increased with economy. A further increase in weight of locomotives, and in the length of trains, means increased expenditures on tracks, bridges, yards, sidings, roundhouses, turntables, and in numerous other directions, and the increased difficulties attending a further increase in the length of our present trains. An increase in speed will lessen the cost for motive power by reducing the number of engines necessary to handle the traffic. There is a growing conviction in Europe that the economical length of train has been reached, and there is, therefore, a movement towards increasing speed.

Although most freight trains moved slowly, speed mattered for certain types of merchandise. The Santa Fe introduced Red Ball priority freight on parts of the system in 1892, expanding it over the whole railroad in 1902.[195] Other railroads offered similar services. The ultimate fast freights were the silk trains from the Pacific coast ports to the eastern seaboard; the demand for speed was financial—the interest payable on the value of the cargo. In 1911, a silk special, carrying $2 million worth of silk, ran from Seattle to New York, 3,178 miles over Great Northern, Burlington and New York Central tracks, in 82 hours 15 minutes, a sustained average speed of 38 miles per hour.[196]

The railroads obtained fast passenger service more by maintaining high average speeds over long distances than by exceptionally high speeds over short runs. In 1905, on the Pittsburgh, Fort Wayne & Chicago, a four-car special, hauled by a 4-4-2, averaged 75 miles per hour over the 257 miles between Crestline, Ohio, and Clarke Junction, Indiana.[197] As companies upgraded track and signaling over greater lengths of railroad, minutes, even hours, could be shaved off passenger schedules between major cities. Maximum speeds remained at 70 to 80 miles per hour, although occasional short runs were recorded at 90 to 100 miles per hour, specifically 108 miles per hour for 5 miles by a 4-6-0 on the Savannah, Florida & Western on March 1, 1901.[198] On June 12, 1905, a Pennsylvania 4-4-2 was clocked at 127 miles per hour over 3 miles near Elida, Ohio.[199] The eminent authority, William Withuhn, casts doubt on these records: he points out that, not only were the timing methods inexact, but the locomotives were insufficiently powerful to do what was claimed. Indeed, test engineers in the late 1930s, using vastly more powerful and better designed locomotives, were discovering just how much power it took to accelerate a train to and past 100 miles per hour.

On occasion, high speeds were maintained over great distances. On September 7, 1905, a Santa Fe express covered the 2,246 miles between Chicago and Los Angeles in just under 45 hours—an average speed of 50 miles per hour. On May 5, 1906, an express ran the 3,255 miles between Oakland and New York in 71½ hours (45 miles per hour) on Southern Pacific, Union Pacific, Chicago & North Western, Lake Shore & Michigan Southern and New York Central tracks.

Railroads whose track and other conditions allowed trains to reach high speeds, notably in the northeastern states, built long troughs between the rails to hold water, typically 6 to 7 inches deep, 18 to 28 inches wide and 1,400 to 2,000 feet long. The crew could lower a scoop under the tender into the troughs ("track pans"), the force of the moving locomotive scooping water into the tender tank.[200] The London & North Western Railway in England started to use track pans in 1857; the New York Central was probably the first American user in 1870. Much ingenuity and expense went into preventing the pans from freezing in winter. Originally they were for fast passenger trains but, as the value of keeping freight trains moving became more apparent, railroads began fitting scoops to freight engines as well. The substantial cost of the track pans and the power needed to plough through them—as much as 590 horsepower at 60 miles per hour— were set against the cost of stopping a train to take on water and restarting it.[201] If track pans were available, locomotives could be built with tenders carrying more coal and less water, providing greater range between servicing stops.

In the boom conditions of the early 1900s, management science and traffic demand both pointed to the economic benefits of very heavy freight trains moving at low average speeds, with locomotives loaded to their maximum capacity. By 1910–15, this idea had run its course. Employees and government organizations were objecting to the increasing size of trains that the 5- or 6-man crews had to handle. The 1913 firemen's arbitration award, and other similar wage negotiations, tied wage rates to locomotive adhesion weight, so that bigger engines cost more to crew.[202] Operating economy deteriorated when helper engines had to be put on to overcome local grades. A study made in 1913 suggested that lighter trains moving faster might cost

more in total, but less per ton moved. During World War I, rumors spread of superintendents clearing their blocked divisions by sending out lighter trains that moved faster, even though this contravened the rule of maximizing train tonnage.

In the early 1920s, managers came to realize that true fuel efficiency lay in moving trains quickly and that the ton-mile per hour was the true measure of railroad output. Wages had to be paid by the hour; labor had to generate revenue by the hour accordingly. Overtime rates were so costly that the avoidance of overtime became a factor in train scheduling. With the threat of nationalization in 1920[203]: "More ton miles per hour is the only salvation of the railroads." Even after the return to corporate operation, doctrine two years later was: "From the standpoint of locomotive efficiency, the main object to be attained is an increase of ton-miles per locomotive hour."[204]

Super-power design had, perhaps, more impact than any other single advance in steam locomotive technology. In 1925[205]:

We need and we have locomotives today that take the heavy "drag" freight at higher speeds without increasing but actually reducing fuel consumption. They are locomotives of great power and high efficiency. These locomotives start heavier trains, accelerate them quicker and pull them faster. They are properly called *super-power steam locomotives.*

Considering that engineers and managers had been thinking for decades that the steam locomotive had reached its limits, the performance of these new engines was astonishing.

Intense efforts to improve the speed and comfort of passenger service enabled the railroads to claw back some of their lost revenues in the mid–1930s. The new, diesel-powered unit trains of 1934–5 were an outstanding success, but steam fought back, responding, not only with the new 4-8-4 and 4-6-4 steam locomotives but also with rebuilds of existing power. Between 1914 and 1940 the Santa Fe reduced its passenger schedule between Chicago and the Pacific Coast by 24 hours, an astonishing feat, considering that it was still using the same basic technology.[206] It achieved this, not only with more powerful locomotives—including diesels, but also through improvements in passenger cars, braking systems, track, signaling and terminal facilities.

Some engineers were happy to oblige[207]:

Nerves and fear were not a part of Walter's baggage; nor was prudence. He had the throttle of the F6 Baltic[208] against the back curtain most of the trip and on a 55-mile an hour curve east of Le Claire, one side of the locomotive briefly took leave of the rails before coming back down with a resounding thump. Walter's reaction was a sly grin and a couple of "heh, hehs."

These faster and more powerful locomotives dragged behind them a vast fleet of aging freight cars, sometimes with disastrous results. In October 1941, the fifth car of a Grand Trunk Western freight, running at 60 miles per hour, derailed on a crossing at Lansing, Michigan; twenty-seven cars derailed and hit a station building, killing a newspaper boy and injuring thirteen people in a waiting room.[209]

All this would have been useless without strict management by superintendents and executives with decades of experience behind them. By 1940[210]:

The Grand Trunk Western has an overnight train from Chicago to Detroit that is popularly known as the "cuckoo train" for the reason that, if there is even so much as a few minutes delay in getting this train started, the supervisory officers are reported to "go cuckoo." … These important, high-speed freight trains are receiving just as much attention from railway operating officers, and the executives, too, as the fastest streamlined passenger trains. The days when the yardmaster or other local dignitary was permitted to hold trains until tonnage, power and a lot of other things suited his convenience are definitely over. Competitive service conditions have changed all that, and freight train schedules are now watched and supervised so carefully, that on some railroads, everyone up to and including the president knows very promptly if any of these important trains are delayed.

In the early 1940s, railroad executives were talking of multiple-unit diesel locomotives developing 10,000 horsepower and capable of speeds of 140 to 150 miles per hour; even conceptually, this was beyond the limits of steam power.

1.3.5 Track and Substructures

Improved locomotives were only one aspect of faster trains. Signaling systems, track maintenance, bridges, curves and gradients, the location and design of passing loops and locomotive and car maintenance, all had to be improved to increase train speeds.

Heavier trains needed heavier track. Rolling stock will damage itself unless the rail flexes slightly as train wheels pass over it; excessive flexure, however, leads to breakage of rails and joints. Heavier rail is not only stiffer than light rail, it provides more steel in the head of the rail to wear away before the rail has to be replaced.

In the 1890s, many of the railroads were still lightly built, reflecting their cash-strapped origins and their often difficult construction through sparsely populated country. The earliest American railroads used track made of timber rails surfaced with iron flat bar. This weak and unsatisfactory material was replaced with rolled-section iron rails but, even so, the strap rails continued in use in lightly trafficked areas into the 1890s.[211] Rolled-section iron rails weighing 56 pounds to the yard were common in 1870; in the next twenty-five years new track was laid and old track was replaced with steel rails increasing in weight to 60, 65, 70, 75, 80 and 90 pounds to the yard. By 1893, the New Haven and the Pennsylvania were using 100-pound rail.[212]

Track will distort unless the ties lie in a bed of ballast, consisting of coarse gravel, cinders or crushed slag. Many of the early railroads were thrown down on the bare formation without ballast: ballasting was a part of ongoing track improvement.

Timber trestles were vulnerable to fire, rot and washouts and were backfilled or replaced by steel bridges over the years, as and when the railroads could afford to do so.

In 1905, 50,000 pounds was the commonly accepted maximum axle load in the U.S. By 1915, Mikado locomotives were being produced in quantity with axle loads of 57,000 pounds; the Pennsylvania was running 4-4-2s with axle loads of 66,500 pounds; the Philadelphia & Reading was building others of this wheel arrangement with axle loads of 73,000 pounds. Gigantic locomotives and massive trains depended on the continual upgrading of track and substructures.

In the early 1900s, railroads were replacing 65-pound rail, typical of original construction in the 1880s, with the stiffer 80-pound rail.[213] Apart from cost, the introduction of heavier rail was inhibited by the difficulty of producing steel of adequate quality in the heavier sections. The new, heavy rail sections showed a worse breakage rate than the older, lighter ones, indicative of manufacturing problems. The pressure of traffic in 1906–7 showed up in derailments due to defects of track—the 1,528 derailments in 1906 were three times the number of derailments from that cause in 1902. Between 1902 and 1911, 10,797 derailments due to defective track killed 106 people.[214]

Ninety-pound rail remained the most common. By 1912, only 13% of U.S. railroad mileage was of heavier rail; 70 to 90-pound rail made up 55% of mileage, with 31% less than 70 pounds.[215]

This timber trestle on the Tionesta Valley line was still supporting the weight of 2-6-0, No. 10, built by Alco in 1904, as late as June 14, 1941 (Denver Public Library, Robert W. Richardson Collection, RR-1508).

Massive locomotives, such as this Union Pacific class FEF-2 4-8-4, No. 823, built by Alco in 1939, photographed near Ogden, Utah, on July 5, 1949, needed equally massive sub-structures; contrast with the ramshackle timber trestle shown in the previous photograph (Denver Public Library, Otto C. Perry collection, OP-17644).

The coal and ore haulers were the first to introduce really heavy rail. In 1915, the Pennsylvania designed its own 125-pound rail section and began to order it from steel mills. The Lehigh Valley started using its proprietary 136-pound section the same year. The Chesapeake & Ohio and the Pennsylvania introduced 130-pound rail in 1916, the Bessemer & Lake Erie in 1917, the Norfolk & Western in 1918. The Central of New Jersey used 135-pound rail to accommodate wear on heavily used curves.[216] In 1921 8,800 miles of the Class I railroads used rail heavier than 100 pounds per yard, including 2,650 miles of 130-pound rail; by 1929 this had increased to 38,400, including 14,750 miles with 130-pound rail.[217] The Delaware, Lackawanna & Western's standard rail weight was 105 pounds, but it began laying 130-pound rail in 1925; between then and 1932, it put down 93,000 tons, equivalent to 400 track miles, nearly half its mileage.[218] Western railroads without the heavy coal traffic standardized on lighter rail, 110 pounds per yard being standard on the Santa Fe in the 1930s.[219]

American railroad engineers worked on both sides of the interaction between locomotives and track. Especially in the 1930s, improved design resulted in engines that were heavier than before, but exerted less dynamic augment. (Dynamic augment was the cyclic increase in the locomotive's apparent weight resulting from unbalanced rotating masses.) The Americans were less willing than the Europeans to accept civil engineering limitations on axle loadings. The French railroads limited axle loadings to 41,000 pounds, while British railroad civil engineering departments vetoed some locomotive designs because they were too heavy for the track. The enormous weight, and hence tractive effort, of American locomotives and the immense tonnages they were able to pull went back to their high axle loadings. Even so, in the 1920s some American locomotives were

built without such innovations as stokers, feed water heaters and boosters so as to stay within weight limits.[220]

In 1930, the Pennsylvania announced the first use of 152-pound rail, probably the heaviest section ever used on a mainline railroad.[221] The company considered that existing 130-pound rail would withstand 80,000-pound axle loads at 80 miles per hour; the new rail, designed in cooperation with U.S. Steel and Bethlehem, was to support 100,000-pound axle loads at 100 miles per hour—such were the new expectations of train speeds.

1.3.6 Signaling Systems

When trains were infrequent, light and slow, they could run in opposite directions on single-track lines with only passing loops and timetables to avoid collisions. In 1844 Samuel Morse used the Baltimore & Ohio Railroad to install a telegraph line between Baltimore and Washington; railroads and the telegraph system were symbiotic.[222] In 1851, Charles Minot, Superintendent of the New York & Erie, made the first—albeit *impromptu*—use of a telegraph to control train movements. This became a universal system of train control by dispatchers, linked by telegraph and issuing written train orders to be picked up by enginemen. The system worked well enough most of the time but became increasingly error-prone with increasing traffic density; it is surprising that it worked as well as it did.[223] In the 1890s American railroads were introducing block signaling systems, which allowed only one train at a time in a section or "block" of track. Automatic block signals and electric color lights were in use on the Philadelphia & Reading and the Lehigh Valley as early as 1894.[224]

Increasing traffic density, especially in the northeast and around Chicago, demanded block signaling, both manual and automatic. Dense traffic and a necessarily dense signal network added to the demands on enginemen. By 1912, in the 114 miles of the Pennsylvania between Pittsburgh and Altoona, each engineman passed 1,800 signals, with a further 259 within Pittsburgh station limits. Bigger boilers obscured the engineer's view across the left front of the engine. The fireman became more important as a lookout on the left side of the engine, even as his task of shoveling coal became more arduous and took more of his time. Even with block signaling, fog, heavy rain or snow, darkness, drifting smoke and steam, system failure and crew inattention or incapacitation could all result in a train passing a stop signal and colliding with another train.

Automatic train control, designed to apply the brakes automatically if a locomotive passed a stop signal, was invented late in the nineteenth century, with more than 5,000 patents for such devices by 1920.[225] The first permanent installation in America was on the Boston Elevated Railway in 1899, followed by another on the Interborough Rapid Transit, New York, in 1903, and the Philadelphia Rapid Transit and the Hudson & Manhattan in 1908. The first mainline installations were on the Pennsylvania and the Chicago & Eastern Illinois in 1911, soon followed by the Burlington and the New York Central.[226] By the 1920s, the Chicago & Eastern Illinois had more experience with this technology than any other railroad and pronounced it to be a complete success, contributing to efficient traffic handling. In 1922, the ICC required forty-nine railroads to show cause why they should not install automatic train control by July 1, 1924.[227] In 1923, the Pennsylvania installed the first automatic cab signal as an adjunct to automatic train control, making the enginemen aware of signal indications, even if the trackside signals were obscured.[228]

The U.S. railroads could not have handled the volume of traffic that they did without these advances in traffic control.

1.3.7 Integrated Improvement Programs

Higher-performance locomotives were only one aspect of long-running, integrated programs to increase traffic capacity, requiring the investment of tens of millions of dollars.

In a single year, 1897–8, the Northern Pacific increased its average freight train payload by 45% from 182 tons to 264 tons, at the same time making significant improvements to its permanent way—209 miles relaid with 72-pound rail, and 10 miles of wooden trestles backfilled or replaced with steel bridges.[229] The same year, the company scrapped ninety-five of its 225 4-4-0s, decreasing its locomotive fleet from 582 to 547, and replaced them with forty-three new, heavier locomotives. The company also strengthened 5,586 freight cars, increasing their capacity from 40,000 pounds to 50,000.

Up to 1906, all Santa Fe traffic between the prairies and California had to go over the Raton Pass with grades up to 3.5%. Even with helpers, the maximum train weight was 1,000 tons. In that year, the company completed the Belen cut-off via Amarillo, bypassing the Raton altogether and providing a route of 928 miles from Belen, New Mexico, to Kansas City with no grades in excess of 0.6%, apart from a short helper grade of 1.2% near Belen. New 2-6-6-2 Mallets hauled 2,250-ton trains on this route at speeds up to 45 miles per hour.[230]

Between 1902 and 1915, the Erie spent $12 million on grade reduction on its New York division alone, reducing grades westbound from 1.5% to 1% and eastbound from 1.4% to 0.5%, at the same time replacing 2-8-0s of 25,000 pounds tractive effort with Mallets developing 58,000 pounds. These two measures combined to increase the maximum trailing load westbound from 520 tons to 1,812 tons, eastbound from 556 tons to 3,193 tons.[231] In the flatter terrain of the Susquehanna division, new 2-8-0s with 32,000 pounds tractive effort

This typical pre-1900 Northern Pacific 4-4-0 survived programs of scrapping older locomotives and was still in action when photographed at St. Paul, Minnesota, on July 30, 1934 (Denver Public Library, Otto C. Perry collection, OP-13897).

One of the Chicago, Burlington & Quincy's new 2-8-2s, class O-1, No. 5036, built by Baldwin in 1910–11, photographed at Denver, Colorado, on July 14, 1940 (Denver Public Library, Otto C. Perry collection, OP-3852).

One of the Norfolk & Western's class M-2 4-8-0s, No. 1148, built by Baldwin in 1910, photographed at Hagerstown, Maryland, on August 24, 1938. The locomotive behind is No. 547, a class E-2b 4-6-2, one of ten built at the company's shops in 1913–14 (Denver Public Library, Otto C. Perry collection, OP-13798).

replaced the lighter 2-8-0s just mentioned, increasing trailing loads eastbound from 2,642 tons to 3,812 tons and westbound from 1,941 tons to 3,071 tons.

The history of the Burlington between 1901 and 1912 illustrates the multi-faceted approach of an aggressive management to maintain profits in an increasingly hostile environment.[232] In that time freight ton-miles increased 98% for 10% fewer train-miles; payload per train increased from 200 tons to 438. The company spent large sums of money flattening grades and straightening curves on its most heavily used lines; flattening the ruling grade over the 331 miles between Centralia, Illinois, and Savanna from 1.2% to 0.3% allowed an increase in trailing load from 800 tons to 3,800. Great efforts to improve maintenance standards and keep freight cars moving achieved a daily freight car mileage of 32, compared to a national average of 24. The company bought new, high-capacity freight cars, scrapping the older ones; in 1901, the company owned 42,821 freight cars with an average capacity of 23 tons; in 1912, it owned 58,967 cars with an average capacity of 38 tons, more than doubling total capacity. In 1901, the company's most powerful engines were 2-8-0s with 38,000 pounds tractive effort and they were few in number; in 1910–11 the company added sixty 2-8-2s, each with a tractive effort of 60,000 pounds.

Between 1923 and 1925 the Norfolk & Western reballasted track, replaced ties, installed new 100-pound rail, strengthened bridges, lengthened passing loops and installed automatic block signaling on the 100 miles between Portsmouth, Ohio, and Cincinnati.[233] Following these improvements, Z-1a 2-6-6-2s and M-2 4-8-0s double-headed trains weighing up to 4,800 tons, reducing train time over the division by 22%, increasing ton-miles per train hour by 33% and saving 22% in fuel with no change to motive power.

The Southern Pacific main line from California to Oregon, completed in 1887, followed easy grades in the Sacramento and Willamette valleys but, between them lay 300 miles of sharp curves and heavy grades across east-west drainages. Toughest of all were the 3.3% grades over the Siskiyou Mountains between Ashland and Dunsmuir. Around 1920, a booster-equipped 2-10-2, developing 84,750 pounds of tractive effort, could haul only 625 tons over that stretch. To move a forty-eight-car train, four 2-10-2s were put on at Ashland for the 17 miles of 3.3% grade to Siskiyou Summit. There two engines were cut off; the other two took the train 59 miles to Snowden. One engine took the train across the Shasta valley; two were added for the 9 miles of 2.2% grade to Black Butte; one took the train down grade for 22 miles to Dunsmuir. This arrangement was so costly that, starting in 1923, the Southern Pacific spent $16 million on the 110-mile Natron cut-off between Kirk and Oakridge, and a further $8 million on flattening grades between Klamath Falls and Kirk and between Eugene and Oakridge and a new line between Weed and Grass Lake. Even this route required nineteen tunnels and could not avoid 1.8% grades over the Cascades, necessitating three 2-10-2s on a seventy-one-car train. Over the decades, civil engineering works became cheaper with mechanization, while locomotives, fuel and crews had become more expensive; grade reductions and realignments were economic in the 1920s that had not been so previously.

The Denver & Rio Grande Western was built in the 1870s and 1880s as a narrow-gauge line serving the then booming Colorado mining industry. Regauging, the decline of mining and the natural difficulties of operating in the Colorado mountains led to bankruptcy; in the mid–1920s the railroad reinvented itself as a through hauler between Denver and Salt Lake City. After trying to operate 534,000-pound Mallets and 2-10-2s with 70,000-pound axle loadings on worn, bent, 85-pound track, the company spent $27 million between 1925 and 1928 on wholesale upgrading of 780 miles of main line.[234]

A Norfolk & Western class Z-1a 2-6-6-2, No. 1472, one of a class built by Alco and Baldwin in 1912-18, being fired up with a draft inducer over the stack, photographed at Roanoke, Virginia, on August 3, 1936 (Denver Public Library, Otto C. Perry collection, OP-13808).

This train is stopped at Dunsmuir, California, on the Southern Pacific route through the Siskiyou Mountains on July 25, 1938. A class F-3 2-10-2, No. 3666, built by Baldwin in 1921, is the helper with the unidentified road engine behind it (Denver Public Library, Otto C. Perry collection, OP-15869).

Of this, $9 million went for new locomotives and rolling stock, but the program also comprised $1 million on ballasting, $2 million on new rail, $1.5 million on bridges, $2.3 million on new yard tracks and branch lines, $2.4 million on flattening and straightening alignments and the balance on signaling, shops and shop machinery, station buildings, eliminating grade crossings, repairing tunnels and other general improvements.

Coal was 80% of Chesapeake & Ohio freight, 31 million tons in 1922, doubling to 62 million tons in 1927, tapping coalfields in Ohio, West Virginia and Kentucky so successfully that net revenue increased from $20 million (20% of gross) in 1922 to $53 million (33% of gross) in 1929.[235] Rising demand justified massive investment in civil engineering works—including thirteen tunnels worth $10 million in 115 miles through the Alleghenies, a program started in 1923 and completed ten years later—and new rolling stock—284 new locomotives and 21,650 new freight cars. A new low-grade line to Toledo, Ohio, enabled a 2-8-8-2 to haul 12,500 tons, while one of the company's new 2-10-4s could handle 12,250 tons; 2-8-2s regularly handled 10,000 tons from Clifton Forge. These measures enabled the company to force down its fuel consumption from 122 pounds of coal per thousand gross ton-miles in 1924 to only 87 in 1929.

Responsibility for efficient operations lay firmly with management; conversely, it was remarkable what energetic management could achieve. Following a reorganization in 1916, the new management of the Gulf, Mobile & Northern achieved major improvements in several apparently unrelated areas. Coal consumption dropped 44% from 181 pounds of coal per thousand gross ton-miles in 1921 to 121 pounds in 1926 with only minor improvements to the locomotive fleet. Gross ton-miles per train hour increased 134% from 6,656 in 1920 to 15,589 in 1926. Engine failures totaled 104 in 1926, down

70% from 347 in 1924. Reportable accidents declined 74% between 1923 and 1926. All of these had beneficial effects on the company's balance sheet.[236]

By the end of the 1920s the railroad industry could look back on a decade of achievement; the following figures were nation-wide averages for the Class I railroads.[237] Freight train speeds increased 20% from 10.6 miles per hour in 1920 to 12.6 miles per hour in 1928; the tonnage in each train increased by 27%. Gross ton-miles per train hour increased 57%. Coal consumption per thousand ton-miles went down by 23% from 167 pounds in 1921 to 129 pounds in 1928; coal per passenger car mile went down by the same amount, from 19.5 pounds in 1920 to 15.2 pounds in 1928. Between 1920 and 1928, in spite of a 20% increase in ton-miles hauled, coal consumption declined absolutely by 14%, from 148 million tons in 1920 to 128 million tons in 1928. The railroads got more out of their ever more expensive labor; freight ton-miles per employee per year increased from 142,000 in 1906 to 234,000 in 1926 and 300,000 in 1929.

Between 1923 and 1929 the railroads spent six billion dollars on capital improvements of all kinds; planned capital expenditures for 1930 alone totaled $1.2 billion. These improvements included civil engineering works, electrification, multi-tracking, better track, better maintenance of infrastructure and rolling stock, better signaling and better terminal facilities; new locomotives were only one component among many. These programs were in full swing when the depression hit.

The relentless drive for efficiency in all aspects of railroad operations, not least the introduction of superpower locomotives, could produce remarkable results on a well-managed railroad. Norfolk & Western gross earnings were $105 million in 1925 and 1940; the two years were therefore directly comparable.[238] In spite of the depression,

The Denver & Rio Grande Western needed what the Mallets could deliver, such as this class L-96 2-8-8-2, No. 3404, built by Alco in 1913 and photographed on September 28, 1938, still in as-built compound configuration. Note the blast deflector on the stack, the enormous low-pressure cylinders with slide valves and the high-pressure cylinders with piston valves. The location of this photograph is not recorded, but the dual-gauge track on the left places it somewhere in the narrow-gauge territory of southern Colorado (Denver Public Library, Otto C. Perry collection, OP-10634).

This Denver & Rio Grande Western class F-81 2-10-2, No. 1402, was built by Alco in 1917, photographed near Helper, Utah, on April 14, 1939 (Denver Public Library, Otto C. Perry collection, OP-10216).

Part of the Chesapeake & Ohio's power upgrade in the late 1920s, this class T-1 2-10-4, No. 3022, came from Lima in 1930, photographed near Columbus, Ohio, on May 5, 1940 (Denver Public Library, Robert W. Richardson collection, RR-1203).

the company went on investing in improvements, totaling $150 million in that time—new rolling stock, expanded terminals and freight yards, heavier rail, better ballast, up-to-date signaling systems.[239] As a result, the company hauled 12% more gross ton-miles in 1940 than in 1925 with 47% fewer locomotives (347 vs. 653) of 47% higher average tractive effort (89,000 pounds vs. 61,000 pounds). These locomotives hauled 47% heavier freight trains (3,800 tons trailing load in 1940, up from 2,600 tons in 1925) 25% faster, producing 80% more gross ton-miles per train hour. Fuel consumption was down 39% from 147 pounds per thousand gross ton-miles to 89. Maintenance had so improved that miles run per locomotive failure were up 230% to 115,000 miles from 35,000 in 1925, while the cost of locomotive repairs per mile and pound of tractive force was down 32%. As a result, in spite of all political and economic pressures, the company's net earnings were 18% higher in 1940 than in 1925.

In spite of the depression, the 1930s saw a revolution in the productivity of American railroads.[240] More powerful locomotives, better-designed cars, improved braking systems, stronger track and sub-structures, better signaling, more efficient switching, terminal plant capable of faster coaling, watering and ash handling and more efficient dispatching all played their part.[241] Average freight train speeds increased 60% from 10 miles per hour in 1920 to 16 miles per hour in 1936, at the same time as gross tonnage per train increased 29% from 1,443 tons in 1920 to 1,859 tons in 1936.[242] This combination doubled the gross ton-miles moved per train hour. Bigger engines played their part, evidenced by an increase in average locomotive tractive force from 41,000 pounds in 1920 to 55,000 pounds in 1936. The national average fuel consumption decreased from 172 pounds per thousand net ton-miles (197 pounds per thousand gross ton-miles) in 1920 to only 117 in 1938 (134 pounds per thousand gross ton-miles), declining still further to 120 pounds per thousand

gross ton-miles in 1946.[243] The vital statistic, gross ton-miles per freight train hour, first recorded in the mid–1920s, continued to climb all through the depression, from 20,000 in the mid–1920s to 34,000 by 1940, an increase of 70% in fifteen years. Freight train speeds flattened off at 16 or 17 miles per hour in the late 1940s, but increased to more than 18 miles per hour in the early 1950s—diesel-powered.[244]

1.3.8 Maintenance and Availability

The coal-burning steam locomotive must be one of the dirtiest machines ever invented. It showers itself with its own cinders thrown out from its exhaust. Its moving parts depend on generous lubrication but dust and grit picked up from the trackbed mix with lubricants to form a black, sticky mass. Parts exposed to the fire and flue gases become coated with soot and rust. Scale, sludge and corrosion form inside the boiler. The exterior is exposed to the weather. Pounding reciprocating parts and twisting, bending and vibration from irregularities in the track cause the locomotive to shake itself to pieces even as the violence of its internal functioning wears out its interior. Its ash pan must be emptied at frequent intervals and it must be replenished with fuel, water, lubricants and sand. Apart from appearance, if a locomotive is not cleaned, dirt abrades moving parts and conceals cracks and other damage. Servicing, cleaning and maintenance are critically important and consume much time and labor.

In the early days one, or at most two, crews operated each locomotive and took pride in keeping it clean and maintained. A passenger engine commonly ran for two years between major overhauls, running 100,000 miles in that time, while a freight engine might run eighteen months to two years between overhauls, covering 75,000 to 100,000 miles.[245] This system was replaced in the 1880s, through economic necessity and the pursuit of efficiency, by "pooling," whereby crews ran whatever locomotives were available. This change

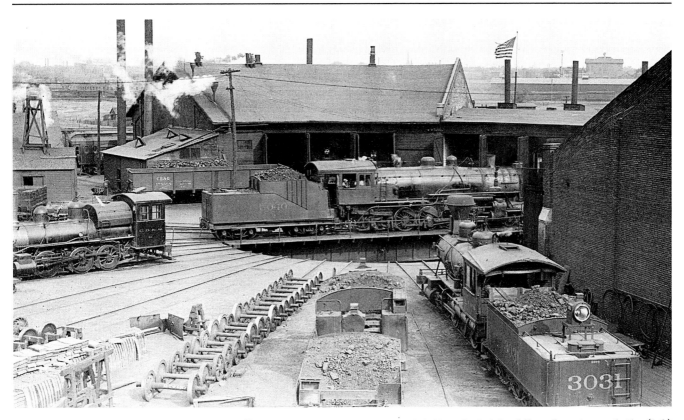

This is the Chicago, Burlington & Quincy roundhouse at Denver as it was in May 1918. Note the 0-6-0 saddle tank engine yard pilot (left) and a 2-8-2 that just fits on the turntable (center). No. 3031 (right) is a Baldwin 2-8-0, built in 1903 and bought from the Iowa & St. Louis (Drury, 106) (Denver Public Library, Otto C. Perry collection, OP-4882).

removed pride of ownership; by 1905, 75,000 miles between overhauls had become typical for passenger engines, 45,000 for freight engines. Pooling contributed to a depersonalized, alienated workforce.[246] Maintenance was given over to full-time roundhouse and shop crews; indeed, as locomotives became bigger—and more tiring to operate, it became increasingly impractical for their crews to maintain them as well as running them. After sixteen hours shoveling coal, few firemen were in any condition to clean or repair their engines. The 1913 arbitration award to firemen on railroads in the eastern United States specifically relieved them of the duty to clean engines.[247] The argument between assignment and pooling went on, however, and railroads that studied the matter found that assigned engines cost less to maintain and were more reliable in service than pooled engines.[248]

Locomotives were serviced between runs at terminals set up at the ends of the divisions on which they were stationed, comprising a roundhouse, plant for handling coal, water, sand, lubricants and ash, a backshop, inspection pits and storage tracks.[249] The roundhouse consisted of tracks arranged radially around a turntable. Shop facilities varied from company to company and place to place, ranging in capability from running repairs, through major overhauls and rebuilds, up to manufacturing complete locomotives. A shop with a single turntable would service 100 to 150 engines per day; twin-turntable roundhouses would service as many as 350 engines per day. The fifty-two-stall roundhouse built by the Pennsylvania at Altoona in 1902 was servicing 250 to 350 engines per day in 1915–20.[250]

Fast turnaround was a major economic objective. In 1914, the Rock Island found that a typical freight locomotive spent half its time being maintained and serviced, a further 17% standing under steam at terminals and only 29% of its time hauling freight.[251] In that time it ran

68 miles per day at an average speed of 10 miles per hour. By 1915–20, the handling of ash, coal and sand at the larger terminals was extensively mechanized; in 1917, the Philadelphia & Reading commissioned a plant at Philadelphia holding 2,000 tons of coal with space to fuel six locomotives at a time.[252] Engine wiping by hand was laborious and time-consuming; by 1918, the Delaware, Lackawanna & Western and the Erie were using compressed-air oil/water sprays to cut this time to 7 to 10 minutes, even for a large engine.[253] Non-moving parts were left with their coating of dirt.

By the early 1920s, cleanliness was at a low ebb; one Briton commented[254]:

> The engines and rolling stock would bring discredit upon any company in Britain. Dirt seems to be the watchword. Paint, soap and water are displaced by grime and rust, yet it is noteworthy that the engine drivers and firemen wear gloves at their work.[255] The running of the coaches, however, is much smoother than in England, due undoubtedly to the longer and heavier rolling stock.

Big engines cost more than their smaller predecessors and consequently wasted more money when idle. In the first decade of the twentieth century a locomotive cost $14,000-$17,000 to buy and $1,500-$3,000 per year to maintain. By 1913, a new 2-8-2 cost $23,000.[256] By 1915, this had increased to $25,000 to $30,000 for a big freight locomotive capable of generating $75 to $100 in revenue per hour hauling freight.[257] By 1919, prices had soared to $36,000 for a USRA switcher and $100,000 for a USRA heavy Mallet.[258] In 1937, locomotive prices ranged from $62,000 for an 0-6-0 switcher to $160,000 for the Southern Pacific's cab-forward 4-8-8-2s; a 4-8-4 cost $110,000 to $130,000.[259]

These capital investments had to be kept working. Even before the

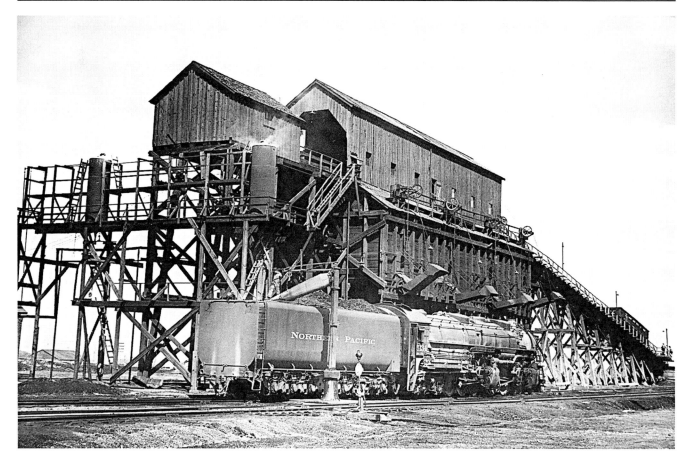

Coal-burning steam locomotives needed massive coaling plants which, themselves, had to be supplied with millions of tons of coal from the mines. This Northern Pacific class Z-8 4-6-6-4, No. 5134, built by Alco in 1943–4, is taking water at one such plant at Missoula, Montana, date unknown. This plant was built of timber; others, built of steel, are visible in other photographs in this book. Four coal chutes are visible above the locomotive, supplied by cars winched up the ramp to the right of the photograph. The cylindrical tank near the top of the plant may be a sand furnace (courtesy *Classic Trains* magazine collection, 20120712).

abnormal demands imposed by World War I, the scramble to move tonnage was already such that, on some railroads, every day was an emergency.[260] Managers demanded that every locomotive went out loaded to its maximum. Continuous maximum loading and pooling of engines drove up the cost of repairs and reduced a locomotive's availability for service.

Bigger engines had heavier parts, requiring increasing shop mechanization. Between 1897 and 1907, the railroads spent more than $80 million on repair shops and equipment, including seventy major shops across the country. Even so, maintenance facilities had difficulty keeping pace with the growing size and number of locomotives.[261] One frustrated railroadman wrote in 1916[262]:

Railway presidents and vice-presidents have got to be brought to realize that Mallet, Mikado and 2-10-2 type locomotives cannot be repaired in the same time and with the same tools that were used in repairing Eight-wheel and Mogul type locomotives 15 or 20 years ago.

"Fast turn-around was a major economic objective." A 1930s Milwaukee 4-6-4 being pressure-greased, using the locomotive's compressed-air system. Location and date unknown (courtesy *Classic Trains* magazine collection, 20121008).

The bigger railroads paid increased attention to the layout of back shops and the organization of shop work[263]; efficient management could control maintenance costs. The Santa Fe forced down the average annual repair cost per locomotive from $2,300 in 1905 to $1,600 in 1907, in spite of bigger locomotives, rising wages and materials costs and the severe service to which its engines were subjected. Between 1903 and 1912, the Pittsburgh & Lake Erie similarly reduced the cost of repairs from $1,936 per locomotive per year to $1,762.[264]

Not only were maintenance costs controlled by improving shop design and organization, but improvements in locomotive construction led to greater mileage between overhauls. ICC data from 1913 showed that the new, big engines cost less to maintain per ton-mile hauled than the smaller engines that they replaced.[265] On the Cleveland, Cincinnati, Chicago & St. Louis, a 4-6-2 ran for 200,580 miles with only minor repairs between November 1907, and December 1909. On the Santa Fe, a Baldwin 4-4-2 balanced compound ran for 227,900 miles from delivery to its first overhaul.[266] On the same railroad a similar engine was operated by the same crew for four years and five months, from the time it was new until its first overhaul after running 241,335 miles.[267] More normal figures at that time were 120,000 miles between overhauls for passenger engines and 95,000 miles for freight engines.[268]

Although bigger and more numerous locomotives were hauling heavier trains than before, the mileage run per locomotive per year declined by one fifth between 1903 and 1921.[269] In 1921, one railroad, operating 3,000 locomotives, expected them to run 22,000 miles a year, a marked decline from typical figures twenty years previously; this average had increased to 38,000 miles in 1944—still only midrange for the figures quoted for 1902. Industry analysts suspected that terminal facilities to ash out, replenish fuel, water and sand and carry out minor repairs and boiler washing had failed to keep pace with the maintenance demands of the new power. These facilities were notoriously neglected and the huge engines of 1920 were often maintained in cold, dark, wet, dirty, ill-ventilated shops built before 1900. Some railroads responded with major investments in new terminals; the Union Pacific built six new roundhouses and five new coaling plants and upgraded many of its other shops in a three-year program from 1917 to 1919.[270] In 1923, the company began a preventive maintenance program; by 1931, this program had produced 10% to 15% more locomotive miles per month, 80% more mileage between shoppings for general repairs and 100% more mileage per locomotive failure in service.[271]

Hot-water boiler washouts, direct steaming from stationary boilers, mechanical drafting during firing up, using an extractor fan placed over the stack, wheel drops, power tools, improved materials handling equipment, better lighting and ventilation and better coal and ash handling equipment were all features of the new locomotive terminals of the 1920s.[272] Improvements in maintenance and turn-around efficiency would continue as an unseen factor in the effectiveness of the American steam locomotive until the end of steam.

Obscure improvements had disproportionately large effects. Ash and clinker on the grates limited the length of engine runs on the Burlington to about 200 miles. Introduction of the Hulson shaking grate in 1922 extended this to more than 400 miles; longer engine runs between servicing released engines for other duties and cut out intermediate terminals.[273] Fuel was wasted every time the fire was replaced; with the Hulson grate the same fire could be kept burning for a week.

In the new conditions after World War I, the railroads realized that a typical freight locomotive cost 26 cents a minute when it was in steam, almost regardless of whether it was pulling a train or not.[274] Something like 21 cents a minute was fuel, yet typical utilization was

only 7 hours in the 24. By 1921, the U.S. locomotive fleet was burning 137 million tons of coal a year, 27% of total U.S. coal production.[275] The cost to the railroads was $595 million, or $4.35 a ton. Fuel made up 13% of the railroads' operating cost; 27 million tons per year, worth $119 million, was burned when locomotives were being fired up, awaiting assignment or disposal and standing in passing loops.

Longer engine runs between servicing were a feature of the 1920s, with a surprisingly wide range of effects.[276] Traditionally, a locomotive would run over a single division of 75 to 150 miles with a terminal at each end. A fresh locomotive and crew would take the train on over the next division. During the 1920s, several companies extended engine runs to 500 to 900 miles, changing crews as necessary, reaching extremes of 1,000 to 1,300 miles in Canada. Oil-burning locomotives were an advantage in this respect, having no need to ash out; in 1924, the Missouri-Kansas-Texas ran an oil-burning 4-6-2 with fifteen cars over the 872 miles from Franklin, Missouri, to San Antonio, Texas, bringing locomotive mileage up to 10,500 miles per month.[277]

Better manufacturing standards and design for maintainability made this possible. Other than mechanical failure, a steam locomotive had to drop its fire for four reasons: to clean the grates, to clear plugged fire tubes, to replace broken staybolts and to wash the boiler. The longer it could be kept in steam, the smaller the proportion of time lost in preparation and disposal, the less the damage caused by expansion and contraction of parts and the more miles the engine ran per month. As 15% to 30% of total fuel consumption was at terminals, the longer an engine could be kept on the road, the more fuel would be saved. Fewer engines were needed and intermediate terminals were closed down, to the regret of the obscure little towns where they were located.

The Union Pacific was a leader in this area, helped by non-clinkering, low-ash coal.[278] The key element for the Union Pacific was water treatment that lengthened the time between boiler washouts, even though the company operated in an area of notoriously bad water. For the whole system east of Ogden, Utah, water treatment doubled the service life of fireboxes from sixty-eight months (average 188,000 miles run) in 1916 to 121 months (average 284,000 miles run) in 1923. For switch engines at fixed locations, such as North Platte and Grand Island, Nebraska, water treatment increased flue life from 7 or 8 months to four times that duration.

By 1928, the Missouri Pacific was running locomotives up to 485 miles between servicings, cutting out intermediate terminals with large savings in fuel, labor and the number of engines used.[279] Some railroads with access to non-clinkering coal, achieved this to an extreme degree.[280] In 1929, the St. Louis & San Francisco ran a 2-8-2 for 587 hours and 7,350 miles on the same fire; at the end of that time the engine was found to have nothing worse than an accumulation of cinders in the combustion chamber, four plugged fire tubes and one leaking staybolt. The same year the Rock Island ran a coal-burning 4-8-2 for 1,000 miles between Chicago and Limon, Colorado, on one fire. By 1930, the Denver & Rio Grande Western was running individual passenger locomotives 754 miles between Denver and Salt Lake City.[281]

In December 1937, a Santa Fe oil-burning 4-6-4 ran 2,227 miles from Los Angeles to Chicago.[282] By 1943, this was standard practice[283]; Santa Fe passenger trains ran between Chicago and Los Angeles in 48 hours, using only two locomotives, changing at Kansas City; previously, the company needed fifteen locomotives and the journey took 70 hours. Diesel locomotives reduced this to one locomotive and 40 hours with fourteen crews.

In 1897, the Chicago & North Western expected a locomotive to run 36,000 miles a year. In 1902, locomotives on twenty-three major U.S. railroads averaged 41,400 miles per year,[284] ranging from 58,931 miles on the Missouri, Kansas & Texas down to 30,050 miles on the Norfolk & Western. By 1932, locomotive construction, maintenance and scheduling had so far advanced that, when the New York Central put a new 4-6-4 into service in October 1931, it ran 98,900 miles in its first seven months of use, including 16,900 miles in the month of May 1932, alone.[285] This prodigy was not typical of the locomotive fleet as a whole. J. R. Macken of the Canadian Pacific reckoned in 1940 that 25% to 30% of the locomotive fleet handled 50% to 60% of total locomotive mileage.[286] The other 70% to 75% of the fleet seldom exceeded 30,000 to 40,000 miles per year. This figure was affected markedly by economic conditions and, in some parts of North America, by crop yields. Seven Canadian Pacific 2-8-2s averaged 55,000 miles each in 1928, a year of good harvest and a booming economy, falling to only 27,000 miles in 1931–1933 which were years of economic depression and poor harvests.

Even though the railroads bought fewer new locomotives during the depression than at any time in living memory, the engines that were built were both more powerful and easier to maintain than their predecessors. One company compared 4-8-2s built in 1921–3 with 4-8-4s built in 1931–8. The differences in dimensions were slight; the difference lay in the monthly mileage made by each locomotive and the miles between overhaul. The 4-8-2s recorded 4,100 miles and 125,000 to 166,000 miles, respectively; the 4-8-4s averaged 6,900 miles, up 70%, and 183,000 to 235,000 miles, up 50%. The last steam locomotives, built in the 1940s, ran 250,000 miles a year.

Individual diesel-electrics ran as much as 390,000 miles in a single year.

In the later years of steam, improvements in maintenance and availability were a real—if obscure—revolution in American railroading.

1.3.9 Working Conditions

Central to this industry were the men who ran the steam locomotives. Their dedication to their work was total, transcending all other considerations.

> He spent the weekend with his family, who were pleased that he had been promoted, because they knew he was pursuing a career he liked. However, it turned out to be a different matter when he informed his bride-to-be of his promotion. She was pleased that he was now an engineer, but she refused to get married and accompany him to Williamsport. She wanted to stay at home on the farm and wait until he got a job in Bellefonte again. O.P. tried to explain that he wouldn't be able to return to the area for quite a while, but this attempt was futile. It almost seemed, he thought, that she was giving him a choice: Either take me or go to Williamsport as an engineer.

O.P. went to Williamsport.[287]

European engine crews were a stable, highly trained and plentiful workforce with a slow progression through skill grades from engine cleaner to express passenger driver that might take a lifetime. In America, a man could walk in off the street and, provided he could

One of 161 Canadian Pacific class N-3 2-8-0s built between 1909 and 1914, with its two-man crew of engineer and fireman, at Revelstoke about 1914. 2-8-0 locomotives in their thousands, and engine men in their tens of thousands, provided the backbone of North American freight haulage for fifty years. The crew shown faced some of the toughest railroading conditions in North America in the mountains of British Columbia (Revelstoke Museum and Archives, photograph #1344 Engine 3868).

The fireman's task: over the years, hundreds of millions of tons of coal went into locomotive fireboxes in this way. This photograph, taken in 1905, shows a fireman firing a small switching locomotive. Doing the job efficiently was not as simple as it looks and demanded years of experience. The engineer's seat and controls are on the right. The fireman's seat is on the left. The fireman's job was also the learner position to become an engineer (Smithsonian Institution Archives, image #MAH-48190F).

The engineer's task was a demanding one, requiring long hours of constant alertness at all hours of the day and night and in all weathers, learned only by years of experience (courtesy Catskill Archive).

convince the road foreman that he had usable experience, could go out on an engine that same night.

> I'll never forget the first trip I made as an oil burner fireman. It so happened that I got out on my first trip with a young engineer who had just

been set up, and he was making his first trip as an engineer, and to make things all the worse, we caught an old tramp engine which should have been in the back shop being overhauled instead of trying to pull a train over the mountains....

> Well we started out and the young hogger was a little bit nervous and excited, but he did not have anything on me, for this was one time that the old boomer did not seem to just fit in somehow or other, for I did not know just where to grab a hold at, for there were so many little valves to be twisted, turned and set ... and all in all there were so many little doodads to fool around with that it kept me guessing where to grab next.[288]

The engine was a 2-10-2 on the Santa Fe, working out of Needles, California, in December 1909.

Train crews worked long hours, at all times of the day and night, all days of the week. One Pennsylvania freight train crew—in 1904—decided to work non-stop for a week, sleeping in the caboose between trips. The fireman had to watch the engine and wake the rest of the crew when their next train was ready; he got less rest than anyone else.

> On the seventh day, while traveling down the main to Enola, O. P. began to feel odd. Although he was wide awake, he couldn't coordinate his body's motions. It took desperate concentration for him to push a shovelful of coal through the fire door. When the train was spotted on the assigned track in the Enola yard and the engine was placed on the pit, O. P. removed his traveling bag from the bulkhead and announced to the engineer that all the trips were over. He was marking off.[289]

Life was easier most of the time.

> Payday was once every month, and as a fireman Oscar averaged nearly $75 a month—a small fortune to a young man who was enjoying his work. Eight to twelve hours a day completed most runs.

Problems could stretch a trip—in one instance to as long as 70 hours to cover 100 miles.

In the more settled conditions of the eastern U.S. after 1900, the "boomer" railroadman was disappearing, replaced by the long-serving (and unionized) company employee, his pay and working conditions negotiated by increasingly powerful unions backed by a growing body of Federal legislation. In 1909, the Pennsylvania employed 4,800 engineers; averaging 44 years of age with 21 years of service, appointed engineer at age 31. The company was paying pensions to 134 enginemen whose average age was 72.[290] In 1914, the Pennsylvania had seventy-seven employees with more than fifty years of service each, including two who had worked for the company for more than fifty-six years.[291] Labor conditions varied from region to region, however. On the Missouri, Kansas & Texas in 1913:

This is the type of engine that Charles P. Brown ("Brownie the Boomer") worked on out of Needles, California, in 1909, an Atchison, Topeka & Santa Fe, 1600 class, 2-10-2 tandem compound. This one, No. 1601, was built by Baldwin in 1905 and photographed at Raton, New Mexico, in 1920 (Denver Public Library, Otto C. Perry collection, OP-494).

With a business that varies so widely in volume as between different seasons, the M. K. & T. in Texas is to a certain extent at the mercy of a floating class of very undesirable employees.[292]

Out West, the railroads had to take what labor they could find:

Because the Tonopah & Tidewater (Nevada) was a desert road, it was difficult to get (let alone keep) the engine crews, and the men knew it well. Consequently the train and engine crews became an independent lot and virtually ran the road to suit themselves. "Rule G" was frequently violated, and many stories circulated of engine crews famous for bringing their train into Beatty purely because the flanged wheel followed the steel rail.

One crew arrived in Beatty so drunk that the engineer ran the locomotive off the end of the track while going for water. The crew managed to rerail the engine, but the fireman fell off the tender while filling the tank. The engineer then collided with the train, demolishing a flat car in the process.

The train was "a little late" leaving town, but for the passengers standing on the platform, the free show had been ample recompense for the delay.[293]

When engine crews were running heavy locomotives and trains at high speeds, crew ergonomics took on an increasing importance. As early as 1905, the Traveling Engineers' Association called for numerous improvements to locomotive cabs and controls.[294] Many of these improvements were small, but significant in total: design of the cab roof and windows to provide better shelter in bad weather, windows giving a clear view ahead and to the top of the stack, convenient placement of controls, pneumatic bell ringers and sanders, pedal-operated pneumatic fire doors that closed automatically, tenders designed so that the motion of the engine would shake the coal forward, shielding of the fire door so that the glare of the fire would not blind the engineer at night and ash pans that could be dumped without the fireman

having to go under the engine. This last was such a safety issue that it was eventually legislated.

Another issue was the high-intensity electric headlight. Fought out for years between the railroads and the unions, with crew men taking both sides and facing union intimidation, the ICC ruled that, effective July 1, 1917, a locomotive had to be equipped with a headlight powerful enough that the engineer could see a dark-clad man standing at a distance of 800 feet on a clear night.[295] Many crew men complained that, on a multi-track railroad with dense traffic, the headlight of an oncoming locomotive blinded them and made it difficult to see signals. Noticeable in the photographs in this book are the enormous kerosene headlights of early years, as late as 1903–05, displaced by smaller acetylene lights about 1912, and, increasingly after about 1906, by the even smaller electric lights, powered by an electric generator or batteries.[296]

Even though a federal law passed in 1907, limiting enginemen's working hours to sixteen without rest, enginemen's work was still arduous. In the 1920s[297]:

The trip back to Denver (from Cheyenne) also took sixteen hours, with stops along the way to shunt cars into sidings, set out empties, and pick up loaded cars while the fireman shoveled twenty-four tons of coal, took on coal and water, cleaned the fire and dumped the ashes. The fireman's job on the North End (of the Colorado & Southern) was so tough that eighteen of the twenty men hired in the fall quit by spring.

One exhausted fireman sat down on the sidewalk between the roundhouse and his lodgings, only to be accosted by a policeman.

"Let me give you some advice," he said, as we walked along Fifteenth Street. "I put in a few trips as a fireman on the C & S before I got smart and quit. You ought to quit too. It's a killer job." Poking me again with his stick, he said, "Say, I could put in a word for you at the police department. It's a lot easier." I thanked him and said I would probably stick with railroading.

A Colorado & Southern 600 class 2-8-0 of the type worked on by Sam Speas in Margaret Coel's book, *Goin' Railroading*. No. 600 was built at Rhode Island in 1901, photographed at Denver, Colorado, on January 18, 1921 (Denver Public Library, Otto C. Perry collection, OP-6604).

It is difficult to escape the reflection that some railroad managements were unworthy of the loyalty that their employees gave them.

Plenty of engineers welcomed the easier working conditions on the diesels, but not all.[298]

> I've rode those old steam engines sometime above 80 miles an hour. They ruined the whole works when they took my steam locomotive away from me. The romance of railroading was gone. No, the diesel's all right as far as…. But to me, I told them when I started runnin' the diesels, I said, "Well, I could have got a job a-runnin'a streetcar forty years ago."
>
> I can recall meeting Red Standefer, him sitting in his chair in the living room, listening to deafening steam locomotive sounds from the stereo, and a shop drawing of a Mountain was behind Red on the wall. And the sound was turned up all the way because C. W. Standefer had sacrificed his hearing to his job and his love for the steam locomotive. He loved that sound as it was music to his ears.

Many others felt this way[299]:

> having a locomotive at your command exceeded any other excitement there could ever be. The romance of railroading in those times (c.1940) was stupendous and inconceivable. As engineer Lee Nelms once said to me, "a good engine is like a good woman, you pet 'em, you pamper 'em and treat 'em nice and they'll do anything for you." … When the diesels replaced the steam locomotives, Lee faded out; diesels held no romance for him and it was not long before he took his pension.
>
> In retrospect, the coming of the diesel meant that working conditions were so much better than with steam locomotives. The skill that steam required from an engineer is gone, as well as the lonely wail of the far off steam whistle that once could be heard across the land. We have lost much of our heritage, but that is part of progress.

From another life-long railroadman[300]:

> My experience spans the best and the worst of the world of steam and diesel. I saw the death of the great beasts of fire, smoke and steam and then the advent of the "stink buggy." The old steamers are gone now … no more of their sharp, staccato exhaust barking their way through the rocky canyons … no more proud plumes of smoke blasting and blackening the eternal blue sky, or shining silver-white under a frosty moon.
>
> If you never fired or ran a steam engine, or even rode on one, you will never know the thrill of being a part of those sounds, scents and motion. I can still feel the wind whipping around me, and the sensation of those mighty drivers pounding, reeling off the miles.
>
> What a sad, mournful thing to see them go, those great, black and silver monsters, fire breathing dragons, with personalities all their own. Steam locomotives were responsive to your touch and feel, one developed a kinship and affection for them .. they are gone now, and they will never return. To hell with progress!

The British fascination with steam locomotives is well known, so perhaps a last word can come from a British Railways fireman[301]:

> To me the fascination of railways began and ended with steam locomotives. Take away these and there was very little left….
>
> Looking back over those nine years one is bound to ask the question—was it all worthwhile? The tremendous physical strain, the acquisition of a vast amont of specialized knowledge, the dirt, the privations, the battle with the elements, being roasted, soaked or frozen and, above all else, the long hours of working all round the clock.
>
> The answer always comes out the same. Yes, it most certainly was…. Few other occupations offered the same excitement, satisfaction and sense of achievement as that of operating a steam locomotive, and added to this was the wonderful spirit of comradeship that existed on the footplate. Furthermore, the work developed an iron self-discipline that, once acquired, stood one in good stead for the rest of one's life."

1.3.10 Safety

Steam locomotive crewmen ran the continual risk of sudden and violent injury or death.[302]

This wreck on the Northern Pacific on August 11, 1908, near Glendive, Montana, was due to a burned-out trestle. The fireman and a tramp were killed; the engineer survived; thirty passengers were injured (Denver Public Library, Ogden collection, Z-5913).

In the late nineteenth century, that era of non-existent safety standards, railroading in the U.S. was more dangerous than other, obviously dangerous industries, such as mining. In 1893, 2,727 American railroad employees were killed out of 873,602 employed—3.1 fatalities per thousand employees. This compared to a fatality rate of 1.3 per thousand employees in the notoriously dangerous British coalmining industry of that time, 5.2 per thousand on British merchant sailing ships.[303] The economic recovery of the late 1890s brought an increased number of accidents with increased traffic, but also some signs that the accident rate was being brought under control.[304]

Collisions, derailments, bridge collapses, landslides, floods, wandering livestock and brake or coupler failures caused 24,700 accidents between 1873 and 1898.[305] This does not include accidents on railroads other than common carriers. Most accidents had nothing to do with the type of motive power. Fifty three percent of the fatalities on American railroads between 1890 and 1909 were neither train crews nor passengers, but trespassers walking on the track or stealing rides on trains.[306] Of all the accidents between 1873 and 1898, only 2% were attributable to the steam locomotive as such, mostly boiler explosions and breaking side rods.

Boiler explosions are discussed elsewhere in this book, but broken side rods were another inherent danger of the steam locomotive. The flailing ends often derailed the engine, pierced the boiler, wrecked one side of the cab and injured the crew. This was a dangerous occurrence because it usually happened with no warning when the engine was running at speed.

11th March (1893) on Delaware, Lackawanna & Western, near Moscow, Pennsylvania, the engine of a passenger train was damaged by the breaking of a parallel rod, the boiler being ruptured. The escaping steam

forced the three men in the cab to jump off, and they were badly injured.[307]

The steam locomotive was a source of danger in a wreck. Boiler explosions in the wreck were surprisingly rare, but not unknown, but locomotive fires often set fire to combustible wreckage; escaping steam was a hazard to anyone nearby; the cab of a steam locomotive was a bad place to be in a wreck.

Prosperous times put increasing loads on old, light rail and rotting ties; trackmen were in short supply; with deteriorating economics, the railroads skimped on track maintenance. The annual total of derailments almost doubled from 1909 to 1913, with an especially rapid increase from 1911 to 1913.[308]

During the boom years, especially between 1900 and 1907, the demand for labor was so great that men with minimal experience were put into responsible positions, working long and irregular hours, resulting in serious accidents. Management and labor were equally responsible: management needed the work done; the men were eager for the pay that resulted.[309] Train crews and dispatchers worked almost continuously for days on end until they fell asleep on the job.

On the Central of New Jersey, December 28 (1892), there was a considerable freight wreck, which resulted from a rear collision caused by an engineman going to sleep on his engine, and sleeping so soundly that a brakeman's lantern thrown into the cab window did not disturb him. His defense, as reported in the papers, was that he had been on duty for 30 hours continuously.[310]

On April 2, 1905, on the Southern Railway, a freight train and a passenger train collided at 4 a.m. in dense fog at Branchville, South Carolina, killing both engine crews. The crew of the freight engine had been without sleep for 40 hours and without food for 30 hours.[311]

This and similar accidents were among the reasons behind the 16-Hour Law of 1907.

Confusion in failing to follow written train orders continued as a fertile source of collisions. Block signaling was supposed to alleviate this problem, but the engineer of a fast-moving locomotive often had very little time in which to spot a signal that could be obscured by fog, snow or drifting steam. Disastrous collisions resulted.

No amount of legislation ever defeated what would be called "pilot error" today. Heavier, faster trains were more difficult to stop; the problem became more dangerous and attracted more public attention. Investigation of the disastrous July 1911, derailment on the New Haven at Bridgeport, New York, showed that the train had gone through a crossover at four times the maximum permitted speed. As both enginemen were killed, no one ever knew their physical or mental condition at the time of the accident.[312]

Improved safety programs resulted in a lower fatal accident rate in 1915 than any year since 1900, even though the railroads were carrying twice the volume of freight and passengers.[313] Rigorous routine and surprise checks on employees to test for knowledge and compliance with rules, signals and operating procedures contributed to this. In 1915 the Pennsylvania carried out 4.4 million such checks; 1915 was the Pennsylvania's third successive year with no passengers being killed in train accidents.[314] Even so, the total number of accidents on U.S. railroads was still large—4,770 collisions and 7,904 derailments in the year ending June 30, 1916, causing $10 million in damage and repair costs, 180,375 injuries and 9,364 fatalities.[315]

The engineman's task demanded ceaseless vigilance and the ability to react instantaneously to sudden emergencies. One engineer on the Pennsylvania related in 1913[316]:

The sub-conscious mind (or instinct) should be trained to act promptly. While running about 35 miles an hour with a heavy passenger train on a dark night, I ran through a boxcar that had been derailed on the adjoining track and had fallen in my path. This was on the Horse Shoe curve. From the time the pilot struck, until the cab of the engine struck was about ½ second; in that time I shut the throttle, applied air brake, opened sand valve, reversed engine, jumped down behind boiler and whistled brakes for the second engine. We stopped in a little over 130 ft., as we were going up hill. As I had no warning I could not have thought and acted so quickly; neither could the other engineman have done his part, if it were not a part of a runner's nature to be eternally on the lookout for trouble—trouble which we don't want to find.

Another on the Burlington[317]:

I saved trains from collision by noticing the reflection of a headlight on the outside rail of a left hand curve round a high bluff. An instantaneous thought flashed the conviction that nothing but a headlight could make light enough to cause a reflection so strong, in such a place; and the result was the escape from a very bad head end collision. ...

I noticed, on my going trip, that a stone quarry was shut down and not working. On my return trip I saw smoke just where the quarry was located about a mile ahead from where I was, the quarry being around a curve. Instantly I knew that something was wrong and immediately stopped my train. Before I had fully stopped I could see an approaching freight train, through a break in the timber; and before they had rounded the curve I had my train backed up about half a mile to a place of safety.

Truly[318]:

Modern railroading, the 200-ton engines, steel cars, and automatic signals have changed conditions very materially. It is now, more than ever, a serious business, especially on the head-end of an express train.

This wreck on the Denver & Rio Grande resulted from a head-on collision near Petersburg, Colorado, on July 17, 1916 (Denver Public Library, Otto C. Perry collection, OP-11090).

The crew would be lucky to survive a wreck such as this on the Denver & Rio Grande Western, East Portal, Colorado, July 13, 1941 (Denver Public Library, Otto C. Perry collection, OP-11099).

From the dismal accident record of the 1890s, railroad safety became a decades-long national campaign. In 1931, the Santa Fe considered it newsworthy that no employee had been killed for eighty-five days; in 1912 an average of thirty-three employees would have been killed in that time.[319] Fewer people were killed in railroad accidents in 1932 than in any year since 1888, in spite of large increases in traffic.[320] The railroads could look back on a remarkable improvement in safety in thirty years.[321] In 1900–04 the chances of getting killed were 1 in 384 for railroad employees generally, 1 in 130 for trainmen, 1 in 1,987,000 for passengers; by 1934 this had improved to 1 in 1,821, 1 in 743 and 1 in 12,582,000 respectively.[322]

Haste made waste in the rush of World War II traffic, often worked by inexperienced new employees; high train speeds increased the dangers of inexperience and meant that accidents, if rare, were often disastrous.[323] No matter how diligent and experienced they might be, the engine crews always faced the possibility of sudden and violent death; in June 1940, two enginemen were killed when their locomotive derailed near Farmingdale, New Jersey, where heavy rain had washed the track out.[324]

Thirty people died when the New York Central's *Lake Shore* express derailed at 60 miles per hour on a curve in April 1940[325]; five died a year later when saboteurs derailed a Pennsylvania train traveling at a similar speed.[326] In August 1943, a Delaware, Lackawanna & Western 4-6-4, traveling at 70 miles per hour, clipped a freight engine on a switch and overturned; steam from the damaged freight engine killed twenty-seven passengers.[327] Seventy-five passengers were killed and 187 passengers and employees injured in December 1943, when a diesel-hauled Atlantic Coast Line train derailed on a broken rail at 85 miles per hour and another train, also moving at about 80 miles per hour, hit the derailed cars.[328] Investigators estimated that the Santa Fe's *Chief* was doing 90 miles per hour

behind a 4-8-4 when it derailed on a curve with a speed limit of 55 miles per hour one night in July 1944, killing three people and injuring 126.[329] The train was 37 minutes late; the engineer was trying to make up time and had no means of knowing the speed restriction on the curve.

It is not clear what role the new diesels played in improving railroad safety, but improve it did, regardless of motive power. No hazard of diesel or electric locomotives was as dangerous as a steam locomotive boiler explosion. All things pointed to the diesel; safety was one of them.

1.3.11 The Motive Power Dilemma and the End of Steam

The depression caught the railroads partway through modernization programs with insufficient numbers of the new locomotives and an aging and increasingly obsolete fleet of pre-existing engines.

In 1934, W. H. Winterrowd, having moved from Lima to a vice-president position with Franklin, commented[330]:

> There may be reasons for such a situation where approximately 60 per cent of the locomotives are over 20 years of age, but such a condition cannot continue indefinitely. There will come a time when locomotive replacements are imperative and when that time comes the replacements should be of such a kind that the investment will produce the maximum return to the purchaser.

The time would come, indeed, but the replacements would not be steam-powered.

In the mid–1930s Westinghouse Electric appointed an engineer, Charles Kerr, jr., specifically to study and develop the company's transportation business. In February 1936, Kerr presented a paper to the New York Railroad Club that shone a brilliant, cold light on

This photograph, taken on August 16, 1940, on the Chicago, Burlington & Quincy at St. Louis, Missouri, goes far to illustrate the railroads' motive power dilemma. The steam locomotive in the foreground is a class S-2 4-6-2, No. 2914, built by Baldwin in 1910, now thirty years old, although retrofitted with an Elesco feed water heater and possibly other upgrades. Traffic conditions result in inefficient underloading with only two cars; meanwhile, at least seven other steam locomotives are awaiting assignment, burning coal and doing nothing. In the background is the train of the future, a diesel-powered unit train (Denver Public Library, Otto C. Perry collection, OP-4208).

the whole transportation issue.[331] Some of his audience may have dismissed him as an arrogant whippersnapper; others more percipient may have felt a profound unease. Westinghouse had nothing to do with the steam locomotive, everything to do with its alternatives, whether diesel engines with electric drive or electric locomotives as such. Westinghouse did have a vested interest in rail transportation, as neither the automotive nor the aircraft industries used heavy electrical equipment as a significant portion of the vehicle's total weight or cost. Kerr coldly informed those who had devoted their lives to the steam locomotive of the changes that were about to overtake them. The steam locomotive in America had ten years to live.

Kerr led off, in management-speak recognizable today:

> The favorable reception accorded to non-rail transport agencies can be traced to the fact that they have brought to the transportation field certain new concepts of comfort, convenience and service. We feel confident that the railroads can meet this competition and that by doing so they will continue to be the dominant form of transport for some 75–80 per cent of the ton miles moved in this country. However, they can only maintain this ratio by providing standards of comfort, speed and service never approached in the past. When this fact is fully appreciated, we may look for these developments to take place at an accelerated pace commensurate with the present accelerated pace of all mechanical developments.

Here was an engineer, not a railroadman, telling railroad executives that their current troubles were their own fault. He had the further insolence to tell them what they had to do about it. Executives who

had spent millions installing 130-pound rail were now being told they had to provide better facilities for ladies to powder their noses.

> The elements of this improved rail service will be many, among which are air conditioning, improved conveniences, easier riding vehicles, better roadbeds, etc. But however extensive these may be, they will not completely provide the standard of transportation demanded by the American public unless they be accompanied by greatly increased speeds, both passenger and freight.

Shattering though this culture shift may have been, Kerr spoke the truth and the writing was on the wall for the steam locomotive in consequence. The man from Westinghouse went on to tell them that the answer was locomotive horsepower and that the steam locomotive was not about to provide it.

Kerr predicted that, in the near future, the railroads would have to run passenger trains at 100 to 110 miles per hour and freight trains at 60 to 70 miles per hour to meet public demand, pointing out that the rolling stock was already available to run at those speeds. So where was the motive power? According to his calculations, a 1,500-ton passenger train would need 5,500 drawbar horsepower at 100 miles per hour, while a 5,000-ton freight train would need 8,500 drawbar horsepower to run at 60 miles per hour.

With a certain smugness:

> In anticipation of these developments, the railway department of the Westinghouse company has been engaged continuously in making an analysis of the various factors which determine the economic application of motive power to the railroad network of this country.

Unctuously, considering his audience:

As would be expected, this analysis has indicated a field for steam, for electric and for Diesel-electric power, and furthermore that there is ample use for all.

But, with a sting in the tail:

An entirely new conception of the requirements of a locomotive is necessary to meet the higher operating speeds of the future. Motive power capacity will be greatly increased. In many cases, the requirements will exceed the capacities which can be economically developed with certain forms of existing motive power.

Kerr was dismissive of the diesel-electric locomotive, failing to comprehend the rapidity of its development:

The largest Diesel electric locomotive in main line service is a 3,600 hp. locomotive, built in two cabs. This type of power is in the development stage, and larger units will undoubtedly be produced in the future. However, we do not expect to see units comparable in capacity to the electric locomotive.

In its present state of development, the Diesel electric locomotive is a competitor of the steam locomotive, but wherever the traffic concentration is sufficient to justify electrification, we do not believe that in general the Diesel locomotive is economically justified. However, this statement is on no way intended to minimize the importance of the Diesel locomotive which has a tremendous field in switching service alone, supplemented by other applications for it where the traffic is too light to justify electrification.

Kerr had to admit that the high capital cost of electrification would continue to limit its extension, where the matter rested.

The breakthrough in diesel-electric power came with technology that ganged multiple diesel-electric power units under one throttle. By this means it became possible to build diesel-electric locomotives developing more than 5,000 horsepower; the first were built in the late 1930s, competing with anything that steam technology could produce. The more the steam locomotive was studied, the more obvious and incurable its disadvantages; the opposite was true of the diesel-electric.

In spite of World War II, diesels continued their advance into road service. In 1944[332] the railroads operated 43,297 steam locomotives and 5,139 other than steam.[333] Diesels hauled more tons faster than steam. In 1947, an average diesel-hauled freight train weighed 2,921 gross tons and moved at 22 miles per hour, the equivalent figures for steam being 2,028 tons and 16 miles per hour; diesel power doubled gross ton-miles per train hour. The steam figures, however, were the average of a much larger and older fleet than the diesels that still hauled 88% of freight ton-mileage. When modern steam power was compared with diesel power, the advantage of the diesel was less marked.

The Norfolk & Western remained committed to steam. The company's 2-6-6-4s turned in a gross ton-mileage per train hour twice the average for diesels quoted above and, thus, four times the national average for steam, and that over three mountain ranges with sharp curves and steep grades.[334] The company supported its locomotives with fully updated maintenance and repair facilities. By the early 1950s, a single 2-6-6-4 was hauling 13,000 tons of loaded coal cars westbound from Williamson, West Virginia, 112 miles to Portsmouth, Ohio, and 175 empty cars eastbound over the same route. Even this figure was improved in 1951 to 14,500 tons hauled westbound in 14% less time, increasing gross ton-miles per train hour by 31%, by adding a 16,000-gallon water tender and eliminating a water stop. In 1954, two of the company's 4-8-4s, built in 1941, reached a total mileage of 2 million miles each.[335] By contrast, a 2-8-0 built by Alco for the

Union Pacific Challengers relegated to pushing behind a diesel, photographed near Spencer, Idaho, June 23, 1949. Note the caboose attached behind the pushers; if the caboose was in front of the pushers, they could crush it in the event of a sudden stop or derailment (Denver Public Library, Otto C. Perry collection, OP-19547).

Western Pacific in 1909 accumulated just over 1 million miles by the time it was scrapped in 1955.[336] In spite of its self-sufficiency in steam locomotive construction and maintenance and its association with the coal industry, the Norfolk & Western suddenly dieselized in 1958.[337]

The rest of the railroad industry dieselized as fast as it could. By 1949, the locomotive fleet had changed to 33,866 steam and 12,692 other types. The rate of change accelerated, with 29,743 steam locomotives and 15,179 other types in service in 1950.[338] The crossover point came with 20,490 steam locomotives and 22,716 locomotives of other types in service in 1952.[339] Steam locomotive numbers continued to dwindle, 12,135 in service in 1954.[340]

The issue was as much quality as quantity. By 1945, the railroads had combed out anything that would run from the locomotives idled by the depression; the first superpower locomotives were already twenty years old. Only 4,200 out of 21,800 freight locomotives—one fifth—were newer than that.[341] The rest were obsolete in performance and availability if not actually worn out. Of them it was harshly written[342]:

> Any road that had a considerable number of 25- and 30-year-old locomotives out behind the shop awaiting disposition when this war broke out in 1941 can console itself with one thought—the war emergency with its attendant inability to get new power and almost complete disregard of costs will cover up that page in motive power history on which is recorded one of the most costly decisions in modern railroading; namely the decision to get along with what we've got and put the old power back in service. Every mile that is run by a modern locomotive serves emphatically to prove what a serious error it is to perpetuate the existence of a 30-year-old unit. By no stretch of the imagination can their use in the post-war period be justified in the handling of main-line traffic on a busy railroad. Like the ox cart on a post-war super-highway they will only stand in the path of progress and tie up traffic.

These engines in their thousands were going to be replaced as soon as the war was over; the only question was the type of power that would replace them. In the post-war world, the demand for diesel-electric locomotives exploded into a procurement vacuum.

The U.S. railroads dieselized between 1944 and 1954, the diminishing role of steam is shown clearly by the following figures[343]:

Steam-hauled	1944	1952	1954
Freight gross ton-miles	95%	33%	16%
Passenger car-miles	86%	22%	14%
Switching locomotive-hours	77%	23%	11%

Electric locomotives occupied their own niche throughout that time, working only 2% of freight, 6% of passenger car-miles and 1% of yard service.

By 1951, when dieselization was half complete, the Class I railroads operated 17,493 diesel-electric locomotives; 97% of these had been built since 1939. By contrast, they operated 21,747 steam locomotives, 32% built before 1915, 85% before 1930, only 2% built since 1945.[344] The diesel-electric locomotive was the right product at the right time, built by first-class engineering and manufacturing and aggressively marketed.

The Class I railroads more than doubled their productivity between 1920 and 1944, averaging 14,900 gross ton-miles per train hour in 1920, 24,500 in 1929 and 37,300 in 1944.[345] This parameter had alarming implications when applied to steam vs. diesel traction. In 1944, one railroad recorded 29,700 gross ton-miles per train hour for steam haulage, 53,000 for diesel.

The first Class I railroad to dieselize entirely was the Texas Mexican in 1939 with the purchase of six diesel-electrics from Baldwin. In 1945 the railroad built two 3,200-horsepower diesel-electrics in its own shops.[346] The next Class I railroad to convert entirely to diesel haulage was the New York, Susquehanna & Western in 1945.[347] The steam locomotive advances of the 1920s and 1930s passed the railroad entirely by; its newest locomotives were sixteen Russian decapods built in 1918, next before them were some 0-6-0 switchers built in 1912. The first diesels, acquired in 1941, therefore competed against well-worn and obsolete steam power. The new diesels were all 1,000-horsepower road and switching locomotives, built by Alco-GE and capable of multiple-unit operation. The New York, Susquehanna & Western was a small railroad, owning only sixteen diesels

End of the road: this Big Boy, No. 4006, awaits scrapping at Cheyenne, Wyoming, in 1958. Rescued, it now resides at the St. Louis Museum of Transportation in Missouri (Denver Public Library, Otto C. Perry collection, OP-17069).

and with an abnormal history of steam locomotive procurement, but other and bigger railroads would soon follow.

The frenetic pace of freight development continued after the war; gross ton-miles per train hour reached new—and previously undreamed-of—levels.[348] Only the Baltimore & Ohio, the Delaware & Hudson, the Louisville & Nashville and the Norfolk & Western bought new steam locomotives. Twenty other railroads had already dieselized the majority of their freight operations by 1947, or planned to do so, or attributed their improved performance to diesel power.[349] Gross ton-miles per freight train hour not only reached new levels, but increased faster after 1945 than ever before—diesel-hauled.

The pace of dieselization took everyone by surprise. Looking back from 1956[350]:

> Not even the most optimistic proponents of the diesel-electric would have dared predict that the change from steam would take place so rapidly.

On the other hand:

> Changes have a habit of occurring fast these days, and with today's developments in research there is no assurance that some new form of motive power may not come into the picture in the next few years that will cause the diesel to become obsolete.

This never materialized. The gas turbine, whether coal- or oil-fired, failed as a locomotive engine. The atomic locomotive was too far-fetched ever to get beyond the speculation stage.

By early 1958, 1,377 steam locomotives remained on railroad rosters in the U.S., 1,709 in Canada, 1,914 in storage or under repair in both countries, for a total of exactly 5,000.[351] A slump in business in 1957–8 caused the scrapping of many of these. Remaining major U.S. steam users were the Norfolk & Western, the Illinois Central, the Baltimore & Ohio, the Nickel Plate, the Union Pacific and the Duluth, Missabe & Iron Range. All of these had dieselization plans which they put into effect in the next few years. The ICC mandatory flue repairs would be a further deadline, when the railroads would scrap their steam engines, even those few retained as stationary boilers, rather than repair them. By the end of 1957, "the steam locomotive has virtually passed out of the picture."[352] And so it remained.

The following table shows the roster of North American steam locomotives in service in 1958 and preserved operable in 2001.[353] The 1958 figures are for Class I railroads only; a substantial but indeterminate number of steam locomotives continued to operate on Class II, III and industrial lines. The 2001 figure includes narrow-gauge locomotives.

Type	1958		Total 1958	2001		Total 2001
	U.S.	Canada		Standard Gauge	Narrow Gauge	
0-4-0	1	0	1	21	38	59
0-4-2	0	0	0	1	4	5
0-4-4	0	0	0	1	4	5
0-4-4-0	0	0	0	0	1	1
0-6-0	29	94	123	20	2	22
0-6-2	0	0	0	0	1	1
0-6-4	0	0	0	1	0	1
0-8-0	225	103	328	0	1	1
0-10-0	3	0	0	0	0	0
0-10-2	9	0	9	0	0	0
2-4-0	0	0	0	3	10	13
2-4-2	0	0	0	2	3	5
2-4-4	0	0	0	0	4	4
2-6-0	1	10	11	5	3	8
2-6-2	5	0	5	13	6	19
2-6-6-2	10	0	10	1	0	1
2-6-6-4	40	0	40	0	0	0
2-6-6-6	0	0	0	0	0	0
2-8-0	80	339	419	22	4	26
2-8-2	286	302	588	20	21	41
2-8-4	62	0	62	1	0	1
2-8-8-2	155	0	155	0	0	0
2-8-4	35	0	35	0	0	0
2-10-0	60	7	67	2	0	2
2-10-2	73	39	112	0	0	0
2-10-4	44	1	45	0	0	0
4-2-0	0	0	0	1	0	1
4-4-0	0	2	2	7	40	47
4-4-2	0	0	0	0	2	2
4-4-4	0	5	0	0	0	0
4-6-0	1	181	182	10	4	14
4-6-2	25	395	420	9	4	13
4-6-4	3	58	61	1	3	4
4-6-6-4	40	0	40	1	0	1
4-8-0	13	0	13	1	0	1
4-8-2	106	56	162	2	0	2
4-8-4	45	117	162	10	0	10
4-8-8-4	25	0	25	0	0	0
6-6-6-6	1	0	1	0	0	0
Shay	?	?		11	11	22
Climax	?	?		5	0	5
Heisler	?	?		5	2	7
						0
Total	1,377	1,709	3,078	183	168	351

PART TWO

Compounds and Mastodons, 1895–1905

This period in American locomotive development opens with the controversy as to the merits and demerits of the compound locomotive in full swing and with the construction of the first giant engines in quantity; it closes with the building of the first American Mallet articulated compound. Power stokers, piston valves, new types of valve gear, superheating and feedwater heaters made their first tentative appearance in this period and, more important, the first large fireboxes supported on unpowered trailing axles. These developments set the stage for the transformation of the American locomotive that took place between 1905 and 1920. Although compounds and mastodons comprised only 7% of the U.S. locomotive fleet as it was in 1902, they symbolized what the American locomotive industry was trying to achieve in the economic boom that followed the depression of 1893–5.

The 1890s were a period of rapid advance in understanding of the steam locomotive but, at the same time, a growing awareness of certain almost impenetrable complexities in its functioning. The steam locomotive was still at the forefront of science. New information was coming to light all the time, month by month. This is sometimes difficult for us to realize at this distance in both time and technology.

2

General Steam Locomotive Development, 1895–1905

"The whole thing gets to be quite a complicated question, and the more I think about it the more I think that I do not know anything about it." J.N.Barr, Chicago, Minneapolis & St. Paul, October 1895, meeting of Western Railway Club, RRG December 13, 1895, 818

"The theories offered do not harmonize, and in many cases differ from the facts." RRG March 29, 1895, 201

By 1895 the American steam locomotive had matured into a standard form. Its origins were empirical; the empirical tradition was strong in those who built and operated it. The time was coming, however, when devices would be designed from engineering principles and calculations before they were ever built. The Wright brothers, for example, built the first powered aircraft in 1903 according to a design developed from years of experiments, measurements and calculations. Yet in the 1890s the steam locomotive was leading-edge technology, capable of moving faster than any other manmade object, except for a bullet or an artillery shell. Developments in test procedures led to an increased understanding of how it worked, leading in turn to locomotives that were designed rather than built empirically.

These advances collided with aspects of the steam locomotive that baffled those seeking to understand it.

The typical American steam locomotive of the late 1800s was the 4-4-0, the so-called "American" type or "Eight-wheeler." For most of the last half of the century, 60% of the locomotives in the U.S. and Canada were 4-4-0s—80% between 1860 and 1875.[1] The dominance of the 4-4-0 began to end in the mid–1880s, as the 2-6-0, 4-6-0 and 2-8-0 wheel arrangements, illustrated here, became increasingly common to provide hauling power that the 4-4-0s could not. Angus Sinclair remarked[2]:

About 1885 the eight-wheel engine was rapidly disappearing from the front of freight trains, and its place was taken by ten-wheel (4-6-0) and mogul engines (2-6-0). Ten-wheel engines were decidedly in favor, probably because they had such a close resemblance to the favorite 4-4-0. In many quarters there was a decided prejudice against the mogul on the ground that a pony truck was not so safe in leading the engine as a four-wheel truck.

This Boston & Maine class A-41, No. 987, one of a class built by Baldwin and the Manchester Locomotive Works between 1900 and 1911, typifies the multi-purpose American-type locomotive of the late 1800s. This one was still at work when photographed at Boston, Massachusetts, August 17, 1937, still in as-built condition with slide valves and inside valve gear (Denver Public Library, Otto C. Perry collection, OP-2684).

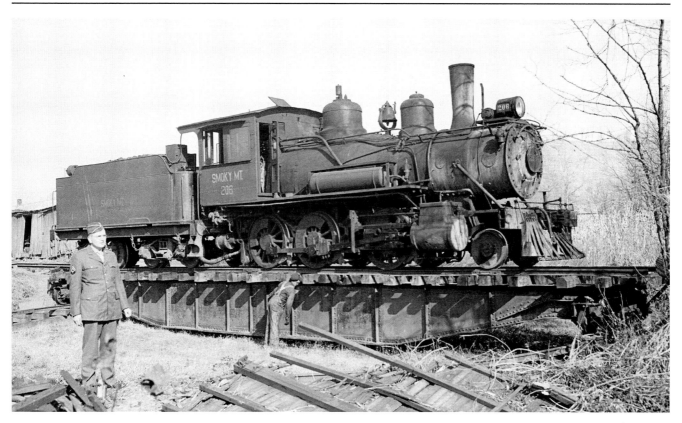

The 2-6-0, or Mogul, was the heavy power of its day, but that day was already passing when Baldwin built No. 206 for the Smoky Mountain Railroad in 1910, still more so when it was photographed at Sevierville, Tennessee, on November 17, 1942 (Denver Public Library, Robert W. Richardson collection, RR-1465).

This 4-6-0, or Ten-Wheeler, was photographed on the Roscoe, Snyder & Pacific at Roscoe, Texas, on January 13, 1947. We do not currently know who built No. 3, or when. General appearance suggests a construction date between 1900 and 1910. Walschaert valve gear and piston valves could be original or retrofits (Denver Public Library, Robert W. Richardson collection, RR-1418).

The specialized switching engine appeared, commonly with an 0-4-0 or 0-6-0 wheel arrangement.

The locomotives of 1895 were of the same wheel arrangements as in the 1870s—4-4-0, 4-6-0 and 2-8-0—but they were much bigger. The average 4-4-0 of 1875 had a 15-square foot grate, 900 square feet of heating surface, developed a tractive effort of 10,500 pounds and weighed 64,000 pounds without its tender.[3] In 1882, Theodore N. Ely, superintendent of motive power for the Pennsylvania, brought out the class K 4-4-0 with the firebox on top of the frames, providing 35 square feet of grate area. By 1895, the 4-4-0 had doubled in weight to 120,000 pounds.

A 2-8-0 built in 1870 had 20-inch × 24-inch cylinders, 1,500 square feet of heating surface, a boiler pressure of 140 pounds per square inch and weighed 100,000 pounds. A 2-8-0 built in 1894 had the same cylinder dimensions, but weighed 150,000 pounds with 2,200 square feet of heating surface and a boiler pressure of 180 pounds per square inch. The 2-8-0 of 1870 hauled a trailing load of 530 tons; this increased to 1,120 tons twenty-five years later.

Locomotives with only a single pair of driving wheels had mostly disappeared from America by the 1880s. The 0-4-0, 0-6-0 and 0-8-0 wheel arrangements originated before 1850; although 0-6-0s and 0-8-0s were common in Britain as road engines, the Americans used them only as switchers, in which role they continued until the end of steam. Norris built the first 4-6-0 in 1847, for the Philadelphia & Reading. Baldwin built the first 2-6-0, with a swiveling bogie rather than a radial truck, in 1860, for the Louisville and Nashville.[4] The first 2-8-0 was built in 1866 for the Lehigh & Mahanoy Railroad to the design of Alexander Mitchell, the company's master mechanic.[5] The Schenectady Locomotive Works built the first successful

4-6-2 in 1887 for the Chicago, Milwaukee & St. Paul.[6] (The first-ever 4-6-2 was probably the Strong locomotive built at Wilkes Barre in 1886 with a duplex, corrugated firebox. It was not a success.[7]) The first two 2-8-2s apparently came from the Norris works in 1867.[8] Baldwin built another in 1890 for the narrow-gauge Interoceanic Railway in Mexico; an early American standard-gauge user was the Chicago & Calumet Terminal Railway in 1893.[9] The 2-4-2 originated in 1893 with an engine that Baldwin built as a demonstrator. The same year Baldwin built the first 4-4-2 for the Atlantic Coast Line.[10]

The American 4-4-0 was a wonderfully perfect design. The two driving wheel axles carried the firebox between them, with space to dump the ash pan. The firebox was large in relation to the size of the boiler. The four-wheel leading truck supported the front of the boiler, the smokebox and the cylinders, and guided the engine around curves and over irregularities in the track. Three sets of springs supported the engine: the truck, the left-hand driving wheels and the right-hand driving wheels. The truck and the two pairs of driving wheels were each sprung as units by means of equalizing levers. This three-legged stool effect gave the engine stability. The cylinders, their steam chests and the rods were on the outside where they were easily accessible, leaving the space between the frames for the Stephenson valve gear. The connecting rod drove the front driving wheel; the long distance between the cylinders and the front driving wheel made a small fleet angle for the connecting rod, which minimized wear on the crosshead. The boiler was small enough in diameter that the engineer had a reasonable view over the left front of the engine. The departure from this perfect design brought with it an array of problems. John H. White's *American Locomotives* is the story of how the American

The 2-8-0, or Consolidation, became one of the most numerous of all locomotive types. Baldwin built 729 class, No. 755, for the Atchison, Topeka & Santa Fe in 1900. By the time it was photographed at Albuquerque, New Mexico, on December 4, 1937, it had been rebuilt with piston valves, although retaining the Stephenson inside valve gear; the original would have had slide valves (Denver Public Library, Otto C. Perry collection, OP-85).

This Illinois Central 0-6-0, No. 328, one of 132 built by Alco in 1913–18, is a typical switcher, photographed at Council Bluffs, Iowa, on May 29, 1938 (Denver Public Library, Otto C. Perry collection, OP-12215).

railroad industry arrived at this design; this book is the story of what happened when it had to be left behind.

From the perspective of 1902, Professor Goss, of Purdue University, pointed out that the American 4-4-0 was the product of railroad expansion in the second half of the nineteenth century.[11] Most railroad companies, unlike those in Britain, had no facilities for building their own engines; their energies and finances were completely absorbed by expansion.[12] The companies that went into the business of building locomotives were keen to supply the enormous demand with as few different types as possible. The qualities required were ability to run over rough track, cheapness, reliability and ease of maintenance. High power and fuel efficiency were not of great significance or, at any rate, received little attention.

> The merits of these (4-4-0) machines of 20 and 30 years ago should not be underrated. With their 16 in. and 17 in. cylinders and 120 or 140 lbs. of steam, they carried good loads and ran at fair speeds. They responded perfectly to the demands of a mixed service, sometimes doing switching, sometimes pulling a freight, sometimes a passenger train. They were sufficiently flexible to be but little affected by roughness of track, and their parts, being few and strong, were not often deranged or broken. The efficiency of these engines, both as to boiler performance and cylinder action, is probably not exceeded by that of the modern simple locomotive. When to these obvious advantages, there is added a low first cost and a low cost of repairs, the preference which has been accorded to the American type is readily explained.

According to Professor Goss, the supremacy of the 4-4-0 ended in about 1890. He explained both the supremacy and the decline of the 4-4-0 in detail, almost a lament, in 1904.[13]

> As a response to early conditions, the (American 4-4-0) type was almost perfect. By the exclusion of other types the problems of the

builder were simplified and the cost of manufacture was kept down; and when track mileage was increasing at enormous bounds this was important. As the same patterns were used over and over again every detail was proven in service upon hundreds of locomotives, hence the cost of maintenance was low. The design was well adapted to the rough track common in pioneering work and, considering the character of the service rendered, the type was and still is remarkably efficient as a power plant. But, while the type still has an important place in service, few locomotives of its kind are now being built. Its decline is due to the fact that as a type it cannot take on the proportions which the modern locomotive must possess. One reason for this is to be found in the fact that it will not admit a grate of sufficient size for present day requirements and another is in its limited tractive power. The grate of the locomotive lies very near the source of its power, and if restricted then the power of the locomotive cannot expand. Originally the fire-box of the American type locomotive was limited in width by the space between the side frames and in length by the distance between the driving axles. In locomotives common in the eighties the width of the grate was not more than 34 in., and the length generally less than 72 in. Various means have since been employed to increase its size. The spacing between the driving axles was increased in order that the fire-box might be made longer; the boiler was raised to allow the fire-box to rest on top of the frames, instead of between them, allowing the width of the two side frames to be added to the width of the grate, and in some cases the grate was inclined upward and allowed to extend back over the rear driving axle. By means such as these the American type locomotive of '76 came to be the American type locomotive of '93, greatly augmented in proportions and power, but nevertheless defining severe limitations to be met by the designer.

> The second limitation affecting the American type concerns its tractive power. Assuming adhesion, or, better, the coefficient of friction between wheel and rail, to be equal to one fifth of the weight on drivers, the American type engine of the eighties, carrying from 14,000 to

16,000 lbs. upon each driver was capable of exerting a tractive force of from 10,000 to 12,000 lbs. Wheel loads have since so increased that the modern engine may be depended upon to develop a tractive force of 5,000 lbs. per driver, or a maximum of 20,000 lbs. for the American type locomotive.

Until harder materials can be found for rails and tires, it is not likely that wheel loads can be further increased, so that greater tractive power must involve more than four coupled wheels, and therefore a departure from the American type.

At a firing rate of 150 pounds of coal per square foot of grate per hour—too high for efficient combustion—and a probable resulting coal consumption of 5 pounds per indicated horsepower-hour, an 18-square foot grate can produce no more than 540 indicated horsepower, while the strength of track, sub-structures and journal bearings combined to limit the maximum axle loading permissible in a locomotive design.

As the nineteenth century ended, locomotive designs for freight and passenger service diverged. The 4-4-0 became a passenger engine, built for speed, while heavier, six- and eight-coupled engines took over as freight engines. Leading-edge express passenger power of the 1880s was the New York Central's 800 class, designed by William Buchanan, Superintendent of Motive Power. The 800's weighed 126,150 pounds, with 19-inch × 24-inch cylinders, 1,834 square feet of heating surface, 78-inch driving wheels and a 28-square foot grate. The 900 class followed, with 86-inch driving wheels and a 31-square foot grate.

In 1902, an average 4-4-0 had a grate area of 20 square feet, 1,225 square feet of heating surface and weighed 90,000 pounds, providing a tractive effort of about 14,000 pounds. Steel passenger cars and 50-ton boxcars were too much for it. In 1884, 60% of new locomotives were 4-4-0s, declining to 50% in 1886 and 14% in 1891.[14]

Speed was not the issue. With light loads, good track and an absence of sharp curves or grades, the New York Central's 800-class 4-4-0s were capable of 70 miles per hour.[15] The New York Central and the Lake Shore planned, in 1893, to put on a passenger train that would cover the 965 miles from New York to Chicago in 19 hours, an average speed of 50 miles per hour, including stops.

The speeds attained by express passenger engines were avidly measured, hotly debated and widely publicized on both sides of the Atlantic.[16] Passionate arguments and vehement rebuttals notwithstanding, it is clear that large-drivered, lightly loaded American passenger engines often reached speeds of 80 to 100 miles per hour and may have reached 100 miles per hour on certain documented occasions. On May 9, 1893, William Buchanan's New York Central class N 4-4-0 locomotive #999, built at the railroad's West Albany, New York, shops,[17] was said to have achieved a speed of 102.8 miles per hour with a trailing load of 181 tons.[18]

These reports of fast runs came from the northeastern States with their heavy passenger traffic, good track and easy curves and gradients. High average speeds depended on more than locomotive capability; trailing loads, track, rolling stock, signaling, curves, grades, passage through towns and yards, conflicting traffic, civil engineering work in progress, number of stops, indeed the whole railroad had to be organized for sustained high speeds, assuming that it was, in fact, worthwhile to do so. The available locomotives, the light, nimble 4-4-0s, were capable of the highest speeds that were possible in routine service, considering these other factors.

Obvious to all those involved in railroading in the 1890s was the growth in size of American freight locomotives. As early as 1893, when it had hardly begun, the trend to big engines in America was known, as were its causes.[19]

The main difference between locomotives used here and in other countries is a necessary result of the difference in environment. In other countries, generally speaking, the distances are short, competition small, wages low, and money rentals moderate; in some a governmental control removes all competition. In the United States, long train runs, high wages, sharp competition and high rates of interest define the method of railroad operation so clearly that it is practically beyond the power of any individual company to vary much from the universal practice of running heavy trains. It is this necessary policy of heavy trainloads that gives rise to the wide difference which is found in maximum hauling power of the American and foreign locomotive. This increased power demands more weight for adhesion and greater steaming capacity; therefore, one finds the American engines heavier and the boilers larger for similar classes of work.

The cost per useful ton-mile for train wage is, in general, the controlling element here, and it decreases as the trainloads are increased. This reduction in the cost of transporting useful loads goes on, even after the load is increased to a point where the scientific steam engineer would deem the locomotive to be too much overloaded for the economical use of steam. So much bearing does the environment of condition and cost of wages have on the policy of locomotive operation that in extreme cases where the fuel is less than $1 per ton the most economical trainload is the maximum load that can be hauled by one engine almost regardless of the economy with which the steam is used. So, then, in the United States, heavy trains, high wages, sharp competition and high rates of interest fix the main distinctive feature of American locomotive practice, which is the greater hauling power of the locomotives. The greater power is obtained in two ways; first by using locomotives of greater weight, and second, by forcing the boilers to a degree almost unknown elsewhere.

European and American freight locomotives of the early 1890s were of similar size. In 1893, the New York, Ontario & Western arranged a test comparing a freight train on their railroad and one on the London & North Western Railway in England.[20] Route length and profile, train load, total work done by the locomotives and maximum speeds achieved were closely similar. The American engine was a 126,000-pound camelback 2-8-0 with an 80-square foot grate in a Wootten firebox for burning waste anthracite, 180 pounds per square inch boiler pressure and 1,630 square feet of heating surface. Two 20-inch × 24-inch cylinders and 50-inch driving wheels produced 29,400 pounds of tractive effort. The British engine was only slightly smaller—an 0-8-0 with inside cylinders, weighing 110,000 pounds. A 21-square foot grate, burning bituminous coal, fired a 160-pounds per square inch boiler with a total heating surface of 1,245 square feet. Two 19½-inch × 24-inch cylinders and 53½-inch driving wheels produced a tractive effort of 23,200 pounds.

The 2-8-0 freight engine was obsolescent in America by 1910–15, replaced by more powerful types. By contrast, those British LNWR 0-8-0 freight engines, improved but externally identical, were still in mainline freight service in the 1960s, hauling trains of four-wheeled, loose-coupled cars of 30,000-pound capacity with no continuous train braking. (A loose-coupled freight car was coupled to its neighbor by a three-link chain joining two open hooks. Although each car had a pair of sprung buffers at each end to prevent the car bodies from striking each other, when the chain was stretched the buffers were 6 to 12 inches apart, leaving large amounts of uncontrolled slack in the train. Slack was enough of a problem with MCB couplers; with this primitive arrangement, the problem was multiplied many times over and restricted freight train capacity.)

Outsized engines worked in America before 1890 with mixed success, but they were so few in number that they can be mentioned individually. A few 0-10-0s ran during the 1890s on the Burlington

& Missouri River and Grand Trunk Railroads. The Philadelphia & Reading built an 0-12-0 in 1863 but rebuilt it in 1870.[21] The Lehigh Valley's Alexander Mitchell, having built the first 2-8-0 in 1866, built two 2-10-0s in 1867, one or both being built by Norris. Both, however, were rebuilt as a 4-8-0 and a 2-8-2.[22] The Central Pacific built a 4-8-0 at its Sacramento shops in 1882, nicknamed *The Mastodon*.[23] The name stuck. The company bought twenty-five more from Cooke in 1882–3. The Lehigh Valley built another in 1883, weighing 102,000 pounds, with a boiler pressure of 130 pounds per square inch and developing 24,000 pounds of tractive effort. In 1884 the Central Pacific built a 4-10-0 at its Sacramento shops for helper service in the Sierra Nevada, weighing 148,000 pounds. The engine was too cumbersome and was rebuilt. The Central Pacific 4-8-0s and 4-10-0 are abundantly described by Robert J. Church in *Southern Pacific Ten-Coupled Locomotives* (Berkeley, CA: Signature, 2013). The same year, Baldwin built two 2-10-0s for the Northern Pacific.[24]

More successful were the 2-10-0 Vauclain compounds that Baldwin built for the New York, Lake Erie & Western (reor-

The Central Pacific built the unsuccessful 4-10-0 locomotive, *El Gobernador*, at its Sacramento shops in 1884. The location and date of this photograph are unknown (courtesy California State Railroad Museum, Negative 17966).

This was one of the 2-10-0s that Baldwin built for the New York, Lake Erie & Western in 1893, as No. 801, photographed at Susquehanna, Pennsylvania, on December 27, 1915, as Erie No. 2501, class J-1. Single-expansion cylinders with slide valves have replaced the original Vauclain compound cylinders; note also the camelback cab and Wootten firebox and the Santa Fe boxcar in the background (courtesy California State Railroad Museum, Gerald M. Best collection, Negative 900/20360).

ganized as the Erie Railroad in 1895), five in 1891, a sixth in 1893.[25] Engine weight at 195,000 pounds, grate area at 89 square feet, heating surface at 2,421 square feet and boiler pressure at 180 pounds per square inch were all huge for their day, as was the tractive effort of 26,850 pounds working compound, 35,000 pounds single-expansion. All six engines were rebuilt to single-expansion in 1904–5. After a service life of thirty-five years, they were scrapped in the mid–1920s.

The trend toward giant engines had barely begun. Even so, a typical American freight train weighed 1,350 tons while a typical European one weighed 450. The Americans drove their engines harder than the Europeans, wore them out and replaced them. In the early 1890s German express passenger trains typically weighed 140 to 190 tons (trailing load), pulled by 50-ton engines. A Chicago, Burlington & Quincy express weighed 265 to 350 tons, or even more, pulled by 50- to 55-ton 4-4-0s and 2-6-0s. The German express passenger engines operating between Hanover and Bielefeld averaged 4,650 miles per month, while the Chicago, Burlington & Quincy engines on the Chicago-Earlville division averaged 8,300.[26]

The 1890s brought a new analytical approach to steam locomotive engineering. Until then locomotive builders designed them empirically, built them and sent them out to their users, but little came back in the way of measurements from properly conducted tests. As of 1893:

> The American Society of Mechanical Engineers is quite apathetic toward railroad engineering, being much more concerned with stationary engines and pumps, and the Master Mechanics' Association has failed to take advantage of its opportunity to make scientific tests; hence there is not now a society or association in this country that has given to

locomotive engineering the attention which the importance of the subject demands. The most important work has been done by the several railroad clubs. It is perhaps unnecessary to call attention to the fact that locomotive designers have to proceed blindly in new work because of the lack of accurate data about existing types.

> It was a realization of this which prompted the Massachusetts Institute of Technology to start a course of locomotive engineering several years ago. This course has been hampered from the start by the want of information; that is, data that are reliable and on which it is safe to base the instruction of students. With a true Western spirit and boldness, Professor Goss conceived the idea of gathering his own data in a way that could not be bettered, and single-handed he succeeded in winning over to his project the faculty of the University at Purdue. It required the expenditure of a large sum of money to get a full size and complete modern locomotive across the prairies into the college grounds and mount it with a complete outfit of testing apparatus, but the locomotive is there, and has been doing good work in giving students a better idea of locomotive action than can be given, or has been given, in any other institution in this country.[27]

The locomotive was a 4-4-0 provided by the Schenectady Locomotive Works. Its installation at Purdue University, Lafayette, Indiana, in 1891 was a landmark in worldwide locomotive design, to which the Purdue laboratory contributed immensely valuable information for the next thirty years.

Within a few years, the Purdue laboratory had uncovered the relationships between speed, cut-off, boiler pressure losses, mean effective pressure, power output, specific fuel consumption, firing rate, smokebox temperature, evaporation rate and friction losses between

The Purdue University steam locomotive laboratory with the captive 4-4-0, *Schenectady*, built by the Schenectady Locomotive Works in 1891. The man with the black beard and moustache on the left of the photograph is Professor Goss. *Schenectady* was known retrospectively as *Schenectady No. 1* to distinguish it from its replacements (Purdue University Libraries, Karnes Archives and Special Collections, PSD00002024).

cylinder and drawbar, as shown in the table at the end of this chapter. Perhaps these results could have been obtained from road tests; perhaps they already had been, but the steam locomotive was a such a mass of independent variables that the value of tests in controlled conditions was enormous.

Mechanical engineers debated the relative merits of static tests versus road tests; both could yield ambiguous results. Apparently, the first locomotive testing laboratory in the world was built at Kiev, Russia, in 1882.[28] Purdue was the first such plant in the U.S.[29] It was, however, a laboratory built around a full-sized locomotive; it was not able to accept locomotives from outside for testing. A testing plant built by the Chicago & North Western followed in 1895 and another by Columbia University in 1899. The Pennsylvania built a testing plant at St. Louis, Missouri, for the exposition of 1904 and then moved it to Altoona, Pennsylvania.[30] The Altoona test plant provided an immense volume of accurate information over a period of fifty years. The first testing plant in Britain was built by the Great Western Railway at Swindon in 1904, but with a limitation of 500 horsepower. The French opened a test plant at Vitry-sur-Seine in 1933; current research has not revealed whether a test plant was in operation in France before that date.[31] World War II thwarted a British plan to build a bigger test plant[32]; the nationalized British Railways built a test plant at Rugby, capable of accepting the biggest British locomotives, but it did not go into service until 1950. The Purdue test plant went out of use, due to lack of student interest, in 1938.

In 1902 the ICC published a census of locomotives by wheel arrangement.[33] At that time 11,280 4-4-0s were at work in the U.S., and still accounted for 30% of the 37,516 engines included in the census. The 4-4-0, 0-6-0, 2-6-0, 2-8-0, and 4-6-0 wheel arrangements accounted for 93% of the engines in the census. The census excluded a further 3,709 engines of unclassified types, such as Shay, Climax or Heisler, or engines working on private or single-use lines. Any numbers given for the size of the American locomotive fleet are approximate; sources disagree and the inclusions and exclusions are so many and so confusing that no completely accurate number may ever be known.

In just four years the major railroad locomotive fleet increased by one third, to 50,954 in 1906. The fleet composition changed as bigger engines were built to meet increasing demands. The 4-4-0 was obsolescent and by 1906 comprised only 20% of the fleet. The more powerful 4-6-0 held its position at 20%. Favored by some railroads, the 2-6-2s more than tripled in numbers, but remained rare at 1.4% of the total. In passenger service, the fast, powerful 4-4-2s quadrupled their numbers between 1902 and 1906 but still comprised only 3% of the fleet. The new 4-6-2s, of which only three were in service in 1902, increased in numbers to 521. In freight service, the workhorse 2-8-0s doubled in numbers to 28% of the 1906 fleet. The 2-8-2s and 2-10-2s, almost unknown in 1902, crept into railroad procurement with 178 and 140 in service in 1906, respectively. The 4-8-0 Mastodons held their own, but offered insufficient advantage as a freight engine over the 2-8-0 wheel arrangement to make good their earlier promise. In switching service, the 0-6-0 gained slightly at the expense of the 0-4-0. The heavy 0-8-0 switcher maintained constant, and small, numbers throughout the period.

Throughout the 1890s American engineers continued to express pessimism that the steam locomotive had reached the limits of its development. In 1896[34]:

> It appears to be the opinion of many persons well informed in locomotive engineering, that unless ways and means are discovered for increasing the "heating surface" in locomotive boilers, the engine in its present most advanced development has about reached the limit of its capacity.

The grate area in locomotives has been enlarged until it is virtually impossible to increase its size, the driving wheels limiting the width, and bridges and the center of gravity the height of the boiler; and it appears to be conceded that no advantage would result from making the boiler longer.

By 1900 many were wondering what directions the locomotive's future progress would, or could, take.[35]

From the standpoint of 1898[36]:

> By far the most striking feature of modern locomotive construction has been the building of heavy freight engines, notably the twelve-wheelers for the Great Northern Railway, and the new consolidation engine of the Pennsylvania Lines. These heavy engines are, partly at least, the outcome of rating locomotives and trains on a tonnage basis, and it is not possible to say where the maximum limit of economical weight and capacity will be found. The engines built a few years ago and considered at that time to be as large as could well be used, are now small in comparison with these latest productions.
>
> "On both of the above roads, the big engines are used only on heavy grades, and at low speeds are able to exert enormous tractive effort. They are, however, in the nature of special machines for a special service, and it is safe to say that it will be a number of years before such heavy engines can be used to advantage on any considerable number of roads in general freight service."

The dimensions of the Pennsylvania Railroad H-3a of 1889 and the H-4 that replaced it in 1897, both 2-8-0s, illustrate this trend. The H-3a had a boiler pressure of 140 pounds per square inch, 1,500 square feet of heating surface, 21,500 pounds of tractive effort and 124,000 pounds total weight. The H-4 had the same grate area of about 30 square feet, but 2,470 square feet of heating surface (65% more), 185 pounds per square inch boiler pressure, 35,800 pounds tractive effort (up 67%) and 174,300 pounds total engine weight (up 40%). The tractive efforts were 18% and 21% respectively of the adhesion weights.

Looking ahead:

> In view of the past experience it is quite likely that some plan may be devised for building locomotives of still greater tractive power, although the exact way of doing this is not yet apparent. The reduction in the cost of handling freight, made possible by the big engines, is such an incentive to greater efforts that the outcome cannot be predicted.

Into this arena stepped the Mallet articulated compound.

The Americans became used to publicizing their mastodons and consolidations of the late 1890s as the biggest locomotives in the world which, for the most part, they were. It therefore came as a surprise that engines of similar size were being used in Belgium. In 1898 the heaviest locomotive in America was a 2-8-0 built for the Union Railroad by the Pittsburgh Locomotive & Car Works.[37] It weighed 230,000 pounds and, with 200 pounds per square inch boiler pressure, developed 62,000 pounds of tractive effort. The Belgian engine was a compound weighing 218,000 pounds and developing a tractive effort of 56,000 pounds when working single expansion. The American view of this engine was:

> The heaviest grade on which the American engine must work is 2.4 per cent, and that for the Belgian engine 3.1 per cent. While the American is of the consolidation type, the Belgian has six driving axles. The first three are on a truck, with the cylinders connected by means of flexible joints (as in the old Fairlie engines), and the rear three axles are rigid in the frames. Thus, while the services required are similar, the Belgian engineers have adopted an entirely different and more expensive method of attaining their results. The engine is really a four-cylinder compound, the two high-pressure cylinders being applied to the rear set of drivers, and the low-pressure to the drivers set in the truck. This has

The class R, reclassified H-3, were among the earlier members of a long and numerous line of Pennsylvania 2-8-0 freight locomotives. The Pennsylvania built the H-3's in its own shops at Altoona in the late 1880s (Reprinted by permission, Pennsylvania Historical and Museum Commission and Railroad Museum of Pennsylvania, General Negative 24871).

the advantage of using solid steam pipe connections for the high pressure, and the flexible joints for the reduced pressure, bringing the exhaust under the stack as desired.

The Mallet articulated compound thus gained the awareness of the American railroad industry. Anything that could haul a useful load up a gradient of 3.1%, steeper than what was normally either practical or safe on a main line, was worth looking at. When American concepts were combined with the Mallet design, the results would astonish the steam locomotive world.

American railroadmen continued to surprise even themselves with the size of new engines.[38] The insatiable demand for freight haulage in the late 1890s emphasized tractive effort. Tractive effort could not exceed 25% of adhesion weight; more tractive effort meant more adhesion weight. The strength of track and substructures limited the weight on each driving axle, so more tractive effort also meant more driving axles. It was that simple.

Almost every year, some new American locomotive would be hailed as the biggest in the world. In 1901 Baldwin built a Vauclain compound 2-8-2 for the Bismarck, Washburn & Great Falls. This engine was designed to haul an 890-ton train up a 1% grade with 9 degrees of curvature. Under test it hauled 940 tons at 18 miles per hour on the level, topping the grade at just 2 miles per hour. In 1902 a 2-10-0 that Baldwin built for the Santa Fe held the title, a 267,000-pound monster with 5,366 square feet of heating surface. The same

year Baldwin built a 260,000-pound 2-8-2 for the Santa Fe, using the same boiler design. Alco built a 2-8-0 tandem compound for the New York Central with 4,117 square feet of heating surface. The adhesion weight was similar to the Santa Fe 2-8-2 but the compound cylinders allowed the New York Central to use a smaller heating surface. Baldwin built a 4-6-2 passenger engine for the Chicago & Alton weighing 219,000 pounds with a boiler carrying 220 pounds per square inch, 73-inch driving wheels, a 54-square foot grate and 4,078 square feet of heating surface.

Bigger locomotives and tonnage rating tables to load them to their maximum put new emphasis on the water capacity of the tender tank.[39] In flat country, water stations were placed about 20 miles apart, 10 to 15 miles in hilly country. In the early 1890s tender tanks had capacities of 3,000 to 4,300 gallons, 4,000 being the most common. Bigger engines consumed water faster in the distance between water stations, while heavier loads meant more time at full throttle and long cut-off, necessitating more water capacity. By 1898 the Chicago, Burlington & Quincy was using 5,000-gallon tender tanks. The Pennsylvania was leading the way with 6,000-gallon tanks on their H-5 2-8-0s.

The cost curves for freight haulage in American conditions all bottomed out at speeds of 15 to 20 miles per hour which was the speed range at and below which the reciprocating steam locomotive produced its greatest tractive effort without the complicating factors of steam friction, valve events and counterbalancing. The engine

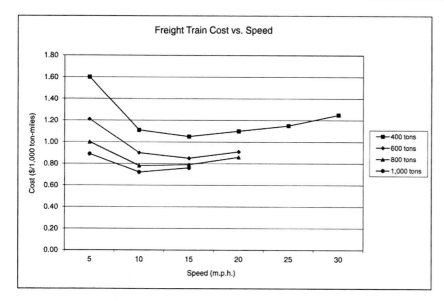

Freight train cost curves all pointed to the heaviest possible tonnage, hauled at low speeds. "Tons" are trailing loads hauled against a continuous 1% grade (figures from Henderson, G. R., *The Cost of Locomotive Operation*, Part XX, *RRG*, January 12, 1906, 39).

designed for fast passenger service, where speed was at a premium, ran into a whole different set of design problems.

Developments in American locomotive engineering were well summarized in the locomotives exhibited at St. Louis, where the 1904 World's Fair displayed an exuberant and increasingly self-confident America. "Large boilers, wide fireboxes and high pressures are features of the locomotives at the World's Fair which are most prominent and which most clearly point the progress that has been made since 1893."[40] (1893 was the year of the World's Fair at Chicago.) Notable among the exhibits was a locomotive testing plant built by the Pennsylvania.

Compounding was already on the way out:

> High pressure has in part taken the place of compound cylinders. Compounding is still appreciated, but the Vauclain four-cylinder compound of 1892 has not swept the field as some thought probable in 1893.

Of the thirty-nine standard-gauge engines exhibited at St. Louis, only three had narrow fireboxes between the wheels. Of the wide fireboxes, only one was of the extra-wide Wootten type. The Wootten retained its popularity on the anthracite-burning Philadelphia & Reading, Delaware, Lackawanna & Western, Lehigh Valley and Erie Railroads. Otherwise the wide firebox, extending above small driving wheels or supported on a two-wheel trailing axle or truck, had become a permanent part of American locomotive construction.

Attracting much attention at St. Louis was the Baltimore & Ohio's enormous 0-6-6-0 Mallet articulated compound. At 334,500 pounds, it really was the biggest locomotive in the world. The grate area was 72 square feet and the boiler contained 5,586 square feet of heating surface. Not far behind was the Santa Fe 2-10-2 weighing 287,240 pounds with 4,796 square feet of heating surface, 59 square feet of grate and a tractive effort of 62,000 pounds. Yet the demand for greater pulling power went on.

> We gaze in wonder at the elephantine proportions of these huge machines, and yet, for the service for which they are designed, why should they be considered large? On a two per cent ascending grade, the Atchison engine propels about 1,100 tons at a speed of five miles an hour. The articulated engine is expected to move about 1,500 tons. In

other words, the Atchison engine, if hitched to a train, such as an 85-ton engine hauls on a level at 20 miles an hour, it could not keep it going up a steeper grade than about 35 feet to the mile (0.7%), even at the lowest practicable speed. To take up such a grade one of the 80-car trains now becoming common, the leviathans will have to be even larger yet.

By the end of the nineteenth century American locomotive design was following a rational procedure.[41] The customer specified the train weight that the engine was required to haul, the ruling adverse grade and any abnormally sharp curves, areas of strong winds and the like. The ruling grade was not necessarily the steepest, as the customer might choose to assign helper engines to long, steep grades. Knowing this information, the designers could use formulae for train resistance to estimate the drawbar pull required. Multiplying this by 4 gave the adhesion weight. Taking 50,000 pounds as the maximum axle loading for most track and substructures gave the number of driving axles. The designers then determined the size of the driving wheels, according to whether the engine was for freight or passenger service. They next calculated the cylinder dimensions from the boiler pressure and the required tractive effort. They could then design and proportion the boiler and firebox.

As an example, test data available by 1900 showed that the resistance of a 13-car, 500-ton passenger train, moving at 50 miles per hour, was about 14.5 pounds per ton of trailing load on straight, level track, requiring 960 horsepower at the drawbar. The internal friction and rolling resistance of the engine and tender consumed about 30% of the cylinder horsepower. Typical water consumption rates had been measured at 26 pounds per cylinder horsepower-hour, so that 960 drawbar horsepower required a steaming rate of 35,600 pounds per hour. Typical evaporation rates were 10 pounds per square foot of heating surface per hour, so that the required heating surface for this power output was 3,560 square feet, from which the boiler and grate could be designed. By the first years of the twentieth century, enough data had accumulated for engines to be designed according to engineering principles with every likelihood that the result would perform as intended.

The numbers and engineering details in this book—so neat, so rational—can never tell the whole story. It is essential to be aware of the true inwardness of the steam locomotive—irrational, frustrating, temperamental, dangerous and with an infinite capacity for things to go quickly and seriously wrong—and the interaction with its crew.

This light-hearted account of a day's work when a lot of things went wrong is reproduced from *The Red Devil and Other Tales From the Age of Steam* by kind permission of the author, Mr. David Wardale. This took place as recently as 1979, on a little used 3-foot, 6-inch gauge line with grades up to 2.5%—which accounts for the relatively small trailing loads quoted—in South Africa.[42] South Africa, with abundant coal and cheap labor, was one of the last bastions of the steam locomotive. But, if the coal was bad and the crew did not care...

The original text uses SI units only; Imperial conversions are added here for the convenience of North American readers.

> It was mid winter and an unusually cold day for Pretoria—below zero with a howling southerly wind blowing straight, it seemed, from Antarctica and filling the air with dust. I should have stayed in bed but I had made the arrangements and thought I ought to stick to them, so off I

went to Capital Park. The locomotive for the Magaliesburg train that day was, of course, not a 19D. It was a 24 class 2-8-4 (no. 3683) which was a smaller locomotive. However the boiler was very similar to that of a 19D, differing only in having a shorter barrel, and as I had bothered to get up so early I thought I had better make the trip. I climbed onto the locomotive. The crew had not been informed that I was going with them but agreed to take me all the same. We left the depot at 06.15 and, sheltering as best we could from the wind which blew through the cab, headed light engine to Pretoria station for the two coaches forming the passenger part of the mixed train, and from there to Hercules yard on the northern outskirts of the city to pick up the rest of the load. This turned out to be nine bogie wagons, the total trailing load from Hercules being 326 tonnes (359 short tons).

A look around the locomotive discovered just a few minor irregularities. The authorized maximum working boiler pressure for this class was 1 380 kPa (200 pounds per square inch) but, according to the boiler pressure gauge, the first safety valve lifted at 1 420 kPa (205 pounds per square inch) and closed at 1 320 kPa (190 pounds per square inch), contravening the boiler code. There was no steam chest pressure gauge, but the driver claimed it was not worthwhile to book this as the store at Capital Park did not have any. By timing the kilometer posts, the speedometer was found to be reading a wee bit too high, 90 km/h (56 miles per hour) on the meter being about 55 km/h (34 miles per hour) in reality. The right-hand piston rod packing and left-hand cylinder drain cocks were leaking.

Before leaving Hercules the fire was built up thickly at the back and then off we went. Nothing exceptional happened in the first 29 km (18 miles) to Meerhof. Steaming was not too good and the boiler pressure never rose above 1 200 kPa (175 pounds per square inch) when the engine was under power, the preferred cut-off being no less than 50% with (of course) partially open throttle. The blower seemed to be on most of the time. At Meerhof water was taken and the fire cleaned, there being a considerable amount of clinker despite the relatively short distance travelled. Most of the clinker manhandled through the drop grate fell into the ash pan sides but the short irons for pushing ash and clinker transversely into the central chute were missing and the fireman had to laboriously push the clinker into the drop grate opening, then climb down and rake the ash pan with the fire iron. This took some time but, in due course, the fire had been cleaned and water taken and we could set off. The throttle was opened, the locomotive went forward a few millimeters, and then stopped. Full boiler pressure, full throttle, full forward gear, full brake vacuum, (South African trains were braked using the British vacuum system, rather than the American compressed-air system) no movement. Neither would it go in reverse. An inspection of the train revealed that the brakes on every vehicle behind the tender were on, despite having the correct vacuum on the locomotive, and it was eventually discovered that the vacuum hose between the tender and the first vehicle was entirely blocked by ice due to water spillage getting into the hose at the connection, which was drawing air. The hose was removed, sprayed with hot water from the coal watering pipe, and replaced, after which a more successful start was made.

Boiler pressure hovered around the 1 200 kPa (175-pound) mark until the climb to Hekpoort, 33 km (20 miles) from Meerhof, when heavy priming occurred at full throttle, about 50% cut-off, and ¼ glass of water. The priming lasted approximately two minutes, pulling the fire to the front of the grate and lowering the boiler pressure to 950 kPa (140 pounds per square inch). The train just made the grade, speed falling to about 10 km/h (6 miles per hour) with full throttle and 70% cut-off. The boiler had not been blown down at Capital Park, nor during the trip, nor after the priming, and the driver said he was not aware what the blowdown schedule was. The coal pulled to the front of the fire was replaced by firing to the back of the grate and, after this the fire was thick all over, up to the arch tubes at the front. Now the boiler pressure

did not rise above 1 050 kPa (150 pounds per square inch) when steaming and most times when the throttle was opened it fell to as low as 780 kPa (115 pounds per square inch).

At Hekpoort one truck (car) was dropped off, reducing the load to about 290 tonnes (320 short tons), and the grate was shaken to bring the level of the fire down. Further on, one gradient brought speed down to as low as 10–15 km/h (6–9 miles per hour) with the locomotive working at full throttle and full forward gear and with 900–950 kPa (130–140 pounds per square inch) boiler pressure. Then on the final 2.5% climb to Magaliesburg heavy priming occurred a short distance from the summit and the locomotive stalled by slipping after speed had fallen to a walking pace. Still the boiler was not blown down. The train was reversed onto straight track from which to re-attempt the climb, and the sanding gear was checked. No sand was flowing on either side and it was found that the sand in the sandboxes was damp (the driver said the sands were working at Capital Park but this claim seemed dubious). The sand valves and pipes were hammered but this failed to produce a continuous flow of sand. A second attempt at the grade was then made; no priming occurred but again the locomotive slipped to a standstill. The fireman was told to put ballast stones on the track at the critical point (in lieu of sand) and the train was run back again. As the sanding gear was still not working, sand was taken from one sandbox and put in a bucket: the fireman and I sat on the front buffer beam with the bucket between us and sanded the rails by hand, but all to no avail. The third attempt ended in a mighty bout of slipping, accompanied by a shower of sparks from the chimney which managed to set fire to the adjacent farm field—right behind the farmer's house. Once more the train was set back, and it was only then that anyone thought about the boiler water level. We looked at the glasses. There was no water in sight, on a 2.5% rising grade. On went one injector and we waited for either the water to appear or else a big, big bang—it was over five minutes before water showed at the bottom of the glass. The boiler pressure was then raised to about 1 250 kPa (180 pounds per square inch) and, with ¼ glass of water showing, the train was restarted but, before the summit, the priming began again and this time we stalled without slipping. Four tries were enough and the driver decided to part the load. As we left with half the train, the smoke and flames rising from the field on our left parted to reveal a figure glaring rather angrily at us.

The boiler primed badly for most of the short distance to Magaliesburg and we reached there with no water showing in the glass, which was not surprising as by that time there was no water in the tender either. On arrival water was taken and the fire cleaned, the latter task taking some thirty minutes as huge pieces of clinker (up to about 600 mm × 600 mm × 300 mm (2 feet × 2 feet × 1 foot)) had to be broken up to a small enough size to pass through the drop grates. The hydrostatic lubricator had run out of oil and the reverser had stuck in full forward gear, requiring much hammering of one radius rod to get it to move. The lubricator was still not working as we headed back to pick up the load we had left behind, and that was where we got the good news. The guard, a white-haired and largely toothless old-timer with several days' growth of stubble around his chin and who looked like he had been a fixture on that train ever since the line was built, was waiting for us. Translated from the original Afrikaans, his message went something like this: "Hee hee hee, that f … g farmer wasn't half f … g mad. He took the f … g engine number and said he'd report you to the f … g station master for setting him on f … g fire…" (at least I now knew what engine numbers were really for). We worked the remainder of the load forward to Magaliesburg: it included the passenger coaches although I think all the passengers had long since concluded it would be quicker to walk and had left.

The return journey was made with only the two passenger saloons—operating probably did not trust us with anything more. Before leaving Magaliesburg, the boiler was finally blown down, after which there was no priming, which was just as well as the lubricator did not function until we had gone about ten km (6 miles). Clinker formed, even with a relatively thin fire, and consequently the boiler pressure could not be maintained above 1 200 kPa (175 pounds per square inch). It got dark before we reached Pretoria and the operation of the turbo-generator became so erratic we had to proceed with no headlight over a section of track with a fair number of ungated level crossings. Fortunately the whistle was working (yes, really), so what we lacked in light we made up for in sound. Approaching Hercules, we were diverted into a loop and the outside-framed engine trucks hit some sleepers piled too close to the track, but by that time the driver just wanted to get home and he did not stop to inspect the damage. We dropped the two coaches at Pretoria station and finally arrived back at Capital Park at eight o'clock, having

taken almost fourteen hours for a 200 km (125-mile) round trip. As I said good-bye to the crew, I made some remark to the driver about it being rather an eventful day, to which he muttered that it was "just another trip."

The years between the depression of the 1890s and about 1905 saw major developments in American locomotive practice. The 4-4-0 was not powerful enough for traffic demands and became obsolete. The rigid-frame compound was vigorously promoted but, by 1905, its heyday was over. The giant freight engine became a permanent and increasingly numerous participant in the railroad scene. Compounding lived on in the Mallets which dwarfed the mastodons that they replaced.

Representative Test Results, Purdue University Locomotive Test Plant, 1892–3

Test	Drivers (rpm)	Speed (mph)	Cut-off %	Boiler (psi)	Dry pipe (psi)	MEP (psi)	Ihp	Lb. coal/ ihp-hr.	Lb. coal/ sq.ft. grate/hr.	Smokebox temp., deg.F	Lb. water/ lb. coal	Dbhp	Lb. coal/ dbhp-hr	Friction loss (%)
1	80	15	77	129	32	27	118	7.4	50	609	7.7	104	8.4	11.9
2	82	15	18	129	104	29	128	4.8	40	590	7.9	106	5.8	17.2
3	130	25	47	130	105	58	412	5.0	119	760	6.6	338	6.1	18.0
4	127	25	18	128	118	31	212	4.2	51	615	8.3	166	5.4	21.7
5	130	25	77	123	79	56	393	6.7	147	825	5.9	335	7.8	14.8

Notes:
MEP   =   Mean effective pressure
Ihp   =   Indicated horsepower
Ihp-hr   =   Indicated horsepower-hour
Dbhp   =   Drawbar horsepower
Dbhp-hr =   Drawbar horsepower-hour

3

Locomotive Engineering, 1895–1905

Section 3.1 Fuels, Firing and Fuel Economy

3.1.1 Coal

By the 1890s, most American locomotives burned bituminous coal. Wood had become scarce, while the rise of coal mining in the Appalachians and the Midwest made coal—of higher calorific value than wood—available at an affordable cost. If supply and cost had not caused coal to replace wood, demands for power would have done so.

A good bituminous locomotive coal consisted of less than 5% moisture, 35% volatiles, 2% sulfur, 10% ash and more than 48% fixed carbon. The calorific value of American bituminous coals ranged from 11,500 BTU per pound to 15,500 BTU per pound.

Some typical compositions were:

Component (%)	Pennsylvania bituminous	Illinois bituminous	Pennsylvania anthracite	Wyoming lignite
Moisture	0.5–2.5	2.1–15.5	1.4–3.8	6.0–16.2
Fixed carbon	52.0–74.0	40.0–56.0	77.0–88.0	36.0–48.0
Volatiles	17.0–36.0	28.0–38.0	3.0–7.0	34.0–42.0
Sulfur	0.2–2.7	0.9–5.3	0.3–0.8	0.4–7.9
Ash	4.5–10.8	8.3–23.8	4.0–13.7	3.2–16.0

Coal quality varied from region to region, mine to mine, even seam to seam and was influenced by mining methods.

Fuel made up about 30% of locomotive operating costs. As these were 20% to 25% of a railroad's operating cost, the coal bill was about 7% of the total. Shipping could double the pithead cost of coal, so railroads fueled their locomotives with whatever was nearest at hand, designing the firebox to suit the fuel. Anthracite, from mines in the Appalachians, burned with a slow, dark fire and needed more grate area than bituminous coal. Huge deposits of lignite were found in the northwestern prairies, although its low calorific value entailed high firing rates. The American railroads were fortunate in that coal is widely distributed in the U.S.; by 1905, it was mined in at least twenty States.

As soon as they started to burn coal, the railroads met the problem of ash. This material could not be allowed to fall onto the track where it would build up between the rails. It had to be collected in an ash pan under the firebox, which had to be emptied at intervals in suitable places with facilities for handling the ash. A locomotive burning 2 to 3 tons of coal per hour could easily deposit ½ ton of ash in an hour or two. The size of the ash pan therefore limited the range of the locomotive between service stops.

Components of the ash, such as iron, alumina, silica and calcium carbonate formed clinker, which blinded the air openings in the grate with plates of sticky material, reducing the steaming rate. At best, clinker was absent or easily removed; at worst, it had to be chipped from the grates with hammer and chisel after the fire had been dropped and the firebox had cooled.[1] This impacted the real value of coal from any particular source. The clinker-forming minerals could be solid, liquid or gaseous in the temperature range of the firebox, depending whether the engine was working hard or lightly; the engine crew's management of the fire thus also affected the formation of clinker.

In the 1890s, American locomotives burned 50 million tons of bituminous coal and anthracite each year, one third of total U.S. consumption. In 1893, the Chicago, Burlington & Quincy burned 925,270 tons of coal, costing $1,291,108 ($1.40/ton).[2] This was twice the coal consumption, for all purposes, of the city of Chicago. So important were the supply, cost and quality of coal that major railroads appointed specialists to procure, analyze and inspect it. The Wabash fuel department, appointed in 1896, saved $200,000 in its first year of work.

In the 1890s the Boston & Maine and the Boston & Albany experimented with coke, which produced less smoke and sparks than bituminous coal, but was more expensive because of competing demand from smelters.[3] Coke had serious disadvantages as locomotive fuel. Because of its spongy texture, it could absorb 15% of its own weight in water if it was stored in the open. The firing technique was the opposite of that for bituminous coal, with a deep fire and large, infrequent additions of fuel; this resulted in much blowing off through the safety valves and waste of fuel. Coke was less dense than bituminous coal; bigger volumes had to be carried, which demanded bigger tenders or shortened the range of the engine between fueling stops. The benefits of coke were quickly recognizable in fewer complaints from passengers and lineside residents and fewer lineside fires, but the Boston & Albany found that they burned coke at 20.65 pounds per passenger car mile compared to 14.70 pounds for coal. Coke was never a significant locomotive fuel.

3.1.2 Oil

Some of the first experiments with oil as locomotive fuel took place in France in 1870. The oil flowed down grooves in sloping grate bars, but this did not allow fast enough combustion for adequate steam generation.[4] The Russians experimented with oil as locomotive fuel in 1874 but success did not come until 1883 when Thomas Urquhart was locomotive superintendent of the Grazi-Tsaritsin railway. By 1885 he had converted all 143 engines to burn oil. Urquhart's breakthrough was to use steam to atomize the oil in a burner of his own design. This concept has been used ever since.[5] The Pennsylvania experimented with oil firing in 1887, but the Pennsylvania's requirements, alone, would have consumed one third of the petroleum production of the U.S. Supply increased with the discovery of oil in Texas and California.

In the early 1890s, Standard Oil of Indiana converted five switching locomotives at its refinery at Whiting, Indiana, to burn oil. Oil was carried in a tank in the tender coal space. The firebox was easily converted by mounting four to six burners in its back sheet below the fire door. Each burner consisted of an oil tube surrounded by a steam tube. Steam from the boiler entrained and atomized the oil. A lighted rag thrown into the firebox ignited the atomized oil jet as soon as it was turned on. No separate oil pump was necessary. The grate was floored with fire brick, leaving air gaps. The front of the firebox was lined with a checkerwork of firebrick to protect the metal from the hot flame. If the fireman manipulated the oil, atomizer and blower valves correctly, the fire burned without smoke. The switch engines at Whiting burned 27 to 30 gallons per hour.

Oil became attractive during the coal miners' strike of 1894, when the railroads had to use whatever fuels they could find.[6] One source[7] asserted:

> The first attempt in the United States to burn crude oil in the firebox of a locomotive was made at Santa Paula, California, in October, 1894.

That year, Baldwin experimented with oil firing so as to use oil in southern California.

Superheated steam was more effective as an atomizer than saturated steam. Air was better yet but needed a separate air pump. Most oil-burning locomotives were converted from coal-burners with nothing more than atomizers and fire brick added to the firebox and the necessary piping and tankage for the oil. In cold climates a steam line was led through the oil tank to warm the oil and make it flow more easily. Although oil firing could be practically smokeless, the oil left a sticky deposit in the fire tubes.[8] At intervals the fireman had to throw sand into the firebox when the engine was working hard. The draft sucked the sand through the fire tubes, scouring them out.

Oil firing had several advantages. Firemen found it easier to control the steaming rate with oil than with coal, losing less steam through the safety valves. Oil eliminated the labor of shoveling coal; in the heat of the American southwest this could be decisive. Even in the temperate climate of the UK, one July day in 2013, the Welsh Highland Railway measured temperatures of 95°F in the open air, 125°F in the cab of a steam locomotive. Because an oil-burner fireman needed only to manipulate the valves, he could keep a lookout ahead, with benefits to safety. Handling coal and ash at terminals could amount to 50 cents per ton of coal burned; oil firing eliminated this cost.[9] Cinders from coal-burning locomotives choked the track ballast, interfering with drainage; this did not occur with oil firing.

Between 1896 and 1900, Baldwin built 450 oil-burning locomotives, many of them for export, including several for Russia.[10] In 1901, the company built a locomotive for the Santa Fe with a new type of firebox, purpose-designed for burning oil. Three tubes, 32 inches in diameter and 86½ inches long, each with a burner inside, ended in a cylindrical combustion chamber 60 inches in diameter and 40 inches long, abutting against the back tube sheet. Each burner consisted of two slots, one above the other. Steam under boiler pressure blew through the bottom slot, entraining and atomizing the oil flowing through the top one.

Oil has a higher calorific value than coal, close to 22,000 BTU per pound. The economy of oil, however, depended not only on the relative prices of coal and oil but on the landed cost to the railroad after transportation. The shipping cost could be decisive in any comparison between the two. Oil from Beaumont, Texas, for example, cost $1.26 a barrel at St. Louis, Missouri, in 1901: $1.05 for transportation and 21 cents for the oil. Oil firing became common in Texas and the southwest because of remoteness from sources of coal and because of locally available oil.[11]

By 1903, the railroads were coming to realize that "the size of the locomotive has increased at a greater rate than the size of the fireman," or, stated in another way:

> the amount of fuel burned in a modern locomotive is in excess of the quantity that can be shoveled into the firebox by one man. A locomotive with 5,000 square feet of heating surface when working at maximum power will evaporate about 75,000 pounds of water an hour, which represents a coal consumption of about 10,700 pounds, or more than 5 tons. Even if two firemen are employed, it is questionable if efficient combustion is possible under these conditions. On the other hand the use of oil can be controlled merely by the turning of a few valves and the amount of fuel burned is easily and quickly regulated to meet the varying demands for power. By keeping close watch on the character of the smoke, it is possible to always maintain practically perfect combustion.

In spite of its general benefits, oil firing always occupied a niche in American steam locomotive practice, dependent on local supply. Most American steam locomotives burned bituminous coal to the end of the steam era.

3.1.3 Coal Firing

Firing a coal-burning steam locomotive is—obviously—crucial to its functioning and—less obviously—a difficult art in which proficiency is acquired only through years of practice.

The fireman or roundhouse crew lit the fire in a locomotive firebox with layers of coal, kindling and oily rags spread evenly over the grate. A necessary preliminary was to insure that the boiler contained enough water to cover the crown sheet. Over a period of hours the fireman would build this to an evenly burning fire bed 6 to 8 inches thick. This filled the cab with smoke until the heat of the fire boiled water and produced enough steam pressure to use the blower to draw smoke through the fire tubes and out through the stack. The fireman continued to build the fire until nearly full boiler pressure had been reached, at which point the locomotive was ready to go about its business. The fireman could increase the heat of the fire by opening the firebox dampers and the blower or quieten it down by closing those two devices.

When the engine was working steam, the exhaust nozzle induced a negative pressure in the smokebox which, through the fire tubes, induced a negative pressure in the firebox, sucking air through the fire from below, but also through any other available entrances. Flaps ("dampers"), fitted to the ash pan, allowed the fireman some control of the amount of air that was sucked into the fire.

As long as the engine was in steam, the fireman's work consisted of a cycle, the frequency of which was proportional to the power demand. He first added coal to the fire, a few shovelfuls at a time. This coal would heat up and start to burn after a period of time ranging from less than a minute with a wide open throttle and long cutoff—thus a strong firebox draft—to several minutes when the draft was quieter, as when the locomotive was drifting downgrade. The newly generated heat caused the boiler pressure, visible on the steam pressure gauge, to rise faster than it was being lowered by the engine's use of steam. As the pressure approached the maximum working pressure, either the fireman or the engineer would turn on the injector. Running the injector caused a fall in the boiler pressure, both due to its use of steam and because it injected relatively cool water into the boiler. If the engine was working steam, the engineman might allow the pressure to drop by no more than 5 pounds per square inch before shutting off the injector; if he wanted to keep the engine quiet, as when drifting downgrade or preparing to stop, he might drop the pressure by as much as 20 pounds. When the boiler pressure had dropped by the desired amount, the engineman would shut off the injector and observe the rate at which steam pressure recovered.

When the steam pressure recovered slowly or not at all, the fireman added more coal, repeating the cycle, adding coal to the fire in a regular pattern so as to cover the full area of the grate. Because of the need to control distribution as well as firing rate, the design of an effective power stoker was not easy.

When the engine was working hard, the cycle would be practically continuous. The ash pan dampers would be open and the fire door closed, except when adding coal, forcing the maximum amount of air through the fire from beneath. Soon after being added to the fire, the coal released its volatiles and black smoke would come from the stack. Leaving the fire door slightly open, admitting "secondary air" over the top of the fire, would burn the volatiles and reduce the smoke. If the fire door was open too wide or too often, cool air struck the back tube sheet, causing uneven expansion and contraction and leaking fire tube joints.

To combat this problem, some fireboxes were built with a steel deflector plate over the fire door inside the firebox, angled downward to deflect air down into the bed of the fire, rather than letting it strike the tube sheet. The deflector also heated the air that passed along its hot underside before striking the fire. William Smith, Superintendent of Motive Power and Machinery on the Chicago & North Western, mentioned this device at the 1893 Master Mechanics' Convention as an innovation.[12] It is also attributed to Matthew Kirtley and Charles Markham of the Midland Railway in Britain in 1859.[13] Some manufacturers put small air slots in the fire door to improve the ventilation of the firebox.

When the engine was working lightly or drifting downgrade, it might run for several miles, keeping the boiler pressure constant with only infrequent additions of coal and running of the injector. The fireman could keep the fire quiet by closing the dampers and slightly opening the fire door, using the blower to prevent flames and smoke from entering the cab and to reduce smoke from the stack. In theory, the injector could be run continuously so that the rate of addition of feed water matched the rate of consumption by the engine. In practice this was rarely achievable.

On occasion the boiler would refuse to steam for several reasons. Holes in the fire, where the grate was not covered by coal, would allow air to short-circuit through the firebars instead of passing through the firebed. At high drafting rates, where the firebox was filled with white-hot flame, holes were difficult to see and their presence could only be suspected. The fireman could check the fire by opening the fire door and using his shovel to direct cold air through the flames, but the heat and glare of the fire discouraged all but the briefest inspection. If the fireman suspected holes in the fire, but could not find them, he could only fire vigorously all over the box in the hopes of blocking them. Clinker could blind the firebars, detectable by blue flames when the fire was quiet. Shaking grates could break up clinker; otherwise the fireman had either to put up with the problem or try to break up the gooey clinker with a pricker iron. Depending on the arrangement inside the smokebox, trapped cinders could blind the spark arrestor netting. If the enginemen suspected this problem, they had to stop, open the smokebox door and bang or brush the cinders from the netting. The common solution to these prob-lems was to throw in more and more coal until there was an opportunity to stop and find out what was wrong.

If, for whatever reason, the fireman was unable to maintain boiler pressure, the crew had to stop the train and wait for it to recover. The alternative, and a dangerous one, was to omit running the injector and risk uncovering the crown sheet.

If the fireman added too much coal, the boiler would generate steam faster than the engineer could use it. The enginemen could then either allow steam to waste through the safety valves or try to hold the pressure down with the injectors, risking overfilling the boiler. This could cause water to be drawn through the dry pipe, with the risk of damaging the cylinders and pistons. A superheater might evaporate this water but at the cost of a serious loss of boiler pressure, leaving the blowdown valve as the only means of lowering the boiler water level.

The fireman had to understand the route well enough to foresee and provide for the power demanded by the various curves and grades in the light of trailing load, weather and the habits of his engineer. The skill of the engine crew affected performance and efficiency as much as the design and construction of the engine itself. The skill and temperament of the crew could frustrate the best efforts of design and test engineers, masking the effects of their improvements to the engine itself. The same engine would perform differently in the hands of different crews, or in different weather conditions. Weather and the seasons had marked effects on fuel consumption, especially in the northern States where bearings tightened in the winter cold. The Chicago Great Western burned 25% more coal per ton-mile in winter than in summer.[14]

The time lag between firing and steam generation and the resulting inconsistency between power demand and fuel burn contributed to the gross inefficiency of the coal-burning steam locomotive. Oil firing alleviated this problem but, the bigger the engine, the longer the time lag in either case. Only the diesel-electric locomotive, still decades away in the future, would match power demand and fuel burn precisely and instantaneously—and sweep the steam locomotive from the rails.

Arguments on how to fire a steam locomotive have gone on since

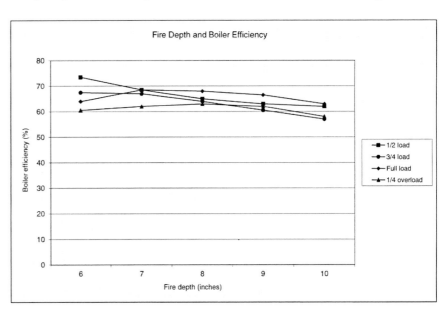

Locomotive loading, fire depth and boiler efficiency (graph drawn from Harding, J. W., *Steam Locomotive Home Study Course*, International Text Book Co., Scranton, Pennsylvania, 1923-46, republished Little River Locomotive Co., Townsend, Tennessee, 2002, Vol. 3, 154).

fireboxes were wider and longer than a shovel blade. Some firemen favored a level firebed ("level firing"); others favored piling coal around the sides or back of the firebox ("bank firing").[15] Too thin a fire would burn the grate, warp the ash pan and make holes in the firebed. Too thick a fire would choke the air flow through the fire.[16] The dividing line between "thick" and "thin" here was a fire depth of 8 to 10 inches. Many enginemen believed that the fire needed to be 10 to 12 inches thick. Tests at Purdue in 1902 showed maximum power output being achieved with a fire depth no more than 3 or 4 inches.[17] Experience showed that, the stronger the draft, the thicker the fire depth for maximum boiler efficiency.

With typical thoroughness, the Pennsylvania ran a test at Altoona in 1908 to compare level and bank firing, building a ridge of coal just inside the fire door, level with the top of the fire door.[18] Coal thrown over the top of the bank gave off its gases and slid down to the center of the fire to be burned. This method was certainly easier on the fireman. The tests found that neither method evaporated more water per pound of coal than the other.

The fireman's skill was so important that the Pennsylvania kept records of the coal usage of more than a thousand enginemen.[19] The company found variations up to 40% between the heaviest and lightest coal users, with as much as 15% going to waste. Comparisons were difficult to make and not necessarily reliable because of variations in grade and curvature between one division and another and daily variations in train load, weather and engine condition.

Railroads appointed experienced enginemen as "traveling engineers" and "traveling firemen" to monitor and instruct engine crews and to spread the doctrines of efficient firing and operation. By 1892, the traveling engineers were numerous enough to form their own trade association. These associations—Traveling Engineers, Master Mechanics, Master Car Builders, to name but a few—with their annual national conventions, played an important part in sharing and developing the skills of the trades that they represented.

The early 1900s brought the fireman's situation to something of a crisis. His task had become so arduous that, especially in a labor-hungry economy, the railroads found it increasingly difficult to attract good men. As firing was the training position for engineers, this boded ill for the future. The more skilled senior firemen were bidding runs on the smaller engines, leaving the big, new engines—the pride of the company's fleet—to the most junior and least skilled firemen. One railroadman[20] wrote that he loved working on the footplate, but that the big engines were such "man-killers" that he avoided it.

Some railroads had to put two firemen on an engine.

During the very hot weather of the first week in July (1900) the Superintendent of the Central of New Jersey employed an extra fireman on each of the large new twelve-wheel locomotives in order to lighten the burden of the regular fireman, and it is said that the helpers will be kept on during July and August.[21]

By 1904, locomotive designers were beginning to realize that locomotive development was being stunted as long as it depended on a human fireman. This problem was ill-defined because some runs were more demanding than others and some engineer-fireman crews were more efficient than others. Nevertheless:

it will be found that under favorable conditions, each pound of coal burned will sustain one indicated horsepower for a period of from 12 to 15 minutes. Within certain limits the power developed is nearly proportional to the amount of coal burned. In the development of the modern locomotive, grates have been enlarged and heating surface extended that larger amounts of fuel may be burned. In one direction only has the designer found the way blocked against his ingenuity. He has not been

able materially to augment the strength of the fireman, and, consequently, when running under constant conditions, the power of the modern locomotive has not increased in proportion to its dimensions. A laborer is working at a fair rate when, in unloading coal from a gondola car, merely dropping it over the side, he handles 6,000 lbs. of coal per hour. At the limit, a locomotive fireman will handle an equal amount, standing upon an unsteady platform, placing it upon some particular part of the grate, and usually closing the door after each scoopful. This rate will serve to develop approximately 1,200 indicated horsepower and cannot be exceeded under sustained conditions of running, though for short intervals the rate of power may outrun the rate of firing. Because of the limitations of the strength of the fireman it is probable that further growth in locomotives will probably await the coming of an automatic stoker which will serve to remove its operation from dependence upon the physical condition of a single man.[22]

The railroads dragged their feet on installing power stokers for decades.

3.1.4 Mechanical Stokers

A mechanical stoker seems an obvious solution to the limited ability of a human fireman to keep pace with the coal demand of a big engine, but developing such a device suitable for locomotives was not easy. The first mechanical stokers were the chain grates used in stationary steam plants; they were not suitable for locomotives.[23]

In 1900–01, J. H. Day & Co., Cincinnati, brought out the Kincaid steam-powered locomotive stoker. Two parallel spirals drew coal from a hopper and moved it into a trough where a steam-driven plunger pushed it through the fire door. The fireman could adjust the force of the plunger and, hence, the distance to which coal was thrown into the firebox.[24] The fireman still had to shovel coal into the hopper, which negated the purpose of the stoker, although he had only to lift the coal 30 inches as opposed to throwing it the length of the firebox. The manufacturers claimed that, because the fire door did not have to be opened to admit coal, the temperature inside the firebox would be more constant than with hand firing, reducing the maintenance on fire tubes.

The new engines coming into service in 1900–05 needed enormous firing rates that the early versions of the Kincaid stoker could not match.

On the ordinary American type of engine there is no necessity for the stoker, as the work is such that an ordinary man can do it with ease, but with the long fire-box type of engine on a long run over a division comparatively free from grades, where the engine is loaded to its maximum capacity all of the time, is where the stoker will be found most valuable. The present type of stoker will throw about 3,000 lbs. of coal per hour. A modern type of passenger engine with 46 sq. ft. of grate surface and burning 200 lbs. of coal per sq. ft. of grate per hr. will require about 9,200 lbs. of coal per hr. The stoker, as it is built at present, will not serve such a fire-box.[25]

The Great Northern in 1902 and the Chesapeake & Ohio in 1904 were probably the first railroads to test power stokers.[26] They acknowledged that the stoker reduced fire tube maintenance because the fire door stayed closed, with no cold air striking the back tube sheet, but doubts existed whether a power stoker could distribute the coal with the same skill as a human fireman and, therefore, if it was as efficient. P. A. Peck of the Chicago & Western Illinois expressed the truth of the matter:

Our engines are getting bigger every day, burning more coal, but the men are not any bigger than they were twenty years ago. We have got to come to some mechanical stoker in the near future.

3.1.5 Firing Rates

Extracting ever more power from locomotives of restricted dimensions resulted in firing rates unknown in other steam plant, as measured by pounds of coal per square foot of grate per hour.

Coal on an open grate in the open air burns at about 3 pounds of coal per square foot of grate per hour; this can be increased by forcing air through the grate. A stationary boiler with a stack draft of 0.1 to 1.4 inches of water gauge increased this rate to 10 to 20 pounds. A fan-drafted marine engine, drafted at 1 to 4 inches of water gauge, increased this rate farther to 50 pounds. European locomotives were built for firing rates up to 50 to 100 pounds of coal per square foot of grate per hour; in America rates as high as 150 to 200 pounds were common. These combustion rates were achieved by intense drafting. In American locomotives the smokebox vacuum was 3 to 10 inches of water gauge, usually higher than 6 inches. Only smelting furnaces used a similar draft intensity.[27]

Experiments on the Purdue test plant in about 1900 showed the following results at 130 pounds per square inch steam pressure, full throttle with the rollers braked to 35 miles per hour.

Cut-off* (Inches)	Cut-off (Percent)	Horsepower (Indicated)	Firing Rate (Lbs. coal/sq.ft. grate/hr.)
6	25%	300	72
8	35%	434	113
10.5	50%	495	179

*Cut off at (inches) of piston stroke. Percent cut-off based on 24-inch stroke.[28]

The researchers measured the smokebox vacuum needed to achieve these combustion rates:

Smokebox Vacuum (Inches water gauge)	Firing Rate (Lbs. coal/sq.ft. grate/hr.)
2.0	64
3.3	113
4.3	147

The smokebox vacuum needed for combustion at high firing rates came at the cost of a constricted exhaust nozzle, hence high back pressure in the cylinders and, hence, lower mean effective pressure (the pressure drop across the cylinders). As mean effective pressure drove the engine, this was counter-productive. Higher firing rates also lowered the evaporative efficiency of both the coal and the heating surfaces. These findings had long-term implications for the power density (power-to-bulk ratio) of the steam locomotive.

On occasion, British locomotives were fired at American firing rates. This narrative is reproduced by kind permission of Oakwood Press, UK. Here, a 2-6-0 has been substituted for a failed 4-6-0 on a heavy train in the 1940s[29]:

> I had had little opportunity to pay any real attention to the state of the fire but when I did my heart sank because it was just half a box of very dull to black fire. The guard gave us the "right away," I turned the blower on full and got the pricker down off the tender and attempted to spread what fire we had more evenly over the grate. I then grabbed the shovel and found that there was just a mish-mash of small coal and rubbish on the front of the tender. Clearly it wasn't anticipated that this engine would be travelling very far. Edgar wasn't going to have any time booked against him and was giving the engine "the gun" in getting our 11 coaches out of Reading. The regulator was wide open and the reversing lever was set in the 40 per cent cut-off notch. All I could do was shovel coal as fast as possible. No fancy "haycock" fire now, just keep that roaring furnace fed. I reckoned that each shovelful held about 15 lb. of coal and I was firing these at a rate of about six shovelfuls a minute into the

firebox of this hungry brute. Most of the small coal went straight out through the tubes and up the chimney leaving a black plume behind us. There was no time to notice familiar landmarks, I just kept my back bent and my head down and shoveled whatever sort of coal I could find into a firebox that resembled Dante's Inferno. I caught a glimpse of Ealing Broadway and realized that the fire was still no higher than when we had left Reading. The exhaust injector had been on all the way and the boiler water gauge still registered no more than half a glass. Anticipating that Edgar would soon be shutting off to run into Paddington I put on the right-hand injector as well and stopped shovelling coal. The palms of my hands were red and sore from the couple of tons of small coal I had shifted during the past 40 minutes, and clearly this engine was incapable of keeping time with such a load. As we ran into No. 8 platform I was glad to see our relief and when we got off the footplate I noticed that the bottom of the smokebox door was red hot and sizzling with the heat.

Engineers were not all paragons of virtue in this regard. The following excerpt is quoted by kind permission of the author, Margaret Coel, as told by Sam Speas.[30]

> I was firing a beet train out of Fort Collins with thirty-five empty cars bound for Wellington and with a hot-tempered engineer no fireman liked. Just out of the west yard, he and the brakeman got into a heated argument. Suddenly, the engineer threw the throttle wide open and pushed down the Johnson Bar, and we took off like a cyclone in Oklahoma with the exhaust tearing up the fire. I was shoveling as fast as I could while coal was blowing out the stack. With the steam pressure dropping, I yelled to the engineer, "Close her down." We hurtled down the track with the throttle open and the pressure still dropping. "Close her down," I shouted again, but he was bent over the throttle, holding it wide open.
>
> Finally, I put the clinker hook into the firebox, waited until it was red hot, took it out, and pointed it at the engineer's seat, I had no intention of poking him, but he didn't know that. He glimpsed the hook out of the corner of his eye, jumped up, and fled out the narrow door in front of his seat. I reached over and flipped the lock on the door. Then I closed down the throttle and notched back the Johnson Bar. Back and forth I went between the right and left sides of the engine cab, shoveling coal, checking the water and running the engine. Gradually, I brought the engine under control, while the engineer was outside on the running board, holding onto the bar.

Heavy drafting and high firing rates carried a penalty in fuel economy that was ultimately unsustainable.

3.1.6 Fuel Economy

Economic conditions and management science resulted in sharply increased interest in fuel economy; the Purdue and Chicago & North Western test plants made it possible to study this matter under controlled conditions as never before.

Fuel economy could be measured in three ways: pounds of water evaporated per pound of coal, pounds of coal per horsepower-hour and pounds of coal per thousand ton-miles hauled. Because the boiling point of water increased with increasing boiler pressure, these figures were calculated for evaporation "from and at 212°F."

Coal burned in a calorimeter will evaporate 13.5 to 14.5 pounds of water per pound of coal, depending on the quality of the coal; steam boilers can be judged against this benchmark.

British and European locomotives sometimes ran on firing rates as low as 20 to 70 pounds of coal per square foot of grate per hour, resulting in evaporation rates of 8.5 to 12.5 pounds of water per pound of coal—the evaporation rate being in inverse proportion to the firing rate. The 150- to 200-pound firing rates on American locomotives dropped the evaporation rate to only 6 pounds of water per pound of coal.

In the spring of 1898, the Cleveland, Cincinnati, Chicago & St. Louis made a series of road tests, supported by tests at Purdue, to compare five types of coal available to it. The test locomotive was a 2-8-0 on the 107-mile run between Indianapolis and Cincinnati with trailing loads of 1,450 tons eastbound, 800 tons westbound, the difference being due to grades. The locomotive evaporated 5.0 to 6.8 pounds of water per pound of coal; the Purdue test locomotive evaporated 5.1 to 6.4 pounds. Of the coals tested, the best—and most expensive—proved to be worth its higher price in the final cost per ton-mile, not only because it generated more steam, but also because it required the handling of the least amount of coal, ash and clinker. The replies to an 1899 survey conducted by the Master Mechanics' Association suggested evaporation rates ranging from 3.1 up to 10.8 pounds of water per pound of coal.[31]

The Purdue work produced the disquieting result that, the harder the boiler was worked, the less efficient it became. At an evaporation rate of 5 pounds of water per square foot of heating surface per hour, one pound of dry coal evaporated 6.5 to 9.0 pounds of water. If the fire was drafted more strongly, the evaporation rate increased to 10 pounds of water per square foot per hour but the water evaporated by a pound of coal dropped to only 5.3 to 6.5 pounds.[32] The tests showed that a surprising amount of coal went out through the stack as incandescent coal and ash, ranging from 6.2% to 6.6% of the coal at the lower evaporation rate to 15.6% to 21.2% with the stronger draft needed at the higher evaporation rate.

These findings boded ill for the future of the steam locomotive: the harder it worked, the less efficient it became. Lump coal needed a certain dwelling time on the grate in order to burn; therefore the combustion process itself limited the weight of coal that could be fed onto each square foot of grate per hour, regardless of the capacity of any power stoker. High combustion rates needed such an intense draft that fine coal would not lie on the grate long enough to burn before being picked up by the draft and blasted out through the stack. Clearance dimensions limited the width of the grate. Therefore the coal-fired steam locomotive faced certain ultimate limits as to the power that it could produce. In the 1890s these limits were still far from being reached, but they existed, nonetheless.

Tests at Purdue in 1902 produced three related benchmarks:

- firing rate: 150 to 160 pounds of coal per square foot of grate per hour;
- evaporation rate: 13 pounds of water per square foot of heating surface per hour;
- coal consumption: 6.0 to 6.5 pounds of water evaporated per pound of coal per hour.[33]

Another measure of fuel efficiency was coal consumption per horsepower-hour. The Newcomen atmospheric engines of the eighteenth century consumed 17 to 22 pounds of coal per horsepower-hour.[34] They were so costly to fuel that they found little use away from the coal mines that they drained and whose waste coal they burned. Watt's double-acting, high-pressure engine with separate condenser reduced this to 6.6 pounds per horsepower-hour. By the early 1890s, non-condensing, single-expansion, high-speed, stationary engines reduced this further to 3.9 pounds. Compounding and condensing dropped this figure to 2.4 pounds. The ultimate in stationary reciprocating steam power in the 1890s was a triple-expansion compound, low-speed, condensing engine with a coal consumption of only 1.8 pounds per horsepower-hour. In more recent years, coal-burning steam turbines used for generating electricity have advanced in efficiency to about 0.5 pounds per horsepower-hour.

In 1896, the Purdue locomotive, working in controlled, ideal conditions, provided the following figures for coal and steam consumption in pounds per indicated horsepower-hour at 180 pounds per square inch boiler pressure with the throttle wide open.

Speed (mph)	Driving Wheel rpm	6" cut-off (25%)		8" cut-off (33%)		10" cut-off (42%)	
		Coal	Steam	Coal	Steam	Coal	Steam
15	81	4.5	29.9	4.2	27.7	—	—
25	135	4.2	28.1	4.5	26.6	5.1	28.6
35	188	4.2	26.9	4.5	26.3	6.3	30.1
45	242	4.3	28.6	5.6	28.5	—	—
55	296	5.1	30.6	6.0	32.0	—	—

Based on 24-inch stroke.

These figures shows clearly the effect of short cut-off and expansive working of the steam.

Some of the big engines of 1900 consumed 6.5 pounds of coal per horsepower-hour. Some freight engines consumed as much as 12 to 13 pounds per horsepower-hour, burning 11,000 to 13,000 pounds of coal per hour while developing 800 to 900 horsepower—barely more efficient than a Newcomen engine, although this may have reflected the uneven and intermittent power demand of any steam locomotive.[35]

Stationary engines had none of the size, weight and arrangement limitations of steam locomotives. They ran at constant speed and load for long periods of time. They could therefore be set up to run with an efficiency unachievable in a steam locomotive with its constant changes in speed and power demand. The ever bigger locomotives being built around 1900 suffered from their empirical design methods and a lack of test data. As late as 1915, engines were still being built in which the main components were poorly proportioned in relation to each other.

The third measure of efficiency was coal consumption per thousand freight ton-miles hauled. This was a useful measure of locomotive performance but was affected by coal quality, terrain, weather and many other aspects of railroad operations.

The coal consumption of the Cleveland, Cincinnati, Chicago & St. Louis 2-8-0, mentioned above, ranged from 118 pounds per thousand ton-miles hauled to 157, depending on the type of coal. An enormous Baldwin compound 2-10-0, built for the Minneapolis, St. Paul & Sault Ste. Marie in 1900, demonstrated the economy of giant engines. Pulling 2,000-ton trailing loads over a 111-mile division, this engine averaged 100 pounds of coal per thousand ton-miles hauled.[36] A true comparison needs the grades and curvatures of the two runs, but this serves as an indicator for locomotive design.

Even in the short space of six years—1885–1891—the effect of bigger engines was apparent. On one division of one (unnamed) railroad, the average payload per train increased 52% from 219 tons to 333 tons. Coal consumption per freight engine-mile increased 18% as bigger engines hauled heavier trains. The cost of coal per ton-mile decreased 19%, even though the price of coal rose 8% at the same time.[37] Between 1897 and 1903, another railroad increased the average tractive force of its engines by 31%, while increasing its freight ton-miles hauled by 87% and freight ton-miles per engine per year by 35%. The company had to burn 79% more coal to do this, but coal consumption per ton-mile dropped by 4%.[38] All of this pointed to the economy of big engines.

Although the railroads demanded giant engines capable of unprecedented tractive effort, the engineering of these monsters was venturing into unknown territory, even without the complexities of compounding or articulation. The design methods available at the time permitted little in the way of prediction of results before the engine was built and proved itself, or failed, in service. In 1900:

> As we have authentic records of 1,800 horsepower having been developed for three or more hours, we are confident that it can be done for any reasonable time. We will admit that some of the modern locomotives of ordinary design have reached a point where the capacity of one man to keep them properly supplied with coal has more than been reached, and such large quantities of coal are consumed that one tankfull does not cover a very long distance or a very long period of time; but we are fully convinced that these exceptionally large locomotives, having from 2,500 to 3,000 square feet of heating surface and with the same grate area as engines of one half the heating surface, are a great mistake, and that high-pressure compound locomotives with 22 × 28 inch cylinders and carrying 200 to 225 pounds pressure, are a greater mistake. Such engines are and must necessarily be very wasteful of fuel and beyond the capacity of men constructed on ordinary lines to either fire them or properly handle them, and, what is worse, they do not perform the work on fast and heavy trains any better than the lighter engines. These, however, are mistakes of designers and builders in trying to achieve a much desired result, in the wrong way and do not in the least detract from the possibilities of the locomotive as a machine.[39]

In 1904, G. R. Henderson[40] assembled the results of road and static tests on the Chicago & North Western, using the railroad's standard 2-8-0 freight engine. Henderson showed that the evaporation rate varied with the type of coal and the ratios between heating surface, grate area and firing rate, using this information to chart the fuel consumption of this class of engine for various speeds, trailing loads and grades. This was an advance on any previous means of estimating the fuel consumption of a particular class of engine on a specified route with a specified load. Henderson also pointed to the maximum economical firing rates per square foot of grate area per hour which were: bituminous coal, 200 pounds; coarse anthracite, 100 pounds; fine anthracite, 60 pounds. This was valuable information for locomotive designers.

The more the steam locomotive was studied, the more its inefficiencies and undesirable features came to light and the more closely they were measured in terms of cost. In 1903–4 the Santa Fe made tests to find out how much coal was used in firing up and standing still.[41] Firing up consumed 515 pounds per thousand square feet of heating surface, while an engine standing still with steam up consumed 140 pounds of coal and 282 pounds of water per thousand square feet of heating surface per hour just to maintain boiler pressure, burning more than 400 pounds of coal per hour heating the atmosphere, feeding steam leaks and maintaining air pressure in leaking brake systems. Later analysis of operations on a division of the Pennsylvania showed that a typical freight engine spent 51% of its time in steam working steam, 16% drifting down grade and 33% standing still. This was a substantial loss, the more so as engines became bigger.

Even in the mid–1890s, even when the depression was at its worst, the weight of opinion on efficiency versus effectiveness was shifting. While a mechanical engineer might look at fuel economy in terms of efficient combustion, railroad operators had to look at it in terms of cost per ton-mile. In 1894:

> It is evident to anyone who has watched the progress of locomotive construction and operation, that less fuel is being used now per ton mile than formerly, but, on the other hand, locomotives are forced so much more than they used to be, that, except in the case of those with large fireboxes, the efficiency of the boiler is less. The increasing weight of trains gives a greater ton mileage and the weight of the locomotive is less in proportion to the weight of the train, therefore on a ton-mile basis less fuel is now used, but so far as the fuel burning of the locomotive itself is concerned, it is a question whether there has been any material advance in average practice for sometime past. About all that has been gained by better design of boilers has been lost by the greater forcing of boilers arising from the increased demand for steam. The exception to this is found in the boilers with large fireboxes and grates.[42]

This underlying disquiet would remain at the heart of steam locomotive development over the next fifty years.

Section 3.2. Fireboxes and Combustion

3.2.1 Fireboxes

The firebox was the most important heating surface, the most difficult part of the boiler to design and the main cause of boiler explosions. It consisted of a rectangular box inside the back part of the boiler, made of iron or steel in America, but made of copper in Britain and some European countries. A space between the firebox and the boiler exterior formed a water jacket, called the "water leg." Steam pressure tended to blow the water legs apart, but was prevented from doing so by staybolts. This general arrangement is shown in the accompanying drawing.

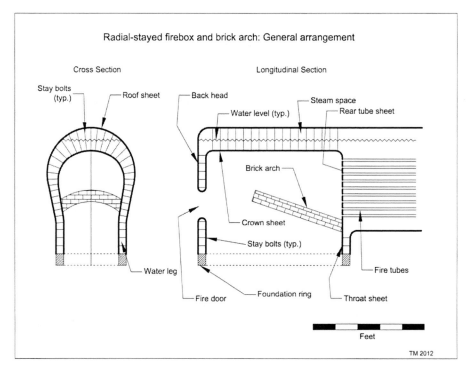

Schematic sections through a typical locomotive firebox with a brick arch (redrawn from Ringel, C., *History, Development and Function of the Locomotive Brick Arch*, RLHS, New York, January 1948. Printed *Journal RLHS*, October 1956, 79).

The firebox rested on the foundation ring. The floor of the firebox was the grate on which the fire lay, with an ash pan underneath. The front of the firebox consisted partly of the back tube sheet, from which the fire tubes went through the main body of the boiler, and partly of a throat sheet between the bottom of the tube sheet and the front of the foundation ring. The back of the firebox was the backhead, containing the fire door. Some of the wide-firebox engines of the early 1900s had two fire doors. The roof of the firebox was the crown sheet. Water covered the crown sheet, above which was a steam space.

The firebox was one of the inherently unsatisfactory features of the steam locomotive. Made from steel that would soften at 600°F to 700°F, it had to contain a fire burning at 1,500°F to 1,700°F while under pressure from the steam in the boiler. Only the water, at about 390°F, prevented it from softening and collapsing under the steam pressure, which it was ill-shaped to withstand. Scale and mud on the water side of the firebox shell could interfere with cooling, resulting in overheating, damage and possible failure.

Angus Sinclair describes the many designs of firebox and boiler that were tried and failed during the nineteenth century in *Development of the Locomotive Engine*. By the 1890s four types of locomotive firebox were current[43]: crown bar, radial-stayed or wagon top, Wootten and Belpaire, illustrated schematically in the accompanying drawing.

expand more than the wrapper sheet, although both were riveted to the foundation ring. This tended to lift the crown sheet against the crown bars, slackening the sling stays and leaving the downward force of the steam pressure on the crown sheet to be supported by the firebox side sheets. Although the staybolts prevented the side sheets from buckling, it was impossible to install them so that they would all take their correct loads when they were hot and the boiler was under pressure. It was difficult to inspect or replace broken stays. The crown bar firebox gave way to the radial-stayed and Belpaire fireboxes.[44]

The radial-stayed firebox was better shaped to resist the various forces. The firebox shell acted as an arch to resist the steam pressure. Its weak point was at the reverse curve where the narrow bottom part of the firebox widened into the cylindrical top part. Here upward expansion of the lower firebox sheets, anchored at the foundation ring, met downward expansion of the top sheets, anchored by the arched crown sheet, causing buckling.

The Belpaire firebox had the advantage that the crown stays were directly loaded in tension because the firebox and wrapper sheets were parallel. Long cross-stays counteracted the force tending to blow out the side walls. Because the firebox and wrapper sheets were almost exactly parallel over most of the cross-section, expansion and contraction was more even than in other designs. Many different Belpaire cross-sections were possible; one railroad used at least seven.

The Belpaire firebox was heavier and more expensive than the radial-stayed version. Stress problems occurred where the rectangular firebox joined the cylindrical boiler shell. Some railroads, such as the Pennsylvania and the Great Northern, favored the Belpaire firebox; others did not. It became standard on the engines that the Pennsylvania built in its own shops.

John E. Wootten patented his wide, shallow firebox in 1877 while in charge of the Philadelphia & Reading shops at Reading, Pennsylvania, to burn cheap waste anthracite. A wide, fixed grate made of water tubes and iron bars, beneath a shallow firebox with two fire doors, extended over the back driving wheels which were limited in size accordingly. The original Wootten firebox had a firebrick wall half its height at the front of the grate with a combustion chamber ahead of it.[45]

The Wootten firebox left little space for the crew. The engineer worked in a cab halfway along the boiler, while the fireman worked in a rudimentary shelter behind the firebox. Such engines were known as "Mother Hubbards," "double cabs" or "camelbacks."[46] This arrangement prevented the engineer and fireman from working as a crew and left the engineer fatally exposed in the event of a collision, derailment or a broken side rod. Even so, camelbacks were common in the eastern U.S., some surviving until the end of steam. One fireman recalled: "We couldn't talk to each other. Heck, I couldn't even see him. We did get off the engine for lunch, and got along great."[47]

Wootten fireboxes were typical of the anthracite country. The Erie had Baldwin rebuild forty-eight 4-4-0s with Wootten fireboxes in 1896–7, having previously retrofitted this type of firebox to nearly one hundred 2-8-0s. Most locomotives built new for the Erie between

Schematic cross-sections through the four common firebox types (redrawn from Bruce, A. W., *The Steam Locomotive in America: Its Development in the Twentieth Century*, New York: Bonanza, 1952, and *RRG*, July 23, 1897, 520).

The crown bar firebox was the earliest type still current in the 1890s. Staybolts held the side sheets together, but the crown sheet was held by crown bars, themselves held by sling stays. Unless the sling stays and crown bars were perfectly dimensioned, they supported the crown sheet unevenly; this worsened under the forces of thermal expansion and steam pressure. The firebox, being exposed to the fire, would be far hotter than the boiler wrapper sheet which was exposed to the outside air. The firebox shell would therefore

A Philadelphia & Reading class P-3a 4-4-2, No. 323, built by Baldwin in 1900, photographed at Philadelphia, Pennsylvania, on October 31, 1927, waiting for its next assignment – and burning coal while doing so. The locomotive has a wide firebox for burning anthracite and a "Mother Hubbard," "double" or "camelback" cab. The Walschaert valve gear would have been a retrofit, although the rebuild retained slide valves (Denver Public Library, Otto C. Perry collection, OP-14504).

1886 and 1902 had Wootten fireboxes; Erie policy changed to single-cab engines in 1903.[48]

The Northern Pacific tried Wootten fireboxes with lignite in 1880–1. This was not a success because of the immense quantities of lignite needed and because alkaline water made it difficult to maintain the large numbers of staybolts needed for that size of firebox.

In the Wootten firebox expansion forces and steam pressure both tended in the same direction, to straighten out the side legs. They proved difficult to maintain as a result. In a long Wootten grate, transverse bracing was needed to prevent the firebox from spreading in the middle.[49] In 1893, the Wharton Railroad Switch Co., Philadelphia, which owned the patents to the Wootten firebox, developed a hybrid design which added the Belpaire top to the wide-skirted Wootten firebox.

The success of the wide grate depended substantially on the fireman.

Not long ago an important Western road built a large-grate engine at its own shops, and with a good fireman, who knew what he was expected to do with this particular engine, she was a success and gave a good saving. But when the road got a lot of them all in a bunch trouble commenced. The engines would not steam and the men did not want them. This made things look black for the mechanical engineer and he grew desperate, with the result that a traveling fireman was put on and the men were told that they would have to make the engines steam if the expert could, and they did, and instead of carrying from 12 to 28 inches of fire on the grates the thickness was reduced to six or eight inches, the engines steamed well, and are the standards of the road today and give an increased efficiency over the small-grate engines of 20%.[50]

Large numbers of staybolts held the water jacket together, ranging from 300 to 400 in an 0-6-0 switcher up to 1,000 to 1,400 in a 2-8-0.[51] Uneven relative movement of the firebox sheets put bending loads on the staybolts which eventually broke. One railroad, operating 249 engines, had to replace 9,446 staybolts in one year. Broken staybolts took the engine out of service for time-consuming repairs. Railroads found a correlation between water quality and staybolt breakage.

Broken staybolts could be detected by tapping or by visual inspection when the boiler was washed out. Another solution was an axial hole in the staybolt that would leak water and steam if the staybolt broke. As early as the 1890s some states, such as Massachusetts, required them by law; staybolts with axial tell-tale holes were almost universal by 1895.[52]

Rigid staybolts were stressed in a destructive combination of tension, shear and reverse bending. Flexible staybolts, allegedly invented on the Pennsylvania,[53] accommodated lateral movement between the sheets. A flexible staybolt had a spherical head seated in a socket in the wrapper sheet. Flexible staybolts were used in those parts of the firebox where expansion and contraction caused lateral movement of the sheets in relation to one another. The Tate flexible staybolt, made by the Flannery Bolt Co., Pittsburgh, was introduced into railroad service in the U.S. about 1897.[54]

The forces acting on a locomotive firebox from expansion and contraction alone, even without the dynamic forces caused by twisting, bending and vibration of the moving locomotive, would be a demanding exercise in present-day computer analysis. In the 1890s it was just one more problem in locomotive design that could be solved only by trial and error. Steam locomotive design never escaped from the staybolted firebox.

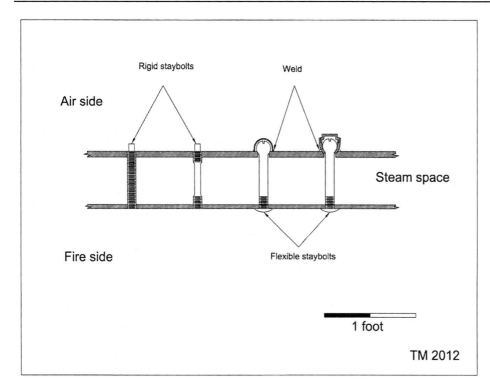

Staybolts (redrawn from Harding, J. W., *Steam Locomotive Home Study Course*, 2002 reprint, Vol. I, 333-5).

The firebox had also to be inspected from inside[55]:

Terminal firebox inspection on large steam locomotives is a sight that once seen is not likely to be forgotten. Immediately after the fire is dumped, the firedoor is opened and planks laid over the still-hot grates. An inspector, swathed in heavy insulated coveralls and wearing shoes wrapped in asbestos and heavy gloves and head protection, enters the firebox through the fire door. Within the firebox, hot steam is now spurting from the end joints of numerous staybolts, caused by the sudden cooling of the firebox itself. Though the fiery interior seems to be a steaming inferno in which no human being could long survive, the intrepid inspector must, however, chalk-mark the leaky staybolts and get out as soon as possible.

Hardly less arduous was inspecting the inside of the boiler:

Occasionally, dome caps are removed, and the inspector crawls into the boiler between the top row of tubes and the inside of the boiler shell. Cases have actually been reported where, through unpardonable oversight, the dome cap was replaced with the inspector still inside the boiler. Fortunately, in every instance the inspector was able to make his presence known in time by hammering furiously or shouting at the top of his lungs. Nevertheless, his feelings in the matter may well be imagined in view of the restricted space and the narrowness of the exit.

Design engineers knew as early as the 1890s that the firebox was the main producer of steam. They believed that the fire tubes extinguished the flames, like the school physics experiment where a flame will not pass through a sheet of metal gauze. This had two implications. Only the rearmost 2 to 3 feet of the tubes boiled water, the remaining tube length serving only as a water heater. Combustion took place only inside the firebox; anything not burned in the firebox went through the fire tubes as cinders, carbon monoxide and soot. They estimated that one square foot of firebox surface evaporated as much water as 6 to 8 square feet of tube surface, later increasing this estimate to 8 to 12 square feet.[56] For this reason, the water jacket,

with its weakness, maintenance problems and thousands of staybolts, was essential to the steam locomotive. A brick-lined firebox with no water jacket would be safer, and possibly more efficient as a combustion chamber, but impractical. Combustion inside the firebox was therefore of prime importance to fuel economy.[57]

Strong drafting and high firing rates produced high power output from limited firebox dimensions, but at the cost of increasing losses in efficiency. Fifty pounds of coal per square foot of grate per hour evaporated 500 pounds of water per square foot of grate per hour; increasing the firing rate to 200 pounds of coal per square foot of grate per hour increased the evaporation rate to 1,200 pounds. A 400% increase in firing rate produced only a 240% increase in evaporation rate. These figures, moreover, were achieved with average British and best American coals. With the poorer coals obtainable in the American West, the evaporation rate dropped to only 4 pounds of water per pound of coal at a firing rate of 200 pounds of coal per square foot of grate per hour.

Bigger grates would avoid these diminishing returns. However, the longest grate that a fireman could tend was 10 feet 6 inches from front to back and, if the firebox had to fit between the frames, its width was limited to about 42 inches, limiting the grate area to 37 square feet.[58] At 150 pounds of coal per square foot of grate per hour, such a grate limited the firing rate to 5,550 pounds per hour. If the engine consumed 5 pounds per horsepower-hour, the grate limited its power output to 1,110 horsepower. Higher firing rates produced only diminishing returns as combustion efficiency declined.

Several factors caused this loss of efficiency. Air shortage prevented the volatiles in the coal from burning fully before going into the fire tubes. The fierce draft needed to burn coal at very high firing rates required a high smokebox vacuum. A wide open throttle, long cutoff and small nozzle produced this intensity of draft, but was expensive in steam and caused high back pressure in the cylinders. The strong draft sucked fine coal through the fire tubes and blasted it out through the stack, at the same time causing high exhaust gas temperatures and high heat losses through the stack.[59]

From the viewpoint of 1896:

The most important of all the changes in dimensions of boilers is probably the change in firebox area in proportion to the work and service required. The small, deep fireboxes formerly used, in which the firebox was dropped between the axles and frames, are no longer adequate. The rate of combustion reaches frequently 220 lbs. per square foot of grate per hour. This is a higher rate of combustion than is used in any class of boiler, not even excepting fire engines and torpedo boats, and is beyond a reasonable limit. Inasmuch as one must expect that locomotive boilers will be crowded, owing to the limit that is placed upon the dimensions and the weight, it must be accepted that the rate of combustion will be very high: but there is a limit which must not be exceeded. Just what is this limit is not yet determined. Officers of the Baldwin Locomotive Works have made many experiments in this matter, and say that the rate should not be higher than 100 lbs. per square foot of grate per hour, but it is probable that the rate can frequently reach 150 lbs. without serious loss in efficiency. The rate for stationary boilers ranges from 15 to 25 lbs. per square foot of grate per hour and seldom exceeds that amount. This is one reason why locomotive boilers cannot be as economical as stationary boilers.[60]

Bigger grates were an urgent need. Paradoxically, a bigger grate could ease the fireman's task by increasing efficiency and reducing total fuel burn. Building a wider firebox above the frames meant that the sum of the driving wheel diameter and the firebox depth had to fit within clearance height, restricting the size of both. Restricting the firebox depth limited both heating surface and combustion space. Alternatively, the frames could be extended rearward and let down as a "Milholland frame," but supporting the firebox on a cantilever caused rough riding. A wide grate and a deep firebox needed the firebox to be let down behind the driving wheels, supported on trailing wheels. This major advance in locomotive design occurred in the 1890s, beginning with the Baldwin 2-4-2 locomotive *Columbia* in 1893 and subsequent 4-4-2s, and later with the Chicago, Burlington & Quincy 2-6-2s that the company built in its own shops in 1900.[61]

In December 1900, the Chicago, Burlington & Quincy made exhaustive tests, comparing a new 2-6-2, having a 38.5-square foot grate 72 inches wide, with a narrow-firebox 2-6-0 with a 30-square foot grate 40 inches wide, with trailing loads of 1,300 to 1,650 tons. The 2-6-2 had a clear advantage with a coal consumption of 110 pounds of coal per thousand ton-miles, compared to 138 for the 2-6-0.

By the end of the nineteenth century, locomotive designers were starting to pursue the ideal ratios between grate area, heating surface and cylinder volume, but the subject was of the most daunting complexity.[62] Mechanical engineers were groping in the dark, grappling with a machine whose physical structure was simple enough, but whose internal working was subtle in the extreme. The possibilities for design without actual construction were meager and, when a device was built it was all too often a mystery why it did or did not work.

3.2.2 The Vanderbilt Boiler

The staybolted firebox was such a problem that inventors on both sides of the Atlantic tried to design a firebox that minimized the use of staybolts or dispensed with them altogether. The best-known and most successful American attempt was a boiler designed by Cornelius Vanderbilt jr., son of the well-known railroad magnate, "Commodore" Vanderbilt, and first manufactured in 1899.[63]

Vanderbilt boilers were recognizable from the outside by the large-diameter cylindrical rear section around the firebox, tapering sharply toward the front. The main innovation was the cylindrical, corrugated firebox, 60 inches in diameter, made of ¾-inch rolled steel plate, called a Morison furnace. The Continental Iron Works, Brooklyn, NY, made the fireboxes of the first Vanderbilt boilers; they were the biggest cylindrical furnaces built to date. The axis of the firebox sloped slightly downward to the back, while the grate sloped slightly downward to the front. The firebox hung from the inside of the boiler by a single row of stays and was held at its ends by the backhead and the back tube sheet. Long diagonal stays held the backhead and both tube sheets. The grate and a brick arch were built inside the cylindrical firebox. In the original version an 18-inch pipe in the bottom of the firebox admitted air to the underside of the grate; this and an 8-inch pipe allowed ash to be removed from the bottom of the firebox which served as the ash pan.

The first Vanderbilt-boilered locomotive, a 4-6-0 built by the New York Central & Hudson River at its Albany shops, went into service in August 1899. A 35-square foot grate fired 2,355 square feet of heating surface, comprising 2,165 square feet in the 332 2-inch tubes and 192 square feet in the firebox (making no allowance for the corrugations). The boiler pressure was 185 pounds per square inch. In initial tests the boiler evaporated 10.3 pounds of water (at and from 212°F) per pound of coal. The locomotive burned only 94 pounds per 1,000 ton-miles, hauling a 2,000-ton train over the 140 miles between West Albany and De Witt. After a year's work, in which it ran 54,650 miles, this engine was taken out of service for overhaul. The overhaul cost 2.66 cents per engine-mile, compared to 3.97 cents average for the Mohawk division where the engine was used.

Road tests against a standard-boiler locomotive of similar dimensions in November 1900, showed a 3% to 5% advantage in favor of the Vanderbilt boiler. Firing rates—which would have affected evaporative efficiency—were 73 to 78 pounds of coal per square foot of

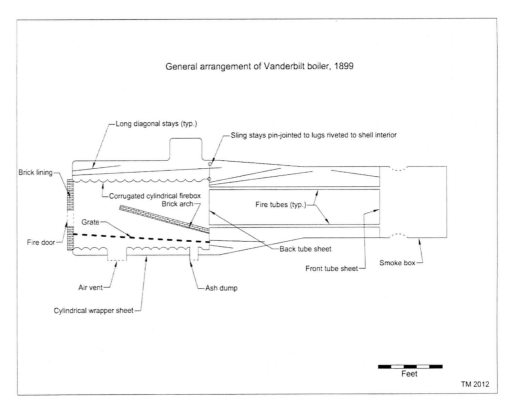

General arrangement of the Vanderbilt boiler (redrawn from *RRG*, September 1, 1899, 612; May 10, 1901, 316).

grate per hour on both engines. The Vanderbilt engine used 3.82 pounds of coal per horsepower-hour and evaporated 8.85 pounds of water per pound of coal vs. 4.04 and 8.56 pounds, respectively, for the standard boiler. This small difference was within test error and did not point to any decisive advantage.

By May 1901, eleven Vanderbilt-boilered locomotives were at work in the U.S.; four others were being built. Other users besides the New York Central (original 4-6-0 and five 2-6-0s, three by Schenectady and two by Baldwin), were the Baltimore & Ohio (two 2-8-0 Vauclain compounds), the Union Pacific (two 2-8-0s) and the Illinois Central (one 4-6-0). Under construction were two 4-6-0s for the Missouri Pacific, one 2-8-0 for the Buffalo, Rochester & Pittsburgh and one 2-8-0 for the Chicago Great Western.[64]

The Vanderbilt boiler did not become widely used, probably due to lack of space for combustion and ash, and the difficulty of removing ash and clinker.

3.2.3 Water-Tube Boilers

Always seductive to locomotive designers was the water-tube boiler. Most so-called water-tube boilers were fireboxes where water tubes made up the firebox sides and crown with a conventional fire-tube boiler ahead of the firebox. A few designs consisted of a conventional firebox with a boiler occupied by water tubes instead of fire tubes. Over the years, many designs for water-tube boilers were invented; none achieved any widespread acceptance. They were complicated to build and difficult to maintain.

John Christiansen, a railroad master mechanic, invented a water-tube boiler in 1895. The locomotive was a camelback with the smoke-box and stack behind the engineer's cab. The firebox was large, wide and of conventional design, except for 52 water tubes passing longitudinally through the fire space, sloping forward and downward at about 20°, connecting the water spaces at the front and back of the firebox. The fire gases went through the boiler in two 12-inch flues into what would be the smokebox in a conventional locomotive, reversing direction to pass through a set of conventional fire tubes and into the actual smokebox. A short flue led from the firebox directly into the smokebox to burn off any unburnt gases and reduce smoke.[65] It is not known if any locomotives were built to this design.

The Perkins water-tube boiler went into experimental service on the Chicago, Milwaukee & St. Paul (three engines) and the Chicago & North Western (one engine) in 1893–6, patented by G. J. Perkins, president of the Perkins Water-Tube Boiler Co. of La Crosse, Wisconsin. In the Perkins boiler a single large flue replaced the fire tubes of a conventional boiler. Water tubes at right angles to the boiler centerline crossed the flue, one set of tubes vertical, the other two sets forming an X when viewed along the boiler. The first Perkins locomotive had 392 of these tubes, increasing to 565 in the fourth locomotive.[66] By the autumn of 1896, the first Perkins engine had been working on the Chicago, Milwaukee & St. Paul for three years, the second for twenty-one months, while the third had just entered service. The Chicago & North Western engine had been in service for six months. This study has not revealed any further outcome.

Samuel S. Riegel of the Alco Brooks Works, and later mechanical engineer with the Delaware, Lackawanna & Western, invented a water-tube boiler in 1902. The device comprised an array of water tubes inside a wide firebox of modified cross-section, the rest of the boiler being of the conventional fire-tube type. The Riegel firebox of a 2-10-0, built for the Santa Fe, contained 518 1¾-inch tubes, providing 6,540 square feet of heating surface, compared to 4,680 square feet with a conventional firebox.[67] In 1915, Alco applied a Riegel firebox to one of a class of five new 4-6-2s for the Lackawanna.[68]

One of the more successful designs of water-tube boiler was the

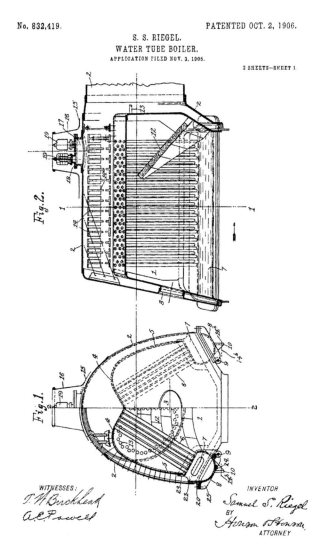

The Riegel water-tube firebox (from U.S. Patent 832419).

Brotan which first went into service in Austria in January 1901, and was popular in that country.[69] A water ring, connected to the boiler water space, paralleled the foundation ring; steeply inclined water tubes formed the sides and backhead of the firebox, joined at the top to a steam collector drum in the firebox crown. Heat from the fire caused steam bubbles to form in the water tubes. The steam bubbles streamed upward into the collector drum, replaced by water flowing from the boiler water space into the water ring. The Brotan contributed to later American designs.

3.2.4 Grates

For something so apparently simple, locomotive grates took on an astonishing number of different forms. The grate supported the fire as it burned; it was made of cast iron, later steel, and was supported by the foundation ring. The grate was slotted, with about 50% air gaps, to admit air to the fire from beneath and to allow ash to fall out.

Wood burns down to a soft, fine ash which will fall through fixed grates. Coal, however, leaves a residue of ash and clinker. Ash and fine clinker will fall through a fixed grate, given sufficient openings, but, when the locomotive is disposed of, the remains of the fire must be laboriously worked down through the grate and oversized pieces of ash and clinker must be shoveled out. A grate that could be shaken while the fire was burning offered great benefits in breaking up clinker and discharging ash. For this purpose steel grate bars 2 to 3 inches in diameter were mounted in trunnions in the foundation ring, connected by levers, so that the fireman could shake them, using a piece of pipe over a stub bar projecting through the cab floor. Steel fingers that supported the fire, either cast integrally with the grate bars or as replaceable elements, were mounted on top of the grate bars.

Shaking grates could be either transverse, with 6 to 12 shaker bars mounted across the firebox, or longitudinal, with 6 to 8 shaker bars mounted lengthwise. In spite of being more complicated than the longitudinal shaking grate, its mechanism exposed to extremes of heat and dirt, the transverse shaking grate allowed the fireman to clear the front and back of the fire independently. Drop grates were a further advance; complete sections of the grate dropped open, dumping the remains of the fire into the ash pan.

When railroads began to burn anthracite, the heat of the fire quickly burned out the cast iron grates then in use. In 1858 Samuel Milholland of the Philadelphia & Reading designed a grate made of twelve water tubes, 2 inches in diameter each, sloping upward from the front of the grate to the back, connected to the water legs.[70] This solved the problem of grate bars burning out but added new problems of maintenance. In particular, the tubes had to be cleaned out whenever the boiler was washed out as, if they filled with mud, they would burn out like a solid iron bar. Problems also arose in making the connection to the water space steam tight, while allowing for differences in expansion and contraction.

The Philadelphia & Reading, the Delaware & Hudson, the Lehigh Valley and the Pennsylvania used fixed water-tube grates for anthracite. Problems with this type of grate, however, led several anthracite-burning railroads to combine shaking elements and water tubes in the grate structure. Examples were the New York, Ontario & Western, the Delaware, Lackawanna & Western, the Pennsylvania, the Lehigh Valley and the Erie in the period 1889–1895.[71] The Hancock Inspirator Company of Boston also built water-tube shaking grates for bituminous coal, such as the Hancock grate of 1900. The water tubes acted as spacers between the shaker elements, resulting in a lighter grate.[72]

A 1904 report by the American Railroad Master Mechanics Association (ARMMA) summarized the findings of a questionnaire on grates for bituminous coal.[73] Preferred was a cast iron finger grate with fingers 6 or 7 inches long. The design of a grate had to follow five main principles: (a) It had to support the fire properly; (b) It had to admit enough air from beneath for the fire to burn properly (c) It had to allow the fire to be stirred and the ashes shaken down into the ash pan; (d) It had to allow for quick dumping of the fire when required at the end of a run; (e) The ash pan had to have

capacity for several hours' running and had to admit enough air through its sides to the underside of the grate. In passing through the 1,500°F fire, the air would expand thermally by a factor of seven. The air openings in the grate had, therefore, to be not less than one seventh of the total cross-sectional area of the fire tubes. Seven railroads with access to good coal low in ash and clinker used fixed grates. Among railroads using shaking grates, transverse grates were the more common, but almost every railroad had its own design. Several railroads used drop grates; ability to dump the front and back sections independently was an advantage. The ARMMA summarized these findings in its own design of transverse shaking grate.

3.2.5 Brick Arches

The brick arch, first used on both sides of the Atlantic in the 1850s,[74] was a structure of firebrick built inside the firebox, angled backward and upward from the bottom of the rear tube sheet for half to two thirds the length of the firebox, originally as a means of smoke prevention. Fire gases swept backward and looped around the brick arch before entering the fire tubes; the longer flame path allowed time for more complete combustion of the gases released by the coal. The brick arch also moderated the effect of the draft lifting the fire off the grate.

One of the earlier railroads to measure the effect of a brick arch found that it saved 5% in coal consumption, compared to engines not so equipped, besides reducing the amount of smoke from the stack. In the 1890s, brick arches were by no means universal, although they became increasingly common and could be retrofitted. The first brick arches were costly to install and had a short life before the brick broke up and collapsed into the fire. Each railroad had its own brick patterns, inhibiting mass production and raising costs. As late as 1910, engines were still being built without them.

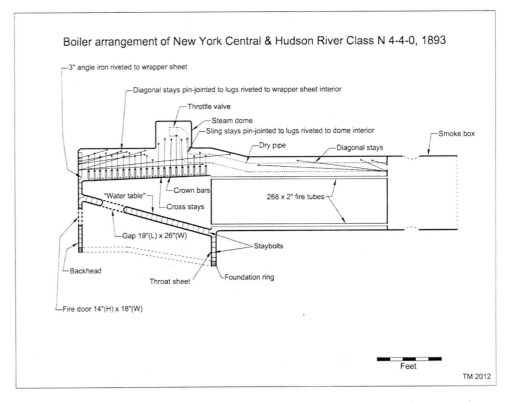

Longitudinal section through the boiler of New York Central locomotive No. 999, showing Buchanan firebox and boiler staying (redrawn from *RRG*, May 19, 1893, 368).

William Buchanan, Superintendent of Motive Power on the New York Central, took this idea further, substituting a "water table" sloping upward and backward from below the rear tube sheet to above the fire door, for the brick arch. This water space was about 4½ inches thick between two steel sheets held together by staybolts and connected to the water legs. A hole only 19 inches front to back and 26 inches wide allowed the fire gases to pass through the water table and into the fire tubes. This added to the firebox heating surface and conducted water through the hottest part of the fire. The Buchanan firebox was widely used on the New York Central in the mid–1890s.[75]

C. E. Taber, Master Mechanic on the Montana Central, used a similar device and called it a "water arch," using an injector and a check valve to force water through the water space. It was installed in an engine in 1902 and ran for 30,000 miles.[76] Water arches did not catch on, probably because of the difficulty of keeping them clear of mud and scale.

A self-supporting brick arch between studs in the firebox side sheets was limited to narrow grates. In 1893–4, the Chicago & North Western installed two lengthwise steel bars to support the brick arch, adding a second arch at the back of the firebox; the steel bars supported both arches. Although good results were reported, including a fuel saving of 5 to 7 miles to each ton of coal and still better control of smoke and sparks, the two-piece brick arch never caught on.[77]

An advance was three or more "arch tubes"—2- to 3-inch water tubes extending from the throat sheet to the back head, adding to steam generation as well as supporting the fire bricks, accessible for cleaning through matching plugs in the wrapper sheet. The earliest arch tubes known from this study were 3-inch tubes installed in 4-4-0s built by the Union Pacific in its Omaha shops in 1893; the idea seems not to have been new then.[78] In some designs the arch tubes terminated in the crown sheet which made it difficult to clean them out.[79] Arch tubes had to be cleaned and could burn out due to the formation of steam pockets. Bad water made it difficult to keep them clean, in which case solid steel supports were used.

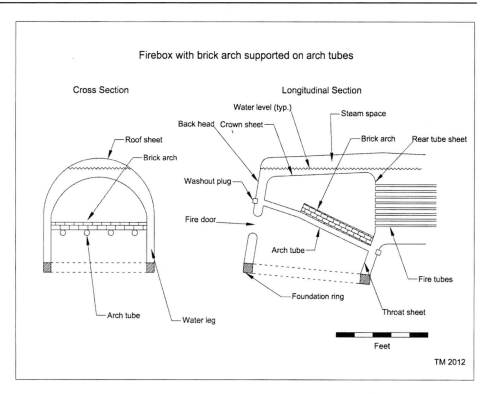

Schematic longitudinal section showing brick arch supported on arch tubes (redrawn from Ringel, C., *History, Development and Function of the Locomotive Brick Arch*, RLHS, New York, January 1948; printed *Journal RLHS*, October 1956, 79).

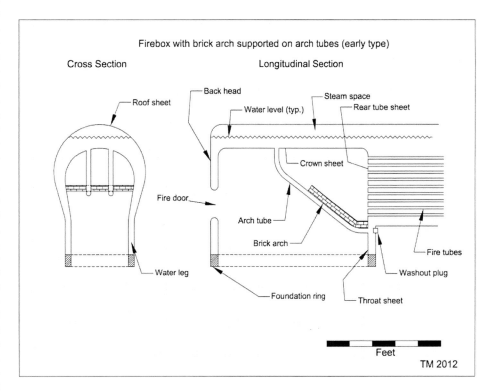

Schematic longitudinal section showing early form of arch tubes (redrawn from various drawings in *RRG*).

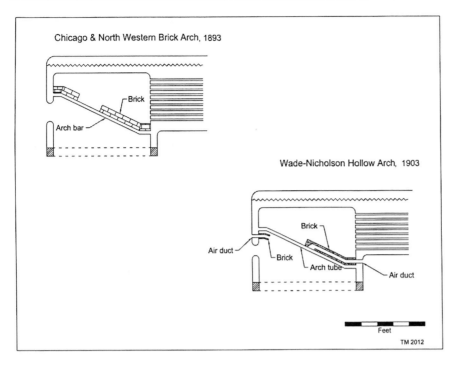

The Chicago & North Western brick arch and the Wade-Nicholson hollow arch (redrawn from *RRG*, July 27, 1894, 521; *RRG*, September 25, 1903, 694).

The Wade-Nicholson Hollow Arch was invented in 1903, with air ducts inside the bricks connecting to air passages through the throat sheet and backhead. Although good results were obtained in tests between 1905 and 1908, this arrangement was expensive and fragile and it was difficult to keep the ducts aligned.[80]

3.2.6 Crown Sheet Failures and Boiler Explosions

By the 1890s, boiler explosions due to excessive pressure were a thing of the past because of conservative design and construction standards and effective safety valves. One report suggests that a factor of safety of 4.5 was used in boiler design.[81] Thus, a boiler rated for 180 pounds per square inch would have safety valves set to lift at that pressure, but would withstand pressures up to 810 pounds per square inch. Boiler maintenance standards, however, varied from railroad to railroad. In one fatal boiler explosion case, where the fireman's widow sued for damages and the railroad company blamed the fireman for letting the water get too low, "The jury decided that the large cracks, extending between several staybolts, horizontally, and

Effects of a boiler explosion. Slide valves, small driving wheels, connecting rod end, inside valve gear and socket for link-and-pin coupler date this 2-8-0 locomotive from before 1900. Initials on the tender of the camelback locomotive in the right background are believed to be "N.Y.O.& W." (New York, Ontario & Western). The location, date and source of this photograph are unknown.

which had been closed temporarily by a cold chisel were the more probable cause and the widow got a verdict."[82]

The devastating violence of boiler explosions resulted from the instantaneous evaporation of the water when a large rupture occurred. The boiling point of water is proportional to pressure; water boiling in a boiler under 180 pounds per square inch steam pressure will be at a temperature of about 380°F. If the pressure is suddenly reduced to that of the outside atmosphere, the whole mass of water—at a temperature well above its boiling point at atmospheric pressure—will instantly evaporate, causing a violent explosion. The operation of the throttle, or even the blow-down valve, is not sufficient to trigger this event. Even if the boiler shell was punctured, as by a broken side rod or even gunfire, this did not cause an explosion. In experiments, boilers were exploded by the sudden opening of a large valve or the sudden failure of a man-hole plate. This danger remained—and remains—inherent to the steam locomotive.

The critical area was the firebox; the surrounding water kept it from burning or melting and the staybolts kept it in place. If the firebox cracked, if enough staybolts failed or if the water level in the boiler fell low enough to uncover the crown sheet, allowing it to overheat and soften, the firebox would rupture inward under pressure, allowing precisely the sudden release of pressure that would trigger an explosion. If the crown sheet overheated and softened only to the extent that staybolts pulled out one by one, gradually releasing boiler pressure through the staybolt holes, an explosion might not occur but, all too often, the crown sheet tore and an explosion resulted.

Incredibly to us, now, on one railroad:

> In several cases no explosion followed an overheated crown sheet and the firemen became careless, and that road has now returned to the use of heads and nuts on crown stays in order that the explosion may be severe enough to emphasize the need of watching the water level. The road now has fewer hot crown sheets, but very much more disastrous results.[83]

From the viewpoint of 1897:

> During boom times when there was an immense increase in traffic and train movement, it was not possible to get enginemen in sufficient numbers of ripe experience, and firemen had to be promoted to the right-hand side rather faster than was good for the service. During this time quite a number of scorched, burned and blown-out crown sheets of the crown bar, radial stay and Belpaire types were carefully examined and reported on. It was very noticeable that the more instantaneous the giving way of the crown sheet was, the more disastrous were the results and some cases where the crown sheets were well supported with large-headed crown bolts, they had held together too well, and finally given way with explosive violence, blowing the boilers clean off the frames by the recoil. In other cases where the crown sheets were more or less supported by screw-stays riveted over, the crown sheet gave way sooner at some one point, from which point the sheets bagged or tore away, but not with the suddenness which produced explosive results, so that beyond blowing out the ash pans and grates, or in some very bad cases wrapping the crown sheet around the back driving axle, the rest of the boiler and the engine were not materially injured, and the engines seldom left the rails. There is not much danger in a gradual blow-down unless the fire door be open or not firmly latched, in which case the blast of steam and hot water from the door may cause fatal injury to the fireman or the front brakeman riding on the leading box car.

Enginemen on early American engines could tell the boiler water level only by means of three try cocks set into the backhead, one above the other. Provided the bottom try cock squirted water when opened, the crown sheet was supposedly covered. Glass water gauges were an innovation of the late 1800s.

Uncovering the crown sheet was alarmingly easy. In the 1890s, locomotive builders allowed only 3 to 4 inches of water between the crown sheet and the bottom try cock. High firing rates could evaporate enough water to uncover the crown sheet a mere 4½ minutes after the bottom try cock went dry. A super-elevation of 6 to 7 inches on the high rail of a curve could uncover one side of a 4½-foot-wide crown sheet, even though the gauge glass or try cocks showed plenty of water on the low rail side. As boilers became longer, the possibility of uncovering the crown sheet as the engine crested a summit or started onto a descending grade increased.[84] A grade change of 2% will cause the water level over the firebox of a 20-foot-long boiler to change by 2½ inches.

Crown sheet failure could to some extent be guarded against by fusible plugs set into the crown sheet. These were already in use before 1860.[85] Excessive heat would melt the soft metal alloy in the plug before the crown sheet failed; a jet of steam into the firebox would at least warn the crew. Fusible plugs were by no means in universal use; scale could prevent them from functioning; boiler explosions still occurred on engines with fusible plugs.[86]

Typically an explosion tore the boiler and firebox loose from the smokebox and frame, threw them end over end for as much as 300 feet, wrecked the engine and killed the crew. After a boiler explosion on the Escambia Railway, Florida, in 1911, the bell was found a mile from the site of the explosion.[87]

> 20th January (1903), 1.20 p.m., Pennsylvania Lines, Philadelphia Road, Ohio, the engine of an eastbound freight train exploded and the boiler was completely lifted from the frame, turned end over end, striking the north rail of the westbound track. It continued to rebound, turning over two times, and landed with the firebox upward on the north side of the right of way 120 yds. from the point of explosion. At the time of the explosion a freight train was approaching from the east; and the boiler of the exploded engine either broke a rail of the westbound track or depressed the track to such an extent that, although the engine passed over the damaged track, 23 cars were derailed and fell down the bank. The wheels of the exploded engine all remained on the track, and its cars were not damaged. The engineer of the exploded engine was injured so that he died later, the front brakeman was instantly killed, and the front brakeman on the westbound train was injured so that he died two hours later.[88]

In one month, January 1896:

> 4th, 2 a.m. on the Columbus, Sandusky & Hocking, near Fultonham, Ohio, the engine of a freight train was wrecked by the explosion of its boiler and the engineman, fireman, conductor and one brakeman were killed.
>
> 9th, on Toledo & Ohio Central, near Rushville, Ohio, the locomotive of a freight train was badly damaged by an explosion due to the rupture of the crown sheet: fireman and one brakeman injured.
>
> 16th, on Pennsylvania road, at Camden, New Jersey, the locomotive of a freight train was badly damaged by an explosion due to the rupture of the crown sheet, and the engineman was fatally scalded.
>
> 17th, 2 a.m. on Delaware, Lackawanna & Western, at Halstead, Pennsylvania, the locomotive of a freight train was badly damaged by the explosion of its boiler and the fireman was fatally injured. It is said that the water in the boiler had been allowed to become too low.
>
> 22nd on Pittsburgh, Cincinnati, Chicago & St. Louis, near South Charleston, Ohio, the locomotive of a passenger train running at high speed was wrecked by the explosion of its boiler and the whole train of 9 cars was derailed and ditched, making a bad wreck. The engineman and fireman were killed and 7 passengers were injured. The smallness of the last mentioned number is attributed to the fact that the cars had Pullman vestibules.[89]

On February 20, 1896, a 2-8-0 of the Nashville, Chattanooga & St. Louis Railway exploded at Bridgeport, Alabama.

> This engine was … built by the Baldwin Locomotive Works in 1884. It was overhauled in January 1895; and in January 1896, when it was in the shop for the purpose of having the boiler cleaned out, 42 broken stay-bolts were replaced. The engineman and fireman were instantly killed by the explosion. At a point some 17 miles north of Bridgeport, a short time before the explosion, as appears from what they told a brakeman, they "heard something pop," a noise so loud that they stopped and tried to find the cause of it, but discovered nothing wrong…. The rear driving axle of the engine was bent by the shock, and one of the frames was broken in two places. A heavy rail in the track beneath the engine was broken in three places.[90]

Crown sheet failure was often suspected but the cause of an explosion was not always known.

> 11th March (1896), 1 p.m. on Delaware, Susquehanna & Schuylkill, at Gum Run, Pennsylvania, the locomotive of a freight train was wrecked by the explosion of its boiler and the engineman, fireman and 2 brakemen were killed and the conductor injured. The engine was a Wootten type, built in 1891. A coroner's jury decided that the explosion was due to low water, but others think that the cause was defective staybolts.[91]

Burst fire tubes and blow-backs from the firebox were a further source of danger.

> 9th May (1895), 4 a.m. on New York, New Haven & Hartford, at Hyde Park, Massachusetts, the locomotive of a freight train was damaged by the rupture of a tube and the consequent escape of steam, and a brakeman who was riding in the cab, who jumped off, was killed. The engineer and fireman were injured, the latter fatally.[92]
>
> 11th April (1897) on Grand Trunk, near Stratford, New Hampshire, the cab of the locomotive of a freight train was burned and many of the fixtures within it melted, by the flames from the firebox, which were driven out in consequence of a stoppage in the smokebox due to the falling down of the deflector sheet. The engineman, in attempting to shut off the steam, was badly burned.[93]
>
> 26th June (1897), on Atchison, Topeka & Santa Fe near Bazine, Kansas, a rupture or explosion of the firebox of the locomotive of a freight train blew the engineman and fireman off into the ditch and both of them were badly injured, the fireman fatally.[94]

Crown sheet failures and the resulting boiler explosions would dog the steam locomotive to the end of its days.

Section 3.3. Boilers and Steam Generation

3.3.1 Boilers

The fire-tube locomotive boiler continued from the first days of the steam locomotive to the last. Builders tried other designs; none

succeeded. During the 1840s and 1850s, at least nine different configurations of boiler and firebox were tried in the northeastern U.S. alone, aimed at the efficient and smoke-free combustion of bituminous coal, including the Phleger, Gill, Norris, Dimpfel, Boardman, Dewrance, Craig, Beattie, McConnell and Head types.[95] Complexity, maintenance difficulties, leakage and the limited metallurgy obtainable at the time put paid to them all. In the end nothing replaced the conventional fire-tube boiler.

The first locomotive in North America with a steel boiler was on

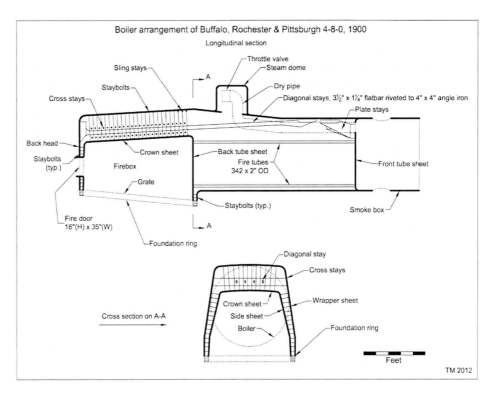

A typical large locomotive boiler, c.1900 (redrawn from *RRG*, October 12, 1900, 667).

the Great Western Railway of Canada in 1892.[96] This material quickly took over from wrought iron. A typical American locomotive boiler of the 1890s had an exterior shell made of rolled steel plates, ½-¾ inch thick, riveted together. The plates were arranged in courses, lap-jointed so that each course fitted inside the course behind it. There was thus a slight diminution of diameter from the back end of the boiler to the front. Each course was about 50 inches long; three courses made up the parallel section of the boiler. The smokebox was a fourth course, lapping over the front boiler course. Long diagonal stays, about 1⅛ inch in diameter and up to 20 feet long, pin-jointed to lugs riveted to the inside of the boiler shell and the tube sheets, helped to restrain the front tube sheet and the backhead against the boiler pressure. Sixty inches was a typical diameter, 12 to 14 feet over tube sheets. The 72-inch-diameter boilers built by the Schenectady Locomotive Works for the Central Pacific Railroad in 1895 were considered large. Typically, 265 to 275 fire tubes, 2 to 2½ inches in diameter, carried the fire gases through the water space.[97]

Higher boiler pressure was one way to get more power from any given size of locomotive. Pressures increased from 130 to 140 pounds per square inch in the 1870s to 180 to 200 pounds per square inch at the end of the century. While opinion favored boiler pressures of 200 pounds per square inch for compounds, operators believed that, in a single-expansion engine, no improvements in economy were to be expected at boiler pressures higher than 160 pounds per square inch.

Increasing the boiler pressure required only slightly greater heat input per pound of steam but brought diminishing returns in efficiency and higher costs for boiler construction and maintenance. The Purdue *Schenectady No. 1* had a maximum boiler pressure of 150 pounds per square inch. In 1897 the university acquired a new engine, *Schenectady No.2,* with a boiler built for 250 pounds per square inch. Purdue was able to show that increasing the pressure from 150 to 200 pounds per square inch reduced the steam consumption per indicated horsepower-hour by 9%; a further increase to 250 pounds per square inch reduced it by only another 6%. In 1898, Baldwin estimated that a 60-inch diameter boiler built for 150 pounds per square inch, weighing 33,100 pounds, would weigh 18% more if built to contain 240 pounds per square inch. The boiler pressures of new locomotives remained between 180 and 220 pounds per square inch for twenty years. As the railroads and their surrounding structures matured, lateral clearances limited the diameter of locomotive cylinders. Increased piston thrust could therefore come only from higher steam pressure.

3.3.2 Water Quality

Locomotives depended on large quantities of water, the quality of which varied markedly from region to region of the U.S.[98] Higher boiler pressures meant higher temperatures and increased reactivity of feed water. Water that caused no problems around 1880, when boiler pressures were 125 pounds per square inch, was causing costly problems by 1900 with boiler pressures of 175 to 200 pounds per square inch.[99]

Unless the water was clean and soft, water quality could cause three types of problem: scale (from hard water), foaming (from alkaline water) and corrosion (from saline water).

Scale is a cement-like deposit forming on heating surfaces exposed to hard water, resulting from the deposition of dissolved calcium and magnesium carbonates. In one test in 1898 the Illinois Central removed 485 pounds of scale from the boiler of a 2-6-0 that had been in service for 21 months. After cleaning, the boiler evaporated 7.0 pounds of water per pound of coal, compared to 6.4 pounds in the same engine before cleaning.[100]

Some people refused to believe that scale caused problems. W. S. Raidler, Master Mechanic of the Green Bay & Western, stated robustly in 1900[101]:

> It is a common experience for locomotives to come into shops with a space between the tubes choked solid with scale, but without any deterioration either in capacity or fuel economy having been noticed.

This remark is significant to our story. The American railroads of the late 1800s and early 1900s were run by empirically trained foremen and officials. Their conservatism, lack of a sense of inquiry or accurate measurement—in fact, a distrust of science in general—was a potent factor in the rejection of improvements in locomotive design. Their attitudes had to disappear as the railroads tried to protect profit margins that had become razor-thin.

More dangerous than scale formation was foaming, which occurred when the steam was unable to break free of the water; steam bubbles and water remained as an inseparable mass. Foaming was dangerous because it obscured the true water level in the boiler, with the risk of uncovering the crown sheet, and because steam being drawn off through the dry pipe entrained water, with the risk of damage to cylinders, pistons and rods. Foaming had several causes, alkaline water being the most common.

The third problem affecting boilers was corrosion, accentuated by saline water. Corrosion concentrated around heavily stressed areas of the boiler around rivet heads, along joints and at those places where the boiler and its components flexed the most under pressure and thermal expansion.[102]

A boiler fed with pure, soft water would last for 25 to 30 years, whereas boilers in areas of bad water had to be extensively repaired in 4 or 5 years or less. The ARMMA appointed a committee to study this problem as early as 1870. In 1899, this committee estimated that the use of hard, dirty water cost about $750 per engine per year, comprising $50 for extra boiler washing, $360 for boiler repairs due to scale formation and $340 in wasted fuel. The committee estimated that 20,000 of the 35,000 locomotives in service in the USA suffered from these problems. At $15 million a year for the nation's railroads, this problem justified substantial investment in reaching a solution. As an average locomotive used 1.5 million gallons of water per year, $750 per year represented 50 cents per 1,000 gallons. Any plant capable of treating water for less than that cost represented a profit to the railroads.

Distillation would be an obvious way of obtaining pure water, but one study in Arizona predicted a cost of 90 cents per 1,000 gallons, which was therefore unattractive.[103] Some companies tried putting chemicals into the tender. The Southern Pacific abandoned this because of the difficulty of adding an amount of chemical that was correct for the point from which the engine was taking water. Adding the wrong amount of chemical caused more problems than it solved. The Green Bay & Western were: "…certainly not partial to boiler compounds and purges, which have been tried for years and abandoned by our best engineers as ineffectual, injurious and in very many cases positively dangerous."[104]

Water treatment plants at watering points were the ultimate solution; chemicals could be added in the correct dosage; solids, whether present in the original water or precipitated by treatment, could be filtered or settled out. The first such was a batch-type lime-soda ash plant, installed by the Oregon Short Line in 1891.[105] This went unnoticed and five years went by before the Southern Pacific installed a similar plant. The Denver & Rio Grande Western installed a continuous-type plant in 1900.

The new plants treated water for far less than the break-even cost quoted above. The Southern Pacific plant at Los Angeles treated water for 4 cents per 1,000 gallons.[106] In 1902–3, the Union Pacific installed thirty-eight water softening plants in Nebraska, Wyoming, Colorado and Kansas. When the program was complete, the Union Pacific was treating 3 million gallons per day for 2.32 cents per 1,000 gallons.

3.3.3 Steam Generation

No one doubted that the steam locomotive generated steam but all certainty ended at that point. No theory existed; all experimentation had to be by trial and error from an infinite range of possibilities. As late as 1900, G. L. Fowler[107] pointed out that:

> The subject is certainly a complex one, and is so filled with variables that it seems all but impossible to formulate any hard and fast rule for the proportioning of the length of tubes and least of all to state that some one particular length is the most economical and efficient. …
> Take for example an engine running under normal conditions: if the rate of combustion is increased the smokebox temperature rises and the evaporative efficiency of the tubes falls. If these are increased in length to meet this emergency the vacuum fails to meet the draft and the rate of combustion drops. If the vacuum is raised by decreasing the area of the exhaust nozzle, there is an increase of back pressure on the piston

involving an increased steam consumption to perform the given amount of work. This puts an increased demand upon the boiler and the efficiency gained by the increase in the length of the tubes may be more than neutralized by the greater waste in the cylinders. Just where the nice adjustment of balance occurs that a variation in tube length in either direction means an increased consumption of coal for the work to be done is a problem of no mean proportions.

These issues were quite sufficiently complicated in static tests. In road service, with changing loads, grades and curves, their complexity was daunting.

French experiments between 1885 and 1890 showed that a brick arch had only a slight effect on the evaporation rate per pound of coal. The tests did, however, show that the evaporation rate per hour

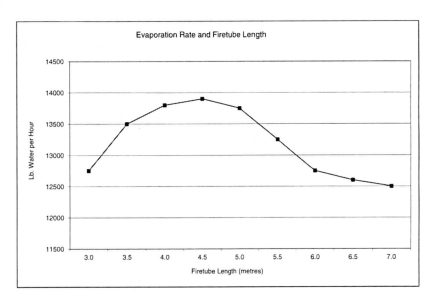

Evaporation rate, pounds of water per hour *vs.* firetube length, from tests carried out in France, 1885–90 (from *Relative Steam-Making Capacity of Firebox and Tube Surface, RRG*, December 4, 1896, 847).

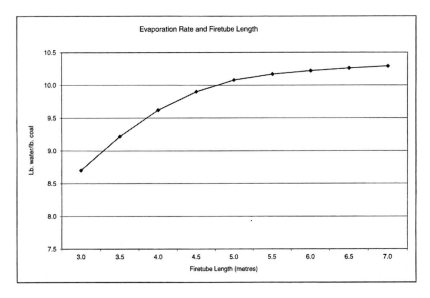

Evaporation rate, pounds of water per pound of coal *vs.* firetube length, from tests carried out in France, 1885–90 (from *Relative Steam-Making Capacity of Firebox and Tube Surface, RRG*, December 4, 1896, 847).

increased to a maximum with a tube length of 14 to 15 feet but declined at greater lengths. The evaporation rate per pound of fuel increased rapidly as fire tube length increased from 9.5 feet to about 17 feet but increased only slightly for greater tube lengths. The Americans took note of this study; it had disquieting implications for the long-term future of the steam locomotive.

Fire tube density was limited by the need for water circulation; in American practice the fire tubes occupied 22% to 37% of the boiler cross-section.[108] To increase the steam generating surface, the boiler had to be longer or fatter or both. Increasing the boiler length ran into diminishing returns, while clearance dimensions and the permissible height of the locomotive's center of gravity limited its diameter. Certain ultimate limits to the steam locomotive were already beginning to appear some sixty years before its demise in America.

The French tests showed that smokebox vacuum was a potent factor in all the parameters measured. Increasing the smokebox vacuum from 1 inch of water gauge to 2.95 inches increased the combustion rate by 80%, the evaporation rate by 75% and the smokebox temperature by 16%. The evaporation rate per pound of coal suffered, being reduced by about 8%. American practice was to use a much higher smokebox vacuum than the Europeans—2 to 8 inches of water gauge.[109]

Mechanical engineers searched for ratios between one parameter and another—square feet of grate area per square foot of heating surface, weight on driving wheels per square foot of heating surface, evaporation rate vs. cylinder consumption, evaporation rate per square foot of heating surface. At the end of the nineteenth century, they measured and compared every parameter they could. Their next task was to discover which of these ratios expressed fundamental truths for locomotive design. Gradually, research showed that the maximum obtainable evaporation rate per square foot of heating surface was 15 pounds of water per hour. Steam consumption averaged 26 pounds per indicated horsepower-hour for a single-expansion engine, 20 pounds for a compound. This information could be used for design.

Many empirical formulae emerged. Research during the late 1890s showed that the necessary drawbar horsepower to pull a train on straight, level track could be estimated as $0.00266LRV$, where L was the trailing load in tons (including tender), R was the train resistance in pounds resistance per ton of weight and V was the speed in miles per hour. The figure of 0.00266 was empirically derived. Train resistance (R) was estimated at $(V/4)+2$ for speeds above 10 miles per hour. Thus drawbar horsepower = $0.00266L((V/4)+2)V$. Drawbar horsepower was estimated at 70% of indicated horsepower after internal friction, rolling friction and wind resistance. This calculation made it possible to estimate the heating surface required in a locomotive required to perform a given service.

Thus, to haul a 700-ton train at 50 miles per hour on straight, level track took $0.00266 \times 700 \times ((50/4)+2) \times 50 = 1,350$ drawbar horsepower.

This required 1,350/0.7 = 1,928 indicated horsepower. At 26 pounds of steam per indicated horsepower-hour, this required 26 × 1,928 = 50,143 pounds of water evaporated per hour. At 15 pounds of water evaporated per square foot of heating surface per hour, this required a heating surface of 50,143/15 = 3,343 square feet. Taking the calculation further, if the evaporation rate was only 6.5 pounds of water per pound of coal, evaporating 50,143 pounds of water per hour took 7,700 pounds of coal per hour, needing 51 square feet of grate area if the firing rate was to be kept down to 150 pounds of coal per square foot of grate per hour. By 1903, locomotives of these dimensions already existed in the USA. The performance of a contemporary 4-4-2 on the Michigan Central verified this calculation, hauling a 650-ton train at an average speed of 56 miles per hour with a heating surface of 3,505 square feet.

Common to most sciences is the question: if predicted and experimental results do not match, is the difference significant and, if so, does it result from experimental error or from a defect in the theory? This conundrum arose often in steam locomotive design, development and testing. Here, in the early 1900s, were the beginnings of a crude thermodynamic model of a steam locomotive, but discrepancies and divergent or absurd results in tests at various speeds suggested unmeasured or immeasurable factors.[110]

This book can barely even sketch the wandering, groping progress in locomotive design of those years. These studies were, however, the beginnings of the American belief in the locomotive firebox as the real energy producer.

3.3.4 Water Gauge Glasses

Enginemen had to have some means of observing the water level inside the boiler. The American traditional method was three try cocks—three small valves penetrating the boiler backhead, one above the other and emitting either hot water or steam when opened. The disadvantage of this method was that it gave no continuous reading and only a vague indication of water level.

The tubular glass gauges, used in Britain since before 1850, at first made no headway in America. A gauge glass consists of a glass tube 8 to 12 inches long, mounted vertically between metal fittings at top and bottom, connected to the boiler water and steam space above and below the normal water level. Shut-off valves at the connections allow it to be isolated to change the glass and serve as a means to test that the entries to the gauge are clear. The glass tubes required higher standards of manufacture than were commonly available in early-day America. Enginemen objected to gauge glasses because from time to time they burst, spewing broken glass, steam and hot water into the cab. The hazard of flying glass was alleviated by placing a shield of thick glass round the gauge tube, but the breaking of a gauge glass was still frightening and somewhat dangerous.

Sometimes this had its uses.

Well, I will give you my first trip on the Union Pacific in 1869. I was ordered from Omaha to the Cheyenne division and there got orders to return to Grand Island and take engine 4126 from Grand Island back to Cheyenne. Going over the road both ways in the night I did not learn much of the lay of the land, and stations at that time were a good ways apart. I got my engine fired up and started west along in the middle of the afternoon and run about 60 miles and I thought it was about time to fill up my tank with water. The first tank my headlight shone on, I stopped, my boy pulled down the spout to fill the tank, and I took the packing hook, tied some waste around it, poured oil on the waste and used that for a torch to oil my engine with. When I finished I knocked the fire off from my packing hook, climbed back into the cab and found I had a visitor. There stood a big buck Indian looking at the steam gauge. Well! I was so taken by surprise that I could not speak for a

moment. He turned around and nodded to me, and as I did not recognize him as an old acquaintance I did not return the bow. I turned around and saw that my fireman had thrown the water spout up and had lain down on the back end of the tank. I then turned a good look at my company in the cab. He had on a dirty big white blanket with a strap on it and a "navy" in the belt on one side and a knife on the other. I motioned to him to get off, he said "No," in broken English, patting the seat, "me ride." I said: "No, you cannot ride here." He patted his revolver and said: "Me ride." I did not have anything on the engine to defend myself with, there was nothing where we stopped but a section man's house and a water tank, and I did not know how many bucks might be on the outside, or on each side of the engine, as it was dark: but I thought I could scare him off, so I threw my oil can against the water glass, breaking the glass with a loud report. The hot water and steam was too much for my frontier friend: he let out a yell louder than my whistle could make and made a jump for the prairie. I pulled the throttle open and got down by the furnace door until the engine went over the west switch on a keen run. By that time I had the water glass cock closed and was wet and scared.[111]

As late as 1898, the ARMMA convention produced some surprising comments[112]:

On the Norfolk & Western several years ago it was decided to omit the gauge glasses entirely. This was followed by a number of crown sheets coming down. After that we put on two glass tubes, one where the fireman could observe it, and since then there has been comparatively little trouble.

* * *

The water glass is a good thing if it is taken care of. If it is not taken care of, it is a very dangerous article.

* * *

I attended a law suit recently in Buffalo where an engine had exploded, killing the engineer and fireman. The case was that there was no water glass and no fusible plug in the firebox. A number of master mechanics were there from different roads to testify, and it was finally decided that water glasses were not necessary. If we put ourself on record that the water glass is absolutely necessary there will be some suits based upon that.

* * *

I have been connected with the road I am on now for 30 years; we have in the neighborhood of 400 locomotives, and during all that time we have used no water glasses and I cannot see the necessity for them.

* * *

We have two water gauges on most of our engines, one for the fireman and one for the engineer, and it struck me at first that it was a little unnecessary to have those two glasses; but I was told that it was very necessary to have two glasses; so that in case anything should happen— if the fireman should be hurt—you would have some excuse, that he had a gauge which he could see; he was not dependent on the engineer at all…. I investigated the thing a little further. I did not find a single water glass on 40 engines which I examined on the fireman's end of the boiler that were in working order. (This refers to camelback locomotives.) They were all stopped up. Most of them had the glass broken. I found that some of the firemen talked very forcibly about that glass. They didn't want it there they said; they might be shoveling coal into the furnace and the glass might break and they would be scalded. I have no objection to the water glass, but I don't think we want too many of them on the engine. I think it would be a good idea for a master mechanic to find out just how many of his water glasses are operating, especially if he has bad water.

Even in 1903, opinion was shifting only slowly in favor of gauge glasses.[113] In 1912, however, new ICC boiler safety legislation mandated one gauge glass with a safety glass shroud and three try cocks.[114]

3.3.5 Injectors

By the 1890s, the injector had replaced the pump as the means of forcing feed water into the boiler against the pressure of the steam and hot water already there. Invented by the French engineer, H. Giffard, in 1859, the injector used a steam jet from the boiler to entrain feed water from the tender tank through a combining nozzle and force it through an evasée which converted the velocity of the combined jet into sufficient pressure to force its way into the boiler through a check valve. Animations can be found on the internet.

Injectors had defects which improved versions sought to cure. They would not function below a certain steam pressure or above a certain feed water temperature. They were often difficult to start, temperamental in action and wasteful of water which overflowed onto the ground. The engineman operated the injector by sound and by observing the boiler pressure gauge and the escape of steam and water. Especially at night, he could be unaware that the injector had failed to start or had stopped working; we will never know how many boiler explosions this caused.

In the mid–1890s at least nine different models of injector were available to the American steam locomotive industry.[115] Different types varied in the pounds of water injected per pound of steam used.

The Sellers 1887 model, size 10½, allowed the enginemen to adjust the water flow rate so as to leave it running continuously at certain rates of steam consumption, rather than continually turning it on and off.[116] Efficiency of this model peaked at 26 pounds of water per pound of steam with 30-pounds per square inch steam, falling to only 10.3 pounds with 200-pounds per square inch steam. The maximum flow rate was 4,000 gallons per hour at a steam pressure of 200 pounds per square inch.

In 1890, Messrs. Holden & Brooke of Manchester, England, produced an injector in which the steam venturi could be moved back and forth by means of a screw thread, simultaneously altering the steam and water openings in inverse proportion to each other. This device would function at steam pressures from 15 to 200 pounds per square inch and could deal with hot feed water. The manufacturers received large orders from American railroads and engine builders.[117]

With the basic form of injector, the engineman had to operate the steam and water valves separately. The Ohio injector of 1894, developed by the Ohio Injector Co., of Wadsworth, Ohio, used a single lever to control steam and water.[118] The first backward movement of the lever admitted a jet of steam to the injector body, inducing a partial vacuum inside it and lifting water through the supply pipe. A second backward movement of the lever admitted steam to the main steam jet and started the injector. Moving the lever fully forward stopped the injector.

Injectors came to be divided into two types: lifting and non-lifting. A non-lifting injector needed positive water pressure at its supply; a lifting injector could lift from a water surface lower than the injector itself. A non-lifting injector had to be placed below the footplate, where it could draw water from the tender by gravity, with the controls in the cab. A lifting injector could be placed in the cab with the controls on the injector itself and was thus a more compact arrangement.

A direct descendant of the Ohio injector was the Hancock Type E, a fixed-cone, lifting injector brought out by the Hancock Inspirator Co., New York, in 1904.[119] It became one of the standard locomotive injectors in America.[120] By nothing more than changing the nozzles,

its capacity could be adjusted from 2,500 gallons per hour to 5,000 gallons per hour, based on 200-pounds per square inch steam pressure, 75°F feed water and 4 feet of suction head. The Type E would function at all steam pressures from 35 pounds per square inch to 350 pounds per square inch and could handle hotter feed water than its predecessors.

Although augmented by feed water heaters and exhaust-steam injectors, the conventional live-steam injector remained an essential part of the steam locomotive.

3.3.6 Feed Water Heaters

The idea of recovering waste heat by heating the feed water dates back to the earliest days of the steam engine.[121] John H. White records the use of feed water heaters on American locomotives during the nineteenth century. Those used, however, did not produce sufficiently obvious fuel economies to offset their manufacturing and maintenance costs. There was no point heating feed water to a temperature that an injector could not handle; any feed water heater had, therefore, to incorporate a pump, bypassing the injector. Nevertheless, a trickle of invention went on.

In 1897, J. B. Barnes, Motive Power Superintendent of the Wabash, piped exhaust steam from a locomotive air pump through pipes in the tender tank and thence to atmosphere. By this means, the water in the tank could be heated to 100°F or more. A three-way valve allowed the air pump exhaust to be directed to the tank or to atmosphere as required.[122]

An American tubular feed water heater, called the Rushforth, existed in 1900, but nothing else is known of it.[123]

The Forney feed water heater of 1902 comprised a "fire heater" and an "exhaust heater."[124] The fire heater was a set of fire tubes in a water space occupying a forward extension of the smokebox, heated by fire gases. The exhaust heater was a water space curved to match the underside of the smokebox, heated by exhaust steam.

This device was the product of defective engineering; its inventor promoted it with fantastic claims.

> The heater represented has 412 2¼" tubes, 3 ft. 8 in. long and has 890 sq. ft. of heating surface. The temperatures in the smokebox, when a locomotive is working under steam, vary from about 400 deg. to 1,200 deg. With that amount of heating surface and such temperatures a very large amount of heat would doubtless be transmitted to the feed water—how much cannot, of course, be determined, except by actual test, but, as already pointed out, these figures indicate not only the possibility, but the probability, of saving a very large percentage of fuel, and, in places where bad water is used, a very material saving in the cost of boiler repairs, by arresting the solid constituents of the water and depositing them in the heaters, and thus excluding them from the boiler.

Further:

> There can be no question of the fact that every 12 deg. of heat added to the feed-water will save 1 per cent of fuel. With temperatures in the smokebox varying from 400 deg. to 1,200 deg., and over 1,000 sq. ft. of heating surface in the heater, it does not seem over sanguine to expect that the temperature of the feed-water can be increased 360 deg., or raised from 60 deg. to 420 deg., which would give an economy of 30 per cent and increase the capacity of the boiler in like proportion.

Water boils at 420°F at a pressure of 300 pounds per square inch, almost twice the working pressure of the locomotive boilers in use at that time.

Also:

> The cost of the heater has not yet been ascertained, but if it will lessen the consumption of coal from 25 to 30 per cent, increase the capacity of the boiler in like proportion, arrest the solid constituents of the water

before they enter the boiler and consequently materially reduce the cost of boiler repairs, and keep the engine in service a greater proportion of the time, these advantages should be some indication of its value to railroad companies.

In 1903, T. C. McBride of the Worthington Pumping Engine Co., Philadelphia, installed a heater inside a dome on top of the boiler, supplied with exhaust steam from one of the cylinders.[125] A small steam engine used live steam to drive two pumps in tandem on a single piston rod. This assembly was mounted on the side of the engine, above the driving wheels and below the running board. One pump took water through a supply pipe from the tender and pumped it into the heater dome. The second pump took the hot water from the dome and pumped it into the boiler. An overflow pipe from the dome returned surplus water to the feed line. The device was controlled by a throttle in the cab. The Worthington feed water heater became one of the three most commonly used feed water heaters, the others being the Elesco and the Coffin.

3.3.7 Superheating

The boiling point of water is in proportion to the pressure of the atmosphere above its surface. At 180 pounds per square inch, water boils at 380°F. The steam at that temperature is said to be saturated or "wet." If the steam is heated to a temperature higher than its boiling point, it is said to be superheated. If steam at 180 pounds per square inch and 380°F is heated further to 500°F, it is said to have 120°F of superheat.

Like feed water heating, the use of superheated steam in both stationary and locomotive engines had a long history of attempted use throughout the nineteenth century.

> The earliest recorded attempt at superheating was that reported in 1828 by Richard Trevithick, at the Binner Downs Mine in Cornwall, on a condensing pumping engine making eight strokes per minute, with a boiler pressure of 45 lbs., in which the cylinders and steam pipes were surrounded with brickwork and heated from a fire burning on a grate underneath. The results were remarkable, for, while performing the same amount of work, 9,000 lbs. of coal were used per 24 hours without the fire under the cylinder, against 6,000 lbs. when it was in use, the coal for superheating included. This experience led Trevithick to the invention of his tubular boiler and superheater, which was patented in 1832…. Owing, no doubt, to the difficulty in regulating the temperature of the steam…, little seems to have been done in the matter during the next 10 or 15 years.[126]

The size and scope of this book do not permit any description of the numerous and persistent nineteenth-century attempts to use superheated steam; the referenced sources provide considerable detail. These attempts encountered severe manufacturing and maintenance difficulties. Superheated steam was hot enough to warp iron valve castings and damage the currently available lubricants and packings. Higher steam pressures and temperatures made these problems worse. The problems were so bad that:

> While a large amount of evidence was thus created in favor of superheating, and it was employed to a considerable extent, placing it beyond the experimental stage, it gradually gave way before the development of increased boiler pressure and compounding which commenced about 1865.
>
> By employing a higher boiler pressure and avoiding cylinder loss by compounding, the same economy could be obtained as by superheating with a decrease in trouble, and its use gradually declined until about 1870.[127]

Superheating made no further headway until balanced valves, petroleum-based lubricants, forced-feed (rather than gravity) lubrication and better packing materials became available after 1870.

The Chicago, Burlington & Quincy tried a smokebox superheater—with the superheater elements placed in the smokebox, as distinct from a fire-tube superheater with the elements in enlarged fire tubes ("flues")—in a locomotive in 1870, but the economies failed to offset the added costs; most American engineers thought superheating was more trouble than it was worth.[128] From the viewpoint of 1903:

> gradually American engineers have come to believe that while a superheater will unquestionably improve the thermal action of an engine, the cost of its maintenance quite offsets the advantage to be derived from its use. …
>
> American engineers threshed the straw of superheating many years ago, and have since been content to let the matter rest undisturbed.

Not so the Germans, who understood the theoretical advantages and were determined to overcome the practical problems that obstructed their realization. The leader in the field was Wilhelm Schmidt, born in 1858 in Wegeleben, Germany, the son of a farmer. He became a gifted mechanical engineer, inventor and business owner in various towns in central Germany.[129] After fourteen years of experiments, he succeeded, in 1894, in producing an engine using steam superheated to 700°F, applying his work first to stationary engines and achieving fuel consumptions as low as 1.0 to 1.7 pounds of coal per horsepower-hour.

By 1898, some 200 stationary plants were using the Schmidt system; probably most, if not all of these were in Germany. Tests showed that steam superheated by 180°F produced 25% more boiler efficiency, and consumed 33% less feed water and 25% less coal—radical advances when great efforts in other directions produced only small gains in efficiency, if any.[130] The Prussian State Railways equipped two locomotives with Schmidt fire-tube superheaters in 1898 with the stated objective of achieving greater efficiency without the complexity of compounding. These engines, with 125°F to 225°F of superheat, achieved 25% better performance than those using saturated steam. By the end of 1904, the Prussian State Railways had 127 superheated locomotives in service. All of these had Schmidt's smokebox-type superheater; only the original two and the last one used his fire-tube superheater. Introduction of superheat on other European railroads began in 1902.

In America superheating was introduced earlier in stationary practice than in locomotives. Eight 6,000-horsepower two-cylinder compound engines, built by Westinghouse for the New York Waterside power house in 1900–1, used steam at 175 pounds per square inch superheated to 577°F. Additionally, steam was reheated in a receiver between the cylinders.[131]

In 1901, Spencer Otis, in a paper read before the Northwest Railway Club[132]:

> announced his purpose to stimulate, if possible, a line of thought calculated to develop the simple locomotive to its greatest efficiency before it should eventually pass down and out to give place to the compound locomotive and perhaps, finally, to the electric or some other form of locomotive. His idea in brief was based upon the often considered proposition of using the heat of the front end gases in a locomotive to superheat the steam in the cylinders.

Otis's plan led the flue gases through jackets around the cylinders and thence to the stack.

The best configuration for a locomotive superheater was not obvious. The original Schmidt superheater comprised sixty-two steam tubes arranged round the inside of the smokebox and separated from it by a shroud, open at the top, closed at the bottom. A flue, one foot in diameter, supplied hot fire gases to the bottom of the shroud; the gases flowed upward through the shroud over the steam tubes and

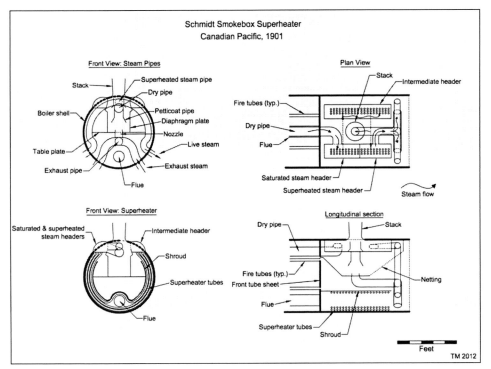

The Schmidt smokebox superheater (redrawn from *RAG*, August 10, 1906, 124).

15% to 20% fuel savings compared to saturated-steam compounds of the same class.[135] As a result of these tests, the Canadian Pacific began to buy new engines with superheat, the first railroad in North America to do so. The fuel economy of the compounds was still acknowledged, even if their total economy did not warrant further orders for new locomotives. The Canadians used their own proprietary design of superheater, known as the Vaughan-Horsey, as well as Schenectady and Schmidt types.

The Schmidt fire-tube superheater used a U-tube inside an enlarged flue, whereas the Schenectady type used an open-ended tube discharging inside a closed-ended tube, the closed-ended tube nesting inside the enlarged flue. Saturated steam, moving rearward through the inmost tube of each element, became superheated and discharged through the open end of the tube, returning forward through the outside tube. The returning superheated steam heated the saturated steam while picking up

through the top of the shroud to exhaust. A header distributed steam from the dry pipe to the tubes, where it was superheated, passing thence to the cylinders. Dampers regulated the flow of gases to prevent the steam tubes from being burned when the throttle was closed and no steam was passing through them. The temperature of the fire gases dropped from about 1,200°F on entry into the shroud to about 600°F at the exhaust, producing a superheated steam temperature of about 575°F.

One design tried by the Prussian State Railways in 1902–3 was the Pielock. Saturated steam from the throttle valve circulated inside a rectangular box under the steam dome. Fire tubes passing through the box superheated the steam before it entered the dry pipe. The Germans exhibited a Pielock superheater in a 4-4-2 at St. Louis in 1904, but found no users in the U.S.[133]

Although the Schmidt smokebox superheater was effective, and the damper arrangement allowed the degree of superheat to be varied, it was too complicated. Schmidt also developed a fire-tube superheater in which a header distributed steam from the dry pipe to looped tubes, installed in flues in the upper part of the boiler. The superheated steam went to a separate part of the header, thence to the cylinders. Schmidt recognized that still higher superheat could be obtained by doubling each superheater tube loop, so that the steam passed through the flues four times instead of two.

The first North American user of superheated locomotives was the Canadian Pacific Railway. The company sent an engineer, A. W. Horsey, to Germany to study Schmidt's work.[134] In 1901, Roger Atkinson, mechanical superintendent, retrofitted a Schmidt smokebox superheater to a single-expansion 4-6-0 freight engine. This engine demonstrated a 25% fuel saving over other engines of the same class, and an 18% saving over two compound 4-6-0s, a Pittsburgh cross-compound and a Vauclain, over a period of several months in 1903–4. In 1903, E. A. Williams, who had taken over as mechanical superintendent, retrofitted Schmidt fire-tube superheaters to two 4-6-0 compound freight engines. The two superheated compounds showed

more heat from the flue gases, this arrangement being known as a Field tube. Other fire-tube superheaters using the Field tube were the Notkine and Churchward. The sources consulted have not revealed the differences between these types.

F. J. Cole, Mechanical Engineer of the American Locomotive Company, brought out the Schenectady fire-tube superheater in 1904, a development of the Schmidt fire-tube type.[136] Cole wanted to eliminate the hairpin bends in the tubes; fire gases and cinders burned and wore through the metal where it was weak. A damper mechanically linked to the throttle prevented the tubes from burning when no steam was inside them to cool them. Cole also redesigned the header in five castings for easier disassembly. The first application of a Schenectady superheater was to a New York Central 4-4-2. Almost at once, the Canadians combined the Schmidt looped superheater elements with the Schenectady modular header. The CPR bought its first new engines with superheat in 1904: forty-one single-expansion 2-8-0s, twenty with the Schmidt type, twenty-one with the Schenectady (Cole) type.

Soon the Canadians were using single-expansion 2-8-0s, 4-6-0s and 4-6-2s and 4-6-0 compounds with superheat. In at least one case, they retained Wilhelm Schmidt himself to design the valves and cylinders appropriately to superheated steam. Because of this quantity and variety of locomotives, operating information built up quickly. Results on the Brandon and Swift Current divisions in Manitoba showed an astonishing 35% coal saving. Superheating, "without any desire to appear too enthusiastic, certainly promises to become one of the greatest steps in the direction of economy that has been introduced for many years past." By the end of 1906, the company had 197 superheated locomotives in use, with another 175 on order. Thereafter, the company ordered all new road engines with superheat. At that time there were only fifteen superheated locomotives in the U.S.

The Americans greeted locomotive superheating with skepticism. As a European invention, it smacked of that complexity which was

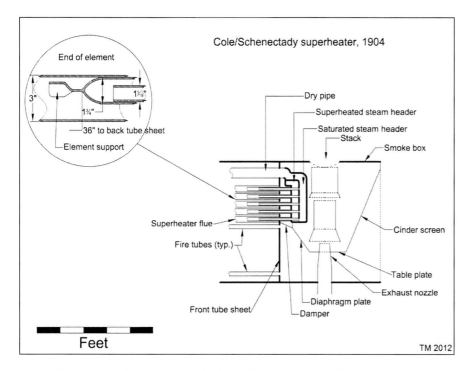

Cole/Schenectady superheater, 1904

The Cole fire-tube superheater (redrawn from *RRG*, September 2, 1904, 293).

anathema to American locomotive builders and operators—one of those "patent economizers" that vied for the attention of engineers and executives. As late as 1901, when the Schmidt smokebox superheater was already proving itself on the German railroads, the American view of this invention was:

> While much thought is being given to the removal of draft obstructions from front ends of locomotives there are yet those who are ready to disregard this consideration by installing complicated economizers.
>
> In the light of the present tendency to simplify draft arrangements, we fear that the inventor's road to success will be more tortuous and difficult than the paths of the gases.
>
> Something may yet come of it, and there are now in use in foreign locomotives some devices which have for their central thought this idea, but there are no available records of increased efficiency, so far as we know.

Measurements dating back more than fifty years, and becoming more voluminous and more reliable year by year, had consistently shown 15% to 25% improvements in fuel economy resulting from the use of superheated steam. This simple device, with no moving parts, harnessing the subtle thermodynamics of steam and capable of substantial fuel economies, was an enormous technical breakthrough. Invisible from the outside, it was probably one of the most important innovations in the history of the steam locomotive.

Section 3.4. Smokeboxes and Drafting

When Richard Trevithick reported in a letter to Davis Giddy, President of the Royal Society, in 1804 that: "…the fire burned very much better when the steam goes up the chimney than when the engine is idle," he was describing one of the most important of all inventions relating to the steam locomotive—the action inside the smokebox. Considering that the smokebox contained no moving parts, its functioning was remarkably complicated.

The "smokebox," or "front end," was an unpressurized cylindrical extension of the boiler ahead of the front tube sheet. The dry pipe from the dome passed through the front tube sheet, bifurcating in the smokebox and passing thence to the cylinders. The exhaust pipes from the cylinders joined in a vertical exhaust pipe, ending in a nozzle. The stack was directly above the nozzle.

As each cylinder exhausted, the steam driven from it by the return stroke of the piston, together with residual pressure from incomplete expansion, forced a blast of steam through the nozzle and up the stack, making the characteristic noise of a steam locomotive. The steam blasts entrained air in the smokebox and threw it out the stack, causing a partial vacuum.

The smokebox vacuum drew gases through the fire tubes from the firebox, creating a negative pressure inside the firebox, drawing air through the fire. The wider the throttle was opened and the longer the cutoff, in other words, the greater the power demand, the stronger the exhaust blast and the stronger the fire draft. The stack acted as a diffuser, converting some of the velocity of the exhaust jet back into sufficient pressure to overcome the pressure of the outside atmosphere. This increased the rate of combustion and made high power output possible from a grate of restricted dimensions. When the throttle was closed, a similar effect could be produced by the blower, a steam jet or ring of jets surrounding the nozzle, drawing steam from the boiler and controlled from the cab. An access door in the front of the smokebox permitted inspection and the removal of cinders. When closed, this door had to be air-tight, otherwise the steam blast could not create a vacuum and the engine would not steam properly.

This was a wonderful discovery at the time; the harder the engine worked, the stronger the furnace draft.[137] A century later, this wonderful invention had become a millstone around the neck of the device it was intended to benefit and the despair of those seeking to improve its dismal thermal inefficiency. Engineers knew that very small adjustments to the exhaust nozzle and stack caused large changes in locomotive performance, but no one knew enough to explain, predict or optimize what went on inside the smokebox. In 1893, A. W. Gibbs of the Pennsylvania was forced to admit[138]:

> Some years ago, I started to figure out the best possible arrangement of draft appliance for locomotives, and I think it took me three or four months to come to the conclusion that I knew less than when I began, and this, too, was very little.

In the mid–1800s American locomotive builders carried the blast pipe effect to extremes with nozzles as small as 1¾ inches for an engine with 15-inch cylinders.[139] This produced an intense fire draft at full throttle and long cut-off and an exhaust almost like gunshots. The tight nozzle, however, produced a high back pressure in the cylinders. Tractive effort and power output depended on the mean effective pressure in the cylinders. The mean effective pressure was the boiler pressure minus all the pressure losses through the throttle, steam pipes and valves, and minus the back pressure in the nozzle. Until mechanical engineers took indicator diagrams, they could not measure these effects. (An indicator diagram was a plot of cylinder pressure against piston position, of which more later in this book.) They also did not know that high combustion rates led to low efficiency in terms of pounds of water evaporated per pound of coal. Yet another problem was the amount of burning cinders thrown out through the stack, causing line-side fires.

In the early 1890s, the Americans wondered why the British used much larger-diameter exhaust nozzles than they did and did not have to use spark arresters,[140] especially as their engines were of similar dimensions to those in America. In Britain, four-coupled engines could haul 700-ton trains over undulating grades at average speeds of 20 to 25 miles per hour, as did American locomotives of that period. Such trains, however, were a quarter mile long and the British found that they were more trouble than they were worth. British locomotives were therefore less heavily loaded than in the U.S. Firing rates up to 110 pounds of coal per square foot of grate per hour produced sufficient power, while the Americans needed firing rates up to 195 pounds to produce the power that they demanded of their engines.

Lower firing rates needed less draft. Bigger-diameter exhaust nozzles allowed British locomotives to run at 2.5 pounds per square inch back pressure in the cylinders, compared to 25 pounds per square inch in the U.S. The lower combustion rates that resulted from the weaker draft produced more steam per pound of coal. With higher mean effective pressure and higher evaporative efficiency, the British achieved better fuel efficiency in pounds of coal per horsepower-hour. The stronger draft used in America caused smokebox temperatures of 950°F to 1,600°F, compared to 600°F in Britain. Not only did American locomotives eject more sparks than their British counterparts, but the sparks were hotter and more likely to start fires, hence the American spark arresters which interfered with the gas flow through the smokebox, and so it went on.

Railroads were always being sued for damage caused by line-side fires; spark suppression had liability implications. Property damage ranged from haystacks to houses and huge tracts of forest where uncontrolled fires wiped out whole communities. Sparks could also set the train itself on fire. Unfortunately, the effectiveness of a spark arrester was in proportion to the complexity of the path into which it forced the gases between the front tube sheet and the stack, and the obstacles that it placed in their way. Much research went into the size, temperature and distribution of sparks ejected from the stack.

Tantalizingly, locomotive designers and operators knew that small changes in the many dimensions of exhaust nozzle and stack had large effects on locomotive performance with thousands of dollars in fuel costs at stake. Yet the only means of investigation was countless experiments by trial and error in the hope that some sort of unifying theory would emerge.

Inventors tried and promoted all sorts of ideas. In 1893:

> The vortex exhaust pipes have been much talked of and written about and not a few who have tried them have said that they produce advantageous results; but so far no one has taken the trouble to investigate and give to the public the facts concerning their operation. No one appears to know just how much in quantity and what is the kind of effect produced in a smokebox by these peculiar exhaust arrangements. It is clear to see, however, that there is some truth in the claims of their promoters, but how much the claims amount to in point of fact is not known.[141]

Furthermore:

> Less is known about the proper arrangement of locomotive exhaust than of any other important detail of locomotive construction. No better proof of this is wanted than is found in the wide variety of designs. Some roads use smokestacks 12 in. in diameter on all classes of engines regardless of the size. Other roads have special stacks for each type of engine. One will find a 3½-in. exhaust nozzle on 18-in. cylinders on one road, and 5-in. exhaust nozzles on the same size cylinder on engines doing the same class of work on another road. Such investigations as have been made by the Master Mechanics' Association have never been anywhere near final. The experiments were non-conclusive and incomplete.
>
> Each individual designer may have a conviction in the matter, but the confliction of prevailing ideas is too great to give much confidence in the ideas of anybody on this subject.

Most American smokebox designs incorporated perforated plates and wire netting in various layouts to break up or trap burning cinders, of the general form shown in the accompanying drawing. A deflector plate, angled downward and forward from the top of the front tube sheet, evened out the gas flow between the upper and lower fire tubes and caused the gases to sweep through the bottom of the smokebox, up past the smokebox door, upward and backward through a sheet of wire netting placed to break up sparks, and then through the stack. Countless designs varied this arrangement in detail, especially in the shape and height of the nozzle, the presence or absence of petticoat pipes, the arrangement of the spark arrester and the length of the smokebox.

The locomotives exhibited at the Chicago World's Fair in 1893, including exhibits from Britain, France and Germany, showed no uniformity in front-end design.

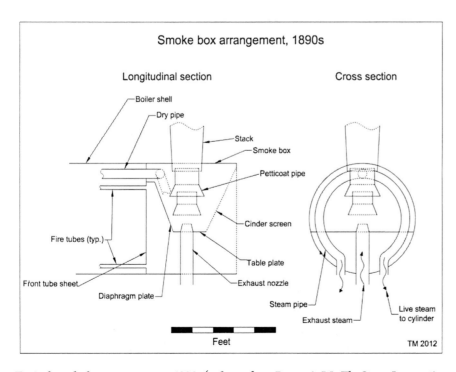

Smoke box arrangement, 1890s

Longitudinal section — Cross section

Boiler shell
Dry pipe
Stack
Smoke box
Petticoat pipe
Cinder screen
Fire tubes (typ.)
Table plate
Front tube sheet
Exhaust nozzle
Diaphragm plate
Steam pipe
Exhaust steam
Live steam to cylinder

Feet

TM 2012

Typical smoke box arrangement, 1890s (redrawn from Bruce, A. W., *The Steam Locomotive in America: Its Development in the Twentieth Century*, New York: Bonanza, 1952).

It seems as if the trouble had been in locomotive designing ever since the development of the locomotive became a study, to grope blindly and ineffectually at the subject of draft appliances.[142]

However:

> That this subject is receiving some attention is evidenced by the appointment of a committee by the Railway Master Mechanics' Association to consider and report on the subject. So far, it is understood that little or nothing has been accomplished. The subject is so large that they hardly know how to commence their work or upon what lines to proceed.

The general consensus was: "As it now stands, it appears that anything works, but how well or how poorly no one knows."

C. H. Quereau, of the Chicago, Burlington & Quincy, pointed out that blowers were more effective when the steam issued from several small jets than when it was in a solid column from a single, large jet, evidencing an initial understanding of how the exhaust blast functioned.[143]

Possibly the first advance in this confusion was a major test program, including more than 30,000 readings from 3,200 combinations of stack length, stack diameter and distance from nozzle to stack, run by the Prussian State Railways at Hanover in 1892–4, managed by A. von Borries; collation of the results took two years.[144] Using a laboratory test rig and locomotives in service, von Borries found that the highest smokebox vacuum was obtained when a diverging steam jet from the exhaust nozzle just filled the stack at its narrowest point. The tests also suggested the proper proportioning of the exhaust nozzle and stack. Von Borries also pointed to the value of a splitter placed across the exhaust nozzle. This was not a new idea; enginemen knew that a splitter would sometimes make an engine steam better, believing that splitting the exhaust caused the steam jet to fill the stack more completely.[145]

This would have been complicated enough if the exhaust jet had been continuous. As it was, the jet was intermittent as each cylinder exhausted and its shape varied with engine speed, throttle setting and cut-off. The spreading of the steam jet varied with pressure and, hence, varied in the course of each exhaust blast.

Under the chairmanship of Robert Quayle, of the Chicago & North Western, an ARMMA committee began to achieve results in 1894, using facilities provided by the Chicago & North Western with its static testing plant built in 1895.

Theories abounded as to why the smokebox functioned as it did but, almost a hundred years after Trevithick's invention, everyone knew that it worked; no one knew why.[146] Every railroad used its own design of front end; the different layouts are too numerous to mention here. The German tests were the first of many experiments on both sides of the Atlantic; the findings were often bizarre, contradicting the tenets of experience and the findings of previous tests. With each advance in the study of the exhaust jet, the problem retreated deeper into obscurity. By 1894, accepted wisdom was that the steam jet had sharp boundaries, that these boundaries diverged after the jet left the nozzle and that the jet had to fill the stack if it was to produce the necessary smokebox vacuum.

In 1895–6, the Chicago, Burlington & Quincy tested a locomotive equipped with an exhaust nozzle which could be raised or lowered while the engine was working and while measuring smokebox vacuum.[147] Researchers at Purdue detected the edge of the jet and measured variations in velocity within the jet by means of pitot tubes passing through the smokebox shell and free to slide in and out, connected to manometers. They found that the jet had sharp boundaries—a tenth of an inch wide—easily detected from the pressure picked up in the tubes. The Purdue researchers discovered that the

steam jet did not expand at a constant angle, but became parallel-sided before entering the stack.

The Chicago, Burlington & Quincy researchers took this further, but with surprising results:

> we had laid special stress on the matter of having the exhaust jet fill the stack at the choke; and of course supposed we had exactly the proper relations between nozzle and stack to secure this result, ... You can imagine our surprise when, making the first trip, we found that the jet did not fill the contracted portion of the stack by from 4 to 5 in.

Professor Goss suggested that, at the higher speeds, the gases that the jet drew with it themselves crowded the jet, preventing it from filling the stack.

> It would also seem to be true that during a trip of 100 to 150 miles, especially over a line with varying gradients, with any given arrangement of draft appliances, the form of the exhaust jet undergoes hundreds or perhaps thousands of changes, being appreciably influenced by every change of cut-off, every variation in speed, or possibly by a change of steam pressure, or difference in the volume of air admitted to the tubes, either owing to the condition of the fire on grates or irregular opening of the firebox door.

This idea destroyed any hopes of a perfect drafting configuration with a single set of dimensions.

The first tests by the ARMMA committee showed that many different designs and dimensions gave adequate results.[148] In 1896, the committee came up with a recommended front end design incorporating the results of the German experiments and within a year several railroads were reporting better fuel economy from using this design.[149]

Efforts went on to design an altogether better nozzle, such as the Sweney nozzle developed at the University of Illinois in 1899 and tested on the Illinois Central.[150] The Sweney nozzle was a star-shaped arrangement of eight separate nozzles, based on the theory that friction along the sides of the exhaust jet drew gases with it. Increasing the total area of the sides of the jet would increase this effect. This idea was prophetic and would be the basis of several successful nozzle designs over the next fifty years. Tests on the Illinois Central detected a benefit in fuel economy from using the Sweney nozzle.

In 1899, the International Railway Congress appointed C. H. Quereau, at that time Assistant Superintendent of Machinery for the Denver & Rio Grande, to report on drafting, spark control and waste heat utilization. His questionnaire to 120 major railroads in the U.S., Canada and Mexico elicited replies from thirty-three, operating 15,000 locomotives.[151] The replies showed that smokebox was still "... a subject that has been repeatedly discussed, and yet there is scarcely another locomotive question in such a chaotic state." American designs were few, compared to the varieties devised in Europe.

Inventions for varying the size, shape or position of the exhaust nozzle to meet the needs of different cut-offs or throttle settings were advocated from time to time but conditions inside the smokebox were so hostile that few succeeded. One exception was the jumper ring used by the Great Western Railway in Britain. Several European railroads used adjustable exhaust pipes but, apart from the difficulties of maintenance, if the enginemen misused them, the resulting fuel economy could be worse than with a fixed exhaust pipe.[152] For a long time, American practice was for each cylinder to discharge through its own nozzle, the two nozzles being mounted side by side in a single casting; neither nozzle was concentric with the stack. This practice changed in the 1890s to both cylinders discharging through a common nozzle.

As in many aspects of steam locomotive design, the number of independent variables was so great that it was difficult to screen out the effects of the controlled variable being studied. Furthermore:

> An engine is often very different in operation from what it was designed and sent out to be, and sometimes there is not enough courage at the division master mechanic's office to report back to the superintendent of motive power the lack of draft; the bushing and bridging is then surreptitiously done. Sometimes even the master mechanic does not share in the secret, and matters are arranged between engineers and the roundhouse men. This is probably one of the chief reasons why front-end questions have remained so clouded with doubt while definite conclusions have been reached on many other questions as complex.[153]

Sometimes the secrecy went farther down the hierarchy. On the Great Western Railway in Britain in the early 1900s:

> One of these old characters, (as of 1935) who witnessed me spilling coal, told me how his driver was a maniac for saving coal and would go berserk if he allowed a lump of coal as small as a golf ball to roll over the side of the footplate. To make matters worse, he would work the engine so lightly, with the regulator (throttle) barely open and very short cut-off, that maintaining a bright fire was nearly impossible. The driver also totally forbade him to touch the blower and he found that life was being made completely impossible for him. One of the other firemen suggested that he should put a "Jimmy" in the blastpipe. This consisted of a piece of ¼-inch iron plate fashioned by the blacksmith which could be dropped edgeways into the blastpipe to spread the blast to fill the chimney. He said that this worked a treat and he used it all the time that he was paired with this particular driver without his knowledge, putting it into position while preparing the engine and removing it during disposal at the end of the shift. This was before the advent of the GWR jumper ring which was fitted to the top of the blastpipe.[154]

By 1900, certain guiding principles were becoming clear:

> A front-end design that sets up a cumbersome or complicated exhaust nozzle, flanks it closely at base and sides with large and heavy steam pipes, obstructs the flue exits with other devices, and shed-roofs the greater part of this apparatus with a diaphragm having abrupt angles in the path of the natural draft, is wrong in principle and proves that fact daily in practice. Yet this description will be recognized by many readers.[155]

The 1902 International Railway Congress reached some conclusions.[156] Complicated smokebox arrangements did not produce worthwhile benefits. The dimensions and positioning of the components could be determined by formulae, but should still be verified by tests. A low nozzle needed a petticoat pipe; a high nozzle, as was common in Europe, should not be above the top row of fire tubes. The smokebox could be as long as 6½ feet if it was to be used as a cinder trap, but only 5 feet if not. If no deflector plate was used, the stack had to be far enough from the front tube sheet to ensure an even distribution of gas flow through the tubes.

Still, in 1902:

> If a person should take the time to look over the hundreds of drawings of front-end arrangements which can be found in different mechanical journals, as well as the papers of different persons which refer to the different ideas on extension front-ends, he will become satisfied at once that such a thing as a standard front-end for locomotives, and one that will be generally adopted throughout the country by the different railroads, is entirely out of the question. No two superintendents of motive power, master mechanics or roundhouse foremen will agree. Two neighboring roads running through the same section of country, using the same grade of fuel, cannot (at least so it is claimed) use the same front-end. In fact, it is safe to say that the different master mechanics on the same road will hardly agree. Each one of them has some idea that is just a little different from the others and which he thinks is superior.[157]

A committee appointed by the Traveling Engineers' Association in 1902 got few replies to a questionnaire on the subject and no original suggestions.

In 1903, the trade journal *American Engineer* experimented at Purdue with a quarter-scale rig designed to provide either a continuous steam jet or an intermittent blast.[158] Although the experiments seemed to produce some useful rules of thumb for smokebox design, the overall conclusion was disappointing:

> The results obtained in these tests have led me to believe that results obtained on any one type of locomotive cannot be duplicated on another locomotive of different design and in different service.

By 1903 at least some of those involved in locomotive design at least knew in some detail what they were trying to achieve. Professor Goss put it plainly:

> The front-end is to be regarded as an apparatus for doing work, receiving energy from a source of power, and delivering a portion thereof in the form of a specific result. The source of power is exhaust steam from the cylinders, and the useful work accomplished is represented by the volumes of furnace gases which are delivered against the difference of pressure existing between the smokebox and the atmosphere. That the power of the jet may be efficient, it is necessary that the engines of the locomotive exhaust against back-pressure. The presence of the back-pressure tends to lower the cylinder performance, and it is for this reason that designers of front-ends have sought to secure the required draft action in return for the least possible back-pressure. In other words, the effort has been to increase the ratio of draft to back-pressure, which ratio has been defined as the efficiency of the front-end.[159]

In most conditions American locomotives ran at 4 to 6 inches water gauge smokebox vacuum. Of this one third was the pressure drop across the ash pan, grate and fire. One third was the pressure loss through the fire tubes. The remaining third was the pressure loss caused by the deflector plate inside the smokebox. Much was to be gained if the deflector plate could be dispensed with.

Professor Goss established several principles on which the steam jet functioned. He confirmed that the jet acted on the smokebox gases by both friction and entrainment, drawing gases to itself from all directions. Especially at high speeds, the exhaust blasts behaved practically as a continuous jet. The resulting draft was nearly proportional to the mass flow rate of the steam exhausted. The form of the jet was influenced by the shape of the passages through which it passed. The jet did not fill the stack until near its top. Interestingly, if the diameter of the stack was changed, the diameter of the jet changed also, confirming earlier suspicions that the jet choked itself with the gases that it entrained. Goss found that the lower the exhaust nozzle was mounted, the better the draft.

Although, by 1900, it was American practice to discharge both cylinders into a common exhaust pipe, it was still necessary to keep the two exhaust passages separate for about 6 to 12 inches after they had joined at the base of the exhaust pipe by means of a steel divider. This prevented the exhaust from one cylinder from adding to the back pressure in the other. Further, whichever exhaust was instantaneously the stronger reduced the back pressure in the other. An ideal dimension of 12 inches for the divider was at least found to be constant for all heights of exhaust pipe. Some builders constricted the exhaust pipe between the junction of the two steam passages and the nozzle. The ARMMA committee found that this was deleterious; no constriction should be tighter than the nozzle itself. The committee was not able to find any shape of nozzle markedly better than any other. Bars or crosses over the nozzle to split the jet improved steaming but increased back pressure. (Curiously, the thirty-three companies replying to the 1899 IRC questionnaire "universally condemned" this practice.)

By 1903:

the investigations already made have served to make clear the action of the exhaust jet, and the condition of pressure which stimulates the currents of air and furnace gases from the ash pan to the top of the stack. Existing data are sufficient, also, to guide in the design of the exhaust-pipe and tip for maximum results. All this is to be accepted as a certainty. In addition, the probability is that we may design stacks for maximum efficiency though the statement must be subject to some qualification until the experiments already made at Purdue have been checked by trials involving larger engines either upon the road or testing plant. This settled, there remains of those elements which characterize the modern front-end, the problem of the draft-pipe, of the inside stack, by which is meant a stack extending downward into the front-end and terminating in a bell-shaped end, and of the inside stack in connection with a false top within the smoke-box. All these questions are now under consideration by a committee of the Master Mechanics' Association, under the chairmanship of Mr. H. H. Vaughan, whose interest in the subject makes it not unreasonable to expect that within the next 2 years all portions of the front-end may be correctly designed by aid of logical formulae.

This hope was to prove illusory.

Section 3.5. Cylinder Arrangements and Compounding

3.5.1 Cylinder Arrangements

Locomotive cylinders were conventionally mounted on the outside of the frames at the front of the locomotive. Nothing was gained by placing them at the back where they would be showered with cinders and grit.

This arrangement had certain disadvantages. Each cylinder had to be cantilevered from the frame; its mounting had to support the weight of the cylinder and valve chest and withstand the piston thrusts. Bigger cylinders and higher steam pressures, in the search for more power, required bigger and heavier mountings and placed the line of the piston thrust farther from the frames.[160] The piston thrusts induced a yawing motion in the locomotive, causing wear and tear to locomotive and track and rough riding at high speeds. The light rail used for original construction, heavy pistons and other reciprocating parts, and increasing train speeds were a poor combination. Although the trend was to heavier rail, both in new construction and replacing worn rail, locomotive builders recognized the need for lighter pistons and began to make pistons of wrought iron or cast steel, weighing only half as much as the older cast-iron pistons.

When the locomotive industry was trying to improve the performance and efficiency of a machine that was not well understood, fads and fashions came and went. One such was to increase the piston stroke from 24 inches to 30 inches.[161] This idea had solid merit. Lateral clearance dimensions limited the diameter of the piston; one way of getting more work from each stroke was to lengthen the stroke.

Locomotive cylinders were conventionally mounted on the outside of the frames at the front, as on this Live Oak, Perry & Gulf 4-6-0, No. 101, still burning wood when photographed at Dowling Park, Florida, on February 20, 1942. The box on top of the cylinder houses the slide valve; the later piston valves are identifiable by a cylindrical housing in that position (Denver Public Library, Robert W. Richardson collection, RR-1361).

This did not increase the size and weight of the piston or the circumference of the piston and its friction against the cylinder wall, and lengthened the lever arm acting on the driving axle. The limit to stroke length was the distance from the driving axle to the crankpin, which had to allow clearance between the connecting rod big end and the ground. Stroke lengths of 28 to 32 inches became standard.

An option much favored by the British was to mount both cylinders between the frames. Two inside cylinders put the piston thrusts close to the centerline of the locomotive, reducing its yawing motion and resulting in smoother riding at high speeds. Inside cylinders were better insulated than outside. The path from cylinder to exhaust was short and straight. Inside-mounted cylinders were supported on both sides. Inside cylinders, however, required crank axles, which were more expensive to build than straight axles and more liable to break, while the internal crossheads and connecting rods were difficult to access for inspection, lubrication and maintenance. For those reasons, the Americans built only a few two-cylinder locomotives with both cylinders mounted between the frames, and those in the early days.[162]

Another possibility was to place a third cylinder between the frames; dividing the piston thrust between three cylinders gave smoother riding, but at the expense of a crank axle. As early as 1846 the Stephensons (J. Snowden Bell (referenced source) says Robert Stephenson; Drury says George Stephenson) built an engine in England with three cylinders, two outside the frames and one inside.[163] This idea made little progress in the U.S. due to bad experience with crank axle breakage and difficulty of access. The advantages of the three-cylinder engine, however, were such that the idea refused to disappear.

The first three-cylinder engines in the United States were two Norris 4-4-0s converted to this arrangement on the Philadelphia, Wilmington & Baltimore in 1848–9. Only twelve other three-cylinder engines were built in the U.S. between then and 1892. In that year, a three-cylinder 2-6-0 went into service on the Erie & Wyoming Valley, patented by the president of the railroad, John B. Smith. The valve arrangement was conventional; all three cylinders exhausted to separate nozzles. The railroad converted two 2-8-0s to this configuration and in 1894 ordered three three-cylinder 2-6-0s from Baldwin.[164] All three 17-inch × 24-inch cylinders were in line beneath the smokebox, driving on the second pair of driving wheels. The cylinders comprised two castings, one containing the left-hand cylinder, the other containing the middle and right-hand cylinders; the middle cylinder was displaced 13 inches to the right of centerline to allow space for the valve gear. These engines later became the property of the Erie and seem to have worked well.[165] Tests in October 1894, showed no discernible thermal advantage for the three-cylinder engine but the cranks, set at 120° from each other, provided a more even tractive force and better counter-balancing than a two-cylinder engine. The designers dispensed entirely with counterweights in the main driving wheels, these being provided by the structure of the crank axle.[166]

Yet another possibility was to mount two cylinders outside the frames and two more inside. Four-cylinder steam locomotives date back at least to 1862, when several were exhibited at the London International Exhibition.[167] In America A. M. Cumming patented a four-cylinder, single-expansion locomotive in 1877, but nothing was built to this design. The same was true of the four-cylinder, single-expansion locomotive patented by M. B. Bulla in 1895. In 1881, H. F. Shaw converted a Hinckley 4-4-0 into a four-cylinder engine to achieve better balancing of the rotating and reciprocating masses.[168] This engine used both inside and outside frames, one connecting rod working inside and one outside the outside frame on each side of the engine. The Chicago, Rock Island & Pacific built two four-cylinder, single-expansion 4-4-2s in 1909 but, otherwise, four-cylinder, single-expansion, rigid-frame engines, although common in Europe, remained rare in the U.S.

One of the few radical departures from the conventional cylinder and valve arrangement was the so-called Cleveland or "uniflow" cylinder, patented by W. F. and E. W. Cleveland of Rounthwaite, Manitoba, and first promoted by A. M. Peterson of Colborne, Ontario, in 1898.[169] The cylinder contained two pistons on the same piston rod, working in a cylinder about twice as long as normal. A piston valve admitted steam to the cylinder. Steam exhausted through ports in the cylinder wall at its mid-length when these were uncovered by the movement of the piston and, secondarily, through the piston valve. The exhaust from the mid-length ports exhausted through the exhaust nozzle; the steam exhausting through the piston valve exhausted through an annulus surrounding the nozzle. The inventors intended to allow the steam to expand more completely than in a normal cylinder, to provide freer exhaust, reduce the back pressure and control compression at the ends of the stroke. The piston valve was set so that, at long cut-off, the piston reached the end of its stroke and opened the mid-length port before the piston valve uncovered the steam port to exhaust. As the engineer shortened the cut-off, this reversed at about 6 inches cut-off in a 26-inch stroke cylinder. A benefit was the reduced temperature cycling in the cylinder ports and reduced condensation.

The Intercolonial Railway of Canada ordered seven 4-6-0s and five 2-8-0s with Cleveland cylinders from the Dickson Locomotive Works, Scranton, Pennsylvania, in 1901. One 4-6-0 and one 2-8-0 were built in May of that year and tested satisfactorily on the Delaware, Lackawanna & Western out of Scranton, the 4-6-0 running at speeds up to 70 miles per hour.[170] The uniflow cylinder never achieved widespread use in locomotive practice.

Temperature cycling in the cylinders was one of the many inefficiencies inherent in the reciprocating steam engine and is one reason why the steam turbine, with steady temperatures in different parts of the engine, is more efficient than a reciprocating engine. Steam entering the cylinder lost heat by conduction and radiation to the cylinder walls and piston face and cooled adiabatically as it expanded. The next charge of live steam entering the cylinders then encountered cylinder walls and pistons cooled by the previous charge. Reduction in this temperature cycling was one of the obscure efficiencies of the compound steam engine. This complex issue, entailing significant heat loss, was studied in road tests at least as early as 1894.[171]

3.5.2 Compounding

Compounding is one of the most complicated and controversial subjects in the whole history of the steam locomotive. For decades the debate raged on amongst locomotive builders and operators whether the compound locomotive was more efficient, all things being considered, than the single-expansion (a.k.a. "simple") version and, if so, whether this justified its increased cost and complexity. On both sides of the Atlantic various designs of compound engine were vigorously, even fanatically, promoted by strong and eccentric characters such as Webb in Britain and Vauclain in the U.S. In some cases, when they retired, their locomotive progeny were quietly set aside. One executive remarked in 1895: "The compound locomotive is without question in my mind the locomotive of the future, but its progress would be much more rapid if the advocates of the compound were more moderate in their claims."[172]

"Compounding" in a reciprocating steam engine means expanding the steam in a series of cylinders (usually two in locomotives, sometimes three in stationary engines) at progressively lower pressures. Compounding dates back to the Hornblower stationary engine, patented in Britain in 1781 as a means of circumventing the Watt

Samuel M. Vauclain. The words and deeds of Samuel Vauclain probably occur more in this book than those of any one individual, warranting a portrait. The work of Professor Goss comes a close second; he appears in one of the photographs of the Purdue locomotive laboratory. The writer has tried to acquire portraits of other significant participants in this narrative, but with disappointing results. The date and location of this photograph are unknown (courtesy California State Railroad Museum, Negative 39078cn).

patent.[173] Most stationary engines exhausted from their low-pressure cylinders into a condenser at less than atmospheric pressure, whereas locomotives depended on exhausting their steam well above atmospheric pressure in order to draft the fire. The total pressure drop available for compounding in a condensing stationary engine was therefore greater than in a locomotive. In stationary power plants, huge, condensing triple-expansion engines were quite common and, in the early 1890s, were regarded as the ultimate in steam engine efficiency.[174]

The irony behind the great effort that went into developing compound locomotives on both sides of the Atlantic was that no theoretical reason existed why a compound engine should be more efficient than one working single-expansion between the same temperatures and pressures. Yet, in certain conditions, compound locomotives were markedly more fuel-efficient. They were, however, heavier and more complicated than single-expansion locomotives and more expensive to buy and maintain; they delivered their promised economies only in certain conditions of service.

Many different types of compound locomotives were built in Europe and the U.S. Most of the main types had variants and derivatives. The proponents of the compound locomotive were men of active intelligence; Anatole Mallet produced at least two different compounding concepts; Samuel Vauclain produced at least three.

The compound locomotive succeeded best in Europe, where con-

struction in quantity began in the 1880s and continued—in France—into the 1950s.[175] One writer estimated that, in 1900, almost one half of the locomotives in service in mainland Europe were compounds. Compounds in Britain, by contrast, were few and short-lived.

In 1901, Samuel Vauclain, of the Baldwin Locomotive Works, predicted that in the twentieth century "compounding of all locomotives upon some system now used, or yet to be invented, will be almost universal." He also predicted the increased use of the high-pressure, water-tube boiler. "Higher pressures will then be common, and we all may live to see triple and even quadruple expansion locomotives almost noiselessly performing their work."[176]

3.5.2.1 Early Compound Locomotives

In 1860, Ebenezer Kemp proposed a double-tandem compound arrangement for an engine on the Caledonian Railway in Scotland.[177] High-pressure cylinders were fitted to each end of a low-pressure cylinder, into which they exhausted. It is not known if this ever worked. The sources are not definite whether one of these three-cylinder assemblies was mounted on each side of the locomotive (for a total of six cylinders), or one assembly between the frames.

The first working compound steam locomotive in the world is said to have been a 4-4-0 tandem compound (high- and low-pressure cylinders mounted one ahead of the other, driving a common piston rod), tried out on a predecessor company of the Erie.[178] This engine was built by the Hinkley Locomotive Works on 6-foot gauge for the New York & Erie in 1851 with 16-inch × 26-inch single-expansion cylinders. The railroad rebuilt it as a compound at their Susquehanna shops in 1868 with 11½-inch high-pressure and 24-inch low-pressure cylinders, 26-inch stroke. The low pressure of the final exhaust produced a weak furnace draft; the high- and low-pressure cylinders were incorrectly proportioned; the result was not a success and the company scrapped it in 1871. Another early American attempt at a compound locomotive was designed by Baxter and ran on the Worcester & Shrewsbury Railroad, Massachusetts, in 1870.[179]

In 1872, William Dawes patented three types of compound: a tandem compound, a four-cylinder cross-compound with cranks at 180° and a four-cylinder compound with each pair of cylinders driving a different axle.

Anatole Mallet (1837–1918) invented the first successful compound locomotive; he built a small, two-cylinder, rigid-frame compound locomotive in France in 1873 and obtained a patent in 1874.[180] Mallet's three 0-4-2T two-cylinder compounds, built in 1876 for the Bayonne-Biarritz Railway in France, followed by two more in 1878, were the first successful compound locomotives anywhere in the world. By 1896, these engines had run 1,366,000 miles and were the oldest compounds still in service.[181]

Also in France, de Diesbach and Garnier patented tandem compounds in 1873 and 1874 respectively. In America, the Boston & Albany built a compound (of unknown configuration) according to Dumbar's patent at its Springfield shops, but converted it to single-expansion after seven months of trials.[182] In France, du Bousquet used the Woolf system, in which the low-pressure cylinder volumes were three times that of the high-pressure cylinders, in the 1880s.

In the 1880s, von Borries in Germany and Webb in Britain took Mallet's work further. Their engines were also two-cylinder compounds. The difficulty of balancing the two piston thrusts resulted in the Webb (Britain, 1889) and Johnson (Britain, 1902) three-cylinder compounds with two high-pressure cylinders and one low-pressure. Apparently, the Russians built three-cylinder Webb compounds at their Kolomna shops. In 1884, a prototype four-cylinder compound locomotive went into service on the Hind, Punjab & Delhi Railway in India. The de Glehn (France) four-cylinder compounds appeared in 1886, (1878, according to Sinclair) driving on two axles, and the Webb (Britain) four-cylinder compounds in 1897 with four cranks all driving on one axle. In 1889, F. W. Johnstone, working in Mexico, designed a four-cylinder compound with the low-pressure cylinders annular to the high-pressure, both driving a common piston rod.[183]

Compounds had their problems. Two-cylinder Worsdell-Von Borries compounds were difficult to start and were laterally unbalanced. Three-cylinder Webb compounds were difficult to start and required "very clever handling, which could only be obtained with experience." Four-cylinder Webb compounds were complicated and sluggish at high speed and needed independent valve gears for the high- and low-pressure cylinders to work well.

High capital and maintenance costs and the skill required of the engine crew never dampened the enthusiasm of such exponents as the British engineer, F. W. Dean[184]:

I now come to the greatest improvement that has been introduced into the motive power department of railroads, viz., the application of the compound principle of using steam in locomotive engines. This is the greatest improvement in such engines that has been made since locomotives were first built, for two reasons; first, because it is the only improvement in principle that has been widely applied, and second, because it is the only fundamental means of economy of fuel and water that can be applied. That it is successful in realizing economy is no more a matter of doubt than that the sun shines.

3.5.2.2 Compounds in America

Samuel Vauclain commented[185]: "About the year 1889, American locomotive designers became deeply interested in the compounding of locomotives." Vauclain patented his cylinder arrangement in that year.[186] A high-pressure cylinder was paired with a low-pressure cylinder, one pair outside the frames on each side of the engine, each pair driving a common crosshead. The same year, A. J. Pitkin of the Schenectady Locomotive Works patented an intercepting valve for a two-cylinder compound. The construction of compound locomotives in the U.S. in quantity apparently began in that year with a Pitkin two-cylinder compound 4-6-0 on the Michigan Central and a Vauclain 4-4-0 for the Baltimore & Ohio and was immediately taken up by several builders.[187]

The Pennsylvania tested a Webb three-cylinder compound in about 1890[188] and built its own two-cylinder compound at Altoona in 1892.[189] This engine had 19½-inch and 31-inch cylinders and a boiler pressure—high for the time—of 205 pounds per square inch.

The same year, the Brooks Works built a tandem compound for the Great Northern and the Pittsburgh Locomotive Works built its first compound, a two-cylinder 4-6-0, as a demonstrator.[190] After trials on several railroads, including the Pennsylvania, the Alabama Great Southern bought it as a freight engine.[191] At the same time, the Richmond Locomotive & Machine Works was building a class of single-expansion 4-6-0s for the Chesapeake & Ohio; the railroad allowed them to build one as a two-cylinder compound. This offered a good test of the compound principle because the compound was one of a class with identical dimensions, all engines of the class being new at the same time. The Chesapeake & Ohio tested the compound in freight service over the 119 miles between Richmond and Gladstone against a single-expansion engine of the same class and estimated that the compound showed a fuel saving of 24%.[192] By mid–1892, 114 compound locomotives were in service in the U.S.

This Chicago, Milwaukee & St. Paul class A-2 4-4-2, No. 3121, built by Baldwin in 1901–03 and photographed at Davenport, Iowa, on July 23, 1923, is a Vauclain compound with the high-pressure cylinder above the low-pressure cylinder (Denver Public Library, Otto C. Perry collection, OP-5023).

This Union Pacific class C-57 2-8-0, No. 449, built by Baldwin in 1900–01 and photographed at Denver, Colorado, in June, 1918, is a Vauclain compound with the high-pressure cylinder below the low-pressure cylinder. Note the uncommon piston- and valve-rod extensions (Denver Public Library, Otto C. Perry collection, OP-16468).

Rogers built their first compound in 1893, a two-cylinder compound, designed by Reuben Wells, the company's shop superintendent, as part of an order for twenty-five single-expansion 2-6-0s from the Illinois Central.[193] The Chicago, Burlington & Quincy found from indicator diagrams that, at 30 miles per hour, a compound was 14% more fuel efficient than a single-expansion engine, but at 45 miles per hour this figure was 18% in favor of single-expansion. This was in passenger service, comparing engines of different dimensions but, as a result, the Burlington began building compound freight engines at its Aurora, Illinois, shops in 1893.[194]

Compounding reached the peak of its popularity in America in the mid–1890s. By mid–1893, 422 compound locomotives were in service in the U.S., with a further 1,088 of twelve different designs being built to domestic orders and another seventy-five being built for export.[195] Although this compares with a total U.S. locomotive fleet of about 35,000, one half of all locomotives built in the U.S. that year were compounds.[196] At the end of 1893 the number of compounds in service or being built worldwide was estimated at 2,200, divided as: Mallet, 150; Worsdell-von Borries (two-cylinder, cross-compound), 1,650; Webb (three-cylinder), 150; Vauclain (four-cylinder), 200; other, 50.[197] America was thus home to about half the world total of compound locomotives at that time.

The Schenectady, Rhode Island, Pittsburgh, Brooks, Richmond and Rogers locomotive works, and the Chicago, Burlington & Quincy

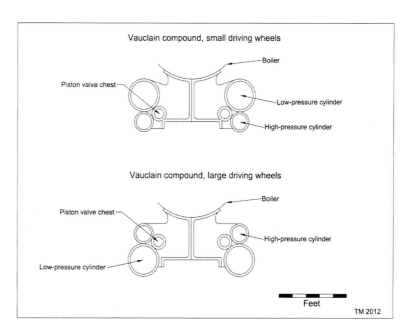

The Vauclain compound cylinder arrangement (redrawn from Bruce, A. W., *The Steam Locomotive in America: Its Development in the Twentieth Century,* New York: Bonanza, 1952).

Railroad were all building two-cylinder cross-compounds, with the high- and low-pressure cylinders outside the frames on opposite sides of the engine.[198] Baldwin promoted the four-cylinder Vauclain type.

Compound locomotives used a starting valve to allow the engineer

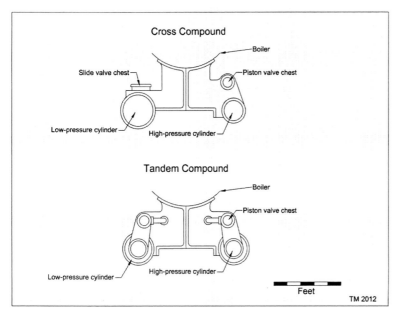

Compound cylinder arrangements (redrawn from Bruce, A. W., *The Steam Loco-motive in America: Its Development in the Twentieth Century*, New York: Bonanza, 1952).

to admit high-pressure steam direct to the low-pressure cylinder for extra tractive effort on starting or on a grade.[199] The Vauclain compound had a three-position starting valve that also controlled the cylinder drains. In the forward position of the lever in the cab, the starting valve and cylinder drains were both open; in the center position, the cylinder drains were closed and the starting valve was open; in the backward position, the cylinder drains and the starting valve were both closed and the engine would work compound.[200] The starting valve let high-pressure steam into the low-pressure cylinder while the engine was stationary until the pressure equalized in both cylinders. As soon as the engine started to accelerate, the amount of steam supplied through the small starting valve soon became negligible in comparison to the total steam flow through the cylinders.

The Richmond Locomotive & Machine Works and Rhode Island Locomotive Works systems allowed the engineer to open the high-pressure cylinder exhaust direct to the exhaust nozzle. In this mode, the steam pressure in the dry pipe opened an intercepting valve that directed live steam to the low-pressure cylinder, so that the cylinders worked in parallel rather than in series. When the engineer closed the exhaust valve, the pressure of steam exhausting from the high-pressure cylinder forced the intercepting valve shut and the engine worked compound.

The Rogers Locomotive and Machine Works (1893) and the Pittsburgh Locomotive & Car Works (1894)[201] used starting valves in which the intercepting valve, directing live steam to both cylinders, opened when the reversing lever was in full gear in either direction. When the engineer shortened the cut-off, the intercepting valve closed. The Schenectady Locomotive Works had yet another starting valve system.

In 1894, the Richmond Locomotive and Machine Works built a cross-compound 4-6-0 demonstrator which toured extensively in the U.S. and Europe, helping to secure orders for more than 150 compounds between 1895 and 1901.[202] The biggest orders came from the Canadian Pacific (38) and the Wabash (43).

In 1897, the Pennsylvania built a 2-6-0 two-cylinder compound on the European Gölsdorf system,[203] distinguished by the absence of an intercepting valve. In the Gölsdorf system, high-pressure steam was piped from the dry pipe to a chamber cast into the low-pressure cylinder wall. Two small ports in the low-pressure cylinder slide valve face admitted high-pressure steam when the engine was in full gear.

The use of high-pressure steam in the low-pressure cylinder(s) was limited by the unbalanced forces that were set up; it was recommended that a compound not be run faster than 4 or 5 miles per hour with the starting valve open, as accelerated wear or outright damage could result. In the two-cylinder and Vauclain compounds, constrictions in the starting valves limited the volume of live steam that could reach the low-pressure cylinders. Even so, hard-pressed engineers worked live steam in the low-pressure cylinders, regardless of any loss of economy or possible damage, and this tendency increased as train loads grew heavier.

High-pressure steam in the low-pressure cylinders increased tractive effort by 20% to 25% at low speeds for as long as the boiler could provide enough steam. Operating departments, forced more and more to load locomotives to their utmost, saw this as extra power with little regard for fuel economy. Compound freight engines, heavily loaded at low speeds, therefore spent significant amounts of time running single-expansion, detracting from their fuel economy.

The fuel economy apparently offered by the compounds was enormously attractive, but several designs failed in service, arousing prejudice against all compounds. This fuel economy resulted from several factors. Compounding offered better utilization of the higher boiler pressures that were being used in the 1890s—180 to 200 pounds per square inch, up from 140 to 150 pounds per square inch in the 1880s. Dividing the expansion between two cylinders reduced the temperature range within each cylinder. A receiver could be placed inside the smokebox, using heat that would otherwise go to waste, to reheat the steam between the high- and low-pressure cylinders. Typically, steam entered the high-pressure cylinder at 370°F and left it at 280°F. The smokebox receiver was surrounded by gases at 550°F to 600°F. The steam, after reheating, exhausted from the low-pressure cylinder at 230°F. Reheating was possible only in cross-compounds. In Vauclain and tandem compounds steam went directly from the high- to the low-pressure cylinders through piston valves.

Shortening the cut-off resulted in shorter port openings and greater steam friction losses. Compounds could be operated at longer cut-off, so reducing this loss. On the other hand, the iterative triangle of firebox draft, exhaust nozzle diameter and back pressure remained unresolved and, in a compound, the back pressure in the low-pressure cylinder—arising in the ports, exhaust pipe and exhaust nozzle—had a bigger piston area to work on than in a single-expansion engine with correspondingly greater effect. By the late 1890s, the performance of the bigger single-expansion engines was becoming limited by the strength of the fireman. A design that produced the same power for a lower firing rate was attractive, especially as this brought the combustion rate per square foot of grate back down to where evaporation was more efficient and the total firing rate more within the capacity of a human fireman.

Enthusiasm for compounding in the 1890s was such that several railroads retrofitted compound cylinders to existing locomotives. In 1894, the Norfolk & Western and the Cleveland, Cincinnati, Chicago & St. Louis bought cylinders and valves to convert single-expansion engines to the Mellin system of compounding. Current research has not discovered any details of this system. In the mid–1890s, the Chesapeake & Ohio, the Cleveland, Cincinnati, Chicago & St. Louis, the Pennsylvania, the Chicago, Milwaukee & St. Paul, and the Chicago, Rock Island & Pacific all retrofitted 4-6-0 single-expansion engines as compounds. The Erie had Baldwin rebuild forty-eight 4-4-0s as Vauclain compounds with Wootten fireboxes in 1896–7.[204]

By mid–1900, Baldwin had 1,200 locomotives of all types built that year and on order—800 for U.S. customers, 400 for export. Of the 800 for domestic use, 500 were compounds. One railroad ordered 165 compounds in a single order, others, 60 and 65.[205]

At that time, three types of compound locomotive were in use in the U.S.[206]: the two-cylinder compound (or "cross-compound") in its various sub-types and the four-cylinder Vauclain compound. The four-cylinder tandem compound was just making a renewed appearance. However:

> The defects of all three types are real, and so great that notwithstanding the generally acknowledged economy in fuel consumption, they are a good ways from superseding the simple engine.

By 1902, the compound locomotive situation in the U.S. was[207]:

> In the past 12 years there have been a great number of patents taken out on compound locomotive cylinders. A number of these have been applied to engines and put into service, only to be removed again for want of real merit. There have only been two styles of compound cylinders that have weathered the storms of active service, namely, the two-cylinder, or cross-compound type, built by the American Locomotive Company at their various works, and the Vauclain four-cylinder type, built by the Baldwin Locomotive Works, and extensively used. To judge by the merits and popularity of these two designs, and from the number of each style that has been built, the Vauclain four-cylinder type would be voted the most desirable and serviceable engine.

At that time, the American mainline locomotive fleet numbered 37,500. Of these, 1,175 were Vauclain compounds; 1,113 were two-cylinder compounds, for a total of 2,288, just 6% of the total.

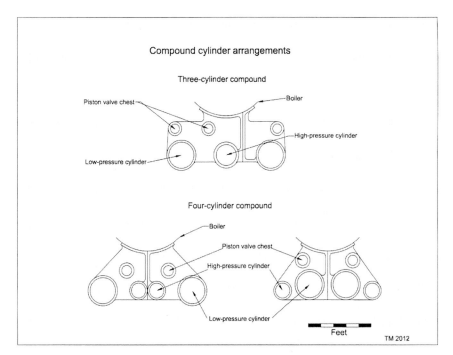

Three- and four-cylinder compound cylinder arrangements. Three-cylinder compounds appeared in the United States in the 1920s (redrawn from Bruce, A. W., ***The Steam Locomotive in America: Its Development in the Twentieth Century,*** **New York: Bonanza, 1952).**

3.5.2.3 Road Tests, Performance and Service Results

Practical difficulties stood in the way of obtaining comparable test results between compound and single-expansion engines. In 1892, the Cincinnati, New Orleans & Texas Pacific road-tested two 4-6-0s, one single-expansion, the other a two-cylinder cross-compound.[208] Both were from Baldwin, the single-expansion engine built in 1889, the compound in 1892. After overhauling both engines, the railroad ran ten tests, totaling 933 miles, hauling trains of about 2,050 tons, with the same crew over the same route. Coal consumption was 321 pounds per thousand ton-miles for the single-expansion engine, 208 for the compound. (By the 1920s, the average coal consumption of U.S. Class I railroads was down to 120 pounds per thousand ton-miles, and that almost entirely with single-expansion engines; clearly, something remarkable happened in American locomotive design and operation in that quarter-century.) Unfortunately for the validity of this apparent 35% fuel saving by the compound, the single-expansion engine ran with 1,565 square feet of heating surface and boiler pressures of 120 to 145 pounds per square inch, compared to 1,820 square feet and 160 to 185 pounds per square inch for the compound. These differences would mask the fuel consumption test results.

Other railroads using compounds turned in less remarkable results. Respondents to an 1893 ARMMA questionnaire estimated coal savings per ton-mile by the compounds[209]:

Northern Pacific	22%
Norfolk & Southern	4%
Kings County Elevated	21%
Norfolk & Western	13%
Chicago, Burlington & Quincy	0%
Pennsylvania & Northwestern	0–24%

The discussion of these findings was remarkable for the emotion that surfaced in—supposedly—a discussion of technical information. With so many variables at work, the comparison between compounding and single expansion was fraught with ambiguity, emotion and prejudice. One western railroad veteran commented on a compound:

> She is a beauty, with cylinders like beer vats, which they say is theoretically more efficient. I am rather cloudy on efficiencies myself, but I know a coal pile, and I tell you them cylinders are steam eaters.[210]

Tiny errors or changes in design, dimensioning and proportions could have large effects on performance. Proponents of compounding argued that individual compound engines could run badly without invalidating the concept itself, an argument unlikely to endear itself to hard-pressed—and hard-headed—executives.

Fuel economy, hotly debated as it was, was not the end of the argument.[211] Train operating costs varied from one part of the country to another, the local, landed cost of coal more than most other cost components. In the early 1890s, coal at $1.10 per ton represented about 25% of the cost of hauling a 20-car train. If a compound used 30% less fuel than a single-expansion engine, the effect on the ton-mile cost was only 7½%, to be set off against the higher capital and maintenance costs of the compound.

The economy of the compound declined with increasing speed; it was better suited to freight than to passenger service. Tests by the Chicago, Burlington & Quincy in 1894 showed that the water consumption of a two-cylinder compound increased from 18.3 pounds per indicated horsepower-hour at 20 to 30 miles per hour to 21.4 pounds at 50 to 55 miles per hour,[212] whereas a single-expansion engine decreased its water consumption from 21.7 pounds per indicated horsepower-hour at 31 miles per hour to 20.0 pounds at 66 miles per hour, concluding that their two-cylinder compound was 30% less economical than similar single-expansion engines in passenger service, but 29% more economical in freight service.

This loss of economy with speed resulted from the longer and more complicated steam path in the compound, causing higher friction losses at high steam flow rates. F. W. Dean, a leading proponent of the compound in Britain, pointed to steam velocities as high as 4,500 feet per second in the ports of some compound engines.[213] If correct, this would suggest trans-sonic and supersonic flow issues that were entirely unsuspected at that time. Pressure losses between the high- and low-pressure cylinders could consume 10% to 40% of the energy contained in the steam leaving the high-pressure cylinder. This choking of the steam flow made some compounds useless at high speeds.

By 1895, Baldwin had built more than five hundred compounds and had standardized on the four-cylinder Vauclain system. The greatest measured gain in fuel economy, compared to single-expansion engines, was 43%, achieved on a 12-mile, 1.9% grade with heavy curvature and where the engines were loaded to their maximum. Another marked success was in slow freight service on the New York, Ontario & Western where the compounds consumed only 17.5 pounds of water per indicated horsepower-hour, compared to 27 pounds for single-expansion engines in the same service.

In 1890s America, the deficiencies of the compound at high speed were more apparent than real as few trains ran at the speeds at which compounds became inefficient. Pulling power and fuel economy at modest speeds was more important for most railroads as they dealt with ever longer and heavier trains. Road tests produced some impressive results. Tests on five railroads (the Chesapeake & Ohio; the Cleveland, Cincinnati, Chicago & St. Louis; the Pennsylvania; the Chicago, Milwaukee & St. Paul; the Chicago, Rock Island & Pacific) over 118,000 engine-miles in freight service demonstrated coal savings by the compounds of 27% and water savings of 25%; nearly 3,000 engine-miles in passenger service showed coal savings of 24% and water savings of 29%.[214]

In 1896, the Northern Pacific rebuilt a class F-1 2-8-0, built by Baldwin in 1890 with 22-inch × 28-inch cylinders to a compound with 15-inch & 25-inch × 28-inch Vauclain cylinders. They tested this engine against an unmodified F-1 on the 16-mile western approach to the Stampede tunnel; Baldwin representatives eagerly participated in the tests. In spite of an apparent saving of 46% in fuel and 30% in water, the Northern Pacific did not order Vauclain compounds, although it bought cross- and tandem compounds for a time. The Northern Pacific retrofitted two other F-1's as Vauclain compounds, but converted one of them back to single expansion in 1906.[215]

In February 1896, the Chesapeake & Ohio bought a batch of two-cylinder, cross-compound 2-8-0s, class G-5, from the Richmond Locomotive Works for the 96-mile division between Clifton Forge and Charlottesville, Virginia. The G-5's were of similar dimensions to the company's existing class G-4 2-8-0s but for 200-pounds per square inch boiler pressure.[216] The G-4's hauled 550 tons over this division; elegant theories and fuel economy were discarded when the railroadmen found that the G-5's would haul 750 tons, working single-expansion, due to their greater adhesion weight and higher

boiler pressure. In spite of extravagant use of coal, they were more productive than the G-4's. The company put a stop to this and assigned 650 tons to the G-5's. Additionally, the Chesapeake & Ohio had had compounds in service on the almost level 119-mile division between Gladstone and Richmond since 1892. Over five years the compounds showed a saving of 10% on repairs and 21% on coal consumption per car-mile hauled. The G-5's were so successful that the Chesapeake & Ohio ordered six more for the Greenbrier division across the Alleghenies. This enthusiasm did not last. The next upgrade, only two years later, was the single-expansion G-6.[217] Time after time, railroads ordered compounds as an experiment in small batches; the initial enthusiasm seldom lasted. Big orders for compounds were few and, mostly, when a company moved on to its next type for a particular duty, it was not a compound.

In 1898, the Wabash was able to make a direct comparison between two-cylinder compound and single-expansion engines in fast freight service. The engines were 4-6-0s differing only in cylinder dimensions and arrangement. The compounds showed fuel savings per car-mile of 23% on one division, 20% on another.[218]

In spite of these favorable results, all three types of compound locomotive—cross-compounds, Vauclain and tandem compounds—suffered from significant mechanical problems. The two-cylinder compounds suffered from the difficulty of balancing the piston thrusts and the limitation on the diameter of the low-pressure cylinder imposed by lateral clearance limits. The Vauclain type suffered from the large and heavy guides and crossheads needed for the thrust of the paired cylinders, while imbalance between the piston thrusts caused racking forces on the crossheads. When the reciprocating masses were properly counterbalanced, the rotating masses were not; as a result, the engines were hard on track and bridges. It was said of the first Vauclain compound[219]:

> This 924 was possibly the roughest riding locomotive ever foaled at the Baldwin Locomotive Works, but she hung to the track, bucking the curves like an unbroken bronco, and taking the straight stretches like a frightened greyhound.

This problem was solved slowly, if at all.

The tandem compound did not have the problem with the crosshead but had the same problem with counterbalancing. All compounds were heavier, more expensive and more complicated than single-expansion engines. They were most economical only when loaded to their maximum tonnage yet, if the engine was so heavily loaded that it had to be worked single-expansion, fuel economy suffered. Operation and maintenance by men who were still unfamiliar with them caused problems and aroused prejudice. As late as 1903:

> Railroad companies have in some cases changed power on an entire division from simple engines, weighing 75 tons, to compounds weighing 150 tons. These conditions have been the cause of the compound locomotive being charged with a great many things for which it is not at fault.[220]

Putting high-pressure steam into the low-pressure cylinder to start a train was an urgent need that was addressed early on but another problem was encountered when the engine was drifting downgrade with steam shut off. The low-pressure cylinder discharged blasts of air through the exhaust nozzle, thus drawing the fire and making more steam than was wanted, wasting fuel. This problem was solved by an automatic bypass valve in a connection between both ends of the low-pressure cylinder. Now, however, soot and smokebox gases were sucked into the low-pressure cylinder. This problem was solved by plumbing a connection between the exhaust pipe and the outside air with a check valve. Vacuum in the high-pressure cylinder was another problem encountered when drifting downgrade, solved by installing a vacuum breaker.

Performance at high speeds was ultimately improved by adapting the Allan-ported slide valve, providing better exhaust opening and steam admission. This produced increases in tractive effort ranging from 5% at 15 miles per hour to 44% at 40 miles per hour.

Users discovered that two-cylinder compounds were less prone to slipping than single-expansion engines, resulting in an effective adhesion factor of 0.33 on starting, compared to 0.25 for a normal single-expansion engine. If the wheels started to slip, the intercepting valve would choke off pressure in the low-pressure cylinder and the slipping would stop, allowing the driving wheels to regain their grip on the rail.

Some large railroad operators came down unequivocally in favor of the compound for certain types of service, although much depended on the views of the Superintendent of Motive Power. In 1899 E. M. Herr, Superintendent of Motive Power on the Northern Pacific stated:

> From my experience on the Northern Pacific road my judgment is that it is advisable to use the compound locomotive in heavy freight service. I say advisable, because of the economy in fuel, and, as far as our experience went, no appreciable, or, at least, no important increase in the cost of repairs. It certainly seems advisable to use a machine that shows a saving of from 15 to 20 per cent of fuel in regular service and no very great, or even appreciable increase in cost of maintenance.[221]

Even so, in spite of convincing evidence of fuel economy, the construction of new rigid-frame compounds in America ceased in the early 1900s; many of the compounds built at that time were rebuilt to single-expansion or scrapped.

3.5.2.4 Reappearance of the Tandem Compound

The potential of the two-cylinder cross-compound was limited by the lateral clearance dimensions. One way ahead was the four-cylinder tandem compound. After its lack of success on the Erie in 1868, the tandem compound idea came back to life with a design by John Player for the Iowa Central in 1886.[222] Player left the Iowa Central before his design was ever built, moving from there to the Wisconsin Central. There, in 1890, he produced a design to convert a single-expansion 2-6-0 into a 4-6-0 tandem compound but, again, Player left before his design was put into effect. By 1899, Player was Superintendent of Machinery for the Santa Fe and introduced his design there. According to the German authority, Gustav Reder, two men, both named John Player, were associated with the development of the tandem compound in America. The first John Player has just been mentioned; the second rose through the ranks of the Brooks Locomotive Works, and subsequently Alco, as a draftsman and engineer.[223]

In 1901, the Santa Fe ordered forty tandem compounds to a design produced by the Schenectady Locomotive Works, then part of Alco. (It is not clear how closely Player's design was followed—or which Player.) At the same time, the Baltimore & Ohio ordered one from Alco and, in late 1901, Schenectady was building tandem compounds for the Northern Pacific.[224] In 1903, Baldwin brought out its own tandem compound to Vauclain's design. In all of these designs, the high-pressure and low-pressure cylinders were joined end-to-end. A large piston valve assembly mounted parallel to the cylinder pair controlled steam admission to the high-pressure cylinder, transfer to the low-pressure cylinder and release to exhaust.[225] The tandem compound became popular in the early twentieth century, reaching its apogee in the Baldwin 2-10-2 freight engines built for the Santa Fe.

3.5.2.5 The Four-Cylinder Balanced Compound

Two European compounds attracted particular attention in the U.S.: the de Glehn four-cylinder, balanced compound and the Mallet four-cylinder, articulated compound.

The American search for a "balanced" locomotive began at least as early as 1895.[226] As engines of 1,000 horsepower were built, the production of all the power in two cylinders, and its transmission to the driving wheels through two main rods and crank pins, was resulting in heavy pistons, rods, crossheads and crank pins, posing increasingly serious counterbalancing problems. Probably the earliest four-cylinder, balanced engine was built by John Haswell in 1862 for the Austrian state railroad.[227] Probably the first four-cylinder compound was an engine belonging to the Hind, Punjab & Delhi Railway in India, originally built as a four-cylinder single-expansion engine and rebuilt in 1884 as a compound. The need for a balanced locomotive and the fuel economy of the compound went together.

The de Glehn principle made its first appearance in France in 1885.[228] Two high-pressure cylinders were mounted on the outside of the frame, driving the second driving wheel axle. These exhausted to two low-pressure cylinders mounted side by side inside the frame, driving on the cranked front driving wheel axle and exhausting directly to the exhaust nozzle through a short steam path. The low-pressure cylinders were set forward of the high-pressure cylinders so that the connecting rods of both pairs of cylinders were the same length. Each cylinder had its own connecting rod and independently controllable valve gear. This multiplicity of parts and the inside cylinders at first discouraged the Americans from using it; its advantages offset these objections. The big advantage was that the cranks could be set in relation to each other so as to optimize the counterbalance of the rotating and reciprocating masses. The Henry-Beaudry or Henry system was a minor variation on the de Glehn system.

F. F. Gaines, Mechanical Engineer on the Lehigh Valley, commented:

> remove the frills from the De Glehn compound, and incorporate in its design, American simplicity and strength, and we will then have our fuel economy minus the drawbacks of the existing types of compounds.[229]

Interest in the four-cylinder balanced compound grew apace. Both Mallet and the Hagan Locomotive Works of Erfurt, Germany, tried to improve on the de Glehn principle with high- and low-pressure cylinders outside the frame and driving on separate axles, but this entailed complicated rodwork and made no headway in the U.S.[230]

American inventiveness produced an indigenous version. In 1891, George S. Strong patented a four-cylinder compound locomotive with all four cylinders in the same transverse plane, the high-pressure cylinders inside the frames, the low-pressure cylinders outside.[231] All four cylinders drove the same axle, the inside cylinders driving on cranks. In 1892, he patented an arrangement with each pair of high- and low-pressure cylinders in one casting, one piston valve controlling the admission of steam into both cylinders. In 1895, the Balanced Locomotive & Engineering Co., New York, rebuilt a locomotive originally built by the Hinckley Locomotive Works in 1888 for the Strong Locomotive Co. The rebuild used modified Walschaert valve gear with one valve gear for each high-pressure/low-pressure cylinder pair. The steam was to be superheated before entering the high-pressure cylinders and then re-heated between the high- and low-pressure cylinders, aiming for a steam consumption of 18 pounds per horsepower-hour. The rebuild included radical departures from general practice: twin corrugated fireboxes, new valve gear, special ("gridiron") valves and other features. The New York Central tested this engine on their West Shore division in 1899; present researches have not revealed the results. The fact that the engine was rebuilt from an old engine was a handicap; it is not known if any other engines were built to this design.

A product of the 1890s was the Shaw four-cylinder locomotive, in which two cylinders on each side, one above the other with a common piston valve between, drove a rocking arm.[232] The lower end of the rocking arm drove the main rod. The intention was that the two pistons on each side would be moving in opposite directions at the same time and, hence, the reciprocating forces would balance each other. Between 1889 and 1905 Samuel F. Prince developed a compound version of this system, with each pair of cylinders consisting of a high- and low-pressure cylinder. This system did not catch on.

In 1902, Baldwin built a four-cylinder, balanced compound locomotive for the Plant System,[233] which, however, soon sold it to a western railroad. Vauclain patented his own four-cylinder balanced compound in 1904.[234]

The years 1904–5 were the heyday of the four-cylinder balanced compound. In 1904, Alco built one—a 4-4-2—for the New York Central,[235] calculating the counterbalancing to minimize yawing and dynamic augment. On the Pennsylvania's static test plant at St. Louis, this engine developed a maximum power output of 1,640 indicated horsepower at 57 miles per hour. The New York Central did not order more of this type. The same year Baldwin built a 4-4-2 of this type for the Chicago, Burlington & Quincy with the outside low-pressure cylinders driving the back driving wheels and the inside high-pressure cylinders driving the cranked front axle. The same year, the Pennsylvania imported a de Glehn 4-4-2 from France. Although it provided valuable information, it was too light for the Pennsylvania's passenger trains; it was little used and was scrapped in 1912.[236]

The Santa Fe was always bold in its procurement. After buying four Vauclain 4-4-2s in 1903, the company bought fifty-three balanced compound 4-4-2s from Baldwin in 1904, followed by 102 more between 1905 and 1910, and 156 balanced compound 4-6-2s between 1905 and 1914.[237] In this adaptation of the de Glehn system, all four cylinders were in line and all drove on the front driving axle. The high-pressure cylinders were inside the frames, the low-pressure outside. Each pair of high- and low-pressure cylinders shared a common piston valve. This design had the advantage over the de Glehn that the cylinder pairs had only one valve between them, instead of one for each cylinder.

In 1905, Baldwin built a four-cylinder, balanced compound 4-6-0 for the New York, New Haven & Hartford with all four cylinders driving the front driving axle. At the same time, Alco was building engines of this type for the Erie and the Pennsylvania. The same year, W. E. Symons, Superintendent of Motive Power for the Plant System, patented his own design of four-cylinder balanced compound.[238] In the Symons system, the high-pressure cylinders were outside the frames, driving the rear driving axle; the low-pressure cylinders were inside the frames, ahead of the high-pressure cylinders, driving the cranked front driving axle. The four cylinders were not aligned; the low-pressure cylinders were mounted ahead of the high-pressure cylinders. This seems to have come full circle back to the de Glehn layout, so it is not clear how Symons's system was an innovation.

Symons arranged the valve gear so that the high- and low-pressure cylinders could be used independently, with their own separate valve gear and cut-off control. The valve gear was the conventional Stephenson link motion. There were two reversing levers, a primary and an auxiliary. The primary reversing lever drove two reach rods, one controlling the high-pressure valve gear, one controlling a starting valve. When the primary reversing lever was in full gear, the second reach rod opened the starting valve, admitting live steam to the low-pressure cylinders, closing it as soon as the engineer shortened the cut-off. The auxiliary reversing lever controlled the valve gear of the low-pressure cylinder. The engineer could control the cut-off of both pairs of cylinders independently; stop bars limited the movement of the auxiliary reversing lever, relative to the primary, although these could be removed if the engineer wanted to use only one pair of cylinders.

While devices such as these, along with controllable exhaust valves

This Atchison, Topeka & Santa Fe 4-6-2 balanced compound, 1226 class, No. 1249, built by Baldwin in 1905–06, was still in as-built condition when photographed at Fresno, California, on May 3, 1934. The left-hand inside high-pressure cylinder and valve chest can just be seen beside the large-diameter outside low-pressure cylinder (Denver Public Library, Otto C. Perry collection, OP-337).

and adjustable nozzles, found favor in Europe, their promised fuel economy materialized only if the enginemen fully understood them and made the fullest possible use of them, and if they were maintained in perfect order. The rugged conditions of American railroading were not conducive to this, leaving only the higher manufacturing and maintenance costs without the promised fuel economy.

3.5.2.6 The Mallet Four-Cylinder Articulated Compound

In parts of Europe, curves, grades and traffic densities were as demanding as those in America; the Europeans were more willing than the Americans to step outside established practices in devising motive power to deal with these situations.[239] The Belgian railroad system was particularly dense and heavily used; an American observer of the European railroad scene commented in 1899:

> European engineers have already had to consider this question, (of the number of driving axles) and as a result some engines have been built for the Belgian State Railroads having six driving axles, that weigh in working order 238,000 pounds. These axles are arranged in groups of three each, the rear group, driven by two high-pressure cylinders, are fixed rigidly in the frames, while the forward group supports a truck which carries the low-pressure cylinders. These engines … show a design that might be followed if it should ever become necessary to greatly depart from present types in order to get great tractive power.

This was the Mallet articulated compound.

Anatole Mallet patented his articulated compound locomotive in 1884. The first one was built in 1888, an 0-4-4-0T for a railroad in Corsica. This configuration spread to Switzerland, Belgium, Prussia, Baden, Saxony and Bavaria and later to a total of fifty-two countries. Britain was not among them, although several British colonies and protectorates were. By 1896, sixty-five Mallet compounds were in service in France out of a total of 320 compounds of all kinds. By 1900, 395 Mallet articulated compounds were in use in Germany (119), Russia (107), France, Switzerland, Austria-Hungary, Turkey, Sweden and Spain; of these 218 were standard-gauge. Although the engine was at its best on steep grades and sharp curves, it was easy on the track and offered low resistance on lines of normal grade and curvature where its benefits were less obvious.[240]

The Americans were aware of this type of engine,[241] but saw it as a special-purpose engine more akin to the Shay than to the uncomplicated engines then in use on their main lines. In particular, they shied away from its complexity. European frame construction was better suited to the Mallet than American methods. The American view in 1900 was:

> It should be clear that the Mallet engine can never in any large sense become a general purpose machine. Its flexible wheelbase allows it to pass short curves, and it may be so designed that it will draw heavy loads, but it can only move at low speeds.

As far as is known, Mallet's earlier, two-cylinder, compound was not used in the U.S. but the American Mallet articulated compounds are well known as the biggest and most powerful steam locomotives ever built.

The four-cylinder Mallet had two power units, each with two outside cylinders. The back power unit, with two high-pressure cylinders, was built on the frame that supported the boiler and firebox. The front power unit, with two low-pressure cylinders, was built on its own sub-frame, connected to the main frame by a flexible joint. The sub-frame supported the front of the boiler, but was not rigidly attached to it.

Steam had to pass from the high-pressure cylinders to the low-pressure cylinders, and from the low-pressure cylinders to exhaust, through pipes with flexible joints. Today this would be easily accomplished with flexible tubing or large-diameter hoses, ending in pipe joints made of matching flanges bolted together with gaskets between. At that time the necessary materials were not available. Pipe joints had to be made individually with two flanges bolted together, sealed with an iron ring ground to fit each face of the joint.[242] Swiveling steam pipe joints were, therefore, a major concern to inventors of articulated steam locomotives. It was a significant benefit of Mallet's design that these joints had only to deal with low-pressure and exhaust steam. The first Mallet four-cylinder, articulated compound built in the U.S. was an enormous 0-6-6-0, built for the Baltimore & Ohio in 1904. This was the biggest locomotive in the world at that time; it launched the Mallet era in America.

Section 3.6. Valves and Valve Gear

The reciprocating steam engine required steam to be admitted alternately to opposite ends of the cylinders. Behind this apparently simple fact lay one of the most recondite of all the features of the steam locomotive.

The first Newcomen atmospheric engine of 1712 required the engineer to manipulate valves by hand for every stroke of the engine, a task so tedious that engineers tried to automate it, the first being a boy named Humphrey Potter, culminating in Henry Beighton's valve gear in 1718, an early example of industrial automation.[243] Something like one hundred valve gears for reciprocating steam engines followed over the next two hundred years. Of these only three became widespread in locomotives: Stephenson, Walschaert and Baker, although others were used in small numbers. Valve gears are so well described in published work and by animations on the internet that no description is needed here.

3.6.1 Valves

One of the more difficult parts of a locomotive to design and analyze were the valves controlling the admission and exhaust of steam to and from the cylinders, and the valve gear that drove them.

> What the human heart is to the body, the valves are to the locomotive. It is their function to control the circulation of the energizing vapors throughout the organism of the machine. When they perform well their functions, the locomotive is prompt and precise; if they are faulty, it limps on its course, or allows its energies to run to waste. From the early days of locomotive operation, valves and their gears have challenged alike the skill of practical mechanics and of the professional engineers. Most men who have had to do with the operation of locomotives and whose abilities have been such as to make them responsive to their surroundings, have at some time in their life, been interested in the introduction of some new type of valve or valve-gear. It goes without saying that much of this effort has been misdirected and it has not infrequently happened that proposed improvements have involved misconceptions concerning fundamental principles.[244]

3.6.1.1 Slide Valves

The standard means of controlling steam flow to and from locomotive cylinders in the nineteenth century was the slide valve, invented in about 1800 by William Murdoch, employee and later partner of Boulton and Watt.[245] If this valve was wrongly proportioned or maladjusted, the engine would work inefficiently, if at all. At high speed and short cut-off, a cast-iron slide valve body weighing 150 to 250 pounds might open by exactly ⅜ inch, 3 to 5 times a second. Driven by a mechanical valve gear with its own elasticity, looseness and wear, this motion had to be extremely precise. The valve body was an iron casting; if it was made wrong, it was not easily

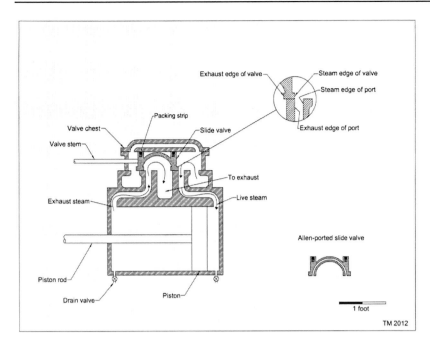

Exhaust edge of valve
Steam edge of valve
Steam edge of port
Packing strip
Slide valve
Valve chest
Exhaust edge of port
Valve stem
To exhaust
Exhaust steam
Live steam
Allen-ported slide valve
Piston rod
Drain valve
Piston
1 foot
TM 2012

Longitudinal section through slide valve and cylinder (drawn from a cutaway on a locomotive at Steamtown USA, Scranton, Pennsylvania, this diagram shows a Richardson-balanced slide valve).

corrected. The means available to ensure its correct adjustment were graphical methods, models, rule of thumb, trial and error and the sound of the exhaust. In common with much else to do with the steam locomotive, the slide valve and the Stephenson link motion were wonderful things when invented but, the more they were studied, the more apparent their defects became.

The box on top of the cylinder in several of the accompanying photographs is the slide valve chest. The accompanying drawing shows a sectional view, with the slide valve at the back end of its stroke, connecting the head-end cylinder port to live steam and the crank-end port to exhaust. When the valve was at the front of its stroke, the connections were reversed. That much was simple. What happened between those two positions baffled the finest minds in the industry.

The first slide valves were shaped like the letter C. As soon as the valve body shut off the steam supply to a cylinder port, it connected the port to exhaust almost immediately, giving the steam no time to expand. Consequently, the valve was modified to the shape of an omega (Ω); the time taken for the feet of the omega to slide across the cylinder ports provided time for the steam to expand.

The ideal valve event would be an instantaneous and complete opening of the port, the port remaining fully open for a controllable period of time independent of any other port, followed by instantaneous and complete closing. The slide valve fulfilled this ideal poorly. As the valve body shuttled back and forth at a sinusoidal velocity, the ports were continually in the process of opening and closing. As the valve gear did not hesitate, keeping a port fully open or fully closed for any length of time depended on the geometry of the valve body. Because the valve body was a single piece, sliding over fixed ports, the inlet and exhaust valve events were inseparable.

The valve gear invented by A. J. Stevens, Master Mechanic at the Central Pacific's Sacramento shops, in the 1880s, overcame this problem by means of separate inlet and exhaust valves but at the cost of greater complexity.[246] The valve gear did not long outlive its inventor and seems to have been forgotten.

The datum setting of the valve was "line-and-line." Line-and-line on the exhaust side meant that the exhaust edges (inset in the accompanying drawing) of the valve and ports matched when the valve was at mid-run. Line-and-line on the steam side meant that, when the piston was at the end of its stroke, the steam edge of the valve matched the steam edge of the port.[247]

If the valve was made, or chiseled out, so that the distance between its exhaust edges was greater than the distance between the exhaust edges of the steam ports (with the valve at mid-run, both ports would be partly open to exhaust), this was called "exhaust clearance." Exhaust clearance allowed a freer escape of exhaust steam and reduced the compression that occurred as the piston moved against a closed port before it opened to steam. Compression wasted energy but cushioned the piston at the end of its stroke and reduced the amount of steam needed to fill the clearance between the piston at the end of its stroke and the cylinder head. On the other hand, the earlier the exhaust opened, the less time the steam had to expand. Decreasing the distance between the exhaust edges of the valve body past line-and-line was called "exhaust lap" and had the opposite effects.

The distance between the steam edge of the port and the steam edge of the valve body when the valve body was at mid-run was called "steam lap." The greater the steam lap, the longer the time between the closing of the cylinder port after the end of admission and its opening to exhaust.

"Lap" was a built-in dimensioning of the valve and ports. The length of the valve stroke was built into the valve gear. Once a locomotive was built, these could not be changed without modifying the locomotive. "Lead" was a setting that placed the valve events at certain points in the piston stroke; mechanics set the valves by experience and by the sound of the locomotive in operation. None of these adjustments were under the engineer's control.

With the valve set line-and-line on the steam side, the piston would reach the end of its stroke, compressing the remaining steam against the closed port, just as the steam edge of the valve slid past the steam edge of the port, opening it to steam. The valve gear could be adjusted in the shop so that the port was already opening as the piston reached the end of its stroke, called "steam lead." This was meant to ensure that the piston received the highest possible steam pressure as early as possible in its power stroke and that the port was as wide open as possible as early as possible. The distance by which the port was open when the piston reached the end of its stroke was "positive lead." It was also possible to set "negative lead," which had certain advantages.

All but the earliest valve gears allowed the engineer to shorten or lengthen the valve travel from the maximum in full forward gear, through a neutral position in which the valve did not move and the engine would not run, to full reverse gear by means of a lever in the cab. Shortening the valve travel shortened the period of steam admission for each piston stroke and allowed the steam to expand in the cylinder, diminishing in pressure as it did so, called "shortening the cut-off" or "hooking up." For an emergency stop, the engineer could put the engine into reverse gear while it was running, although the benefits of doing so were much argued over.

Running a locomotive in full gear is the equivalent of running a car in first gear—hard on the engine and wasteful of fuel. If two engineers run the same route with the same load, one using shorter cut-offs than the other, the difference in steam consumption is immediately noticeable as soon as the water tank is refilled. Anecdotes come to us from the late nineteenth century. One old engineer was renowned for high fuel consumption and being hard on his firemen. This went on until an alert fireman plucked up the courage to tell him that the reversing lever had other uses than reversing the direction of the locomotive.

The British engineer F. W. Dean tabulated the work contained in a pound of steam at various cut-offs[248]:

Cut-off	Work value of 1 pound of steam
Full gear	1.000
50%	1.659
25%	2.207
13%	2.532
6%	2.560

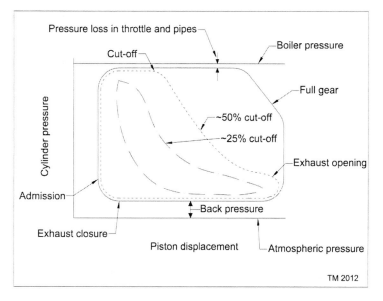

Indicator diagram.

Valve events could be analyzed by an "indicator," producing a trace called an "indicator diagram." This device was not a permanent fixture; it was installed only for test purposes. In the 1800s a needle scribed the diagram on a metal plate; later a pen marked the trace on paper.[249] Small tubes, plumbed into each end of each cylinder, traced cylinder pressure on the y-axis. A pantograph attached to the crosshead traced piston position on the x-axis. Test engineers, riding in a makeshift shelter on the front of the locomotive, obtained diagrams for each end of each cylinder, thus four diagrams for a two-cylinder locomotive.

The indicator diagram enabled engineering and maintenance staff to analyze the valve events and to detect problems more accurately than by any other means. It was also a means of calculating the power output of the cylinders, hence the term "indicated horsepower." An experienced mechanic could tell from the shape of the diagram if something was wrong, such as leaking piston rings or maladjusted valves.

W. E. Symons, Superintendent of Motive Power for the Plant System, reported instances where locomotives never performed well until indicator diagrams were obtained from them.[250]

I had some experience recently with an 18-in. passenger locomotive, which had given continual trouble since coming from the builders, in the way of breaking driving boxes, rocker arms, rocker boxes, piston rods, rod straps, etc. It also caused much annoyance on account of running hot, was very extravagant in fuel, water and oil, and had scarcely rendered a successful month's service in the ten years of its existence. Much time and money had been spent in following the usual orthodox methods of adjusting the valve gear.

An indicator test suggested overhauling the valves and valve gear, whereupon the problems disappeared. Coal economy improved from 28 to 30 miles per ton to 43 to 55 miles.

Errors in valve setting could make a mockery of savings achieved by advances in locomotive design.[251] Taking indicator cards was a costly and time-consuming exercise but, in one case, the Southern found that a 2-8-0 with Stephenson gear was working at 87.5% cut-off in full forward gear, when 85% would have been correct. The indicator card showed that the engine was burning 15% more coal than needed in full forward gear, while its tractive effort was reduced by about 3,000 pounds. An experienced eye could read an indicator card and instantly detect wrong valve settings and slack motion. Deficiencies as small as a few percent of cut-off at a particular notch of the reversing lever could waste 10% of fuel and cause a 5% loss of tractive effort. Tiny changes in a valve event recurring four or five times every second could have large effects on performance.

Valve setting was rife with prejudice; valve lead was an example. In the 1890s, "Probably 90 per cent of the men in the mechanical departments of our railroads believe a locomotive must have positive lead that it may be 'smart.'"[252]

Some railroad master mechanics questioned this[253]:

The rule on this road, at least on this division, is to give the valves of all engines ⅛ in. positive lead in full gear. Most of them are hard riding and pound themselves to pieces badly; will run about so fast and no faster, regardless of train. I reduced the lead at 6 in. cutoff to 3⁄16 in. on one of these engines, and turned her out on the rounds. She did such excellent work that she was the cause of general remark among all the engineers who ran her. Would ride very smoothly, run faster, and do her work easier than before.

These engines, which had 7⁄16 in. lead at 6 in. cut-off, were pounding badly, and, even with a light train, had to be worked at 8 in. cut-off with a light throttle. I had the lead reduced to ¼ in. in the same cut-off and found a very remarkable improvement in their working. We had had a great deal of trouble because of hot main pins, and were unable to overcome this till we reduced the lead.

An engine that broke 5 or 6 piston rods every eighteen months was still running with the same piston rod nine months after the lead was reduced.

With one of our 18 in. × 24 in. engines, handling our limited scheduled at 40 miles an hour, including stops, each of three engineers was unable to make running time. Since the full gear lead was reduced from 3⁄32 in. positive to 1⁄32 in. negative they can make up considerable lost time with the same engine.

Opinion changed against valve lead accordingly.

Adjusting the lead with the Stephenson gear, however, also changed the cut-off for any position of the reversing lever. Engineers had the tools and knowledge to make their own adjustments. C. H. Quereau commented:

It has been a favorite plan with locomotive runners for a number of years to make their engines "smart" by increasing the lead of the back-up eccentric, believing this was warranted by the fact that their engines had greater power than before when working in the same notch. Had they understood that they were lengthening the cutoff by this change in the lead, and that they were using as much or more steam to do the same work, it is quite probable that this adjustment would not be as popular as it is.

The ideas of the maintenance department ran into the prejudices of the enginemen.

> it should be borne in mind that the prejudices of enginemen are important factors in determining the success or failure of any detail with which they are not familiar. An engineer once lost 40 minutes because the cutoff for the notch where he usually worked the engine had been reduced from 6 in. to 4½ in. by changing the full-gear setting from the first to the second method. Naturally both he and the master mechanic were not favorably impressed with the innovation.[254]

As late as 1900:

> The old subject of lead for locomotives was discussed at the April meeting of the Pacific Coast Railway Club. As usual, a wide diversity of opinion was expressed and many by ways of the subject were entered upon which might well have been left untraveled.[255]

Lengthening the valve travel by adjusting the valve gear achieved beneficial effects as the longer travel provided a longer opening time for the ports. In one engine on the Chicago, Burlington & Quincy, in 1892–3, increasing the valve travel from 5 inches to 5½ inches increased the engine's average train-miles per ton of coal from 12.8 to 17.2, an astonishing 34% gain in efficiency.[256]

A problem inherent to slide valves was steam pressure in the valve chest bearing down on the valve body, increasing wear on the valve and its seat and increasing the power used in moving the valve. The first balanced slide valves are attributed to John Grey on the Liverpool & Manchester Railway in Britain in about 1838.[257] Many inventions followed during the nineteenth century, attempting to balance this force by springs or steam pressure applied to the underside of the valve, lifting it against a plate.

Bigger valves and higher steam pressure made this problem worse. Tests on the Chicago, Burlington & Quincy by Philip Wallis, Engineer of Tests, in 1886 showed that, at 40 miles per hour, unbalanced valves needed 6 horsepower to move them; balanced valves needed only one-third as much. It also became more difficult for the engineer to alter the cut-off while the engine was under steam—a disincentive to fuel efficiency; the first steam-powered reversers were invented for this purpose. Otherwise enginemen had to close the throttle before altering the cut-off while the engine was running in order to relieve the pressure on the top of the valve.[258] Researchers discovered that significant gains in efficiency came from running with the throttle wide open, using cut-off to control power, but: "Most runners persist in running with a partially opened throttle because it is so much easier to handle the throttle than the reverse lever."[259]

Balanced slide valves were more common in America than in Europe because the engines were bigger and more difficult to handle. In 1896, a census of 10,934 locomotives on fifty railroads (about a third of the U.S. fleet) showed that 7,241 had balanced valves. Another 145 had the newly introduced piston valve. Of the balanced valves, the following types were represented:

Richardson (patented 1872)	5,945
Morse (patented 1870)[260]	482
Barnes	288
American (invented 1893)	287
Delaney	42
Margach	30
Leeds	8
Other/not specified	159

Most common was the Richardson type. George W. Richardson, a locomotive engineer on the Troy & Boston in the 1860s, invented

a spring-loaded safety valve in 1867 that became standard on American locomotives and patented his balanced slide valve in 1872.[261] Spring-loaded packing strips in the valve body bore against a plate fixed to the roof of the valve chest as in the accompanying drawing. Steam flowed around the plate and thus did not bear down on the valve. Springs held the valve to the valve seat against the steam pressure tending to lift it off. The sources consulted have not revealed anything about the other types of balancing. Balanced valves wore only half to one-third as much as unbalanced valves.[262]

Tests at Purdue in 1896 showed that at a 6-inch (25%) cut-off the mean effective pressure decreased from 43 pounds per square inch at 15 miles per hour to only 18 at 55 miles per hour because of the shorter port opening and increased friction losses.[263] Efforts to obtain better steam admission, especially in express passenger engines, resulted in the Allen valve—a slide valve with a steam passage running through the valve body, intended to provide more port area and higher mean effective pressure. The Allen port allowed steam from the valve chest on the far side of the valve seat into the cylinder port at the same time as the valve was opening the cylinder port to steam. At that time, only 513 engines in the U.S. had Allen valves.

The Allen valve doubled the speed of port opening and the port dimensions at short cut-off; indicator diagrams showed that this resulted in a substantial increase in power at short cut-off.[264] A discussion on this subject at the 1896 ARMMA convention between Vauclain, Goss and Henderson—three of the most eminent American authorities on the steam locomotive of that time—revealed, not only the alarming number of independent and uncontrolled variables that affected indicator diagrams, but also the bafflement of these three pre-eminent engineers with the subtleties of something as apparently simple as a slide valve. Vauclain ended the argument by declaring: "It is hard to believe the variation is due to the Allen valve. We will not be any nearer a solution of the matter if we discuss it all day and I move the matter be closed."

3.6.1.2 Piston Valves

Higher boiler pressures increased the problems of the slide valve; the solution was the piston valve, first used in marine and stationary engines, working in the vertical direction. Prejudice delayed its introduction on locomotives; many master mechanics believed that it would not function properly when working in the horizontal direction but it was also more expensive than a slide valve.

Apparently, the first piston-valved locomotive was in France in the late 1880s.[265] The first in the U.S. were Vauclain compounds in 1889[266]; in that application, the piston valve made possible a single valve between the high- and low-pressure cylinders.[267] The first piston valves in single-expansion engines were retrofitted in place of slide valves on the Flint & Pere Marquette in 1889. In about 1891, the Brooks Locomotive Works used them in 4-8-0s built for the Iron Range & Huron Bay Railway. In 1895, Brooks contracted to build 4-8-0s for the Great Northern, at the time the biggest engines in the world with 21-inch × 34-inch cylinders and 210 pounds per square inch boiler pressure. Piston valves were installed to avert problems with the sheer size of the slide valves that would be needed. Brooks considered a two-part slide valve, each with its own exhaust cavity, but opted for piston valves instead. "We became satisfied that the piston valve was the proper thing to apply to high-pressure locomotives."

By 1898, 30 to 40 locomotives had given satisfactory results with piston valves and prejudice was disappearing.[268] Piston valves offered benefits in steam distribution; they were lighter and took only half the power needed for even a balanced slide valve. Size for size, a piston valve offered more port area for less weight than a slide valve and the reversing lever was easier to operate, a point of increasing importance

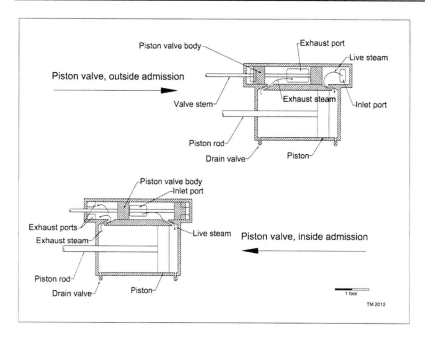

General arrangement of piston valve (redrawn from *RRG*, January 7, 1898, 3).

as valves and valve gear became bigger and heavier in the course of time.

One of the earlier major railroads to use piston valves was the Chicago, Burlington & Quincy, starting with two 2-6-0s built in its own shops in 1898, followed by sixteen more in 1899. The main problem was the packing rings and that was soon solved.[269] By mid–1900, the Chicago, Burlington & Quincy had sixty-five single-expansion engines with piston valves and had adopted it as standard for all new engines.[270] By the end of 1901, most orders placed with Brooks were for piston-valves.

Piston valves also leaked less than slide valves.[271] They did, however, need blow-off valves to get rid of water condensing in the valve chest or entrained into it by priming or foaming, while slide valves released water by a slight lifting of the valve from its seat.

Acceptance of the piston valve and the gradual disappearance of the slide valve, both in new construction and through retrofitting, was a feature of the early 1900s.

Regardless of valve type, the 1890s brought new suspicions about the effects of steam friction (known as "wire-drawing") in long, sinuous and constricted steam passages on locomotive performance. In 1893, R. P. Sanderson, Division Superintendent of Motive Power on the Norfolk & Western, stated:

> The power of a locomotive at high speeds is limited not so much by the boiler, many locomotives having more than sufficient steam, as by the reduction of cylinder power due to wire drawing, compression and internal friction.[272]

In 1904, G. R. Henderson put numbers on the effect of friction losses and different slide valve port sizes on the steam pressure available in the cylinder, based on work on the Chicago & North Western Railway.[273] Even with the throttle wide open and the engine in full gear (90% to 92% cut-off) the pressure available in the cylinder dropped by 20% at 30 miles per hour, and further if the ports were too small.

All of the foregoing contributed to a growing awareness that steam distribution was one of the factors limiting locomotive performance at high speed. This problem remained one of the besetting problems of the reciprocating steam locomotive.[274]

3.6.2 Valve Gear

During the nineteenth and early twentieth centuries, the Stephenson link motion was universal on American locomotives. Conservatism and unawareness of its disadvantages maintained its supremacy. The gear, mounted between the frames, necessarily became heavier with the increasing size of locomotives, weighing up to 1,500 pounds, including the valve body, and adding to counter-balancing problems. Inertia and flexure of the gear could affect steam distribution. It was difficult to access for lubrication and inspection and, when individual parts weighed as much as 250 pounds, it was difficult to remove and replace them underneath the locomotive.[275] Due to its geometry, Stephenson gear increased lead as cut-off was shortened—in the extreme, causing a violent jarring and breakage of piston rods.[276] It was therefore unsatisfactory for high speeds and short cut-offs.

Angus Sinclair describes some of the many valve gears that were devised during the nineteenth century in *Development of the Locomotive Engine*. About the turn of the century, at least four attempts to improve on the Stephenson motion went as far as installation on American locomotives. The Lewis valve gear, produced and promoted by the Lewis Valve Gear Co., St. Louis, Missouri, dated from 1892.[277] The gear took its motion from the crosshead, not from an eccentric like the Stephenson. G. H. Prescott, Superintendent of Motive Power and Machinery on the Terre Haute & Indianapolis, noted that lead did not change with cut-off and that the reverse lever was easy to work, even at high power and high speed. The Lewis gear was fitted to a new 4-4-0, built for the Terre Haute & Indianapolis by the Pittsburgh Locomotive Works in 1892, and used in both freight and passenger service. After eighteen months, no significant problems had appeared and the valve gear was "really working into favor against a strong prejudice." It was also tried on the Wabash, the Illinois Central and possibly a western railroad.

Railroads were not necessarily averse to innovations, but they were a harsh testing ground, offering few second chances. W. C. Arp, a later Superintendent of Motive Power on the successor to the Terre Haute & Indianapolis (the Terre Haute & Indianapolis was incorporated into the Vandalia in 1905) commented:

> This gear was placed on engine 39 in the summer of 1892 and removed in the fall of 1895. The working parts of the gear were poorly constructed and gave continuous trouble in the matter of repairs. It would frequently break when the engine was in heavy service, necessitating the engine being towed back to the shop for repairs of broken parts. When this valve gear was in good condition it gave very good results.

Not good enough, as it "failed to demonstrate its superiority over the shifting link."

At about the same time, the New York, Ontario & Western tried the Lamplough valve gear, retrofitted to a Baldwin 4-4-0 built in 1872.[278] Like the Lewis gear, the Lamplough gear dispensed with eccentrics and provided a constant lead, regardless of cut-off. It was more compact and had fewer moving parts than the Stephenson gear. Like the Lewis gear, it disappeared.

The Haberkorn Engine Co., a manufacturer of stationary engines in Fort Wayne, Indiana, adapted their valve gear to locomotives in 1902–3.[279] This resembled the Stephenson gear, but steam admission was through a piston valve, while a separate, parallel piston valve controlled cut-off. E. F. Needham, Master Mechanic of the Wabash, retrofitted this gear to one of his engines in 1903. Indicator diagrams showed a freer steam admission, sharper cut-off, better expansion and later release to exhaust than with Stephenson gear. Over three months, pulling a 360-ton train daily over a 105-mile division, the engine used 4 tons of coal and 4,400 gallons of water per trip, compared to 6 tons of coal and 6,600 gallons of water for Stephenson-gear engines. The Haberkorn valve gear also vanished.

O. W. Young, working for the Chicago & North Western, invented a new valve system, including a new valve gear, in 1900–4, derived from the Corliss valves used in stationary engines and meant for high speeds and short cut-offs.[280] The company retrofitted and tested Young's gear on two engines, a 4-4-0 in 1901 and a 4-4-2 in 1903.

Each cylinder had two valves. Each valve consisted of a slotted cylindrical valve body oscillating between two positions inside a cylindrical valve chest, one position for admission, one for exhaust. The axis of rotation was horizontal and at right angles to the locomotive's centerline. Eccentrics drove the valves; mechanical linkages allowed adjustment of cut-off. An important advantage of this gear was that both steam and exhaust lead could be varied independently of cut-off through ingenious mechanical linkages.

Road tests at speeds up to 95 miles per hour produced indicator diagrams comparing favorably with those from Stephenson-gear locomotives. In comparative tests between two similar engines, one with piston valves, one with Young valves, the Young-valve locomotive showed 40% less back pressure, 40% higher mean effective pressure, 34% greater indicated horsepower and 25% fewer pounds of steam per indicated horsepower-hour. In spite of this triumph, the Young system did not achieve widespread popularity. Higher initial cost than its alternatives and the difficulty of retrofitting existing engines were probably among the reasons. This should not be confused with Young's later and better known valve gear, first used in 1915.[281]

Growing dissatisfaction with the Stephenson gear around the turn of the century led to this comment in 1904[282]:

> The Stephenson link motion has been the standard valve gear on American locomotives since the beginning of railroading in this country, the chief reason for this being that it combines simplicity and reasonable efficiency. Simplicity has been the keynote of all progress in locomotive design in the United States rather than extreme economy either of fuel or water. Because of this fact, the deficiencies of the Stephenson valve gear, with its irregularity of steam distribution under various conditions and its excessive weight of moving parts, are complacently put up with, and, of course, freely admitted; nevertheless it is used to the practical exclusion of every other kind.

For decades, the Americans had been aware of an alternative to the Stephenson gear, widely used in Europe, invented by Egide Walschaerts (1820–1901), a shop foreman with the Belgian State Railways, in 1844–8.[283]

Confusion exists whether the name was Walschaert or Walschaerts, further complicated by the English possessive "s." M. J. Boulvin, professor at the University of Ghent in Belgium, writing in 1905 and therefore authoritative, spells the name as "Walschaerts." References to this valve gear in *Railroad Age Gazette* for 1905–14 are about evenly divided between "Walschaert" and "Walschaerts." One author writes[284]: "the Walschaert radial valve gear … since its invention, in 1844, by Egide Walschaerts, of Belgium," acknowledging the spelling of the name but indicating that American usage was "Walschaert." The Pennsylvania Railroad Technical and Historical Society Publications Style Manual, 2006, confirms this.

Use of the Walschaert gear spread in Europe during the nineteenth century, but made no impression in America. Locomotive builder William Mason, of Taunton, Massachusetts, exhibited a locomotive with Walschaert gear at the Centennial exposition of 1876 and is said to have built about one hundred locomotives with this gear; otherwise it was ignored for another thirty years.[285]

Dissatisfaction with the Stephenson gear paved the way for a second introduction of Walschaert gear into the U.S. in 1904.

Section 3.7 Frames and Running Gear

3.7.1 Frames

The frame is one of the least visible and most important parts of a steam locomotive, supporting the boiler and keeping the cylinders and wheels aligned with each other. Originally, the boiler was a more important structural element than the frame.[286] This changed in the 1860s to a more massive, purpose-built frame.

The earliest locomotive frames were built from timber beams. Replacement of the timber with iron bars led, conceptually, to the bar frame. During the 1800s, frames were built up of progressively larger wrought iron members until the original "bar" construction became hard to visualize. Toward the turn of the century the frame consisted of two massive longitudinal members made of wrought iron. During construction, the two members were carefully aligned and then bolted together by spreaders.

From the 1890s onward, cast steel gradually replaced wrought iron. The first American steel casting was a switch frog, made for the Philadelphia & Reading by the Midvale Steel Works in 1867; for many years, the new technology was poorly understood. American cast steel in the mid–1890s had a tensile strength of about 71,000 pounds per square inch, compared to 48,000 to 50,000 pounds per square inch for wrought iron and 20,000 to 30,000 pounds per square inch for cast iron.[287] As a steel casting cooled, however, shrinkage stresses built up in the metal, which had to be relieved by heat treatment; the bigger the casting, the worse the problem. If a casting was not properly heat treated, it could be weaker and less reliable than wrought iron.

Cast steel in locomotive construction started with small items, such as pistons, wheel centers, driving boxes and crossheads. Schenectady put its first cast steel driving wheels into service in 1895. Acceptance by the railroads was slow, due to poor quality and high cost, until the problems were overcome; the economic conditions of the late 1890s increased the demand for stronger and lighter parts.

The bigger and riskier task was to cast the frames in steel. Krupp was doing this in Germany by the mid–1890s, but the Americans were still hesitant.[288]

> Mr. James Smith, of the Boston Forge Co., after forty-nine years' experience in working iron, would hesitate long before trying steel for locomotive frames, this principally for the reason that you cannot tell certainly whether or not you get a sound casting, and the first intimation of unsoundness would be the breaking of the frame.

Some of the early cast steel frames were "very defective, as they are simply full of blow-holes. I have run a piece of wire 18 inches into a blow-hole in a frame we had down for the purpose of welding, and I have seen some of them, when we took them apart where they were broken, have chunks as large as hen eggs drop out, dross and dirt."[289]

Such failures reinforced natural distrust.

A new company, the American Steel Casting Co., willing to take risks and unhindered by prejudice, was set up to exploit this new technology and find ways round the doubts of older men. This company made the first cast steel locomotive frame in America in 1896.[290]

The first substantial order for cast steel locomotive frames came when Baldwin built twenty-five 2-8-0s for the Santa Fe. Standard Steel supplied some of the frames; American Steel Casting supplied the majority. By the end of 1898, American Steel Casting had supplied 195 locomotive frames.

The manufacture of cast steel frames by specialty manufacturers left existing builders wondering what to do with their huge forging shops and the equipment and skilled workforce making wrought iron frames. This may have delayed the introduction of cast steel frames which found their first application in the heaviest engines, where their advantages were most needed.[291] In 1901, Baldwin decided on cast steel frames for engines with 20-inch cylinders or bigger. In the first eight months of that year they built 874 locomotives; 550 had cylinders of 20-inch bore or bigger. Of these, 336 had cast steel frames. (The Baltimore & Ohio [64]; Pennsylvania [64]; Philadelphia & Reading [50]; Chicago, Burlington & Quincy [15]; Lehigh Valley [40]; Rio Grande Western [5]; Erie [32]; others [66])

By then, the railroads felt that the earlier quality problems had been solved. A 1904 ARMMA questionnaire drew responses from forty-one railroads, representing 21,440 locomotives. Railroads representing 54% of the locomotives favored steel frames; railroads representing 26% of the locomotives still favored wrought iron frames; the remainder were non-committal.[292]

3.7.2 Accommodation to Curvature

All American road engines during the period with which we are concerned had two or four free wheels, mounted ahead of the driving wheels and of smaller diameter, both to support the front of the locomotive and to guide it around curves and over rough track, omitted only on switchers and small industrial locomotives that moved over short distances at low speeds. In Britain, where short distances and dense traffic justified heavy investment in track quality, 0-6-0 and 0-8-0 road engines were common throughout the steam era.

The earliest American steam locomotives had only centrally pivoted four-wheel leading trucks. As these had no lateral movement, they in effect extended the rigid wheelbase, requiring blind flanges on the leading driving wheels. Self-centering lateral motion through swing links was developed in the 1860s, as shown in the accompanying drawing, shortening the rigid wheelbase to the driving wheels only.

This made it possible to build locomotives with more than six driving wheels with a four-wheel leading truck.[293] This was not a simple problem; resistance to the sidewise movement of the truck had to be strong enough to damp out yawing on straight track, but not so strong that the truck would climb the rail on a curve. The Europeans used centering springs, but this did not allow enough lateral movement for American conditions.

In 1857, Levi Bissell developed and patented a two-wheel truck

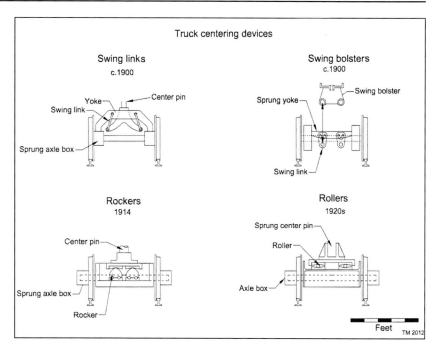

Centering devices used on locomotive trucks (redrawn from Bruce, A. W., *The Steam Locomotive in America: Its Development in the Twentieth Century,* New York: Bonanza, 1952; *RAG*, October 23, 1914, 741).

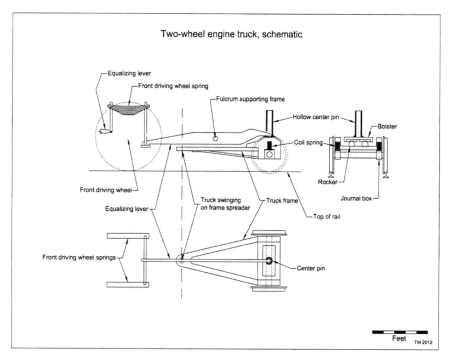

Two-wheel engine truck (redrawn from Harding, J. W., *Steam Locomotive Home Study Course,* 2002 reprint, Vol. 1, 63-8).

pivoted on the locomotive frame at a point behind the truck itself.[294] A radius bar connected the truck to a pivot point on the frame. A center pin above the center of the truck transmitted the engine weight to the truck wheels through swing links. (The center pin was an addition to the original design, where the weight of the locomotive rested on opposing inclined plates.) When a curve in the track deflected the truck wheels to one side, the swing links lifted the front of the

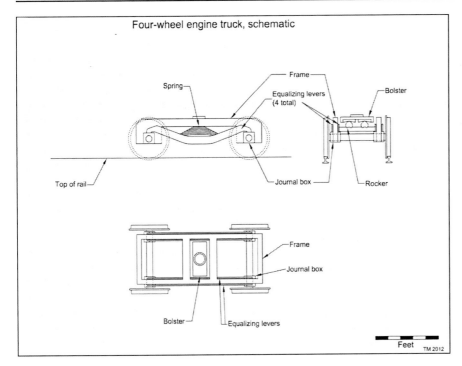

Four-wheel engine truck (redrawn from Harding, J. W., *Steam Locomotive Home Study Course*, 2002 reprint, Vol. 1, 70-2).

engine slightly. The weight of the engine tended to recenter the engine over the truck, turning it into the curve.[295] This had the disadvantage of briefly lifting some of the weight off the driving wheels and could cause them to slip.[296] The Bissell truck came to fruition when William S. Hudson devised a means to make its center point a part of the locomotive suspension through an equalizing lever, patented in 1864.[297] With minor developments to improve strength, stability and cheapness of construction, the Bissell truck continued in use until the end of steam.[298]

Railroads distrusted the two-wheel leading truck for high speeds, favoring four-wheel leading trucks instead. Two-wheel leading trucks were therefore typical of freight locomotives, and four-wheel leading trucks of passenger locomotives, for most of the twentieth-century steam era.

The leading truck led the locomotive into a curve but six, eight and ten driving wheels posed additional problems as the rigid wheelbase entered the curve. This problem was addressed in several ways. Track on curves was spiked to a slightly looser gauge than on straight sections. The tires on the endmost driving wheels could be set slightly closer together than the tires on the middle drivers. Sometimes blind flanges were used on the middle driving wheels. The driving wheels were able to move slightly from side to side in the driving boxes. All of these tolerances were of the order of ⅛ to ¼ inch but together they sufficed for long-wheelbase locomotives to negotiate curves in the track.

With rare exceptions, the application of steam power to more than ten driving wheels entailed articulation. The Europeans invented several articulated locomotive types; very few were used in America; only the Mallet became widespread and that not until after 1905.

During the 1890s, increasing numbers of locomotives were built with a pair of free wheels supporting the firebox. At first the axles ran in axle boxes capable of sprung vertical movement between pedestals in the rear of the frame, but at the cost of extending the rigid wheelbase. The first flexible trailing trucks appeared in the first years of

the twentieth century with the combined purpose of supporting a large, deep firebox and guiding long-wheelbase locomotives while backing.

The Player truck, developed by Alco Brooks, comprised a pair of rigidly connected axle boxes capable of moving sidewise against centering springs; the pedestals in the frame were curved so that the wheels swiveled under the locomotive as well as moving from side to side.[299] Early 4-4-2s, 4-6-2s, 2-6-2s and 2-8-2s, built by Alco Brooks between 1902 and 1907, used this device. It suffered from being difficult to manufacture and providing poor lateral stability. The Rushton truck, developed by Kenneth Rushton, chief draftsman at Baldwin, in 1902, was a true truck with a radius bar and self-centering lateral movement through swing links. The Wells truck, built by Rogers between 1904 and 1907, allowed the trailing wheels to move sidewise against swing links, although the wheels apparently only moved from side to side without swiveling. The De Voy truck of 1905 was similar, but used rollers and inclined planes instead of swing links.[300]

Alco Schenectady introduced the Cole truck in 1903 with a radius bar, spring centering and outside axle boxes which distinguish its appearance from other designs. Springs, bearing on sliding pads, supported the weight of the firebox; rollers and inclined planes provided additional centering action. In particular, whereas the Player, Rushton and Wells trucks were independently sprung, the suspension of the Cole truck was equalized with that of the driving wheels. Yet another form of trailing truck, built in about 1904, had the bearings outside the wheels, supporting the frame through rollers between opposed concave inclined planes.

In 1912, Baldwin brought out the Hodges trailing truck, similar to the Cole truck, except that swing links provided centering action.[301]

In 1916, the Commonwealth Steel Co. brought out the Delta trailing truck with a massive, cast-steel frame capable of accommodating a booster. The design did not include an effective centering mechanism, leading to lateral instability. The Delta Type B truck, introduced in 1921, solved this problem by using rockers.

3.7.3 Suspension

A locomotive driving wheel consisted of a hub, spokes and rim onto which a tire was shrunk-fit. The tire could be machined back to shape as it wore, and eventually replaced. The driving wheels were keyed onto axles; the axles ran in plain bearings, mounted in driving boxes. The driving boxes were free to slide up and down between pedestals in the frame, against springs, so as to accommodate unevenness in the track. Suspension had important effects on the riding of the engine and, indeed, was essential to safe riding without damage to both engine and track.

In the 4-4-0 locomotive three sets of springs supported the engine. The front point of suspension was the center pin of the four-wheel leading truck. The two back points of suspension were the left and right driving wheel pairs. The front and back driving wheels on each side were sprung as a unit, sharing loads and shocks by means of springs and equalizing levers. This three-point suspension provided the stability needed to run over uneven track. There was no cross-equalization.

This Southern class Ms 2-8-2, No. 4532, built by Alco or Baldwin, 1911–14, and photographed at Glens, Mississippi, on October 17, 1929, has a Cole-type trailing truck (Denver Public Library, Otto C. Perry collection, OP-15222).

This Southern Pacific class SP-2 4-10-2, No. 5034, built by Alco in 1926, and photographed at Los Angeles, California on May 1, 1934, has a Commonwealth trailing truck (Denver Public Library, Otto C. Perry collection, OP-15753).

The principle continued to be used in 6- and 8-coupled engines. In the 4-6-0s of the 1890s, the springs on the three driving wheels on each side of the engine were connected by equalizing levers; the left and right driving wheel sets and the truck provided three-point suspension.[302] In 2-6-0s the truck was equalized with the front pair of driving wheels, the front two pairs of driving wheels in 2-8-0s. The back two pairs of driving wheels were equalized separately in both cases.

Satisfactory in theory, this was difficult to achieve in practice.[303]

When the late Mr. J. B. Collin of the Pennsylvania Railroad designed the first consolidation engine (RRG Editor's note: Our understanding is that the *first* "consolidation" locomotive was built in 1866 by the Baldwins from the designs of Mr. Alexander Mitchell of the Lehigh Valley) for that railroad he endeavored to equalize its weight in a manner based on the principle of equalizing then and now in vogue on the American type of engine. It is simple enough to distribute the weight of an engine equally on two pairs of drivers, where the centers of the two equalizers form the base of a tripod with the center of the truck, but with the introduction of the ten-wheel engines complications arose, and still more so with the consolidation type, where the weight had to be distributed between four pairs of drivers. As long as these engines were built of a comparatively light design the correct distribution of weight was of minor importance, but as the engines grew into their present proportions the faulty balance was multiplied until to-day it is rare to find even upon the foremost roads, a consolidation engine which had not one pair of drivers loaded greatly in excess of the pair that carries the minimum load.

The result was excessive numbers of broken springs. The Europeans did not use this suspension system because they could rely on better track.

Some nineteenth-century locomotives had a "traction increaser," which lifted some or all of the leading, trailing or tender wheels to throw more weight onto the driving wheels, increasing the adhesion weight.[304] Supposedly, the engineer could use this device to start a heavy train or get over a hill. Engineers, however, were liable to use the device at other times, increasing the axle loading beyond safe limits on old, light track, bridges and soft roadbed. The New York Central and the Santa Fe experimented with them but, like many such devices, unforeseen problems had to be set off against claimed benefits.

Equalization became more complicated with increasing numbers of driving wheels. The accompanying drawing shows both the general principle and some of the options available with eight-coupled locomotives.

The top drawing shows the conventional arrangement of spring

rigging, as applied to a 2-8-2. The leading truck and front two pairs of driving wheels form one point of the system; the leading truck is equalized to a yoke between the front driving wheel springs. The back two driving wheels and the trailing truck wheels on each side are equalized lengthwise, but with no connection between the springs on opposite sides of the locomotive, forming the other two points of the triangle.

The bottom drawing shows an alternative method, as applied to a 4-8-2. The four-wheel leading truck, alone, forms the front point of the three-point suspension. The driving wheels and trailing truck wheels on each side form the other two points of the triangle.

Other variations will be mentioned in this book.

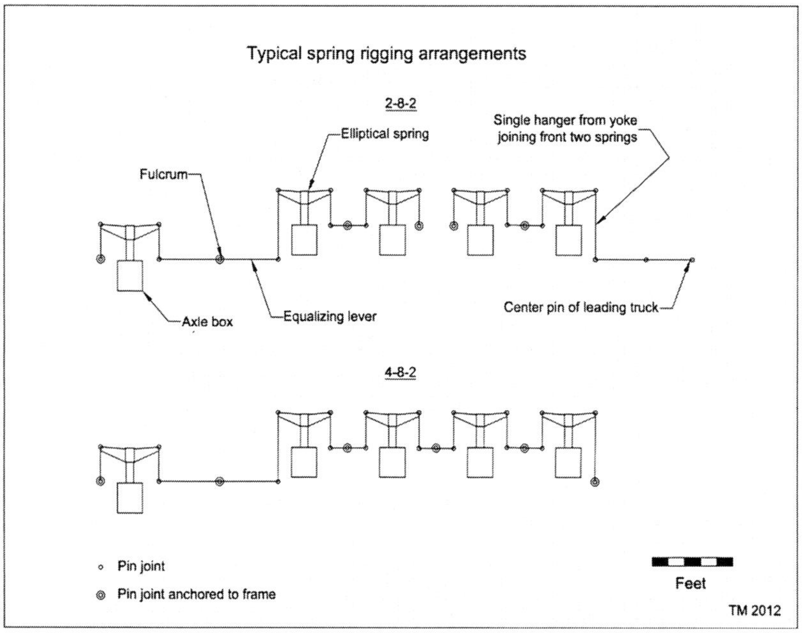

3.7.4 Counterbalancing

Counterbalancing was an inherent problem of the reciprocating steam locomotive.

When the locomotive was moving, the connecting rods exerted a centrifugal force on the crankpins. When the crankpins were at the top of their rotation, this force tended to lift the driving wheels off the track against gravity and locomotive weight transmitted through the springs while, at the bottom half, it combined with gravity to add to the static wheel load. This was called "dynamic augment." Furthermore, the centrifugal force of the rods acted outside the plane of the wheel as a lever, with the driving box as its fulcrum, tending to rock the engine from side to side.[305] As each piston reversed its stroke, the inertia of the piston, crosshead and rods caused a lengthwise shock, through the crank pins, axles and driving boxes, into the frame. This stressed the frame and caused yawing and pitching of the locomotive that increased wear and tear on both locomotive and track.

These problems became apparent only gradually during the nineteenth century as locomotive speeds and weights increased. The problem appeared first in Britain.[306]

With few exceptions, the original outside cylinder engines were fairly steady at moderate speeds, in spite of the fact that they were not counterbalanced, but as speeds were increased and working parts made heavier, some surprising and dangerous movements of the engine soon developed, which confounded our mechanical predecessors and called for immediate and close study—for at that time the behavior of unbalanced revolving and reciprocating masses was imperfectly understood, it being generally believed that the alternate action of the steam on the cylinder covers was wholly accountable for unsteady motion, and there being no known remedy for the evil, matters were allowed to take their course, until at last certain outside cylinder engines on being urged a little beyond the usual speed, made a vigorous protest by actually throwing themselves off the track, and the engine drivers declined to run them. The erratic movements of early locomotives became so marked that the British government had to take cognizance thereof, and Major-General Pasley, Inspector-General of Railways, sharply criticized them, affirming that their oscillation was positively alarming, and that something would have to be done in the matter. It was found that outside connected engines with outside frames were the most vicious of all, and this led to the deduction that the more closely the cylinders could be placed together about the center line of the engine, the steadier the engine would run. The truth of this having been established by practice, an additional advantage of the inside cylinder engine

Typical spring rigging arrangements

2-8-2

Elliptical spring

Single hanger from yoke joining front two springs

Fulcrum

Axle box   Equalizing lever

Center pin of leading truck

4-8-2

∘ Pin joint
⊚ Pin joint anchored to frame

Feet

TM 2012

Spring rigging arrangements (redrawn from Harding, J. W., *Steam Locomotive Home Study Course*, 2002 reprint, Figs. 71, 72).

was found to arise from the fact that the cylinders could be kept at a higher temperature inside the smokebox than outside, which meant an economy of fuel—always a matter of prime importance to British engineers. For these reasons the cranked axle and inside cylinders came to be standard in British practice, and a solution of the counterbalancing problem was thus postponed for a little season.

As early as the 1830s, builders began to counterbalance the rotating mass of the rods by putting weights in the wheel rims opposite to the crank pins. In the 1840s, both Robert Stephenson and Thomas Crampton realized that the reciprocating mass of the pistons, crossheads and rods could be counterbalanced by putting an additional counterweight in the wheel rim whose centrifugal force would counteract the effect of piston reversal. This counterbalance to the reciprocating masses, however, acted only twice in each wheel rotation, at piston reversal. At other times, it was an unbalanced mass that added to the dynamic augment.

Many attempts were made on both sides of the Atlantic throughout the last half of the nineteenth century, to circumvent this problem by rearranging the whole configuration of the locomotive.[307] Various designs of side lever engines were arranged so that the pistons and connecting rods moved in opposite directions by means of levers or intermediate crankshafts. Another idea was to place two pistons, moving in opposite directions, in the same cylinder. These attempts are outside the scope of this book, but we should be aware that they continued throughout the nineteenth century—all to no avail.[308]

Locomotive speeds and weights in mid-nineteenth century America caused few counterbalancing problems. Photographs show the ubiquitous 4-4-0s with no counterweights in the wheels, or with small ones bolted between the spokes. Bigger counterweights were fitted to the small-drivered freight engines with their higher rotation speeds and heavier rods. As locomotive designers looked for more power, entailing heavier pistons and rods, the counterbalancing problem crept up on them. As centrifugal force increases as the square of the speed, higher running speeds quickly intensified this problem. Thicker rods, farther from the plane of the main driving wheel, added transverse unbalanced forces to the problems of the reciprocating and rotating masses. Increasing track damage in the 1880s and early 1890s highlighted this problem, which was worse in America than in Europe because the Americans built their reciprocating parts cheaper, less exactly designed and, as a result, heavier. In 1893, the Purdue researchers estimated that, in spite of efforts by American builders to lighten their reciprocating parts, the average weight of the pistons, piston rods, crossheads and connecting rods on an American engine was 2.4 times that on equivalent European engines.[309]

In the 1880s, railroad men made the connection between 70-mile-per-hour passenger trains and track damage caused by "hammer blow."[310] At worst, hammer blow kinked the rails downward by ½ inch and, surprisingly, inward by ⅛ to ½ inch for 6 to 18 inches at intervals equal to the circumference of the wheel that caused it. The inside foot of the rail displaced the spikes inward; the outside foot pulled out from under the spike heads. Damage extended from ¼ mile to more than a mile. The engines identified as causing the damage were 4-4-0 express passenger locomotives with 68-inch driving wheels, reaching speeds of 80 miles per hour. Investigation revealed that sometimes the wheel lifted off the rail high enough to bring the flange above the head of the rail. When the wheel came down again, the flange struck the top of the rail with an obvious risk of derailment. In a 4-4-0 the back driving wheels lifted more than the front ones because the connecting rod thrust, directed obliquely downward, helped to keep the front wheels on the rail. Even without such extreme damage, hammer blow accelerated wear on locomotives and track.

Much was suspected, but little was known. Some of the first experimental work was done in the Purdue locomotive laboratory in 1893. When researchers fed wire between the driving wheels of the test locomotive and the dynamometer rollers, the weight of the driving wheel flattened the wire. When the wheel speed reached 59 miles per hour, test wires came out with lengths showing no flattening at all, proving that the driving wheels lifted off the track altogether. This was the first solid evidence on what had hitherto been a matter of speculation, provoking discussion, comment and published articles.

If hammer blow could damage track on a solid road bed, its effect on bridges must be still more dangerous, yet in the 1890s bridge engineers knew nothing about it.[311] In one case:

> an engine with one car running at a high rate of speed commenced jumping on a pin-connected bridge, and the drivers were actually seen to leave the rails by a person who stood on the bridge at the time the train passed. The marks on the rails, and the bends in the rails, together with the testimony of the persons on the engine, corroborated the story of the observer.

The usual method of counterbalancing engines at that time was rule of thumb and trial and error.

> When the _____ works first began building engines for this company, we required them to balance the wheels on trestles and pour in an amount of (lead) weight in the counterbalance pockets to correspond with the whole weight of reciprocating parts in addition to the revolving parts. This has been standard with us for many years, and has made our engines run with remarkable smoothness. Of course it makes a heavy blow, but we cannot say that we have had any special trouble with broken rails; certainly none has been traced to this cause. The locomotive works kicked about the extra work, and finally we gave them the weight of lead to be used, as derived from our experience. The work was rushed out and they failed to put any counterbalance in at all, and the result was we could hardly get the engines over the road, and finally I had to take them all into the shop and counterbalance them.[312]

Furthermore:

> Probably "Bridge Engineer" does not know that some railroad master mechanics guess at the amount of counterbalance required in locomotive driving wheels, and then ride on the engine to test the accuracy of their guesses. The way in which the engines ride upon the bridges decides whether more or less counterbalance is required.[313]

The rule of thumb was to counterbalance the whole of the rotating masses and two-thirds of the reciprocating masses. With driving wheels less than 72 inches in diameter at speeds above 65 miles per hour, the counterweight balancing the reciprocating masses was liable to damage the track. The only way to reduce this effect was to reduce the weight of the reciprocating parts or to increase the driving wheel diameter. The heavier the engine in relation to its reciprocating parts, the less the tendency to pitch or yaw. Heavier driving wheels and stiffer springs inhibited the tendency of a driving wheel to lift off the rail but, ultimately every locomotive had a maximum safe running speed which could be calculated from the masses of its reciprocating parts and counterweights. For example, Professor Goss calculated that a driving wheel imposing 14,000 pounds static load on the rail with a counterweight of 400 pounds to balance the reciprocating parts would lift off the rail at 310 revolutions per minute.[314] Surprisingly, an engine could be counterbalanced so that it rode smoothly, as felt by the enginemen, yet still impart a heavy hammer blow to the track.

In view of these tormenting problems, the four-cylinder balanced compound seemed to offer wonderful possibilities, accounting for the vogue that such engines enjoyed in the first years of the twentieth century. In 1897 the Balanced Locomotive & Engineering Co. of New

York tested a Strong-type four-cylinder balanced compound locomotive for hammer blow on the Purdue static test plant, using the same procedure (crushed wire) as Professor Goss had used in his 1893 experiments. The test was a great success, with no hammer blow, pitching or yawing of the engine.[315]

Unlike the process inside the smokebox, counterbalancing was within the theory and computing power available in the 1890s. As early as 1894, R. A. Parke of the Westinghouse Air Brake Company produced a rigorous mathematical analysis.[316] Parke's analysis made it possible not only to calculate the correct amount of counterweight, but also to predict the speed at which the driving wheels would lift from the rail and how high they would lift at any given speed thereafter. The analysis also predicted the dynamic augment that would result from any given combination of weights, speeds and counterbalancing.

G. R. Henderson, at that time Mechanical Engineer on the Norfolk & Western, published several practical guidelines in 1896.[317] Each driving wheel should be balanced for all rotating weights attached to it. The connecting rod should be considered part rotating weight, part reciprocating weight, the rotating weight portion ranging from 0.57 for a connecting rod 5 feet long, down to 0.51 for a 12-foot rod. This portion should be wholly balanced on the main driving wheel. He also suggested that reciprocating weights, including the "reciprocating" portion of the connecting rod, up to a maximum of $\frac{1}{360}$ of the total engine weight, could be left unbalanced without adverse effect. Considering the trouble caused by the counterweight for the reciprocating weights, this was an important finding.

The reciprocating counterbalance problem was serious and difficult to solve.[318] Methods for apportioning the weight for counterbalancing between reciprocation and rotation remained arbitrary until Parke produced a further mathematical analysis in 1903.[319] He also pointed out that the counterweights in the wheels were in a different vertical plane from the rods whose weight they were counterbalancing, resulting in a disturbing effect on the wheel on the opposite side of the engine. This effect had also to be counterbalanced. This may have been the first time this particular problem was identified.

Although the counterbalancing issues were well known by 1905, and the mathematical tools were available to resolve them, bigger engines brought worse and more complicated problems of counterbalancing. During the early twentieth century counterbalancing was a serious and limiting factor in American locomotive development.

3.7.5 Internal Friction

By the 1890s, engineers had long been aware that a locomotive must consume some of its power overcoming its own internal friction. No one knew how much.

> The internal friction of locomotives has long been a matter of conjecture. The only locomotive tests that approach reasonable accuracy as to internal friction are those made at Purdue University, by Professor Goss; but these results vary considerably from each other, and, … there is good reason for such variation, arising mostly from difference in lubrication, it being exceedingly difficult to maintain anything like uniform lubrication on locomotives with the ordinary oiling apparatus.[320]

The Purdue test plant was especially valuable in these investigations because indicated and drawbar power could be compared directly without wind resistance, the internal friction of the tender, and rolling resistance. A rail vehicle is always climbing out of a depression in the track caused by its own weight. This rolling resistance is distinct from the friction resistance in axle bearings. The shape and depth of the depression depends on wheel loading, distance between axles, stiffness of the track and firmness of the road bed. Tests continued at

Purdue for several years and were the first to throw real light on the actual internal friction of the locomotive.[321] Results ranged from 23.3% of indicated horsepower at 55 miles per hour down to 5.5% at 25 miles per hour.

This discovery led to investigations how to reduce internal friction. Proper alignment when the engine was being built prevented moving parts from binding while, as an engine aged, clearances loosened and moving parts wore to fit, reducing internal friction. Winter cold in the northern states increased friction as parts contracted against each other and lubricants stiffened. Lubrication was vital—proper design of oil and grease channels, the new technology of lubricants and regular and conscientious oiling.[322]

Road tests by the Pennsylvania in 1899–1900 showed that the loss of power between cylinder and drawbar depended on the relative weights of engine and train. In the extreme, if an engine was running light, the cylinders would be developing little power, all of which went to overcome the engine's internal friction, rolling resistance and air resistance.[323] Therefore, comparisons between indicated and drawbar horsepower were misleading without knowing how much the engine was loaded. The determination of internal friction was difficult because so many different items contributed to it; without the Purdue test plant, it would have been impossible.

3.7.6 Brakes

While most of this book is concerned with making the engine go, devices to make it stop were equally important.

Braking was by means of a friction shoe applying calculated forces against the rim of each driving wheel, sometimes against truck and tender wheels as well, through a system of levers known as brake rigging. Force was applied to the brake rigging, both from a compressed-air piston and from a hand-operated mechanism for use when the locomotive was dead. Compressed air was supplied by a steam-driven, reciprocating compressor mounted on one side of the boiler. This compressor also pressurized the train pipe and car reservoirs. Although varying in detail, this concept remained unchanged throughout the period with which we are concerned.

Section 3.8. Performance Testing and Design

> We had a mass of commendatory and condemnatory testimony bundled together and uttered simultaneously, because the conditions under which the contradictory opinions were formed were, in themselves, contradictory. *RAG*, July 21, 1911, 109

The steam locomotive was well developed, and many thousands were in use all over the world, before anyone knew how or why it worked. Steam locomotive performance in road service was subject to so many uncontrolled and independent variables that it was difficult to measure reliably, making it difficult to compare different locomotives of the same class, locomotives of different classes, or to assess the effects of changes in design, construction or operation.

Over a period of about fifteen years, testing methods developed enough to unlock a large body of reasonably accurate numerical information on locomotive performance, giving mechanical engineers a sound basis for design. By 1900, a locomotive could be designed for its intended task and rated for the tonnage it was supposed to haul. This engineering development advanced against the opposition of rugged personalities steeped in a strong empirical tradition. Argument broke out at the 1891 ARMMA convention[324]:

Mr. Forney stated that he could not recall a single case of any person who had found out by a steam indicator anything that was worth knowing. This statement made the pot boil and the discussion proceeded fast and furiously. One member stated that he designed locomotives to draw cars and not to draw indicator diagrams.

3.8.1 Road Tests

The two main tools of the road test engineer were the indicator and the dynamometer car, both of which were in use before 1890. We have already mentioned the indicator. The dynamometer car was placed behind the engine as a part of a train. It was equipped to measure and record speed and drawbar pull but could also be equipped with devices to measure and record boiler pressure, steam chest pressure, brake system air pressure, exhaust gas temperature, cut-off, driving wheel rotation speed and even the speed and direction of the wind.[325] Road tests were expensive and not lightly undertaken.

As an example, in the summer of 1892, the Chicago, Burlington & Quincy, looking for the next step in express motive power, road tested five instrumented engines on a 350- to 400-ton passenger train, including a dynamometer car, running to a fast schedule between Chicago and Galesburg. The engines were a two-cylinder, single-expansion 4-4-0, two two-cylinder, single-expansion 2-6-0s, a two-cylinder, cross-compound 2-6-0 and a four-cylinder Vauclain compound 4-6-0.[326]

The 2-6-0 compound results had to be discarded because the engine had a leaky safety valve and, after the test, "a bad leak was found in the high-pressure cylinder caused by cracks in the casting, out of which one or more pieces of iron fell."[327]

To Baldwin's fury, their supposedly more efficient compound used 25% to 38% more coal and 13% to 22% more water than the single-expansion engines during this test but, for some reason, the 4-6-0 compound was run at long cut-off, using the throttle to control steam flow to the cylinders, which would have adversely affected fuel economy. Discussion of the results never referred to the loops at the compression ends of the indicator diagrams from the Vauclain compound, indicative of excessive steam lead and compression. This valve setting problem was not even recognized until about 1895. The indicator diagrams from the other engines in the tests showed these loops either not at all or to a much lesser extent.

The test report commented:

Inside a dynamometer car on the Nickel Plate, 1949 (courtesy *Classic Trains* magazine collection, ctr_j1206_01, GE photo).

One lesson, therefore, to be learnt from these tests is that a boiler, grate and draft appliances which generate steam freely are of even greater importance than the compound principle, and that the disadvantages entailed by bad steaming will more than offset any advantages conferred by compounding.

The truth of this prescient comment would pervade steam locomotive history.

Whatever the ambiguities, the Chicago, Burlington & Quincy tests produced substantial amounts of information. The lowest recorded coal consumption per drawbar horsepower-hour was 5.7 pounds for the 4-4-0; the highest was 40% higher at 7.9 pounds for the Baldwin 4-6-0. The single-expansion 2-6-0s ranged from 5.8 to 7.1 pounds, differing by 40% between one run and another. The lowest recorded water consumption per drawbar horsepower-hour was 31.3 pounds in the 4-4-0; the highest was 39.2 pounds in the 4-6-0. The single-expansion 2-6-0s ranged from 32.0 to 35.2 pounds. The single-expansion 2-6-0s recorded both the lowest and the highest specific evaporation, from 6.0 pounds to 6.9 pounds of water per pound of coal. Firing rates ranged from 90 pounds of coal per square foot of grate per hour in a single-expansion 2-6-0, with 27 square feet of grate area, up to 122 in the 4-6-0 with its 28-square foot grate.

As a benchmark, in 1924, a British Great Western Railway 4-6-0 in express passenger service tested at 2.1 pounds of coal per indicated horsepower-hour, 2.8 pounds per drawbar horsepower-hour, evaporation rate 9.25 pounds of water per pound of coal. The rest of the British locomotive industry greeted these figures with an astonishment verging on disbelief, 3 to 4 pounds of coal per drawbar horsepower-hour being more normal.[328]

In 1894, a committee of the Master Mechanics' Association pointed to the importance of complete and uniform road test procedures. Without these, it was impossible to make objective comparisons between types of locomotive. Parameters to be measured were: weight of coal burned, its chemical analysis and calorific value, weight of cinders and ash, weight of water evaporated, weight of water lost through safety valves and injector overflow, moisture in steam, exhaust gas temperature and composition, smokebox vacuum, boiler and steam chest pressures, driving wheel rotation speed, indicated horsepower and drawbar pull. The committee recommended that the results should be reported as pounds of standard coal per drawbar horsepower-hour. "Standard coal" meant a calorific value of 12,500 BTU per pound, which was the average value of American coal. Drawbar horsepower was ambiguous because of the large differences that could result from differences in oiling and the percentage of power used in moving the engine, which varied both with grade and curvature and with the degree to which the engine was fully loaded.[329]

Tests by the Northern Pacific in 1895 between Tacoma, Washington, and St. Paul, Minnesota, provided information, not only for traffic and motive power planning and scheduling, but also guidance on where civil engineering works offered the best returns on investment.[330]

Railroads cooperated in road tests with university mechanical engineering departments; the whole industry benefited from publication of the results.[331] In 1898, the Louisville & Nashville allowed a party of four mechanical engineering students from Rose Polytechnic Institute, Terre Haute, Indiana, supervised by their professor, to road-test a newly shopped 2-8-0 with a 25-square foot grate, 1,810 square feet of heating surface, 20-inch × 26-inch cylinders, 51-inch driving wheels and nominal tractive effort 29,000 pounds. The engine was instrumented with indicators on both cylinders, pyrometers in the firebox and smokebox and a steam calorimeter plumbed into the dry pipe.

The tests repeated a 5- to 6-hour, 86-mile freight run between Decatur and Birmingham, Alabama, seven times with as nearly as possible the same crew throughout. The trailing load was 21 to 28 cars, totaling about 620 tons. The Chicago, Milwaukee & St. Paul made its dynamometer car available for the tests.

The test results were as follows:

Coal analysis	
Volatiles	31.3–36.2%
Carbon	55.7–59.1%
Ash	5.9–8.0%
Moisture	1.4–1.6%
Firing rate (lb. coal/sq.ft. grate/hr.)	100–115
Evaporation from & at 212°F (lb. water/lb. coal)	6.5–7.2
Evaporation rate (lb. water/sq.ft. heating surface)	10
Smokebox vacuum (ins. water gauge)	2.9–3.7
Smokebox temperature, average (deg. F)	650–680
Smokebox temperature, maximum (deg. F)	800–1,000
Boiler pressure (psi.)	145–165
Steam loss through safety valve (lb./min. when open)	200
Average ihp.	580
Steam consumption (lb./ihp.-hr.)	25–26
Coal consumption (lb./ihp.-hr.)	4.3–4.7
Coal consumption (lb./1,000 ton-miles)	185–200

This coal consumption was in the flat country of Alabama. On the Great Northern in Montana, this figure ran as high as 440 to 530 pounds.[332]

Comprehensive benchmark figures, such as these, were essential to locomotive design; we will see how these figures evolved over the next fifty years.

As early as 1900, road tests on the Northern Pacific were revealing some bleak facts about what happened to the thermal energy in a pound of coal[333]:

the efficiency of the ordinary locomotive engine is low at best, in striking contrast with the theoretical potential energy in the fuel, and it becomes very important to use the available power to the best advantage.

The engine investigated was a class D-2 2-6-0 with 140 pounds per square inch boiler pressure, producing 380 indicated horsepower while moving a 550-ton (including engine) train at 16 miles per hour. Energy distribution was as follows:

Wasted, used in firing up, left in firebox, idling	10.0%
Lost in heated air, gases, vapor	17.0%
Evaporating moisture in coal	0.9%
Heating coal to ignition	2.0%
Heat and unconsumed coal in ashes	1.8%
Unconsumed gases	6.0%
Lost in sparks	5.7%
Radiation from boiler, firebox, etc.	4.5%
Heat lost in entrained water	0.4%
Heating feedwater	7.0%
Latent heat of evaporation	34.2%
Friction in ports and steam passages	0.3%
Clearance space at cylinder ends	0.2%
Cylinder condensation	1.0%
Back pressure	1.2%
Lost through incomplete expansion	3.6%
Machinery friction and wind resistance	0.4%
Traction of engine	0.6%
Traction of cars	1.9%
Traction of load (net useful effect)	1.4%

The engine burned 5.9 pounds of western coal with a calorific value of 10,000 BTU per pound and used 27.7 pounds of water per indicated horsepower-hour. The fact that one third of the fuel energy went into the latent heat of evaporation limited the efficiency of all forms of open-circuit, non-condensing steam engines. Worse, the steam locomotive threw half the total fuel energy out into the atmosphere, or wasted it in other ways that were inherent in what it was and how it worked. Test results from elsewhere confirmed these findings.[334] Steam leaks inflicted enormous penalties in loss of power and made nonsense of efficiency calculations.

Road tests continued to improve with better dynamometer cars and instrumentation. Road tests on the Hocking Valley in 1904 listed ninety-two dimensions and 123 parameters and calculated results.[335] Three figures remained depressingly familiar: 6.0 to 6.8 pounds of water evaporated per pound of coal, 27 to 28 pounds of water per indicated horsepower-hour and 4 to 5 pounds of coal per indicated horsepower hour. In the flat country of Ohio, between Columbus and Toledo the engines reached speeds of 70 to 80 miles per hour with indicated horsepower as high as 1,380, 630 to 680 continuous. The evaporation rate was 8.5 to 8.8 pounds of water per square foot of heating surface at firing rates of 90 to 100 pounds of coal per square foot of grate per hour. High speeds carried a penalty in fuel cost: 360 to 400 pounds of coal per 1,000 ton-miles.

As of 1904, the new, big engines were being introduced faster than reliable tests could be made.

> Few reliable tests of modern locomotives have been made and it is difficult to get accurate data as to their performance.[336]

3.8.2 Static Test Plants

Road testing, no matter how carefully done, was full of ambiguities. Only a static test plant, where a locomotive ran on braked rollers or carrying wheels, could produce repeatable measurements under controlled conditions. The information that started to come from Purdue in the 1890s was news to the railroading and engineering world.

To make a test, the Purdue test crew brought the engine up to operating temperature and pressure, running it slowly under light load for an hour or more. They then ran each test for 2 to 3 hours before shutting the engine down. Besides the two-man engine crew, eleven observers took indicator cards and measured fuel supply, water supply and temperature, boiler pressure, steam quality, smokebox temperature and vacuum, driving wheel revolutions per minute, brake force and drawbar pull, using coal analyzed and tested for calorific value.

Work at Purdue came to a temporary halt when a fire destroyed the laboratory in January 1894.[337] The university built a bigger and better laboratory, connected by a siding to the Lake Erie & Western Railroad and built for four- and six-coupled locomotives. The locomotive was repaired. Professor Young, writing in 1933, lists four locomotives at Purdue, *Schenectady No. 1* (1891–1897), *Schenectady No. 2* (1897–1902), *Schenectady No. 3* (1903–1923) and *Vauclain-Purdue No. 4* (1924–).[338] The Purdue test plant went out of use in 1938, when *Vauclain-Purdue No. 4* was declared unsafe, due to lack of funding and student interest.[339]

Professor Goss designed a second test locomotive, built at Schenectady in 1897 as *Schenectady No. 2* to replace *Schenectady No. 1*.[340] *Schenectady No. 2* was a conventional 4-4-0 but with interesting variations. The boiler was built for 250 pounds per square inch, well above any pressure used in new construction. The cylinders were designed to be interchangeable, for configuration as either single-expansion or compound, and bushed so that in single expansion they could be either 16-inch or 20-inch bore, with pistons to match. The alternative left-hand cylinder for compound working was of 30-inch diameter but could be bushed down in decrements to 16 inches. But

for the fact that it had no tender, the locomotive was in all respects complete, down to the bell and headlight.

High power at high speed was one of the besetting problems of the reciprocating steam engine. The work at Purdue was breaking fresh ground and we must take into account just how little was known of the working of the steam locomotive at the time.[341] It was a new finding in 1896 that:

> with the throttle fully open and the cut-off constant the power of the locomotive increases as the speed is increased up to a certain point, after which the power does not increase, even though the speed is increased.

Researchers found that the Purdue locomotive was capable of up to 500 indicated horsepower at 35 miles per hour; power increased up to that speed but thereafter showed no further increase. This type of information could be found out only in the controlled conditions of a static test plant.

Professor Goss called this speed the "critical speed," a term whose choice "sprang from a desire to give emphasis to a series of relationships which…, so far as I am informed, have not before received attention." Goss noticed that fuel and water efficiency were greatest at this critical speed; the existence of this speed and its implications were important to locomotive designers. Goss at first thought that it was to do with valve settings, apparently not realizing that the boiler was running out of steam.

In 1894, Robert Quayle of the Chicago & North Western set up a simple static test plant at the railroad's Kaukauna shops.[342]

> Having selected a passenger car truck, Mr. Quayle lengthened the frame to make the wheel spacing equal to the distance between the drivers of the locomotive which he proposed mounting. Selecting an unused side track, he next removed a short section of the rails, and in their place excavated a shallow pit into which the truck turned upside down was placed. The wheels of the truck were thus brought in line with the rails of the side track. The wheels of the locomotive were next placed upon the wheels of the inverted truck, and loaded cars with brakes tightly set were coupled before and behind the locomotive to hold it in place. Load was supplied by the application of the usual brakes both to the wheels of the supporting truck and to the wheels of the locomotive, while jets of water were applied to carry off the heat. By these means Mr. Quayle was able to operate his experimental locomotive under fairly constant conditions, and to duplicate conditions with a fair degree of certainty.

The railroad built a more permanent test plant at its West Chicago shops in 1896. While the Purdue plant was a laboratory built around a locomotive, the Chicago & North Western plant was built to accept operating locomotives with four or six driving wheels.

Although the plant was originally built to run engines in after shopping, increasing amounts of experimental work followed.[343] This plant started to produce useful, if disquieting, information. Indiana coal fired at 62 to 65 pounds per square foot of grate per hour evaporated 8.25 to 9.0 pounds of water per pound of coal, but the test engineers noticed that evaporation efficiency deteriorated with increased firing rates. An inferior grade of Illinois coal, fired at 125 to 135 pounds per square foot per hour evaporated only 6 pounds of water per pound of coal. Coal consumption per indicated horsepower-hour also increased with higher power output from 3.6 pounds at 250 indicated horsepower to 4.6 pounds at 450 indicated horsepower. The highest power output from a 4-4-0 with a 16-square foot grate, 975 square feet of heating surface and 17-inch × 24-inch cylinders was 477 indicated horsepower at 43 miles per hour.

Demand on the plant rose rapidly and a wider variety of tests followed, including some with unexpected results. On one locomotive the eccentric rods were so springy that it was impossible to obtain

The Purdue locomotive *Schenectady No. 2*, showing the test plant mechanism (Purdue University Libraries, Karnes Archives and Special Collections, PSD00001989).

duplicate indicator cards in identical running conditions. The plant highlighted an obscure, but significant (0.5% to 15.0%) error introduced by the long steam pipes necessarily used for indicators mounted on moving locomotives. On a stationary locomotive the indicator could be mounted so that the pipes were less than 6 inches long, compared to more than 3 feet on a moving engine.

In 1901, the Pennsylvania considered a test plant at its huge shops at Altoona; the same year the Baltimore & Ohio donated a 4-4-0 locomotive to West Virginia University at Morgantown for installation in a laboratory like that at Purdue. The Chicago & North Western likewise donated a 4-4-0 to Iowa State College at Ames for the same purpose. At the same time the Santa Fe was planning a test plant at its Topeka shops.[344] In 1903, the Pennsylvania built a test plant at the Louisiana Purchase Exposition at St. Louis, Missouri, which it later moved to Altoona. The Pennsylvania plant was designed by A. Vogt, the railroad's mechanical engineer, assisted by W. F. Kiesel, Jr., who later took over that position.[345] This study has not revealed which of the other planned plants went into service. By 1904 the Chicago & North Western plant was not big enough for the biggest engines then entering service. The Pennsylvania plant at St. Louis was. The plant's first test took place on May 25, 1904, with a Pennsylvania H6a 2-8-0 freight engine. By October, six engines had

been tested, including an enormous Santa Fe 2-10-2 tandem compound.

Purdue was a powerhouse of research into many different aspects of railroad operations.[346] Railroading was at that time a leading-edge technology and was the road to fame and fortune for many of the brightest and most ambitious young men in the country. The Purdue researchers were confident that their test results held good for any currently operating steam locomotive. Using their measurements, and the formulae derived from them, they believed that graphs of net available horsepower, speed and tractive effort could be drawn for any class of engine from its dimensions. Unfortunately these formulae made too many assumptions, required too many and too large correction factors and were found to be inaccurate in actual conditions. Even though they were ahead of their time, they indicated what could be done and the usefulness of the result. The Purdue results were valid only insofar as they applied to all steam locomotives but in this capacity the plant discovered some fundamental truths and its value was enormous.

3.8.3 Tonnage Rating

In 1881, the Pittsburgh, Cincinnati & St. Louis published a tonnage rating sheet to allow yardmasters to maximize train loads based on

A Pennsylvania class L-1s 2-8-2 No. 1752 on the test plant at Altoona. The maker's plate on the side of the smokebox bears a date of 1914; otherwise the date of the photograph is uncertain (Pennsylvania Historical and Museum Commission and Railroad Museum of Pennsylvania, General Negative 41468).

locomotive power and the number and contents of freight cars.[347] This may have been the first attempt at what became a standard practice.

In the mid–1890s, the Great Northern, the St. Louis Southwestern and the Northern Pacific were among the earlier American railroads to introduce locomotive tonnage rating. Faced with soaring traffic demand, superintendents had to know what their locomotives could haul to optimize train scheduling and power allocation. The old, homespun wisdom was: "It is a very simple matter. Find out what your engines can haul and then see that they haul it." In the days of sparse, slow-moving traffic, if a train stalled on a hill, the train crew divided the train into two, hauled the two parts to the nearest passing loop after the top of the hill, reconnected them and went on their way ("doubling the hill"). This played havoc with scheduling and was a hazard to other traffic. Engine rating by direct experiment was slow and disruptive and had to be repeated on each division with each class of engine, and had to be repeated each time a new type of engine appeared on the division. Some predictive method was needed.[348]

The earliest of all the train resistance formulae was published by K. Clark in England in 1855, giving a constant resistance of 8 pounds resistance per ton of car weight, increasing with speeds as $V^2/171$. American engineers changed the Clark formula to $(V^2/171) + 6$. As early as 1892, however, Angus Sinclair took indicator diagrams on the Empire State Express, operated by the New York Central, when the engine was hauling a 300-ton train at 70 miles per hour and the entire available power of the locomotive was consumed in maintaining speed. This test showed that total resistance was 17.6 pounds per ton when the Clark formula predicted 34.6 pounds per ton. Had that

been so, no locomotive in America could have hauled a 300-ton train at 70 miles per hour.

In 1893, the Chicago Great Western was still making physical tests with weighed trains and: "A theoretical determination of the capacity upon any basis of the computed traction of the engine and the resistance of the train would seem to be entirely unreliable,...."[349] The railroad was forced to use rules of thumb, reckoning the rolling resistance of the train on straight, level track at 6 pounds of resistance per ton of trailing load for a full car, 8 pounds for an empty car, prorating train resistance according to the percentage of empty and loaded cars and adding ½ pound for each degree of curvature, although grade and curve resistance were "too indeterminate a quantity to say much about." They also used telegraphed weather and track condition reports when making up trains and added a factor to the train resistance for bad conditions of weather and track, or for fast freight and stock trains. By this means they calculated the tonnage to be assigned to a locomotive of known tractive effort. After this system went into effect in January 1894, a 21% increase in cars per train resulted. Efforts to ensure the efficient loading of cars increased the average train weight by 40%, hauled by the same locomotives.

Much was unknown about train resistance, necessary information if locomotives were to be designed in any rational manner. Engineers drew curves between test readings and fitted formulae to them, but formulae that provided realistic predictions at one speed produced nonsense at another.[350] In the late 1890s, the Northern Pacific produced a set of theoretical speed: tractive effort curves for different locomotive power outputs in order to tonnage rate its engines. When actual curves were plotted for seven classes of Northern Pacific locomotive, from dynamometer car tests, none followed the theoretical curves.[351]

An 1898 questionnaire from an ARMMA committee on tonnage rating received replies from forty-three railroads operating 66,000 line miles. Some had been using tonnage rating since 1883, but most only since 1896.[352] All agreed that this led to more efficient operations. Tonnage rating by direct experiment was impractical for a railroad operating seventy-five classes of locomotives and 5,000 line miles. Theoretical methods allowed a division of 500 miles to be tonnage rated in 3 to 5 hours; a newly built division could be tonnage-rated before traffic ever ran on it. More important yet, it was now possible to design locomotives for their intended tasks.

By 1900:

> Tonnage rating is no longer a mere experiment. It must be applied specifically for each road.
>
> The day is past when the so-called practical railroader can decry the modern system of tonnage rating as a fad of the times. Closer profit margins are rapidly forcing railroad administration to a science. Results are severely scrutinized by comparative and statistical methods as never before. Railroad officials rise and fall by results accomplished. The key in a large measure to the operating efficiency of a road to-day is the tonnage hauled for each potential unit of power furnished.

Those words were written in the benign political and economic environment in which the railroads operated around 1900. They would attain greater force in the more hostile conditions of the early twentieth century.

The Great Northern was among the earlier railroads to develop formulae of general application. By direct experiment, they determined that the train resistance as:

$$R = 7 + 20a + 0.5b$$

Where R was the train resistance in pounds per ton of trailing load; a was the adverse grade percent; b was the degrees of curvature.

Thus, to haul a 1,000-ton train up a 1% grade and around a 2° curve took 28,000 pounds of tractive effort. This ignored the force needed to accelerate the train, the momentum favoring the locomotive as a train decelerated up a hill and the effect of empty cars, but it was a start.

In 1901, G. R. Henderson produced a more exhaustive analysis than anything done previously, taking into consideration the issues omitted from the Great Northern formula, and more.[353] He first estimated the tractive force developed by the engine. He estimated a 5% loss of steam pressure in the throttle and dry pipe, and a further loss of 9% in the valves and ports, giving a "mean effective pressure" of $0.86 \times$ boiler pressure. Internal mechanical friction was estimated at a further loss equivalent to 8% of boiler pressure, resulting in a "mean available pressure" of $0.8 \times$ boiler pressure. This resulted in the well-known formula: $T = (0.8Pd^2s)/D$ where T is the tractive effort in pounds; P is the boiler pressure in pounds per square inch (gauge); d is the cylinder diameter in inches; s is the piston stroke in inches; D is the driving wheel diameter in inches.

He derived a more complicated formula for compounds. For a two-cylinder compound working compound: $T = (0.8Pd_l^2s)/(D(r+1))$ where d_l was the diameter of the low-pressure cylinder in inches and r was the ratio of cylinder volumes between the high-pressure and low-pressure cylinders. For a two-cylinder compound working single-expansion: $T = (0.8Pd_h^2s)/D$ where d_h was the diameter of the high-pressure cylinder in inches. For a four-cylinder compound, the figure of 1.6 was substituted for 0.8, otherwise the formulae were the same.

Using a 4-6-0 on the Chicago & North Western test plant, Henderson next derived a curve of tractive effort against speed. From the fact that power equals force × velocity, a power:speed curve was easily

drawn from drawbar pull and speed measurements. While this eventually filtered back into locomotive design, the power:speed curve was not a part of Henderson's original concept of matching engine tractive effort to train resistance.

Using work done by *The Engineering News*, Baldwin and others, Henderson drew curves for train resistance in pounds resistance per ton of rolling load (train + engine).

Rolling resistance	(*Engineering News*)	$2 + (V/4)$
	Baldwin	$3 + (V/6)$ where V is the speed in miles per hour.
Grade resistance		$0.38M$ where M is the rise in feet per mile.
Curvature resistance		$0.7c$ where c is the degrees of curvature
Acceleration resistance		$0.0132A^2$ where A is the speed change in miles per hour per mile.

He also drew curves to predict the effect of momentum in helping a train up a hill, assuming that the force favoring the engine was $70((V^2\text{-}25)/x)$ pounds force per ton of rolling load where the train decelerated from an initial speed, V, in miles per hour to 5 miles per hour in a distance, x, in feet.

Thus, if a 1,000-ton train (including engine and tender) decelerates from 30 miles per hour to 5 miles per hour up a mile-long hill rising at 100 feet per mile (1.9%) with a constant 2° curve, the required tractive effort is 32,675 pounds (using the average of 30 and 5 for the rolling resistance calculation). Henderson combined all these calculations to produce a set of curves for one "standard" class of locomotive with adjustments for other classes. The final result was a table giving the maximum tonnage that could be assigned to each class of engine on a division. Many railroads came up with their own methods of tonnage rating but, whatever the method, the aim was to enable a yardmaster to assign the maximum tonnage to each class of engine in any type of weather.

3.8.4 Design

At the turn of the century, with rising demands for both power and fuel efficiency, steam locomotive design had reached a frustrating impasse. The steam engine was a weird device that mystified the designers of all its forms on both sides of the Atlantic. From the viewpoint of 1901[354]:

> James Watt knew absolutely nothing of the science of thermodynamics as now understood; yet it is impossible to make any advance on the principles of construction which he laid down. If we add to his work that of Hornblower, who invented the compound engine, we may say at once that no advance whatever has taken place in the working of steam engines. Superior materials and workmanship enable us to use steam of a pressure that would have terrified Watt. But the normal counsel of perfection is the same—expand steam in a hot cylinder. If, again, we turn to the explosive engine, it will be found that it has been developed without much regard for thermodynamics; and that for its success it mainly depends on the observance of certain principles of construction which have been discovered by practice with the engine, and not by mechanical investigations. Not the least instructive lesson taught by the events of the last century is that we have mainly reached our present position by trial and error, and that little or nothing has originated by the aid of mathematical science.

One informed, but anonymous writer is worth quoting at length.[355]

It is a noteworthy fact that a decade's progress in locomotive designing, significant as it has been, has been confined chiefly to structural matters. To satisfy demands for greater power, locomotives have been made larger and heavier. Each proposed increment in size has presented difficult problems for the designer. In many cases he has been required to re-arrange important members and give new form to many details, but in accomplishing this he has succeeded in preserving in his design those elements of strength and simplicity which have hitherto characterized the American locomotive. At the same time he has greatly improved the general character of his design. Parts have been made stronger and at the same time lighter, materials entering into their construction have come to be more carefully chosen, and the workmanship expended upon them is of a higher character than ever before. The result is that the modern locomotive is not only marvelously certain in action but it is a machine of so high an order that the service required of it is continually more exacting.

From this brief review of results accomplished, it will be seen that progress in locomotive design has been finding expression entirely in the domain of mechanism. Nothing to which reference has been made can improve or in the least degree affect the thermodynamic action of the machine. Except for such progress as has been achieved in the matter of compounding, it is impossible to show that the locomotive of today delivers more work per pound of coal consumed than the locomotive of twenty years ago. Moreover, the conditions affecting the thermodynamic efficiency of a locomotive are so little understood that it happens not infrequently that a new engine is even less economical in its action than the engines of an older type. Referring to this matter, a prominent superintendent of motive power recently defined the situation by saying that he could point to a number of new locomotives, the cylinders, ports and valve gears of which had, in the working out of the designs, received unusual attention, but which now in service were "proving to be regular coal eaters." The adoption of the compound principle opens the way to important thermodynamic improvements, but the number of compound locomotives now running is still relatively small. The slow progress which has attended their introduction is in part, at least, due to a lack of definite information concerning their performance.

It not infrequently happens that locomotives of a new type when put into service fail to give the results that those responsible for their design had anticipated. The new engine may be larger than those previously employed and, if worked to its full power, may demand greater exertion on the part of its crew. Firemen may argue that if the new engines are forced to their full capacity the whole equipment of the road may soon be composed of similar engines, a change which would greatly increase the severity of their labor. Engineers sympathizing with their firemen, may run with a partially open throttle or with the reverse lever close to the center. When the engine tugs lazily up a slight grade they may refuse to drop the lever a few notches, saying, "She's doing all she'll do now. If the lever is dropped she doesn't seem to free herself," and the word goes around that the new engine, although heavier and larger than those of an older type, will do no more work. The purchaser perhaps withholds payment, disputes arise, time passes, effort is lost, and ill feeling engendered before the real facts are apprehended and a proper remedy applied.

E. H. McHenry, Chief Engineer of the Northern Pacific, writing in 1900, commented[356]:

it is quite certain that the opportunities for improvements in engine design are much greater than generally supposed. It is improbable that the specifications supplied to builders ever specify the engine horse-power desired and very rarely contain any information concerning the physical characteristics of the districts on which such engines are to be operated. Engine builders are usually better able to furnish engines of proper design than their customers are to furnish proper specifications

for engines best adapted to the kind of service and the local conditions in and under which they are to be operated. Attempts have been made from time to time to fix a definite relation and proportion between the weight on drivers, cylinder tractive power, heating surface and grate area but … the wide differences in physical operating conditions have never been taken into account.

Professor Goss summarized his hopes for the American locomotive of the future in muted terms[357]:

I look forward, then, to the representative American locomotive of the future, as an engine capable of exerting even greater power than the modern engine. I predict that it will be automatically supplied with fuel; its thermodynamic performance will be made high through the adoption of compound cylinders, and its mechanical action perfect, through the balancing of its reciprocating parts. With such a locomotive and with a track which is in keeping with the improved action of the locomotive which is to run upon it, the present generation will not need to blush when called upon to give over its responsibilities to that which is to follow.

A more nuts-and-bolts assessment was made in 1903.[358]

The development of the locomotive has been chiefly along the lines of increased size and power in response to the demands for heavy train loads and high speeds. The power of the boiler has increased at a greater rate than the power of the cylinders, so that the modern locomotive has a high steaming capacity. In order to keep the total weight of each engine within certain fixed limits, it has been necessary to pay close attention to the detailed design of the several parts so that the greatest possible weight could be placed in the boiler. Cast steel has been substituted for cast and wrought iron and wheel arrangements have been modified to accommodate the powerful boilers with their large grates and wide fireboxes.

The improvement of the steam locomotive's fundamentally poor fuel efficiency was a never-ending concern. An ARMMA survey in 1901 drew thirty-nine suggestions from twenty-six respondents.[359] Some of the replies come across as home-spun; most show little ability to "think outside the box"; generally they show frustration that only minor improvements were possible. The really big fuel economizer, superheating, was not mentioned, nor was the other source of future economy, longer trains and bigger engines. Also unconsidered was any alternative source of power to the steam locomotive itself.

The committee's discussion did mention superheating in guarded terms:

Superheating of steam is much in favor in stationary practice in Europe, and is beginning to receive considerable attention in this country. We understand that to some extent efforts have been made to apply the principle to locomotives with economical results and that tests are now under way in this country along the same lines.

On the other hand, by 1903, enough numerical information had accumulated that locomotives could be designed according to rational procedures.[360] Computational methods, however, were limited to the slide rule, tables of previously calculated results, nomograms and other graphical techniques.

This database enabled a designer to calculate the drawbar pull needed to haul a train of given weight against a given ruling curvature and adverse grade. Detailed design and the preparation of shop drawings could then follow.

Let us suppose that a railroad wanted an engine to accelerate a 2,000-ton train from rest to 10 miles per hour in 2 miles up a 1% grade with 5° of curvature, unassisted. This is no mean task and the result will be a big engine. The sum of rolling resistance, grade resistance, curvature resistance and acceleration effort, from the formulae quoted earlier, is about 57,000 pounds. Therefore the necessary adhesion weight, using a 25% adhesion factor, is 228,000 pounds. Restricting the axle load to (typically) 50,000-pounds necessitates five driving axles; the result will be a 2-10-0 or a 2-10-2, weighing about 268,000 pounds (taking adhesion weight as 85% of engine weight, the other 15% being supported on the trucks). We can select 57-inch driving wheels, boiler pressure 200 pounds per square inch and 30-inch piston stroke. Using the tractive effort formula, we can calculate the cylinder bore as 25 inches. [$T=(0.85Pd^2s)/D$, where T is the tractive effort in pounds, P is the maximum boiler pressure in pounds per square inch, d is the cylinder bore in inches, s is the piston stroke in inches and D is the driving wheel diameter in inches. So $d = \sqrt{((TD)/(Ps))} = \sqrt{((57,000 \times 57)/(0.85 \times 200 \times 30))} = 25$ inches.]

This engine will need to develop 1,520 drawbar horsepower ((57,000 pounds × 880 feet per minute)/33,000), 2,170 indicated horsepower (1,520/0.7). At a steam consumption rate of 27 pounds per indicated horsepower-hour, this will require a steaming rate of 58,590 pounds per hour. At an evaporation rate of 10 pounds per square foot of heating surface per hour, this requires 5,700 square feet of heating surface. A coal consumption rate of 4.5 pounds per indicated horsepower-hour and a firing rate not higher than 150 pounds of coal per square foot of grate per hour, implies a fuel burn of 9,765 pounds of coal per hour on a 65-square foot grate. Such an engine could not develop its maximum power with a human fireman.

By 1905–10, the Americans were building engines of these dimensions. Two or three smaller engines would supply similar performance, but at a cost in wages and other expenses. To increase the speed to 15 miles per hour, however, required only 4% more tractive effort but 57% more horsepower. This change would require an engine with 9,200 square feet of heating surface, burning 7½ tons of coal per hour on a 100-square foot grate. No such engine existed in 1905; this performance was unattainable with saturated steam. As long as it was restricted to saturated steam, human firemen and rigid-frame engines, the industry could be excused for thinking that the limits of steam locomotive performance had been reached. The breakthrough that superheating, power stokers and articulation achieved in the period 1905–1920 will become apparent in the next section of this book.

4

Locomotive Construction, 1895–1905

The American locomotive building industry of the 1890s had a productive capacity of about 2,000 locomotives a year, of which up to one third went for export. Of these, we may usefully examine particular locomotives and classes of locomotive, either because they were typical of their time and type or because they in some way advanced locomotive technology. The great majority differed from each other only in detail and did not advance technology. George H. Drury's *Guide to North American Steam Locomotives*, and his references, provides greater detail of the design and procurement histories of individual railroads and the composition of their locomotive fleets. Where a class of locomotive was built, the sources quoted here provide only the size of the initial order. Some orders were reduced or canceled; others were increased or repeated over a period of years. Drury provides the numbers of each class ultimately built.

Section 4.1 Development of the 4-4-0

New 4-4-0s were still being built in the 1890s, although more for passenger service than for their earlier general-purpose role. Railroads went on ordering them because they sufficed for the more lightly trafficked lines. Railroads with established 4-4-0 designs improved their details and increased their size as time went on. The Pennsylvania class P of 1894 originated in the class K of 1886, differing mainly in its dimensions.[1] Boiler pressure was 175 pounds per square inch, up from 140 pounds per square inch in the K, with a slightly smaller grate and more heating surface. The P had the Belpaire firebox favored by the Pennsylvania. Tractive effort was 16,100 pounds, up from 14,400 pounds in the K and, with driving wheels increased from 68 inches to 80, the P would have been a faster engine.

Some of the 4-4-0s built at this time were express locomotives, built for sustained fast running. In 1892, William Buchanan, Superintendent of Motive Power on the New York Central, designed the 800 class and ordered them from Schenectady.[2] A 27-square foot grate fired a 180-pounds per square inch boiler with 268 2-inch (outside diameter) fire tubes, giving a heating surface of 1,820 square feet. Two 19-inch × 24-inch cylinders drove 78-inch wheels for a tractive effort of 17,000 pounds. The tender carried 6¾ tons of coal and 3,500 gallons of water; the empty tender weighed 38,000 pounds. At 126,000 pounds engine weight, these were the heaviest and most powerful 4-4-0s of the time. They influenced the management of the New York Central and the Lake Shore to schedule a train from New York to Chicago in 19 hours—965 miles at 51 miles per hour, including stops. On the Empire State Express, the 800s "make the highest average speed for long distances on regular schedule time of any engine in this country," averaging 60 to 65 miles per hour for 100 to 120 miles.

Buchanan followed up with a one-off, high-speed 4-4-0, the No. 999, in 1893. The 190-pounds per square inch boiler contained 1,930 square feet of heating surface; 19-inch × 24-inch cylinders drove 86-inch driving wheels. Total engine weight was 124,000 pounds. This engine made the New York Central's controversial 100-mile per hour speed records, including one at 112 miles per hour on May 11, 1893; 4-4-0s would not surpass its dimensions for several years.

A 4-4-0 class I-6 on the Baltimore & Ohio was said to have made 92 miles per hour for 10 miles with a six-car train. These engines were built in 1892 to the design of G. B. Hazlehurst, General Superintendent of Motive Power, assisted by F. J. Cole, of whom we will hear more in his subsequent career with the American Locomotive Co.[3]

In 1894, Schenectady built two 4-4-0s for the Boston & Albany, similar in dimensions to the New York Central 800s, for the Boston-Chicago expresses between Springfield, Massachusetts, and Albany, New York. This section of the route totaled 103 miles through hilly country, scheduled for 183 minutes including one stop and, westbound, 12 miles of 1.5% adverse grade. The heating surface of these engines was 1,845 square feet, slightly more than the 800s. With 190 pounds per square inch boiler pressure, 19-inch × 24-inch cylinders (almost standard dimensions for this type) and 69-inch driving wheels, tractive effort was 20,250 pounds.[4]

The 4-4-0s built at Schenectady for the Chicago & North Western in 1895 were for fast running, hauling eleven-car passenger trains between Chicago and Council Bluffs.[5] A 30-square foot grate, with a brick arch supported on 3-inch water tubes (among the earlier known installations of arch tubes), fired a 190-pounds per square inch boiler with 1,900 square feet of heating surface; 19-inch × 24-inch pistons with balanced, Allen-ported slide valves powered 75-inch driving wheels. Cast steel reduced the weight of the running gear.

The two powerful 4-4-0s that Schenectady built for the Cleveland, Cincinnati, Chicago & St. Louis that same year may have been the first 4-4-0s with more than 2,000 square feet of heating surface and 200-pounds per square inch boilers. These were built for heavy passenger service over the 80 miles between Cleveland and Galion which included a 595-foot climb. The New York Central 800 class were built with crown bar fireboxes, but in just two years new construction shifted to Belpaire or radial stays.[6]

Recovery from the depression of 1893–5 brought new types of locomotive to challenge the dominance of the 4-4-0, even in the passenger service which had become its territory.

Several decided changes have been made recently in the construction of passenger locomotives and the later types are so varied in design that the question of the most suitable locomotive is a very interesting one. The Chicago, Burlington & Quincy has received from the Baldwin Locomotive Works an engine of the "Columbia" type, with a large firebox (45 square feet) and piston valves. This is one of the most novel locomotives built in this country for a long time…. The Baldwin Locomotive Works have built for the Philadelphia & Reading a locomotive

133

The New York Central's one-off 4-4-0, No. 999. Built at West Albany company shops. The location and date of this photograph are unknown (courtesy *Classic Trains* magazine collection, 20100322).

This Boston & Albany 4-4-0, No. 254, built at Schenectady in 1894, was a typical express passenger locomotive of the 1890s. When photographed at Boston, Massachusetts, on August 22, 1933, it was still in as-built condition with inside valve gear and slide valves (Denver Public Library, Otto C. Perry collection, OP-2644).

This Chicago & Alton 4-4-0, No. 504, was a predecessor to the class built by Brooks in 1900. Otto Perry photographed it at Kansas City, Missouri, on June 6, 1924 (Denver Public Library, Otto C. Perry collection, OP-2981).

This is one of the Pennsylvania's class D-16d's, No. 8167, built at Altoona in 1900, photographed at Cincinnati, Ohio, in May, 1919 (courtesy California State Railroad Museum).

with a large Wootten firebox and a single pair of drivers. This locomotive carries 200 lbs. steam pressure, has Vauclain compound cylinders, and is probably the most economical locomotive in America, judging from the results in actual service.[7]

Cast steel, instead of cast or wrought iron, was a big improvement in construction, resulting in lighter parts for the strength required. In 1896, W. Renshaw, Superintendent of Machinery for the Illinois Central, designed a 4-4-0 passenger engine; Brooks built eight.[8] Cast steel back cylinder heads, pistons, driving wheel centers and driving boxes cut the weight of these parts by one-quarter. The Illinois Central expected that these engines would reduce the time between Chicago and New Orleans by two hours.

The earlier compounds performed poorly in fast service; the great majority of these 4-4-0s were single-expansion. In 1895, however, Pittsburgh built a two-cylinder compound 4-4-0 for the Alabama Great Southern.[9]

Dimensions of heating surface and cylinders gradually increased. In 1899, Schenectady built four 4-4-0s for the Vandalia to run expresses between Indianapolis and St. Louis.[10] Although the grate area was still 30 square feet, firing a 190-pounds per square inch boiler, 320 2-inch fire tubes provided a total heating surface of 2,240 square feet. The cylinders were of 20-inch bore × 26-inch stroke, driving 78-inch driving wheels. The rated tractive effort of 21,500 pounds was the highest of any 4-4-0 to date. The Chicago & North Western 4-4-0s, built the same year to haul mail and passenger trains between Chicago and Omaha, were of similar dimensions to the Vandalia engines but managed to fit 2,500 square feet of heating surface into the 190-pounds per square inch boiler, the biggest boiler used on a 4-4-0 to date.[11]

The Chicago & Alton pushed the possibilities of the type still further with a class of twelve built by Brooks in 1900.[12] The grate area was now increased to 32 square feet, firing a 210-pounds per square inch boiler with 2,180 square feet of heating surface. The total engine weight was 139,000 pounds, while the tender, loaded with 12 tons of coal and 6,000 gallons of water, weighed another 120,000 pounds. The headlight was electric, powered by a steam-driven generator. Ten-inch piston valves replaced the earlier slide valves. Steel castings were used extensively in place of cast or forged iron. The engine weighed 139,000 pounds with a tractive effort of 23,000 pounds.

The American type soldiered on in some surprising situations. In 1900 the Pennsylvania started building its class D-16-d at Altoona, a class of 4-4-0s with dimensions and appearance that would not have been out of place ten years earlier.[13]

By 1905, the 4-4-0's days as a mainline engine were numbered and they were displaced to branch lines where the track and substructures would not support heavier engines. The Boston & Maine bought some new, but clearly old-style 4-4-0s as late as 1909–11.[14]

Section 4.2. *Fast Passenger Locomotives*

4.2.1 The Last 4-2-2s

Possibly the first 4-2-2 was built in Germany in 1841, but the wheel arrangement became common with British express passenger locomotives.[15] A single, huge driving wheel made high speeds possible with low cycling rates, while the single, fixed trailing wheel was capable of supporting a large firebox, although it is unclear whether the builders of the day sought, or were aware of those benefits. Tractive effort was, however, fatally limited.

In 1895, the Philadelphia & Reading bought a single, camelback, Vauclain compound 4-2-2 from Baldwin.[16] Earlier, in 1880, Baldwin had built another 4-2-2 for the Reading and during 1894–5 the Reading had been running one of its 4-4-0s with the side rods disconnected, making it, in effect, a 4-2-2. There was no doubt that the new engine was powerful; it hauled 430-ton passenger trains. It was also fast, reaching speeds of 75 miles per hour. It seems to have been a success in the service for which it was designed but

it was found to be practically impossible to find a service for which this type of engine was adapted. It might have a suitable train one way over the road but on the return trip the load or number of stops would almost invariably render schedule time an impossibility. Also when shortage of power exists (a chronic condition in American railroad service) and the engine pool is resorted to, an engine of this type is utterly unfitted for the service.

The Philadelphia & Reading bought a second 4-2-2 in 1896, but both were rebuilt as 4-4-0s in 1903–4, first with 84-inch driving wheels and later with 78-inch drivers.[17]

The 1902 ICC census lists no 4-2-2s at all but, as late as 1921, the Boston & Maine was still running at least one that, from its appearance, must have been built in the 1870s or 1880s. The company rebuilt it as a 4-4-0 in that year.[18]

4.2.2. The Abortive Columbia Wheel Arrangement

The first departure from the 4-4-0 wheel arrangement in fast passenger service was the experimental locomotive *Columbia*, built by Baldwin as a demonstrator with a 2-4-2 wheel arrangement and exhibited at the 1893 World's Fair at Chicago.[19] As the grate area was only 25 square feet which was later exceeded in 4-4-0s, the benefit of the trailing axle is not clear. A 4-4-0 carried the firebox between the two driving axles; the connecting rods drove the front driving axle. The *Columbia* firebox was placed behind the enormous 84-inch driving wheels, supported on a fixed trailing axle; the connecting rods drove the rear driving axle. The front and rear carrying wheels were 54 inches in diameter, as large as the driving wheels of some freight engines. The driving wheel suspension was not connected by equalizers; the suspension was equalized between the front driving wheels and the front truck and between the back driving wheels and the trailing axle. Firebox and tube surface totaling 1,480 square feet heated a 200-pounds-per-square inch boiler. The engine was a Vauclain compound, with 13-inch high-pressure and 22-inch low-pressure cylinders with 26-inch stroke and weighed 126,650 pounds. In April 1894, the Baltimore & Ohio tested it between Baltimore, Jersey City and Washington. The engine was able to make schedules that existing power could not. Although its dimensions were similar to those of existing engines, the combination of a deep firebox, high boiler pressure and large driving wheels may have been the source of its greater speed. For many of these runs the engine burned coke with the brick arch removed from the firebox.[20]

Baldwin built eleven similar engines for the Philadelphia & Reading in 1893, but with a 35-square foot grate, Wootten firebox, camelback cab and 129,700 pounds engine weight.[21] These engines were fast, but unstable at high speed; serious maintenance problems began to appear after only a year in service.[22] The Reading rebuilt them as 2-6-0s in about 1904 but, even so, soon scrapped them.[23]

The first order for this type of engine after the Philadelphia & Reading's was not until 1895 when the Chicago, Burlington & Quincy ordered their class N from Baldwin.[24] G. W. Rhodes, Superintendent of Motive Power, selected the general arrangement, leaving detailed design to Baldwin. The design retained the 84-inch driving wheels and large carrying wheels of the *Columbia*, but used the trailing axle to install a 44-square foot grate, intending to get the firing rate down to a combustion-efficient 100 to 125 pounds of coal per square foot of grate per hour. The firebox was radially stayed with a combustion chamber extending 34 inches forward of the throat sheet. The boiler pressure was 200 pounds per square inch with 1,580 square feet of heating surface, driving single-expansion 19-inch × 26-inch pistons,

The Philadelphia & Reading's 4-2-2 Vauclain compound, No. 378, built by Baldwin in 1896. The location and date of the photograph are unknown (courtesy California State Railroad Museum, Negative 16945).

The Baldwin demonstrator 2-4-2 locomotive, *Columbia*, built in 1893 (Pennsylvania Historical and Museum Commission and Railroad Museum of Pennsylvania, General Negative 58067).

supplied through one of the earlier applications of the piston valve in American locomotives. The suspension followed *Columbia* practice. The tender departed from American practice in having three rigidly mounted axles, rather than the usual two four-wheel bogies, carrying 7 tons of coal and 4,200 gallons of water. Total engine weight was 138,000 pounds, developing a rated tractive effort of 18,900 pounds. This engine was of advanced design for its time.

The 2-4-2 wheel arrangement had a short life in America. It was

immediately superseded by the 4-4-2 which was more stable at high speeds and better suited to carrying a big boiler.

4.2.3 Pursuit of High Power at High Speed: The First Atlantics

The 4-4-2 design originated with a Baldwin locomotive built for a high steaming rate within a limit of 72,000 pounds on driving

One of the first Atlantics, Atlantic Coast Line's 4-4-2, No. 153, built by Baldwin sometime between 1894 and 1900 (courtesy *Classic Trains* magazine collection, 20120702).

wheels. Neither the 2-4-2 nor the 4-4-0 could meet this requirement. The four-wheel leading truck supported the longer boiler needed for the necessary 2,400 square feet of heating surface.[25] Vauclain, never shy about his own achievements, was generous enough to attribute the idea to J. N. Barr of the Chicago, Milwaukee & St. Paul.[26]

Orders for 4-4-2s got off to a slow start in the depression years after Baldwin built the first one in 1893 for the Atlantic Coast Line, hence the type name "Atlantic." The Atlantic Coast Line bought ten more between 1894 and 1900, also two 2-4-2s as an experiment.[27]

The next order came from the Central of New Jersey in 1896. This engine was a camelback 13- & 20-inch × 26-inch Vauclain compound with a 76-square foot grate under a Wootten firebox. The boiler contained 278 1¾-inch fire tubes, 13 feet over tube sheets, for a heating surface of 1,835 square feet. Total engine weight was 141,000 pounds.[28] The same year the Philadelphia & Reading put two Baldwin 4-4-2s into service on passenger expresses between Philadelphia and Atlantic City of similar dimensions to the Jersey Central engine, including a Wootten firebox and 84½-inch driving wheels.[29]

At the same time Baldwin built two 13- & 22-inch × 26-inch Vauclain compound 4-4-2s for the Chicago, Milwaukee & St. Paul. These engines had conventional cabs and 30-square foot grates for bituminous coal. With the firebox, the 264 2-inch × 15-foot fire tubes provided 2,245 square feet of heating surface. Total engine weight was 140,700 pounds.[30] These engines illustrate the purpose of the 4-4-2 wheel arrangement, to carry a bigger firebox and boiler than existing 4-4-0s. One of the Chicago, Milwaukee & St. Paul engines hauled a 500-ton train over the 85 miles from Chicago to Milwaukee in 1 hour, 55 minutes, reaching 80 miles per hour, having clearly solved earlier problems with the high-speed performance of compounds.

With improving economic conditions, orders for 4-4-2s followed more quickly. Later in 1896 the Lehigh Valley ordered five from Baldwin; the Lehigh Valley's Superintendent of Motive Power directed the design.[31] These were single-expansion, camelback, anthracite-burners with Wootten fireboxes and 64-square foot grates. The trailing axle was rigidly mounted in sprung journal boxes in a rear extension of the frame. The 76-inch driving wheels and trailing axle were

suspension-equalized. The leading truck was independently sprung. Seventeen manufacturers supplied parts, such as cast-steel wheel centers, injectors, safety valves, brake parts and piston packings.

In 1898, the Wabash ordered twenty-five engines, comprising 4-6-0 freight engines and 4-4-2 passenger engines designed by J. B. Barnes, Superintendent of Motive Power,[32] incorporating the greatest possible number of interchangeable parts. The company split the order between Baldwin (five single-expansion 4-4-2s, five single-expansion 4-6-0s), Pittsburgh Locomotive Works (five single-expansion 4-6-0s) and Richmond Locomotive Works (five single-expansion 4-6-0s, two two-cylinder compound 4-6-0s). Both types weighed 137,000 pounds. The 4-4-2s had 32-square foot grates, 200-pounds per square inch boilers, a large heating surface of 2,425 square feet and 19-inch × 26-inch cylinders powering 73-inch driving wheels for a tractive effort of 21,850 pounds.

The two 4-4-2s that Baldwin built for the Chicago, Burlington & Quincy in 1899 set new records for size and power in passenger locomotives.[33] They were substantially heavier, at 159,000 pounds, than their predecessors. A 35-square foot grate fired a 210-pounds per square inch boiler with 2,500 square feet of heating surface. The Vauclain compound 13½-inch & 23-inch × 26-inch cylinders drove 84½-inch driving wheels. The Chicago, Burlington & Quincy ordered them for comparison with the 2-4-2 *Columbia*, at the same time ordering a 2-6-0 with piston valves and two 2-6-0s with slide valves as a guide for future procurement.

The year 1899 saw the first appearance of the Pennsylvania's class E-1 4-4-2 designed and built at Altoona.[34] The Pennsylvania class E 4-4-2s, culminating in the E-6, were among the finest of the type. First came three engines for fast passenger service between Philadelphia and Atlantic City—single-expansion camelbacks with Wootten fireboxes, combustion chambers and 69-square foot grates. The 185-pounds per square inch boilers contained 2,320 square feet of heating surface, including 353 1¾-inch fire tubes. The 20½-inch × 26-inch cylinders drove 80-inch driving wheels, providing a tractive effort of 21,500 pounds. The engines were heavy for the type at 173,450 pounds with over 50,000 pounds axle loading. Tested with a 410-ton

The Wabash 4-4-2; the class G's were built by the Baldwin, Pittsburgh and Richmond locomotive works in 1898. Otto Perry photographed No. 603 at Moberly, Missouri, on October 26, 1929 (Denver Public Library, Otto C. Perry collection, OP-19665).

The Pennsylvania Class E-1 4-4-2, No. 820, built at Altoona in 1899 and photographed at Atlantic City, New Jersey, the same year. The E-1's were the first of a line of successful Pennsylvania 4-4-2s (Pennsylvania Historical and Museum Commission and Railroad Museum of Pennsylvania, Harris Negative 08703).

The Pennsylvania class E-2 4-4-2, No. 1984; Altoona shops and Alco built the class between 1901 and 1909. The date of this photograph is 1915, location unknown (Pennsylvania Historical and Museum Commission and Railroad Museum of Pennsylvania, Railroad History Corporation Negative 04773).

trailing load, one of these engines covered the 33 miles from Philadelphia to Trenton in less than 35 minutes.

The E-1 was followed by the E-2 in 1900, built at first as a single example.[35] The Pennsylvania recognized the disadvantages of the camelback cab in preventing the engineer and fireman from working as a crew. Accordingly, the cab was placed at the back behind a 51-square foot grate, a wide, standard-type firebox and 2,430 square feet of heating surface. The Pennsylvania put a modified version of the E-2 into production in 1901, reclassing the original E-2 as E-1a. The new E-2 had 2,640 square feet of heating surface and a 205-pounds per square inch boiler. On June 12, 1905, an E-2 was clocked at 127 miles per hour over 3 miles near Elida, Ohio, hauling the *Pennsylvania Special* between Crestline, Ohio, and Fort Wayne, Indiana.[36] Altoona built 102 of them between then and 1909.[37]

The E-3 followed immediately with 22-inch cylinders instead of 20½-inch and in 1902 the Pennsylvania brought out the E-2a and E-3a with Belpaire fireboxes. Strong track and substructures enabled the company to build up to axle loads of 60,000 pounds. In 1903, Alco built thirty-two 4-4-2s for the Pennsylvania, nine with piston valves (E-2b) and twenty-three with Richardson-balanced slide valves (E-2c).

Robert Quayle, Superintendent of Motive Power and Machinery on the Chicago & North Western, designed a 4-4-2, of which Schenectady built an initial six in 1900.[38] A large, 46-square foot grate brought firing rates and draft down to levels permitting efficient combustion and evaporation and fired a 200-pounds per square inch boiler with 3,015 square feet of heating surface, including 338 2-inch fire tubes. The new engines used 20% less fuel than 4-4-0s in the same service with their smaller boilers and grates. The firebox contained a brick arch supported on water tubes. As a concession to the width of the grate, the backhead had two fire doors. The water legs were 4 to 5 inches wide at the sides, 3½ to 5 inches wide at the back and 3½ to 4½ inches at the front—generous dimensions for the time. All staybolts were drilled with telltale holes. Piston valves supplied steam to 20-inch × 26-inch cylinders driving 80-inch wheels. Wheel centers, crossheads, pistons, driving boxes and the pedestals for the trailing axle were of cast steel. The trailing axle was still mounted rigidly in a frame extension, as distinct from the trucks that would come later. Total engine weight was 158,000 pounds. A further eighty-five followed from Schenectady between then and 1908.[39]

The Chicago & North Western called their 4-4-2 the *Northwestern* type. The Burlington, Cedar Rapids & Northern called theirs the *Chautauqua*. Brooks built three for the latter company in 1900.[40] The Belpaire firebox, with its 45-square foot grate, was supported between the back driving wheel axle and the trailing axle, unlike previous designs where the firebox was above the trailing axle. The boiler was built for 210 pounds per square inch with 2,550 square feet of heating surface. Piston valves supplied steam to the 19½-inch × 26-inch cylinders, driving 75-inch wheels. Tractive effort was 23,500 pounds.

The New York Central endorsed the 4-4-2 on a large scale, ordering twenty from Schenectady for completion in 1901, following design and consultations between the two companies going back to early 1900.[41] These engines were to replace the highly developed 4-4-0s mentioned earlier. When their performance became known, four other railroads with work in progress at Schenectady asked for their orders to be changed to this type.

The firebox was 6 feet 4 inches wide—thus about 7 feet wide over the wrapper sheet, including the water legs. This allowed for a 50-

The Chicago & North Western class D 4-4-2. Alco built this class between 1900 and 1908. Otto Perry photographed No. 1091 at Chadron, Nebraska, on April 12, 1936 (Denver Public Library, Otto C. Perry collection, OP-3111).

Alco built the New York Central class I 4-4-2s between 1901 and 1907. No. 856 had been retrofitted with Baker valve gear by the time Otto Perry took this photograph at Cleveland, Ohio, on November 3, 1927 (Denver Public Library, Otto C. Perry collection, OP-13337).

square foot grate, while the fireman had to throw coal over no more than 8 feet of grate length. The radially stayed firebox contained a brick arch supported on arch tubes. The 200-pounds per square inch boiler contained 396 2-inch fire tubes contributing to a heating surface unprecedented in a four-coupled engine: 3,505 square feet. Twelve-inch piston valves admitted steam to the 21-inch × 26-inch cylinders, driving 79-inch wheels. Tractive effort was 24,650 pounds. Already heavy at 176,000 pounds, the engines had a compressed-air-powered lever in the suspension equalizer between the back driving axle and the trailing axle that could increase adhesion weight by shifting 10,000 pounds onto the drivers. Production of this class and its variants between 1901 and 1907 totaled 213, all from Schenectady.[42]

These engines were as remarkable in performance as in design.[43] Under test, one of them averaged 46 miles per hour over the 143 miles between New York and Albany with a 685-ton trailing load of thirteen cars. The highest recorded power output was 1,452 indicated horsepower.

The next substantial order for 4-4-2s was from the Chicago, Milwaukee & St. Paul.[44] Baldwin built nine in 1901 as Vauclain compounds with cylinders of 15-inch & 25-inch bore × 28-inch stroke and 84-inch driving wheels. The total heating surface was 3,200 square feet. Each engine weighed 170,000 pounds. They were soon hauling 490-ton trains between Chicago and Milwaukee at average speeds close to 60 miles per hour.[45]

Later in 1901, Brooks, by then a plant of the American Locomotive Co., built a pair of 4-4-2s for the Buffalo, Rochester & Pittsburgh. Dimensions were intermediate between the earlier Brooks 4-4-2s and the New York Central class I. The important innovation was a trailing axle mounted in a spring-centered radial truck, patented that year by John Player, Mechanical Engineer at Brooks.[46]

Orders for 4-4-2s increased. Late in 1901, Brooks delivered three

to the Central of New Jersey, three more in 1902.[47] At 190,000 pounds, these were the heaviest 4-4-2s built to date—anthracite-burning, single-expansion camelbacks with Wootten fireboxes supported on Player trucks, 82-square foot grates, 210-pounds per square inch boilers, 2,970 square feet of heating surface, 20½-inch × 26-inch cylinders and 85-inch driving wheels. The tender carried 12 tons of coal and 6,000 gallons of water. Alco built twenty 4-4-2s for the Chesapeake & Ohio between 1902 and 1916, of similar dimensions to the New York Central class I.[48] Brooks built forty for the Cleveland, Cincinnati, Chicago & St. Louis between 1902 and 1904.[49] Baldwin built nine oil-burning Vauclain compounds with Vanderbilt boilers for the Southern Pacific in 1903. These were unusual in having the connecting rods driving on the front driving axle.[50]

Ominous for devotees of the compound was the Baltimore & Ohio's decision in 1903 to go with single expansion in its new 4-4-2s. Baldwin built the B & O's first 4-4-2s in 1901—six 149,600-pound Vauclain compounds with 43-square foot grates, 200-pounds per square inch boilers and 2,665 square feet of heating surface. Only two years later the company decided to upgrade with a bigger version. The result weighed 180,000 pounds with a 56-square foot grate, a 205-pounds per square inch boiler and 2,640 square feet of heating surface. Cylinders measuring 22 inches × 26 inches provided a tractive effort of 27,400 pounds, the highest to date for a 4-4-2. This was a slap in the face for Baldwin because the engines were single-expansion and Schenectady got orders for twenty.[51]

Alco Schenectady built a 4-4-2 balanced compound speculatively to the design of their Mechanical Engineer, F. J. Cole, adapting the French de Glehn four-cylinder balanced compound to American practice.[52] The New York Central bought the engine in 1904, displayed it at the St. Louis World's Fair and put it into fast, heavy passenger

A Chicago, Milwaukee & St. Paul class A-2 4-4-2, No. 3121, built by Baldwin in 1901, photographed at Davenport, Iowa, on July 23, 1923 (Denver Public Library, Otto C. Perry collection, OP-5023).

A Buffalo, Rochester & Pittsburgh class W 4-4-2, No. 160, built by Alco in 1901, photographed in 1928—location unknown (Denver Public Library, Otto C. Perry collection, OP-2770).

A Baltimore & Ohio class A-2 4-4-2, No. 1470, built by Alco in 1903, photographed at Cincinnati, Ohio, in September, 1919 (Denver Public Library, Otto C. Perry collection, OP-2424).

Baldwin built the Atchison, Topeka & Santa Fe's balanced compound class 507 4-4-2s, in 1904, including No. 537, photographed at Palmer Lake, Colorado, on July 20, 1919 (Denver Public Library, Otto C. Perry collection, OP-50).

service. A 50-square foot grate fired 3,445 square feet of heating surface—including 390 2-inch × 16-foot fire tubes and 3½-inch-5½-inch water legs, producing steam at the abnormally high pressure of 220 pounds per square inch. The two 15½-inch high-pressure cylinders were between the frames (opposite to the de Glehn layout), slightly forward of the smokebox, driving the front, cranked, driving axle. The two 26-inch low-pressure cylinders, mounted outside the frame, drove the back driving axle. Steam admission was by tandem piston valves, with the high- and low-pressure valves on the same stem. The 79-inch driving wheels were suspension-equalized with the trailing axle; the front truck was independently sprung. Because the balancing did away with hammer blow, the New York Central accepted a 55,000-pound axle load on the driving wheels, 50,000 pounds being the usual maximum, and that was high by American standards of the time, reflecting the New York Central's heavily built, heavily used roadbed. This was the biggest 4-4-2 to date, weighing 200,000 pounds. Working single-expansion, the engine would have had a tractive effort of 27,850 pounds. No further engines of this type followed on the New York Central.

Baldwin was also building 4-4-2 four-cylinder balanced compounds. One class that they built for the Santa Fe had the inside-mounted high-pressure cylinders and outside-mounted low-pressure cylinders all driving on the front driving axle. These were a big success and, including modified versions, Baldwin supplied 132 to the Santa Fe between 1904 and 1910. Baldwin also built a class of twenty for the Chicago, Burlington & Quincy with the outside-mounted high-pressure cylinders driving on the back driving axle.[53]

By 1905, the 4-4-2 still had years of fame ahead of it as an express passenger locomotive, especially on the New York Central and the Pennsylvania. About twenty other railroads used it in substantial numbers in areas of dense passenger traffic and flat terrain. The

biggest user was the New York Central with total procurement of 329, followed by the Pennsylvania with 246. Others were the Santa Fe (172), the Boston & Maine (41), the Baltimore & Ohio (65), the Chicago, Milwaukee & St. Paul (57), the Chicago, Burlington & Quincy (91), the Chicago & Eastern Illinois (26), the Chicago & North Western (91), the Chicago, Rock Island & Pacific (30), the Erie (57), the Illinois Central (37), the Lehigh Valley (30), the Missouri Pacific (40), the Philadelphia & Reading (51), the Southern Pacific (87), the Union Pacific (66) and the Wabash (28).

The 4-4-2 went the way of the 4-4-0 in the end because it did not have the pulling power for ever longer trains of steel cars, especially where heavy adverse grades stood in its way, while keeping axle loadings within acceptable limits. It was displaced by the 4-6-2.

Section 4.2.4 Heavy Passenger Power: The First Pacifics

For one of the most successful types in locomotive history, the 4-6-2 had inauspicious beginnings. The unsuccessful Strong locomotive of 1886 with a duplex firebox was probably the first 4-6-2 in America.[54] The Chicago, Milwaukee & St. Paul bought a 4-6-2 from Schenectady in 1887; in 1893, the Rhode Island Locomotive Works built three more for the same company.[55] The trailing axle was intended to spread the locomotive's weight so that it could haul heavy passenger trains at high speeds over light track.

The three built in 1893 were two-cylinder compounds with 21-inch & 31-inch × 26-inch cylinders and 78-inch driving wheels. A 24-square foot grate fired 1,790 square feet of heating surface, producing steam at the abnormally high pressure of 200 pounds per square inch. The weight was modest for an engine of that size—

One of the first 4-6-2s, Chicago, Milwaukee & St. Paul No. 796, built by Schenectady or Rhode Island. The date and location of the photograph are unknown (courtesy *Classic Trains* magazine collection, 20121206).

143,000 pounds—with an axle loading of only 29,500 pounds. In the absence of any classification system, they were called a "ten-wheeler with a trailing axle," also described by Angus Sinclair, as "...an odd type of engine, being a big ten-wheeler with a pair of trailing wheels extra placed behind the drivers."

Surprisingly for engines with such apparent chances of success, they were a failure. The Chicago, Milwaukee & St. Paul returned all three to the manufacturer because they could not do the work required of them. Rhode Island sold them to the Plant System (the Savannah, Florida & Western Railway and its subsidiaries). W. E. Symons, Superintendent of Motive Power with the Plant System remarked, in October 1901: "I purchased these engines, however, at a time when we were badly pinched for power, and I was compelled to take them in the condition I found them in, except that I had two of them changed from compound to simple." So much for compounding, even at that early date! In 1902, the Atlantic Coast Line took over the Plant System—and the three 4-6-2s with it—and converted them to 4-6-0s in 1912, reducing the driving wheel diameter at the same time.[56]

This wheel arrangement did not reappear in U.S. domestic service for nearly ten years. In 1902 two railroads adopted it.[57] W. S. Morris, Superintendent of Motive Power on the Chesapeake & Ohio, designed one and had it built at Alco Schenectady. Morris put the

wheel arrangement to good use with a 47-square foot grate and 3,535 square feet of boiler heating surface; steam at 200 pounds per square inch produced 32,000 pounds of tractive effort. Piston valves admitted steam to 22-inch × 28-inch cylinders, driving 72-inch wheels. This engine weighed 187,000 pounds. Assuming an evaporation rate of 10 pounds of water per square foot of heating surface per hour and a steam consumption rate of 26 pounds per indicated horsepower-hour, such an engine would have been capable of 1,360 indicated horsepower. Alco built twenty-seven of these engines for the Chesapeake & Ohio between 1902 and 1911; they were the Chesapeake & Ohio's most numerous class of 4-6-2.[58]

The Missouri Pacific was another early user; Alco Brooks built twenty-one smaller 4-6-2s for the company in 1902–3. The fireboxes had brick arches supported on arch tubes. Brooks used steel castings for some parts but retained wrought iron for the frames. These engines weighed 173,000 pounds with 69-inch driving wheels and 2,955 square feet of heating surface.[59]

With increasing demands for fast, heavy passenger trains, often to be hauled through hilly country, the 4-6-2 soon caught on. The new wheel arrangement gave ample scope for big boilers and fireboxes and the industry made full use of it. Baldwin named the new wheel arrangement *Pacific*, a name it has borne ever since.[60] The two that Baldwin built for the Chicago & Alton in 1902 were the biggest

An early 4-6-2 was the Chesapeake & Ohio class F-15, built by Alco between 1902 and 1911. No. 451 was still in service when Otto Perry photographed it at Clifton Forge, Virginia, on August 4, 1936. The Walschaert valve gear may be original or retrofit (Denver Public Library, Otto C. Perry collection, OP-2870).

A Missouri Pacific class P-69 4-6-2, No. 6516, built by Alco in 1902–03, photographed at St. Louis, Missouri, on October 24, 1921 (Denver Public Library, Otto C. Perry collection, OP-13025).

passenger engines built to date. These potent locomotives decisively broke out of the restrictions of the four-coupled passenger locomotive. They weighed 230,000 and 236,000 pounds, one having 80-inch driving wheels, the other 73-inch. Large 54-square foot grates fired 220-pounds per square inch boilers, 20 feet long over tube sheets, containing 4,065 square feet of heating surface. The 22-inch × 28-inch cylinders provided 34,700 pounds of tractive effort and theoretically 1,500 indicated horsepower. Even so, the Chicago & Alton did not order 4-6-2s in quantity until 1909 and then from Brooks and not Baldwin.[61]

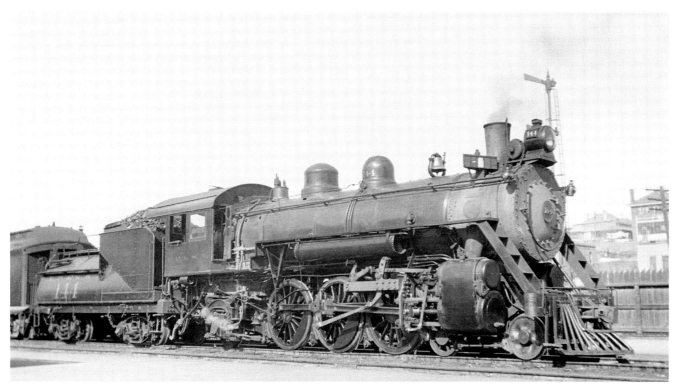

A photograph in the *Railroad Gazette* shows that El Paso & Southwestern 4-6-2, No. 144, built by Baldwin in 1903, had been retrofitted with Walschaert valve gear, piston valves and a Vanderbilt tender by the time Otto Perry photographed it at El Paso, Texas, on January 21, 1919 (Denver Public Library, Otto C. Perry collection, OP-11565).

Another early 4-6-2 on a New York Central subsidiary, the Cleveland, Cincinnati, Chicago & St. Louis, was class Kb, No. 6401, built by Alco in 1905 and photographed at Indianapolis, Indiana, on September 22, 1930 (Denver Public Library, Otto C. Perry collection, OP-13444).

In 1903, Baldwin delivered four 4-6-2s to the El Paso & South-western of slightly smaller dimensions than the Chicago & Alton engines.[62] With 63-inch driving wheels, these engines were intended for fast freight rather than passenger service, hauling 1,000-ton trains at 10 miles per hour up 1% grades.

The New York Central commissioned its first 4-6-2 from Schenectady in 1903; the New York Central and its subsidiaries procured 1,033 between then and 1930.

When the Michigan Central bought its first 4-6-2 in 1904, innovations were a cast steel frame and a trailing truck, as distinct from a trailing axle fixed in a frame extension.[63]

Even the first American 4-6-2s were bigger than the ultimate British 4-6-2 development in the 1950s; the *Britannia* class there had 42-square foot grates, 2,470 square feet of heating surface, weighed 214,580 pounds and were rated at 32,000 pounds of tractive effort.

While the 4-4-2 was starting to reach the limits of its usefulness in America by 1905, the glory days of the 4-6-2 were just beginning. Although later outclassed by the 4-8-2s and 4-8-4s, they sufficed for the passenger needs of many railroads until the end of steam.

Section 4.3 Six-Coupled, Multi-Purpose Locomotives

As early as the mid–1800s, railroads began to look for power that the 4-4-0s could not provide. Engines with six coupled driving wheels and leading trucks were an answer to this problem, putting a higher percentage of weight into adhesion, spread over more axles to run on light track. The 2-6-0s ("Moguls") and 4-6-0s ("Ten-Wheelers") flourished in the 1890s and early 1900s in both passenger and freight service but were superseded by the 4-6-2s in passenger service and the 2-8-0s and 2-8-2s on freight. They were not the biggest or the fastest, but they unobtrusively took over where the 4-4-0s left off as versatile, multi-purpose engines offering a good compromise between speed and pulling power. In 1902, they comprised 33% of the U.S. locomotive fleet. A trailing axle, supporting a wide, deep firebox, developed the briefly popular 2-6-2 wheel arrangement.

4.3.1 Multi-Purpose Ten-Wheelers

The 4-6-0s of the early and middle 1890s differed remarkably little from contemporary 4-4-0s. The four that Schenectady built for the Chicago & North Western in 1893 were 4-4-0s with a third pair of driving wheels squeezed into the space between the front driving wheels and the cylinders. At 120,000 pounds engine weight, 18-square foot grate, 1,800-square foot heating surface, 170-pounds per square inch boiler pressure and 19-inch × 24-inch cylinders, the dimensions were similar to those of 4-4-0s that were being built at the time. The advantage lay in spreading the adhesion weight over more axles, lightening the axle loading and making the locomotive easier on light track. Western railroads favored the 4-6-0 for this reason.[64] Because the weight of a 4-4-0 bridged the gap between the driving wheels and the truck, only about 65% of the engine weight was available for adhesion. The 4-6-0 raised this figure to 80%, the 2-6-0 still further to about 87%. The extra weight that the axles could carry while staying within load limits went into longer boilers and more heating surface.

In the Delaware, Lackawanna & Western's hilly territory heavier passenger trains outmatched the pulling power of the 4-4-0s. In 1893, the company built a 4-6-0 for this service in its own shops, a camelback anthracite-burner with a Wootten firebox and an 84-square foot grate.[65] The driving wheels were only 62 inches in diameter, so the firebox could extend over them. The total heating surface was 1,935

square feet; boiler pressure was only 160 pounds per square inch. Three driving axles kept the axle loading down to 36,650 pounds for a total engine weight of 137,000 pounds. The anthracite-burning, camelback 4-6-0 with a Wootten firebox became common in the northeastern U.S. during the 1890s.

The 4-6-0 that the Pittsburgh Locomotive Works built for passenger service on the Terre Haute & Indianapolis that same year was a good compromise between speed and hauling power.[66] A typical 4-4-0, weighing 126,000 pounds, might have an adhesion weight of 83,000 pounds and an axle loading of 41,500 pounds. The Terre Haute & Indianapolis 4-6-0, weighing 137,000 pounds with a 32-square foot grate and 2,235 square feet of heating surface, had 110,000 pounds of adhesion weight, but an axle loading of only 36,650 pounds. According to the available drawings, the firebox was stayed in a transitional manner between crown bars and radial stays with stiffening bars partway between the crown sheet and the wrapper sheet.

The twenty 4-6-0s that the Southern Pacific ordered from the Cooke Locomotive & Machine Co., Paterson, New Jersey, in 1894 demonstrated the multi-purpose nature of this wheel arrangement. Some were for passenger service, some for freight, differing only in driving wheel diameter.[67]

The German electrical engineering manufacturer, Siemens & Halske, made a brief and unsuccessful foray into American steam locomotive building when it bought the bankrupt Grant Locomotive Works in Chicago. On the books was an order from the Chicago, Burlington & Quincy for fifty-five locomotives. The Burlington reduced their order to twenty 4-6-0s. There was nothing special about these engines; the venture failed.[68]

In 1895, the Chesapeake & Ohio worked with the Richmond Locomotive & Machine Works to build a two-cylinder compound version of the company's class F-1 4-6-0s to haul 350-ton passenger trains on a 3 hours 10 minutes schedule over the 96 miles between Charlottesville, Virginia, and Clifton Forge, crossing the Blue Ridge and North Mountain with adverse grades up to 1.6%.[69] A 33-square foot grate fired 1,950 square feet of heating surface. The brick arch was supported on water tubes; these went up through the crown sheet at their back ends instead of through the back firebox sheet. Boiler pressure—high for the time at 200 pounds per square inch—powered 20-inch and 32-inch × 24-inch cylinders. Driving wheels 62 inches in diameter emphasized pulling power over speed. The resulting engine weighed 145,000 pounds, of which the 115,000-pound adhesion weight would have permitted a tractive effort of about 29,000 pounds.

With increasing passenger train weights and increasing traffic after the depression, the 4-6-0 encroached on the fast-passenger territory hitherto occupied by the 4-4-0. Orders came apace in 1896–7. In 1896, the Lake Shore & Michigan Southern put 4-6-0s into service on expresses between Buffalo and Chicago.[70] Cast steel was used extensively to meet weight limits of 118,000 pounds total engine weight and 90,000 pounds on driving wheels. Three years later, Brooks built eleven 4-6-0s for the Lake Shore, much bigger at 171,600 pounds engine weight, to haul 14-car passenger trains at sustained speeds of 60 miles per hour. A 34-square foot grate fired a 210-pounds per square inch boiler with 2,915 square feet of heating surface. Slide valves, Richardson-balanced and Allen-ported, supplied 20-inch × 28-inch cylinders, powering 80-inch driving wheels.

The split was typically, but not always, between 2-6-0s for freight and 4-6-0s for passenger service. E. M. Herr, Superintendent of Motive Power for the Northern Pacific, and an advocate of compounding, designed a 4-6-0 cross-compound freight engine in consultation with Schenectady, the first of which came out in 1897.[71]

The Northern Pacific bought the class P-2 4-6-0s from Alco as cross-compounds between 1900 and 1902. No. 240 had been converted to single-expansion with piston valves, although retaining inside valve gear, by the time Otto Perry photographed it at Tacoma, Washington, on October 2, 1931 (Denver Public Library, Otto C. Perry collection, OP-13891).

These engines were the biggest 4-6-0s built to date, weighing 172,500 pounds with 200-pounds per square inch boiler pressure and 2,895 square feet of heating surface. The two cylinders were 22 and 34 inches bore × 26 inches stroke. With 63-inch driving wheels and Allen-ported slide valves, these engines were built for speed as well as pulling power. At the same time Schenectady built some 4-6-0 compound passenger engines for the Northern Pacific similar to the freight engines, but lighter at 155,000 pounds engine weight, with less heating surface (2,485 square feet) and bigger driving wheels (69 inches diameter).[72] Schenectady built a further 4-6-0 passenger engine for the Northern Pacific of closely similar dimensions, but single-expansion and hence 5,000 pounds lighter.

One of the less known builders of steam locomotives was the Dickson Manufacturing Co. of Scranton, Pennsylvania. In 1897, Dickson built eight 156,800-pound 4-6-0s for the Santa Fe, to a design by John Player, the Santa Fe's Superintendent of Machinery. These class B-13's were for heavy passenger trains between Topeka, Kansas, and Las Vegas, New Mexico.[73] This route included open prairie, where side winds added substantially to train resistance—side winds pushed the train sideways so that the downwind wheel flanges ground on the downwind rail, and the Raton Pass between Trinidad, Colorado, and Raton, New Mexico, with grades up to 3.5% with heavy curvature. Even so, these engines were of unremarkable dimensions and were built with the obsolete crown bar firebox.

The 4-6-0s built at Schenectady for the Chicago & North Western in 1897 were typical of the many 4-6-0s being built at that time.[74] A 29-square foot grate fired a 190-pounds per square inch boiler; 295 2-inch × 14-foot fire tubes contributed to a total heating surface of 2,310 square feet. Cylinders measuring 19 inches × 26 inches drove 63-inch driving wheels for a tractive effort of 24,000 pounds. The

engine weighed 156,000 pounds, of which 118,000 pounds (76%) was adhesion weight. The tender held 8 tons of coal and 4,500 gallons of water.

In 1898, the Great Northern bought powerful 4-6-0s from Brooks. These engines, with 63-inch driving wheels, were for both passenger and freight service.[75] A 34-square foot grate fired 2,450 square feet of heating surface in a 210-pounds per square inch boiler. The firebox contained a brick arch supported on three 3-inch arch tubes. The cylinders were 20 inches bore and of abnormally long 30-inch stroke, providing 34,000 pounds of tractive effort. Twelve-inch piston valves and the Belpaire firebox were innovations. Total engine weight was 166,000 pounds of which 129,500 pounds (78%) went into adhesion.

Baldwin was confident enough of their designs to offer performance guarantees. They built two 4-6-0s for the Fitchburg Railroad, one single-expansion, the other a Vauclain compound, with a guarantee that each engine would haul a 325-ton train up 10 miles of 1.1% grade at 40 miles per hour.[76]

In 1899, the Northern Pacific upgraded their 4-6-0 freight engines with fourteen two-cylinder compounds from Schenectady.[77] These had slightly more than 3,000 square feet of heating surface, making steam at 200 pounds per square inch, fired by a 34-square foot grate. They were slightly heavier than their predecessors at 175,500 pounds.

The 4-4-0s and 4-4-2s did not have enough pulling power for the Pennsylvania's heavy passenger trains, except in flat country. Consequently the company developed the class G 4-6-0s; the class G-4 was built in 1900. These engines had the very high boiler pressure for that time of 225 pounds per square inch and, hence, 38% more tractive effort than the class E-1 4-4-2s.[78]

The Lehigh Valley had a problem with helper service on the

This Atchison, Topeka & Santa Fe class B-13 4-6-0, No. 454, was built by Dickson in 1897 and photographed at La Junta, Colorado, on January 23, 1919 (Denver Public Library, Otto C. Perry collection, OP-33).

Baldwin built this 4-6-0 as Fitchburg Railroad No. 5 in 1898. A photograph on the Boston & Maine website shows the locomotive at Boston, Massachusetts, on July 3, 1937, after the Fitchburg had been taken over by the Boston & Maine, retrofitted with piston valves and Walschaert valve gear (courtesy California State Railroad Museum, Railway & Locomotive Historical Society Collection, Negative 39073cn).

passenger run between Easton, Pennsylvania, and Wilkes-Barre.[79] Not only the helper service cost money, but time and competitive advantage were lost putting the helpers on and cutting them off. The offending stretch of track was 10 miles of 1.1% grade between White Haven and Glen Summit, but helpers were put on at Mauch Chunk and cut off at Glen Summit, 35 miles away. In 1900, the company ordered five massive 182,000-pound, anthracite-burning 4-6-0 Vauclain compounds with 17-inch & 28-inch × 26-inch cylinders from Baldwin to run passenger trains over this route without helpers. Railroads would often order small classes of locomotive to solve a specific problem.

Persistent users of six-coupled engines bought bigger ones as their power needs increased. Only a year or two after buying the B-13's, the Santa Fe replaced them on the Raton Pass in 1898 with the 158,600-pound B-14's from Baldwin and again, in 1900, with thirty 162,200-pound B-15's from the International Power Co., Providence, Rhode Island. Only three years separated them from the B-13's, yet they had piston valves, cast steel frames, 200-pounds per square inch boiler pressure (up from 180), 6% more heating surface, longer-stroke pistons and 27% more tractive effort—22,300 pounds in the B-13's to 28,400 pounds in the B-15's.[80]

The Santa Fe competed with the Southern Pacific for traffic between the Midwest and California. Traffic was increasing fast and the Santa Fe wanted to increase its share, especially San Francisco traffic which included ocean freight from across the Pacific. The B-13's hauled four cars of the *California Express* over the Raton Pass without a helper, but five cars or more needed a helper from Trinidad, Colorado, to Lynn, New Mexico. The "Nine-Mile Hill" from Colmore

The Pennsylvania built their class G-4 4-6-0s at Altoona in 1900. This is No. 558, date and location unknown (Pennsylvania Historical and Museum Commission and Railroad Museum of Pennsylvania, Railroad History Corporation Negative 04695).

The Atchison, Topeka & Santa Fe bought their class B-15 4-6-0s from the Rhode Island Locomotive Works in 1900. No. 476 is shown at San Bernardino, California, on April 30, 1934 (Denver Public Library, Otto C. Perry collection, OP-36).

to Levy was the limiting factor for westbound trains between Raton and Albuquerque; a B-13 could handle eight cars over this hill, making a scheduled speed of 30 miles per hour, including stops. The B-15's increased this to five cars over Raton without a helper and ten cars up the Nine-Mile Hill while keeping to schedule. Even the B-15's could handle no more than 280 tons over the Raton Pass unassisted.

In 1901, a 4-6-0 on the Savannah, Florida & Western ran with three cars from Fleming, Georgia, to Jacksonville, Florida, 149 miles, at an average speed of 69 miles per hour, including one stop. Those on the train, timing the mileposts, thought that it reached 120 miles per hour on one 5-mile stretch. The engineer was A. H. Lodge; W. E. Symons, Superintendent of Motive Power, supported the claim.[81]

Most railroads were still cautious about committing themselves to compounds, ordering them in trial batches of ones and twos; few of these orders were repeated. Thus, when the Cleveland, Cincinnati, Chicago & St. Louis ordered six 4-6-0s from Baldwin in 1901, two were Vauclain compounds, four were single-expansion. The company then canceled the compounds and ordered no more 4-6-0s.[82] The Big Four put these engines onto passenger trains between Cleveland and Indianapolis, 283 miles scheduled for an average speed of 40 miles per hour including ten stops. The engines ran 7,000 to 8,000 miles per month in this service.

The Santa Fe was never shy about trying new inventions; many failed. In 1901, Baldwin built five oil-burning 4-6-0s for them with Vanderbilt boilers, otherwise of normal 4-6-0 dimensions for that time. The order was not repeated.[83]

The first four-cylinder balanced compounds were 4-4-2s. Baldwin's 20,000th locomotive, however, was a 176,500-pound four-cylinder balanced compound 4-6-0 for the Plant System designed by Samuel Vauclain and W. E. Symons, the Plant System Superintendent of Motive Power, for passenger and fast freight service and built in 1902.[84] A 27-square foot grate fired a 200-pounds per square inch Vanderbilt boiler; 341 15-foot fire tubes contributed to 2,665 square feet of heating surface. Opposite to the de Glehn system, the high-pressure cylinders were inside the frames, the low-pressure outside. A single piston valve with three pistons on a single stem, patented by Vauclain, controlled the steam flow to the high-pressure cylinders, from the high-pressure to the low-pressure cylinders and from the low-pressure cylinders to exhaust. One valve controlled each pair of cylinders. All four cylinders — 15-inch & 25-inch × 26-inch — drove on the 73-inch front driving wheels.

In 1904, the New York, New Haven & Hartford ordered twenty-two 4-6-0 passenger engines from Baldwin. Two were Vauclain four-cylinder balanced compounds similar to that built for the Plant System in 1901.[85] The use of 4-6-0s for passenger service was new on the New Haven which had hitherto used 4-4-0s. Following a familiar pattern, no further orders for balanced compounds followed. The New Haven bought a total of seventy-five 4-6-0s between 1903 and 1909.

Construction of new 4-6-0s faded as they were overtaken in power by 4-6-2s for passenger service and 2-8-2s for freight. In Britain, however, the 4-6-0 remained one of the standard mixed traffic types, with new construction into the 1950s.

4.3.2 Mogul Freight Locomotives

In the early 1890s, the 2-6-0 was a freight hauler second only to the 2-8-0. A two-cylinder compound 2-6-0 that the Pittsburgh Locomotive & Car Works built for the Columbus, Hocking Valley & Toledo in 1893 was designed to haul a 1,900-ton train at 20 miles per hour on straight, level track, 215 tons up a 3% grade at 10 miles per hour.[86] The grate area was 24 square feet, firing 1,470 square feet

of heating surface in a 180-pounds per square inch boiler. The engine weighed only 116,200 pounds. The available drawings seem to show a steam jacket around the high-pressure cylinder; steam jackets were experimented with in locomotives, but without success.

As early as the mid–1890s, some railroads recognized the need for speed in freight service, both to compete with their neighbors and to maximize revenue when freight rates were falling. In the northeastern U.S., traffic was dense, but so was the railroad network and competition was fierce. Instead of moving 50-car trains at average speeds of 18 to 20 miles per hour, engines were now needed that would do so at 30 to 35 miles per hour. The Pennsylvania set out to find, by experiment, a locomotive that would do this; the class R (H-3) 2-8-0s wore out too quickly at such speeds.[87] The company selected the 2-6-0 wheel arrangement, building the first class F-1's in 1895,[88] with 62-inch driving wheels, 185-pounds per square inch boilers and 20-inch × 28-inch cylinders, for a tractive effort of 28,400 pounds—16% more than the class R 2-8-0s, enabling the F-1's to handle 2,700-ton trains faster than the 2-8-0s.[89]

This was only a temporary solution; bigger 2-8-0s soon followed. The Pennsylvania built five experimental 2-6-0s: one single-expansion and one each on the Pittsburgh, Richmond, von Borries and Gölsdorf compound systems. The four compounds were designated class F-2. All were two-cylinder compounds differing in detail. The Pennsylvania would have made rigorous comparative tests; the compounds did not survive the process and were rebuilt to single-expansion a few years later.

Other railroads that did not have the Pennsylvania's engineering resources still needed the same results. In 1896, the New York, New Haven & Hartford bought ten 2-6-0 freight engines from Schenectady, built to the specifications of John Henney, the railroad's Superintendent of Motive Power.[90] A 30-square foot grate fired a 190-pounds per square inch boiler with 2,110 square feet of heating surface, 20-inch × 28-inch cylinders and 63-inch driving wheels for a tractive effort of 28,700 pounds. Total engine weight was 144,000 pounds.

Although the six-coupled engine evolved slowly during the 1890s, evolve it did.[91] William Buchanan of the New York Central favored the 2-6-0 for freight service; in 1889–90 Schenectady built 137 of the 120,000-pound class J to his design. A 30-square foot grate fired 1,765 square feet of heating surface—large for that time, although the boiler pressure was a traditional 160 pounds per square inch; 19-inch × 26-inch cylinders powered 64-inch driving wheels for 20,000 pounds of tractive effort, also high for 1890.

Eight years later, the company upgraded to the 2-6-0 class P, also designed by Buchanan and built by Schenectady. These engines weighed 152,000 pounds. The grate area was still 30 square feet but the heating surface was increased to 2,585 square feet and the boiler pressure to 180 pounds per square inch. The cylinders were bigger—20 inches × 28 inches, powering 57-inch driving wheels, so that the tractive effort increased to 30,000 pounds. As a result, the class P hauled 50% more cars than the J.

With rolling stock of lower rolling resistance than European equivalents and powerful locomotives, the Americans were able to haul spectacular tonnages. On October 12, 1898, with indicators plumbed in and the test crew riding on the engine, the prototype New York Central class P was on the last of seven test runs between Albany and De Witt, with increasingly heavy loads. Eighty-one loaded grain cars and a caboose were on the drawbar for a trailing load of 3,428 tons. The engine got up the 0.5% grade out of De Witt with a helper but thereafter was on its own for the 139-mile run which took 12 hours 49 minutes. Speeds were never higher than 30 miles per hour, even on the downgrade into Albany. The boiler pressure stayed at 170 to

The Pennsylvania's class F-1c 2-6-0. The available information suggests that No. 923 was built in June, 1897, and photographed at this unknown location in 1910 (Pennsylvania Historical and Museum Commission and Railroad Museum of Pennsylvania, General Negative 24806).

New York, New Haven & Hartford 2-6-0, No. 426, was built at Schenectady in 1896. By the time Otto Perry photographed it at Boston, Massachusetts, on October 11, 1930, it had been retrofitted with piston valves and Baker valve gear (Denver Public Library, Otto C. Perry collection, OP-13691).

The Chicago, Burlington & Quincy built this class H-4 2-6-0, No. 1227, in company shops in 1899, photographed at Sterling, Colorado, on July 27, 1927, retrofitted with piston valves but retaining inside valve gear (Denver Public Library, Otto C. Perry collection, OP-3551).

180 pounds per square inch with 25% cutoff; speeds were 15 to 20 miles per hour most of the way. The maximum adverse grade after the helper was cut off was a mile of 0.5%, which was surmounted at 15 miles per hour. The highest recorded power output was 815 indicated horsepower at 19 miles per hour.

For much of the 1890s, the Chicago, Burlington & Quincy's standard freight locomotive was the class H 2-6-0. The company also used 2-6-0s for passenger service, passenger and freight engines differing only in driving wheel diameter (68 inches and 63 inches respectively).[92] This class was modified in new construction until, at the end of the 1890s, the newest (fifteen class H-4 built in 1899) weighed 143,000 pounds and had 30-square foot grates and 2,048 square feet of heating surface.

In the first years of the twentieth century the Pennsylvania's demand for motive power outran even the company's formidable manufacturing capability at Altoona. At one time the Pennsylvania could also build locomotives at Fort Wayne, Indiana, where it built a 4-6-0 passenger engine, class X, in 1892.[93] The present study has not revealed how many locomotives the Pennsylvania built at Fort Wayne or when.

In 1901, the company ordered 180 locomotives from Baldwin. Of these, seventy-eight were 2-6-0s, class F-3.[94] The fifty-four F-3b's had the Belpaire firebox, sloped down toward the backhead, that became a hallmark of Pennsylvania designs. The F-3's and F-3b's differed slightly in firebox, heating surface and weight but were in most respects identical. Even though the grate was between the frames, a long firebox provided 49 square feet of grate in the F-3b, firing 2,470 square feet of heating surface in a 205-pounds per square inch boiler; 20-inch × 28-inch cylinders drove 62-inch driving wheels for a tractive effort of 31,500 pounds.

In 1901, Baldwin built five oil-burning 2-6-0s for the Southern

Pacific with Vanderbilt boilers and Vauclain compounding. These must have been successful as an order for ten more followed in 1902.[95] Baldwin were also building forty-five coal-burning Vauclain compound 2-6-0s for the Southern Pacific of almost identical dimensions and these were followed by another twenty-three in 1902. The Southern Pacific used these and similar medium-sized 2-6-0s for a long time; the first were built in 1899, the last were retired in 1958.

On the Southern Pacific and many other lines, unspectacular 2-6-0s and 4-6-0s in their thousands were continuously at work throughout the first half of the twentieth century, although superseded in mainline service by more powerful types. They remained common in Europe into the mid-twentieth century. In common with the 4-4-0, the 4-6-0 and the 2-8-0, the 2-6-0 was ultimately limited by the size of the firebox that would fit between its frames or above its driving wheels. The trailing axle provided the solution.

4.3.3 Further Pursuit of High Power at High Speed: The First Prairies

Rumor suggests that Baldwin built the first American 2-6-2 in 1899 for the Williamsville, Greenville & St. Louis Railway; the engine went to the Munising Railway, Michigan, in 1905 and was rebuilt as a 2-8-0 in about 1920.[96]

A more definite beginning came in 1900, when Chicago, Burlington & Quincy Superintendent of Motive Power, F. A. Delano, and Mechanical Engineer, F. H. Clark, planned a locomotive with a wide, deep firebox mounted low to keep the center of gravity low. The company built a class of the resulting 2-6-2 wheel arrangement at their West Burlington shops and called the new engines "Class R, Prairie Type."[97]

The first batch consisted of four engines, weighing 140,000

The Pennsylvania went to Baldwin for this class F-3b 2-6-0, No. 1949, built in 1901; the location and date of the photograph are currently unknown (Pennsylvania Historical and Museum Commission and Railroad Museum of Pennsylvania, General Negative 24981).

Baldwin built this class M-7 2-6-0, No. 1776, for the Southern Pacific as a Vauclain compound with a Vanderbilt boiler in 1901–02. By the time Otto Perry photographed it at Marysville, California, on August 2, 1935, it had been converted to single-expansion, although retaining inside valve gear. The electric headlight, powered by the generator just above the cab front, was also a later addition (Denver Public Library, Otto C. Perry collection, OP-15446).

pounds, for fast freight service over flat terrain.[98] A 42-square foot grate fired a 190-pounds per square inch boiler with 2,075 square feet of heating surface. Cylinders measuring 19 inches × 24 inches with piston valves drove 64-inch wheels with blind flanges on the center pair. The new locomotives were unremarkable, except that the firebox had broken out of its restricted space between the driving wheels. The trailing axle was rigidly mounted in a rear frame extension.

The next 2-6-2 user was the Lake Shore & Michigan Southern in 1901. The company bought two from Brooks; another seventy-nine followed from Brooks between then and 1905.[99] The trailing axle permitted a 49-square foot grate; although this was no larger than that of the Pennsylvania's F-3b, it would have been shorter and easier to fire. It also allowed a longer boiler and more heating surface. The 200-pounds per square inch boiler measured 19 feet over tube sheets and contained 3,345 square feet of heating surface. Cylinders measuring 20½ inches × 28 inches drove 80-inch driving wheels. The purpose of these class J's was to handle heavy trains in bad weather better than the existing 4-6-0s. Engine weight was 174,500 pounds.

The same year, Schenectady built some 2-6-2 switchers for the Colorado Springs & Cripple Creek District Railroad. The trailing wheels were more likely to guide the locomotive when backing round sharp curves than to support a large firebox.[100]

The Santa Fe's class B-15 4-6-0s were still not powerful enough and, in 1901, the Santa Fe ordered the most powerful passenger locomotives built hitherto. Baldwin got the order; the engines were 190,000-pound Vauclain compound 2-6-2s. A 54-square foot grate fired a 200-pounds per square inch boiler with 3,740 square feet of heating surface, including 318 fire tubes 19 feet long. Fifteen-inch piston valves admitted steam to 17-inch and 28-inch cylinders with 28-inch stroke, powering 79-inch driving wheels. The trailing wheels

were mounted in a truck, instead of rigidly in a frame extension. These engines would have had a tractive effort of 26,000 pounds, working compound, 34,000 single-expansion; the large grate and heating surface would have produced close to 1,400 horsepower. The Santa Fe intended them for the *California Limited* between Chicago and San Francisco. Even on level track high power was necessary in bad weather, even to the extent of double heading. These engines were a big success and the Santa Fe bought 143 of them from Baldwin between 1901 and 1903.[101]

One was equipped with traction increasers, shifting 8,730 pounds to the driving wheels from the front and back trucks, applied automatically at long cut-off by a connection to the reversing lever, although the engineer could override this and cut out the traction increaser. This particular engine weighed 210,800 pounds. Axle loadings with the traction increaser applied increased to a maximum of 53,340 pounds on the middle driving wheels from a normal loading of 51,800 pounds. After this experiment, the traction increasers were built into forty-five Santa Fe 2-6-2s in 1902. These forty-five were for freight with driving wheels reduced in diameter to 69 inches.

At this time, the Santa Fe also bought two 2-6-2 tandem compounds from Schenectady in 1902, rebuilt four 2-6-2s from 4-6-2s in 1903 and, the same year, bought eighty-eight 2-6-2 balanced compounds from Baldwin.[102] The purchase of 233 2-6-2s with three different compounding systems is remarkable. Although these locomotives continued in service into the 1950s, the company bought no more 2-6-2s.

In 1902, the Illinois Central bought two engines for comparative tests in fast passenger service—a 4-4-2 from Baldwin and a 2-6-2 from Rogers.[103] The 2-6-2 had a tractive effort of 25,500 pounds and a total engine weight of 203,000 pounds; the 4-4-2 was rated at 24,400 pounds tractive effort and weighed 178,000 pounds. Both

An early 2-6-2 built at Schenectady for the Colorado Springs & Cripple Creek District in 1901, No. 103, photographed at Colorado Springs, Colorado, on June 22, 1919 (Denver Public Library, Otto C. Perry collection, OP-7275).

Once the pride of the Santa Fe's express passenger fleet, this 1050 class 2-6-2, No. 1079, built by Baldwin in 1902–03, was still at work on a branch line at Homewood, Kansas, on July 1, 1950. First built as a Vauclain compound, it has long since been converted to single expansion and Walschaert valve gear and retrofitted with an electric headlight (Denver Public Library, Otto C. Perry collection, OP-251).

boilers were built for 200 pounds per square inch; both were fired by 51-square foot grates. The 2-6-2 wheel arrangement allowed 2½ feet more boiler length than the 4-4-2, allowing 3,335 square feet of heating surface compared to 3,190. The 2-6-2's trailing wheels were mounted in a Rushton truck, a self-centering device with 6 inches of side play but no radial motion, suspension-equalized with the back driving wheels. The tenders were enormous for that time, with capacity for 15 to 18 tons of coal and 7,000 gallons of water. At 147,000 pounds loaded, they weighed almost as much as the engines themselves. The 2-6-2 lost the contest, but Rogers got the order for twenty-five 4-4-2s in 1903–4, while the Illinois Central built a further eleven in its own shops.[104] The company soon went to 4-6-2s for passenger service, of which they bought and built 235 between 1902 and 1920.

By 1904, the class J 2-6-2s built by Brooks for the Lake Shore & Michigan Southern were already inadequate for the demands of passenger service. The company liked the Brooks 2-6-2s well enough to want the same again, only bigger, for 13 to 15-car trains. At 233,000 pounds, the resulting class K's were the heaviest passenger engines built in the U.S. to date, heavier than the Michigan Central 4-6-2s (221,000 pounds). They had the advantage that the 2-6-2 wheel arrangement put 71% of the engine weight into adhesion, compared to 63% for the Michigan Central 4-6-2s. In the class K's a 55-square foot grate fired a 200-pounds per square inch boiler with an abundant 3,905 square feet of heating surface; 21½-inch × 28-inch cylinders powered 79-inch driving wheels. The two back pairs of driving wheels were suspension-equalized with each other and with the trailing truck. The front driving wheels were equalized with the leading truck. The axle loading on the driving wheels was up to 55,333 pounds. Like the Illinois Central engines, the tenders were large for the time, holding 15 tons of coal and 7,800 gallons of water. Brooks

built forty-six J's in 1901–3 followed by thirty-five K's in 1904–5.[105]

Of the sixty-eight most important American railroads and amalgamations, only three did not at some time use the 4-6-0, the 2-6-0 or both. The 2-6-0 was less universal than the 4-6-0 but, even so, some 11,000 were built between 1860 and 1910; one of the last was built by Alco for the Green Bay & Western in 1924.[106] These two wheel arrangements were superseded by engines with trailing trucks supporting big fireboxes and, to that extent, they went the way of the 4-4-0 and for the same reason. New construction faded out between 1900 and 1920. The Southern Pacific built some of the last of both types in its own shops, the T-32 4-6-0s in 1917–20, the M-2 2-6-0s in 1927–8.[107] Many survived until the end of steam in the 1950s. The last steam locomotive in regular service on an American common carrier railroad was an antique 2-6-0 on the Mobile & Gulf Railroad, replaced by diesel power in September 1970.[108] The 2-6-2 was a multi-purpose locomotive, but was not widely used and was soon superseded by the 4-6-2 and 2-8-2 types.

Section 4.4. Heavy Freight Locomotives

They have replaced the little old eight-wheel engines, with their ear-splitting, staccato bark, with compound steel mountains, with cylinders like hogsheads and nozzles so big that the exhaust is gentle as a lover's whispered nothings, for no better reason than a desire to keep down coal consumption. Trains, instead of being made up of a dozen or so of pill boxes, now consist of a string of warehouses on wheels so long that the when the front end is arriving at its destination the hind end is just pulling out at the other end of the division.

Ah, no! Railroading isn't what it used to be.[109]

The American railroads drew more of their revenues from hauling freight—in limitless variety and ever-increasing quantity—than from the ever more costly and troublesome passenger service. The effort that went into the design, construction and development of freight locomotives was correspondingly great.

The fifty-two American locomotives exhibited at the 1893 World's Fair in Chicago were probably a fair sample of what was being built at the time: fifteen 4-4-0s, five 2-6-0s, twelve 4-6-0s, six 2-8-0s, two 4-8-0s, one 2-10-0, three 0-6-0s and seven 0-4-0s.[110]

Demand for freight power led to desperate expedients. On the New York Central in 1899, a freight train broke in two and the sudden automatic application of the air brakes caused a derailment. This train was being pushed by another which, itself, had three engines, one at the front, one cut into the middle of the train and one pushing at the back.[111] Such an arrangement was inefficient in crew labor, fuel consumption and time spent cutting locomotives into and out of the train. The answer was stronger freight cars, hauled by ever more powerful locomotives.

4.4.1 Consolidations

The prime American heavy freight engine of the 1890s and early 1900s was the 2-8-0; more were built than any other type. Freight locomotive driving wheels were typically small, so a wide grate could be built out over them, while keeping the firebox and boiler within height limits for center of gravity and clearance dimensions. A high percentage of engine weight was available for adhesion. By 1902, 2-8-0s comprised one-fifth of the U.S. locomotive fleet. Although superseded in heavy freight service after 1905, 2-8-0s remained in use until the end of steam.

Typical of contemporary 2-8-0s were ten that Rhode Island built for the New Haven in 1895.[112] Total engine weight was 156,850 pounds when a typical new 4-4-0 weighed 100,000 to 120,000 pounds. In a 4-4-0 about 65% of engine weight was available for adhesion. In these 2-8-0s, 92% of engine weight went into adhesion for an axle loading of 36,000 pounds. A 33-square foot grate fired a 180-pounds per square inch boiler with 2,115 square feet of heating surface, including 310 fire tubes 13 feet 8 inches long; 21-inch × 26-inch cylinders and 51-inch driving wheels with blind flanges on the second and fourth pairs provided 34,000 pounds of tractive effort.

With improving economic conditions in 1895–6, the demand for

such engines increased and new orders came apace. The new iron mines in northern Michigan demanded the most powerful locomotives available; compounds excelled in this kind of slow freight service. In 1896, Pittsburgh built four 147,600-pound 2-8-0 two-cylinder compounds for the Lake Superior & Ishpeming for $11,381 each while the railroad was still under construction from the Ishpeming iron mines to the docks at Marquette, twenty miles away.[113] A 32-square foot grate fired a 180-pounds per square inch boiler with 2,200 square feet of heating surface; 20-inch and 31-inch × 28-inch cylinders with Richardson-balanced slide valves drove 56-inch driving wheels, producing 22,000 pounds of tractive effort, compound, 31,000 pounds, single-expansion. Experience with the compounds was not good; the railroad's next two 2-8-0s were single-expansion[114]; the compounds were rebuilt to single expansion in 1910.

In 1897, the Pennsylvania brought out its class H-4 2-8-0s, building the first ten at Altoona.[115] A 30-square foot grate beneath a Belpaire firebox fired a 185-pounds per square inch boiler with 2,470 square feet of heating surface; 22-inch × 28-inch cylinders and 56-inch driving wheels produced 38,000 pounds of tractive effort.[116] Total engine weight was 174,300 pounds. One hundred and eleven H-4's followed.[117]

Within a year, the Pennsylvania brought out the more powerful H-5 which rivaled even the Great Northern 4-8-0s in size.[118] The turntables at Altoona were not long enough for the first H-5, which served as a helper west of town, and the scales were not big enough to weigh it. Fifteen were built.[119]

The H-6 followed in 1899; the H-6 and its variants were one of the most numerous classes of 2-8-0 ever built, with 2,029 built by Baldwin and the Pennsylvania between 1899 and 1909. The long, narrow grates of the original H-6's were hard to fire. Accordingly, in 1901, the Pennsylvania put the wide firebox from their E-1 and E-2 4-4-2s over the back driving wheels of the H-6 to produce the H-6a with 47% more grate area (49 square feet vs. 33 square feet) but a firebox shortened from 10 feet to 9. Between 1902 and 1905, Baldwin built 1,017 H-6a's for the Pennsylvania. The Pennsylvania gained control of the Baltimore & Ohio in 1901; the B&O bought 197 copies of the H-6a from Pittsburgh, Rogers and Richmond (class E-24). In 1905, the Pennsylvania ordered H-6's with Walschaert valve gear—the H-6b. In addition to its own needs, the Pennsylvania built fourteen H-6b's for other railroads between 1907 and 1913. Engine weight

The Pennsylvania's class H-5 2-8-0, No. 1431, built at Altoona, 1898 (Pennsylvania Historical and Museum Commission and Railroad Museum of Pennsylvania, General Negative 24910).

A Pennsylvania class H-6a 2-8-0, No. 8038, at Carnegie, Pennsylvania, in 1924. The H-6a differed from the H-6 in its wider firebox, but retained the inside motion and slide valves (Pennsylvania Historical and Museum Commission and Railroad Museum of Pennsylvania, General Negative 25743).

A Pennsylvania Class H-6sa (the "s" denoting superheat) 2-8-0, No. 576, built by Baldwin and photographed at an unknown location in 1918. Note wide firebox, inside motion and piston valves (Pennsylvania Historical and Museum Commission and Railroad Museum of Pennsylvania, General Negatives 24733).

climbed from 186,500 pounds in the H-6 to 200,700 in the H-6b for an axle loading of 45,000 pounds in the latter; tractive effort remained at 42,000 pounds.[120] From 1905 onward, the H-6 was displaced by the larger H-8. The last H-6 (an H-6sb—"s" denotes super-heat) on the Pennsylvania ran in 1955. An H-3 and an H-6sb are preserved in the Pennsylvania State Railroad Museum, Strasburg, Pennsylvania.

Railroads still ordered light 2-8-0s if that was all that they needed.

The Pennsylvania class H-6b 2-8-0, followed the H-6a in 1905, built by Altoona and Baldwin. This H-6sb, with Walschaert valve gear and piston valves, No. 6539, was photographed at York, Pennsylvania, in March 1939 (Pennsylvania Historical and Museum Commission and Railroad Museum of Pennsylvania, Railroad History Corporation negative 05082).

This Union Pacific 2-8-0, No. 119, photographed at La Salle, Colorado, on April 20, 1930, may have been one of those ordered from Brooks in 1898. If not, the appearance would have been similar (Denver Public Library, Otto C. Perry collection, OP-16389).

At the end of the 1800s, the Union Pacific was still struggling with vast mileage, difficult operating conditions and sparse traffic—it went bankrupt in 1893. In 1898, it ordered ten light (145,000-pound) 2-8-0s designed under the direction of J. H. McConnell, Superintendent of Motive Power.[121] Brooks built eight of these with single expansion; Schenectady built two as two-cylinder compounds. These engines were of modest dimensions with 32 square feet of grate, 180 pounds per square inch boiler pressure, 2,110 square feet of heating surface, 20-inch × 24-inch cylinders and 51-inch driving wheels, producing 29,000 pounds of tractive effort.

The 2-8-0 wheel arrangement allowed plenty of scope for growth. Even as they were being built, the Great Northern 4-8-0s were outclassed by even bigger 2-8-0s, built for railroads in Pennsylvania. Baldwin built a 225,000-pound camelback anthracite-burner for the Lehigh Valley in 1898, a Vauclain compound with 18-inch & 30-inch × 30-inch cylinders; 511 fire tubes 14 feet 8 inches long contributed to 4,105 square feet of heating surface, fired by a 90-square foot grate under a Wootten firebox.[122] Many mammoth engines were built to do battle with some particular steep grade; this engine was for pusher service on the climb out of Wilkes-Barre. The following year, S. Higgins, Superintendent of Motive Power, designed a lighter engine of the same configuration. The company ordered two from Baldwin, one single-expansion with 21-inch × 30-inch cylinders, the other a Vauclain compound with 17-inch & 28-inch × 30-inch cylinders. Whichever design was the most successful, the company planned to build another twenty-four to haul 2,000-ton freight trains between Buffalo and Sayre, Pennsylvania, hitherto double-headed.

The 2-8-0 had an advantage over the 4-8-0 in the percentage of engine weight available for adhesion. The Northern Pacific followed its 4-8-0 design with a class of 189,200-pound 2-8-0s, class Y, of which Schenectady built fourteen in 1898.[123] These were two-cylinder compounds, indicating the Northern Pacific's confidence in Schenectady compounds. A 35-square foot grate fired a 225-pounds per square inch boiler with 2,925 square feet of heating surface; 23-inch & 34-inch × 34-inch cylinders and 55-inch driving wheels produced 43,000 pounds of tractive effort (25% of adhesion weight), compound, 63,000 (37% of adhesion weight), single-expansion—enormous for those days. The company's track and substructures permitted an axle loading of 42,000 pounds.

The Southern Pacific did not follow up on its 1898 Schenectady Mastodon, but in 1899 ordered six engines from Schenectady, following the same design, but improved and changed to the 2-8-0 wheel arrangement, putting 90% of the total weight into adhesion instead of 80%.[124] The boiler pressure was also substantially higher, at 220 pounds per square inch. The cylinders were of the same bore, but longer stroke at 34 inches.

The Santa Fe faced the continuing problem of hauling increasingly heavy freight trains over the Raton Pass. In 1898, it started building single-expansion 2-8-0s at its Topeka shops to the design of John Player, Superintendent of Machinery.[125] By mid–1899, sixty were in service, known as class C-17—twenty-five from Topeka shops, twenty-five from Baldwin, ten from Dickson. Considering the task and what was being built elsewhere, this design was surprisingly small and retrograde. The boiler pressure was 180 pounds per square inch with 1,840 square feet of heating surface. The firebox was still of the crown bar type with no brick arch.

After trying without success to get his tandem compound idea adopted on other railroads where he had worked, Player was finally able to do so on the Santa Fe in 1898. Topeka built five 2-8-0 Player compounds in 1898–9. An auxiliary throttle allowed the engineer to feed live steam direct to the low-pressure cylinders through a pre-set reducing valve. Player patented a method of adjusting the cut-off of

Schenectady built this Northern Pacific class Y 2-8-0 in 1898. No. 39 had been rebuilt to single-expansion with piston valves by the time Otto Perry photographed it at Billings, Montana, on July 31, 1939 (Denver Public Library, Otto C. Perry collection, OP-13889).

Rogers built this Illinois Central 2-8-0, No. 638, in 1899, believed to be at Sabinas, Texas, when photographed on October 28, 1928 (Denver Public Library, Otto C. Perry collection, OP-20609).

the high-pressure piston valves independently of the low-pressure valves. In comparative tests the compounds showed savings of 18% in coal and 13% in water. They doubled the freight train tonnage that one engine could haul between La Junta and Albuquerque and achieved substantial savings in fuel.

At the same time as buying the 4-8-0 from Brooks, the Illinois Central ordered a 2-8-0 from Rogers that was almost as heavy at 216,000 pounds with an almost identical tractive effort.[126] Both these engines went into service on the same run, hauling 2,000-ton trains up 0.7% grades. The Illinois Central did not repeat the 4-8-0 order but, between 1902 and 1911, the company bought 280 2-8-0s in several different classes from Cooke, Rogers, Schenectady, Brooks and Baldwin.[127]

By 1900, the Lake Shore & Michigan Southern was in search for more freight power, ordering twenty-five 2-8-0s from Brooks, 12,000 pounds heavier than those it bought in 1898 with higher boiler pressure and bigger cylinders which increased tractive effort from 32,000 pounds to 36,000.[128] In 1904, a Lake Shore 2-8-0 hauled a coal train, weighing 5,800 tons, from Youngstown to Ashtabula, 63 miles in 4 hours.[129]

In 1900, the New York, Ontario & Western ordered a 198,000-pound 2-8-0 from Cooke, designed by the Superintendent of Motive Power, G. W. West, to be used as a pusher on coal trains.[130] It was an anthracite-burning camelback with an 87-square foot grate beneath a Wootten firebox, firing a 200-pounds per square inch boiler with 3,290 square feet of heating surface; 21-inch × 32-inch cylinders, powering 55-inch driving wheels, provided 43,600 pounds of tractive effort.

After buying twelve 4-8-0s from Cooke, the Oregon Short Line next bought four 2-8-0s from them.[131] These were big for 2-8-0s at the time, weighing 196,000 pounds with 200 pounds per square inch

boiler pressure, 21-inch × 32-inch cylinders and 55-inch driving wheels for a tractive effort of 44,000 pounds. A 33-square foot grate fired 2,975 square feet of heating surface. The company bought these engines for a specific task. A single 4-8-0 was to haul 1,650- to 1,700-ton trains from Pocatello, Idaho, north to Dubois on the Snake River Plain. The ruling grade on that 100-mile stretch was 0.9%. From Dubois, two of the 2-8-0s would push them up 2.5% grades for 35 miles to the crest of the Monida Pass, whence they would go on their way north into Montana.

Baldwin scored a commercial success in 1900 by selling 235 compound 2-8-0s to three different companies with only minor alterations to a standard design.[132] The engines were typical 2-8-0s of the period with a total engine weight of 182,300 pounds, 200 pounds per square inch boiler pressure, 15½-inch & 26-inch × 30-inch Vauclain cylinders, 2,345 square feet of heating surface, 34-square foot grates and 54-inch driving wheels. The biggest order, 165, went to the Baltimore & Ohio; of these, twenty-four had Wootten fireboxes and two had Vanderbilt boilers. The Union Pacific ordered sixty, two with Vanderbilt boilers. The ten for the Kansas City, Pittsburgh & Gulf had minor modifications to suit their requirements.

The engines that set a new record for size and tractive effort, records that would now be broken several times each year, were neither Mastodons nor Decapods, but a pair of 2-8-0s built by Pittsburgh for the Pittsburgh, Bessemer & Lake Erie.[133] Grate area—37 square feet—and heating surface—3,805 square feet—were large but not startling for that time. The boiler, however, was built for 220 pounds per square inch; 24-inch cylinders and 54-inch driving wheels produced 64,000 pounds of tractive effort, 28% of adhesion weight. Adhesion weight was 90% of the total engine weight of 250,300 pounds. The company's track and substructures permitted an axle loading of 56,000 pounds. These engines received widespread pub-

This Baltimore & Ohio 2-8-0, No. 1786, was probably one of class E-19, built by Baldwin in 1900–01, rebuilt to single expansion by the time Otto Perry photographed it at Benwood, West Virginia, on August 17, 1933 (Denver Public Library, Otto C. Perry collection, OP-2432).

licity for their extensive use of Pittsburgh steel. The frames (American Steel Castings), cylinder heads, crossheads and valve gear rocker arms (Reliance Steel Casting) and main driving wheel centers (Pittsburgh Steel Foundry) were all of cast steel. The other driving wheel centers were of "steeled cast iron." The 406 fire tubes, 2¼ inches × 15 feet, were also of steel. The rocking grates were still of cast iron, but steel was used extensively elsewhere, such as the firebox, the boiler, and the tender frame which was built up from steel channels. The tender held 14 tons of coal and 7,500 gallons of water.

The Pittsburgh, Bessemer & Lake Erie's business was to haul Michigan iron ore from the Lake Erie port of Conneaut, Ohio, to Pittsburgh, 150 miles including 1% grades; the tonnage requirement was immense. Each 2-8-0 was expected to haul a trailing load on straight, level track of 7,850 tons. Two more were built in 1900–02, class C-3a, remaining in service until 1936–43. Between 1900 and 1913, the Bessemer & Lake Erie procured 110 2-8-0s, mostly from Pittsburgh (99), but also from Brooks (2) and Baldwin (9). Curiously, the company never used Mallets, or anything bigger than a 2-8-0, until it bought 2-10-2s in 1916.

Early in 1901, Schenectady started on a big order of 2-8-0s for the New York Central. The initial order comprised thirty single-expansion engines and twenty two-cylinder compounds.[134] The New York Central increased the order for compounds to fifty-five as the first one went to work, ordering them with 63-inch driving wheels and steam heat supply as backup passenger power. A 50-square foot grate fired 3,215 square feet of heating surface. The firebox contained a brick arch supported on water tubes. The high-pressure cylinder had a piston valve, while the low-pressure cylinder had an Allen-ported, Richardson-balanced slide valve. To solve the old problem in compound locomotives of vacuum-formation in the low-pressure cylinder when drifting downhill, these engines had relief valves that

dropped open under gravity when the engine was drifting and lifted shut when steam was admitted to the cylinder. Schenectady built eighty-three of these compounds for the New York Central in 1901–03, classes G-1 (two-cylinder compounds) and G-2 (tandem compounds), thirty of the class G-3 single-expansion 2-8-0s and a further fifteen class G-4 compounds in 1903. Total procurement of 2-8-0s by the New York Central, including engines acquired through mergers, between 1900 and 1914 was 1,744.

These engines hauled some startling tonnages.[135] The first one hauled an 80-car train, weighing 3,225 tons, from De Witt 140 miles to West Albany in 13 hours, 35 minutes in winter temperatures of 10°F to 12°F. In May 1901, a G-1 hauled a train of 92 cars, 4,017 tons, over the same route. In 1902, a G-2a tandem compound hauled 87 cars over this route, 4,019 tons gross, at an average 12 miles per hour. The same year, a Lehigh Valley 2-8-0 Vauclain compound hauled 104 cars, weighing 4,014 tons, from Sayre, Pennsylvania, to Weldon.

In 1901, Schenectady built twelve 200,000-pound 2-8-0 two-cylinder compounds for the Southern Pacific.[136] A 55-square foot wide grate fired a 220-pounds per square inch boiler containing 3,600 square feet of heating surface. High-pressure cylinders of 23-inch bore × 34-inch stroke and enormous 35-inch low-pressure cylinders powered 57-inch driving wheels. Lateral clearance dimensions limited the size of the low-pressure cylinders. As in the New York Central compounds, steam was admitted to the high-pressure cylinder by a piston valve and to the low-pressure cylinder by a balanced slide valve. The Southern Pacific bought fifty-four Vauclain compound 2-8-0s from Baldwin in 1901–3 but no more compounds after that date. The company eventually converted most, if not all, to single-expansion, in which form both types went on working until the 1950s.

The four-cylinder tandem compound made a fresh start in about 1900. In that year Schenectady started building 2-8-0s to this design

Otto Perry photographed this Southern Pacific Class C-4 2-8-0, No. 2617, built at Schenectady in 1901, at Los Angeles, California, on July 27, 1937 (Denver Public Library, Otto C. Perry collection, OP-15534).

Schenectady built this Northern Pacific class Y-2 2-8-0, No. 1275, in 1901–02, rebuilt to single expansion by the time Otto Perry photographed it at Spokane, Washington, on July 31, 1938 (Denver Public Library, Otto C. Perry collection, OP-13914).

A Northern Pacific class Y-3 2-8-0, No. 1204, built at Schenectady in 1901, after rebuilding to single expansion. The wide firebox extending over the back driving wheels is clearly visible in this photograph, taken at Spokane, Washington, on July 31, 1938 (Denver Public Library, Otto C. Perry collection, OP-13912).

The next Northern Pacific freight locomotives were the Class W 2-8-2s, built by Alco in 1904–07. No. 1575 emerges from a tunnel in the Lapwai Canyon, Idaho, on September 18, 1953. Note the crude timber structure to prevent the portal from sloughing in (Denver Public Library, Henry R. Griffiths collection, Z-5949).

for the Northern Pacific. After tests on a prototype, the Northern Pacific ordered another twenty-six.[137] The twenty-seven engines were divided into classes Y-2 (13) and Y-3 (14). The Y-3's were built for mountain service with smaller driving wheels and bigger boilers than the Y-2's. Both classes had the same large grate area—52 square feet, the same high boiler pressure—225 pounds per square inch, the same cylinder dimensions—15 inches & 28 inches × 34 inches and cast steel frames. The Y-2's had 2,995 square feet of heating surface; the Y-3's had 3,670 square feet. The Y-2's developed tractive efforts of 36,000 pounds compound, 46,000 pounds single-expansion.

The prototype had piston valves for the high-pressure cylinders and balanced slide valves in a separate steam chest for the low-pressure cylinders. The production version had tandem piston valves on both cylinders.

Schenectady completed thirty Y-2's, and the fourteen Y-3's, in 1901–2.[138] The fourteen Y-4's and ten Y-5's that the Northern Pacific bought from Schenectady in 1903 were, however, single-expansion, whereupon the company stopped buying 2-8-0s altogether. The next Northern Pacific freight engines were 160 class W 2-8-2s from Brooks in 1904–7.

While searching for ever bigger engines, the Santa Fe had to make do with what was reasonably available. In 1902 it bought forty 201,000-pound 2-8-0 tandem compounds from Alco.[139] The Alco plants on Rhode Island and at Pittsburgh filled the order. These engines cannot have been a big success because thirty-five of them were later rebuilt as 0-8-0 switchers.

By 1902, a typical medium-weight 2-8-0 was the class built for the Minneapolis, St. Paul & Sault Ste. Marie by Alco Schenectady.[140] This engine was a two-cylinder 22½-inch & 35-inch × 30-inch compound weighing 177,000 pounds. A 46-square foot grate fired a 210-pounds per square inch boiler with 2,635 square feet of heating surface,

including 326 2-inch × 14-foot 6-inch fire tubes. The grate was 5 feet 5 inches wide, extending over the back driving wheels, achieving the desired grate area without an excessively long firebox (8 feet 6 inches). The frames were still of wrought iron. The Soo Line bought fourteen of these class F-8's in 1902–3 and thirty more cross-compound 2-8-0s from Schenectady between then and 1909. The Soo Line had a long involvement with compounds, beginning in 1893, but the company's next and later 2-8-0s, built by Schenectady from 1910 onward, were single-expansion. In the end, all the compounds were rebuilt to single-expansion and retrofitted with super-heating.

More and bigger 2-8-0s redefined "average" dimensions. In 1901, the Southern Pacific bought a new class of 205,000-pound Vauclain compound 2-8-0s from Baldwin.[141] The 55-square foot grate for bituminous coal fired a 200-pounds per square inch boiler containing 3,600 square feet of heating surface. Vauclain cylinders, 17 inches & 28 inches × 30 inches, powered 57-inch driving wheels. The 442 2-inch fire tubes were of steel, as were the driving wheel centers, although the frame was still of wrought iron. Baldwin built fifty-four of these class C-5's in 1901–3; some lasted into the 1940s and 1950s. Subsequent Baldwin 2-8-0s for the Southern Pacific, from 1904 onward, were single-expansion.

Not all railroads were equally pressed for engine size. Some, such as the Norfolk & Western, found a design that suited their needs and built large numbers of them over a period of years. The Norfolk & Western ordered their first 2-8-0s from Baldwin in 1898.[142] In 1900 the railroad started building these engines at its Roanoke shops, but with piston valves instead of slide valves. By 1902 seventy-five had been built and the company ordered forty-eight more; Roanoke was to build five, Baldwin nineteen and Alco Richmond twenty-four. Total procurement reached 276 by the end of production in 1905.

An Atchison, Topeka & Santa Fe, 825 class tandem compound 2-8-0, No. 834, built by Alco in 1902 and photographed at Pueblo, Colorado, in 1920 (Denver Public Library, Otto C. Perry collection, OP-120).

An oil-burning (evident from the shape of the tender) Southern Pacific class C-5 2-8-0, No. 2642, built by Baldwin in 1901–03. It had been rebuilt to single expansion with piston valves, but retaining the inside valve gear, by the time Otto Perry photographed it at Los Angeles, California, on May 1, 1934 (Denver Public Library, Otto C. Perry collection, OP-15536).

The Norfolk & Western divided production of its class W-2 2-8-0s between Baldwin and the company shops at Roanoke between 1901 and 1905. No. 794 is shown at Roanoke, Virginia, on August 6, 1932 (Denver Public Library, Otto C. Perry collection, OP-13787).

The Chicago, Rock Island & Pacific bought their class C-39 2-8-0s from Alco in 1903. No. 1653 is shown at Denver, Colorado, on June 9, 1925 (Denver Public Library, Otto C. Perry collection, OP-5411).

Some of the last class W 2-8-0s were still in service in 1950. The next new Norfolk & Western freight engines were 4-8-0s; a big program of 4-8-0 construction began in 1906.

Operating in flat country, the Rock Island was interested in speed as much as pulling power. In 1903, it ordered 135 2-8-0s from Alco Brooks with 63-inch driving wheels for speeds up to 60 miles per hour.[143] The silk trains, with their enormously valuable cargoes (and carrying charges), crossing the continent from California to markets in the northeastern States, may have driven the Rock Island's interest in hauling freight at such high speeds. These engines weighed 202,500 pounds with 50-square feet of grate area, 3,245 square feet of heating surface, 200 pounds per square inch boiler pressure and 22-inch × 30-inch cylinders supplied through piston valves. Based on an evaporation rate of 10 pounds of water per square foot of heating surface per hour and a steam consumption rate of 26 pounds per indicated horsepower-hour, these engines would have developed 1,250 indicated horsepower. Brooks built 193 of them for the Rock Island in 1903–4.

As a footnote to the American 2-8-0, the British brought out their own 2-8-0s for the first time in 1903.[144] These were the Great Western Railway freight engines, designed by G. J. Churchward, Chief Mechanical Engineer. But for superheating and a new class with bigger boilers, they remained in service unchanged until the end of British steam in the 1960s. They narrowly missed being the standard freight engine selected for mass-production in World War II, this place being taken by an engine of 1930s origin, designed by a former Churchward subordinate. The GWR engine weighed 153,000 pounds. A 27-square foot grate under a Belpaire firebox fired a 200-pounds per square inch boiler with 2,145 square feet of heating surface, powering 18-inch × 30-inch cylinders and 55½-inch driving wheels to produce 30,000 pounds of tractive effort. These dimensions were not greatly

exceeded in any engines built in quantity for service on British railways over the next fifty years.

4.4.2 Mastodons

The name *Mastodon* was first applied to a new locomotive with a 4-8-0 wheel arrangement, rolled out at the Central Pacific's Sacramento shops in April 1882.[145] The name stuck to that wheel arrangement.

In early 1893, Schenectady built nine 4-8-0s for the Duluth & Iron Range to the design of A. J. Pitkin, Superintendent of Motive Power.[146] This was one of the earlier orders for a giant engine in quantity. With 180 pounds per square inch boiler pressure, 22-inch × 22-inch cylinders and 54-inch driving wheels, tractive effort was 30,150 pounds, twice that of a contemporary 4-4-0.

By comparison, the British never built any locomotives in quantity for domestic service capable of more than 41,000 pounds of tractive effort. Holden's 0-10-0 tank engine, built for the Great Eastern Railway in 1903, developed 44,500 pounds of tractive effort, but the cost of strengthening bridges to take its concentrated weight was prohibitive; it was rebuilt as a 2-8-0 tender engine. *Big Bertha,* an 0-10-0 that worked as a pusher on the London, Midland & Scottish Railway between 1919 and 1959, developed 42,650 pounds. The biggest locomotive ever built for British domestic service was the London & North Eastern Railway's sole 2-8-0+0-8-2 Garratt articulated, weighing 356,000 pounds and developing 72,940 pounds of tractive effort, built in 1924 and scrapped in the mid–1950s.

The year 1897 saw significant developments in freight power; the explosive growth in demand for freight haulage was underway and the era of the American giant freight engine began. The Northern Pacific bought four 186,000-pound, two-cylinder compound 4-8-0s from Schenectady.[147] A 35-square foot grate fired a 200-pounds per square inch boiler with 2,940 square feet of heating surface. The fire-box was radial-stayed and contained a brick arch supported on water tubes. Cylinders measuring 23 inches & 34 inches × 30 inches powered 55-inch driving wheels. The Northern Pacific wanted these engines for hauling freight up 17 miles of 2.2% grade, expecting them to develop 35,000 to 40,000 pounds drawbar pull and 1,200 horsepower for 3 hours at a time at 16 miles per hour. In tests on the New York Central, one of them developed 1,190 indicated horsepower at 15 miles per hour.

In these locomotives, the 332 fire tubes were 14 feet long over tube sheets. Experiments in France in the late 1880s showed that the heating effect of the fire tubes did not increase in proportion to their length beyond about 15 feet. Beyond that length, other problems became apparent as fire tubes expanded, contracted and sagged under their own weight. A boiler 15 feet over tube sheets fitted an eight-coupled wheelbase well. When designers looked for increased pulling power by increasing the number of driving axles, they were left with the problem of what to do with the greater length available for the boiler. We will encounter some bizarre solutions to this problem.

The Great Northern, operating in similar conditions to the Northern Pacific, followed their lead and bought enormous 4-8-0s from Brooks with several innovations.[148] Brooks delivered the first two in December 1897. They were the biggest locomotives built hitherto, weighing 212,750 pounds, 80% of which went into adhesion. A 34-square foot grate in a Belpaire firebox fired a 210-pounds per square inch boiler containing 376 2¼-inch fire tubes 13 feet 10 inches long for a total heating surface of 3,280 square feet. The water legs were 4 inches wide, front, sides and back, 3½–4 inches being common. Instead of round rod, the boiler long diagonal stays were made of plate at the front and 4-inch × 4-inch angle-iron at the back. Piston valves 14½ inches in diameter admitted steam to 21-inch cylinders

with the long stroke of 34 inches. This long stoke was intended to obtain full expansion of steam supplied at a pressure 30 pounds per square inch higher than was normal in locomotives of that time. Piston valves were used because of the difficulty of balancing slide valves at such pressures. These features and 55-inch driving wheels resulted in 48,650 pounds of tractive effort. The first and third driving wheel pairs were blind-flanged. Axle loadings were 42,000 to 45,000 pounds.[149] These Mastodons were a breakthrough in size and power, exceeding anything else built in the U.S. hitherto and, as far as is known, elsewhere in the world.

The Great Northern followed through with an order for fifty more from Rogers in 1899–1900 and another ten from Brooks in 1900.[150] Rogers retained slide valves.

In 1898, the Southern Pacific followed the lead of the Northern Pacific and Great Northern and ordered a 192,000-pound Mastodon from Schenectady.[151] This engine was a two-cylinder compound with 23-inch & 35-inch cylinders × 32-inch stroke. The low-pressure cylinder was one of the biggest made for a locomotive hitherto. The boiler pressure was 200 pounds per square inch with a total heating surface of 3,025 square feet, fired by a 35-square foot grate. Tractive effort was 37,000 pounds, compound, 52,000 pounds single-expansion.

A Brooks 4-8-0 for the Illinois Central in 1899 set a new record for size at a total engine weight of 232,000 pounds, with 83% on the driving wheels; everything about the American steam locomotive was growing bigger with new construction.[152] A 38-square foot grate beneath a Belpaire firebox fired a 210-pounds per square inch boiler. The boiler diameter measured 82 inches in its parallel course ending at the smokebox; 50 to 60 inches was common only five years before. This doubled cross-section contained 424 2-inch × 14-foot 8 inch fire tubes for a total heating surface of 3,500 square feet. Steam went through 12-inch piston valves to 23-inch × 30-inch cylinders,

The Rogers Locomotive Works built this class G-3 4-8-0 for the Great Northern in 1899–1900. No. 748 was still in service at Spokane, Washington, on July 31, 1938, still with slide valves and inside valve gear (Denver Public Library, Otto C. Perry collection, OP-11792).

powering 57-inch driving wheels, resulting in a tractive effort of 49,700 pounds.

Herein lay a problem. At 10 pounds of water evaporated per square foot of heating surface per hour, this boiler could generate 35,000 pounds of steam per hour. At an evaporation rate of 7 pounds of water per pound of coal, the fireman had to shovel 5,000 pounds of coal per hour to maintain full power, beyond the sustainable rate of an unaided fireman. Things were starting not to add up. The 4-4-2 passenger engines with their big grates supported on trailing wheels had shown the way. The eight-coupled freight engine was about to follow.

By 1900, locomotive designers were becoming aware that a firebox needed volume, as well as grate area—in other words, depth, for efficient combustion. This was especially true if the fuel was poor-quality bituminous coal. This limited the scope of engines, such as 2-8-0s and 4-8-0s, which could have wide grates extending above the wheels or deep fireboxes between the wheels. For this reason, the railroad industry observed with interest the performance of a 4-8-0 built by Brooks in 1900 for the Buffalo, Rochester & Pittsburgh.[153] At 172,000 pounds engine weight, it broke no records for size, but the grate was abnormally large—59 square feet—9 feet long × 6 feet 8 inches wide. The Belpaire firebox contained no brick arch. Brooks built seventeen more for the company, class S-3, in 1900–01. Although the Buffalo, Rochester & Pittsburgh acquired forty-six 4-8-0s between 1898 and 1901,[154] they were only moderately successful because the weight carried by the leading truck reduced the weight available for adhesion. Some were rebuilt as 2-8-0s.[155]

The same year, the Chicago & Eastern Illinois improved on this with a Pittsburgh 4-8-0 with a 72-square foot grate and camelback configuration. Even though the engine looked like an anthracite-burner, it was intended for bituminous coal. It was also a two-cylinder compound with 21½-inch & 33-inch × 30-inch cylinders. The frames were of cast steel. The order was not repeated.[156]

By 1900, the Union Pacific was needing heavy power. Accordingly, the company bought eight 4-8-0s from Brooks with 35 square feet of grate, 3,010 square feet of heating surface, 200 pounds per square inch boiler pressure, 21-inch × 30-inch cylinders, 57-inch driving wheels, and 39,500 pounds of tractive effort.

The task was to haul a 750-ton train between Ogden, Utah, and Evanston, Wyoming, in 5 hours.[157] Hitherto, the company used class 1200 2-8-0s with 160-pounds per square inch boiler pressure, 20-inch × 24-inch cylinders, 51-inch driving wheels, an engine weight of 104,200 pounds and a tractive effort of 25,600 pounds. Eastbound, the maximum load for one engine was 450 tons, with a pusher on the 5 miles of 1.7% grade between Uintah and Devil's Gate and another on the 8 miles of 1.7% between Echo and Wahsatch. Two 1200s, double-heading, increased the load to 650 tons. The new 1500-class 4-8-0s hauled 70% more tonnage and dispensed with the helpers.

The 4-8-0 wheel arrangement and compounding were both in favor around 1900 but, for both, orders were typically small and were not repeated. That year, the Chicago & Eastern Illinois ordered a two-cylinder compound 4-8-0 from Pittsburgh that year and Cooke built twelve for the Oregon Short Line.[158] These orders were not repeated. Total American construction of 4-8-0s was only 600, compared to more than 33,000 2-8-0s.

4.4.3 The First Mikados

Considering that the 2-8-2 replaced the 2-8-0 as the prime freight hauler, its introduction into America was tentative and indirect. The

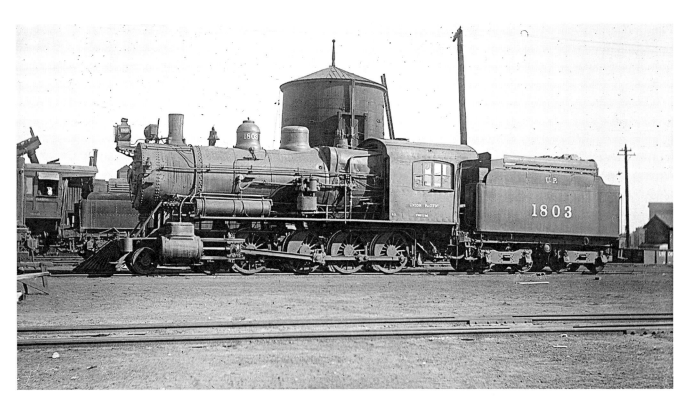

A Union Pacific 4-8-0, No. 1803, built in 1900 by Brooks Locomotive Works, photographed at Denver, Colorado, in 1916. Drury does not mention any Union Pacific 4-8-0s; the referenced source calls them the 1500 class; the photograph shows the number 1803, whereas the class number might be expected to begin "15." Notwithstanding these discrepancies, it is fair to assume that the photograph shows the locomotives described in the text (Denver Public Library, Otto C. Perry collection, OP-16618).

first-ever 2-8-2 may have been the Lehigh Valley's rebuild of one of two unsatisfactory 2-10-0s built in 1867.[159] The first 2-8-2s built as such were probably four locomotives that Brooks built for the Chicago & Calumet Terminal Railway in 1893, for which reason the first locomotives of this type were known as *Calumets*.[160] The leading and trailing axles were both mounted in radial trucks; their purpose was to carry part of the engine's 150,000-pound total weight. With 180-pounds per square inch boiler pressure, 19-inch × 26-inch cylinders and 51-inch driving wheels, the locomotives had a tractive effort of 28,200 pounds when most engines then in use had tractive efforts less than 20,000 pounds. The freight transfer service for which they were built demanded high pulling power at low speeds over short distances. Two went to the Wisconsin & Michigan Railway in 1903 to haul construction trains.[161] The traditional origin of the 2-8-2 wheel arrangement was a metre-gauge class that Baldwin built for the Japan Railway Company in 1897, for which reason they became known as *Mikados*. The trailing wheels supported a wide grate for burning low-grade coal.[162]

F. W. Johnstone, Superintendent of Motive Power on the Mexican Central Railway, designed another early 2-8-2, built by Brooks in 1897, to haul 210-ton trains up 30 miles of 3% grade with curves as sharp as 18 degrees.[163] The driving wheels were of 49-inch diameter and closely spaced for the shortest possible rigid wheelbase, with blind flanges on the two middle pairs of driving wheels. The boiler and Belpaire firebox were set high above the frames with a total heating surface of 2,805 square feet, including 412 fire tubes 2 inches in diameter. The leading and trailing trucks were used more to carry some of the 193,450-pound engine weight than to support a large firebox; in spite of the trailing axle, the 31-square foot grate and foundation ring were set between the driving wheels.

The 2-8-2 idea began to catch on in the U.S. with an engine built by Baldwin in 1901 for the Bismarck, Washburn & Great Falls.[164]

This engine was similar in size to, or smaller than many contemporary 2-8-0s, but it had a 56-square foot grate, supported on trailing wheels, to burn lignite, firing a 200-pounds per square inch boiler with 2,495 square feet of heating surface. The Vauclain compound 14-inch & 24-inch × 26-inch cylinders powered diminutive 50-inch driving wheels to produce 35,000 pounds of tractive effort, single-expansion, 26,000 pounds, compound. The Bismarck, Washburn & Great Falls tested the engine in December 1901, on maximum grades of 1% and curvature of 9° in temperatures close to freezing with snow on the rails. With a trailing load of 940 tons, the engine made a maximum speed of 18 miles per hour, cresting the summit at 2 miles per hour. As the company intended it to haul 890 tons over this route in a temperature of 55°F, it performed better than expected. The Northern Pacific tested it between Jamestown and Mandan, North Dakota. Lignite evaporated only 2.1 to 2.4 pounds of water per pound of lignite and "it is evident that without a mechanical stoker one man cannot throw the amount of fuel consumed in the average run." The Jamestown-Mandan run, with 1,564 tons trailing load, took 15¾ hours; the fireman shoveled 25 tons of lignite, including 2½ tons firing up the engine.

The year 1903 was a banner one for Santa Fe and American freight power. In that year the 2-8-2 and 2-10-2 types made their real debut in America, both on the Santa Fe, both from Baldwin. The Santa Fe ordered fifteen Vauclain compound 2-8-2s for use on the Raton Pass.[165] The engines weighed 260,000 pounds, of which 77% was adhesion weight, with John Player's traction increaser. These engines weighed little less than the company's 2-10-0s, with a closely similar heating surface at 5,365 square feet. The grate area was 59-square feet; the cylinders measured 18 inches & 30 inches × 32 inches, developing up to 55,000 pounds of tractive effort. From the available drawings, the leading truck was suspension-equalized with the front two pairs of driving wheels; the trailing truck was equalized with the back

The Bismarck, Washburn & Great Falls 2-8-2 built by Baldwin in 1901 as a Vauclain compound. This looks like a manufacturer's photograph, taken when the locomotive was new. This view highlights the potential for unpowered trailing wheels to support a wide, deep firebox, a possibility that American locomotive designers exploited to an extreme degree over the next fifty years (courtesy California State Railroad Museum, Gerald M. Best Collection, Negative 39085cn).

One of the first 2-8-2s, Atchison, Topeka & Santa Fe 825 class, No. 895, built in 1903 by Baldwin, seen in 1918 at an unknown location after rebuilding to single-expansion with Baker-Pilliod valve gear (Denver Public Library, Otto C. Perry collection, OP-158).

The same locomotive as the previous photograph (Atchison, Topeka & Santa Fe, 2-8-2, 825 class, No. 895, Baldwin, 1903) at Belen, New Mexico, on December 5, 1937, further rebuilt with new cylinders, rebuilt valve gear and an additional sand dome (Denver Public Library, Otto C. Perry collection, OP-159).

two pairs of driving wheels. The order was not repeated and the Santa Fe converted them to single-expansion in 1908–9.

The Lehigh Valley was an early user of the 2-8-2, ordering its first in 1903 and taking delivery of forty-seven from Baldwin and Alco Schenectady between 1903 and 1907. These were the only camelback 2-8-2s ever built, using saturated steam, Stephenson link motion and slide valves.[166]

4.4.4 Decapods and the First Santa Fes

As far as is known, no decapods were built in the 1890s after the New York, Lake Erie & Western Baldwins of 1893. If the strength of the American economic recovery, and its effects on the railroads, surprised many in the late 1890s, it only accelerated after 1900. That year, Baldwin built a 2-10-0 Vauclain compound for the Minneapolis, St. Paul & Sault Ste. Marie.[167] The total engine weight was planned at 214,000 pounds with 190,000 pounds supported on the five pairs of driving wheels, the middle pair being blind-flanged, providing 4-8-0 size and 2-8-0 weight distribution. The 39-square foot grate area was achieved at the cost of a firebox 11 feet long. Boiler pressure was 215 pounds per square inch with 3,000 square feet of heating surface; 17-inch & 28-inch × 32-inch cylinders powered 55-inch wheels for a tractive effort of 31,000 pounds, single-expansion, 22,000, compound. The company planned to use this engine on 2,000-ton trains between Minneapolis and Pennington, Wisconsin, 165 miles including 0.8% adverse grades that the engine was to surmount unaided. Doubling was anticipated on one stretch of 10 miles with grades up to 1.2%. The engine as built weighed 207,210 pounds in working order, without fire or crew; Baldwin guaranteed that it would haul 2,000 tons up a straight 0.8% grade at 6 miles per hour. This order was not repeated.

Besides the Raton Pass, the Tehachapi Mountains, between Mojave, California, and Bakersfield, were especially demanding of Santa Fe motive power. In October 1901, the company ordered seventy-five 260,000-pound, oil-burning, Player tandem compound 2-10-0s from Baldwin with 5,800 square feet of heating surface.[168] Apparently,

Baldwin built only one of these engines, weighing 268,000 pounds, capable of an astonishing 57,000 pounds tractive effort, compound, 77,000 pounds single-expansion. A 59-square foot grate fired a boiler with 5,390 square feet of heating surface. This locomotive was fitted with a Le Chatelier brake.[169] A Le Chatelier brake functioned by closing the exhaust nozzle and admitting steam to the cylinders through the exhaust port; as the pistons compressed the steam they produced a braking action. The engineer could vary the amount of braking by opening a relief valve. A safety valve guarded against excessive pressure developing in the cylinder. At the time this engine was the heaviest locomotive in the world—but not for long.

The company asked Baldwin to drop one of the 2-10-0s that it had ordered and add one to the order of thirty-five 2-8-0s that they were building, with a Player oil-burning boiler. The Player boiler had three cylindrical, corrugated fireboxes, with a burner in each, combining in a combustion chamber. Oil-burning opened up new possibilities in locomotive size because heating surfaces were outrunning the capacity of a hand-fired, coal-burning grate, especially in summer in the southwestern U.S.

At the same time, the Santa Fe ordered two 260,000-pound coal-burning 2-10-0 tandem compounds from Alco Schenectady. These were the heaviest and most powerful engines built to date. The Santa Fe's clearance limits were generous; the engine was 15 feet 6 inches high to the top of the stack. The grate area was 59 square feet, firing a 225-pounds per square inch boiler with 4,680 square feet of heating surface. Steam went to 17½-inch & 30-inch × 34-inch cylinders through piston valves and powered 57-inch driving wheels, developing 70,000 pounds of tractive effort, single-expansion, 52,000, compound. The fireboxes were designed for easy conversion between bituminous coal and oil. Surprisingly for this time, the engines were fitted with speed recorders. The frames and several other parts were of cast steel. Building a steam locomotive took Alco surprisingly little time; the two tandem compound 2-10-0s were at work near Bakersfield in January 1902.[170] All three of the 2-10-0 tandem compounds were converted to single-expansion in 1911 and 1915.

The first of a new series of freight power, the Atchison, Topeka & Santa Fe tandem compound 2-10-0, No. 989, built by Alco Schenectady in 1902 (Stephen Hart Library, William H. Jackson collection, History Colorado, CHS.J1818).

One of the first Atchison, Topeka & Santa Fe 2-10-2s, a tandem compound, 900 class, No. 963, built by Baldwin in 1903–04. The missing main rod shows that this locomotive was in storage, probably for rebuilding to single expansion, when Otto Perry photographed it at Topeka, Kansas, on October 13, 1921 (Denver Public Library, Otto C. Perry collection, OP-209).

G. R. Henderson replaced the inventive but unfortunate Player as Superintendent of Motive Power on the Santa Fe and cancelled the order for the 2-10-0s. Henderson then worked with Baldwin to come up with the 2-10-2, known as the Santa Fe type, of which the first was built in 1903. Apparently, the reason for adding the trailing truck was to improve tracking while backing downgrade after a helper run[171]; the Santa Fe's first 2-10-2s had the same grate area as the 2-10-0s that they replaced.

The Santa Fe boldly placed an initial order of seventy with Baldwin. Eighty-five were built in 1903–4; a further 267 followed in successive classes between then and 1927. The first 2-10-2s were tandem compounds. The order was not repeated and the company rebuilt them to single-expansion in 1916–23.[172] Of the first seventy, twenty-five were to burn coal, the rest oil. They were the heaviest engines built to date, weighing 287,000 pounds, of which 82% was adhesion weight; spreading the weight among five axles kept the axle loading down to 47,000 pounds. The grate area was 59 square feet, like the 2-8-2s, but the heating surface was less at 4,795 square feet. Both types had the high boiler pressure of 225 pounds per square inch. Like the 2-8-2s, the cylinders were 19-inch & 32-inch × 32-inch stroke. The middle pair of the 57-inch driving wheels was blind-flanged. Tractive effort for both types was 78,000 pounds, single-expansion, 57,000, compound. The designers of the 2-10-2s reduced the percentage of boiler cross-section occupied by fire tubes from 38%, in the 2-10-0s and 2-8-2s, to 32% so as to obtain better circulation and for easier boiler washing. The tubes in the 2-10-2s were 20 feet long, compared to 19 feet in the 2-8-2s. The current study has not discovered why the Santa Fe bought two different types of such similar dimensions, but the 2-8-2 and, to a lesser extent, the 2-10-2 would become the standard rigid-frame American freight engine for more than twenty years.

Adding to the momentous developments of 1903, the Baltimore & Ohio placed an experimental order with Alco for the first American Mallet. The engine went into service in May 1904; the eyes of the American railroad industry were upon it. The operational debut of the 2-8-2, the 2-10-2 and the Mallet in 1903–4 ushered in a new era in American freight power.

Section 4.5 Switchers, Suburbans, Geared and Special-Purpose Locomotives

4.5.1 Switchers

Locomotives purpose-built for making up and breaking down trains at marshalling yards first appeared during the 1850s, replacing first horses and then obsolescent road engines. By the 1870s, the 0-4-0 switcher was common; by 1890, switchers made up 28% of the U.S. locomotive fleet. In areas of dense traffic, railroad companies built huge classification yards with multiple parallel tracks and capacities for hundreds of freight cars.[173] As freight trains grew longer, so did the cuts of cars that the switchers had to move. Moving slowly over short distances, the switchers did not need leading trucks; the whole engine weight was therefore available for adhesion.

The 0-6-0, with its greater pulling power, replaced the 0-4-0 in switching service. By 1902, 0-4-0s comprised only 3% of the U.S. locomotive fleet; 0-6-0s made up 10%. The 0-4-0 continued around docks, industrial plants and large civil engineering works, usually as tank engines, 0-4-0 tender engines becoming increasingly rare. Equally rare were compound switchers; compounding offered no benefits in switching service to offset its higher cost.

Probably typical of switchers of the early 1900s were the 0-6-0 oil-burners that Alco Schenectady built for the Southern Pacific in

This Atchison, Topeka & Santa Fe 900 class 2-10-2, No. 934, built by Baldwin in 1903–04, had already been rebuilt to single expansion with piston valves and Walschaert valve gear, although retaining the tandem compound low-pressure cylinder, by the time Otto Perry photographed it at Trinidad, Colorado, on October 28, 1920 (Denver Public Library, Otto C. Perry collection, OP-197).

An Atchison, Topeka & Santa Fe 900 class 2-10-2, No. 934, further rebuilt with new cylinders and Baker valve gear when photographed at Wootton, Colorado, on July 21, 1929. Additionally, a power reverser shows above the back driving wheel (Denver Public Library, Otto C. Perry collection, OP-198).

A Southern Pacific class S-57 0-6-0, No. 1120, built by Alco Schenectady in 1904 and photographed at Oakland, California, on July 30, 1940 (Denver Public Library, Otto C. Perry collection, OP-15389).

1904.[174] These engines weighed 147,000 pounds. A 30-square foot grate fired a 180-pounds per square inch boiler with 1,805 square feet of heating surface. Cylinders measuring 20 inches × 26 inches powered 57-inch driving wheels and provided 27,900 pounds of tractive effort. Schenectady built twelve; they lasted until 1935–52. Between 1900 and 1924, the Southern Pacific bought 239 0-6-0s, new and used. Five built by Baldwin in 1903 had Vanderbilt boilers.

Every major railroad used 0-6-0 switchers. The New York Central and its subsidiaries bought 1,252 of them between 1900 and 1916. In new construction they were superseded on some lines by 0-8-0s; even so, they stayed in service until the end of steam in the 1950s. Construction of new 0-6-0s continued throughout the steam era; an estimated 15,000 were built, rivaling the Ten-Wheelers and Mikados.[175]

4.5.2 Suburban Locomotives

The so-called "Suburban" locomotive—also known as a "tank engine"—carried its coal and water in tanks on the engine frame with no separate tender. Such locomotives were intended to run equally well in either direction, dispensing with turntables and wye-tracks for local services. Their coal and water capacity was small and they depended on short runs in areas of dense infrastructure.[176] This type of locomotive had a long history in America; only a few examples can be given here.

The first suburban locomotive was a steam car built by Baldwin for the Pennsylvania in 1860. Similar cars were built in the 1870s, but the idea lapsed in favor of separate locomotives.

The Pennsylvania rebuilt a Baldwin 4-4-0 as a 2-8-0 tank engine at Altoona in 1864; it derailed on curves.[177] At the same time the Altoona shops rebuilt a 4-4-0, replacing the tender with a rigidly attached passenger car. In 1865, Altoona rebuilt a Baldwin 4-6-0,

placing a small coal and water bunker on a rearward extension of the frames, the extension being supported by an additional driving wheel, making a 4-8-0 wheel arrangement. This design was unsuccessful.

In about 1873, M. N. Forney obtained a patent for a suburban locomotive and such engines were also known as "Forneys" for that reason. The tender was carried on a rear frame extension supported by a four-wheel truck. In 1874, D. W. Wyman designed an 0-4-0 for the New York elevated railroad, carrying water in a saddle tank over the boiler. The elevated railroad subsequently bought both this type and Forneys. In 1876, the Mason Machine Works, Taunton, Massachusetts, built an engine on the Fairlie principle with one powered drive unit free to swivel under the boiler, while the tender, as in the Forney, was built on a rear frame extension supported on a four-wheel truck.

In 1881, Altoona built a 2-4-6 "double-ender" with the tender on a rearward frame extension, supported on a six-wheel truck. The Pennsylvania had the best facilities of any railroad in the country for experiments of this nature. Other railroads would have had to order such creations from established builders at greater expense and risk of failure. As far as is known, the builders themselves did not promote engines of this type.

In 1889, the Chicago, Burlington & Quincy started to build its class I 0-6-2T (the suffix "T" denotes "tank engine") engines which were still in use in the early 1900s. In 1891, the New York Central brought out a 2-6-6T, but they were prone to derail and were rebuilt as 2-6-0 tender engines. At the same time Brooks built a class of 4-4-4Ts for the Chicago & Northern Pacific with side tanks and a rear coal bunker. The Illinois Central built three types of Forney engine, the standard being a 2-4-4T.

H. K. Porter & Co., of Pittsburgh, was the dominant builder of small steam locomotives, such as the 0-4-4ST (saddle tank) for the Munising Railway in 1895. Its price, new, was $5,725.[178] Porter was apparently able to charge a better price per pound of locomotive than its competitors, as evidenced by the $11,380 price for the Lake Shore & Ishpeming's much bigger 2-8-0s quoted earlier. This may have influenced the company's decision to stay out of the Alco merger of 1901. Between 1866 and 1952, Porter built 8,200 locomotives, 4,200 before 1901, 4,000 after.[179]

Late in 1901, the New York Central bought a large 2-6-6T suburban engine from Schenectady.[180] It performed so well that the company at once ordered fifteen more. These engines weighed 216,000 pounds. A 62-square foot anthracite-burning grate fired a 200-pounds per square inch boiler containing 2,435 square feet of heating surface. Piston valves admitted steam to 20-inch × 24-inch cylinders powering 63-inch driving wheels, for 25,900 pounds of tractive effort. The two-wheel leading truck was conventional; the coal and water bunker behind the cab was mounted on a rear frame extension supported on a six-wheel truck, center-pivoted and capable of sidewise movement. The coal and water spaces held 5 tons and 3,700 gallons respectively. These were the biggest suburban engines built to date. In the long run they were not a success and were later rebuilt as 2-6-0 tender engines. A later batch of 2-6-6Ts, built by Schenectady for the Boston & Albany in 1906–7 enjoyed better success.

In 1903, the Philadelphia & Reading bought six 2-6-4T suburban engines from Baldwin.[181] These were lighter than the New York Central engines, at 201,700 pounds. Like the New York Central engines, they were built to burn anthracite on 68-square foot grates. The 1,980 square feet of heating surface was concentrated in a short, fat boiler, only 9 feet over tube sheets, containing 447 1¾-inch fire tubes. Like the New York Central engines, the coal and water space was in a bunker at the back of the cab. The final number built was ten in 1903–4, but the order was not repeated.

Tank engines continued to be built in small numbers until the late 1920s. The Boston & Albany 4-6-6T illustrated here represents the American tank engine in its final form.

The history of the tank engine in America is obscure, but the Otto C. Perry collection of photographs includes sixty such locomotives of several different configurations, distributed among twenty-five users; Class I railroad users included the Boston & Albany, the Central of Georgia, the Chicago, Burlington & Quincy, the Milwaukee, the Chicago & North Western, the Rock Island, the Canadian National, the Denver & Rio Grande Western, the Illinois Central, the Norfolk & Western, the Philadelphia & Reading, the Santa Fe, the Southern Pacific and the Union Pacific. The present study has not discovered how many were used in total. Some diverse examples are illustrated here.

4.5.3 Geared Locomotives

The Americans developed three successful types of steam locomotive for the steep, sharply curved and rough track of mountain railroads and logging sites: Shay, Climax and Heisler. Their cylinders drove power trucks through gearing and jointed drive shafts, giving them great flexibility to follow uneven track. Reduction gearing enabled them to climb steeper grades than any other type of locomotive, other than those with toothed wheels engaging a toothed rail ("rack-and-pinion") but this feature so limited their speed that they were not usable on main lines. The Geared Steam Locomotive Works website (www.gearedsteam.com) lists nearly forty other types of geared steam locomotives that were built in small numbers for limited periods of time.

The Shay was the longest-lived and most successful also known as "Limas," "Limeys," "stem-winders" and "Shay-gears."[182] Its cylinders

This Boston & Albany class D-1a 4-6-6T, built at Schenectady in 1928, was the ultimate development of the American tank engine. Otto Perry photographed No. 401 at Boston, Massachusetts, on October 15, 1930 (Denver Public Library, Otto C. Perry collection, OP-2652).

This 2-4-4T belonged to the Morristown & Erie, builder unknown, probably built before 1900. The missing connecting rod suggests that this locomotive awaited scrapping when Otto Perry photographed it at Morristown, New Jersey, on August 20, 1933 (Denver Public Library, Otto C. Perry collection, OP-13261).

The Norfolk & Western rebuilt a class W-1 2-8-0, one of a class originally built by Roanoke company shops, Baldwin and the Richmond Locomotive Works in 1900–1, as this 0-8-0 saddle tank engine, No. 830, for hostling duties. Photographed at Roanoke, Virginia, on August 4, 1936 (Denver Public Library, Otto C. Perry collection, OP-13789).

The Baltimore & Ohio bought four of these class C-16 0-4-0T's from Baldwin in 1912. No. 98 at Baltimore, Maryland, on August 19, 1937 (Denver Public Library, Otto C. Perry collection, OP-2395).

The Denver & Rio Grande Western owned this 2-6-0T, No. 578, builder unknown, photographed at Salt Lake City, Utah, on August 7, 1935. Slide valves and inside valve gear suggest a construction date before 1905. This tank engine may have been built as such or may have been converted from a 2-6-0 tender engine (Denver Public Library, Otto C. Perry collection, OP-9323).

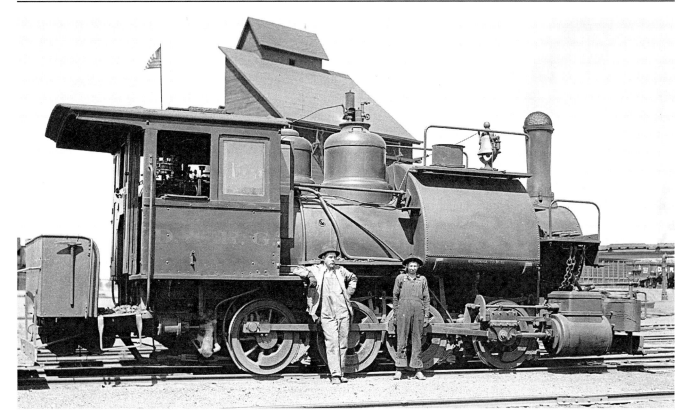

This Denver & Rio Grande Western 0-8-0T, No. 800, builder unknown, could have been built as such or could have been rebuilt from a 2-8-0 tender locomotive, photographed at Denver, Colorado, in July 1918. Slide valves and inside valve gear suggest a construction date before 1905 (Denver Public Library, Otto C. Perry collection, OP-9473).

The Union Pacific owned this 0-6-0 tank engine, No. 010998, builder unknown, probably built before 1905, photographed at Pocatello, Idaho, on November 13, 1936. This locomotive may have been converted from a tender engine (Denver Public Library, Otto C. Perry collection, OP-17374).

A typical Shay, Uintah Railway No. 7, photographed at Atchee, Colorado, on September 3, 1934 (Denver Public Library, Otto C. Perry collection, OP-16340).

were mounted vertically on one side of the laterally offset boiler. The pistons drove a jointed, lengthwise drive shaft which drove the power bogies through bevel gears. Hirsimaki (*Lima: The History,* Edmonds, WA: Hundman, 1986) describes how the Shay reached its ultimate form by way of several experimental arrangements of cylinders, shafting and gearing. Manufacture began at the Lima Locomotive Works, Lima, Ohio, in 1880.[183] By 1895, 500 had been built and were in use in North and South America.

Main line railroads used a few big Shays on steeply graded branch lines. The Buffalo & Susquehanna owned seven in the mid–1890s.[184] The El Paso Rock Island Route operated a logging branch line from Alamogordo, New Mexico, to Cox Cañon.[185] The line gained 6,000 feet in elevation in 31 miles. Grades ranged from 3% to more than 6½% with one 8-mile stretch of 4.5% to 5.2%, including ½ mile at 6% with tight curves. In 1902, the company bought the biggest Shay built to date, weighing 291,000 pounds, for this line. A 36-square foot grate fired a 190-pounds per square inch boiler with 1,990 square feet of heating surface, supplying steam to three 15-inch × 17-inch cylinders. Because the coal and water space contributed to the adhesion weight, the adhesion weight diminished as the 9 tons of coal and 6,000 gallons of water were consumed. The locomotive compressor supplied Westinghouse air brakes for the train only. The engine carried steam and Le Chatelier brakes for itself. Under test, the engine took a train of twenty-seven empty logging cars and a caboose up the line, a trailing load of 222 tons.

In 1905, the Chesapeake & Ohio put a Shay into service, hauling coal cars on its Keeney's Creek branch, 7 miles long with grades up to 4.2%.[186] The complete engine, including tender, weighed 330,000 pounds in working order. Grate area was 43 square feet; steam pressure was 200 pounds per square inch. Tractive effort could not be calculated in the same way as for a conventional reciprocating engine,

but under test, the engine developed 814 indicated horsepower at 116 revolutions per minute and a drawbar pull of 40,100 pounds. At a slower speed at 44 revolutions per minute, drawbar pull was 53,000 pounds. Typical speeds were 5 to 7 miles per hour.

The Western Maryland inherited some of the biggest Shays ever built when it took over the 88-mile Greenbriar, Cheat & Elk line in 1927.[187] These engines developed 52,000 pounds of tractive effort from 200 pounds per square inch of boiler pressure and 17-inch cylinders driving four four-wheel trucks. They weighed 302,000 pounds. The Western Maryland found them expensive to maintain and replaced them with conventional 2-8-0s in 1934, even though the line climbed grades up to 3.7%; one 2-8-0 could handle only ten cars.

Probably the last Shay ever built was a 324,000-pound monster for the Western Maryland, built in 1945 to replace an older Shay, built in 1918, on a coal mine branch that joined the Western Maryland at Chaffee, West Virginia.[188] The branch was built narrow gauge by a mining company in 1904, rebuilt to standard gauge in 1912 and acquired by the Western Maryland in 1929. This line included grades up to 10% with 7% being common.

The design of the new locomotive was primitive by 1945 standards. The frame was built up from girders. High power was not an issue, so a 49-square foot hand-fired grate fired a 200-pounds per square inch boiler with a Type A superheater. Three 3-inch arch tubes supported the brick arch. Evaporative heating surface totaled 1,850 square feet with another 430 square feet of superheating surface. Stephenson valve gear, with Alco power reverse, controlled 9-inch piston valves to three vertical 17-inch × 18-inch cylinders. These drove a line shaft that in turn drove three four-wheel trucks through universal jointing. The engine developed 60,000 pounds of tractive effort. Even that insignificant branch line could accept a 54,000-pound axle loading. The engine hauled 5,600 tons on straight, level

Western Maryland Shay, No. 6, built by Lima in 1945, may have been the last Shay to be built (courtesy *Classic Trains* magazine collection, _e0305_02, Lima photo).

track but at no more than 10 miles per hour; it made the same speed with 156 tons against a 7% grade.

From the time when Ephraim Shay licensed his 1881 patent to Lima until the last one went to the Western Maryland in 1945, Lima built 2,761 Shay locomotives.[189] Production peaked at 223 in 1907. Truck logging pushed rail logging aside in the years after World War I; only eight Shays were built after 1929. The Climax and Heisler geared locomotives suffered a similar fate.

In the Climax locomotive, one steeply inclined cylinder was mounted on each side of the boiler; the pistons drove a cross-shaft running under the boiler. Bevel gears drove a lengthwise drive shaft. The drive shaft drove the trucks through more bevel gears. Manufacture of the Climax began at the Climax Manufacturing Co., Corry, Pennsylvania, in 1884. Between 1884 and 1934, the company built 500 locomotives, ranging in weight from 16,000 pounds to 100,000 pounds.[190] The biggest was probably the 100,000-pound locomotive built in 1897 for the Colorado & Northern Railroad, operating out of Boulder, Colorado.[191]

In the Heisler, the cylinders were mounted in a V, converging underneath the boiler, where the pistons drove a lengthwise drive shaft. The Heisler locomotive resulted from seven years' work by Charles Heisler of New York.[192] The first Heisler locomotive was built in March 1898, by the Stearns Manufacturing Co., Erie, Pennsylvania, a three-truck, 120,000-pound locomotive for the McCloud River Railway Co., Mount Shasta, California. Heisler later formed the Heisler Locomotive Works at Erie to manufacture these engines and built 850 of them between 1898 and 1941.[193]

Annual construction of geared locomotives was already insignificant, compared to conventional locomotives for the common carriers, in the early 1900s. Orders for geared locomotives of all types totaled only 561 between 1908 and 1928, divided as 298 Heisler, 259 Shay and only 4 Climax. Trucks and automobiles took over the logging sites and mountainous areas from the 1920s onward, ending the role of the geared locomotive.

4.5.4 Other Unconventional Locomotives

Among the more grotesque, or comical, manifestations of the steam locomotive was the so-called inspection car, or observation car. This looked like a steam locomotive trying to hide under a passenger car. These devices were for the use of senior employees on

The Crown-Willamette Paper Co., Longview, Washington, owned this Climax-type locomotive, photographed on July 26, 1936 (Denver Public Library, Otto C. Perry collection, OP-7281).

The Tionesta Valley Railway operated both rod and geared engines over 80 miles of narrow-gauge line in northern Pennsylvania. Heisler No. 19 is shown near Sheffield, Pennsylvania, on July 12, 1947 (Denver Public Library, Robert W. Richardson collection, RR-1511).

The Rapid City, Black Hills & Western's Heisler No. 7, photographed at Rapid City, South Dakota, on September 2, 1935 (Denver Public Library, Otto C. Perry collection, OP-14533).

A typical inspection locomotive, the New York Central's *Mohawk*, photographed near Ilion, New York, on August 23, 1933 (Denver Public Library, Otto C. Perry collection, OP-13507).

tours of inspection. The one that Cooke built for the Erie & Wyoming Valley Railroad in 1899 was designed by the company president, George B. Smith, and built for his personal use.

This vehicle was of the 4-2-2 wheel arrangement. A small, vertical boiler inside the car provided steam at 165 pounds per square inch to 8¼-inch × 8½-inch cylinders. The car carried 1 ton of coal and 600 gallons of water.[194] Other railroads, such as the Lake Shore & Michigan Southern, the Chicago, Burlington & Quincy and the Philadelphia & Reading also built such vehicles, either from scratch or using obsolete locomotives.

Builders on both sides of the Atlantic tried to build steam engines into self-propelled passenger cars. The idea failed because, when the engine was down for repair, the passenger accommodation was lost as well, and for reasons of passenger comfort and safety.

Articulated locomotives were a European specialty, originally conceived as special-purpose engines for extreme grades and curvatures. Of the many articulated locomotives invented in Europe, only the Fairlie, the Mallet and the Garratt were extensively used world-wide.

The Fairlie comprised two boilers set firebox-to-firebox with a common steam space. The first was built in 1865. Engineer and fireman worked in restricted spaces on opposite sides of the twin fireboxes. A powered truck, supplied with steam through flexibly jointed pipes, swiveled under each boiler. Some 200 were built in America in the 1870s and were the first use of Walschaert valve gear in America.[195] They were used on the New York & Manhattan Beach, the Wheeling & Lake Erie, the Boston, Revere Beach & Lynn and the Denver, South Park & Pacific. Although they performed well on this latter railroad, they were unpopular due to their complexity. By the 1890s, the Fairlie was no more than a memory in America.

The Garratt was a British invention of 1907 that never gained a foothold in North America. Some of the Garratts were the biggest steam locomotives ever manufactured outside America; some are still running in Africa at the time of writing.

These unconventional locomotives are the tip of an iceberg of diverse and sometimes exotic locomotives outside the scope of this book—geared, rack, fireless, compressed-air, electric trolley and battery locomotives, and the like. Among these small and exotic engines in the 1890s, however, were the electric and internal-combustion locomotives that would eventually displace steam from the main lines.

5

Traction Other Than Steam, 1895–1905

ENGINEER: "What's wrong with this engine?"
MECHANIC: "It's a steam locomotive. That's what's wrong with it."
Welsh Highland Railway, UK, 2011

Even as the American steam locomotive was reaching its greatest ascendancy, the seeds of its demise were not only sown but sprouting. Completely different forms of motive power were coming into existence that would eventually replace it.

Section 5.1 Electric Traction

The first of these new forms of traction was the electric motor. The history of electric traction goes remarkably far back in time.[1] Experiments on the generation and application of electricity had been going on for much of the nineteenth century. In 1834, Thomas Davenport, a blacksmith of Brandon, Vermont, exhibited a toy running on a circular track, powered from a battery. In 1842, Robert Davidson built and tested an electric locomotive on the Edinburgh & Glasgow Railway (Reference 1 gives the date as 1838).[2] In 1847, Moses G. Farmer exhibited a small model at Dover, New Hampshire. In 1850, Charles G. Page's electric locomotive ran for 5 miles between Washington and Bladensburg. None of these experiments had immediate results. In 1879, Siemens & Halske exhibited a 3-horsepower electric locomotive at Berlin, taking remotely generated 150-volt power from a third rail. The first railroad to offer a scheduled commercial passenger service, powered by electricity, followed at Berlin in 1881.

In the 1880s and 1890s, electric traction took over urban and interurban transit systems on both sides of the Atlantic, hitherto powered by horses and steam locomotives. In 1883, Leo Daft began experiments at Greenville, New Jersey, followed by small experimental electric tramways at Saratoga and other places. Bentley and Knight installed an experimental tramway at Cleveland in 1884, followed by Van Depoele at the Toronto Exhibition. Van Depoele installed electric tramways at South Bend and Minneapolis, as did Short at Denver and Henry at Kansas City. In 1885, Daft began operations at Baltimore on the Union Passenger Railway and on the Manhattan Elevated in New York. Frank J. Sprague, after some previous successes, electrified the street railway system of Richmond, Virginia, between 1887 and 1888.[3] In 1892, the Baltimore & Ohio contracted for the electrification of a tunnel in Baltimore, completed in 1895. In 1896–7, the New York, New Haven & Hartford electrified branch lines around Boston and Hartford. In 1897, Frank Sprague invented a system to put multiple units under the control of one person. This would ultimately revolutionize locomotive technology and would set the seal on the demise of the steam locomotive. In 1887, there were less than 60 miles of electrically operated tramway in Europe and North America combined. By 1905, 30,000 miles of electric railway were in service in the United States alone.

Westinghouse built its first electric railcar in 1894 and teamed up with Baldwin the following year to form a partnership that would last for more than fifty years.[4] The first Baldwin-Westinghouse electric locomotive went into service on the Lackawanna & Wyoming Valley that year.

The benefits of electric traction were many. When not in use, it consumed no power; when needed, it was ready for use as soon as it was switched on, unlike a steam locomotive which took hours to start up and then consumed fuel keeping hot. The electric motor was clean and quiet. It provided uniform tractive effort, whereas the steam locomotive's tractive effort fluctuated with piston and crank positions. Electric traction was capable of faster acceleration than steam power. Power could be supplied from a large, efficient, stationary generating plant and picked up by the locomotive through a shoe sliding on a third rail or from an overhead trolley wire. Battery-powered locomotives became common in mines and industrial plants, but lacked the power needed for railroad work. The power of an electric locomotive was limited only by the size of the power supply and the motor itself, and by the maximum acceptable temperature of the windings. Engineers realized early on that one throttle could control more than one motor. The limiting factor was the capital high cost of the power generation and distribution system. This would restrict the electric locomotive to areas where high traffic density justified the capital investment.

The nub of the argument in favor of electrification came through clearly when the Manhattan Elevated Railroad was considering the matter in 1897.[5]

The cost of fuel for operating a steam locomotive amounts to about 20 per cent of the total operating expenses of these roads, the fuel consumption being about 7 to 8 lbs. of coal per horse-power per hour.

With good compound condensing engines driving electric generators at a station, the coal consumption is reduced to about one-third that amount.

Were steam locomotives discarded it would be possible to replace the high priced skilled labor necessary for their operation by ordinary trustworthy men who are not skilled mechanics; whose rate of wages is about one-half that of a locomotive engineer, and only one man would be necessary to operate the electrical propelling mechanism. We believe that the repair account will be materially lessened both in the units of motive power and in the permanent way were the trains equipped with motors. The care of a steam locomotive is very onerous, the average run being about one hundred miles, when it must be thoroughly overhauled and inspected by skilled mechanics before being used again. Contrast with this the all-day service of most electric motors two or three hundred miles a day for days.

Electric traction was particularly well suited to suburban service with frequent stops and fast acceleration. In switching service, where the steam locomotive was particularly inefficient, an electric locomotive consumed no power when it was not working. Against this, the cost, complexity and danger of overhead wires or third rails in a yard was a deterrent.

An attempt to circumvent this cost was the Heilmann steam-electric locomotive, invented, built and tested in France in 1892–3, foreshadowing the diesel-electric locomotive. J. J. Heilmann's original idea was to power each car in a train electrically, the power being supplied from a steam-powered generator car at the front of the train which was also a locomotive.[6] In 1893, a huge, 200,000-pound Heilmann locomotive was under construction in France, designed solely as a locomotive. A 500-horsepower, two-cylinder, horizontally opposed, compound steam engine was coupled directly to a 400-volt, 1,025-amp generator. A separate 20-horsepower steam engine drove the generator exciter. Each of the eight driving axles had its own electric motor.

By 1896, this engine had run 1,250 miles on a French railroad without mishap and a second prototype was built. The efficiency was said to be 65% to 70% in terms of tractive effort at the rail as a percentage of the steam engine power output; this was no higher than the efficiency of a steam locomotive, comparing cylinder and drawbar horsepower. The second prototype had a 1,300 to 1,400-horsepower, six-cylinder, vertical steam engine. The steam-electric locomotive did not catch on because it retained the disadvantages of the steam locomotive with no gain in efficiency.

The "first substantial attempt to put an electric locomotive in the same service as a steam locomotive"—at least in the U.S.—was the electrification of the Baltimore & Ohio's Belt Line tunnel under Baltimore in 1893.[7] General Electric at Schenectady built the locomotives to push 500-ton trains at 30 miles per hour up a 0.8% grade, running on 625-volts. Tunnels, where the heat and smoke of steam engines was objectionable, even dangerous, were the first electrification projects. The Baltimore & Ohio's tunnel went into operation in 1895, soon followed by the St. Clair and Hoosac tunnels. One locomotive reached 60 miles per hour, running light. These were full-sized, potent, railroad locomotives; one developed 63,000 pounds of tractive effort, pulling a 1,900-ton train. In 1895, the Pennsylvania electrified the 9-mile branch line from Burlington to Mount Holly, New Jersey, hitherto worked by steam.[8]

The late 1890s and early 1900s saw rapid growth of "interurban" electric railroads.[9] Now forgotten, although immortalized as the Toonerville Trolley, these lines, using trolley and third rail power systems, were built around such cities as Cleveland, Grand Rapids, Buffalo, Chicago, Detroit, Toledo and Cincinnati. The area of greatest activity in the early 1900s was northern Ohio and southern Michigan.[10] In 1902, in Michigan, alone, twenty-four lines were in operation, with franchises for forty-seven more being applied for. Some were substantial operations. The Aurora, Chicago & Elgin Railway was built with 80-pound rail and designed for schedule speeds of 40 miles per hour, maximum speeds of 70 miles per hour, powered by 26-kilovolt, 3-phase AC. On the Buffalo & Lockport, 72,000-pound trolley locomotives hauled 350-ton freight trains. Connecting networks, such as one in upstate New York, stretched for 100 miles. All offered passenger and parcel freight service; some offered sleeping car accommodation and such services as a 6-hour run between Columbus, Ohio, and Cincinnati.

The interurban lines were feeders to the steam-powered railroads, but also competed with them directly, offering a quality of local service that the steam-powered railroads did not. The Detroit, Ypsilanti & Ann Arbor carried 4,000 passengers a day, while a steam railroad passing through the same towns carried only 200. The interurban lines were superseded by cars and buses, but they were the forerunners of today's urban rapid transit systems.

The electric locomotive was the first form of motive power to challenge the steam locomotive. Its immediate and outstanding success led some to prophesy the wholesale electrification of American railroads and the disappearance of steam.[11] At that time, however, there was no widespread power grid; each project needed its own, coal-fired, steam-powered generating station; conductors and switchgear, alone, cost $3,000 per mile of track.[12]

Cooler heads remarked in 1897[13]:

> The man who watches human affairs with a little memory and some sense of proportion, and who keeps his bearings cool, can find a certain entertainment in the frequent "relegation of the steam locomotive to the scrap heap" by the electric motor. For four or five years we have had detailed statements of hundred-mile-an-hour railroads and 200-mile-an-hour railroads between Chicago and St. Louis, or New York and Chicago or New York and Philadelphia.... Within a few months all of the railroads reaching New York have been on the eve of abandoning the steam locomotive for their suburban travel at least. Several transcontinental railroads have been on the point of equipping their heavy grade divisions for electric working any time in the last four years.
>
> But in reality what has happened? ... out of about 184,000 miles of railroad some 30 miles have been converted to electric working, and more than half of this is experimental....
>
> From all this it does not follow that we are not on the eve of a revolution. Perhaps we are, but it is evident that the men who are responsible for the financial results of administering the great railroad properties entrusted to their charge are looking at the possible change with very proper caution.

In 1901, the New York Central investigated electrifying the 5 miles of line leading into Grand Central station, which included 2 miles of tunnels.[14] With 600 train movements a day, the noise and smoke of steam locomotives was a great nuisance. The study indicated a slight saving in operating costs through electrification, although this was based on many assumptions and a meager data base. These investigations bore fruit; by 1904, the company was electrifying the lines from Grand Central Station to Croton and White Plains with a 600-volt third rail.[15] With a rail as the conductor, there was practically no limit to the amount of power that could be supplied. The locomotives were built by General Electric and Alco at Schenectady—another partnership that would stand the test of time.

The motors were wonderfully simple, the armature being mounted directly on the driving axle. Each of the four driving axles was rated at 550 horsepower (continuous). The 190,000-pound, double-ended locomotive's maximum power output was 2,800 horsepower, 50% more than the railroad's most powerful steam locomotive. The company planned to build 30 to 50 locomotives, hauling trains of 250 to 875 tons at speeds up to 70 miles per hour. For trains heavier than 450 tons, two engines were to be coupled together, controlled from the cab of the front one with a Sprague–General Electric control system.

The first test was on a 4-mile stretch of electrified track at Hoffman's Ferry on November 12, 1904—a momentous event, attended by the company's Fifth Vice-President.

> The occasion marks a new era in the development of transportation facilities in this country. Although the Baltimore & Ohio has for a number of years been hauling its trains through the tunnel at Baltimore with electric locomotives the New York Central's electrification scheme is the first radical change on the part of an existing steam road to electric operation for comparatively long distances.

The locomotive reached 60 miles per hour, running smoothly with no yawing, pitching or hammer blow. It raced a scheduled mail train hauled by a 4-4-2; the electrically hauled train was more than half a mile ahead of the steam-hauled one at the end of the 4 miles.

While some of the best engineers in the country wrestled with the steam locomotive, here was a locomotive that was more powerful than any existing steam locomotive, more efficient in fuel and labor and had none of the steam locomotive's built-in problems. But for the high cost of electrification, the steam locomotive might have disappeared by 1920. But for the increasing political hostility facing the railroads, and their resulting loss of profit, funds might have been available to bring this change about.

Section 5.2 Internal Combustion Traction

By the late 1890s, the internal combustion engine existed in three forms, fueled by coal gas, gasoline and diesel oil. All such engines were started by filling the cylinder(s) with an explosive mixture of fuel and air and igniting it. The force of the resulting explosion drove the piston, but the engine depended on a flywheel to complete the return stroke and cycle the valves until the next explosion. For this reason, the engine could not be started under load, as could a steam or electric motor. It had to be connected to its load by a clutch and a variable-speed drive. Although its power:weight ratio was high, enabling the Wright brothers to make their first powered flight in 1903, in its early years its power output was too small to be usable in a locomotive.

An early appearance of internal combustion on U.S. railroads took the form of gasoline-powered inspection cars, first built by the Kalamazoo Railroad Velocipede & Car Co. in 1895.[16] They were powered by two-stroke engines developing up to 6 horsepower and were capable of speeds up to 20 miles per hour.

The steam railroads' answer to the interurban electric lines was a self-propelled passenger car. The first of these were powered by small steam engines but, in 1899, the Pennsylvania and the Cleveland, Cincinnati, Chicago & St. Louis experimented with a car driven by a 45-horsepower, two-stroke, gasoline engine, built by the Jewett Car Co. of Jewett, Ohio.[17] The car reached 40 miles per hour in trials.

The more was known about the steam locomotive, the more obvious its disadvantages and the more frustrating its problems. Wholesale electrification was barred by installation costs. The internal combustion engine was too immature to offer competition. For the time being, the steam locomotive reigned supreme over the world's railroads and would do so for another fifty years.

PART THREE

Transformation, 1905–1920

This period in American locomotive development opens in 1905 with the entry into service of the first American Mallet and closes with the USRA standard locomotives of 1918–20. In that period, several innovations, some of them small in themselves and externally invisible, transformed the American steam locomotive into a much more efficient machine, as well as a bigger and more powerful one, than it was in 1905. Freight and passenger traffic doubled in the period, hauled by a locomotive fleet that doubled in numbers at the same time.

The Baltimore & Ohio's Mallet ignited a craze for that type of locomotive in an industry hungry for tractive effort—something that Mallets produced in abundance—and spawned locomotives of fantastic dimensions that were never equaled elsewhere in the world. By 1920, the American steam locomotive had reached the limits of its size; improvements had to advance in other directions.

This period is bounded by political events as well as by landmarks in technology. The political climate of 1905 produced the first biting legislation against the railroads, culminating in their takeover by the government in 1918. These political events did much to drive and shape American locomotive development.

6

General Steam Locomotive Development, 1905–1920

The booming economy of the early 1900s placed huge demands on the railroads.[1] At the end of 1906:

> Operating officers everywhere are trying to move the enormous amounts of freight offered and keep down the cost of transportation to the lowest limit. Locomotives and men are being overworked and the one solution seems to be bigger locomotives and bigger train loads. The saving in time and in wages by doubling the number of cars in a train is a strong incentive for using the heavier power.

On the other hand:

> Not a single railroad in the country has shops or roundhouses big enough to hold the heaviest types of locomotives now being turned out. They cannot be turned on any turntable in existence. Many, if not most, of the bridges are overloaded when they run over them. When they exert their maximum power, the cars and draft attachments in the train are strained to the breaking point. In case of a wreck or derailment no wrecking equipment could put them on the track or clear them off the track possibly for days after the accident. The present track structure was not designed for carrying such loads. Yards and terminal facilities are inadequate to care for the trains these heavy engines can and should haul.

Bigger engines kept coming; engineering and management had to scramble to keep up.

Over the years, railroad companies strengthened their track and substructures until, by the early 1900s, allowable axle loadings were as high as 48,000 to 52,000 pounds, especially in the industrial northeast. By 1912, the Pennsylvania's motive power engineers were pressing their civil engineers for axle loadings up to 70,000 pounds. At that time, allowable axle loadings in England were 38,000 to 40,000 pounds, in France 34,000 to 36,000 pounds, in Germany 32,000 pounds and in Austro-Hungary 28,000 to 31,000 pounds.[2,3] As the friction between wheel and rail limited a locomotive's tractive effort to 25% of its adhesion weight, the higher the permissible axle loading, the higher the possible tractive effort. Stronger track and substructures gave American locomotives an advantage over their European counterparts. The British accepted the limits imposed by their civil engineering infrastructure; the Americans were more willing to rebuild their infrastructure to accommodate bigger engines and heavier trains.

American locomotive builders benefited from the biggest domestic market of any country in the world.[4] They designed their locomotives to be simple to build and maintain, applying similar design features to large numbers of locomotives differing only in detail. In the early 1900s, Alco and Baldwin had a combined capacity of about 5,000 locomotives per year.[5] This contrasted with a German capacity of 2,000 locomotives per year from fourteen manufacturers and a French annual capacity of only 400 locomotives from six manufacturers which were not even specialized locomotive builders. In

Britain, the major railroads built their own locomotives, forcing independent manufacturers to rely on export markets. In the days of the British Empire, these were extensive, although not immune to German and American competition.

In 1900–10, inclusive, manufacturers in the U.S. and Canada built 49,000 locomotives. About 95% of these were single-expansion, rigid-frame locomotives, running on saturated steam. Many of them were inefficiently proportioned because no one knew any better. The Mallet articulated compounds were a major innovation but, by 1910, no more than 350 had been built.

In the early 1900s, compounding and superheating were widespread in Europe; Alco engineer George Basford acknowledged that the Americans had much to learn from the Europeans[6]:

> As yet, comparatively little has been done in the improvement of the locomotive in this country in the direction of superior economy and efficiency. In Europe the high price of coal has led to care in design and in operation of locomotives which is unknown here. The French are a generation ahead of us in locomotive operation. In France, locomotive engineers use devices such as double valve gears and variable exhaust nozzles, which we do not intrust to our engineers and firemen.

At that time, the Americans were disillusioned with compounding and unconvinced of the benefits of superheating. Distrusting steel, they continued to use heavy wrought iron parts; the French were making reciprocating parts one-third lighter than the American equivalent in the same size of locomotive.

From the viewpoint of 1906, the American attitude was[7]:

> The single-expansion locomotive, after all the efforts which have been made to supplant it, still stands as an acceptable device for handling railroad trains. Many years have passed since compound cylinders were first used in locomotive service and a considerable period has elapsed since the advent of superheating locomotives but neither compounding nor superheating have yet gained themselves a place of real security in the railroad practice of this country, while single-expansion locomotives are being built at a rate never before known.

The Americans acknowledged that they increased locomotive power by increasing size and weight. In particular, the strength of a human fireman had become a real limitation on power output, but the railroads remained antagonistic to power stokers and saw many innovations only in terms of their ability to extend the power that a human fireman could produce.

> The greatest need is for that which will extend to the utmost the capacity of the fireman and render the limited physical strength of a man capable of supplying the requisite power.

This could not go on indefinitely. Power density had to increase as well as power output. By 1911[8]:

A typical freight locomotive of the early 1900s, a Chesapeake & Ohio class G-7 2-8-0, built by Alco and Baldwin in 1903–07. Otto Perry photographed No. 919 at Clifton Forge, Virginia, on August 4, 1936 (Denver Public Library, Otto C. Perry collection, OP-2891).

In the construction of these gigantic machines there appears to be little effort made to obtain the most powerful machine with the least weight per horse-power, but, on the contrary, there is a strange pride on the part of both locomotive builders and railways in the production or ownership of the "heaviest locomotive in the world."

This sluggish approach to design ended quite suddenly in about 1910 with a sharp increase in the use of several innovations: trailing trucks supporting big fireboxes, cast steel parts, superheating, feed water heaters, power stokers, improved valve gear, power reversing gear, brick arches, powered firedoor openers, coal pushers and powered grate shakers. Of limited effect individually, their combination in new locomotives produced some remarkably potent machines.

In June 1912, the Buffalo, Rochester & Pittsburgh road-tested 2-8-0s hauling 2,350-ton freights to determine the efficiency of the brick arch, the superheater and the power stoker.[9] The superheater and brick arch combination showed an astonishing 43% coal saving and 47% water saving. These two devices had been in use for more than fifteen years before the Buffalo, Rochester & Pittsburgh adopted them, yet comparative tests were still news.

As an instance of this distinct period of advance in American locomotive practice, the Chesapeake & Ohio upgraded its motive power in 1910–11 with 131 new locomotives: twenty-five 2-6-6-2 Mallets, twenty-four 2-8-2s, three 4-8-2s and seventy-nine 2-8-0s, all from Alco, all superheated.[10] The Mallets, each with 73,000 pounds of tractive effort, displaced forty-four 2-8-0s on the Alleghany district for use elsewhere.

The 2-8-2s were designed to haul 4,000 tons at 15 miles per hour up a 0.3% grade. The Chesapeake & Ohio dynamometer-tested them in late 1911.[11] One hauled a 112-car train, weighing 7,590 tons, over a division with an 8-mile ruling grade of 0.2% at an average speed of 15 miles per hour, including 9 miles per hour up the hill. The maxi-

mum tonnage hauled by the company's older 2-8-0s over the same division was 4,246 tons. The 2-8-2 developed a tractive effort of 27,000 pounds at 33 miles per hour, equivalent to 2,378 drawbar horsepower, and hauled 77% more tonnage than the 2-8-0s. For comparison, the highest recorded power output of a British steam locomotive was 3,300 indicated horsepower by a London, Midland & Scottish Railway *Coronation* class 4-6-2 in 1939.[12]

The 4-8-2s were for fast passenger service between Clifton Forge and Charlottesville with 1.5% grades in both directions. These 330,000-pound engines were fully equipped with superheaters, brick arches and power stokers. Capable of 58,000 pounds of tractive effort, they handled 600- to 700-ton passenger trains on the same schedule that the company's existing 4-6-2s could barely make with a 350-ton train.

By the end of 1912, new, superheated 2-8-2s on other railroads were hauling 45% to 50% more tonnage than the 2-8-0s that they replaced, while burning the same amount of coal.[13]

This sudden combination of new devices caused an extraordinary advance in locomotive performance in the three years 1911–13. Key to this development was a growing acceptance of increased complexity and the abandonment of a curmudgeonly conservatism. From the viewpoint of 1914[14]:

Only a few years ago motive power men were practically a unit against adopting any appliance on a locomotive that would add to its complication ... the modern locomotive, with its superheater, power reverse gear, improved air brake equipment and a host of other features which add to its complication, would have made a superintendent of motive power of 15 or 20 years ago hold up his hands in horror.

Testing was already pointing to yet further advances. The 1912 Coatesville tests (described in Chapter 7, Section 2) showed that

This Chesapeake & Ohio class K-1 2-8-2, No. 1107, built by Alco between 1911 and 1914, photographed at Charlottesville, Virginia, on August 8, 1932, was a part of the company's 1910–11 power upgrade. The Chesapeake & Ohio mounted the air brake compressors on the smokebox front, giving their locomotives a distinctive appearance. Note the power reverser above the third driving wheel (Denver Public Library, Otto C. Perry collection, OP-2901).

Part of the transformation of American steam power, a Chesapeake & Ohio class H-4 2-6-6-2. Alco built the H-4's between 1912 and 1918. No. 1332 was still in service forty years later when photographed near Hinton, West Virginia, on July 10, 1953. This huge fleet of ancient steam power influenced the rapid dieselization of the American railroads (Denver Public Library, Otto C. Perry collection, OP-2958).

40% to 48% of evaporation was from the firebox sheets; understanding of this fact, alone, produced huge, long-term advances in American locomotive design.

The Pennsylvania was the acknowledged leader in American steam locomotive technology, designing and building its own locomotives, or supervising their construction by others, testing them exhaustively on the road and on the Altoona test plant, probing the limits of steam locomotive performance and putting numbers on characteristics that were unknown or unsuspected only a few years before.

For years, data streamed from the test plant at Altoona, freely published in Pennsylvania technical bulletins, and from the Purdue laboratory. The Coatesville tests of 1912 produced information whose importance was out of all proportion to their short duration. Engineers realized that the numbers were universally valid for all reciprocating steam locomotives; F. J. Cole, a senior engineer with Alco, produced a set of ratios in 1912–14 that could be used for design. If the numbers were universally valid, so were the restrictions that they placed on steam locomotive performance.[15] These were the Cole ratios:

- Maximum efficient firing rate (pounds of coal per square foot of grate per hour):
  Bituminous coal   120
  Anthracite   55–70
- Evaporation rate (pounds of water per square foot of heating surface per hour):
  Firebox sheets   55
  Fire tubes   7.5–14.0
  (Tubes 10–24 feet long, 2-inch, 2¼-inch and 5½-inch OD, spaced ⅞₆-inch and 1-inch apart.)
- Steam consumption (pounds of steam per indicated horsepower-hour):
  Single-expansion   Saturated steam 27.0
  (At piston speeds of 700–1,000 feet per minute.)

(More than 200°F superheat)	Superheated	20.8
Compound	Saturated steam	23.5
	Superheated	19.7

These figures were supported by voluminous tables and graphs. Cole's work was so important to locomotive design that his words, spoken in 1914, are quoted at length as Appendix C to this book.[16]

Although the evaporation rate per square foot of tube surface declined with increasing length, so did the smokebox temperature, indicating better total heat recovery. For this reason alone the new big engines were more thermally efficient than their smaller predecessors.

Test plant figures could not be matched in road service, but they pointed the way ahead; the resulting improvements had real effects on the ability of the embattled railroads to stay in business.

Two design features made World War I the heyday of the American 2-10-2: a floating front axle and ball-jointed connecting rods, used in 2-10-2s built in 1915 for the New York, Ontario & Western and the Erie. Even so, 2-10-2 development was limited by the clearance dimensions of the two outside cylinders, the weight of reciprocating parts and the resulting counterbalancing problems.

No amount of human labor could hand-fire a 2-10-2 or a Mallet to its full power for any length of time. Building these monsters without power stokers was a waste of money; this realization, slow and late as it was, brought the railroads around to power stoking, one of the most important developments in the development of the American steam locomotive. By the end of 1915, 1,300 locomotives were stoker-fired in a U.S. fleet of about 65,000. Most of the 2-8-2s, 2-10-2s and Mallets built at that time had power stokers.

In spite of the proven success of the superheater and brick arch, only 75% of new-builds in 1915 were ordered with superheaters and 58% with brick arches. Both these devices were suitable for retrofitting; two older engines were retrofitted for every one built new.

The 4-8-2 made its mark, combining speed, power and low axle

The Chicago, Rock Island & Pacific's class M-50 4-8-2, No. 4000, built by Alco in 1913, was the Rock Island's first 4-8-2 and one of the first 4-8-2s ever built, photographed at Topeka, Kansas, October 29, 1929 (Denver Public Library, Otto C. Perry collection, OP-5794).

Mallet gigantism was well under way when the Chicago, Burlington & Quincy bought this class T-3 2-8-8-2, No. 4200, from Baldwin in 1911. It was already on the scrap line, evidenced by the missing rods, when Otto Perry photographed it at Denver, Colorado, on January 16, 1927 (Denver Public Library, Otto C. Perry collection, OP-3837).

Alco built this 2-6-6-0 for the Denver & Salt Lake sometime between 1913 and 1916, shown after acquisition by the Denver & Rio Grande Western and renumbering to 3373. This locomotive was still in its original compound configuration with slide valves on the low-pressure cylinders when Otto Perry photographed it at Craig, Colorado, on April 25, 1948 (Denver Public Library, Otto C. Perry collection, OP-9853).

loading. By the end of 1915, only forty-seven 4-8-2s had been built, following their introduction on the Chesapeake & Ohio in 1911. In 1916, alone, 180 were ordered. Although improvements in track were allowing 4-6-2s to be built with axle loadings as high as 67,000 to 68,000 pounds, the 4-8-2s developed more tractive effort, while keeping axle loadings below 60,000 pounds.

Mallet construction accelerated after 1910. The American steam locomotive reached its ultimate size limits in the Santa Fe 2-10-10-2s of 1911, three triplex Mallets built for the Erie in 1914–16, the Virginian triplex Mallet of 1916 and the Virginian 2-10-10-2s, also of that year. These were the biggest steam locomotives ever built, anywhere in the world. Their limited success forced design engineers to search for higher power density and better proportioning of parts, while improvements in steel metallurgy, design, manufacture and stronger track improved the prospects of rigid-frame locomotives. The idea of power density continued to gain ground.[17]

> While the building of large locomotives continues, there is not the tendency that there was a few years ago to build large engines without due consideration being given to economical features as well as maximum capacity.

Alco graduate George Basford, President of the Locomotive Feed Water Heater Co., New York, stated this concept in plain terms: the problem facing the locomotive designer of 1916 was "forcing every pound of weight to justify itself in terms of power."[18] The innovations mentioned above contributed to this goal. Last of these was the feed water heater, which did not become widespread until after 1920.

In spite of their immense facilities and experience, the major builders were still capable of producing locomotives with serious defects.[19] In 1916, the New Haven took delivery of fifty 4-6-2s from Alco. Poor weight distribution placed too little weight on the leading truck; as a result, the engines yawed so badly at their scheduled speeds that frames and driving wheel spokes broke. The Ragonnet power reverser could not prevent the Baker valve gear from creeping, annoying the engineers; the injectors could not keep the boiler filled. These problems were solved, but not for several years.

Before 1920, steel metallurgy was developing rapidly. With ever bigger locomotives, American engineers were increasingly concerned with the destructive effects of unbalanced rotating and reciprocating parts on the whole fabric of the engine and track.[20] If these parts could be made lighter, counterbalance weights in the wheels could be lighter. The French were using forged steel to build pistons half the weight of equivalent American parts using cast iron. If axles could be made with higher tensile strength, they could be bored out to save weight. If the frames did not have to withstand such destructive forces, they could be built lighter. Weight savings could go into greater boiler capacity, while remaining within the axle load limits imposed by bridges and track—all of which meant more revenue for an increasingly desperate industry.

The year 1916 was the apogee of the old-time American railroad industry; route mileage reached its maximum before abandonments exceeded new construction. From 1916 comes this perceptive view[21]:

> Eight or ten years ago there was a widespread belief that the end of a comparatively short period would see the steam locomotive largely replaced by electric power. Today the steam locomotive in America has reached a point of development which even the greatest visionary would not have attempted to predict fifteen years ago. Moreover, the highest point in this development has not yet been reached; there is no question that the steam locomotive will gain much in both sustained power and economy within the next few years.

One of the defective class I-4 4-6-2s supplied by Alco to the New York, New Haven & Hartford in 1916. Otto Perry photographed No. 1381 at Springfield, Massachusetts, on August 22, 1933, retrofitted with an Elesco feed water heater (Denver Public Library, Otto C. Perry collection, OP-13699).

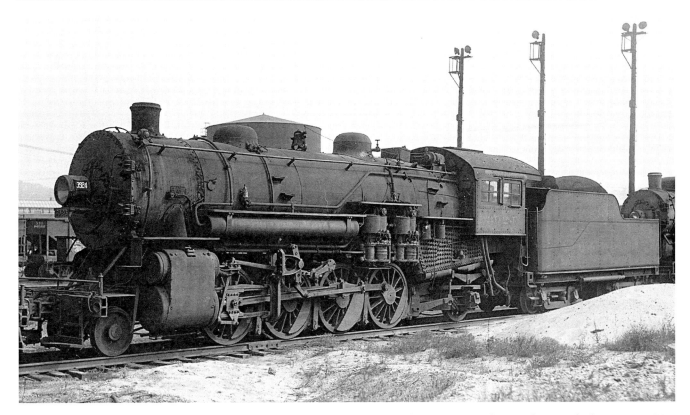

The New York Central rebuilt a 2-8-0 to produce this class H-5p 2-8-2, No. 3924, between 1915 and 1918, photographed at Harmon, New York, on October 17, 1930 (Denver Public Library, Otto C. Perry collection, OP-13378).

Many of the innovations of the early 1900s could be retrofitted to locomotives originally built without them; railroad shops began to rebuild existing engines with superheaters, power stokers, new valve gear and bigger cylinders. The numerous 2-8-0 freight engines lent themselves readily to this.[22] The New York Central converted 462 of them into superheated 2-8-2s in 1912–16; the new, deeper firebox made space for a brick arch. Moving the firebox back behind the main frame and supporting it on a trailing truck made room for a longer boiler. Many were retrofitted with outside Walschaert or Baker valve gear. Superheating allowed the use of a smaller, lighter piston valve for any given cylinder diameter.

When the Cleveland, Cincinnati, Chicago & St. Louis converted eighty-nine 2-8-0s into 2-8-2s, the new engines developed 4% more tractive effort than the originals on starting, increasing to 78% more tractive effort at 35 miles per hour as superheating took effect. Curiously, only one railroad, the Norfolk & Western, considered power stokers as a retrofit. The steam locomotive was amenable to rebuilding into configurations never planned by its makers.

The rigid-frame compound did not survive in America because its economies did not offset its complexity, rough riding in some designs, difficulty of operation and maintenance costs. By the time of World War I, the rigid-frame compound was so dead that many were being rebuilt as single-expansion. Compounding survived with the Mallets because their vast size allowed space for a steam reheater between the high- and low-pressure cylinders; their construction allowed monstrous low-pressure cylinders. Their enormous tractive effort, without excessive axle loading or weight of reciprocating parts, compensated for their complexity and high maintenance costs.

Developments in locomotive design, and in railroad operation generally, had the extraordinary result that in a single year, from 1915

to 1916, the ton-miles hauled per freight locomotive increased by 26%, averaged over the entire United States,[23] followed by a further 20% increase from 1916 to 1917.

As the demand for motive power intensified, every means was explored to maximize the time that each locomotive spent in service. Ease of maintenance started to become a design and construction issue in about 1917.[24] In the culminating years of the American steam locomotive that were yet to come, design for maintainability and efficient maintenance procedures would be among the obscure contributors to the tonnage hauled by the steam-powered railroad system.

In spite of their enormous hauling power, all had not been rosy with the coming of the Mallets[25]:

A comparison with the number of Mallet locomotives being ordered today with the number which were placed in service six or seven years ago, might lead to the inference that the Mallet locomotive is discredited as a road unit, and that its usefulness is confined to certain special operating conditions only. But the facts hardly justify such an inference. There are a number of railroads on which the requirements for heavy freight service are being met by the use of Mallet locomotives, in some cases to the exclusion from consideration of the 2-10-2 type.

Much of the early experience with Mallet locomotives was unfortunate. This type, when introduced into America, was a decided innovation under our conditions of maintenance and operation. It is not at all surprising, therefore, that its use was not always highly successful at the outset. One of the greatest difficulties, and probably the one which now most frequently eliminates it from consideration, was the high cost of maintenance. The more recently built of these locomotives are operating in road service and offering no difficulty in maintenance, and it is doubtful whether the prejudice generally entertained against the type, based on experience with the earlier designs, is justified under present conditions.

Based on testing at Altoona, the Pennsylvania began to build locomotives with the cut-off in full forward gear limited to 50%. The intention was to restrict the cut-off to the 50% to 25% range, where steam consumption was more nearly constant, and where the expansive force of the steam was more fully applied, than the normal 85% to 25% range. The Pennsylvania tested this concept on a new 2-10-0, and followed it up with an order for 122 engines of the same type in 1917. The concept spread to other new construction in the 1920s.

Although feedwater heating was by no means new, 1917 also saw "the first practical development of locomotive feedwater heating in America." Like the superheater, this device entailed no moving parts, requiring only the substitution of a pump for the injector. Initial optimism forecast fuel savings of at least 10%. Feed water heaters could be retrofitted. Hitherto, economizing devices—notably compounding and superheating—were aimed at reducing fuel consumption as a means of increasing locomotive capacity. In wartime conditions a real scarcity, as well as high cost, of coal made fuel saving an object in itself, especially when retrofitting existing engines.

> The fuel situation is rapidly becoming such that improvements in existing locomotives which might not be justified from the standpoint of increased capacity, may be fully justified by the resulting decrease in fuel consumption.

As the railroad fuel bill for 1918 totaled $750 million, these economies were well worth pursuing.

By 1917, with traffic demand still increasing, the railroads had to do everything they could to maximize the availability of the engines they had.[26] Wartime conditions focused unprecedented attention on maintenance and maintainability which would become a permanent contributor to the total performance of the steam locomotive in America.

The hot issue of 1918 was the USRA crash program of locomotive building to standard designs.[27] Standardization was instigated by Director General William McAdoo, a lawyer, politician, member of the Woodrow Wilson cabinet and son-in-law of the President.[28] This massive—and controversial—program was not lightly to be undertaken; each new design required a new set of drawings, dies, templates and patterns.

McAdoo instructed Samuel Vauclain, then executive vice-president of Baldwin, to form and chair a committee; Vauclain selected four senior officials from Alco and two from Lima. The committee reached its conclusions quickly, by the end of March 1918.[29] There were to be twelve designs: light (55,000-pound axle loading) and heavy (60,000-pound axle loading) classes of 4-6-2, 2-8-2, 4-8-2 and 2-10-2, with a "light" 2-6-6-2 Mallet, a "heavy" 2-8-8-2 Mallet, a "light" 0-6-0 switcher and a "heavy" 0-8-0 switcher. The "light" classes had axle loadings heavier than the heaviest allowed by the biggest railroads, such as the Pennsylvania, only a few years before. The American type, the Atlantics, Ten-Wheelers, Moguls, Consolidations, once the commonest American locomotives, and the rarer Decapods, were all of the past.

Comment from the railroads and builders fell on deaf ears[30]: if the introduction of standard engines was truly a war emergency measure, there should be just one standard locomotive, the multifarious 2-8-2, and five standard freight and passenger cars. The 4-6-0 and 2-8-0 were not among the standard types, even though they were better suited to certain conditions than the proposed standards. The Pennsylvania, the Harriman lines, and other extensive railroads in Canada, Australia, Brazil and Argentina had tried to standardize their

Chicago, Burlington & Quincy class T-2 2-6-6-2, No. 4107, built by Baldwin in 1910, still working as a compound in 1933, retrofitted with an Elesco feed water heater (on the smoke box brow). Otto Perry took this shot near Mystic, South Dakota, on September 4, 1933 (Denver Public Library, Otto C. Perry collection, OP-3829).

locomotive fleets, but with so little success that the effort diminished to a standardization of parts at best. Elaborate arguments expounded the virtues of the 2-8-0 and 2-10-0, some by E. F. Givin of the Pittsburg, Shawmut & Northern, distinguished by the longest time in receivership of any railroad in North America.[31] The lapse of time needed to realize any benefit from standardization was so long that some people suspected that it was part of a secret plan to nationalize the railroads permanently.

Perversely, the USRA forbade the railroads to place orders for the new engines that it said they needed, leaving a gap between the completion of current orders and the first deliveries of the new standards. Having issued a specification for each of the twelve types in April 1918, the USRA asked each railroad how many of the standard engines it required, without inviting any discussion of the specifications.[32] Railroads that could not handle the axle loadings of the new engines were to have their motive power needs made up with lighter engines displaced from other railroads by the standards, adding to their maintenance problems. Any modifications to meet local conditions, such as coal quality, would have to be made by the railroads themselves.

Standardization was never popular and did not survive the end of government control.[33] The introduction of the new designs delayed production, instead of accelerating it. The USRA placed orders for 2,030 locomotives with Alco, Baldwin and Lima, of which only 628 were delivered before the end of 1918, by which time the war was over. The Toledo & Ohio Central refused outright to pay for the engines that were foisted on it. On another railroad, the new engines started arriving before the company knew it was to receive them. Although the engines performed well, unfamiliarity, different sets of

drawings and spare parts from those that the railroads already possessed and—we may suspect—resentment, resulted in engine failures and downtime. As soon as the war ended, the railroads began to demand the return of their property and standardization ended.

Baldwin delivered the first USRA engine, a light 2-8-2 for the Baltimore & Ohio, on July 1, 1918.[34] The last engines were delivered in late 1919. They comprised:

0-6-0	255
0-8-0	175
2-8-2 (light)	625
2-8-2 (heavy)	233
2-10-2 (light)	94
2-10-2 (heavy)	175
2-6-6-2	30
2-8-8-2	106
4-6-2 (light)	81
4-6-2 (heavy)	20
4-8-2 (light)	47
4-8-2 (heavy)	15
Total	1,856

Ninety percent were freight locomotives, reflecting the needs of the time. Of these engines, 775 were ordered with power stokers, comprising the Duplex (570), Standard (170) and Hanna (35) types. The majority of these locomotives went to the hard-pressed railroads of the northeastern U.S. Current research has not discovered a distribution of USRA locomotives by railroad that will reconcile with the above listing by type.

In spite of controversy, the USRA designs were good and several years passed before new designs overtook them. One author[35] esti-

The "light" Mikado 2-8-2 was the most numerous of all the USRA types. Otto Perry photographed Chicago, Rock Island & Pacific, class K-55, No. 2314, built by Alco or Baldwin in 1919, at Colorado Springs, Colorado, on July 4, 1934 (Denver Public Library, Otto C. Perry collection, OP-5488).

mates that more than 5,000 locomotives were built to USRA designs, distributed among most of the major railroad companies of the U.S., many continuing in service until the end of steam in the 1950s.

By 1918, 95% of all new engines were built with superheat, although only 21,800 of a fleet of 65,000 were so equipped. Between 1910 and 1918, 5,000 2-8-2s, 4,000 4-6-2s and 900 2-10-2s were built. These engines were not only bigger and faster than their predecessors, but the relentless drive for efficient management had produced better maintenance standards and higher availability and utilization.

The American rigid-frame locomotive went through a remarkable metamorphosis in the period covered by this chapter.[36] In 1904, a Pennsylvania 2-8-0 freight engine was capable of 1,035 indicated horsepower at a thermal efficiency of 5.2% and weighed 187 pounds per horsepower. Twenty years later a Pennsylvania 2-10-0 developed 3,485 indicated horsepower at a thermal efficiency of 8.1% for a specific weight of only 107 pounds per horsepower. A locomotive twice as heavy produced more than three times the power output for a 55% gain in thermal efficiency.

Even so, the reciprocating steam locomotive remained dismally and irredeemably inefficient. By 1920, its heat balance was as follows[37]:

Thermal content of coal, per pound		14,000 BTU
Absorbed by firebox heating surface	3,780 BTU	
Absorbed through boiler tubes	5,810 BTU	
Sub-total to water		9,590 BTU
Absorbed by steam in superheating		1,050 BTU
Total to steam		10,640 BTU	76%
Lost to ash pan, live coal and ash		280 BTU	2%
Lost through stack, gases, cinders, moisture in coal, incomplete combustion		3,080 BTU	22%
Total		14,000 BTU	100%

The 10,640 BTU that went into steam was distributed as:

	BTU	% of energy in coal
Discharged in exhaust steam	8,260	59%
Used by air pump	840	6%
Radiated from whole locomotive	420	3%
Locomotive friction	140	1%
Useful traction at drawbar	980	7%
Total	10,640	76%

Astonishing developments in the 1920s would prove wrong those that thought the steam locomotive had reached the end of its development.

7

Locomotive Engineering, 1905–1920

Section 7.1. Fuels, Firing and Fuel Economy

7.1.1 Coal

By 1910, 70,000 steam locomotives were at work in the United States and Canada, 120,000 in the rest of the world combined. Locomotives burned one quarter of U.S. coal production; North American locomotives burned one tenth of world coal production.[1] By 1917, American railroads were burning 175 million tons of coal every year, worth $438 million.[2] Added to this was 48 million barrels of oil, worth approximately $80 million.

Coal was such a cost for any railroad that the majors set up whole departments for its procurement, analyzing calorific value, clinkering, burning rate, the cost of screened vs. mine-run coal, anthracite vs. bituminous coals and lignite, ash content and shipping cost. Experimenters found that 1- to 3-inch lumps of coal provided the best compromise between a large burning surface and a free and even flow of air through the fire; worst was a mixture of large lumps and dust.[3] Burning fines fell through the grates, contributing to ash pan damage, or were sucked through the fire tubes and thrown from the stack, causing lineside fires.[4] Mine-run coal was cheaper to buy than coal screened into sizes, but included more shale and dust.

The quality and cost of coal to any one railroad company resulted from a web of interactions between the mining companies, their miners, the miners' unions and even state legislatures—Kansas, Arkansas and Oklahoma legislated their coal mine operators to pay the miners equally for all sizes of coal,—as well as the quality of the coal in the ground which varied from coalfield to coalfield, indeed mine to mine and seam to seam.[5]

The demand for more power, less smoke and lower fuel costs drove the railroads to the point of desperation, considering any form of fuel or fuel preparation that promised to solve these problems. Much effort went into utilizing slack and dust. By 1913[6]:

> Everywhere the demand is for more motive power; every day the problem of smoke is becoming more urgent, and we have about come to a standstill in the development of our steam power.

Briquetting is a means of combining fine coal and dust with a binder, such as tar, into small blocks for convenient handling. Believed to have originated in China, briquetting began in Europe in the 1600s and was undertaken on an industrial scale from the 1840s onward. By 1905, plants in Europe were producing 30 million tons of coal briquettes annually. In particular, it was a method of upgrading lignite as a fuel. At the same time, American annual production of coal briquettes was about 175,000 tons, the difference being attributable to the abundance of cheap coal.[7]

The Rock Island was the first railroad in the U.S. to try coal briquettes, followed by the Missouri Pacific, the Chicago, Burlington & Quincy, the Chesapeake & Ohio, the Atlantic Coast Line and the Seaboard Air Line.[8] In 1908, the Pennsylvania tested a 4-4-2, burning coal briquettes, at Altoona,[9] seeking to use a low-volatile, friable coal from Lloydell, Pennsylvania, which was unsuitable for locomotives in its raw state. The briquettes showed higher evaporation of water per pound of coal at all firing rates than the raw coal and the briquettes performed notably better at high firing rates, where the friable coal was wasted through the stack. The Rock Island built its own briquetting plant at Hartshorne, Oklahoma, with a capacity (as of 1908) of 8 tons per hour, using slack that could be bought cheaper than lump coal.[10] In spite of the many advantages claimed for briquettes—reductions in smoke, cinders and clinker and the use of otherwise unusable material—by 1911, it was already apparent that the cost of briquetting made it uneconomic.[11]

Pulverized coal, so fine that, when forced through a nozzle, it burned like oil or gas, was another attractive possibility; its first use in the U.S. was in a cement plant in 1895.[12] By 1916, American cement making and metallurgy consumed 7 million tons of pulverized coal per year.

The possibilities for locomotive application were so tempting that experimenters persevered for many years. Pulverized coal reduced smoke, eliminated cinders and expanded the resource base, including mines that would otherwise be uneconomic. Ash pans, smokebox netting, grates, coal handling equipment, the manual labor of the fireman and the time and effort in preparing and dumping fires and handling ash could all be eliminated. As with oil-firing, the fire could be turned down or shut off when the engine was idling. Experience between 1890 and 1910 showed that the cost of drying and pulverizing could be brought down to about $0.10 to 0.20 per ton in a plant with a capacity of 25 tons per hour.[13]

Possibly the first experimental use of pulverized coal in a locomotive was on the Manhattan Elevated in the early 1900s.[14] The firing device incorporated a steam turbine, pulverizer and blower. The cylinder exhaust was not used for furnace draught, the coal was relatively coarse and no provision was made for dealing with clinker; the experiment was unsuccessful, as was an experiment on the Chicago & North Western at about the same time.

The first full-sized railroad locomotive burning pulverized coal successfully was a New York Central 4-6-0, modified in 1914. As with oil burning, pulverized coal did not need the strong furnace draught of a normal coal-burning firebox. Accordingly the locomotive's original 5-inch diameter exhaust nozzle, giving a back pressure of 8 to 10 pounds per square inch, was modified to a rectangular 5½-inch × 8-inch nozzle, giving a back pressure of only 1 to 3 pounds per square inch. A steam-powered turbo-generator drove two electric motors which drove the coal handling equipment. Firebox temperatures were recorded at 2,600°F to 2,850°F, with smokebox temperatures of only 425°F to 490°F. At firing rates of 2,500 to 4,000 pounds per hour, the evaporation rate was 9½ to 12¾ pounds of water per pound of coal. The system apparently saved 15% to 25% of coal consumption, compared to hand-fired lump coal, for a coal consumption of about 75 to 85 pounds per thousand ton-miles, significantly more economical than conventionally fired locomotives. The only solid combustion residue was clinker. The New York Central converted a 4-6-2 to burn pulverized coal in 1916.[15]

These experiments produced some interesting comparative manufacturing costs; the cost of a 2-8-0, developing 50,000 pounds tractive effort, was:

Coal-fired, hand-firing	$22,000
Oil-fired	$22,750
Coal-fired, mechanical stoker	$24,000
Pulverized-coal-fired	$26,500
Equivalent electric locomotive	$50,000

The small but innovative Delaware & Hudson bought a 2-8-0, fitted for burning pulverized coal, from Alco in 1915–16, intending to use the large amounts of fine anthracite waste generated in the railroad's Pennsylvania anthracite-mining territory.[16] The Locomotive Pulverized Fuel Co., New York, built the firing equipment. Its president was J. E. Muhlfeld, formerly Superintendent of Motive Power on the Baltimore & Ohio, and responsible for the first American Mallet in 1903–4. The Delaware & Hudson used a mixture of half anthracite dust and half bituminous coal dust; the anthracite flame tended to go out because the volatile content was too low. Fired at rates up to 6,000 pounds per hour, this locomotive reportedly hauled 13% more tonnage than its conventional equivalent.

At the same time, the Chicago & North Western retrofitted a 4-4-2, using coal pulverized to 95% passing 100 mesh and dried to less than 1% moisture.[17] Screw conveyors, driven by a steam turbine, moved the pulverized coal from a tender tank to feeders where it was aerated, through a nozzle into a mixing chamber, where more air was added, thence to three burners in the firebox, handling 500 to 4,000 pounds per hour, each. The fireman controlled the rates of firing and air addition, according to the engineer's use of the throttle. Dynamometer tests against a conventionally fired engine of the same class in passenger service between Chicago and Milwaukee showed a 6% saving in coal per horsepower-hour and a 13% improvement in water evaporated per pound of coal (from 8.1 to 9.2 pounds of water per pound of coal). Tests with pulverized lignite were also successful.

In 1919, the Hocking Valley equipped a camelback 4-6-0 for pulverized coal.[18] The tender tank was divided to contain bituminous coal and anthracite, the mixing proportions being under the control of the fireman. Feed screws, driven by a reciprocating steam engine, moved the pulverized coal to the front of the tender tanks. A steam-turbine-powered fan collected the pulverized coal from the ends of the screw conveyors and blew it through a flexible hose to the burners. The fan supplied 15% to 20% of the combustion air, the balance being drawn in by the action of the exhaust nozzle which, however, could be so enlarged as almost to eliminate back-pressure in the cylinders.

By 1919, five railroads had experimented with pulverized coal: the Santa Fe, the Chicago & North Western, the Delaware & Hudson, the Missouri, Kansas & Texas and the New York Central. Under the stress of wartime conditions, the experiments were discontinued and the locomotives were refitted to conventional firing.[19] One railroad found that their pulverized-coal locomotive burned 23% less coal when directly compared with a conventionally fired locomotive, negated, however, by increased repairs to the brick arch and the pulverizing and handling cost. Although poorer-quality coal could be used, the price difference between the better and poorer coal had to equal or exceed the $0.45 to $0.50 per ton processing and handling

cost. Pulverized coal made a user vulnerable to plant failure, explosion and spontaneous combustion and, in railroad operating conditions, was impossible to keep dry. As soon as the overall economics were examined, the outlook was less promising and experiments ceased.

The railroads of the Pacific Northwest were so remote from sources of coal that they found it worthwhile to ship oil 1,300 miles from California.[20] Their attention turned to the huge deposits of lignite being discovered in the northwestern plains and foothills. For best results, locomotives had to be built to burn lignite, particularly with a large grate, up to 70 square feet, so that fuel could be burned at a high rate with a light draught. The brick arch was especially important in ensuring that light particles of fuel lifted from the fire were burned before entering the fire tubes. Long fire tubes and a long smokebox with plenty of spark arrester netting inhibited sparks and the risk of lineside fires.

In 1911, bituminous coal from Iowa cost the Chicago & North Western $5.20 a ton on its divisions in Wyoming and western Nebraska, compared to a mine-site cost of $2 for Wyoming lignite.[21] Alco developed a long smokebox to enable Chicago & North Western locomotives to burn this material, containing netting, deflector plates and an exhaust nozzle that swirled the gases to break up and extinguish cinders before they were blown from the stack.

A clean lignite could have a calorific value as high as a bituminous coal, although with a high water and ash content, but tended to break down on exposure to air. Several western lignites from Wyoming, Montana and New Mexico had calorific values of 10,000 to 13,000 BTU per pound with low clinkering and sulfur content. Unlike briquetted and pulverized coal, lignite firing was a long-term success.

Anthracite seems gradually to have gone out of use as locomotive fuel because of its slow burning and the consequent impossibility of installing big enough grates. The Delaware, Lackawanna & Western bought seven 4-6-2s designed for anthracite in 1912 but even these locomotives, which were already being overtaken in size and power, needed 95-square foot grates to use this fuel.[22] The Lehigh Valley 4-6-2s of 1913 were also built to burn anthracite as were the Lackawanna 4-6-2s of 1915 with 91-square foot grates.

7.1.2 Oil

Oil developed as locomotive fuel in America in response to local availability, becoming most common in the Southwest, distant from sources of coal, but where the Californian oilfields were being developed. The Southern Pacific used oil from Kern River, near Bakersfield, and Summerland, near Santa Barbara.[23] Typical calorific values were 18,500 BTU per pound, compared to 13,340 BTU per pound for the coal that the company was using. At temperatures less than 100°F, this oil was too viscous to be sprayed through a burner; steam coils in the tender tank kept it at 120°F. The Southern Pacific used two types of firebox: "back-fired," with the burner near the backhead, and "front-fired," with the burner farthest from the cab. The bottom and lower sides of both types of firebox were of firebrick.

The maximum useful oil flow rate was the amount that could be fully burned within the firebox. If the oil flow exceeded this rate, unburned gases passed into the fire tubes, where they were cooled below their combustion temperature, depositing soot, causing smoke and wasting fuel. At full power, a Southern Pacific 2-8-0 freight locomotive burned 350 to 420 gallons of oil per hour, a Mallet could burn 600. After making a start with oil-burning in 1900, apparently the first in the U.S., by 1905, the Southern Pacific had about 750 oil-burning locomotives in service and could compare oil- and coal-burning locomotives of the same type on the same service. Even though the oil had 37% more calorific value than the coal, the oil-burning locomotives evaporated 49% to 73% more water per pound

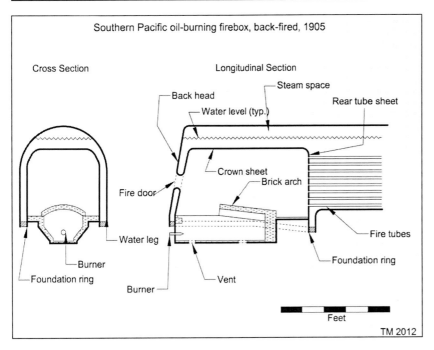

Southern Pacific oil-burning firebox, back-fired (redrawn from *RRG*, May 19, 1905, 558).

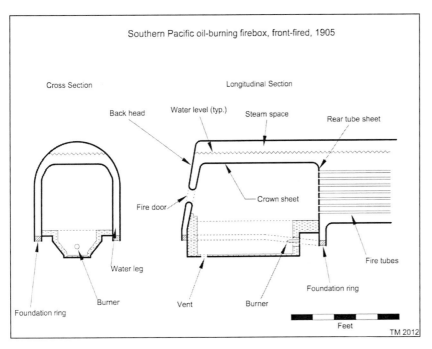

Southern Pacific oil-burning firebox, front-fired (redrawn from *RRG*, May 19, 1905, 558).

ther the length of the firebox nor the volume of oil burned were limited by the strength and dexterity of the fireman. No ash or clinker had to be removed. The stack emitted fewer sparks to cause lineside fires. Steam generation was closely under the fireman's control. Oil was cleaner and easier to handle than coal; fuel handling costs were less. A particular benefit was the reduction in fuel consumption when the engine was drifting or standing still.[24] Against this, oil-burning fireboxes cost twice as much in repairs as coal-burning ones due to the fierce, but unevenly distributed heat and the repeated heating and cooling of the firebox as the fireman increased or decreased the oil supply.[25] Although coal-burning fireboxes were easily converted to oil, a purposely designed firebox was needed if the best results were to be obtained.

The Santa Fe's Thomas W. Neely designed a solution to these problems. Oil burned in a brick furnace before exposing the firebox metal to the hot gases. Gas flow in the furnace helped ensure complete atomization and vaporization of the oil before it burned. By mid–1907, the Santa Fe had eighteen 2-10-2s with Neely furnaces. Reduced maintenance enabled them to make 20% more mileage per month than oil-burners with conventional fireboxes.

By 1911, oil was 4% of the locomotive fuel burned in the U.S.[26] The Southern Pacific had 991 oil-burning steam locomotives in service at that time, comprising all the company's California divisions and its lines as far east as El Paso.[27]

The use of oil fuel doubled between 1907 and 1914, when fifty railroads were oil-fired over 31,000 route miles.[28] The railroads used whichever fuel was most easily available. The Missouri-Kansas-Texas ran through the oilfields of Kansas, Oklahoma and East Texas; by the 1920s, all of its 400 engines, except those based in Missouri, were oil-burners.[29] In 1910, oil-burners numbered 3,000 in a total U.S. locomotive fleet of 59,000. By 1915, this had increased to 4,250 oil-burners in a fleet close to its ultimate maximum at 65,000 locomotives.[30]

By 1915–16, the distillation of gasoline from crude oil for use in the growing numbers of automobiles, trucks and aircraft was threatening to raise the price to a point that inhibited its use as locomotive fuel.[31] Nevertheless, oil continued as a locomotive fuel until the end of steam.

7.1.3 Coal Firing

The skill and strength of the fireman were essential to the functioning of the steam locomotive. This had three implications, all unfortunate. First, differences in skill between one fireman and another could mask any performance parameter that test engineers might try to measure. Second, as locomotives were built bigger, the fireman's task in firing them became so arduous that the railroads found difficulty recruiting men with the intelligence to make, either, efficient firemen or, ultimately, efficient engineers. Third, the potential power output of the new, big engines so far outran any improvements in their efficiency that it became physically

of fuel, probably due to the possibility of adjusting oil flow to steam demand more closely than the coal firing rate. Even so, the determining factor between coal and oil throughout the U.S. was availability and cost, delivered to the tender.

Oil had great advantages over coal as locomotive fuel. It had a higher calorific value and burned hotter than coal, typically 2,700°F compared to 1,300°F. Not only did oil need less combustion air than coal, the smokebox vacuum did not have to draw air through a fire bed, hence a lower smokebox vacuum and lower back pressure. Nei-

impossible for a human fireman to keep them fueled at maximum power for any extended length of time.

> For a number of years I was a locomotive engineer, and I always felt if I had a good fireman I was a good engineer, and that if I had a poor fireman I was a poor engineer. It did not make any difference what the quality of the fuel was, the success of the engine steaming depended entirely on the fireman. …
>
> One of the greatest difficulties encountered in any effort to extend knowledge regarding the subject of fuel consumption is the fact that it is difficult in the case of the old engineers and firemen, who have been on an engine for years, to get them to understand there is anything you can teach them.[32]
>
> However well a locomotive may be designed its operating economy will be low, unless it is handled intelligently and fired with care and skill. A really good fireman will effect greater economies than any apparatus on the locomotive…. His work can spoil or render ineffective the best coal and the most efficient design of locomotive; on his intelligence and industry depends largely the expenditure of $188,735,868.00 (paid by the railways of the United States for coal in 1909) which is 12¾ per cent of the operating costs of the railways.[33]

Tests put numbers on what was already known, that experienced firemen did their work with better fuel economy than inexperienced ones.[34] When the Pennsylvania tested a 2-8-0 at Altoona, inexperienced firemen burned 5.2 pounds of coal per dynamometer horsepower-hour; experienced firemen burned 3.9 pounds, a 25% saving. Efficient firing took effort, as well. In tests on two major eastern railroads in 1915–16, one group of firemen knew that they were under observation; the other did not. For the same tonnage hauled over the same route, the firemen who knew that they were being observed burned 30% less fuel than those that did not.[35]

Railroads made great efforts to save fuel by educating engine crews. The Erie appointed a supervisor of locomotive operation to the Allegheny division in 1910 as an experiment. The appointee, V. C. Randolph, immediately began a system of training and record keeping with the result that coal consumed per thousand freight ton-miles fell by 15% from 320 pounds to 275 in one year alone.[36]

The fireman's task became ever more arduous. In 1916, on one (unnamed) representative American railroad, switch engines burned 13 pounds of coal per mile run, passenger engines 105 pounds, freight engines 229 pounds. The fireman on a freight engine on a 100-mile division therefore had to shovel 11 tons of coal through the firebox door in the course of his run, placing it accurately where it was needed on the grate. In addition, he had to pull the coal forward in the tender, wet it to lay dust, break up lumps, shake the grates, clean the fire if necessary, watch the steam gauge, inject feed water, keep the cab floor clean and, when he was not doing all that, watch for signals, especially on left-hand bends where the big-boilered engines left the engineer blind. At stops, he had to clamber about on the locomotive to take on fuel and water and sometimes open the smokebox door to clean the spark arrester netting.

> Besides being laborious these duties are sometimes attended by severe physical hardships. The heat thrown out by the fireboxes of the extremely large locomotives now coming into use is intense, especially when a long freight is barely moving up a heavy grade, devouring fuel as fast as it can be piled upon the fire and making practically no breeze through the cab by its own motion. Firemen on runs of this kind sometimes have to protect themselves with leather aprons to keep the heat from igniting their clothing. When we add to these conditions an outside temperature of 100 deg. or more, such as not infrequently occurs in the southern and prairie states during the summer, a situation is reached that taxes the limits of physical endurance. At such times heat prostra-

tions become frequent—as railway men say, the firemen "burn out" or "the monkeys get them." They suffer undue strain when a badly clinkered fire has to be cleaned in the middle of a heavy run, for this is rated exceptionally exhausting labor. Firemen are also exposed to more or less suffering from smoke and from gases thrown back from the firebox in passing through tunnels or long snowsheds, especially where more than one locomotive is attached to a train. They sometimes lose consciousness and even die under these conditions.

The head-end brakeman rode in the cab but might or might not help the fireman. ("all these interchanges of service are voluntary, and are more or less the exception.") The increasingly powerful unions frowned on this in their attempt to increase manning levels; some results were extra men to clean fires and doubled or relief firemen, locally or seasonally. The poor quality of both fuel and maintenance that became current during World War I added to the enginemen's difficulties.

> Oil-burning locomotives have made possible firing heavy trains through the south-western deserts, where the mercury reaches 120 deg. or more in the shade and the temperature of the breezes through the cab window almost rivals the blast from the firebox door.

Some devices helped with this situation, but they were few and their effects slight. Brick arches and superheaters reduced the amount of fuel per ton-mile, but fresh demands appeared at once. Power grate shakers and power-operated firebox doors attempted to ease the fireman's lot—or add to his productivity. A forward-sloping floor to the tender coal space slid the coal forward as the fireman took it, but limited the coal capacity and increased the number of coaling stops required. A flat floor added to capacity but meant, either that the fireman had to spend time raking coal forward, or that a second man had to be employed for that task. Tender coal spaces were so huge by 1910–14 that a steam-powered coal pusher, pushing coal forward to where the fireman could reach it, paid for itself.[37]

On one recorded 79-mile run with a 3,150-ton trailing load, the fireman was on duty 14 hours, spending 7 hours in manual labor, shoveling coal, pulling it forward, breaking up lumps, cleaning the fire and shaking the grates, handling 11.2 tons of coal. Stoker firing by no means eliminated manual labor; on a 115-mile run on a stoker-fired engine, the fireman still shoveled 2.5 tons of coal of the 22.5 tons burned. The stoker, when used, was noisy and dirty, filling the cab with coal dust. Even so, the total number of locomotive power stokers in America increased from six in 1910 to 1,418 in 1916, when the locomotive fleet numbered close to 65,000.

By 1920, the fireman's situation was at a crisis.[38] Notwithstanding the amount of effort that had gone into the development of power stokers, by 1918:

> A very few large locomotives of recent construction have mechanical stokers, but they form an inappreciable fraction of the motive power in use on American railways.

Railroads were slow to adopt the power stoker. After 1920, it would make possible the most powerful locomotives in the world.

7.1.4 Mechanical Stokers

When mechanical stokers were first considered in the 1890s, hand-firing, though arduous on certain routes, was not the limiting factor that it later became. The first stokers were intended to save fuel rather than labor.[39]

By 1905, however:

> In all of this growth (in locomotive size) we have heard much of the strength of material, the efficiency of heating surface, the proper loading

of bridges and track, and the economy of high steam pressures and heavy loads, but hardly a word about the man.

Unfortunately, he remains the same as in the days of small engines, while the only consideration that he has received is in the limitation of the length of the firebox. Practical working with extra long fireboxes showed them to be impossible when considered from the physical standpoint of the man; firemen were found to be incapable of throwing coal to the front of such a box with any certainty of placing it where it was needed. So there has been a limit placed on the length of this part, though in other respects the modern locomotive seems to have been developed regardless of the man who is to feed its furnace.[40]

In twenty-five years, from 1880 to 1905, typical heating surfaces in American locomotives grew by a factor of three and a half, demanding a corresponding increase in firing rates if steam pressure was to be maintained when the locomotive was putting forth its full power. The ability of the fireman to throw coal through the fire door to the front of the firebox placed an absolute limit on firebox length but, even so, wide grates, fierce drafting and enormous firing rates placed ever-increasing demands on the fireman. Physical exhaustion was becoming a problem; labor unions were demanding a second fireman on some types of locomotive.

The industry view in 1905 was[41]:

> The overworked fireman has been a favorite theme for the labor leaders and the legislators who would compel three men to be in the cab. Firing a modern locomotive is no child's play, for it requires the exercise of much brawn to feed three or four tons an hour into the firebox, and the man who is attending to the many other duties on the left side of the engine does not have much time to look out of the window at the passing scenery.

Grade, curvature, train load, the skill of engineers, the strength and skill of individual firemen, weather conditions, the willingness of head-end brakemen to help with firing, locomotive maintenance, quality of coal and other factors all varied from division to division, railroad to railroad, season to season and year to year. The loss of locomotive efficiency was hard to measure and the railroads showed no great inclination to do so.

The development of effective power stokers was slower and more difficult than might be supposed.[42] After conveying coal across the flexible connection between locomotive and tender, the stoker had to distribute coal over the grate under the fireman's control. The fireman had to be able to control firing rate and distribution. The stoker had to maintain any set firing rate, regardless of changes in the steam pressure driving the stoker engine. It had to be simple, easy and cheap to lubricate, inspect and maintain. It had to be simple enough that an average fireman could learn to operate it without undue difficulty. It had to handle various sizes of coal, including wet material, rocks, timber and scrap metal. It had to be quiet enough in operation that engineer and fireman could talk to each other across the cab and it must not obstruct movements of the crew about the cab. It had to be extremely reliable, of rugged construction and so designed that, if it broke down, the fireman could hand-fire

without it getting in the way. Parts of it had to withstand the full heat of the fire.

The first mechanical locomotive stokers delivered coal into the firebox from a hopper. The fireman still had to shovel coal into the hopper, although he was no longer exposed to the direct heat of the fire and had only to lift the coal from the tender floor about 30 inches to the hopper. On the other hand, keeping the fire door closed cut down the supply of air to the top of the fire, resulting in the continuous emission of black smoke. These devices were short-lived as they failed to solve the underlying problem that human firemen could not sustain the firing rates demanded by the new locomotives. One example was the Kincaid stoker, mentioned earlier. The Cleveland, Chicago, Cincinnati & St. Louis installed an improved version of the Kincaid, the Victor, on seven locomotives in 1905.[43]

Another early mechanical stoker, the Ideal, developed by the Ideal Stoker Co., New York, and dating from 1904, was intended more for efficient combustion and smoke prevention than as a power stoker.[44] Again, the fireman shoveled coal into a hopper. The stoker fed coal onto the top end of a reciprocating grate sloping downward and forward. Coal already burning on the grate heated the coal fed onto the top end of the grate, causing it to release volatiles. Air jets, drawn in by the firebox draft, mixed with these gases which were then ignited by a red-hot firebrick brow. The reciprocating grate moved the burning coal downward and forward, until only ash and clinker remained to be disposed of at the lower end of the grate. It is not known if this device was ever used in a locomotive.

The first true locomotive mechanical stoker, feeding coal from the tender to the fire, was the Hayden, developed by the N. L. Hayden Manufacturing Co., Columbus, Ohio in 1905.[45] Coal fell through a grating in the tender floor onto a bucket conveyor running across the tender. This conveyor ran in a housing up one side of the tender, across the top and down the other side, dropping coal into a screw conveyor at its top center position. The screw conveyor ran forward under the cab roof with 6 feet of headroom between the bottom of the conveyor trough and the cab deck. The screw conveyor was can-

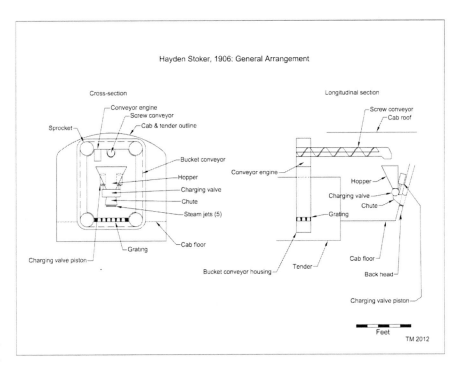

The Hayden mechanical stoker, 1906 (redrawn from *RRG*, March 2, 1906, 211, 212).

tilevered forward from the tender and was not connected to the engine, being free to move under the cab roof with the relative movement of engine and tender. The screw conveyor dropped coal into a hopper fixed to the boiler back head. The bottom of the hopper was closed by a rotating, hollow cylinder cut open on one side. When the open side was uppermost, the cylinder took a charge of about 12 pounds of coal from the hopper. As the cylinder rotated, it dropped the charge of coal into a chute leading into the firedoor. Steam jets under the fire door distributed the coal over the fire. A small (4-inch × 4-inch) reciprocating steam engine drove the tender conveyors. Two small (5-inch × 6¼-inch) steam cylinders on the back head rotated the charging cylinder with an oscillatory motion through rack and pinion drives. The speed of operation of these two cylinders was governed by a valve which, itself, was driven by a small (1½-inch × 1½-inch) reciprocating steam engine. Additionally, this valve supplied a steam blast to the jets, pulsating in time with delivery of coal by the charging cylinder. The firedoor could still be opened for hand firing. The first installation was on a Pennsylvania H-6a.

The 1907 ARMMA convention was apathetic toward power stokers, although[46]:

> On large engines the work of firing by hand is so hard that intelligent men do not seek that grade of employment, and the result is that the supply of material for firemen who are to be future engineers is declining in quality.

In the year following, several new stokers made their appearance and much experimentation went on.[47] The Kincaid was used experimentally on the Chesapeake & Ohio, purpose-built for long fireboxes. With the introduction of shorter, wide fireboxes, the immediate need disappeared; so did the stokers. The Crosby stoker, developed on the Chicago & North Western, used a fan to blow coal through a spout which could be pointed at different parts of the fire. It was unsuccessful.

The Strouse stoker was invented by an engineer on the Iowa Central; the first tests were on two locomotives in 1907.[48] The Chicago & Alton ordered the device for twenty new locomotives in 1909. Like the Kincaid, the Strouse stoker consisted of a hopper, mounted on wheels, into which the fireman shoveled coal. A steam-powered plunger took coal from the hopper and threw it into the fire, the forward stroke feeding the front of the fire, the backward stroke feeding the back of the fire. This action depended on the design of the distributor and the speed and stroke length of the plunger. Much was claimed in terms of combustion efficiency but the power output of the locomotive still depended on the fireman. A conveyor from the tender was added in 1911. Between 1907 and 1912, seventy-six Strouse stokers were built and tested on sixteen railroads but, by early 1913, none survived.[49]

By 1908–9, certain facts were becoming bluntly apparent. The biggest new engines were not delivering value for money as long as they depended on a human fireman. A typical 1909 Mallet with a 78-square foot grate could burn 9,300 pounds of coal per hour at 120 pounds of coal per square foot of grate per hour. An average fireman could fire no more than 3,000 to 4,000 pounds per hour. The British reckoned that a grate larger than 50 square feet could not be effectively hand-fired; this figure is worth bearing in mind when when we discuss the locomotives built between 1905 and 1920. Even existing locomotives were running into this problem. One western railroad found that, at a firing rate of 150 pounds of coal per square foot of grate per hour, its 2-8-0s exerted their maximum tractive effort up to 10 miles per hour; a human fireman could sustain no more than 135 pounds of coal per square foot of grate per hour, restricting this speed to 7½ miles per hour. More and more reports came in of stoker-

fired engines maintaining full steam pressure while hauling more than their rated tonnage.[50] During tests with the Strouse stoker on the Chicago & Alton in 1909, a 2-8-0, rated at 2,800 tons, hauled 3,300 tons using run-of-mine coal, maintaining full steam pressure over an 88-mile run.

In 1908–9, new designs of stoker appeared in increasing abundance.

The Black was an overfeed stoker developed on the Erie. ("Overfeed" stokers scattered coal over the top of the fire; "underfeed" stokers pushed coal through the grate from beneath.) Two screw conveyors in series conveyed coal from the tender and dumped it into a hopper above the fire door. The hopper discharged onto a plate swept by two four-bladed rotors which distributed coal over the surface of the fire.

The Barnum was an underfeed stoker developed on the Chicago, Burlington & Quincy, first applied to switchers in Chicago where it reduced smoke. Two screw conveyors ran longitudinally beneath the grates, diminishing in diameter from back to front and driven by a worm shaft running transversely beneath the cab deck, powered by two small steam engines. A coal crusher, mounted on the tender and driven by a separate steam engine, was a later option.[51] The Chicago, Burlington & Quincy continued to develop the Barnum, using it on a switching engine in Chicago, five new 2-10-2s and a 2-6-2. It proved unsatisfactory and trials had ceased by early 1913.

The Marshall was invented in Canada in 1909. A screw conveyor in the cab, driven by a small steam engine, took coal spilling from the tender door and elevated it to a hopper discharging into the fire door.[52] The coal spilled onto a plate, where two steam jets distributed it over the fire.

The Americans looked in vain to other countries for progress in mechanical stoking. No other country had engines as big as the Americans or drove them so hard. The chief locomotive superintendent of the British Great Western Railway remarked that, over his whole system, the average consumption of coal per engine-mile was 40 pounds, yet the new American Mallets could burn 1,000 pounds per mile.[53] In 1910, only six locomotive stokers were in use on the entire American continent.

The new stokers failed in several respects. They caused the fire to produce great volumes of smoke and they were less economical in coal consumption than hand-firing. Smoke consisted largely of unburned volatiles; smoke and loss of economy were part of the same problem. The early stokers obstructed the cab and, when they broke down, the frustrated crews threw them over the side and left them beside the track. To be fully effective, the stoker had to do all the work, conveying coal from the tender to the firebox. It had to be capable of being built into new locomotives and retrofitted to older ones.

The Street stoker, invented by Clement F. Street of Schenectady, New York, appeared in 1909 and was first used on the Lake Shore & Michigan Southern and then on the New York Central.[54] Coal in the tender fell through a jaw crusher, down a chute and into a hopper beneath the cab deck. A bucket conveyor ran in a pipe up one side of the back head, across the top and down the other side. This conveyor picked up coal from the hopper and dumped it into a second hopper above the fire door; a movable deflector plate allowed the fireman to adjust the coal feed to left, right or center. The bucket conveyor discharged coal over a cylindrical screen. The screen had four quadrants with different screen openings, selectable by the fireman. Fine coal falling through the screen went to the back center of the firebox where it would be less likely to be picked up by the draught before it could burn; the coarser coal went to a distributor which directed it to the right or left side of the firebox. Coal fell from this second hopper into three distributors with pulsating steam jets. By

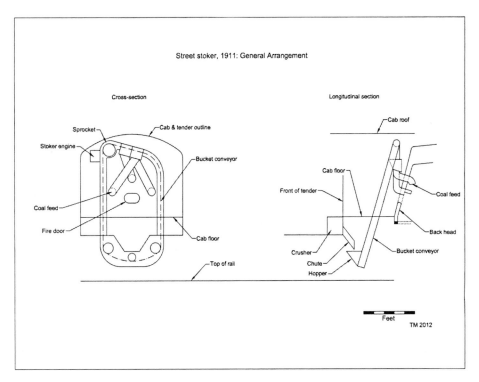

The Street mechanical stoker, 1911 (redrawn from *RAG*, May 26, 1911, 1197).

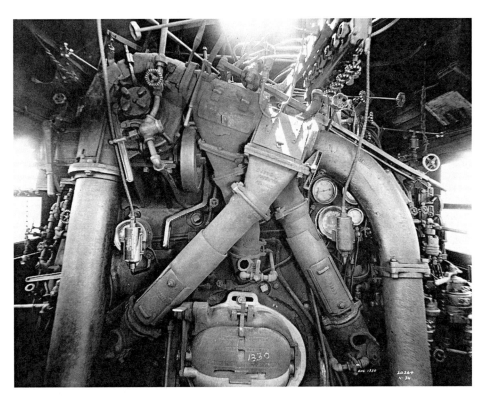

A Street stoker on the backhead of a Norfolk & Western class Z-1a 2-6-6-2, No. 1330, taken in November 1934 (courtesy Norfolk Southern Corporation, ns1007).

adjusting the steam jets, the fireman could direct coal to the left, right or center of the fire. The stoker was clear of the fire door, so that the engine could still be fired by hand when building up the fire or if the stoker broke down. The crusher and the stoker were driven by sep-

arate small (3½-inch × 3-inch) steam engines. Coal supply to the jaw crusher by gravity was unsatisfactory so, in 1911, the company added a screw conveyor to the tender floor for use with coal already crushed before being put into the tender. In that year, the Street stoker was in service on the St. Louis & San Francisco, the Santa Fe, the Lake Shore & Michigan Southern, the Norfolk & Western, the New York Central, the Chesapeake and Ohio and even on the Pennsylvania in competition with the Pennsylvania's Crawford stoker.[55]

D. F. Crawford, General Superintendent of Motive Power of the Pennsylvania lines west of Pittsburgh, analyzed the problems of existing stokers and brought out his own underfeed stoker in 1910, after several years of development. Introducing coal into the bottom of the fire ensured that the gases were liberated inside the fire and were fully burned. Crawford also set out to build a stoker that was at least as fuel efficient as the best hand firing.

Coal in the bottom of the tender fell through a shearing crusher into a conveyor trough. The conveyor consisted of a trough containing a reciprocating structure with fingers that folded on the back stroke, but dug into the coal and moved it forward on the forward stroke. The conveyor ended under the cab deck, where it discharged coal into the stoker. Linkages allowed the conveyor to accommodate all the relative movements between engine and tender. The stoker itself consisted of two parallel troughs rising up under the grates and opening into the firebox. Three plungers in each trough pushed the coal upward into the fire. The whole device was driven through mechanical linkages by a small steam engine bolted to the frame beneath the cab. A significant advantage was that the whole, substantial mechanism was beneath the tender and cab floors, leaving the cab unobstructed. The first installation was on an H-6b.

By 1911, the Pennsylvania had made 2,000 trips with the Crawford stoker; twenty were in service, of which seventeen were on H-6 2-8-0s. On the test plant at Altoona, the stoker fired at up to 6,300 pounds of coal per hour with better fuel economy than hand-firing. The Crawford was widely used on the Pennsylvania, including 2-8-0s and 4-6-2s which were typically hand fired on other lines.[56] Although Crawford rose to be General Manager of the Pennsylvania lines west of Pittsburgh, he eventually left the company for a senior position with the Locomotive Stoker Co.

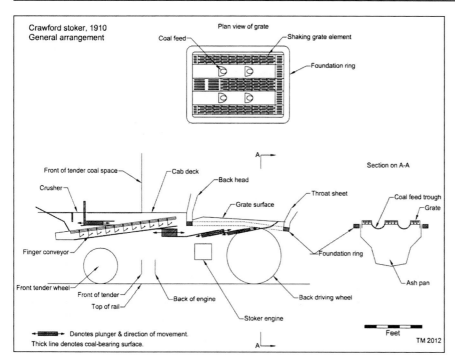

The Crawford mechanical stoker, 1910 (redrawn from *RAG*, June 10, 1910, 1413).

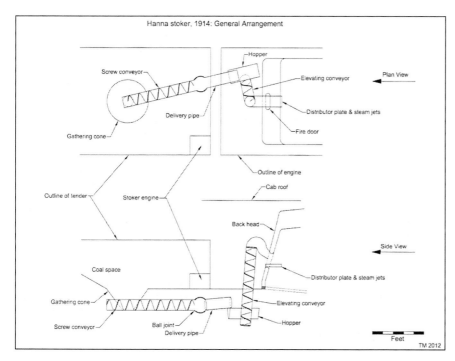

The Hanna mechanical stoker, 1910 (redrawn from *RAG*, April 3, 1914, 792).

Another new design of 1910 was the Hanna, first used by the Cincinnati, New Orleans & Texas Pacific on Mallets running between Oakdale and Danville, Kentucky. On this heavily graded route, even two firemen could not keep steam up and flues leaked every trip. The Hanna stoker not only maintained steam pressure, but did so with slack coal costing $0.90 per ton instead of $1.35 and, additionally, solved the leaking flue problem. The Cincinnati, New Orleans & Texas Pacific found that they could use cheaper coal with the Hanna stoker, resulting in a 30% saving in the cost of coal per ton-mile.[57]

Curiously, this was achieved in spite of the fact that the fireman still had to shovel coal into a hopper and the Mallets burned as much as 6,000 pounds per hour. The railroad also used this stoker on 4-6-2s and 2-8-0s. The Hanna was an overfeed type.[58] From the hopper, a short screw conveyor pushed coal upward to where it fell onto a ridge plate. There, moving wings with adjustable motion swung the stream of coal from side to side. Coal fell off the ridge plate onto distributor plates whence steam jets blew it onto the fire. The Hanna stoker did not live up to earlier promise and only one was still in use in early 1913, on a Mallet of the Clinchfield. The Hanna Locomotive Stoker Co. brought out a modified version in 1913 with a conveyor moving coal from the tender to the bottom of the screw conveyor. The tender conveyor crushed oversize coal by shearing it against fixed blades in the tender.[59] The modified Hanna stoker was first fitted to a 2-6-6-2 Mallet on the Clinchfield and a 4-8-0 on the Norfolk & Western.

The turning point in the application of the mechanical stoker came in 1910.[60] In that year, the Chicago, Burlington & Quincy ordered five Class M-1 2-10-2s for delivery in 1911. These engines weighed about 375,000 pounds with 88-square foot grates and 72,500 pounds of tractive effort. They were designed from the outset with Barnum stokers. The stokers failed and the locomotives were placed on divisions where they could be hand-fired; 25% of the grate area had to be blocked with firebrick. These engines were later fitted with Street stokers and returned to their intended use. The company later ordered sixty more with Street stokers. Between 1914 and 1919, 95% of the new engines ordered by the Burlington were stoker-fired, the highest percentage of any railroad in the country.

Opinions still differed on mechanical stokers. The Santa Fe, for example, tried the Hanna, Street and Strouse stokers and had little success with any of them. With the Strouse, the firemen complained of the noise and that they had as much work to do as before, feeding the hopper by hand. The Hanna and Street stokers banked coal at the back of the firebox. All types gave poor fuel economy.[61] It became apparent, however, that many stoker failures were attributable to defective training and maintenance.[62]

The Erie introduced two new stokers in 1911, the Dickinson overfeed and the Brewster underfeed types. The Dickinson was a development of the unsuccessful Hayden stoker, using a coal crusher, a screw conveyor and a separate bucket conveyor lifting the coal to the distributor.[63] Two small steam engines drove the mechanism. In the Brewster, a screw conveyor moved coal from the tender, through a flexible coupling to a point beneath the firebox. There a second screw conveyor forced the coal upward through the grates to where steam jets distributed it over the fire. At the same time, the grates were tilted slightly forward, moving the fire and keeping it free of ash.[64] The Brewster failed because of the difficulty of operating the vertical conveyor inside the firebox.[65] The Erie failed in its attempts to develop the Hayden, Brewster, Hervey, Dickinson and Erie stokers and work on all of them had ceased by early 1913.[66] Management attitudes may have had something to do with it; W. C. Hayes grumbled[67]:

> I believe that if we were to bend our energies more in the direction of perfecting the work that can be performed by the fireman, we will do more than can possibly be done by the perfection of the stoker.

By 1912, 265 stokers were in service or being built—150 overfeed, 115 underfeed—in a locomotive fleet approaching 60,000.[68] The Pennsylvania was the biggest user, with the Crawford on sixty-five new K-2 4-6-2s and H-8c 2-8-0s in service or being built. The Baltimore & Ohio was testing one on a Mallet.[69] The Pennsylvania used very few Mallets, but one of these was a 2-8-8-2 built by Alco Schenectady in 1911 with a Crawford stoker. At full power climbing the 13 miles of 2% grade between Altoona and Gallitzin it burned 11,000 pounds of coal per hour. The Pennsylvania also hauled some of the heaviest high-speed passenger trains in the country on runs that included severe grades. The Crawford stoker found an application here, too. By early 1913, the Pennsylvania had 153 locomotives equipped with Crawford stokers and another 140 on order.[70]

Between 1911 and 1912 the number of Street stokers in service increased from eight to thirty, with a further sixty-nine in locomotives being built. By early 1913, 189 Street stokers were in use, mostly on the Norfolk & Western, the Chesapeake & Ohio and the Baltimore & Ohio, with another 173 on order.[71]

In 1912, the Norfolk & Western equipped several Mallets with stokers. Between Portsmouth, Ohio, and Columbus, these engines hauled 6,000 tons, the same as two 4-8-0s, at the same speed, for 25% less coal.[72] At about the same time the Chesapeake & Ohio bought fifty 2-8-2s with a tractive effort of 60,000 pounds, rating them at 4,800 tons hand-fired, 6,000 tons stoker-fired on one Kentucky division, between Russell and Silver Grove.

Opinions and experience differed as to the amount of coal that a fireman could shovel in an hour, ranging from 3,000 pounds to as high as 9,700 pounds on a locomotive testing plant. One Pennsylvania fireman fired 8,400 pounds per hour for three hours on a fast test run between Fort Wayne and Valparaiso—and said that he would do the same again—but this was held to be a record impossible to maintain in normal service. A fireman would pace himself, so that 3,000 pounds per hour was the best that could be expected on a 6–8-hour run. Even so, firemen on continuous, hard runs could not work day after day, but had to take time off to rest. Hot weather further reduced the amount of work a fireman could do; by 1914, some railroads had to employ two firemen on big engines on some runs for the five hot months of the year.[73]

New in 1913 was the Gee overfeed stoker, developed by a mechanical engineer working on the Pennsylvania at Altoona.[74] The Gee stoker was simpler than other types, but at the expense of having the coal conveyor running up through the cab floor, discharging onto a plate in the firedoor. Wings and steam jets, both adjustable by the fireman, controlled the discharge of coal into the firebox. The conveyor and the coal crusher were both driven by an 18-inch × 11½-inch steam engine under the cab deck. Claims for this device were a firing rate up to 18,000 pounds of coal per hour and the ability to work on as little as 40 pounds per square inch steam pressure.

By 1913, the Crawford and Street types were dominant, but other new designs continued to appear, such as the Standard, developed by the Standard Stoker Co., New York, in 1913.[75] A screw conveyor moved coal from the bottom of the tender, under the cab deck to a point beneath the back center of the firebox. There a vertical screw conveyor pushed it up to a height of 12 inches above the grates where steam jets, controlled by the fireman, blew it across the grates. A flexible section, consisting of two ball joints, allowed for relative movement between the locomotive and tender.[76] A distinctive feature was the use of a steam turbine as power. The first users were the New York Central and the Norfolk & Western.

The same year, the Baltimore & Ohio experimented with a stoker invented by D. F. Hervey of Logansport, Indiana. This device used a screw conveyor to force coal up through a duct which ran up the back head inside the cab, opening at the fire door where a rotor threw the coal into the firebox. A tender-mounted crusher and conveyor common to the Crawford stoker moved coal from the tender to feed the screw conveyor.[77]

By 1914, 418 Street stokers were in service on twelve different railroads. The Norfolk & Western, the Chesapeake & Ohio and the Baltimore & Ohio were the main users. The Crawford stayed on the Pennsylvania, where 301 were in use on nine different classes of locomotive.[78] The Hanna, Standard and Gee were still in experimental service. New designs continued to appear: the Ayers (chain grate) on the New York Central, the Elvin (overfeed) and the Rait. The Elvin used shovels, rather than steam jets, to distribute the coal over the fire.

After initial distrust, engine crews began to take to the stoker, with unforeseen results.

you all know that the engineer with a hand-fired engine operates his locomotive in accordance with the operations of the fireman. His eyes are constantly, or at any rate, frequently, on the steam

The Standard mechanical stoker, 1913 (redrawn from *RAG*, October 10, 1913, 647).

Locomotives, such as the Pennsylvania's class K-4s 4-6-2s, could not be fired to their full capacity without a mechanical stoker. Altoona and Baldwin went on building the K-4s from 1914 to 1928. Otto Perry photographed No. 623 near Harrisburg, Pennsylvania, on August 19, 1933 (Denver Public Library, Otto C. Perry collection, OP-14337).

gauge. In the case of a stoker operated engine, he learns that the gauge is always at the same point. Then he begins to take interest in how much power he can get out of his locomotive. The results are, in some cases, rather surprising—you will have more power in that machine than you have imagined it possible to get out of it. They haul more cars and go over the road faster.[79]

Successful retrofitting showed the extent to which big engines were falling short of their full potential.[80] Keeping the fire door shut kept temperatures and combustion inside the firebox constant; enginemen did not have to open the fire door, blinding themselves at night with the glare of the fire. The Baltimore & Ohio found that they could use lower-grade coal on their stoker engines; consumption increased, but so did the amount of work done. Stoker firing reduced the wide variations in efficiency between one fireman and another that characterized hand-firing.

By 1914, more and more locomotives were entering service that depended on power stoking, unable to develop their maximum power hand-fired. Indicator diagrams showed the Pennsylvania's K-4s 4-6-2s developing 2,600 horsepower at 60 miles per hour, while the 2-10-2s acquired by the Baltimore & Ohio, the Burlington and the Erie could develop up to 3,100 horsepower at 35 miles per hour. At 2.7 pounds of coal per indicated horsepower-hour, these engines needed to burn 7,000 to 10,000 pounds of coal per hour on their 100-square foot grates to develop maximum power; restricting the firing rate to the capability of a fireman cost 30% to 40% of their maximum power output.[81] The Norfolk & Western was using its 2-6-6-2 Mallets in service that would have been impossible without power stokers.[82]

One railroad ran 2-8-2s originally rated to haul 4,750 tons on one of its divisions; superheating increased this to 5,000 tons, stokers to 6,000 tons. The stoker-fired locomotives moved so much faster that the remaining hand-fired engines delayed traffic. On another division, the same 2-8-2s were rated at 5,000 tons, hand-fired; after retrofitting with stokers, they hauled 8,900 tons at 18 miles per hour at full throttle in full forward gear with both injectors on, while still maintaining full steam pressure. Fast freights with stoker-fired engines could run over two divisions with the same crew. The stokers so reduced clinkering that fire-cleaning time was halved. Coal, that was so poor that it could not be hand-fired successfully at all, could be used on stoker-fired engines. The stoker may have sacrificed evaporative efficiency but it maximized power output.

By 1916, 1,418 power stokers were in service with a further 379 on order. Of these, the Street (866), the Crawford (413), the Hanna (39) and the Standard (100) were the survivors of many abortive designs.[83] The main users were the major eastern railroads—the Norfolk & Western, the Baltimore & Ohio, the Chesapeake & Ohio, the Pennsylvania, the Philadelphia & Reading, the Delaware & Hudson and the Erie.

Even so, some managements fell over their own feet. In 1916, the New Haven bought twenty-five 252,000-pound 2-8-2s from Alco Schenectady, developing 50,600 pounds of tractive effort, hand-fired.[84] The same year the company bought eight bigger 2-8-2s, weighing 310,000 pounds and developing 59,000 pounds of tractive effort. These engines, bought at great cost, were beyond the capacity of a human fireman to keep in steam and impractical to retrofit with power stokers; after three years of unsatisfactory road service, they were assigned to pusher duties. These were the only 2-8-2s the company ever bought.

Those railroads that espoused the mechanical stoker enjoyed many benefits. The four biggest users increased their average locomotive

The New York, New Haven & Hartford's first and last 2-8-2s were the class J-1, built by Alco in 1916. Otto Perry photographed No. 3015 at Providence, Rhode Island, on August 17, 1937 (Denver Public Library, Otto C. Perry collection, OP-13709).

tractive force by 30% to 40% between 1904 and 1915 while increasing their average freight train tonnage by 50% to 80%,[85] handling more tonnage at higher speeds. Second firemen or tonnage restrictions in hot weather were no longer needed. The firemen's working conditions were improved, attracting better men to the position with better potential for training as engineers. Crews tried to stay with the same engine, resulting in better maintenance and more careful operation. Mechanical stoking could compensate for steam leaks in a poorly maintained engine or one that developed defects on the road. Small coal could be used that would otherwise go to waste because it could not be hand-fired in the quantities required; loss of partly burned fine coal through the stack was immaterial with the almost limitless firing rates that mechanical stoking provided. This fuel was cheaper than sized lump coal. Stoker firing facilitated a thinner fire, with almost all combustion air being drawn through the grates and heated, rather than cold air being drawn through the fire door over the top of the fire.

In some places, locomotives could be run over two divisions, which was impossible with hand-firing due to exhaustion of the fireman. The economic benefits of running engines through two divisions was startling, whether the crews changed at the division point or not. One railroad found that freight engines run through two divisions ran 155% more miles per month and saved 11% on fuel per ton-mile. Avoidance of hostling at intermediate division points reduced labor costs. Fewer engines were needed, allowing those released to be used elsewhere. This revision of operating practices was among the factors underlying the transformation of the American railroad system from its frontier origins to one that handled more tonnage more efficiently than any other system in the world.

The Street stoker was so successful that the Street Stoker Co. was unable to finance the expansion needed to support demand. In 1915,

Westinghouse bought the company and formed the Locomotive Stoker Company.[86] In 1917 the company developed the new Duplex stoker, which superseded the Street. The Duplex had two vertical conveyors, one each side of the fire door, instead of one. The same year Westinghouse recruited D. F. Crawford from the Pennsylvania as Vice-President and General Manager. The retirement of both the president, W. S. Bartholomew, and Crawford in 1927 led to Westinghouse selling the company to DuPont, where it was merged with the Standard Stoker Co., Erie, Pennsylvania. Manufacture of the Street stoker ceased in 1917; about a thousand were still in use in 1926.

New in 1917 was the Locomotive Stoker Co., Duplex Type D stoker.[87] Novel features were a two-stage coal crusher and duplex vertical conveyors. A screw conveyor drew coal from the tender and forced oversize against a plate, crushing it to size. This horizontal conveyor moved the coal from the tender to a transfer hopper under the cab deck, where there was another crusher, whence vertical screw conveyors elevated it to slightly above the level of the fire door and discharged it into tubes passing through the backhead and into the firebox. There, steam jets blew the coal past distributors which spread the coal over the fire. The device was so designed that the coal conveyor moved with the engine, loosely supported on the tender, although, when the engine was separated from its tender, the conveyor could remain on the tender. One 11-inch × 17¾-inch steam engine drove the whole device. This type of stoker was quieter and more compact than its predecessors, occupying very little cab space.

While the Baltimore & Ohio, the Chesapeake & Ohio, the Norfolk & Western, the Burlington and the Pennsylvania embraced the power stoker whole-heartedly for their larger engines, the rest of the American railroad industry dragged its feet, installing them for particular, rather than general reasons.

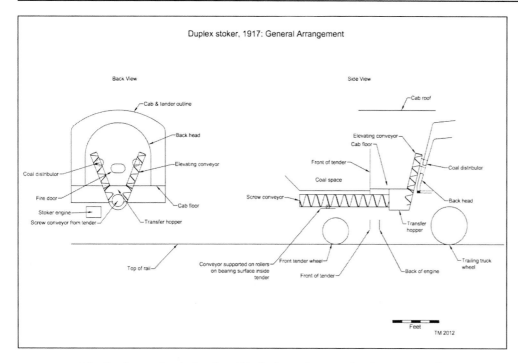

The Duplex mechanical stoker, 1917 (redrawn from *RAG*, July 13, 1917, 73).

A Duplex stoker on a Norfolk & Western class Y-3a 2-8-8-2, No. 2070, photographed on July 11, 1934 (courtesy Norfolk Southern Corporation, ns973).

The Santa Fe installed a large number in 1918, to use slack that could not be hand-fired in the quantities required. One of the railroads in the Pacific Northwest, with only poor coal available locally, converted to oil firing because the firemen could not keep up, but then installed 400 stokers. The El Paso & Southwestern applied stokers to twenty-one of its 2-8-0s because it was almost impossible to find men able or willing to hand-fire these engines in the heat of the deserts where they operated.

The specifications for the Virginian 2-10-10-2 Mallets, new in 1918, called for power stoking with a capacity of 15,000 pounds per hour. By that date the Baltimore & Ohio's experience with more than 400 stoker-fired 2-8-2s influenced the application of stokers to the USRA standard Mikados.[88] The Pennsylvania originally intended its I-1s 2-10-0s, the first of which was built in 1916, to be hand-fired, and to be operated only up to the limits of hand-firing. This idea did not last; 122 of these locomotives were built in 1918–19, all with stokers, and the prototype was retrofitted with a stoker as well.

The USRA ordered stokers for all locomotives under construction developing more than 50,000 pounds tractive effort and coal pushers for the smaller locomotives then being built. Of the 1,856 engines built for the USRA, 775 were built with power stokers.

The Elvin stoker reappeared in developed form in 1918, manufactured by the Elvin Mechanical Stoker Co., New York.[89] A universally jointed screw conveyor moved coal from the tender to the backhead. There, an elevator plate pushed the coal up to where two horizontally swinging shovels picked it off the plate and threw it into the firebox. The shape of the shovels and the mechanism that moved them caused the coal to be distributed over the grate. The Erie tested the device successfully on a 2-10-2.

By 1919, 3,717 locomotives on American railroads were stoker-fired, out of a total locomotive fleet of about 65,000.[90] By type these were distributed as Street, 1,522; Duplex, 1,294; Standard, 731; Hanna, 169. Use of the Crawford never spread beyond the Pennsylvania. Of these stokers, 3,325 were in use on Mallets, 2-8-2s and 2-10-2s. Installations on 4-6-2s, 4-8-2s, 2-10-0s, 2-8-0s and 4-8-0s made up the remainder.

Power stokers increased coal consumption. Their use resulted in a less efficient evaporation of water. Nevertheless, the total economy of the locomotive improved because it could move more tons, faster, for the same crew wages, sometimes burning cheaper coal. The later developments of the American steam locomotive could never have been contemplated without the mechanical stoker.

7.1.5 Fuel Economy

The years between 1905 and 1920 witnessed a transformation of American locomotive efficiency. Not only was the locomotive of 1920 more efficient internally than its predecessor of 1905; its greater size improved its total fuel economy.

As of 1905, the rule-of-thumb fuel efficiency of a saturated-steam, single-expansion locomotive was commonly taken as 5 pounds of coal per indicated horsepower-hour, 7 pounds per drawbar horsepower-hour. Comparisons between steam and electric traction caused engineers to look more closely at actual consumption.[91] Detailed calculations from company annual reports suggested that the real, all-inclusive coal consumption of steam locomotives in the United States, including firing up, drifting downgrade and standing still, was 10 to 15 pounds per drawbar horsepower-hour.

The ways in which coal could be wasted were alarmingly numerous.[92] Some of these were external to the locomotive itself, such as spillage, space taken up by dirt and shale, theft and excessive amounts of time standing under steam. Others contributed directly to the gross inefficiency of the reciprocating steam locomotive. They included improper firing, excessive grate shaking, steam leaks, improper drafting, steam lost through the safety valves, improper valve setting, lack of lubrication, brakes set too tight. Because the engine went on burning fuel, whether it was working or not, all inefficiencies of turn around, assignment, crewing or delays on the road resulted directly in wasted fuel. This was a major disadvantage of the conventionally fired steam locomotive, that the fire had to be kept burning for many more hours than power was required. One investigation suggested that the railroads were spending $3 million a year in coal, merely to supply compressed-air leaks in train braking systems. Seasons and weather affected fuel economy; fuel consumption was always heavier in winter than in summer.[93] By 1916, the railroads of America were spending $300 million a year on coal. J. E. Muhlfeld, at that time president of the Locomotive Pulverized Fuel Co., estimated that $75 million to $100 million of this was spent in lighting, building up and cleaning fires and in keeping the engines in steam when they were standing still, drifting or running light.[94]

Superheating and other design and manufacturing improvements had the effect that a locomotive built in about 1912–15 burned about 2.5 pounds of coal per indicated horsepower-hour, 4 pounds per drawbar horsepower-hour. Under test at Altoona in 1917, a Pennsylvania L-1s 2-8-2 achieved the extraordinarily low specific fuel consumption of 2.1 pounds of coal per indicated horsepower-hour, 2.3 pounds per drawbar horsepower-hour.[95]

In 1905, the Chicago & North Western found a direct correlation between engine and train weight and fuel economy[96]:

Type	Engine weight (lb.)	Train weight (tons)	Coal per 1,000 ton-miles (lb.)
4-4-0	90,000	390	268
4-6-0	126,000	460	247
4-6-0	153,000	620	194

The biggest engine hauled 60% more tons for 15% more fuel per mile, 28% less fuel per ton-mile than the smallest.

By 1915, the comparison had changed yet more markedly. Test results from the Seaboard Air Line, published in 1915, comparing an unsuperheated 4-6-0 with a superheated 2-8-2, demonstrated that the new locomotives being built offered immense gains in both effectiveness and efficiency.[97]

Type	Engine weight (lb.)	Train weight (tons)	Coal per 1,000 ton-miles (lb.)
4-6-0	?	700	244
2-8-2	?	1,580	102

The 2-8-2 hauled 126% more tons for a 58% reduction in unit fuel consumption. As two men crewed all three types of locomotive, the wage cost per ton hauled dropped in proportion to the train weight.

These figures go far to explain the genesis of the American giant steam locomotive.

Section 7.2. Fireboxes and Combustion

But, while assumptions and theories were as plentiful as autumn leaves, there was no data on the subject and no one knew. (Fowler, G. L. *Deflections of Staybolts in Locomotive Boilers,* RA December 5, 1919, 1088)

7.2.1 Combustion

The ever-increasing demand for power and efficiency, together with improving analytical techniques, focused attention on what really happened inside a locomotive firebox.[98] High temperatures and violent reactions made this difficult to study; knowledge could advance only as better instrumentation became available.

Large grates, supported on trailing wheels, became increasingly common from the 1890s onward but, as late as 1908[99]:

The relative advantages of large and small grates for locomotive boilers has not been definitely settled by any accurately measured tests … the Pennsylvania Railroad tests at St. Louis covered such a large field that there was not time during the exposition to deal with the effect of different grate areas in the same locomotive.

Having moved their test plant to Altoona, the Pennsylvania ran tests in 1907–8 to investigate the effect of grate area on combustion.[100] They ran a 4-4-2 with a grate area of 56 square feet with its grate blocked off, first to 40 square feet of grate area, then to 30 square feet. The tests pointed to the importance of firebox volume to combustion efficiency. These and other tests showed that, for efficient combustion at high rates, grates had to be large enough to admit the necessary amount of air, while keeping the fire thin enough so that this air could be drawn through the fire without excessive smokebox vacuum. At the same time, the firebox volume had to be large enough for complete combustion of the gases released from the coal before they entered the fire tubes—it was known by then that combustion ceased when the gases entered the fire tubes. Designers began to recognize the firebox as the true source of locomotive power.

As air came through the grate, the oxygen reacted with the carbon in the burning coal to form carbon dioxide. Unless excess oxygen was present, it was then reduced to carbon monoxide on passing through the fire. If this carbon monoxide was not then burned to carbon dioxide as it passed through the firebox above the fire, 70% of the energy contained in the carbon was lost through the stack, besides causing a smoke nuisance. The carbon-carbon monoxide reaction produced only about 4,400 BTU per pound, of a possible 14,600 BTU per pound from the full carbon-carbon dioxide reaction. The other source of heat was the volatile hydrocarbons, such as methane, that were driven off very soon after fresh coal was added to the fire. If insufficient oxygen to burn them was available above the fire, they, too, went out through the stack unburned. The volatiles coming off the coal had to be thoroughly mixed with air; sufficient space had to be provided for all gases to be completely burned before they reached the back tube sheet.

Secondary air could be admitted above the fire through the open fire door, but air supply by itself was not enough. Hydrogen would not react with oxygen below 600°F; carbon would not react below 800°F. Cold air admitted through the firebox door into a strongly drafted fire would therefore not react as required, cooled the fire and caused thermal shock to the back tube sheet. Higher firing rates and stronger drafting merely exacerbated these problems.

The addition of secondary air remained erratic as long as its only source was the open fire door. In 1912, the Santa Fe added over-fire air jets to its switchers in Chicago to induct secondary air through the firebox sides above the fire and reduce smoke.[101] The enormous Chicago railroad yards became a focal point of public objection to locomotive smoke. In 1912, locomotives around Chicago burned about 2.5 million tons of coal; if 15% of this went out through the stack, locomotives showered the city with 375,000 tons of coal and cinders each year. By 1913, public complaints against locomotive smoke were so vehement that the elimination of the steam locomotive was seen as a possible solution. Electrification was, however, the only alternative offering sufficient power at that time; capital costs prevented this solution.

At the time, the overfire air jet was referred to as "time-honored"; M. W. Ivison was granted a British patent on such a device in 1838.[102] Tubes, set into the firebox walls and passing through the water legs, provided air passages from the exterior into the firebox. As the firebox was at a negative pressure, compared to the atmosphere, air was sucked in through the tubes; 2-inch steam jets entrained additional air and forced it into the firebox. This action provided additional mixing of the burning gases released from the fire.

The same year, the ARMMA appointed a committee to investigate the role of over-fire steam jets in smoke prevention.[103] The Pennsylvania made the Altoona testing plant available; an 0-6-0 switcher was used for the tests. The firebox contained a brick arch, supported on two 3-inch water tubes, with a 5-inch gap between the front of the brick arch and the back tube sheet. Eight 2-inch air tubes were set into each side of the firebox, about 18 inches above the grate, with another ten tubes in the back head, four below the fire door and six above. Steam jets were set inside the tubes, blowing into the firebox so as to entrain additional air and blow it into the firebox. The fire door was fitted with a damper and a deflector plate. Seventy-five tests, with and without the brick arch, showed that the brick arch alone reduced smoke by 50% but, when 4 to 6 pounds of air was injected into the firebox per pound of coal fired, with not less than 13 pounds of total air per pound of coal, smoke was reduced by 75%; filling the gap between the brick arch and the back tube sheet resulted in 87% smoke reduction. Reduction of smoke improved evaporative efficiency.

Much depended on grate design and firing rates. Test engineers at Altoona in 1913 noticed that steam pressure increased when the fire door was opened[104]:

> We have noticed the same characteristic when the grate surface is being forced to a burning rate of 135 to 150 lbs. of coal per sq. ft. of grate. With probably 15 in. of draught in the front end, there is an insufficient air supply through the grate, and therefore it is necessary to supply that air for proper combustion. If the fire door is closed under these high burning rates with the tremendous draughts, it immediately results in a fall in the steam pressure, due to the failure of the coal to burn. By opening the door wide and permitting the air to pass into the firebox from the door, the pressure is quickly regained.

This kind of information was difficult to obtain because:

> These tests are made for one hour duration, and you can readily understand that under a test of this kind your attention and that of your people is taken up with noting a number of details, and it is impossible to make a close study of the efficiency of the increased quantity of air that comes in at that time. But I am convinced we could demonstrate that our monoxide was running very high until we opened the door, when it would change to dioxide.
>
> It is difficult to make an examination of the firebox under conditions of this kind. The box is incandescent, due to the depth and brilliancy of

the fire; and the introduction of the air gives a black cone from the point of entry, indicating quite clearly what it is. There is so much air in the inside of the box that I question very much whether under these forced firing rates, there is any drop in temperature due to the admission of the cold air.

These investigations were timely. American locomotives were being fired at such enormous rates that the normal means of supplying air to the fire were insufficient, resulting in strong smoke generation and losses in efficiency. Boilers that, from their heating surface, would be rated at 400 horsepower in stationary plant were producing 2,000 horsepower on locomotives.[105]

The gaps in the ash pan needed to be a certain size to admit air to the underside of the grate. Opinions differed. Tests by Professor Goss at St. Louis in 1914 revealed that this area needed to be between 11% and 14% of the grate area. If this figure was less than 11%, greatly increased draft was required; if it was more than 14%, no further decrease of draft occurred.[106] The dimensions of some engines currently being built showed that they had insufficient ash pan air inlet area, wasting energy in fire drafting.

The air openings in the grate also needed to be a certain size, so as not to choke off the air supply to the fire. A 1915 survey conducted by the International Railway Fuel Association[107] found that American locomotive grate air openings averaged 38% of the grate area, although designs ranged from 25% to 50%.

Although enormous firing rates, approaching 200 pounds of coal per square foot of grate per hour, were common in American locomotives, by 1912–15 an increasing body of test results forced the industry to recognize that firing rates had to be kept below 100 to 120 pounds per square foot per hour; at higher rates, combustion efficiency dropped and the flow of heat and cinders out through the stack increased rapidly.[108] Ultimately, beyond about 200 pounds of coal per square foot of grate per hour, no amount of firing produced any increase in power. This understanding drove the tendency to bigger grates, although they cost more to fire up and consumed more coal when the engine was idle.

The Pennsylvania ran comparative tests at Altoona in 1914–15 between a 2-8-0 with a 55-square foot grate and 4,200 square feet of heating surface, and a 2-8-2 with a 70-square foot grate and 5,765 square feet of heating surface.[109] Burning 2,000 pounds of coal per hour (36 pounds per square foot of grate per hour for the 2-8-0, 29 pounds for the 2-8-2) steam generation was the same for both engines: 17,000 pounds per hour, 8.5 pounds of water evaporated per pound of coal. When the firing rate was increased to 8,000 pounds per hour, however, (145 pounds of coal per square foot of grate per hour in the 2-8-0, 114 pounds in the 2-8-2), the 2-8-0 produced 34,500 pounds of steam per hour (only 4.3 pounds of water per pound of coal), while the 2-8-2 produced 52,500 pounds of steam per hour (6.6 pounds of water per pound of coal). The 2-8-2 produced 52% more steam from the same amount of coal.

Locomotive construction shows how trailing axles and big fireboxes caught on in the short space of five years, 1910–15. In 1910, new construction comprised 38% 2-8-0s while 2-8-2s comprised only 3%. By 1915, 38% of new locomotives built were 2-8-2s; only 11% were 2-8-0s. The USRA standard designs set the seal on this concept; all USRA locomotives, except switchers, had large fireboxes supported on trailing trucks.

By 1915, engineers were realizing just how violent were the reactions inside a typical, strongly drafted locomotive firebox.[110] A 60-square-foot grate, under a 200-cubic foot firebox, fired at only 60 pounds of coal per square foot per hour required an air supply of 20 pounds of air per pound of coal and carried a fire burning at 2,000°F.

This fire evolved gases at the rate of 1,200 cubic feet per second, replacing the gaseous contents of the firebox six times per second; combustion had to be complete in ⅙ second. Firebox volume, brick arches and combustion chambers took on an enhanced importance in the light of this finding.

More became known about the combustion process as instrumentation developed.[111] A typical coal was about 26% volatiles, containing 40% of the heat energy of the coal, and 58% solids, mostly carbon, containing 60% of the heat energy. Ash and water made up the remaining 16% and not only contained no heat energy but absorbed heat from the fire. As soon as the coal temperature reached 500°F, its structure broke down, releasing volatile hydro-carbons. These burned at temperatures above 800°F in the firebox space above the fire. At 1,600°F the solid component of the coal started to burn. Gas sampling inside the fire showed that 25% to 45% of the total combustible material was burned on the grate, while the remaining 55% to 75% was burned in the firebox space above the fire. These proportions depended on firing rate, fire bed thickness and other factors. This assumed a fire bed of even thickness with an even distribution of oxygen flow, which was often not the case. This finding was enormously important to subsequent locomotive development.

7.2.2 Ash Pans

One of the many hazards of working around steam locomotives was emptying ash pans. Many designs of ash pan had evolved since the burning of coal, rather than wood, became widespread. Two basic types were a flat pan or a hopper with hinged or sliding doors. The flat pan guarded against live coals falling onto timber trestles, but ashes had to be hoed out by hand, or blown out with steam jets. The hopper needed doors which warped under the heat and weight of ashes, jammed open or shut, or froze and clogged with snow and ice. Many of these problems required a fire cleaner to go under the engine, risking burns from hot ashes and other injuries. On January 1, 1910, it became compulsory for all locomotives engaged in interstate commerce to be fitted with ash pans capable of being opened and shut without anyone going beneath the engine.

Several designs fulfilling this requirement had been in use since the 1880s with levers and steam pistons to open and close the doors[112] but, even so, the railroads blustered at this legislation—without effect.[113]

> One of the most serious problems we have ever had on the Milwaukee road has been the ash pan question, and if this convention does not do anything else, it should enter a protest at this time against the passage of bills making railways apply devices which are an absolute detriment, not only to the locomotive, but to the country in general. The idea of making a railway spend $50,000 or $75,000 for a device, in connection with the use of which there is no return, to my mind comes pretty near being confiscatory, if that is the proper term. I do not know if we can prevent such bills being passed, but the least we can do is voice our sentiment against such things.
>
> They (the Chicago & Northwestern) operate nearly everything in the line of an ash pan that can be dug up in any institution in the world. The Smithsonian Institute should get hold of everything they have, because I want to tell you now they are gems, some of them; some are all right. I do not know that I can say anything appropriate on the ash pan question; it is a shame to make a railway company go into anything like that, and it is pretty nearly time that a commission or something of that kind be appointed to determine what is the proper thing to do, because when we were compelled to go into this the federal authorities knew nothing about it, and we knew less.

The railroads growled[114]:

Again the self-cleaning ash pan that has been required by law. It has cost the Pennsylvania Railroad alone about $600,000, and all of this is an absolute waste and would not have been needed, if the men would only be careful.

As late as 1919, the Master Boiler Makers' Association had to admit that: "Your committee has failed to locate a recognized rule for designing ash pans."[115]

7.2.3 Brick Arches

In the absence of a brick arch, air entering the front of the grate went direct to the fire tubes, much of its contained oxygen performing no useful purpose, while hydrocarbons emitted by the fire at the back of the grate remained unburnt. A brick arch forced air entering through the front of the grate to pass over the full length of the fire, mixing the gases and increasing their dwelling time in the firebox.[116] The results were better combustion of fine coal sucked off the fire, a hotter fire and less emission of carbon monoxide and sparks. As a secondary benefit, the arch protected the back tube sheet from draughts of cold air entering through the firebox door, reducing fire tube leakage.

Tests at Altoona in 1904 proved these benefits.[117] The Pennsylvania tested two identical 2-8-0s, one with a brick arch, the other without. Test engineers measured a fire temperature of 2,200°F with the brick arch, 1,980°F without. They calculated that, without the brick arch, 16% of the heat energy of the coal was lost due to imperfect combustion of carbon monoxide; with the brick arch, this figure fell to 2%. Further tests in 1913 demonstrated a 10% fuel saving due to the brick arch alone, 4.3 pounds per dynamometer horsepower-hour without a brick arch, 3.9 with a brick arch.[118]

Even with a brick arch, smoke still increased as the firing rate per square foot of grate increased; here the combustion chamber became increasingly important, both as an economizer and as a smoke preventer. All the calculations and test results pointed to bigger fireboxes.

Although the brick arch dated back to the mid-nineteenth century, in the early twentieth century its use was still far from universal in spite of its known benefits. In 1904[119]:

> a somewhat careful canvass of the situation in regard to this subject on American railroads revealed that very few roads were consistently using brick arches; a much larger number were tolerating them in a very small percentage of their engines, and a still larger number had discarded them entirely.

Why was such a beneficial device so slow in being adopted?

The bricks lasted only 10 to 14 days. When shop forces dropped the fire, they turned the blower on to cool the firebox as quickly as possible for maintenance. Thermal shock destroyed the bricks. Large stocks of brick had to be kept on site but bricks deteriorated under the weather and often suffered high breakage rates in handling. The design of both the brick itself and the brick arch left much to be desired, contributing to high maintenance costs.[120] Cinders accumulated on top of the arch, so that about once a week, the fire had to be dropped and the firebox allowed to cool so that a man could go inside and shovel out the accumulated cinders; otherwise they would block the fire tubes. A shallow firebox left little room for an arch. Where water was bad and fire tubes needed frequent maintenance, the brick arch had to be destroyed to gain access to the fire tubes and arch tubes could not be kept clean.[121] Stoker firing and higher firing rates added to the abrasive wear on the brick arch and demanded stronger designs of brick. The longer grates permitted by stoker firing demanded stronger arch tubes.[122]

These problems were gradually overcome and J. P. Neff, Vice-

President of the American Arch Co., reck-oned that at least 12,000 locomotives were equipped with brick arches in the five years 1910–1915, although it is not clear whether this was retrofitting, new construction or both. The American Arch Co. was formed in 1910 and achieved some degree of stan-dardization in brick shapes between rail-roads.

By 1910, the increasingly obvious econo-mies of the brick arch were gradually spread-ing its use. Improvements in design and construction were overcoming earlier main-tenance problems; some of its most vocal opponents became its most ardent support-ers.[123] More and more railroads making tests, such as the New York Central, the Santa Fe and the Erie, found fuel savings of 5% to 15%. With locomotive size pushing the limits of the human fireman, anything that would increase his effectiveness was desirable. The 1910 ICC rate hearings told the railroads that their profitability would have to come from improvements in efficiency and not from increased rates, adding further force to argu-ments for fuel efficiency. Public objections to smoke and cinder nuisance tended in this same direction.[124]

By 1915 the benefits of the brick arch were becoming fully recognized.[125] The by then abundant test data showed that fuel saving efficiency increased as 1% per 10 pounds of coal per square foot of grate per hour, accom-panied by a large reduction in sparks and smoke. By 1916, some 30,000 locomotives were equipped with brick arches, roughly half the U.S. locomotive fleet.[126]

The Pennsylvania ran a particularly com-prehensive set of tests on locomotive per-formance with and without the brick arch at Altoona in 1917, using a superheated Class L-1s 2-8-2.[127] Besides justifying the use of the brick arch, the figures are of additional inter-est, showing the capabilities of engines of this type and period. Maximum power output was achieved at 29 miles per hour, full throt-tle and 64% cut-off, with the following fig-ures.

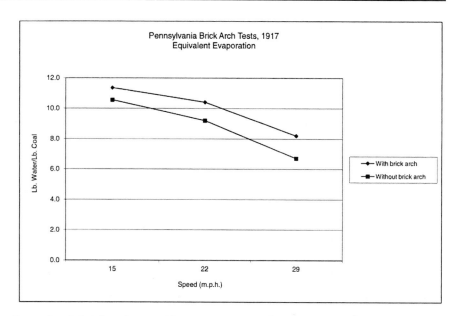

Pennsylvania brick arch tests, Altoona, 1917: equivalent evaporation (graph drawn from numbers in *Pennsylvania Locomotive Brick Arch Tests*, Pennsylvania Railroad Bulletin #30, 1917; abstracted *RAG*, May 4, 1917, 933).

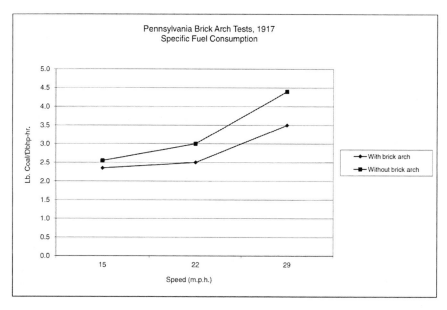

Pennsylvania brick arch tests, Altoona, 1917: specific fuel consumption (graph drawn from numbers in *Pennsylvania Locomotive Brick Arch Tests*, Pennsylvania Railroad Bulletin #30, 1917; abstracted *RAG*, May 4, 1917, 933).

Item	Without brick arch	With brick arch
Boiler pressure (lb./sq.in.)	185	204
Firing rate (lb. dry coal/hr.)	13,018	9,332
Firing rate (lb. coal/sq.ft. grate/hr.)	185	133
Fire temperature (°F)	2,050–2,610	2,360–2,820
Evaporation rate (lb. water/lb. coal)	5.5	8.2
Smokebox temperature (°F)	425–530	455–610
Maximum steaming rate (lb./hr.)	53,898	58,227
Maximum indicated horsepower	2,551	2,790
Steam consumption (lb./dbhp.-hr.)	22.5	22.0

Item	Without brick arch	With brick arch
Fuel consumption (lb. coal/dbhp.-hr.)	5.4	3.5
Locomotive thermal efficiency (%)	3.6	5.5

The tests showed that a brick arch, alone, combined an increase of 9% in maximum drawbar horsepower with a 46% saving in specific fuel consumption.

In the first of the accompanying graphs, evaporation efficiency deteriorates with increasing power output with and without a brick arch. With a brick arch, however, efficiency is higher and declines less rapidly than without. In the second graph, specific fuel consumption increases with increasing power output but, with a brick arch, it is lower and increases more slowly than without.

Even so, by 1918, only about 60% of the locomotives in the U.S. had brick arches, even though they could be retrofitted to existing fireboxes. Most—but not all—new locomotives were built with brick arches. The 164 locomotives built in 1919 for logging and industrial lines, other than USRA orders, had neither superheaters nor brick arches. By 1921 most new locomotives were built with brick arches;

with new construction and retrofitting, 43,000 locomotives were so equipped.[128]

Among the frustrations facing those who designed, built and operated the steam locomotive was that its performance and efficiency were affected by unknown variables whose importance no one could reasonably suspect. It was not discovered until 1949–50—in South Africa—that, for any combination of smokebox design and fire tube layout, the best gas flow distribution depended on the angle between the brick arch and the grate; this angle was critical to ±1°.[129]

A variant on the brick arch was invented in 1908.[130] F. F. Gaines, Superintendent of Motive Power on the Central of Georgia, invented a hollow brick wall, instead of a brick arch, standing vertically at the front of the grate and providing a combustion chamber between the wall and the back tube sheet.[131] Air ducts led from the underside of the firebox, up through the firebrick wall and into the firebox. Air, sucked into the firebox, was heated as it passed through the ducts in the white-hot firebrick. A hopper collected cinders accumulating in front of the wall. After experimental use on a 4-6-0 freight engine in 1909, Gaines walls were added to other locomotives on the Central of Georgia and on railroads in the northern U.S. In a conventional firebox, the grate had to be well below the bottom of the back tube sheet, otherwise the fire would plug the lowest fire tubes. This required a deep firebox which sacrificed ash pan volume. A brick arch did nothing to solve this problem. The wall prevented the fire from encroaching on the back tube sheet, permitting a shallower firebox and a more capacious ash pan.

The Gaines wall and the American Arch Co. standard brick arch were combined in 1914, the result being known as the "Gaines locomotive furnace," which enjoyed long-term success in American locomotive design.

7.2.4 Combustion Chambers

The combustion chamber, known since the mid–1800s, began to receive increased attention in 1905–10. This forward extension of the firebox ahead of the throat sheet allowed the more complete mixing and combustion of the gases rising from the fire. Where engines of the same type could be compared, one with a combustion chamber, one without, the engine with the combustion chamber produced more steam, better fuel economy and less smoke than the one without, even though the combustion chamber took up space that could have been occupied by fire tube heating surface.[132]

The earliest use of a combustion chamber in America is obscure. White points to the use of combustion chambers in the 1830s.[133] Church tells us that the Central Pacific's *El Gobernador* had one.[134] Union Pacific company-built express 4-4-0s of 1893 and Baldwin's class N 2-4-2s, built for the Burlington in 1895, had them, as did Alco's 40,000th locomotive, a 4-6-2 balanced compound built for the Northern Pacific in 1906.[135] Increasing numbers of fireboxes had combustion chambers in the years that followed.

The Gaines wall (redrawn from *RAG*, June 16, 1913, 1220-1221).

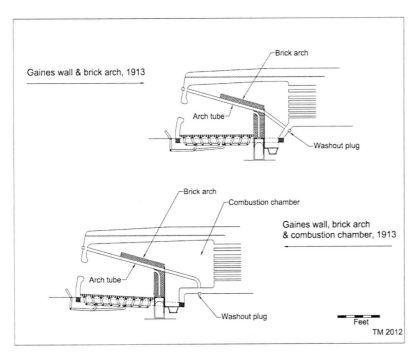

Gaines wall and brick arch combinations (redrawn from *RAG*, June 16, 1913, 1220-1221).

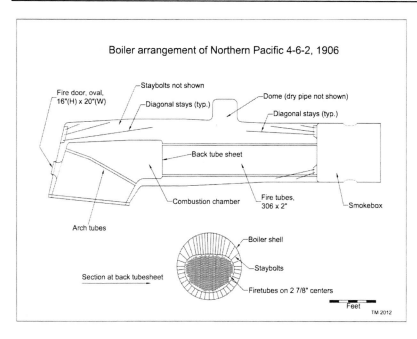

Northern Pacific boiler with combustion chamber (redrawn from *RAG*, March 12, 1915, 445–6).

When Alco built six 2-10-0s for the Buffalo, Rochester & Pittsburg in 1907, comment referred back to the Northern Pacific, rather than to general experience[136]:

> The introduction of the combustion chamber, of course, reduces the amount of tube heating surface, but experience on the Northern Pacific has proven that the increase of firebox heating surface more than offsets this loss, and that engines with a combustion chamber and less actual or even equated heating surface, steam fully as well as those without the combustion chamber and more heating surface. Assuming the Vaughan formula to be correct, the larger firebox, by causing a better rate of combustion, delivers more heat to the tubes proportionately than the ordinary firebox can do, and so raises their efficiency per foot of length.

This understanding was fundamental to American locomotive development over the next forty years.

Nevertheless, introduction was slow; by 1914, only a few companies were using it to any great extent. One of these was the Milwaukee, which had 605 locomotives with combustion chambers.[137] In the company's opinion, better steam generation and decreased firebox maintenance costs more than offset the increased construction cost and difficulty of access.

The combustion chamber was almost an unintended benefit of the new Mallets. The combined length of the two power units exceeded the maximum useful length of fire tubes. A combustion chamber fitted well between the throat sheet and the back tube sheet.[138] By 1915, engineers were becoming aware that engines then being built with very long fire tubes would perform better if the fire tubes were shortened and a combustion chamber added to the front of the firebox.[139]

Acceptance increased rapidly; by 1919 some 6,000 American locomotives had combustion chambers, ranging in length from 18 inches to 11 feet, with fire tubes 9 to 25 feet long.[140] These extreme variations in relative dimensions pointed to much experimentation but little calculation or real understanding. The correct ratios of firebox volume to grate area and firebox heating surface to fire tube heating surface remained unknown, a problem made more difficult by variations in coal quality.

The U.S. Bureau of Mines ran extensive tests on this subject at their Pittsburgh laboratories for stationary plant, based on a firing rate of 60 pounds of coal per square foot of grate per hour with 25% excess air. The ratio of firebox volume to grate area needed to be 13:1 for Illinois coal, 10:1 for Pittsburgh run-of-mine coal and 5:1 for Pocahontas low-volatile coal. In locomotives, however, firing rates were much higher, air was not so freely available and dimensions were more limited than in stationary plant, so these figures were not directly transferable. One new Mallet class, with a brick arch on water tubes, a Gaines wall and a 7-foot long combustion chamber, had a ratio of firebox volume to grate area of 7:1.

Tests were made on two 4-6-2s, one measuring 22 feet over tube sheets with no combustion chamber, the other with a 3-foot combustion chamber and 19-foot fire tubes. The referenced source does not identify the railroad. At low firing rates, there was no difference between the two in boiler efficiency or evaporation rate. As the firing rate increased, the evaporation rate in both boilers increased but efficiency decreased. However, the efficiency of the boiler with the combustion chamber declined more slowly and its evaporation rate increased more rapidly than those of the boiler with no combustion chamber. In particular, the evaporation rate peaked in the conventional boiler at a firing rate of 130 to 140 pounds of coal per square foot of grate per hour, while the evaporation rate of the combustion chambered boiler continued to increase. At a firing rate of 150 pounds of coal per square foot of grate per hour, the combustion chambered boiler evaporated 32% more water (83,000 pounds per hour vs. 63,000 pounds) and was 13% more efficient (53% vs. 40%) than the boiler without the combustion chamber.

By 1917, several railroads were using a combination of brick arch, Gaines wall and combustion chamber. The total length of the firebox and combustion chamber was in some cases as much as 18 feet.[141]

7.2.5 Thermic Siphons

New in 1918 was the Nicholson Thermic Syphon, patented by J. L. Nicholson of the Locomotive Firebox Co., Chicago, and first road tested on the Chicago, Milwaukee & St. Paul.[142] Each siphon consisted of a 6-inch pipe angled backward and upward from the throat sheet, opening out into a lengthwise water space between two triangular plates, connected to a slot in the crown sheet. The pipes supported the brick arch. A wide firebox could contain two siphons and two arch tubes. Steam boiling inside the siphon welled up through the slot in the crown sheet, drawing in fresh, cooler water through the throat sheet.

The Milwaukee tested two similar 2-8-0s, one with siphons, one without, hauling 2,000- to 2,500-ton trains over the 90 miles between Milwaukee and Portage, Wisconsin. In the 7-hour run the engine without the siphons burned 12¼ tons of coal; the engine with the siphons burned only 10 tons. The engine with the siphons evaporated 18% more water per pound of coal than the one without (7.7 vs. 6.5 pounds of water per pound of dry coal). The engine with the siphons saved 25% of coal burned per thousand gross ton-miles hauled. Like brick arches, superheating and combustion chambers, thermic siphons could be retrofitted in the course of a major overhaul. The success of the first tests induced the Milwaukee to install three siphons in the firebox of a Mallet, two in the firebox of a 4-6-2 and one in the firebox of a 4-6-0, in 1919.[143]

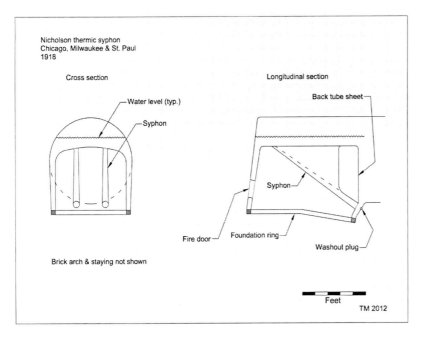

First application of the Nicholson thermic syphon, Chicago, Milwaukee & St. Paul (redrawn from *RA*, January 10, 1919, 151).

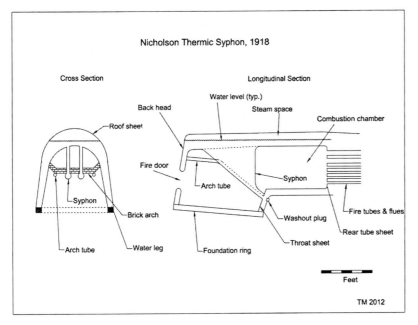

Schematic longitudinal section through a firebox with siphons and a combustion chamber. Staybolts not shown (redrawn from Ringel, C., *History, Development and Function of the Locomotive Brick Arch*, RLHS, New York, January 1948, article reprinted *Journal RLHS*, October 1956, 79).

Large grates, brick arches, superheating, combustion chambers and siphons were wonderful devices. They had no moving parts and their effect increased with increasing power output. In this they were ideally suited to locomotives and contributed enormously to their development.

7.2.6 Problems of the Staybolted Firebox

The firebox was the most problematical of the component structures of the steam locomotive. It required endless maintenance. Bad water caused scaling and corrosion. Sheets buckled and cracked due to uneven expansion; the joints, where the fire tubes came through the tube sheet, leaked. Thermal shock, caused by rapid heating or cooling was a main culprit; the need for slow heating and cooling of the boiler at engine turn-arounds received scant attention in the economic stress of the times.

It is manifestly impossible to correct the handling of engines at terminals so that these irregular temperatures and stresses will be done away with. Availability of power is the first consideration and terminal forces are under extreme pressure to get engines turned in the shortest possible time, and engines which they are not in a hurry for get the same treatment generally in respect to the matters which contribute to staybolt breakage and firebox cracking.[144]

A great deal of our boiler trouble is due to the handling of the engine. I can take an engine off of a run, put it over the cinder pit and handle it so roughly that when it goes over to the roundhouse it will leak like a sieve. If it goes out on the road there will be an engine failure. This is due to allowing the cold air to rush in when it is over the pit. The hostler pulls the throttle right open, drawing fresh air through the flues. That is where a great deal of the boiler troubles start. It is a man failure and not an engine failure.

The British were careful to raise steam from cold over a period of about 8 hours, without using the blower, giving the expanding boiler parts ample time to adjust to each other. At least as early as 1905, American engines had an attachment for connecting the roundhouse compressed air supply to the engine's blower to accelerate fire raising.[145] This made it possible to raise steam from the first kindling of the fire to boiler working pressure in a mere 50 to 90 minutes, but at the cost of accelerated damage to the boiler.

The more that was known about locomotive fireboxes, the more alarming, frustrating and intractable these problems became.[146] Firebox life varied widely from railroad to railroad in response to factors that were poorly understood.[147] The British had long used copper for fireboxes and fire tubes in both domestic-service and export locomotives. Copper transmitted heat more efficiently than steel and the softer metal withstood the stresses caused by uneven expansion and contraction better. In Argentina, where both copper and steel fireboxes were used, copper fireboxes lasted 10 to 12 years while steel lasted only four. In America, high firing rates caused unacceptably rapid erosion of the soft copper by flying cinders.

In the days of the 4-4-0s, with their narrow, deep fireboxes, low boiler pressures and modest firing rates, steel fireboxes lasted 20 years and more in areas of good water. The new locomotives, fired to their limits, carrying 180 to 200 pounds per square inch boiler pressure, and working in areas of bad water, used up their fireboxes in as little as 2–4 years. Some steel formulations gave better service than others, but the information available to the industry was vague and opinions differed. The experience of one railroad was often diametrically opposite to that of another without anyone knowing why. Advocates of softer steel were vindicated with time, as fireboxes made with this material corrugated in response to thermal shocks without cracking, whereas harder steel cracked.[148]

George L. Fowler began a study in 1915, which he continued for several years, on locomotives of the Lake Shore & Michigan Southern and the Delaware & Hudson with both radial-stayed and Wootten fireboxes, using beams of light reflected from two small mirrors and projected onto a screen to achieve the enormous magnification needed to detect the tiny, but nonetheless destructive, relative movements between the inner and outer firebox sheets, expressed by the angular movement of staybolts.[149] The tests revealed continual and unexpected differential movements between the firebox and wrapper sheets, caused both by thermal expansion and contraction and by pressurization and depressurization of the boiler. These movements began as soon as the fire was lit and continued for as long as heat remained in the firebox, even when the boiler was at constant pressure, further complicated by expansion and contraction of the fire tubes, pushing the tube sheet back and forth. The greatest relative motion was around flexible staybolts. Where rigid staybolts constrained this motion, it was taken up by flexure of the staybolts. Where proximity to major structural components further constrained the motion, the firebox sheets themselves buckled.

The results were baffling. Any neutral zones, where the movements canceled each other out, were transient in time and location. Movements relative to some fixed datum, such as the foundation ring, remained unknown. In the course of hundreds of tests, no two traces were the same. These findings, moreover, were from static tests with no contribution from the bending and twisting of a moving locomotive. The main conclusion was that, as these differential movements could not be resisted, they had to be accommodated, both by means of flexible staybolts and by trying to incorporate flexibility into boiler design.

In spite of persistent efforts to replace the staybolted firebox, almost all steam locomotives were built with this type of firebox and continued so until the end of steam.

7.2.7 The Wood Corrugated Firebox

A new and bold attempt to circumvent the problems of the conventional firebox was William H. Wood's corrugated firebox which appeared in 1908.[150] This firebox was built of corrugated sheets, allowing the firebox to flex with steam pressure and thermal expansion. Flexure of the tube sheet was intended to prevent the seal between the fire tubes and the tube sheet from leaking. The design used fewer staybolts than a conventional firebox and increased the heating surface. The New York Central, the Pennsylvania and the Union Pacific experimented with Wood fireboxes.

Another firebox using corrugated sheets was the Cour-Castle, used experimentally on some western railroads in 1907.[151]

Neither of these designs achieved widespread or lasting success.

7.2.8 The Jacobs-Shupert Firebox

In 1909, Messrs. Jacobs and Shupert of the Santa Fe brought out a radically new design of corrugated firebox which dispensed with staybolts altogether, designed for oil firing. The corrugations were so designed that the riveted joints were inside the water legs and were not exposed to the fire itself. Instead of staybolts, the firebox sheets were held in place by ⅜-inch diaphragm plates spaced at 10-inch

intervals along the firebox.

The first application was to a 2-10-2 tandem compound on the Santa Fe in April 1909.[152] The results were so successful that, by November 1910, thirty-two of the Santa Fe's engines were equipped with it with a further sixty-six on order. Tests showed that the new firebox evaporated nearly 30% more water per square foot of heating surface per hour than a conventional firebox, this figure increasing from about 12 pounds of water to 15.5. The locomotive fraternity greeted these figures with indignant disbelief, especially in view of the greater obstruction to water circulation around the firebox that the stay sheets must present.[153]

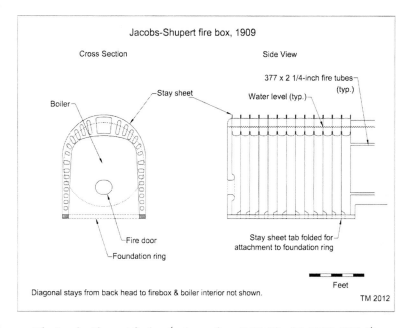

The Jacobs-Shupert firebox (redrawn from *RAG*, May 28, 1908, 1125-6).

One of the design objectives was safety against explosions resulting from uncovering of the crown sheet. In September 1910, the Santa Fe tested an oil-fired Jacobs-Shupert firebox and a 225-pounds-per-square-inch locomotive boiler in an instrumented stationary rig, making every attempt to simulate the conditions in which a conventional firebox would rupture, causing a boiler explosion. The water level was allowed to fall to 6 inches below the top of the crown sheet and cold water was injected into the boiler (often surmised as a cause of boiler explosions) while the safety valves, set at 225 pounds per square inch, were blowing. Pyrometers set into the firebox crown recorded a temperature of 1,125°F; after the test, discoloration showed that other parts of the crown sheets had been hotter still. Even so, there was no explosion. In spite of these merits, the Jacobs-Shupert firebox proved vulnerable to flexure of the locomotive and soon leaked.[154]

Tests at Coatesville, Pennsylvania, home of the Jacobs-Shupert United States Firebox Co., in 1912 under the supervision of Professor Goss, produced further interesting results.[155] In both the test boiler and a conventional boiler, the back tube sheet was extended as a diaphragm separating the body of the boiler from the firebox so that evaporation by the firebox could be measured separately from that of the fire tubes. The tests showed that the Jacobs-Shupert firebox was somewhat more efficient than the conventional firebox. More important than this finding was that, although the firebox heating surface was only about 10% of the total heating surface of the boiler in both types, the firebox accounted for 30% to 50% of the heat transfer in the boiler. The percentage decreased as the firing rate and drafting increased, spreading more heat through the fire tubes.

The tests also emphasized the familiar, but depressing fact that boiler efficiency diminished as firing rates increased. When the Jacobs-Shupert firebox was fired at 1,390 pounds of coal per hour (24 pounds per square foot of grate), the boiler absorbed 72% of the thermal energy of the coal. Increasing the firing rate to 6,300 pounds of coal per hour (109 pounds per square foot of grate), dropped this to only 50%, the difference being lost in stack gases and cinders. Nevertheless a 350% increase in firing rate did produce a 215% increase in steam generation and the American railroads were everlastingly hungry for power.

One phase of the Coatesville tests was arranged as a public spectacle with the deliberate intention of causing a crown sheet failure. The radial-stayed boiler failed in the expected manner while the Jacobs-Shupert boiler remained intact.[156]

In 1916–17, the Texas & Pacific bought fourteen new oil-fired 2-10-2s from Baldwin. At least some of these were equipped with Jacobs-Shupert fireboxes containing Gaines walls.[157] Tests with and without the Gaines wall showed that use of the Gaines wall produced an improvement in boiler efficiency of about 10%.

The understanding of the importance of the firebox in steam generation that resulted from the Coatesville tests was a major advance in the development of the American steam locomotive with important implications, both for the design of conventional boilers and for the development of water-tube fireboxes. Even so, as late as 1919[158]:

> The ratio of firebox volume to grate area has never received any careful or scientific investigation.

7.2.9 Water-Tube Fireboxes

The water-tube firebox retained its seductiveness, both as a means of reducing the everlasting maintenance of staybolts, and as a means of generating steam at higher pressures than were possible with conventional boilers.

Samuel S. Riegel patented his water-tube firebox in 1902 while working for the Brooks Locomotive Works. By 1914 he had become Mechanical Engineer to the Delaware, Lackawanna & Western and in that year the railroad bought a 4-6-2 from Lima equipped with his firebox.[159] Sixty-six 2½-inch water tubes were set in two groups inside the firebox, passing between the side and crown sheets at an angle of about 60° to the horizontal. The brick arch and its supporting tubes were fitted between the groups of water tubes. The heating surface of the tubes totaled 471 square feet; the Riegel boiler had a total heating surface, excluding the superheater, of 3,960 square feet, 14%

more than similar conventionally equipped engines. This increase, moreover, was placed in the firebox, where it could have the greatest effect.

After several years of development, including an experimental application on the Boston & Maine, the McClellon water-tube firebox was built into two of an order of fifteen 2-8-2s for the New York, New Haven & Hartford in 1917.[160] The firebox side sheets and back head were entirely replaced by 5- to 6-inch diameter vertical water tubes connecting the foundation ring to three horizontal drums. The foun-

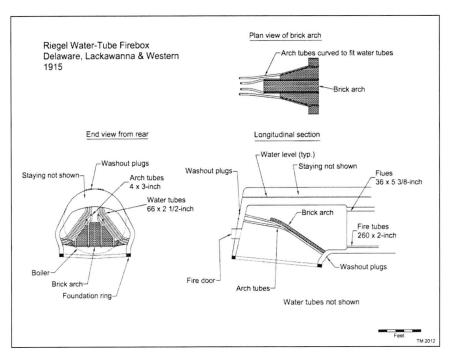

The Riegel water-tube firebox (redrawn from *RAG*, March 12, 1915, 445–6).

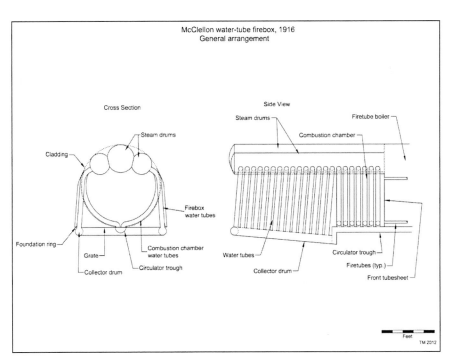

The McClellon water-tube firebox (redrawn from *RA*, February 25, 1928, 453–4).

dation ring was a hollow chamber, made of 1½-inch plate and constrained by staybolts. The drums formed the crown of the firebox and extended forward over a 44-inch long combustion chamber. The two outer drums were 23 inches in diameter; the center drum 32 inches. The foundation ring and the drums all formed part of the boiler water space. The water tubes were caulked and lagged with steel-reinforced cement. This was covered with insulating felt, the whole being covered by a steel jacket.

Neither of these two designs made any lasting headway in locomotive construction.

7.2.10 Boiler Explosions

In five years from June 1904, to June 1909, locomotive boiler explosions on American railroads killed 265 people and injured another 3,656.[161] The ARMMA estimated that 768 boiler explosions occurred in the five years, 1905–10.[162] Almost all were attributed to failure by the crew to keep water over the crown sheet; as the explosion usually killed the crew, they were not available to contest that assertion. Bad water, depositing mud and causing scale and corrosion, played its part, as did insufficient maintenance. Boiler explosions due to weakness of the boiler shell itself were far fewer, averaging six per year—one for every ten thousand locomotives in service. A still greater number of boiler failures occurred which did not cause loss of life; these instances only encouraged enginemen to take chances when no water was showing in the gauge glass or bottom try cock. The enormous demands that the railroads had to cope with, resulting in the employment of inexperienced men for excessive hours of duty, played its part in this apparent carelessness.[163]

The boilers themselves were strong enough; there was no merit in designing them stronger. Low-water alarms were still unreliable and could produce a false sense of security. Some railroads used staybolts without heads on the fire side, threaded into the firebox sheets, so that an overheated crown sheet would fail gradually and blow the fire down before an explosion could occur. Gauge glasses were still so problematical that, even in 1910, only half of the new locomotives being built were equipped with them. Try cocks and gauge glasses alike were prone to blockage with scale and mud unless they were regularly blown down and reamed out.

Calculations showed that even a small locomotive boiler, weighing 25,000 pounds and containing 7,000 pounds of water at 125 pounds per square inch, contained enough energy to throw the boiler to a vertical height of 2,850 feet.[164] By 1910, locomotive boilers of much greater size and pressure were in common use in the U.S.

Inspection reports on the causes of boiler explosions revealed disastrously bad maintenance practices on some railroads.

Improperly located water glass and gauge cocks; lowest reading of water glass one-eighth inch above highest point of crown sheet; bottom gauge cock 1⅛ inches above highest point of crown sheet; locomotive received new firebox nine months before accident and had evidently been operating in this dangerous condition for that length of time.

Both injectors defective; injectors reported 14 times previous to accident.

Mud ring cracked and leaking badly; reported 18 times and crown bolts reported leaking badly 16 times within 30 days prior to the accident.

Crown sheet failure, overheated; water foaming badly; reported six times by different engineers prior to accident, but boiler not washed.

This is the merest selection from a great number of such reports between 1912 and 1918.[165] These excerpts suggest how a crusty road foreman and an overworked or indifferent shop crew could easily force an engineer and fireman to balance the possible loss of their lives against the certain loss of their jobs. If enginemen were used to taking chances with defective engines, they would tend to take that chance. Viewed in this light, the fatality rate from boiler explosions may be easier to understand.

The first legislation on the inspection and construction of boilers came, not from the federal government, but from the New York State Railroad Commission; this legislation went into effect in 1905. Predictably, the railroad industry pilloried it:

Up to the present time (1905) the railroads of the country have been remarkably free from any legislative interference in the care and operation of their locomotives. This has been due to the fact that no regulation has been necessary, for the very obvious reason that all railroads pay the greatest possible attention to the inspection and maintenance of their boilers, thus rendering outside supervision unnecessary.... Still, the legislative desire to have a finger in every pie, where there is the slightest prospect of finding a plum, has led the lawmakers of New York to add one more official to the list of incumbents and to create an office that is useless in the extreme.[166]

Nevertheless, the record of injuries and fatalities caused by boiler explosions and less spectacular failures, and also by visibility impaired by leaking steam, built up against the railroads and their blustering could not stem the tide of legislation that swept over them during the first decades of the twentieth century.

The New York boiler legislation was extended in 1907 to cover inspection, construction standards and test frequency.[167] (For brevity, minimum standards are given here, although the regulations read "at least" in each case.) Boilers had to be hydrostatically tested to 25% above working pressure on entering service and then once a year, washed out every thirty days and inspected every three months. Every three years, the fire tubes had to be removed and the interior of the boiler thoroughly cleaned and inspected. Boilers had to be fitted with a water gauge glass and three try cocks, the bottom of the glass and the lowest try cock being 3 inches above the highest part of the crown sheet. The engine had to be sufficiently steam-tight that leaking steam did not obscure the engineer's vision. Staybolts had to be tested by tapping once a month. Staybolts shorter than 8 inches had to be drilled with weep holes. If two adjacent staybolts were broken, or three within a 4-foot circle, they had to be replaced before the boiler could be returned to service. Boilers had to be fitted with steam gauges and these had to be tested once a month. Each boiler had to have two safety valves capable of preventing the pressure from rising more than 5 pounds per square inch above working pressure. Fire tubes could be plugged, provided the plugs were tied together by a ⅝-inch rod. All of this had to be recorded. The language of this legislation was the forerunner of the safety regulations of today.

In 1911, Congress passed legislation on boiler inspection substantially the same as the earlier New York State legislation. Congress assigned enforcement of the new law to the ICC, developing its early involvement with safety, having recorded accidents since 1888. From 1912 onward, all boilers had to be designed to a safety factor of 4.

In 1912, the Southern Pacific introduced a low-water alarm. If the boiler water level fell below a predetermined minimum safe level, steam escaping through the mechanism caused a whistle to blow. In a coal-burning locomotive, water could be sprayed onto the fire; in an oil-burning locomotive, the oil valve would be closed. The device proved successful; the Southern Pacific installed it on all new locomotives and its use spread to other railroads.

The first annual report of the chief inspector of locomotive boilers appeared in January 1913.[168] This report showed that 90% of the fatalities caused by boiler explosions resulted from low water, causing crown sheet failures. Before the new legislation came into effect, the fatality rate due to boiler explosions had increased faster than the locomotive fleet. Comparing two periods, 1905–9 and 1911–12, boiler shell explosions ran at only three per year throughout the period, while firebox explosions almost doubled from 51 per year in 1905–9 to 94 per year in 1911–12—eight fatal locomotive boiler explosions every month.

Spot the gauge glass! The backhead of this Norfolk & Western Class Z-1a Mallet, No. 1409, photographed in November, 1934, shows how bigger boilers placed the boiler water level higher above the cab floor, making it increasingly difficult to observe the gauge glasses, especially at night. Two gauge glasses can be seen near the top center and top right of the back head (courtesy Norfolk Southern Corporation, ns1011).

Unfortunately for the credibility of the railroads' regulation of their own safety, the new boiler safety legislation and the rigorous investigation of accidents had an immediate effect.[169] Fatalities caused by failures of locomotive boilers and their attachments dropped by 60% in a single year between 1912 and 1913. Crown sheet failures dropped from 18 in the first quarter of 1913 to 9 in the last quarter, burst water glasses from 36 to 16; other boiler-related accidents declined similarly. The Federal locomotive inspectors, headed by Frank McManamy, inspected 90,346 locomotives (the entire fleet 1½ times over); 54,522 (60%) had defects that had to be remedied before the locomotive went out on the road; 4,676 (5%) were ordered out of service. Of these, 472 were ordered to run with reduced boiler pressure to insure the required factor of safety; a further 553 had to have the gauge glass or lowest try cock raised to provide a proper safety margin. The inspectors exceeded their authority by reporting a wide range of common defects, especially of running gear, that could cause derailments but were not covered by law. Some railroad officials told the inspectors to mind their own business, which boded ill for the railroads and heralded the all-encompassing regulation that would eventually overcome them. In 1914, only 23 fatalities resulted from boiler-related accidents, compared to 91 in 1912, a decline of 74%.[170]

The ICC proposed a boiler factor of safety of 4, the current average being about 3.75. Investigations over a two-year period revealed 11,153 locomotives, about 17% of the fleet, with boiler factors of safety less than 4. Some railroads were running on lower factors of safety; 212 boilers were found with factors of safety less than 2.5 and a further 1,224 with factors of safety less than 3—all of which was grist to the regulatory mill.

Federal boiler inspection was not only a breakthrough in safety, but also a contributor to improved efficiency, although the railroads were unlikely to acknowledge it. The railroads'

Effects of a boiler explosion on the Chicago, Milwaukee & St. Paul at Kellogg, Minnesota, on July 20, 1920, killing the engineer, fireman and brakeman. The locomotive was a class K-1 2-6-2, built in company shops, 1908–9 (courtesy Wescott family).

own regulations for improved construction practices became subject to government approval.

The railroads blamed practically all boiler explosions on crown sheet failures and all of these on enginemen. The vast reduction in these accidents, coincident with the new inspectorate, disproved this assertion. Government inspection included rigorous and objective accident investigations, revealing defects that some railroads would have preferred to remain undiscovered. One of the culprits was the position of the water gauges, relative to the crew working positions. The backheads of the huge boilers on new engines were so high that an engineman could not see the water level in a gauge glass when even the minimum water level was above his head.

> A recent investigation of a crown sheet failure showed that the cab arrangement was such that the water glass and gauge cocks were 9 in. above the engineer's head and that he regularly carried a small keg to climb upon to try the gauge cocks.

The boiler safety record went on improving. Between 1912 and 1915 the number of boiler-related accidents and injuries resulting from them decreased by 50%; the number of fatalities decreased by no less than 86%.[171] In 1915, the federal government extended the authority of the boiler inspectors to cover all parts of the locomotive and tender.

The explosions went on, however. On July 20, 1920, a boiler explosion on the Chicago, Milwaukee & St. Paul killed the engineer, fireman and brakeman. A local newspaper reported[172]:

> A frightful explosion took place half a mile north of Kellogg on Friday morning of last week in which Wells J. Wescott and Joseph Homola of Farmington and a man by the name of Schrafer, of Minneapolis lost their lives.
>
> It was the boiler of a K-1 engine, No. 5604, while pulling an extra, bound from La Cross to Farmington.
>
> The cause of this accident will never be known, as the entire engine crew were killed. The only evidence as to what happened lies buried with the victims and the entire engine almost entirely blown to pieces. The boiler was lifted from the tracks and carried 400 feet up the track, blowing the cab to atoms.
>
> According to a statement made by a hobo who was riding in a car next to the engine, Wescott rode with him for several stations and had only left the car and gone into the engine when the explosion occurred. He was found in a field 600 feet away from the wreck, but still alive. He died an hour later. The body of the engineer, stripped of all clothing, was found lodged in the telegraph wires. Joseph Homola was firing and he and the engineer were killed instantly.
>
> The engine had recently been sent out from the shops and was supposed to be in good condition. Although no one knows the cause of the explosion trackmen believe it was caused from low water.

Boiler explosions would dog the steam locomotive as a major, inherent safety hazard until the end of its days. These explosions were rare in Britain. The British attitude was—and is—that uncovering the crown sheet would cause the fusible plugs to melt, dousing the fire and failing the engine—nothing more. Possibly British locomotives were universally fitted with bigger and more numerous fusible plugs; otherwise the reasons are unclear.

Section 7.3. Boilers and Steam Generation

7.3.1 Boiler Pressures

The years 1880–1905 saw a marked increase in locomotive boiler pressures, from 160 pounds per square inch, typical in the 1880s, to as high as 220 pounds per square inch in the first decade of the twen-

tieth century. Higher boiler pressure led directly to higher tractive effort, but was it more thermally efficient?

Theoretically, the efficiency of a heat engine increases in proportion to the range of temperatures and pressures between which it operates. As the temperature of saturated steam increases with pressure, the efficiency of a saturated-steam locomotive should increase in proportion to its boiler pressure. Raising the boiler pressure, however, increased leakage losses, radiation heat losses, capital and maintenance costs and the chemical activity of impure feed water. If a boiler had to weigh more, was it more cost effective to increase its size and steam generating capacity, than its strength?

The Carnegie Institution sponsored a series of tests at Purdue to examine whether there was a net benefit in increasing boiler pressures. Beginning early in 1904, the tests went on for eighteen months; publication of the results began late in 1906.[173] Opportunely, the Purdue locomotive, *Schenectady No. 2*, had a boiler designed for pressures up to 250 pounds per square inch; it ran the equivalent of 14,000 miles in more than a hundred tests.

The tests showed that increased steam pressure produced a gain in efficiency, with coal consumption per indicated horsepower-hour declining from 30 pounds at 125 pounds per square inch to 25 pounds at 240 pounds per square inch. The gains, however, diminished with each increment in pressure and were very small beyond 220 pounds per square inch.

The Carnegie and Goss[174] publications resulting from these tests concluded that, up to 180 pounds per square inch, increasing boiler pressure was justifiable; beyond 180 pounds per square inch, increased pressure offered no savings when compared to greater capacity and: "no possible excuse can be found for increasing pressure above the limit of 220 lbs."

The total cost of higher boiler pressure was so great that by 1912 a contrary trend had set in and[175]: "there is a marked tendency toward pressures below 200 lbs. Passenger engines are now designed for boiler pressures of 185 lbs., while recent large freight engines have a working pressure of only 160 lbs. per sq. in." Superheating and large cylinders offered compensating advantages.

Boiler pressures in new locomotives remained between 180 and 200 pounds per square inch until the 1920s when demands for ever more power combined with improved steel metallurgy to allow firetube boilers to be built for pressures up to 350 pounds per square inch.

The last mainline steam locomotives ever built were the QJ-class 2-10-2s built in China up to the 1980s, with a boiler pressure of 215 pounds per square inch. Even this was less than the boiler pressure of the last British Railways locomotives, built in the 1950s, of 250 pounds per square inch.

7.3.2 Water Circulation

> Into a boiler we put water and take out steam, but of the inwardness of the process practically nothing is known. Things are taken for granted, and when phenomena present themselves which are out of the common we are told either that they have no real existence, that they are quite usual, or that it is not worthwhile to pursue the inquiry. Pendred, V. in *The Locomotive*. Quoted *RAG*, April 9, 1909, 784

If the structure of the fire-tube boiler was simple, its functioning was not and was only gradually understood. As early as 1906, D. Van Alstyne, Mechanical Superintendent of the Northern Pacific, understood several subtle interactions that influenced boiler design over the course of time.[176]

As designers improved the efficiency of combustion inside the firebox, their efforts increased the temperature of the fire. Increased fire temperature increased the evaporation rate around the firebox; this, in turn, demanded better water circulation, including generously sized water legs as, otherwise, the firebox sheets would burn out, warp and crack. Van Alstyne realized that water circulation was not merely an interesting phenomenon; it was essential to the steaming rate. He realized, too, that there could be limits to the circulation rates that could be induced naturally by heating and evaporation, but that no practical means of forcing circulation were in sight.

The bigger the firebox, the greater the volume of the water legs and the greater the volume of water required to circulate through them. The water legs were encumbered with staybolts; if they were narrow as well they resisted free circulation. It was therefore desirable that the firebox be short from front to back, but deep with wide water legs. This was achievable if the firebox was behind the driving wheels and supported on a trailing truck. Van Alstyne foresaw that this requirement would lead to fireboxes supported on four-wheel trailing trucks twenty years before such engines were built.

> The locomotive firebox in its fullest development should be much larger and heavier in proportion to the barrel than it is now. It is quite likely that it will be necessary to carry the overhanging weight back of the drivers on a four-wheel trailer truck.

In the first decade of the twentieth century those involved with the steam locomotive suspected that water circulation in a locomotive boiler was both more important and more complicated than they had hitherto realized. The new, wide fireboxes were giving trouble and had lives as short as one to three years due to cracking of the side sheets, incurring heavy cost for their replacement. Design engineers felt that the water circulation resulting from the shape of the firebox sides must be a factor, but agreed that almost nothing was known about how the water behaved in the water legs and how the water and steam interacted.

Common opinion held that water injected near the front of the boiler flowed rearward along the bottom of the boiler to the water spaces around the firebox, where it flowed upward as it evaporated, with a strong flow upward within two feet of the back tube sheet. Experiments by G. J. Churchward of the Great Western Railway in England in 1903–4, using vanes inside the boiler with spindles passing through glands in the boiler shell to telltales on the outside, confirmed this.[177]

In the 1860s, the injector check valve had been located near the firebox. Expansion and contraction caused by the injection of cool feed water damaged the back end of the boiler so much that the check valve was moved farther and farther forward with successive new construction until the same effects started to appear at the front tube sheet, whereupon it was moved back a short distance to about 18 to 24 inches from the front tube sheet, at which compromise position it remained.

On the Duluth, Missabe & Northern[178]:

> Some three and one-half years ago (1905–6) we received two locomotives from a locomotive builder. After putting them in service we found it impossible to make a round trip of one hundred and fifty miles in passenger service because of tubes leaking. This continued until the transportation department condemned them and ordered them off the road until they could be put in shape to do business. We then turned the engines over to the builder, advising them to either overcome the difficulty or take the engines back. They sent an expert who worked for six weeks trying every possible thing he could think of to overcome the trouble, and finally he gave it up as a bad job.

The Motive Power Superintendent moved the position of the injector feed into the boiler, spraying feed water into the steam space, whereupon the problems ceased. The reason for this was that feed water injection caused cool water (at about 175°F after passing through the injector) to sink down to the bottom of the boiler, cooling the lower tubes and causing them to contract and leak where they passed through the tube sheets. The leaks were most common on the same side as the most-used injector. In 1907, the company began to convert all its engines to this system and found that better steam generation and economies in fuel and maintenance resulted. This practice became widespread on other railroads, but not universal. Current research has not shown whether this was the first application of "top feed." All the locomotives illustrated in White's book show feed water check valves on the side of the boiler.

In 1911 the situation was still[179]:

> The speaker was challenged to show any data whatever that could demonstrate in any way either the direction or velocity of the currents of water in a firebox. Much as such data was to be desired, and valuable as it would be, no one knew of any such experiments that had ever been made and any statements as to the character of the circulation of water in a locomotive boiler were purely a matter of deduction based on general principles and not on actual measurements made in the field.

Claims for the efficiency of the Jacobs-Shupert firebox, introduced on the Santa Fe in 1909, were dismissed by some as extravagant, but sparked further research into water circulation.[180] The Santa Fe conducted road tests in 1911, comparing the Jacobs-Shupert firebox with conventional fireboxes, using a comprehensively instrumented, oil-fired 2-10-2. Of these tests, it was said:

> The investigation is interesting and of value, but we know so very, very, little about boiler circulation and what it means in the generation of steam that it is decidedly unsafe to draw any generalizations from such meagre data as that which is presented here.
>
> That there is an upward circulation in the water leg, there can be no doubt, but as to its rapidity, actual direction and complication of counter currents we know about as little as can be imagined. The one thing promising is that there is a prospect of its being actually measured in the near future, and then we may be able to design fireboxes with some idea of what actually goes on within them.

Over the years, such features as thermic siphons, Security Circulators and various arrangements of channels and baffles improved boiler water circulation, but the shape and arrangement of the locomotive boiler and firebox remained too severely constrained by other factors for water circulation to be a major design feature.

7.3.3 Boiler Washing and Water Treatment

Boiler washing and water treatment have no obvious or compelling historical interest, yet improvements in these two areas during the early twentieth century had surprising effects on the economics of a desperate industry.

Railroads had to accept whatever water they could find for their locomotive boilers. In New England and the Pacific Northwest, water was clean and soft; in the early 1900s, the New Haven washed its boilers out every thirty days, and that was only for the staybolt inspections required by New York state laws. Elsewhere, the available water was in varying degrees charged with mud and chemicals. As such water evaporated into steam, it left mud, precipitates and scale behind it which accumulated in the boiler and had to be washed out. In the Mid-West, feed water from muddy rivers was so silty that 100 to 120 pounds of mud could be taken into a locomotive boiler on a single run, resulting in "mud burns" where mud settled out in areas of slack circulation, allowing patches of the firebox sheets to overheat and causing costly damage and even boiler explosions. On the Louisville & Nashville, where the water was muddy and brackish, boilers had to be washed out every 220 to 280 miles and the water changed at lesser intervals. General experience ranged between these extremes.

A typical locomotive boiler had 30 to 50 wash-out plugs. After the fire was dropped and the steam pressure reduced to nothing, they could be unscrewed to drain the water. Blow-down valves in the underside of the boiler allowed water to be released while still under steam pressure. Increasingly common by 1905 was the practice of opening the blow-down valves a little and often while the engine was working, allowing the steam pressure in the boiler to force a blast of hot water out onto the ground, taking accumulated sludge with it.[181] The blow-down valve controls on many locomotives were not accessible from the cab, being intended for use when the engine was stationary, so that the fireman had to crawl out along the running board to open them, which discouraged their use. In 1907–8, the Louisville & Nashville fitted its engines with blow-down valves for use when the engine was working and started introducing oil into the boiler; this increased the company's monthly locomotive mileage in districts of muddy and brackish water by one-third.[182]

Blowing down locomotive boilers wasted coal at about 50 pounds for each minute a 1¼-inch blow-down valve was open; the noise was a public nuisance and the violent blast of hot water threw debris over nearby property. Another possibility was more or less continuous blowing down through a ¼-inch valve. In 1912, the Chicago, Burlington & Quincy made detailed calculations as to the relative costs of water treatment, boiler washing, blowing down and the breakdown and maintenance costs that were otherwise incurred.[183] The cost balance was so complicated and so much affected by local operating conditions that no general recommendation was possible.

When cold water was used to wash out and refill a boiler, 7 to 8 hours were needed to blow down the boiler, wash it out, refill it, heat the water and raise steam pressure to 100 pounds per square inch. Accelerating this process damaged the boiler but the frantic demands on the railroads in the early 1900s swept away such concerns.[184]

Under good water and coal conditions, fires are seldom dumped and leaks are almost unknown. Most of this, of course, is due to the water, but most of us have known of engines that have given trouble on account of leaking every day; when placed in the hands of certain engineers, they would run day in and day out for a long time and be absolutely dry, the secret of the man's success being in the uniform temperature maintained, by insisting on careful firing, proper handling of dampers, and a scientific use of the injector. If such a condition can be obtained, and we know it is possible, it speaks volumes for maintaining the same temperature as far as possible in firebox and boiler; yet, how many are there of us who, when an engine is coming in from a run, will stand by and see all sorts of things done that, in our thinking moments, we know to be absolutely wrong. We apply cold water through the injector, while no circulation is taking place in the boiler, we then blow the steam off by letting it escape to the atmosphere, after which the blow-off cock is opened, and a boilerful of hot water runs down the sewer; and then, as if not satisfied with wasting such a large amount of heat that we will have to replace later on at a cost of probably 800 to 1,000 pounds of coal, we turn on a stream of cold water and go through the washing-out process, so that the firebox is at a temperature of 45 to 50 degrees, and the top of the boiler and some of the upper flues are still hot. Then is the time when some boilermakers get their work in; and we are surprised to have someone tell us that a report like a cannon was heard and a crack developed in the side sheet that has put our engine out of commission for a time, or if we are fortunate enough to miss the cracked side sheet, we fill our boiler up with cold water and reverse the process that has just taken place; a large fire is put in the box and blower applied, so that we have steam on, before the water around the mud ring is hot, and often after the engine has gone a short distance on the road

we get word from the train dispatcher that the fruits of our abuse has shown itself in a dead locomotive that is blocking traffic. This is not an exaggerated picture.

Thermometers placed inside the water legs showed that, if a boiler washer connected the wash-out hose to the blow-down valve and injected 60°F water into a hot boiler, the hot and cold water would hardly mix at all, resulting in a temperature gradient of as much as 150°F across a line as little as 3 inches wide. This could corrugate the firebox sheets.

One of the first places to wash out boilers with hot water was the Pittsburgh & Lake Erie terminal at McKee's Rocks, Pennsylvania, in 1905. Using waste heat from locomotives and shop stationary engines, a boiler could be blown down from 150 pounds per square inch in 20 minutes, washed out with hot water in 1½–2 hours and refilled with water close to boiling. The temperature of the wash-out water was limited to about 130°F for the safety of the boiler washers. Steam pressure could be raised to 100 pounds per square inch 30 minutes after washing was complete.[185]

Washing with hot water halved the amount of coal needed to regain working pressure; savings in coal and labor soon paid for the heat recovery plant. No matter how carefully a boiler was cooled and heated, some degree of damage resulted from uneven expansion and contraction; railroads reported that washing boilers with hot water halved their boiler repairs and doubled the mileage of their boilers and fire tubes.

Equipment was quickly refined. As early as 1908, one railroad found that they could blow down a large boiler in 35 minutes, wash it out with 150°F water in 22 minutes and refill it with 190°F water in 13 minutes, for a saving of 1,000 pounds of coal and 2,500 gallons of water, compared to washing with cold water.[186] Steam pressure could be brought up to 100 pounds per square inch in another 25 minutes, reducing boiler washout time from 4 to 6 hours to less than 2. The payback period on the necessary plant was one year, with added savings in maintenance costs and increased locomotive availability.

The steam locomotive community held varied opinions on the effects of scale, but by 1918 few doubts still existed.[187] Researchers estimated that ¹⁄₁₆ inch of scale on all the heating surfaces increased fuel consumption by 15%; ¼ inch of scale would increase fuel consumption by 40%. Frank McManamy, Manager of the Locomotive Section, USRA, reckoned that 40% of the locomotives in service were running with ¹⁄₁₆ inch of scale.

We will pay, therefore, during the year of 1918 more than $50,000,000 for fuel on account of the scale in locomotive boilers that many men do not consider of sufficient importance to warrant its removal.

Railroads without water treatment plants found that scale could be reduced by putting sodium carbonate ("soda ash") into the tender tanks,[188] turning scale into soft mud which was ejected by blowing down. In the early 1900s, the Chicago & North Western had to wash boilers or change water at each end of a 150-mile division; soda ash and blowing down increased this to 1,050 to 1,500 miles.

The Great Northern faced a wide range of water conditions in Montana and North Dakota, mostly bad.[189] Good water was obtainable from shallow gravel beds and small lakes, but water from deep wells was so saline as to be unusable for locomotives in its raw state. Some rivers were saline or alkaline; chemical content and turbidity varied from season to season. The increase of farming caused long-term changes in water quality. The Great Northern began to build water treatment plants in 1912. By 1919, 1,100 route miles were supplied with treated water, with satisfactory reductions in boiler problems.

The Missouri Pacific started building water treatment plants in 1905.[190] By 1918, the company had spent $154,000 which was returned many times over in reduced boiler repairs, better fuel economy and all the effects of improved locomotive availability. That year, the Missouri Pacific's fifty-two treatment plants precipitated nearly 2,000 tons of material that would otherwise have been deposited as scale in the boilers of 700 locomotives.

A 1914–15 ARMMA study of boiler washing practices drew replies representing 80% of the U.S. locomotive fleet.[191] Of these, 40% made more than 1,500 miles between wash-outs, 60% made less; 25% made less than 500 miles. Fifty-four railroads used hot water for boiler washing; they reported a 36% saving in water, a 36% saving in fuel used during wash-outs, a 42% saving in time and a one-third reduction in boiler problems. Thirty-one railroads used lineside water softening plants, with 100% to 300% increases in mileage between boiler repairs. Forty-five railroads added water treatment chemicals to their tender tanks.

Engine crews had to be educated in this new approach—easier said than done with men who had been running engines for decades.[192]

> I have run engines thirty years ago, before we ever heard of water treatment, and I can see no advantage at this late date in using soda ash. It is all rot.

7.3.4 Superheat

Superheating was one of the most important advances ever made in the thermal efficiency of the steam engine, marvelously simple, capable of retrofitting and invisible from the engine's exterior. The seminal development work was done in Germany. Introduction in America was slow against barriers of skepticism.

The histories of compounding and superheating are curiously entwined. Early experiments with superheated steam encountered trouble with lubricants and packings; compounding seemed to offer more immediate benefits. While compounding was successful in marine and stationary plant, it aroused virulent controversy when applied to American locomotives[193]:

> In the compound controversy there was scarcely a superintendent of motive power in the country who took the slightest interest in making it a success; while the hostility in all quarters was intense almost to bitterness.

During the 1890s, American locomotive builders saw compounding as a means of obtaining a competitive edge over their rivals; this drove much of the effort that went into its promotion. Superheating lacked the vigorous and eccentric champions of compounding and so was not promoted in the same way. In the early 1900s, construction of rigid-frame compounds was fading, although the Mallet articulated compound was just beginning its American career. Seen from 1906:

> It does not seem likely that the superheater will be extensively used upon the compound, as the composite saving of the two systems is not enough in excess of the superheater alone to make the combination of the two worthwhile.

In spite of the early success of the first superheated locomotives in Canada, in 1906 there were still only fifteen superheated locomotives in the whole of the United States; the superheater was an interesting curiosity[194]:

> Superheated steam offers a very attractive field in connection with locomotive development. In German practice it has been remarkably successful and the Canadian Pacific Railway has practically duplicated the satisfactory results obtained in Germany. A number of experiments are now being made in this country, promising very satisfactory results. In

short, superheating is one of the fundamental questions in locomotive practice which is worthy of most careful attention at this time.

Even the form it would take was still uncertain[195]:

> As to the final form that the superheater will take, there is, as yet, no certainty. It seems now as though it would be of the smokebox type, though the tube superheaters are rendering a good account of themselves. This statement is based more upon the results obtained abroad than upon any evidence forthcoming in this country.

The Canadian superheated compounds performed well in freight service, but in passenger service the superheated single-expansion locomotives outperformed them.[196] The compounds were difficult to maintain in extreme cold weather; superheat offered economies equal to or better than compounds but without this problem.

The Schmidt fire-tube superheater needed an automatic damper, connected to the throttle, to prevent fire gases from passing through the superheater flues unless the steam tubes were full of steam. If the damper was not used or properly maintained, the U-bends burned out. The importance of the damper was not realized at first, but:

> The writer sees no reason whatever for abandoning a valuable and important principle such as the use of superheated steam because troubles have been incurred through neglect in maintaining a small attachment which could easily have been attended to had its importance been appreciated, and after three years' experience feels justified in stating that if the dampers are properly maintained the trouble through the destruction of the ends of the superheater pipes will not occur.

The Canadians found that the lubrication problem could be overcome, using hydrostatic lubricators, lubricating the pistons as well as the valves. Previously, condensation of saturated steam had sufficed for this purpose. Improved packing materials solved the problems of leaking glands.

The real beginning of superheating in American steam locomotives was a New York Central 4-4-2, retrofitted with a Schenectady superheater in 1904. The following year, the Chicago & North Western tested a second locomotive, also retrofitted with a Schenectady superheater and using only 30°F of superheat.[197] Tests recorded 7% more work per pound of coal. Researchers noticed that efficiency was lowest at long cut-offs, with heavy steam draw and short dwelling time in the superheater elements.

The fifteen superheated locomotives in trial service in the United States by the end of 1906 were on the New York Central (1 Schenectady), Burlington (1 Schenectady, 2 Schmidt), Rock Island (6 Schenectady), Soo Line (1 Schenectady), Chicago & North Western (1 Schenectady), Boston & Maine (1 Schenectady) and the Lake Shore & Michigan Southern (11 Schenectady, 1 Vaughan-Horsey).

Only a year later, fifty-four additional American locomotives were superheated.[198] Always bold in its locomotive policy, the Santa Fe had forty-nine of these with the Vauclain superheater. Four other railroads experimented with single engines so equipped: the Central of Georgia, the Rock Island, the Chicago & Alton and the Pittsburgh, Shawmut & Northern. The Union Pacific experimented with a Vaughan-Horsey superheater and a smokebox superheater of its own devising. The Great Northern had two engines with Schmidt smokebox superheaters. Tests indicated a saving of 13% in water, 14% in coal per car-mile in passenger service, while the superheated 2-6-2 freight engine saved 30% in water and 28% in coal per ton-mile. The Boston & Maine and the Soo Line each had one engine with a Schenectady superheater. The Lake Shore & Michigan Southern was experimenting with a Schenectady superheater and a Vaughan-Horsey. Formidable gains in locomotive power and efficiency and the ability to use poorer grades of coal more than offset temporary and solvable problems of leaks, cracked fittings, superheater flues plugged with cinders, soot deposition on tubes, and cylinder lubrication.

Opinions differed as to the best degree of superheat.[199] The Germans favored the highest possible temperature. The Canadian Pacific found that the 20°F to 30°F of superheat produced by the smokebox superheaters did not produce worthwhile economies after the tubes had become coated with soot, and removed them. The firetube superheaters that they retained produced 100°F to 150°F of superheat. H. H. Vaughan, by then Superintendent of Motive Power, commented in 1908:

> I do not wish to take any position against the Baldwin superheater, but I think the Germans have been on the right track in going to high superheat.

The Vauclain/Baldwin superheater comprised an array of steam tubes in two 90-degree arcs on each side of the smokebox interior.[200] Sheets directed the fire gases forward through these arrays, reversing their direction to exit the stack. Baldwin claimed that the device used only waste heat and took up no tube space inside the boiler shell. Smokebox superheaters, however, produced only low superheat; in the Baldwin design, the intricate tube arrays would have offered high resistance to gases and would have been vulnerable to erosion and plugging by cinders. This and other smokebox superheaters, such as the Hagans and Deeley types, failed to produce useful superheat and were difficult to construct and maintain.

Vauclain acknowledged the German ideas but maintained that the goal of superheating in American conditions was a single-expansion engine of improved efficiency, high availability and low maintenance costs, with a boiler pressure of only 160 pounds per square inch and without the complexities of compounding or the material problems of high superheat. Vauclain persuaded the Santa Fe to allow him to build one of an order of tandem compounds as a low-pressure, low-superheat, single-expansion engine, using the large-diameter low-pressure cylinders and omitting the high-pressure cylinders; the result was so successful that further orders followed, both from the Santa Fe and from other railroads. The increase of boiler pressure in saturated-steam locomotives from 160 pounds per square inch to 210 pounds had so increased the costs of leakage and boiler maintenance that a return to lower boiler pressures offered real benefits.[201]

Professor Goss had experimented with superheated steam at Purdue in 1902, but followed up with detailed tests in 1906–07.[202] Purdue rebuilt the boiler of *Schenectady No. 2* with a Schenectady superheater in 1903 and renamed it *Schenectady No. 3*. Tests on *Schenectady No. 3* at boiler pressures of 120 to 240 pounds per square inch with 150°F superheat resulted in efficiency as high as 3 pounds of coal and 22 pounds of steam per indicated horsepower-hour. Four pounds of coal and 26 pounds of steam were typical for saturated-steam engines. *Schenectady No. 3* produced more power at lower smokebox vacuum than *Schenectady No. 2*. The Purdue tests predicted that, for any given power requirement, superheated steam would save 15% to 20% in water and 8% to 12% in fuel. Alternatively, superheat would increase maximum power output by 10% to 15%, with a 5% water saving and no increase in fuel consumption. The researchers also predicted that superheat would allow a return to the 160-pound per square inch steam pressures of former times.

In 1908, Schmidt devised yet a third form of superheater. The dry

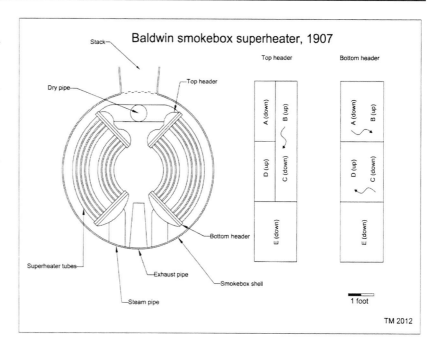

The Baldwin smokebox superheater (redrawn from *RRG*, June 7, 1907, 780-1; March 27, 1908, 454).

pipe ended in a header toward the back of the boiler interior. From this, tubes coaxial to the topmost fire tubes passed saturated steam along their exterior, ending in a header in the smokebox.[203] The disadvantages of this and other superheaters inside the boiler barrel, such as the Pielock and Clench, was that irregular heating weakened the fire tubes, removal of the fire tubes for repair was more difficult, and the superheater itself was inaccessible for maintenance.

Several different types of superheater appeared in America; the sources consulted have not in every case revealed the differences between these types. These were the Schmidt from Germany, the Vaughan-Horsey from Canada, the Cole/Schenectady from Alco and the Vauclain from Baldwin, but also the Emerson, Union Pacific, Jacobs, Buck and Buck-Jacobs types.[204] George H. Emerson was later famous as the innovative superintendent of motive power for the Baltimore & Ohio from 1920 to 1941. The Emerson superheater was a double-loop fire-tube type, comprising twenty-eight elements in four vertical rows with a header on each side of the smokebox.[205] The Union Pacific superheater was a smokebox type with two vertical, crescent-shaped headers, connected by 108 2-inch horizontal tubes.[206] Jacobs was co-inventor of the Jacobs-Shupert firebox. An early diversity of arrangements showed that the fire-tube superheater with U-bends in the tubes was the only practical and effective form. This arrangement offered the double advantage that the exterior of the superheater flues heated water in the boiler, even as the heat passing through them heated the steam in the superheater elements. The benefits of superheating more than offset a very small loss of primary heating surface—because the 5- to 5½-inch flues offered a smaller circumference, relative to the cross-section area that they occupied. By 1910, 90% of the locomotive superheaters in service were of the fire-tube type.

Alco discarded the Field tube in 1909.[207] Each element of their new Cole superheater fitted inside a flue and comprised four tubes and three return bends so that steam passed through the flue four times. Successive design changes to the header made it easier to manufacture, install and dismantle for maintenance. An automatic damper

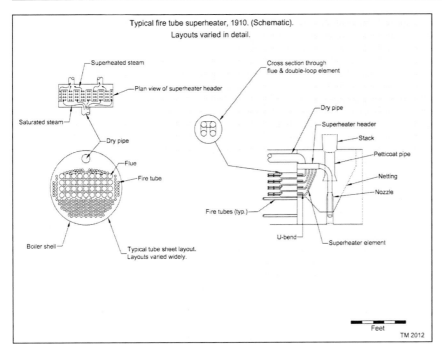

Typical fire tube superheater, 1910. (Schematic).
Layouts varied in detail.

Typical firetube superheater, 1910 (redrawn from *RAG*, January 26, 1912, 156–7).

in the smokebox prevented fire gases from passing through the flues when the engine was not using steam. The accompanying drawing shows the general arrangement which became typical; other arrangements were tried[208] but did not become widely current.

The benefits of superheating in locomotives became more apparent with increasing use.[209] Since the 1880s, increased power had come from higher boiler pressure, bringing higher construction and maintenance costs and diminishing benefits to thermal efficiency. Saturated steam at 160 pounds per square inch has a temperature of 370°F, increasing by only 17°F at 225 pounds per square inch. A smokebox superheater added 35°F to 40°F; a fire-tube superheater with a single-loop element added 100°F to 125°F; a double-loop element added 175°F to 200°F, producing large increases in energy without the cost of containing higher pressure. As superheating took place downstream of the throttle valve, this increased energy appeared as an increase in volume at constant pressure, allowing shorter cut-off and greater expansion. With saturated steam, a cyclic condensation and re-evaporation of water vapor took place in the cylinders, accompanied by the release and absorption of latent heat and the exchange of heat between the steam and the cylinder walls; superheated steam remained as steam throughout the cycle. Designers of saturated-steam engines had to limit cylinder diameters to limit the condensation surface; cylinders could be built 20% bigger for superheated steam than for saturated steam, not only to use the greater expansive power of the steam, but because condensation no longer occurred in the cylinder. Cylinder size was limited only by clearance dimensions and the need for the tractive effort produced by the pistons to remain within the limits imposed by adhesion weight. Coincidentally, slide valves were being replaced by piston valves at this time, easing the problems of lubrication with superheated steam. Savings in water consumption as much as 40% were being predicted, with a 25% saving in fuel. The lower fuel saving was due to fuel used in firing up and keeping the engine hot while it was drifting downgrade or standing still. Astonishingly, any engine could produce one-third more power with nothing more than a retrofitted superheater. One railroad found that superheating enabled an engine previously capable of haul-

ing 3,600 tons to haul up to 4,000 tons, even with boiler pressure reduced from 200 to 185 pounds per square inch.[210] The limitations of the human fireman were beginning to worry management; any device that increased the power extracted from a pound of coal increased what a hand-fired locomotive could do.[211] Engineers testing a new Lake Shore & Michigan Southern superheated Alco 4-6-2 in 1911 identified a 17-pounds per square inch pressure loss through the superheater but this was more than offset by the gain in thermal efficiency. The throttle accounted for another 10 pounds per square inch, with 3 pounds per square inch pressure loss through the steam pipes and cylinder valves.[212]

Far from adding to maintenance costs, some railroads found that their superheated engines cost less to maintain than those running on saturated steam. This was no mere reflection of newer engines. The Santa Fe retrofitted five engines with superheaters, reduced their boiler pressure from 225 pounds per square inch to 160 pounds, converted them from compound to single-expansion and found that their maintenance cost dropped by 23% to 33%.

In 1908, the Santa Fe retrofitted a tandem compound with a two-stage, smokebox-type Jacobs superheater, providing 90°F to 125°F of superheat. Two heat exchangers were placed in the smokebox ahead of and behind the stack. Baffles directed gases through the rear heat exchanger, past the stack and through the front heat exchanger; the gases then reversed direction and exited through the stack. Steam from the dry pipe went through the front heat exchanger to the high-pressure cylinders. The rear heat exchanger reheated the steam before it went to the low-pressure cylinders, thence through the nozzle to exhaust. Labyrinth plates inside the front heat exchanger ensured the even distribution of steam. Although this superheater provided only 20°F of superheat ahead of the high-pressure cylinders, it reheated the steam to 95°F of superheat between the high- and low-pressure cylinders. Like all smokebox superheaters, the heat exchangers would have added to the difficulty of clearing cinders from the smokebox and replacing fire tubes.

Direct comparison of two 2-10-2 tandem compounds, one with superheat, one without, produced some remarkable results: 20% coal saving working upgrade, 12% down-grade, 16% less coal and 13% less steam per indicated horsepower-hour, 14% less coal per drawbar horsepower-hour, 12% more steam per pound of coal, 11% more water evaporated and 20% more drawbar horsepower per square foot of heating surface, 10% more horsepower per cubic foot of cylinder volume. On the demanding run between Raton, New Mexico, and La Junta, Colorado, the superheated engine burned 200 to 205 pounds of coal per thousand ton-miles, compared to 245 to 275 pounds for a saturated-steam locomotive of the same class.

Other railroads reported similar results. The Pennsylvania reported the smallest savings, using the Baldwin superheater. Although Baldwin went on promoting their smokebox superheater, 160-pounds per square inch boiler pressure, low superheat and enlarged cylinders, the tide was against them and demands for raw power swept their arguments aside.[213]

The motive power department should forever keep in mind that the stockholder is not so much interested in the economy of the motive power department as he is in the economy of transportation as a whole. If with higher superheat and higher steam pressure combined there should result greater hauling capacity or speed per ton of locomotive, thus gaining economy of transportation as a whole, then the motive power department will have to accept the higher pressures, rather than to take a retrograde step towards the lower pressures—a retrograde position, let us say, from the point of view of efficiency of transportation, though apparently not retrograde from the point of cheapening the cost of boiler maintenance.

By 1910, opinion favored the highest obtainable superheat; locomotive and stationary plant tests showed increasing fuel and water savings as superheat increased.[214] Opinion was that a superheater would not pay to install unless it developed more than 50°F of superheat. Slide valves, however, were marginally usable with superheat; at the higher temperatures the valves warped. The Union Pacific was able to use slide valves at 130°F superheat, but with bronze valve seats instead of cast iron and improved lubrication; road tests demonstrated savings of 14% in coal and 23% in steam. Superheat as high as 500°F was being used in stationary plant; the practical limits were still not in sight. L. Hoffman, representing the Schmidt Superheating Co. in England, summarized European development as:

> When superheat on locomotives first came up, many experts believed that it was quite sufficient to get only dry steam in the cylinders. Later on it was believed that the steam would be superheated sufficiently high to remain dry during the cut-off, and now experts are glad if they have still some superheat in the exhaust steam.

Purdue tested the effects of superheat temperature by installing superheater elements of three different lengths[215] and running tests at boiler pressures between 120 and 240 pounds per square inch. The lowest steam consumption occurred at 180 to 220 pounds per square inch at all superheat temperatures, the lowest being 21.6 pounds per indicated horsepower-hour at the highest superheat temperature and 200 pounds per square inch for a coal consumption of 3.0 pounds per indicated horsepower-hour. With saturated steam, the lowest steam consumption was 25 pounds per indicated horsepower-hour at 240 pounds per square inch for a coal consumption of 3.3 pounds per indicated horsepower-hour. Superheating thus provided 14% better steam economy and 9% better coal economy at 17% lower boiler pressure than the best results obtainable with saturated steam.

By 1910, 805 locomotive superheaters were in use in North America on nineteen railroads. Four hundred and eighty-seven of these were in Canada, leaving 318 superheaters in an American locomotive fleet of about 59,000. By contrast, the Europeans had more than five thousand superheated locomotives in service or being built for 130 railroads; the Belgian state railway had more superheated engines than all the railroads of the U.S. The only American railroads with significant quantities in service were the Santa Fe (168), the Great Northern (61), the Northern Pacific (36) and the Southern Pacific (21). These four had also been enthusiastic users of compounds. Other trial users were the Boston & Maine (1), the Chicago & North Western (1), the Burlington (5), the Central of Georgia (1), the Rock Island (9), the Erie (1), the Soo Line (1), the Lake Shore, Michigan & Southern (2), the Oregon Short Line (2), the Pennsylvania—for all its engineering skill and technical leadership—(1), the Pittsburgh, Shawmut & Northern (1), the Wheeling & Lake Erie (1) and the Union Pacific (3).

The Canadian Vaughan-Horsey type accounted for 57% of numbers installed, followed by the Baldwin (9%), Churchward (7%), Cole (2%), Emerson (7%), Jacobs (12%) and Schmidt (7%). The Baldwin type equipped seventy-nine engines on twelve railroads.

The Great Northern's sixty-one engines had the British Churchward type. The Cole, Emerson and Schmidt types were scattered over eleven railroads. The Santa Fe used 104 examples of its own Jacobs superheater. The Union Pacific experimented with a single example of its own design. The Canadian Pacific used its own design, the Vaughan-Horsey.

The Santa Fe was thus the biggest American user of superheated locomotives and also, for a time, the only railroad in America with superheated compounds, having installed their Jacobs superheater in tandem, balanced and Mallet compounds. They found reheating the steam between the high- and low-pressure cylinders more advantageous than superheating ahead of the high-pressure cylinders only. European superheated compounds superheated only the steam ahead of the high-pressure cylinders because of the bulk of the reheater and the friction losses that it caused.

It took more than ten years for the American railroads to accept superheating, but the 1910 ARMMA convention was a milestone. Hard-headed practical men whole-heartedly endorsed the high-temperature fire-tube superheater. Obstacles to its introduction remained, but they were few, small and easily overcome.[216]

The meeting paid tribute to the Canadians for introducing locomotive superheating to North America:

> In 1901 the Canadian Pacific, under the leadership of Roger Atkinson, of the Canadian Locomotive Works, introduced the use of superheated steam on locomotives in America. A few years later H. H. Vaughan extended its use, and the success of the superheater is due in a great measure to his push and energy.

Mass retrofitting of older engines was impeded by the fact that most had slide valves. Although slide valves could be used satisfactorily at low superheat, problems increased in proportion to temperature. H. W. Jacobs of the Santa Fe said installing a superheater was was not worthwhile at less than 90°F of superheat (480°F at 180 pounds per square inch) but the Europeans found that slide valves warped above 450°F.

H. H. Vaughan of the CPR stated categorically:

> We do not use slide valves on superheaters. It has been tried many times, and in every case it is found to give trouble.

The Canadian Pacific managed to lubricate slide valves up to 190°F of superheat (580°F). Whatever the valve type, forced lubrication became increasingly necessary with increasing superheat temperatures and experience on the Central of Georgia and the Southern Pacific finally established that low-temperature superheat—so vigorously promoted by Vauclain—offered no worthwhile benefits.

Besides improved fuel economy, superheating provided 20% to 30% more power from each ton of engine weight. By 1910, the Americans, having focused on fuel and water economy, were only just becoming aware of this issue of power density. F. J. Cole, Chief Engineer with Alco, pointed out:

> One of the most important possibilities of locomotives equipped with superheat has not received the attention it justly deserves; namely the increased hauling capacity and the greater efficiency which can be obtained than from locomotives using saturated steam. There is no doubt that this is the most important feature of all, and while great economies in fuel and water are obtained, yet the fact that for a given weight of locomotive having a high factor of adhesion it is possible to make a machine of at least 20 per cent greater hauling power, overshadows all other considerations. This is a fact of obviously more importance than the mere question of economies in coal and water.

As the strength and stamina of the human fireman was a limiting factor in locomotive performance; a device that increased power output without increasing the fireman's labor was a great benefit, especially as it functioned without increasing the engineer's work load. Experience showed that superheated engines cost only slightly more to maintain than saturated-steam engines to any marked degree, while fuel and water savings reduced the number of servicing stops.

For compounds, the Canadian Pacific was firmly in favor of a single superheater ahead of the high-pressure cylinders, rather than a low-temperature superheater ahead of the high-pressure cylinders with a reheater between the high- and low-pressure cylinders. They rebuilt a compound accordingly and "It made a different engine of it." The Canadian Pacific also saw no point in using less than 200 pounds per square inch boiler pressure.

In spite of remarkable successes, a coolness toward the superheater remained. Dr. Goss explained in 1911[217]:

> The ideal underlying practice in the development of the modern American locomotive has placed power-capacity and continuity of service upon a higher plane than thermodynamic efficiency. This ideal has on the whole not been misleading. It has produced locomotives of unprecedented power; it has satisfied a legitimate demand for service; and it has resulted in the development of a machine which must always be regarded as a mechanism of remarkable quality. It is, therefore, not discreditable to the railways of America that their interest in superheating has thus far been hardly more than academic, for the advent of the superheater brings complications of mechanism with it, and introduces new problems in maintenance.

But:

> The time is approaching when, in the natural order of development, the railways of the United States will leave no stone unturned in their efforts to increase the thermodynamic efficiency of the American locomotive.

Dr. Goss had earlier pointed out that 20% of total locomotive coal was burned in firing up, keeping the locomotive hot while waiting for assignment, stopped at stations, waiting to cross with other trains, drifting downgrade, left burning in the firebox at the end of a run and other loss and waste that had nothing to do with thermal efficiency. These were abiding defects of the coal-fired steam locomotive. Improvements to thermal efficiency therefore benefited less than 80% of total fuel consumption and had to be regarded in that light.

Locomotive superheating was, however, an engineer's dream: the harder it worked, the more effective it became. Heavy drafting and high smokebox temperatures in American locomotives suited them to superheating even better than their European counterparts because of the high superheat temperatures that were readily obtainable, offsetting the loss of boiler efficiency at high firing rates. Chicago & North Western superheated express passenger 4-6-2s, early in 1911, demonstrated coal savings of 26% to 35% and water savings of 32% to 37%.[218] Chesapeake & Ohio superheated, compound Mallets saved 43% in fuel consumption per ton-mile, compared to saturated-steam, single-expansion 2-8-0s.[219]

In 1911 Purdue gave *Schenectady No. 3* a Schmidt superheater instead of the Cole type and achieved 200°F to 275°F of superheat.[220] Researchers expected trouble with slide valve lubrication and diminishing gains in economy with increasing superheat; neither materialized. The new Schmidt superheater provided 324 square feet of superheating surface, compared to a maximum of 193 square feet with the Cole type. The lowest coal consumption obtained with the Cole superheater was 3.0 pounds per indicated horsepower-hour. The Schmidt superheater reduced this to 2.5 pounds at a boiler pressure of 180 pounds per square inch. Steam consumption with the Schmidt superheater bottomed out at 180 to 200 pounds per square inch boiler pressure with a steam consumption of 19 pounds per indi-

cated horsepower-hour. Purdue found that economies, compared to saturated steam, continued to improve with increasing superheat; at 180 pounds per square inch boiler pressure, 80°F of superheat produced coal savings of 3%, increasing to 29% at 240°F.

By the time the American railroads became interested in superheat, earlier lubrication problems had disappeared because of high-temperature mineral oils developed for other industries.[221] Designers piped oil direct to the steam chests; operators used 10% to 20% more oil than with saturated steam engines. New materials for piston valve rings alleviated earlier problems with accelerated wear.[222] When a superheated engine was drifting downgrade, a slight flow of steam had to be maintained through the cylinders, either by keeping the throttle slightly open or by means of a drifting valve; otherwise oil would carbonize to a hard deposit. In the absence of a slight positive pressure in the cylinders, the steam passages and relief valves would ingest dirt which combined with carbonized oil and accelerated wear. In 1919, the Lewis Valve Co., New York, brought out an automatic drifting valve, controlled by the valve gear.[223]

Retrofitting gained momentum; by the end of 1911, more than 2,000 U.S. locomotives had fire-tube superheaters.[224] The worldwide total was about 12,000. As of mid–1912, 2,222 superheated locomotives were in service in North America on thirty-two railroads— 1,748 with fire-tube superheaters, 474 with smokebox superheaters.[225]

That year, the chairman of the ARMMA remarked:

> Since the introduction of superheated steam on locomotives by the Prussian State Railways in 1898, the whole railway world has been much interested in the development of the superheater on locomotives.

This hardly reflects the dismissive attitudes prevalent in America in the first years of the new century.

Acceptance was still uneven. On the Burlington:

> We now have about 200 of our largest locomotives equipped with the superheater, and we are adding to that number as rapidly as we can do so.

The Pennsylvania was sluggish in introducing superheat. As of 1912:

> The Pennsylvania Railroad have not had very long experience with a high degree of superheat on locomotives. Some years ago they tried a low temperature superheater, but it did not prove very satisfactory, and it was not until about a year ago (i.e. 1911) that investigation was made into the application of superheated steam to our equipment.

Introduction was rapid, once begun, and the Pennsylvania soon had 200 superheated locomotives in service.

Railroads whose enthusiasm for superheat was still lukewarm, such as the Erie, were those that encountered nagging problems of leaking joints, lubrication and materials for bushings and packing rings that caused superheated engines to fail in service. But the Erie also had trouble with power stokers, suggesting a pervasive management attitude.

Newcomers, such as the Illinois Central, suddenly introduced 125 superheated engines in 1911–12 and had very little trouble with them. They recorded 25% to 30% savings in water consumption and 20% savings in fuel and, additionally were able to improve on their schedules by omitting water stops that had been necessary previously. In districts where the water caused foaming, superheating evaporated the water carried over through the throttle and dry pipe.

The superheated fleet quadrupled in a year. By mid–1913, 8,822 superheated locomotives were in service in the U.S. and Canada.[226] Most new engines were built with superheat; retrofitting continued apace.

Reports from the users indicate that they have been uniformly satisfactory. The troubles that were feared with packing and valves, due to the high temperature of superheated steam, have not developed to any great degree, and where there has been any trouble it has been overcome largely, if not entirely, by the use of good material for the parts in question.

The committee has not been able to determine any definite figure in the comparative cost of maintaining superheated and saturated steam locomotives, but the general consensus of opinion seems to be that the increase, if any, in the cost of maintenance is not going to be of sufficient moment to influence the question one way or the other.

With predictable thoroughness, the Pennsylvania ran a series of tests in 1912–13, comparing saturated-steam and superheated engines of the same classes: a pair of E-6 4-4-2s, a pair of K-29 4-6-2s and a pair of 2-8-0s.[227] Figures given hitherto have been average values over a range of power outputs, but at high power, the fuel economy and power increase achieved by superheating was astonishing. The fuel economy of the superheated E-6 reached 46% at maximum power output, compared to the unsuperheated engine; the superheated E-6 developed a maximum of 1,850 dynamometer horsepower, 32% more than the unmodified engine. Thus was created the Pennsylvania's E-6s, one of the legendary express passenger locomotives of American railroad history. (The suffix "s" to a class number denoted superheat, not plural.) Superheat had no effect on starting or low-speed pulling power, but the effect became apparent at high power where the saturated-steam engine ran out of steam. The Pennsylvania tests produced the first indicator diagrams drawn in America, directly comparing superheated and saturated-steam engines of the same class and dimensions; the company published the results as a 192-page bulletin.

The benefits of superheating affected many aspects of design, construction and operation. Designers were freed from the restrictions on cylinder diameter imposed by condensation. Even with no increase in boiler pressure, the stoker-fired, superheated engine was a markedly different machine from its hand-fired, wet-steam predecessors. The builders of the mastodons of the 1890s knew that big engines could haul more tons for each dollar spent than small ones, but this was something different. From 1912:

Mr. Beyer[228] has shown that locomotives of large capacity are more economical in operation than smaller units. He particularly cited the case of large superheater mikado locomotives which haul trains of 45 and 50 per cent. greater tonnage with the same amount of coal that was consumed by the consolidation locomotives they replaced. In order to develop the specified tractive effort these mikado locomotives had to be equipped with cylinders of 27 in. diameter. What would have become of these poor engines without the superheater! The cylinder condensation would have been so large as to make the operation of the engines a practical impossibility. There is no other means existing to entirely prevent cylinder condensation but superheaters, and superheating has made the most powerful locomotives with big cylinders possible.

On Mallet engines built during the last two years (1910–12) superheaters have been quite generally applied, as the large surface to which the steam is exposed in the four cylinders and long steam pipes makes the application of this device even more necessary than in ordinary simple engines in order to prevent the increased amount of condensation. In most cases the superheater has been applied in front of the high-pressure cylinder and the steam has been superheated sufficiently high to leave at least 30 or 50 deg. of superheat in the receiver steam. This remaining superheat makes it possible to use slide valves on the low-pressure side; high-pressure cylinders using steam of a high degree superheat cannot successfully be used with slide valves.

Road tests went on confirming the success of superheat. In the summer of 1913, the Norfolk & Western tested two M-2 4-8-0s, one superheated, the other using saturated steam, on the same run.[229] Loading differed only in that the unsuperheated engine pulled 15 cars, weighing 1,030 tons, while the superheated engine pulled 17, weighing 1,200 tons, this being necessary to work the superheated engine to its maximum while remaining within speed restrictions. The superheated engine developed 36% higher indicated horsepower—26% more at low speeds, 53% at high speeds, reflected in a 19% average decrease in coal consumption per indicated horsepower-hour, 12% at low speed, 27% at high speed. The superheated engine consumed 19 to 20 pounds of steam and about 3.5 pounds of coal per indicated horsepower-hour; the saturated-steam engine consumed 28 to 29 pounds of steam and about 4.3 pounds of coal. Greater fluidity of the superheated steam resulted in a 20% reduction in cylinder back pressure. Thermal efficiency at the drawbar increased from 3.7% with saturated steam to 4.6% with superheating, a 24% improvement in what remained a miserably low figure. Coal consumption per thousand ton-miles went down from 334 pounds with saturated steam to 244 pounds with superheating, a 27% saving.

Retrofitting the huge fleet of 4-4-0s, 4-4-2s, 4-6-0s, 2-6-0s and 2-8-0s with superheat, as they passed through the shops for routine overhaul, had enormous potential.[230] Superheating added very little weight to such engines, giving them increased power without the need to strengthen track and substructures. Many of these engines already had piston valves, either new-built or retrofitted. The rebuilds could be put onto train schedules that had become too much for them with increasing car and train weights. The potentially useful locomotive fleet therefore expanded just when it was about to be most urgently needed.

The effects of superheating were extraordinarily pervasive.[231] The higher power of superheated locomotives could influence decisions on whether grade reduction and line straightening programs were necessary or profitable. Superheating increased the amount of heat lost through the stack; this begged for a feed water heater to recover some of the lost heat. Studies in Germany indicated that about 15% of the exhaust steam could be drawn off and passed through a feed water heater with no effect on drafting.

In one limited area, superheating had no effect; when an engine was slogging up a long grade at low speed, exerting its maximum tractive effort, a superheated engine would not haul any more tons than one working on saturated steam, nor would it start a heavier train.[232] The difference lay in the speed at which the engineer first had to shorten the cut-off; a superheated locomotive could accelerate to higher speeds in full forward gear than one using saturated steam. The reciprocating steam locomotive had three speed regimes: 0 to 15 miles per hour where boiler pressure and cylinder diameter limited performance; 15 to 60 miles per hour where steaming rate was the limiting factor; above 60 miles per hour where steam flow through the valves limited power output. Drawbar pull and drawbar horsepower were the same for saturated-steam and superheated engines up to about 15 miles per hour, diverging in favor of superheating at higher speeds.[233]

By 1915[234]:

The fire-tube superheater has come to be almost universally considered as an essential part of the locomotive. The superheater locomotive may be worked at longer cut-offs and at higher speeds, making possible longer trains and faster schedules than is possible with identical saturated locomotives under the same conditions.

At the beginning of 1916, there were 15,666 superheater locomotives in the U.S. and Canada, almost all with fire-tube superheaters[235]; of these, 5,766 were retrofits, the balance new construction. Superheating was practically standard on all new road engines and most switchers. Locomotives as old as 10 to 15 years had been retrofitted. The large and increasing volume of information available from tests was showing fuel savings of 15% to 25% and water savings of 20% to 30%. Superheating reduced the road time of some freight trains by 10% to 15%, with significant implications in view of the 16-Hour Law restricting crew working hours. Operators felt that superheated engines cost slightly more to maintain than those using saturated steam, but this was more than offset by fuel savings and increased performance. With mineral oil lubricants and piston valves, lubrication practically ceased to be a problem, although a drifting valve, passing saturated steam to the cylinders, was beneficial while the locomotive was drifting downhill. Passengers liked superheat as saturated steam engines often threw sooty water from the stack. For this reason the New York Central superheated their slide valve switchers working around passenger terminals. With properly designed lubrication and drifting valves, even the problem of superheat and slide valves practically disappeared.

The Locomotive Superheater Co., later known by its abbreviation—Elesco, achieved a dominant role in the manufacture of superheaters.[236] The standard Elesco superheater was the Type A. Each superheater flue contained an element, consisting of four tubes with three U-bends—two at the back end of the flue, one at the front—so that steam passed through the length of the flue four times. In 1916, the company brought out the Type E.[237] Each element comprised two four-tube bundles in parallel. Each bundle comprised two single loops; each loop occupied its own flue.[238] This arrangement provided more superheating surface than the Type A and better exposure to hot gases and was a significant advance in steam technology.

By 1918, about 25,000 American and Canadian locomotives were equipped with superheat, out of a total fleet around 65,000, increasing to 35,000 only a year later.[239]

Although slide-valve locomotives were successfully retrofitted with superheat, new construction between 1900 and 1910 had gone over to piston valves and the railroads had been retrofitting piston valves to slide-valve engines. Retrofitting with superheat encouraged retrofitting with bigger-diameter cylinders with piston valves. By 1919, the ARMMA reckoned that no more than ten superheated slide-valve engines remained in the United States and: "The use of superheated steam with slide valves is a dead subject."

7.3.5 Feed Water Heaters

The possibility of recovering waste heat by heating the boiler feed water was recognized since the early 1800s, possibly as far back as 1802.[240] Feed water heaters were tried on locomotives in the UK as early as 1827–8 and on the Baltimore & Ohio in 1836.[241] Their use failed to develop for several reasons. Until sophisticated means of measuring fuel economy and thermal efficiency became available, there was no way of telling what effect they had, if any. Railroad staff saw them as more trouble than they were worth. Many different designs were possible; some worked, some did not.

The injector was a feed water heater of sorts, but it took heat directly from the boiler and was limited, both in the maximum water temperature at which it would function and in the temperature to which it could heat the feed water. A typical injector would not function at water temperatures above 120°F to 125°F. At boiler pressures of 180 pounds per square inch, it supplied 11 pounds of water per pound of steam used, heating 65°F feed water to 160°F. The small gain in economy obtainable by heating the water above 160°F between the injector and the boiler check valve barely warranted the cost of the necessary equipment, although several companies experimented along this line.

In 1908, the Milwaukee experimented with a feed water heater designed by W. H. Brown.[242] The injector forced feed water into a drum, 6 feet long and 27 inches in diameter, mounted on top of the boiler, containing a heat exchanger consisting of 269¾-inch tubes. Exhaust steam, tapped from the exhaust cavities of the cylinders, passed through these tubes, condensate being returned to the tender tank. The pressure developed by the injector sufficed to force water into the boiler. An engine equipped with this device showed a 24% saving in coal in its first month of operation, burning 229 pounds per thousand ton-miles, compared to 300 for an engine not so equipped.

About 1912, some locomotive builders used a forward extension of the boiler to heat feed water from the injector.[243] This was a pressurized space connected to the boiler itself. Designs ranged from a separate space connected to the boiler by pipes to a mere baffle plate separating the feed water reception area from the boiler proper. Conceptually, there was only a vague distinction between this and injecting the feed water directly into the front end of the boiler.

In 1914, the New Orleans Great Northern experimented with a feed water heater in conjunction with an ordinary injector, similar to the Milwaukee experiment.[244] Water from the injector passed through a heat exchanger, picking up heat from the exhaust steam from the air brake compressor. The water then passed through a hollow diaphragm installed in place of the normal smokebox diaphragm plate, picking up more heat from the smokebox gases, passing thence into the boiler through a check valve. The company claimed a fuel saving of about 6%. Valving allowed the smokebox heater to be bypassed.

The combined length of the drive units on Mallet locomotives allowed all manner of equipment to be placed in extensions of the boiler barrel. A number of Mallets, especially those on the Santa Fe, were equipped with feed water heaters interposed between the injector and the boiler check valve, placed in a forward extension of the boiler barrel and using the smokebox gases. Such devices typically heated the feed water from the temperature at which it left the injector to 245°F at the boiler check valve, effecting a fuel saving of about 6%.

Exhaust steam injectors, using exhaust instead of live steam, were an advance in economy; at 180 pounds per square inch boiler pressure, these devices were about 9% more economical than a live steam injector. A locomotive could not, however, function entirely on an exhaust steam injector because of the need to inject feed water when the engine was not working steam; a live steam injector had to be installed anyway. Additionally, the steam supply to the exhaust steam injector was at a lower pressure than to a live steam injector, requiring a bigger device to deliver a given volume of water. A practical feed water heater therefore had to use a pump and replace the injector altogether.

The Canadian Pacific began experimenting in 1908 with open-circuit heaters in the tender tank as well as exhaust steam injectors. The company obtained fuel savings of 6% by heating the water to 120°F before it entered the injector, but a feed water heater with a pump instead of an injector, supplying water to the boiler at 200°F, doubled this saving. In 1914, H. H. Vaughan commented:

> This is a subject which American railroad people have largely neglected. It has the advantage of not only saving in coal, but increasing the capacity of the boiler. In careful experiments we found an economy of 12 per cent in the use of the heater, and we feel that this justifies our going into the device more thoroughly. I feel that we will see feed water heating coming into larger use, not only with waste steam, but with waste gas.

In 1910, the Chesapeake & Ohio installed a high-pressure feed pump on a freight engine, using an exhaust steam bleed to heat the feed water to 280°F to 300°F, injecting it into the boiler close to the foundation ring.[245] They noticed that, not only did this result in substantial coal savings, but troubles from broken staybolts and leaking fire tubes practically disappeared.

The Pere Marquette persisted with an older system, routing the compressor exhaust through the tender tank. This was limited by the maximum temperature that the injectors could handle.

The Americans acknowledged that feed water heating had received more attention in Europe than in America. The Europeans replaced the injector with a steam-driven pump; exhaust steam from the cylinders and the pump heated the feed water. The Burlington was an early American experimenter with this device, claiming a fuel saving of about 12%. The Central of Georgia, the New York Central, the Central of New Jersey and the Canadian Pacific were other early experimenters with feed water heating in North America.[246]

F. F. Gaines of the Central of Georgia echoed this comment:

Feed water heating in this country is confined to a limited number of cases, and cannot be said to be generally recognized as a factor on fuel economy.

On the other hand:

While American railroad practice is averse to adding any complicated apparatus to the locomotive, it seems that the demand for the utmost economy will eventually bring about a satisfactory method of feed water heating so that in connection with superheating, liberal firebox heating surface and possibly compounding we can obtain the maximum possible economy from the fuel used.

The Central of Georgia began experiments in 1911, substituting a feed water pump for one injector. The feed water was pumped through heat exchangers taking exhaust steam from the air brake compressor and the feed water pump to a tube array inside the smokebox, thence into the boiler. The pump was unsuitable; the smokebox tube array plugged with soot and cinders; steam exhausted from the heat exchangers condensed in clouds around the engine in cold weather, interfering with visibility, but fuel savings of about 10% resulted. The Central of Georgia abandoned feed water heating for the time being due to maintenance costs and because they felt that the smokebox space could be better used for superheating than for heating feed water.

As experimental evidence on feed water heaters accumulated, the experimenters realized that a steam-driven pump moved 5 to 6 times as much water per pound of steam as an injector.[247] The boiler pressure drop caused by injecting cold feed water was well known to generations of enginemen. Where sustained maximum performance was required, this was something they could ill afford.

Two heat sources were available: exhaust steam and smokebox gases. Exhaust steam could not heat feed water beyond its own temperature, typically about 250°F, but contained more heat per pound than waste gas which it gave up as latent heat when condensed in a feed water heater. Back pressure in the exhaust nozzle sufficed to drive exhaust steam through a heat exchanger, but the steam blast needed to draft the furnace limited exhaust diversion to about 16% of the total exhaust steam flow. The smokebox gas temperature was typically 600°F to 700°F, but heat extraction was more difficult and required more heating surface. An adequately sized heat exchanger impeded the free exit of the gases, demanding a stronger exhaust blast, and was subject to plugging and abrasion by the cinder-laden gases.

By 1917:

both methods are more or less in the experimental stage. The exhaust steam method is being rapidly developed and developments are planned for the waste gas method. There is one thing assured, and that is, that feed water heating is practical, and that it is the next important refinement to be added to the locomotive. If a combination exhaust steam and waste gas heater is found practical there is hardly a question but that savings of 20 to 25 per cent or more may be made. Tests so far have shown that savings over 10 per cent may be expected by the exhaust heater alone.

One of the first feed water heaters offered commercially came from the Locomotive Feed Water Heater Co., New York, in 1917, known as the Type E.[248] A steam-driven reciprocating pump, with a 9½-inch steam cylinder and a 6½-inch water cylinder, mounted on the side of the locomotive at running board height, sucked water from the tender tank and pumped it to a heat exchanger mounted immediately beneath the front of the smokebox. Walls in the domed ends of the cylindrical heat exchanger forced the feed water to pass four times through the tubes, thence into the boiler through a check valve. Spiral agitator strips inside the water tubes improved heat transfer. Exhaust steam from the pump went into the body of the heat exchanger, along with steam bled from the exhaust side of the steam chest. Curiously, in view of the economizing purpose of the device, condensate was wasted onto the track. The normal rate of water supply was 6,500 gallons per hour to the boiler, up to a maximum of 8,400 gallons per hour. The pump handled 50 pounds of water for every pound of steam that it consumed, compared to only 11 pounds for a typical live-steam injector. The Delaware, Lackawanna & Western was one of the first users of this device which became the Elesco feed water heater. The referenced source includes a photograph of an installation on a Wootten-firebox 4-6-2, No. 1135, belonging to an unidentified railroad. The Lackawanna owned such an engine, built at Schenectady in 1915. Drury (p.151) confirms that Lackawanna No. 1135 was used to test feed water heaters.

The American railroad industry took more than ten years to accept superheating; it accepted feed water heating much more quickly and on far less evidence.[249] This acceptance resulted from World War I. Coal, mined with great danger, cost and difficulty, was the life blood of American industry. In the eastern and mid-western states, railroads were clogged with freight that they could not move, much of which was coal, much of which they needed for their locomotives. Yet, when the coal went into the locomotive, a mere 7% of its heat value went through the drawbar. This awareness intensified the demand for improved efficiency and caused feelings of guilt that ultimately condemned the steam locomotive itself. And so:

Preheat is a fundamental necessity, easily within our grasp, which can no longer be overlooked. The failure of American railways to utilize preheat is an economic mistake which may be expressed in terms of millions of dollars of lost earnings.

Section 7.4. Cylinder Arrangements, Valves and Valve Gear

7.4.1 Compounding

The popularity of the compound locomotive in America peaked during the 1890s and early 1900s. A new variant at the beginning of the twentieth century was the four-cylinder balanced compound, originating with de Glehn in France; Baldwin delivered the first such engine in America to the Plant System in 1902.[250]

From the viewpoint of 1905, this type of locomotive seemed like a dream come true. Some passenger services ran to schedules so demanding that speeds close to 90 miles per hour had to be maintained for forty miles at a stretch.[251] Counterbalancing two-cylinder, single-expansion engines for such speeds was difficult and the necessary firing rates approached the limits of a human fireman. The four-cylinder balanced compound seemed to solve these problems.

By early 1905, a hundred were in service with another hundred for construction during the year.[252] Baldwin sold twenty 4-4-2 Vauclain balanced compounds to the Burlington in 1904–5 and another twenty-two to the New Haven.[253] The Santa Fe had sixty balanced compound 4-4-2s in service by 1905. The Burlington and the Santa Fe found that their balanced compounds rode smoothly, accelerated fast and used 20% less water than equivalent two-cylinder, single-expansion locomotives, besides causing less track damage at high speed. Prejudice still existed against crank axles, but operators reasoned that the more even division of forces, compared to a two-cylinder engine, led to lighter main rods and reduced repairs.

Static tests by the Burlington at Aurora, Illinois, demonstrated a steam consumption of 23 pounds of steam per horsepower-hour, 25% less than an equivalent single-expansion locomotive. The engines were popular with those who ran and maintained them. The Burlington proved the reduction in dynamic augment in the most direct way possible—by measuring the deflection of a bridge girder when various locomotives ran over it at high speed. The compound produced 25% less dynamic augment than a single-expansion engine, even though its axle loading was 15% greater. As experience accumulated, Maintenance of Way engineers rated balanced compounds the same as single-expansion engines weighing 20% less. One problem of the conventional locomotive was fore-and-aft pounding of the journal boxes in the frame pedestals. If these were a loose fit, the pounding could break the frame. The balanced compound alleviated this problem because two piston pairs moved in opposite directions.[254]

In 1905, W. E. Symons, Superintendent of Motive Power for the Plant System, devised a new type of four-cylinder balanced compound and valve gear. The high-pressure cylinders were outside the frames, driving the rear driving axle; the low-pressure cylinders were inside the frames, ahead of the high-pressure cylinders, driving the cranked front axle. The high- and low-pressure cylinders had their own separate valve gears, independently adjustable by separate reversing levers in the cab. A linkage connected the reversing levers to a valve so that, in full gear, high-pressure steam was supplied direct to the low-pressure cylinders. This design came to nothing.

By the summer of 1906, Baldwin had built or was building 265 four-cylinder, balanced compounds for fourteen American railroads.[255] The company was well equipped to build these engines which were the consummation of the four-cylinder compound that Vauclain had been promoting for more than ten years. Crank axles were essential to the balanced compound; whether cast and forged as a unit or built up from components, they had a history of breakages that had caused lasting prejudice against them in America but Baldwin showed that design by calculation and rigorous quality control could solve this problem.

The Santa Fe was the biggest buyer: forty-one 4-6-2s, ninety-six 4-4-2s and fifty-six 2-6-2s.

> The progressiveness of the Atchison, Topeka & Santa Fe Railway, however, is largely responsible for the rapid growth in favor of these engines, as this road alone has in operation, or in the course of construction, 193 engines of this type of locomotive with various arrangements of wheel base, and it was the first railroad in the United States to fully appreciate the value of the balanced compound locomotive. They have divisions where balanced compound passenger engines are exclusively used, and the quiet assurance of their roundhouse men responsible for the maintenance of these engines is in strong contrast to the excitement usually prevalent when a new type of power is being used.

Other, more cautious, buyers were the Oregon Railroad & Navigation (four 4-6-2s), the Associated Lines (fifteen 4-4-2s), the Great Northern (ten 4-4-2s), the Rock Island (eight 4-4-2s), the North Carolina

& St. Louis (three 4-6-0s), the Chicago & Eastern Illinois (two 4-6-0s), the Erie (two 4-4-2s), the Pennsylvania (two 4-4-2s), the New Haven (two 4-6-0s), the Missouri, Kansas & Texas (two 4-6-0s), the New York Central (one 4-4-2) and the Chicago Short Line (one 4-6-0). These wheel arrangements were typical of express passenger engines; the balanced compound was a high-speed engine that finally overcame the limitations that had previously limited compounding to slow freight service.

By 1908, superheating was adding a new element to the controversy about compound engines. Even as trenchant a promoter of the compound as Samuel Vauclain admitted[256]:

> I think that balanced compound and Mallet compounds will still continue to be built—but that the superheater locomotive will perhaps take the place of the majority of locomotives in railroad service.

The balanced compound had improved on the speed limitations of the compound locomotive, but had not removed them; growing American experience with superheating was highlighting high power at high speed as one of its most decisive benefits.

The debate on compound performance raged on.

> I am satisfied that the friends of the compound had done it more harm than all other people put together. Mr. Vauclain made the statement yesterday that a Mallet compound would do a horsepower on 20 pounds of dry steam per hour. I do not believe that the engine has ever been built or ever will be built that will do it.

This hidebound prediction would prove to be rash, such were the achievements of American locomotive builders over the next forty years.

> I read in the report: "The saving of the compound over the simple locomotive is shown to be about 24 per cent." There would not be a simple locomotive on the American railroads today if this were the case. A compound locomotive will save, generally, from 18 to 25 per cent in fuel under all conditions.

A landmark series of tests at Altoona made the demise of the compound all the more surprising. The Santa Fe and the New York Central each tested a four-cylinder balanced compound on the plant while it was still at St. Louis in 1904. After the Pennsylvania moved the plant to Altoona, the company tested two of its own two-cylinder, single-expansion engines of similar dimensions in 1906.[257]

The compounds came out very markedly superior. Steam consumption for both types of engine was lowest at 1,100 indicated horsepower, 24 pounds per indicated horsepower-hour for the single-expansion engines, 20 pounds for the compounds. Lowest coal consumption was at 800 indicated horsepower, 3.75 to 4.00 pounds per indicated horsepower-hour for the single-expansion engines, 2.50 to 2.75 pounds for the compounds. At that power output the compounds were 44% more coal efficient than the single-expansion engines. Equally remarkable, at a steaming rate of 31,000 pounds per hour, the single-expansion engines developed 950 drawbar horsepower, while the compounds developed 1,200, 25% more power for a given steaming rate. In the single-expansion engines, coal consumption rose rapidly above 800 horsepower. In the compounds, not only was coal consumption lower, it rose more slowly with increasing power output. For a railroad industry demanding high power at high speed, while limited by the strength of a human fireman, this was a wonderful development.

Unfortunately for the proponents of the compound, questioning revealed that the very low specific fuel consumption of the compounds was obtained at speeds of 20 miles per hour; the resistance of the test plant was therefore simulating pulling a train uphill. At speeds of 55 miles per hour, the compounds burned 4.5 pounds per drawbar horsepower-hour, compared to 5.8 pounds for the single-expansion engines, a saving of 23% instead of 44%—substantial, nonetheless.

To everyone's surprise, in 1908, the Milwaukee, after many years of tests, ordered twelve 4-4-2 compounds of the original Vauclain type (all four cylinders outside the frames) from Baldwin to haul 600-ton expresses at high speeds between Chicago and Milwaukee.[258]

Between 1889 and 1904, Baldwin built about 3,000 Vauclain compounds for domestic use and export, but:

> Since 1902 the orders for this type of compound locomotive have been rapidly growing less, and in more recent years the species has been generally thought to be almost extinct. The recent order from the St. Paul road is as much a surprise to the builders as to the railroad public.

Baldwin did not have it all their own way; Alco built substantial numbers of balanced compounds. By 1908, however, the four-cylinder balanced compound had gone the way of the other compound types, with the exception of the Mallet. Operating experience failed to prove significant economies in fuel or water in high-speed service. Roundhouse crews disliked the extra mechanism inside the frames. Locomotive builders charged much higher prices than for single-expansion locomotives of similar size. Even if the balanced compounds were easier on the track than single-expansion engines, track repairs were governed by the far more numerous single-expansion engines. Locomotives were, in any event, far from being the only determinant of repairs needed to the track. The railroads therefore did not see this benefit as justifying the extra cost.

A supposed benefit of compounding lay in the reduced temperature cycling that took place inside each cylinder when expansion was divided into two stages. George Hughes, Chief Mechanical Engineer of the Lancashire & Yorkshire Railway in England, pointed out in 1910 that, at high speeds, steam remained in the cylinders for so little time that compounding provided no benefit over single expansion in this respect.[259] A piston speed of 600 feet per minute seemed to be the critical point, below which compounding caused a useful reduction in temperature cycling, above which it did not. With a 30-inch piston stroke and 62-inch driving wheels, this translated into a speed of 25 miles per hour. This discovery accounted for the American experience over a period of years that compound locomotives built for fast passenger service had not shown better fuel economy than single-expansion engines of similar dimensions in similar service.

In America, compounding became discredited before superheating came in. What, then, might have been achieved by combining compounding and superheating?[260] The French found that single-expansion, superheated engines used 19 to 22 pounds of water per horsepower-hour; superheated, four-cylinder compounds used only 13 to 15 pounds. In Germany, superheated, single-expansion 4-6-0s used 23 pounds of water per horsepower-hour; superheated, three-cylinder compounds of the same type used only 18 pounds. The Midland Railway in England, testing engines that were similar but for the presence or absence of superheating and compounding, found coal savings from superheating alone, 15%, compounding alone, 25%, superheating and compounding, 38%. Yet, in both Britain and America, the superheated, rigid-frame compound locomotive made no headway at all.

A rare American user of superheated, rigid-frame compounds, in 1915, the Michigan Central had ninety compounds on one division, of which twelve were superheated. The superheated compounds hauled 15% more freight tonnage, and passenger trains 10 to 12 miles per hour faster, than the saturated-steam compounds. The company planned to superheat its remaining compounds at a time when most others had rebuilt their compounds to single-expansion.

In 1918, when the rigid-frame compound was a dead issue in America, John E. Muhlfeld looked back on what its real market penetration had been.[261]

Year	2-cylinder	4-cylinder	Mallet	Total fleet	% compounds
1900	1,000	900		38,500	5
1905	900	1,800		51,650	5
1910	875	1,500	200	59,000	4
1915	650	1,300	800	64,750	4

Muhlfeld, however, could be well pleased with the progress of what he had begun. While, the rigid-frame compounds reached their apogee in 1904, doomed by difficulties of design, operation and maintenance, the compound Mallet, numbering 1,500 locomotives on more than fifty railroads by 1918, was an outstanding success. High boiler pressure, superheating, compounding, single-expansion for starting, enormous adhesion weight within prevailing axle load limits and carried on a flexible wheelbase, all these combined to provide 25% to 35% fuel and water savings per ton-mile, compared to a superheated, single-expansion engine. Commenting generally on steam locomotive performance, Muhlfeld asserted that American steam locomotives of 1918 were capable of a fuel consumption of only 2¼ pounds of coal per drawbar horsepower-hour. If possible in theory, this would not be borne out in practice until the American steam locomotive reached its ultimate development twenty years in the future.

Muhlfeld (at that time President of the Locomotive Pulverized Fuel Co.) prophesied:

> The steam locomotive is still in its infancy so far as economy per ton-mile is concerned. The atomization and burning of liquid or solid fuels in suspension will enable the elimination of grates and other metal work from the combustion zone and permit of higher furnace temperatures and more complete and effective combustion, which, in combination with higher steam pressures, compounding, higher superheating of both high and low pressure steam, utilization of waste gases and steam for feed water heating and purification, better boiler water circulation, reduced cylinder clearances and back pressure, improved steam distribution, lower factor of adhesion, higher percentage of propelling to total weight, less radiation, elimination of unbalanced pressures and weights, application of safety and labor-saving devices, and the greater refinement and perfection of general and detailed design, equipment and control throughout, will yet enable it to produce a drawbar horsepower hour per pound of coal. Furthermore, it is not inconsistent now to predict that a self-contained steam-electric articulated compound locomotive, combining the advantages of both steam and electric motive power, will shortly find a useful field in services where maximum power and efficiency at high speeds, greater utilization of existing waste heat, high starting and low-speed torque and rapid acceleration are required and where an exclusive electrification system would not be permissible from the standpoint of first cost, or justified on account of the combined expense for operation and maintenance.

We will see how this bold prophesy played out over the next thirty years.

7.4.2 The End of Compounding in America

Argument for and against compounding went on, but the railroads voted with their pocket books. Even in the 1890s[262]:

> Judging from the orders for very heavy freight locomotives within the past three years, (1896–9) it would seem that there is a decided preference for simple locomotives for very heavy service on steep grades.

The verdict of American railroad officials continued negative[263]:

> It may seem strange, in view of the superior economy of compound locomotives, that they have not been adopted generally in place of single expansion locomotives. Compounds are apparently increasing in favor at the present time (1905), and this is to be explained rather on the ground of the increased capacity which they render available rather than because of their superior economy. It is claimed by those who have used compounds and discarded them that the additional cost of maintenance, because of the somewhat increased complication, more than offsets the advantage gained by saving a little fuel.

Even when compounds were at their most popular, the railroads were ambivalent—at best—in their procurement; over the ensuing years, many companies reckoned it money well spent to rebuild them to single-expansion. The Otto Perry photographic collection shows that, by the 1920s, most locomotives known to have been built as rigid-frame compounds had either been rebuilt to single-expansion or scrapped.

In the mid–1890s, the Pennsylvania built five prototype 2-6-0 freight engines, including four different types of two-cylinder compound (von Borries, Gölsdorf, Richmond and Pittsburgh)[264] and one single-expansion engine. On the Pennsylvania the comparative tests would have been rigorous. The company rebuilt all four compounds to single-expansion and settled for single-expansion in the production engines that followed.

As early as 1899, the Norfolk Southern sent an 1892-built Vauclain compound to the Richmond Locomotive Works for rebuilding to single-expansion.[265]

Between 1899 and 1904, the Wabash bought 131 2-6-0s from the Baldwin, Richmond and Rhode Island locomotive works; seventy were compounds and were eventually rebuilt to single-expansion.[266] The company received its last compound 2-6-0s in 1904; large purchases of ninety 2-6-2s, forty-seven 2-8-0s and twenty-eight 4-4-2s between 1901 and 1907 were all single-expansion.

The Soo Line entered the new century with the purchase of three 2-8-0 cross compounds from Schenectady and a single 2-10-0 (probably a Vauclain) from Baldwin in 1900. Current research has not revealed whether the Soo Line bought compounds before 1900. Between then and 1909, however, the company bought sixty-five 2-6-0s, ten 2-6-2s and another forty-four 2-8-0s, all cross compounds from Schenectady. The company also, however, bought twenty-nine single-expansion 2-8-0s between 1903 and 1909 and the ten 2-8-0s that the company bought from Schenectady in 1910 were single-expansion.[267]

In 1904, the New Haven bought twenty-two 4-6-0s from Baldwin.[268] Twenty were single-expansion engines; two were Vauclain compounds. Compounding added 5 tons to an otherwise identical design. The company rebuilt the compounds to single-expansion in 1907, after less than three years' service.

The Lake Superior & Ishpeming went into business with four 2-8-0 cross-compounds, built at Pittsburgh in 1896, but converted them to single-expansion in 1910.[269]

The Chicago Great Western acquired a small mixed fleet of compounds—six Baldwin 4-6-0 Vauclain compounds in 1899 and one more in 1902, ten Baldwin 2-8-0 Vauclain compounds in 1900 and twenty Alco 2-6-2 tandem compounds in 1902. All were converted to single-expansion between 1908 and 1913.[270]

The motive power history of the Erie delivers a particularly crushing judgement on the rigid-frame compound locomotive.[271] After buying and building large numbers of locomotives in the 1880s, the company bought only 290 in the whole decade of the 1890s; one-fifth of these were compounds. The first compounds were six

2-10-0 Vauclains from Baldwin in 1891–3; these were converted to single-expansion in 1904–5 and scrapped between 1924 and 1926. In 1893, Baldwin built ten 4-6-0 compounds for the Erie; these were converted to single-expansion in 1904–7 and scrapped between 1912 and 1924. In 1896–7, the company took forty-seven engines from its large and varied fleet of 4-4-0s built in the 1880s and sent them to Baldwin for conversion to Vauclain compounds. All but two of these were reconverted to single-expansion in 1904–5. All had been sold or scrapped by 1920. Fifty-eight 4-4-2 Vauclains, built by Baldwin in 1899–1903, were all converted to single-expansion in 1904–6, running as such until they were scrapped in 1927. Twenty 2-8-0 Vauclains built in 1902 were converted to single-expansion between 1904 and 1911 and scrapped in 1927. A single Alco 2-8-0 tandem compound built in 1902 was converted to single-expansion in 1908 and scrapped in 1927. Baldwin built two 4-4-2 four-cylinder balanced compounds in 1905; they were converted to single-expansion in 1917 and scrapped in 1942 and 1947. Alco built another in 1905; it was converted to single expansion in 1919 and scrapped in 1942. The company increased its compound fleet to a maximum of 142 in 1903; almost all were converted to single-expansion in 1904–7, running as such for many years. The last hope was the 4-4-2 balanced compound, but the company bought only three and eventually converted them. In 1900, the Erie was running 1,040 locomotives, so at best the compounds numbered no more than 10% to 15% of the total fleet.

The Great Northern was bitten only lightly by compounding, to the tune of two 4-6-0 and five 2-8-0 Vauclains built in 1892 and five cross compounds from Rogers in 1901. All were converted to single-expansion.[272]

The Wheeling & Lake Erie sent five locomotives a month to Lima for overhaul between 1908 and 1910. Converting compounds to single-expansion was a part of the overhaul work.[273]

This ambivalence was the epitaph of the rigid-frame, compound locomotive in America. Whatever fuel savings may have been reported in the first flush of enthusiasm, in the long run the compounds did not live up to expectations. Executives were unimpressed by a locomotive that delivered its promised economies in only a narrow range of conditions. Railroads that bought compounds in ones and twos typically did not follow up with bigger orders. Sometimes a railroad bought a class of compounds for a specific duty previously performed by single-expansion engines, but, when the company needed an upgrade, usually bigger, the result was a new class of single-expansion engines, not bigger compounds. Historians have asserted that the superheated engine replaced the compound because superheat achieved the same fuel savings by simpler means. Superheating had no impact on American locomotive engineering before 1910, while the railroads had turned away from the rigid-frame compound five years before that date. Nothing prevented the American railroads from combining superheating and compounding in rigid-frame locomotives—as the Europeans did—but, even when desperate for anything that would save fuel and labor, they converted their compounds to single-expansion.

W. S. Morris of the Chesapeake & Ohio commented in 1901, during his presidency of the ARMMA[274]:

> The compound locomotive has been with us for several years, and as lately as 1897 it was pronounced by a former President of the Association as "still in the balance." We cannot be proud of the fact that its status has not changed since then, and that its place has not been defined and established.

It never was.

"Epitaph of the rigid-frame, compound locomotive in America." Alco built this 825 class 2-8-0, No. 845, for the Atchison, Topeka & Santa Fe in 1902 as a tandem compound. By the time Otto Perry photographed it at Pueblo, Colorado, on February 17, 1929, the Santa Fe had rebuilt it to single-expansion with piston valves driven by inside Stephenson valve gear. Even the Santa Fe, one of the most enthusiastic users of compounds, rebuilt them to single-expansion (Denver Public Library, Otto C. Perry collection, OP-129).

7.4.3 Valves and Valve Gears

In 1905, the Stephenson link motion, mounted between the frames, was universal in American locomotives. Within five years it was displaced by Walschaert and Baker gears, mounted outside the frames. Why?

As engines were built bigger, the parts of the Stephenson motion had also to be bigger and heavier to maintain the necessary strength and stiffness, becoming harder to access for lubrication, inspection and maintenance, more difficult to remove from under the engine and occupying more of the space between the frames that was increasingly needed for axles and frame bracing. In the early 1900s, the moving parts of the Stephenson gear on a typical 2-8-0 weighed 4,800 pounds, compared to 4,270 pounds for Walschaert gear on the same engine. Frame bracing made the whole locomotive stronger and more rigid, helping to control maintenance costs. It was as much ease of access and the need for frame bracing as any other characteristic that favored the Walschaert gear.

In about 1906–07, the Purdue laboratory made possible an unprecedented analysis of the apparently simple action of the slide valve, advancing the art of valve setting from guesswork, experience and opinion to more definite knowledge.[275] The geometry of the Stephenson gear increased valve lead as the engineer shortened the cut-off. Opinions as to whether this was good or bad, diametrically opposed and vehemently expressed, surfaced wherever engineers and mechanics discussed it. Careful work in the laboratory under controlled conditions showed that this feature adversely effected steam economy; at worst, it could cause a violent jarring and breakage of piston rods. The Purdue work hastened the introduction of the Walschaert gear in which lead was constant with varying cut-off.[276]

The geometry of the Walschaert gear is illustrated elsewhere, including internet animations; only a few of its subtleties may be mentioned here. A crank rod imparted motion to the valve gear. This rod was fixed rigidly to the main crank pin, but at an angle such that its free end described a circle smaller than that of the crank pin, but concentric with it. This free end drove the eccentric rod which drove one end of an oscillating link, pivoted at its center, which provided cut-off and reversing functions, imparted to the valve stem through a radius rod. The valve stem was driven, both by the radius rod and by a combination lever connected to the crosshead, causing the valve to hesitate at each end of its travel, keeping the valve open for slightly longer than was achieved by the sinusoidal motion of valves driven by the Stephenson gear. While the shortest cut-off at which the Stephenson gear could be used was 25%, the Walschaert gear could be worked at cut-offs as short as 15%. With the Walschaert gear the valves could be set either so that the engine ran forward with the link block in the lower half of the link (direct setting) or with the link block in the upper half of the link (indirect setting). On Mallets, the valves on each power unit were set oppositely so as to balance the loads on the reversing lever.

One cynical commentator pointed out:

> I hear more or less semi-surprised comment, in view of the recent (1907) rapid extension of the use of the Walschaerts valve gear, that it has been neglected in this country for so long a time. There is really nothing surprising about it. In the first place, it was not protected by a patent, so no one had a pecuniary interest in its development.

The first locomotives to reintroduce Walschaert gear in the U.S. were at the opposite ends of the performance spectrum. One was the 0-6-6-0 Mallet articulated compound that Alco Schenectady built for the Baltimore & Ohio in 1904. The other was the de Glehn four-cylinder balanced compound built in France for the Pennsylvania.

The Pennsylvania was one of the first American railroads to use the Walschaert gear with a new H-6b 2-8-0, received from Baldwin in June 1905, followed by 107 more by the end of 1905.[277] Another early user was the Chicago, Rock Island & Pacific. By mid–1907, more than a thousand American locomotives were fitted with the Walschaert gear.[278] Countless locomotives, built in the early 1900s with Stephenson gear and slide valves, were rebuilt with Walschaert gear and piston valves, noted in the captions to many of the photographs in this book.

Other inventors tried to emulate the success of the Walschaert gear/piston valve combination.

A. J. Stevens supervised the Central Pacific Sacramento shops from 1869 to 1888. In that capacity, he invented a valve and valve gear system that would have overcome the failings of the Stephenson gear by means of a duplex slide valve. A power reverser controlled cut-off. Robert J. Church describes this system in *Southern Pacific Ten-Coupled Locomotives* (Berkeley, California: Signature, 2013, 15). Apparently, the Central Pacific built the first locomotive equipped with this valve gear in 1884 and other locomotives equipped with it continued in service until the early 1900s. It failed, however, to obtain wider acceptance.[279]

In 1904–5, the Allfree-Hubbell gear, under development since 1901, began to attract attention.[280] It consisted of an addition to the Stephenson link motion and a new valve. A combination lever, linking the crosshead with the existing valve gear, drove the valve stem. The inventors recognized that, at short cut-off, existing slide or piston valves trapped exhaust steam by closing the exhaust port before the piston reached the end of its stroke. This had some value in cushioning piston reversal, but also cost power. The inventor, E. H. Allfree, intended his new valve to contain the steam for as long as possible, release it quickly at the end of the power stroke, and delay the closing of the port to exhaust. The main valve was, essentially, an inside-admission piston valve. A small additional valve chamber in each end of the cylinder casting communicated with the exhaust port, providing additional exhaust port area. Each housed a small piston valve, driven by an arm projecting from the main valve. The arm was free to slide along the valve stem between two points of contact so that the movement of the compression valves lagged that of the main valve, delaying closure of the exhaust. The valve could be operated by any type of valve gear. The noise and impact wear of the arm striking the contact points would have militated against this valve gear.

The Pittsburgh & Lake Erie installed this gear on a freight engine in 1904. Three months of tests convinced the company that the new gear resulted in 2% heavier loads hauled 3% faster for 5% less coal; they installed it on a passenger locomotive in June 1905. Between 1903 and 1906, Alco Cooke built forty-two 2-6-0s with Allfree-Hubbell valves, driven by Stephenson motion, for the Kansas City, Mexico & Orient. Most of these engines were refitted with piston valves and Walschaert valve gear.[281] By mid–1907, the Allfree-Hubbell valve system was under test on several railroads. Reports indicated a 6% reduction in fuel consumption and a 5% to 6% increase in train loads for locomotives equipped with this valve system. These results were within testing error and, so, were not significant.

By 1909, the valve gear part of the system had been discarded; development work by the Locomotive Appliance Co., Chicago, focused on the cylinder, valve chamber and valve. In 1910, the Allfree valve was paired with the Hobart valve gear, installed on a Kansas City Southern 2-8-0.[282] The Hobart valve gear replaced the expansion links of the Stephenson and Walschaert gears with a system of levers, intended to provide better valve events than the Stephenson gear and to eliminate back-force on the reach rod. By mid–1911, the Pittsburgh & Lake Erie had twenty engines retrofitted with Hobart Allfree cylinders and gear and, the same year, took delivery of five new engines from Alco with this gear. The Norfolk & Western adopted the device and, by the end of 1913, was installing it on all new locomotives and was retrofitting older engines as they became due for cylinder replacement.[283] The Hobart Allfree Co. modified their design so that it could be retrofitted to either slide-valve or piston-valve engines.[284] By 1915, the Central of New Jersey had four high-speed passenger locomotives in service with this valve arrangement, two with piston valves, two with slide valves. The performance of one of the Hobart Allfree slide-valve engines indicated a 12% fuel and water saving, compared to an unmodified slide-valve engine of the same type. Tests on Mallets showed a 13% increase in tonnage hauled for the same coal consumption, a 4% increase in speed and an 11% saving in water. By 1915, 162 locomotives had been equipped with Hobart Allfree slide-valve cylinders driven by various types of valve gear. Another thirty were in service with Hobart Allfree piston-valve cylinders: twenty with Baker valve gear, ten with Walschaert gear. In spite of this success, the device made no further headway.

New in 1908 was the Baker-Pilliod valve gear.[285] Resembling the Walschaert gear in its eccentric crank, rod and combination lever, but replacing the expansion link with a system of rods and a bell crank, the Baker-Pilliod gear came closer than the Stephenson gear to achieving the ideal of a quick and wide valve opening, both for admission and exhaust, with a constant lead at all cut-offs, and placed no back-loading on the reach rod, an important benefit with bigger and heavier valve gears. Like the Walschaert gear, the Baker-Pilliod gear could be retrofitted to older engines, allowing the frames to be braced in the space vacated by the Stephenson gear. The new gear was an immediate success. First applied to a Toledo, St. Louis & Western 4-6-0, within a year it was in use on the Chicago & Alton and on a 4-4-2 on the Chicago & North Western. The Chicago & Alton ordered twenty 2-8-0s, five 4-6-2s and five 0-6-0s with Baker-Pilliod gear.[286]

In 1910, the Pilliod Co., New York, manufacturers of the gear, made changes to the motion that improved its balance and wear characteristics.[287] By the end of 1911, Pilliod Brothers Co., Toledo, Ohio, was marketing a gear known by the name "Pilliod" alone, dispensing with the eccentric crank and rod entirely.[288] The motion was derived from the crosshead and was transmitted to the valve stem by mechanical linkages, a bell crank and a combination lever. A cross shaft transmitted motion to the valve stem on the other side of the engine.[289] This version did not become current.

A further modification, known as the "Baker" valve gear, was patented in 1911 and, by 1933, equipped 13,000 locomotives, rivaling the Walschaert gear until the late 1930s.[290] When locomotive building resumed after the depression, fewer of the new locomotives were equipped with Baker gear for reasons that this study has not revealed.

We mentioned the Young valve gear earlier. The Chicago & North Western, first users of this gear when they installed it on one of their passenger engines in 1903, found it so satisfactory that in 1908 they ordered it for ten locomotives then being built by Alco Schenectady.[291] The original system comprised a new valve gear, as well as the Corliss-type valves. In 1908, however, the inventor modified the Walschaert gear to drive the rotary valves. This arrangement was applied to an engine on the Delaware, Lackawanna & Western. In comparative tests with an engine equipped with Stephenson gear and piston valves, the Young-valve engine showed an 8% saving in water, and was well liked by the crews.

At the end of 1905, the Delaware & Hudson built two 4-6-0 freight engines with Young oscillating valve gear at its own shops, the first freight engines to be so equipped.[292] A feature of this valve gear was that it was adjustable for steam and exhaust lead. While the steam lead was constant for all cutoffs, the exhaust lead increased as the cutoff was shortened, giving a freer exhaust. Only small numbers of engines were equipped with this valve gear. The Delaware & Hudson, though small, would emerge as an innovator over the years.

This Atchison, Topeka & Santa Fe 1050 class 2-6-2, No. 1062, built by Baldwin in 1902–3, has Baker-Pilliod valve gear. First built as a Vauclain compound, it has been converted to single-expansion. When Otto Perry photographed it at Albuquerque, New Mexico, on October 23, 1920, it was less than twenty years old and already on the scrap line (Denver Public Library, Otto C. Perry collection, OP-245).

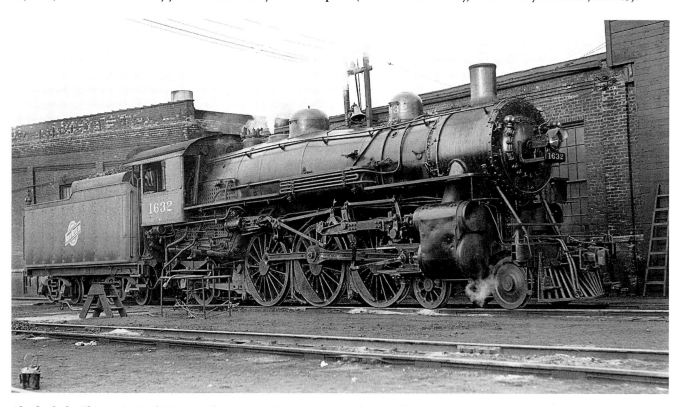

Alco built the Chicago & North Western Class E 4-6-2s between 1909 and 1923. This one, No. 1632, photographed at Council Bluffs, Iowa, on May 29, 1938, shows the right-side view of Young valve gear with a power reverser (Denver Public Library, Otto C. Perry collection, OP-3193).

This photograph, of another Chicago & North Western Class E 4-6-2, No. 1645, at Marshalltown, Iowa, on September 27, 1935, shows the left-side view of Young valve gear (Denver Public Library, Otto C. Perry collection, OP-3197).

Confusing to the historian is the appearance, in 1915, of another "Young" valve gear.[293] The inventor was O. W. Young "who for some years was in charge of valve gear design for the American Locomotive Company," presumably the same O. W. Young who invented the rotary valve system mentioned earlier. The new Young valve gear was clearly (from a photograph) driven by the crosshead, driving a piston valve.

The first experimental use of this gear was on a 4-6-2 of the Grand Trunk Railroad in Canada. Design improvements lightened the Young valve and gear by 40%, compared to the Walschaert equivalent. It was reported to allow freer inlet and exhaust for the steam, resulting in higher mean effective pressure, lower back pressure and better power output at high speed. Better hauling power and fuel savings of the order of 10% to 15% were also claimed. Construction details have not come to light in the course of this study.

Of these devices, only the Walschaert and Baker gears were widely used.

7.4.4 Power Reversers

Traditionally, the engineer controlled the direction and cut-off of the valve gear by means of a long lever in the cab, held in position by a latch engaging a notched quadrant. As engines became bigger, and their valve gear heavier, the force needed to move the reversing lever became greater. In a big engine, working hard, the backlash in the valve gear was so strong that releasing the latch and trying to move the reversing lever could cause injuries. Briefly closing the throttle while changing the cut-off was a necessary precaution, although this discouraged the frequent adjustments of cut-off that were desirable for efficient performance.

The British and French commonly used a hand wheel and a threaded rod to control the valve gear, offering more precise cut-off control and better mechanical advantage than the reversing lever, and suppressing backlash. A locomotive with this type of control could not be thrown into reverse in an emergency as quickly as one with a lever, although the value of this practice was debated. Although in common use in Europe, the screw valve gear control initially made little headway in the U.S.

The first power reversers were invented to overcome the friction between the slide valve and its seat. In 1882, W. E. Good designed a steam-powered reverser that was used on fast passenger engines of the Philadelphia & Reading. The same year, Theodore N. Ely, superintendent of motive power for the Pennsylvania, brought out the class K 4-4-0; the slide valves were so heavy and hard to control that he added a steam-powered reverser. At about the same time, W. P. Henszey of the Baldwin Locomotive Works invented another such device that was used on the Central of New Jersey.[294] These devices were superseded by the numerous slide-valve balancing systems.

Power reversing reappeared with a compressed-air powered reverser on the first American Mallet; the double sets of valve gear were too heavy for the engineer to control unaided. The Great Northern and Erie Mallets of 1906 had compressed-air powered McCarroll reversers.[295] The Santa Fe Mallets of 1910 had Ragonnet power reversing gear, as did the 2-10-2s that Baldwin built for the Burlington in 1912.

The design of a power reverser was not as simple as might be supposed. Most, if not all, such devices comprised a cylinder and piston arrangement, using steam or compressed air to drive the reach rod. The piston controlling the reach rod had to move not only full stroke, but repeatable, set distances to set the cut-off as desired by the engineer, remaining in that position without creeping until the engineer wanted to change the cut-off again.[296] It was also necessary to move the valve gear when the engine was dead.

The Ragonnet, patented by Eugine L. Ragonnet in 1909, was the most successful of the early power reversers. It retained a direct mechanical link between the engineer's reversing lever and the reach rod, but through a combination lever. The combination lever pivoted on a rocker arm which activated a slide valve, admitting steam or compressed air to either end of a cylinder, where a piston drove the reach rod. When the engineer relatched the reversing lever, the piston continued to move slightly until air pressure equalized on both sides of the cylinder. The Ragonnet was thus an augmenter, as distinct from a control system, augmenting the force that the engineer put into moving the reversing lever, while suppressing unwanted movement of the reach rod. When the engine was dead, a stop block at each end of the slide valve's travel acted as a fulcrum, the system having sufficient mechanical advantage for someone in the cab to move the valve gear. Other systems were less successful because they were more complicated and susceptible to wear and leaks causing creeping or jumping of the valve gear.

Other power reversers were interesting, ingenious but, ultimately unsuccessful; space does not permit their description. The Canadian Locomotive Co., Kingston, Ontario, brought out the Casey-Cavin in 1913.[297] Two new power reversers came out in 1916, the Snyder, from the Pittsburgh Locomotive Power Reverse Gear Co., Pittsburgh, and the Brown, from the Southern Locomotive Valve Gear Co., Knoxville, Tennessee.[298] M. F. Cox, assistant superintendent of machinery on the Louisville & Nashville, invented another power reverser, first used in 1916.[299] The Ragonnet Type B appeared in 1917, marketed by the Economy Devices Corp., New York.[300] The Lewis power reverser, marketed by the Commonwealth Supply Co., Richmond, Virginia, was of this same general type and was also air-operated.[301]

The Franklin Railway Supply Co. made a start in business with the Franklin automatic fire door opener, applied to the Erie Mallets of 1908, but expanded to other locomotive appliances and brought out a series of compressed-air power reversers.[302] The Franklin Types B and E so closely resembled the Ragonnet that Franklin probably licensed the manufacturing rights. The later Alco Types G and K and Barco Type M-1 resembled the general arrangement of the Ragonnet, differing in detail.[303]

The Franklin Types F and G Precision Power Reverse Gear of the 1920s comprehended the essential feature of the Ragonnet as an augmenter, rather than a control system; they were power-assisted screw reversers with a hand wheel in the cab, enabling the engineer to set and hold a more precise cut-off than was possible with the Ragonnet and its derivatives. The hand wheel turned a threaded rod inside a block which moved along the threads; an arrow on the block showed the percentage of cut-off against a scale.[304] Shafting and two universal joints transmitted the rotary motion to a sleeve inside the power reverser. An axial rod was formed at its rear end into a square-section shank, which was a sliding

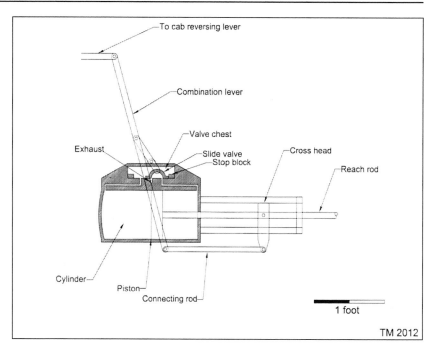

Schematic of the Ragonnet power reverser (redrawn from *RAG*, November 16, 1917, 900).

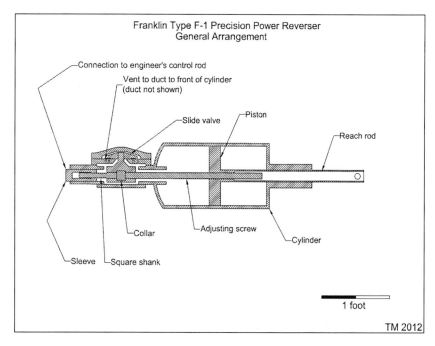

Schematic of the Franklin Type F Precision Power Reverser (redrawn from Harding, J. W., *Steam Locomotive Home Study Course*, 2002 reprint, Vol. 2, 65–9).

fit in the sleeve. Farther forward, the rod carried a slide valve body. Its front end was formed as a thread which turned inside a piston. The piston rod drove the reach rod which adjusted the valve gear.

When the engine was dead, and no compressed air was supplied to the reverser, turning the rod moved it into or out of the piston until the slide valve body butted against one end of its travel. If the rod was turned more, the thread forced the piston forth or back. When the engine was live, and compressed air was supplied to the reverser, movement of the slide valve body opened ports which supplied compressed air to one side of the piston, while opening the other side to atmosphere. This augmented the force applied by the engineer to the screw thread, making it possible to move heavy valve gear to a precise point of cut-off in either forward or reverse gear. When the engineer stopped turning the rod, the piston continued to move slightly, taking the rod with it and moving the slide valve body until air was admitted to both sides of the piston and the vent to atmosphere was closed.

Power reversers were among the devices that made the giant American steam locomotive possible.

Section 7.5. Front Ends

By the early 1900s, designers thought that they had uncovered the secrets of the front end. From the standpoint of 1906[305]:

Gradually the mysteries of the locomotive front end have been disclosed. Ten years ago experiments on the testing plant developed the proper form and character of the exhaust jet and the fundamental principles involved in the design of exhaust pipes. Later the stack received attention, first as applied to a small locomotive and more recently as applied to larger and more modern locomotives. Last of all, the petticoat, or draft pipes, have been scientifically investigated. The only parts of the front end which have not yet been carefully studied are the netting and the diaphragm. These two details have no active part in bringing about the draft action, and have naturally been left till the last.

An ARMMA committee summarized the results of many years of studies and tests in a front end design that they believed to incorporate some optimum dimensions, shown here in a drawing, known as the Master Mechanics' Front End.[306] Actual dimensions, as applied to a Pennsylvania 4-4-2, are shown in the accompanying drawing.

Curiously, the committee did not comment on the critical dimension between the nozzle tip and the bottom of the petticoat pipe. The findings of the ARMMA committee were accepted as authoritative and, for a time, were widely adopted. Nevertheless, the design and dimensions of smokeboxes remained a mystery; small changes in dimensions produced large changes in performance. Tests with E-2a and E-3a 4-4-2s at Altoona in 1910, using the actual dimensions shown in the drawing, led the Pennsylvania to the depressing conclusion that, with coal firing, the performance of the front end varied so much with the condition of the fire that no meaningful results were obtainable. ARMMA tests at Purdue on a New York Central 4-4-2 had been conducted with oil firing, which enabled the condition of the firebox to be more completely controlled. (The Purdue test plant had been modified to accept locomotives other than its own captive locomotive.) After trying many different combinations, the Pennsylvania found that a petticoat pipe with very little flare

and a long parallel-walled section, projecting below the smokebox centerline, obtained the best results—markedly different from the ARMMA findings. The Pennsylvania experimented with an adjustable diaphragm plate, but conditions inside the smokebox were too hostile for such a device which was found, in any event, to be unnecessary.

Fifteen years after the Purdue tests, the International Railway Fuel Association Standing Committee on Front Ends, Grates and Ash Pans circulated a questionnaire to find out whether the locomotives then being built were using the Master Mechanics' Front End. It

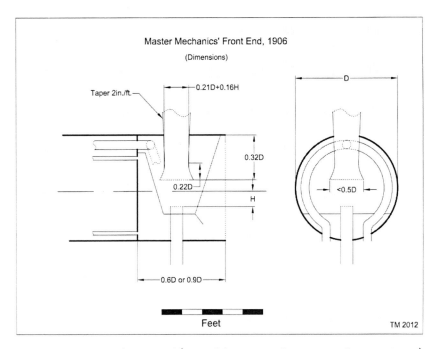

The Master Mechanics' Front End (general dimensions from *RAG*, July 15, 1910, 124).

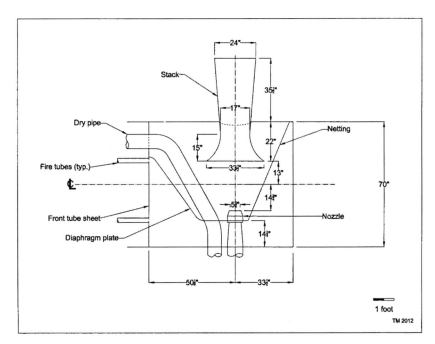

The Master Mechanics' Front End as applied to a Pennsylvania 4-4-2, 1910, actual dimensions (redrawn from *RAG*, July 15, 1910, 125).

turned out that there was no "standard" front end. Each railroad was using its own designs.[307]

Much disagreement existed about the desirability of a bridge, or splitter, placed across the exhaust nozzle as a means of spreading the steam jet.[308] The 1896 ARMMA report on front ends condemned this practice as obstructing the jet and increasing back pressure for no beneficial effect on drafting. Mechanics and enginemen knew that it would sometimes improve steaming and its use persisted. The locomotives current in 1896 were small enough that their stacks could be long in relation to the smokebox diameter. The locomotives being built ten years later had much larger-diameter smokeboxes and short, wide stacks. A splitter ensured that the steam jet completely filled these stacks.

Operators tried many different shapes of nozzle over the years— round, square, single, double, star-shaped, dumb-bell shaped.[309] A significant body of opinion held that the jet should be split to entrain more of the exhaust gases.

In 1914, F. A. Goodfellow, foreman of the Pennsylvania's Altoona test plant, came up with a design of nozzle with four fingers projecting into the interior of a circular outline.[310] This invention, of extraordinary simplicity, produced a spectacular 27% increase in indicated horsepower in the first locomotive on which it was tested.

> There has recently been developed on our locomotive testing plant a nozzle having four internal projections which appears to be more satisfactory than some of the irregularly formed nozzles. With these nozzles, having other than a circular outlet, an increase in the evaporative capacity of the boiler of from 15 to 25 per cent has been obtained and in recent tests on a large Pacific type locomotive a nozzle with four internal projections has given a maximum capacity in equivalent evaporation from and at 212 deg. of 87,414 lb. per hour. In the locomotive in question, this is an evaporation of 18.0 lb. of water per square foot of heating surface per hour and with this quantity of steam an indicated horsepower of 3,184 was obtained; whereas, the circular nozzle on this same locomotive developed a maximum equivalent evaporation of but 62,719 lb. of water per hour, resulting in an indicated horsepower of 2,501. It should be understood that no change was made in the locomotive other than in the exhaust tip.

The Pennsylvania tested an E-6s 4-4-2, a K-4s 4-6-2 and an L-1s 2-8-2, all with 7-inch circular nozzles, changing nothing but the addition of the four small projections. These had astonishing effects. By more than doubling the smokebox vacuum from 6 to 8 inches of water gauge to 15 to 19 inches, they affected the combustion rate, hence the steaming rate and superheat temperature, with spectacular effects on power output.

| Class | Type | Maximum power | | |
		Circular nozzle (ihp)	Goodfellow nozzle (ihp)	Increase %
E-6s	4-4-2	1,900	2,300	21
K-4s	4-6-2	2,240	3,180	42
L-1s	2-8-2	2,365	2,835	20

The Goodfellow exhaust nozzle was a breakthrough and is still in use today.

Over the years many mechanisms were invented on both sides of the Atlantic, enabling the engine crew to vary the exhaust nozzle while the engine was running; some dated back to 1803.[311] The interior of the smokebox was an extremely hostile environment for such mechanisms; if the device was out of repair or improperly used, the effect on performance would be worse than if it was not there at all. For an engine crew, it was just one more gadget that had to be kept in adjustment. As such, they were likely to set it for one set of conditions and then neglect to reset it when conditions changed. In par-

ticular, if an adjustable nozzle was left in one position for any length of time, it was liable to become stuck with soot, cinders and rust.

The Pere Marquette and the Duluth & Iron Range used the Wallace and Kellogg variable exhaust of 1903. Two hinged plates widened or narrowed the sides of a square nozzle. One of the inventors claimed that it was used for several years with good results.

In the Baker variable exhaust of 1912, two opposing threads moved the sides of a split collar together or apart. The St. Joseph & Grand Island experimented with the device for about 18 months but C. E. Slayton, assistant superintendent, reported:

> The adjustable feature worked well, that is, we were able to keep it in working order without any trouble. They did not effect saving enough to warrant us in applying them to more locomotives.

The French were probably the main users of variable exhausts. The jumper ring used by the Great Western Railway in England was also successful as it was extremely simple and automatic in its action.

Fierce drafting on American locomotives threw out large quantities of cinders—as much as 1,000 pounds an hour. The resulting lineside fires were a continual problem, costly in compensation claims for property damage, while cinders burned and dirtied passengers and increased wear and tear on cars. Countless spark-suppressing front-end designs resulted. Tests at Purdue in 1910 showed that gas flow velocities in the center fire tubes could reach 4,150 feet per minute with a pressure drop of 1.1 inches of water gauge along the tube.

The Van Horn–Endsley spark arrestor of 1910 retained cinders for extraction through a hopper in the bottom of the smokebox.[312] A spiral swirl plate in a lengthened smokebox threw cinders to the bottom of the smokebox while the gases themselves passed through a hole in a diaphragm plate. The Chicago & North Western tried this device, but the problem was the very long smokebox, the difficulty of keeping the hopper door airtight and the locomotive's limited range—about 30 miles—before the cinder hopper had to be emptied.

In 1911 a new device appeared in experimental service on the Chicago & North Western, the Slater front end.[313] A vertical diaphragm plate was placed immediately behind the stack. The space between the nozzle tip and the base of the petticoat pipe was boxed in. Gases and cinders passed around the exhaust nozzle under this box, reversing course in the front bottom of the smokebox, passing backward and upward through a perforated sheet containing a square hole covered with netting. In the 1910–11 fiscal year the Chicago & North Western paid out $129,250 in compensation for lineside fires, halved to $63,787 in the following year. Much of this was attributed to the Slater front end, which equipped 70% of all the company's locomotives by the end of 1912.

Another attempt was the Brooks spark arrester of 1911.[314] The device was, in effect, a diamond stack, inverted and placed between the nozzle and the petticoat pipe. The Chicago, Milwaukee & Puget Sound, using a soft semi-lignite from Montana, equipped seventy-five locomotives with it that year and planned to equip more.

I. A. Seiders, Superintendent of Motive Power on the Philadelphia & Reading, invented a successful spark arrester in 1915,[315] replacing the diaphragm plate with a plate made of baffles. The exhaust nozzle was surrounded, front and back, by netting extending the full width of the smokebox. This much reduced the resistance to gas flow, while enhancing the extinction of sparks. Between 1915 and 1918, the company equipped 474 locomotives with this device and estimated that compensation claims for lineside fires dropped by 40%.

Unfortunately, spark suppressors consumed a large proportion of the energy of the draft. Measurements on a locomotive under test at Altoona showed a smokebox vacuum as high as 19.6 inches of water

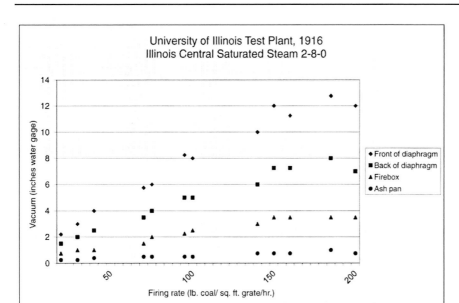

Typical magnitude and distribution of smokebox vacuum (figures from *Tests of a Consolidation Type Locomotive*, RAG, March 10, 1916, 437).

gauge in the front of the smokebox.[316] At the front tube sheet the vacuum was 10.2 inches of water gauge, 3.7 inches in the firebox. Only 19% of the draft went to the task for which it was intended, drafting the fire. The balance went into overcoming friction losses in the fire tubes and at the diaphragm plate. These losses increased, both with increased firing rates and with increasing tube length. The accompanying graph shows the smokebox vacuum needed for increasing firing rates in a typical locomotive and where the vacuum was distributed.

In 1911–12, H. B. MacFarland, Engineer of Tests with the Santa Fe, estimated that the power consumed by the exhaust blast in drafting the fire could reach 1,000 horsepower in some of the company's Mallets—more than the power exerted at the drawbar. MacFarland expressed these findings in an 85-page paper, resulting from extensive road tests on every class of locomotive used by the Santa Fe. MacFarland's reasoning and method of calculation were erroneous.

The power consumed in producing the draft was the power that the pistons had to exert against the back pressure. In a two-cylinder locomotive, with 28-inch × 30-inch cylinders, at a back pressure of 15 pounds per square inch, at 100 wheel revolutions per minute (26 miles per hour for a 60-inch driving wheel), the power consumed would be the back pressure in pounds per square foot × the piston area in square feet × twice the stroke in feet × the driving wheel revolutions per minute, divided by 33,000 foot-pounds per minute to convert to horsepower. ($15 \times 144 \times 3.1415 \times 1.17^2 \times 2.5 \times 2 \times 100)/33,000 = 140$ horsepower for each piston, or 280 horsepower in total. In a Mallet, with the back pressure acting on 40-inch pistons in the low-pressure cylinders, the total would be 573 horsepower. MacFarland's calculation may have been wrong, but his finding was valid.

Nevertheless, the report seems to have gone unquestioned—the myth was still current in 1920[317]; it led the company to experiment with fan drafting over the next 2 to 3 years.[318] Later, MacFarland arrived at a more reasonable set of results, but still one that pointed to the inefficiency and high power consumption of exhaust blast drafting.

Fan drafting was already standard practice in marine and stationary plant, although drafting was less important to such plants with their lower firing rates per square foot of grate area. The Santa Fe carried out its fan drafting experiments at Topeka with a test plant built around a locomotive. The fan was a 25-horsepower, 48-inch diameter, constant-speed fan, driven by an electric motor; drawing 20 horsepower at 715 revolutions per minute, it developed a smokebox vacuum of 3 inches of water gauge. The first tests were made in February 1912.

In January 1913, the company installed a 24-inch fan, directly connected to a 40-horsepower steam turbine, in the smokebox. The fan was too small and had to be extensively redesigned; in its final form, it developed a smokebox vacuum of 4 to 6 inches of water gauge—insufficient to maintain boiler pressure. Road tests showed cylinder back pressures of 11 to 24 pounds per square inch with exhaust blast drafting; fan drafting, with direct exhaust to atmosphere, dropped the cylinder back pressure to 4 pounds per square inch or less. The New York Central tried a MacFarland draft fan on a switching engine in an attempt to reduce engine noise in residential areas. Fan drafting in non-condensing locomotives never succeeded; the steam locomotive was too demanding and too hostile an environment. For all its mysteries, exhaust blast drafting remained unchallenged until the end of steam.

The front end continued to frustrate locomotive designers.[319] Smokebox leaks developed gradually, especially where the steam pipes passed through the smokebox shell. As the steaming capacity of the locomotive gradually deteriorated, maintenance shops responded by bushing the exhaust nozzle to improve the draft, which increased the back pressure in the cylinders. Tests by the USRA showed that this process could be reversed by properly sealing the smokebox. Increasing nozzle diameters by as little as ¼ inch decreased fuel consumption by 14% to 21%. Raising the diaphragm, causing a better distribution of drafting over the fire, could save another 3%. The steam locomotive continued to harbor obscure details, such as these, apparently insignificant but with extraordinary effects on performance. When multiplied over the U.S. locomotive fleet, they implied the waste of millions of tons of coal.

Section 7.6. Frames and Running Gear

7.6.1 Frames

By 1905, the problems of manufacturing cast steel locomotive frames had largely been overcome. Shrinkage cracks were the worst problem; even if shrinkage cracks did not appear during manufacture, shrinkage stresses remaining latent in the steel could cause cracking in service. Many railroads refused to accept this hidden hazard so the use of wrought iron frames went on. Low-phosphorous steel, carefully annealed to release shrinkage stresses, eventually solved this problem[320] but, even when railroads did adopt cast steel frames, the drawings previously used for wrought iron frames continued in use so that the greater strength of steel was wasted.[321]

Each railroad used its own frame design. The complete absence of uniformity is surprising as few railroads built their own locomotives. It might be supposed that railroads would leave the frame design to the manufacturer and that the manufacturer would seek to standardize one frame design for each wheel arrangement, but this was not the case.

In spite of the increasing success of cast steel frames, frame breakage continued to be a widespread and serious problem, typically after two years in service.[322] Bending a long rigid wheelbase around sharp curves was recognized as a fruitful cause of frame breakage. Poor-quality metal, poor frame design and deficient quality control in manufacture contributed further. A poorly maintained locomotive could pound itself to pieces, frame breakage being one result; allowing axle boxes to work loose in their pedestals could break the frame.

About 1910, cast steel and wrought iron frames were in service in roughly equal numbers, including the first vanadium-steel frames. In about 1913, the American Vanadium Company produced a carbon-vanadium steel with a 60,000-pounds per square inch yield point, about 25% higher than annealed carbon steel; longer delivery times inhibited the use of more sophisticated steels, a problem that intensified during World War I.

The life of cast steel frames was still, on average, slightly shorter than that of wrought iron, but this was due to residual problems with the quality of large steel castings, which was still improving. By 1912, most new locomotives were being built with cast steel frames, although steel specifications and methods of calculating the proper dimensions of the frame members lagged behind their widening use.

Frame design was easy to criticize but, until 1911, no rational guidelines existed. Of concern:

> all of the heavier power is more liable to breakage than the lighter engines, which would seem to indicate that the strength of frame has not increased in the same ratio as the power of the engine.

An ARMMA committee, formed in 1910 to address these problems, recommended the metal cross-sections needed at various places in the frame in terms of square inches of metal cross-section in relation to piston thrust. This was a start but did not take into account the complex bending and twisting to which the frame was subjected. The question of why frames broke as and when they did remained a mystery. It seemed that some frames broke because they were too stiff, others because they were not stiff enough. Frame breakages were still being traced to expansion of the boiler. The sliding shoes fitted to relieve this movement sometimes failed to do so, due to poor design or lack of lubrication. Vertical plates, mounted crosswise and fixed both to the boiler and to the frames, and capable of flexing with the expansion of the boiler, were found to be a better solution than the shoes. Breakage was noticed at bolt holes and sharp corners, but the modern-day science of stress analysis had not even reached infancy.

T. H. Curtis of the Louisville & Nashville admitted:

> I cannot give you any light on how to construct frames to keep them from breaking, but I will mention that the Louisville & Nashville have 150 consolidated [*sic*] locomotives with the Stephenson link motion. These locomotives were not troubled with frame breakage, but we built some fifty or more locomotives with the same frame, the locomotives are practically interchangeable, except that these last engines were equipped with the Walschaert valve gear. We have been troubled a great deal by the breaking of the left frame near the front pedestal, in the case of these engines. I have looked the engines over and cannot see any reason for the breaking of the frame. It breaks in a very strong place, and everything seems to be in a good condition, and I know that the engines are well kept up. ... Therefore I attribute the trouble to the Walschaert valve gear. As to why it should cause this breakage of frames I cannot give any reason.

Others considered that outside Walschaert valve gear reduced frame breakages because of the stronger frames and cross-bracing that this arrangement allowed. At the same time, it was realized that the cylin-

der castings for piston valves were stronger than those for slide valves, so taking some of the load off the frame.

A major development in locomotive construction was the one-piece, cast steel engine bed. In 1919, the New Haven ordered ten new electric locomotives. A frame built up by bolting and riveting would have made the complete locomotive too heavy. Accordingly the New Haven approached the Commonwealth Steel Co. of St. Louis to produce a one-piece cast frame. The result was 32 feet long and weighed 17,000 pounds.[323] Besides saving weight, this innovation eliminated the numerous bolted connections which loosened in service, allowing pounding and ultimately frame breakage.

7.6.2 Counterbalancing

The new 2-10-2s brought all the problems of dynamic augment into focus. Their enormous pulling power came from heavy piston thrusts requiring strong and heavy main rods. Of all the locomotive types in service, the 2-10-2s had the greatest total weight of parts rotating and reciprocating simultaneously. Although the Mallets were bigger and heavier, their moving parts were divided between two, out-of-phase power units.

In 1914–15, the Chicago, Burlington & Quincy bought seventeen 2-10-2s using carefully designed main and side rods made of heat-treated Nichrome steel.[324] Heat treating meant that the rods could be designed safely for loads closer to their ultimate strength than could be done with normal steel. By this means they reduced the dynamic augment at 40 miles per hour from 27% of the axle load to only 12%. These design measures carved nearly 10,000 pounds off the locomotive weight. Dynamic augment was also a problem with the 4-6-2s because of their combination of heavy weight and high speed. In 1915, the Burlington bought fifteen 4-6-2s with light-weight reciprocating parts which permitted higher axle loadings and a more powerful locomotive. Light-weight reciprocating parts made the Pennsylvania's hugely successful E-6 4-4-2s possible, in spite of their exceptionally heavy axle loading of 66,500 pounds. Careful design reduced dynamic augment to 30% of the driving wheel static weight, compared to 42% for a typical 2-10-2. The Pennsylvania followed through by applying these principles to their 4-6-2s and 2-8-2s.

The counterbalancing problem was inherent in the reciprocating steam locomotive; the only available solution was a compromise between the reciprocating and rotating masses. When these parts weighed several tons, even this compromise became less and less satisfactory, especially as dynamic augment came closer to the ultimate strength of the track. Although locomotive builders might use steel of higher tensile strength for the reciprocating parts, most railroad back shops lacked heat-treating equipment. Advanced types of steel might be supplied with a new locomotive, but parts had to be repaired in the user's back shop with the facilities that were available there.

From the viewpoint of 1918[325]:

> In no decade in the history of the American locomotive have here been more and greater improvements in design than in the last 10 years. What is rightly called the American locomotive is a very different machine from that of 10 years ago. Through the development of correct boiler and cylinder proportions; by the application of fuel-saving and capacity-increasing devices, and by refinements in detail design, the modern locomotive has been brought to a high degree of efficiency in operation and maintenance.
>
> Through these means and the introduction of new types of wheel arrangements, tremendous progress has been made in the construction of more and more powerful units to meet the never-ceasing demand for greater hauling capacity.
>
> But in one respect there has been, generally speaking, no progress; on the contrary, approved practice is not on a par with that of 10 years ago.

This is in regard to the weights of the reciprocating and revolving parts per unit of load.

The problem was urgent; its solution was one of the triumphs underlying the superpower design movement.

Section 7.7. Performance and Performance Testing

7.7.1 Performance Testing

Testing the performance of a steam locomotive was difficult, time-consuming and costly. Static test plants were so expensive to build and operate that few existed in the world. Dynamometer cars cost so much that even a large railroad was unlikely to own more than one, limiting the amount of information that could be obtained. Performance testing was money well spent, however; without it the American steam locomotive could never have been developed to the extent that it was. Industry associations and railroad companies supported the testing process and helped to disseminate the results.

Test plants allowed performance to be tested under constant, ideal conditions, but road tests, using instrumented locomotives and dynamometer cars, were an essential counterpart; direct comparisons between static and road tests were few.[326] H. H. Vaughan pointed out that, during one month of freight operations on the Canadian Pacific, locomotive efficiency came no closer than 25% to that derived from a test plant. Locomotive performance on the road was poorer than on a test plant because conditions were never constant.

Reports of locomotive performance tests, published in the 1890s and before 1905, give the impression that the test engineers measured everything they could think of, hoping to discern some pattern in the results. The key parameters and ratios had been identified by about 1905 but, as late as 1911, test engineers conducting road tests on the Lake Shore & Michigan Southern's new, superheated, Alco 4-6-2 came up with fifteen ratios, including such obscure relationships as "weight on driving wheels divided by total equivalent heating surface." Some of these served no useful purpose, yet such was the thirst for any knowledge that could show the way to improved locomotive design.[327] F. J. Cole, chief consulting engineer to Alco, collected and studied a mass of performance data; Alco published the results, known as the Cole ratios, in a landmark pamphlet, *Locomotive Ratios*, in 1914. (Refer to Appendix C to this book.)

7.7.1.1 Static Test Plants

By 1907, the industry was realizing the importance of the Purdue and Pennsylvania static test plants[328]:

It seems curious in the light of the recent experimental information that has been obtained regarding the action of the several parts of the locomotive, that the world should have waited for it so long. It is not so very long ago that the use even of the indicator upon the locomotive was rare or unknown, and our only means of testing, if it could be called testing, was to ride upon the engine and observe general results. This was followed by road tests that involved so many variables that the real object of the work was sometimes buried beneath a mass of uncertainties. So when it was proposed by Purdue University to build a laboratory plant upon which a full-sized locomotive could be tested under constant conditions it was received with the warmest acclaim by the railroad world and the greatest interest was at once manifested in the probability of obtaining valuable results. Whether the promoters of the scheme had a clear idea of what was to be the outcome, we are not informed, but if they had they must have been endowed with a most remarkable foresight.

The Purdue testing plant has given rise to others, and the results of the investigations that have been made have been so prolific of good that this method of testing has now come to be recognized as the only one upon which reliance can be placed, and the records of Purdue and St. Louis form the most valuable contributions to the literature of the locomotive extant. When it is remembered that in 1890, before the opening of the Purdue laboratory, we had no definite idea of how the draft of a locomotive was produced and that every engine driver was a law unto himself as to the adjustment of the smokebox details; that the action of the fire was almost unknown; the influence of tube length a mystery; the quality of steam supplied to the engine a pure guess, and the economical efficiency of the machine, as a whole, a matter upon which there was a general agreement to the wrong, namely that it was extravagant in the use of coal and steam, we can see that much was to be learned, much more than was realized at the time.

Seventeen years of constant, painstaking effort has borne fruit a hundredfold, and we have learned so much that we are realizing more and more every day how much there still remains to be done."

By 1913, only six static test plants existed in the world. They were, with their construction dates:

> Purdue University, 1891, captive-locomotive laboratory, later modified to accept non-captive locomotives;
> Chicago & North Western, South Kaukauna, Wisconsin, 1894, test plant;
> Columbia University, 1899, laboratory incorporating a Baldwin 4-4-2;
> Pennsylvania, St. Louis, 1904, test plant, moved to Altoona 1905;
> Great Western Railway, Swindon, England, 1904, test plant;
> St. Petersburg, Russia, 1904, test plant.

In 1913, the University of Illinois, Urbana, approved funding for a test plant, making three static test plants in the U.S.[329] The Chicago & North Western and Columbia University plants seem to have gone out of use.

By 1921, there was also a test plant at Oi in Japan[330] and, by 1926, there was a plant at the Hohenzollern Locomotive Works, Düsseldorf, Germany.[331] Current research has not revealed when these plants were built.

No test plant was ever built that accommodated a Mallet. Only road tests revealed their performance.

7.7.1.2 Development Work on the Pennsylvania Test Plant

The Pennsylvania test plant was the first to produce test results from operating locomotive types. Results from Purdue were valid only insofar as they applied to all steam locomotives. The Chicago & North Western plant seems to have produced only meager results, probably because of its crude design.

The testing of a newly built H-6a 2-8-0 in May 1904, the first locomotive to be tested on the new plant at St. Louis, was a landmark in steam locomotive development.[332] In one month, the company ran seventeen tests, each lasting about three hours. Thirty-five people instrumented and recorded the tests with typical Pennsylvania thoroughness.

The test engineers took indicator diagrams and measured nearly thirty parameters: atmospheric pressure, boiler pressure, pressure downstream of the throttle, ambient and feedwater temperatures, firing rate in pounds of coal per hour (the coal was analyzed for combustible and water content and calorific value), water evaporated in pounds per hour, steam quality, weight of trapped cinders and sparks and their calorific value, draft in the ash pan, firebox and smokebox (both sides of the diaphragm), firebox and smokebox temperatures, mean effective pressure, indicated horsepower, smokebox gas oxygen, carbon monoxide, carbon dioxide and nitrogen content, drawbar pull, drawbar horsepower, driving wheel revolutions per minute and cut-off. All tests were run at full throttle.

They averaged this information for each test and derived nearly twenty ratios: combustion rate (pounds of coal per square foot of grate per hour and per square foot of heating surface per hour), evaporation rate (pounds of water per hour, per square foot of grate per hour and per square foot of heating surface per hour), boiler horsepower (total, per square foot of heating surface and per square foot of grate), boiler efficiency, evaporation efficiency (pounds of water per pound of coal as fired, dry coal and combustible), heat loss in carbon monoxide, fuel efficiency (pounds of coal per indicated horsepower-hour and drawbar horsepower-hour), friction horsepower, mechanical efficiency and steam consumption (pounds per indicated and drawbar horsepower-hour).

The accompanying graphs show some of the findings of these tests. Although the numbers were specific to this class of locomotive, the conclusions were of general application.

The test results provided a complete picture of the functioning and efficiency of the locomotive.

The Pennsylvania tested eight locomotives in 1904—four passenger and four freight, comprising:

- one de Glehn four-cylinder balanced compound;
- one "Hannover type with Pielock superheater" four-cylinder balanced compound;
- two American four-cylinder balanced compounds (presumably one Baldwin, one Alco);
- two single-expansion freight engines;
- one two-cylinder cross-compound freight engine;
- one four-cylinder tandem compound freight engine.

None were superheated.

Firebox temperatures ranged from 1,400°F to 2,000°F at low combustion rates to 2,100°F to 2,300°F at high rates. Smokebox temperatures for all boilers ran at 500°F at low power, increasing to 600°F to 700°F at high power. Smokebox vacuum ranged from 1 inch of water gauge at low power to as much as 8.8 inches at high power.

At maximum power, steaming rates varied from boiler to boiler, from 12 pounds of steam per square foot of heating surface to as much as 16 pounds. The tests did not shed light on what design features led to these results but did confirm the efficacy of the brick arch. A large grate area, relative to heating surface, produced the greatest boiler capacity.

The tests confirmed the depressing fact

that evaporative efficiency declined as power output increased, from 10 to 12 pounds of water per pound of coal at low power to only 6 to 8 pounds at high power. The single-expansion freight engines burned 3.5 pounds of coal per drawbar horsepower-hour, increasing with speed to 5 pounds; the compound freight engines burned as little as 2 pounds. The four-cylinder compound passenger engines burned as little as 2.2 pounds per drawbar horsepower-hour at low speed to 5 pounds at high speed. This was an unfortunate finding, considering the effort that had gone into developing the four-cylinder balanced compound as the apparently ideal fast passenger engine. The figures of 2.0 to 2.2 pounds of coal per drawbar horsepower-hour were among the lowest ever achieved by any reciprocating steam locomotive anywhere, but they were obtained by running the compounds for long periods of time at constant speeds and loads and were not reproduced in road service.

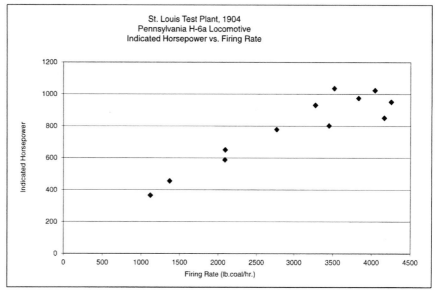

Increase in power output with increasing firing rate, but with diminishing returns beyond 3,000 pounds per hour (figures for the next five graphs from *Locomotive Tests at St. Louis, RRG*, April 7, 1905, 324–5).

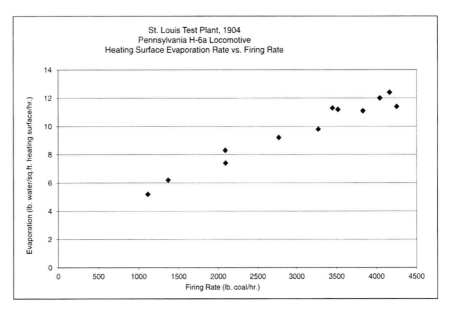

Improved use of heating surface with increasing firing rate.

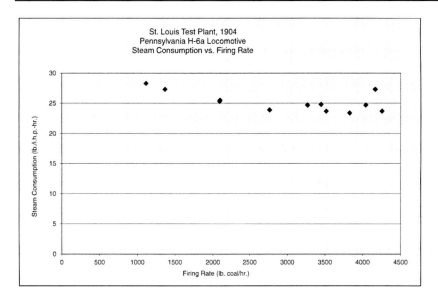

Efficiency of steam consumption with increasing firing rate. No improvement beyond 3,000 pounds per hour.

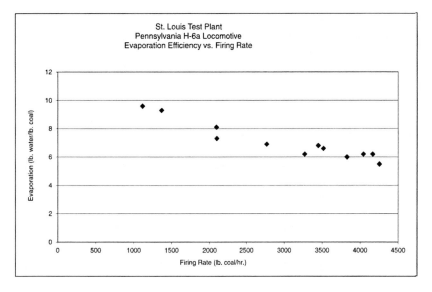

A decrease in evaporation efficiency with increasing firing rate.

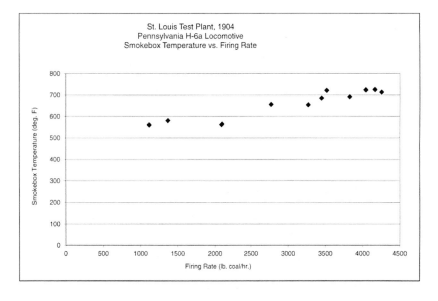

An increase in heat loss through the stack with increasing firing rate.

A 750-page technical bulletin, published eighteen months after completion of the 1904 St. Louis tests, provided a complete description of the test plant, methods, test results and conclusions; a 700-page bulletin documented the 1905 test program. These bulletins were landmarks in locomotive testing and design.[333]

> This work is perhaps the most exhaustive treatise of its kind ever published ... the record of (the tests) will doubtless endure as an intellectual monument to the enterprise and scientific spirit of the Pennsylvania Railroad System.
>
> The art of locomotive construction has been materially advanced by reason of these tests. They have demonstrated the practicability of the testing plant as a means of studying the performance of locomotives; they have established a logical method of conducting tests and of making the necessary observations; and they have determined the efficiency and limits of power which may be expected from the modern locomotive ... it is the purpose of the Pennsylvania to establish this testing plant at Altoona and make it a part of the permanent organization of the testing department.

The results were widely used by mechanical engineers on both sides of the Atlantic.

More than two years of testing and development went into the Pennsylvania's legendary E-6s 4-4-2 express locomotive, a process that was not available to any other railroad in the U.S., or even to Baldwin or Alco. Both companies must have considered building such a plant but, turning out 5,000 locomotives a year for hundreds of customers, they had neither the opportunity nor the motivation to do so.

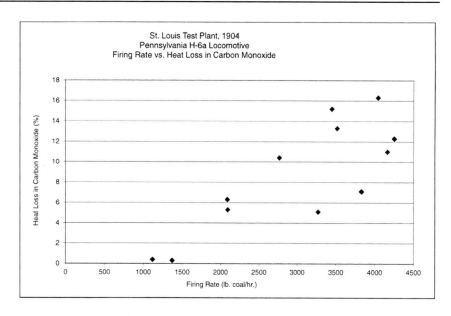

An increase in heat loss in unreacted carbon monoxide with increasing firing rate.

The E-6s was the first American locomotive to be developed in this way. The company built the first, unsuperheated prototype in 1910, adding a superheater in 1912. Quantity production of the E-6s began in 1913, eighty-two being built in 1913–14.[334]

While developing the E-6s, the Pennsylvania found that fire tube length could be usefully increased until its length reached 100 times its diameter (20 feet for a 2½-inch tube), beyond which friction resistance to gas flow inhibited drafting. The prototype E-6s measured 13 feet 9 inches over tube sheets and recorded a smokebox temperature of 770°F; lengthening the fire tubes to 15 feet in the production E-6s dropped the smokebox temperature to 435°F to

This photograph, taken in 1916, shows one of the Pennsylvania's legendary class E-6s 4-4-2s, No. 5142, at Jersey City, New Jersey (Pennsylvania Historical and Museum Commission and Railroad Museum of Pennsylvania, General Negative 25366).

665°F. This temperature difference went into higher steaming rates, higher thermal efficiency and more power. The steaming rate peaked at 44,000 pounds per hour.

The greater fluidity of superheated steam allowed the diameter of the piston valves to be reduced from 14 inches in the E-6 to 12 in the E-6s, resulting in lighter valves and lower power consumption by the valve gear.

Evaporation rate was something the Pennsylvania could do little about—9 pounds of water per pound of coal at firing rates of 35 pounds per square foot of grate per hour, decreasing to 6 pounds at 135 pounds per square foot per hour.[335] At a maximum firing rate of 8,000 pounds per hour (145 pounds per square foot of grate per hour), the total pressure drop from ash pan to exhaust was 15 inches of water gauge, distributed as 20% across the ash pan, grate and firebed, 40% across the fire tubes and 37% across the diaphragm plate. The highest recorded fuel efficiency was 2 pounds of coal per indicated horsepower-hour while producing 1,400 to 1,600 indicated horsepower; power outputs were obtained up to 2,375 indicated horsepower. At a maximum drawbar power output of 2,200 horsepower, steam consumption was 20 pounds per horsepower-hour. For comparison, the highest power output ever recorded for a steam locomotive in Great Britain was 3,348 indicated horsepower, obtained during a dynamometer test of a Coronation class 4-6-2 express passenger engine on the London, Midland & Scottish Railway on February 26, 1939.[336]

Steaming rates set at 37,000 to 38,000 pounds per hour produced 1,545 indicated horsepower in the E-6, 2,130 in the E-6s, a 37% improvement as a result of superheating and design development. The best obtainable efficiency improved through development from 24 pounds of steam per indicated horsepower-hour in the E-6 to 18 pounds in the production E-6s. The ultimate achievement of the E-6s was a coal consumption of 3.8 pounds per drawbar horsepower-hour.

Development of the 2-8-0 freight engine from the H-6 to the H-9s was still insufficient for the Pennsylvania's freight haulage; in 1914 the company brought out the L-1s 2-8-2, developed at Altoona and benefiting from work on the E-6s.[337]

The maximum steaming rate achieved in the H-9s boiler was 34,000 pounds per hour at a firing rate of 8,000 pounds per hour, although forcing the boiler to that extent drove evaporative efficiency down to only 4.25 pounds of water per pound of coal. The L-1s, with a bigger boiler, reached 60,000 pounds per hour; somehow the test plant crew managed to throw 12,000 pounds of coal per hour into the firebox, although evaporative efficiency was down to 5 pounds of water per pound of coal. Here, however, was an almost inexhaustible boiler, able to supply steam at full throttle and 80% cut-off at speeds up to 18 miles per hour. Maximum power output of 2,837 indicated horsepower in the L-1s was achieved at 60% cut-off and 30 miles per hour.

The L-1s and H-9s both achieved a fuel efficiency of about 2.5 pounds of coal per indicated horsepower-hour, but this was at 1,700 indicated horsepower in the L-1s, compared to only 750 indicated horsepower in the H-9s. Both locomotives were highly efficient, the L-1s consuming 19 pounds of steam per indicated horsepower-hour at 2,300 indicated horsepower; the H-9s achieved 18 pounds at 1,200 indicated horsepower.

The vast engineering and manufacturing complex at Altoona, employing 15,000 men, lay behind the Pennsylvania's legendary success in locomotive engineering. Among its outstanding successes were the E-6s 4-4-2, the K-4s 4-6-2, the H-class 2-8-0s, the L-1s 2-8-2, the I-1s 2-10-0 and the M-1 4-8-2. The test plant enabled the Pennsylvania to develop locomotive designs in ways that even Alco

A Pennsylvania class L-1s 2-8-2 at Wilkinsburg, Pennsylvania, on September 30, 1930. The massive structure of the Commonwealth trailing truck is plainly visible (Denver Public Library, Otto C. Perry collection, OP-14270).

and Baldwin could not match, but were glad to imitate. The USRA construction program does not seem to have used the Altoona plant directly but certainly the USRA designs owed much to both Purdue and Altoona.

7.7.2 Performance Calculations

7.7.2.1 Locomotive Performance[338]

The increasingly vast body of test data from static and road tests, gathered at great cost from the 1890s onward, had two very concrete purposes: locomotive development, as we have seen, but also the calculation of what tonnage an existing locomotive should haul over a given route and how much fuel it would burn in doing so.

The American Railway Engineering and Maintenance of Way Association produced a landmark report on tractive effort and train resistance at their 1910 annual meeting as part of a study of the economics of railroad location. By then, enough information had accumulated for the Association to publish a single table of steam generation in pounds per square foot of heating surface per hour for various firing rates, ratios of heating surface to grate area, boiler pressures and calorific values of coal. Enough was known about the ability of various types of locomotive to convert pounds of steam into horsepower-hours for the complete chain of parameters from firing rate to tractive effort to be worked out by calculation and tables.

Tractive effort was easily calculated from the locomotive's dimensions. The speed, typically 5 to 10 miles per hour, beyond which the boiler could not supply steam fast enough to fill the cylinders at full throttle and full forward gear, was also easy enough to calculate. Beyond that, dynamometer and static tests told the story of what happened to tractive effort at higher speeds, but predictive formulae were lacking or produced results unsupported by experience.

Data from many sources increased awareness of the locomotive's own resistance, caused by internal friction, power consumed in overcoming the inertia of reciprocating parts, and the rolling resistance of driving wheels, trucks and tenders.[339] These losses consumed roughly 5% to 15% of the tractive effort delivered by the cylinders. Here the Mallets performed poorly. They were too big to be tested on any of the static test plants, so their internal resistance could be determined only from road tests. A Pennsylvania 0-8-8-0 tested at 5,100 pounds of drawbar pull just to overcome its own friction, the Norfolk & Western and Erie 0-8-8-0s at 7,300–7,600 pounds, the Norfolk & Western 2-8-8-2s at 10,350 pounds. This contrasted with 1,500 to 3,000 pounds for rigid-frame engines. These losses increased with speed. At 40 revolutions per minute (7 miles per hour for 56-inch driving wheels) 77% to 94% of the cylinder power appeared at the drawbar (depending on the type of locomotive), declining to 62% to 87% at 280 revolutions per minute (47 miles per hour for 56-inch driving wheels). This power loss was unpredictable, as it could be halved or doubled by nothing more than the viscosity of lubricants (which varied with temperature) and the quality of lubrication.

By the time of World War I, enough was known to plot the steam locomotive's characteristic relationship between speed, tractive effort and horsepower.

This issue took on increased importance as railroad officials became aware of the importance of the ton-mile per hour as a measure of productivity.

The Rock Island may have been one of the developers, in 1915, of a means of calculating "sustainable drawbar pull," the tractive effort that a locomotive could develop at any speed and ruling grade. This could be expressed as:

$$TE = ((0.8FPd^2S)/D) - W_G(20g + C) - 22.2W_D - 6W_T - Tr, \text{ where}$$

F was a speed factor to allow for the loss of mean effective pressure with increasing piston speed,

P was the maximum boiler pressure in pounds per square inch,

d was the cylinder diameter in inches,

S was the piston stroke in inches,

D was the diameter of the driving wheels in inches,

W_G was the loaded weight of the engine and tender in tons,

g was the percent of adverse grade,

C was the number of degrees of curvature,

W_D was the adhesion weight in tons,

W_T was the weight of the engine on the trucks,

T was the weight of the tender in tons and

r was the tender resistance per ton of its weight.

The Rock Island tabulated values of F and r.

By 1916, four formulae were current: the Baldwin, Kiesel, Williamson and American Railway Engineering Association. Of these, the Williamson formula came closest to replicating the tractive effort developed by a Pennsylvania H-8b on a dynamometer run. This formula considered heating surface, evaporation rate, steam consumption per horsepower at various speeds, quality of fuel and resistances. These calculations were worthwhile because:

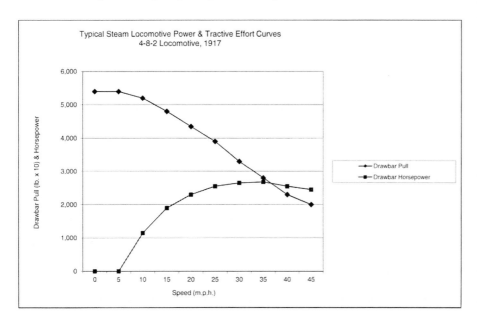

Typical Steam Locomotive Power & Tractive Effort Curves
4-8-2 Locomotive, 1917

Typical curves of steam locomotive power and tractive effort against speed. The example is a New York Central 4-8-2 (figures from *New York Central 4-8-2 Type Locomotives, RAG,* December 28, 1917, 1167).

If there is one thing which will decrease the pounds of coal per ton-mile it will be to get proper tonnage behind the locomotive.

Even so, for everything that mechanical engineers discovered about the steam locomotive, some further mystery receded into obscurity ahead of them.

B. B. Milner, Engineer of Motive Power on the New York Central, commented in 1919[340]:

> It is a fact recognized upon most divisions that with the same engine and the same train, some enginemen are able to handle trains over ruling grades or other difficult places, while others generally fail to do so. The successful men are unable to very clearly state how the successful performance is accomplished, while the unsuccessful men cannot explain any reason for failure, although they make every effort possible.

Milner pointed out that some engineers ran with the throttle fully open, some with partial throttle; at low speeds the throttle opening made little difference but this changed at higher speeds as steam friction took effect. The only other performance control available to the engineer was the reversing lever; Milner focused his attention on the effects of cut-off.

> It should be rather apparent that there is, for each speed, a cut-off at which the drawbar pull developed will be a maximum and that the drawbar pull developed for any other cut-off, either longer or shorter, will be less than that developed by the cut-offs which should be used under conditions where the maximum drawbar pull is necessary.

Throttles and cut-off levers were coarse controls, lacking fine adjustment, markings or calibration. The actual cut-off provided by any setting of the reversing lever was not necessarily what it was thought to be. Locomotives had no speedometers and almost no instrumentation.

Milner circulated a questionnaire to eighteen road foremen as to the best cut-off for each speed range, what was the recommended cut-off for 10 miles per hour and what was the actual percent cut-off in the first and ninth notches of the reversing lever. This produced eighteen different sets of answers, indicating only the vaguest understanding.

In 1919 Milner was a voice crying in the wilderness. Sixty thousand locomotives of hundreds of different types had no speedometers and no calibration or constancy between reverse lever settings and cut-offs. There was no means of calculating by formula the information that he had obtained from road tests and no possibility of running road tests for the diversity of conditions prevailing across the United States.

Milner's ideas led, not only to an examination of the best cut-off for each speed range, but to experiments in the 1920s with automatic cut-off control—a degree of sophistication that, though promising in economic benefits, never found its way into locomotive operation.

In parts of the northeast and the midwest, the railroads had developed far beyond their primitive beginnings to well-maintained, heavy-railed, straight, level, multiple tracks and signaling systems where trains could make very high speeds in safety. But now the steam locomotive was increasingly the obstacle to high-speed service.

The saturated steam boilers available in the early 1900s developed about ½ horsepower per square foot of heating surface. Thus, a boiler with 4,000 square feet of heating surface would develop 2,000 horsepower in the cylinders. At 100 miles per hour, this was equivalent to a tractive effort of only 7,500 pounds. Tests in Germany, where high-speed electric railcars reached speeds of 124 miles per hour between Berlin and Zossen, showed that air resistance increased as the square of the speed. The steam locomotive had an extremely poor aerodynamic shape and the German test results suggested that at 100 miles per hour a large passenger engine would encounter 3,500 pounds of air resistance. The internal friction of the engine added another 1,000 pounds, while the rolling friction of the engine and tender added a further 2,000 pounds, only 1,000 pounds remaining to overcome train resistance. If the friction and rolling resistance of a passenger car equaled 18 pounds per ton of weight, the locomotive could haul just one 55-ton car at 100 miles per hour on level track. Saturated steam imposed a practical limit of 70 to 80 miles per hour due to steam viscosity and extremely short valve events, leading to a build-up of back pressure and low mean effective pressure in the cylinders. All reciprocating steam locomotives had inherent problems reaching speeds much beyond 70 miles per hour (327 revolutions per minute for an engine with 72-inch driving wheels). When steam locomotives did reach very high speeds, pulling useful loads, it was achieved with superheated steam, as well as being a significant feat of engineering in other respects. The performance of the ultimate American steam locomotives of the 1930s and 1940s was all the more remarkable when viewed in this light.

7.7.2.2 Train Resistance[341]

Mirror image to tractive effort was the train resistance that the locomotive had to overcome. If train resistance could be estimated, then it was a simple matter to match the results against tractive effort. This was a large "if."

Train resistance could supposedly be calculated from empirical formulae with corrections for temperature, grade and curvature. By balancing locomotive tractive effort against train resistance, any type of locomotive could be rated for the tonnage it was supposed to be capable of

University of Illinois Test Plant, 1916
Illinois Central Saturated Steam 2-8-0
Two lowest speeds at 16% cut-off and two highest speeds at 48% cut-off extrapolated for graph generation.

The relationship between speed and steam consumption for different cut-offs. The speed/cut-off relationship for best economy was difficult to analyze and even more difficult to control (figures from *Tests of a Consolidation Type Locomotive*, RAG, March 10, 1916, 437).

hauling over any particular route. Train resistance, however, was a morass of complexity; something like a hundred different formulae attempted to describe and predict it. From the viewpoint of 1906:

> Many attempts have been made to determine a rational expression or formula for train resistance, but none has yet been devised, nor is it probable that any simple formula ever will be devised, that shall, correctly, give the quantity known as train resistance.

Too many independent and unpredictable variables applied—condition of journal bearings, weight on bearings, rail condition, weight on rail, condition of trackbed, temperature, wind speed and direction and train speed—for train resistance to be calculable easily, or indeed at all. A study in 1909 pointed to a surprisingly large number of independent and unpredictable variables governing even something as apparently simple as journal friction. It was not directly proportional to load; it also varied with speed, temperature, track curvature and lubrication.

Rolling resistance—each wheel of each moving car and locomotive was always climbing out of a depression in the track of its own making—varied with the relationship between car weight and rail weight. The New York Central found that freight train resistance on 65-pound rail was 7 to 8 pounds per ton, decreasing to 3½ pounds per ton on 80-pound rail. Although heavier cars supposedly had lower resistance per ton than lighter ones, in 1900, the New York, Ontario & Western was dismayed to find that engines hauling 55-ton cars stalled when loaded with the same tonnage in 70-ton cars. If heavy cars were hauled over light rail, rolling resistance could so increase as to negate the otherwise reduced resistance of the new, bigger car.

According to investigations by Professor Goss at Purdue, air resistance alone could consume 10% to 20% of the tractive effort of the locomotive when freight trains were moving at high speeds. In one case, with a freight train in western Kansas on a light grade:

> The wind was blowing about 25 miles an hour, but the train being protected from the full force of the wind by the bluff and foothills, made fairly good speed. Upon running out into the open country and crossing a trestle where the wind had a fair sweep at the train the resistance was sufficient to momentarily stall the train. For a few seconds there would be a lull in the wind and the engine would make some headway until a stronger gust of wind would strike the train and the engine would stall again. This was repeated for at least five times in the distance of 200 yds.

The speed:resistance relationship changed with the percentage of empty cars in a train. The resistance per ton was acknowledged to be higher for empty cars, but each railroad had its own ideas as to what allowance to make, ranging from 8% to 25%. This issue was so complicated that many railroads ignored it.[342]

The investigation of curve resistance turned out to be so complicated that the findings cannot be quoted here, but they included factors such as the swiveling forces on trucks, the grinding of rails and wheel flanges, the effects of rail super-elevation, centrifugal forces, endwise play between wheels and track and others.

In 1909, F. J. Cole produced a study of train resistance so detailed that even the general results were too voluminous to quote here.

Dynamometer test results were flawed when it came to predicting train resistance. As late as 1913:

> Many miles have been run with dynamometer cars, but few real results have been obtained which give reliable data concerning train resistance…. The verdict is, generally, that the only way to make a rating is to try different loadings until the correct one is found, and then use it.

The detailed formulae were either erroneous or unusable. By 1915, railroadmen responsible for tonnage rating were using a crude approximation:

$$R = V + 20g + C$$

where R was the train resistance in pounds per ton of train weight, V was the rolling resistance in pounds per ton weight of car, g was the percentage of adverse grade and C was the number of degrees of curvature. Where the train resistance exceeded the locomotive's tractive effort, helper service would be necessary. Railroads using tonnage rating also used adjustment actors to allow for the effects of wind, weather and low temperatures.

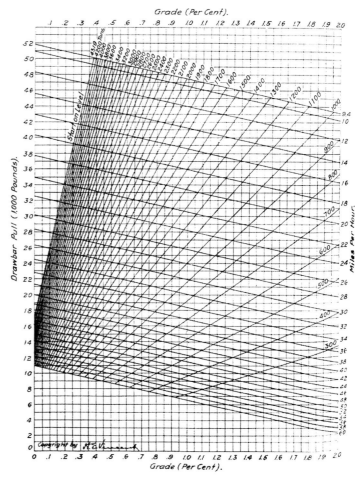

Typical tonnage rating chart, for a 1918 USRA light Mikado (Vincent, H. S., *Tonnage Rating of the Standard Locomotives,* **RA, October 4, 1918, 627. RA published a tonnage rating chart for each USRA class).**

The ever-increasing volume of data on train resistance and tractive effort permitted an increasingly wide application of tonnage rating systems and a correspondingly smaller margin left to judgement. The war effort and nationalization of the railroads brought with it the hope that standard locomotives and freight cars would lead to all-encompassing systems of tables, graphs and formulae. By 1918 the tonnage rating of locomotives had progressed far enough so that a tonnage rating chart was issued for each of the USRA standard types.

8

Locomotive Construction, 1905–1920

The years between 1905 and 1920 witnessed the all-time numerical peak in U.S. locomotive construction.

The Alco merger was a big success, increasing market share from 40% at the time of the merger to 57% only nine years later; Baldwin retained 38% of the market, while 4% of orders went to company shops. (Figures are for locomotives ordered; numbers ordered and built would differ in any one year.) Lima supplied 1% of the market. This period was Lima's nadir; the Shay was losing its competition with the Heisler for the geared-engine market; in 1910, Heisler sold thirty-two of their geared engines, while Lima sold but eight Shays. This state of affairs probably drove Lima's determined irruption into the rod engine market that was to bear such brilliant fruit fifteen years away in the future.

Lima had built rod engines in ones and twos since 1879, typically narrow-gauge for coal, quarry, logging, smelter and factory systems, increasing in size and number after 1900.[1] In 1909, it built a 148,000-pound 2-8-0 for the Southern Utah Railroad.[2] Its first order from a Class I railroad was five 0-6-0s for the Erie in 1911. Companies, such as the Pennsylvania, the Erie, the Delaware, Lackawanna & Western and the New York Central began to figure in the company's order books from then onward, culminating with five 2-8-8-2 Mallets for the Western Maryland in 1915–16. Lima bankrupted itself trying to undercut Alco and Baldwin; the Mallets, vast and unfamiliar to the company, may have contributed to this condition. Hirsimaki writes[3]: "What had begun as a bold venture into big-time locomotive building had turned sour," but offers no elaboration. The company went through two reorganizations in 1916, emerging as the Lima Locomotive Works, with William E. Woodard as Vice-President of Engineering. This laid the foundations for the company's future success.

A minority of railroad companies built their own locomotives, notably the Pennsylvania. The old Altoona shops built 2,289 locomotives between 1866 and 1904; the new Juniata shops built a further 4,584 between 1891 and 1946.[4] In one year (1910) the Pennsylvania built 105 locomotives of six different classes,[5] while the Milwaukee built a hundred of its own engines the same year, including twenty-five 2-8-0s and twenty-five 2-8-2s, while ordering fifty more from Alco and another fifty from Baldwin. The Louisville & Nashville built full-scale construction capability into its new South Louisville shops between 1902 and 1905, building 400 locomotives between 1905 and 1923.[6] These engines—2-8-0s, 0-6-0 switchers converted from older 2-8-0s, new 0-8-0 switchers, 4-6-2s and 2-8-2s—were as advanced in design and as powerful in service as anything produced by Alco or Baldwin.

In 1910, 38% of new construction was still 2-8-0s; another 17% was 4-6-2s; 12% was 0-6-0 switchers and 7% was Mallets.[7] Smaller railroads and industrial lines continued to order new 4-4-0s (2%), 4-4-2s (1%), 2-6-0s (2%) and 4-6-0s (6%), although they also could buy used engines of these types as the majors discarded them. The Norfolk & Western continued its adherence to the 4-8-0. No

2-10-2s were built in that year; 2-8-2s comprised only 3% of new construction. Construction of rigid-frame compounds had ceased, except for a single 4-10-0 built by Alco for the Butte, Anaconda & Pacific. (This could be a misprint; the 4-10-0 wheel arrangement is practically unknown.)

This profile changed markedly by 1915. In that year Lima secured 18% of a far smaller market, building 247 engines; thirty-two Shays outnumbered Heislers by four to one. Company shops built 12% of new construction. In five years, one quarter of the market had gone to Lima and company shops; Alco took the brunt of this shift, possibly because of Alco engineers going to Lima, while Baldwin retained a 37% market share. Of new construction, 38% was now 2-8-2s and 11% 2-8-0s; no other wheel arrangement accounted for more than 10% of the new-build total. 2-10-2s were beginning to appear in force (75 engines, 5% of total). New Mallets were only half as numerous (120, 8%) as they were in 1910 (243).

While the Class I railroads ordered locomotives in batches as large as 25 to 30, most orders were for ones and twos. In 1915, 234 U.S. companies ordered locomotives, ranging from the Pennsylvania to the Quanah, Acme & Pacific. Mining, logging and construction sites ran railroad systems powered by surprisingly large locomotives. A 2-8-2 built by Baldwin in 1914 worked for a logging company and then for the Carlton & Coast Railroad, before being bought by the Tonopah & Goldfield in 1945. It probably still had life in it when it was scrapped on closure of the line in 1948. In 1928, Alco built a 259,000-pound 2-8-2 for Denkmann Lumber, fully the equal of locomotives being built for the Class I railroads.[8] Denkmann sold this engine to the Louisiana & Arkansas in 1934.

While World War I raged in Europe, the years 1915–18 saw a remarkable flowering of American locomotive design and construction. From a peak of 7,362 engines built in the U.S. and Canada in 1907, construction fell by two thirds in the wake of the 1907 financial panic, rising to a new peak of 5,332 in 1913 with the recovery in business. Again, slack economic conditions in 1914 cut production to only 2,085 in 1915. Increasing American involvement in the European war drove production to 4,075 in 1916 and a new high of 6,475 in 1918.

There was also a large trade in used locomotives in ones and twos. A steam locomotive had a useful life of thirty to forty years; some of the 4-4-0s, 2-6-0s and 4-6-0s that hauled the light traffic of small railroads outlasted the bigger engines that were worn out in Class I service. The small companies supplied their needs with a mixture of new and used engines. When they were finished with them, they sold them on to factories, logging lines or construction contractors.

The Wisconsin & Michigan, for example, bought a new 4-6-0 from Baldwin in 1895, but returned it when it turned out to be too heavy for the company's track. Baldwin resold this engine to the Randsburg Railway in Nevada which, in turn, sold it to the Santa Fe; the Santa Fe sold it to the Tonopah & Tidewater in 1905 (two different sources give three different dates; 1905 seems the most probable), where it was scrapped in 1941. The Wisconsin & Michigan bought a used 2-6-0 in 1918 and sold it to a local logging company in 1926. In 1922, the company bought two new 4-6-0s from Baldwin and sold them to the Atlantic & East Carolina in 1937.[9]

It is not easy from the available records to see what a typical company's locomotive fleet consisted of at any one time; the Northern Pacific roster for 1909–1910 is therefore instructive.[10] In 1909, the company owned 1,353 locomotives. They still owned three 0-4-0 switchers; the 183 0-6-0s were more typical; the NP also owned nine big 0-8-0 switchers. The older 4-4-0 and 2-6-0 types were well represented, respectively 137 and 142 being on the company's books, although ten 4-4-0s and three 2-6-0s were disposed of during the year. One hundred forty-five 2-8-0s hauled freight, two being disposed of during the year. By far the most common type was the multi-purpose 4-6-0 with 292 in service. The Northern Pacific was also a big user of 2-6-2s, owning 150. The curiosities were two 2-10-0s, four 4-8-0s and six 4-4-2s. The 2-10-0s and 4-8-0s may have been experiments or were taken over with acquired lines. The company bought the 4-4-2s for fast passenger service over its limited areas of flat terrain. Procurement in 1909–1910 showed where the company was going. Forty-four 4-6-2s for fast, heavy passenger service over the mountains were added to the eighty already owned. The 2-8-2s were already well established for heavy freight haulage, with 180 owned and forty added. For freight service in the mountains, six 2-6-6-2 Mallets were added to the sixteen already owned, while five 2-8-8-2s set new standards in heavy power. In twelve months the Northern Pacific added 120 large locomotives to its fleet, with 1,456 engines in service by mid–1910.

In 1912, the company owned 1,433 engines.[11] Most numerous were still the 4-6-0s (289) and 2-8-2s (220). Besides these, 2-6-0s (138), 2-8-0s (142), 4-4-0s (103, twenty-one disposed of during the year), 4-6-2s (142) and 2-6-2s (150) made up the bulk of the road engine fleet. Of these engines twenty-one were oil burners; only ninety-nine were superheated. Even though new types came on apace in the early 1900s, the bulk of the company's fleet dated back ten years or more.

By 1914, although the company was retrofitting superheaters, still only 17% of its fleet was superheated.[12] In two years, forty-three 4-4-0s, thirty-three 2-6-0s, twenty-four 2-8-0s and twelve 4-6-0s disappeared—sold, scrapped or withdrawn pending sale; fifty 2-8-2s and ten 2-8-8-2s were added, bringing the fleet down to 1,357.

Similar to the Northern Pacific in the size of its locomotive fleet (1,165 locomotives), but very different in its traffic characteristics was the New Haven,[13] hauling dense traffic over relatively level terrain. As late as 1915, small 4-4-0s averaging only 17,300 pounds of tractive effort, were still the most numerous type, 367 in service, followed by 2-6-0 freight engines, 343 in service, averaging 28,000 pounds tractive effort. Besides the 4-4-0s, passenger types predominated with 106 4-6-0s, twelve 4-4-2s and eighty-eight 4-6-2s. Heavy freight power was represented by only thirty-five 2-8-0s, with twenty-eight 2-8-2s added in 1915–16. The 4-6-2s averaged 36,000 pounds tractive effort, but the company had no need for the massive freight engines in service elsewhere. Even though most newly built engines were superheated, the great majority of the fleet predated superheat and had never been retrofitted, only 10% of the New Haven's fleet being superheated. The Northern Pacific was slightly more active in this regard, with 22% of its fleet superheated by 1916.[14]

The Missouri, Kansas & Texas, with 678 locomotives in 1916, was probably typical of many railroad companies all over the U.S. that did not have to cope with extremes of grades or traffic[15]:

Type	Quantity	Tractive effort (lb.)
4-4-0	32	15,400
4-6-0	87	27,000
4-6-2	39	36,200
2-6-0	204	28,900
2-8-0	70	35,100
2-8-2	105	55,500

The company rebuilt a total of 586 engines in 1915–16, a large number compared to the total fleet size.

U.S. builders produced enormous numbers of locomotives during World War I to U.S. Government orders for overseas service and to orders from foreign railroads. Between 1915 and 1918 inclusive, these orders totaled 10,857 locomotives, compared to only 9,800 from domestic buyers.

By 1920, Lima's share of the 1,930 engines built had slipped slightly to 15%; Alco made a comeback to 45%; Baldwin remained steady with 35%. The 2-8-2s dominated new construction at 33%, followed by 4-6-2s (11%), 0-6-0s (11%) and 2-10-2s (9%). Heavy 0-8-0 switchers now accounted for 8% of construction; 2-8-0s still accounted for 7%. After a complete slump in 1920, locomotive building picked up as companies went back to specifying their own designs to deal with the rising traffic demands of the 1920s.

Even though a locomotive was built at a single plant, it could incorporate components, such as brakes, brake shoes, safety valves, headlights, bell ringers, sanders, lubricators, firebox doors, even boiler lagging, from as many as fifteen to twenty different specialty suppliers. This supply industry increased in size and diversity over the years.

Section 8.1. Passenger Locomotives

In 1905, the 4-4-0 was still the most numerous passenger locomotive type. The two-wheel trailing axle, at first rigidly mounted in the frame, later a truck, supporting a big firebox, brought about the 4-4-2 which remained an important passenger type in areas of level terrain and numerous short trains. Long trains, steel cars, heavy grades and fast schedules outclassed the four-coupled locomotive, producing an insatiable demand for high power at high speed. The 4-6-2 became the standard heavy passenger engine; heavy and light 4-6-2s were among the twelve standard classes designed by the USRA. The ultimate high-power locomotive of the time was the 4-8-2, first introduced on the Chesapeake & Ohio in 1911.

8.1.1 Obsolescent Types:
4-4-0s, 4-6-0s, 2-6-0s and 2-6-2s

The 4-4-0 and 4-6-0 continued to meet the demands of some railroads, while the 2-6-2 continued its brief vogue. Construction of these types continued, but in declining numbers.

Large areas of America were served by little-known railroads, hauling light trains over flat country. Thus, in 1904, the Chicago Southern ordered forty engines from Alco, comprising twenty 4-6-0s, twelve 2-6-0s and eight 4-4-0s.[16] The 2-6-0s had boiler pressures of only 160 pounds per square inch, while the other two classes used 180 pounds per square inch steam.

In 1905, the Delaware, Lackawanna & Western bought two 4-4-0s from Alco, soon increased to twelve.[17] These were camelback engines with Wootten fireboxes, but they were equipped with Cole superheaters. A high-set Wootten firebox with an 85-square foot grate, extending over the small driving wheels, bypassed the need for a trailing truck, allowing more weight to go into adhesion; heavy track accommodated axle loadings of 50,000 pounds.

In 1905, the New Haven ordered twenty-two four-cylinder, balanced compound 4-6-0s from Baldwin. The New Haven suddenly lost faith in this arrangement; it reduced the order for balanced compounds to two[18]—and rebuilt them to two-cylinder, single-expansion in 1912 and 1924—but bought fifty conventional 4-6-0s between 1904 and 1907.

In 1905, the Delaware, Lackawanna & Western bought five super-heated 4-6-0s from Alco, said to be the first engines of the type to develop 35,000 pounds of tractive effort[19]; the Lehigh Valley bought ten 4-6-0s from Alco, of similar appearance but not superheated.[20]

The Central of New Jersey bought three heavy (158,000 pounds)

Alco built this 4-4-0, No. 950, for the Delaware, Lackawanna & Western 4-4-0 in 1905, photographed at Hoboken, New Jersey, on October 29, 1927 (Denver Public Library, Otto C. Perry collection, OP-7325).

Alco built this 4-6-0, No. 1013, for the Delaware, Lackawanna & Western in 1906, photographed at Hoboken, New Jersey, in 1917 (Denver Public Library, Otto C. Perry collection, OP-7328).

camel-back 4-4-0s with Wootten fireboxes to replace 4-6-0s on 67 miles with grades up to 1.2% and sharp curves between Bethlehem and Scranton, Pennsylvania, because of the track damage caused by the 4-6-0s.[21] These engines were equipped with Walschaert valve gear. The frames were of cast steel. The back head and tube sheets were stayed to the boiler shell by diagonal plates, rather than long stay rods. Water tubes were incorporated into the grate structure ("water grates"). The unsuperheated boilers contained 2,005 square feet of heating surface.

The Burlington favored the 2-6-2. The class of fifty that they ordered from Alco in 1905 had some different features, however.[22] The 54-square foot grate was intended to burn lignite. To obtain proper combustion, 24 fire tubes in the top of the boiler were of 5 inches diameter, the same size as superheater flues, but no superheater was installed. The water legs widened from 4 inches at the mud ring to 9 inches at the top of the firebox to enhance water circulation.

By 1905, the New York Central already had 4-6-2s, but chose to

A Chicago, Burlington & Quincy class R-4 2-6-2, No. 1940, built by Alco in 1905, photographed at Derby, Colorado, in July 1918. The tender tank shows that this was an oil-burner (Denver Public Library, Otto C. Perry collection, OP-3616).

Alco built this class F-2 4-6-0, No. 2166, for the New York Central in 1908, photographed at Montreal, Quebec, on October 4, 1930 (Denver Public Library, Otto C. Perry collection, OP-13349).

order additional 4-6-0s from Alco; the 4-6-0s developed 9% more tractive effort than the 4-6-2s (31,000 pounds vs. 28,500 pounds) because, although they were lighter by 13½ tons (and probably cheaper in proportion), the adhesion weight was greater.[23] The New York Central was in an area of good water. Accordingly, the water legs were only 3½ inches wide at the foundation ring and 4 inches wide at the crown sheet. Four hundred fire tubes provided 3,100 square feet of heating surface in a 200-pounds per square inch boiler. Procurement increased to 102 of these engines by 1908.

The landmark Great Northern order for five 2-6-6-2 Mallets for delivery in 1906—the first user after the Baltimore & Ohio, and the first Mallets intended as road engines—was part of a larger order with Baldwin for fifty 2-6-2s, twenty 4-6-2s—all single-expansion— and ten balanced compound 4-4-2s.[24] The 2-6-2s and 4-6-2s had Walschaert valve gear. Cautiously, the Great Northern ordered one engine of each class fitted with a Baldwin smokebox superheater, which could be installed with minimal design changes. The 2-6-2s went to work hauling iron ore trains in Minnesota.

Engines with 2-6-0 and 4-6-0 wheel arrangements continued to be built because the absence of a trailing truck put a higher percentage of the engine weight into adhesion, typically 80% to 85%, compared to as little as 60% in a 4-6-2. This reasoning lay behind the construction of three heavy 2-6-0s for the Vandalia by Alco in 1906.[25] The 187,000-pound engines had the high axle loading of 53,100 pounds and developed 33,300 pounds of tractive effort. These engines were transitional in design: no superheat, no brick arch, Walschaert valve gear and 200 pounds per square inch boiler pressure. A shallow, but wide firebox provided 52 square feet of grate area.

In contrast with the Northern Pacific's cautious order for two engines in 1906, the Santa Fe bought fifty-six balanced compounds from Baldwin the same year.[26] These were 2-6-2s and, at 248,000 pounds, were the heaviest six-coupled engines built by Baldwin to date. Balancing the piston thrusts allowed the high axle loading of 58,230 pounds. With 225 pounds per square inch steam pressure, the engines developed 37,850 pounds of tractive effort. Total heating surface was 4,020 square feet. All four pistons drove the second driving axle, all four cylinders being in the same fore-and-aft line. This seems to have been Baldwin practice by contrast with Alco which built its four-cylinder compounds with the inside cylinders driving a different axle from the outside cylinders. These engines were intended to handle the growing traffic in Californian fruit and Oriental goods, such as silk, that demanded freight service through the mountains on schedules faster than express passenger trains only a few years before. Although these engines worked well enough for the company to increase orders to a total of eighty-eight, the Santa Fe rebuilt them to single expansion in the 1920s.

While companies such as the Great Northern were ordering 150 locomotives at a time, others functioned on a more modest scale[27]:

The Yosemite Valley has ordered one simple eight-wheel passenger locomotive from the Rogers Works of the American Locomotive Co. for April 15 (1907) delivery, and is considering the purchase of an additional locomotive.

This engine weighed 110,000 pounds. The oil-fired, unsuperheated boiler produced steam at 165 pounds per square inch from 1,700 square feet of heating surface. Tractive effort was a modest 17,650 pounds.

For comparison to American types, some of the most powerful express passenger engines in Britain at the time (1907) were the 4-cylinder 4-6-0s built by the Great Western Railway.[28] A 27-square foot grate fired a 225-pounds per square inch boiler containing 2,140 square feet of heating surface. Four 14-inch × 26-inch cylinders developed 23,780 pounds of tractive effort. Engine weight was 172,000 pounds. Engines of this type remained in mainline service with only minor development until the 1960s.

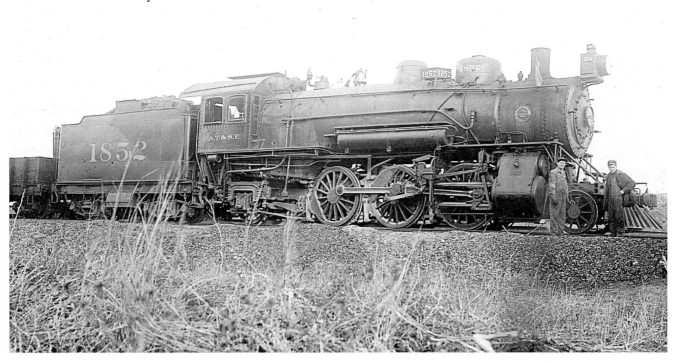

Baldwin built this 1800 class 2-6-2, No. 1852, for the Atchison, Topeka & Santa Fe in 1906 as a balanced compound. Otto Perry photographed it at Littleton, Colorado, in 1918 (Denver Public Library, Otto C. Perry collection, OP-581).

Small companies and light traffic still needed new 4-4-0s.[29] The Atlanta, Birmingham & Atlantic ordered six of them from Baldwin in 1909. These were substantial engines. Steam pressure was 200 pounds per square inch. A 34-square foot grate fired 2,215 square feet of heating surface. Total engine weight was 143,000 pounds;

tractive effort would have been 22,400 pounds. Four were ordered with Walschaert valve gear and two with Pilliod gear.

The 4-6-0 wheel arrangement continued well liked in the years around 1910. Both the Chicago Great Western and the Great Northern ordered them from Baldwin at that time.[30] The Chicago Great

A Great Northern class E-14 4-6-0, No. 1084, built by Baldwin in 1909, photographed at Shelby, Montana, on May 13, 1934 (Denver Public Library, Otto C. Perry collection, OP-11816).

One of the last new 4-4-0s, the Philadelphia & Reading class D-11s, No. 419, built by Baldwin in 1914, photographed at Bridgeport, Pennsylvania, in 1938 (courtesy California State Railroad Museum, Negative 900_26201).

Western ordered four with Emerson superheaters. The Great Northern ordered heavy and light versions, twenty of each. All three batches were superheated; all had boiler pressures of only 150 pounds per square inch. Baldwin believed that the increased power provided by a superheater made it possible to lower the boiler pressure and obtain the benefits of a lighter boiler.

Philadelphia & Reading traffic in the New York area consisted of numerous, light passenger trains, hauled over short distances with slight gradients and demanding schedules. Here the nimble 4-4-0 still reigned supreme.[31] When the company bought 4-4-0s in 1883, most other railroads were doing the same; when the company was still buying this type in 1914, eyebrows were raised and the 4-4-0 was an unusual design for a particular purpose.

The Philadelphia & Reading 4-4-0s of 1883 were typical of their time, using saturated steam at 140 pounds per square inch, weighing 93,000 pounds and developing 14,600 pounds of tractive effort. A 68-square foot grate, sized for anthracite, fired 1,015 square feet of heating surface. The 1914 version was just under twice the weight and developed twice the tractive effort. An 86-square foot grate fired 1,520 square feet of heating surface, supplying superheated steam at 210 pounds per square inch. Cylinder and driving wheel dimensions were closely similar. The new 4-4-0s made extensive use of steel components and were visibly different in having Walschaert valve gear. Although the valve gear weighed nothing like as much as the 2-10-2s and Mallets of other lines, a Ragonnet power reverser eased the engineer's task and made for a nimble engine.

The last 4-4-0s to be built were for the Chicago & Illinois Midland in 1928.[32] The last 2-6-0s were built at that time, by the Southern Pacific at its Houston shops. By contrast, the last 2-6-2s were built in 1909 for the Milwaukee. One 4-6-0 was built in 1925, but this must have been among the last of its kind.

The Canadian Pacific Railway ran its last regularly scheduled steam-hauled passenger train in 1960; the engine was a 4-4-0 built in 1887. Considering their formerly vast numbers, few of this type remain in operating condition.

8.1.2 Heyday of the Atlantics

The early 1900s were the heyday of the 4-4-2; although a significant advance over the 4-4-0, the increasing weight of passenger trains soon made four-coupled locomotives obsolete.

The four-cylinder balanced compound 4-4-2 that Alco built for the Erie in 1905 was the heaviest of its kind built to date, at 206,000 pounds engine weight.[33] Axle loading reached a new high at 57,500 pounds, prompted by the balanced compound's low dynamic augment. Tests on a Cole-type four-cylinder balanced compound 4-4-2 on the Pennsylvania's test plant at St. Louis in 1904 had shown that dynamic augment was so reduced by this new arrangement that this very high axle loading was permissible.

The Philadelphia & Reading had a long-standing reputation for fast passenger service. In 1909 the company built an atypical, three-cylinder single-expansion 4-4-2 at its Reading shops to the design of the Motive Power Superintendent, H. D. Taylor.[34] Typical of anthracite-burners, the engine had a Wootten firebox and camelback cab. The outside piston valves were driven by Walschaert valve gear, while the inside cylinder's piston valve was driven by Joy gear, a rare instance of two different valve gears being employed on the same engine. The engine was heavy for a 4-4-2 at 207,000 pounds and had 80-inch driving wheels.

Four-cylinder, rigid-frame, single-expansion locomotives were common in Britain, but in America they were extremely rare. The two built by Alco for the Chicago, Rock Island & Pacific in 1909 were advanced for their time.[35] The Rock Island had already adopted superheating and had eight 4-4-2 four-cylinder balanced compounds, acquired from Baldwin in 1905–6.[36] Seeking to combine the benefits

The Philadelphia & Reading built this class P-6s three-cylinder 4-4-2, No. 300, in company shops in 1909 (courtesy California State Railroad Museum, Negative 900_26180).

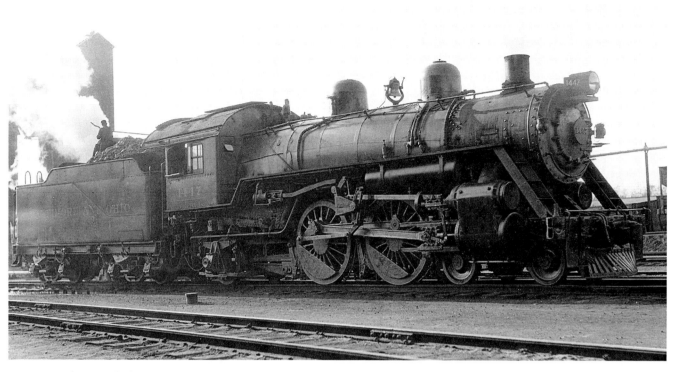

Otto Perry photographed this Baltimore & Ohio class A-3 4-4-2, No. 1447, built by Alco in 1910, at Washington, DC, on October 20, 1930 (Denver Public Library, Otto C. Perry collection, OP-2423).

of superheating and balancing, the company bought two superheated, four-cylinder engines, notably abandoning compounding.

As a type, 4-4-2s were fast, used for hauling express passenger trains over flat country. At speed, however, dynamic augment was severe, especially as high axle loadings were needed to obtain tractive effort sufficient for the new steel passenger cars. In a conventional 4-4-2 running at 85 miles per hour, a static axle loading of 52,900 pounds ranged between 30,140 pounds and 75,660 pounds with each revolution of the driving wheels (± 43%), due to dynamic augment. The effect was even worse when considering the action of each driving wheel separately as the locomotive rocked from side to side. At 85 miles per hour, a static wheel loading of 26,450 pounds varied between 10,350 and 42,550 pounds (±61%) with each revolution. The four-cylinder balanced 4-4-2s reduced these percentages to 2% and 23% respectively.

The Rock Island compared their new 4-4-2s in regular service with a two-cylinder, unsuperheated, single-expansion 4-4-2 and a four-cylinder balanced compound of the same wheel arrangement. They were 17% more fuel efficient than the single-expansion engine and 8% more efficient than the balanced compound. Maintenance costs were similar for all three classes of engine. The order was not, however, repeated.

The 4-4-2 continued in favour for its simplicity and low internal friction, accompanied by ever-rising axle loads, wherever traffic permitted. In 1910, the Baltimore & Ohio, its heavy traffic and heavy grades notwithstanding, bought twenty-six from Baldwin.[37] The trailing axle supported a 56-square foot grate. Twenty-six-inch cylinders were supplied through 14-inch piston valves, driven by Walschaert valve gear. All four driving wheels were equalized with the trailing truck; the leading truck was independently sprung. Engine weight was 190,000 pounds, a remarkable 58,000 pounds on each axle; with

a boiler pressure of 205 pounds per square inch, tractive effort was 27,400 pounds.

Never shy about ordering innovative engines in large numbers, the Santa Fe owned 171 balanced compound 4-4-2s by 1910, including twenty-three received from Baldwin in that year.[38] The engines of this type built in 1909 were fitted with both superheaters and reheaters; the batch delivered in 1910 curiously had no superheaters, but retained the reheaters.

The Buck-Jacobs reheater was a 48-inch long section let into the boiler immediately behind the smokebox, containing 417 fire tubes. A space, 30 inches long, was let into the boiler between the reheater and the front tube sheet to provide maintenance access to the front tube sheet, although this reduced the possible length of the fire tubes to 14 feet 6 inches. The engines were built with Jacobs-Shupert fireboxes. H. W. Jacobs was Assistant Superintendent of Motive Power at the time.

The boiler was fitted with two steam domes and a sand dome. Live steam, at the high pressure of 220 pounds per square inch, was collected in the rear dome and conveyed by two parallel 5-inch dry pipes to the front dome where the throttle valve was located. From the front dome, an external dry pipe mounted over the boiler centerline ran forward to just behind the stack, where it split in a T, with branches running down to the high-pressure cylinders. The front driving axle drove Walschaert valve gear, but reversed, with the expansion links between the two driving wheels.

In a typical four-cylinder balanced compound, one piston valve sufficed to control the flow of steam into the high-pressure cylinder, directly from the high-pressure into the low-pressure cylinder and from the low-pressure cylinder to exhaust, with no reheater between the cylinder pairs. In these engines, an ingenious design of the piston valve and steam passages controlled steam flow through the reheater

Baldwin built the 1452 class 4-4-2s for the Atchison, Topeka & Santa Fe in 1909–10. By the time Otto Perry photographed No. 1457 at Albuquerque, New Mexico, on April 28, 1934, it had been rebuilt to single-expansion with Walschaert valve gear. Note the coal pusher on the tender and the Ragonnet power reverser above the rear driving wheel (Denver Public Library, Otto C. Perry collection, OP-463).

AnAtchison, Topeka & Santa Fe 1480 class 4-4-2, No. 1480, built by Baldwin in 1910, photographed at Topeka, Kansas, on October 13, 1921. By that date, it had been rebuilt to single expansion. Note the reversed Walschaert valve gear (Denver Public Library, Otto C. Perry collection, OP-476).

as well. The valve body had six sets of piston rings, four on one piston, two on the other, but grooved between piston rings so that the effect was of six pistons. The steam chest was pierced by seven ports, four at one end, three at the other. At each end of the valve stroke live steam passed through an annular space between piston rings into the 15-inch high-pressure cylinder. At the same time, steam exhausting from the opposite end of the high-pressure cylinder passed through the valve body to the reheater. Steam from the reheater went past the end of the valve body into the 25-inch low-pressure cylinder. Exhaust from the opposite end of the low-pressure cylinder passed through another annular space between piston rings to exhaust.

These were substantial engines for their wheel arrangement. A 48-square foot grate fired a boiler containing 2,500 square feet of heating surface. The 231,700-pound engines developed 23,800 pounds of tractive effort.

The Pennsylvania's E-6 4-4-2 express engine first emerged from the company's Juniata shops in December 1910,[39] with immediate success. A 55-square foot grate fired a large boiler with 460 fire tubes providing 3,580 square feet of heating surface, generating steam at 205 pounds per square inch. A small combustion chamber extended 42 inches ahead of the firebox. Tractive effort was 25,800 pounds. Water legs 5 inches wide at the mud ring flared to 8 inches at the crown sheet of the Belpaire firebox, allowing for a free escape of steam and circulation of water. Cylinders of 22-inch bore, driving 80-inch wheels, made for a fast engine. The Pennsylvania tested the first and only E-6 at Altoona. In 1912, the engine went back to Juniata for the addition of superheating and an increase in cylinder diameter to 23 inches. The same year, the company built two more prototypes: an

E-6s similar to the modified E-6 and an E-6sa with rotary valves and Young-Averill valve gear (subsequently removed).[40] These three prototypes were the basis for the E-6s.

The year 1914 saw the first series production of the E-6s.[41] The new engines, designed at Altoona and built in the Juniata shops, were hailed as "The most advanced locomotive design in America at the present time…." The engine weighed 240,000 pounds, 133,100 pounds on driving wheels, for an axle loading of 66,550 pounds. This very high axle loading was made possible partly by the Pennsylvania's track construction on the routes where the engines were to be used, but also by careful counterbalancing and design to reduce the weight of reciprocating parts to less than 1,000 pounds per side. The piston rods and crank pins were made of heat-treated steel, bored hollow to save weight. On most 4-4-2s the suspension of the driving wheels and trailing truck were equalized, with the front truck being independently equalized. In the E-6s, the front truck was equalized with the front pair of driving wheels, the trailing truck with the rear pair. The E-6s class totaled only eighty-two locomotives, compared to 425 K-4s 4-6-2s, but their fame outran their numbers.

The 4-4-2 was effective enough in the service for which it was designed that such users as the Pennsylvania, the Santa Fe and the Southern Pacific kept them in service into the 1950s. Last to be built were the Milwaukee's in 1937.

8.1.3 The 4-4-4

At the 1915 ARMMA convention at Atlantic City, New Jersey, the Philadelphia & Reading unveiled an astonishing leap in locomotive design.[42] This engine was a 4-4-4 express passenger locomotive built

The Philadelphia & Reading's revolutionary but unsuccessful class C-1a 4-4-4, No. 110, built in the company shops at Reading, Pennsylvania, in 1915. The locomotive is obviously new and on display at Reading (courtesy California State Railroad Museum, Negative 900_26137).

by the Reading in its own shops at Reading, Pennsylvania. A Wootten firebox with a 108-square foot grate was supported on a four-wheel trailing truck, interchangeable with the leading truck. Even for burning anthracite, this was the biggest grate area ever applied to a passenger locomotive. A combustion chamber extended 39 inches ahead of the throat sheet. The axle loading was 73,100 pounds, allowing the development of 36,600 pounds of tractive effort. With 80-inch driving wheels, the engine was built for speed. In spite of great effort put into lightness of construction, the engine weighed 231,000 pounds. For the first time, aluminum was used to save weight in the crosshead shoes, main steam valves, valve stem crosshead, hand reversing wheel, cab window frames and smokebox door clips. Heat-treated chromium-nickel steel was used for rods, axles, crosshead guides, pistons, piston rods and other small parts. Axles were hollow. Weight saved in rotating and reciprocating parts reduced dynamic augment and allowed extra weight to be put into the boiler. With a boiler pressure of 240 pounds per square inch, one of the highest ever used in America, this was an important consideration. The reverser for the Walschaert valve gear was cable-operated by a hand wheel. The company built four of these engines in 1915; even though the Reading rebuilt them as 4-4-2s the following year, the American locomotive industry took note of the new design features.

8.1.4 Growth of the Pacifics

John E. Muhlfeld, Superintendent of Motive Power with the Baltimore & Ohio, designed a handsome 4-6-2; the company ordered a prototype from Alco in 1905.[43] A 56-square foot grate with a brick arch fired a boiler carrying the abnormally high pressure of 225 pounds per square inch, with 3,415 square feet of heating surface.

The 20 feet over tube sheets was long for that time. Stephenson valve gear drove piston valves supplying 22-inch × 28-inch cylinders. Weighing 229,500 pounds, these engines developed 35,000 pounds of tractive effort.

Designed for fast acceleration, while hauling heavy, long-distance passenger trains through the mountainous country on the Maryland-Pennsylvania border, these engines were the biggest and most powerful of their type in existence at the time. The generously sized grate was for burning cheap grades of bituminous coal. The boiler was designed for the free circulation of water and passage of gases, concepts that were still little understood at the time. They were also of rugged design with reliability and ease of maintenance in mind and were capable of hauling a 950-ton train at 10 miles per hour up a 1% grade, developing 924 horsepower. The company ordered thirty-five of these engines.

On a more modest scale, the Louisville & Nashville took delivery of five 4-6-2s, class K-1, from Alco Rogers in 1905.[44] These resembled the class G-13 4-6-0s that they were designed to replace, themselves a new class in 1903, only two years before. The 4-6-2s provided an immediate 37% bigger grate by supporting the firebox on a trailing axle.

Buying locomotives from a manufacturer was only a hiatus in the company's policy to build its own; the new shops at South Louisville built a further twenty K-1's in 1906–07, followed by twenty class K-2's in 1909–10. Both classes used saturated steam; the K-2's differed from the K-1's mainly in having Walschaert valve gear and piston valves, instead of Stephenson gear and slide valves.

Most of these engines were later retrofitted with superheaters; the K-1's were retrofitted with piston valves and Walschaert gear and had

First of a line of handsome Baltimore & Ohio express locomotives, this class P 4-6-2, No. 5000, was built by Alco in 1906. By the time Otto Perry photographed it at Washington, DC, on October 20, 1930, it had been rebuilt, Walschaert valve gear and an electric headlight being noticeable upgrades (Denver Public Library, Otto C. Perry collection, OP-2472).

This Louisville & Nashville class K-1 4-6-2, No. 157, one of 25 built by Alco and company shops in 1905–07, was still in as-built condition with slide valves and inside Stephenson valve gear when Otto Perry photographed it at Birmingham, Alabama, on July 31, 1936 (Denver Public Library, Otto C. Perry collection, OP-12491).

The Louisville & Nashville built this Class K-2 4-6-2, No. 175, in its own shops in 1909–10, shown at Mobile, Alabama, on October 15, 1929 (Denver Public Library, Otto C. Perry collection, OP-12493).

Louisville & Nashville class K-1 4-6-2, No. 151, after rebuilding with piston valves and Walschaert valve gear, photographed at Birmingham, Alabama, on July 31, 1936 (Denver Public Library, Otto C. Perry collection, OP-12490).

The Louisville & Nashville built this Class K-3 4-6-2, No. 201, in its own shops in 1912, shown at Memphis, Tennessee, on October 18, 1929 (Denver Public Library, Otto C. Perry collection, OP-12497).

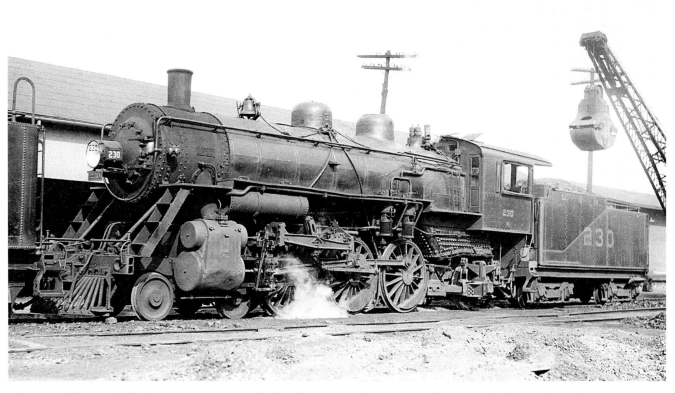

This Louisville & Nashville class K-4 4-6-2, No. 230, built at the company shops in 1914, is being coaled with a mechanical grab at Louisville, Kentucky, on October 3, 1929 (Denver Public Library, Otto C. Perry collection, OP-12498).

The Louisville & Nashville classified its USRA light Pacifics, built by Alco in 1919, as class K-5. Otto Perry photographed No. 243 at Cincinnati, Ohio, on August 16, 1933 (Denver Public Library, Otto C. Perry collection, OP-12500).

their cylinders bored out by ½ inch. Seventeen class K-3's followed in 1912–13. Twenty-eight class K-4's followed in 1914–18. The company built eighteen more K-4's in 1920–22 with power reverse and coal pushers, even though they were outclassed by the six USRA light Pacifics assigned to the railroad in 1919, classified K-5.

The Chicago, Milwaukee & St. Paul built a 4-6-2 at its West Milwaukee shops in 1905.[45] This competed with the Chicago & Alton's as the heaviest 4-6-2 in the world at a weight of 218,000 pounds. In the 200-pounds per square inch boiler, the long diagonal stays of other designs were replaced by large plates staying the tube sheets and back head to the boiler interior. A brick arch was installed, but no superheat.

The Erie competed with the New York Central for the dense passenger traffic of the northeastern U.S. and demanded the highest-performance passenger engines obtainable. Accordingly, they ordered four 4-6-2s from Alco, cautiously specifying two with superheaters, two without.[46] A 56-square foot grate fired 3,300 square feet of primary heating surface, with another 760 square feet of superheating surface in a 200-pounds per square inch boiler. Inside Stephenson valve gear drove piston valves. The 230,500-pound engine developed 28,000 pounds of tractive effort. Unusually, the suspension of all three driving axles and the trailing truck was equalized, leaving the leading truck independently sprung.

An issue in superheater design was the fire tube heating surface in the boiler that the superheater flues displaced. Alco had supplied a class of superheated 4-4-2s to the New York Central, in which each Cole-type superheater element consisted of a 1 1⁄16-inch OD inner tube discharging inside an 1 3⁄4-inch OD outer tube ("Field tube"). Each Field tube was placed inside a 3-inch flue tube, of which there were

fifty-five. The superheaters in the Erie engines were of the same type, but a 7⁄8-inch OD inner tube discharged into a 1 1⁄2-inch OD outer tube. These were nested in fours inside 5-inch flue tubes, of which thirty-two were mounted in the upper center of the boiler. Whereas the arrangement in the New York Central engines provided 300 square feet of superheating surface; this apparently small change in design provided 760 square feet of superheating surface in the Erie engines, while occupying the same boiler cross-section.

An increasing number of railroads were accepting 50,000-pound axle loads on main lines. The Santa Fe bought twenty-eight four-cylinder balanced compound 4-6-2s from Baldwin in 1905, weighing 226,000 pounds, 50,000 on each axle.[47] These were oil-burners with 220-pounds per square inch boiler pressure. This class ultimately numbered forty-one. Although the company rebuilt many of its compounds to single-expansion, a photograph shows one of these engines in its original condition as late as 1934.

Alco completed its 40,000th locomotive in October 1906,[48] presumably counting the total contribution of all its constituent companies. The engine was one of two 4-6-2 Cole balanced compounds for the Northern Pacific. The cylinders were 16 1⁄2-inch and 27 1⁄2-inch × 26-inch, with the high-pressure cylinders inside the frames, supplied by a 220-pounds per square inch, unsuperheated boiler with 2,900 square feet of heating surface, fired by a 44-square foot grate. The inside cylinders drove the cranked front axle; Alco thought it worthwhile to obtain the crank axle from the German steelmaker, Krupp. Outside Walschaert valve gear drove the piston valves for all four cylinders. The piston valves for each high- and low-pressure cylinder pair were mounted in tandem on a common valve stem; the space between them acted as a receiver. A combustion chamber extended 3 feet ahead of the firebox; the Northern Pacific had such

One of the Erie's 59 Class K-1 4-6-2s, built by Alco and Baldwin in 1905–08. Otto Perry photographed No. 2553, retrofitted with Walschaert valve gear, at Jersey Heights, New Jersey, on October 30, 1937 (Denver Public Library, Otto C. Perry collection, OP-11576).

The Pennsylvania's new 4-6-2, Class K-28, No. 7067, built by Alco in 1907 (Pennsylvania Historical and Museum Commission and Railroad Museum of Pennsylvania, General Negative 25656)

success with combustion chambers, not least in reducing maintenance work on the back tube sheet, that they forthwith adopted them as standard on all new engines.

These two engines developed 30,340 pounds of tractive effort; the reduction in dynamic augment resulting from the balanced compound arrangement allowed 11,000 pounds more adhesion weight than a single-expansion engine of similar dimensions. Total engine weight was 240,000 pounds. Tests on the New York Central had shown that a balanced compound developed 20% to 30% more horsepower than a single-expansion engine of the same size and that, more-

over, at speeds of 65 to 75 miles per hour. Great hopes were entertained for the Northern Pacific 4-6-2s accordingly. The old problem with compounds of poor performance at high speed seemed to have been solved.

The year 1907 saw the birth of some of the most famous of all American express passenger locomotives, the Pennsylvania 4-6-2s.[49] The first example was built by Alco Pittsburgh, unsuperheated and with no brick arch, but with piston valves driven by Walschaert valve gear, classified K-28. At 269,200 pounds, this was the heaviest passenger engine built to date. Increasing train weights were exceeding

The Pennsylvania's second class K-21s 4-6-2, No. 8702, built by Alco in 1910. Alco built this class until 1913. The photograph was taken at Indianapolis, Indiana, in 1920 (Pennsylvania Historical and Museum Commission and Railroad Museum of Pennsylvania, General Negative 25820).

the capabilities of the company's E-3d 4-4-2s; the demand for higher tractive effort, while keeping the axle load below the limit of 60,000 pounds, necessitated a six-coupled engine; the new engine's axle loading was 59,000 pounds.

Cylinders 35% bigger than the E-3d's were supplied from a boiler with 67% more heating surface: 4,427 square feet provided by 343 fire tubes 2¼ inches in diameter and 21 feet over tube sheets. A boiler pressure of 210 pounds and 24-inch × 26-inch cylinders provided 31,000 pounds of tractive effort. The boiler was fired by a 62-square foot grate.

This is undoubtedly ample for the heating surface, but the question of firing so large a grate with the engine hauling a heavy passenger train at high speed will probably prove a tax of physical endurance, for at a rate of combustion of only 100 lbs. of fuel per square foot of grate per hour, it will involve the handling of more than three tons of coal in that time.

The frames were still of wrought iron. The design was ripe for the addition of a brick arch, a superheater and a power stoker, invisible from the exterior, which would add significantly to its performance.

A Pennsylvania class K-2 4-6-2, No. 3327, photographed at Louisville, Kentucky, on August 6, 1934. Altoona and Alco built the K-2's in 1910–13 (Denver Public Library, Otto C. Perry collection, OP-14347).

This is the Pennsylvania's legendary class K-4s 4-6-2. Altoona and Baldwin produced these locomotives from 1914 to 1928. Otto Perry photographed No. 2112 at Altoona on August 19, 1933. The Belpaire firebox helps to give this locomotive a characteristic Pennsylvania look (Denver Public Library, Otto C. Perry collection, OP-14264).

A New York Central class K-2 4-6-2, No. 3490, photographed at Harmon, New York, on October 17, 1930. Alco built this class between 1907 and 1910 (Denver Public Library, Otto C. Perry collection, OP-13376).

Alco Schenectady built twelve more 4-6-2s for the Pennsylvania in 1910–1913, class K-21s.

The Pennsylvania built 153 K-2's in 1910–11; these were followed by 72 K-2a's from the Pennsylvania's shops and Alco Schenectady in 1911–13 and thirty K-3s's from Baldwin in 1913.[50]

The design lessons learned from the E-6s went into developing the K-4s 4-6-2s that first emerged from the Juniata shops in 1914.[51] There followed 425 K-4s's between 1914 and 1928. The boiler and firebox were common with the L-1s 2-8-2s with 70 square feet of grate, 205 pounds per square inch working pressure and 4,035 square feet of heating surface—hand fired. The permissible axle loading between Altoona and Pittsburgh was now up to 65,000 pounds. The 4-6-2s developed 41,850 pounds of tractive effort. These engines had the increasingly common screw reversing gear. Many of the K-4s class were retrofitted with power stokers and power reverse after World War I.[52]

Meanwhile (1907–8), the Lake Shore & Michigan Southern was replacing its 2-6-2s with twenty-five Alco 4-6-2s only slightly smaller than the future Pennsylvania K-4s.[53] The New York Central replaced its 4-4-2s with 4-6-2s of similar size, again because the 4-4-2s could no longer exert the necessary tractive effort.[54]

At the same time, the New York Central ordered 275 locomotives from Alco in a single order. These included 110 4-6-2s in five different classes, differing in driving wheel diameter and cylinder diameter and ranging in weight from 234,000 to 266,000 pounds. The order also comprised ninety-five 2-8-0s in three different classes, forty-five 0-6-0s in two different classes and twenty-five 2-6-6-2 Mallets.

In July 1910, the Chicago & North Western took delivery of twenty 4-6-2s from Alco; five had Alco Type A (Schmidt) double-loop fire-tube superheaters.[55] They were an immediate success, saving 4 tons of coal on a 217-mile run from Chicago, eliminating a stop for water

and delivering high power at high speed. As a result, the company specified superheaters in a new order for fifty 2-8-0s—but in only thirty of the total.

The New York Central watched the performance of the Alco 4-6-2s on its Lake Shore & Michigan Southern subsidiary with interest.[56] Between 1907 and 1910 the Lake Shore ordered ninety-five from Alco, class K-2 and, as a result of Lake Shore experience, the New York Central ordered ninety-seven from the same source.[57] However, as still greater power was demanded, and the boilers were as big as they could be, the next step was to add superheating; a superheated 4-6-2 was tested on the Lake Shore in 1910. This was only indirectly a matter of fuel economy; the real issue was power density—the power that could be developed by a boiler of fixed size.

In 1911, the New York Central placed an initial order for twenty superheated 4-6-2s with Alco Schenectady, class K-3, differing only slightly from the K-2's, particularly in ease of access for maintenance. Cylinder diameter was increased from 22 inches to 23½ inches and the stroke shortened from 28 inches to 26 inches, these dimensions favoring the use of superheated steam. The company ordered another sixty 4-6-2s, of which only ten were superheated, with bigger cylinders (24 inches for unsuperheated, 26 inches for superheated) and smaller driving wheels (79 inches to 69 inches), for fast freight service. The company's faith in superheating was still tentative. It is interesting that, as early as 1910, a major eastern railroad was so concerned with fast freight trains as to order a class of slightly modified express passenger engines for this duty.

All three batches had 57-square foot grates. The superheated passenger engines and the saturated-steam freight engines used steam at 200 pounds per square inch; the superheated freight engines used only 180 pounds per square inch. The saturated-steam freight engines had 4,650 square feet of primary heating surface; the other two superheated classes had about 3,500 square feet. All classes weighed about 265,000 pounds.

In 1910, Alco built an experimental 4-6-2 at its own expense, incorporating F. J. Cole's ideas, to see just how much power and efficiency could be wrung from a standard-sized locomotive when the design was free of the prejudices, requirements and procurement policies of any individual railroad.[58] The engine was the 50,000th built by Alco and its component companies and was numbered accordingly.

The experimental engine was superheated and single-expansion, weighing much the same as other 4-6-2s at 269,000 pounds. This engine, however, was capable of 2,215 drawbar horsepower with 25% better fuel economy than existing engines of the same type. Alco achieved this success by attending to numerous design details, small in themselves, but of large cumulative effect.

A 60-square foot grate with two firedoors (but no power stoker), fired a boiler containing 4,050 square feet of heating surface with an additional 900 square feet of superheating surface in a fire-tube superheater. The boiler pressure was only 185 pounds per square inch, but the large superheating surface produced up to 340°F superheat (728°F steam); Alco believed this to be one cause of the engine's

The New York Central's next 4-6-2s were the class K-3, built by Alco and Baldwin between 1911 and 1913. Otto Perry photographed No. 3416 at Harmon, New York, on October 17, 1930 (Denver Public Library, Otto C. Perry collection, OP-13374).

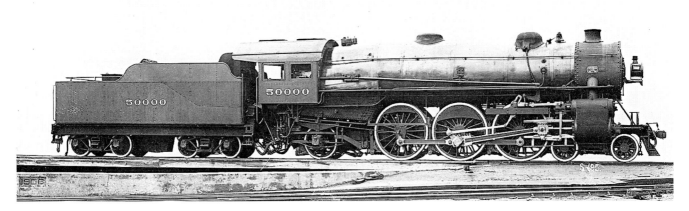

Alco's 4-6-2 demonstrator, No. 50000, built in 1910 (courtesy California State Railroad Museum, Negative 39069cn).

superior thermal efficiency. The firebox had a brick arch, but no arch tubes or combustion chamber. A photograph dating from 1941 shows a Worthington feedwater heater mounted under the running board on the left side of the engine; this was almost certainly added later.

Screw reversers were widely used outside North America, but the Americans persisted in the use of the reversing lever, supposedly because it was the quickest means of putting the engine into reverse in an emergency. On big engines the backlash in the lever made engineers reluctant to change the cut-off, so Alco fitted this engine with a screw reverser, worked by a hand wheel in the cab, encouraging finer and more frequent adjustment of cut-off, leading to better fuel economy. The engineer could completely reverse the gear in 4 to 6 seconds.

Part of the engine's success lay in its high power:weight ratio. Cast vanadium steel cylinders, used for the first time, saved 4,000 pounds, compared to conventional cast iron cylinders of the same size. Pressed, rather than cast, steel for the bumper and pilot saved 1,500 pounds. Other parts using vanadium steel were the frames, driving wheel centers, rods, piston rods, valve gear, springs and crank pins.

The Erie was the first railroad to host trials of this engine; several others tested it, including the New York Central. The Erie was so impressed that it bought the engine in September 1912, designating it class K-3, No. 2509.[59] The engine pulled the Erie's express passenger trains until superseded by the yet more powerful USRA "heavy Pacific" 4-6-2s that entered service in 1919 as class K-5. No. 50000 continued in passenger service until retired, worn out, in March 1949, and scrapped at Warren, Ohio, in March 1950.

After the Erie bought the engine, it must have been a disappointment to Alco when the Erie ordered five new 4-6-2s, based on the 50000 design, from Lima in 1913, a sign of that company's increasing competitiveness with the two established builders.[60]

A trailing truck gave scope for depth as well as width in the Wootten fireboxes that characterized engines for the Pennsylvania anthracite country. In 1912, the Delaware, Lackawanna & Western bought seven 4-6-2s from Alco Schenectady with 95-square foot grates, to replace 4-6-0s with 103-square feet of grate.[61] The new 4-6-2s were built for passenger service between New York and Elmira, crossing northeastern Pennsylvania over Pocono Summit, between Stroudsburg, Pennsylvania, and Scranton, with 21 miles of 1.6% grade. With increasing train weights, the company's 4-6-0s could not keep schedule reliably without helper service. The new, superheated 4-6-2s, with a tractive effort of 41,000 pounds, were expected to handle 530 tons with no helper. These were the company's first 4-6-2s; the company would order eighty-three between 1912 and 1924, mostly from Alco; the fourteen built by Lima in 1914 signified that company's growing presence in the large engine field.

The Chesapeake & Ohio was still having to double-head passenger trains between Clifton Forge and Hinton, West Virginia. Schedules demanded that westbound 10-car, 692-ton trains, be hauled up 13 miles of 1.1% ruling grade at 24 miles per hour. This took two of the company's existing fleet of twenty-seven class F-15 4-6-2s, built by Alco between 1902 and 1911. Accordingly, the company bought eight 4-6-2s from Baldwin, class F-16, in 1913, substantially more powerful and developing 44,000 pounds of tractive effort.[62] A 60-square foot grate with a brick arch and arch tubes fired 3,785 square feet of primary heating surface with another 880 square feet of superheating surface. Steam at 185 pounds per square inch went to 27-inch × 28-inch cylinders through 16-inch piston valves. Extensive use of vanadium steel kept weight down to 282,000 pounds.

The Lehigh Valley built many of its own locomotives at its Sayre, Pennsylvania, shops. By 1912 the company's first 4-6-2s, built in 1905, already needed a 4-6-0 helper to haul passenger trains over Wilkes

Delaware, Lackawanna & Western 4-6-2, No. 1101, photographed at Hoboken, New Jersey, on October 29, 1927. Alco built these locomotives between 1912 and 1914. Note the wide firebox for burning anthracite (Denver Public Library, Otto C. Perry collection, OP-7333).

Even in the depression the Chesapeake & Ohio kept its passenger locomotives clean. Baldwin built this class F-16 4-6-2, No. 460, in 1913. Otto Perry photographed it at Washington, DC, on August 10, 1932 (Denver Public Library, Otto C. Perry collection, OP-2871).

The Lehigh Valley built this Class K-2½ 4-6-2, No. 2014, in company shops in 1913–14, shown at Bound Brook, New Jersey, on October 18, 1930 (Denver Public Library, Otto C. Perry collection, OP-12467).

Built by Baldwin in 1914, the Atchison, Topeka & Santa Fe superheated balanced compound 3500 class 4-6-2s were among the most technically advanced steam locomotives of their time. No. 3515 is shown, still in as-built condition, at Raton, New Mexico, on October 28, 1920. The inside high-pressure cylinder valve chests are just visible. A power reverser is visible above the back driving wheel (Denver Public Library, Otto C. Perry collection, OP-861).

Barre Mountain, including 19 miles of 1.8% grade eastbound which limited trains to 360 tons. In 1913 the company introduced new, bigger 4-6-2s, capable of carrying out this task unassisted.[63] These engines, weighing 262,000 pounds and developing 42,000 pounds of tractive effort, used superheated steam at 215 pounds per square inch, controlled by Walschaert valve gear with screw reverse and 14-inch piston valves. The trailing truck supported a Wootten firebox with two fire doors and 87 square feet of grate surface. The ever-rising demand for power could no longer afford the luxury of a low boiler pressure in exchange for superheating.

The Santa Fe carried on with the balanced compound principle after other railroads had given it up. In 1914, the company bought thirty-five balanced compound 4-6-2s from Baldwin, making a total of 115 of this type, all from Baldwin with progressive improvements. Twenty were built to burn bituminous coal; fourteen were oil-burners; one was built to burn lignite mined at Gallup, New Mexico.[64] They were substantial engines, weighing 277,700 pounds and developing 34,000 pounds of tractive effort. A straightforward design of firebox and boiler comprised a 58-square foot grate with a brick arch firing 3,475 square feet of heating surface in tubes 21 feet over tube sheets.

The cylinder arrangement was first introduced in the company's 2-6-2s, built for fast freight service in 1906. The 17½-inch high-pressure cylinders were mounted inside the frames, elevated so as to drive the center driving axle; the main rods passed above the front driving axle without the need for a bifurcated main rod. The 29-inch low-pressure cylinders, mounted externally, also drove the center driving axle.

In America of the early 1900s, compounding went out of favor

before superheating gained a foothold. These Santa Fe engines were high-pressure (210 pounds per square inch), superheated compounds with Baker valve gear, Ragonnet power reversers, generously sized 15-inch piston valves and extensive use of vanadium steel. They were the first balanced compounds to be built by Baldwin with Baker valve gear. Probably they were the most thermodynamically advanced rigid-frame design before the superpower locomotives of the 1920s; disappointingly, the present study has uncovered no records of their performance.

> The Santa Fe has long recognized, not only the advantages to be derived from compounding, such as increased capacity and economy, but also the fact that compound locomotives must be suitable for the service, intelligently handled and properly maintained. This policy has been persistently carried out, and to it the success of the balanced compounds is largely due.

This human issue was, no doubt, the crux of the success or failure of compounds: employees from managers downward had to dedicate themselves to getting the best out of them. Even so, these were apparently the company's last new compounds and probably among the last new rigid-frame compounds built for any railroad in America.

One way out of the railroads' economic dilemma was to increase the speed of freight movement. In 1913, the Delaware, Lackawanna & Western bought seven 4-6-2s from Alco specifically for freight haulage.[65] These took over from older 2-6-0s; in tests between Scranton, Pennsylvania, and Hoboken, New Jersey, the new engines burned 75 pounds of coal per 1,000 ton-miles hauled, compared to 103 pounds for the 2-6-0s, a saving of 25%. This concept was so successful that the company ordered a second batch of fourteen engines for

This photograph, taken at Washington, DC, on August 3, 1939, shows Chesapeake & Ohio class F-17 4-6-2, No. 470, built by Alco in 1914, retrofitted with Boxpok driving wheels. This shows the pride that the C&O took in its passenger power (Denver Public Library, Otto C. Perry collection, OP-2875).

delivery in 1914.[66] Lima won the contract, signifying the company's growing presence in the big-engine market, and its growing position as a builder of engines for high speed and high power.

The 4-6-2 continued to grow in size and power; the six built by Alco for the Chesapeake & Ohio in 1914 had the highest tractive effort of any 4-6-2 to date: 46,600 pounds.[67] The Chesapeake & Ohio ran 675-ton passenger trains to demanding schedules over the sinuous and steeply-graded route through the Appalachians between Charlottesville, Virginia, and Hinton, West Virginia, servicing mountain resorts, such as Virginia Hot Springs and White Sulphur Springs, along the way. These engines applied the best available practice with few innovations. Almost for the first time in a passenger locomotive a Street Type C stoker fired an 80-square foot grate burning bituminous coal. Boiler pressure was only 185 pounds per square inch, but steam was supplied from 4,480 square feet of heating surface with 990 square feet of superheating surface. Ragonnet power reverse controlled the Walschaert valve gear. To meet the massive racking forces applied to the bar frames, themselves 6 inches thick, Alco braced them with box castings. The engines weighed 312,600 pounds with axle loadings of 63,000 pounds.

The Union Pacific had used 4-6-2s since 1904, totaling eighty in nine classes built between 1904 and 1913. In 1914, the company took delivery of a new class of twenty-five, built by Lima for high power at high speed.[68] Weighing 273,500 pounds, the new engines were 24% heavier than their most recent predecessors, developing 29% more tractive effort (38,500 pounds) with 50% greater heating surface. Cylinder diameter was increased from 22 inches to 25 inches, both with 28-inch stroke. Both older and newer types worked on 200 pounds per square inch boiler pressure. High boiler pressures had come to stay; the demand for power was too urgent for it to be oth-

erwise. The new engines were fully up to date with brick arches, superheat and power reversers. One of the new engines hauled a mail train over the 291 miles from North Platte, Nebraska, to Omaha in 290 minutes, including six stops.

The Santa Fe finally gave up on compounding when it ordered a single-expansion 4-6-2 from Baldwin in 1915.[69] This engine was a superheated oil-burner, designed for the maximum tractive effort available within a 58,000-pound axle loading limit—41,000 pounds. The engine was built with Baker valve gear and Ragonnet power reverse. Its up-to-date construction notwithstanding, this engine remained the only one of its class; the Santa Fe ordered no new 4-6-2s until 1927, heavy passenger power being made up by fifty-one 4-8-2s built by Baldwin between 1918 and 1924.

The 4-6-2 continued to grow in size. Both Baldwin and Alco turned out engines in 1915 capable of 47,500 pounds of tractive effort for the Richmond, Fredericksburg & Potomac[70] and the Delaware, Lackawanna & Western.[71] These engines used 200-pounds per square inch steam and weighed 290,000 to 300,000 pounds with axle loadings of 60,000 to 65,000 pounds. Ragonnet power reverse and Walschaert valve gear were typical. New types of steel (Nikrome) and careful design maximized boiler power and minimized dynamic augment. Clearly, however, the tractive effort of a six-coupled engine was limited to about 48,000 pounds with an adhesion factor of 4 and a maximum permissible axle loading of 65,000 pounds. The adhesion factor was an inescapable fact; major civil engineering work was needed to increase the permissible axle loading. Given these constraints, the future for increased passenger power lay with the 4-8-2 and, ultimately, the 4-8-4.

The Philadelphia & Reading came late to the 4-6-2 but when it did, the engines that it built in its Reading shops were as fast and

Union Pacific Class P-10 4-6-2, No. 2884, built by Lima in 1914 and photographed at Denver, Colorado, in 1920. This locomotive signifies Lima's growing position in the large-engine market (Denver Public Library, Otto C. Perry collection, OP-16846).

An Atchison, Topeka & Santa Fe 3600 class 4-6-2, No. 3600, built by Baldwin in 1915 and photographed at San Bernardino, California, on April 25, 1933 (Denver Public Library, Otto C. Perry collection, OP-878).

The Philadelphia & Reading built the class G-1sa 4-6-2s at its own shops between 1916 and 1923. Otto Perry photographed No. 108 at Communipaw, New Jersey, on November 30, 1927. Note the wide firebox for burning anthracite (Denver Public Library, Otto C. Perry collection, OP-14501).

powerful as anything in America.[72] Reading shops turned out an initial batch of five in 1916, followed by five more each year up to 1926, except for 1920 and 1922. Reading track permitted a 60,000-pound axle load. With 200 pounds per square inch of boiler pressure, 25-inch × 28-inch cylinders and 80-inch driving wheels, the 274,000-pound engines developed 37,000 pounds of tractive effort. The Wootten firebox had 95 square feet of grate and a 48-inch combustion chamber.

Bigger and more powerful engines not only moved freight faster, but in fewer, longer trains. In 1916–17, the Lehigh Valley bought fifty 4-6-2s and seventy-six 2-10-2s from Baldwin.[73] This was in addition to twenty 2-8-2s built in 1916. The 4-6-2s were for both fast freight and heavy passenger service in the relatively flat country of northwestern New York and northern Pennsylvania. The 2-10-2s were for heavy, if slow-moving, freight trains in the same area.

In the 4-6-2s a 75-square foot grate with a 48-inch combustion chamber fired 3,734 square feet of primary heating surface, made up of 254 2¼–inch fire tubes, 17 feet 6 inches over tube sheets, with an additional 980 square feet of superheater surface, producing steam at 205 pounds per square inch. The Lehigh Valley ordered twenty of the 4-6-2s with Walschaert valve gear, the remaining ten with Baker gear. The Lehigh Valley had decided against any further camel-back engines, regardless of firebox width. They weighed 301,500 pounds and developed 48,700 pounds of tractive effort, 55% more than the 4-6-0s that they replaced.

Although USRA locomotive designs were mainly concerned with hauling freight, the Administration designed heavy and light 4-6-2s with 60,000-pound and 55,000-pound axle loadings respectively,[74] ordering fifty-nine light 4-6-2s, twenty-six from Alco and thirty-three from Baldwin, and twenty heavy 4-6-2s, ten from each supplier. Com-

mon to both types were the 10,000-gallon standard tender, 200-pound boiler pressure, brick arches supported on arch tubes and 14-inch piston valves driven by Baker valve gear with power reverse.

All twenty heavy Pacifics went to the Erie; the eighty-one light Pacifics were distributed between the Louisville & Nashville (6), the Atlantic Coast Line (70) and the Union Pacific (5).

The Louisville & Nashville built most of its own power during the early twentieth century, building 291 locomotives at its South Louisville shops between 1909 and 1922.[75] This came to an end with the voluntary purchase of USRA types in 1919. First of these were six light Pacifics; a further twenty 4-6-2s built by Alco Brooks and Baldwin in 1923–4 copied the USRA design. These engines were bigger than the L&N's home-built 4-6-2s; with power stokers, they were popular with the crews. The company bought a single three-cylinder version of the USRA light Pacific from Alco Brooks in 1925. It was unused during the 1930s, then rebuilt as a two-cylinder engine in 1940. The only 4-8-2s that the L&N ever owned (sixteen built in 1926 and six in 1930, all by Baldwin) were all based on the USRA light Mountain. The influence of the USRA designs lived on after the demise of the organization itself.

8.1.5 The First Mountains

The Chesapeake & Ohio's successive 4-6-2s were still not powerful enough for the company's needs. The company accordingly approached Alco for an engine that could maintain 25 miles per hour, hauling 600 tons up a 1.4% grade. In 1911, Alco Richmond built two engines of a 4-8-2 wheel arrangement, new to America and named the Mountain type.[76] The first-ever 4-8-2s were a class of 100 tank engines built by Dübs, Glasgow, UK, between 1888 and 1900 for South Africa. Preserved there, the sole survivor was repatriated to

The Atlantic Coast Line received 70 USRA light Pacifics from Alco and classified them P-5a. Otto Perry photographed No. 1510 at Jacksonville, Florida, on August 1, 1932 (Denver Public Library, Otto C. Perry collection, OP-2352).

the UK in 2010.[77] The trailing trucks on British-built tank engines, however, were to support the coal bunker, not to support a large firebox.

At 330,000 pounds, the Chesapeake & Ohio's new locomotives were the heaviest rigid-frame engines built to date; their 29-inch × 28-inch cylinders were the biggest ever fitted to a single-expansion engine. Even with only 180 pounds per square inch boiler pressure this, and a 60,000-pound axle loading, developed 58,000 pounds of tractive effort. A 67-square foot grate fired 4,130 square feet of heating surface, with a Schmidt-type fire-tube superheater. The firebox had a brick arch, a 42-inch combustion chamber and a power-operated grate shaker, but no power stoker. The engineer controlled the Walschaert valve gear with a screw reverser worked by a hand wheel.

The new engines hauled 10- and 12-car trains on routes where the company's 4-6-2s could handle only six. One hauled a 4,200-ton train at 23 miles per hour up a 0.3% grade, developing an estimated 2,480 horsepower. Although speeds up to 72 miles per hour were achieved, the 69-inch driving wheels proved too small for passenger service. Although the company bought a third 4-8-2 in 1912, it bought only another seven between 1918 and 1923. The Chesapeake & Ohio, originator of the type, was one of its least enthusiastic users; the New York Central, by contrast, bought 600 between 1916 and 1944.

In 1913, the Rock Island completed a major upgrade of its motive power, ordering 137 new engines from Baldwin and Alco: seventy-five 2-8-2s, thirty 0-6-0 switchers, thirty 4-6-2s and two 4-8-2s.[78] Hauling passengers for long distances across the prairies, the company was concerned to maximize the size of each train. The 4-8-2s, built by Alco, were designed to haul 16-car, 1,000-ton passenger trains up 247 miles of rising grades from Phillipsburg, Kansas, to Limon, Colorado, including ruling grades of 1%, at an average speed of 31 miles per hour, including ten stops. These engines were superheated

with brick arches, Baker valve gear and screw reversers. They were also an early application of over-fire steam jets. Engine weight was 333,000 pounds with 50,000 pounds of tractive effort. All of this order, except the switchers, had 63-square foot grates and 180 to 185 pounds per square inch boiler pressure. In service, these engines routinely handled eleven all-steel passenger cars, weighing 750 tons, between Phillipsburg, Kansas, and Limon, Colorado, as many as nineteen cars, weighing 1,175 tons.

Another early user of the 4-8-2 was the St. Louis, Iron Mountain & Southern, merged with the Missouri Pacific in 1917, which bought seven from Alco in 1913.[79]

Lima was gaining a good reputation for full-sized engines capable of high power and high speed.[80] In 1913, the company delivered twenty-five 4-6-2s and fifteen 4-8-2s to the Great Northern. The 251,000-pound 4-6-2s, developing 40,500 pounds of tractive effort, went into service along the 1,072 miles between St. Paul, Minnesota, and Cut Bank, Montana, maintaining all-inclusive average speeds of 30 to 35 miles per hour. The engine districts were 300 to 400 miles long with crew changes at the halfway points.

The 4-8-2s went into service in the mountains between Cut Bank and Whitefish, Montana, and through the Cascades. These 326,000-pound engines developed 62,000 pounds of tractive effort. A 78-square foot grate, still hand-fired, fired 4,540 square feet of heating surface with a further 1,075 square feet of superheating surface. A combustion chamber extended 41 inches ahead of the throat sheet, keeping the fire tube length to 20 feet 6 inches. Boiler pressure was still only 180 pounds per square inch, working through 28-inch cylinders. The front two pairs of driving wheels were equalized with the front truck, the two back pairs of driving wheels with the trailing truck, which was of a Lima design called the Austin truck, designed to simplify maintenance and improve lateral stability. In Montana the 4-8-2s eliminated helper service on the 18 miles of 1.8% grade eastbound between Essex and Summit, maintaining 17 to 20 miles per hour uphill. The engines working in the Cascades were oil-burners capable of maintaining 15 miles per hour against the 2.2% grades on both sides of the Cascade tunnel.

The 4-8-2 gained ground in the Appalachians, where heavy passenger traffic was combined with steep grades. The eight 4-8-2s that the Norfolk & Western built at its Roanoke shops in 1916 were similar in size to the Great Northern's but all eight had power stokers to fire their 80-square foot grates, four with the Hanna, four with the Standard.[81] Baker valve gear with Ragonnet power reversing was becoming the norm for large engines. At 347,000 pounds, they were the heaviest 4-8-2s built to date; their 70-inch driving wheels gave them slightly less tractive effort, at 57,000 pounds, even though the boiler pressure was higher, at 200 pounds per square inch. An innovation was a low-water alarm to warn crews of low water levels in the boiler. These engines were capable of hauling eleven steel passenger cars at 30 miles per hour up a 1.6% grade.

A competitor of the Chesapeake & Ohio in this same territory was the Seaboard Air Line. They achieved a similar solution with a lower axle loading, replacing 4-6-2s with ten 4-8-2s from Alco in 1914.[82] In 1913, the company's biggest passenger engine was a 4-6-2, developing 36,000 pounds of tractive effort, limited by an axle loading of 47,000 pounds.[83] The volume of passenger traffic and resulting length of trains necessitated double-heading. Many of the design principles of Alco's demonstrator, No. 50000, went into the new 4-8-2s. The new engines weighed 316,000 pounds and developed 48,000 pounds of tractive effort for an axle loading of 52,600 pounds, 40% more than the 4-6-2s that they replaced, achieving an 11% saving in fuel consumption per car-mile. Boiler pressure was 190 pounds per square inch, generated from a 57-square foot grate and 3,700 square feet of heating surface. In particular, they were capable of continuous high power output, with single locomotives, unaided, maintaining 22 to 25 miles per hour against 1.1% ruling grades with thirteen 75-ton steel passenger cars for a trailing load of 975 tons. The new engines typically ran 95,000 miles between overhauls. They were so successful that the company bought five more in 1917 and ten more in 1922.

One way to prevent the enormous wartime demand for freight haulage from clogging the railroads was to move freight trains faster. In 1916 the New York Central took delivery of thirty 4-8-2s from Alco with that in mind—the fast movement of freight trains over relatively level grades. This was the New York Central's first use of this type, which would increase to 600 by 1944 in four successive classes, mostly from Alco Schenectady, but also from Lima.[84] With 69-inch driving wheels, these engines were designed for a maximum of nearly 2,700 horsepower at 33 miles per hour. The grate was sized for a consumption rate of 4 pounds per indicated horsepower-hour at a firing rate not to exceed 120 pounds per square foot of grate per hour. However, at that rate the 67-square foot grate could burn up to 8,000 pounds of coal per hour. In most respects, the engines were of up-to-date design, with a brick arch on arch tubes, 40-inch combustion chamber, superheating and Walschaert valve gear with Ragonnet power reverse, yet with bizarre logic, the New York Central had the engines built so that power stokers could be retrofitted, but did not actually fit them. Although they moved trains of up to ninety-five cars and 3,500 tons over a 139-mile division faster than before, "As the locomotives are hand fired, they have never developed their full capacity in regular road service." Boiler pressure was 190 pounds per square inch. They developed 51,000 pounds of tractive effort, while limiting axle loadings to 60,000 pounds.

The USRA heavy 4-8-2 was the most powerful of its type built to date, developing 58,000 pounds of tractive effort and only a

The Norfolk & Western built their own class K-1 4-8-2s in 1916. No. 101 is shown at Roanoke, Virginia, on August 14, 1936 (Denver Public Library, Otto C. Perry collection, OP-13756).

One of the New York Central's original 4-8-2s, class L-1, built by Alco in 1916. No. 2631 had been retrofitted with an Elesco feed water heater by the time Otto Perry photographed it at Elkhart, Indiana, on September 25, 1930 (Denver Public Library, Otto C. Perry collection, OP-13353).

The Atchison, Topeka & Santa Fe received its 3700 class 4-8-2s from Baldwin in 1918, just before the USRA ban on non-standard locomotive production. No. 3728 had received an Elesco feed water heater, with the heat exchanger below the smokebox, by the time Otto Perry photographed it at San Diego, California, on July 28, 1935 (Denver Public Library, Otto C. Perry collection, OP-914).

USRA light Mountains went to the New York, New Haven & Hartford as class R-1, built by Alco in 1919. No. 3305 had been retrofitted with an Elesco feed water heater when Otto Perry photographed it at Providence, Rhode Island, on August 17, 1937 (Denver Public Library, Otto C. Perry collection, OP-13711).

ton lighter than the Santa Fe's massive 3700 Class 4-8-2s, built in 1918.[85]

It also had a record adhesion weight, with an axle loading of 60,750 pounds. The stoker-fired grate measured 76 square feet and fired 4,665 square feet of primary heating surface and a further 1,085 square feet of superheating surface. A combustion chamber extended 60 inches ahead of the throat sheet. The 247 2¼-inch fire tubes and forty-five 5½-inch flue tubes measured 20 feet 6 inches over tube sheets. The boiler was closely similar to that of the USRA light 2-10-2; working pressure was 200 pounds per square inch. Clearance dimensions had to fit the widest possible range of railroads that had track strong enough to accept the 4-8-2's axle loading; the figures used were 15 feet 0 inches high and 10 feet 3⅞ inches wide. The British Railways equivalent figures were 11 feet 0 inches high at the sides, 13 feet 6 inches in the center and 9 feet 0 inches wide.

Last of the USRA designs to appear in service was the light 4-8-2.[86] The USRA assigned the first ten of these to the New Haven. These were the first 4-8-2s used by that company, which put them into service on fast freight trains. So well did this type match the company's needs that it ordered thirty-nine more for delivery in 1920 and 1924; between 1919 and 1928 successive classes of 4-8-2 totaled seventy engines, all built by Alco. While remaining within a 50,000-pound axle loading limit, these engines developed 54,000 pounds of tractive effort from 200 pounds of boiler pressure and an engine weight of 327,000 pounds. A combustion chamber extended 60 inches forward of the 70-square foot grate. The firebox was hand-fired, with a power-operated firedoor, while the tender was equipped with a powered coal pusher. The 216 2¼-inch fire tubes and 40 5½-inch flue tubes extended for 20 feet 6 inches over tube sheets, providing 4,120 square feet of primary heating surface, augmented by

700 square feet of superheating surface. Baker valve gear with power reverse drove the 14-inch piston valves.

The 4-6-2s and 4-8-2s, rigid-frame, single-expansion locomotives capable of high power at high speed, were the forerunners of the superpower locomotives of the 1920s.

Section 8.2. Rigid-Frame Freight Locomotives

In 1905, three freight locomotive types were still new: the 2-8-2, the 2-10-2 and the Mallet. The 2-8-0 was the most common type of freight engine at that time; when a two-wheel trailing truck was added, supporting a large firebox, the result was a remarkably potent locomotive that became one of the standard American freight haulers and displaced the 2-8-0. The 2-10-0 was rare in America, although built in large numbers in Europe. On the other hand, the 2-10-2, with its large, stoker-fired firebox supported on a two-wheel trailing truck, brought the ten-coupled locomotive to fruition in American conditions. Although less common than the 2-8-2s, the 2-10-2s built from 1905 onward were the most powerful rigid-frame locomotives of their time. The USRA program endorsed these developments.

8.2.1 The Consolidation Becomes Obsolete

In the years before the financial panic of 1907, railroad procurement was on a vast scale. In 1904, the Baltimore & Ohio placed an order with Alco for the prototype of a new 2-8-0.[87] Three committees, led by John E. Muhlfeld, the master mechanic and the road foreman of engines, examined every detail of its construction and operation, even to the extent of taking it apart. When testing was complete, the

This Baltimore & Ohio class E-27 2-8-0, No. 2741, was part of a huge order built by Alco in 1905–10. Although five of the initial order were built with Walschaert gear, this may be a retrofit. Otto Perry photographed No. 2741 at Zanesville, Ohio, on August 20, 1937 (Denver Public Library, Otto C. Perry collection, OP-2445).

company ordered 210 in April 1905; Alco Richmond built seventy engines, Alco Schenectady built 140; delivery was completed in February 1906.

These engines were built with Stephenson link motion and slide valves. Following the success of the Walschaert gear on the company's new Mallet, five were built with this gear. These were conventional engines, weighing 208,500 pounds and developing 41,000 pounds of tractive effort. A 56-square foot grate area was achieved with a high-set, wide firebox above the rear driving wheels. The axle loading, at 46,500 pounds, was the maximum that the company's track would permit. Even though little was known about water circulation at that time, the water legs were designed to widen from 4½ inches at the mud ring to 6 and 7 inches. "The inward slope of both sheets gives the steam an opportunity to free itself from the surface on which it is formed." Boiler pressure was 200 pounds per square inch. Sixty-inch driving wheels were aimed at speed as well as hauling power. These engines could haul a 1,180-ton freight train at 10 miles per hour up a 1% grade, developing 1,125 horsepower. They were designed for the maximum interchangeability of parts with the company's class of 4-6-2s.

In making this massive investment, totaling $14 million and including 10,000 freight cars, the Baltimore & Ohio deliberately stepped back from the new Mallets, 2-8-2s and 2-10-2s, on the grounds that their exaggerated dimensions caused excessive breakages. At the same time, they felt that efficient design could circumvent the problems with high steam pressure that had been experienced elsewhere.

At the same time, Alco was building twenty-four 2-8-0s for the New York Central that only a skilled eye could distinguish from the Baltimore & Ohio engines.[88] While each railroad claimed that its engines were unique, and the industry poured abuse on the USRA's attempted standardization, the vast American locomotive building industry, concentrated in two huge firms, produced thousands of engines differing from each other only in detail.

In 1905, Walschaert valve gear was still new to America, making headway against Stephenson link motion. Accordingly, it was news when the New York Central ordered a 2-8-0 with this gear.[89] The firebox, with its 56-square foot grate, had a brick arch supported on arch tubes. Setting the firebox above the frames and rear driving wheels allowed a width of 75 inches. Because of its width, the firebox had two fire doors. Because of the high-set firebox and the diameter of the boiler, the dome was only 15 inches high, causing unease about the amount of water that might be carried into the cylinders with the steam. Tractive effort was 45,600 pounds; engine weight was 221,500 pounds. The twenty-four production engines from Alco in 1906 were heavier than the prototype at 232,500 pounds, developing 45,680 pounds of tractive effort.[90] This was produced by steam at 200 pounds per square inch working in 23-inch × 32-inch cylinders. The boiler to feed these cylinders contained 3,700 square feet of heating surface.

The standard New York Central freight engine of 1880 used a boiler pressure of 125 pounds per square inch, 1,175 square feet of heating surface and 16-inch × 24-inch cylinders. The power output of the new 2-8-0s was 4½ times that of the engines of twenty-five years previously.

Back in 1901, the Soo Line had bought a class of 180,000-pound two-cylinder, cross-compound 2-8-0s, developing 37,000 pounds of tractive effort.[91] The 22½-inch high-pressure cylinder took steam from the boiler at 210 pounds per square inch and exhausted to a 35-inch low-pressure cylinder; Stephenson valve gear drove slide valves. In 1905, the company ordered some more that were practically identical, but for Cole-type superheaters and other upgrades that added 20,000 pounds to the engine weight. The superheated engines sacrificed a mere 53 square feet of primary heating surface to add 261 square feet of superheating surface. Superheated, rigid-frame compounds were rare in the U.S.; it is disappointing that we know nothing of their performance.

Increasing traffic on the Pennsylvania outclassed the company's H-6 2-8-0s and in September 1905, Alco Schenectady delivered two 2-8-0s of a new design, class H-28, with 200-pound boiler pressure, 23-inch × 32-inch cylinders, 63-inch driving wheels, 222,000 pounds engine weight and 46,000 pounds of tractive effort, significantly bigger than the H-6. These engines inspired Altoona to design a still bigger 2-8-0, the H-8 (apparently, there was no Pennsylvania class H-7) with 24-inch cylinders and 43,000 pounds tractive effort, the first being built in 1907. Even so, H-6 production continued until 1913.

The year 1908 saw the birth of the H-8b at the Juniata shops.[92] An observer commented:

> It is probable that in these engines the Pennsylvania has reached the maximum weight on drivers which will be used by that company in simple locomotives for regular road service, and that when greater power is required resort will be made to the articulated type.

The axle loading was indeed high, at 52,750 pounds, but the Pennsylvania was never a significant user of Mallets.

The H-8b's relied on conventional, but rugged construction. The company sought to overcome the common problem of cracked frames by building wrought iron frames thicker and heavier than usual. These supported a likewise abnormally large boiler, containing 465 2-inch fire tubes 15 feet long, providing, with the firebox, 3,840 square feet of heating surface. In other respects, with its 238,000-pound engine weight and 42,660-pound tractive effort, the H-8b was a conventional and successful design.

In June 1909, an H-8 set a new record for freight train weight by hauling eighty-five 100,000-pound coal cars over the 124 miles between Altoona and Harrisburg at an average speed of 17 miles per hour. The payload was 4,450 tons of coal; the trailing load was 6,150 tons.[93] Four days later the same engine hauled ninety-four cars over the same route, carrying 5,040 tons of coal and weighing 6,920 tons. Grade reduction and line straightening played their part in achieving these records, the maximum adverse grade faced by this train being 0.2%. The Pennsylvania, Alco Brooks, Pittsburgh and Baldwin between them built 686 H-8's between 1907 and 1913.

The H-8 was followed in 1913 by the superheated H-9s with 25-inch cylinders and the H-10s with 26-inch cylinders; 205-pound boiler pressure was common to both. The H-9s developed 49,000 pounds of tractive effort; the H-10s developed 53,000 pounds. Baldwin and Altoona supplied 274 new H-9s's in 1913–14, while a further 312 H-8's were upgraded to H-9s standards.

Pittsburgh, Alco Brooks, Baldwin and Lima supplied 273 H-10's's between 1913 and 1916, while a further 200 H-8's were upgraded to H-10s standards. Some of these engines continued in service until the late 1950s.[94]

Exemplifying the design differences between Alco and Baldwin, in 1907, the Santa Fe took delivery of seven 4-6-2s and forty-two 2-8-0s from Baldwin, all single-expansion oil burners, all with Baldwin smokebox superheaters. Walschaert valve gear drove piston valves. In the 2-8-0s, large-diameter (24-inch), long-stroke (32-inch) pistons and an engine weight of 212,400 pounds converted a remarkably low boiler pressure of 160 pounds per square inch into 44,000 pounds of tractive effort.

In some cases, superheating was used as a means to compensate

This class H-8sc 2-8-0, No. 9959, was one of the Pennsylvania's many 2-8-0 freight locomotives. The class H-8 came from Alco and Altoona between 1907 and 1913. Otto Perry photographed this one at Buffalo, New York, on August 7, 1939 (Denver Public Library, Otto C. Perry collection, OP-14318).

The Pennsylvania class H-9s 2-8-0s came from Baldwin and Altoona, including H-8 conversions, between 1913 and 1914. Otto Perry photographed No. 685 at Camden, New Jersey, in June 1957 (Denver Public Library, Otto C. Perry collection, OP-14259).

The Pennsylvania's demand for freight power was such that Alco, Baldwin and Lima all built Class H-10s 2-8-0s, including H-8 conversions, between 1913 and 1916. Otto Perry photographed No. 7239 at Valparaiso, Indiana, on August 9, 1936 (Denver Public Library, Otto C. Perry collection, OP-14298).

This Atchison, Topeka & Santa Fe 1950 class 2-8-0, No. 1976, came from Baldwin in 1907 and was photographed at Los Angeles, California, on June 14, 1935 (Denver Public Library, Otto C. Perry collection, OP-616).

for a reduction in boiler pressure. In 1909, Alco built a class of 2-8-0s for the Wabash-Pittsburgh Terminal, some superheated, some not.[95] The saturated-steam engines had 210 pounds per square inch boiler pressure, while those with Cole superheaters had the boiler pressure reduced to only 160 pounds per square inch. The cylinder diameter was increased from 22 inches to 24 inches. The cylinders of the saturated-steam engines were bushed to the smaller diameter, to allow for retrofitting superheat, if warranted. The frames were of cast steel. At 236,000 pounds, the engines were heavier than typical 2-8-0s and developed a high tractive effort of 47,000 pounds.

In 1914, Alco delivered twenty 2-8-0s to the Western Maryland.[96] These engines were designed for the maximum possible tractive effort at low speeds, intended to haul 4,725 tons between Cumberland and Hagerstown against a maximum grade of 1%. With driving wheels only 51 inches in diameter (compared to 62 inches in the Pennsylvania's H-9s and L-1s), 200 pounds per square inch boiler pressure and 25-inch × 30-inch cylinders, these 244,500-pound engines developed 62,500 pounds of tractive effort. The small driving wheels made room for a 61-square foot grate without a trailing truck, so maximizing adhesion weight. In May 1914, one of these engines left Cumberland, Maryland, with 114 loaded cars weighing 7,014 tons. It ran the 74 miles to Williamsport in 7 hours, surmounting adverse grades up to 0.3%. Fifteen cars were set off; the train attacked the six miles of 1% grade to Hagerstown with two Mallet helpers, completing the run in 1 hour.

The entry of the United States into the European war in 1917 caused a paroxysm in the American railroad industry.[97] The War Department ordered 1,064 locomotives from Alco and Baldwin, 8,997 freight cars and 155,000 tons of rails for shipping to France. Baldwin completed its first engine of this order, a 2-8-0 of conventional dimensions, twenty days after receiving the order; production

followed at a rate of four per day. The initial order for 300 standard-gauge 2-8-0s was divided evenly between Alco and Baldwin; the next order, for 764 locomotives, was given entirely to Baldwin. This order comprised 380 standard-gauge 2-8-0s and 195 1-foot 11⅝-inch (600-millimetre) gauge 2-6-2 tank engines and included 189 narrow-gauge locomotives powered by gasoline engines. In July 1918, the U.S. Government placed an order with Baldwin for 1,010 2-8-0s for service overseas, known as "Pershings." Baldwin completed 750 of these by the end of November 1918.

Twelve companies got engines built to their own design under USRA management: the Santa Fe, the Philadelphia & Reading, the Baltimore & Ohio, the Virginian, the Boston & Maine, the Pennsylvania, the Chesapeake & Ohio, the Norfolk & Western, the Lehigh Valley, the Southern Pacific, the Union Pacific and the Kansas City Southern.[98] At this stage we cannot distinguish between the placement of new orders under USRA management and the completion of orders placed in 1917.

The Southern Pacific was able to build a few locomotives of various types in its own shops.[99] The Philadelphia & Reading was able to buy its own design of 2-8-0 from Baldwin, a class that totaled seventy-five engines built between 1918 and 1921.[100] Although the Wootten firebox with a Standard power stoker had a grate area of 95 square feet, continuous high power output was less important on the routes where the engines were to be used than low-speed pulling power. Consequently the company adopted the 2-8-0 wheel arrangement which put a higher percentage of engine weight into adhesion. A boiler pressure of 200 pounds per square inch, 55½-inch driving wheels and an engine weight of 281,000 pounds contributed to a tractive effort of 61,300 pounds. The company contrasted the new design with engines of the same wheel arrangement built in 1880. The 2-8-0s of that earlier time had a boiler pressure of only 120

Baldwin built this Philadelphia & Reading class I-9sb 2-8-0, No. 1646, as one of 75 built between 1918 and 1921. The location and date of the photograph are unknown (courtesy California State Railroad Museum, Negative 900_26267).

pounds per square inch, weighed 104,000 pounds and developed 19,600 pounds of tractive effort.

Construction of new 2-8-0s for domestic service declined during World War I, with only a few built for special purposes thereafter. Significantly, the 2-8-0 was not among the USRA standard designs.

8.2.2 Reign of the Mikados

The 2-8-2 wheel arrangement was gaining popularity when compounding was at the peak of its favor in the early 1900s. The Northern Pacific operated in terrain as demanding as any in the country; its demands for freight power were correspondingly immense. The company was the first user of 2-8-2s in quantity, receiving the first order for twenty-five, of which six were tandem compounds, from Alco Brooks in 1904.[101] Forty-three square feet of grate fired a 200-pounds per square inch boiler; in the single-expansion engines, 24-inch × 30-inch cylinders produced 44,000 pounds of tractive effort. Total engine weight was 259,000 pounds. The Northern Pacific ran through districts where the water was bad, so heating surface (4,010 square feet with 374 2-inch tubes) was sacrificed to the free flow of water and steam inside the boiler. The water legs were generous for the time at 4 inches. The two rear pairs of driving wheels were equalized with the trailing truck, while the two front pairs were equalized with the pony truck. In other respects, the engines were conventional, with internal Stephenson link motion, no superheat and piston valves. The first Northern Pacific 2-8-2s were:

> almost the pioneers of this type in this country, so far as modern heavy power is concerned ... the heaviest on the road and among the heaviest in the country.

The company took a total of 160 of this initial class by 1907, including some more tandem compounds. By 1913, it had 270 2-8-2s in service,

more than any other railroad in North America. Twenty of the tandem compounds were rebuilt to single-expansion in 1912. As the Northern Pacific was an enthusiastic user of compounds, this abandonment of compounding spoke volumes. Procurement of 2-8-2s by the Northern Pacific totaled 335 in three variants, all from Alco, between 1904 and 1923.

The Virginian was among the last major new railroads built in the United States, merging two smaller companies and completed in 1909. From the outset, it was a coal hauler from Appalachia to the sea. Management took the opportunity to use novel designs from the outset, such as 100,000-pound capacity, all-steel coal cars. Some of the first new locomotives ordered by the company were 2-8-2s from Baldwin.[102] Conventional practice was to cast a cylinder, steam chest and half the boiler saddle in one piece for bolting to the frame. If one part of this massive casting was damaged, the whole had to be replaced. Uneven expansion and contraction caused cracking and loosening of the bolted connection to the frame. The Virginian's new engines, therefore divided the steam chest, cylinders and saddle into several smaller parts which could be replaced individually. A 51-square foot grate fired 4,530 square feet of heating surface, producing saturated steam at 180 pounds per square inch. These 269,000-pound engines developed 50,350 pounds of tractive effort.

In 1909, the Virginian set a new record; one of the new 2-8-2s hauled a hundred steel coal cars, carrying 5,500 tons and weighing 7,560 tons, for 124 miles between Victoria, Virginia, and Sewall's Point in 8½ hours. Opposing grades were less than 0.2%. The engineer had to use the slack in the train to get it moving, a tribute to the strength of the cars and draft gear.[103]

An early user of the 2-8-2 was the Milwaukee, which built a class of twenty for its Chicago, Milwaukee & Puget Sound subsidiary at its Milwaukee shops in 1909.[104] These engines were only slightly big-

The Northern Pacific was an early user of 2-8-2s; Alco built the Class W in 1904–07. Otto Perry photographed No. 1640 at Minneapolis, Minnesota, on August 3, 1937 (Denver Public Library, Otto C. Perry collection, OP-13932).

A Virginian Class MB 2-8-2, No. 457, built by Baldwin in 1909–10 and photographed at Roanoke, Virginia, on August 6, 1932 (Denver Public Library, Otto C. Perry Collection, OP-19636).

Baldwin built 160 Baltimore & Ohio class Q-1 2-8-2s in 1911. No. 4089 is shown at Benwood, West Virginia, on August 17, 1933 (Denver Public Library, Otto C. Perry collection, OP-2454).

ger and more powerful than existing 2-8-0s, weighing 260,500 pounds and developing 46,600 pounds of tractive effort. A deep fire-box, with a 48-square foot grate, combustion chamber and brick arch supported on 3-inch arch tubes, fired a 200-pounds per square inch boiler containing 3,615 square feet of heating surface. The boilers were unsuperheated. The locomotives were designed by J. F. De Voy and incorporated his design of trailing truck with roller bearings for lateral movement. Walschaert valve gear drove piston valves. The engines were intended for use in pairs to haul 1,500 tons up a 2% grade, but they were also intended for passenger service in the mountains.

The Baltimore & Ohio began its extensive use of the 2-8-2 in 1910, ordering the first fifty from Baldwin in July 1910, for delivery in only six months.[105] These were 270,000-pound engines with 5,014 square feet of total heating surface. Still unsuperheated, boiler pressures of 205 pounds per square inch and 24-inch × 32-inch cylinders developed 47,000 pounds of tractive effort. The Baltimore & Ohio ordered a total of 320 Q-1's, all from Baldwin, delivered in 1911–13. The company acknowledged the growing importance of speed in freight engines by equipping twenty-five of the 64-inch drivered 2-8-2s with compressed-air operated scoops to draw water from track pans. The Q-1's were the first of 664 2-8-2s that the company acquired between 1911 and 1923. Many lasted into the 1950s.

Fully in the Baldwin style were two 2-8-2s built for the Atlanta, Birmingham & Atlantic in 1910,[106] combining some curious features. An unsuperheated boiler, containing 5,365 square feet of heating surface and fired by a 59-square foot grate, produced steam at only 170 pounds per square inch. The grate was small in relation to the heating surface. Baker-Pilliod valve gear drove slide valves. An adjustable pet-ticoat pipe was an unusual feature of the smokebox. An axle loading of 50,000 pounds allowed these engines to develop 50,000 pounds of tractive effort.

The Pacific Northwest offered some of the toughest railroading in the country, combined with unparalleled remoteness from supplies of high-grade coal, giving the railroads every incentive to mine the lignite of Centralia, Washington, and Kemmerer, Wyoming. In 1910, the Oregon Railroad & Navigation Co. ordered a 2-8-2 from Baldwin, purpose-built to burn lignite.[107] With 180-pounds per square inch steam, an engine weight of 263,000 pounds and 45,500 pounds of tractive effort, the dimensions were unremarkable. To handle lignite, however, a grate area of 70 square feet was provided; the unsuper-heated boiler contained 5,560 square feet of heating surface. An extra-long smokebox, well equipped with spark-arresting netting was also a necessary feature. The results were satisfactory. This success was soon followed by an order for 196 locomotives, placed by the Harri-man lines with Baldwin in early 1911, comprising eight different wheel arrangements for nine different railroads. Of these, ninety 2-8-2s and two 4-6-2s were built to burn lignite.[108]

In 1911, the Illinois Central was added to the growing number of railroads using 2-8-2s.[109] These engines from Baldwin weighed 284,000 pounds; even with the low boiler pressure of 170 pounds per square inch, 27-inch cylinders provided 51,700 pounds of tractive effort, 30% more than the company's 2-8-0s. Seventy square feet of grate fired 4,070 square feet of heating surface. Although the engines were superheated, there was no brick arch in the firebox which, how-ever, was fitted with over-fire steam jets, an early application of this device. A Baldwin power reverser controlled the Walschaert valve gear. The company ordered fifty of these engines as an initial order and bought a total of 517 from Baldwin, Alco Schenectady and Lima between 1911 and 1923.[110]

The Great Northern bought its first 2-8-2s from Baldwin in 1911.[111] An initial order of twenty was followed by another 125, class O-1; the company would buy a total of 200 of this type, mostly from Bald-win, up to 1920. The new 2-8-2s went for low boiler pressures—170

Illinois Central 2-8-2, No. 1511, was one of 517 built by Baldwin in 1911–23, photographed at Mattoon, Illinois, on August 15, 1933 (Denver Public Library, Otto C. Perry collection, OP-12260).

Otto Perry photographed this Great Northern class O-1 2-8-2, No. 3128, built by Baldwin sometime between 1911 and 1918, at Spokane, Washington, on September 29, 1931. The Great Northern, like the Pennsylvania, was a devotee of the Belpaire firebox (Denver Public Library, Otto C. Perry collection, OP-11934).

pounds per square inch—and big cylinders—28-inch bore, developing 57,500 pounds of tractive effort. They were equipped with firetube superheaters, but no brick arches over their 78-square foot grates. The Great Northern built an additional eighty-nine 2-8-2s in its own shops between 1922 and 1931 by rebuilding its fleet of 2-6-

6-2 and 2-6-8-0 Mallets built by Baldwin between 1907 and 1911. The 2-6-8-0s had already been converted to single expansion before being rebuilt as 2-8-2s. This was the real epitaph of the compound Mallet—too complicated, too slow and replaced by rigid-frame engines with new design features.

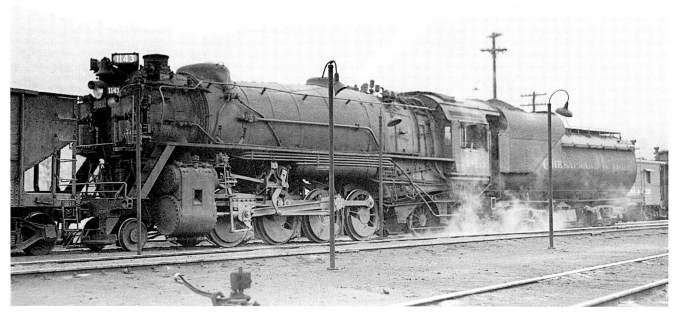

This Chesapeake & Ohio class K-1 2-8-2, No. 1143, was one of 68 built by Alco between 1911 and 1914, shown at Rainelle, West Virginia, on June 27, 1950. The huge fleet of steam locomotives, dating back thirty and forty years, influenced the sudden and rapid dieselization that took place after 1945 (Denver Public Library, Otto C. Perry collection, OP-2903).

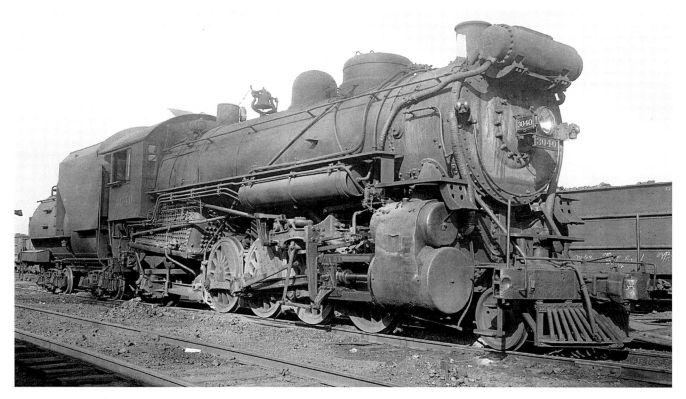

Erie class N-1 2-8-2, No. 3040, at Buffalo, New York, on October 1, 1930. Alco, Baldwin and Lima all contributed to this class of 155 locomotives between 1911 and 1913. The Elesco feed water heater was a post-1920 retrofit (Denver Public Library, Otto C. Perry collection, OP-11580).

Twenty-two percent of all new locomotives built in the U.S. in 1911 were 2-8-2s, setting new records for size and tractive effort.[112] The Chesapeake & Ohio commissioned its first 2-8-2 from Alco Richmond that year, followed by sixty-seven more between 1912 and 1914, designed for the maximum interchangeability of parts with the company's new 4-8-2s. The engines were superheated and stoker-fired, but boiler pressure was only 170 pounds per square inch. With a tractive effort of 60,800 pounds and 315,000 pounds engine weight, the 2-8-2s were designed to move 4,000 tons up a 0.3% grade at 15 miles per hour. A 60,750-pound axle load pointed to massive track construction on the company's main lines. The company intended the 2-8-2s to replace Mallets; performance test results were awaited with interest. Dynamometer tests showed the new engines developing 2,390 drawbar horsepower at 33 miles per hour.

Even after much grade reduction and double-tracking, the Erie still had significant grades on its Cincinnati division between Marion and Kent, Ohio. New trackbed and bridges allowed axle loadings up to 60,000 pounds. In the search for more power than the existing 2-8-0s could provide, the company considered both 2-8-2s and Mallets. In 1911, the Erie ordered twenty-five 2-8-2s from Baldwin and another fifteen from Alco.[113] These engines were built as state of the art, although without power stokers. Cast vanadium steel frames were 6 inches thick. A brick arch was supported on four 3-inch arch tubes above a 70-square foot grate. Heating surface was 4,155 square feet, with another 845 square feet in the Schmidt-type fire-tube super-heater. Boiler pressure was only 170 pounds, applied to 28-inch × 32-inch cylinders. Baker-Pilliod valve gear, controlled by a Ragonnet power reverser, drove 16-inch piston valves. The new 2-8-2s developed 57,000 pounds of tractive effort, 35% more than the company's

saturated-steam 2-8-0s without the complexity of the Mallet design. They were designed to haul 1,450 tons westbound, 1,520 tons eastbound, 38% more than the 2-8-0s.

Although the Chesapeake & Ohio's first 2-8-2s had power stokers, many 2-8-2s were built for other railroads with 60 to 70-square foot grates and hand firing. A sustainable hand firing rate of 4,000 pounds of coal per hour spread 57 pounds per hour on each square foot of grate. While this promoted efficient combustion, it did not allow the locomotive to maximize its power output; reasonably efficient combustion was still possible up to 120 to 150 pounds per square foot of grate per hour—8,400 to 10,500 pounds per hour, which was beyond the strength of most human firemen.

In 1913, the Rock Island completed a major upgrade of its motive power with 137 new engines from Baldwin and Alco[114]: seventy-five 2-8-2s, thirty 0-6-0 switchers, thirty 4-6-2s and two 4-8-2s. The sixty-five 2-8-2s from Baldwin were thoroughly modern and free from design quirks, equipped with brick arches, superheating, power reverse and Baker valve gear. The ten 2-8-2s from Alco had Walschaert gear and screw reverse. The frames were of cast vanadium steel, 6 inches thick. A 63-square foot grate, beneath a brick arch supported on four arch tubes, fired a 180-pounds per square inch boiler containing 4,265 square feet of primary heating surface and a further 848 square feet of superheating surface. The steam thus generated drove 28-inch × 30-inch cylinders through 16-inch piston valves driven by Baker valve gear with a Ragonnet compressed-air operated reverser. The result was an engine weighing 319,000 pounds, developing 57,000 pounds of tractive effort. On the El Paso division in Kansas, the 2-8-2s took over from saturated-steam 2-8-0s and increased train tonnage from 1,650 to 2,400 tons, hauling 45% more

Alco and Baldwin built the 143 Chicago, Rock Island & Pacific Class K-60 2-8-2s between 1912 and 1923. No. 2610, photographed at Liberal, Kansas, on May 26, 1940, is probably a Baldwin engine, identified by its Baker valve gear (Denver Public Library, Otto C. Perry collection, OP-5502).

tonnage while reducing coal consumption per 1,000 ton-miles from 96 to 66 pounds, a saving of 31%. Even the switchers saved 20% in fuel over their saturated-steam predecessors. In 1913, one of the 2-8-2s hauled a 99-car train, weighing 3,770 tons, for 111 miles at an average speed of 28 miles per hour.[115]

In 1913, the Lake Shore & Michigan Southern division of the New York Central ordered twenty 2-8-2s from Alco to replace superheated 2-8-0s that were, themselves, only a few years old.[116] With an engine weight of 322,000 pounds and developing 56,000 pounds of tractive effort from 190-pounds per square inch steam, the new engines offered 22% more tractive effort than the 2-8-0s that they replaced. Under test, the new engines hauled 100-car trains weighing 6,345 tons against a 0.3% grade. On the routes in Ohio, for which the new engines were built, the 2-8-0s turned in a fuel economy of 104 pounds of coal per thousand ton-miles; the new 2-8-2s reduced this to only 62 pounds per thousand ton-miles, a saving of 40%. So cautious were the railroads in adopting new technology that the company ordered half of the engines with the extensive use of vanadium steel components, half with conventional metallurgy. Cylinders were still of cast iron, but with vanadium added. A force-feed lubricator, automated with the throttle, and pneumatic firedoors were minor innovations of which American locomotive development now included a great many. The company reckoned that, as tire wear would reduce driving wheel diameter by 4 inches before they were replaced, and cylinder diameter by ½ inch before they were bushed, the nominal tractive effort would increase to nearly 60,000 pounds, reducing a deliberately high factor of adhesion of 4.4 when the engine was new to 3.95 in its worn state.

The design lessons that the Pennsylvania learned from the E-6s went into developing the L-1s 2-8-2s that first emerged from the Juni-

ata shops in 1914.[117] There followed 574 L-1s's between 1914 and 1919. The 2-8-2s developed 25% more tractive effort (57,850 pounds) than the H-9s 2-8-0s that they supplanted.

The railroads had huge fleets of 10- to 20-year old engines and looked for all possible means of extending their usefulness. The Southern put the complete running gear of a scrapped 2-6-0 or 2-8-0 under the tender of a 2-8-2.[118] The 2-8-2 cylinders were reduced in diameter from 27 inches to 26; the cylinder diameter on the tender engine was reduced to 19 inches; as a result, the 2-8-2's boiler could supply them all. A 3-inch pipe supplied superheated steam to the tender engine; a second pipe supplied saturated steam to it for short-term use; the engineer controlled both steam lines independently of the throttle on the main engine. The 2-8-2 boiler pressure was 175 pounds per square inch. The reversing gear on the tender engine was also separate from the main engine. The modification reduced the 2-8-2's tractive effort from 51,600 pounds as manufactured to 47,900 pounds, but the tender engine contributed an additional 28,600 pounds for a total of 76,500 pounds. The duplex engines hauled 39% more tonnage than the original 2-8-2s on the 68-mile run between Asheville, North Carolina, and Hayes, South Carolina, increasing the maximum freight train tonnage from 1,160 tons to 1,600 tons. Loss of adhesion when the tender ran low on coal and water proved not to be a problem.

A steam locomotive could be so extensively rebuilt that few of the original components were left. At the time of writing, a preserved 0-6-2T steam locomotive is in service in the UK, originally built in 1888. Only the two top slide bars remain of the original locomotive. The side rods originally belonged to another locomotive, built in 1876.[119] In 1918–19, the Northern Pacific, faced with aging power and the scarcity and high cost of new locomotives, rebuilt six 1906-built

The Northern Pacific rebuilt this class W-4 2-8-2, No. 2503, from a Class T 2-6-2 in company shops in 1919, photographed at Glendive, Montana, on September 23, 1931. This rebuild surprisingly retained the inside valve gear (Denver Public Library, Otto C. Perry collection, OP-14115).

class T 2-6-2s at their Brainerd shops into 2-8-2s for freight service in Montana.[120] The company replaced the frames with new, stronger, cast steel frames, extended to add a fourth driving axle and provision for a trailing truck. The 2-6-2s' short wheelbase, with the connecting rod driving the rear axle, allowed the company to retain the rods, wheels, valve gear and much of the spring rigging with only minor modifications, adding a fourth driving axle with the main rod driving on the third axle as before. This not only provided more adhesion weight, but improved the hitherto defective riding qualities. Lengthening the boiler barrel by 57 inches allowed the combustion chamber to be lengthened from 32 inches to 50 inches. Otherwise the firebox remained the same with 44 square feet of grate. The 306 2-inch fire tubes, 13 feet 3 inches over tube sheets were replaced by 173 2-inch fire tubes and 28 5⅜-inch flue tubes containing a superheater, 16 feet 6 inches over tube sheets, increasing the primary heating surface from 2,360 to 2,400 square feet and adding 525 square feet of superheating surface. Boiler pressure was reduced from 200 pounds per square inch to 185. The smokebox was lengthened to reduce spark emission. The 21-inch × 28-inch slide valve cylinders on the 2-6-2s were replaced with 24-inch × 28-inch cylinders with 14-inch piston valves on the 2-8-2s. As a result, engine weight increased from 204,500 pounds to 249,000 pounds and tractive effort from 33,000 to 40,000 pounds. While the 2-6-2s were capable of hauling 1,600 tons between Glendive and Billings, the 2-8-2s could handle 2,600 tons, an increase of 62%.

The 2-8-2 was one of the types endorsed by the USRA; 46% of the total USRA locomotives were of this type—more than any other. The light Mikado was the first of the USRA locomotives to appear— "light" because their axle loading was limited to 55,000 pounds.[121] The first order placed by the USRA was for 575 of these engines. The USRA placed the order on April 30, 1918; Baldwin outshopped the first one on July 1, destined for the Baltimore & Ohio. The frames were of cast steel 6 inches thick; cast steel was used extensively in numerous components. The USRA had a sense for the most efficient possible use of scarce labor; a Duplex power stoker fired the 67-square foot grate with its brick arch on arch tubes, 24-inch combustion chamber and powered grate shaker; the railroad companies typically did not order stokers with engines of this size. The primary heating surface provided by the firebox and 216 2¼-inch × 19-foot fire tubes totaled 3,785 square feet; the Schmidt-type elements contained in 40 5½-inch flue tubes provided 880 square feet of superheating surface. The boiler assembly combined welding and riveting. Boiler pressure was high, but not unusually so, at 200 pounds per square inch. Walschaert valve gear with a Ragonnet power reverser controlled steam supply to the 26-inch × 30-inch cylinders; these and 63-inch driving wheels produced 54,600 pounds of tractive effort. Engine weight was 290,800 pounds. These engines were still in service on many railroads during World War II; in the flat terrain of the Texas & Pacific's Louisiana division, one of them hauled 10,100 tons in a scheduled freight train of 126 cars.[122]

At the same time the USRA ordered 157 heavy 2-8-2s.[123] These were only slightly larger than the light version, with a fatter boiler, 59,750-pound axle loading and 60,000 pounds of tractive effort. The boiler pressure was only 190 pounds per square inch. A slightly bigger grate, at 70 square feet, fired 4,295 square feet of primary heating surface, with 995 square feet of superheating surface. A Lewis power reverser was used for the Walschaert valve gear instead of Ragonnet. Cylinders measured 27 inches × 32 inches. Many parts were interchangeable with the lighter engines. Engine weight was 320,000 pounds.

At 14,100 built between 1905 and 1930, the 2-8-2 was the fourth most numerous of all American locomotive types, after the 4-4-0, 2-8-0, 4-6-0 and 0-6-0.

The Chicago, Burlington & Quincy classified its USRA heavy Mikados O-4. Otto Perry photographed No. 5509, built by Baldwin in 1919, at Alliance, Nebraska, on April 12, 1936 (Denver Public Library, Otto C. Perry collection, OP-3943).

8.2.3 Decapods

The 2-10-0 was uncommon in U.S. domestic service, typically being used on the smaller railroads to provide high pulling power with low axle loading.

In 1907, the Buffalo, Rochester & Pittsburg bought six 2-10-0s from Alco Brooks for pusher service on Clarion Hill, between Clarion Junction, Pennsylvania, and Freeman, 17 miles away up a 1.1% grade with sharp curvature.[124] The rated train load for Clarion Hill was 3,350 tons with a 2-8-0 road engine and another as a pusher. Track improvements and the new decapods were intended to increase train loads to 4,000 tons with a 2-8-0 road engine and a decapod pushing.

The decapods weighed 268,000 pounds and developed 55,350 pounds of tractive effort. The wheel arrangement allowed an adhesion weight of 243,000 pounds while keeping axle loading down to 48,600 pounds. Fifty-two-inch driving wheels kept the rigid wheel base within acceptable limits, while making for high tractive effort. The firebox, with its 56-square foot grate, had a 3-foot combustion chamber but no brick arch. The 210-pounds per square inch boiler was unsuperheated. Walschaert valve gear drove slide valves. The suspension was equalized between the pony truck and the first two driving axles and between the rear three driving axles. The tender was unusually large, containing 9,000 gallons of water and 14 tons of coal, bringing the total weight up to 432,000 pounds.

The company ordered two more 2-10-0s from Alco in 1909.[125] A 56-square foot grate, with a combustion chamber, fired 3,535 square feet of heating surface. Two hundred ten pounds of steam pressure, working through 24-inch × 28-inch cylinders, developed 52,750 pounds of tractive effort in these 268,000-pound engines.

During the summer of 1915, the American locomotive industry received an immense order from the Russian State Railways for 400 2-10-0s. The order was divided between Baldwin (250), Alco (100) and the Canadian Locomotive Company (50).[126] Apart from the size of the order, nothing was remarkable about these engines. With 51,500 pounds of tractive effort, they were designed to haul 1,300-ton trains at 8 to 10 miles per hour up a 0.8% grade. Design details were part American, part Russian. The engines were fitted with the relatively rare Le Chatelier cylinder brakes. New orders in 1917 brought the total of Russian Decapods to 1,231, of which 1,057 were built.[127] Production was in full swing at the time of the Russian Revolution. Payment difficulties with the Soviet government caused shipments to cease, with the result that 200 of these locomotives became available to the American railroads at a time of acute need. Passed on from one user to another, Russian Decapods worked on forty-two different railroads. During World War II, the Americans built more than 2,200 similar engines for the Soviet government. A Russian Decapod is preserved on the Strasburg Railway, Strasburg, Pennsylvania.

The Pennsylvania's engineers pulled a rabbit out of the hat with the enormous I-1s 2-10-0. Juniata shops built a prototype in December 1916, followed by 122 in 1918–19.[128] A 70-square foot grate with a Duplex stoker fired a boiler, 19 feet over tube sheets, with 4,043 square feet of primary heating surface. The power potential of this size limitation was increased by using the unprecedented boiler pressure of 250 pounds per square inch, applied to 30-inch × 32-inch cylinders. To remain within the maximum steaming rate of the boiler, the designers limited the cut-off in full gear to 50%; this flow rate allowed the piston valves to be only 12 inches in diameter. Small auxiliary steam ports, 1½ inches × ⅛ inch,[129] admitted steam to the cylinders on starting from any crank position—so small that no significant amount of steam flowed through them when the engine was moving. To improve the ability of the 62-inch driving wheels to accommodate

A 2-10-0 Russian Decapod, built by Alco or Baldwin in 1915–17, acquired by the Charleston & Western Carolina as No. 400 and photographed at Spartanburg, South Carolina, on October 22, 1930 (Denver Public Library, Otto C. Perry collection, OP-2856).

Baldwin and Altoona built the Pennsylvania class I-1s 2-10-0s between 1917 and 1923. No. 4246 is shown, at Cleveland, Ohio, on September 28, 1930 (Denver Public Library, Otto C. Perry collection, OP-14275).

curves, the middle three driving wheels were blind-flanged. The prototype weighed 366,500 pounds and developed 80,600 pounds of tractive effort. Changes for production brought the engine weight up to 371,800 pounds and tractive effort up to 90,000 pounds.

The prototype was not fitted with a power stoker initially; early tests were hand-fired at up to 13,225 pounds of coal per hour. Limiting the maximum cut-off to 50% was successful.[130] Road tests recorded 3,080 indicated horsepower at 40% cut-off, consuming an astonishingly low 2.9 pounds of coal and 15.4 pounds of steam per indicated horsepower-hour. Lowest coal consumption was 2.0 pounds per indicated horsepower-hour while developing 1,780 horsepower at 30% cut-off, for a total thermal efficiency of 8.1%. Maximum recorded power output was 3,480 indicated horsepower. A road test recorded a drawbar pull of 81,000 pounds at 7 miles per hour. Compared to an L-1s, the I-1s saved 38% in coal consumption while developing 46% more tractive effort. The Pennsylvania bought 475 I-1s's from Baldwin in 1922–23 with Worthington feed water heaters.

North American locomotive builders manufactured about 4,100 2-10-0s between 1870 and 1945, comprising:

For domestic service (29 railroads)	869*
Russian Decapods shipped during World War I	857
Russian Decapods retained in U.S., 1917	200
Russian Decapods, World War II	2,200

*As 597 of these were Pennsylvania I-1s's, the remainder were few.

8.2.4 Heyday of the Santa Fe

"A maximum theoretical tractive effort of 71,500 lbs. is obtained with one group of drivers and two simple cylinders."[131] The writing was on the wall for the ponderous Mallets. The engines thus described were a class of five 2-10-2s built by Baldwin for the Burlington, put into service in 1912. Superheating, stoker firing and track that allowed axle loads as high as 60,000 pounds meant that single-expansion, rigid-frame engines could be as powerful as the early Mallets. A seldom-acknowledged factor in the ultimate triumph of the high-performance, rigid-frame locomotive was the railroads' civil engineering programs, providing ever stronger track and substructures and permitting a rapid increase in permissible axle loadings.

At 379,000 pounds engine weight, the Burlington 2-10-2s weighed more than the company's 2-6-6-2 Mallets; 80% of this was available as adhesion weight. Driving wheels 64 inches in diameter meant that maximum power, typically delivered at 700 feet per minute piston speed, was achieved at 25 miles per hour. The designers calculated that, at an evaporation rate of 8 pounds of water per pound of coal and a steam consumption of 21 pounds of steam per indicated horsepower-hour, the firebox would demand 7,200 pounds of coal per hour. The intended service in the Illinois coalfields would require continuous maximum performance and "while there are some firemen capable of handling this amount of fuel, the average fireman cannot do so." To achieve the design power output therefore required either oil firing or a power stoker. The result was a Barnum underfeed stoker firing an 88-square foot grate.

A combustion chamber extended 27 inches forward of the throat sheet. Instead of a brick arch, a Gaines wall between the firebox and the combustion chamber left a 38-inch space between the top of the wall and the crown sheet. Total primary heating surface was 5,160 square feet in 285 2¼-inch fire tubes just under 23 feet long. A fire-tube superheater provided a further 970 square feet of heating surface. The thirty 6-inch superheater flues were arranged in four vertical rows, rather than being clustered in the top of the boiler, as was more usual. Walschaert valve gear with a Ragonnet power reverser drove

"The 2-10-0 was uncommon in US domestic service." Otto Perry photographed Alabama, Tennessee & Northern No. 402 at Mobile, Alabama, on October 15, 1929. Drury (p. 351) identifies this locomotive as a type that Baldwin promoted in the 1920s and sold to several short lines (Denver Public Library, Otto C. Perry collection, OP-7).

Baldwin built this Chicago, Burlington & Quincy class M-2 2-10-2, No. 6106, in 1914, shown at St. Joseph, Missouri, on September 16, 1930 (Denver Public Library, Otto C. Perry collection, OP-3973).

15-inch piston valves. Cast steel was used extensively for the frames, pistons and the main driving axle and crankpin. The suspension equalization was divided between the third and fourth driving axles. Because the routes of intended use were sharply curved, side play was built into the front and back driving wheels, requiring knuckle pins on the side rod connections; the center driving wheels were blind-flanged. Such massive counterbalancing was needed that two flyweights had to be pressed and keyed onto the main driving axle between the frames.

These five class M-1's were followed by five more classes of 2-10-2s, progressively improved as technology became available, totaling a further eighty-six engines up to 1921. By comparison, the company's Mallet purchases totaled only nineteen, beginning in 1908 and ending in 1911.

The rigid-frame locomotive crept up on the Mallet, even though the frame was an increasingly complex and massive structure, demanding of design, metallurgy and fabrication and sometimes not as rigid or as durable as might be desired. As companies strengthened their track and substructures, the centipede-like grip of the Mallets was no longer the virtue it once was.

Baldwin was adept at satisfying its customers, ranging from the Santa Fe with its subtle and sometimes weird designs, to those like the Baltimore & Ohio and the Burlington that demanded raw power. There was little subtlety about the thirty-one 2-10-2s that Baldwin built for the Baltimore & Ohio in 1914: 406,000-pound monsters with an axle loading of 67,360 pounds.[132]

A Street stoker threw coal onto an 88-square foot grate, firing a 200-pound per square inch boiler with 5,575 square feet of heating surface, 23 feet over tube sheets. At the economic maximum of 120 pounds of coal per square foot of grate per hour, the stoker would be handling 10,000 pounds per hour, more than the sustained capability of two human firemen. Walschaert valve gear with a Ragonnet power reverser drove 16-inch piston valves supplying 30-inch × 32-inch cylinders. The 21-foot rigid wheelbase accommodated the Baltimore & Ohio's curves in three ways. The center driving wheels had blind flanges. The flanges on the front and back driving wheels were under-gauged by 1 inch, the second and fourth driving wheels by ¾ inch. All driving wheels had ¼-inch play in their axle boxes. All of these tolerances would have loosened with wear; track was typically laid slightly over-gauge on curves anyway. The result was 84,500 pounds of tractive effort, more than many Mallets that had been in service less than ten years.

The Erie soon followed suit, ordering a trial 2-10-2 from Baldwin in 1915.[133] These engines, of closely similar dimensions to the Baltimore & Ohio's, were so successful that the company ordered a class of forty-two, soon followed by thirty more slightly smaller engines divided between Baldwin, Alco and Lima. The Erie 2-10-2s were designed with relatively high speeds in mind; Baldwin built them with 63-inch driving wheels and gave special attention to designing the lightest possible reciprocating parts.

Even though ten years had elapsed since the first 2-10-2s were built for the Santa Fe, they were still few in number as railroads settled for Mikados or Mallets according to traffic and route demands. Now, however, track capable of accepting unprecedented axle loadings, insatiable demand for freight power and disillusionment with the construction and operating costs of the Mallets gave new life to the rigid-frame engine. The years 1915–18 were the glory days of the massive American 2-10-2.

The 2-10-2's long rigid wheelbase limited its usefulness. When Alco delivered twelve to the New York, Ontario & Western at the end of 1915, and five to the Erie, they took special pains to get around this problem.[134] The front driving axle ran through a pair of driving

Impressive, even in decay, this Baltimore & Ohio class S 2-10-2, No. 6020, built by Baldwin in 1914, awaits scrapping at Cumberland, Maryland, on August 7, 1936 (Denver Public Library, Otto C. Perry collection, OP-2522).

boxes which transmitted its thrust to the frames. A spacer held the pair of driving boxes at the correct lateral spacing but they were free to move 2 inches from side to side in the frames. The spacer supported its fraction of the engine weight through a cross member attached to the springs and capable only of vertical movement. Between the spacer and the cross member was a pair of rockers, so that engine weight tended to centralize the driving boxes. The front end of the front side rod was pin-jointed; the front crank pin had a spherical bushing to accommodate this motion. The front driving wheel suspension was equalized with the front truck. Both the truck and the front driving axle combined to guide the engine through sharp curves.

The Erie engines weighed 401,000 pounds and developed 83,000 pounds of tractive effort. A Street stoker fired a 95-square foot grate with a Gaines wall and brick arch to heat 317 2½-inch fire tubes which, together with the firebox, provided 4,960 square feet of primary heating surface. Sixty flue tubes, 5½ inches in diameter, added 1,274 square feet of superheating surface. Steam at 200 pounds per square inch drove 31-inch × 32-inch pistons. Driving wheels 63 inches in diameter provided a compromise between speed and hauling power. Power stokers, Baker valve gear with Ragonnet power reversers and cast vanadium steel frames were increasingly typical of new big engine construction.

By 1916, power stokers were common on the heaviest new freight engines. When Baldwin built two 2-8-8-2 Mallets and six 2-10-2s for the Duluth, Missabe & Northern, all had Street stokers.[135] A modified trailing truck by Baldwin, with the rear driving wheel springs decoupled from the back equalizer, addressed a problem with crosswise rocking of the trailing truck. As both rigid and total wheelbases increased in length, more complicated suspension arrangements became necessary.

The Lehigh Valley's Baldwin 2-10-2s of 1916–17 had 100-square foot grates with 60-inch combustion chambers, designed for mixed anthracite and bituminous coal, fitted with Street stokers and air-operated fire doors.[136] The firebox had always been a complicated and problematic structure. The inner and outer fireboxes in these 2-10-2s were held together by 2,913 staybolts of four different types: expansion, radial, rigid and flexible. The boiler pressure was 200 pounds per square inch; the long wheelbase allowed 21 feet over tube sheets, hence 4,485 square feet of primary heating surface. Of the first forty 2-10-2s, thirty were fitted with Walschaert and ten with Baker valve gear. Ragonnet power reverse and Nikrome steel for the larger reciprocating parts were common to both groups.

These engines weighed 370,000 pounds and developed 73,000 pounds of tractive effort; each one displaced two 2-8-0s. They made the 88-mile run between Manchester, New York, and Sayre, Pennsylvania, with a 4,000-ton train in 6½ hours against adverse grades up to 0.4%. In spite of their enormous pulling power, they were slow and cumbersome; the company sold sixteen of them to the Hocking Valley in 1920 and rebuilt twenty as 2-8-2s in 1928–9. The remainder survived until they were scrapped in 1947–51.[137]

The Denver & Rio Grande set new records with ten 2-10-2s bought from Alco in 1917. At 428,500 pounds engine weight, they were the heaviest 2-10-2s built up to that time.[138] Boiler pressure was still only 195 pounds per square inch. Heating surface was maximized by very low-profile stack and domes and a length of 23 feet over tube sheets, providing 5,000 square feet of primary heating surface, with a further 1,330 square feet of superheating surface. The firebox included an 88-square foot grate, fired by a Street stoker, and a 50-inch combustion chamber. An Alco power reverser controlled Baker valve gear. The front two driving axles were equalized with the leading truck; the rear three driving axles were equalized with the trailing truck. These engines developed 81,000 pounds of tractive effort, almost twice that of a 2-8-0. To accommodate curvature, Alco used a Wood-

This Denver & Rio Grande Western class F-81 2-10-2, No. 1405, was built by Alco in 1917 and photographed at Helper, Utah, on July 4, 1949. The objects along the side of the firebox are overfire steam jets (Denver Public Library, Otto C. Perry collection, OP-9751).

Baldwin built this Union Pacific class TTT-1 2-10-2, No. 5006, in 1917, shown at Wilson, Kansas, on August 22, 1937. Smoke fills the cab as this engine is fired up, before steam pressure suffices to bring the blower into action (Denver Public Library, Otto C. Perry collection, OP-17152).

ward floating front driving axle; all driving wheels were flanged but the flanges were set just over 3 inches less than the nominal track gauge. Between January and March 1917, the traffic between Denver and Salida increased by 1.2%; the first five 2-10-2s reduced engine-miles by 11% in the same period.

For decades the Union Pacific had suffered—to the point of bankruptcy in 1893—from the cost of maintaining a vast track mileage in uniquely hostile conditions of terrain, climate and water quality, paid for by a sparse market. This changed for the better as the Far West developed in the early 20th century, with increasing commerce between the Pacific coast and the prairies, the mid-west and the eastern States.

The twenty-seven massive 2-10-2s, designed under the supervision of C. E. Fuller, superintendent of motive power, and ordered from Baldwin in 1917, heralded a new—and legendary—era in Union Pacific motive power.[139]

They weighed 357,000 pounds, 285,000 pounds of adhesion weight. A Street Type C stoker fired the 84-square-foot grate with a combustion chamber extending 4 feet ahead of the throat sheet; a brick arch was supported on arch tubes. A Ragonnet steam- and air-power reverser controlled Walschaert valve gear, driving 15-inch piston valves.

Two hundred sixty 2¼-inch fire tubes, 22 feet long, provided 4,774 square feet of heating surface, with another 378 square feet in the firebox sheets and 1,262 square feet in the superheater, supplying steam at 200 pounds per square inch to two 29½-inch × 30-inch cylinders. These produced 70,450 pounds of tractive effort, an order of magnitude greater than any other Union Pacific rigid-frame engine and equaling some of the Mallets. Driving wheels 63 inches in diameter imparted speed as well as tractive effort. The resulting maximum

power output was 2,940 horsepower at 30 miles per hour—higher power at higher speed than most other rigid-frame engines. Lugging trains up the eastbound grades brought coal consumption to 358 pounds per thousand gross ton-miles.

The front driving axle ran in axle boxes permitting sideplay to deal with curves; all the driving wheels were flanged. The leading truck was of the Economy constant-resistance type, of which no details are to hand. The combination of a Commonwealth rear frame cradle and a Delta trailing truck served the purposes of a frame, radius bar and equalizer. The trailing truck was equalized with the two back pairs of driving wheels through a central, vertical heart-shaped link suspended from a transverse beam hung from the rear driving wheel springs. This link was not only the equalizer connection, but also the radius bar pivot. The bearing between the equalizer frame of the truck and the locomotive frame was made with a spherical surface to provide flexibility.

The Union Pacific assigned fifteen of these monsters to the stretch between Ogden, Utah, and Evanston, Wyoming, 76 miles with a ruling grade of 1.14% eastbound, intended to haul the same 1,800-ton trains—without helpers—that the company's 2-8-2s handled over the 400 miles east of Evanston, where the ruling grade was only 0.8%.

In 1917, the Wabash received twenty-five 2-10-2s from Alco, planned to handle 5,000-ton trains northbound against a 0.4% ruling grade between St. Louis and Chicago, compared to the 3,500 tons hauled by 2-8-2s hitherto, hiking tonnage by 43% and cutting train mileage by 30%.[140] The company found that their 64-inch driving wheels could handle 30-car troop trains at speeds up to 35 miles per hour. Peak power output was estimated at 2,950 cylinder horsepower. A Street Duplex stoker fired an 80-square foot grate, firing 5,370 square feet of primary heating surface, 23 feet over tube sheets, gen-

The biggest engines ever built for the Wabash were these class L-1 2-10-2s, built by Alco in 1917. No. 2519 is shown at Decatur, Illinois, on September 19, 1930 (Denver Public Library, Otto C. Perry collection, OP-19739).

erating steam at 195 pounds per square inch. This was superheated in a 1,129-square foot superheater. Applied to 29-inch × 32-inch cylinders, the result was 69,700 pounds of tractive effort. Engine weight was 395,000 pounds. A Mellin power reverser controlled the Walschaert valve gear. The order was not repeated; these were the biggest engines ever built for the Wabash.

In 1918, the Pennsylvania took delivery of sixty 2-10-2s, thirty-five from Alco, twenty-five from Baldwin, class N-1s.[141] They were similar in size to those built by Alco for the Denver & Rio Grande the previous year, except that greater attention was paid to flexibility on curves. For this purpose the front and rear driving wheels were fitted with a Woodward floating axle, details of which this study has not revealed. The center driving wheels had blind flanges. The suspension was new; the front and rear driving wheels were equalized with their respective front and rear trucks, while the center three driving axles were equalized independently. A Crawford underfeed stoker fired the 80-square foot grate. A combustion chamber extended nearly 5 feet forward of the throat sheet. The boiler was built for 250 pounds per square inch, but working pressure was restricted to 205 pounds for reasons unknown. Weighing 435,000 pounds and developing 81,000 pounds of tractive effort, these engines handled 85-car trains weighing 6,000 tons over level country between Pittsburgh, Erie, Pennsylvania, and Ashtabula, Ohio. The Pennsylvania subsequently received 130 USRA heavy 2-10-2s, class N-2s. (Drury, 328, quotes 130; Fisher, C. E., *The Steam Locomotives of the Pennsylvania Railroad System, Part III,* Journal RLHS, October 1954, 130, quotes 125.) Only 1 or 2 years after receiving them, the company rebuilt them with Belpaire fireboxes.

The 2-10-2 was one of the types selected by the USRA as a standard and was built in heavy and light versions, the light version being the first to appear.[142] Like other "light" USRA locomotives, the light

2-10-2 was limited to a 55,000-pound axle loading. The USRA 2-10-2 was fitted with a Duplex power stoker and powered fire doors. Cast steel frames 6 inches thick were common to the USRA engines. The firebox and boiler were of identical dimensions to the USRA heavy 4-8-2 with a 60-inch combustion chamber ahead of the 76-square foot grate, 4,665 square feet of primary heating surface, 1,085 square feet of superheating surface, 20 feet 6 inches over tube sheets and 200 pounds per square inch boiler pressure. With 27-inch × 32-inch cylinders, the resulting tractive effort was 69,400 pounds.

The first USRA heavy 2-10-2 was completed by Alco Brooks in early 1919.[143] These engines were designed for a 60,000-pound axle load. At 380,000 pounds engine weight and 74,000 pounds tractive effort, they were smaller than some earlier 2-10-2s. However, like all the USRA engines, the designers made sure that the boiler could generate more steam than the cylinders could demand at peak power output at a piston speed of 1,000 feet per minute. Curiously, boiler pressure was kept at 190 pounds per square inch, generated from an 88-square foot stoker-fired grate, 5,155 square feet of primary heating surface and 1,230 square feet of superheating surface.

The USRA standard locomotives were a snapshot of best American practice, as it was in 1918. In 1920, the railroads returned to corporate management, and to their own design and procurement practices, in some cases significantly influenced by USRA design. William D. Edson offers this trenchant epitaph on the USRA locomotives[144]:

Without a doubt the most universally accepted steam locomotives ever built were the U. S. R. A. standard locomotives designed during the regime of the United States Railroad Administration of World War I. A total of 1856 were built to twelve distinct designs for the Administration itself, and almost twice that number were built for the individual

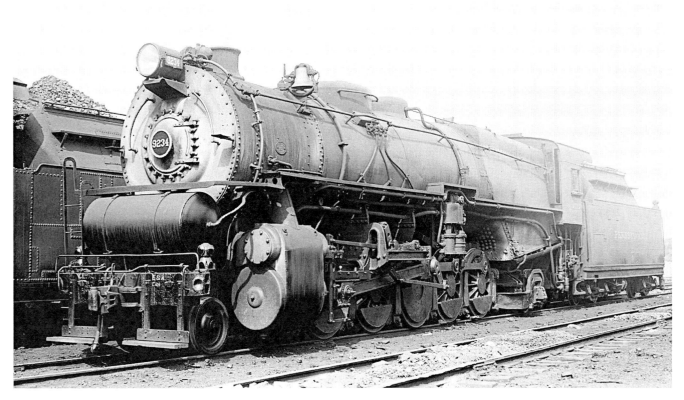

The Pennsylvania's 2-10-2 was the class N-1s, built by Alco and Baldwin in 1918. Otto Perry photographed No. 9234 at Erie, Pennsylvania, on August 9, 1937 (Denver Public Library, Otto C. Perry collection, OP-14316).

The Pennsylvania received USRA heavy Santa Fes from Alco and Baldwin in 1919 and classified them N-2s. No. 7284 is shown at Cincinnati, Ohio, on June 28, 1950. These two photographs illustrate the difference between the Commonwealth (N-1s) and Alco (N-2s) trailing trucks (Denver Public Library, Otto C. Perry collection, OP-14299).

railroads following their return to private ownership when the war was over. In fact, new steam locomotives built to U. S. R. A. designs have been ordered in recent years, even after the growth in popularity of the diesel locomotive. Well over 5000 of these U. S. R. A.-design locomotives were built, distributed among almost all the major railroads of the country, and it is safe to say that a very high percentage of these engines is still in existence (1953).

Eighty years later, on the threshold of the twenty-first century, the Chinese were still building standard-gauge steam locomotives. Only a skilled eye could detect any difference between their 2-8-2s and an American 2-8-2 of 1920. The Chinese QJ 2-10-2s differed from American style slightly in appearance, not at all in dimensions or performance. From our current perspective, we can see that the year 1920 was a turning point in worldwide steam locomotive design, even though this was not apparent at the time. Remarkable developments were in store for the steam locomotive in America after 1920; only in rare instances did these innovations extend to the outside world.

Section 8.3. Mallets

Anatole Mallet's articulated compound locomotive found its truest application on the railroads of America. Sadly for its inventor, this was after his patent had expired. Its incarnation on the Baltimore & Ohio in 1904 was a visionary experiment, at once the biggest Mallet built to date and the biggest steam locomotive anywhere in the world. American motive power superintendents soon realized that this was a dream come true, offering almost limitless tractive effort to haul immensely long freight trains over the Appalachians and the western mountains. The craze for Mallets that followed produced monstrosities as well as monsters. The USRA endorsed the saner Mallet designs.

The new engine was "designed according to the well known system of A. Mallet. This type of locomotive has been received with much favor in Europe, there being about 400 in use in 1900."[145] John E. Muhlfeld, the Baltimore & Ohio's Superintendent of Motive Power, was behind this innovation, wanting a locomotive to eliminate pusher service on the steep, curving grades that were a legacy from the Baltimore & Ohio's early construction in mountainous terrain. It is not clear whether the company designed it, or Alco—probably both.

This locomotive was a radical departure from anything built in America hitherto, a bold, expensive experiment, incorporating a mass of new features and posing new design problems; it would change the nature of American freight power. Alco's C. J. Mellin modified the Mallet compounding system, although the details have not come to light. The articulated frame, the absence of truck wheels, Walschaert valve gear, flexibly jointed steam pipes, power reversing gear, steam-balanced piston packing rings, a single-disc balanced throttle valve and the abnormally high boiler pressure were all new to America. No difficulties were experienced with any of these innovations; the new design was acclaimed as a complete success.

Everything about the locomotive was on a gigantic scale. The 0-6-6-0 wheel arrangement put the whole 334,500-pound engine weight into adhesion with an axle loading of 55,750 pounds. The boiler pressure, at 235 pounds per square inch, was higher than had ever been used in the U.S. in a locomotive (other than at Purdue). The 72-square foot grate, above the back 56-inch driving wheels, was the biggest built hitherto for bituminous coal. Two fire doors opened

The Baltimore & Ohio's 0-6-6-0, No. 2400, built by Alco in 1904—the first American Mallet. The boy wearing knickerbockers and the spotless condition of the locomotive suggest that it was photographed when new (courtesy California State Railroad Museum, Negative #900/19947).

into a firebox 9 feet long × 8 feet wide. The boiler contained 436 2¼-inch × 21-foot fire tubes—5,585 square feet of heating surface.

A new throttle valve opened by lifting an umbrella-shaped member off a seat, changing the flow direction of the steam and throwing entrained water against the walls of the valve, whence it dripped back into the boiler. Steam passed through 5-inch pipes down each side of the boiler exterior through piston valves into the 20-inch × 32-inch high-pressure cylinders. The high-pressure cylinders were in two castings, with their match-line offset from the boiler centerline so that one casting accommodated a flexible pipe joint.

Steam exhausted from the high-pressure cylinders into a 9-inch longitudinal receiver pipe beneath the boiler centerline; the back end was ball-jointed in one high-pressure cylinder casting; the front end was ball-jointed to a Y pipe, the two branches of which were rigidly connected to the low-pressure cylinder castings. Allen-ported, Richardson-balanced slide valves controlled steam flow to the 32-inch × 32-inch low-pressure cylinders. From the low-pressure cylinders, steam exhausted through a common exhaust pipe to the 5½-inch nozzle. Because the low-pressure cylinders had to move relative to the boiler, the exhaust pipe ended in ball joints with a slip joint between.

Today, this would be achieved by hoses and flexible tubing that did not exist then. Flexible pipe joints were the bugbear of all articulated steam locomotives. Keeping them lubricated and steam-tight and taking up wear was a maintenance nightmare. If they were not properly maintained, leaking steam obscured the view of the enginemen and caused alarming losses in power and efficiency. A particular benefit of the Mallet design was that the high-pressure steam pipes were all rigidly connected; only the low-pressure steam needed flexible pipe joints. This piping, varying in detail, was common to all Mallets.

Housed in the high-pressure cylinder castings was the Mellin interceptor valve, first used in the two-cylinder cross-compounds built by the Richmond Locomotive Works, a complicated device that, nevertheless, maximized the potential of the Mallet. The valve was a sleeve with three annular surfaces of different areas, A, B and C. Rings

A and C pushed in one direction under steam pressure; ring B pushed in the opposite direction. Ring B had a greater area than ring A, but less than rings A and C combined. Therefore, when the engineer opened the throttle, live steam pressure acting on ring B moved the valve to open a port, admitting steam to the receiver pipe. This pressure acted on ring C. As soon as pressure built up, the steam pressure on rings A and C overcame the force exerted by the pressure on ring B and closed the valve. The valve thus floated as steam acted on it, to produce a desired pressure in the receiver pipe.

This valve admitted live steam to the receiver pipe on first opening of the throttle, closing automatically when the pressure in the receiver pipe and the low-pressure cylinders built up to the design level. The engineer could also activate an "emergency valve," supplying live steam direct to the receiver pipe; in this mode, a pipe led the high-pressure cylinder exhaust direct to exhaust.

Each drive unit had its own Walschaert valve gear. The engineer controlled cut-off with a single power reverser with a flexible linkage to the front drive unit. The power reverser was an augmenter working directly from the engineer's reversing lever in the cab. A second lever, pivoted on the main lever, operated the valves controlling this augmenter. The augmenter comprised two pistons in separate cylinders on a common piston rod. One piston was driven by compressed air; to move the gear, the second lever admitted compressed air to one side of this piston. The other piston ran in a cylinder filled with oil. Normally, oil could not flow between one side of this piston and the other, so locking the gear in its set position. When the engineer worked the second lever, it opened a connection between the two sides of the piston, which allowed oil to flow between one side and the other, but damped out backlash.

Articulation and suspension were the product of much thought, both by Alco and by the Mallet's European originators.[146] The two drive units had separate frames, joined by a hinge which had to allow some relative vertical movement, bending and twisting between the two units. The back driving wheels supported the main frame, to which the firebox and back half of the boiler were fixed. The front driving wheels supported the front frame; a large pedestal just behind the center of gravity of the front drive unit supported the front of the boiler in a cradle which slid from side to side on the pedestal, centered by springs. To lighten the load on this slide, a pair of vertical hanger bolts between the front and rear frames took some of the weight of the boiler.

The suspension of the front drive unit was equalized by a cross-equalizer between the front springs. The rear drive unit was equalized separately, but without cross-equalization. The principle of triangular suspension was thus preserved, and the locomotive was able to accommodate itself to both cross-wise and lengthwise irregularities in the track.

When the locomotive was drifting downgrade, the large low-pressure cylinders sucked in cold air, thermally shocking the cylinders and valves and drafting the fire strongly when it was not needed. To prevent this, by-pass valves were fitted into the cylinder castings which opened automatically when the throttle was closed, making a direct connection between both ends of the cylinders.

The new locomotive was exhibited—before it was ever used—at the Louisiana Purchase Exposition, St. Louis, Missouri, in the summer of 1904. It went into regular service on January 6, 1905, as a

Typical Mallet steam piping (redrawn from *RRG*, August 16, 1907, 171, 173; October 4, 1907, 386, 388).

helper on freights between Cumberland, Maryland, and Connellsville, Pennsylvania, a division characterized by heavy freight traffic, sharp curves and steep grades.[147] The tractive effort of the new engine was 66,000 pounds compound, 91,000 pounds single expansion; this compared with 42,000 pounds for one of the company's 2-8-0s. A pair of 2-8-0s could move a 2,025-ton train over the division. With the new Mallet as a helper, a 2-8-0 road engine could move a 3,210-ton train over the same division at speeds up to 10 miles per hour on the steepest grades, in good weather and with reasonably good coal. The Mallet developed up to 2,435 horsepower, working single-expansion, 1,905 horsepower working compound, compared to 965 horsepower for a 2-8-0.

Railroadmen were quick to notice the enormous power of a Mallet working single-expansion. The engine was so heavy that it could be designed for a tractive effort that would merely produce wheel slip in existing, lighter engines. Helper duty was particularly hard on locomotives; periods of maximum effort, alternating with periods of drifting down-grade and waiting for the next train, caused wide fluctuations in firebox temperature, dirty fires and the leakage and failure of fire tubes but, in five months of hard service, no significant wear, maintenance problems or track damage appeared. Early statistics on trains averaging 2,190 tons showed firing rates of only 62 pounds of coal per square foot of grate per hour, resulting in a respectable 8 pounds of water evaporated per pound of coal. Coal consumption was 215 pounds of coal per thousand ton-miles—not surprising on steep grades. Over three years, the operating cost was 27 cents per engine-mile, compared to about 20 cents for a conventional locomotive, but the added performance more than paid for this.

The first of more than 3,000 American Mallets, *Old Maude* was never replicated. Sad to say, this historic locomotive, exhibited in spotless condition at the Baltimore & Ohio centenary in 1927, was scrapped in 1938.[148]

It is no coincidence that the Baltimore & Ohio, with its legacy of steep grades and sharp curves dating back to the earliest days of American railroading, was the first to use the Mallet in America. This is so important to the history of American locomotive development that the words of C. J. Mellin, a senior official with Alco, are quoted here as they were spoken in December 1908[149]:

> In striving to meet this demand (for greater power), the locomotive designers and builders were brought face to face with an unsurmountable barrier to further progress in the enlargement of engines on the old lines; and in 1902 the American Locomotive Company decided to work out a design of a heavy, powerful locomotive for the Baltimore & Ohio Railroad, having two sets of engines under one boiler, capable of adjusting themselves independently to the alinement of roads with curvatures up to 30 deg. on the principle developed by the prominent French engineer, M. Anatole Mallet, of Paris.
>
> Mr. Loree, then President of the Baltimore & Ohio Railroad, considered the question seriously; but it was first thought that it would be of no advantage to the Baltimore & Ohio Railroad, even if it proved successful, and the subject was left undecided for some time. In the latter part of 1903, on the recommendation of J. E. Muhlfeld, who in the meantime had become General Superintendent of Motive Power, the Baltimore & Ohio ordered one engine of this type, which was built at the Schenectady Works of the American Locomotive Company during the winter of 1903 and 1904, to suit the conditions of that railway.
>
> Propositions for building the Mallet type of engine had been made both by S. M. Vauclain, General Manager of the Baldwin Locomotive Works, and by the writer, several years prior to the above date, but the one under consideration is, so far as the writer is aware, the first engine of this type completely designed and built in the United States.

Vauclain's reply showed that the American Mallet had a longer pre-history than this. In building the first one, Alco had stolen a competitive advantage from Baldwin which Vauclain strove to regain. Vauclain said that Baldwin had carefully examined the Mallet displayed at the Paris Exposition of 1889 and tried to promote the idea throughout the 1890s without success.

In 1892, Baldwin built an 0-6-6-0 for the Sinnemahoning Valley Railroad, named the *Edward T. Johnson,* using the Meyer type of articulation. Engine and tender rested on a single frame. Two six-wheel drive units swiveled beneath the frame, one under the tender, one under the boiler. Conventionally, a Meyer had four single-expansion cylinders set back to back under the center of the locomotive. Baldwin's modification was to set a pair of Vauclain compound cylinders at the rear end of each drive unit.[150] The railroad merged with two others to form the Buffalo & Susquehanna which returned the locomotive to Baldwin in 1893. Unable to resell it, Baldwin scrapped it.[151] Thereafter, Baldwin promoted the Mallet design.

In the depression of the mid–1890s, there was little interest in a locomotive capable of hauling more freight than existing designs; a locomotive of very high tractive effort would have damaged rolling stock in long trains when most freight cars were of relatively weak construction. In 1898, Baldwin approached the Erie with a design but the Erie was put off by the size of the locomotive. In 1904, at the same time that Alco was building its first Mallet for the Baltimore & Ohio, Baldwin placed four of this type with the American Railroad of Porto Rico. Baldwin then spent several years trying to interest the Santa Fe, but without success. After the success of the Baltimore & Ohio engine was proven, Baldwin wiped out Alco's competitive advantage by placing more than a hundred Mallets with the Great Northern and the Northern Pacific over the next five years.

Baldwin stole a march on Alco with a connection between the front and rear frames that allowed the front frame to move laterally as well as radially in relation to the rear frame. Baldwin also omitted the by-pass valves, the double-ported slide valves and the interception valve; for starting they gave the engineer a valve to allow live steam direct into the receiver pipe. The builders of the first Mallets deliberately omitted superheat until the new design should have proved itself in service.

The Great Northern took note of the B&O's success and, less than a year after *Old Maude* went into service, placed an order with Baldwin to build a 2-6-6-2, with leading and trailing trucks, for use as a road engine.[152] Whoever made the first approach, Samuel Vauclain persuaded the company president and legendary railroad builder, James J. Hill, to take five locomotives, delivered in 1906.[153] George H. Emerson, of whom more will be heard later, was the Great Northern's Superintendent of Motive Power at that time.

A 78-square foot grate fired a boiler containing 441 2¼-inch fire tubes, 21 feet over tube sheets, producing steam at 200 pounds per square inch from a total heating surface of 5,660 square feet. This powered two 21½-inch × 32-inch high-pressure and two 33-inch × 32-inch low-pressure cylinders. Walschaert valve gear with a McCarroll compressed-air reverser drove slide valves on both pairs of cylinders. The frames were of cast steel. Steam consumption was 21.8 pounds per indicated horsepower-hour; the enormous grates permitted a low firing rate of only 74 pounds per square foot per hour.

Developing 71,600 pounds of tractive effort, compound, these engines hauled trains weighing up to 1,390 tons over the 32 miles from Leavenworth to the Cascade Tunnel, including adverse grades averaging 1.3% and as steep as 2.2%, burning 13½ tons of coal in the 7 hours that it took to make the run—4 hours running, 3 hours in passing loops.[154] Compared with the existing 2-8-0s, which hauled only 454 tons over the route, burning 12 tons of coal, the Mallets

The Great Northern was the first Mallet user after the B&O. Baldwin built this Class L-1 2-6-6-2, No. 1903, in 1906, shown at Everett, Washington, on June 19, 1920 (courtesy California State Railroad Museum, Negative 39089cn).

slashed coal consumption on this route from 164 pounds of coal per thousand ton-miles to 90, a saving of 45%. The operating cost of the first five engines over three years came to 94 cents a mile. This difference from the Baltimore & Ohio experience resulted from a fuel cost which was five times higher.

The new engines were so successful that the company ordered more of the same wheel arrangement; seventy were in service by the end of 1908 in two sizes, classes L-1 and L-2. The smaller L-2's, for service in eastern Washington, differed in having 53-square foot grates, 3,900 square feet of heating surface and 20-inch × 30-inch high-pressure cylinders. In flat country, they reached speeds up to 30 miles per hour.

The Mallets made possible a 35% increase in train weight between Minot, North Dakota, and Seattle. Compared to the 2-8-0s used previously, this halved fuel consumption and reduced crew cost per ton-mile. In spite of the heavier trains, the Great Northern found that coupler breakages were less frequent than with the 2-8-0s, attributing this to the smoother traction provided by the two sets of driving wheels. The company considered that firing these monsters was within the capacity of one fireman, but they considered power stokers because of the heat from the open fire door. Difficulties with the new design were few and minor.

The next Mallet user was the Erie. Perversely, in view of Baldwin's earlier efforts to interest the company, the Erie placed an order with Alco in 1906 for three monstrous 0-8-8-0s for use in pusher service on the 1.3% climb from Susquehanna, Pennsylvania, to Gulf Summit.[155] With a Mallet pushing, a 2-8-0 road engine was supposed to haul 2,660 tons up this grade. Alco Schenectady delivered the three 0-8-8-0s in September 1907.

A Wootten firebox, a camelback cab and gigantic 39-inch × 28-inch low-pressure cylinders, projecting 10 to 12 feet ahead of the smokebox, gave these engines a strange appearance. For a short time, they were the biggest locomotives in the world.

The boiler was the biggest locomotive boiler built hitherto, weighing 97,200 pounds empty, 139,900 pounds including water, made of plate up to 1 3/16 inches thick and containing 404 2¼-inch × 21-foot fire tubes for a total heating surface of 6,110 square feet. The Wootten firebox was 10 feet 6 inches wide, including 5-inch water legs. At first, the Erie put two firemen to fire the 100-square foot grates, but then reckoned one man could do it by himself.

At 215 pounds per square inch boiler pressure to supply the 25-inch × 28-inch high-pressure cylinders, the Erie backed off from the boiler pressure used by the Baltimore & Ohio but, even so, these engines developed 89,000 pounds tractive effort, compound, 125,000 pounds, single-expansion. They weighed 410,000 pounds, all of which went into adhesion weight for an axle loading of 51,000 pounds. Walschaert valve gear with compressed-air-assisted reversing gear drove piston valves on the high-pressure cylinders, slide valves on the low-pressure cylinders. The Erie Mallets had the Mellin automatic starting valve.

The three locomotives replaced nine 2-10-0s and 2-8-0s. Tested after six months in service, they turned in the uneconomical result of 37 pounds of steam per indicated horsepower-hour.[156] C. J. Mellin grumbled that the tests had been made on a leaky engine by engineering students from Cornell University. Samuel Vauclain suggested that the engineer may have been so frightened of uncovering the crown sheet on the long boiler that he allowed the engine to prime. The Erie superintendent responsible for the engine said that it consumed only 18% more coal than any one of the three engines it replaced, indicating a massive coal saving, regardless of how inefficient the

The Erie's class L-1 0-8-8-0, No. 2602, built by Alco in 1907. The location and date of the photograph are unknown (courtesy *Classic Trains* magazine collection, 20101108).

engine itself might have been. In 1921, the Erie sent them to Baldwin for rebuilding as 2-8-8-2s with power stokers.[157]

Another early Mallet user was the Northern Pacific, which took delivery of sixteen 2-6-6-2s (class Z) from Baldwin in 1907.[158]

Soon after, in 1908, the Burlington acquired a Baldwin 2-6-6-2, soon followed by two more.

In 1909, Baldwin delivered two oil-burning 2-8-8-2s to the Southern Pacific for one of the toughest routes in North America, the Donner Pass between Sacramento and Reno.[159] Eastbound, this was a continuous climb for 87 miles, rising from 163 feet above sea level at Roseville, California, to 7,018 feet at Summit, culminating in 40 miles of 2.2% grade, one of the severest grades in the United States. At the time, the company's most powerful freight engines were 2-8-0s of 43,000 pounds tractive effort. It took four of these to run a train of 45 to 50 cars, 2,300-feet long and weighing 1,900 tons, up the west slope of the Sierra Nevada.[160] Two locomotives were at the head end, with two more cut into the train eleven cars ahead of the caboose. A locomotive that could replace two 2-8-0s was highly attractive.

Developed from the Great Northern design, the two MC-1's established a new record for weight at 430,000 pounds. Eight-coupled

Mallets brought to light a new design issue with potential benefits in thermal efficiency. Extending fire tubes beyond 20 feet in length added little to their evaporative capacity but caused problems with expansion, contraction and sagging under their own weight. Mallet running gear could carry a boiler shell 50 feet long, longer than the sum of an 8-foot firebox, a 20-foot pressure vessel and a 6-foot smokebox. Designers put this space to use in various ways. Baldwin championed various configurations of multi-tubular heat exchangers to preheat the feed water before it entered the boiler, to superheat the live steam and to reheat steam between the high- and low-pressure cylinders. A profusion of firebox designs also appeared, with and without combustion chambers, brick arches and Gaines walls. (Besides a chamber extending ahead of the throat sheet, the term "combustion chamber" was also used for spaces let into the boiler shell for maintenance access, even though no combustion took place inside them.)

The MC-1 boiler shell contained a feed water heater, supplied by an injector, with a Baldwin reheater in the smokebox. Baldwin provided a simple by-pass valve for admitting high-pressure steam to the low-pressure cylinders. McCarroll compressed-air reversing gear controlled the Walschaert valve gear, driving piston valves. The boiler

Northern Pacific class Z 2-6-6-2, No. 3001, built by Baldwin in 1907, was still in its original condition, compound with slide valves on both cylinder pairs, when Otto Perry photographed it at Livingston, Montana, on June 26, 1937 (Denver Public Library, Otto C. Perry collection, OP-14020).

The Chicago, Burlington & Quincy was another early Mallet user. Baldwin built this Class T-1 2-6-6-2, No. 4002, in 1908, photographed at Galesburg, Illinois, in the 1920s (Denver Public Library, Otto C. Perry collection, OP-3816).

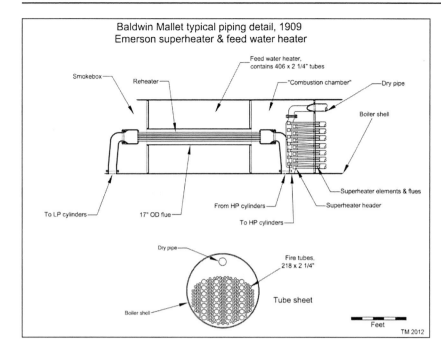

Baldwin Mallet typical piping detail, 1909
Emerson superheater & feed water heater

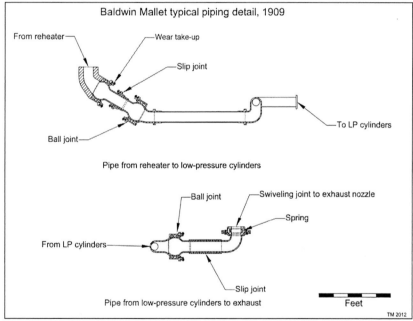

Baldwin Mallet typical piping detail, 1909

Top: **Baldwin Mallet typical piping detail, Emerson superheater and feed water heater.**
Bottom: **Baldwin Mallet typical piping detail (both figures redrawn from *RAG* April
30, 1909, 936; November 26, 1909, 1023; May 13, 1910, 1215–1216).**

der trailing the boiler and drive units. Oil firing
made this arrangement possible and also made it
possible to fire a total heating surface of 6,395
square feet. The Southern Pacific Mallets were even
bigger than the Erie 0-8-8-0s, at 425,900 pounds.
Baldwin delivered fifteen of these 2-8-8-2s, class
MC-2, the same year as part of an order for 105
locomotives placed by the Harriman Lines.[161] The
order included six conventionally arranged coal-
burning 2-8-8-2s, three for the Union Pacific, three
for the Oregon Railroad & Navigation.

In late 1909, the Southern Pacific ran comparative tests between a new MC-2 Mallet and an older
2-8-0 on the Sacramento division up the west slope
of the Sierra Nevada. Both locomotives were oil-
fired, which enabled long periods of full-throttle
operation that would not have been sustainable
with coal firing by hand. Both locomotives, too,
were without superheat.

The 2-8-0 weighed 208,000 pounds; 89% went
into adhesion (187,000 pounds). The 200-pounds
per square inch boiler contained 3,400 square feet
of heating surface; 22-inch × 30-inch cylinders and
55-inch driving wheels provided 46,000 pounds of
tractive effort. Moving at 5 miles per hour, at full
throttle and 75% cut-off, with the boiler pressure
at 195 pounds per square inch, the mean effective
pressure was 168 pounds per square inch (86% of
boiler pressure). The back pressure was 5 to 10
pounds per square inch, increasing to 20 pounds
per square inch at 35 miles per hour as the steam
flow choked in the exhaust nozzle. At 35 miles per
hour and 38% cut-off, the mean effective pressure
was only 59 pounds per square inch. The measured
tractive effort was very close to the theoretical
value, confirming the usual method of calculating
tractive effort from dimensions. The 2-8-0 developed 1,470 indicated horsepower at 35 miles per
hour, hauling a 480-ton train.

The Mallet weighed 426,000 pounds; 93% went
into adhesion (394,150 pounds). Its heating surface was double that of the 2-8-0 at 6,395 square
feet; boiler pressure was also 200 pounds per
square inch. Tractive effort was 89,000 pounds.
Moving at 5 miles per hour, at full throttle and 83%
cut-off, with 200 pounds per square inch boiler
pressure, its actual tractive effort was 86,000
pounds. The mean effective pressure in the high-
pressure cylinders at that speed was only 59% of
boiler pressure. The maximum power output was
2,485 indicated horsepower, obtained at 18 miles

per hour, full throttle and 72% cutoff, hauling a 1,105-ton train. The
maximum speed reached in the tests was only 20 miles per hour. At
that speed, power was beginning to fall off (2,245 indicated horsepower); mean effective pressure was a surprisingly low 49 pounds
per square inch in the high-pressure cylinders and only 30 pounds
per square inch in the low-pressure cylinders, an effect of the long,
convoluted steam path. The steam typically lost 15 to 20 pounds per
square inch between high-pressure exhaust and low-pressure intake.

The comparison strongly favored the Mallet. Everything about it
was twice the size of the 2-8-0, including fuel consumption; the Mallet burned 7,700 gallons of oil on the run, compared to 4,300 gallons

pressure was 200 pounds per square inch, supplying 26-inch (high-
pressure) and 40-inch (low-pressure) × 30-inch cylinders.

These engines developed 94,600 pounds of tractive effort, intended for hauling 1,200-ton trains up a 2.1% grade. From a traction
point of view they were successful. However, visibility ahead was
poor due to the extreme length of the boiler and the exhaust came
close to asphyxiating the crews in the tunnels and snowsheds of the
Sierras. As a result, the Southern Pacific ordered the first of the cab-
forward Mallets. The MC-2's were arranged with the firebox at the
front of the boiler and the smokebox at the rear; the cab was built
around the front of the firebox. Fuel and water were carried in a ten-

Southern Pacific class MC-1 2-8-8-2, No. 4000, built by Baldwin in 1909. By the time Otto Perry photographed it at Sacramento, California, on October 10, 1931, it had been rebuilt to cab-forward and single expansion, as evidenced by both cylinders being the same size. The cab-end cylinder receives live steam through a front-end throttle and an exterior dry pipe. A Worthington feed water heater has been added above the stack-end driving wheels. A power reverser is visible above the cab-end driving wheels (Denver Public Library, Otto C. Perry collection, OP-15653).

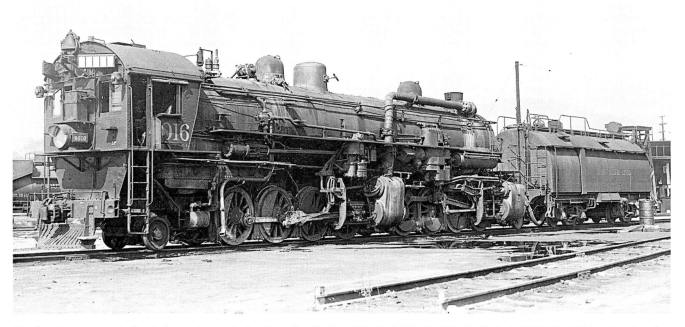

The first locomotives built cab-forward were the Southern Pacific class MC-2 2-8-8-2s, built by Baldwin in 1909. No. 4016, at Los Angeles, California, on August 10, 1940. The same notes apply to this locomotive as to No. 4000 in the previous photograph (Denver Public Library, Otto C. Perry collection, OP-15658).

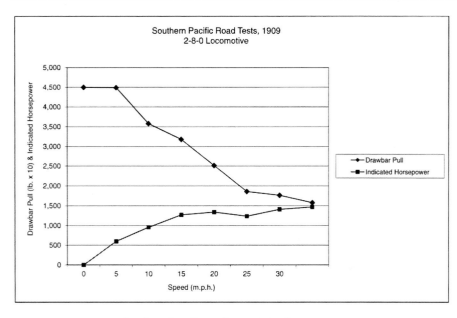

Southern Pacific road tests, 2-8-0 locomotive.

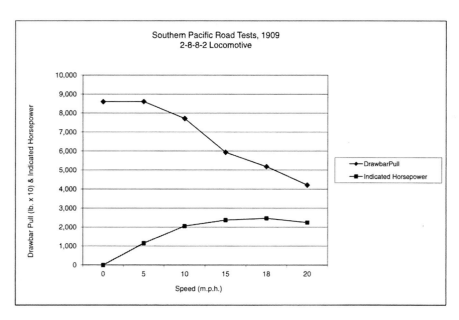

Southern Pacific road tests, 2-8-8-2 locomotive.

maintain than existing types of locomotive. Bigger boilers and fireboxes offered lower firing rates for similar steam generation, hence greater boiler efficiency. The greater number of driving wheels put more of the engine weight into adhesion. The bigger boiler did not need such a strong exhaust blast to draw the fire; the steam pressure that otherwise went into back pressure to create a high smokebox vacuum could go into the low-pressure pistons. Space was available at the front of the engine for low-pressure cylinders of diameters unprecedented in other compounds. Distributing power between more numerous moving parts reduced the wear and tear on each one. Two unsynchronized drive units made for less tendency to slip, better counterbalancing and reduced dynamic augment. As long as the theory prevailed that the most efficient movement of freight lay in fewer and longer trains, regardless of speed, the Mallet was extremely attractive. The total labor cost of running, servicing, maintaining and dispatching a locomotive did not increase in proportion to its size or tractive effort; the Mallets were therefore more efficient in terms of labor cost per unit of tractive effort. In effect, they offered two engines for the price of one crew. Hauling longer trains over existing routes could obviate the need for costly civil engineering works to make those routes flatter or straighter.

Resistance to slipping was a valuable feature of the Mallets. The low-pressure drive unit received steam only as fast as the high-pressure unit supplied it. If the low-pressure drive unit started to slip, the high-pressure unit throttled its steam supply with the result that it slowed down and regained its grip. If the high-pressure unit started to slip, its more rapid exhaust increased the back-pressure in the receiver pipe, forcing it to slow down and regain its grip. It was unlikely that both engines would slip at the same time. Even when working single-expansion, the interception valve throttled the supply of high-pressure steam to the low-pressure cylinders so that slipping of the low-pressure unit caused a reduction in pressure. The automatic control of slipping, however, was at the cost of violent pressure fluctuations which contributed to the high maintenance costs that bedeviled the Mallets.[162]

These features enabled Mallets to be loaded closer to their ultimate capacity than conventional locomotives and they were easier on draft gear. They could also be designed to higher adhesion factors than conventional locomotives. Although the Mallets were ideal for drag freight, unstable riding of the front drive unit limited maximum safe speeds; this was not finally overcome until 1940.

Already, American development of the Mallet was becoming grotesque. Samuel Vauclain, who should have known better, patented a design in which the boiler was flexible, and not the drive units. The front and rear drive units were connected rigidly to front and rear

for the 2-8-0. The Mallet, however, hauled 130% more tons than the 2-8-0 for 23% less fuel per ton-mile, although the Mallet took 18 hours for the 87 uphill miles, compared to 13 hours for the 2-8-0, for similar crew wages. The Mallet evaporated 8% more water per gallon of oil; the Mallet's exhaust gas temperature—450°F, compared to 740°F in the 2-8-0—indicated better heat recovery in the feed water heater and steam reheater.

John E. Muhlfeld, C. J. Mellin and George H. Emerson were among the first to serve on an ARMMA committee studying the new Mallets. Their first report, published in 1908, put operating results before the American railroad industry that were nothing short of astonishing. No one ever saw a great future for the Mallets as fast passenger engines but, as road and helper engines in freight service over steep grades and sharp curves, their possibilities were enormous.

Per unit of tractive effort, the Mallets cost less to build, run and

boiler halves which were separate pressure vessels. The joint in the boiler was made of overlapping flexible plates; the unpressurized space inside the joint contained a superheater and reheater. The Santa Fe was the only railroad to fall for this design; only seven were built, all 2-6-6-2s, six from Baldwin, one from Santa Fe shops.[163]

In 1909, the Great Northern started a trend by converting a 2-8-0 into a Mallet.[164] With exaggeration but justifiable surprise, an editor commented:

> The recent decision to convert these consolidations into articulated locomotives is one of the most surprising and far-reaching movements in locomotive practice ever witnessed in this country.

The first application was to a 2-8-0 originally built by Baldwin in 1907.[165] Baldwin built a new front drive unit with a leading truck and six driving wheels. The boiler shell was extended and occupied by an Emerson-type superheater and a feed water heater.

The 20-inch × 32-inch cylinders on the original locomotive became the high-pressure cylinders of the new engine. They exhausted through a Y-pipe into a 7⅝-inch receiver pipe running through an 11-inch flue in the center of the boiler extension. This reheated the steam which then went out of the underside of the new smokebox, through a flexible pipe, into the new, front, low-pressure cylinders. Exhaust from the low-pressure cylinders went through another flexible connection to the exhaust nozzle and stack. Both drive units had Walschaert valve gear, controlled by a Ragonnet power reverser.

The railroad expected that the improvement in economy from the compound cylinders, superheating and feed water heating would off-set the fact that the 59-square foot grate and 2,770 square feet of primary heating surface remained the same. The new 2-6-8-0 was evidently successful; Baldwin delivered thirty-five more in 1910, class

M-1, apparently built new in their entirety.[166] Although the Erie (1), the Chicago Great Western (3) and the Santa Fe (4) bought new front drive units, it appears that the Great Northern did not convert any more existing 2-8-0s.

By 1909, demand for Mallets was growing apace. The Northern Pacific ordered two classes at the same time from Baldwin, five 2-8-8-2s and six 2-6-6-2s.[167] The 2-8-8-2s were monsters, weighing 425,900 pounds with 40-inch low-pressure cylinders. A 68-square foot grate fired 5,175 square feet of heating surface, with a large feed-water heater, supplied by an injector, but no superheating. These engines would have developed 85,000 pounds of tractive effort compound, 121,000 pounds single-expansion.

American engineering triumphed when the Eastern Railway of France ordered two 2-6-6-0 Mallets from Alco in 1909.[168] The French invented the Mallet, but when it came to truly large engines, they went to Alco to build them, ordering an engine as like as possible to the Baltimore & Ohio original, except for the leading truck. At 206,000 pounds, the engines were smaller than many rigid-frame engines being built in the United States.

The locomotive designs espoused by the Santa Fe were at least original, sometimes bizarre, none more so than when the Mallet craze took root among its senior management. One of the company's Vice-Presidents, Kendrick, ordered two 2-8-8-2 Mallets from Baldwin in 1909, incorporating some of his patented inventions.[169] The Jacobs-Shupert boiler was to have an 89-square foot grate and 7,840 square feet of heating surface, including a reheater between the high- and low-pressure cylinders. As conceived, the high-pressure cylinders were to be mounted conventionally at the front of the rear drive unit, but the low-pressure cylinders were to be mounted back-to-back with the high-pressure cylinders at the rear end of the front drive unit.

The referenced sources suggest that the two 2-8-8-2s were deliv-

A Great Northern class M-1 2-6-8-0, No. 1951, built by Baldwin in 1910. The location and date of the photograph are unknown (courtesy *Classic Trains* magazine collection, 20120802).

This Northern Pacific class Z-1 2-6-6-2, No. 3101, built by Baldwin in 1910, was still in original condition but apparently disused when Otto Perry photographed it at Missoula, Montana, on September 27, 1931 (Denver Public Library, Otto C. Perry collection, OP-14022).

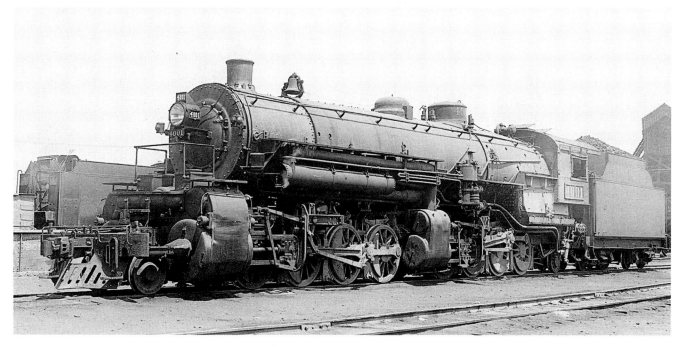

Baldwin built the Northern Pacific's class Z-2 2-8-8-2s in 1910. No. 4001 was still in original configuration when photographed at Livingston, Montana, on June 26, 1937 (Denver Public Library, Otto C. Perry collection, OP-14025).

ered with a conventional Mallet cylinder arrangement, 70-square foot grates and 8,365 square feet of heating surface, incorporating a live-steam superheater as well as a reheater. A boiler pressure of 220 pounds per square inch drove 26-inch & 38-inch × 34-inch pistons and 63-inch driving wheels for a tractive effort of 108,000 pounds. Engine weight was 462,000 pounds; engine and tender combined weighed 350 tons. The Santa Fe rebuilt these engines to single-expansion in 1924.

Baldwin proposed a conventionally arranged 2-4-4-2 passenger Mallet to the Santa Fe; the Santa Fe did not order any locomotives of this type, but ordered two 4-4-6-2s instead. The idea was to use 73-inch driving wheels, but to keep the rigid wheelbases short enough to follow 16-degree curves. The front drive unit was equalized like a 4-4-0; the rear driving wheels were equalized with the trailing truck. These engines were intended for heavy passenger service on a division rising in elevation by 5,000 feet with adverse grades up to

The Atchison, Topeka & Santa Fe 2-8-8-2, No. 1700, built by Baldwin in 1909—probably the company's first Mallet. Note the Jacobs-Shupert firebox. The location and date of the photograph are unknown (courtesy *Classic Trains* magazine collection, 20120510).

1.8% with schedule speeds of 25 miles per hour. Tractive effort was 57,000 pounds; engine weight was 376,000 pounds. The order was not repeated and the Santa Fe rebuilt these engines as 4-6-2s in 1915.

The boiler of the 4-4-6-2 was 52 feet long from the backhead to the front of the smokebox and contained 5,880 square feet of heating surface, subdivided as follows:

Item	Length	Heating surface (sq.ft.)
Jacobs-Shupert firebox	11 ft. 0 ins.	200
Boiler	19 ft. 2 ins.	3,275
Superheater		325
Reheater		800
"Combustion chamber"	10 ft. 9 ins.	—
Feed water heater	7 ft. 0 ins.	1,280
Smokebox	5 ft. 0 ins.	—

The 2-8-8-2 freight Mallet boiler was similarly configured, but with 8,365 square feet of heating surface and differing in detailed dimensions. These engines were all oil-burners, eliminating the labour of firing this enormous heating surface. The passenger Mallet 53-square foot grate and the freight Mallet 70-square foot grate could generate more power than a coal-burning grate of the same size because of the higher calorific value of oil. In both types Walschaert valve gear, powered by a Ragonnet reverser, drove piston valves.

Hauling coal through the Appalachians, the new Virginian immediately demanded the heaviest available power. Apart from obsolete locomotives taken over from its predecessor companies, the new company went to work with new 2-8-2s, with Mallets for pusher service on the 14-mile, 2.07% Clark's Gap grade.[170]

The superintendent of motive power, R. P. C. Sanderson, specified 2-6-6-0s, capable of 70,800 pounds of tractive effort, compound, 85,000 single-expansion. A 56-square foot grate fired 5,065 square feet of heating surface, generating steam at 200 pounds per square inch. Working single-expansion, the exhaust from the low-pressure cylinders exhausted through an annulus around the main exhaust nozzle, so that the exhausts from the two pairs of cylinders did not interfere with each other. Alco Richmond built the first four in 1909 with cast steel frames, supplying another eight the following year.

A single 2-8-8-2 followed in 1910.

The heaviest locomotive built during 1910 was of the 2-8-8-2 type and was constructed for the Virginian. It weighs 448,750 lbs. in working order and develops a tractive effort of 97,200 lbs. It is capable of hauling 20 cars, each weighing 78 tons, and a caboose up a grade of 2.07 per cent.

This Alco class AB could haul a 1,600-ton train up to Clark's Gap. Alco Richmond built six more, class AD, in 1912–13. We have not heard the last of Clark's Gap.

The only Canadian application of the Mallet configuration came in 1909, when the Canadian Pacific designed and built one of unusual configuration, a compound 0-6-6-0 of modest dimensions, weighing 262,000 pounds and capable of 54,700 pounds of tractive effort.[171]

The Virginian's Class AB 2-8-8-2, No. 600, built by Alco in 1910. The date and location of the photograph are unknown (courtesy Norfolk Southern Corporation, ns1383).

One of the few Canadian Mallets, Canadian Pacific class R-1 0-6-6-0, No. 1950, at Field, British Columbia, in 1908 (Revelstoke Museum and Archives, photo #253 Engine 1950).

The boiler was divided into three compartments: an 8-foot feed water heater at the front, a 5-foot superheater and a 9-foot boiler at the back. Two 4-inch equalizing pipes connected the front and rear compartments. The high- and low-pressure cylinder pairs were set back-to-back, providing a short steam path; because of the proximity of the low-pressure cylinders to the pivot point between the front and rear frames, the movement that had to be taken up in the low-pressure exhaust pipe was slight. The Walschaert valve gear was arranged so that cut-off in the high- and low-pressure cylinders could be varied independently, using a steam-powered reverser.

Boiler pressure was 200 pounds per square inch; friction losses dropped this by about 20 pounds per square inch between the boiler and the high-pressure steam chest. Steam entered the high-pressure cylinders at 540°F. While the engine was running, typical mean effective pressure in the high-pressure cylinders was 90 to 110 pounds per square inch, 70 pounds per square inch and 340°F in the receiver pipe, 55 to 60 pounds per square inch in the low-pressure cylinders. Piston work was typically split as 45% by the high-pressure pistons, 55% by the low-pressure, for a total of about 850 horsepower.

The engine went into service as a pusher eastbound from Field, British Columbia, to Stephen on 2.2% grades through the Kicking Horse Pass spiral tunnels. The CPR built five more, including one with single expansion, in 1911, but rebuilt them all as 2-10-0s in 1916–17.[172] In spite of its apparent advantages, the back-to-back cylinder arrangement never caught on. One problem was excessive flange wear caused by the distance between drive units imposed by the cylinder arrangement.[173]

By 1910, the strengths of the Mallet were plainly apparent but so, too, were its limitations.[174]

When it is claimed, or even suggested, that a Mallet articulated compound locomotive can be maintained as cheaply as an ordinary simple engine of half its capacity, the statement must be attributed to enthusiasm or ignorance. The Mallet is, to all intents and purposes as far as repairs are concerned, two complete and independent locomotives. That it should be possible to maintain these two engines as cheaply as one does not stand to reason and is not borne out in practice.

Railroadmen considered their availability low at 75% to 80%. They cost 2½ to 3 times as much to maintain per mile run as a rigid-frame locomotive, although this favored the Mallets when measured against ton-miles hauled. Repairs to steam pipe joints offset the cost of maintaining one boiler, rather than two. Articulation joints gave trouble in the early Mallets because they were not strong enough to withstand surging between the two drive units. Experience supported claims that the Mallets were easier on track than rigid-frame locomotives. Human firemen could sustain the violent, but intermittent exertions needed to hand-fire a coal-burning Mallet on short runs up steep grades but, even so, the heat through the open fire door scorched their clothes (it is not clear why this problem affected Mallets more than rigid-frame engines, if it did) and railroadmen knew that a power stoker would be necessary if the Mallets were to be used as road engines. Oil firing eliminated this problem but its economy was limited to those areas of the U.S. that produced oil or were remote from sources of coal.

The Mallets were slow.[175] Long, tortuous steam passages choked steam flow at speeds faster than about 15 miles per hour. One mechanical engineer pointed out that, as mean effective pressure in the low-pressure cylinders declined with increasing speed, a point would come when the low-pressure drive unit would not produce enough tractive effort to overcome its own resistance.[176] Tests on the Southern Pacific supported this, suggesting that, at 20 miles per hour, the front drive unit would produce only 6,350 pounds of tractive

effort. The internal resistance of a Mallet was more than twice that of a rigid-frame locomotive; the Great Northern found that the internal resistance of their Mallets was equivalent to a drawbar pull of 11,850 pounds, compared to 4,675 pounds for their 2-8-0s and 3,880 pounds for their 4-6-2s; the Mallets had to work steam on down grades as steep as 1.25%.[177] Nevertheless, H. B. MacFarland, Engineer of Tests on the Santa Fe, said that the new 4-4-6-2s had run as fast as 60 miles per hour in flat terrain.[178]

Fuel and crew savings meant that the Mallet was a fixture where heavy loads had to be hauled on steep grades[179]:

During 1910 the increasing use of the Mallet locomotive was notable, 169 being built by the Baldwin Locomotive Works. These locomotives are now being used to a considerable extent in heavy road service, especially on lines where grades are severe and speeds are necessarily slow. In common with other compound locomotives, the Mallet shows its greatest economy at comparatively slow speeds and does its best work on heavy pulls where a high tractive effort is exerted for a maximum period of time.

An early and obvious Mallet user, the Clinchfield was unique in buying more Mallets than rigid-frame locomotives from its formation in 1905 to its last purchase of a steam locomotive in 1947. A syndicate of Virginia and Kentucky coal owners formed the 250-mile Carolina, Clinchfield & Ohio Railroad from predecessor lines in 1905, rebuilt it and put it into operation in its new form in 1910, starting out with twenty-one 2-6-6-2s.[180] In 1914, the railroad's Mallets and 2-8-0s ran one 6,400-ton train the full length of the line each day. A Mallet took the train from Dante to Kingsport, 58 miles; two Mallets took it from Kingsport to Johnson City, 27 miles, three Mallets took it from Johnson City up 16 miles of 1.0% grades to Erwin, 12½ hours from Dante. Erwin was the division point where crews changed. Two Mallets and two 2-8-0s took the train up the 1.5% grade from Erwin to Poplar, 13 miles, two 2-8-0s and a Mallet from Poplar to Alta Pass, 38 miles, and one 2-8-0 and one Mallet from Alta Pass to Bostic where the trains were broken up, 11½ hours out of Erwin. A Mallet fireman shoveled 12 tons of coal during his 12-hour run; training, high wages and a positive management attitude provided the Clinchfield with a stable workforce of engine crews capable of moving these tonnages.

The Mallet craze hit hard in 1910. Railroads bought complete locomotives of increasingly fantastic dimensions, while significant numbers of companies bought Mallet front drive units and rebuilt existing locomotives as Mallet articulated compounds.

Only three years after building the Erie's monster 0-8-8-0s, in 1910, Alco built six more, even bigger at 445,000 pounds.[181] Delaware & Hudson coal trains faced six miles of 1.4% grades northbound from Carbondale, Pennsylvania, followed by 14 miles with 0.9% ruling grades to Ararat Summit, before running downgrade to Oneonta, New York. A single 252,000-pound E-5—large for a 2-8-0—developing 49,700 pounds of tractive effort, could haul a 2,600-ton train over the route, but needed two more E-5's pushing from Carbondale to Ararat summit, making 10 miles per hour for the first six miles, 15 miles per hour for the next fourteen. The company borrowed one of the Erie's Alco Mallets, and found that it could replace both the E-5 pushers. Accordingly, the Delaware & Hudson ordered six even bigger 0-8-8-0s from the same supplier. Pusher service needed no trucks, putting the whole 445,000-pound engine weight into adhesion, based on massive cast vanadium steel frames.

The firebox, with a 100-square foot grate, had a combustion chamber 48 inches long, but neither power stoker nor brick arch. Four hundred forty-six 2¼-inch × 24-foot fire tubes provided 6,630 square feet of heating surface (including firebox surface) with no superheat. To support the long fire tubes, a plate was set into the boiler 5½ feet

Delaware & Hudson class H 0-8-8-0, No. 1611, built by Alco in 1910–12. The location and date of the photograph are unknown (courtesy California State Railroad Museum, Negative 900_21193).

behind the front tube sheet. The front section of the boiler received injected feedwater and acted as a preheater before the water overflowed the support plate into the main part of the boiler.

A single dry pipe ran into the smokebox, where it divided into two. Twin high-pressure steam pipes ran back to the high-pressure cylinders, with ball and slip joints for expansion and contraction. The designers intended that this arrangement would improve the engineer's vision by removing the steam pipes running circumferentially outside the boiler. Even so, the firebox was so wide that the engineer had to lean out the side window to see ahead.

Steam at 220 pounds per square inch went to 26-inch × 28-inch high-pressure cylinders and enormous 41-inch low-pressure cylinders. Walschaert valve gear with power reverse drove 14-inch piston valves on the high-pressure cylinders and Mellin, double-ported, balanced slide valves on the low-pressure cylinders. The result was 99,000 pounds of tractive effort compound, 139,000 pounds single expansion.

Road tests showed a 39% saving in coal consumption per ton-mile, compared to the paired 2-8-0s; further tests—and, no doubt, operating experience—increased this figure to 44%.[182] The single Mallet, with tender, weighed 97 tons less than the pair of 2-8-0s with their tenders, saving that much dead weight to move. The bigger engine was also a more efficient evaporator of water. The 2-8-0s evaporated 5.5 pounds of water per pound of coal; the Mallets increased this to 7.1 pounds. Astonishingly, these engines were hand-fired. The railroads reckoned that one man could hand-fire 4,000 pounds of coal per hour, but this was a sustained rate; firemen achieved far higher rates on short pusher runs. The run up the Ararat grade took 2½ hours. In that time the two 2-8-0 firemen fired 10,000 pounds of coal; one unaided Mallet fireman handled 12,000 to 14,000 pounds. The only labor-saving device was a Franklin powered firedoor.

Only a year later, the Delaware & Hudson bought four more of these engines with fire-tube superheaters. A specialist crew maintained the Mallets; they were run stack-first upgrade for a month, then turned and run tender-first upgrade so as to equalize wear. Speed up or down grade was strictly limited to 15 miles per hour, monitored by speed recorders. This contributed to their longevity into the 1950s.

Baldwin built forty 2-6-6-2 Mallets for the Santa Fe at this time, of which two had jointed boilers—one with two ball-and-socket pairs, the other with a Vauclain bellows joint. Maintenance problems precluded any widespread use of jointed boilers.

The 392,000-pound engines developed 62,500 pounds of tractive effort, compound, 87,000 pounds, single expansion, from a 220-pounds per square inch boiler, fired by a 54-square foot grate. With 69-inch driving wheels, these engines were for fast freight service on the Belen cut-off, where they hauled 2,700-ton trains up 0.6% grades at 15 miles per hour.

Baldwin built ten 2-6-6-2s for the Burlington with boilers that could be taken apart, designed to burn lignite.[183] The boiler shell extended 40 feet ahead of the firebox. The back 16½ feet was the boiler with a double-loop fire-tube superheater in twenty-eight 5-inch flues; the superheater header occupied a 5-foot "combustion chamber." A 9-foot section of the boiler shell contained a feedwater heater, supplied by injectors. The receiver pipe between the high- and low-pressure cylinders passed through a 17-inch flue in the center of the feed water heater, divided into nineteen 2-inch tubes, reheating the steam in the process. Heating surface totaled 5,661 square feet, divided as: firebox, 210; boiler, 2,708; feed water heater 2,172; superheater, 464; reheater, 107. Baldwin applied this same arrangement to thirty-five 2-6-8-0 Mallets for the Great Northern.

With 65-square foot grates, 200-pound boiler pressure, 23-inch

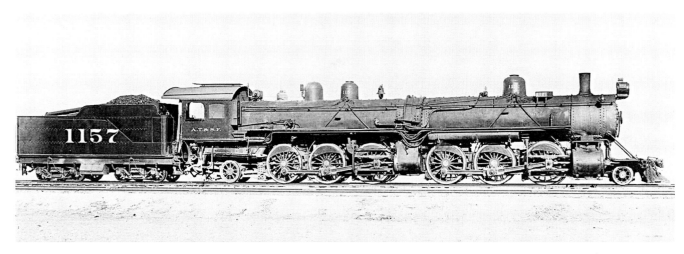

The sole Atchison, Topeka & Santa Fe 1157 class 2-6-6-2, No. 1157, built in company shops in 1910. Note the jointed boiler (courtesy *Classic Trains* magazine collection, 20110926).

Atchison, Topeka & Santa Fe 1170 class 2-6-6-2, No. 1179, built by Baldwin in 1910 with a conventional rigid boiler, photographed at Albuquerque, New Mexico, on October 23, 1920 (Denver Public Library, Otto C. Perry collection, OP-289).

& 35-inch × 32-inch cylinders and 64-inch driving wheels, these 362,000-pound engines developed 71,000 pounds tractive effort.

The Chesapeake & Ohio bought a single 2-6-6-2 from Alco for tests in 1910.[184] After this engine had been in service for only a few months, the company ordered another twenty-four, designed from experience with the first. The hand-fired grate measured 72 square feet. Alco used the length of the two sets of running gear to extend a combustion chamber 6½ feet forward of the firebox. Arch tubes supported a brick arch. The prototype had no superheat, but the boilers of the production locomotives contained a fire-tube superheater in thirty-six 5½-inch flues, 24 feet long. Total heating surface was 5,041 square feet, of which 911 square feet was superheater surface, generating steam at 225 pounds per square inch. As was common, piston valves controlled the steam flow to the 22-inch high-pressure cylinders; the 35-inch low-pressure cylinders were fitted with slide valves. These engines weighed 400,000 pounds and developed 82,000 pounds of tractive effort compound, 98,400 pounds, single-expansion.

Before the Mallets, a 2-8-0 would handle a 1,800-ton coal train eastbound between Handley, West Virginia, and Allegheny, with pusher service on the 13 miles of 0.6% grade between Ronceverte and Allegheny. A 2-8-2 could have increased this tonnage to 2,250,

Chicago, Burlington & Quincy class T-2 2-6-6-2, No. 4108, built by Baldwin in 1910, photographed near Dumont, South Dakota, on September 2, 1935 (Denver Public Library, Otto C. Perry collection, OP-3832).

A Chesapeake & Ohio 2-6-6-2, No. 873, possibly a class H-2, built by Alco in 1911, shown coaling with a mechanical grab at Newport News, Virginia, on January 10, 1919 (Denver Public Library, Otto C. Perry collection, OP-2889).

but still with a pusher being put on at Ronceverte. Eighty-two thousand pounds of tractive effort enabled the new 2-6-6-2 Mallets not only to handle 3,000 tons over the division but to dispense with the pusher as well, making 12 miles per hour unaided up the grade from Ronceverte. One of these engines handled a train weighing 3,492 tons unaided.

The company reported a reduction of 43% in train crew wages per ton-mile when the twenty-five Mallets replaced forty-four 2-8-0s on the Hinton division between Clifton Forge, Virginia, and Thurmond, West Virginia, resulting in a 43% saving in coal per ton-mile. Between 1912 and 1948, the Chesapeake & Ohio would purchase another 336 Mallets of three different wheel arrangements.[185]

Alco favored a simple boiler with a combustion chamber ahead of the throat sheet and a high-temperature fire-tube superheater. The complicated multi-element boilers and low-temperature smokebox superheaters, championed by Baldwin, had an unhappy history. The Virginian rebuilt its 1910-built Baldwin 2-8-8-2s with Alco-type boilers in 1922.[186] The Duluth, Missabe & Northern found the Baldwin feed water heaters so unsatisfactory that they removed them and put 6 to 7 tons of steel in the vacant space for adhesion weight. These engines were ultimately retrofitted with fire-tube superheaters, Elesco feed water heaters and power stokers, continuing in service until the early 1950s.[187]

In addition to new construction, 1910 saw significant numbers of Mallets assembled from existing rigid-frame engines. The Chicago Great Western built three 2-6-6-2s from three 2-6-2s in its shops at Oelwein, Iowa, under the direction of J. G. Neuffer, Superintendent of Motive Power.[188] The company bought three new front drive units from Baldwin with 35-inch × 28-inch low-pressure cylinders. The original 2-6-2s developed 33,000 pounds of tractive effort; the conversions developed 52,000 pounds. Tenuously:

The steam generating portion of the old locomotive remains the same; that is, the firebox and boiler shell with the tubes remain as they were; the additional steam required for the larger engine will be obtained from the economy resulting from the compound cylinders and the large amount of heating surface provided in the feed water heater.

The Santa Fe combined two Vauclain compound 2-6-2s as a 2-6-6-2 at its Topeka shops.[189] New cylinders, 24-inch and 38-inch bore, replaced the originals. The new boiler measured 60 feet from the backhead to the smokebox door, providing space for a feed water heater 12 feet long, a superheater 3 feet long and a reheater 5 feet long, all of the drum type inserted into the overall length and diameter of the boiler. The boiler itself was a conventional boiler taken from one of the 2-6-2s with fire tubes 18 feet long. The total heating surface comprised 3,740 square feet for the boiler and firebox, 485 square feet in the superheater, 1,063 square feet in the reheater and 2,216 square feet in the feed water heater, for a total of 7,500 square feet. The boiler was articulated, with a ball-and-socket joint between the superheater and the reheater, designed (and patented) by one of the company's draftsmen, W. J. Leighty. The engine retained the Stephenson link motion, but added Ragonnet power reversing gear. The complete engine weighed 358,000 pounds and was expected to develop 68,000 pounds of tractive effort.

The Santa Fe carried these measures to the extreme. In 1910–11, the company worked with Baldwin to convert ten 1903-built 2-10-2s to 2-10-10-2 Mallets.[190] Baldwin built the ten front drive units. The boilers were jointed and had oil-burning Jacobs-Shupert fireboxes. The total heating surface of 8,465 square feet comprised 3,920 square feet of primary heating surface, 580 square feet in the superheater, 1,305 square feet in the reheater and 2,660 square feet in the feed water heater. Boiler pressure was 225 pounds per square inch. The original 32-inch cylinders were bushed down to 28 inches as the

This Atchison, Topeka & Santa Fe 3000 class 2-10-10-2, No. 3001, was built jointly by Baldwin and company shops in 1911. The location and date of this photograph are unknown (courtesy California State Railroad Museum, Railway & Locomotive Historical Society Collection, Negative 39074cn).

high-pressure cylinders of the new Mallets; the new front sections had 38-inch low-pressure cylinders. The rebuilt engines weighed 616,000 pounds and developed 109,000 pounds of tractive effort compound, 168,000 pounds single expansion. Although these figures seem incredible, they are calculated from the ARMMA 1923 formula for the tractive effort of compounds.

The first two of these bizarre monsters went into service west of Winslow, Arizona. They had to be run backwards, otherwise the locomotive blocked most of the engineer's forward view. The tenders were built low for this reason and were curved to reduce wind resistance. Initially successful, they ran in this form for several years but the Santa Fe converted them back to 2-10-2s in 1915–18. At the same time, Baldwin built front sections to convert four Santa Fe 2-8-0s to 2-8-8-0s. They were rebuilt to their original configuration in 1923.[191]

The Erie rebuilt one 2-8-0 to a 2-6-8-0, purchasing the front unit from Baldwin and doing the rebuild at its Meadville shops.[192] The 2-8-0 boiler could not produce enough steam to supply the extra cylinder capacity, limiting speed to 2 or 3 miles per hour. The company rebuilt it to a 2-8-0 in 1916, eventually rebuilding it again as an 0-8-0 switcher. The Chicago Great Western similarly rebuilt three 2-6-2s.

By March 1911, Alco and Baldwin between them had built or under construction 539 Mallet articulated compounds. Of these, 449 were for buyers in the United States, the balance were for export to Puerto Rico, Brazil, South Africa, Ecuador, Japan, China, Santo Domingo, Natal, Colombia, France and Mexico. Five had been ordered by logging companies, most of the remainder by twenty-four Class I railroads:

Atchison, Topeka & Santa Fe (44), Baltimore & Ohio (11), Boston & Albany (1), Boston & Maine (4), Chesapeake & Ohio (25), Chicago & Alton (3), Chicago, Burlington & Quincy (18), Chicago Great Western (10), Chicago, Milwaukee & St. Paul (25), Delaware & Hudson (6), Denver & Rio Grande (8), Duluth, Missabe & Northern (8), Erie (3), Great Northern (102), New York Central (25), Norfolk & Western (10), Northern Pacific (27), Oregon Railroad & Navigation (3), St. Louis & San Francisco (7), Southern (2), Southern Pacific (41), Union Pacific (3), Virginian (13), Western Maryland (4).

Biggest user was the Great Northern with 102. The 2-6-6-2 wheel arrangement was the most popular, with 290 examples bought for U.S. domestic use. This was followed by sixty-three 2-8-8-2s, thirty-eight 2-6-8-0s (thirty-five on the Great Northern), 2-6-6-0s (twelve on the Virginian), 0-8-8-0s (twenty-six on five railroads) and 0-6-6-0s (thirteen on three railroads, the biggest user being the Denver, Northwestern & Pacific with ten).

The smallest Mallets were those built for the logging companies, such as the single 2-4-4-2 built for the Little River Company, weighing 142,000 pounds with 14 & 21-inch × 22-inch cylinders, 44-inch driving wheels and 23,500 pounds of tractive effort. The logging companies accepted the complexity of the Mallet design, as they accepted the Shay, Climax and Heisler types, for the sake of a sure-footed locomotive, capable of running over steep, rough and sharply curved track, while offering a relatively high tractive effort. The 2-6-6-2 tank locomotive built by Baldwin in 1910 for the Booth-Kelly Lumber Co. was designed to develop 37,800 pounds tractive effort on 56-pound track with 6.5% grades and 35 degrees of curvature.

The railroads made extensive comparisons between Mallet and conventional locomotives. The Norfolk & Western went a step far-

Otto Perry photographed this Western Maryland 0-6-6-0 Mallet, No. 954, at Cumberland, Maryland, on August 18, 1933. Drury (p. 426) tells us that it originated as a class M-1 2-6-6-2 from Baldwin in 1911 but was rebuilt as an 0-6-6-0 for switching service sometime between 1927 and 1931. The rebuilt locomotive retained its compound cylinders and slide valves (Denver Public Library, Otto C. Perry collection, OP-19830).

Otto Perry photographed the Crown-Willamette Paper Co.'s 2-6-6-2T logging Mallet, No. 12, manufacturer and construction date unknown, at Longview, Washington, on July 26, 1936 (Denver Public Library, Otto C. Perry collection, OP-7282).

ther and made rigorous comparative tests between Alco and Baldwin Mallets.[193] In 1910, the company received five 0-8-8-0s from Alco Schenectady and five 2-8-8-2s from Baldwin. The Baldwins had the three-part boiler described above. Apart from boiler and the wheel arrangement, the dimensions were almost identical. It is a comment on the empiricism of those days that a railroad would order ten of the biggest locomotives on earth, in two batches of five, so that it could compare them in service. The Baldwins were slightly better than the Alcos in boiler performance, but suffered a greater loss in steam pressure between the high- and low-pressure cylinders. The Alcos developed a maximum of 1,600 indicated horsepower, of which 84% went to the drawbar, compared to 1,400 indicated horsepower in the Baldwins, of which 78% went to the drawbar. As a result, the Alcos hauled 4% more tonnage 19% faster for 1.6% less coal per thousand ton-miles (273 pounds vs. 278 pounds).

By 1911: "The growth in favor of the Mallet locomotives in this country has been phenomenal."[194] Meanwhile, superheating and power stokers had been making their slow entry into American locomotive practice. Railroadmen knew that the saturated-steam Mallets were working far below their maximum power output, simply because no human fireman could keep them fueled. Oil firing, power stokers and superheating were the means to increase power in the face of this limitation.

Enthusiastic reports continued from the Baltimore & Ohio, the Chesapeake & Ohio, the Great Northern and the Santa Fe.[195] The Chesapeake & Ohio and the Santa Fe recorded Mallet road engines reaching speeds of 45 miles per hour. The Santa Fe did everything it could for its Mallet enginemen—short of installing power stokers—with compressed-air powered reversing gear, fire doors, bell ringers, cylinder drains and coal pushers. Operating experience continued to prove that a Mallet was two engines under the control of one crew, with fuel savings of 25% to 35%, compared to the two rigid-frame engines (typically 2-8-0s) that it replaced.

The New York Central bought twenty-six superheated compound 2-6-6-2 Mallets from Alco Schenectady in 1910–11 to solve a specific problem.[196] The single-track line between Williamsport, Pennsylvania, and Corning, New York, was at its maximum capacity, with still more needed. It took sixty 236,000-pound class G6G 2-8-0s, developing up to 45,700 pounds of tractive effort, to move 1,000 cars a day over this line in trains of 3,500 tons each. Thirty-one of these engines were used as road engines, the other twenty-nine as pushers. Increasing the capacity of the line required costly double-tracking or bigger engines. The arrival of the Mallets was opportune. By no means the biggest Mallets yet built, the 354,000-pound Alcos developed 67,500 pounds of tractive effort compound, 81,000 pounds single-expansion. These twenty-six engines replaced the sixty 2-8-0s, moving 1,400 cars per day over the line in 70-car trains weighing 4,000 tons each, with no pusher service required. Train length was limited by the available passing loops. This increase in capacity was achieved with a 40% saving in coal consumption per ton-mile. The freight trains averaged speeds of 10 to 14 miles per hour, although during the tests, the Mallets ran as fast as 30 miles per hour with no damage to engines or track. The heaviest train that a single Mallet moved over the division was 4,465 tons, made possible by the interceptor valve to work the engine single-expansion. Total thermal efficiency was still only 5.5%; even that was better than the 3.5% efficiency of the 2-8-0s that the Mallets replaced. The New York Central would order another forty-seven 2-6-6-2s from Alco between 1913 and 1921. The New York Central was never a big Mallet user, totaling no more than ninety-one throughout its whole system.

The Pennsylvania, with its heavy traffic in mountainous country, might seem an obvious Mallet user. Such was not the case. The company dabbled in Mallet designs in 1911 with a monstrous 2-8-8-2, built by Alco and put into experimental service at Altoona (class HH-1s). This locomotive had the biggest locomotive boiler built to date, 24 feet over tube sheets, containing 6,120 square feet of primary

Norfolk & Western class X-1 0-8-8-0, No. 990, built by Alco in 1910. The location and date of the photograph are unknown (courtesy Norfolk Southern Corporation, ns953).

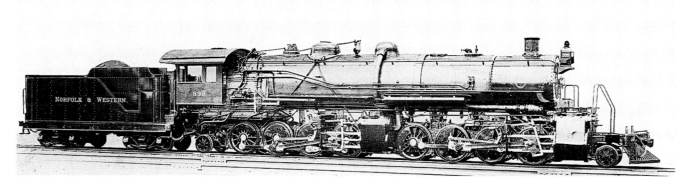

Norfolk & Western class Y-1 2-8-8-2, No. 999, built by Baldwin in 1910 (courtesy Norfolk Southern Corporation, ns956).

heating surface and a further 1,260 square feet in a Schmidt superheater. Boiler pressure was only 160 pounds per square inch. Compound cylinders big enough to use the boiler capacity would not have fitted within clearance limits. As a result, this was the first American Mallet using single expansion only, with four 27-inch × 28-inch cylinders. The jointed steam pipes had to carry high-pressure steam, but the builders hoped that careful design and maintainence would minimize leakage. The engine weighed 482,500 pounds and was expected to develop 99,200 pounds of tractive effort. The Pennsylvania did not repeat this order. The company bought one 0-8-8-0 from Baldwin the following year (class CC-1s). The Pennsylvania ordered no more Mallets for seven years.

The Canadian Pacific revisited the 0-6-6-0 articulated locomotive with cylinder pairs back-to-back with five locomotives completed at Angus shops, Montreal, in 1911.[197] One of these was built with single expansion. Single expansion would enable the locomotive to reach speeds up to 50 miles per hour without the choking effect of compounding. At the same time, bridge strength limited axle loading to 44,000 pounds. The company therefore put great effort into designing light-weight moving parts to obtain the biggest possible boiler, while remaining within bridge strength limits. Cast steel cylinders saved 3 tons, compared to cast iron. The 262,000-pound locomotive produced 57,000 pounds of tractive effort, already within the capacity of many rigid-frame locomotives which, we must assume, overtook

Otto Perry photographed this New York Central Class NE-2A 2-6-6-2, No. 1392, built by Alco in 1911, at Corning, New York, in 1919. All over the United States facilities, such as turntables, had to be enlarged to handle the new locomotives (Denver Public Library, Otto C. Perry collection, OP-13343).

Alco Schenectady built this sole class HH-1s 2-8-8-2 Mallet for the Pennsylvania in 1911 (Pennsylvania Historical and Museum Commission and Railroad Museum of Pennsylvania, General Negatives 44081).

this design, because nothing more is heard of it. Robert D. Turner confirms that maintenance problems that increased with age caused the CPR to lose interest.[198]

Having been the originator of the Mallet in America, the Baltimore & Ohio was tardy in adding to its fleet of one. In 1911, the company built a single 2-6-8-0 by adding a Baldwin front end to an existing 2-8-0,[199] but this was no more successful than similar rebuilds on other lines and was converted back to its original configuration six years later. The same year, however, the company bought thirty monster 0-8-8-0 Mallets from Alco Schenectady for pusher service on the heavy grades—up to 2.2%—eastbound from Grafton, West Virginia.[200] These 461,000-pound engines developed 105,000 pounds

of tractive effort. A 100-square foot grate fired 5,525 square feet of heating surface, generating steam at 210 pounds per square inch. This was superheated in a fire tube superheater before going to 26-inch & 41-inch cylinders. The boiler contained a rudimentary feed water heater in the form of a weir 54 inches behind the front tube sheet extending 25 inches above the boiler centerline. Water was injected ahead of this weir, circulating around the front parts of the 24-foot fire tubes before overflowing into the main part of the boiler. Notwithstanding the 100-square foot grate, just one locomotive was fitted with a Crawford stoker. At the maximum economical firing rate of 120 pounds of coal per square foot of grate per hour, these engines could have burned 12,000 pounds per hour, three times the com-

Baldwin built this sole class CC-1s 0-8-8-0 Mallet for the Pennsylvania in 1912 (Pennsylvania Historical and Museum Commission and Railroad Museum of Pennsylvania, BLW negative 03980).

Alco built this Baltimore & Ohio Class LL-1 0-8-8-0, No. 7021, in 1911, photographed at Cumberland, Maryland, on August 7, 1936 (Denver Public Library, Otto C. Perry collection, OP-2535).

monly reckoned maximum shoveling power of a human fireman. Even allowing for the intermittent nature of pusher service, we may wonder how—or if—this was achieved. With one of these Mallets pushing, a 2-8-0 could handle 2,035 tons over the 2.2% grades. Rugged in the extreme, they lasted until 1950 when they were replaced by diesels.

Having tested five Alco 0-8-8-0s against five Baldwin 2-8-8-2s in 1910, the Norfolk & Western bought forty 2-6-6-2s from Alco in 1912

and another forty the following year.[201] These engines were among the first of a new generation of Mallets with power stokers, combustion chambers and fire-tube superheaters. Fifteen had Walschaert valve gear, twenty-five Baker, all with power reversers.

The company intended that these new engines would increase the tonnage of each train and reduce the number of trains, saving crew wages. On the 105-mile division between Bluefield and Roanoke, Virginia, pusher service was retained on a 10-mile stretch of 1.0%

Alco and Baldwin built 175 class Z-1a 2-6-6-2s for the Norfolk & Western between 1912 and 1918. No. 1435 was still in its original, compound condition when Otto Perry photographed it at Bluefield, West Virginia, on June 25, 1950 (Denver Public Library, Otto C. Perry collection, OP-13806).

grade, but the Mallets increased train tonnage from 2,800 tons to 4,000. The company put twenty of the new Mallets onto the 130-mile route over the Blue Ridge between Roanoke and Crewe. Before the Mallets arrived, two 4-8-0s, developing 52,500 pounds of tractive effort each, would leave Roanoke with a 3,500-ton train. After 9 miles, at Bonsack, Virginia, a third 4-8-0 was added to push the train up the 6 miles of 1.2% grade to Blue Ridge, returning light to Bonsack. At Phoebe, 56 miles from Blue Ridge, the lead 4-8-0 was cut off and the other engine took the train the 59 miles to Crewe, except for 16 miles of 0.45% grade from Farmville to Burkeville with pusher service by another 4-8-0. A single 2-6-6-2, developing 73,000 pounds of tractive effort, hauled a 5,000-ton train from Roanoke to Crewe, double-headed with a 4-8-0 as far as Phoebe, with a Mallet pusher from Bonsack to Blue Ridge and a 4-8-0 pusher from Farmville to Burkeville.

The Virginian demanded the biggest engines it could find, receiving eighty Mallets between 1909 and 1923. Being one of the last major railroads built in the United States, Virginian locomotives could be built to more generous clearance dimensions than for most other lines, 16 feet 10 inches from rail to top of stack, 12 feet wide. The six class AD 2-8-8-2s built by Alco in 1912–13 were the most powerful locomotives in the world at that time[202]; Alco photographed one of its 0-4-0 tank engines inside the Mallet's firebox.

Much thought went into the design of this enormous firebox. The 99-square foot grate was 133 inches long with a Gaines wall, 10 inches thick and 40 inches high, at its front end. Ahead of the Gaines wall, a space of 26 inches to the throat sheet provided a cinder hopper. A combustion chamber extended 39 inches ahead of the throat sheet to the back tube sheet. Five 3½-inch arch tubes extended from the bottom of the combustion chamber, midway between the throat sheet and the back tube sheet, arching through the top of the Gaines wall to the top of the backhead. These supported a brick arch extending

rearward from the Gaines wall. Six vertical 3-inch air ducts inside the Gaines wall allowed air to be drawn from beneath the firebox, heated inside the Gaines wall and discharged beneath the brick arch. Only 22 inches separated the top of the brick arch from the crown sheet. Firebox and fire tubes provided 6,760 square feet of heating surface; the 24-foot tubes permitted 1,310 square feet of superheating surface in a Schmidt superheater.

Steam at 200 pounds per square inch went to 28-inch × 32-inch high-pressure and 44-inch × 32-inch low-pressure cylinders. Vanadium steel was used extensively for heavily stressed parts, including the frames. Weighing 540,000 pounds, these engines were expected to develop 138,000 pounds of tractive effort single-expansion, 115,000 pounds compound. The Virginian planned to use two as pushers behind an older Mallet road engine, increasing the maximum train tonnage through Clark's Gap from 3,340 to 4,230 tons.

About 1914, the Virginian was handling 100-car, 7,500-ton trains on the descending grades of its Victoria to Norfolk division and was lengthening its sidings to accommodate 120 cars. Loaded coal trains from the mountains of West Virginia, however, faced the 14-mile, 2.0% grade from Elmore to Clark's Gap. Up to 1912, one 2-8-2 and two 2-6-6-0 Mallets moved 2,775-tons up this grade. After the AD's arrived, a 2-6-6-0 on the head end, with two 2-8-8-2s pushing, moved 4,330 tons up to Clark's Gap. Even so, the AE 2-10-10-2s were welcomed when they arrived in 1918.

These feats of haulage with multiple locomotives took great skill on the part of the enginemen if the trains were not to break in two. Starting a heavy train upgrade was especially demanding. The front and rear engines might be out of both sight and sound of one another. Accordingly, the head end engines backed slowly down, letting the slack in the train bunch against the pusher which was using either brakes or steam against the train. At this point the pusher engineman

This Great Northern class N-1 2-8-8-0, No. 2009, built by Baldwin in 1912, had been converted to single expansion by the time Otto Perry photographed it at Shelby, Montana, on May 13, 1934 (Denver Public Library, Otto C. Perry collection, OP-11878).

opened his throttle against the train; the head end engines started forward, taking up slack until sufficient load was taken off the pusher engine that it was able to move forward, whereupon the whole train started to move.[203]

Baldwin ultimately accepted Alco practice, exemplified by twenty-five 2-8-8-0s for the Great Northern in 1912.[204] These were super-heated compounds in which the great length of the boiler accommodated a 58-inch combustion chamber ahead of the firebox and 24-foot fire tubes. The 78-square foot hand-fired grate fired a 210-pounds per square inch boiler containing 6,445 square feet of primary and 1,370 square feet of superheating surface. A forty-two-element double-loop Emerson superheater provided high superheat. Walschaert valve gear with Ragonnet power reverse drove 15-inch piston valves; Baldwin added an arrangement allowing the engineer to control the cut-off in the 28-inch high- and 42-inch low-pressure cylinders independently. Weighing 450,000 pounds, the new 2-8-8-0s were rated at 98,000 pounds tractive effort, compound, 142,000 pounds, single expansion—37% more than the company's first 2-6-6-2s built only six years before. Seventeen were coal-burners, the remainder burned oil.

The impact of these Mallets was immense. In 1906, the Eastern Railway of Minnesota was using eight-year-old 2-6-0s and 2-6-2s to haul 1,400-ton ore trains from iron mines on the Mesabi to the Lake Superior docks. The Great Northern absorbed the Eastern; Great Northern Mallets hiked train tonnage to 8,800 tons. In 1923, one of these hauled a 150-car train of iron ore, weighing 16,360 tons, for 64 miles from Baden, Minnesota, to the ore dock at Allouez.[205] This became standard practice during the 1920s; by 1929 the average trailing load of an ore train on this route was 13,350 tons behind a single 2-8-8-0 Mallet, representing an increase of 86% in gross tonnage, 91% in net since 1920: 213,000 ton-miles per train hour, 19.4 million tons of ore during 1929.[206]

Mallet gigantism reached its limit when George R. Henderson patented the idea of a triplex Mallet in 1912, assigning the patent to Baldwin.[207] Henderson reasoned that Mallet tenders already weighed as much as some complete locomotives and that this weight could be used as adhesion weight, if only the tender could be powered. The high-pressure cylinders were positioned as normal, rigidly attached to the rear frame. The right-hand high-pressure cylinder exhausted through a receiver to the front pair of low-pressure cylinders. The left-hand high-pressure cylinder exhausted through another receiver to a pair of low-pressure cylinders beneath the tender, using its adhesion weight and exhausting through a stack at the rear of the tender. Three sets of Baker valve gear, all controlled by the same Ragonnet power reverser, drove 16-inch piston valves. All six cylinders were of the same 36-inch diameter and 32-inch stroke. Articulating steam pipes between engine and tender differed little from the articulation under the front of the boiler. Only four triplex Mallets were ever built—three for the Erie and one for the Virginian.

Baldwin built the first of these remarkable machines for the Erie in 1914. The heaviest locomotives built to date were the Santa Fe's 2-10-10-2 Mallets, weighing 850,000 pounds complete with tender. The first Erie 2-8-8-8-2 triplex Mallet weighed 853,000 pounds in running order, of which 761,500 pounds was adhesion weight. The highest tractive effort to date when running compound was 115,000 pounds developed by the Virginian 2-8-8-2s. The new triplex Mallets were expected to develop 160,000 pounds of tractive effort, running compound; they had no provision for running single-expansion. The Erie intended them for pusher service on the eight miles of 1% grade east of Susquehanna, Pennsylvania. The company ran maximum-tonnage trains up this grade with a 2-8-0 road engine and three pushers—two 2-8-0s and an 0-8-8-0. The triplex was to replace all three pushers.

A Street stoker fired the 90-square foot grate. A Gaines wall was

The Erie's class P-1 2-8-8-8-2, No. 5014, built by Baldwin in 1914, was the first triplex Mallet and one of the biggest steam locomotives ever built. The location and date of this photograph are unknown (courtesy California State Railroad Museum, Railway & Locomotive Historical Society Collection, Negative 39076cn; D. L. Harding photograph).

The Virginian 2-8-8-8-4 triplex Mallet, class XA, No. 700, built by Baldwin in 1916. The location and date of the photograph are unknown (courtesy California State Railroad Museum, Negative 17343).

placed at the front end of the 10-foot-long grates. For a further 2 feet ahead of the Gaines wall, the bottom of the firebox sloped upward slightly to the throat of a 54-inch-long combustion chamber. The Gaines wall contained seven vertical 3-inch ducts which drew in and heated combustion air. Six 3½-inch arch tubes supported a brick arch extending backward and upward from the top of the Gaines wall; the arch tubes themselves arched upward from the floor of the combustion chamber, ending in the backhead. This arrangement and 326 2¼-inch fire tubes, 24 feet over tube sheets, provided 6,885 square feet of heating surface, with another 1,585 square feet of superheating surface, supplying steam at 210 pounds per square inch. This was the biggest Schmidt superheater ever applied to a locomotive to date. To maximize drafting, the exhaust nozzle was made rectangular, 7 inches wide but controllable in length from 3 to 9 inches.

The center engine received high-pressure steam. The arrangement differed from Henderson's layout in that the right-hand high-pressure cylinder supplied the two low-pressure cylinders under the tender; the left-hand high-pressure cylinder supplied the two front low-pressure cylinders. Exhaust steam from the rear cylinders passed through a tender feed water heater. The crossheads drove two piston pumps continuously, pumping hot water from this heater into the boiler. The engineer controlled the water flow rate. Two 7,500-gallons per hour injectors were also installed, drawing cold water from the tender tank, for use when the engine was standing still or if the pumps malfunctioned. All six cylinders measured 36 inches × 32 inches. Baldwin made extensive use of steel parts, in particular, cast vanadium steel frames 6 inches thick.

On July 23, 1914, the triplex Mallet broke all previous records, hauling a 250-car train, 8,550 feet long, weighing 17,912 tons, 23 miles from Binghamton, New York, to Susquehanna, Pennsylvania.[208] This was slightly upgrade, the worst condition being 0.9% adverse grade with 5° of curvature. The train achieved a maximum speed of 14 miles per hour. Pushers helped to get the train started, but were then uncoupled. Telephones were installed between the front and back of the train. Trains this long never became standard practice during the steam era. Even so, the Erie returned the triplex to Baldwin to have its grate enlarged to 122 square feet.

After two years, the Erie judged this locomotive so successful that they ordered two more.[209] In the new engines, the grates, with power shakers, were lengthened to the full 13-foot 6-inch length of the firebox, providing 122 square feet of grate. The Gaines wall was moved forward to the throat of the combustion chamber, with the foot of the brick arch joining the top of the wall as before. The two new triplexes weighed 860,000 pounds, with 766,000 pounds of adhesion weight. Dimensions were otherwise similar to the first. The Erie's three triplex Mallets ran until 1927; a service life of thirteen years is hardly the failure asserted by some railroad historians.

Baldwin built a single 2-8-8-8-4 triplex Mallet for the Virginian in 1916.[210] This engine had a four-wheel trailing truck under the back of the tender. A 108-square foot grate fired a 215-pounds per square inch boiler, supplying six 34-inch × 32-inch cylinders. Valving allowed the engine to be worked single-expansion for starting. Vanadium steel frames, Baker valve gear and Ragonnet power reversers were common to this and many other engines built at this time. Also increasingly popular in Mallet construction were spherical bushings for the hinge pins joining the frames, allowing the front frame to pitch and yaw at the same time without binding. The 365 2¼-inch fire tubes were 25 feet long; with the firebox, superheater flues and arch tubes, they provided 8,120 square feet of heating surface, to which was added 2,059 square feet of superheater surface. Like the Erie triplexes, this engine had a feedwater heater under the tender, heated by the exhaust from the back cylinders. Total engine weight was 844,000 pounds.

The engine had smaller driving wheels than the Erie triplexes; while this gave it a higher tractive effort, the higher cycling rate consumed more steam and the boiler had insufficient steaming capacity for the cylinders. If the engineer shortened the cut-off, there was insufficient draft for the fire; if he did not, the engine ran out of steam. The engine could not, therefore, maintain its maximum 166,000 pounds of tractive effort for any useful length of time. After four years of frustration, the Virginian returned it to Baldwin in 1920; Baldwin rebuilt it into a 2-8-8-0 and a 2-8-2 which continued in service until they were scrapped in 1953.[211]

Between 1915 and 1918, Lima built twenty-five 2-8-8-2s for the Western Maryland to deal with the 20 miles of 1.75% grades northbound from Cumberland, Maryland.[212] The company that had started out building small logging and industrial locomotives was now building engines as big as any on the continent. It seems, however, that Lima bankrupted itself trying to undercut Baldwin and Alco on this job and never built any more Mallets for twenty-five years. According to Drury (p. 427), Lima built fifteen 2-8-8-2s for the Western Maryland in 1915–16, then another ten in 1917–18. Lima did go through bankruptcy at that time, but the exact cause-and-effect relationship between these events is not currently known.

The Baltimore & Ohio became one of the biggest Mallet users in America, ordering 250 between 1904 and 1945, including sixty 2-8-8-0s in three classes from Baldwin in 1916–17 alone.[213] On the Cumberland division, the company was moving coal traffic over 2.4% eastbound and 2.3% westbound grades. Even the 2-10-2s could not handle it and the company replaced them with 486,000-pound 2-8-8-0 class EL-1 compound Mallets capable of 103,000 pounds of tractive effort. A Street stoker fired an 88-square foot grate; a combustion chamber extended 60 inches ahead of the throat sheet. The boiler contained 5,836 square feet of primary heating surface with another 1,415 square feet of superheating surface. Steam at 210 pounds per square inch supplied 26-inch & 41-inch cylinders. The low-pressure cylinders had Allen-ported slide valves, while 14-inch piston valves admitted steam to the high-pressure cylinders. Walschaert valve gear with Ragonnet power reverse drove both sets of valves. A Baldwin starting valve admitted high-pressure steam to both pairs of cylinders under the engineer's control. Baldwin catered to the Baltimore & Ohio's sharply curved routes by allowing a nominal 1 inch of play between flange and rail on the front and back driving wheels of each drive unit,¾ inch on the middle driving wheels. The Baltimore & Ohio was one of only a dozen companies to get engines built to their own design under USRA management; the company managed to place an order with Baldwin for twenty-six 2-8-8-0 Mallets, improved EL-1's.[214]

The Norfolk & Western ordered its first five 2-8-8-2s from Baldwin in 1910 as class Y-1. After five years of observation, 222 more of this type followed between 1918 and 1952, classes Y-2 to Y-6. Of these the company built 112 in its own shops at Roanoke[215]; Alco and Baldwin built the remainder. The USRA heavy Mallets followed the Y-2 design.

Clearance dimensions restricted the Y-2's' low-pressure cylinders to 39 inches diameter. To maximize power output within this limitation, boiler pressure was an unprecedented 230 pounds per square inch. A Duplex stoker fired the 96 square feet of grates with steam-

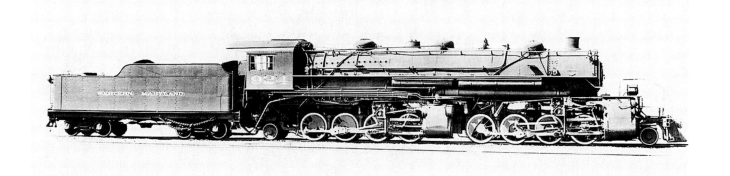

Western Maryland class L-2 2-8-8-2, No. 924, built by Lima in 1917–18 (courtesy *Classic Trains* photographic collection, 20110110).

Baldwin built the Baltimore & Ohio's class EL-1 2-8-8-0s in 1916. No. 7133 is shown at Cumberland, Maryland, on August 7, 1936, after conversion to single expansion (Denver Public Library, Otto C. Perry collection, OP-2539).

Baldwin built Norfolk & Western class Y-2 2-8-8-2, No. 1715, in 1919, shown at Radford City, Virginia, on August 3, 1936, still in compound configuration (Denver Public Library, Otto C. Perry collection, OP-13809).

Otto Perry photographed one of the biggest steam locomotives of all time, Virginian class AE 2-10-10-2, No. 801, built by Alco in 1918, at Roanoke, Virginia, on August 7, 1932 (Denver Public Library, Otto C. Perry collection, OP-19642).

powered grate shakers. A combustion chamber extended 62 inches ahead of the firebox; the whole firebox structure was arc-welded, then a new technique. Tubes, flues, firebox and arch tubes provided 6,800 square feet of primary heating surface, while the 24-foot tube length permitted 1,510 square feet of superheating surface. Two injectors, each capable of 7,500 gallons per hour, supplied feed water to the boiler. Railroad companies were finding that superheater efficiency increased if the crew carried a slightly low water level in the boiler, although this decreased the safety margin against uncovering the crown sheet. Accordingly, the Norfolk & Western equipped its Y-2's with the new Sentinel low-water alarm. Piston valves, driven by Baker valve gear with the Norfolk & Western's own KY power reversers, controlled steam flow to the cylinders. Even the cylinder drains were compressed-air-operated. The engine weighed 535,000 pounds and developed 104,000 pounds of tractive effort compound, 136,000 pounds, single-expansion within an axle loading of 59,000 pounds. The tender was a massive structure, carried on six-wheel trucks, with a capacity of 12,000 gallons of water and 20 tons of coal. The tender alone weighed 212,000 pounds, loaded—375 tons for the complete locomotive.

The Virginian's demand for tractive effort to haul eastbound coal trains up to Clark's Gap was insatiable. The triplex Mallet was a failure; by 1918, a 2-6-6-0 road engine and two 2-8-8-2 pushers with a combined tractive effort of 320,000 pounds were moving 4,500-ton, sixty-car trains over that route. This was still not enough and other parts of the railway were equally demanding. The Virginian went to Alco for a locomotive capable of moving one hundred 120-ton cars from Princeton, West Virginia, to the coal port at Sewall's Point with helper service restricted to 10 miles of 0.6% adverse grade. The result was ten 2-10-10-2s, developing 177,000 pounds of tractive effort, single-expansion, 147,000 pounds, compound, probably the highest tractive effort ever developed by a steam locomotive.[216]

This colossal power came from several sources. Boiler pressure was 215 pounds per square inch, applied to 30-inch × 32-inch high-pressure cylinders; the 48-inch low-pressure cylinders were probably the biggest ever applied to a steam locomotive. Total engine weight was 684,000 pounds, of which 617,000 pounds went into adhesion through 56-inch driving wheels. Ten driving axles kept axle loads to 61,700 pounds.

Engines that size were of no use if the boiler could not supply them with steam. The stoker-fired 109-square foot grate was 12 feet long × 9 feet wide with a brick arch, arch tubes and a Gaines wall. From the Gaines wall to the throat sheet was another 3 feet, while a combustion chamber extended 3 feet ahead of the throat sheet. This grate heated 8,605 square feet of primary and 2,120 square feet of superheating surface. The Virginian's clearance dimensions allowed a 113-inch-diameter boiler, probably the biggest ever built for any steam locomotive anywhere in the world. Regardless of efficiency, the 381 fire tubes were 25 feet long over tube sheets, supported by an intermediate tube sheet. The resulting steaming rate allowed the engine to work compound continuously at full power. Walschaert valve gear drove 16-inch piston valves on the high-pressure cylinders; the Virginian retained slide valves on the low-pressure cylinders. Because of their size, the locomotives had to be transported from Alco's Schenectady plant to Princeton, West Virginia, dead and partly dismantled. They were probably the biggest steam locomotives ever built. They were also highly efficient, showing a coal consumption of only 127 pounds of coal per thousand ton-miles hauled in the service for which they were designed.

A 2-8-8-2 road engine, with two 2-10-10-2s pushing, moved seventy-eight-car trains, weighing 5,850 tons, up to Clark's Gap. In 1921, a single AE hauled a 120-car train weighing 17,050 tons from Princeton, West Virginia, to Norfolk, Virginia, against maximum grades of 0.3%. Three 0-8-0 switchers got the train moving at Princeton; a

The ten Virginian class AE 2-10-10-2s set astonishing records for train length. No. 801 enters Roanoke, Virginia, on August 7, 1932 with a long train of coal empties (Denver Public Library, Otto C. Perry Collection, OP-19653).

One of the USRA 2-6-6-2 light Mallets, assigned to the Wheeling & Lake Erie (courtesy California State Railroad Museum, James E. Boynton Collection, Negative 39080cn).

2-8-8-2 pushed it up 9 miles of 0.6% grade from Whitethorne to Merrimac. Although replaced by electric power on the route for which they were built, the 2-10-10-2s remained in service until 1952.

On May 25, 1921, the Virginian assembled a train of 100 cars at Princeton with a gross weight of 16,000 tons. Three 4-4-0s pushed the train to get it going and a 2-8-8-2 was added for the short grade between Rich Creek and Merrimac but, otherwise, a single 2-10-10-2 handled the train. Although the train was successfully controlled down the 1.5% grades east of Princeton and Merrimac, it broke in two twice. By 1928, the AE's were routinely moving 13,500-ton coal trains eastbound against a maximum adverse grade of 0.2%.[217] On June 24, 1928, a 2-10-10-2 moved 180 empties and nine loads from Victoria, Virginia, westbound to Roanoke; the train was 7,850 feet long and weighed 4,500 tons. This record was broken on July 16, 1928, on the same route with a single 2-10-10-2 pulling 201 cars (197 empties) westbound, 8,480 feet long, weighing 4,573 tons.[218]

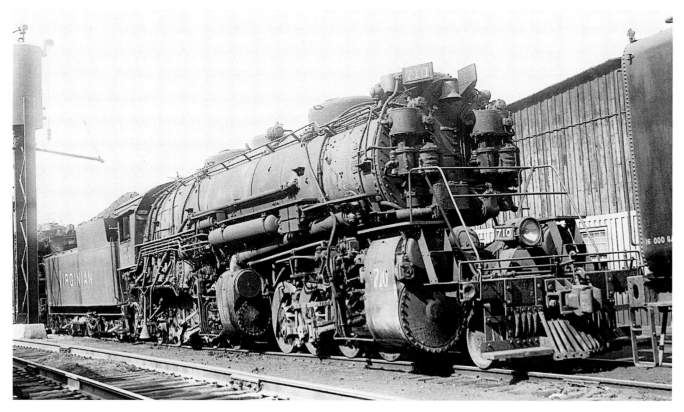

The Virginian class USA 2-8-8-2 was the USRA heavy Mallet. No. 710, built by Alco in 1919, was still in service, in original compound configuration when Otto Perry photographed it at Page, West Virginia, on July 9, 1953 (Denver Public Library, Otto C. Perry collection, OP-19639).

The USRA produced two Mallet designs, "light" 2-6-6-2s and "heavy" 2-8-8-2s, with an initial order of thirty 2-6-6-2s and twenty 2-8-8-2s from Alco Schenectady in 1918.[219] The 2-6-6-2s were light in name only; they were the heaviest 2-6-6-2s built to date at 448,000 pounds engine weight with an axle loading of 60,000 pounds. Compared to some of the arrangements mentioned earlier, the boilers were large and straightforward. The firebox, with power-operated fire doors and grate shakers, had a 76-square foot stoker-fired grate, a brick arch supported on five arch tubes and a combustion chamber extending 7 feet ahead of the throat sheet. The water legs were 5 to 6 inches wide. The fire tubes were 24 feet long; 247 2¼-inch fire tubes and forty-five 5½-inch superheater flues were common to the light Mallet, the heavy 2-8-2, the light 2-10-2 and the heavy 4-8-2. The 225-pounds per square inch boiler pressure meant that piston valves needed to be only 12 inches in diameter, driven by Baker valve gear with Lewis power reverse, supplying 23-inch and 35-inch cylinders. High boiler pressure and enormous engine weight enabled the USRA light Mallets to deliver 80,000 pounds of tractive effort, compound, 96,000 pounds, single expansion.

The USRA designers used much ingenuity to make parts common to more than one type, although the commonality was not obvious. Thus, the piston valves to the 2-6-6-2 high-pressure cylinders were the same as those on the 0-6-0 switchers, while some of the axle boxes and axles were common with the heavy 4-8-2. Those engines, in turn, had parts that were common to other USRA designs.

The USRA increased its initial order for twenty 2-8-8-2 "heavy" Mallets to 110, sixty-five from Alco, forty-five from Baldwin.[220] These engines were derived from the Norfolk & Western Y-2's. Boiler pressure was 240 pounds per square inch, hitherto exceeded only by the Pennsylvania I-1s 2-10-0s. A Gaines wall was built ahead of the 96-square foot stoker-fired grate; a space of about a foot extended forward of the Gaines wall to the throat sheet, with 3 feet of combustion chamber ahead of the throat sheet. The fire tubes were 24 feet long; primary heating surface totaled 6,120 square feet with another 1,475 square feet of superheater surface. Tractive effort was 101,000 pounds, compound, 122,000 pounds, single expansion. The USRA built their 2-8-8-2s 15 feet 9 inches high and 10 feet 9 inches wide over cylinders, acknowledging that they would have limited route availability.

The Pennsylvania revisited the Mallet concept at the end of World War I. In 1919, it bought ten more 0-8-8-0s from Baldwin, class CC-2s. The same year, it was force-fed by the USRA with seven reassigned 2-8-8-2s (known as class HH-1), bought by the Buffalo, Rochester & Pittsburgh.[221] These only later went to their rightful owner.

The Pennsylvania chose the 1919 ARMMA convention to unveil a gigantic 575,000-pound, single-expansion 2-8-8-0 Mallet of advanced design, just completed at its Juniata shops.[222] The design was based on axle loadings up to 68,000 pounds. The wide, but shallow Belpaire firebox contained a 112-square foot grate, apparently without a brick arch. The grate was 14 feet long; ahead of it, a combustion chamber extended 11 feet, so that the distance from the backhead to the back tube sheet was 25 feet. A folded and welded joint between firebox and combustion chamber dealt with expansion. The great length of the firebox and combustion chamber increased the risk of uncovering the crown sheet on a change of grade, even when the water at the backhead was above the top of the gauge glass. For this reason, the gauge glass was fitted with sampling pipes extending forward to points 4, 7½ and 11 inches above the front of the crown sheet. Additionally, a mechanical water level indicator was installed at the neutral point of the boiler water level. The firebox had a Duplex

No. 2-8-8-2, class HH-1, No. 375, one of six built at Schenectady in 1919 for the Buffalo, Rochester & Pittsburgh, temporarily assigned to the Pennsylvania by the USRA. The date and location of the photograph are unknown, but the Worthington feed water heater above the fourth driving wheel was probably a retrofit (Pennsylvania Historical and Museum Commission and Railroad Museum of Pennsylvania, Railroad History Corporation Negative 04678).

Pennsylvania 0-8-8-0, class CC-2s, No. 9358, one of ten built by Baldwin in 1919. The 0-8-8-0 wheel arrangement was not one of the USRA standard designs; it is not known by what arrangement they were built. This photograph was probably taken at Columbus, Ohio, where all ten were stationed for pusher and hump service, date unknown (Pennsylvania Historical and Museum Commission and Railroad Museum of Pennsylvania, Railroad History Corporation Negative 05184).

The Pennsylvania built this class HC-1s 2-8-8-0 at Altoona in 1919. No. 3700 was the only one of the class ever built, scrapped in 1929. Otto Perry photographed it on display when new at Atlantic City, New Jersey, on June 22, 1919 (Denver Public Library, Otto C. Perry collection, OP-14271).

stoker and power-operated grate shakers. The boiler, 19 feet over tube sheets, was built for the new Type E superheater, with 137 2¼-inch fire tubes and 284 3¼-inch flue tubes. The primary heating surface was thus 6,655 square feet, with an additional 3,135 square feet of superheating surface. Boiler pressure was 205 pounds per square inch. High-pressure steam went to both sets of 30½-inch × 32-inch cylinders, but the longest cut-off was 50%, following the I-1s 2-10-0s. Auxiliary ports bled enough steam to the cylinders to move the locomotive to where the main ports opened, so that it could be started from any crank position. When the engine was running, the steam flow through these ports was too slight to have any significant effect. Each pair of cylinders exhausted to a separate exhaust nozzle and into a divided stack.

Power reverse systems using steam or compressed air allowed the control piston to move against an elastic medium, and hence the cut-off to change slightly, unless a mechanical lock was added. The Pennsylvania introduced a new power reverser with a combined steam or compressed-air and hydraulic activator, so that the piston controlling the valve gear was held in place by an inelastic liquid.

The second and fourth pairs of driving wheels on the front drive unit and the second and third pairs on the rear drive unit were blind-flanged. The suspension of the front driving wheels was equalized both longitudinally and transversely and with the front truck. The suspension of the rear driving wheels was equalized longitudinally only.

The result of this monstrous engine was an estimated tractive effort of 135,000 pounds, but this study has not discovered any records of its performance and it remained unique for reasons unknown.

Gradually, the mighty Pennsylvania, the standard against which other railroads were measured, lost its way. Employee morale faded.[223] After producing such locomotives as the H-series 2-8-0s, the E-6s, the

G-5s and K-4s passenger engines and the L-1s, I-1s, M-1s and N-1s freight engines, the Pennsylvania design engineers produced nothing for twenty years and then wandered off into increasingly exotic designs with diminishing success. The brilliant technical leadership of the early 1900s was not maintained; the superpower designs of the 1920s passed the Pennsylvania by with the exception of a class of 2-10-4s—designed by the Chesapeake & Ohio and forced on it by World War II. One of the world's great railroad companies was settling into a long decline.

Espousal of the Mallet was a fundamental shift away from the simplicity that had governed locomotive design since the beginnings of American railroading. The American Mallets were rugged beyond belief, but their enormous tractive effort was achieved at the expense of a huge leap in complexity which brought maintenance difficulties with it. The plodding compound Mallets of 1905–20 were side-tracked by civil engineering programs resulting in ever-stronger track and substructures, allowing axle loadings that permitted rigid-frame locomotives of the 1920s to offer similar tractive effort, but at higher speeds and with easier maintenance. Mallet development went on, even so; in the latter years of steam railroading, the American Mallets were the biggest and most powerful steam locomotives on the face of the earth.

Section 8.4. Switchers

The marshalling of long freight trains and transfer service between yards demanded a purpose-built locomotive—the switcher. In the early 1900s, they needed to be substantial engines, typically of short wheelbase and with no leading or trailing trucks so that the whole engine weight went into adhesion. They did not need to

Alco built this Lake Shore & Michigan Southern class M-1 0-10-0, No. 4597, in 1905, photographed at Cleveland, Ohio, on September 28, 1930 (Denver Public Library, Otto C. Perry collection, OP-13385).

move fast, but they did need to negotiate the sharp curves of yard turnouts.

A new and demanding application for switchers in the early 1900s was the hump classification yard. Exceptional power was needed to push long trains over the hump, beyond which the cars ran by gravity—and adroit switching—into the required tracks. The Lake Shore and Michigan Southern had several such yards and ordered a class of large 0-10-0 switch engines from Alco Brooks in 1905.[224] The 270,000-pound engines had all their weight on ten driving wheels for an axle loading of 54,000 pounds. In spite of working close to sources of fuel and water, these engines had tenders carrying 12 tons of coal and 8,000 gallons of water. A boiler containing 4,625 square feet of heating surface provided steam at 210 pounds per square inch through piston valves driven by Walschaert valve gear to 24-inch × 28-inch cylinders, providing a tractive effort of 52,000 pounds.

The forty 0-6-0 switchers that Alco built for the Illinois Central in 1913 represented a marked update in switcher design.[225] They were the first superheated American-built switchers. Even though the effects of superheating were most marked over long periods at high power, and therefore inapplicable to switch engines, the Illinois Central yard crews found the new engines quicker and more responsive than older switchers using saturated steam. Superheat greatly reduced the amount of sooty water thrown from the stack, a great benefit around passenger terminals. A Ragonnet power reverser saved time with the frequent reversing in switching service. Yard crews reckoned that this combination of features enabled them to handle 20% to 25% more cars per day than with older engines. With the whole 166,000-pound engine weight on the driving wheels, even with the low steam pressure of 170 pounds per square inch, these engines developed 32,000 pounds of tractive effort.

By 1913–14, thirty American railroads had ninety-five hump yards in service. Hump shunting was a task commonly given to obsolete Mallets. The Lake Shore & Michigan Southern found that even the 0-10-0 switchers mentioned earlier were not powerful enough to handle the trains that its road engines brought to the hump yards without dividing them, and bought three 0-8-8-0 Mallets from Alco in 1913 to shunt the hump yard at Elkhart, Indiana.[226] Sharp curves gave Mallet-type flexibility a premium, while the 0-8-8-0 wheel arrangement put the entire engine weight into adhesion. These three 466,000-pound engines developed 120,500 pounds of tractive effort, single-expansion, 100,500 pounds compound with their 26-inch high-pressure and 40-inch low-pressure cylinders. A Street stoker fired an 81-square foot grate with a Gaines wall, a short combustion chamber and a brick arch. Five thousand three hundred square feet of heating surface supplied steam at 220 pounds per square inch, with an additional 1,235 square feet of superheating surface.

Although the duty for which Alco built these engines was prosaic and their speeds rarely greater than 5 miles per hour, their design is full of interest. The low-pressure cylinders were supplied through Allen-ported, Richardson-balanced slide valves. This is doubly curious, not only because, by 1913, the slide valve was rare in new construction, but also because the Allen ports were developed for the short valve events of fast passenger engines; hump shunting was the slowest of all slow service. Ragonnet reverse gear and controls for use on either side of the cab eased the engineer's task when he had to be able to see signals from the hump crew from either side of the engine with the engine running boiler first or tender first, with frequent reversals of direction. Nickel and vanadium were the new wonder steel alloy metals; while Alco made extensive use of cast vanadium steel in the structural parts of these engines, they made the cylinder castings of vanadium-alloyed cast iron. The company tried the engines in road service, but their top speed was 20 miles per hour;

A typical switcher, Illinois Central 0-6-0, No. 328, built by Alco in 1913 and photographed at Council Bluffs, Iowa, on May 29, 1938 (Denver Public Library, Otto C. Perry collection, OP-12215).

Lake Shore & Michigan Southern class NU-1a 0-8-8-0, No. 5897, built by Alco in 1913. The boarded-up cab window and capped stack suggest that this engine was stored serviceable when Otto Perry photographed it at Cleveland, Ohio, on September 28, 1930. (Denver Public Library, Otto C. Perry collection, OP-13424).

The Louisville & Nashville built this class C-1, 0-8-0, No. 2115, in company shops in 1916, photographed at Louisville, Kentucky, on August 6, 1934 (Denver Public Library, Otto C. Perry collection, OP-12534).

The USRA heavy switcher, as supplied to the New York Central (classified U-3a), built by Baldwin in 1919. Otto Perry photographed No. 307 at Cleveland, Ohio, on September 28, 1930 (Denver Public Library, Otto C. Perry collection, OP-13330).

The USRA light switcher, as supplied to the Chicago, Rock Island & Pacific (classified S-33), built by Alco and Baldwin in 1919. Otto Perry photographed No. 277 at Rock Island, Illinois, on September 28, 1929 (Denver Public Library, Otto C. Perry collection, OP-5273).

the Street stokers were ineffective and it was impossible to maintain steam pressure by hand firing, so they merely obstructed traffic.

The New York Central and its subsidiaries bought sixteen 0-8-8-0s for this specialized service in five variants between 1913 and 1921, all from Alco.

Demands for switching power increased with increasing freight traffic and longer trains. In 1916, the Louisville & Nashville built eight 0-8-0s at its South Louisville shops, weighing 219,000 pounds and, with all of this weight going into adhesion, capable of 46,900 pounds of tractive effort.[227] Although boiler pressure was only 170 pounds per square inch, they were in other respects fully up to date with brick arches, superheat and power reverse. The new engines moved three times the hourly tonnage of the older, saturated-steam 0-6-0s because they could move long freight trains whole and accelerated faster.

By 1916, the Boston & Albany's 0-6-0 switchers were not powerful enough to handle trains brought to the yards by Mallets and 2-8-2s.[228] New 0-8-0 switchers were costly and hard to obtain. At the same time, it owned a number of 1901-built 2-8-0s that could not make scheduled speeds with the freight trains then being run. The company rebuilt twelve of them as 0-8-0 switchers in its West Springfield shops. The rebuilt engines were provided with new, superheated boilers (although with pressure reduced from 195 pounds per square inch to 180), air-operated fire doors, Baker valve gear with Ragonnet power reverse and 23-inch instead of 20-inch cylinders. By this means, with the whole engine weight going into adhesion, the tractive effort was increased from 37,000 pounds to 45,000. The front frames were cut off and replacements thermite-welded in place. The center of gravity had to be adjusted by mounting the new boiler 14 inches rearward of the old one. The frames were strengthened. A steel cab replaced the original wooden one; there were other detailed modi-

fications. The rebuilds gave satisfactory service. The Chicago & Eastern Illinois did the same thing in 1917, converting sixteen 4-8-0s, built in 1897–9, into 0-6-0 switchers.[229] Other railroads likewise built obsolete or unsatisfactory road engines to switchers.

In early 1918 the USRA ordered 150 0-8-0 switchers for distribution among seventeen railroads.[230] These were substantial engines. The frames were of cast steel 5 inches thick. The firebox contained a brick arch supported on arch tubes, but no combustion chamber. A 47-square foot grate fired 2,780 square feet of primary heating surface, with a further 675 square feet of superheating surface. Although boiler pressure was only 175 pounds per square inch, the engines weighed 214,000 pounds, all of which went into adhesion, while remaining within a 55,000-pound axle loading. The resulting tractive effort was 55,000 pounds. The engines were fitted with Baker valve gear and Ragonnet power reverse. Steam was admitted to the 25-inch × 28-inch cylinders by 14-inch piston valves which were interchangeable with those of the light and heavy USRA 2-8-2s.

The USRA 0-6-0 switchers were smaller and lighter than the 0-8-0s, but with 190 pounds per square inch boiler pressure, 165,000-pound engine weight and 39,000 pounds of tractive effort. Like the 0-8-0s, these had Baker valve gear, but with Lewis or Mellin power reverse. The USRA designed three standard tenders, of 8,000, 10,000 and 12,000-gallon water capacity with Locomotive Stoker Co. coal pushers. Both switchers had the smallest of these.

The 0-4-0 was obsolete for Class I railroad purposes, construction having ceased in 1890. The 0-6-0 was the typical switcher, with 15,000 built. The 0-8-0 was common, with 3,200 built. The 0-10-0 was rare, only 50 to 60 being built between 1905 and 1925. Construction of 0-6-0s and 0-8-0s continued throughout the first half of the twentieth century.

9

Traction Other Than Steam, 1905–1920

Between 1905 and 1920, the elimination of steam locomotives became an objective in itself for some railroad managements on the grounds of noise, dirt and inefficiency, even though the means of achievement did not exist.[1] The electric locomotive was already fully developed, but the high capital cost of electric power generation and distribution restricted it to areas of particularly dense traffic. Although an internal combustion engine powered the Wright brothers' first flight in 1903, the technology was too immature for railroad service.

Section 9.1 Electric Traction

The electric locomotive was by far the most efficient of all available forms of traction.[2] Power output was limited only by the systems for electricity generation and distribution and by heat in motor windings; an electric locomotive consumed power only when it was working. Multiple units allowed high traction without high axle loading. The electric locomotive produced no dynamic augment. It could be run in either direction. It accelerated faster and to higher speeds than a steam locomotive.[3] Evenly applied torque permitted a lower adhesion factor than did the uneven torque of the reciprocating steam locomotive. It needed almost none of the vast amount of roundhouse labor needed for steam engines; experience proved that it was cheaper to maintain. Nascent control technology promised to put several locomotives under the control of a single throttle. It produced no noise, smoke, soot or cinders—increasingly important factors in congested city terminals. Power stations could use lower-grade, cheaper coal than steam locomotives; with its higher thermal efficiency, an electric power station could produce energy at half the cost of a steam locomotive. Even if steam power generated the electricity, driving the generators by turbine, rather than reciprocating, steam engines increased efficiency.

The problem lay in the high capital cost of the distribution system, which restricted these benefits to areas of high traffic density, or where air quality in tunnels was a major safety issue. Economic growth in the early twentieth century increased the number of railroads reaching the requisite traffic density. Not only did the electric railroads take short-haul passenger traffic from their steam-hauled counterparts; their very convenience built their own traffic and brought about the suburban way of life.

W. S. Murray, consulting engineer to the New Haven, described the electrification issue succinctly[4]:

Experience with the movement of billions of ton-miles in freight, passenger and switching service has justified the early predictions that one pound of coal burned under the boilers of a central power station and converted into electrical energy and transmitted to an electric engine will develop twice the drawbar pull at the same speed as a similar pound of coal burned in the firebox of a steam locomotive; and, second, that

the maintenance and repairs on electric locomotives of the straight alternating-current type are on the order of one-half of those required for steam locomotives of equal weight on drivers. It is thus seen that the problem of electrification merely revolves around the question of the density of traffic in which the economies aforesaid can be practiced, and, therefore, the denser the traffic the greater the requisite motive power for its movement, and hence the greater the saving to be effected.

Volition came not only from the railroads themselves. For reasons of smoke abatement, the New York State Legislature required the New York Central and the New Haven to electrify their trackage within the city of New York before July 1, 1908.

The New Haven, with some of the highest short-distance passenger volumes in America, was among the most aggressive companies in developing electric traction under the leadership of President Mellen.[5] Two acquisitions in 1906 gave this steam railroad 1,350 miles of electrified line, including inter-urban and street railways, as well as the means of public power supply. The company started running an all-electric passenger service between New York and Stamford in 1907.[6] Electric passenger service between New York and New Haven began in 1914; electric haulage spread to freight and switching service. Power came from an 11,000-volt overhead wire. By 1915, the company had 100 electric passenger, freight and switching locomotives and sixty-nine multiple-unit, self-propelled passenger cars in service,[7] displacing 150 steam locomotives. Utilization was intense; individual locomotives ran 500 miles per day; self-propelled units averaged as high as 2,100 miles per day. Slight as their maintenance requirements were, electric locomotives still required training in operation and maintenance.

The Long Island electrified its first lines in 1905; in 1906 the Southern Pacific began electrification around San Francisco.[8] The same year, the Spokane, Coeur d'Alene & Palouse was built from the outset with overhead-wire electric traction.[9]

In 1908–9, the Great Northern electrified operations through the Cascade tunnel with four 230,000-pound trolley-wire locomotives, using power generated thirty miles away on the Wenatchee River.[10]

Justified by high traffic density, the Pennsylvania began tests on electric traction in 1908.[11] In 1911:

The Pennsylvania, it is said, will build the frames and the running gear for 20 2,000-h.p. electric locomotives at its Juniata shops. The brakes and the motor equipment for these locomotives will be made by the Westinghouse Electric and Manufacturing Company.[12]

By 1912, seven major U.S. railroads were using electric traction on one or more main line divisions.[13] These were: the Baltimore & Ohio, the New York Central, the Pennsylvania, the New Haven, the Great Northern, the Grand Trunk and the Michigan Central.

Other than the Pennsylvania, the Butte, Anaconda & Pacific was one of the first railroads to electrify for reasons of economy, rather than smoke abatement.[14] Built in 1892 to haul copper ore from the mines at Butte, Montana, to the smelter at Anaconda, the line was only 26 miles long. The company started electrification work in 1912 and completed it the following year. Electric power was already available from the Montana Power Co. Taking 2,400-volt DC power from overhead lines, seventeen electric locomotives replaced twenty-eight Mastodons, hauling 4,600-ton trains at average speeds of 16 miles per hour, compared to 3,500 tons at 13 miles per hour for the steam locomotives. Maintenance cost one-third as much as the steam locomotives. The conversion was a complete success.

In 1913, the Norfolk & Western began electrification of a 30-mile stretch between Bluefield and Vivian, West Virginia.[15] The N&W was moving 40,000 to 60,000 tons of coal per day over the Elkhorn grade; this justified the capital expenditure. Eastbound ruling grades were 1.5% to 2.0%, climbing almost continuously from Vivian to Bluefield, with sharp curves and the 3,000-foot, single-track Elkhorn tunnel. Three Mallets moved 3,250-ton coal trains over this section, averaging 7½ miles per hour; ventilation in the tunnel was so bad that the company imposed a 6-miles per hour speed limit to control locomotive emissions. With a 24,000-kilowatt steam turbine powerhouse supplying 25-cycle, single-phase power at 44 kilovolts, transformed to 11 kilovolts in overhead wires, one electric road engine, with an electric pusher on the grades, doubled the speed of the Mallets. The N&W put its electric locomotives on the coal drags, hauling passenger and other freight trains by steam. The first twelve electric locomotives, built by a Baldwin-Westinghouse joint venture, weighed 540,000 pounds and developed 133,000 pounds tractive effort. Under test, one locomotive developed 170,000 pounds at the drawbar and moved a 5,200-ton train at 32 miles per hour against a 0.4% grade. Regenerative braking allowed engines drifting downgrade to return power to the grid and reduced brake wear.

By 1914, 463 electric locomotives were in service in the U.S.— and fifty-nine on order—compared to 262 in service—148 on order—in the whole of Europe.[16] Approximately 1,750 miles of steam railroad track had been electrified; electrification projects about to begin comprised another 900 miles. Biggest of these was the Chicago, Milwaukee & St. Paul project to electrify 440 miles, inspired by the success of the Butte, Anaconda & Pacific. These figures conceal the magnitude of interurban railroad development in that time; 20,000 self-propelled electric railroad cars went into interurban service in the U.S. between 1900 and 1914.

The Milwaukee's program—estimated at $15 million—took advantage of existing hydroelectric power and coal-fired power stations, using coal that the company mined, to electrify haulage across three mountain ranges between Harlowton, Montana, and Avery, Idaho.[17] Working against 1% grades, passenger locomotives were to haul 800-ton trains at 35 miles per hour; freight locomotives were to haul 2,500-ton trains at 16 miles per hour with electric pusher service for 2% grades. The Milwaukee ordered forty-three locomotives; General Electric delivered the first in 1915. The freight engines were 568,000-pound monsters, rated at 3,000 continuous horsepower and developing 135,000 pounds of tractive effort. Steam freight engines were removed from the electrified sections in January 1916. Main transmission was at 100 kilovolts, 60-cycle, 3-phase, transformed to 3,000 volts for the locomotives. The first construction contract was let in November 1914, for the 113 miles between Three Forks and Deer Lodge; all 440 miles were electrified by February 1917, a year ahead of schedule.

Even before the program was complete, it was so successful that the Milwaukee decided, in January 1917, to electrify 225 miles of main line from Othello, Washington, through the Cascades to Seattle and Tacoma.[18] Besides steep grades and heavy curvature, this section included the 12,000-foot Snoqualmie tunnel. A Mallet would haul

A Chicago, Milwaukee & St. Paul electric locomotive, No. 10300, built by General Electric in 1915, photographed at Three Forks, Montana, on August 9, 1938 (Denver Public Library, Otto C. Perry collection, OP-5234).

2,100 tons eastbound from Seattle to Cedar Falls, with a second Mallet pushing from Cedar Falls for the 17 miles of 1.7% grade to the Snoqualmie west portal. With electrification, the combination of road engine and pusher would remain, but the eastbound tonnage would increase to 3,000 tons at twice the speed. The new engines would weigh 564,000 pounds with a starting tractive effort of 126,000 pounds. This work was forecast to cost $6.25 million.

Electrification was expensive. Whereas a typical steam locomotive cost $25,000 in 1915, before wartime inflation took effect, an electric locomotive of equivalent capacity cost $45,000.[19] The average operating cost of a steam locomotive was about $0.26 per engine-mile at that time; the equivalent cost for an electric locomotive was still $0.21 per mile, if all variable costs were taken into account. Taking fixed costs into account, these figures became $0.30 per engine-mile for steam, $0.60 per mile for electric. Each electric locomotive averaged 85 miles per day, compared to 150 miles per day for a steam locomotive. The New York Central's initial electrification program around Central Station cost $12 million. (The source states $120 million, but this is probably a misprint, as the New Haven spent $15 million on its electrification system.)

The economic challenges surrounding the electric locomotive were never overcome; consequently, electric traction never replaced steam over the vast areas of the U.S. where traffic density never warranted electric power. The form of traction that would banish the steam locomotive comprised an internal combustion engine, powering an on-board electric generator which, in turn, drove an electric motor that powered the driving wheels. The pioneers of internal combustion-engine locomotives in the United States were two railroads, so obscure as to delight the historian.

Section 9.2 Internal Combustion Traction

In 1905, the internal combustion engine in railroad service resembled the first mammals in the age of dinosaurs.[20] The gasoline-engine railcar offered the advantages of the electric train, but was independent of costly power generation and transmission systems. However, a gasoline engine cost two to three times as much to build as an equivalent steam engine; the most powerful of them developed only one-tenth the power of existing steam locomotives. Fuel was expensive. A gasoline engine needed clutched and geared transmission to the driving wheels; substituting an electric transmission doubled the initial cost and increased operating costs. If a railcar engine failed, it disabled passenger accommodation as well as motive power. In the early 1900s, the gasoline-powered car or locomotive attracted little attention.

The Union Pacific pioneered the railroad use of gasoline engines; in 1905, it bought three self-propelled passenger cars from the McKeen Motor Car Co., followed by six in 1906, ten in 1907 and one in 1908.[21] These cars were powered by 100-horsepower, later 200-horsepower, gasoline engines with mechanical transmission. By 1909, the Union Pacific was operating fifteen of these cars in Nebraska, Colorado and Kansas.

In 1908, General Electric brought out a self-propelled passenger car, powered by a gasoline engine driving a 600-volt motor-generator set.[22] This had profound implications for the railroads. It was much more economical than a steam locomotive hauling one or two passenger cars over a lightly traveled branch line; it could also operate on interurban lines.

On April 30, 1912, Dr. Rudolph Diesel gave a seminal lecture to the American Society of Mechanical Engineers in New York.[23] That same month, the German firm, Borsig, of Berlin, completed a loco-

motive of 1,000 to 1,200 horsepower, powered by a Sulzer diesel engine. A V-4, two-stroke diesel engine drove two pairs of driving wheels through a blind axle and connecting rods. There must have been a clutch and transmission, although the referenced source does not mention them. An auxiliary engine supplied compressed air to the main engine intake for a temporary increase of power. The Americans gave no further thought to the diesel locomotive until the 1920s.

Self-propelled passenger cars offered an alternative to cars hauled by a steam locomotive; several types were tried.[24] Self-propelled cars with a built-in reciprocating steam engine achieved little success because the power density of the steam engine was insufficient for the required service of fast acceleration and frequent stops. Battery-powered electric cars required excessively heavy and bulky batteries. Compressed air-powered cars had insufficient power and range for useful service. The only promising design was the gasoline-engine railcar with either a mechanical or an electric transmission. By 1913, the McKeen car with a mechanical transmission had 138 units in service on fifty railroads, while General Electric had fifty gasoline-engine cars with electric transmission in service. Other manufacturers of mechanical-transmission railcars were Fairbanks-Morse, P. H. Batten, Stover Motor Car and Hall-Scott.

As far as is known, the first locomotive (as distinct from a railcar), powered by an internal combustion engine, to enter service in the U.S. was built by General Electric at its Erie, Pennsylvania, works for the Minneapolis, St. Paul, Rochester & Dubuque Electric Traction Co., (the Dan Patch Line), running from Minneapolis 107 miles south to Mankato.[25] The company ran a heavy passenger service between Minneapolis and Northfield with gasoline-engine, electric-transmission railcars; indeed it contributed to suburb development south of Minneapolis by selling land. Freight and passenger traffic grew so much that the company decided to buy a gasoline-powered locomotive.

This 114,000-pound locomotive developed 30,000 pounds tractive effort, reaching 45 miles per hour with a five-car train. The power plant comprised two units; each unit consisted of one 175-horsepower and one 225-horsepower V-8 gasoline engine, running at 550 revolutions per minute. Each engine drove a 600-volt electric generator which drove a 100-horsepower electric motor directly connected to a drive axle; the driving wheels were in the form of two 4-wheel trucks with an electric motor on each axle. With the electric motors mounted on the trucks, only flexible power cables were needed to connect the trucks to the rigid frame. Each power unit was cross-connected electrically so that either or both generators could drive either or both motors; the motors were connected in parallel but could be switched to series connection. Load sharing was automatic in that, if one motor took more load than the other, it would slow down until it matched the other. Reversing was accomplished by switching the electric motors; the gasoline engines ran in a constant direction. One power unit was started by compressed air; the first started the second electrically. A separate, 5-kilowatt gasoline engine drove a generator for electric lighting in the locomotive and train. A coal-fired water heater provided train heating. This engine went into service in July 1913. It was so successful that the company ordered three more which went into service in 1915, slightly larger than the prototype at 120,000 pounds. The locomotives were built to be driven in either direction. The Dan Patch Lines ran thirteen gasoline-electric passenger cars and, with these four locomotives, was said to be the first railroad in the world to be powered entirely by gasoline-electric means.

From self-propelled railcars, it was a short step for McKeen to build gasoline-powered locomotives. In 1915[26]:

The Motley County (Tex.) Railway recently purchased a 300-horsepower gasoline switching locomotive from the McKeen Motor Car Company, Omaha, Neb., to be used in freight and switching service between Roaring Springs Junction on the Quanah, Acme & Pacific and Matador, Tex. It has a tractive effort of 12,000 lb. at a speed of six miles an hour.

A box-shaped body contained a 6-cylinder in-line gasoline engine with 11-inch × 15-inch cylinders, apparently with a direct drive to two driving axles with wheels connected by rods.

The Erie[27] followed in 1916 with a 44,000-pound gasoline-engine switching locomotive for transfer service in Chicago, built by Baldwin. Engine power was applied through a clutch and a two-speed chain drive.

World War I inhibited the development of these new forms of motive power as the manufacturing plants turned to war materials.[28]

Part Four

Superpower, 1920–1930

"In spite of all our battles, most of we American railroad men are loyal and want to see the operation at the highest possible standard. We wouldn't quit the game if we could. It's a he-man's job and we love it, with all of its dirt, long hours, poor grub, hard beds and grief, but we would like to see some of our operating officials get on the job—have less talking and more doing." (Letter from "Locomotive Engineer," *RA*, April 8, 1922, 861)

The Transportation Act of 1920 returned the railroads from the USRA to private operation after a Senate investigation lasting for most of 1919, but under new and more pervasive restrictions, administered by the ICC. Economic and political turbulence, influenced by the Russian revolution, continued for several years after the end of World War I, with a sharp contraction in business in 1921. Only in 1923–4 did the nation's affairs return to normality, indeed, prosperity. Passenger traffic went into permanent decline as more and more people traveled by car and bus; demand for freight haulage continued to intensify. Even as rate restrictions and rising costs for taxes, labor and materials suppressed profit margins, the sheer volume of traffic forced the railroads to move freight through their systems faster than before. Into this arena came the super-power steam locomotive, first produced by Lima and at once imitated by Alco and Baldwin, offering immense gains in speed, power and efficiency. These new locomotives had more effect on railroad operations and economics in a shorter space of time than any previous improvement in locomotive design.

The comment was made in 1920[1]: "If the railroads are to stay out of the hands of the government, a lot of people have got to wake up." They did.

The full extent of this "waking up" is shown in the following graphs. Considering that these are national averages, the achievement that they reflect is astonishing.

What locomotive developments contributed to this achievement?

10

General Steam Locomotive Development,
1920–1930

"If we are to save the race against government ownership we must regard the locomotive in a new light." (Basford, G. M., Lima Locomotive Works, *As to the Locomotive—What Next?* Pacific Railway Club, March 1923. Reported RA March 10, 1923, 553)

The 1920s were a time of fertile locomotive development in America, not only the reciprocating steam locomotive but also new forms of power.[1] This took place against a background of burgeoning new technologies, such as the internal combustion engine, the aviation and automotive industries and advances in the use of electricity. One commentator, A. F. Stuebing, remarked:

> The year 1922 is likely to go down in history as marking one of the turning points of locomotive development … because of the distinct tendency toward a departure from what has been considered standard in every-day equipment.

Stuebing pointed out that the basic steam locomotive configuration established in 1829 had remained unchanged, but for greater size. Over the years, various inventors had tried radically new types of power, albeit without success, but never in such number and variety as in 1922. These included steam-turbine and internal-combustion locomotives. He prophesied:

> Probably it is too early for anyone to predict the outcome, but the new designs recently brought out are worthy of the closest attention by both mechanical and operating officers.

The steam locomotive had retained its basic configuration for a hundred years because no one had come up with anything better. "Some very able men have devoted their energies to designing substitutes for the steam locomotive without success."[2] But now a shadow fell across the conventional, reciprocating steam locomotive.

In the early 1920s, locomotive designers stood at a cross-roads in their search for ever-higher tractive effort in drag freight service.[3] The ultimate rigid-frame freight power was now the 2-10-2 or the less common 2-10-0. To avoid the maintenance problems of the compound Mallets, some railroads—such as the Pennsylvania—clung to these types, even though they had reached the limits of their development. Other railroads, with similar topography and traffic, felt no inhibitions toward the compound Mallet which, in spite of the abuse directed at it, was still the ultimate American freight hauler. Its numerous driving

wheels produced more tractive effort for a given axle loading than any rigid-frame engine—and that by a large margin. It was easier to counterbalance than a large rigid-frame engine, resulting in less track damage. Compounding resulted in lower steam consumption. The rigid-frame locomotive had fewer parts than a Mallet, but these parts were stressed to the limits of existing steel metallurgy and were harder to maintain in consequence. In summary:

> Many heavy simple locomotives give trouble due to excessive heating and wear in the driving box and rod bearings, but there is a question whether this is not offset by the reduction in the number of parts. The connection between the front and rear frames and the joints in the steam pipe prove troublesome in many designs of Mallet engines. The crux of the whole matter seems to be that the Mallet permits of hauling heavier loads while the increased cost of maintenance may or may not outweigh this advantage.

During the 1920s, locomotive designers resolved this impasse in three ways. First, the inventive genius gathered in the Lima Locomotive

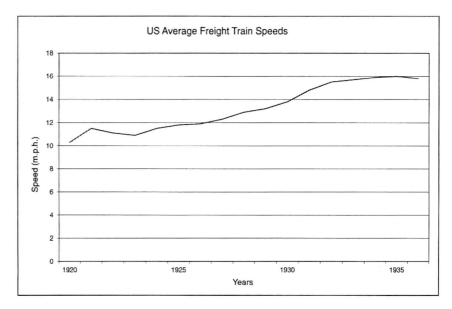

U.S. average freight train speeds from 1920 to 1936. Acceleration during the 1920s increased during the worst years of the Depression (figures for these ten graphs come from the American Railroad Association Mechanical Division 1937 convention, reported as *Utilization of Locomotives and Conservation of Fuel, RA*, June 21, 1937, 1040D22).

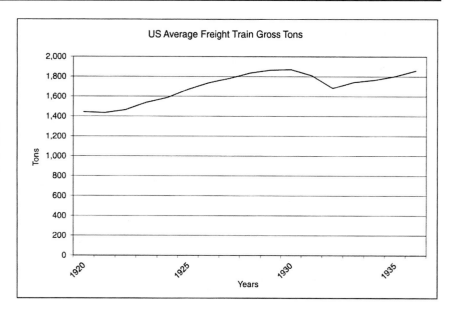

U.S. average freight train gross tons from 1920 to 1936. The decrease during the depression resulted from lack of traffic, but note the continuous rapid increase in the 1920s. The bottom of the depression in 1932 shows clearly.

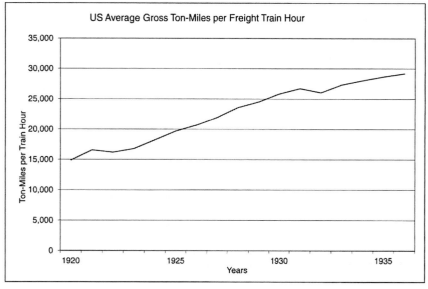

U.S. average gross ton-miles per freight train hour from 1920 to 1936. The 1920s brought recognition that this was the real measure of railroad production.

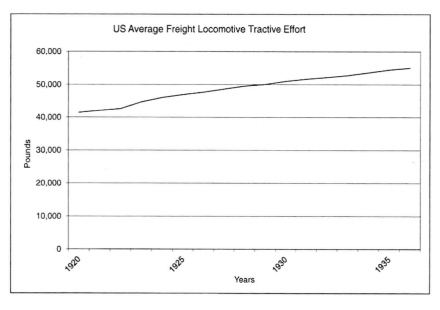

The U.S. average freight locomotive tractive effort from 1920 to 1936. This increase, in spite of the huge fleet of older freight engines, highlights the enormous tractive effort of the locomotives built in the 1920s.

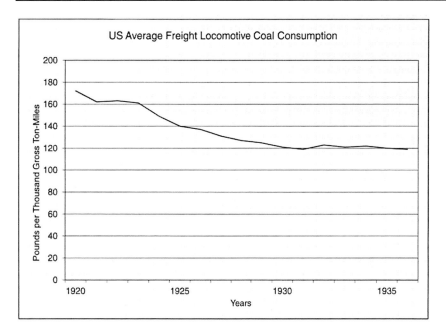

U.S. average freight locomotive coal consumption from 1920 to 1936. Coal consumption can be looked at in several ways. This trend shows the rapid gain in efficiency during the 1920s in terms of pounds of coal burnt per thousand gross ton-miles hauled.

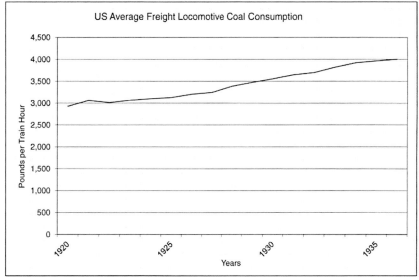

U.S. average freight locomotive coal consumption from 1920 to 1936 in terms of fuel burn per train hour. The increase highlights the effect of bigger grates and power stokers.

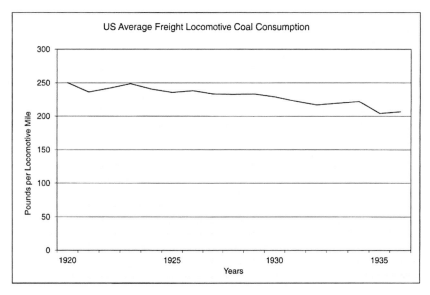

U.S. average freight locomotive coal consumption from 1920 to 1936 in terms of fuel burn per locomotive mile. The decrease highlights increased locomotive efficiency.

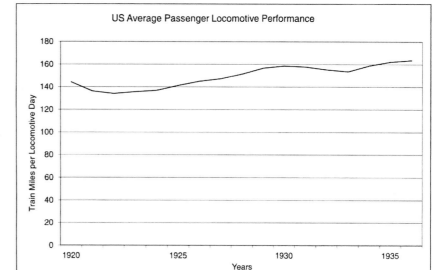

U.S. average passenger locomotive performance from 1920 to 1936. The increase in train miles per locomotive day shows the effects of better locomotive design, manufacturing, maintenance and dispatching.

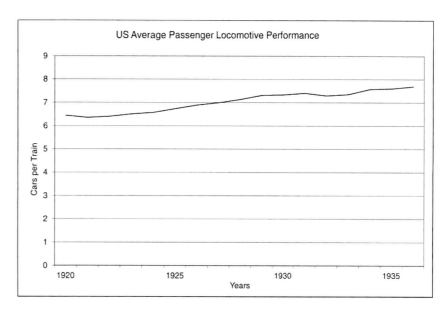

U.S. average passenger locomotive performance from 1920 to 1936. Train length continued to increase in spite of the depression and declining passenger numbers.

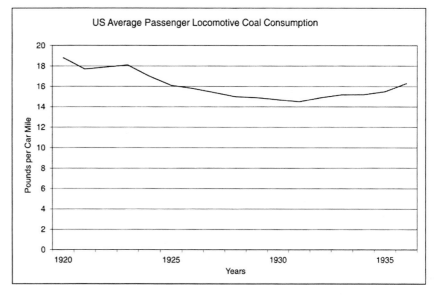

U.S. average passenger locomotive coal consumption from 1920 to 1936. The weight of passengers and baggage made up a small proportion of passenger train weight and the railroads had to haul trains to schedule, whether they were full or empty. The decrease in fuel burn per car mile is therefore the passenger-service equivalent of freight ton-miles per train hour.

"The compound Mallet was still the ultimate American freight hauler." Denver & Rio Grande Western class L-107 2-8-8-2, No. 3501, built by Alco in 1923, sits simmering and leaking steam at Helper, Utah, on July 4, 1939 (Denver Public Library, Otto C. Perry collection, OP-9875).

Works produced rigid-frame engines of unprecedented power and efficiency, quickly emulated by Alco and Baldwin. Second, the Mallet never lost its place in American freight power; single-expansion Mallets were the most powerful steam locomotives ever built, anywhere in the world. Third, the diesel locomotive came of age.

Any radically new form of power had to match existing infrastructure. It had to produce the same or greater power than a steam locomotive and had to do so reliably and at a lower cost. Ruggedness and reliability were prime virtues of the conventional steam locomotive; the big manufacturers could turn out new orders astonishingly quickly.[4] The first locomotives of a new design would leave the shops 90 to 120 days after receipt of order. The 1920s brought, not only several radically new designs in practical forms, but also, a new willingness on the part of operators and designers to consider possibilities that they would previously have rejected.[5]

The steam-turbine locomotive offered high thermal efficiency. The Swedish State Railways measured a thermal efficiency of 14.7% on a Ljungstrom engine and found that it burned only half as much fuel as a modern reciprocating engine. It produced only 1,800 horsepower, however; its power output was limited by the size of the condenser that would fit within clearance dimensions. A turbine locomotive cost three times as much as a conventional one; its delicate and complicated mechanism was ill-suited to railroad service and was difficult to maintain.

The most promising competitor to the steam locomotive was the diesel-electric. A. I. Lipetz of Alco pointed out that, while the first two decades of the twentieth century had produced substantial improvements in steam locomotive power and efficiency, these were slight, compared to the inherent efficiency of the internal combustion engine.[6]

If we built a three-cylinder single expansion locomotive with the idea of obtaining one-half per cent more efficiency under the 7½ to 8 per cent efficiency for the whole locomotive, and compare that with the 20 or 28 per cent efficiency which can be obtained from a Diesel locomotive, the possibilities are so vast and so attractive that we cannot help but think that if we would not develop this it would be of great significance to civilization and the transport problem.

Other leaders of the steam locomotive industry were unaware of the rapidity of diesel development. Samuel Vauclain growled[7]:

There is an idea in many places, not only in this country but abroad, that something should be invented, something should be devised, that would supersede the steam locomotive. It is my opinion, after a thorough examination of everything that has been done, not only in this country but abroad, that we can save more money in the operation of our railroads by giving our attention more closely to the development of the steam locomotive. I assure you that you are going to have it with you not only the rest of your lives, but that your children will have to deal with this means of locomotion.

C. E. Brooks of the Canadian National commented:

Some of us have been working for some time past in the development of the oil engine. We may be wrong or we may be right, but there is one thing we can take for granted, and that is that we are never going to know whether we are right if we do not go to it and try it.

I cannot say that the attitude of some of the locomotive builders is a great encouragement or assistance to the young railroad man who is trying to do something new, such as the oil engine.

There, in 1926, stood the locomotive that would sweep the steam locomotive away only twenty years in the future.

Meanwhile, the railroads demanded that steam locomotives haul heavier trains at higher speeds. Freight train cost curves still bottomed out at 20 miles per hour. These graphs assume a 100-mile run by a 2-8-2, 3 hours terminal and road delays, crew wages $27.32 for 8 hours or 16 hours with overtime, coal cost $5 per ton on the tender, firing rate during delays 750 pounds per hour.

Economics still favored the heaviest possible trains. Moving these heavier trains faster demanded enormous increases in power; the graph is for straight, level track. Grades and curves demanded even more power. In the early 1920s, only a tiny minority of the U.S. locomotive fleet was capable of more than 2,500 drawbar horsepower. High power at high speed, with high availability, was the breakthrough achieved by the superpower designs.

By the 1920s the steam locomotive's characteristic relationship between speed, drawbar pull and power was generally known. In 1923, H. A. F. Campbell, working for Baldwin, and George Basford, working for Lima, both sketched out a concept for a conventional steam locomotive of advanced design.[8] The resulting "superpower" design was one of the biggest advances in performance and efficiency ever made in the history of the steam locomotive.

Campbell proposed a 2-8-4 compound passenger locomotive

capable of developing 4,000 indicated horsepower for extended periods; at that time the highest horsepower recorded in a steam locomotive was 3,500 by a Union Pacific 4-8-2, and that for a short period. A power stoker would fire an 88-square foot grate in a Belpaire firebox with thermic siphons and a combustion chamber extending 5 feet in front of the throat sheet. The boiler, 19 feet over tube sheets, would contain 5,000 square feet of primary heating surface with another 1,000 square feet of superheating surface, generating steam at 250 pounds per square inch. The boiler would fill the 15-foot clearance height; instead of a steam dome, a perforated dry pipe would draw steam from directly above the crown sheet. The throttle valve in the dome would be replaced by a front-end throttle, downstream of the superheater. Steam would be used in one 25-inch × 30-inch high-pressure cylinder centrally mounted between the frames and two 28-inch × 30-inch low-pressure outside cylinders, limited to 60% cutoff. Baldwin was still pursuing the benefits of compounding, elusive though they might be in practice. The counterbalance provided by the three cylinders would so reduce yawing that a two-wheel leading truck would suffice, instead of the four-wheel truck currently believed essential for a passenger locomotive. This power would be applied

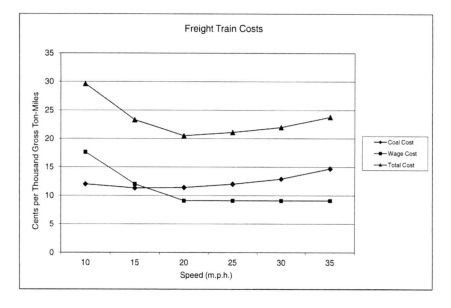

Wage, coal and total cost (cents per 1,000 gross ton-miles) for a 3,000-ton train at various speeds (plotted from figures provided in Davenport, J. E., New York Central, *Effect of Tonnage and Speed on Fuel Consumption*, RA, July 8, 1922, 71).

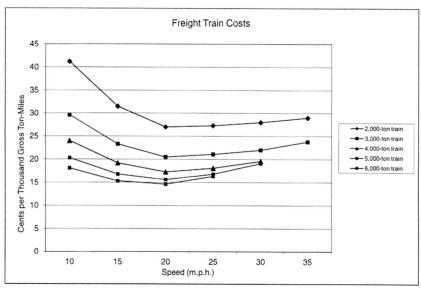

The total cost per 1,000 gross ton-miles hauled for various train weights and speeds (plotted from figures provided in Davenport, J. E., New York Central, *Effect of Tonnage and Speed on Fuel Consumption*, RA, July 8, 1922, 71).

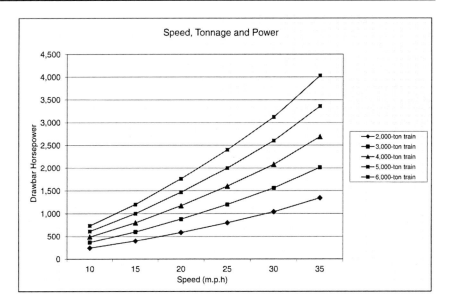

The power required to haul various train
weights at various speeds (plotted from figures
provided in Davenport, J. E., New York Central,
*Effect of Tonnage and Speed on Fuel Consump-
tion, RA, July 8, 1922, 71,* assuming resistance
characteristics of 40-ton cars).

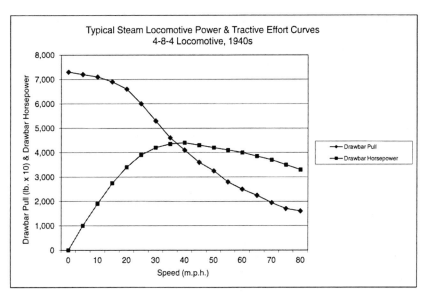

Typical steam locomotive speed, drawbar pull and power characteristics. Up to 1920,
the dominant design objective was to increase tractive effort; after 1920, the main objective was to increase peak power output and the speed at which this was developed. The
numbers happen to be from a 1940s 4-8-4, representing the culmination of this process.

already being fired beyond their economical firing rates. Even with big grates, power stokers
were firing 130 pounds of coal per square foot of
grate per hour, to the detriment of efficiency; 120
pounds per square foot per hour was the
acknowledged maximum for economical combustion; still lower rates were desirable. Fireboxes
had reached the weight limit of a two-wheel trailing truck, yet still bigger fireboxes were needed,
requiring a four-wheel trailing truck. Locomotive
designers were trying to increase heating surface
in parts of the boiler not supported by the trailing
truck but, in the end: "To sum the matter up, further development and extension of locomotive
power is dependent upon adequate methods of
taking care of larger grate areas and firebox heating surfaces than present construction allows."

Basford sketched out a 2-8-4 improved locomotive: "a proposed solution to the problem
which has not yet been worked out in practice."
A stoker-fired 76-square foot grate with a short
combustion chamber would fire 3,540 square
feet of primary heating surface and 915 square
feet of superheating surface in a Type A superheater; it is interesting that Basford ignored the
Type E superheater. A feedwater heater would
add to boiler efficiency. A front-end throttle would
admit steam to 26-inch × 30-inch cylinders through 14-inch piston valves, driving
eight 63-inch driving wheels. An adhesion weight of 212,000 pounds
(54,000 pounds axle loading) would permit 53,000 pounds of tractive effort, augmented on starting by a booster. Total engine weight
would be 322,000 pounds.

The year 1925 was a landmark in American motive power development with the appearance of the 2-8-4 and 2-10-4 types from Lima
and three-cylinder 4-10-2s from Alco.[9] The particular potency of
these locomotives lay in the reduction of the adhesion factor from
the conventional 4.0–4.25 to 3.6–3.7. Limited cut-off made this possible by smoothing the torque produced by each revolution of the
driving wheels, while boosters added 10,000 pounds to the starting
tractive effort. New arrangements of the valve gear permitted long
valve travel which increased the effective valve opening at high speed

to 70-inch driving wheels, of which the rear three axles would be
mounted rigidly in the frame; the front driving axle and the leading
truck would be combined in a Zara or Krauss truck. Campbell noted
that maximum practical piston speeds were limited to 1,000 to 1,200
feet per minute by existing valves and valve gear; in other words, the
steam valves were the limiting factor in locomotive speeds. Whether
this concept influenced 1920s locomotive development or not, it certainly foretold several aspects of it.

George Basford's landmark paper to the Pacific Railway Club was
remarkably succinct in sketching out the origins of the superpower
design. He pointed out that nationalization of the railroads was still
possible; keeping them out of the hands of the government depended
on the fullest possible development and utilization of the steam locomotive in all its aspects of design, construction, operation, scheduling
and maintenance. Locomotives with two-wheel trailing trucks were

Otto Perry photographed this early superpower 2-8-4, Illinois Central No. 7006, built by Lima in 1926, near Ferber, Illinois, on August 15, 1940 (Denver Public Library, Otto C. Perry collection, OP-12356).

One of the first superpower 2-10-4s, Texas & Pacific class I-1, No. 601, built by Lima in 1925, photographed at Fort Worth, Texas, on October 25, 1930 (Denver Public Library, Otto C. Perry collection, OP-16260).

and short cut-off.[10] The superpower locomotive did, in fact, have a pre-history that we will consider later.

The new superpower locomotives shared ten common design features[11]: (i) high boiler pressures of 225 to 275 pounds per square inch; (ii) stoker-fired grates, measuring 65 square feet or more to burn coal at high rates without excessive firing rates per square foot of grate; (iii) large fireboxes supported on four-wheel trailing trucks; (iv) limited cut-off in full gear to enforce steam economy in normal running conditions with auxiliary steam passages to allow the engine to exert its maximum tractive effort on starting; (v) boosters; (vi) Type E superheaters; (vii) feed water heaters; (viii) front-end throttles; (ix) powering auxiliaries with superheated steam; (x) cast-steel engine beds.

The new engines were an astonishing advance over even recent pre-existing types.[12] Lima pointed out that the 2-8-4 halved the coal consumption of a 2-8-2 built only four years before: 3.0 pounds per drawbar horsepower-hour, compared to 5.7 pounds for a 1921-built 2-8-2. The new 2-8-4s, first used on the Boston & Albany, developed 81,000 pounds of tractive effort with the booster cut in—this in an eight-coupled, rigid-frame engine on massive track with none of the complexities and maintenance problems of the Mallets. The performance of the new engines might have gone unrecognized without the management tools of an increasingly sophisticated industry. The Boston & Albany estimated the gross ton-miles hauled during each train-hour on all its routes on May 1, 1925, and the same day a year later. On the latter date, ten 2-8-4s hauled 42% more ton-miles than the combined efforts of one Mallet, nine 2-8-0s and four 2-8-2s only a year previously.

When the Texas & Pacific compared their new 2-10-4s with their 2-10-2s, themselves less than ten years old, they found that the 2-10-4s hauled 44% more tonnage 33% faster for 42% less fuel (oil in both cases) per thousand gross ton-miles, while remaining within a 60,000-pound axle load limit. The 12% heavier 2-10-4 developed 42% more starting tractive effort with the booster cut in than the 2-10-2s which had no booster. Limiting the cut-off to 60% allowed Lima to reduce the adhesion factor from 4.1 to 3.6, while 25% higher boiler pressure worked on a 7% bigger piston. Contributing to the extraordinary advance in fuel economy were 43% more grate area, 35% more primary heating surface, a Type E superheater, an Elesco feed water heater and thermic siphons. In fact, the large, stoker-fired fireboxes would have been under-utilized without these ancillaries.[13]

The new engines not only performed better, they were easier to maintain, so increasing their availability and lowering their maintenance costs. Cast-steel engine beds eliminated highly stressed bolted frame joints which worked loose and caused the engine to pound itself and the track to pieces. Larger driving wheels with lower rotation rates, compared to earlier freight power, reduced the counterbalancing problem at the same time as engineers were designing better counterbalancing systems. New methods of lubrication reduced wear and tear.

The following year, 1926, was as momentous with the construction of the first 4-8-4s, the Union Pacific 4-12-2s and the Baldwin No. 60000 high-pressure, three-cylinder compound 4-10-2.[14]

By 1929, some two hundred 2-8-4s were in service. Their effects on fuel economy were extraordinary, even when compared to 2-8-2s of recent design. For a firing rate of 6,000 pounds of coal per hour, the 100-square foot grate dropped the firing rate to 60 pounds per square foot of grate per hour, producing a 27% increase in steaming rate from 42,600 to 48,000 pounds per hour and a 50% increase in drawbar horsepower from 1,350 to 2,030. Correspondingly, for a power output of 1,600 drawbar horsepower, steam consumption dropped 15% from 30 pounds per drawbar horsepower-hour to 25; coal consumption dropped 33% from 4.4 pounds per drawbar horsepower-hour to 3.0.

One of the first 4-8-4s was Northern Pacific class A, No. 2605, built by Alco in 1926, photographed at Missoula, Montana, on September 27, 1931 (Denver Public Library, Otto C. Perry collection, OP-14006).

Shown is the first of the famous Union Pacific 4-12-2s, class UP-1, No. 9000, built by Alco in 1926, photographed at Laramie, Wyoming, on August 21, 1927 (Denver Public Library, Otto C. Perry collection, OP-17293).

W. E. Woodard, Vice-President of Lima, pointed out that most railroads had branch lines where axle loadings were limited to 55,000 pounds or less, operating with old and inefficient engines. He suggested that the railroads could obtain good returns on capital by investing in light-weight, standardized, multi-purpose, superpower 4-6-4s for such lines. In twenty years, American locomotive design had come so far that these engines could save 30% to 50% on fuel consumption with easier maintenance and higher availability. The basic design would provide passenger train speeds, while a booster would provide the low-speed tractive effort of a freight engine. The economic events of 1929 swept away all thoughts of investment in new locomotives.

Switch engines comprised 15% to 20% of a typical railroad's locomotive fleet; during the late 1920s their performance came under unprecedented scrutiny and many superpower design features were applied to them.[15] At the same time, because of the nature of their work, it was difficult to measure their performance and few railroads did so. Movements of switch engines were typically too short for the engineer to take the trouble to shorten the cut-off and so they ran in full gear most of the time. Several railroads bought new switchers with limited cut-off and high boiler pressures. In 1929 the Seaboard Air Line owned 101 0-6-0 switchers. Fifty-one of these were USRA engines (class F-5); fifty were new builds with cut-off limited to 65% (class F-7). The F-5's had 190 pounds per square inch boiler pressure and developed 39,000 pounds of tractive effort; the F-7's had 205 pounds per square inch boiler pressure and developed 46,000 pounds of tractive effort. The company recorded the mileage and coal consumption of the two classes in December 1928, assuming reasonably that the two classes would haul the same loads. The F-7's burned 98 pounds of coal per engine-mile, a 20% saving over the F-5's (121 pounds). Switch engines were a natural application for tender boosters.

The 1920s were noteworthy for the rebuilding of obsolescent locomotives. Many of the improvements of the previous twenty years—brick arches, siphons, combustion chambers, power-operated fire doors, coal pushers, superheating, new valve gear, piston valves, feed water heaters, power stokers, power reversers, boosters and light-weight reciprocating parts—were eminently suitable for retrofitting. The scope was enormous. In 1920, roughly 65,000 steam locomotives were at work on American railroads.[16] Of these, 43,000 had brick arches; 37,000 had automatic fire doors; 35,000 were superheated; 15,000 had power reversers; 6,000 had combustion chambers; one hundred had thermic siphons; only thirty had feed water heaters.

The Delaware, Lackawanna & Western had retrofitted superheaters to all its wet-steam road engines by 1922 and at that time was equipping all of its sixty-two 2-8-2s with power stokers.[17] One railroad spent $22,000 to rebuild an obsolete engine, obtaining the equivalent of an engine that would have cost $50,000 to buy new. The result was a more powerful and more efficient engine that placed no extra loads on the track and substructures.[18]

In 1920 the Boston & Maine began to rebuild 250 old engines[19]; their widespread network of lightly built and lightly trafficked branch lines offered no scope for locomotives bigger than their existing fleet. The first step was to install superheaters in 150 2-8-0s and forty 4-6-2s bought in 1911. Engines of these types built after 1911 were already superheated; the company had already installed superheat in some of its 1911-built K-8 2-8-0s, reducing the boiler pressure from 220 pounds per square inch to 180 and replacing the 22-inch cylinders with 24-inch. The next step was to upgrade 110 older 2-8-0s in six different batches built between 1901 and 1911; the older the engine, the more extensively it was modified. These included ten saturated-steam cross-compounds built in 1901–2; the company sent six to Alco Schenectady, the original builder, for conversion to single-expansion with superheat; Walschaert gear and piston valves replaced

Alco and Baldwin built the Boston & Maine Class K-8 2-8-0s between 1911 and 1916. No. 2610 is shown after rebuilding; note the Elesco feed water heater, at Boston, Massachusetts, on October 12, 1930 (Denver Public Library, Otto C. Perry collection, OP-2699).

Stephenson gear and slide valves. Drury (p. 57) records that the Boston & Maine bought 110 2-8-0s, classes K-6 (34), K-7 (10) and K-8 (66) between 1901 and 1911; therefore all of these were modernized. Drury records that the K-7 compounds were converted to single-expansion between 1910 and 1919. The *Railway Age* article, dated January 21, 1921, records that this did not take place until 1920. This work cost only half the price of new locomotives in the revised configuration. Alco replaced the 22-inch high-pressure and 35-inch low-pressure cylinders with new 20-inch cylinders and shortened the stroke from 32 inches to 30, probably replacing the driving wheels at the same time. The boiler pressure remained the same at 200 pounds per square inch. Having made the improvements that were easiest to make, they rebuilt eighteen 4-8-0s as 0-8-0 switchers. The 4-8-0s suffered from high maintenance costs; reconstruction extended to complete new frames. Next, the company had about ninety 4-4-0s, dating from 1900–1911; they planned to install superheaters in these and replace crown-bar fireboxes with bigger, radial-stayed replacements. The company also owned at least one ancient 4-2-2, dating—by its appearance—from the 1870s or 1880s. This, too, was swept up and modified to a 4-4-0.

The Baltimore & Ohio took rebuilding to extremes, taking a class S 2-10-2 into the Mount Clare shops on May 16, 1925, and turning out a 4-8-2 on June 20.[20] The well-known and somewhat eccentric chief of motive power and equipment, George H. Emerson, instigated and supervised the work. The frame, wheels, connecting rods, guides and valve gear were built new, Baker valve gear being substituted for Walschaert. The boiler and heating surfaces retained the same dimensions but an increase in boiler pressure from 180 to 210 pounds per square inch and an 18-inch increase in the length of the combustion chamber suggest that a new boiler was built as well. It is difficult to see what remained from the original engine. The company intended to use the new 4-8-2 to haul passenger trains over the hills from Washington, D. C., to Grafton, West Virginia, and Pittsburgh.

Between 1917 and 1919, Baldwin built thirty-one 2-8-8-2 compound Mallets for the Reading.[21] By the end of the 1920s, these engines no longer suited the company's needs. The company therefore rebuilt one as a 2-10-2 to its own design at its own shops at Reading, Pennsylvania. The result was one of the heaviest 2-10-2s ever built, at 340,000 pounds. The engine was satisfactory and by mid–1930 the company had converted ten. The rebuilds required new frames, cylinders and wheels and were fitted with exhaust steam injectors and thermic siphons; the boiler pressure was 220 pounds per square inch. Caprotti poppet steam valves were applied to at least one of these engines; this must have been one of the earliest locomotive applications in America. Like the Baltimore & Ohio rebuild, the referenced source is not, in fact, clear how much of the original engine remained.

The Lehigh Valley was dissatisfied with the seventy-six 2-10-2s it bought from Baldwin in 1917 and 1919. It sold sixteen to the Hocking Valley in 1920. In 1928–9 it rebuilt twenty as 2-8-2s. The Wootten firebox remained common in the anthracite country that the Lehigh Valley served.

All through the 1920s, the Great Northern rebuilt sixty-seven 2-6-6-2 Mallets—out of an original seventy built between 1906 and 1908 and twenty-two 2-6-8-0s—out of an original thirty-five built in 1910—to 2-8-2s.[22] After fifteen to twenty years of hard service, the old compound Mallets must have been worn out, hard to maintain and otherwise ready for the scrap yard.

The benefits of these retrofits could be startling, as one unnamed major western railroad found out through detailed tests on its 2-8-0 freight engines. These engines typically ran 40,000 miles per year. An engine with no superheating, brick arch or thermic siphons burned 7,500 tons of coal in the process. Adding a brick arch saved 10% of this; superheating saved a further 26%; adding siphons saved a further 15%, so that the fully modified engine burned only 4,260 tons of coal, a total saving of 43%. As the company was paying $4.50

The Great Northern rebuilt this class O-7 2-8-2, No. 3391, from a 2-6-8-0 Mallet sometime between 1929 and 1931. The date and location of the photograph are unknown (courtesy *Classic Trains* magazine collection, 20120503).

for coal on the tender, this saved nearly $15,000 a year, paying back in a few years at most. As a typical freight locomotive earned $135,000 in revenue per year,[23] this was no minor sum. Not only this, but the modified engines hauled 20% more tonnage.

Scrapping and replacement was often a deliberate and aggressive policy. When the Pennsylvania was returned to corporate operation in 1920, it operated 7,600 locomotives. Between 1920 and 1929 the company scrapped 2,200 and bought or built 1,500 new ones, leaving 6,800 in operation. As of 1929, the company planned to scrap a further 3,300 and procure 1,300 so as to run the railroad with 4,800 locomotives, of which 2,800 would have been built since 1920.[24]

Upgrading motive power was often multi-faceted. As soon as the Van Sweringens took over the ailing Erie in 1926, they spent $25 million on upgrading its equipment. Their manager, J. J. Bernet, bought fifty new 2-8-4s from Lima and Alco, retrofitted power stokers to 125 2-8-2s and scrapped 327 old locomotives, reducing the fleet to 1,217.[25] Between 1924 and 1927, the Rock Island bought eighty new locomotives and retrofitted existing engines with superheaters, brick arches, thermic siphons and improved valves and valve gear.[26]

It is quite difficult to discover the composition of any one company's locomotive fleet at any one time. Those few examples that are available are therefore of interest. It is also important to realize the huge technological inertia of the existing locomotive fleets.

The Northern Pacific fleet is shown below for 1923 and 1927.[27] The older 2-6-0s, 4-6-0s, 2-8-0s and 4-4-0s were gradually sold or scrapped, also half the first-generation Mallets. The 4-6-2s, 2-6-2s, 2-8-2s, switchers and bigger Mallets held their own. The 4-8-4s were the only additions.

Type	Number in 1923	Number in 1927
0-4-0	1	0
0-4-2	1	0
0-6-0	147	141
0-8-0	38	34
2-6-0	58	20
2-8-0	135	108
2-10-0	2	2
4-4-0	40	19
4-6-0	230	130
4-8-0	4	4
4-4-2	6	5
4-6-2	182	182
2-6-2	144	137
2-8-2	386	384
4-8-4	0	12
2-6-6-2	22	12
2-8-8-2	30	30
Total	1,426	1,220
Average tractive effort (lb.)	37,930	41,236
Oil burners	4.2%	1.7%
Superheated	50.1%	66.1%
Power stokers	9.5%	23.1%
Boosters	0%	3.1%

As late as 1927, still only two-thirds of the fleet was superheated.

In 1927, the national average tractive effort of new locomotives was 50,600 pounds; the engines being scrapped averaged 31,300 pounds. As a result, the average tractive effort of the locomotive fleet increased from 41,800 pounds to 42,600 pounds.[28] Fuel efficiency improved as a result. By the mid–1920s nation-wide locomotive fuel consumption ranged from 173 pounds per thousand gross freight ton-miles in January down to 134 pounds in the summer months. A new level of economy at 118 pounds was reached in July–August 1927.[29]

The railroads' enforced obsession with efficiency in every aspect of operations paid dividends as a 35% reduction in their direct cost per gross freight ton-mile between 1920 and 1925.[30] This resulted, however, from causes other than locomotive design. Coal prices were falling, in spite of increased demand, possibly as a result of improvements in coal mining methods and equipment. A 14% reduction in train-miles due to longer trains triggered a 25% reduction in wage costs per gross ton-mile hauled and a 40% saving in fuel cost. Improvements in the equipment and organization of maintenance facilities contributed a 40% reduction in enginehouse expense and 30% in locomotive repair costs.

By 1925 these improvements had run their course. The new super-power locomotives produced economic effects out of proportion to their small numbers. Then the depression hit and the railroads were left with whatever they had. The financial crisis of 1929 and the ensuing depression brought new locomotive construction to a halt.

11

Locomotive Engineering, 1920–1930

Section 11.1. Fuels, Firing and Fuel Economy

11.1.1 Coal

By 1919, annual U.S. coal consumption was 530 million tons, of which 125 million went into locomotives. In 1923 the railroad fuel bill for coal and oil was $507 million, divided as 61% for freight service, 21% for passenger service and 18% for switching.[1]

Of total U.S. coal reserves of 3.5 trillion tons known at the time, one third was lignite, mostly in the Dakotas and eastern Montana.[2] Each year 2 million tons of bituminous coal were shipped a thousand miles from the eastern U.S. into this area. Railroads such as the Northern Pacific and the Great Northern had every incentive to use lignite as locomotive fuel.

The lignite from Rosebud, Montana, that the Northern Pacific started to burn in the 1920s had a calorific value of only 8,700 BTU per pound, with 39% fixed carbon, 28% volatiles, 7% ash and 26% moisture. Enormous, stoker-fired grates made the efficient use of this material possible.

In spite of early promise, neither briqueted nor pulverized coal made any further progress as locomotive fuel because of processing costs for briquets and handling problems for pulverized coal.

11.1.2 Oil

By 1921, U.S. crude oil consumption of 1.4 million barrels per day exceeded domestic production by 81,000 barrels per day; this was made up by imports from Mexico.[3] Geologists estimated that 60% of total U.S. reserves had already been burned and that reserves existed for only a few years' consumption. This did not encourage the use of oil as locomotive fuel. Even so, forty-one railroads in twenty-one states ran at least some oil-burning locomotives. In 1924, locomotives on forty-five American railroads burned 57.6 million barrels of oil—one-tenth of U.S. consumption. Considering that an oil burner is not a complicated device, it is astonishing that more than 3,000 different types had been patented.[4] Standard American practice placed the burners at the front of the firebox, spraying oil backward toward a brick flash wall which turned the flames forward again toward the rear tube sheet.[5] Typically, there was no brick arch. Locomotives could be converted back and forth between coal and oil firing with little difficulty.

In 1920, the Santa Fe operated 3,160 locomotives. Two thirds burned coal; one third burned oil.[6] Burning 11,500-BTU per pound coal and 19,000-BTU per pound oil, the Santa Fe found that oil was 25% more cost efficient than coal for hand-fired locomotives, 40% more for stoker-fired engines. A 2-10-2 at full power burned 550 gallons of oil per hour, equivalent to 5,400 pounds of coal.[7] The Santa Fe found that an oil-burning 4-4-2 hauled 750 tons, compared to 578 tons for a coal-burning engine of the same class in the same service.

Oil firing had many advantages over coal. Engines could be worked at maximum power for extended periods, even in hot weather, with no exertion on the part of the fireman. Closer control of steaming rate wasted less steam through the safety valves. Oil produced no cinders; smoke and the risk of lineside fires were reduced. Gas flow through the front end was unobstructed by netting and cinder-catching devices. The fireman could keep a better lookout. Without ash and clinker handling, hostler service and turn-around times were reduced. Fuel consumption could be measured more accurately than with coal. Even so, transportation costs governed and steam locomotives continued to be designed around the closest fuel source, whether oil, bituminous coal, anthracite or lignite. Even oil firing could not compensate for the abiding deficiency of the steam locomotive: fuel consumption while standing still. An oil-burning engine consumed 35 to 45 gallons of oil per hour to keep it in steam.

Oil firing had its problems. Steam had to be bubbled through the oil in the tender to heat it to 100°–180°F (depending on the viscosity of the oil), ensuring a steady flow to the burner. This had to be done carefully; too much steam caused the oil to give off flammable gases and could result in enough condensation to put the fire out. Immediately before the burner, the oil was superheated to improve atomization. Oil typically flowed to the burner by gravity, except that some Mallet tender tanks were pressurized with compressed air at 6 pounds per square inch. Pyrometer tests showed that gas temperature in the fire tubes dropped below the minimum efficient combustion temperature within 18 inches of the rear tube sheet. Combustion therefore had to be complete before this point; unburned oil was deposited as soot.

Although oil firing enabled the fireman to produce more or less steam on demand, fluctuating firing rates caused rapid changes in temperature with deleterious effects on the boiler and firebox. An oil-burning firebox lasted nine years on the Santa Fe, compared to ten years, burning coal. The fireman had to adjust the oil flow, atomizer pressure and blower to match the engineer's every change in throttle and cut-off, watching the exhaust. Black smoke indicated too much oil, but an absence of smoke could indicate anything from a correct firing rate to such an excess of air over oil that the fire would go out. Blue smoke meant that the fire had gone out. If the fireman instantly increased the oil flow and turned on the blower, the hot firebrick would reignite the oil; otherwise, oil pooling in a hot firebox could explode. The fireman had therefore to keep a light smoke from the stack. Cinders scoured the fire tubes of coal-burning engines, but oil firing allowed the fire tubes to soot up, cured by dumping sand into the firebox when the engine was working hard. The furnace draft sucked the sand through the fire tubes, scouring them and producing an impressive plume of black smoke. Some footplate crews on oil-burning engines must have become aware of the fine points of oil firing early on, but a general awareness did not develop until the 1920s.[8]

One of the few innovations to the simple, oil-burning firebox was the so-called Martin water table, built by the Locomotive Boiler Economizer Co. of Los Angeles and first installed by the Texas & Pacific on a 2-10-2 in 1927.[9] This consisted of a pair of water legs, curved convexly upward, installed along the bottom side corners of the firebox. These could be installed in an oil-burning firebox because there was no need for a horizontal grate to support the fire, provided only that enough space remained for the burners. A slotted pipe drew water, either from ahead of the back tube sheet ("outside connection") or through the throat sheet ("inside connection") and supplied it to the bottom of each water table. The top of each water table connected with the water leg through a slot in the side sheet. Steam bubbles forming in the water tables and along the side sheets caused an upward flow of water which was replaced by cooler water drawn through the pipe. These additional water legs not only increased the heating surface in the firebox, where it could do the most good, but also promoted water circulation. The test locomotive evaporated 14% more water per pound of fuel oil than a locomotive of the same class without this modification and saved 11% in fuel per ton-mile hauled. The Chicago, Burlington & Quincy also tested this device and found that it saved 7% of the time normally needed to fire up to a 200 pounds per square inch pop off pressure, but at a 29% saving in the fuel required to do so.[10]

As the last new steam locomotives were being built in 1946, the U.S. Class I railroads owned 41,600 locomotives, of which 37,570 were steam; about 7,000 of these burned oil.

11.1.3 Firebox and Grate Design

The steam locomotive never escaped from the staybolted firebox with its dangers and maintenance problems. The waggontop and Belpaire designs continued in use until the end of steam, albeit of increasingly vast dimensions, stayed with more than 3,000 staybolts. Great efforts put into water-tube boilers and other alternatives ultimately failed.

Since the beginning of systematic testing, engineers realised that combustion and steam generation efficiency declined with increasing firing rates. In the 1890s, they knew that firing rates went as high as 180 to 200 pounds per square foot of grate per hour. In the early twentieth century, 120 pounds of coal per square foot of grate per hour came to be accepted as the maximum rate for reasonably efficient combustion. By the late 1920s, designers had dropped this figure to 60 to 100 pounds.[11] Very large grates, supported on four-wheel trailing trucks, made this possible.

The firebox was the main power source; its heating surface was only 5% to 10% of the total heating surface, but it evaporated 25% to 50% of the steam. Power requirements and combustion efficiency demanded the biggest possible firebox, but this had to respect limitations of weight and clearance dimensions. Already, in 1923, fireboxes were outrunning the weight limits of a two-wheel trailing truck, demanding a four-wheel truck.

George Basford may have been the first to enunciate an idea that influenced the latter years of steam locomotive design: "Coal does not burn on the grates. The fire itself is mainly a gas producer." Combustion in a locomotive firebox was almost a gas explosion in slow motion. Even at typical firing rates in a typical

firebox, gas generation could reach 2,000 cubic feet per second, replacing the volume of the firebox six and a half times a second. Air velocity through the grate could be as high as 100 to 300 feet per second.

Even so, by the early 1920s, there was still no consensus on the design of grates and ash pans.[12] A 1923 survey of sixty-two grate designs revealed air openings in the grates varying from 26% to 50% of grate area. George Basford fulminated: "Differences in the character of coal do not explain this variety of figures. Who is in a position to defend such chaotic practice?" Closer attention to grate design produced some remarkable improvements in combustion and operating efficiency.

Shaking and dropping grates were a big advance over fixed grates in keeping the fire clean and dropping it at the end of a run. Such grates comprised a section that could be shaken and a section of fixed grate bars that could be hinged downwards, when the fire was dropped, to discharge stone and clinker that would not pass through the grate openings. Ash, stone and clinker, however, built up on the fixed section, blocking air flow through that part of the grate and reducing the effective grate area until the engine could be shut down in the terminal and the fire dropped.

In 1920, the Hulson Grate Co., of Keokuk, Iowa, designed a new type of grate with transverse shaking elements.[13] Nine shaking elements underlay the whole grate area, with no fixed section that could not be shaken. The front three elements were mounted in a sub-frame that could be tilted. After dropping the fire, the hostler could rake oversized debris that had accumulated on the front three elements to the rear of the firebox and could then tilt the sub-frame and push the oversize forward, dropping it into the ash pan. This obscure innovation enabled the Burlington to double engine mileage between fire droppings from 200 miles to 400.

Stoker firing brought with it the possibility of using large amounts of poor-quality coal, either bituminous coal screenings or soft lignite which broke down to fines easily.[14] With conventional finger grates, suitable for burning lump coal, it was difficult to keep this fine mate-

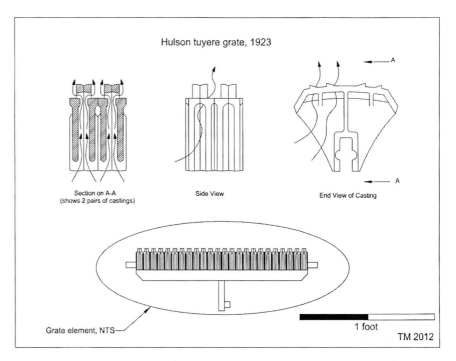

The Hulson tuyere grate (redrawn from *RA*, June 20, 1923, 1420D35-6).

rial on the grate for long enough for it to burn. Either the draft would lift it off the grate and blow it out through the stack, or it would fall through the grate into the ash pan unburnt. As free oxygen was still showing up in smokebox gas analyses, design engineers reasoned that the grate opening could be cut down.

Hulson took this idea a step further in 1923 by modifying the grate castings so that each pair of castings formed a tuyere which discharged into the firebed between adjacent pairs.[15] This indirect air path through the grate reduced the velocity of the air stream, preventing tearing of the fire, while preventing fine coal from falling into the ash pan and, at the same time, allowing a 42% total air opening through the grate. The grates worked equally well with fine anthracite, bituminous coal screenings and lignite. One early installation was in stoker-fired 2-10-2s, burning screenings. With conventional grates, these engines had needed their combustion chambers cleaned out every trip; with the tuyere grates, the combustion chambers were still clean after a month.

The Santa Fe had problems with fine coal falling through their finger grates and being wasted in the ash pan. In 1925, the company introduced table grates with ¾-inch round holes cast into them, providing an air opening of only 16%.[16] The holes flared to 1¹⁄₁₆ inch in the thickness of the grate casting to allow free passage for ash. Smokebox gases showed a marked reduction in free oxygen and the company attributed a 6% fuel saving to this innovation.

The Northern Pacific had a similar problem burning lignite which broke down as it burned. The same year they introduced table grates with air holes only ½ inch in diameter, flaring to ⅞ inch at the bottom of the casting, and providing only 12% air opening. This type of grate was a necessity for burning lignite, whereas the conventional finger grate worked best with lump bituminous coal.

During the 1920s, the standard grate on the Milwaukee was a shaking, slotted table grate 10 inches wide with ¾-inch slots providing a 30% air gap.[17] The company realized, however, that significant amounts of fine coal were falling through the grate into the ash pan while the fire was being built up. As the company built a thousand fires every day, they estimated that they were losing 11,000 to 12,000 tons of

coal a year due to this cause. In 1926–9 the company experimented with a table grate perforated with ½-inch holes making an air gap of only 16%; this worked well with all except clinkering Iowa coal. Using these grates, the company ran 4-6-2s for 354 miles between Omaha, Nebraska, and Savannah, Illinois, with no trouble.

11.1.4 Power Stokers

By the 1920s the power stoker was an accepted necessity.[18] The railroads had to accept that locomotives of more than 50,000 pounds tractive effort could not reach their full power with hand firing. Even on a smaller engine, provided the crew were properly trained, stoker firing was more economical than hand firing as well as producing higher power output. In the heat of the southern United States summer, firemen became so exhausted that one company had to station replacement firemen every 50 miles along a 156-mile division. Another company, with a division comprising 117 miles of continuous 1% grade, had to reduce the maximum train tonnage from 1,500 tons trailing load to 1,150 tons in summer. An assured market for power stokers made it more worthwhile to invest in their development.

Retrospection indicated 1910 as the year when the power stoker came into its own, coincident with the large-scale introduction of very large locomotives.[19] Ten years later, five thousand stoker-fired locomotives were at work on seventy-one American railroads. This development, unmatched elsewhere in the world was the product of economic logic: "The expense of moving freight does not increase in proportion to the weight of the train, and therefore the larger the train the lower the cost per ton mile."[20]

As early as 1913, D. F. Crawford on the Pennsylvania was studying the annual reports of other railroad companies and noticing that, although the tractive effort of company locomotive fleets was increasing, the tons hauled per pound of tractive effort was decreasing. Beyond a certain point, increasing the size of locomotives had no effect on their hauling power.

The maximum firing rate for acceptable fuel economy was 120 pounds of coal per square foot of grate per hour; conversely, if a steam locomotive was not fired up to that rate, it was not producing the maximum power of which it was capable. A Mallet with 90 square feet of grate could burn 10,000 pounds of coal per hour; even a 2-8-2 with 70 square feet of grate could burn more than four tons of coal per hour. If a fireman could fire only two tons per hour, such engines could never reach their maximum power. The sticking point was the human fireman.

The firemen themselves were no mere silent victims of these cold facts.

In 1903, with locomotives of about 40,000 lb. tractive force and 50 sq ft of grate area, from time to time complaints were received from the firemen regarding their arduous work, and frequently men left the railroad service, preferring to seek a more congenial occupation. This, of course, embarrassed the service, as at times it was difficult to obtain sufficient men to supply the demands, and I well remember the concern of those responsible on account of the large turnover and its effect on the operations. As the size of the locomotives continued to increase, the difficulties and complaints grew apace, and it may be said that the climax occurred in 1912, when the firemen in the Eastern Wage Application demanded two

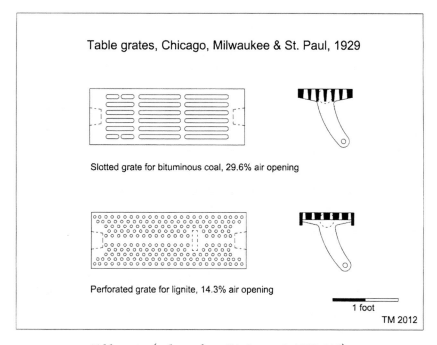

Table grates, Chicago, Milwaukee & St. Paul, 1929

Slotted grate for bituminous coal, 29.6% air opening

Perforated grate for lignite, 14.3% air opening

1 foot

TM 2012

Table grates (redrawn from *RA*, August 3, 1929, 346).

firemen on locomotives weighing over 200,000 lb. on the driving wheels.

Not only were the railroads disinclined to employ two firemen on one engine, increasing the number of firemen would tend to increase the length of time a fireman would have to work as such before being promoted to engineer.

Union agitation for power stokers became more vocal.[21] In 1924, the Brotherhood of Locomotive Firemen and Enginemen petitioned the Labor Board to force the railroads, either to install stokers or to employ two firemen, on engines between 170,000 and 279,000 pounds adhesion weight. The Board denied this request.

The railroads found it increasingly difficult to recruit men with enough intelligence to become engineers, but who were willing to spend the necessary years of apprenticeship as firemen.[22] Easier and better paid work was available elsewhere.

> Granted that we set out to employ a man who can think. We place him on a large hand-fired engine to learn the art of firing. When he looks back he sees from 16 to 20 tons of coal staring him in the face. On the deck he sees a large scoop, a coal pick and a clinker hook. He turns around and sees a fire-door which, when opened, pours out a stream of heat that will burn his overalls off if he gets too close and near the door a shaker bar and a bunch of shaker levers. He is told that all he has to do is crack the coal, throw it into the firebox, and then shake down the ashes.

In the early days, boilers were small enough that the engineer could see across the left side of the engine. By 1920, that possibility was long gone; the fireman was more and more needed as a lookout. If the fireman was exhausted by his labor, he was incapable of taking the intelligent interest in how the engine worked that was necessary to his promotion to engineer. Stoker firing went far to solve these problems.

The Traveling Engineers' Association hoped that stoker firing would improve the quality of men the railroads were able to attract as firemen and future engineers and would give them the chance to apply themselves intelligently to their work, without being too exhausted by coal-shoveling to do so.[23] While this may have had some validity, with no more than 10% of the locomotive fleet stoker-fired, the idea must have remained a pious hope.

The Hanna stoker had lagged behind its competitors in acceptance; attempting to remedy this state of affairs, the Hanna Locomotive Stoker Co., Cincinnati, brought out their H-2 model in 1922.[24] The H-2 was powered by an 11-inch × 16-inch steam cylinder and piston mounted transversely under the footplate. The piston rod extended as a rack which drove two pinion gears. The two pinion gears drove a screw-type coal conveyor inside a tube. A clutching system caused the pinions to alternate in driving the screw conveyor with the out and return strokes of the piston so that the conveyor turned in a constant direction, although the fireman could reverse it to clear blockages in the coal feed. The screw conveyor drive shaft extended rearward of the drawgear and drove a horizontal screw conveyor in a trough in the bottom of the tender through a universal joint. The conveyor tube terminated at its back end in a socket engaging a ball mounted rigidly to the tender. At the front end of the tube a ball engaged a socket mounted rigidly on the engine. This arrangement catered to all likely movements of the tender relative to the engine. The screw conveyor delivered coal to the bottoms of two elevating screw conveyors, mounted one on each side of the fire door. These deposited coal through two oscillating chutes onto a distribution plate where steam jets blew it into the fire. By controlling the steam jets and the oscillation of the chutes, the fireman could scatter or concentrate the flow of coal onto the grate as well as controlling the speed of the conveyor and, hence, the firing rate. The Norfolk & Western was among the first users of the H-2.

Meanwhile, Du Pont had acquired the Standard Stoker Co.; in 1922, the company brought out a new stoker called the du Pont-Simplex of the same general arrangement as the Standard.[25] Ruggedness, simplicity and freedom from maintenance were its design objectives. As in other types of stoker, a screw feed working in a trough under the tender coal space moved coal forward to the locomotive, forcing it against teeth which crushed it to size. The screw conveyor under the tender was able to force coal through a multi-part tube to a point beneath the firebox without a screw conveyor inside the tube itself, which the Hanna H-2 required. Telescoping and ball-and-socket jointing of the tube parts provided for relative movement between engine and tender. A vertical screw conveyor moved the coal from the front of the tube up through the bottom of the firebox. A cast-iron grate of the approximate size and shape of an inverted bathtub both protected the vertical screw conveyor and provided a horizontal surface above the main grate, onto which the vertical screw conveyor discharged coal. Steam jets, controlled by the fireman, blew coal off the horizontal surface to those parts of the fire where it was needed. A two-cylinder steam engine drove the two screw conveyors through drive shafts with universal joints.

Soon after introducing the du Pont–Simplex, the company brought out the Simplex Type B.[26] The screw conveyor was

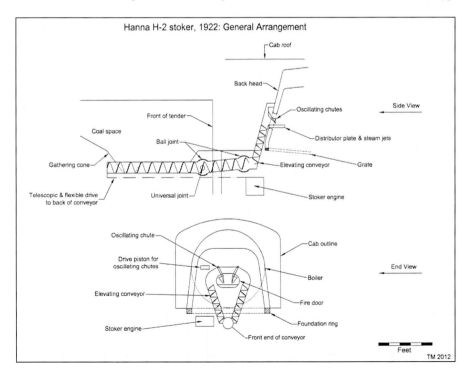

The Hanna H-2 stoker (redrawn from *RA*, February 18, 1922, 430).

extended forward through the delivery tube by two segments, connected by universal joints, the frontmost of which ended below the backhead. The vertical screw conveyor was deleted from this design; instead, the screw conveyor forced coal through an elbow and up to the top of the inverted-bath-shaped grate, where the steam jets dispersed it over the fire.

By 1923, 6,714 locomotives on American railroads were equipped with power stokers.[27] The Locomotive Stoker Co. Duplex model was the clear winner, with 4,142 installed. The company's Street model came next, with 1,458 installed. The Standard Stoker Co. had 711 stokers installed (Types A-1, A-1M, Du Pont and Du Pont Simplex). Next came the Elvin (Types A and B), with 247 installed. Last came the Hanna Stoker Co. (Types V-H, H-2 and S-1) with 151 installed. One thousand stokers were on order: 772 Duplex, 102 Elvin Type B, fifty-nine Du Pont Simplex, fifty-seven Hanna H-2 and ten Elvin Type A. In spite of earlier success, no orders were placed for the Street stoker. Thus the Locomotive Stoker Co. had built 83% of the stokers installed and had 77% of new orders.

In 1926, the Locomotive Stoker Co. brought out the D-3 and D-4 models which were smaller and lighter than the earlier D-1 and D-2 types, looking to extend stoker firing into smaller engines and a possible export market.[28]

In 1924, the Northern Pacific discovered an immense deposit of lignite.[29] Because this material had a lower calorific value than bituminous coal, the company decided to equip all of its road engines with power stokers. Some of its engines were so close to the maximum allowable axle loading that the Standard Stoker Co. produced a variant of its du Pont–Simplex model with the stoker engine mounted on the tender, instead of under the footplate. As an additional benefit, the stoker exhaust bubbled through the water in the tender tank one third of the tank height from the bottom of the tank, pre-heating the water and returning condensate to the tank. If the water was low, the stoker exhaust would not heat it to a temperature that the injectors could not handle. This is quoted as an example of the extreme ingenuity and attention to detail that American railroadmen put into every aspect of the locomotives in their charge.

Although a power stoker was an obvious retrofit, the actual installation could be a problem. Accordingly, in 1927 the Locomotive Stoker Co. brought out the K-2, subsequently redesigned by the Standard Stoker Co. and marketed as the B-K.[30] The B-K was similar in principle to the Type B, described above. However, instead of passing beneath the foundation ring and rising abruptly into the bottom of the firebox, the conveyor tube rose through the footplate to an enlargement of the fire door opening, opening out into a discharge box inside the firebox. The coal discharged over the front of the discharge box, falling in front of two steam jets which blew it to wherever the fireman wanted it. Grooves in the distributor plate discharged coal into the back of the grate. The device was so arranged that it did not interfere with hand-firing or entry into the firebox. The stoker engine was a two-cylinder steam engine, mounted on the tender. The complete stoker weighed 5,300 pounds.

The locomotive power stoker was an American achievement made possible by the combined efforts of the railroad industry over thirty years. At this distance in time, it is difficult to appreciate the magnitude of this achievement and its effects. F. P. Roesch of the Standard Stoker Company pointed out that the development of the locomotive stoker entailed the elimination of all unnecessary or troublesome parts and the construction of a machine that was rugged, dependable, fully controlled by the fireman and that could be maintained by existing mechanical skills. It also had to be adaptable to any type of locomotive.[31] In summary:

The whole job required a lot of time, patience, study, money, and (last but not least) the full and hearty cooperation of the railroad officers and employees, but, nevertheless, the end justified the means, and in the stoker of today you will find incorporated and combined the best thoughts of all the stoker designers, manufacturers and operators developed during the past thirty years.

By 1929, power stokers were firing the biggest steam locomotives in the world, including one type with 184 square feet of grate, capable of burning 15 tons of coal per hour. With these grate areas, power stokers had to throw coal reliably as far as 17 feet. They were also being applied to engines with grates as small as 21 square feet, burning 1 ton per hour; naturally, the manufacturers hoped that power stokers would extend into these smaller sizes of engine.

11.1.5 Fuel Efficiency

The weight of coal required to move 1,000 freight ton-miles varied widely with the terrain over which a railroad passed, the climate and the season of the year. However, by the early 1920s, data gathering and transmission was such that a national average could be compiled and used as a measure of efficiency from year to year—a figure with economic, technical and political connotations. The national average for 1921 was 168 pounds. Such was the attention paid by the railroads to fuel efficiency that, by 1923, this figure had been forced down to 160 pounds,[32] decreasing still further to 131 pounds in 1927, a decrease of no less than 20% in five years.[33] As a result, the railroads hauled 40% more freight for very little increase in fuel consumption.

In the absence of any alternative power, some railroads achieved extraordinary increases in fuel efficiency during the 1920s. It would be difficult to better the record of the Texas & Pacific, largely achieved by the superintendent of motive power, A. P. Prendergast, supported by a forward-thinking management.[34] At the end of 1917, the railroad operated 353 locomotives with an average tractive effort of 26,200 pounds. In the next ten years the company scrapped 148 engines and bought 165 new ones, fifty-five of which were 2-10-4s. At the end of 1928, the company ran 370 locomotives with an average tractive effort of 49,100 pounds, an 88% increase over 1917. These engines were equipped with every available fuel-saving device. These acquisitions were supported by an aggressive maintenance program, including a new terminal at Fort Worth where engines could be steamed up from a central steam plant, saving 20% in the fuel used in terminals. The result was a saving of 47% in freight service, 50% in passenger service and 30% in switching service. The efforts of management would have had limited effect, were they not supported by every employee of the company.

Between 1927 and 1928, alone, the Milwaukee reduced fuel consumption in freight service by 8 pounds per 1,000 ton-miles, in passenger service by 0.9 pounds per car-mile and in switching by 7 pounds per yard locomotive mile, saving 270,200 tons of coal in the process.[35] This was attributed both to small things, such as an improved blower that consumed less steam and better grate designs, and to a wide appreciation of fuel saving throughout the organization.

At that time the most efficient stationary steam power plants, with condensers, were consuming about 1.7 pounds of coal per shaft horsepower-hour (12% thermal efficiency). The objective of steam locomotive design and operation was 2.3 pounds of coal per drawbar horsepower-hour. By the late 1920s several of the new superpower engines were achieving fuel efficiencies of 1.9 pounds of coal per indicated horsepower-hour, 2.5 to 2.7 pounds per drawbar horsepower-hour (8% thermal efficiency) and 15 pounds of steam per indicated horsepower-hour.[36] In this, they were approaching the ultimate in efficiency achieved by the ocean liners, *Mauretania* and *Lusitania*, which recorded steam consumptions of 14.4 pounds per shaft horsepower-hour in 1907.

The foregoing figures focus on the efficiency of the locomotive when hauling a train. Total fuel economy was yet more complicated. In 1928 an ARMMA committee on utilization of locomotives identified 124 items affecting fuel economy, ranging from the design, maintenance and operation of the locomotives themselves to the length of passing loops and the inspection and testing of fuel.[37] The reduction of the national average coal consumption per thousand freight ton-miles during the 1920s was the result of a coordinated effort by railroad employees of all grades and trades.

Section 11.2 Boilers and Steam Generation

11.2.1 Steam Generation

By 1920, mechanical engineers knew enough about the generation of steam to rely on a figure of 55 pounds of water evaporated per hour per square foot of firebox heating surface, but only 10 pounds per square foot of tube heating surface.[38] The temperature inside the firebox was typically 2,000°F. As soon as gases passed the back tube sheet, their temperature dropped rapidly to only 1,250°F after the first foot of tube length and to 750°F after 10 feet. Gases emerged from the front tube sheet of a 20-foot long boiler at 600°F, although radiation losses quickly dropped this to 450°F to 500°F in the front end. This brought the depressing certainty that, structural factors apart, there was little merit in a tube length longer than 20 feet. There was also no hope of superheating steam hotter than 600°F to 750°F in a fire-tube superheater. The weight of water evaporated per pound of boiler weight dropped markedly with a longer boiler. One of the few areas where boiler efficiency could be improved was in water circulation; the 1920s brought both an unprecedented awareness of this issue and the means to investigate it.

We saw earlier how a prolific Chicago inventor, John L. Nicholson, morphed the arch tube into a vertical water leg, called the Nicholson Thermic Syphon. After an initial installation on the Milwaukee in 1918,[39] the Rock Island installed siphons experimentally the following year.[40] The first large-scale application came with an order for ten 4-8-2s, ten 2-8-2s and fifteen 2-10-2s placed by the Rock Island with Alco in 1920, specifying siphons for the whole order.

The thermic siphon was ideal for retrofitting. In 1923, the Nashville, Chattanooga & St. Louis replaced two of the four arch tubes in the firebox of a 2-8-2.[41] Dynamometer tests, comparing the siphon-equipped engine with another engine of the same class without siphons, showed a remarkable improvement in performance; the siphon-equipped engine burned 11% less coal per ton-mile hauled and averaged 19°F higher superheat than the unmodified engine.

By 1926, thermic siphons were in service in 1,906 locomotives on seventy-eight domestic and foreign railroads.[42] Siphons were applied to fireboxes with combustion chambers by building three siphons in the firebox and a further two in the combustion chamber.

As early as 1921, siphons prevented a boiler explosion.[43] The crew of a 2-8-0 allowed the water level to drop 5 to 8 inches below the crown sheet. The crown sheet just behind the back tube sheet soft-ened enough to pull away from two rows of staybolts, and buckled between staybolt rows the length of the crown sheet; steam blowing into the firebox alerted the crew, who were able to pull into a siding. The structural reinforcement provided by the siphons, and water boiling up through them and spilling over the crown sheet, prevented a catastrophic failure. Increasing numbers of cases were reported.

In 1933, the American Arch Co. patented the Security Circulator.[44] Each circulator consisted of water tubes arranged in an inverted T. The cross arms connected to the water legs; the vertical arm connected to the water space above the crown sheet. The cross arms were typically 5½ inches in diameter and supported the brick arch; the vertical riser was typically 7 inches in diameter. As many as seven could be installed in a long firebox. This device gained in popularity when locomotive construction resumed in the late 1930s.

Between 1910 and 1921 the railroads installed 33,000 superheaters in new locomotives and retrofits.[45] By the early 1920s, 90% of new locomotives were built with superheaters. By 1924, the estimated total investment in superheaters was $125 million, $7 million worth being installed in 1923 alone.[46] By mid-decade 44,000 steam locomotives of a total U.S. fleet numbering 65,000 were superheated (68%), reaching 75% by the end of the decade.[47]

An important innovation was the Elesco Type E superheater.[48] In the Type A, each element comprised four tubes with three U-bends nested inside a 5½-inch flue tube, so that the steam ran the length of the flue tube four times, gaining 200°–250°F of superheat. In the Type E, each element split into two four-tube elements in parallel, each loop occupying a separate 3- to 3½-inch flue tube. Each element occupied four flue tubes and the superheater occupied most of the tube sheet. Although any individual water molecule passed through the superheater four times, as in the Type A, the arrangement provided better exposure to hot gases, resulting in 250°–300°F of superheat. The change in the diameter and layout of tubes and flues provided 8% to 10% more flue evaporative surface, a 3% to 6% increase in the total gas cross section through the boiler and 35% to

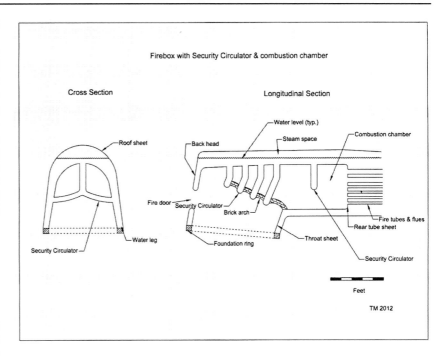

The Security Circulator (redrawn from Ringel, C., *History, Development and Function of the Locomotive Brick Arch*, RLHS, New York, January 1948. Printed *Journal RLHS*, October 1956, 79).

50% more superheating surface than a boiler with a Type A superheater.[49]

The Pennsylvania's 2-8-8-0 Mallet, built in 1919, was an early application. Although by no means universal, the Type E became increasingly common in new construction during the 1920s.

Superheating inserted a substantial steam space between the throttle valve and the cylinders. When the throttle was first opened, this space had to fill with steam before the engine would move; when the throttle was closed, the steam would continue to expand, resulting in a sluggish throttle response. The bigger the engine, the worse the problem. The solution was to place the throttle valve in the front end, downstream of the superheater. The first modern locomotive built with a front-end throttle seems to have been the Michigan Central's high-performance 2-8-2, built by Lima in 1922, although Wilson Eddy built his first engine, the *Addison Gilmore,* domeless, with a perforated dry pipe and a front-end throttle, in 1851.[50] At first, superheated steam warped the valve; the Bradford Draft Gear Co., New York, brought out the Chambers throttle valve in 1923, designed to solve this problem.[51] A front-end throttle permitted a smaller dome, significant when boiler dimensions pressed hard on clearance height. An unexpected gain was the ability to supply superheated steam to the compressor, generator, stoker engine and feed water pump when the throttle was closed, estimated to save 2% to 4% of the fuel used by the locomotive.[52] Front-end throttles became typical of large locomotives, although smaller superheated locomotives continued to be built with throttles in the dome.

The double-beat throttle valve had been standard since the 1800s and, at first, this was merely displaced to the front end.[53] On bigger engines, this still offered insufficient sensitivity at low speeds. In 1926, the American Throttle Co., New York, brought out a valve assembly for attachment to the front of the superheater header, comprising a small pilot valve which opened first and closed last, with three double-beat valves that opened in sequence as the engineer opened the throttle.[54] Cams operated all four valves. This device gained widespread currency in large locomotives. Front-end throttles can be identified in photographs by the control rods running along the upper right-hand side of the boiler. The valve control crank occupied a distinctive small, cylindrical dome immediately in front of or behind the stack.

By 1930, mechanical engineers could look back on three decades of remarkable advances in the steam generation capacity of steam locomotive boilers.[55] The figures given in the table below are typical for their time; higher rates were achieved.

11.2.2 Pressures in Fire-Tube Boilers

Work at Purdue University in 1904 showed gains in efficiency with increasing boiler pressure, up to 180 pounds per square inch. Increasing boiler pressure beyond that produced diminishing returns; the test reports asserted that "no possible excuse can be found for increasing pressure above the limit of 220 lbs." The higher the pressure, the more a boiler cost to build and maintain and the greater its weight. Not only that, but valves, pipes and steam fittings had to be stronger; leakage losses were higher. A survey by the Master Boiler Makers' Association in 1920 showed that a sample of saturated-steam engines running at 220 pounds per square inch broke up to four times as many staybolts as a sample of superheated engines running at 185 to 200 pounds.[56] When ICC inspectors were finding defects in two thirds of the engines that they inspected, and shutting down engines that leaked steam so badly that the engineer's view was obscured, operating officials may well have been disinclined to pursue higher boiler pressures. Designers felt that capacity was more valuable than pressure. For twenty years, boiler pressures in newly built engines ranged from 180 to 205 pounds per square inch; typical boiler pressures in the USRA engines were 200 pounds per square inch.

The front-end throttle (redrawn from *RA*, February 10, 1923, 385).

Year	Steam pressure	Superheat temperature	Steam energy	Steam rate	Steam rate	BTU/hr.	BTU/hr.	Boiler weight	Boiler weight	BTU/hr./lb boiler weight	BTU/hr./lb boiler weight
	(p.s.i.)	(°F)	(BTU/lb.)	(lb./hr.)	(lb./hr.)	('000)	('000)	(lb.)*	(lb.)*		
				Passenger	Freight	Passenger	Freight	Passenger	Freight	Passenger	Freight
1900	180	—	1,198	23,200	35,000	27,793	41,930	70,000	85,000	397	493
1905	200	100	1,260	32,000	38,000	40,300	47,880	80,000	92,000	504	520
1910	200	150	1,287	37,000	47,000	47,600	60,500	88,000	104,000	541	581
1915	200	225	1,327	39,000	53,000	51,700	70,300	97,000	120,000	533	585
1920	210	225	1,328	48,000	62,000	63,700	82,300	107,000	136,000	595	605
1925	225	250	1,343	52,000	71,000	69,800	95,300	117,000	155,000	597	615
1930	250	300	1,373	63,500	82,000	87,190	112,600	128,000	175,000	680	643

*Weight of boiler and superheater with two gauges of water.

An early perceived benefit of superheating was a retreat from the high boiler pressures used in the attempt to extract more power from saturated-steam engines. The 1920s brought a new questioning of this constraint. Developments in metallurgy, engineering and manufacturing made it possible to build boilers capable of containing higher pressures. Even if such boilers were heavier than before, stronger track permitted higher axle loadings and, hence, higher concentrated weight. The Mallets had reached the limit in the number of driving axles; clearance dimensions and stability considerations limited a locomotive's height and width. The only term in the tractive effort equation that had not reached its limits was boiler pressure. The new demand of the 1920s was for increased power per pound of locomotive—power density. Stationary plants were using steam at 300 to 500 pounds per square inch, so why not locomotives? Designers realized that, at higher pressures, less steam was needed for a given amount of work, with some saving in coal consumption as a result. The thermodynamics of heat engines showed that thermal efficiency increased in proportion to the spread between initial and final steam pressures and temperatures.

The pressure in a cylindrical boiler barrel was limited by the thickness of mild steel plate that could be cold-rolled; this limited the pressure of locomotive boilers to 400 pounds per square inch, unless special steel were used. Indeed, beyond 250 pounds per square inch, conventional locomotive boilers were prohibitively expensive to manufacture.[57]

A. I. Lipetz, consulting engineer to Alco, pointed out that the advantages of higher pressures delivering greater tractive effort and more power had long been recognized. The use of higher pressures had been constrained only by the difficulties of building and maintaining boilers for those pressures. Compounding called for the highest obtainable pressures. When interest in compounding waned and superheating became accepted, one of the perceived benefits of superheating was the possibility of lower boiler pressures, saving in construction and maintenance costs. This did not last long, as the demand for more power caused a new trend to higher pressures. This remained limited by steel metallurgy and manufacturing techniques.

The Pennsylvania was one of the leaders toward high steam pressure and by 1926 operated more than 600 2-10-2s and 200 4-8-2s with boiler pressures of 250 pounds per square inch. That same year,

the Canadian Pacific put some new locomotives into service, using a new nickel steel that made it possible to increase boiler pressure from 200 pounds per square inch to 250 with no increase in the thickness or weight of the steel.[58]

In 1927, Lawford H. Fry calculated theoretical cylinder thermal efficiencies for various boiler pressures.[59] Expanding steam from 220 pounds per square inch down to the 25-pounds per square inch back pressure in the nozzle needed for drafting gave a theoretical thermal efficiency of 15.1%, increasing to 17.5% for a 350-pound boiler pressure and 21.6% for an 800-pound boiler pressure. Tests on existing locomotives gave results of 11% for a 205-pound inlet pressure, 12.5% for a 250-pound inlet pressure and 13.5% at 350 pounds. Although increasing pressures brought diminishing returns in thermal efficiency, any increase in efficiency still made very high boiler pressures attractive.

By the late 1920s, stationary plants were running on steam at its critical pressure of 3,200 pounds per square inch.[60] Only a few locomotives were ever built with boiler pressures as high as one tenth of that figure. From the viewpoint of 1928:

> In the near future, we may expect to see experimental locomotives operating with boiler pressures up to 1,000 lb., with three cylinders, probably compounded; with water-tube fireboxes using coal burned on grates; with improved draft apparatus and developing up to perhaps 7,500 i.h.p.; with a steam consumption not exceeding 14 or 15 lb., and a coal consumption probably less than 1½ lb. per i.h.p. If this cannot be done, it would hardly seem worthwhile to go to the necessary complication and expense.

The Baldwin 4-10-2 compound, described below, came close to these fuel economy figures; its maximum power was never measured because it exceeded the 4,500-horsepower capacity of the Altoona test plant.

The Delaware & Hudson, one of America's oldest railroads, with its own locomotive building capability at Colonie, New York, had a long and somewhat eccentric history of developing both the efficiency and the appearance of its locomotives; several instances appear in this book. The driving force behind some of these efforts came from the energetic Pennsylvania Railroad graduate, L. F. Loree, and his forceful henchman and Superintendent of Motive Power, the Englishman, George S. Edmonds.[61]

The Delaware & Hudson built three experimental 4-6-2s with high-pressure conventional boilers.[62] The first was built in 1929 with 260 pounds per square inch boiler pressure and conventional cylinders. The second was built in 1930 with 275-pound boiler pressure and Dabeg poppet valves. The third was completed in 1931 with uniflow cylinders and 325-pound boiler pressure; the company experienced excessive staybolt breakage and reduced the boiler pressure, first to 295 pounds, then to 275. We will look at these locomotives in a later section of this book.

Boiler pressures of 240 to 250 pounds per square inch became well established in the 1920s and were among the distinguishing features of the superpower designs.

11.2.3 Water-Tube Boilers

Improved metallurgy and manufacturing techniques and the pursuit of higher boiler pressures intensified the work being done on water-tube boilers. Some of these were water-tube fireboxes

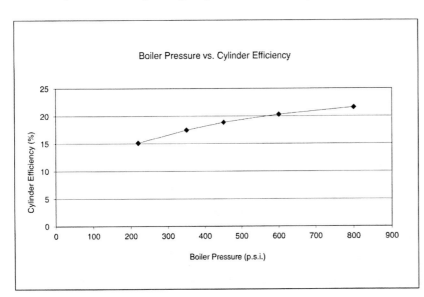

The effect of steam pressure on cylinder efficiency (drawn from Fry, L. H., ASME, spring meeting, 1927. Reported in *Locomotive Efficiencies*, RA, August 11, 1928, 250).

behind conventional, fire-tube boilers; other experiments reconfigured both boiler and firebox. Experiments they remained, doomed by high manufacturing and maintenance costs.

In 1916, the New Haven put two 2-8-2s into service with McClellon water fireboxes, manufactured by the McClellon Boiler Co., of Boston, but with inconclusive results.[63] The company's Mechanical Manager, W. L. Bean, felt that the idea had sufficient merit to work on its defects and modified the two boilers in 1920.

The McClellon firebox was externally indistinguishable from a normal firebox. A collector drum paralleled the sides and back of the foundation ring and opened into the boiler water space at the firebox throat. The firebox crown consisted of three parallel, longitudinal drums opening into the boiler water space through the back tube sheet. Each side of the firebox consisted of fifteen 4-inch water tubes connecting the collector drum with the shoulder drums. The backhead consisted of 2-inch tubes, apart from the fire door surround, which was a stayed structure. A combustion chamber, also surrounded by water tubes, extended forward of the firebox. The combustion chamber water tubes drew water from a central circulator trough open at one end to the boiler water space. Protection plates, lagging and wrapper sheets surrounded the firebox and combustion chamber. Ahead of the combustion chamber, the boiler was of the conventional fire-tube type. The McClellon firebox provided 458 square feet of heating surface with a further 3,603 square feet in tubes and flues for a total evaporative surface of 4,061 square feet, with a further 1,009 square feet of superheating surface. The fire caused steam to form in the water tubes; steam bubbles streamed upward into the shoulder drums. The center drum was an independent steam generator with no connection to the shoulder drums.

A defect of the original firebox design was that the water tubes were structural members. A massive web of steel girders took over this function in the modified version and provided mounting points for the cab fittings. For such a complicated structure, the McClellon firebox heated up surprisingly uniformly, while rapid circulation kept the tubes clean. Boiler washing was easier than with a conventional

boiler. Ten years of experience on the New Haven showed that the maintenance cost was only half that of a normal boiler and that availability was better.

In 1924, the New Haven had ten 4-8-2s on order from Alco—equipped with the rare Southern valve gear—and had the company equip one of them with a McClellon boiler, to generate steam at 250 pounds per square inch. The rest of the order was delayed, pending test results from this engine. The new 4-8-2s closely resembled the company's existing USRA 4-8-2s; the McClellon-boilered engine was therefore dynamometer-tested against one of these. The McClellon boiler evaporated 12% more water per pound of dry coal (8.75 pounds, compared to 7.81 pounds), although the evaporation per square foot of heating surface was practically the same. The USRA 4-8-2 burned 2.95 pounds of dry 13,500 BTU-per-pound coal per dynamometer horsepower-hour; the McClellon-boilered engine reduced this to 2.50 pounds, a saving of 18%. The McClellon-boilered engine was 30,000 pounds heavier than the USRA engine and, because of its higher boiler pressure, developed 63,400 pounds of tractive effort, compared to 53,900 pounds in the older engine. Cut-off in full gear was limited to 70%, compared to 85% in the older engine.

Apparently, Alco completed the remaining nine 4-8-2s with conventional boilers—probably to avoid delay, but the test results were so satisfactory that the New Haven ordered ten new 4-8-2s with McClellon boilers, delivered in 1926, and a further ten, with three cylinders and McClellon boilers, delivered in 1928. In the long run, the McClellon boilers developed increasing maintenance problems and were impossible to keep steam-tight. In 1929, Bean left the company and all twenty-one McClellon boilers were replaced with conventional boilers. The two 2-8-2s received new McClellon boilers in 1928, but were reboilered with conventional boilers in 1942.[64]

In 1922, the Delaware & Hudson started building a 2-8-0 of grotesque appearance with a 350-pounds per square inch (?Brotan) water-tube firebox and a fire-tube boiler.[65] This was also one of the last rigid-frame compounds to be built in the U.S., a cross-compound,

The Delaware & Hudson high-pressure 2-8-0, No.1400, *Horatio Allen*, built in the company shops in 1924. The date and location of the photograph are unknown (courtesy California State Railroad Museum, James E. Boynton Collection; Harold K. Vollrath photograph; Negative 39084cn).

and used the rare Southern valve gear. John E. Muhlfeld, consulting engineer, designed the engine in collaboration with G. S. Edmonds, Superintendent of Motive Power. Construction by Alco at Schenectady went ahead slowly; in December 1924, the company president, L. F. Loree, named the engine—with much ceremony—the *Horatio Allen* after the man commissioned by the Delaware & Hudson to go to England in 1828 to buy steam locomotives. The engine went into service on freight trains between Oneonta, New York, and Mechanicville. With an axle loading of 74,600 pounds, it developed 70,300 pounds of tractive effort, working compound, 84,300 pounds single-expansion. The back tender truck was replaced with a four-wheel booster, adding 10,000 pounds of tractive effort.

By 1926, the engine had been running for two years with good results.[66] In road tests the boiler evaporated 10.7 pounds of water per pound of coal. The engine consumed 2.2 pounds of coal and 17.9 pounds of steam per indicated horsepower-hour—2.3 pounds of coal per drawbar horsepower-hour, developing an average of 1,800 indicated and 1,700 drawbar horsepower. Total thermal efficiency was estimated at 8%.

The company had Alco build another experimental engine, also a 2-8-0 cross-compound, with 400 pounds per square inch pressure in the water-tube boiler, completed in 1927 and called the *John B. Jervis* after the one-time chief engineer of the Delaware & Hudson, friend and mentor of Horatio Allen and designer of the locomotive *DeWitt Clinton*.[67]

In April 1930, the company took delivery of a third high-pressure 2-8-0 two-cylinder cross-compound locomotive from Alco, called the *James Archbald* after an associate of John B. Jervis.[68]

The boiler comprised a fire-tube boiler with a water-tube firebox, generating steam at 500 pounds per square inch. Two water drums 20 inches in diameter and 12½ feet long paralleled the bottom corners of the firebox. Five rows of vertical 2½-inch water tubes, totaling 286 tubes, formed the sidewalls of the firebox, joining the lower water drums with 29-inch diameter steam drums, 25 feet long, paralleling the shoulders of the firebox and extending 12 feet ahead of it. The boiler, 15 feet over tube sheets, contained 155 2-inch fire tubes and 52 5½-inch flue tubes. Unlike some high-pressure boilers of this configuration, this was not a dual-pressure boiler, but comprised a con-

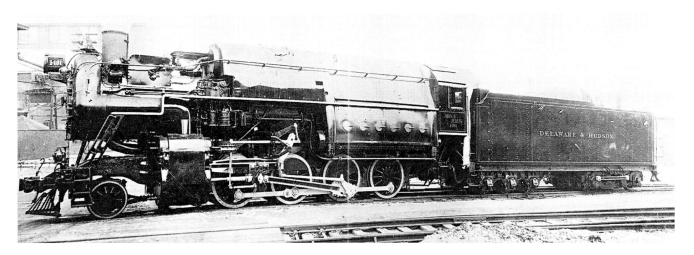

The Delaware & Hudson high-pressure 2-8-0, No. 1401, *John B. Jervis*, built by Alco in 1927. Note the size of the water-tube firebox in relation to the rest of the boiler. The date and location of this photograph are unknown (courtesy California State Railroad Museum, Negative 39083cn).

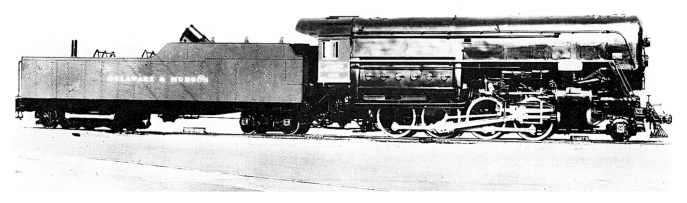

The Delaware & Hudson high-pressure 2-8-0, No. 1402, *James Archbald*, built by Alco in 1930. The date and location of the photograph are unknown. Note the coal pusher projecting above the tender. All three locomotives have boosters in place of the rear tender wheels (courtesy California State Railroad Museum, Paul Darrell Collection, Negative 39087cn).

tinuous water space supplying 500-pounds per square inch steam to the high-pressure cylinder.

The high-pressure steam went to a 20½-inch high-pressure cylinder and a 35½-inch low-pressure cylinder, both of 32-inch stroke, which powered 63-inch driving wheels. Total engine weight was 356,000 pounds. The engine developed 84,300 pounds of tractive effort working single-expansion, 70,300 pounds working compound,

the engineer being provided with a control valve permitting either mode of working. A Bethlehem auxiliary locomotive under the tender added another 18,000 pounds of tractive effort.

These three locomotives had no further impact on steam locomotive development because the demand was for speed, to which they were ill-suited.

In 1926, Baldwin built a high-pressure, three-cylinder compound

The Baldwin 4-10-2 high-pressure compound demonstrator locomotive, No. 60000, at Philadelphia in 1926. The inside cylinder and valve chest are plainly visible. Note the two radius rods, one to drive the valve gear of the middle cylinder. Note also the front-end throttle, housed in the small dome behind the stack (courtesy California State Railroad Museum, James E. Boynton Collection, Negative 39081cn).

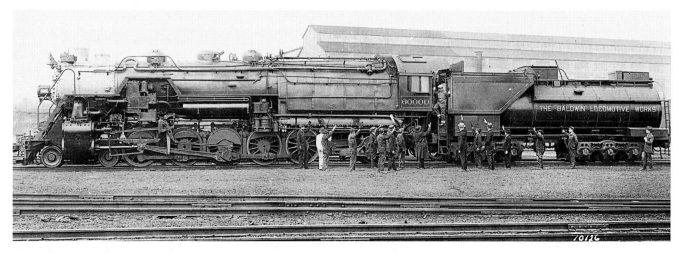

The Baldwin 4-10-2 high-pressure compound demonstrator locomotive No. 60000. Note the Worthington feed water heater above the front driving wheel. The location and date of the photograph are unknown but something is clearly cause for celebration (courtesy California State Railroad Museum, James E. Boynton Collection, Negative 39079cn).

4-10-2, numbered 60000, and tested it at Altoona.[69] A modified Brotan water-tube firebox surrounded an 83-square foot grate, fitted with a brick arch on arch tubes; the boiler was built for a steam pressure of 350 pounds per square inch. The Brotan design was used more for strength than for efficiency. The firebox and arch tubes provided 772 square feet of evaporative surface, with a further 4,420 square feet in flues and tubes, and 1,357 square feet of superheating surface. Superheated steam went to a central 27-inch × 32-inch high-pressure cylinder, which exhausted to two low-pressure cylinders of the same dimensions. All three cylinders, their valve chests and the smokebox saddle were one casting. The total engine weight was 457,500 pounds, developing 82,500 pounds of tractive effort.

On the test plant this locomotive achieved a steam efficiency of 14.2 to 15.4 pounds per indicated horsepower-hour. Coal consumption ranged from 1.9 pounds per indicated horsepower-hour to 2.7 pounds when the engine was developing 4,500 indicated horsepower and burning 11,900 pounds of coal per hour (144 pounds per square foot of grate per hour). This power output was the maximum capacity of the test plant; the engine's maximum power was never measured. Sophisticated and comprehensive temperature measurements showed that, of the total heat absorbed by the boiler, the firebox absorbed 38%, the fire tubes 52% and the superheater 10%. Tests in road service on the Pennsylvania and the Baltimore & Ohio confirmed the test plant results. At the time, there was only one other locomotive in the U.S. with 350 pounds per square inch steam pressure. Fuel efficiency compared favorably with marine and stationary plant.

In 1904, a typical freight locomotive developed one horsepower per 175 pounds of weight. By 1924, this figure had improved to one horsepower per 110 pounds. The new engine developed one indicated horsepower per 100 pounds. The French at this time had a 4-6-2 developing one indicated horsepower per 85 pounds of weight.[70] The French also persevered with compounding, long after the Americans had given it up; French compounds of the 1920s achieved steam efficiencies as high as 13.5 to 14.5 pounds of steam

per indicated horsepower-hour, developing 2,400 indicated horsepower.[71]

Nevertheless, the Altoona tests demonstrated the inefficiency of the reciprocating steam locomotive. Each pound of steam reached the cylinders at 322 pounds per square inch and 652°F, containing 1,338 BTU. That same pound of steam went out through the stack at 11 pounds per square inch and 248°F, containing 1,164 BTU. Only 174 BTU (13%) went into useful work in the cylinders and some of that was lost in friction before going to the drawbar.

C. D. Barrett, engineer of tests at Altoona, pointed out that, as the heat content of the steam could be calculated from its temperature and pressure, the difference between initial and final temperature and pressure gave the energy per pound of steam used by the cylinders. The steaming rate in pounds per hour gave the total energy used in the cylinders. The thermal equivalent of one horsepower was 2,547 BTU per hour, allowing the indicated horsepower to be calculated without a mechanical indicator. This method assumed that steam passed through the system without significant heat losses through the steelwork.

No. 60000 went on demonstration visits to the Pennsylvania, the Baltimore & Ohio, the Burlington, the Santa Fe, the Southern Pacific, the Great Northern and the Erie. On the Burlington's Beardstown, Illinois, division it hauled a 7,500-ton freight train for a coal consumption of only 57 pounds per thousand gross ton-miles—when the national average was about 130 pounds. On the Pennsylvania, boiler evaporation was measured at 5.3 to 6.7 pounds of water per pound of coal; the engine used 2.9 to 3.4 pounds of coal and 18 to 20 pounds of steam per drawbar horsepower-hour, hauling freight trains up to 7,500 tons between Enola, Pennsylvania, and West Morrisville.[72] On the Baltimore & Ohio, coal consumption was measured at 2.1 to 3.4 pounds of coal per drawbar horsepower-hour—16% to 18% less coal and 20% to 22% less water, with a 9% better evaporation rate, than the company's class S-1 2-10-2s. The test on the Burlington showed similar advantages over 2-10-2s. On the Santa Fe, the 60000 showed fuel and water economies of 20% to 25%, compared to

Baldwin built the Baltimore & Ohio's class T-1 4-8-2, No. 5510, with an Emerson water-tube boiler in 1930, shown at New Castle, Pennsylvania, on September 15, 1940 (courtesy California State Railroad Museum, Negative 900_19947).

2-10-2s. The railroads, however, all shied away from its weight and complexity. Superpower engines simpler than No. 60000 were turning in some astonishing results; a water-tube boiler, three cylinders and compounding were a nightmare for maintenance crews already struggling to keep power on the road. No. 60000 was stored in Philadelphia from 1928 to 1932 and then placed in the Franklin Institute, where it remains, surviving the majority of its more successful contemporaries.[73] We can only surmise what this engine might have achieved with a booster, automatic cut-off control and other refinements that were proved separately elsewhere. Its further improvement must remain one of the great unpursued avenues of steam locomotive development. A strange echo of this locomotive came in 1935 when Alco built four 4-10-2 three-cylinder compounds for the Sorocabana Railway in Brazil.[74]

George H. Emerson became Superintendent of Motive Power on the Baltimore & Ohio in 1920, retiring from that position in 1941. With massive experience as a mechanic, boilermaker, engineman, foreman, superintendent and manager, his inventive mind made significant—and bold—innovations to the design of locomotives and other rolling stock. One of his inventions was the Emerson water-tube firebox, first applied to a Baltimore & Ohio locomotive in 1927.[75] In 1930, Baldwin built two experimental locomotives for the Baltimore & Ohio with Emerson fireboxes—a 4-8-2 (class T-1) and a 2-6-6-2 (class KK-1).

Directly comparable with the class T-2 4-8-2 and KK-2 2-6-6-2, which were fitted with conventional fireboxes and thermic siphons, the Emerson firebox provided 82% more heating surface and could be supported on a two-wheel truck; a conventional firebox with the same amount of heating surface would have required a four-wheel truck. As applied to the T-1 and KK-1, four 5½-inch × 7½-inch hollow rectangular-section water spaces connected the backhead water space with that of the conventional fire-tube boiler. The lower spaces paralleled the sides of the foundation ring. The upper spaces were placed at the shoulders of the firebox, each being joined by thirteen 4-inch connections to a 40-inch diameter steam drum in the crown of the firebox. The four water spaces provided a structurally strong frame. A total of 190 2½-inch water tubes, connecting the top and bottom water spaces, formed the sides of the firebox. The firebox was made airtight with fire brick, magnesia lagging and a steel jacket. Other Emerson fireboxes varied in detail from these dimensions.[76] A combustion chamber extended ahead of the firebox.

The efforts devoted to unconventional high-pressure boilers intensified, in spite of economic conditions, in the 1930s.

11.2.4 Feed Water Heaters

The economically benign nineteenth century gave no incentive to pursue a device so complicated and so ambiguous as a feed water heater. The American railroads of the 1920s not only faced the grinding need for all possible economies, however slight, but also had the means both to design a truly effective feed water heater and to test its performance. The introduction of the feed water heater from 1920 onward was "the most fundamental improvement to locomotive economy since the advent of superheating."[77]

Photographs of locomotives of this period show the Worthington type, mounted on the left side of the engine high up under the running board, while the heat exchanger of the Elesco type appears as a cylinder mounted transversely on the smokebox brow. The heat exchanger of the less common Coffin type was sometimes mounted invisibly inside the smokebox, sometimes outside, concentrically with the smokebox brow. These devices contributed to the performance of superpower locomotives.

If the ability to test new devices existed, the will often did not.[78]

The speaker recalls that about ten years ago (i.e. 1915) he had occasion to investigate the performance of a Caille-Potonie feedwater heater that had been tested on a southeastern railroad some years prior. This is a closed type of heater which was developed in France many years ago and is now extensively used in that country. One of the directors of the American railroad had become interested in the possibilities of such equipment and a heater of this type together with the pump and accessory apparatus had been imported for test on the railroads in this country. The only record of this test disclosed in the files was a report to the superintendent of motive power to the effect that the road foreman had made two round trips on the locomotive and had not noticed any improvement in performance due to the application of the feedwater heater. As a result of this exhaustive test the apparatus was dismounted from the locomotive without further investigation and shipped back to France. "Tests" of this general character have cost American railroads a good many millions of dollars.

The railroad referred to may have been the Baltimore & Ohio; the contrast between this and the exhaustive tests carried out by the Pennsylvania at Altoona could hardly be greater.

By 1920, four main types of feed water heater were available: waste gas/gas-tube; waste gas/water-tube; exhaust steam/closed and exhaust steam/open.[79] Development of an effective feed water heater for locomotives was more challenging than might be supposed. Existing live steam injectors were simple, reliable and easily maintained, as well as being a form of feed water heater in themselves. Feed water heaters had to compete with them in terms of total economy. Feed water heaters used a pump instead of an injector. This pump was heavier, more complicated, more costly and less reliable than an injector; the design of the pump was therefore a major challenge to be overcome in developing an effective feed water heater, extracting heat from exhaust steam. A big incentive to develop an effective feed water heater was the ease with which it could be retrofitted to existing locomotives.

An injector used live steam to force feed water into the boiler, heating the water from the ambient temperature to about 160°F in the process, but was relatively inefficient as a pump.[80] A feed water heater separated these two functions, using a smaller amount of live steam to drive a pump and using waste heat to heat the water from the ambient temperature to above 200°F. Compared to an injector, therefore, a feed water heater used less live steam to supply the required amount of water and supplied hotter water to the boiler, using waste heat to do so. A feed water heater using exhaust steam also recycled the condensate, further adding to its economy.

When the Baltimore & Ohio installed a French-built Caille feed water heater of the closed, exhaust steam type in 1913 they found that it was not built strongly enough and was difficult to maintain in consequence. The device was too small for the engine on which it was used and was damaged by water hammer from the pump. The quotation shown above suggests that the employees entrusted with the tests were not interested in the outcome.

As we have seen earlier, some Mallets already incorporated feed water heaters of the waste gas/gas-tube type in their immensely long boiler casings. These devices, supplied by the injector, could add a further 70°F to the water temperature before it went into the boiler, but were bulky and were badly affected by scale formation. This type of heater offered little potential in the shorter boiler casings of rigid-frame locomotives because of the limited space available and the large heating surface needed to produce any worthwhile effect.

Attempts were made, as in the Thompson type tested on the Santa Fe, to place an array of water tubes in the smokebox as a feed water heater. This idea did not succeed earlier as a steam superheater; it enjoyed a similar lack of success as a feed water heater. Either the heating surface was too small to be useful, or it obstructed the exhaust gases. These devices were also vulnerable to the effects of scale formation.

The exhaust steam/closed-type heater bled steam from the exhaust pipe and passed it through heat exchanger tubes surrounded by water. In 1920, the Southern Railway was testing the Weir type; the New York Central, the Delaware & Hudson and the Delaware, Lackawanna & Western were testing a type made by the Locomotive Feed Water Heating Co., with further test units soon to be installed on the Central of New Jersey, the Fort Smith & Western, the Canadian Pacific, the Grand Trunk and the Erie. Water hammer, caused by the pump, and leakage, caused by expansion and contraction, were problems to be overcome.

Exhaust steam was a more promising heat source than waste gas because the rate of heat transfer from steam to a heating surface was ten times that from waste gas, probably because steam condensed on the heating surface, releasing latent heat, and because exhaust steam contained six times as much energy as waste gas.[81] Further development of waste gas heaters ceased.

The Pennsylvania installed a McBride exhaust steam/open-type heater, built by the Worthington Pump & Machinery Corp., on a 2-8-2 in October 1918, and tested it at Altoona before putting it into service. The company fitted three more engines with Worthington heaters in early 1919.[82] The open-type heater injected steam directly into the feed water. Bleeding steam from the exhaust nozzle reduced the firebox draft; the company reduced the nozzle diameter from 7 inches to 6¾ inches to compensate. Even so, the reduced draft resulted in a lower steaming rate and 30°F to 40°F lower superheat. The feed water heater did, therefore, exact a penalty and the company had to consider the overall thermal efficiency with this in mind.

Overall, however, the tests were an outstanding success. In one one-hour test at a wheel speed of 22 miles per hour the engine took 39,900 pounds of water from the tender tank at 40°F; the feed water heater heated it to 208°F. Back pressure in the exhaust nozzle forced

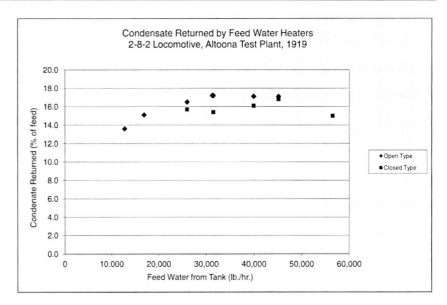

This scatter graph plots the condensate returned by feed water heaters from tests on a Pennsylvania 2-8-2 at Altoona, 1919 (figures from *Report on Feed-Water Heaters for Locomotives,* 1920 ARMMA convention, reported *RA,* June 12, 1920, 1739).

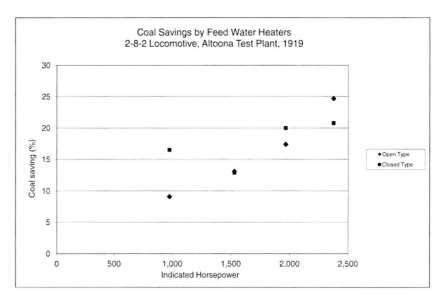

This scatter graph plots coal savings by feed water heaters from tests on a Pennsylvania 2-8-2 at Altoona, 1919 (figures from *Report on Feed-Water Heaters for Locomotives,* 1920 ARMMA convention, reported *RA,* June 12, 1920, 1739).

exhaust steam into the heater at 6 pounds per square inch. The heater condensed 6,820 pounds of exhaust steam and lost only 90 pounds of water to the atmosphere, so that a total of 46,640 pounds of feed water was pumped into the boiler. The pump used 875 pounds of steam, and that exhausted into the exhaust steam line going to the feed water heater. The heater caused a loss of only 3% in power output, but saved 17% in coal consumption. With the heater, the efficiency of the engine improved with increasing power output so that, at 2,400 horsepower, the coal saving was 25%. A year of tests on four Worthington heaters in road service showed a coal saving of 14%.

The Pennsylvania also installed a closed-type water heater on the same 2-8-2 locomotive and tested it at Altoona. The feed water was pumped through 180⅝-inch brass tubes, providing 113 square feet

of heating surface, causing the water to loop back and forth through the steam space; each tube contained a crimped and twisted brass strip to mix the water in its passage. This unit may have been the later well-known Elesco heater. At similar steaming rates to the tests on the Worthington type, the closed-type heater raised the water temperature by 150°F, compared to 170°F for the open type. The closed-type heater condensed water from the exhaust steam equivalent to 16% of the feed, compared to 15% in the open type. Coal savings were similar between the two types. The accompanying graphs show the test results of both types.

The Boston & Albany was unenthusiastic. For them, the feed water heater was more complicated and costly to maintain than an injector. When the engine was drifting down grade with the throttle closed, the temperature of the feed water dropped, causing undesirable fluctuations in feed water temperature, compared to the injector which mixed live steam with the feed water at all times. Bleeding off exhaust steam reduced the draft but, unlike the Pennsylvania, the Boston & Albany found this an irremediable objection. The performance of the pump varied with boiler steam pressure and needed more attention from the crew than the injector, as well as being less reliable. They concluded that a feed water heater added to maintenance costs for no offsetting savings in fuel.

The Canadian Pacific experimented with both waste gas and exhaust steam feed water heaters from about 1905 onward but by 1920 had not had any success.

As with superheating, the U.S. lagged behind Europe. By 1920, more than 10,000 German locomotives had feed water heaters with 2,000 added each year, compared to seven in the U.S. Of the Dutch fleet of 1,000 engines, 300 had feed water heaters. In both these countries, the Knorr type was dominant. Heaters were used in small numbers in Belgium, France, Tunisia, Turkey and Rumania. The British had only trial quantities in service, apart from one railway that had fifty-three. Even so, the American railroads accepted feed water heaters and thermic siphons much more quickly than had been the case with superheating twenty years before.

In 1920, seven railroads used five different types of feed water heaters: the Locomotive Feed Water Heater Co. (later called the Elesco), Weir, Worthington, Caille and Simplex Blake-Knowles.[83] Only a year later, eighteen of the country's bigger railroads were experimenting with ones and twos, totaling thirty-five Elesco units, twelve Worthington, four Weir, one Caille and three Simplex Blake-Knowles. Keeping the Elesco clean was difficult in districts with bad water. Several railroads were pushing the limit of permissible axle loadings; the weight of the heater was an obstacle to its use.

In tests on the Erie, a closed-type heater dropped the superheat temperature by about 20°F, but heated the feed water to 200°F, compared to 174°F from the injector, and produced an 18% saving in coal consumption. On the Delaware, Lackawanna & Western a closed-type heater produced a coal saving of 21% and evaporated 28% more water per pound of coal.

The use of feed water heaters spread quickly. Between 1920 and 1922, the number of railroads with feed water heaters in use or on order increased from seven to twenty-eight, with a total of 234 units.[84] The Worthington (136) and the Elesco (ninety-three) types had taken over the market. Trial applications included locomotives of every size, type and service. The Worthington functioned best in bad water districts because the Elesco was vulnerable to scale formation and required frequent washing with muriatic acid to maintain its effectiveness. The Elesco was preferred where water conditions favored its use; the Worthington was open to atmospheric pressure and could not, therefore, heat the water above 212°F, whereas the Elesco heated the water to 235°F to 240°F, close to the temperature of the exhaust steam. Teething problems with the new equipment were remarkably few and were resolved by minor changes in design and materials. Of the new engines built in the last half of 1922, 28% had feedwater heaters or exhaust steam injectors (discussed below).[85]

In early 1923, 319 feed water heaters were in service, with a further 678 on order.[86] However, 78% of the units in service were on only five railroads—the Pennsylvania, the Southern Pacific, the New Haven, the Cleveland, Cincinnati, Chicago & St. Louis and the Canadian National—one third on the Pennsylvania alone. Twenty-three other railroads were experimenting with small numbers.

Only a year later, 2,123 feed water heaters were in use or on order by American railroads, including twenty-one on switch engines where the application was unexpectedly successful.[87]

The feed water heater did not replace the injector. Engine crews were instructed to use the feed water heater only when the engine was working steam; otherwise the pump would supply cold water to the boiler, causing thermal shock and maintenance problems. Users found that condensation from the feed water heater amounted to 10% to 15% of the feed water, enough to reduce the number of water stops.

Ongoing tests showed fuel savings of 4% to 11% per ton-mile. Not only that, the feed water heater was an engineer's dream because its effectiveness increased with power output, making it an ideal partner to superpower design. Engines with feed water heaters not only developed higher maximum power but delivered their maximum power at higher speeds than engines not so equipped. One series of dynamometer tests showed an engine developing 2,800 indicated horsepower at 25 miles per hour using an injector only; this increased to 3,000 indicated horsepower at 36 miles per hour with a feed water heater. This was achieved by passing only 12% of the exhaust steam through the feed water heater, the balance being needed to draft the fire.

In 1925, Elesco brought out a duplex pump, delivering up to 10,000 gallons per hour against 225 pounds per square inch, with pistons phased to provide a steady flow of water, eliminating water hammer and keeping the boiler check valve open while the pump was running.[88] Adding chemicals to the feed water by an automatic drip feed reduced the need to de-scale the Elesco heater, extending its use into areas of hard water. Corrosion-resistant coatings reduced the effects of acid washing or saline water.

Worthington heaters numbered 1,400 out of the 2,551 heaters in service or on order in 1925. The Pennsylvania reported a 14% average fuel saving after applying the Worthington to their I-1s 2-10-0s.

During the 1920s some railroads, such as the Union Pacific and the Boston & Maine, persevered with an older and cheaper method of feed water heating, passing exhaust steam from stoker and air compressor engines through the tender water tank. Even this small amount of steam was quite capable of heating the water to the point where the injector could not handle it; its usefulness was limited accordingly.[89] The Boston & Maine estimated a fuel saving of 3% to 4% due to this innovation.

The Coffin, a closed-type heater, appeared in 1923. A centrifugal pump, driven by live steam and mounted under the cab floor, forced feed water through a heat exchanger.[90] This heat exchanger was arranged in an arc, concentric with the smokebox and mounted either inside the smokebox or around the smokebox brow.

This arrangement allowed longer tubes than the Elesco version and permitted expansion without expansion joints. Condensate returned to a pre-heating chamber in the front of the tender, which acted as a settling tank and oil skimmer, where the condensate heated the water immediately before it entered the pump suction line. For reasons unknown, the exhaust steam from the centrifugal pump was piped all the way forward to exhaust through the stack or immediately adjacent to it.

By the end of 1928, 5,854 feed water heaters were in service or on order in the U.S. and Canada combined—less than 10% of the total fleet.[91] The following table allows a comparison between numbers installed and new locomotive orders.

Year	Elesco	Worthington	Coffin	Total*	Locos built*
1920	17	33		50	2,022
1921	40	64		104	1,185
1922	319	105		424	1,303
1923	242	730		972	3,505

continued on page 374

Year	Elesco	Worthington	Coffin	Total*	Locos built*
1924	432	292		724	1,810
1925	357	307		664	994
1926	565	339	3	907	1,585
1927	456	461	68	985	1,009
1928	449	362	209	1,020	636

*U.S. and Canada

This table counts only the replies received to a questionnaire; actual numbers installed may be higher. From 1922 to 1926, probably about one-quarter of all new locomotives were built with feed water heaters, allowing for retrofitting to existing engines. In 1927–8, however, installations equaled or exceeded locomotive construction, pointing to a significant retrofitting effort.

11.2.5 Exhaust Steam Injectors

The exhaust steam injector, first patented in 1867 and already widely used by the British, was first tested on a U.S. railroad in 1921,[92] on a New York, Ontario & Western 2-6-0 in November of that year. Comparative tests on a run between Middletown, New York, and Weehawken, New Jersey,[93] showed that the exhaust steam injector saved 20% in fuel, compared to an engine not so equipped. The water temperature going into the boiler averaged 198°F and use of the injector caused a noticeable drop in back pressure. Forthwith live steam injectors were applied to four new 4-8-2s.

This device used exhaust steam, bled from the exhaust nozzle, instead of live steam, drawn from the boiler, to inject water into the boiler, supplemented by live steam, thereby recovering heat from the exhaust steam.[94] It was sensitive to feed water temperature and to back pressure in the exhaust nozzle, which changed with throttle setting and cut-off. It was more complicated to operate than a conventional injector, a problem that was eventually overcome by internal automation and a pressure gauge that told the engineman when the injector was properly adjusted. Observations showed that an exhaust steam injector could inject water into a boiler against 225 pounds per square inch with as little as 4 pounds per square inch back pressure from inside the nozzle and no supplementary use of live steam. The exhaust steam injectors handled feed water at temperatures between 45°F and 85°F.[95] By 1924, twenty-four were on trial on nine railroads, with good results reported, increasing to thirty-seven in use or on order a year later.

An innovative design by the Sellers Co. of Philadelphia, introduced in 1927, comprised two sets of nozzles in series. The exhaust steam nozzles supplied hot water under pressure to the live steam nozzles which forced the water into the boiler. A steam pressure line from the valve chest caused a pair of valves to open and close simultaneously, according to whether there was pressure in the valve chest or not. This automatic valving supplied live steam to the exhaust steam nozzles when the throttle was closed, so that the supply of steam to the injector was unaffected by opening and closing of the throttle.[96] The Sellers device delivered steam to the boiler at temperatures of 250°F to 300°F, compared to 160°F to 235°F for existing exhaust steam injectors.

By the end of 1928, 676 exhaust steam injectors were installed or on order on the railroads of the U.S., Canada and Mexico, compared to 5,854 feed water heaters.[97] Indeed, after peaking at 225 new units in 1926, installations fell back to only fifty-three in the following year, apparently because the exhaust steam injector was more complicated to operate than either a conventional injector or a feed water heater.

> The exhaust-steam injector is an English device and when it was first brought over here there were more keys for its operation than there are keys on a piano.[98]

11.2.6 Boiler Washing and Water Quality

Railroads gained important benefits in areas of bad water by supplying boilers with clean water, either by treating water in fixed plants or by adding chemicals to tender water tanks.

Operating through notoriously bad water areas in Kansas, Oklahoma and East Texas, the Missouri-Kansas-Texas was particularly aggressive in this regard, appointing a full-time water engineer in 1917.[99] Between 1921 and 1923, the company spent $281,000 on ninety-four water treatment plants and, by 1925, was treating 65% of all its locomotive boiler water. Success was immediate; engine miles per boiler failure increased from 89,000 miles in 1923, when the program was completed, to 403,000 miles in 1924. This was one of the factors that enabled the MKT to achieve an extraordinary 31% decrease in fuel consumption, from 157 pounds coal equivalent per 1,000 freight ton-miles in 1922 to 107 pounds in 1927.[100]

There was a strong correlation between scale formation and leaking boilers. Adding soda ash (typically 0.6 pounds per 1,000 gallons of water) deposited the scale-forming ingredients of the water as sludge in the bottom of the boiler, where it could be disposed of by blowing down. Blowing down wasted about 1% of fuel, but the Wabash felt that this was good value. The Wabash began water treatment by this method in 1912 and expanded it to cover its whole territory by 1916,[101] practically eliminating engine failures in service due to leaking flues and boiler joints. Operating officials surmised that the elimination of scale saved fuel as well, but it was not possible to break out this figure from other gains in fuel efficiency.

Pitting and corrosion of fire tubes continued to be a problem, quirky and difficult to predict or cure. It took the Milwaukee twelve years to track down the causes.[102] Water service engineers noticed that the tubes in a stationary boiler at Havre, Montana showed no signs of pitting, whereas locomotives working in the area suffered endless pitting problems. The stationary boiler was fitted with an open-type feed water heater; they theorized that pitting could be cured by the deoxygenating effect of this heater. In April 1925, the company fitted a locomotive with a feed water heater of this type and new fire tubes and tested it for two years in South Dakota in parallel with another engine with no heater. The engine with the heater had no pitting problems in more than two years.

The railroads had to take whatever water they could get:

> In 1918, on the Great Northern, the boilermen established the fact that in water slightly acid from any cause, either coal-mine, swamp or sewage, the pitting commenced at the hot end of the boiler and gradually worked forward until, sometimes, it reached the front end before the tube became useless.

During the early 1920s, the Chicago & Alton installed soda ash plants to combat scale formation, but immediately found that increased and destructive pitting and corrosion occurred instead. An employee, L. O. Gunderson, developed an electro-chemical process, named for him, that proved successful in tests on seventy-five engines between 1924 and 1929.[103] A tube, containing a soluble arsenic compound (not named in the available sources) was placed in the boiler, where the arsenic gradually dissolved. Two lengths of iron pipe were attached to the inside of the boiler shell with insulated brackets. Connections to the headlight generator and a battery made these anodes, with the boiler shell as the cathode, causing arsenic to plate out on the boiler shell and tubes. The arsenic compound was replaced at the rate of five pounds a month; the anodes lasted four years. The saving in tube replacements was large in relation to the cost of the system.

By 1925, some 9,000 locomotives, out of a total U.S. fleet numbering 65,000, were serviced at shops that washed and refilled boilers with water heated by blown-down water and steam. The same year L. G. Plant, of the National Boiler Washing Co., Chicago, suggested that locomotives in shops could be steamed up from a central steam plant.[104] Keeping a locomotive in steam throughout its time in the shop burned 375 pounds of coal per hour; the fire needed continual tending; corrosive smoke cost money in building maintenance and made life arduous for mechanics working on the engines. To fire an engine up from a cold boiler refill took nearly 3 tons of coal. With a central steam plant, the fire could be dumped outside the shop and the engine moved into the shop under residual steam pressure. Inspections and repairs could then be carried out with no fire in the grate; when work was complete, the locomotive could be steamed up from the shop boilers and moved out into the open for firing up and return to service. If the boiler had to be washed out, the central steam plant could recover heat from the hot water blown down from the boiler. The boiler could be washed with hot water and could then be refilled with hot water and enough steam to move the locomotive outside and fire it up in the open. This improved working conditions for employees inside the shop, saved fuel, minimized thermal shock to the boiler and kept the building warm in winter. Open smoke jacks, wasting heat to the atmosphere, could be closed over. Several direct steaming plants were installed at new terminals being built in 1925.[105] The Santa Fe made comprehensive tests at Newton, Kansas. An installation at the Grand Trunk Western Chicago shops in 1927 supplied steam from a 300-pound per square inch shop boiler plant.[106] The Cleveland, Cincinnati, Chicago & St. Louis used this system in its new terminal at Cincinnati, completed in 1928.[107]

11.2.7 Water Gauges

Every advance in steam locomotive performance seemed to bring with it frustrating and unsuspected problems. As of 1920:

> The development of the locomotive has created new difficulties in design, construction, operation and maintenance. One of the perplexing problems which has presented itself is that of securing a correct indication of the height of water over the crown sheet under all conditions of service. The grave importance of this matter is evidenced by the number of crown sheets damaged, due to low water, where careful investigation fails to disclose any contributory cause.

One of the worst dangers in steam locomotive operation was uncovering the crown sheet. It was therefore alarming when accident investigations suggested that the means of measuring the water level in the boiler were misleading and only the fusible plugs—if installed—saved the crew and engine from destruction. Surging of the water in the boiler due to acceleration, deceleration and changes in grade was a known problem but now the basic assumption that, at least, the water surface would find its own level turned out to be alarmingly flawed.[108]

After the ICC Bureau of Locomotive Inspection became aware of this problem, they made tests on fourteen different railroads with various arrays of try cocks and water glasses.

The first tests showed that, when the throttle or safety valves were open, the top try cock would discharge water, regardless of the water level indicated by the gauge glass. A second water glass, installed at the back tube sheet, showed a higher water level at the back of the firebox than at the front.

Next, they installed the three try cocks on a verti-

cal "water column," standing free of the backhead, instead of plumbing the try cocks directly into the backhead. The top of the water column was connected to the steam space above the firebox, while the bottom was plumbed into the backhead, well below the level of the crown sheet. In this arrangement, however, stagnant water in the bottom connection caused erratic readings.

Finally, they installed four try cocks, each with an extensible tube, plumbed into the backhead, so that the forward extent of the disturbance of the water surface could be determined.

The tests showed that, in the new locomotives being built, the brick arch threw the heat of the fire onto the backhead, while the arch tubes poured steam bubbles out into the same area. As a result, when the throttle was opened, or even if the safety valves lifted, steam generation in the backhead could cause the water to boil up as much as 8 to 10 inches higher than the general level of water in the boiler; the toe of this disturbance could extend as far as one foot ahead of the firedoor sheet. The bottom try cock could therefore show water, even when the top of the crown sheet was uncovered.

The Bureau was able to confirm this by placing an electric lamp inside the steam space of a boiler and fitting sight glasses, through which the water surface could be observed. The ICC carried out this test on an old switch engine with a vertical backhead, no brick arch and thus no arch tubes. The rods and valves were disconnected and blocked so that, when the throttle was opened, steam flowed straight through the cylinders and out the exhaust nozzle. The observers found that the water surface was level only when the throttle and safety valves were closed. They saw water welling up from the water legs, converging over the crown sheet, and moving toward the front of the boiler. As soon as the throttle was opened, the upwelling of water in the water legs increased to 1 to 2 inches, with accelerated circulation and the water surface throughout the boiler rose by 1 to 1½ inches; this appeared in the gauge glass. The upwelling around the firebox increased to as much as 4 inches; the try cocks registered this upwelling; the gauge glass did not. A brick arch, arch tubes and a forward-sloping backhead led to even stronger upwelling.

Arch tubes contributed to this problem, as did any foaming tendency of the water. The position of the connections to the try cocks

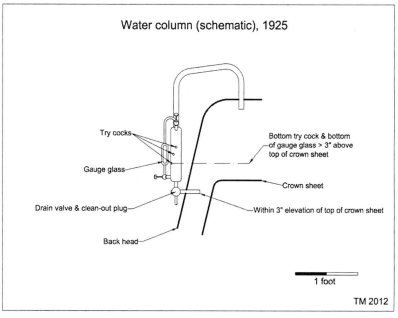

A schematic view of a water column (redrawn from *RA*, June 20, 1920, 1552).

and water glasses was therefore critical. The only saving feature was that the water boiling up the backhead above the general water level in the boiler lacked sufficient mass to force a falsely high reading in a gauge glass.

As a result of these tests, the USRA Committee on Standards recommended, not only a water column with three try cocks but a gauge glass connected to the top and bottom of the water column with a second, independently connected gauge glass as well. These three devices were set to read over an 8-inch range, the bottom of which was about 3 inches higher than the highest point on the crown sheet. The top connections of both were piped into the highest point of the wrapper sheet, rather than into the backhead, so that the top connections could never take water boiling up the backhead.

From 1921 onward, most new engines were built with water columns, and retrofitting of older engines began. The 1922 report of the ICC Bureau of Locomotive Inspection called for all locomotives showing a discrepancy of more than 2 inches between try cock and water glass readings to be fitted with a water column with three gauge cocks and a water glass and a separate water glass.[109]

Low water alarms began to appear in 1925–6, which blew a whistle if the boiler water level was too low.[110]

11.2.8 Boiler Explosions

Boiler explosions went on; the bigger the boilers, the more disastrous their explosions. A typical locomotive boiler of the 1920s contained 3,750 gallons of water and a steam pressure of 200 pounds per square inch and weighed 50 to 60 tons. If the crown sheet ruptured, 700 million foot-pounds of energy would be released, capable of tearing the boiler loose from its mountings and throwing it end over end for hundreds of feet.

Low water uncovering the crown sheet remained the dominant cause; the entry holes to try cocks and gauge glasses could plug with scale, rendering them useless or misleading. Undetected corrosion could have disastrous results. More worrying, explosions were traced to unpredictable rupture of the firebox side sheet, usually midway along its length, due to a crack running suddenly upward from the foundation ring, or just above it, sometimes reaching the crown sheet. Such fireboxes typically exhibited no other defects or signs of abuse.[111]

In the 1920s, welding was still a new process; boiler and firebox joints were riveted. The first commercial use of both oxy-acetylene and thermite welding was in 1903; arc welding followed in 1907. World War I forced on the development of welding technology, but the process remained experimental and of ill repute. In 1918, the Boiler Code Committee of the American Society of Mechanical Engineers appointed a Subcommittee on Welding; the American Welding Society was founded the following year. By 1920, little was known about welding, and even less about the quality control of welds. In that year, the ASME Boiler Code Committee considered a petition to allow welded joints in boilers generating steam up to 15 pounds per square inch; intensive efforts by the ASME and the AWS resulted in a welding code for pressure vessels other than boilers in 1925. Nevertheless, some railroads welded joints or patches in boilers containing more than ten times that pressure; defective welds contributed to boiler explosions and to the bad reputation of welding in general. The welding referred to was "autogenous," using only the metal to be joined without adding metal from a welding rod.

The first full year of locomotive boiler inspection by the ICC was 1912.[112] In that year 856 accidents resulted from the failure of some part of the boiler, killing ninety-one people and injuring 1,005. After ten years of ICC inspections, the accident rate from this cause had dropped by 60% to 342, in spite of the bigger locomotive fleet; fifty-one people were killed and 379 injured. Disturbingly, where crown

sheets with welded joints failed, 80% of the welds failed compared to only 17% of riveted joints. In 1922, the Bureau of Locomotive Inspection recommended that welding technology was too immature to be applied to safety-critical parts of the engine. This led to an ICC prohibition against the welding of pressurized parts of the boiler, although the ICC still permitted the welding of fireboxes, possibly on the grounds that fireboxes were loaded more in compression than tension, but no higher than 14 inches below the top of the crown sheet.[113]

In the 1921–2 fiscal year, the number of fatalities caused by failure of some part of the locomotive showed a gratifying year-on-year decrease of nearly 50%. Even so, there were still thirty-three boiler explosions, still mostly caused by exposure of the crown sheet. Welded joints continued to be suspect. Unfortunately, substantial numbers of fireboxes with welded joints or patches were already in service; the ICC was not able to demand that they all be withdrawn and replaced, leaving the engine crews to a kind of Russian roulette. In one instance in 1923, a 21-inch crack in the backhead that had been repaired by welding opened up, filling the cab with steam and scalding water. The fireman and engineer were forced out of the cab without being able to close the throttle or apply the brakes. Badly scalded and terrified that the whole boiler would explode, they climbed round to the front of the moving locomotive and opened the angle cock, thereby applying the brakes. The engineer died of his injuries.

The downward trend in engine-related accidents was reversed in 1923, when fifty-seven boiler explosions caused forty-one fatalities[114]; that year, no less than 65% of locomotives inspected by the ICC were defective in some way. In fiscal 1924, locomotive defects caused 1,005 accidents, resulting in sixty-six fatalities and 1,157 serious injuries.[115] Traditionally, the blame for boiler explosions was placed on the crew for allowing the crown sheet to become uncovered; closer investigation revealed that half the incidents had some contributory cause.

Detailed testimony revealed practices that are incomprehensible to us today.[116] In 1924, crown sheet failure caused the explosion of the boiler of an engine on the Baltimore & Ohio, killing the engineer, fireman and a brakeman who was in the cab at the time. The crown sheet had no fusible plugs; seven staybolts had broken before the date of the explosion. The relatives of one of the enginemen sued the company. The brakeman from another train visited the doomed crew before the explosion, while they were taking on water. He testified that:

> while there, he observed that water and steam were escaping from the boiler into the firebox; that he heard the sizzling of the water upon the fire; that, when he opened the firebox door, steam gushed out; that the fire was dead; that the steam gauge showed 160 lb. pressure, and that water was being put into the boiler by the two injectors.

The crew were evidently used to working engines in that condition because they somehow drove it another three miles before the crown sheet ruptured and the boiler exploded. The location of the broken staybolts in relation to the rupture showed that they did not cause the explosion. The case went to the Supreme Court; the plaintiff lost.

As the crew were usually killed in the explosion, they took the blame for allowing the boiler water level to fall too low. This was not always the case.

One day in July 1925, a Maine Central freight left Rigby Yard, Portland, with two locomotives on each end and class W 2-8-0 No. 505, built by Alco in 1910, cut into the middle of the train. The crew of No. 505 complained that the throttle "felt mushy" but were told to take the locomotive anyway. A few miles from Bartlett, New Hampshire, the boiler exploded. The force of the explosion threw the locomotive end over end; it destroyed the telegraph wires, landed on the embankment inverted and slid into the trees. The explosion destroyed the surrounding foliage and coated the ground with a crust of coal, ballast and cinders. The engineer lived for an hour after the event, in which time he said that the throat sheet had failed at the foundation ring. The company sent men into the woods to pick up as much debris as they could find, disposed of the engine before the ICC could investigate the accident, lost documentation and sued the engineer's family; the case was dismissed. It is difficult to imagine a connection between a defective throttle and a failure of the throat sheet, but company managements were not always blameless in the matter of boiler explosions.[117]

The number of boiler explosions halved from 1926 to 1927 but, when they did occur, the explosions of bigger boilers carrying higher pressure than before were devastating. Sixty percent of fatalities due to defects of the engine resulted from this cause. They were not always the fault of the crew. The following narrative is reproduced by kind permission of Golden West Books, San Merino, California.[118] The locomotive involved in the accident was a Class F-81 2-10-2 built by Alco in 1917; the accident took place in August 1934.

On the D&RG's desert division the water carried a lot of alkali, soluble and insoluble salts, and just plain mud. And gas … some kind of carbonation, that when it got hot and under pressure it would not make clean steam, just foam and froth. The carryover from the boiler washed away the lubrication from valves, pistons, cylinders, air pumps, water pumps and stoker engines…. The former sharp, clear exhaust from her stack began to sound like the engine was working oatmeal mush through the cylinders. And stink! Whew! It smelled of stale, dry dust, that which sticks in one's throat. Needless to say, a dry cylinder or valve soon lost its efficiency and the packing became shot and the piston began to leak steam. The worst result of foaming in the steam engine boiler was that you could not get an accurate reading of the water level from the sight glasses on the boiler head. The engineer never knew for certain how much water he might have in a foaming boiler. This is a dangerous condition, because that firebox roof can get red-hot in a damn short time!

The fireman who could keep his engine from foaming had to carry the water level lower than normal working conditions might indicate and use the manual blowoff cock frequently. As the water evaporated the salts and silt settled to the bottom of the firebox mud ring, and this concentration was blown out into the atmosphere through the use of the blowoff cock. This manually operated valve was located in the locomotive cab, usually on the left side, under the fireman's seat, where it would be handy to use.

In the case of the No. 1409, the crew had stopped their westbound drag freight at Green River, Utah, for coal, water, and to eat lunch. The coal chute man doped the rods and filled (the tender tank and water car) while the fireman straightened up his fire and the hoghead oiled around. The next stop would be Woodside, 25 miles west. The train took around two hours en route to that water spout; then stopped to fill both tanks. The water supply for the Woodside tank was a deep well that had been drilled by the railroad in the early 1900's. Prior to drilling the well the D&RG ran a water train out from Helper daily; big wooden

The effects of a boiler explosion on the Charleston & Western Carolina, November 18, 1948, near Clarks Hill, South Carolina. The locomotive was a 2-8-2, built by Baldwin in 1919, No. 853 (ex–Clinchfield No. 405), transferred in February, 1943, to ease a wartime shortage of motive power. The locomotive was hauling a freight train at an estimated speed of 25 to 30 miles per hour. The engineer was killed, the fireman so severely injured that he died a few minutes after reaching the hospital and the head-brakeman was severely injured (courtesy Michael J. Young; information provided by Young and Mike Hopson, locomotive engineer, Johnson City, Tennessee).

tubs mounted on flatcars and filled with pure, mountain spring water to supply the locomotives at that point. The water from the Peace River was too full of alkali to use in steam boilers. The water well was a gasser. Many years later it became famous as a tourist attraction, known as the "Woodside Geyser." It spouted about 15 or 20 feet high due to gas pressure.

For the crew of the ill-fated No. 1409, their next water tank stop was at Farnham. That tank was supplied from the river and was pumped out about where the wash from Desert Lake empties into that stream. The water in the wash runs deep green with a heavy concentration of salts. Now there is a mixture of carbonation and alkali salt in both tanks of the locomotive consist.

It was just about dark when the train topped the grade a mile west of Wellington and entered a little sag. The hoghead hooked her up and eased off on the throttle and "BLAM…" There was a horrible roar of an explosion and a bright, blinding flash!

The entire firebox tore away from the boiler and turned inside out, its heavy metal sheets ripped like so much paper, its stay bolts projecting like the quills of a giant porcupine; it flew to the right of the track and landed in the middle of U.S. Highway 50. The boiler and running gear remained on the rails and continued on west for a mile. It looked like a big tube mounted on wheels as the front end door had been blown off and had sailed like a huge plate, circular to the left across the river, where it came to rest in a field one hundred yards away. The Vanderbilt tank went up in the air and turned over, facing back towards the east, falling behind the auxiliary water car that once was trailing. The locomotive bell, which hung on the smokebox door was never found, or if it was, whomever found it kept it as a souvenir.

Examination of the left front boiler leg at the mud ring disclosed an area of about two square feet of rusty looking metal. It appeared that mud had settled there a foot deep, and then probably dried; there was no water circulation … so the metal got red-hot. The mudded space was burned, and it dried, the mud swelled and cracked open. When water poured into that void of heat and gas, the overheated metal cracked and the adjacent stay bolts failed. A tremendous explosion ripped the mighty Santa Fe–type asunder in one flashing instant.

A friend of mine, who was living in Helper and working on a track gang at Woodside that scorching day in August 1934, was riding on top of an empty stock car 15 cars deep from the head end of the train; about 750 feet behind the No. 1409. He had climbed aboard to ride home for the weekend. He told me later of his experience. He said that he was riding along, enjoying the cool evening breeze as he sat there on the running board of the swaying car, when suddenly there was a brilliant flash and a terrific roar such as he had never heard before, and he next found himself sitting in the willows along the river, the train was standing on the track nearby."

The outlook was not good. In spite of a decrease in the overall accident rate caused by locomotive defects:

Explosions may be expected to increase in violence with the increasing size of locomotive boilers and the higher pressure carried therein, and accidents of this nature may be expected to increase as the duties and responsibilities of enginemen become more complex and exacting.

In fiscal 1929, there were only twenty-two boiler explosions, killing ten people. It was the government's opinion that the reduction in crown sheet failures was "largely, if not entirely, brought about through better maintenance, better water-indicating appliances, visibility of water glasses, proper and accessible location of gauge cocks, and better and more dependable feedwater appliances."[119]

Boiler explosions continued to worry railroad officers enough to be an underlying factor favoring the diesel locomotive.[120]

Section 11.3 Cylinders and Valve Gear

11.3.1 Three-Cylinder Locomotives

The 1920s brought an increased willingness to experiment with the three-cylinder configuration, promoted with some success by Alco.[121] The possible advantages were already well known, but became more desirable with the increasing size and power of American locomotives. Dividing the piston thrust among three pistons permitted lighter individual reciprocating parts, offering benefits in counterbalancing and reduced dynamic augment and yawing. Three-cylinder engines could be built to adhesion factors as low as 3.7–3.8 (compared to the hitherto sacrosanct 4.0), increasing the tractive effort that was possible within the limits of a given axle loading by as much as 15%. Six exhaust blasts per driving wheel revolution smoothed out the draft and promoted efficient combustion; more effective drafting allowed a wider exhaust nozzle and lower back pressure. The standing objections to the three-cylinder configuration were the difficulty of manufacturing reliable crank axles and the inaccessibility of the mechanism between the frames; like the advantages, these objections also took on greater significance with increasing locomotive power.

According to Robert J. Church,[122] the Philadelphia & Reading rebuilt three 4-4-0s, one 4-6-0 and one ten-coupled locomotive to the three-cylinder configuration between 1909 and 1912 (according to Drury, four 4-4-2s and two 4-6-0s new-built in company shops), but Drury points out that they were soon converted to the conventional two-cylinder configuration.

The first of a new generation of three-cylinder locomotives was a 4-8-2, belonging to the New York Central, rebuilt by Alco in 1922. All three cylinders drove the same axle.[123] At the same time, Alco retrofitted this engine with an Elvin power stoker, a feed water heater and a booster and changed the superheater from the Type A to the Type E. Steam was supplied to the inside cylinder by means of a conjugate valve gear based on the British Gresley gear developed for this purpose; this helped to solve the problem of an inaccessible mechanism between the frames. These alterations made it difficult to evaluate the actual effects of changing the cylinder configuration. Even so, the engine was immediately hauling 8,000 to 8,500-ton trains over the 140 miles between Albany and Syracuse in less than eight hours, convincing the New York Central that a three-cylinder engine could deliver 12% to 15% more power than a two-cylinder engine of the same size. They attributed this to the more even application of torque to the wheels and a more continuous exhaust blast. "Diametral speed"—the speed in miles per hour equal to the driving wheel diameter in inches—was for long believed to be a limiting speed for steam locomotives for counterbalancing reasons; the rebuilt engine ran smoothly 12% faster than its diametral speed.

The following year, the New York Central had Alco build a new three-cylinder 4-8-2 of similar design to the company's 4-8-2s built in 1917–18.[124] Additions to the original design were an Elesco Type E superheater, an Elesco feed water heater and a booster which brought the basic 51,000 pounds of tractive effort up to 76,000. The 200-pounds per square inch boiler contained 216 3½-inch × 25-foot fire tubes. Of these, 176 contained superheater elements, providing 5,155 square feet of primary and 2,158 square feet of superheating surface—a large heating surface for a rigid-frame engine with a conventional, 80-inch diameter boiler.

Next came a new 4-8-2 built by Alco and delivered to the Lehigh Valley in October 1923.[125] In the New York Central engine, all three cylinders drove the second driving axle. In the Lehigh Valley engine, the two outside cylinders drove the third driving axle, while the inside

One of the six three-cylinder 4-8-2s built by Alco for the Lehigh Valley in 1923–24. The date and location of the photograph are unknown (courtesy California State Railroad Museum, Negative E417).

cylinder drove the second axle. In both locomotives, the inside cylinder had to be set high and inclined so that the connecting rod passed over the front driving axle. The Lehigh Valley engine had neither booster nor feed water heater, but was stoker-fired. It weighed 369,000 pounds and developed 65,000 pounds of tractive effort; the three-cylinder arrangement allowed a low factor of adhesion of 3.8. In other respects, the dimensions were conventional for a 4-8-2, except for an 84-square foot anthracite grate. This engine hauled trains weighing up to 4,275 tons against 0.4% grades, achieving the very low coal consumption of 63 pounds per thousand gross ton-miles, 2.7 pounds per indicated horsepower-hour, and a steam consumption of 20 pounds per indicated horsepower-hour, developing up to 3,000 indicated horsepower. The new engine not only handled more cars in fast freight service on the heavy grades and curvature between Sayre and Lehighton, Pennsylvania, than the two 4-6-2s that it replaced but did so without the time-consuming connection and disconnection of a helper. Savings in time and fuel were substantial, but this was an altogether bigger engine, developing 33% more tractive effort than the engines it replaced and so it was difficult to identify the effect of the three-cylinder configuration as such. The company ordered five more engines of this type.

The most direct comparison between three- and two-cylinder locomotives came from the Louisville & Nashville which placed a three-cylinder 2-8-2 in service in November 1924, with dimensions closely similar to the company's existing 2-8-2s. Tested against a conventional 2-8-2, the three-cylinder locomotive showed 12% to 16%

coal savings per gross ton-mile. In 1925, the company bought a three-cylinder 4-6-2 from Alco, similar in other respects to its class K-5 USRA light Pacifics.

Other early experimenters with this configuration were the Chicago, Rock Island & Pacific (one 4-6-2, Alco, 1924), the Delaware, Lackawanna & Western (five 4-8-2s, Alco, 1925), the Missouri Pacific (a 4-6-2 and a 2-8-2, Alco, 1925) and the Wabash (five of a class of fifty 2-8-2s, Alco, 1925).

Following the success of its five 4-8-2s, the Lackawanna ordered another twenty-five from Alco, which were delivered in late 1926.[126] The company's first five three-cylinder 4-8-2s were for passenger service; the twenty-five were for freight service on the heavy grades out of Scranton. These engines were a slightly heavier development of the first five with smaller driving wheels. With a boiler pressure of 200 pounds per square inch, these engines developed 77,000 pounds of tractive effort; a booster, running at a fixed 50% cut-off, added another 11,000 pounds. The outside cylinders drove on the third driving axle; the inside cylinder drove on the second axle. The three-cylinder arrangement permitted a factor of adhesion of only 3.54.

By the end of 1927, 144 three-cylinder locomotives were in service in the U.S.: nineteen 0-8-0s, seven 2-8-2s, three 4-6-2s, fifty-one 4-8-2s, forty-nine 4-10-2s and fifteen 4-12-2s. This compared to 2,000 three-cylinder locomotives in Germany, 250 in England and 100 in other countries.[127]

Although replies to an ARMMA questionnaire said that three-cylinder locomotives cost less to maintain per ton-mile hauled and

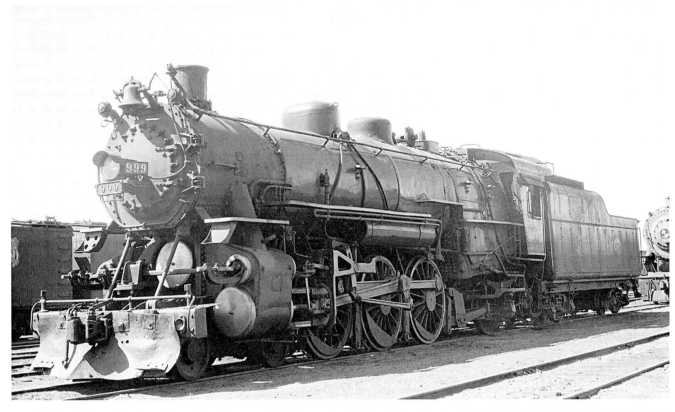

The third cylinder is clearly visible in this photograph of Chicago, Rock Island & Pacific class P-46 4-6-2, No. 999, built by Alco in 1924, photographed at Dalhart, Texas, on May 7, 1934 (Denver Public Library, Otto C. Perry collection, OP-5385).

Otto Perry photographed Wabash class K-5 three-cylinder 2-8-2, No. 2600, built by Alco in 1925, at Decatur, Illinois, on September 19, 1930 (Denver Public Library, Otto C. Perry collection, OP-19742).

were more fuel-efficient than two-cylinder locomotives, the experimenters neither ordered more of them, nor persisted in using the ones they had. The Rock Island scrapped its 4-6-2 in 1939. The Lackawanna rebuilt five 4-8-2s with two cylinders in 1930–31. The Indiana Harbor Belt bought three three-cylinder 0-8-0s from Alco in 1927 and later rebuilt them with two cylinders. Of the Louisville & Nashville's 4-6-2 one writer commented sardonically[128]:

> The three-cylinder Pacific had been a success only in the pages of contemporary Alco literature—and the Shops had been gradually "raiding" her for parts, many of which were interchangeable with those of the K-5 class.

By 1940, the engine was headed for the scrapyard but, faced with renewed traffic demand and shortage of supply, the company rebuilt it as a two-cylinder engine, adding a feed water heater, an air-smoothed skirt and cowl and a high-capacity tender, and put it into express passenger service between Louisville and Montgomery, Alabama, in which role it continued into the 1950s.

The Louisville & Nashville scrapped its three-cylinder 2-8-2 in 1950. The Lehigh Valley reconfigured its six 4-8-2s in 1939. The Missouri Pacific rebuilt its 2-8-2 in 1937 and its 4-6-2 in 1942, using it as a test bed for Franklin poppet valves.[129] The New York Central reconverted its two 4-8-2s in 1936. The Wabash stored its engines, then used the boilers to build 4-6-4s in 1943–4.

Only four railroads used three-cylinder engines in significant numbers and persisted in their use until the end of steam. These were the New Haven, the Denver & Rio Grande Western, the Southern Pacific and the Union Pacific.

Among the boldest of the new users of three-cylinder engines was the New Haven. The company ordered ten 0-8-0 switchers, put into service in 1924, followed by a further six in 1927; the company also bought three 4-8-2s in 1926 and ten more in 1928, all from Alco Schenectady. The ten 4-8-2s were further distinguished by McClellon water-tube boilers, Bean smokeboxes (one-piece steel castings), and Elesco feed water heaters.[130] With 265 pounds per square inch boiler pressure and 71,000 pounds of tractive effort, they were the most powerful engines on the New Haven, bought to haul 100-car, 5,000-ton freight trains at passenger train speeds over the 275 miles between Maybrook, New York, and Boston. Three-cylinder locomotives comprised 30% of the company's heavy switchers and nearly one fifth of the company's 4-8-2s. All these three-cylinder engines remained in service until 1949–52.

The Denver & Rio Grande Western broke the Alco monopoly, buying ten three-cylinder 4-8-2s from Baldwin in 1926.[131] Apart from having three cylinders, these engines comprised design elements which were normal for that time: a Du Pont-Simplex Type B stoker, a brick arch supported on two siphons and three arch tubes, a Worthington feed water heater, 210 pounds per square inch boiler pressure and a conventional arrangement of fire tubes and superheater flues. The grate was abnormally large, at 95 square feet. The cylinders were of cast iron, cast in center, left and right sections and bolted together. Steam flow was controlled by three Walschaert valve gears, of which two were on the right side of the engine; the outer of these was mechanically connected to the center cylinder valve stem. The three cylinders produced the abnormally high tractive effort for an eight-coupled engine of 75,000 pounds, made possible by a very high axle loading of 72,600 pounds. The total engine weight was 419,300 pounds. The engine was designed to operate in Colorado conditions

Baldwin built Denver & Rio Grande Western class M-75 three-cylinder 4-8-2, No. 1603, in 1926 with a Worthington feed water heater, visible above the two middle driving wheels. Otto Perry photographed it at Grand Junction, Colorado, on April 16, 1939 (Denver Public Library, Otto C. Perry collection, OP-9801).

This Denver & Rio Grande Western class M-75 4-8-2, No. 1605, came from Baldwin in 1926. The original Worthington feed water heater had been replaced with an Elesco type by the time Otto Perry photographed it at Grand Junction, Colorado, on August 11, 1935. The third cylinder is just visible (Denver Public Library, Otto C. Perry collection, OP-9804).

Alco built this Southern Pacific Class SP-1 three-cylinder 4-10-2, No. 5004, in 1925. Otto Perry photographed it at Lordsburg, New Mexico, on July 25, 1935. Note the Worthington feed water heater above the middle driving wheel (Denver Public Library, Otto C. Perry collection, OP-15743).

with grades up to 3% and sharp curves. These engines remained in service as such until they were scrapped in 1941–9.

Bolder yet was the Southern Pacific, ordering forty-nine three-cylinder 4-10-2s in 1925–7.[132] The company bought new 2-10-2s in 1924 and was already looking for more power. The 4-10-2s went onto routes with notoriously steep grades, six in the Sierra Nevadas between Roseville, California, and Sparks, Nevada, the other ten in the Siskiyou Mountains between Dunsmuir, California, and Ashland, Oregon. Across the Sierra Nevadas, a 4-10-2 handled seventeen passenger cars, weighing 950 tons, unaided against grades as steep as 2.6% that previously required a 2-10-2 road engine and a 2-8-2 helper. In the Siskiyous, they handled 16% more tonnage than the 2-10-2s and saved 12% on fuel. These engines were limited to a 70% maximum cut-off, but had boosters, providing a maximum of 84,000 pounds of tractive effort at speeds up to 8 miles per hour. They were scrapped in 1953–5.

The Union Pacific's attitude on the eve of its whole-hearted espousal of the three-cylinder locomotive is interesting, as expressed by the company's Chief Engineer, A. H. Fetters[133]:

> The probable increased maintenance of three-cylinder locomotives is a serious matter....
>
> The three-cylinder locomotive has, heretofore, not been successful largely because the time had not yet arrived when American designers had sufficient incentive to refine it into a mechanical success. Until recently, other and more conventional avenues were open by which to increase the power and capacity, but at the present time the field is largely exhausted, and we are confronted with a serious problem if we desire to go further in power and capacity, inasmuch as we have about reached the permissible limits in clearances, wheel arrangements, axle

loads and power economizing auxiliaries. If at this juncture some one should state that he can produce 15 per cent. more tractive force, without increasing the weight on drivers, we are compelled to give the suggestion serious thought, even though it involves another cylinder.

In 1925, the Union Pacific bought ten three-cylinder 4-10-2s; although it rebuilt these engines with two cylinders in 1942, they were the precursors of the biggest and most successful class of all the three-cylinder engines, the eighty-eight famous 4-12-2s, built by Alco between 1926 and 1930. These were never modified and survived until 1953–6.

The four-cylinder, rigid-frame, single-expansion locomotive made no headway in America at all. Yet such locomotives were popular in Europe and the British four-cylinder express passenger engines of the mid–1920s were among their best-known designs, typified by the Southern Railway 4-6-0 *Lord Nelson* class, the Great Western Railway 4-6-0 *King* class and the London, Midland & Scottish Railway 4-6-2 *Coronation* class.[134] The *King* class came out in 1927 and was exhibited at the Baltimore & Ohio centenary. With 250 pounds per square inch steam pressure, an engine weight of 200,000 pounds and 40,000 pounds of tractive effort, these represented the limits of British locomotive design. A *Coronation* achieved the highest power output ever measured in a British steam locomotive.

11.3.2 Compounding

Apart from a few experiments, such as the Baldwin 4-10-2 three-cylinder compound and the Delaware & Hudson 2-8-0 cross-compounds, compounding in the U.S. was dead. Some astonishing animosities ensured that it would remain so. By the 1920s, the generation of senior officers who had espoused it had passed on,

Alco built this Union Pacific class FTT-1 three-cylinder 4-10-2, No. 8000, in 1925. Otto Perry photographed it at Laramie, Wyoming, on July 29, 1928 (Denver Public Library, Otto C. Perry collection, OP-17287).

leaving their juniors—now in positions of authority—to curse its memory[135]:

> There is no disguising the fact that many of the older motive power officers view their former experiences with compound locomotives as a nightmare, which they are perfectly willing to forget, and consequently will hesitate a long time before trying this type again.

Even new Mallets were built with single expansion from the mid–1920s onward. The Duluth, Missabe & Iron Range and the Baltimore & Ohio—and others—rebuilt their compound Mallets to single expansion during the 1920s and 1930s.[136] The Baltimore & Ohio found that the rebuilt engines were more fuel-efficient than they had been in their original compound form.

The French persevered and, by 1927, had a four-cylinder compound, running on 235-pounds per square inch steam and developing 3,000 indicated horsepower.[137] This engine achieved a thermal efficiency of 10.0% (in terms of indicated horsepower) and only 80 pounds of locomotive weight per indicated horsepower while the Americans were still trying to get their specific locomotive weight down to 100 pounds per horsepower and some American engines were reaching thermal efficiencies of 8% on the test plant.

By a quirk of fate, the last steam locomotives that Baldwin built for U.S. service were ten compound 2-6-6-2s for the Chesapeake & Ohio, built in 1949 to the same basic design as that used in 1910.[138]

11.3.3 Boosters

By the 1920s, contempt for innovations such as superheating was long past.

> The demand for efficiency and economy in locomotive design and service is increasing every day. Every new idea that can be worked out successfully along those lines is speedily adopted by railroad managements.[139]

The first locomotive booster was installed on the New York Central in 1919; by 1924, 1,453 were in service on forty-three railroads in the U.S. and Canada.

The booster was the brainchild of H. L. Ingersoll, Assistant to the President of the New York Central. He reasoned that more tractive effort was required to start a train than to keep it moving. At low speeds, the boiler could produce more steam than the cylinders used. Additionally, the weight on the trailing truck was not used for adhesion. The bigger the engine, the smaller the percentage of total weight supported by the trailing truck, so that a booster would increase the tractive effort of a 2-8-2 by 10%, increasing to 36% for a 4-4-2.

In its original form, the booster consisted of a steam engine with two horizontal 10-inch × 12-inch cylinders, mounted on the trailing truck beneath the ash pan and driving its axle. The booster engine drove a shaft, geared to the trailing truck axle. It worked only in the forward direction and at a fixed 75% cut-off. The exhaust was piped to the main exhaust nozzle. The booster was for starting, accelerating to line speed and grades; the engineer disconnected it by means of a compressed-air clutch when the train reached 20 miles per hour.

The New York Central made the first booster installation as a retrofit on a class K-11 4-6-2. The company ran a dynamometer test on this locomotive from Ravena, New York, to Weehawken, New Jersey. A crew with no experience of the booster left Ravena with just under 2,600 tons on the drawbar. They took water at Catskill, where the water plug was located at the bottom of two grades. A K-11 could not restart a tonnage train from this point; the crew had to leave the train at the top of one grade, run light to the water plug, take water, return to the train, restart it and rely on momentum to surmount the 0.4% adverse grade beyond the water plug; this caused a substantial delay. With the booster, the crew were able to take the train down to the

water plug, take water and restart the train against a 0.4% grade, disengaging the booster when the speed reached 8 miles per hour. Adverse grades south of Newburgh meant that a K-11 could handle only 2,100 tons beyond that point, but the booster-equipped engine took the full tonnage through to Weehawken. Hitting the foot of the six miles of 0.5% ruling grade at Haverstraw at 33 miles per hour, the crew cut in the booster when the speed had dropped to 7½ miles per hour after five miles; with the booster, the train accelerated upgrade to 10 miles per hour. At the top of the grade, the crew cut out the booster and continued to Weehawken with 23% more tonnage than this class of engine had ever taken before. Depending on speed, the booster increased the locomotive's tractive effort by 15% to 20% and enabled tonnage increases of 20% to 25%.

This device was an immediate success and had some remarkable effects. Heavily loaded express engines typically had to jerk the slack in a train to get it started, to the discomfort of the passengers and to the detriment of the cars; a booster allowed the engineer to start a heavy train more smoothly than before, or to start a train on grades or curves where the unaided engine could not. Booster-equipped engines could accelerate a train to line speed quicker than unaided engines and maintain speed on adverse grades. They could haul full-tonnage trains across a division where previously cars had to be taken off for some sections. In some places, the engine crew would have to disconnect from their train and run light for some distance to take water because they could not restart the train on the grade where the water plug was located; a booster could eliminate the time so lost. The Franklin Railway Supply Co. was first in the field as a manufacturer; they proved with dynamometer tests that, even at 18 miles per hour—well above the starting case for which the booster was intended—their booster still developed 316 horsepower.[140] It increased the productivity of slow-moving engines in hump and yard service. (Obviously, it could not be applied to switchers having no trailing truck.) All of this was achieved with a device that could be retrofitted to existing engines for a small cost and consumed little or no extra fuel. It speaks volumes, both for the economic plight of the railroads and for their operational research capabilities, that they embraced a device capable of adding seven hundredths of a cent per ton-mile to their earnings.

In 1920, J. A. McGrew and J. T. Loree of the Delaware & Hudson came up with a better idea, using a tender truck as a booster.[141] (It appears[142] that J. T. Loree was the general manager, as distinct from L. F. Loree, the company president; the present study has not revealed whether they were related or not.) Steam was supplied to two 10-inch × 10-inch cylinders through piping with flexible joints; the booster exhaust went through the tender water tank. The booster engine drove a shaft geared to one of the tender truck axles through an intermediary third gear. Connecting rods transferred power to the other axle of the truck. The steam supply to the booster engine forced the intermediary gear into mesh with the drive shaft and the driven axle by means of a small piston, so that clutching and declutching were automatic whenever the engineer engaged or disengaged the booster. The first installation was on a camelback, Wootten-boilered 2-8-0 and increased the engine's rated tonnage by 30%.

Improvements to the booster were not slow in coming. Bethlehem Steel and Franklin both brought out four-wheel boosters that could be clutched into the forward and reverse directions for application to tender trucks.[143]

In early 1927, the Missouri Pacific retrofitted a 2-8-8-2 and a 2-10-2 with high-capacity tenders, each supported on a pair of six-wheel trucks. Each six-wheel truck had four powered wheels, incorporating the so-called Bethlehem auxiliary locomotive. Both these engines were used in the Dupo, Illinois, hump yard where high tractive effort at low speeds was particularly in demand. The tender boosters increased the tractive effort of the 2-8-8-2 from 94,400 pounds to 122,400 (30%) and the 2-10-2 from 81,600 pounds to 111,600 (37%). Steam had to be piped from the boiler to the tender; flexible joints took care of differential movement between engine and tender. Exhaust was piped through the tender tank. As each tender, fully loaded with 18 tons of coal and 14,000 gallons of water, weighed 305,000 pounds, there was no lack of adhesion weight; each Bethlehem auxiliary locomotive added a further 32,000 pounds. These booster-equipped engines moved trains of 4,500 to 5,000 tons over the Dupo hump, eliminating the helpers that were needed previously.

In the summer of 1927, the Norfolk & Western fitted one Y-3 2-8-8-2 with a pair of Bethlehem auxiliary locomotives under its tender and another with two Franklin reversible boosters for service in its hump yard at East Portsmouth, Ohio. In this case, the boosters replaced six-wheel trucks; the tenders weighed 128,000 pounds empty, 264,000 pounds loaded with 18 tons of coal and 12,000 gallons of water and therefore had ample adhesion weight. The powered tenders added 34,000 pounds of tractive effort for a total of 142,000 pounds.

The Norfolk & Western's Scioto division was fairly level, allowing a Y-3 to haul a 95-car train, weighing 9,500 tons, westbound over the 113 miles from Williamson, West Virginia, to Portsmouth, Ohio.[144] The hump yard at Portsmouth, however, forced the company to limit trains to 7,500 tons and these trains needed a Y-3 and a 2-8-0 to handle them over the hump. With the boosters, the Y-3 handled 9,500-ton trains over the hump unaided, including a test train of 127 cars, weighing 10,336 tons.

The same year, Bethlehem Steel tested one of its "auxiliary locomotives" at Altoona.[145] Because the test plant was not long enough to accommodate an engine and tender, where the booster was intended to be, the Pennsylvania modified an L-1s 2-8-2, replacing the trailing truck with the four-wheel booster. The steam pipes were carefully arranged to simulate the resistance of the piping with the booster in its proper place under the tender. The Pennsylvania found that, although the drawbar pull at low speeds was increased by some 10,000 pounds, the booster exhaust was not available for drafting and the blower had to be used to maintain boiler pressure. Although the booster increased drawbar pull by 18%, this was achieved at the cost of a 37% loss of thermal efficiency in the whole locomotive. The locomotive used for the tests had a total thermal efficiency of 4.9% in full forward gear, but only 3.1% with the booster cut in. On the test plant, the L-1s was hand-fired at rates up to 12,500 pounds per hour, generating 62,000 pounds of steam per hour at 620°F and 200 pounds per square inch.

The booster was inefficient in its use of steam, using 46 pounds per indicated horsepower-hour at 2 miles per hour, developing 75 horsepower, down to 29 pounds at 13 miles per hour and 380 horsepower. The locomotive was set up so that the locomotive and booster could be tested separately and in combination. On starting, the total tractive effort of locomotive and booster was close to the sum of the two; as speed increased, friction losses in the steam pipes reduced this total. The crew were able to maintain full boiler pressure in full gear at 80% cut-off with the booster cut in up to speeds of 7 to 10 miles per hour. At higher speeds, demand on the boiler exceeded its steaming capacity and drew the pressure down.

A superheated steam engine developed its highest power at a piston speed around 1,000 feet per minute. The speed on the rail at which this piston speed was achieved resulted directly from the driving wheel diameter. The urgent desire of the railroads to move freight faster therefore demanded freight engines with bigger driving wheels

than before. Tractive effort—the starting force and pulling power at low speeds—declined, however, with increasing driving wheel diameter. The booster offered a wonderful means of retaining high pulling power on starting and at low speeds, while increasing the maximum speed of which the engine was capable.[146] By adding to the number of powered wheels on starting, the booster also made it possible to reduce the factor of adhesion below the accepted figure of 4.0 without undue slipping on starting.

Boosters were among the distinguishing features of the superpower design.

11.3.4 Cut-Off Control

Using steam expansively by shortening the cut-off was essential to fuel economy. The control of this important function, however, was crude in the extreme and offered the engineer no means of knowing if he was using the most efficient possible cut-off, beyond his own feel, experience and intuition. The only measurement of cut-off available to the engineer was by notches on the reversing lever quadrant; the cut-off increment between notches was not constant; the actual cut-off at any one notch was not the same from one engine to another. Except when maximum performance was demanded, an engine could run at an infinite number of combinations of throttle and cut-off. Only one of these was the most efficient in any one set of conditions; the engineer had no means of knowing which it was. This unsatisfactory state of affairs received attention during the 1920s in several different ways.

11.3.4.1 Limited Cut-Off

The traffic demands of the 1920s required the existing freight engines to work for long periods in full forward gear, making little use of the expansive power of the steam, although best efficiency was obtained between 20% and 50% cut-off. In 1916, the Pennsylvania modified a class I-1s 2-10-0 so that the cut-off in full gear was only 55% and tested it in road service and at Altoona against a conventional L-1s 2-8-2.[147] The modified I-1s produced the same power output under normal running conditions for less fuel and water than the unmodified L-1s. The full tractive effort needed to start a train could be obtained through auxiliary ports in the steam chest, providing 80% cut-off. These could be made so small that steam flow through them became negligible, due to friction losses, at speeds higher than 2½ miles per hour, the speed at which train resistance typically dropped from its starting value to its running value. Slipping on starting, and the wear and tear that it caused to the engine, was reduced because the small size of the starting ports would choke off the steam as the wheels accelerated. The Altoona tests showed water savings between 11% and 39%; the 2-10-0 achieved a total thermal efficiency of 8%. The Pennsylvania built 598 I-1s's with limited cut-off between 1916 and 1923. Until 1926, the Pennsylvania was the only American user of this idea. A. W. Bruce points out that engines with cut-off limited to 50% to 60% tended to stall at low speeds because of insufficient overlap between power strokes; he estimates that about 1,000 locomotives were built in the U.S. with this degree of cut-off limitation.[148] Cut-off limited to 60% to 75% was one of the features of the superpower engines of the late 1920s.

11.3.4.2 Cut-Off Instrumentation

The steam locomotive has traditionally been sparsely instrumented, typically fitted with nothing more than gauges to measure boiler pressure and water level. Many parameters that significantly affected performance and fuel economy were unknown, impossible to measure or both. An engineer would run an engine as he had seen it done when he was a fireman, adding his own skill and intuition.

Railroads appointed traveling engineers, both as trainers and inspectors, but engine performance remained very much under the engineer's control for better and for worse. There was no diagnostic instrument that the engineer could watch—even if he had the time and inclination to do so—that would optimize the engine's performance for every combination of throttle and cut-off.

In 1924, the Union Pacific observed ten engineers, running the same locomotive over the same route with as nearly as possible the same load.[149] In these conditions, one engineer burned 17% less coal per ton-mile hauled than the average of the other nine. Another burned 45% more. Such wide variations due to personal factors alone cast alarming doubts on the fuel economy figures quoted in this book.

The Union Pacific came up with the facts that:

> The steam locomotive operates at various cutoffs, which are critically important in economy of fuel. With full throttle there is one best and correct cutoff adjustment for each combination of speed and load, and it is necessary for the engineman to know this at all times; otherwise a large amount of fuel is wasted. Unfortunately, it is impossible for the average engineman to determine and practice this varying degree of cutoff because of the lack of one essential item of information.
>
> The point of economic cutoff by which fuel is saved is known to depend upon the back pressure of the exhaust steam, and when a gauge is located in front of the engineman to indicate this back pressure, and its variations, he is for the first time placed in possession of exact information and knowledge that enables him to operate the locomotive with prescribed economy. It is of equal importance that he be in possession at all times of knowledge concerning the initial or steam chest pressure carried; in other words, an additional pressure gauge warning him if his throttle is not wide open.

Road tests on a 2-8-2 showed a 5% difference in fuel economy between 12 and 17 pounds per square inch back pressure with the same power output, cutoff being the only difference.[150] Repeated over the whole American railroad system, the potential for fuel saving was enormous. Power reversers controlled by small levers or hand wheels enabled the engineer to make repeated, precise adjustments of cutoff—if he was inclined to do so.

The Union Pacific responded to this issue by placing gauges in the cab that measured steam chest pressure and back pressure. Enginemen noticed that small changes in cutoff had disproportionately large effects on back pressure and that their engines used significantly less fuel if they adjusted the cutoff for minimum back pressure.

With two hands on a single gauge displaying steam chest pressure and back pressure, this cheap device had great potential. The engineer could set the cut-off for minimum back pressure, regardless of the actual setting of cut-off against lever position. Engineering staff could easily check the effects of different exhaust nozzles. Irregularities in valve setting and steam distribution would become more readily apparent than hitherto. If too high a water level in the boiler caused water to be carried over into the superheater, this would reduce the temperature of the steam, raising its viscosity and causing an increase in back pressure; the back pressure gauge would give warning of this condition. The back pressure gauge would also reveal a creeping power reverser.

This device caught on rapidly, being cheap to install. Railroads began to install these gauges in 1925 with 918 being installed, totaling 6,400 by the end of 1928.

New in 1928 was the Valve Pilot, developed by a New York-based corporation of the same name.[151] A mechanical linkage from the reversing gear drove a needle on a gauge in the cab, so calibrated that the needle indicated the speed at which the selected cut-off produced the maximum drawbar pull. A linkage to a driving wheel drove a second needle, showing the speed at which the locomotive was moving. With the throttle fully open and the locomotive developing maximum power, setting the cut-off so that the needles coincided ensured the most economical use of steam. If maximum power caused the locomotive to run faster than desired, power could be reduced by shortening the cut-off, in which case the needles would not coincide. A pen recorder charted speed and cut-off.

The first trial installation was on five 4-6-4s in 1928—possibly on the New York Central, an early user of 4-6-4s. The charts showed that no two engineers used the same sequence of cut-offs on any one route. Some used the widest possible throttle opening and cut-off shorter than 35%; others used the throttle to control speed, typically with cut-offs longer than 35%. In 1931, the railroad company tested a 4-6-4 equipped with a Valve Pilot and a coal-measuring device, hauling thirteen Pullman cars over 146 miles. On the first test, the engine was run at an average of 45% cut-off, using the throttle to control speed. On the second test, the engine was run at full throttle, using the cut-off to control speed, averaging 27% cut-off. The second test demonstrated coal savings of 2¼ tons, or about 16%. The company then made it a management responsibility to instruct their enginemen in the use of the Valve Pilot and to run at the shortest possible cut-off. By 1933 locomotive construction was at a low ebb but when demand picked up in the late 1930s many of the new engines were equipped with Valve Pilot.

All was useless if the engineer was not inclined to use it.[152]

> Great military battles have been fought with lesser uproar than that manifested when either "Bean Belly" or Joe took hold of a locomotive throttle. Joe dismissed the back pressure gauge as a device placed on an engine primarily for the hearing impaired or slow of wit. Both worked an engine half stroke and full throttle and if anyone benefited from their noisy activities, it was the coal mine operators.

11.3.4.3 Automatic Cut-Off Control

Fertile minds suggested that cut-off control could be continuously optimized by automation. This idea seems to have originated in tests carried out on the Cleveland, Cincinnati, Chicago & St. Louis in the early 1920s.[153] As the engine accelerated in full forward gear, friction losses caused a decrease in cylinder inlet pressure and an increase in back pressure, to the detriment of both power and economy. Shortening the cut-off reduced these losses because of the smaller amount of steam passing through the system.

This engine under test, a 2-8-2, developed its maximum drawbar pull at:

Lever position	Cut-off %	From (speed) (miles per hour)	To (speed) (miles per hour)
Full gear	89	0	12–14
Third notch	87	12–14	18–19
Sixth notch	80	18–19	28–30
Ninth notch	61	28–30	

Test engineers noted that back pressure reached 12 pounds per square inch at the speeds that dictated a shortening of cut-off for best economy, and that a relationship existed between back pressure and mean effective pressure. Shortening the cut-off each time the back pressure reached 12 pounds per square inch would provide the best possible ratio of mean effective pressure to back pressure.

The researchers also came to the interesting conclusion that:

> Shortening the cutoff to hold back pressure constant as speed increases results in constant draft and, as a result of this regulation of the quantity of steam passing through the superheater, practically a constant amount of superheat is obtained throughout a great range of speed.

Further:

> it would seem that operating an engine to constant back pressure should regulate the cutoff to sustain the maximum drawbar pull at all speeds and consequently develop the maximum drawbar horse power at each speed; and that in developing the maximum drawbar horse power at each speed the required number of pounds of water per drawbar horse power would be supplied, the draft and superheat being so regulated that the boiler would maintain adequate working pressure.

And:

> for any given locomotive, dependent on type, size and boiler pressure, there is a definite constant back pressure which, if maintained constant at all speeds above which it is first reached, will permit maximum rated drawbar pull to be developed. The back pressure is held constant by lengthening the cut-off as the speed decreases and shortening the cut-off as the speed increases. Should the boiler pressure change in addition to a change in speed, the cut-off adjustment will be made accordingly.

The pursuit of this ideal efficiency was beyond the capability of any engineer, no matter how conscientious, while running a train at varying speeds over changing grades and curvatures, yet millions of dollars in fuel costs were at stake.

The Cleveland, Cincinnati, Chicago & St. Louis developed a system of valves, responding to back pressure and linked to the throttle, that drove a power reverser to maintain a constant back pressure.

The Transportation Devices Corporation of Indianapolis developed Automatic Cut-off Control into a marketable form capable of retrofitting to existing engines, incorporating the company's own compressed air-powered reversing gear.[154] The device controlled cut-off in pursuit of a back pressure set point.

The Cleveland, Cincinnati, Chicago & St. Louis and the Nickel Plate tested Automatic Cut-off Control in 1923. Tests on the Big Four, comparing hand and automatic cut-off adjustment over the same run, showed 10% fuel savings per ton-mile, but also a 20% gain in ton-miles per hour due to more efficient operation of the engine. The tests also showed that the automatic device was slower to shorten cut-off during acceleration than the engineer, providing faster acceleration to line speed, but kept the cut-off shorter than the engineer when running. Engineers lengthened the cut-off in anticipation of grades and curves and were slow to shorten cut-off after they were passed; the automatic device sensed resistance from the behavior of the engine and adjusted cut-off only as needed. The engineer had the option to cut the device in or out at will. When cut in, the device operated only when the throttle was more than 60% open.

This remarkably subtle device was a forerunner of modern automation but was ahead of its time as applied to steam locomotives. Promising though it was, it never caught on. We may suspect that it needed near-perfect set-up and adjustment to deliver its benefits. It depended on a known back pressure set point; this would have been difficult to determine and would vary between classes of engine, indeed between one engine and another. By its nature, the device was restricted to locomotives with power reversers; these remained in a minority to the end of steam.

Section 11.4 Front Ends

By the 1920s, when the steam locomotive had been in service for a century, mechanical engineers knew that the dimensioning and placement of exhaust nozzles and stacks had large effects on efficiency but was still a matter of trial and error. Nothing ever replaced this means of drafting a locomotive furnace. Research advanced along two lines: to improve the mysterious inner workings of the smokebox and to replace this method of drafting.

11.4.1 Improved Exhaust-Blast Drafting

As late as 1920, even though locomotive designers and builders had been searching for the best nozzle design for decades, a committee reporting to the Traveling Engineers' Association annual convention was forced to admit that[155]:

> Your committee does not consider the information now available sufficiently complete to justify positive conclusions as to the most efficient shape of nozzle, and is only in position to report that the circular form of nozzle does not result in the highest vacuum and the least back pressure. As to what form will produce those conditions it is impossible to say without an extended investigation involving a long series of test plant observations.

A committee of the American Railroad Association reported a similar lack of success; road tests were affected by too many uncontrolled variables and they did not have access to a test plant. In fact, the task was hopeless until front ends could be designed from gas dynamics theory, using computation methods that would not become available until after the steam locomotive was commercially extinct.

By 1920 only a few railroads adhered to the ARMMA smokebox design standards developed in 1906.[156] The remarkable success of the Pennsylvania's tests on the Goodfellow exhaust nozzle garnered surprisingly little acclaim.

In 1918, the Norfolk & Western obtained improved results with a "waffle-iron" nozzle, the conception of which "was due to the fact that the engine (a class K-1 4-8-2) choked itself from back pressure and we could not get the speed out of it."[157] Compared to a 7-inch split nozzle exhausting though an 18-inch stack, a 14-inch diameter waffle-iron nozzle, exhausting though a 24-inch stack, lowered the back pressure from 11 pounds per square inch to 4.5 pounds, with only a slight reduction in smokebox vacuum from 8.9 inches of water gauge to 8.6, enabling the engine to develop an additional 140 horsepower. The Norfolk & Western engineers confirmed common knowledge, that the exhaust must completely fill the stack for most of its length to obtain the full piston effect of the exhaust jet; a reverse flow round the walls of the stack was to be avoided. The company ran about seventy special trains in developing this nozzle; the locomotive gained 300 horsepower as a result.

At about the same time, the New York Central found good results with two splitters at right angles to each other, slightly arched so as to cross 1¼ inches above the exhaust nozzle itself. This design made it possible to obtain the same draft with a 6⅝-inch nozzle as with a 5½-inch nozzle, so reducing the back pressure. The company also experimented with a nozzle in the shape of a ring, interrupted so as to produce five or six streams of exhaust steam, but two years later the company still had not run dynamometer tests to determine the efficiency of these nozzles.[158]

Meanwhile, the Santa Fe was experimenting with a newly built Baldwin 2-8-2, running between Belen and Gallup, New Mexico, to determine the best means of burning the semi-bituminous coal found in that area.[159] These experiments focused mainly on the design of the grate and the brick arch but also tried out an exhaust nozzle of variable cross-section, invented by one of the company's boilermakers, a Mr. Stevens. This device was ill-suited to the hostile environment inside the smokebox and tended to jam in one position. As with many such refinements, the engineers did not have the time to devote to its efficient operation, with the result that they left it fully open or fully closed, nor did they have any instrumentation to tell them what was being achieved. Only the French had any success with variable exhaust nozzles and adjustable petticoat pipes.

Better success came from automatic devices, such as the jumper ring used on the Great Western Railway in Britain. About 1919, the

Americans experimented with an automatic variable exhaust nozzle based on the premise that only 4 pounds per square inch of back pressure were needed for efficient drafting. This device opened and closed with each exhaust blast, thereby preventing it from jamming. No other details have come to light.[160]

Another attempted improvement at this time was the Lewis system, which used a stack of abnormally large diameter to maximize the contact area between the exhaust steam and the entrained air.[161] The exhaust nozzle was a long slot, extending across the smokebox and entraining the flue gases through a matching, rectangular petticoat pipe. The transverse nozzle spread the draft evenly across the tube sheet, whereas a conventional nozzle concentrated the draft on the center tubes. The petticoat pipe was mounted inside a rectangular outer stack, exhausting below its top and thus entraining more flue gases. Inside the nozzle were vanes, mounted on shafts which were geared together and extended outside the smokebox; at the end of each shaft an arm, carrying a weight, limited the back pressure to 4 pounds per square inch. Road tests suggested that the Lewis was a more efficient draft appliance than existing systems at a lower back pressure and a smokebox vacuum of only 2½ inches of water gauge; like so many other innovations, nothing more is heard of it.

The Southern Pacific used two different drafting methods in its oil-burning engines.[162] The nozzle exhausted through a two-piece petticoat pipe; the top and bottom parts could be raised or lowered independently, so varying the gap between the nozzle and the bottom part (typically 1 inch) and between the top part and the base of the stack (typically 4½ to 6 inches). It is not clear whether the adjustments could be made while the engine was running or whether they had to be made in the shop. The exhaust blast thus entrained flue gases twice, drawing gases from the top and bottom of the tube sheet. This was replaced by a downward stack extension that was also adjustable, drawing from about the centre of the tube sheet.

The Pennsylvania supplied a remarkable series of test results from Altoona in 1920,[163] testing ten different nozzle shapes on a superheated 4-6-2 with a brick arch to determine the maximum equivalent evaporation and least obtainable back pressure. We may assume that these were equated for cross-section area. For each shape the steaming rate was increased until no further increase was obtainable. The maximum steaming rate was therefore a direct measure of the effectiveness of the nozzle.

The nozzles comprised, with the Pennsylvania's ranking: A Goodfellow nozzle (1); a rectangular nozzle consisting of a circular section tapered to a rectangular section (2); a circular nozzle with a triangular-section splitter (3); a circular nozzle (smaller of two sizes) (4=); a circular nozzle with a splitter and a cone projecting downward 6½ inches below the nozzle tip (4=); a circular nozzle (larger of two sizes) (5=); a circular nozzle with four jaws projecting vertically above the nozzle tip (5=); a circular nozzle with four notches in its rim (6); a circular nozzle with two jaws projecting 6 inches above the nozzle tip (7); a circular nozzle with 4-inch projections flaring upward and bored hollow (8); a circular nozzle with two jaws projecting 12 inches above the nozzle tip (9).

The difference in performance between the best and worst of these was extraordinary. The Goodfellow nozzle supported a combustion rate of 9,400 pounds of dry coal per hour, while the four-notched circular nozzle underperformed even the plain circular nozzles, supporting a combustion rate of only 5,000 pounds of dry coal per hour.

William Elmer, of the Pennsylvania, experimented with multiple nozzle tips exhausting through a nest of conduits within the stack, foreshadowing future designs of double and multiple nozzles.

After running extensive tests between 1925 and 1928, the Missouri Pacific[164]:

reached the conclusion that its former standard front-end arrangement was, to an unnecessary extent, wasteful of power and fuel, because the proportions specified for the stack, petticoat pipe, exhaust pipe, table plate, etc., require a highly restricted nozzle tip in order that the locomotives may make sufficient steam. Moreover, the front-end arrangement of similar locomotives in the same class of service was found to differ greatly, indicating anything but a satisfactory condition as regards this important locomotive detail.

Changes indicated by the tests included a bigger stack diameter with the stack reaching as far down as the smokebox centerline, a new exhaust pipe with a bigger nozzle area and a base area at least as large as the exhaust passages in the cylinder saddle, a netting table plate instead of a solid plate and "in certain cases" four short diamond projections over the nozzle opening. The Missouri Pacific tests confirmed the superiority of the Goodfellow exhaust nozzle, but found also that no benefit accrued from increasing the prongs from four to six.

By the late 1920s, informed opinion suggested that big engines were getting rid of as much as 450 horsepower straight through the stack in drafting the furnace, yet there was still no consensus how to reduce this loss and each railroad made its own tests and reached its own conclusions on the subject.

Even the manufacturers had no firm ideas on the best possible design for the front end. In 1925 the Missouri-Pacific ran a three-cylinder 2-8-2, newly built by Alco, straight from Schenectady to the Altoona test plant.[165] Nothing could better describe the almost haphazard, trial-and-error state of knowledge that surrounded locomotive front ends, even as late as the mid–1920s, than the report on these tests.

As received at the test plant, the locomotive was difficult to fire and appeared to have insufficient draft. Because the locomotive was similar to the Pennsylvania L-1s (2-8-2), the test engineers believed that, with proper combustion, the boiler should evaporate up to 59,000 pounds of water per hour or about 12 pounds per square foot of total combined heating surface. After a running-in period, the locomotive was tested at 160 revolutions per minute (30 miles per hour), 50% cut-off, and wide open throttle. The resulting evaporation was only 48,000 pounds per hour, or about 10 pounds per square foot of total combined heating surface. The draft in the smokebox was 9 inches of water gauge. The engineers fitted a basket bridge to the exhaust nozzle, increased the inside nozzle diameter to 6½ inches and extended the stack downwards to about 15 inches above the nozzle. Trials with this arrangement showed little improvement in the strength of the draft. They then replaced the stack with one of the same dimensions as an L-1s, with 50% more area at the top of the stack, and re-ran the test. This produced an evaporation rate of 46,440 pounds per hour. The pressures at the top rim of the stack were small and most of them negative, indicating a vacuum of 4 to 7 inches of water gauge, which showed that the stack was not filled. The exhaust nozzle was then increased in diameter to 7 inches, retaining the basket bridge, after which an evaporation rate of 55,000 pounds per hour was obtained. The locomotive still did not steam freely. The test engineers replaced the basket bridge with a Goodfellow nozzle. These modifications resulted in an evaporation rate of 59,000 pounds per hour and later, 61,680 pounds—12.6 pounds per square foot of heating surface per hour, a 29% higher steaming rate from nothing more than tinkering with the front end.

Very few new locomotives ever went through that kind of testing and optimization, but went out on the road with whatever front end the manufacturer or the owner's designer had given them. This condition was inherent to the steam locomotive and the state of engineering knowledge and computing ability at the time. We can only imagine the loss of performance and waste of fuel that this entailed throughout the industry.

11.4.2 Fan Drafting

Some back pressure in getting rid of exhaust steam was inevitable, but every pound reduced the available power. By the 1920s, stationary steam engines with fan-drafted furnaces, ran on back pressure as low as 1 pound per square inch. By contrast, steam locomotives, relying on exhaust drafting, developed back pressures as high as 25 pounds per square inch. This resulted in long-continued but unsuccessful attempts to find some entirely different method of drafting the fire.[166]

Seguin tried fan drafting in 1835, as did Winans on the Baltimore & Ohio in 1839. Winans used exhaust steam to drive a fan forcing air into the grate from beneath; the steam then passed through a feed water heater. Neither of these experiments produced a result that was cheaper and more effective than the exhaust blast.

Tests carried out by H. B. MacFarland on the Santa Fe in 1911–12 highlighted the inefficiency of exhaust blast drafting.[167] Indicator diagrams taken from a 2-8-2 measured an average back pressure of 13 pounds per square inch when the engine was running at 57% cutoff and 26 miles per hour, losing 302 indicated horsepower. At the same time, the smokebox vacuum was 9.3 inches of water gauge; maintaining the gas flow rate into this vacuum consumed only 70 horsepower. The power consumed by the exhaust blast was thus only 23% efficient in producing draft. This was the first time anyone had estimated the efficiency of the exhaust blast; once again, the more the steam locomotive was studied, the more apparent were its deficiencies.

Engineers reasoned that a fan, driven by a steam turbine, could produce the same draft at a lower back pressure. H. Daubois proposed an annular vent on top of the exhaust nozzle. Exhaust steam flowing through this vent would drive a turbine, rotating on a vertical shaft; the turbine would drive a coaxial fan which would suck gases from the smokebox and exhaust them through the stack. Running the turbine would still require back pressure in the cylinders and the device would be more complex and costly to manufacture and maintain than an exhaust nozzle, assuming it could be kept running at all in the hostile conditions of the smokebox. The alternative was to run the steam turbine with live steam, which took power from the cylinders.

Frans Coppus, President of Coppus Engineering, Worcester, Massachusetts, proposed a substantially reconfigured locomotive.[168] (Coppus still makes fans at the present time.) The premise of Coppus's proposal was:

> In the use of the exhaust steam for drafting the locomotive fires the locomotive power plant differs in principle from the marine or stationary power plant. In the latter the boiler is an independent unit, while in the former the boiler and engine are interdependent inasmuch as the exhaust of the engine creates the draft for the boiler and the shutting down of the engine renders the boiler inoperative. Separate the two by substituting mechanical draft for the exhaust jet and there is no reason why the locomotive power plant cannot be fitted out with the devices that have been responsible for the low cost of power generated in marine and stationary power plant.

This premise was flawed. Exhaust blast drafting matched power demand; shutting down the engine did not render the boiler inoperative because much of the steam in a locomotive was generated around the firebox, which remained hot; the blower provided a substitute draft at such times. Coppus also ignored the fact that marine and stationary power plants ran at constant speed and were not subject to the space limitations of the locomotive engine.

Coppus mounted a fan, with its axis vertical, driven by live steam, at the base of the stack. The fan eliminated the need for back pressure

and allowed a larger-diameter nozzle to be used. A second fan, blowing into the firebox, augmented the exhaust fan. Exhaust steam went to a feed water heater and a condenser, both mounted on top of the boiler, and then to a cooling tower on top of the tender. Coppus's proposal received support from W. L. Bean, Mechanical Manager of the New Haven—father or proponent of several dubious inventions—and Dr. Goss. Railroadmen questioned both its practicality and the need for its supposed benefits. No Coppus locomotive was ever built.

In 1926, the Texas & Pacific modified a 2-10-2 with a Coppus fan, driven by a steam turbine, forcing 34,000 cubic feet per minute against 7 inches of water gauge into a closed ash pan, which was thus under positive pressure by contrast with other fan-drafting systems which replicated the negative firebox pressure of conventional drafting.[169] The fan ducted secondary air into the firebox through the firedoor opening. The company hoped that this device would enable it to burn lignite, without throwing sparks, and would reduce back pressure and increase cylinder power. The company installed Northern Pacific–type table grates with ½-inch holes, totaling 13% of grate area. They enlarged the exhaust nozzle to 9 inches, the stack to 39 inches. The grate was stoker-fired; the firedoor was kept permanently closed. The experiment was apparently successful, adding 400 horsepower to the locomotive's power output and burning lignite economically with no sparks. If repeated at all, this experiment did not gain wide currency.

In 1927, Professor Goss proposed a "turbo-exhauster."[170] Exhaust steam drove a turbine mounted inside the smokebox with its axis horizontal; a fan was mounted on the turbine drive shaft. The device was tested on a locomotive, but it is not clear to whom the locomotive belonged. Immediate problems were abrasion of the fan blades by cinders and reduction of the blade efficiency due to the accumulation of oil.

The smokebox was about as hostile a place as could be imagined; extreme heat, dirt, cinder abrasion, soot and rust all threatened any mechanical appliance. The exhaust nozzle and blower, inefficient though they might be, at least cost almost nothing to manufacture and included no moving parts.

Section 11.5. Frames and Running Gear

11.5.1 Counterbalancing

An abiding problem of the reciprocating steam locomotive was dynamic augment; as engines were built bigger, this problem grew worse. Designers were aware of this and, from the 1890s onward, devoted increasing effort to producing lighter moving parts, using improvements in design and metallurgy. This effort lapsed with the onset of the war; the USRA engines were rushed into service without refinements of design.[171]

Steel mills and railroad civil engineering departments continually tried to keep pace with the destructive propensities of the immense new locomotives[172]:

> The counterbalancing of locomotives has been a source of contention for years, the discussion being renewed with each successive wave of kinked rails.

Broken rails were still more serious, resulting in a witch hunt for the cause and many accusations between steel mill operators, locomotive designers and footplate crews.

Realizing that a complex interaction took place between locomotives and track, the American Railway Engineering Association and the American Society of Civil Engineers organized a Joint Committee on Stresses in Track in 1914. The committee delivered its first progress report in 1918 after four years of tests, followed by a second after another two years of tests.

The St. Louis & San Francisco, using a 2-10-2 and a 4-6-2, and the Illinois Central, using a 2-8-2, ran the tests on behalf of the committee. Of the three types, the 2-10-2 produced the highest dynamic augment—160% of its static weight at 50 miles per hour, compared to 150% for the 2-8-2 and 135% for the 4-6-2—because its main rods had to be heavier than those of the other two types. Curiously, the rail stress under the left-hand driving wheels was 20% higher than under the right-hand wheels; the researchers were unable to suggest reasons for this. The tests showed, further, that each driving wheel tended to both twist and bend the rails outward. The equalized suspension extended the dynamic augment produced by the driving wheels to the trailing and tender wheels. Six years of tests pointed only to the complexity of the problem.

Counterbalancing had to compromise between the rotating and reciprocating masses. This compromise was difficult to achieve in most locomotives but the 2-10-2s, with their massive reciprocating parts, were notorious in that this compromise was practically impossible.[173]

Counterbalancing was further complicated by the fact that the revolving and reciprocating weights acted in different planes. A locomotive therefore needed counterbalancing in roll, pitch and yaw. In 1926, H. A. F. Campbell commented, depressingly[174]:

> our big present-day power is badly balanced, some of it very badly, and this power is hard, both on itself and on the rail. The large Santa Fe type engine is difficult to balance at all, even incorrectly; the Mountain type engine can be balanced, but it is not balanced correctly on any two-cylinder locomotives now running in America.

Even at this late date:

the cross-balancing of the revolving weights has been done here in America on only one locomotive, a Santa Fe type in 1924, and with markedly good results.

Apparently, this locomotive belonged to its eponymous railroad and C. T. Ripley, Chief Mechanical Engineer on the Santa Fe, asserted that cross-counterbalancing was so successful that the locomotive developed almost no hammer blow, even at 45 miles per hour.[175] This was promising for the future.

Help came from developments in steel metallurgy. In 1915, an ARMMA committee recommended that the reciprocating parts on each side of the locomotive weigh no more than $\frac{1}{160}$ of the whole locomotive and preferably $\frac{1}{200}$; more sophisticated design and higher-strength steel brought this goal within reach. These same advances made higher boiler pressures possible which, in turn, permitted smaller-diameter, lighter pistons running in cylinders whose centerlines were closer to the locomotive centerline; this had a large effect on counterbalancing. As early as 1928, Campbell foresaw the four-cylinder, duplex-drive engines that the Pennsylvania built in the 1940s as a means of reducing the weight of revolving and reciprocating parts. The three-cylinder engine needed no counterbalance of the reciprocating parts, leaving only the revolving parts to be counterbalanced, which could be done exactly; even this benefit failed to sway management in favor of the three-cylinder locomotive.

It is no overstatement to say that counterbalancing would determine the future of the steam locomotive in America. The fast, powerful locomotives of the 1920s, 1930s and 1940s could never have reached their potential without effective counterbalancing.

11.5.2 Frames

The Union Steel Casting Co. cast the first vanadium-steel locomotive frame in 1907, using steel with an ultimate tensile strength of

No. 9000 was the first of the famous Union Pacific 4-12-2s, built by Alco in 1926, photographed at Denver, Colorado, on March 11, 1956 (Denver Public Library, Otto C. Perry collection, OP-17295).

The rear engine bed of a Norfolk & Western 2-6-6-4 (courtesy Norfolk Southern Corporation, ns1491).

70,000 pounds per square inch.[176] The same company cast the first high-test vanadium-steel locomotive frame, with 80,000 pounds per square inch ultimate tensile strength, in 1922 for a Norfolk & Western electric locomotive built by Alco and Westinghouse. The two frame members were cast separately; each one was 41 feet long and weighed 23,700 pounds.

In 1924, the New York Central combined the two frame members into a cast-steel "engine bed," comprising both sides of the frame and its internal bracing; cylinders and smokebox cradle were separate castings.[177] The referenced source provides no further information. Given adequate quality control, one-piece engine beds offered immense advantages in ease of assembly, rigidity and freedom from maintenance.

The first engine bed incorporating the cylinder castings, valve chests and smokebox saddle was cast by Commonwealth Steel, St. Louis, in 1926 for an 0-8-0 switcher built by the Terminal Railroad of St. Louis at its own shops, replacing thirty separate parts in the original, built-up frame.[178] This locomotive, No. 318, was donated to the Museum of Transportation, Kirkwood, Missouri, in 1956, where it is currently preserved. The same year, Commonwealth cast engine beds for five 4-8-2s that the Southern Pacific was building at its Sacramento shops. These were some of the biggest and most intricate steel castings produced to date, measuring 52 feet long, 10 feet wide and 4 feet deep, weighing 40,700 pounds.

11.5.3 Trucks

Truck designs proliferated over the years. Reports on locomotive construction from the 1920s mention several different types, such as the Alco, Delta, Woodward, Woodward-Commonwealth, Commonwealth-Franklin, Commonwealth and Blunt types. The sources consulted are not specific as to their design details or differences from previous types.

Two types of two-wheel trailing truck became the most common: the Alco and the Commonwealth.[179]

In the Alco truck, the axle boxes supported the weight of the rear frame extension through elliptical springs. A yoke fixed each spring seat, relative to the frame extension. A ball-and-socket joint accommodated vertical movement against the springs, while a sliding plate on top of each axle box allowed the axle to move from side to side under the spring seats, as shown in the accompanying drawing. The axle boxes were held in the truck sub-frame which was pivoted to the main engine frame. The early Alco trucks were spring-centered. Later models deleted the centering springs and replaced the ball-and-socket joint with a swiveling box containing toothed rollers engaging inclined planes. Harding (*Steam Locomotive Home Study Course*) cites lubrication difficulties as the reason for the change.

The Commonwealth truck supported the weight of the engine frame at three points: the pivot point of the truck sub-frame and a heart-shaped rocker behind each wheel. The axle boxes were sprung vertically within the sub-frame but were otherwise fixed within it.

General Steel Castings, manufacturers of the Commonwealth two-

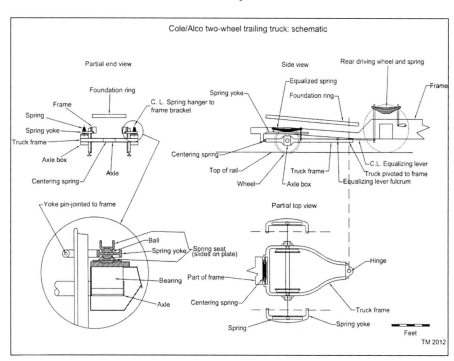

Alco two-wheel trailing truck (redrawn from Harding, J. W., *Steam Locomotive Home Study Course*, 2002 reprint, Vol. 1, 77-82).

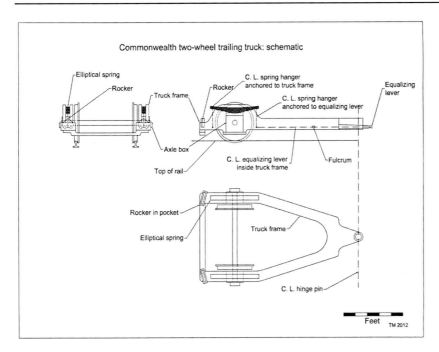

Commonwealth two-wheel trailing truck (redrawn from Harding, J. W., *Steam Locomotive Home Study Course*, 2002 reprint, Vol. 1, 84).

wheel trailing truck, developed the design into a four-wheel trailing truck of the same general configuration as the two-wheel truck. The Lima four-wheel trailing truck of the mid–1920s was, however, a radical innovation, in that the tractive force went through the truck frame, the main frame rear extension being eliminated.

With a booster, the trailing truck was an auxiliary locomotive in itself. These innovations were fundamental to American locomotive development after 1920 and were uncommon outside North America.

The high-speed locomotives of the 1930s were characterized by bigger driving wheels and a deliberate spreading of weight onto the front truck; the two-wheel truck was not strong enough to take the increased weight, favoring the four-wheel leading truck. Harding comments: "As for safety, there is practically no difference between the two-wheel and the four-wheel truck."

11.5.4 Tandem Side Rods

As manufacturers built bigger cylinders within fixed lateral clearance dimensions, the frames had to be placed closer together.[180] The stronger piston thrusts therefore acted on a longer lever arm, doubly increasing the racking forces on the crankpins, journal bearings and frames. In 1925,

Otto Perry photographed the tandem side rods on a Chicago, Burlington & Quincy class S-4a 4-6-4, No. 4004, at Denver, Colorado, on June 29, 1939. Baldwin built this locomotive in 1930, as class S-4; the Burlington rebuilt it in the West Burlington shops in 1938, as class S-4a. Note the Baker valve gear, Baldwin main driving wheel and Elesco feed water heater (Denver Public Library, Otto C. Perry collection, OP-3819).

Lima brought out the so-called tandem side rod to bring the piston centerlines inward toward the frames.

Conventionally, the main rod drove the outer end of the main crank pin; side rods, working inside the main rod, transmitted force from the main crank pin to the other driving wheels. One side rod was shared between two driving wheels, each side rod being connected to its neighbor by a pin-jointed tongue and fork. In Lima's arrangement, the end of the main rod was forked; the side rod behind the main driving wheel fitted inside this fork, transmitting force directly to the back driving wheel and reducing the load on the main crank pin by one-quarter in an eight-coupled engine. The side rod in front of the main driving wheel worked inside the main rod as before. The first locomotives to use tandem side rods were the Boston & Albany 2-8-4 and the Texas & Pacific 2-10-4s, both types delivered in 1925. On locomotives with conventional side rods, the pin joint for the side rod can be seen immediately behind the main crank pin.

On engines with tandem side rods only the main crankpin shows at the main driving wheel, later fitted with roller bearings.

This apparently small innovation made it possible to bring the cylinder centerlines together by as much as 10 inches, from 96 to 98 inches to 88 inches. This lent itself to the insertion of a massive casting between the front ends of the frames, incorporating the cylinder mounts, the smokebox saddle, the bumper mounting and the valve gear and guide supports. It could be expanded further to include the cylinders themselves. Lima considered that this would be impractical with conventional side rods. Tandem side rods even inspired Lima to propose a monstrous, rigid-frame 2-12-6 design with a 151-square foot grate supported on a six-wheel trailing truck.

Improved counterbalancing, engine beds, four-wheel trailing trucks and tandem side rods, themselves invisible or barely so, went far to define the ultimate American steam locomotive of the 1930s and 1940s.

12

Locomotive Construction, 1920–1930

The end of World War I caused uncertainty and unease among railroads and locomotive builders alike.[1] With the end of the war and the railroads still under government control, orders collapsed by 90% in 1919, although the shops were still kept busy with USRA orders from the previous year. New orders totaled a mere 164 engines for logging and industrial lines. The hiatus was short; big orders resumed as soon as the railroads were returned to private operation. In January 1920, the Union Pacific ordered 102 locomotives from Alco, Baldwin and Lima[2] and the New York Central ordered new equipment worth $53 million, comprising 196 locomotives, 265 passenger cars and 11,244 freight cars.[3] Domestic locomotive orders totaled 1,998 in 1920.[4]

This spate of orders crashed to 239 in the slump year, 1921. Orders peaked again at 2,600 as traffic boomed in 1922, but then declined throughout the 1920s. This decline in numbers was no reflection on the condition of the railroad industry, which enjoyed renewed prosperity during the decade, but resulted from the increasing size and power of individual locomotives. Orders of only 603 in 1928 doubled to 1,212 in 1929 as the railroads ordered new, modern power in antic-

ipation of a rosy future. The crash of 1929 and the ensuing slump brought this to an end.[5]

Between 1920 and 1932, orders for new locomotives from the Class I railroads totaled 11,356. "Installations" totaled 20,109; the difference—8,753—was rebuilt locomotives, indicating a huge rebuilding effort. Many of these rebuilds disappointed their owners, unable to stand up to the increased work demanded of them. During the same period, 31,798 locomotives were scrapped. As a result, the Class I railroads' locomotive fleet peaked at about 65,300 in 1923–4 and declined in numbers to 53,300 in 1932. Average tractive effort increased from 36,000 pounds to 46,000.

Section 12.1. Passenger Locomotives

12.1.1 The Last Ten-Wheelers

The 4-6-0 was obsolete as a mainline type, except for special purposes that demanded its particular characteristics.

The Pennsylvania built this class G-5s 4-6-0, No. 1966, at Altoona in 1923–24, photographed at Chicago, Illinois, on July 25, 1940 (Denver Public Library, Otto C. Perry collection, OP-14263).

The Pennsylvania exercised its formidable design and construction capability with a class of forty 4-6-0s, class G-5s, built at its Juniata shops in 1923, followed by another fifty in 1924.[6] The company chose the 4-6-0 wheel arrangement for a powerful locomotive for local passenger services, requiring fast acceleration to meet tight schedules over steep grades. These engines replaced double-heading with 4-4-0s and 4-4-2s. The G-5s was of conventional design with a 55-square foot grate, a superheated 205-pounds per square inch boiler and 68-inch driving wheels, offering a compromise between speed and traction. The engine weighed 237,000 pounds and developed 41,000 pounds of tractive effort.

The Maine Central thought the same when they bought eight 4-6-0s from Lima in 1924 for passenger and freight service on short, steep branch lines, in which they performed well.[7] With an engine weight of 182,000 pounds and 30,000 pounds of tractive effort, they were of similar size to the 4-6-0s used in Europe, particularly in Britain where they were ubiqitous.

Otherwise, construction of 4-6-0s dropped from an insignificant twenty-six in 1920 to only one in 1925.

12.1.2 Twilight of the Pacifics

New construction of 4-6-2s, as powerful express passenger locomotives, continued in the 1920s, although it was no longer leading-edge passenger power, the 4-8-2 having taken that role.

The 4-6-2 still had room for growth; the twenty that the Northern Pacific ordered from Alco Brooks in 1920 were slightly larger than the USRA heavy Pacific, weighing 314,000 pounds and developing 42,000 pounds of tractive effort.[8] The company bought them to haul heavy passenger trains—up to seventeen cars—between Dilworth, Minnesota, and Missoula, Montana, against grades up to 2.3%. Boiler

pressure was moderate at 190 pounds per square inch. A coal pusher was installed in the tender, but no power stoker.

When Lima delivered two 303,500-pound 4-6-2s, each developing 47,500 pounds of tractive effort—one to the Atlanta & West Point, one to the Western Railway of Alabama—in 1926, their 2,625 cylinder horsepower was at the top end of the power range for this wheel arrangement. With 64,000-pound axle loadings, they were also among the heaviest of their kind. These handsome engines were technically retrograde in having hand-fired 70-square foot grates and no feed water heaters or siphons. They were expected to haul fifteen-car passenger trains weighing 1,265 tons over 175 miles of rolling grades between Atlanta and Montgomery, Alabama, in just under five hours.

The 1920s saw attempts by some railroads to beautify their engines in the attempt to prevent further loss of passenger revenue. In 1910, the Chicago Great Western began rebuilding its twenty 1903 Alco 2-6-2s to 4-6-2s. Four at least (905, 915, 916, 917) were restyled in 1924 to resemble British express passenger locomotives, including maroon paint with gold leaf striping and polished steelwork; the result was an American locomotive trying to look like its British equivalent and failing to do so.[9]

The Baltimore & Ohio made no concessions to British style, but bought the handsome P-7 class of twenty 4-6-2s from Baldwin in 1927, named for U.S. presidents, developing 50,000 pounds of tractive effort from a boiler pressure of 230 pounds per square inch and weighing 326,000 pounds.[10] These were the most powerful 4-6-2s built to date. The 70-square foot grate and 3,450 square feet of primary heating surface were hand-fired. The Baltimore & Ohio painted its P-7's Pullman green with gold and maroon striping and gold lettering. These, and a single 4-6-2 built in the company's shops in 1928,

This Maine Central class O-4 4-6-0, No. 384, came from Lima in 1923, among the last new 4-6-0s, photographed at Bangor, Maine, on August 15, 1937 (Denver Public Library, Otto C. Perry collection, OP-12578).

Otto Perry photographed this Northern Pacific class Q-5 4-6-2, No. 2242, built by Alco in 1920, at Bismarck, North Dakota, on August 12, 1938 (Denver Public Library, Otto C. Perry collection, OP-13988).

Lima built this Western Railway of Alabama class P 4-6-2, No. 6689, in 1926, photographed at Birmingham, Alabama, on August 2, 1936 (Denver Public Library, Otto C. Perry collection, OP-15285).

The Chicago Great Western re-styled this 4-6-2, No. 916, in company shops in 1924, photographed at Council Bluffs, Iowa, on May 29, 1938. (Denver Public Library, Otto C. Perry collection, OP-4921).

Baltimore & Ohio class P-7 4-6-2, No. 5315, built by Baldwin in 1927, at Cumberland, Maryland, on August 7, 1936 (Denver Public Library, Otto C. Perry collection, OP-2515).

Otto Perry photographed this supposedly British-styled Delaware & Hudson class P-1 4-6-2, No. 652, built in company shops in 1929, at Montreal, Quebec, on October 4, 1930 (Denver Public Library, Otto C. Perry collection, OP-7307).

brought total Baltimore & Ohio 4-6-2 procurement to 216, of which the company was issued thirty USRA light Pacifics and rebuilt thirty from 2-8-2s in 1924. The company acquired another thirty-two from other railroads.[11]

The P-7's achieved remarkable fuel economy: 2.4 to 2.9 pounds of coal and 19 to 22 pounds of steam per drawbar horsepower-hour while developing an average 20,000 pounds of tractive effort. The 70-square foot grate allowed the firing rate to be kept down to 40 to 60 pounds of coal per square foot per hour.

In 1929:

> The Delaware & Hudson recently placed in passenger service a 4-6-2 locomotive, the general exterior appearance of which is similar in many respects to the general design of passenger locomotives used in de luxe train service in Great Britain.[12]

The company built three of these engines at its Colonie, New York, shops between 1929 and 1931. The boiler pressure established a new high at 260 pounds per square inch, producing 42,000 pounds of tractive effort. Like other similar attempts, the result looked like an American locomotive trying to look like a British one and failing to do so.

The actual British comparison was the 179,000-pound *Castle* class 4-6-0 express passenger engine, built by the Great Western Railway at its Swindon shops from 1923 onward.[13] A 30-square foot grate fired a 225-pounds per square inch boiler with 2,050 square feet of evaporative heating surface and 260 square feet of superheating surface. While the Americans were wary of three-cylinder designs, the British were building many classes of single-expansion, four-cylinder engines, of which the *Castle* class was one. Cylinders measuring 16 inches × 26 inches drove 80-inch driving wheels, providing 32,000 pounds of tractive effort. Hauling six-car trains, weighing 185 to 200

tons, these engines achieved average speeds of 75 to 85 miles per hour, peaking on one occasion at 90 miles per hour for 39 miles.

By the late 1920s, concessions to marketing were such that[14]:

> Several railroads are using color in the exterior finish of their locomotives. No doubt most railroads will continue to adhere to black as the most practicable color for use on locomotives, but it must be conceded that the use of other colors in pleasing combinations has a certain value in attracting favorable attention to the railroad by the public which it serves—at least while the paint is new. Perhaps some favorable attention might be attracted in some cases by the mere expedient of cleaning and polishing the conventional black.

Passenger trains on the Central of New Jersey faced grades up to 1.8% in the hills of eastern Pennsylvania and in 1928 the company bought five 4-6-2s from Baldwin to deal with them, class G-3s's.[15] These were handsome and substantial engines, weighing 326,000 pounds and developing 47,000 pounds of tractive effort from 230 pounds per square inch of boiler pressure. A stoker-fired 84-square foot grate burned fine anthracite and bituminous coal. A combustion chamber extended 3 feet ahead of the grate; three siphons and three arch tubes supported the brick arch. An Elesco feed water heater supplied water to the boiler. Automatic train control was built into these engines from the outset. In 1930 the company bought another five 4-6-2s from the same maker, slightly heavier and more powerful, class G-4s, making four classes of 4-6-2 used by the company, all from Baldwin—the six G-1s's built in 1918, the five G-2s's built in 1923 and the two latter classes mentioned above.[16] The last-built class used a driving wheel diameter reduced from 79 inches to 74 inches and 240 pounds per square inch boiler pressure instead of 230 pounds to develop 52,000 pounds of tractive effort—up from 47,000 pounds in the G-3s's—for a combination of heavy grades and tight clearance dimensions.

Baldwin built this Central of New Jersey Class G-4s 4-6-2, No. 811, in 1930, photographed at Bound Brook, New Jersey, on October 18, 1930 (Denver Public Library, Otto C. Perry collection, OP-2830).

Rutland class K-2 4-6-2, No. 84, built by Alco in 1929, photographed at Montreal, Quebec, on October 6, 1930 (Denver Public Library, Otto C. Perry collection, OP-14995).

Trains from New York to Montreal passed over the tracks of the Rutland Railroad.[17] Bridges, track and motive power combined to limit both tonnage and schedule time in through service. The motive power comprised 4-6-0s of 32,000 pounds tractive effort, the newest of which had been built in 1912, which needed double-heading to move more than nine cars between Troy, New York, and Shaftsbury, Vermont. After strengthening bridges and improving track in the late 1920s, the company bought three 293,000-pound 4-6-2s from Alco in 1929.

These engines were of conventional design and dimensions, with 67-square foot grates firing boilers supplying steam at 215-pounds per square inch to 25-inch × 28-inch cylinders. These and 73-inch driving wheels developed 44,000 pounds of tractive effort. Modern features included Type BK stokers, Type E superheaters, Elesco exhaust-steam injectors, Alco power reversers and cast steel engine beds incorporating cylinders and steam chests. The trailing trucks were designed for the future addition of boosters. The new engines handled 12- and 13-car through trains with no helper service, cutting half an hour off the schedule for trains from New York to Montreal.

Construction of 4-6-2s was down to ninety-three in 1925, from 223 in 1920. They were pushed aside in the search for ever more power by the 4-8-2s, 4-6-4s and 4-8-4s; many continued in service into the 1950s.

12.1.3 The Mountains Hold On

In the early 1920s, the 4-8-2s were the ultimate in fast, heavy passenger power. They found particular favor on the New York Central, which bought 600 of them between 1916 and 1944. The Pennsylvania bought and built another 300; on those two systems, no steam locomotive ever replaced them. Technologically, they were superseded by the 4-8-4s from the late 1920s onward.

The light Mountain was the last USRA design; the first ten went to the New Haven.[18] The company liked the type because it hauled heavier trains than 2-8-2s over territory where the customer base was not conducive to assembling trains heavy enough to make a 2-10-2 worthwhile. The 4-8-2 hauled trains faster than either of these two types. As soon as government control ceased, the New Haven ordered thirty 4-8-2s closely similar to the USRA design, differing mainly in the addition of an Elesco Type E-1 feed water heater and the planned retrofitting of a trailing truck booster. This class used the rare Southern valve gear. On their assigned route, these engines burned only 62 pounds of coal per 1,000 ton-miles between terminals; this figure ignored fuel burned firing up and between runs but, even so, was only half the all-inclusive national average for the time.

As soon as the Rock Island was returned to corporate management, the company ordered ten 4-8-2s, ten 2-8-2s and fifteen 2-10-2s from Alco, which built them at its Dunkirk plant.[19] Nicholson thermic siphons were specified for all of these engines.

The Rock Island was an early user of the 4-8-2 for heavy passenger trains. The design of the new engines left no doubts that they were intended for high power at high speed. Heavier than the original 4-8-2s by 29,000 pounds, the driving wheel diameter was increased from 69 to 74 inches. Although the grate area was the same at 63 square feet, the boiler primary heating surface was increased from 4,115 square feet to 4,690 square feet, most of this increase being provided by three Nicholson thermic siphons. A closed channel along the bottom of the boiler interior supplied the siphon entry tubes with cold water from the front of the boiler. The bottoms of the siphons were bulged into a 6¼-inch tubular cross-section to support a brick arch. A short combustion chamber projected 36 inches ahead of the throat sheet. The boiler heating surface comprised 216 2¼-inch × 22½-foot fire tubes; the superheater elements were

This New York, New Haven & Hartford class R-1a 4-8-2, No. 3334, built by Alco in 1920, was at New Haven, Connecticut when Otto Perry photographed it on August 18, 1937. Note the overhead electric wires (Denver Public Library, Otto C. Perry collection, OP-13712).

Otto Perry photographed this Chicago, Rock Island & Pacific Class M-50 4-8-2, No. 4046, at Liberal, Kansas, on May 26, 1940. Alco built this class between 1913 and 1927 (Denver Public Library, Otto C. Perry collection, OP-5562).

accommodated in forty-five 5½-inch flues. Boiler pressure was increased from 185 pounds per square inch to 200. Baker valve gear with Alco's own design of power reverser controlled steam to 28-inch × 28-inch cylinders. Company clearance dimensions allowed a height over stack of 15 feet 7 inches and an overall width of 10 feet 10 inches. The new engines weighed 369,000 pounds and developed 50,400 pounds of tractive effort, practically the same as the older engines; in tractive effort the bigger driving wheel diameter offset the higher boiler pressure and identical cylinder dimensions, but made for higher speeds. The Rock Island bought fifty-seven 4-8-2s between 1913 and 1927, all from Alco.[20]

The new 4-8-2s could burn more than 7,000 pounds of coal per hour, yet, of the three types ordered by the company, with curious parsimony, only the 2-10-2s were stoker-fired, as

it has been found entirely practical to meet the maximum service requirements on Mountain and Mikado type locomotives by means of hand firing and it was thought that the application of syphons would further improve the free steaming qualities of these locomotives. However, the Mountain type locomotives are designed so that stokers may subsequently be applied if found necessary.

The 4-8-2 was emerging rapidly as the new express passenger engine when 4-6-2s could not cope. The Missouri Pacific had 4-8-2 experience through its subsidiary, the St. Louis, Iron Mountain & Southern, which had been using seven since 1913. After being issued seven USRA light 4-8-2s, the Missouri Pacific bought five in 1921, although these diverged significantly from the USRA design.[21] The new engines were given 73-inch driving wheels for fast passenger service; bridge restrictions limited their weight. An innovation was the Harter circulating plate, a horizontal plate extending the full width of the boiler interior from just behind the feed water inlet to six inches

ahead of the back tube sheet, intended to channel cold feed water along the bottom of the boiler to the water space surrounding the firebox; steam pipes conveyed steam forming beneath the plate directly to the main steam space. It was claimed that this device increased boiler capacity by 10%. So confident was the company in this device that they underdesigned the boiler in the expectation that it would make up the deficiency. Four more followed in 1923.[22]

The reasons for procuring a particular design of steam locomotive were often highly specific. So it was with the Union Pacific's first 4-8-2s, a class of fifty-five bought in 1922 to haul passenger trains between Cheyenne, Wyoming, and Ogden, Utah.[23] The grades demanded that passenger trains be hauled by 2-8-2s; even so, the engine crews had to make up for slow speeds uphill with excessive speeds downhill, wearing out track and locomotives, no doubt with some degree of hazard. To solve this problem, the Union Pacific developed a 4-8-2 capable of faster speeds uphill so as to make schedule without excessive speeds downhill. The company began developing this design in 1920, with help from Baldwin, Alco and Lima, and took it to final design with its own staff; Alco got the contract to build the class.

A Duplex stoker fired semi-bituminous coal onto an 84-square foot grate, supplying a 200-pounds per square inch boiler containing 4,975 square feet of primary heating surface and another 1,240 square feet of superheating surface. With 29-inch × 28-inch cylinders and 73-inch driving wheels, and weighing 345,000 pounds, the engine was expected to produce 55,000 pounds of tractive effort and a maximum power output of 3,030 horsepower. Young valve gear, controlled by an Alco power reverser, drove 14-inch piston valves. The front driving axle ran in lateral motion driving boxes, allowing ¾ inch of play. In spite of all efforts, reciprocating parts for engines of this size had become enormously heavy; each piston weighed 939

Missouri Pacific class MT-73 4-8-2, No. 5308, at Kansas City, Missouri, on October 27, 1929. Alco built this class in 1921–23 (Denver Public Library, Otto C. Perry collection, OP-12979).

The Union Pacific bought this Class MT-1 4-8-2, No. 7010, from Alco in 1922 with Young valve gear, photographed at Cheyenne, Wyoming, on February 11, 1934 (Denver Public Library, Otto C. Perry collection, OP-17230).

pounds; each main rod weighed 864 pounds; each crosshead weighed 640 pounds. Design successfully reduced dynamic augment to 27% at 60 miles per hour, 39% at 73 miles per hour. Exterior pipework was located under the running board, giving an unusually clean exterior. The Vanderbilt tender held 12,000 gallons of water and 20 tons of coal.

The new engines performed better than expected. Design calculations predicted a power:weight ratio of 114 pounds engine weight per cylinder horsepower, comparable to the Alco experimental 4-6-2, No. 50000, at 111 pounds per horsepower. The first, No. 7000, developed 3,500 indicated horsepower on an instrumented run, hauling an eleven-car, 816-ton passenger train up a 0.8% grade at 50 miles per hour, thus 99 pounds engine weight per cylinder horsepower. This was the highest indicated horsepower ever recorded for a single-expansion locomotive in the U.S. up to that time.

As the 4-8-2 developed, dimensions that had been extraordinary only a few years previously became commonplace; twenty-eight 4-8-2s built by Baldwin for the Great Northern in 1923 illustrated the new normality.[24] Ten burned coal for service in Minnesota and North Dakota; the remainder burned oil for service in the Rockies and the Cascades. In the coal-burners, a Standard Dupont Simplex stoker fired an 88-square foot grate with a power grate shaker beneath a firebox with a brick arch and thermic siphons but no combustion chamber. The boiler was 22 feet long over tube sheets; designers tacitly abandoned any restriction of tube length to the 20-foot maximum for efficiency. The boiler contained 5,065 square feet of primary and 1,370 square feet of superheating surface and generated steam at 200 pounds per square inch. A Ragonnet power reverser controlled Walschaert valve gear driving 14-inch piston valves; 29-inch × 28-inch cylinders powered 73-inch driving wheels. The resulting locomotive weighed 365,000 pounds with an axle loading of 61,000

pounds and 55,000 pounds of tractive effort. The engines lacked feed water heaters or boosters, suggesting that acceptance of these devices still had some way to go. The Vanderbilt tender was enormous, carrying 20 tons of coal or 5,000 gallons of oil and 12,000 gallons of water, weighing 252,000 pounds loaded.

The ten 4-8-2s that the Southern Pacific bought from Alco in the same year were all of this and more. The 4-6-2s that the company bought in 1921 were already averaging 10,000 miles per locomotive per month, hauling eleven-car passenger trains over the 536 miles between Ogden, Utah, and Sparks, Nevada, against 1.5% grades, without changing engines.[25] The Southern Pacific sought to better this on the even more demanding route, 816 miles of mountain and desert between Los Angeles and El Paso. The design objectives were the maximum tractive effort within weight limits and sustained high power to haul twelve-car trains at 25 miles per hour against 2% grades. As with the Union Pacific's engines of the same type, a secondary objective was to even out speeds up- and downgrade. The designers paid close attention to minimizing the weight of reciprocating parts and got them down to 1,830 pounds, or 1 pound per 200 pounds of engine weight, 1:160 being considered good. These engines were oil-burners with boosters and Worthington feed water heaters. The dimensions were by no means abnormal—an engine weighing 368,000 pounds and developing 57,500 pounds of tractive effort, 67,700 pounds with the booster.

In 1923, the Pennsylvania built a prototype 4-8-2 at its Juniata shops for fast freight and heavy passenger service.[26] After more than two years of road and static tests, the company ordered 175 similar engines from Baldwin and twenty-five from Lima; this was the M-1, the first of which entered service in late 1926. The stoker-fired grate measured 70 square feet; an abnormally long combustion chamber extended 8 feet 2 inches ahead of the throat sheet, cutting the tube

Otto Perry photographed this well-kept Great Northern class P-2 4-8-2, No. 2507, built by Baldwin in 1923, at Whitefish, Montana, on July 22, 1939 (Denver Public Library, Otto C. Perry collection, OP-11903).

Southern Pacific Class Mt-1 4-8-2, No. 4300, built by Alco in 1923–24, at El Paso, Texas, on July 24, 1935 (Denver Public Library, Otto C. Perry collection, OP-15691).

The Pennsylvania bought 200 class M-1 4-8-2s from Baldwin and Lima in 1926. No. 6891 is shown at Huntington, Pennsylvania, on August 19, 1933 (Denver Public Library, Otto C. Perry collection, OP-14295).

length down to 19 feet. The superheater was an Elesco Type E; the tube layout comprised 120 2¼-inch fire tubes and 170 3½-inch flue tubes containing superheater elements, resulting in 4,700 square feet of primary and 1,630 square feet of superheating surface. The Type A superheater typically occupied 5½-inch flues; 3½-inch flues were typical of the Type E superheater. Boiler pressure followed Pennsylvania practice at 250 pounds per square inch.

So quickly was American locomotive development advancing that 65,000 pounds of tractive effort and an engine weight of 382,000 pounds, which would have been remarkable in 1923, were no longer so for an engine of this type in 1926. One hundred more, class M-1a, followed from Baldwin, Juniata and Lima in 1930.[27] The trend to ever-longer locomotive runs between servicing meant bigger tenders. The Pennsylvania carried this to new extremes with the M-1a's.[28] The original M-1 tenders held 17½ tons of coal and 11,000 gallons of water; the M-1a's had immense tenders, weighing 379,000 pounds loaded—almost as much as the locomotive itself—holding 31½ tons of coal and 22,000 gallons of water, running on two six-wheel trucks with roller bearings. On September 12, 1929, two of these locomotives hauled a 150-car train, weighing 12,600 tons, over the 259 miles from Altoona to Morrisville in 18 hours; the company said that one engine was in transit and the other could have handled the train unaided.

Only six years after buying five 4-8-2s to haul heavy passenger trains against 1.9% grades, the Missouri Pacific bought five more to keep schedules with still heavier trains.[29] As the dimensions of the new engines were almost identical to those of their predecessors, what was the source of their greater power—64,000 pounds of tractive effort, compared to 54,000? The answer lay in a 26% bigger grate, firing 30% more heating surface in an 8-inch-fatter boiler with pressure increased from 210 pounds per square inch to 250.

Alco built ten 4-8-2s for the New York, Ontario & Western in 1929, modeled closely on those of the New York Central.[30] A booster helped them to achieve 72,000 pounds of starting tractive effort. Alco built them with engine beds, contracted out to General Steel Castings; by 1929, engine beds were no longer a novelty, but were specialized enough to be contracted out.

New locomotive construction practically ceased in the depression but, curiously, locomotive development did not. When manufacturing resumed in the late 1930s, the 4-8-4 had consigned the 4-8-2 to obsolescence.

Railroads continued updating their motive power to meet demand that faded as the depression bit; orders placed in 1928–9 were still being filled in 1929–30. The Bangor & Aroostook bought four 4-8-2s from Alco, delivered in 1930.[31] These were quite small, at 303,000 pounds engine weight, with the limited objective of replacing 1924-built 2-8-0s. The 2-8-0s developed 41,000 pounds of tractive effort; the new 4-8-2s developed 50,000 pounds with another 11,000 pounds from the Franklin booster. Apart from 240 pounds per square inch boiler pressure, boosters and thermic siphons, few features distinguished the new engines from engines built ten years earlier, including a 66-square foot hand-fired grate and a Type A superheater. They did include back pressure gauges and superheater pyrometers. A railroad bought only what it needed; this outdated design sufficed for traffic conditions at the end of the 1920s and through the 1930s. Ultimately the company owned twenty-seven 2-8-0s and fifteen 4-8-2s, the last being one of each type built in 1945. In 1946, the company bought two used 2-8-0s and five used 4-8-2s, but dieselized three years later, scrapping its last steam locomotives in 1953.

In 1925, 4-8-2s were the second most numerous type built in America (220) and were among the last steam locomotives built in the U.S. Between 1911 and 1948, construction totaled 2,400.

12.1.4 The First Hudsons

The New York Central had been using a succession of bigger and more powerful 4-6-2 designs on various parts of its system since 1903, when the Boston & Albany installed ten, class K-1, from Alco Schenectady. System-wide procurement totaled 988 in a dozen different classes before the last K-5 was built in 1927. The earlier classes (K-2, K-3) developed up to 1,750 drawbar horsepower at 30 to 40 miles per hour. The K-5, introduced in 1925, was an altogether more powerful machine, with a power stoker and a booster, developing peak power of 2,500 drawbar horsepower at 40 to 50 miles per hour. Even so, in 1926, the company surveyed its passenger operations, and saw the need for a locomotive of higher tractive effort, still more power at much higher speeds and higher thermal efficiency than was obtainable from a 4-6-2. Smoother riding, cleaner appearance and greater reliability were additional requirements. When passenger numbers demanded it, express passenger trains were run in sections; the new locomotive type was to reduce the number of sections by hauling longer trains than the 4-6-2s. Although the company used 4-8-2s on a large scale, the fourth driving axle added materially to size, weight, first cost and maintenance expense. The result of conversations with Alco and Elesco was a new design, a 4-6-4 wheel arrangement with a much bigger firebox supported on a four-wheel trailing truck. Although the Boston & Albany had already received the first-ever 2-8-4 from Lima in early 1925, the New York Central and Alco seem to have arrived at the 4-6-4 wheel arrangement independently of the Lima design.

Alco Schenectady produced the prototype 4-6-4 in 1927 with such success that the New York Central bought fifty-nine more within the next year, and called it the *Hudson* type, class J-1.[32] A Duplex D-3 stoker fired an 82-square foot grate with cast steel grate bars. The 225-pounds per square inch boiler, 20½ feet over tube sheets, was curiously arranged with nineteen 3½-inch fire tubes, thirty-seven 2¼-inch fire tubes and 182 3½-inch flues for the Type E superheater, providing 4,490 square feet of primary and 1,965 square feet of superheating surface in an 83-inch diameter. Cylinders measuring 25 inches × 28 inches and 79-inch driving wheels developed 53,500 pounds of tractive effort with another 11,000 pounds provided by a booster for quick starting and acceleration. Total engine weight was 343,000 pounds. An Elesco feed water heater, a front-end throttle, a compressed-air powered whistle valve, power reverse and a back pressure gauge in the cab filled out the equipment and were typical of advanced locomotive construction at that time. The tender carried 18 tons of coal and 10,000 gallons of water.

The result was a leap in performance; the first of the class developed 4,075 cylinder horsepower at 66 miles per hour, weighing 98 pounds per drawbar horsepower, just below the much sought-after figure of 100 pounds engine weight per horsepower.[33] Fuel economy was excellent; with a train of twenty-six passenger cars over a 140-mile route, the locomotive used 2.3 pounds of coal and 16.3 pounds of steam per indicated horsepower-hour, including all steam-powered auxiliaries at a firing rate of only 67 pounds of coal per square foot of grate per hour.

Production locomotives developed 3,950 indicated horsepower at 65 miles per hour, 3,200 drawbar horsepower at 58 miles per hour, evaporating 57,500 pounds of water per hour at a firing rate of 5,500 pounds of coal per hour (67 pounds of coal per square foot of grate per hour, 10.5 pounds of water per pound of coal). Increasing the firing rate to 8,250 pounds of coal per hour (100 pounds of coal per square foot of grate per hour) increased the evaporation rate to 81,000 pounds of water at only a slight cost in boiler efficiency at 9.8 pounds of water per pound of coal. Coal consumption was a constant

One of the first 4-6-4s, New York Central class J-1, No. 5263, photographed at Buffalo, New York, on August 7, 1939. Alco built 145 J-1's between 1927 and 1931 (Denver Public Library, Otto C. Perry collection, OP-13405).

4 pounds per drawbar horsepower-hour over a power range of 2,000 to 2,300 drawbar horsepower.[34]

The New York Central ordered another 275 4-6-4s between 1927 and 1938.[35] The 4-6-4s were among the big successes of American locomotive design. They spread to several other railroads, typically in the dense passenger traffic of the northeastern U.S. Even so, such apparently obvious users as the Pennsylvania and the Erie were not among them, while the Delaware, Lackawanna & Western went to 4-8-4s.

12.1.5 The 4-8-4: The Ultimate Multi-Purpose Locomotive

Unlike the 2-8-4, 2-10-4 and 4-6-4, the ultimate American multi-purpose locomotive, the 4-8-4, crept onto the scene almost apologetically. The first, built for the Northern Pacific, was of similar dimensions and tractive effort to many of the 4-8-2s being built at the time and needed its four-wheel trailing truck to support a grate big enough to burn large quantities of semi-bituminous coal.

In 1926, the Northern Pacific ordered twelve locomotives from Alco with this new wheel arrangement, called the *Northern* type accordingly.[36] Other railroads gave it their own names: *Confederation* (Canadian National), *Pocono* (Western Maryland), *Dixie* (Nashville, Chattanooga & St. Louis), *Greenbriar* (Chesapeake & Ohio), *Niagara* (New York Central), *Wyoming* (Lehigh Valley). The four-wheel trailing truck was no mere adaptation of the Lima design; its function was to support a stoker-fired 115-square foot grate—it could be reduced to 95 square feet if better coal became available—with a combustion chamber extending 74 inches ahead of the throat sheet. The 210-pounds per square inch boiler and steam passages were designed for 225 pounds per square inch, if required later. An Elesco

exhaust steam injector was a novelty. The 426,000-pound locomotive had a high adhesion factor of 4.5; a booster increased maximum tractive effort to 59,000 pounds. The grate bars were of cast steel to reduce weight; even the stoker engine was placed in the tender for better weight distribution. The Baker valve gear was designed with full-gear cut-off slightly limited to 89%. The first assignment of these engines was to haul nine-car passenger trains unassisted against 2.2% grades between Livingston, Montana, and Missoula and between Jamestown, North Dakota, and Glendive, Montana. The Northern Pacific bought another thirty-seven 4-8-4s between then and 1943.[37]

The second engines of this type to appear were "modified Mountain type coal-burning locomotives of 4-8-4 wheel arrangement." The Santa Fe designed them and Baldwin built fourteen in 1927–9.[38] A boiler pressure of 210 pounds per square inch and 30-inch × 30-inch cylinders with 15-inch piston valves and Walschaert valve gear, working through 73-inch driving wheels, developed 66,000 pounds of tractive effort. Although the mountain service for which the engines were built would make a booster seem obvious, none was provided.

Like the Northern Pacific engines, the four-wheel trailing truck was not merely an adaptation of the Lima concept; the Santa Fe had been working on it since 1919. This truck supported a 108-square foot stoker-fired grate, sized to promote efficient combustion with low firing rates per square foot of grate. Even so, the combustion chamber was only 3 feet long and the boiler measured 21 feet over tube sheets. Two 3½-inch arch tubes and two siphons supported the brick arch; a third siphon was placed in the combustion chamber. Burning low-grade Colorado coal, the boiler evaporated 6.7 pounds of water per pound of coal at a firing rate of 4,125 pounds per hour (only 38 pounds per square foot of grate per hour).

The suspension was equalized and cross-counterbalanced. This permitted axle loadings of 70,000 pounds, 10,000 pounds more than

The Atchison, Topeka & Santa Fe bought fourteen 3751 Class 4-8-4s from Baldwin in 1927–29. Otto Perry photographed No. 3758 at Denver, Colorado, on February 4, 1940 (Denver Public Library, Otto C. Perry collection, OP-953).

the older 4-8-2s, while still placing less maximum stress on the track. The boiler was arranged for a Type E superheater with fifty-seven 2¼-inch fire tubes and 220 3½-inch flues. The Elesco feed water heater had a centrifugal pump, instead of a piston pump. The Walschaert valve gear had a small multiplying lever to lengthen the valve travel to 9 inches. The cylinders exhausted through a Layden four-ported exhaust nozzle. The cylinders were a single steel casting, weighing 25% less than an equivalent iron casting, keyed and bolted to an engine bed incorporating the boiler cradle.

The performance of these engines in the service for which they were designed—fast, heavy passenger service over steep grades and sharp curves—was spectacular. They started twenty-six passenger cars on level track, accelerating to 20 miles per hour in 1,500 feet, and handled nine cars against a 3.5% grade over the Raton Pass. Averaged over five round trips over the 348 miles between La Junta, Colorado, and Albuquerque, the new 4-8-4s burned 39% less coal per ton-mile than the 4-8-2s, themselves of no great age. The company bought another fifty-one 4-8-4s, all from Baldwin, in 1938–44.

Also in 1927, Alco built five 4-8-4s for the Lackawanna.[39] These were high-power, high-speed engines with 77-inch driving wheels, 250-pound boiler pressure and 65,000 pounds of tractive effort, an increase over the company's 4-8-2s, delivered only two years before. The company ordered another fifty 4-8-4s from Alco between 1929 and 1934.[40]

In February 1928, Alco delivered a 4-8-4 prototype to the Rock Island.[41] This was so successful that an order for twenty-four followed in 1929. This engine incorporated many features that were practically standard by the late 1920s: a large, stoker-fired grate, 250 pounds per square inch boiler pressure, Baker valve gear with power reverse, a feed water heater (a Coffin type), front-end throttle, thermic siphons (three in the firebox, two in the combustion chamber), a booster and

an enormous tender carrying 20 tons of coal and 15,000 gallons of water. The result, also common for the time, was an engine weight of 434,000 pounds and 66,000 pounds of tractive force (79,000 pounds with the booster). The company eventually owned eighty-five 4-8-4s, all from Alco, the last being built in 1946, making it one of the biggest users of the type in the U.S.[42]

At 3.3%, the Denver & Rio Grande Western route over the Tennessee Pass between Denver and Salt Lake City must have had the steepest grades on any main line in America. In 1929, the company, finding itself short of passenger power, bought ten 4-8-4s from Baldwin for use on this run.[43] A stoker-fired 88-square foot grate with a 41-inch combustion chamber fired a 240-pounds per square inch boiler, supplied by an Elesco feed water heater and containing 4,920 square feet of primary heating surface; the Type E superheater provided another 2,230 square feet. The locomotive weighed 418,000 pounds and developed 64,000 pounds of tractive effort. The new 4-8-4s shortened the passenger schedule between Denver and Salt Lake City by a whole hour to 25 hours, hauling fifteen cars between Denver and Grand Junction. They were also used in freight service with trains weighing 1,500 tons.

Walschaert valve gear drove 14-inch piston valves with an innovation never seen before and rare in steam locomotives. The radius rod and combination lever were connected through a link and a bell crank. This adjusted the valve travel as the engineer altered the cut-off and altered the lead from zero in full gear to ⅜ inch at 25% cut-off. Locomotive operation had come full circle to a built-in feature of the Stephenson link motion that increased lead as cut-off was shortened. An order of six 4-8-4s that Baldwin built at the same time for the Great Northern achieved a similar result by setting the eccentric cranks to increase the lead from ³⁄₃₂ inch in full gear to ¼ inch in mid-gear. It is a tribute to the specifics of steam locomotive design

Alco built this Delaware, Lackawanna & Western 4-8-4, No. 1504, in 1927, shown at Dover, New Jersey, on August 20, 1933 (Denver Public Library, Otto C. Perry collection, OP-7340).

Chicago, Rock Island & Pacific class R-67B 4-8-4, No. 5055, built by Alco in 1928, photographed at Pratt, Kansas, on September 6, 1937 (Denver Public Library, Otto C. Perry collection, OP-5586).

Baldwin built fourteen class M-64 4-8-4s for the Denver & Rio Grande Western in 1929. Otto Perry photographed No. 1704 near Tolland, Colorado, on November 5, 1939, after it had hit a cement truck near Kremmling (Denver Public Library, Otto C. Perry collection, OP-11096).

Otto Perry photographed Great Northern class S-1 4-8-4, No. 2553, built by Baldwin in 1929, at Spokane, Washington, on September 29, 1931 (Denver Public Library, Otto C. Perry collection, OP-11911).

and the failure of standardization that Baldwin should be building engines of the same wheel arrangement at the same time for two different customers, yet of markedly different dimensions.

The Baldwin Great Northern 4-8-4s were much bigger, with an engine weight of 472,000 pounds, burning oil over a 102-square foot grate with a 44-inch combustion chamber.[44] The firebox and tender were built for retrofitting to coal firing. They were one factor in shortening the previous 70-hour passenger schedule between Seattle and Chicago by seven hours. Impressed by this performance, the company bought another fourteen, class S-2, with 80-inch driving wheels, delivered in 1930; rigorous design made these engines 25 tons lighter than the S-1's. The Great Northern bought twenty 4-8-4s from Baldwin in 1929–30.[45]

The 4-8-4 was avidly accepted in all conditions of terrain and traffic. Widespread purchases between its first introduction in 1926 and the financial crisis of 1929 showed that it filled a pressing need. It became the first all-purpose American locomotive since the 4-4-0.

Section 12.2 Freight Locomotives

In the new economic and political environment after 1920, the railroad companies understood, as never before, that their survival depended on moving freight at unprecedented speeds, blurring the distinction between passenger and freight engines. The fast, powerful 4-8-2 was an agent of this change, first attracting attention in heavy express passenger service on the Rock Island in 1913, going forward in two USRA designs. This was only the beginning.

12.2.1 Last of the Consolidations and Decapods

The Western Maryland faced a combination of traffic, grade and curvature as severe as any, including 3½% grades with sharp curvature. To meet these demands with a locomotive of high pulling power at low speeds, the company ordered a class of forty 2-8-0s from Baldwin in 1920.[46] This wheel arrangement was cheaper to build and maintain than a 2-8-2 and typically put 90% of the engine weight into adhesion, compared to 75% for a 2-8-2. The small, 61-inch driving wheels allowed a firebox deep enough to accommodate a brick arch to be built above them without an unduly high center of gravity. A 75-square foot grate, fired by a Standard stoker, raised steam at 210 pounds per square inch in a boiler 15¼ feet over tube sheets. Total engine weight was 294,000 pounds, resulting in an axle loading of 67,050 pounds—high for the 90-pound rail on which the company planned to run these engines. This combination produced a tractive effort of 68,000 pounds. The new 2-8-0s were 30% heavier than the previous batch and produced 40% more tractive effort. The tenders were unusually large, containing 16 tons of coal and 15,000 gallons of water. The company bought ten more in 1923.

It is noteworthy that the Western Maryland ordered power stokers in these engines for territory where steep grades and sharp curves enforced slow speeds, whereas the Rock Island did not order them for their new 4-8-2s designed for high power at high speed across the prairies, apparently demanding higher firing rates.

Similar conditions prevailed on the Lehigh & New England, which ordered four of the heaviest 2-8-0s built to date at 301,500 pounds, developing 68,000 pounds of tractive effort, from Alco.[47] An 84-square foot grate—hand-fired—fired a 210-pounds per square inch

The Western Maryland hung onto the 2-8-0 wheel arrangement, and carried its virtues to an extreme, like this class H-9, built by Baldwin in 1921–23. No. 813 is shown at Cumberland, Maryland, on August 18, 1933. The small driving wheels allowed space for a wide, deep firebox set above them (Denver Public Library, Otto C. Perry collection, OP-19828).

boiler. The engines went into service in 1922, two being put to hauling 3,500-ton coal trains from Lansford to Pen Argyl, Pennsylvania, covering the 54-mile route at 20 miles per hour. The other two hauled 690-ton trains up a 2¾% grade out of Pen Argyl. The company evidently reckoned that short runs enabled a fireman to fire the enormous grate by hand.

The 2-8-0 type and Wootten firebox carried on in the anthracite country. The Delaware & Hudson procured a class of twelve between 1926 and 1930, building some in its own shops, buying others from Alco Schenectady.[48]

Following the success of their class I-9 2-8-0s, built in 1919, the Reading went to Baldwin for twenty-five more, class I-10sa, in 1923.[49] The company continued to order 2-8-0s because of their need to haul heavy coal trains where speed did not matter. Low-speed pulling power was everything and track and substructures permitted very high axle loadings. These new engines took the virtues of the 2-8-0 type to extremes, resulting in an almost grotesque locomotive, weighing 315,000 pounds and developing 71,000 pounds of tractive effort, made possible by a 71,000-pound axle loading. A Duplex stoker fired a mixture of fine anthracite and bituminous coal onto a 95-square foot grate in a Wootten firebox, with a Gaines wall and a combustion chamber, that hung out over the 61½-inch driving wheels, heating a boiler built for 220 pounds per square inch. The fat boiler, 96 inches in maximum diameter, was only 13½ feet over tube sheets, providing 3,315 square feet of heating surface. Two of the class were equipped with Sellers exhaust steam injectors. With track accepting 71,000-pound axle loadings, a 2-8-0 could now exert as much tractive effort as an early Mallet.

The Western Maryland stuck to its doctrine of maximizing adhesion weight through a two-wheel leading truck and no trailing truck, a vast firebox being set above small driving wheels. Retaining Baldwin as their supplier, they bought twenty immense 2-10-0s in 1927.[50] These engines were designed to run on 3.5% grades, some of the steepest mainline grades in North America at that time. The axle loading was 77,360 pounds. A stoker-fired 105-square foot grate in a wide firebox overhung 61-inch driving wheels. Boiler pressures of 225 pounds per square inch and 30-inch × 32-inch cylinders developed a tractive effort of 90,000 pounds from an engine weight of 419,000 pounds. The tender was one of the biggest ever built, with a coal capacity of 30 tons and a water capacity of 22,000 gallons.

With these special-purpose locomotives, however, the 2-8-0 and 2-10-0 types exhausted their usefulness in America. American manufacturers built substantial numbers of both types, however, during World War II for service overseas.

12.2.2 End of the Line for the Santa Fes

At the beginning of the 1920s, nothing—other than a Mallet—equaled a 2-10-2 for low-speed pulling power. They were in widespread use on major railroads all over North America, although procurement was quirky, some railroads using them in large numbers, others with similar conditions of terrain and traffic not at all.

Since 1914, the Baltimore & Ohio had been using thirty Baldwin 2-10-2s in both road and pusher service with good results.[51] Most of them were used as helpers on the 2% Sand Patch grade on the Connellsville division. The Baltimore & Ohio surprised the industry in

The Philadelphia & Reading Class I-10sa 2-8-0, No. 2005, at Erie Avenue Terminal, Philadelphia, Pennsylvania, on August 2, 1935. Baldwin built this class between 1923 and 1925 (courtesy California State Railroad Museum).

Otto Perry photographed this Western Maryland Class I-2 2-10-0, No. 1130, built by Baldwin in 1927, at Cumberland, Maryland, on August 18, 1933. Small driving wheels and a cantilevered frame extension make room for a huge firebox (Denver Public Library, Otto C. Perry collection, OP-19839).

1923 by ordering seventy-five more 2-10-2s—fifty from Baldwin and twenty-five from Lima—as class S-1. These had no greater tractive effort than the original class S, but were intended to be faster and more versatile. A stoker-fired 88-square foot grate, with a brick arch on five arch tubes, fired an 88-inch diameter boiler with 5,270 square feet of primary and 1,510 square feet of superheating surface, producing steam at 220 pounds per square inch. Supplying this boiler required injectors with a capacity of 6,000 gallons per hour, each. Cylinders, 30-inch × 32-inch, drove 64-inch driving wheels, the biggest diameter ever applied to a ten-coupled engine. The result was an engine weighing 436,000 pounds and delivering 84,000 pounds of tractive effort. Notably absent were a booster and a feed water heater. The enormous Vanderbilt tender carried 23 tons of coal and 15,800 gallons of water. The frames were still of conventional construction, with several members bolted together; the main frames were steel castings 6 inches thick. Orders totaled 125 by 1926.[52]

Of similar dimensions and appearance, but more powerful yet were the thirty oil-burning 2-10-2s that Baldwin supplied to the Great Northern the same year.[53] Baldwin managed to fit a boiler of even greater diameter—102 inches tapering to 90 inches—into the clearance dimensions, 21 feet over tube sheets, and to fit in 5,610 square feet of primary and 1,520 square feet of superheating surface. With 210 pounds per square inch boiler pressure and 31-inch × 32-inch cylinders, these engines weighed 422,000 pounds and developed 87,000 pounds of tractive force; some of the class had boosters, providing another 10,000 pounds. The Great Northern bought them specifically to replace Mallets on freight duty in the Rocky Mountains, planning to double-head 3,000-ton freight trains up 12 miles of 1.8% grade. Enormous Vanderbilt tenders carrying 5,000 gallons of oil and 15,000 gallons of water were intended to eliminate water stops, cutting the fast freight schedule across the mountains by nearly an hour.

Construction of 2-10-2s went on through the 1920s, although the new superpower locomotives outclassed them. Baldwin built the last for the Reading in 1931.[54] Drury records total procurement at 2,295, including 108 in Canada.

12.2.3 The Union Pacific Type

The years 1925–6 were extraordinary for American freight power, equaling 1903–04 and 1910–12 in their impact. Even as the railroads were digesting the superpower 2-8-4s and 2-10-4s, Alco and the Union Pacific unveiled the biggest rigid-frame reciprocating steam locomotive ever constructed in quantity, the famous 4-12-2s.[55]

Union Pacific heavy freight power of the early 1920s comprised 2-8-8-0 Mallets and 2-10-2s. The Mallets had enormous pulling power and good fuel economy but, with a 20 miles per hour speed limit, were so slow that they could not be used as road engines when traffic was heavy. The 1917-built 2-10-2s were faster but lacked the Mallets' pulling power.

In 1925, the company bought two, three-cylinder 4-10-2s, dimensioned as closely as possibly to the 2-10-2s for the most direct possible comparison between two- and three-cylinder configurations. The 4-10-2s handled 20% more tonnage than the 2-10-2s for 16% less fuel per ton-mile.

The Union Pacific then consulted with Alco to develop an engine with Mallet pulling power but good for speeds up to 40 miles per hour. Putting the necessary power into a 59,000-pound axle load limit needed six pairs of driving wheels. This was not possible with two cylinders driving one axle, hence the three-cylinder configuration, driving on two axles and distributing stresses more evenly over the frame. The result was the 4-12-2. The definitive work on these engines is the two-volume study by William Kratville and John E. Bush: *The Union Pacific Type*. Volume I was published by Autoliner Inc., Omaha, Nebraska, 1990. Volume II was published by the authors in 1995.

Accommodating this wheel base to the existing curves needed lateral motion devices on the end driving wheels and a four-wheel

Baldwin and Lima built the Baltimore & Ohio's class S-1 2-10-2s in 1923–26. Otto Perry photographed No. 6153 at Cumberland, Maryland, on August 7, 1936 (Denver Public Library, Otto C. Perry collection, OP-2531).

Great Northern class Q-1 2-10-2, No. 2104, built by Baldwin in 1923, photographed at Wiota, Montana, on August 10, 1938. This one has been converted to coal firing (Denver Public Library, Otto C. Perry collection, OP-11892).

"Union Pacific freight power of the early 1920s." Alco built this class MC-2 2-8-8-0, No. 3606, in 1918. When Otto Perry photographed it at Kamela, Oregon, on July 29, 1938, it was still in compound configuration, but with a Worthington feed water heater added (Denver Public Library, Otto C. Perry Collection, OP-16958).

Alco championed the 3-cylinder locomotive and built the Union Pacific class UP-1 4-12-2s in 1926. No. 9010 is shown near Bosler, Wyoming, on October 8, 1939 (Denver Public Library, Otto C. Perry collection, OP-19086).

leading truck. The crank axle design needed a driving wheel diameter of 67 inches, up from the 63 inches of the 2-10-2 and 4-10-2, which made for a faster engine. A boiler pressure of 220 pounds per square inch, driving through three 27-inch cylinders, resulted in 96,700 pounds of tractive effort with an adhesion factor of only 3.7. The company did not see the need for a booster.

The grate was a monstrous 108 square feet, fired by an Elvin stoker from a 21-ton coal bunker in the Vanderbilt tender. The firebox contained a brick arch supported on five arch tubes, but no siphons. The boiler, 22 feet over tube sheets, contained 5,855 square feet of primary and 2,560 square feet of superheating surface in a Type E superheater. Elements in 222 3½-inch flues provided the very high superheating surface area; only forty 3½-inch flues were unoccupied by superheater elements. A Worthington feed water heater supplied the boiler from a 15,000-gallon tender tank. The resulting engine weighed 495,000 pounds and developed up to 4,900 indicated horsepower. The Union Pacific bought fifteen as a first order; later they totaled eighty-nine.

Eastbound freights were made up at Ogden, Utah, in trains averaging 3,800 tons. A Mallet and a helper took the train up the 1.2% ruling grade as far as Wahsatch, where the helper was cut off, leaving the Mallet to complete the 176 miles to Green River, Wyoming. A 4-12-2 took the train over varying grades, up to 0.8% adverse, for the 250 miles to Laramie. Another Mallet took the train over Sherman Summit to Cheyenne. A 2-10-2 took the train over descending grades to North Platte, Nebraska. The 4-12-2s also handled 6,700-ton coal trains against grades up to 0.5%; when displaced by the Challengers to Kansas and Nebraska, they moved 100 to 150-car trains at 45 to 50 miles per hour.[56] Typical runs were accomplished at very low sus-

tained firing rates of 50 to 77 pounds of coal per square foot of grate per hour, achieving an equivalent evaporation of 8.9 pounds of water per pound of dry coal, resulting in coal consumptions of 65 to 75 pounds of coal per thousand gross ton-miles. Compared to the Mallets, still only seven years old, the 4-12-2s hauled 80% more ton-miles per hour for just under half the fuel per gross ton-mile, with trailing loads of 3,500 to 5,500 tons. According to Kratville and Bush, they were never popular with Union Pacific employees because they were difficult to maintain.

The Union Pacific 4-12-2s were the only twelve-coupled locomotives built in the U.S.; the last were built in 1930. Small numbers of twelve-coupled locomotives were built in Europe.

12.2.4 Mighty Mikados

The USRA did little to slake the railroads' thirst for new power of their own choosing. As early as 1921, the Missouri Pacific bought fifty new locomotives from Alco: fifteen 0-6-0 switchers, twenty-five 2-8-2s, five 4-6-2s, and five 4-8-2s. The switchers and 4-6-2s resembled previous engines of those types; the 2-8-2s and 4-8-2s were markedly developed from the USRA types.[57]

The new 2-8-2s developed 10% more tractive effort than the USRA light 2-8-2s. Innovations included Duplex Type D power stokers, Alco power reversers and Harter plates. Two were built with boosters; the remainder were designed for retrofitting. These engines handled 13% more tonnage than the engines of the same class without boosters and hauled their full rated tonnage up a five-mile grade at full throttle, in full forward gear, and with the booster cut in, with no loss of boiler pressure. Engines without the booster weighed 320,000 pounds and developed 60,000 pounds of tractive effort. The booster

Union Pacific class UP-1 4-12-2, No. 9006, built by Alco in 1926, is shown near Julesburg, Colorado, on June 19, 1938. The air pumps have been moved from the smokebox door to the sides of the locomotive as part of the Third Link revision program of the 1930s, described by Kratville and Bush (Denver Public Library, Otto C. Perry collection, OP-17303).

added 7,000 pounds to the weight and 10,000 pounds to the tractive effort.

Having got through bankruptcy, and having attracted top engineering talent, Lima began to produce innovative designs that would have pivotal effects on the American railroad industry for the next thirty years.

In 1921, the company built six high-performance 2-8-2s for the New York, Chicago & St. Louis, better known as the Nickel Plate.[58] These engines were based on the USRA light 2-8-2, but with innovations. Most important was a booster built into the trailing trucks of two of the engines, with provision to retrofit the other four. The booster added 10,000 pounds of tractive effort, for a total of 64,000 pounds. One of these engines handled a train of 3,850 tons between Conneaut, Ohio, and Buffalo, New York, 23% more than the rated tonnage for an engine of that size without a booster. A Duplex stoker fired a 67-square foot grate beneath a brick arch supported on arch tubes, heating a 200-pounds per square inch boiler with 3,780 square feet of primary heating surface and 880 square feet of superheating surface. Apparently, the originals did not have feed water heaters or front-end throttles. A Ragonnet power reverser controlled Walschaert valve gear. These engines were not radical in their changes from the USRA design, but Lima designed them with engine and shop crews in mind.

In the summer of 1922, the Michigan Central, a subsidiary of the New York Central, put an innovative 2-8-2, No. 8000, into fast freight service, representing a marked advance over previous designs.[59] Although built by Lima,

The locomotive was planned and constructed under the personal direction of President A. H. Smith of the New York Central Lines, who speci-

fied the several most important main accomplishments to be sought by the new design and made provision for the use of every up-to-date improvement of proved worth, brought to the last degree of refinement for economy and efficiency. The engine is of Mikado type, but contains many features never before incorporated in any locomotive.

The design objectives were extravagant:

Locomotive No. 8000 is considered the last word in efficiency and economy in freight motive power. The principal advantages which it is expected to demonstrate are the following:

(1) For its weight, it will deliver more power than any other locomotive in the world.

(2) It will deliver more power per ton of coal consumed than any locomotive ever built.

It will prove a locomotive easier to operate and repair than its predecessors, this making for quick turn arounds and safety.

On June 30, 1922, this engine handled a 147-car train, weighing 10,039 tons, between Detroit and Toledo, unassisted, reaching a speed of 18 miles per hour. The same engine was run light at speeds up to 70 miles per hour. Specific evaporation was 9.7 pounds of water per pound of coal, a high figure for the firing rates being used. Considering that its dimensions resembled those of existing 2-8-2s— indeed the Michigan Central already had a well-designed 2-8-2, class H-7e—how were these ambitions achieved?

The answer lay in a large number of well-considered innovations and refinements, insignificant in themselves but potent in combination. The grate area was 66 square feet, fired by an Elvin stoker, selected for its light weight. An American Arch Co. Type P two-row brick arch was supported on eight 3½-inch arch tubes; this was a

Alco built 170 class MK-63 2-8-2s for the Missouri Pacific between 1921 and 1925. No. 1402 is shown at Pueblo, Colorado, on April 4, 1937 (Denver Public Library, Otto C. Perry collection, OP-12950).

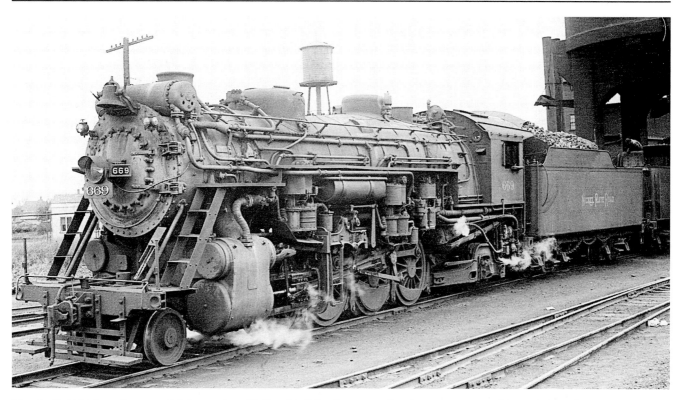

Lima built 61 high-performance 2-8-2s, versions H-6b to H-6f, for the New York, Chicago & St. Louis (the Nickel Plate) between 1920 and 1924. No. 669 is shown at Conneaut, Ohio, on August 24, 1933 (Denver Public Library, Otto C. Perry collection, OP-13679).

Michigan Central 2-8-2, No. 8000, built by Lima in 1922. The location, date and occasion of this photograph are uncertain (courtesy California State Railroad Museum, Railway & Locomotive Historical Society Collection, Negative 39077cn).

novel design of brick arch to promote water circulation by doubling the number of arch tubes. The sources consulted have not supplied details. Steam was generated at 200 pounds per square inch in a boiler containing 4,580 square feet of primary heating surface and 1,780 square feet of superheating surface. The boiler was untapered, 86 inches in diameter and certainly the maximum possible heating surface was fitted into the available cross-section. Starting a new trend, the boiler was fitted with 253 3¼-inch fire tubes, a high proportion of which contained the elements of a Superheater Co. Type E superheater, providing a higher degree of superheat and better heat recovery (evidenced by a lower smokebox gas temperature) than the Type A. (By 1925 the manufacturing company name was being printed as "Elesco"—Locomotive Superheater Co., shortened to L. S. Co.) The 28-inch cylinders were of 1 inch greater diameter than those on the H-7e; this and the acceptance of a lower adhesion ratio than the H-7e (3.9 vs. 4.2) gave the new engine 8% more tractive effort for 2% more engine weight. The new engine weighed 334,000 pounds. Baker valve gear drove generously sized 14-inch piston valves with an extralong 8¾-inch travel. A booster in the trailing truck gave it a maximum tractive effort of 74,500 pounds. The booster exhaust went through the stack, helping to draft the fire. Heat-treated chrome-vanadium steel, hollow axles and hollow crankpins lightened the reciprocating masses, halving the dynamic augment of the H-7e. An Elesco feed water heater, with the heat exchanger mounted across the smokebox brow and the pump mounted above and behind the left-hand cylinders, delivered water to the boiler at 225°F. The throttle control rod, jointed to compensate for expansion, ran along the outside of the boiler to a front-end throttle. The stoker, air pump, feed water pump, booster engine and headlight turbo-generator were supplied with superheated steam; as these could consume up to 25% of total steam generation, this innovation was significant. A square steam dome, containing a water separator, fed steam into an external dry pipe to the superheater. A manual shut-off valve at the steam dome made it possible to access the throttle valve while the boiler was still under pressure. Crew ergonomy was studied; besides the power stoker, the cab was fitted with a power grate shaker, a Franklin Type D screw-type, air-assisted, precision power reverser and even a pneumatic whistle valve. Controls were within easy reach of the crew seats. The tender carried 10,000 gallons of water and 16 tons of coal; a water scoop beneath the tender reduced the number of water stops on routes with track pans. Every detail was thought through; redesign of the brake rigging removed nearly a ton of weight. The New York Central bought another 301 of these engines from Lima and Alco, classes H-10a and H-10b, between 1922 and 1924. They proved capable of sustained high power at high speed; burning 6,000 pounds of coal per hour, they produced 1,350 drawbar horsepower continuously, 35% more than the H-7e. An engine of this class hauled a 77-car train for 90 miles non-stop at an average speed of 47 miles per hour.

In 1925, 2-8-2s were still the most numerous of all types being built (257) and, with 14,100 built between 1905 and 1930, were the fifth most numerous of all American locomotive types. The improved Mikados just described were the springboard for the superpower locomotive.

12.2.5 Superpower: The Berkshires

Lima continued to develop the design of the Michigan Central 2-8-2 and delivered the first of a new type, the 2-8-4, to the Boston & Albany at Selkirk, New York, in February 1925.[60] If the 2-8-2's design goals were extravagant, plans for the new type were even more so. In drag freight service, it was to haul the same trailing load as the 8000, but using 20% less coal; in fast freight service it was to haul

The Cleveland, Cincinnati, Chicago & St. Louis class H-7e 2-8-2, built by Alco in 1920, was common to that railroad and to the Michigan Central. No. 6150 is shown at Indianapolis, Indiana, on November 4, 1927 (Denver Public Library, Otto C. Perry collection, OP-13437).

New York Central class H-10a 2-8-2, No. 5, at Indianapolis, Indiana, on September 22, 1930. Alco and Lima built 190 H-10a's in 1922–23 (Denver Public Library, Otto C. Perry collection, OP-13326).

the same train as the 8000 at the same speed for 12% less coal. The resulting locomotive was among the most revolutionary developments in American locomotive design. The Boston & Albany called it class A-1, No. 1, as heralding a new era in steam locomotive development, which it did.

Many dimensions were the same as the 8000, making the differences especially interesting. A four-wheel trailing truck supported a 100-square foot grate, compared to the 8000's 66-square feet. Cylinder and driving wheel dimensions were the same, indeed the new engine developed only 4% more tractive effort (69,000 pounds) than the 8000; adhesion weight was 248,000 pounds in both engines—62,000 pounds axle loading. The real issues were power and fuel economy. Boiler pressure was up from 200 pounds per square inch to 240. Although both types had the Type E superheater, Lima packed more heating surface into the boiler—12% more evaporative surface in the flues, tubes and firebox, 18% more superheating surface. Lima limited full-gear cut-off to 60% (full stroke in the 8000); the higher boiler pressure compensated for the loss in mean effective pressure. This allowed Lima to reduce the adhesion factor from an already low 3.7 in the 8000 to 3.6 in the new engine. In 1923, the New York Central ran standing tests at Gardenville and starting and acceleration tests at Ashtabula; the results of these tests and the voluminous Pennsylvania test plant bulletins went into the design of the boiler and cylinders of the new engine.[61]

Cast-steel cylinders saved 4,000 pounds weight. As far back as 1911, Alco No. 50000 had cast-steel cylinders, but making high-quality steel castings, incorporating the valve chambers and steam passages, was a project of the most daunting complexity, the success of which was an important precursor to the 2-8-4 design. This casting was a project in itself, which the Ohio Steel Foundry Co. helped Lima to develop.[62]

The four-wheel trailing truck, a massive structure articulated to the frame like the front frame of a Mallet, was an innovation distinct from existing two-wheel trucks. All buffing and pulling forces produced by the locomotive ran through this truck and not through a rear frame extension, as with existing two-wheel trucks. A booster drove the rear axle, which had 45-inch wheels, while the front truck wheel diameter was only 36 inches. The 45-inch diameter increased the maximum booster engagement speed. The four driving wheels on each side were equalized, forming a three-point suspension with the leading truck; the two wheels on each side of the trailing truck were equalized, forming a three-point suspension with the hinge connection to the back of the frame. The trailing truck carried a capacious ash pan; the space between the top of the ash pan and the foundation ring allowed a free flow of air to the underside of the grate.

The articulated main rod was another innovation, barely visible but with significant engineering implications. This, too, was tested on an existing 4-8-2 before being incorporated into the new engine.

Even the limited cut-off came under the scrutiny of Lima engineers; all limited-cut-off engines had auxiliary starting ports, but Lima lengthened two of the front main steam ports by just 7/16 inch to provide an effective 63% maximum cut-off at the front of the cylinders, 60% at the back, slightly stretching the application of full steam pressure on starting and smoothing the transition between starting and running speed.

So critical was space inside the boiler shell that an exterior dry pipe led steam from a dome to the superheater header and the front-end throttle. Two steam turrets were provided; one supplied superheated steam to the air pump, the feed water heater pump, the blower, grate shakers, stoker and electric generator, that benefited from using

Boston & Albany 2-8-4, No. 1, built by Lima in 1925. This was the first 2-8-4. The box on the front of the locomotive is a shelter for test engineers taking indicator diagrams, the plumbing for which can be seen on the cylinder. The location and date of the photograph are unknown (courtesy California State Railroad Museum, Railway & Locomotive Historical Society collection).

superheated steam; the other supplied saturated steam to the injectors and lubricators, that did not. The prototype had a variable exhaust nozzle of French design, not under the engineer's control, but adjustable from outside the engine so that the best exhaust nozzle size could be determined in advance of production.

Although the new 2-8-4 differed little in external appearance from thousands of other locomotives built by Alco, Baldwin and Lima over the previous twenty-five years, it was the product of an astonishing re-engineering of the entire locomotive in which no detail was too trivial to be considered.

After a running-in period, instrumented road tests of this engine began in March 1925. Nine tests were run over 60 miles of the company's Albany division between Selkirk and Washington, climbing continuously at about 1%. This section was running at maximum capacity; only longer trains or higher speeds could achieve any increase in traffic. During the tests, the stoker fired 5,300 pounds per hour—only 53 pounds per square foot of grate per hour on the 100-square foot grate, evaporating 11.4 pounds of water per pound of dry coal. Gone were the days of 180-pound firing rates, bringing evaporation rates down to 6 pounds of water per pound of coal; this approached the efficiency of a calorimeter. Such a low firing rate needed a vacuum of only 5 inches of water gauge in the smokebox, minimizing back pressure. The average steaming rate was 61,000 pounds per hour at 240 pounds per square inch, of which 20 pounds

was lost between the throttle and the steam chest. The Type E superheater achieved a steam temperature of 655°F, while the smokebox temperature averaged only 570°F. Average power output over the whole duration of the tests was 1,923 indicated horsepower at 44% cut-off, 1,480 horsepower at the drawbar. Power was there if needed; the maximum recorded cylinder horsepower was 3,675; maximum recorded drawbar pull was 76,800 pounds, of which the booster contributed 11,800. Thermal efficiency was sacrificed to total effectiveness; coal consumption at 3.5 pounds per drawbar horsepower-hour and steam consumption at 29.7 pounds per drawbar horsepower-hour, resulting in a total thermal efficiency of about 5%, showed no advance over saturated steam locomotives twenty years before. Total effectiveness was unparalleled.

One of the more famous tests in American locomotive history took place on April 14, 1925. A 2-8-2 with 1,691 tons on the drawbar left Selkirk, New York, at 11 a.m. The new engine departed 47 minutes later with a trailing load of 2,296 tons—one third heavier. The 2-8-4 overtook the 2-8-2 on a stretch of multiple track and arrived at North Adams Junction 10 minutes before the other train, at 2 p.m. When both engines were being fired at 6,000 pounds of coal per hour, the 2-8-4 developed 1,750 drawbar horsepower, one third more than the 2-8-2. The 2-8-2 never exceeded 1,650 drawbar horsepower, burning 7,200 pounds of coal per hour.

By March 1926, the Boston & Albany had twenty-five 2-8-4s in

Boston & Albany Class A-1b 2-8-4, No. 1430, at Boston, Massachusetts, on October 15, 1930. Lima built 20 A-1b's in 1926–27 (Denver Public Library, Otto C. Perry Collection, OP-2661).

service. The Illinois Central was one of the earliest users; Lima delivered fifty in the fall of 1926, of similar dimensions to the original A-1.[63]

Orders for the new 2-8-4s came apace. Unfortunately for Lima, the design was not patentable and Alco was soon taking orders—twenty-five for the Erie, twelve for the Chicago & North Western in 1927.[64] The always innovative Santa Fe got on the 2-8-4 band wagon, while remaining loyal to Baldwin, and ordered fifteen 2-8-4s the same year.[65]

J. J. Bernet, the new president of the Erie, tasked with curing the company's financial woes, needed the 2-8-4s urgently to accelerate freight movement between Hornell, New York, and Marion, Ohio, improving the company's position in the fiercely competitive northeastern U.S.[66] The Erie tried them on continuous runs between those two points; the necessary endurance came from a gigantic tender, supported on two six-wheel trucks, itself weighing 310,000 pounds when loaded with 24 tons of coal and 16,500 gallons of water.

The Chicago & North Western engines were close in size to Lima's original A-1, but the Erie engines were bigger than the Lima originals with an engine weight of 443,000 pounds and 70,000 pounds of tractive effort at 80% cut-off in full gear. Erie track allowed a 69,000-pound axle loading. Alco packed 5,700 square feet of primary and 2,450 square feet of superheating surface into a 90-inch diameter boiler, 21 feet over tube sheets, fired by a 100-square foot grate. The firebox contained a brick arch supported on two siphons and two arch tubes, but the available boiler length over four driving axles discouraged the designers from adding a combustion chamber. Two Ohio non-lifting injectors and a Worthington feed water heater supplied the boiler. With 70-inch driving wheels, the Erie 2-8-4s were built for speed.

That same year, the Erie bought another twenty-five 2-8-4s from Lima, heavier than the twenty-five from Alco with 250 pounds per square inch boiler pressure, compared to 225 in the Alco engines and 240 pounds in the original A-1, producing 72,000 pounds of tractive effort.[67]

The Boston & Maine became a 2-8-4 user in 1928, ordering twenty from Lima, closely resembling the A-1, except for a Coffin feed water heater mounted on the smokebox brow.[68]

The Boston & Albany called the 2-8-4s the *Berkshire* type, after the range of hills they were designed to conquer. With less than a thousand built between 1925 and 1949, their impact on the American railroad industry far outran their numbers.

12.2.6 Superpower: The Texas Type

The introduction of the 2-8-4 on the Boston & Albany in early 1925 was followed in the same year by another Lima prodigy, ten colossal 2-10-4s for the Texas & Pacific (hence, called the *Texas* type), where they went into service in November 1925.[69] The 2-10-4 was the ultimate rigid-frame freight power.

These Limas had one predecessor. The first-ever 2-10-4 was one of a batch of 2-10-2s, built by Baldwin for the Santa Fe in 1919. It is not clear whether No. 3829 came from Baldwin with its experimental 4-wheel trailing truck or was modified by the Santa Fe.[70]

Those first Lima 2-10-4s weighed 448,000 pounds and developed 83,000 pounds of tractive effort, with another 13,000 pounds from the trailing truck booster. Burning oil over a 100-square foot grate, the length over the five driving axles allowed space for a 42-inch combustion chamber, adding 40% to the firebox heating surface of the 2-8-4s. Although the total heating surface was the same in both locomotives, the 2-10-4s had 10% more steaming capacity for that reason. The boiler contained eighty-two 2¼-inch fire tubes and 184 3½-inch

Lima built 25 Class T-1 2-8-4s for the Boston & Maine in 1928–29. No. 4009 is shown at Portland, Maine, on August 16, 1937. Note the Coffin feed water heater (Denver Public Library, Otto C. Perry collection, OP-2736).

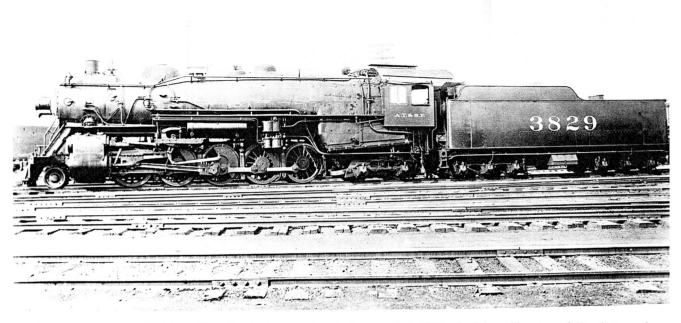

The first 2-10-4, No. 3829, built by Baldwin for the Atchison, Topeka & Santa Fe in 1919. The date and location of this photograph are unknown (courtesy *Classic Trains* magazine collection, ctr_a0907_31, ATSF photo).

flues for a 92-element Type E superheater, thus 2,100 square feet of superheating surface. Other superpower design elements comprised an Elesco feed water heater, a front-end throttle, cut-off in full gear limited to 60% and a low adhesion factor of 3.6. Back pressure gauges allowed the engineer to optimize the cut-off. The Texas & Pacific put these engines on its Fort Worth and Rio Grande divisions, 450 miles between Marshall and Big Spring, Texas, dominated by 1.5% ruling grades.

The performance and fuel efficiency of the Texas & Pacific 2-10-4s was startling. Their predecessors were a ragbag of forty-four Baldwin and USRA 2-10-2s dating from 1916–19. In March 1922, these engines burned 15.5 gallons of oil per thousand gross ton-miles, hauling an average load of 1,370 tons. In 1925, the T&P increased boiler pressures from 185 to 200 pounds per square inch and retrofitted some with boosters and feed water heaters, reducing fuel consumption to 12.7 gallons per thousand gross ton-miles and increasing train loads to 1,595 tons by March 1926. That same month, the 2-10-4s burned 7.4 gallons per thousand gross ton-miles, hauling an average train of 2,350 tons—42% less fuel and 48% more tonnage—developing 4,160 indicated horsepower at 38 miles per hour and 57% cut-off. With only a switcher pushing, a 2-10-4 could move a 91-car train weighing 4,000 tons up 4½ miles of 1.3% grade. Between 1925 and 1929, the company bought seventy of these engines from Lima. Nearly twenty years later, they were still the backbone of the company's locomotive fleet, hauling passenger and freight trains at 60 miles per hour.

The next order for 2-10-4s was for twelve from the Chicago, Burlington & Quincy, placed with Baldwin in 1927—the most powerful two-cylinder locomotives built to date.[71] The company ordered them specifically to haul more tons faster and to reduce over-time wages, compared to a fleet of 2-10-2s, themselves massive engines with superheaters and feed water heaters, built by Baldwin in 1914–15. The new 2-10-4s developed 90,000 pounds of tractive effort and 30% more horsepower than the 2-10-2s. This power came from 107 square feet of Hulson grates, firing 5,900 square feet of primary and 2,490 square feet of superheating surface in a 250-pounds per square inch boiler. Baker valve gear with a Barco power reverser drove 15-inch piston valves, supplying steam to 31-inch × 32-inch cylinders. Cut-off in full gear was limited to 61%; auxiliary steam ports increased this to 80% on starting; a multi-stage front-end throttle helped to prevent the engine from breaking its train apart. Six engines had Elesco feed water heaters, six Worthington. Surprisingly, the locomotives were supplied without boosters, although they were built for retrofitting, if required. Each engine weighed 512,000 pounds, the heaviest rigid-frame engines built to date.

The new locomotives went to work hauling 8,000-ton coal trains from the mines around Centralia, Illinois, 135 miles north to Beardstown. The 2-10-2s hauled 97-car trains weighing 6,800 tons; the 2-10-4s hauled 113 cars, weighing 8,000 tons, under an initial speed restriction of 25 miles per hour. The railroads had long debated the merits of maximizing tonnage or speed; the 2-10-4s enabled the Burlington to maximize both. Compared to the 2-10-2s, the 2-10-4s economized on coal by 16%, water by 22% and crew time by 25%. The enormous tractive effort allowed the engine to maintain speed on grades; the tender, holding 24 tons of coal and 21,500 gallons of water, dispensed with two, or even three, of the water stops needed by the 2-10-2s. For a round trip, 125 empties southbound, 113 loads northbound, the 2-10-4s burned 46 tons of coal (only 43 pounds per square foot of grate per hour) and evaporated 64,000 gallons of water

This Texas & Pacific class I-1 2-10-4, No. 637, built by Lima in 1925, seems to have been making good speed when Otto Perry photographed it near Merkel, Texas, on June 26, 1948, yet note the brakeman perched precariously on the tender (Denver Public Library, Otto C. Perry collection, OP-16292).

No. 6326 was one of eighteen class M-4 2-10-4s built by Baldwin for the Chicago, Burlington & Quincy between 1927 and 1929, shown at Denver, Colorado, on May 2, 1936 (Denver Public Library, Otto C. Perry collection, OP-4021).

(6.9 pounds per pound of coal), hauling 20% more gross ton-miles per round trip, including empties, than the 2-10-2s.

Only 450 2-10-4s were ever built, between 1925 and 1944, but, like the other superpower locomotives, their impact on railroad economics outran their small numbers.

12.2.7 Coming of the Simple Mallets

Describing a Mallet as "simple" seems a contradiction in terms; the American railroads used the word to denote single-expansion.

With their twenty-five class H-7 2-8-8-2 Mallets, built by Alco in 1924, the Chesapeake & Ohio produced one of the true monsters of American steam.[72] Festooned with externally mounted pumps and piping, the smokebox brow surmounted by an Elesco feed water heater, these engines weighed 565,000 pounds and developed 104,000 pounds of tractive effort through their 57-inch driving wheels. The company was already using 2-6-6-2 Mallets, but it now planned to use the new 2-8-8-2s on steeper grades, relegating the 2-6-6-2s to flatter parts, allowing longer trains to be hauled without breaking them up. The challenge was to fit the maximum power density into the existing clearance dimensions of 15 feet 3½ inches height and 10 feet 7 inches width. Compound Mallets had starting valves, supplying live steam to all four cylinders; the enormous tractive effort obtainable by using them this way was a never-ending temptation. Total efficiency and thermal efficiency were not the same thing. The Pennsylvania, with its single 2-8-8-0 Mallet, and some demand from overseas, led the way in locomotives with Mallet articulation but single-expansion cylinders; this was the first American quantity order for a Mallet-articulated locomotive supplying live steam to all four cylinders.

This arrangement placed a premium on steaming rate. A 63,000-pound permissible axle loading helped to make it possible. The overall length of the boiler from backhead to smokebox was 57 feet. The elaborate arrangements occupying the boiler length of the early Mallets were gone. The firebox was 17 feet long with a Gaines wall and a 69-inch combustion chamber. The boiler was 92 inches in diameter and 24 feet over tube sheets. A Duplex stoker fired the 113-square foot grate at up to 12,700 pounds per hour. The primary heating surface, comprising the firebox (467 square feet), 278 2¼-inch fire tubes and sixty 5½-inch superheater flues, was 6,443 square feet, with an additional 1,885 square feet of superheating surface in the Type A superheater. The boiler pressure was 205 pounds per square inch, supplying four 23-inch × 32-inch cylinders, expected to produce 3,900 horsepower. The Vanderbilt tender carried 15 tons of coal and 12,000 gallons of water for an all-up weight of 775,000 pounds. When a locomotive that size was working in a tunnel, the heat and gas in the cab were practically unsurvivable. Two electric fans, each driven by a small steam turbine, drew air from the space between the engine and tender and blew it through ducting to cool and ventilate the cab; three gas masks were also provided, supplied with compressed air from the brake reservoir. The Chesapeake & Ohio bought another twenty 2-8-8-2s, class H-7a, from Baldwin in 1926.[73]

The Great Northern hauled a heavy traffic of forest products and seasonal fruit from the Pacific Northwest.[74] Over the 1,630 miles between Wenatchee, Washington, and St. Paul, Minnesota, the 14 miles of 1.8% eastbound grade between Walton and Summit, Montana, was the bottleneck for this traffic. A 1923-built Baldwin 2-10-2 road engine handled 3,000 tons over this route with a 2-8-8-0 Mallet cut into the train for the Walton grade; management wanted to

Otto Perry photographed this Chesapeake & Ohio class H-7 2-8-8-2, No. 1557, built by Alco in 1924, at Clifton Forge, Virginia, on August 4, 1936 (Denver Public Library, Otto C. Perry collection, OP-2914).

increase this to 4,000 tons. Since the Mallets were built in 1912, the company had strengthened its track and could now accept a 67,000-pound axle loading, which would support a boiler big enough to supply live steam to four cylinders. With this in mind, they converted a 2-8-8-0 to single-expansion in 1924. As this was successful, the Great Northern went to Baldwin for four 2-8-8-2 simple Mallets.

Basis of these was a 108-square foot oil-burning grate with no brick arch, a Gaines wall and a 72-inch combustion chamber. The firebox and tender were built for possible retrofitting to burn coal with a power stoker. The maximum diameter of the slightly tapered boiler was 109 inches, providing space for 310 2¼-inch × 24-foot fire tubes and sixty-eight 5½-inch superheater flues for 7,140 square feet of primary and 1,895 square feet of superheating surface, generating steam at 210 pounds per square inch. The boiler diameter conformed so closely to the railroad's clearance dimensions that the safety valves and whistle had to be set into a recess in the top of the boiler. A Sellers non-lifting injector on the left side of the cab and an Elesco exhaust steam injector on the right side supplied feed water. Live steam went to all four 28-inch × 32-inch cylinders. The exhaust pipe from the rear cylinders ended in an annular nozzle surrounding that from the front cylinders. The engine weighed 594,940 pounds; the tender, containing 5,800 gallons of oil and 16,800 gallons of water, brought this up to nearly a million pounds. With 127,500 pounds of tractive effort, these were the most powerful single-expansion locomotives in the world. Three hundred tons of locomotive developed 3,000 indicated horsepower at 15 miles per hour. For comparison, a 2,800-horsepower Pratt & Whitney radial aero engine powered the World War II P-47N fighter aircraft; the gross weight of the aircraft, complete with fuel, guns and ammunition, was 11 tons. This difference in power density explains why steam never stood a chance against internal combustion.

Winter frost, snow and mist on the rails added to the problems of the Walton grade; slipping of either the road engine or the helper could break a train in two. A high adhesion factor of 4.2, combined with cut-off limited to 65%, made the R-1s particularly sure-footed. One of these as a road engine could handle 4,000 tons in winter, 4,500 tons in summer, with another as a helper on the Walton grade.

The Great Northern was so taken with the single-expansion Mallets that in 1926 it converted the other 2-8-8-0s to single-expansion in its shops at a cost of $27,000 each, saving $100,000 per locomotive per year.[75]

The Denver & Rio Grande Western plan to run 3,000-ton trains over the 3.3% grades of the Tennessee Pass needed new motive power. Eastbound, one locomotive was to run from Grand Junction to Minturn, climbing the Tennessee Pass with two Mallet helpers, taking the train alone to Salida or Pueblo.

As it was impossible to build a rigid-frame locomotive with enough pulling power, the company approached Alco for ten 2-8-8-2 single-expansion Mallets, delivered in 1927.[76]

Track and substructures permitting a 70,000-pound axle loading and abnormally generous clearance dimensions—16 feet high × 10 feet 8 inches wide—made it possible to build a locomotive of enormous power. A stoker-fired 137-square foot grate with arch tubes, siphons and a 72-inch combustion chamber for burning soft coal fired a 240-pounds per square inch boiler of 100-inch diameter, containing 284 2¼-inch × 24-foot fire tubes and seventy-four 5½-inch flues for 7,265 square feet of primary and 2,295 square feet of superheating surface. A 12-inch dry pipe conveyed steam from the dome to the superheater header and front-end throttle. A virtue of the compound Mallets was that the flexible piping conveyed only low-pressure steam. In the new single-expansion Mallets, the flexible

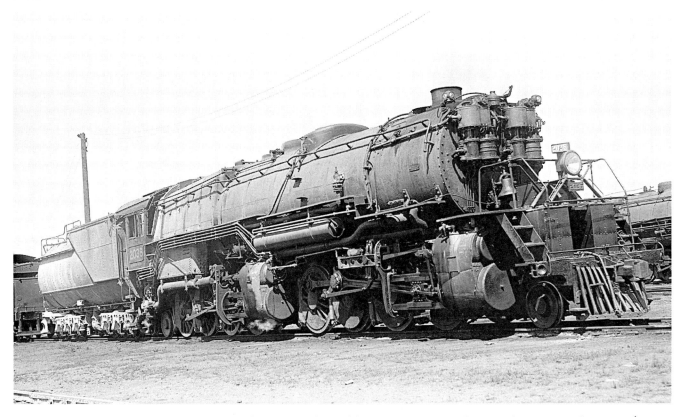

Great Northern class R-1s 2-8-8-2, No. 2036, one of fourteen built by Baldwin in 1925–28, at Spokane, Washington, on July 30, 1938 (Denver Public Library, Otto C. Perry collection, OP-11882).

Alco built this Denver & Rio Grande Western class L-131 2-8-8-2, No. 3602, in 1927, shown at Minturn, Colorado, on April 29, 1938 (Denver Public Library, Otto C. Perry collection, OP-9896).

piping was exposed to almost the full boiler pressure; improved packing materials and joint design solved this problem. Walschaert valve gear with power reverse, 14-inch piston valves, 26-inch × 32-inch cylinders and 63-inch driving wheels produced 132,000 pounds of tractive effort at the 70% maximum cut-off, 140,000 pounds on starting. The tender was of unprecedented size, holding 30 tons of coal and 18,000 gallons of water.

The Sierra Nevada made never-ending demands on motive power.[77] In the early 1920s, trains loaded with California fruit, bound for the eastern U.S., left Roseville, California, 160 feet above sea level, with fifty-six cars behind a Mallet with a 2-8-0 helper thirteen cars ahead of the caboose. This sufficed for the 35 miles to Colfax with grades up to 1.5%. At Colfax a second Mallet was cut in behind the 2-8-0. These three engines tackled the 2% grades to Emigrant Gap, 29 miles farther east and 5,220 feet above sea level. There the 2-8-0 was cut out and the two Mallets took the train to Summit, 7,020 feet above sea level and 20 miles farther on. At Summit, the Mallet helper was cut out and the Mallet road engine took the train on, downgrade, to Sparks, Nevada. Putting the helpers on and off was so time-consuming that the train took 16½ hours *en route*, a point-to-point speed of 8 miles per hour. At peak periods, trains were only 25 minutes apart. Going through the snowsheds, visibility in smoke and darkness was so bad that a brakeman hung two lanterns from the back platform of the caboose and sat there watching the track. "If he sees freshly splintered ties he knows something is wrong and he stops the train with the emergency valve."

In the event the train needed to stop, as in a passing loop, whistle signals from the road engine were inaudible through the roar of the helpers' exhaust; the helper crews therefore ran with wide open throttles until such time as the road engine's engineer applied the train brakes with a force that even they could not overcome and brought the train to a standstill. Immediately, the helper crews set their brakes and the engineer on the road engine released the train brakes, allowing the slack to run back onto the helpers. To restart the train, the engineer on the road engine signaled to the helper crews by means of a full application and release of the train brakes which they could hear and feel. The helper engineers opened their throttles, loading the slack against the road engine. The engineer on the road engine then opened his throttle and the train began to move.

More oil-burning, cab-forward Mallets followed in 1928 with ten 4-8-8-2s from Baldwin, this time single-expansion and rated at 113,000 pounds of tractive effort.[78]

The boiler pressure was 235 pounds per square inch. The 63½-inch driving wheels were small enough to fit beneath an immense firebox with 139 square feet of grate area and a 68-inch combustion chamber. Baldwin crammed 6,505 square feet of primary and 3,000 square feet of superheating surface into a 92-inch diameter boiler, 22 feet over tube sheets. Because of the long distance from the tender to the burner, the oil tank was pressurized from the compressor reservoir. Each pair of cylinders, limited to 70% cut-off, exhausted through a separate nozzle and a double stack. A Worthington feed water heater used steam bled off, both from an annular chamber surrounding the rear exhaust pipe and from the valve chambers of the front cylinders. Like the other cab-forwards, these engines were assigned to the Sierra Nevada.

The same year, the Northern Pacific commissioned a 2-8-8-4, named the *Yellowstone* type, from Alco which truly was the biggest engine in the world.[79] The Northern Pacific hoped that this monster would solve the problem of the 216 miles between Mandan, North Dakota, and Glendive, Montana. The steepest grades were 1.1% but their distribution made helper service impractical. The maximum load that the company's 2-8-2s could handle was 2,225 tons; 4,000-ton trains from either direction had to be broken into two for the passage of this division. The Northern Pacific studied the possibility of flattening and realignment, but concluded that this was impractical.

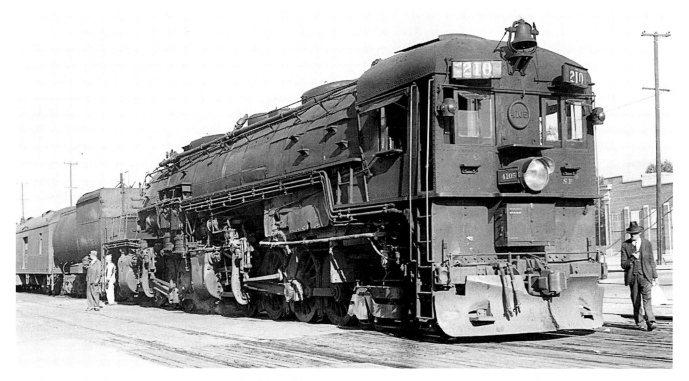

Southern Pacific class AC-4 4-8-8-2, No. 4105, built by Baldwin in 1928, at Reno, Nevada, on August 4, 1935 (Denver Public Library, Otto C. Perry collection, OP-15663).

Baldwin built this Northern Pacific class Z-5 2-8-8-4, No. 5004, in 1930, shown at Bozeman, Montana, on June 24, 1949 (Denver Public Library, Otto C. Perry collection, OP-14037).

Accordingly, they approached Alco for a locomotive that would take 4,000 tons through this district.

The Northern Pacific wanted this engine to burn sub-bituminous coal from Montana and "In order to obtain the required boiler horse-power from the heat developed by this coal, it was necessary to design the largest firebox and boiler ever applied to a steam locomotive."

The grate area was 182 square feet with a combustion chamber extending 6 feet ahead of the throat sheet, stayed with 5,153 staybolts. The firebox and combustion chamber combined were 28½ feet long; the firebox contained three siphons, the combustion chamber a further two. The 103-inch diameter boiler contained ninety-two 2¼-inch × 22-foot fire tubes and 280 3½-inch flues for a primary heating surface of 7,675 square feet with a further 3,220 square feet of Type E superheating surface, generating steam at 250 pounds per square inch. The boiler alone weighed 165,000 pounds (presumed empty but the source is not specific). Firing was by a Standard Type B stoker, designed for up to 40,000 pounds of coal per hour. The smokebox brow accommodated a Coffin feed water heater, supplied by two centrifugal pumps with a combined capacity of 10,000 gallons per hour. Two Hancock injectors were provided in addition, with a combined capacity of 10,400 gallons per hour; the maximum evaporation rate was 12,000 gallons per hour. Even the throttle valve was so big it had to be compressed-air powered, the first such installation on a locomotive. Walschaert valve gear drove 14-inch piston valves, supplying four 26-inch × 32-inch cylinders. The tender held 27 tons of coal and 21,200 gallons of water.

The resulting engine weighed 715,000 pounds. Tractive effort at the maximum 70% cut-off was 140,000 pounds; even this could be increased by 13,400 pounds by a booster driving the back axle of the four-wheel trailing truck. The adhesion weight was 554,000 pounds, for an axle loading of 69,250 pounds. No locomotive had ever been built this big; no one knew if it would function as intended. A reviewer commented, pessimistically: "If it is unsuccessful, it can be assigned as a helper in mountain territory." Over the years, helper service was the means to sweep many an unsuccessful design under the carpet.

After Alco had built the first of these engines, the Northern Pacific went out for tenders on another eleven. Baldwin won the contract and delivered them in 1930. No more were built thereafter; apparently their performance was disappointing.

Lima was not among the builders of the giant Mallets of the 1920s. By contrast, the Great Northern emerged as a builder in its own right, building Mallets for its own use in its Hillyard, Washington, shops which were among the biggest steam locomotives anywhere in the world.[80] After buying four 2-8-8-2s from Baldwin in 1925, the company evidently believed that it could the job cheaper itself and built ten more in 1928. The two engine frames and the trailing truck frame were single castings by Commonwealth Steel. The Puget Sound Machinery Depot Co. built the boilers. The Great Northern bought finished rods from Baldwin and manufactured wheels, axles, driving boxes and crank pins at its St. Paul, Minnesota, shops. All other fabrication and assembly was done at the Hillyard shops near Seattle.

These engines differed from the Baldwins in higher boiler pressure at 225 pounds per square inch, up from 210 pounds, which increased the tractive effort to 136,000 pounds. In 1929, the company built ten more with a still higher boiler pressure, at 240 pounds per square inch, developing 146,000 pounds of tractive effort at the 65% maximum cut-off. These were oil-burners, with 126-square feet of grate area in a Belpaire firebox with no combustion chamber, arch tubes or siphons. The firebox and tubes provided 7,870 square feet of primary heating surface with a further 3,515 square feet of superheating surface. An Elesco exhaust-steam injector supplied water to the boiler.

The Great Northern built this class R-2 2-8-8-2, No. 2056, in its own shops in 1928–29, shown at Summit, Montana, on August 6, 1938 (Denver Public Library, Otto C. Perry collection, OP-11890).

The resulting engine weighed 631,000 pounds. The tender, when loaded with 5,800 gallons of oil and 22,000 gallons of water, weighed 371,000 pounds, heavier than many locomotives.

The Great Northern rated the R-1s's for 4,200-tons eastbound from Whitefish to Walton, but found they could haul 4,400. The first company-built batch was rated for 4,400 tons and hauled 5,000; the second batch was rated for 4,600 tons and handled 5,500.

By the end of the 1920s, power stokers, siphons, combustion chambers, power-operated grate shakers, front-end throttles and superheated steam for auxiliaries, power reversers, Baker valve gear, vanadium steel parts, one-piece engine beds, boosters, feed water heaters and Type E superheaters were common in new construction. Locomotive builders also gave careful thought to crew ergonomics, providing improved and increased instrumentation and controls labeled, lit and easily accessible so that the engineer and fireman could both work from their cab seats. British enginemen appreciated this feature of the S-160 2-8-0s that the Americans provided to them during World War II; their own engines, by contrast, were designed with no thought for crew comfort. Ergonomic design, enormous tenders, multi-tracking and increasingly efficient signaling meant that freight trains could run through division points, covering enormous distances at higher speeds than ever before, without stopping. These advances were vital to American railroad economics.

Section 12.3 Switchers

By the 1920s massive freight trains arriving in classification yards were outrunning the power of the available switching locomotives. The standard 0-6-0 switcher was increasingly supplanted by 0-8-0s, yet even this was not enough and some yards had to use Mallets. The

Chesapeake & Ohio tackled this problem with a class of 0-10-0 switchers, the first of which were built by Alco Richmond to a design arrived at by engineers from both companies.[81] The first went into service in February 1919, somehow escaping the restrictions of the USRA. These engines weighed 295,000 pounds, all of which went into adhesion weight, and developed 63,000 pounds of tractive effort from a 185-pounds per square inch boiler. The driving wheels were only 51 inches in diameter and placed as closely together as possible for the shortest possible wheelbase. The very small driving wheel diameter meant that the valve gear eccentric crank was mounted eccentrically on the main crankpin to avoid hitting the track. A Lewis power reverser controlled the Baker valve gear. A 72-square foot hand-fired grate fired a superheated boiler with 3,700 square feet of primary heating surface and a further 935 square feet of superheating surface. After a year in service, these engines were pronounced a success.

Besides their obvious use in mainline classification yards, switch engines were widely used at steel mills, mines, docks and other industrial plants; here, too, came a demand for greater capability. They tended to be lacking in the fuel-saving refinements adopted by the mainline railroads but, even so, superheating and power reversers proved their worth.

The Pennsylvania built fifty 0-8-0 switchers at its Juniata shops, starting in 1925.[82] The 275,000-pound engines had the classic Pennsylvania look with a Belpaire firebox and tapered boiler with a very high 250 pounds per square inch boiler pressure. Cylinders measuring 27 inches × 30 inches, driving 56-inch driving wheels, resulted in 76,000 pounds of tractive effort. To obtain the optimal three-point suspension, the front driving wheels were cross-equalized and were sprung separately from the rear six driving wheels which were equalized longitudinally. Cut-off was limited to 60% in full gear, although starting ports permitted steam entry at up to 80% of the stroke.

Alco built fifteen of these class C-12 0-10-0s for the Chesapeake & Ohio between 1919 and 1923. No. 143 is shown, location and date unknown (courtesy California State Railroad Museum, Paul Darrell Collection, Negative 11247B).

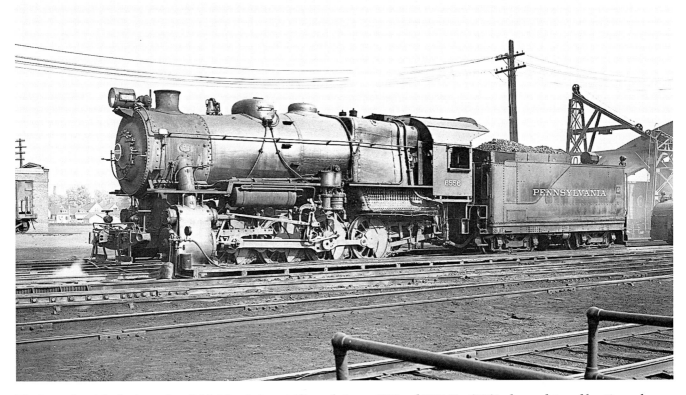

The Pennsylvania built ninety class C-1 0-8-0 switchers at Altoona between 1925 and 1927. No. 6556 is shown, date and location unknown (courtesy California State Railroad Museum, Negative 28363).

Otto Perry photographed Boston & Maine class H-3 0-8-0, No. 649, built by Baldwin in 1927, at Boston, Massachusetts, on August 17, 1937 (Denver Public Library, Otto C. Perry collection, OP-2682).

The innovations applied to superpower road engines found their way to increasingly powerful switchers. In 1927, Lima delivered eight 0-8-0 switchers to the Oliver Iron Mining Company.[83] At 254,000 pounds engine weight, 56,000 pounds of tractive effort, 70,000 with the booster cut in, the switcher was now a massive, special-purpose engine, in modern appliances fully the equal of its road engine counterparts. The mining company evidently built solid track; the axle loading was 63,500 pounds. Rare in a switcher, a stoker fired the 63-square foot grate and a feed water heater supplied the boiler, which had a working pressure of 225 pounds per square inch. Cut-off in full gear was limited to 70%. A booster replaced the front four-wheel tender truck.

Alco followed suit immediately, with three even bigger 0-8-0 switchers for hump shunting over 2.2% grades on the Indiana Harbor Belt at Gibson, Indiana.[84] Alco built these 294,000-pound monsters with three cylinders and 76,000 pounds of tractive effort, 90,000 with the tender booster. The inside cylinder drove the second driving axle; the two outside cylinders drove the third driving axle. The 72-square foot grate was hand-fired, although the engine had other modern appliances, such as a feed water heater and power reverse. The tender had the enormous capacity—for a switcher—of 15 tons of coal and 12,000 gallons of water. Three shift crews ran these engines

24 hours a day. In service they proved capable of moving 6,000-ton trains over the Gibson hump.

The ten 0-8-0 switchers that Baldwin built for the Boston & Maine in 1927 had 250-pounds per square inch boilers with modest-sized 47-square foot hand-fired grates; in eight locomotives the brick arch was supported on four arch tubes, in the remaining two, on two siphons and two arch tubes.[85] These engines had the new Coffin feed water heater, Baker valve gear and Ragonnet power reverse. Weighing 244,500 pounds, they developed 57,000 pounds of tractive effort. Because of the Maine climate, they had live steam jets to blow snow and ice off the track in front of the engine, also flange oilers to reduce the grinding action of the wheels on curved rail; these devices managed to avoid oiling the tire tread and running surface of the rail.

The 0-10-0 switchers remained rare. Baldwin built one for the Alabama & Vicksburg in 1922 specifically to move freight trains out of the Mississippi Valley onto the plateau at Vicksburg.[86] Equipped with the equally rare Young valve gear, the engine weighed 320,000 pounds and developed 78,000 pounds of tractive effort from a 185-pound boiler pressure.

The relative importance of the switcher types shows in the numbers built: 15,000 0-6-0s, 3,200 0-8-0s and only forty to fifty 0-10-0s.

13

Traction Other Than Steam, 1920–1930

The Boston & Maine was a steam railroad throughout, and would remain so until 1956, but as early as 1923 the Assistant General Manager, L. G. Coleman, voiced a groundswell of frustration, even resentment, against the steam locomotive, as if the machine were ungrateful for the care lavished upon it.[1]

> I think there will be no dissent to the statement that the steam locomotive today is probably the most uneconomical and unsatisfactory machine in industry. We have made enormous improvements, that, granting its inherent original weakness, have very much increased its efficiency as far as a power producer is concerned, but these same improvements have so increased the cost and difficulty of maintenance that the time lost in terminals practically wipes out the savings due to fuel economy obtained by modern devices, and increased unit power.

Several of Coleman's audience "took exception to the statements that the steam locomotive is inefficient and out-of-date."

Nevertheless, as soon as World War I was over, the American railroads began to look, not only at new power but at radically new types of power. The superpower design movement grew up in the shadow of these developments; it was only because electrification was too expensive, and the diesel locomotive too immature, that it grew up at all. In 1926[2]:

> There is great activity in Europe and America in developing a more economical form of motive power than that now furnished by the steam locomotive.

Section 13.1 Electric Power

By 1920, electric traction was fully developed; General Electric already had its own Railway and Traction Engineering Department. One of its engineers, A. H. Armstrong, took a hard jab at the steam locomotive itself.[3] The railroad industry keenly felt the disgrace of the war years and government take-over; his comment did not fall on deaf ears.

> During the war period many lessons have been most clearly brought home to us and not the least of these is that there is something inherently wrong with our steam railroads.

He went on:

> During the winter of 1917–18 our railways fell down badly when the need was the greatest in their history. It is true that the cold weather conditions were unprecedented and the volume of traffic abnormal, but the weaknesses of steam engine haulage were disclosed in a most startling and disastrous manner.

The unpalatable truth was:

> In marked contrast to the adjoining steam engine divisions, the 40 miles of electrified section of the Chicago, Milwaukee & St. Paul continued to do business as usual all through that trying winter of 1917–18.

After protesting that he "is not proposing the immediate electrification of all the railways in the United States," Armstrong went on to advocate exactly that, concluding with:

> Accord full honor to the reciprocating steam engine for the great part it has played in the development of our railways and industries, but complete the work by replacing it with the electric motor and enter upon a new era of real railroading.

John E. Muhlfeld, at that time with Railway & Industrial Engineers, Inc., shot back[4]:

> The basis for arriving at these comparative figures is so obviously ridiculous that they warrant comment only for the reason of the general publicity given.

He pointed out that Armstrong had taken the results of "tests made in 1910 on the C. M. & St. P. of some probably long since antiquated types of saturated steam locomotives" and extrapolated them as a measure of nation-wide steam locomotive fuel efficiency. Further, the much-vaunted efficiency of electric traction averaged 100 pounds of coal per thousand gross-ton-miles hauled, when powered by coal-burning power stations; the latest steam locomotives were already achieving that figure. While a powerhouse burned coal more efficiently than a steam locomotive, the steps from the powerhouse to the electric locomotive were so numerous, each with its own losses, that the true thermal efficiency of an electric locomotive was not significantly higher than that of the abused and derided steam locomotive. Proponents of the electric locomotive quoted the maintenance costs of the locomotive but ignored the cost of maintaining the infrastructure.

The rhetoric continued but, over the years, the answer remained simple: electric traction was used to good effect where traffic density or special conditions justified the heavy investment in infrastructure.

Following the success of the Milwaukee and the Norfolk & Western, the Virginian announced its intention in 1923 to electrify 134 miles between Mullens, West Virginia, and Roanoke, Virginia.[5] The Virginian was already using the biggest locomotives on the face of the earth on the grade between Elmore and Clark's Gap and needed still more power to increase tonnage. The triplex Mallet had been a failure; there was no prospect of building any steam locomotive more powerful than the existing 2-8-8-2s and 2-10-10-2s. To move a 5,500-ton train up to Clark's Gap already took three Mallets. More locomotives per train or more trains per day were undesirable or impractical.

The company would generate its own 25-cycle power in a 60-megawatt, steam-turbine powerhouse for transmission at 88 kilovolts. The Virginian adopted the Westinghouse locomotive design then being built for the Norfolk & Western with an initial order of twelve, each consisting of three power units semi-permanently coupled together, picking up power from an 11-kilovolt overhead line, transformed to a lower voltage on the locomotive with drive through jack shafts and side rods. The locomotives were designed to develop 135,000 pounds of tractive effort, up to a 5-minute maximum of 252,000 pounds, and up to 6,000 horsepower.

In 1928, the Pennsylvania built its own electric locomotive at Altoona, with electrical equipment from American Brown Boveri. Control apparatus allowed the engine to run off either 600-volt DC or 11-kilovolt AC power from an overhead wire, developing up to 3,480 horsepower continuously with a maximum tractive effort of 72,000 pounds. Total engine weight was 397,000 pounds.[6] That year the company announced plans to electrify 1,300 track miles.[7]

In contrast to these enormously powerful and highly developed electric systems, internal combustion power for railroads was completely immature, making its eventual development all the more extraordinary.

Section 13.2 Internal-Combustion Power

It may be that the merits of internal combustion will be tested out on our railroads, although the complications involved do not appeal strongly to the maintenance departments. Several locomotives of this type are being developed in other countries.

These words, from an Alco engineer, summarized American attitudes in 1922.[8]

The use of self-propelled passenger cars spread in the early 1920s, powered by 60-horsepower commercial truck engines with automotive transmissions; engines of 120 to 150 horsepower, with fluid transmissions, replaced these as they became available.[9] The Burlington was an early user, putting a 21,000-pound, 53-horsepower unit with a gasoline engine and a mechanical transmission into service between Atchison, Kansas, and Armour, Missouri, in 1923.[10] The company

bought six more in the next three years, followed by the first gasoline-engined car with an electric transmission in 1927. By 1931, the Burlington had sixty units, with 225 to 400-horsepower engines, in service across Illinois, Iowa and Nebraska, replacing forty-year-old 4-4-0s and 4-6-0s at a one-third saving in cost.

More power was an urgent problem as the available gasoline engines ran too close to their maximum power output, resulting in frequent breakdowns.[11] The 1924, an Electro-Motive/General Electric joint venture built rail cars for the Chicago Great Western and the Northern Pacific, each powered by a 175-horsepower gasoline engine. This drove a 110-kilowatt generator, which supplied 700-volt power to two electric motors on a four-wheel power truck, the other truck being unpowered.

As mentioned in an earlier chapter, internal-combustion-powered locomotives, as distinct from railcars, had been built and put into service in North America in very small numbers before 1920. The Canadians built a gasoline-powered switching locomotive in 1922. Steam locomotives twenty times more powerful were common but, even so:

It is not unlikely that from the modest beginning of the small self-propelled passenger car, internal combustion locomotives of considerable power will eventually be developed. A successful Diesel locomotive would reduce fuel consumption so greatly that it would almost revolutionize railroad operation.

The diesel locomotive was a promising development.[12] Fuel consumption per horsepower-hour was one-quarter that of a steam locomotive, with much lower standby losses. Further economies resulted from eliminating coal, water and ash handling. It needed very little water. It reduced the noise, smoke and dirt of a steam locomotive—increasingly important in urban areas. It was free from the hazards

The Virginian's electric locomotives near Roanoke, Virginia, on August 7, 1932 (Denver Public Library, Otto C. Perry collection, OP-19646).

of boiler explosions, overhead wires or live third rails. It was simpler to maintain than an electric locomotive and offered higher availability than a steam locomotive. It achieved all this with a fraction of the capital expenditures needed for electric traction.

Applying internal-combustion engines to locomotives depended on the development of a satisfactory transmission. An automotive-type gearbox could not be built big enough for a mainline locomotive; Dr. Rudolph Diesel gave up on his early attempts to harness his engine to a locomotive because of this problem but the diesel engine was so enormously attractive that efforts to solve the problem continued. By the mid–1920s, experimental diesel locomotives had been built with mechanical, hydraulic and electric transmissions. The Americans settled at once for the electric transmission.

By 1923, diesel engines (as distinct from locomotives) developing up to 3,000 horsepower had been built but they were heavy and bulky, weighing 450 pounds per horsepower, compared to 100 pounds for a steam locomotive. The Germans brought this weight down to 57 pounds in a six-cylinder diesel engine developed for submarines. Even so, this 1,000-horsepower unit was 9 feet high, 4 feet wide and 20 feet long, pressing hard on railroad clearance dimensions; three such engines would be needed to produce as much power as one large steam locomotive.

Even so, as early as 1923:

> It is not unlikely that within the next few years a sturdy reliable Diesel locomotive will be developed which will be a worthy competitor of the steam locomotive.

Within a year, a General Electric/Ingersoll-Rand joint venture built a diesel-electric switching locomotive with a six-cylinder diesel engine and four DC electric motors.[13]

> This has resulted in a remarkably flexible and economical form of motive power and, which, if experience proves its practicability when adapted to units of greater hauling capacity, should materially aid in the efforts being made to utilize the oil engine, with its low operating cost, for the propulsion of railway locomotives.

One of the pioneers of the diesel-electric locomotive was H. L. Hamilton, who founded the Electro-Motive Co. in a one-room office in Cleveland, Ohio, in 1922. John Barhyd, a draftsman then and later an officer of the Electro-Motive Division of General Motors, remembered the company's first stenographer[14]:

> Anyhow, there we were, me at a drafting board and this girl typing letters, nobody coming or going out—no telephone calls, no activity of any kind. Here were these few offices with hardly any furniture, not even a picture on the walls. A dead-looking outfit if ever there was one. The girl finished the letters, laid 'em on Hamilton's desk, then went to the halltree for her hat.
> "I'm quitting," she says.
> I ask her why, and she replies: "I've seen these fly-by-night companies before and I don't want any part of them."
> "You better wait till Mr. Hamilton comes back. You've got half a day's pay coming to you," I told her, but she shook her head.
> "He can keep the money," she replied. "He'll need it." She walked out and I never saw her again.

In 1930, the company became the Electro-Motive Division of General Motors; the technical ability of Electro-Motive and the financial and management clout of General Motors were a winning combination that transformed American railroading. Hamilton became a vice-president of GM.[15]

The view in 1925 was[16]:

> Railroad engineers have watched with much interest the development of the oil engine in the hopes that it will become available for locomotive

use. Not a great deal has been accomplished as yet, either in this country or abroad, but there are good prospects that an oil-engine locomotive can be produced for successful switching service and for main line operation where traffic is light through residential districts. These two fields are, perhaps, the most promising at the present time for this type of locomotive.

Size and weight per unit horsepower, transmission and cooling remained the dominant unsolved technical problems; behind these lay the largely unknown issue of cost. The low power:weight ratio of the diesel locomotive remained a problem. In 1925, Baldwin built a 1,000-horsepower diesel-electric locomotive weighing 275 pounds per horsepower. First costs were high—1½ to 2 times the cost of a steam locomotive.

A 300-horsepower switcher on the Central of New Jersey, built in 1925, was hailed as the first "commercial" diesel-electric locomotive.[17] The following year, the Great Northern put a 216,000-pound locomotive into service with two 300-horsepower diesel engines and electric transmission, built by a consortium of Ingersoll-Rand, Alco and General Electric. It was capable of 60,000 pounds starting tractive effort, but only 600 horsepower, with a maximum speed of 30 miles per hour.[18] The same year, the Chicago & North Western and the Erie both put diesel-electric switchers into service.[19]

By mid–1927, thirty-four diesel-electric locomotives were in service (15), under construction (7) or in builders' stock (12) in the U.S. for ten major railroads, including the Central of New Jersey, the Baltimore & Ohio, the Lehigh Valley, the Chicago & North Western, the Erie, the Philadelphia & Reading, the Delaware, Lackawanna & Western, the Great Northern, the New York Central and the Pennsylvania.[20] Alco built twenty-nine of these with Ingersoll-Rand engines and General Electric transmissions. The Pennsylvania built its own. These locomotives were of 300- and 600-horsepower capacity and were used for switching; even at this early date, they turned in startling performance and economy figures when compared with steam switchers. Apparently, only five other diesel-electric locomotives existed in the world—in Germany, Russia, Austria and Italy. The American railroads had come far from their attitude to new ideas a generation previously, leading the world in this radical new development.

A consortium of General Electric, Alco and Ingersoll-Rand built the first diesel-electric road locomotive for the New York Central in 1928.[21] Electric power came either from a third rail or from the on-board 750-horsepower diesel engine, supplying 600-volt power to four electric motors. Basic locomotive weight was 110,000 pounds; the third-rail operating equipment added another 60,000 pounds. Starting tractive effort was 51,000 pounds.

The first diesel-electric locomotive that really threatened the supremacy of steam was unveiled in 1929 by the Canadian National Railway, comprising two power units, each containing a 1,330-horsepower Beardmore diesel engine.[22] Each engine drove a generator; each generator powered four electric motors, connected by gearing to four driving axles. The electric transmission allowed the diesel engines to be run up to full power while the locomotive was stationary, exerting a starting tractive effort of 100,000 pounds, limited only by wheel slip and overheating of the electrical machinery. This was twice the tractive effort of a 4-8-2 while, at speeds above 20 miles per hour, the speed:tractive effort curves of the two locomotives were closely similar. At the fuel prices currently available to Canadian National ($0.05 per U.S. gallon for diesel oil, $5 per ton for coal), the fuel cost per passenger car-mile was only one-third that of a 4-8-2. The heavy machinery was an advantage, providing 462,000 pounds adhesion weight with an axle loading of 58,000 pounds. Total locomotive weight was 668,000 pounds.

An early diesel-electric switcher on the Baltimore & Ohio, Baltimore, Maryland, August 10, 1932 (Denver Public Library, Otto C. Perry collection, OP-2548).

Designed and built by Baldwin, Westinghouse Electric, Canadian Westinghouse and The Canadian Locomotive Co., the first power unit went into experimental service in late 1928, the second following in 1929, completing the locomotive. The threat to the steam locomotive lay in the control mechanism allowing two power units, totaling 2,600 horsepower, to be ganged together under the control of a single throttle—and that with no need for a fireman. On a publicity run from Montreal to Toronto the locomotive reached 73 miles per hour with a 660-ton train.

Self-propelled passenger rail cars gained popularity during the decade; by 1931 the Lehigh Valley was operating all local passenger services by this means and found that the savings over steam haulage paid for the new units in two years.[23] The diesel engine replaced the gasoline engine as the prime mover in about 1930.[24]

The twelve-year rail car era—from 1924 to 1936—introduced the railroads to high-speed internal-combustion power and gave them an appetite for more, while familiarizing builders such as Electro-Motive with railroad needs and operating conditions.[25] When the new diesel-electric locomotives of the late 1930s underwent the ultimate test—road freight service under the stress of wartime demand, combined with shortages of labor and materials—they could have failed due to inadequate manufacturing standards. The fact that they withstood the test determined the dieselization of the American railroads.

PART FIVE

Finest and Final, 1930–1950

14

General Steam Locomotive Development, 1930–1950

The prosperity of the 1920s fueled an optimism about the future of the steam locomotive that was still evident in 1930.[1] William C. Dickerman, President of Alco, asserted that "no limit has been set to the eventual capacity of the steam locomotive," while J. E. Muhlfeld described the steam locomotive as "still an infant." The main hopes supporting these dreams (for so they turned out) lay in turbine locomotives and very high-pressure (e.g. 850 pounds per square inch) steam. These were still unproven and would ultimately prove abortive. Dickerman also "commented on the possibility of Diesel, steam turbine and unaflow [sic] engines, poppet valves, variable exhaust nozzles, fan draft and many other details of interest."

T. W. Demarest, General Superintendent of Motive Power on the Pennsylvania, Western Region, stated unequivocally that future motive power would have to haul 1,000-ton passenger trains at 90 miles per hour and 5,000-ton freight trains at 60 miles per hour. While this requirement was by no means universal—or even widespread—in America, it made clear the future haulage demands in areas of high traffic density and high-quality infrastructure.

R. A. Black, of the Canadian National, raised a sober voice, pointing out that a typical steam locomotive delivered its maximum gross ton-miles per train hour at only 17 miles per hour, basing his conclusions on tests on a 101-mile subdivision of the Canadian National and on figures published by the University of Illinois for a typical 2-8-2.[2] Either some remarkable developments would have to take place in steam locomotive technology or some other form of motive power was needed. Electric power remained limited to areas of high traffic density, but diesel-electric locomotives that could challenge the steam locomotive, while requiring none of the infrastructure for electric power, were already foreseeable.

As the financial crisis of 1929 took effect, the tone became more muted.[3] Ominously:

> The past year has not been one in which to look for the development of many striking innovations in motive power and rolling stock. The conditions which have prevailed during most of the year on a large part of the railway mileage in America have not been conducive to much interest in innovations of any kind.

In 1933, Dickerman produced a long view of American locomotive development, pointing to some remarkable advances since 1905[4]:

These large increases in power would have been impossible without the massive civil engineering programs that provided track and substructures allowing higher axle loadings. They also resulted from developments, some of which were invisible from outside the locomotive and comprised no moving parts.

Dickerman pointed to a lack of improvement in specific coal and water consumption between 1905 and 1910, which suggested that locomotive design had reached an impasse. The introduction of the high-temperature superheater in 1910 broke this impasse, resulting in sudden, substantial decreases in coal and water consumption from 20 to 25 pounds of water and 4.0 to 4.5 pounds of coal per indicated horsepower-hour to 21 pounds of water and 3.5 pounds of coal. Continuing superheater developments resulted in further decreases in coal and water consumption to 16 pounds of water and 2.3 pounds of coal per indicated horsepower-hour by the early 1930s. Early high-temperature superheaters produced steam at temperatures up to 550°F to 600°F; the Type E increased this to nearly 800°F. Boiler pressures remained at 200 pounds per square inch from 1905 to 1920 but then increased to as high as 300 pounds per square inch as steel metallurgy improved.

In the light of these improvements in efficiency, Dickerman pleaded for the railroads to buy modern locomotives for local passenger traffic, instead of the inefficient, obsolete power that they relegated to this duty. He proposed a 2-4-4 suburban locomotive, but the railroads remained deaf to this proposal; the self-propelled unit passenger train, with diesel or gasoline engines, took on this role.

Two factors inhibited the spread of diesel-electric power: high initial cost and low power. No diesel locomotive built to date even remotely equaled the 3,500 horsepower of a big steam locomotive. Even so, by 1933, more than a hundred such locomotives were at work in the U.S., mostly 300 to 600-horsepower switchers and Dickerman remarked, ambiguously:

> Perhaps, at this time there is very little justification for a Diesel locomotive of high horsepower, but we find considerable interest on the part of our railroad friends. There is more than a possibility that there will be a definite field for a locomotive of this type a little later.

A "diesel locomotive of high horsepower" was exactly what the railroads needed; maybe this attitude opened the gate for completely new companies to develop and market the diesel-electric locomotive and push the steam locomotive builders out of business. Certainly, efforts by Alco, Baldwin and Lima to build diesel-electric locomotives were retroactive, rather than proactive; ultimately they failed.

Type	Year	Tractive effort (lb.)	Maximum i.h.p.	At (speed) (m.p.h.)	I.h.p. per axle	Axle load (lb.)
2-8-0	1905	35,000	1,100	20	275	43,000
4-6-0	1905	25,000	1,500	50	400	40,000
4-6-4	1933	45,000	4,000	60	1,300	60,000
4-8-4	1933	70,000	4,000	40	1,000	60,000

"A typical steam locomotive delivered its maximum gross ton-miles per train hour at only 17 miles per hour." Atchison, Topeka & Santa Fe 1790 class 2-8-8-2, No. 1792, (USRA heavy Mallet), built by Alco in 1919, and 3776 class 4-8-4, No. 3778, built by Baldwin in 1941, near Trinidad, Colorado, on January 16, 1944 (Denver Public Library, Otto C. Perry collection, OP-1352).

Many believed in the future of the steam locomotive, sometimes in radically new forms. In 1933, the International Railway Fuel Association Committee on Steam-Turbine and Condensing Locomotives not only reported on the status of such engines in the world, but proposed a design of their own.[5] Two oil-burning, multi-pressure boilers were to supply steam at 850 pounds per square inch to two eight-cylinder, uniflow, closed-circuit, condensing, reciprocating engines, driving four-wheel trucks through clutched gearing. No locomotive of this type was ever built and this proposal marks the beginning of a trend, culminating in the ACE 3000 designs of the 1980s, whereby terrifying physical problems and monumental development costs stood between a paper sketch and its realization as a functioning, commercially viable locomotive.

W. H. Winterrowd, who by 1934 had left Lima to be a Vice-President of Franklin, pointed to the substantial gains in efficiency that had taken place in twenty years[6]:

Year	Types	Steam per i.h.p.-hr. (lb.)	Coal per d.b.h.p.-hr. (lb.)	Power per driving axle (h.p.)
1912	2-8-0, 2-10-0	27	6.5	475
1922	2-8-2, 2-10-2	22	5.0	575
1932	2-8-4, 2-10-4	16	3.0	1,000

As the 1930s wore on, the country remained mired in a never-ending economic depression and[7]:

> due to curtailments in railroad mechanical organizations and an almost complete absence of any new locomotive construction, progress in the development of new locomotive devices and the general application of proven economy devices has been slow and that, as an indirect result of the depression, railroads generally have devoted the period of adjust-

ment to the elimination of wasteful practices and the utilization of existing equipment to the best advantage.

Earlier optimism for the future of the steam locomotive faded. The American approach to locomotive development was more Germanic than British; after World War I, Germany became a leader in the experimental development of all forms of railroad traction and was, therefore, a bellwether for locomotive developments that might—or might not—take place in America.[8] Unfortunately, these experiments were indicating that high capital and maintenance costs and poor reliability were offsetting improvements in fuel efficiency.

Argument continues to this day, whether the steam locomotive was prematurely abandoned. Remarks such as these suggest that, while the steam locomotive (regardless of configuration) was still capable of development, such developments came at a high cost in construction, maintenance and total economy. Although the conventional reciprocating steam locomotive was still open to subtle development, the writing was on the wall that technically and economically successful major developments were not forthcoming.

W. E. Woodard, Vice-President of Lima, tried to promote a light, fast, superpower passenger locomotive.[9] The proposed 4-4-4 had a 62-square foot grate, a 275-pounds per square inch boiler, 21½-inch × 26-inch cylinders with poppet valves and 84-inch driving wheels for a rated tractive effort of 31,000 pounds, with an extra 12,000 pounds from a trailing truck booster for an engine weight of 300,000 pounds.

An interesting innovation was an air preheater, piping exhaust steam through finned tubing in the ash pan air intakes to preheat

Canadian Pacific class F-2a 4-4-4, No. 2924, built by the Montreal Locomotive Works in 1936, at Brandon, Manitoba, on September 23, 1949 (courtesy California State Railroad Museum, Negative 900_18895).

combustion air. Lima had examples under test with favorable results in fuel economy and reduced firebox maintenance. Woodard claimed that this device would bleed exhaust steam with no additional back pressure and without affecting the supply of exhaust steam to the feed water heater.

The boiler was to be air-smoothed, with a pair of smoke deflectors on each side of the front end merging with a hood encasing the steam and sand domes, safety valves and turret. Particular attention was paid to lightening and counterbalancing the reciprocating parts. The engine was to be designed for 2,200 horsepower at speeds higher than 30 miles per hour and capable of hauling a 250-ton train at 90 miles per hour on straight, level track. The Lima proposal met with as little success as the earlier Alco proposal; only the Canadian Pacific ever took up this design with twenty-five locomotives built in Canada in 1936–8.[10]

Samuel Vauclain suggested that the future road engine was a three-cylinder compound 4-8-4 with 80-inch driving wheels, using 350-pounds per square inch steam, still no doubt regretting the lack of acceptance of the Baldwin 4-10-2 compound of 1926.[11]

F. E. Williamson, Superintendent of the New York Central, announced the streamlined 4-6-4, *Commodore Vanderbilt*, diplomatically:

> The New York Central will present this streamlined engine as evidence of its belief that, despite recent developments in the use of other fuels, the day of the steam locomotive is far from past. It believes that, if present expectations are realized, steam can continue to offer the maximum of travel safety and comfort and speeds as high as most persons would care to travel. At the same time, the Central is watching with interest the operation of the existing new models of streamlined trains operated by other than steam power.

"Watching with interest" aptly summarizes the attitude of railroad management in the mid–1930s. An immense steam locomotive fleet,

backed by an enormous design, manufacturing, operating and maintenance workforce, many of whom had devoted their whole working lives to the steam locomotive, provided the entire motive power of a gigantic and essential industry. The economic conditions of the 1930s forced the railroads into a bunker mentality, not conducive to buying new power of any kind but, meanwhile, the diesel-electric locomotive went through a ten-year gestation, supported by those with boundless—and well-placed—faith in its future potential.

Those musing on the future of railroad motive power in the mid–1930s looked at three alternatives: the conventional steam locomotive with its vast design, performance and cost database; the diesel-electric locomotive with its great promise but limited power, high initial cost and minimal database; and the condensing steam turbine locomotive with direct gear drive, about which even less was known than about diesel-electric power.[12] At that time, no steam turbine locomotives had been built in the U.S., while worldwide economic conditions had brought European developments to a standstill, except for one non-condensing steam turbine locomotive in England.

Although advanced steel metallurgy of the 1920s and 1930s contributed markedly to locomotive development, its application—whether the alloys themselves or the heat treatment applied to them—was not problem-free.[13] Laboratory tests on small billets sometimes failed to replicate the performance of the very large cross sections required for locomotive components. Parts made of advanced steels sometimes behaved worse than existing materials when subjected to unforeseen stress, shock or heat. When such parts had to be replaced, railroad shops were not necessarily able to duplicate their metallurgy.

Proponents of the steam locomotive based their case on the continuing refinement of the conventional steam locomotive—and with good reason. In spite of the depression, American steam locomotive development continued beyond the superpower designs of the 1920s, with corresponding improvements in performance. Improvements in steel metallurgy made higher boiler pressures possible with acceptable weight and cost. Refinements in boiler design, power stoking and still bigger fireboxes increased boiler capacity from 15 to 17 pounds of steam per square foot of heating surface per hour to 21 to 22 pounds. Combustion chambers, brick arches supported on arch tubes, siphons and circulator plates improved the efficiency of combustion and steam generation. Type E superheaters produced higher steam temperatures than the Type A. Feed water heaters further increased power output at high speed. Cast-steel engine beds increased mileage between overhauls from 60,000 to 70,000 miles for engines with bolted frames built in the early 1920s to more than 200,000. Mechanical lubrication was more efficient and reliable than lubrication by hand, reducing maintenance and improving reliability. Water treatment reduced the need for boiler wash-outs. Enormous tenders increased range between fuel and water stops; coal capacity could be increased at the expense of water capacity if the user company had track pans. No matter what the power output, higher speeds would have been dangerous and damaging to the track without improvements to the riding qualities of locomotives, including more sophisticated counterbalancing, bigger driving wheels providing lower rotation rates at high speed, redesigned, lighter reciprocating parts, disc driving wheels and improved suspension. Many of these features could be retrofitted during major overhauls. These improvements, in combination, had the result that the last steam locomotives built in America, in the 1940s, achieved power and efficiency that no one believed possible only a few years before.[14]

Unlike the developments between 1890 and 1920, this came about with minimal increases in size by means of refinements that were for the most part externally invisible; a quiet revolution in power density took place over the years.[15] In 1912, a New York Central K-80 4-6-2 weighed 177 pounds per drawbar horsepower. Twenty-five years of passenger locomotive development by the New York Central produced the J-3a 4-6-4, weighing only 93 pounds per drawbar horsepower. Design for maintainability, better manufacturing standards and better maintenance facilities paralleled this trend. In 1940, a J-3a ran three times as many miles per month as a K-3 fifteen years before, hauling trains twice as heavy.

Four designs bought by one railroad (unnamed, possibly the New York Central) illustrate this point, especially as all were six-coupled; weight and external dimensions increased only slightly over the years and adhesion weight remained almost constant.

Year built	Configuration	Evaporation rate (lb./hr.)	Maximum i.h.p.	Speed of max. i.h.p. (m.p.h.)
1910	4-6-2	45,000	1,870	50
1925	4-6-2	65,000	3,040	54
1927	4-6-4	74,000	4,073	65
1937	4-6-4	84,000	4,700	75

The influence of superpower design is clear from the difference between the 4-6-2 of 1925 and the 4-6-4 of 1927, but the comparison between the 4-6-4 of 1927 and 1937 points to refinements that continued even through the depression years. Not only did maximum power increase, but the speed at which maximum power was developed also increased.

Gains in thermal efficiency did not match these encouraging trends. Depressingly, R. Johnson, Baldwin's chief engineer, pointed out in 1940 that the introduction of high-termperature superheat around 1910 had been the last major improvement in steam locomo-

One of the successes of American steam locomotive design, this New York Central class J-3a 4-6-4, No. 5450, leaves Chicago on August 10, 1939. Alco built fifty in 1937–38 (Denver Public Library, Otto C. Perry collection, OP-13610).

tive thermal efficiency. Since then, typical specific steam consumption had decreased by only 8% and even this came mostly from supplying hotter and higher-pressure steam to the cylinders.[16] The 1926 Baldwin 4-10-2 high-pressure compound achieved a steam consumption of 14 to 15 pounds per indicated horsepower-hour under test at Altoona. The British estimated that the London, Midland & Scottish Railway's single-expansion *Coronation*-class 4-6-2s, built in the 1930s, achieved 14.5 pounds per indicated horsepower-hour with 250 pounds per square inch boiler pressure and 615°F steam.[17] These seemed to be irreducible minima. The French, however, persevered with superheating, compounding and the 4-8-0 wheel arrangement; a locomotive of this type, designed by Chapelon, achieved a steam consumption of only 11.7 pounds per indicated horsepower-hour, using steam at 295 pounds per square inch and 750°F. While the Chapelon engine achieved a cylinder thermal efficiency of 12.8%, this still compared poorly with a steam-turbine power station, using steam at 1,350 pounds per square inch and 950°F, reaching a turbine-shaft efficiency of 34.2%. The steam locomotive was still being improved in various ways; thermal efficiency was not one of them.

These refinements did, however, contribute to ever-lower fuel consumption per ton-mile. In 1921, the average coal consumption of the Class I railroads was 162 pounds per thousand freight ton-miles. By 1931, the railroads had forced this figure down to only 119 pounds, a decrease of 27%. Six years later, this figure was down to 117 pounds, a further decrease of 1%, reflecting the economic and financial stagnation of that time. Most of this decrease occurred, therefore, between 1921 and 1931, a period of major civil engineering works and improved operating efficiencies as well as advances in locomotive design and construction. Renewed investment in overhauls and new locomotives in the late 1930s forced this figure down farther to 112 pounds in 1939, reaching an all-time low of 109 pounds in 1941, but

rising to 115 pounds in 1944. If the railroads had spent as much on modernizing their steam locomotive fleet as they did on diesel-electric locomotives in the late 1940s, this figure might have gone down farther, but such was not to be.

At the beginning of 1937, the locomotive fleet numbered 44,400, with an average age of twenty years. Of these, 71% had been built before 1920, representing an enormous technological inertia; 25% were built between 1920 and 1929; only 4% had been built since 1929. The improved fuel economy mentioned above, therefore, was achieved in spite of an aged and aging locomotive fleet.

The steam locomotive was capable of almost infinite rebuilding. Ralph Johnson remarked in 1945, with little exaggeration[18]:

> The life of a locomotive, if given regular overhaulings, is not based on the wearing out of the machine, for it can be repaired indefinitely and will still haul the same train at the same speed and with the same consumption of fuel, water and oil as when new, though there may not be a single pound of the original material still in it.

Small alterations, externally invisible, could pay surprising dividends in increasing the power of an aging locomotive fleet.[19] The St. Louis & San Francisco increased the power of a 2-8-2 by one-third by increasing steam lap by 1¼ inch and increasing the steam port width by 9⁄16 inch. The company improved the performance of older 4-8-2s with 210 pounds per square inch boiler pressure to match newer locomotives of the same type with 250-pounds per square inch boilers by increasing the number of superheater flues from forty-five to sixty-three, the piston valve diameter from 13 inches to 15, steam lap by 15⁄16 inches and maximum valve travel by 2 inches; they estimated that adding a feed water heater would increase power at the drawbar by 12% to 13%.

Even if locomotive construction ceased in the 1930s, fleet improve-

Technological inertia: The Minneapolis & St. Louis was still running this class G3-22 4-6-0, No. 215, built by Alco in 1900–01, when Otto Perry photographed it at Grand Junction, Iowa, on September 27, 1935 (Denver Public Library, Otto C. Perry collection, OP-12783).

"Scrap that littered the property." This Minneapolis & St. Louis 4-6-0, No. 202, was probably built before 1900, photographed at Marshall-town, Iowa, on September 27, 1935 (Denver Public Library, Otto C. Perry collection, OP-12773).

This Sprague-era Minneapolis & St. Louis class M1-46 2-8-2, No. 649, came from Alco sometime between 1915 and 1921, photographed at Minneapolis, Minnesota, on August 3, 1937 (Denver Public Library, Otto C. Perry collection, OP-12782).

ments still went on—as much because of the depression as in spite of it. The energetic management of L. C. Sprague turned the Minneapolis & St. Louis around from a hopeless bankrupt to an efficient railroad between 1934 and 1939.[20] He sold the scrap that littered the property, including eighty-four locomotives and more than three thousand freight cars, and used the proceeds to finance improvements, including the rebuilding of eighty-two locomotives. Retrofits included boosters, siphons, power stokers, disc driving wheels, mechanical lubricators, improved superheaters and feed water heaters, increasing the tractive effort of thirty-five of these locomotives from 46,000 pounds to 62,000.

While the late 1920s saw the emergence of the 4-8-4 as the new standard, multi-purpose locomotive for freight and passenger service, by 1938 its dominance was complete, and "there is no good reason for making a distinction between passenger and freight locomotives, now no more than a remnant of an age-long custom."[21] For hauling heavy freight trains over severe grades, however, the single-expansion, Mallet-type, articulated locomotive remained supreme.

In 1933, Alco acquired the North American manufacturing rights to the Beyer-Garratt, the only articulated locomotive ever to rival the Mallet in size or popularity. Invented by the English engineer, H. Garratt, the first one was built by the British firm, Beyer Peacock, in 1907. (For complete coverage of the Garratt, see R. L. Hills and D. Patrick, *Beyer, Peacock: Locomotive Builders to the World*, Venture Publications, UK, 1982. Garratts—including the first one ever built—are standard power on the Welsh Highland Railway; see the Welsh Highland Railway website.) Popular in the British Empire, the Beyer-Garratt carried the boiler, firebox and cab on a bridge between two swiveling drive units. The front drive unit carried the water tank; the rear drive unit carried the coal bunker. When the Garratt first appeared, the Mallet was already mature and gaining a foothold in America; the Garratt offered no decisive advantages over the Mallet and some disadvantages. Built in both compound and single-expansion versions, it readily accommodated a fat boiler and a deep firebox, but its adhesion weight changed as fuel and water were consumed. Longer steam pipes and more numerous swiveling joints than the Mallet were another penalty. As far as is known, no Garratt was ever built in the U.S.[22]

The locomotive exhibits at the 1937 American Association of Railroads Mechanical Division convention showed that, for all its immense size and power, and the refinements resulting from decades of invention and attention to detail, the steam locomotive was doomed.[23] The Pennsylvania exhibited an electric express passenger locomotive, weighing 460,000 pounds and capable of 73,000 pounds tractive effort. With almost limitless power available from fixed electric power sources, this locomotive was capable of 7,000 horsepower, continuously rated at 4,620 horsepower at 90 miles per hour. No steam locomotive could match this. Most ominous for the steam locomotive was a diesel-electric locomotive built by Electro-Motive for the Baltimore & Ohio, comprising two separate vehicles, each powered by two 900-horsepower diesel engines—3,600 horsepower controlled from a single cab. Each unit ran on two six-wheel trucks, of which four wheels were drivers and two were idlers. The axle loading on the driving wheels was only 23,400 pounds, with no dynamic augment. Control technology now put the diesel-electric locomotive into direct competition with the steam locomotive.

The steam locomotive was doomed in all its forms. Efforts to develop some radically new and more efficient form of steam locomotive grew ever more costly, the results ever more complex and the gap between concept and actuality ever wider. In 1937, after ten years' work, the Railway Fuel and Traveling Engineers' Association Committee on Steam Turbine and Steam Condensing Locomotives came up with a 4,000-horsepower condensing steam turbine locomotive with mechanical drive, using steam at 1,200-pounds per square inch, generated in an oil-fired boiler with automatic controls.[24] The committee had to admit that a conventional 4-6-4 steam locomotive produced more tractive effort at 60 miles per hour and cost one-third as much to manufacture, both absolutely and per pound of weight and drawbar horsepower, as their proposal.

Some of the sharpest engineering minds in the world gave of their utmost to come up with some more efficient form of steam engine.[25] Steam locomotive design had reached the limits of steam temperature, pressure and heat recovery. To break out of these limits, engineers even considered working fluids other than water, such as mercury or mineral oil but, even in concept, the difficulties of applying them to steam locomotives were too great to contemplate for long. In the 1950s, the University of Utah even considered a nuclear-powered locomotive.[26] Designers of conventional steam locomotives faced other insoluble problems: high speeds required high piston speeds, resulting in undesirably short valve events and heavy reciprocating forces, unless the driving wheel diameter could be increased. Bigger driving wheels increased the boiler height above the track, squeezing the boiler diameter against height clearance limits, raising the center of gravity of the locomotive and reducing maximum permissible speeds on curves. Some of the latest steam locomotives were known to slip to dangerous wheel speeds without the enginemen being aware of it.

The steam locomotive had few supporters as staunch as W. H. Winterrowd, who became a vice-president of Baldwin in 1939. In 1937, he asserted[27]:

> The steam locomotive is the backbone of railroad transportation in this country. It will continue to be that backbone for many years to come.

With some condescension:

> Those statements should not be construed to decry the value of some other forms of railroad motive power which, in more or less restricted service, or under certain conditions of operation, have proved their great value to the railroads. Neither should they be construed to decry the very great importance of continual research, development, and experimentation in connection with other forms of motive power which indicate promise of real value.

He finished off by saying:

> If some form of motive power can be developed that will do as much, do it as cheaply, and net a greater return upon the investment than the truly best steam locomotive, that type of motive power will eventually supplant all steam locomotives. Nothing like that is on the horizon today.

In view of the locomotive exhibits outside the convention hall where Winterrowd was speaking, the last sentence shows a certain lack of imagination, even blindness, to the developments that were going on around him.

Even during the depression, the development and commissioning of diesel-electric locomotives went on—155 new locomotives of this type during 1937, making a total of 389 in service by the end of the year.[28] The majority were 300-, 600- and 900-horsepower switchers (354). Next most common were twenty-seven passenger locomotives, all but three developing more than 1,000 horsepower, including thirteen of more than 2,000 horsepower.

With some economic recovery in the late 1930s, the railroads became obsessed with speed in both passenger and freight service. Some freight trains were averaging start-to-stop speeds of 45 to 50 miles per hour, necessitating maximum speeds up to 70 miles per hour, while the new target for passenger power was a locomotive capable of hauling a 1,000-ton train at 100 miles per hour on straight,

The Baltimore & Ohio built this class N-1 duplex-drive 4-4-4-4, No. 5600, in its own shops in 1937. Otto Perry photographed it on display in New York on August 5, 1939 (Denver Public Library, Otto C. Perry collection, OP-2521).

level track. In 1937, the American Association of Railroads Mechanical Division formed a Committee on Further Development of the Reciprocating Steam Locomotive to study this as one of its objectives. This committee included vice-presidents from Alco, Baldwin and Lima and senior mechanical officers from the Chesapeake & Ohio, the New York Central, the Pennsylvania and the Santa Fe.

The committee's specifications, arrived at in 1938, comprised a conventional, radial-stayed boiler supplying steam at 300 pounds per square inch and 750°F to a four-cylinder engine with a duplex 4-4 driving wheel arrangement and 84-inch driving wheels developing 6,400 cylinder horsepower, 4,000 drawbar horsepower, at a high adhesion factor of 4.5 to enable fast acceleration. J. E. Ennis of the New York Central pointed out that existing 4-6-4s already came close to the performance objective and either a 4-6-4 or a 4-8-4 could reach it with minimal development.

Duplex drive was the last major new configuration of the reciprocating steam locomotive—two pairs of cylinders, each driving two axles, all mounted in a single frame.[29] The Baltimore & Ohio built a 4-4-4-4 of this type with a water-tube firebox in 1937; they removed it from service in 1943 and scrapped it in 1950. The Pennsylvania followed with eighty such engines built between 1939 and 1946. No other railroad took on this idea.

In October 1938, the AAR study developed into a road test of a 1,000-ton passenger train and dynamometer car, provided by the Pennsylvania, on a round trip between Fort Wayne, Indiana, and Grand Island, Nebraska. The Pennsylvania provided a K-4s 4-6-2; the Chicago & North Western provided an E-4 4-6-4, built in 1937; the Union Pacific provided an FEF-1 4-8-4, built in 1938.[30]

Train resistance by itself suggested that 3,400 drawbar horsepower would haul a 1,000-ton passenger train at 100 miles per hour on straight, level track. The problem lay in the excess power needed to

accelerate the train to that speed and sustain it against even slight adverse grades. The highest speed reached during the tests was 102 miles per hour by the Union Pacific 4-8-4 on a slightly descending grade of 0.1%. The test engineers calculated that, on level track, the locomotive could not have accelerated the train beyond 99 miles per hour. The tests showed that locomotives capable of more than 5,000 horsepower would be needed to achieve the stated objectives.

The power output of the locomotives used in the road tests all peaked at 370 to 390 revolutions per minute—70 to 80 miles per hour—as friction losses in steam passages and very short valve events choked off the supply of steam. Poppet valves and very short cut-off might solve this problem, but the committee also pointed out that[31]: "The entire question of counterbalance is in a chaotic condition."

In the summer of 1939, Europe stood on the brink of war and the American railroads were about to replace the steam locomotive with the diesel-electric. A comment from middle management—J. Bjorkholm, Assistant Superintendent of Motive Power with the Milwaukee, who had climbed the career ladder the hard way—is revealing.[32]

> The internal-combustion engine, and more particularly the Diesel, is challenging the steam locomotive for supremacy. Even those of us who have spent a lifetime in close companionship with the steam locomotive, those of us who have learned to look upon it as something alive, something to nurse and caress, even though we may have cussed it at times and called it names that can be found only in the railroad vocabulary, must admit that the newcomer has many advantages and looks like a real competitor.

He made the point that the high initial cost of a diesel locomotive was worthwhile, only if it could be intensively used. Even so, he pointed to "almost phenomenal" progress in railroading, particularly in passenger and switching service. In prospect:

As the demand for this type of power becomes greater, however, and the production becomes higher, it is reasonable to believe that the cost will be reduced and I am looking forward to the Diesels replacing a large number of steam locomotives in the near future.

The 694 locomotives ordered for U.S. domestic service in 1940 was the biggest number since 1929.[33] Of these, two thirds were diesel-electrics, mostly switchers. Electro-Motive built on its earlier success and offered a 5,400-horsepower diesel-electric locomotive. Successful service trials brought orders for eight from three railroads; two railroads ordered two 2,000-horsepower and five 4,000-horsepower locomotives of the same type. These engines were freight power, competing head-on with the steam locomotive in its last undisputed territory. The war distorted the railroads' intentions but did not entirely frustrate them.

Railroads met wartime demand by buying whatever new steam and diesel locomotives they could. The manufacturers could not gear up fast enough, resulting in back order times of a year or more and, in 1942, the War Production Board stepped in to control raw materials. The railroads launched extensive and ingenious rebuilding programs, revealing the manufacturing capability of company shops.

In 1940–2, the Missouri Pacific rebuilt twenty-five Lima 2-8-4s, built in 1930, at its Sedalia, Missouri, shops as 4-8-4s, installing cast-steel engine beds and 75-inch Boxpok driving wheels with roller bearings, instead of the original 63-inch wheels.[34] They rebuilt the boilers for 250 pounds per square inch, up from 230, and added 63-inch combustion chambers and siphons to the fireboxes. The rebuild was 33,750 pounds heavier than the original at 445,950 pounds. The intention was to reduce maintenance costs, improve availability and haul faster trains without excessive wear and tear to locomotives or track. It is particularly interesting that the Missouri Pacific should

have chosen 2-8-4s to rebuild, considering that in the mid–1920s these were thought to be the ultimate in steam power. The rebuild summarized the advances that had taken place in fifteen years. By 1942, the first rebuilds had been in service for nearly two years and were running twice the monthly mileage of the original engines.

The Baltimore & Ohio tried to order twenty-three diesel locomotives in 1942; the War Production Board allowed them only nine.[35] (Perversely, the Louisville & Nashville received eight 4,000-horsepower diesels instead of the 4-8-4s it wanted.[36]) The B&O therefore turned to its fleet of 663 2-8-2s bought from Alco, Lima and Baldwin between 1911 and 1923. They gave one of these engines, built in 1923, a new tender, increasing coal capacity from 17½ tons to 32 and water capacity from 12,000 gallons to 29,000, eliminating several fuel and water stops. They took another, bored out its cylinders by ¾ inch, rebuilt the boiler to increase pressure from 220 to 240 pounds per square inch, replaced the 64-inch driving wheels with 70-inch, improved the counterbalancing and lubrication, added a device to cushion the lateral play of the rear driving wheels and substituted a high-capacity tender. Successful dynamometer tests led to the modification of three other 2-8-2s, built in 1911–13, that were already awaiting heavy repair, including new driving wheels, frames, cylinders and fireboxes.

The B. & O. modified twenty more 2-8-2s from that period more extensively as 4-8-2s. New boilers increased pressure from 190 pounds per square inch to 230 pounds; new 27-inch × 32-inch cylinders replaced the 26-inch × 32-inch originals; 70-inch driving wheels replaced 64-inch. Ten received a half engine bed, replacing the front half of the frame and its attachments; ten received complete new engine beds. Combustion chambers, Baker valve gear, power stokers, feed water heaters and power reversers were also added. New tenders held 26 tons of coal and 27,500 gallons of water. Tractive effort

The Missouri Pacific rebuilt a Lima 2-8-4 in its own shops in 1940–42 to produce this 4-8-4, No. 2107, shown at Horace, Kansas, on November 21, 1941 (Denver Public Library, Otto C. Perry collection, OP-12966).

increased from 54,000 pounds to 65,000 and the new engines saved 17% in fuel, compared to the old ones. The company modernized one engine a month at its Mount Clare shops; the resulting class T-3 ultimately numbered forty; modification went on until 1948. These locomotives were not scrapped until 1960, making them, together with the class EM-1 2-8-8-4s, the last survivors of the Baltimore & Ohio's steam locomotive fleet. Examples abounded from other railroads.

By 1944, the Rock Island was hauling more than twice the freight traffic and five times the passenger traffic that it had in 1939.[37] Between 1943 and 1945, the company bought nineteen passenger diesels, six 5,400-horsepower freight diesels, eleven 1,000-horsepower diesel road switchers and ten oil-burning 4-8-4s. In addition, they rebuilt and upgraded sixty-four 4-8-4s (Alco, 1929–30), eighteen 4-8-2s (Alco, 1913–27) and eighteen 2-8-2s (Alco, 1927).

As the end of the war came into sight, American railroad motive power stood at a crossroads and "Speculation as to the locomotive of the future is always an interesting pastime."[38] No less than five different types of motive power stood poised to challenge or continue the supremacy of the steam locomotive: conventional steam, electric, diesel-electric, steam-turbine and coal-burning gas-turbine. Many senior executives still could not believe that anything would replace the conventional steam locomotive in the foreseeable future.

In 1943, T. V. Buckwalter, vice-president of Timken, pointed to the high capital cost of diesel-electric locomotives—$87.50 per horsepower vs. $35.00 per horsepower for a steam locomotive—and the consequent difficulty of financing them and[39]:

> the weight of evidence gives indications that the steam locomotive is just entering its period of most useful life and, further, that the demise of the steam locomotive has been placed so far into the future centuries as to be utterly unpredictable.

In 1944, Duncan W. Fraser, President of Alco, remarked, complacently[40]:

> Progress in steam locomotives has gone hand in hand with Diesel developments. Modern steam locomotives, capable of 20,000 miles per month are now in use, reflecting a high level of availability similar to that of Diesel locomotives. It is unlikely that there will be any one dominant type of locomotive, at least in the foreseeable future. Steam, Diesel and electric, each have their advantages and the selection of motive power is influenced by operating conditions and needs which vary between railroads, and on the same railroad, so that the final choice may be either one or all three from the standpoint of economy and service.

As late as 1946, the president of a coal-mining company asserted[41]:

> I don't believe for a moment that a diesel locomotive is ever going to be able to pull a train of cars over the road as cheaply as a properly constructed, properly operated, properly fueled coal-burning steam locomotive, ... (as an afterthought) ... a coal-burning locomotive in any case.

Few foresaw that 40,000 steam locomotives would become scrap metal in the next few years.

Diesel-electric locomotives had become standardized to an extent that favored mass-production, whereas buyers of steam locomotives demanded their own designs.[42] Between October 1942 and September 1943, the railroads bought 170 new steam locomotives of eleven different wheel arrangements and twenty-nine different designs; although eighty-two were 4-8-4s, they ranged in weight from 399,000 pounds to 508,000. Both the USRA and the British nationalized railroad system of the 1950s had to provide twelve different classes of "standard" locomotive. Even with government authority over a unified rail system, the steam locomotive could not be standardized beyond a very limited degree.

The new 5,400-horsepower diesel freight locomotives competed head-to-head with existing steam freight locomotives, greatly to the disadvantage of the latter.[43] One western railroad in mountainous country found that its oil-burning steam locomotives burned 24 gallons of oil per locomotive mile, while the diesels burned 6. A sample group of articulated steam locomotives on this same railroad hauled 2,600 tons per train; the diesels hauled 3,325 tons. The steam engines spent 32% of their time on the road, 46% at terminals and 22% available but not being used; these figures for the diesels were 59%, 11% and 30% respectively. Operating costs, including fuel and maintenance were $1.70 per locomotive mile for steam, $0.82 for diesel. This may be skewed by the relative ages of the locomotives being compared, but the writing was on the wall for steam power.

The more the steam locomotive was studied, the more obvious, glaring and frustrating its defects. The more the diesel-electric was studied, the more numerous its perceived advantages.[44] The axle loading of a diesel-electric locomotive did not increase with power. A single-unit, 2,000-horsepower diesel-electric locomotive, running on six axles, might have an axle loading of 52,000 pounds; adding two power units produced 6,000 horsepower with the same axle loading. Increases in steam locomotive power depended on ever-stronger track and sub-structures; in some cases, track strength limited the routes that the new, high-power steam locomotives could use.

The engineer of a 4-8-4 on the head end of a Milwaukee freight train circumvented a traffic jam by using an old branch line, but[45]:

> As I looked at that pea vine, I was aghast that he (the engineer) would risk such an undertaking. It seemed to be a railroad track all right; four feet, eight and one-half inches wide, give or take a couple of inches. The eighty-five pound, spaghetti-like rails were supported on crossties shriveled by the ravages of time and sunk in a ballast of cinders and mud better suited to growing toadstools than carrying the massive weight of an S3 locomotive. Rails that for decades had borne nothing heavier than a C5. (2-8-0 built 1913)
>
> We crept along that perilous path at a rate that should have been monitored by a sun dial and held our breath at each lurch or squeal, fearful that the engine was about to be divorced from the rails. Oran hung far out of the window, listening for sounds of impending disaster, his brow as furrowed as a scrub board, one foot braced against the brake valve pedestal and his left hand wrapped around the automatic brake valve in a grip you couldn't dislodge with a tire iron. Thoughts of how he could plausibly explain a derailment here must have been fevering his brain. The rash move succeeded, however, enabling him to execute a balancing act worthy of the most daring of high-wire performers."

Lower hostling and maintenance labor demand, high availability, the absence of coal and ash handling, reduced demand for watering facilities, the absence of dynamic augment and now increased route availability, were a dream come true for hard-pressed railroad management that more than offset higher capital costs.

> This one fact, alone ... has made it possible for many roads having a considerable proportion of single-track main line, light rail and relatively low bridge capacities to handle a volume of passenger traffic that could not have been handled with motive power other than Diesel without making costly changes to the physical structure of the right-of-way.

Diesel locomotives benefited from heavy automotive developments forced on by the war; more and more powerful diesels became available.[46] In the summer of 1946, the Santa Fe bought a 6,000-horsepower diesel locomotive, built by an Alco-General Electric joint venture, comprising three power units with a single, 2,000-horsepower diesel engine in each. With thirty-six driving wheels—more than a triplex Mallet—axle loading was no more than 51,000 pounds.

Proponents of the steam locomotive fought back, pointing to large advances in power, speed, availability and range between servicing, even though the locomotive of 1945 was—externally—barely distinguishable from that of 1925 or even 1915. Manufacturing executives were confident that innovations of the 1920s and 1930s would be further improved.[47] Still under investigation with varying degrees of promise were poppet valves, pulverized coal, high-pressure water-tube boilers, welded boilers, and turbine and duplex drives. By 1945, however, the diesel-electric locomotive was the new benchmark against which such developments had to be assessed. Worse yet for the advocates of steam power, railroads admitted that they could not have met wartime traffic demands without diesel freight locomotives, small though their numbers were.[48] The proponents of advanced steam locomotives, whether refined or reconfigured, became voices crying in the wilderness.

In spite of major improvements in steam locomotive performance between 1920 and 1945, most steam locomotives were built to sub-optimal designs and were never optimized in service. Copious examples showed that, when even a new locomotive was tested, its performance could be substantially improved by quite minor modifications. Only a tiny fraction of the fleet was ever tested and optimized. One commentator pointed out[49]:

> Locomotive design is not an exact science, and the few roads that have adequate facilities for testing their motive power usually find that some minor changes from the original design are absolutely necessary to secure the best results. In some cases, a new design, though prepared with the utmost care, has proved so uneconomical that the railroad after testing a sample engine has never built another like it.

Testing on the scale required was impossible, yet:

> No better evidence of the loss that railroads are undoubtedly experiencing if they are not using dynamometer cars could be offered than the results which one railroad obtained when it placed a dynamometer car in service. On a Mikado type locomotive, which was performing with no complaint from the crew, an exhaust tip ⅜ in. smaller in diameter increased the firebox temperature 400 deg. F. and resulted in a saving in coal amounting to $57,000 a year.

Fifty-seven thousand dollars a year would buy a new locomotive in two years.

> An adjustment in the valve gear resulted in an increase of 7.8 per cent in the drawbar horsepower. On another locomotive, by making several changes as indicated by the test data, the coal consumption was reduced 9.8 per cent and the engine was enabled to haul three additional passenger cars with less fuel and water than it had formerly used with the smaller train.

The inference is obvious: the vast majority of the steam locomotives in the U.S. never worked as well as they could. Those words were written in 1920; they remained substantially true to the end of steam.

One obscure factor extended the life of the steam locomotive: the symbiosis between railroads and coal mines. In 1943, U.S. railroads carried 774 million tons of coal, contributing one-third of their freight tonnage and one-eighth of their gross revenues, of which they themselves burned 124 million tons.[50] The oil-burning diesel locomotive was such an alarming threat to this relationship that coal-carrying railroads, such as the Pennsylvania, the Chesapeake & Ohio and the Norfolk & Western, tried to sustain the coal-burning steam locomotive—or any locomotive that would burn coal—with a desperation that is now forgotten. The destruction of this *status quo* was foreseen as a "catastrophe." Many people, therefore, had a vested interest in extending the life of the coal-burning locomotive by whatever means and in whatever forms might be possible. It is no coincidence that these three railroads bought the last and among the more bizarre

reconfigurations of the coal-burning locomotive. Other voices warned of shortages of diesel fuel in the face of soaring automotive, aviation and military demand. Even so, a major coal miners' strike in 1946, with the threat of more to come, was "a factor definitely favorable to an increase in the use of Diesel locomotives" and the difference in first cost between steam and diesel locomotives was narrowing.[51]

Urged by R. B. White, President of the Baltimore & Ohio, eight coal-carrying railroads and four coal producers pooled their resources in 1945 to form a Locomotive Development Committee within the existing Bituminous Coal Research Inc. to experiment with new types of coal-burning locomotive.[52] Another joint venture between the coal-carrying railroads, General Electric and Babcock & Wilcox aimed at developing a coal-burning steam turbine locomotive. Yet another joint venture between railroads and equipment companies aimed to develop a coal-burning, gas-turbine locomotive.

In view of the intense effort devoted to new forms of coal-burning locomotive, a remark by J. W. Barriger, President of the Chicago, Indianapolis & Louisville, in 1947 is of great interest[53]:

> One must never forget that when Rudolph Diesel made his great invention, he was really searching for a device to burn coal in an internal-combustion engine. He expected to use liquid fuel in its elementary stages of development, but intended to perfect the device for injection of solid fuel in powdered form. His untimely death and developments in the petroleum industry removed the pressure and incentives to achieve Diesel's full ambition—but the time seems ripe to do it soon. Certainly the problems of solid-fuel injection and disposal of the waste products should not be beyond the possibility of solution by the resourcefulness and talent and scientific ingenuity of industry's engineers.

Diesel's "full ambition" has yet to be achieved; the problems remain unsolved.

The end of the war in 1945 ended the extreme pressures under which the railroads had operated for the previous four years[54]; increasing capacity was not, therefore, an issue. The main issue was the replacement of the huge fleet of old steam locomotives.

The American locomotive building industry stood on the threshold of the most fundamental and disquieting changes in its hundred-year history, with immense commercial rewards for those companies that benefited from the changing environment and extinction awaiting those that failed to do so. Alco, Baldwin and Lima faced the threat that their decades of accumulated experience, their tens of thousands of employees, their millions of drawings, jigs and patterns and their huge investment in plant—all devoted to the reciprocating steam locomotive—could become valueless. They tried to adapt to the new environment, forming partnerships with companies representing the new technology with the result that, in 1945, four entities were building diesel-electric locomotives: the Electro-Motive Division of General Motors, Alco-General Electric, Baldwin-Westinghouse and Fairbanks-Morse. Any one of five fundamentally different types could be the locomotive of the future, perhaps more than one: reciprocating steam, electric, diesel-electric, steam-turbine and gas-turbine, the two latter with either geared or electric transmission. Backing the wrong horse with research, development and marketing dollars could have alarming consequences.

A few railroads did not get the diesel message. By 1945, the Norfolk & Western had one of the most highly developed steam locomotive fleets in the country, mostly built in their own shops, comprising eighty-one passenger locomotives, of which only the eleven J's were of up-to-date design, and 339 freight engines, of which 105 A's and Y-6's were of up-to-date design, supported by equally up-to-date servicing and maintenance plants. Perhaps they could afford to be almost comically blind to diesel locomotive developments[55]:

A Norfolk & Western class Y-3a 2-8-8-2, No. 2064, undergoing heavy overhaul in the company's Roanoke shops, August 27, 1943 (courtesy Norfolk Southern Corporation, ns147).

The Norfolk & Western is not "allergic" to Diesel power plants. We own and operate some Diesel equipment, such as a bunkering barge for refueling ships, and work equipment consisting of bulldozers, shovels, and locomotive cranes. We have an order placed for a 250-ton Diesel wrecking crane.

The writer acknowledged that diesel locomotives had their uses, but, for the Norfolk & Western:

The Norfolk & Western serves the bituminous coal fields of southern West Virginia and southwestern Virginia which produce a great volume of coal. In the year 1945 we handled a total of 47,600,000 net tons of coal other than our own fuel. Naturally, we are interested in the welfare of the coal business. It is our belief that the conventional type of coal-burning steam locomotive can be greatly improved and made at least the equal in efficiency and economy of operation, under most conditions, of any other type of railroad locomotive. Our experience with the operation of the types of locomotive I have just described (Norfolk & Western classes J, A and Y-6) further confirms us in this view.

The Louisville & Nashville spent $7.6 million on twenty-two new 2-8-4s in 1949, adding to an existing class of twenty and scrapping ninety-one older engines.[56] The Western Maryland took pride in[57]

the quality and power of its steam locomotives—some of the world's heaviest Consolidations, the biggest Decapods ever built, and massive 4-6-6-4 Mallets.... Maintained in engine houses and shops at Hagerstown, Knobmount, Elkins and elsewhere, with watchmaker's precision and more-than-housewifely cleanliness, they give every evidence of being able to maintain themselves for years to come as one of the last outposts of steam railroading.

The Chesapeake & Ohio continued its enthusiasm for steam for the same reasons as the Norfolk & Western, ordering sixty 2-6-6-6s from Lima between 1942 and 1948. The company underwent a change of heart in the following year, canceling an order for fifteen 2-6-6-2s and selling thirty 0-8-0 switchers, built in 1948, to the Norfolk & Western in 1950.[58]

At this teeter point between steam and diesel power (1947), Paul W. Kiefer, Chief Engineer Motive Power and Rolling Stock for the New York Central, provided an insight into locomotive procurement, both retrospective and prospective, by one of the country's biggest railroads.[59] As a strategy:

Over the years it has been our unceasing determination and practice to advance the design of the reciprocating steam locomotive, not only to achieve progressively better results therewith, but also to enforce

The New York Central's class S-1 4-8-4s, built by Alco in 1945–46, were among the ultimate developments of American steam power. Otto Perry photographed No. 6015 at Indianapolis, Indiana, on June 30, 1956 (Denver Public Library, Otto C. Perry collection, OP-13428).

constantly higher standards for new and competing forms of motive power which, in turn, has accelerated the development and improvement of reciprocating steam. As a self-contained power plant, it provides horsepower at the lowest initial cost of any type of locomotive now used or under consideration.

Kiefer pointed out, however, that much needed to be done to improve reliability and reduce down time, otherwise the time might come when the steam locomotive could not compete with other forms of power. The company had continually sought to decrease weight per horsepower and increase steam generation, power and thermal efficiency. Roller bearings had improved mechanical efficiency and better counterbalancing reduced track damage. The company's history of achieving its goals for the steam locomotive was long and successful.

Type	Class	Year	Weight lb.	Weight lb./dbhp.	Steam Pressure p.s.i.	Tractive Effort lb.	Maximum i.h.p.	At speed m.p.h.
4-6-2	K-5	1924-6	308,000	123	200	37,600	2,500	45
4-6-4	J-1	1927–31	358,600	115	225	42,400	3,100	54
4-8-4	S-1	1945	471,000	89	290	65,000	5,300	62

Detailed studies showed that the S-1's were fully competitive with diesels. The higher thermal efficiency of the diesel was offset—at that time and place—by the higher cost of fuel and a diesel still cost twice as much to buy as an equivalent steam locomotive. When all costs were fully estimated, the New York Central reckoned the total annual cost per mile at $1.22 for an S-1 and $1.48 for an equivalent diesel. The steam locomotive, however, suffered heavily from qualitative disadvantages that were difficult to estimate. In severe winter weather handling coal, water and ash was difficult and time-consuming. Large variations in performance could result from coal

quality and crew efficiency. The diesel beat the steam locomotive at its own traditional game: high tractive effort at low speed, providing better performance on heavy grades and faster acceleration. Other advantages of the diesel, as seen by the New York Central, were reduction in track stress, a lower center of gravity, better riding qualities, cleaner operation, less time for servicing en route and higher availability.

By the end of 1946, eighty-two railroads had 3,624 diesels in service, including 386 rated at 4,000 horsepower or more and one rated at 8,000 horsepower, equaling the most powerful steam locomotives.[60]

This situation evolved so quickly that, in late 1947, J. W. Barriger remarked[61]:

> It now seems unlikely that any railroads except those so closely linked to the coal industry as the Norfolk & Western, Chesapeake & Ohio, Virginian, and Clinchfield will ever again order any substantial numbers of reciprocating steam locomotives.

Steam locomotive numbers fell below 30,000 in 1949, for the first time since the 1800s.[62] The real massacre of the steam locomotive fleet gathered momentum in 1951 to satisfy a national need for scrap metal, partly to build new locomotives and rolling stock, partly to provide munitions for the Korean War.

Symbolic both of the nation's need for scrap metal and of the declining importance of steam locomotives on many of the nation's railroads was "a retired locomotive being dismembered at the Worcester, Mass., plant of the American Steel & Wire Co,... It takes three men a week to break down the old locomotive and to segregate copper, brass and bronze parts from heavy melting steel scrap—of which this locomotive, plus 12 others, will yield about 2,000 tons."[63]

With glee, the Belt Railway of Chicago

> contributed the biggest single haul—more than 1,000 tons—of steel scrap uncovered up to that time by the special committee on scrap collection of the Chicago Association of Commerce & Industry, when it turned over, in early January (1952), seven 0-8-0 switchers from 24 to 38 years old, plus a 150-ton locomotive coaling plant.[64]

There were ceremonies at Cleveland, Ohio, in 1952, when the Erie sent eleven steam locomotives for 3,000 tons of scrap.[65] The New York Central sent three hundred locomotives to Bethlehem Steel's Lackawanna, New York, plant for 50,000 tons of scrap.[66] The Union Pacific sent nearly a million tons of scrap metal to industry, including 578 steam locomotives, between 1945 and 1951; a locomotive cut up at Pocatello, Idaho, was "the 578th 'old gal' to meet her maker."[67] The Seaboard Air Line kept a hundred steam locomotives in reserve, in case the Korean War should develop into a world conflict but even that reprieve ended with the Korean War.[68] The only steam locomotive news of that time was of last runs and of donations of unwanted locomotives to museums and municipal parks, where they became a liability as they deteriorated in the weather and the municipalities were unwilling to spend money maintaining them.

Inefficient they might be, but steam locomotives were remarkably durable. A 2-8-0, built by Alco for the Western Pacific in 1909, was scrapped in 1955 after running 1,026,875 miles.[69] The greater productivity and more intensive utilization of the later locomotives is illustrated by the 2,200,000 miles that the Timken roller-bearing

demonstrator ran between 1930 and 1957.[70] The Northern Pacific scrapped it in 1958.

In 1949, J. Monroe Johnson of the Office of Defense Transportation, suggested that the government buy steam locomotives at scrap value as the railroads disposed of them and store them for future emergencies.[71] Other jurisdictions had similar ideas in the years to come, none of which took into account the need to maintain infrastructure, the loss of operating and maintenance skills and the difficulty of storing steam locomotives to prevent deterioration. Once replaced by diesels, no large quantities of steam locomotives have ever been returned to service.

Even as the Americans were converting to diesel power as fast as they could, the French were making further progress with the conventional steam locomotive.[72] In 1947, the French National Railways converted a 1932-built, poppet-valve, three-cylinder 4-8-2 into a 4-8-4, three-cylinder compound, intending to apply the results to planned new classes of 4-8-4 and 2-10-4. For comparison with American locomotives, a 54-square foot grate fired a 285-pounds per square inch boiler with 2,700 square feet of evaporating surface and a relatively high 1,290 square feet of superheating surface, the engine weight being 327,000 pounds and starting tractive effort 46,000 pounds. An innovation was the high-efficiency Kylchap (Kylala-Chapelon) exhaust nozzle. In tests this locomotive developed 4,200 drawbar horsepower at 60 miles per hour.

The completion of a 2-8-4 for the Pittsburgh & Lake Erie on June 16, 1948, marked the end of steam locomotive production at Alco Schenectady; domestic orders for steam locomotives had ceased.[73] Lima went the same way in 1949 with a 2-8-4 for the Nickel Plate; Baldwin's last steam locomotive was a 2-6-6-2 compound Mallet for the Chesapeake & Ohio the same year.[74] As the railroads

This Colorado & Southern class F-3b 4-6-2, No. 370, was one of a class of three built by Baldwin in 1918, shown when new in Denver, 1918. Thirty-five years separate these two photographs by Otto Perry (Denver Public Library, Otto C. Perry collection, OP-6536).

Otto Perry photographed the same locomotive as the previous photograph, being scrapped thirty-five years later, Denver, November 29, 1953 (Denver Public Library, Otto C. Perry collection, OP-6539).

Western Pacific class C-43 2-8-0, No 36, built by Alco in 1909, near Portola, California, on July 20, 1938 (Denver Public Library, Otto C. Perry collection, OP-19985).

dieselized, they found huge cost reductions that converted into a 3- or 4-year payback on the investment. Overseas markets for American diesel locomotives also opened up.

During the latter decades of mainline steam haulage, steam locomotive development divided along two paths: reconfiguration and refinement.

The 1930s and 1940s produced radically reconfigured locomotives powered by steam turbines or by compact, high-pressure, multicylinder reciprocating engines. The very few such locomotives that were built can only be regarded as prototypes. Perhaps they might have been developed to success, were it not for the dominance of the diesel-electric.

Refinement of the conventional, reciprocating steam locomotive continued after it was displaced from mainline haulage in North America. Individual engineers, such as Chapelon in France, Porta in Argentina and Wardale in South Africa, continued to make discoveries into the 1980s in the face of an increasing lack of official interest.

With the exception of French developments, steam locomotive development overseas progressed slightly, if at all, beyond the USRA rigid-frame designs. The last standard-gauge steam locomotives in main-line service in the world were the Chinese class QJ 2-10-2s. In 1984, the Chinese state railways ran 7,551 steam locomotives with a manufacturing capacity of six hundred locomotives per year; to this must be added an unknown number on industrial lines.[75] The QJ's were derived from the Russian LV 2-10-2s which, in turn, were influenced by American technology. A 73-square foot, stoker-fired grate fired a boiler containing eighty fire tubes and sixty-nine flues for 2,750 square feet of evaporative heating surface, with 1,600 square feet of superheating surface in a large Type A superheater, generating steam at 213 pounds per square inch. Four arch tubes supported the brick arch, with a combustion chamber but no siphons. A feed water heater and two live-steam injectors supplied water to the boiler. Built-up bar frames supported bolted-on cylinders. Power-operated Walschaert valve gear, limited to 72% cut-off in full gear, drove 12-inch piston valves supplying 26-inch × 31-inch cylinders. Boxpok 59-inch driving wheels produced 63,000 pounds of tractive effort. The tender carried 19½ tons of coal and 13,000 gallons of water. Engine weight was 244,000 pounds for an axle loading of 44,000 pounds. Maximum recorded power output was 4,100 indicated horsepower; rated power output at the wheel rim was 3,000 horsepower. Specific steam consumption was apparently as low as 12.3 pounds per indicated horsepower-hour at 30% cut-off and 40 to 50 miles per hour. Counterbalancing limited the locomotives to 50 miles per hour. Thus, the last mainline steam freight locomotives in the world were at the same technological level as the USRA locomotives of 1918–20.

At the time of writing, a surprisingly large number of steam locomotives are still being built, mostly in Britain, but at a cost of $5 million to $10 million each and 10 to 20 years of construction time. The motivation behind these large expenditures of time and effort, however, is to reproduce extinct classes of locomotive with no thought of producing an optimized design. Mr. David Wardale's 5AT Project to develop an advanced steam locomotive has hitherto come to nothing.

Between 1980 and 1985, the American Coal Enterprises Development Co. produced five concepts for coal-burning steam locomotives. All were highly refined reciprocating locomotives with boiler pressures of 300 to 360 pounds per square inch and various combinations of condensing or open-circuit operation, compound cylinders and duplex or articulated drive with sophisticated combustion, heat recovery and control systems.[76] The venture came to nothing.

If global political, economic and technical factors were to make a coal-burning locomotive an urgent, national-level priority, it is conceivable that such designs could be resurrected and developed. At the time of writing, it seems unlikely that the massive development cost will ever be justified, let alone the even greater cost of re-equipping the railroads and their infrastructure. For present purposes, the steam locomotive has run its course.

15

Locomotive Engineering, 1930–1950

Section 15.1 Fuels, Combustion, Firing and Fuel Economy

15.1.1 Fuels

Coal and, to a lesser extent, oil remained the fuels of the steam locomotive until its demise. After 1930, briqueted and pulverized coal made no further progress as locomotive fuel. By 1945, the Class I railroads were burning 124 million tons of coal each year at a cost of $357 million; oil-burning steam locomotives burned a further 112 million barrels of fuel oil at a cost of $121 million.[1] Of a total fuel cost of $534 million, 67% went to coal, 23% to fuel oil, 4% to diesel fuel, 5% to electric power and 1% to gasoline.

The cost to the railroads varied widely, depending on proximity to coal supplies. In the extreme, the Boston & Maine paid $6.58 per ton in 1945, while the Burlington paid only $2.10. The major railroads in the northeastern U.S. averaged $3.50 to $4.50 per ton.

Even as the railroads demanded ever higher performance from steam locomotives,

> Railroads agree that steam locomotives are greatly handicapped in meeting present motive power requirements because of inferior quality, lack of uniformity and the relatively high cost of coal.

Frustrated by the ever-changing specifications and quantities demanded by the railroads, the coal producers protested[2]:

> But is it fair, proper, or reasonable, to ask us to make a 1⅝-in. by ³⁄₆₄-in. size of coal and then take it up in the air and drop it down onto an empty coal dock, throw it into a locomotive tender, grind it all to smithereens with the screw of the stoker, and then not even use the stoker properly, but build up a big clinker in the back of the firebox and let the engineman blow a hole in the fire at the front end of the grates?

In contrast to careful handling by public utilities, the railroads

> don't get the meat out of the coconut. They blow it up the stack. They throw it out on the right of way. They do everything but turn it into steam.

Every railroad faced the issue of coal size and quality *versus* total real cost with varying degrees of sophistication and varying perceptions of value. There was no general solution; Earl C. Payne, of the Pittsburgh Consolidation Coal Co., pointed out in 1947[3]:

> These intangible factors, in which the steam locomotive has been deficient in its competition with the Diesel locomotive, have also in some measure been responsible for the Diesel preference when purchasing new motive power. Better coal on a modern steam locomotive will give a cost and performance that is

quite comparable with the best Diesel locomotives available. Therefore, if better locomotive fuel is used by the railroads, then the outlook for coal is good. If they continue the purchase of unsuitable coal, the outlook is not at all promising.

Diesel oil was in all respects easier to deal with than coal; this was one of the factors contributing to the dieselization of the railroads.

15.1.2 Fireboxes and Combustion

The railroads had every economic incentive to burn fine coal—whether cheap bituminous coal screenings or friable lignite—and every physical disincentive from doing so. The production of fines was a particular problem with power stokers, especially with friable western coal. The problem was how to keep fine coal on the grates for long enough to burn before it either fell through into the ash pan or was blown out through the stack by the enormous furnace draft needed to provide sufficient combustion air—200 cubic feet of air per pound of coal. The table grates introduced in the 1920s, with a smaller percentage of air opening than finger grates, alleviated but did not entirely solve this problem.

In October 1932, the Firebar Corporation convinced the Union Pacific to install its new grate design in a 4-12-2 and a 4-8-2.[4] Initial results impressed the company sufficiently to convert a second 4-8-2 in March 1933.

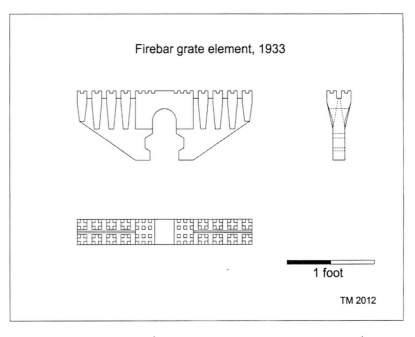

Firebar grate element (redrawn from *RA*, November 18, 1933, 720).

The Firebar grate was a grate element for installation on a conventional transverse shaking grate carrier bar. Each element was apparently a single complex casting, measuring about 18 inches × 3 inches and comprising twenty-four square, turret-like posts; each post had a castellation at each of its four corners. Tuyeres were cast into the element; no point on the grate was more than ⅜ inch from a tuyere exit and the tuyeres distributed air to more than 80% of the grate area. The total air opening was only 12% of the grate area.

The Firebar grate retained fine coal which other grates allowed to fall into the ash pan while still burning, thereby wasting heat, burning and warping the ash pan and causing lineside fires.

Firing up a 4-12-2 to a boiler pressure of 150 pounds per square inch, took 55 minutes and 2,485 pounds of coal with the standard table grates, 37 minutes and 2,295 pounds of coal with the Firebar grate—savings of 33% in time and 8% in coal. (Presumably this would have been with a boiler full of hot water. Firing up a boiler that size from cold would have taken longer than that.) When the time came to drop the fire, the Firebar grate reduced the time spent dropping the fire and cleaning the ash pan from thirty minutes to nine.

A thousand-mile run, Omaha-Cheyenne-Omaha, with a 4-8-2 averaged 4.7 pounds of water per pound of coal with the Union Pacific standard table grate, 5.1 pounds with the Firebar grate, a 7% improvement. Retention of fine coal meant that ash pan space was not taken up by unburnt or half-burnt material. As a result, fewer stops to ash out were needed; the 4-8-2 ran the whole distance without dumping its ash pan, whereas, with the existing table grates, two stops were needed for that purpose each way. The Union Pacific had installed wire netting over the air gaps in the ash pan to guard against lineside fires; in winter the netting plugged with snow and ice, choking off the supply of air and reducing combustion efficiency. By retaining fine coal until it was completely burnt, the Firebar grate reduced the risk of lineside fires to the point where the netting could be removed.

Experience with the two 4-8-2s and the one 4-12-2, averaging ten months per locomotive, convinced the Union Pacific to retrofit Firebar grates to 234 2-10-2s, 4-8-2s and 4-12-2s, plus some others. The Firebar grate came to be widely used when locomotive building resumed in the late 1930s.[5]

In 1933, the Wabash and others discovered that too much air entering the grates could detract from combustion efficiency, as could too little air.[6] If the grate openings allowed more air into the firebox than was needed for combustion, energy from the coal was wasted in heating air that was not used in combustion. In solving the problem of holding fine coal on the grate, table grates solved this problem, too. While testing a new front end design, the Wabash converted three of its 1930 Baldwin 4-8-2s from Hulson finger grates with 43% air opening to Hulson tuyere grates with only 15% opening, at the same time replacing the round, hook-type exhaust nozzle with a Kiesel type. The more efficient nozzle produced the stronger draft needed by the reduced grate opening at lower back pressure with higher superheat temperature; the company estimated a 25% to 30% increase in power.

Simple table grates with holes or slots allowed combustion air to pass through them as vertical jets, lifting fine coal off the firebed. The tuyere-type grates of the 1920s and 1930s, especially those that directed air into the firebed horizontally, were a solution to this problem. The Hulson Grate Co. developed a grate of this type during the 1930s for burning North Dakota lignite in stationary boilers. The same design was later applied to a locomotive burning West Virginia screenings and was successful in keeping a thin fire with fine material and low stack losses.

J. Partington, engineering manager with Alco, commented in 1938[7]:

On one of the western roads, where the coal was rather light and hard to hold under the best conditions, a set of the now well-known pin-hole grates was applied which reduced the air openings to the neighborhood of 15 per cent. Not only was the fire carried better, but actual fuel saving resulted, and the anticipated trouble from clinkering did not materialize. Now it is rare to find a set of grates in a locomotive with more than 25 per cent air opening, 20 percent being the prevailing average.

In 1941, the New York Central succeeded in making the first motion pictures of the interior of a firebox at its Selkirk, New York, test plant.[8] This was not a dynamometer plant, like Altoona, but was equipped for standing tests and other locomotive testing and study methods. The pistons were removed from the cylinders and steam was passed through the valves and cylinders to the stack. This was an effective means of testing the firebox, boiler and front end without the cost and difficulty of tests with a dynamometer car or a static test plant. These motion pictures convinced F. P. Roesch, Vice-President of the Standard Stoker Co., that:

Until quite recently we knew but little about what actually happens to the fuel bed in a locomotive firebox at various rates of combustion. The little we thought we knew was based largely on data obtained from stationary power plant tests, but aside from the fundamentals governing the combustion of solid fuel, there is no similarity whatever.

In Roesch's opinion:

(The New York Central) tests and pictures are to my mind the greatest contribution to the art ever made.

Researchers found out that even large lumps of coal broke down into small pieces as they burned; as soon as a fragment became light enough, the draft through the firebed picked it up as a burning cinder and either deposited it on top of the brick arch or in the smokebox or blew it out through the stack. The New York Central high-speed motion pictures showed coal fragments in flight that were undetectable to the human eye due to heat, glare and their speed of movement.

From the pictures, it is evident that fairly large pieces of coal are picked up from the fuel bed and projected into the zone of high gas velocity where the gas stream passes over the rear end of the arch, a velocity calculated as equal to 2,000 to 3,000 ft. per sec. Naturally, any coal projected into this zone is gone forever insofar as boiling water is concerned, therefore, it should be clear that our problem is to hold these particles of coal as close to the fuel bed as possible until they are burned.

If these calculations were correct, they indicate supersonic gas flows with effects that were unsuspected at the time. Observations at Altoona showed that the lifting action of vertical air jets, coming through holes in the firebed, was proportional to the square of their area, explaining why quite small holes produced a disproportionate loss in steaming.

In the early 1930s, Lima developed a simple device to preheat the air entering the bottom of the grate.[9] This was a heat exchanger consisting of a rack of finned tubes, covering the airway between the ash pan and the foundation ring. When the throttle was open, the device was supplied with exhaust steam; when the throttle was closed, it was supplied with live steam, reduced in pressure to 15 pounds per square inch. The change-over was automatic. Steam condensed in the tubes, giving up its latent heat. In the first applications, condensate was wasted onto the ground. Lima claimed that the withdrawal of exhaust steam had no effect on the supply of steam to the feed water heater. They made the first trial installation in January 1934, in ambient temperatures about freezing and found that air entering the grates averaged 205°F. An 18-month trial on a 2-10-4 showed fuel savings of 7% to 8% and reduced firebox maintenance.

Steam jets, set in the firebox wall to induct additional air into the firebox above the fire as a means of smoke abatement, dated back to the nineteenth century, but, from the viewpoint of 1945: "Since that time, literally hundreds of variations of the original idea have been tried and some of them extensively used, but with rather meager and not entirely satisfactory results."[10] Some American railroads certainly used this idea in 1910–12. In 1943–4 Bituminous Coal Research Inc. developed an improved version which was tested on the Louisville & Nashville. By late 1945, it was in service on 350 locomotives on some seventeen railroads, including the Akron, Canton & Youngstown, the Atlantic Coast Line, the Baltimore & Ohio, the Canadian National, the Central of New Jersey, the Chesapeake & Ohio, the Erie, the Nashville, Chattanooga & St. Louis, the New York Central, the Norfolk & Western, the Pennsylvania, the Richmond, Fredericksburg & Potomac, the Tennessee Central and the Wheeling & Lake Erie.

Additionally, the Batelle Memorial Institute was researching the effects of over-fire jets on boiler efficiency. Switching engines, emitting smoke in urban areas, were a particular target for this device. The Louisville & Nashville found that the necessary nozzle and induction pipe diameters varied markedly with different firing rates; this was probably one reason for its late and limited adoption.

By 1948, the Chicago & North Western had equipped all of its Chicago-based locomotives with over-fire air jets as a means of preventing smoke.[11] The company believed that the air jets both supplied additional oxygen and promoted mixing of the gases inside the firebox. Smoke was unburnt carbon and so efficient combustion and smoke abatement went hand in hand.

These and other efficiency-improving devices cost money to install. They had to be operated and maintained correctly, otherwise they had no effect. Their effects were slight; costly test programs were needed to find out if they had any effect at all.

15.1.3 Power Stokers

By the late 1930s, Standard Type MB stokers on Norfolk & Western 2-6-6-4s were distributing 7 tons of coal per hour, controlled as to both rate and distribution, over a grate the size of a living room. The power stoker was clearly a massive and ingenious machine in its own right.

New in 1929–30 was a power stoker from the Lower Stoker Co. of Pittsburgh, designed to crush oversized coal in a way that minimized the dust produced by other power stokers.[12] A horizontal screw conveyor flexibly mounted on the tender fed coal to an inclined screw conveyor mounted rigidly on the locomotive. The first conveyor was so designed that only those lumps too big to fit inside it were crushed against the back end of the ball joint casing. The inclined conveyor discharged coal onto a ribbed distributor plate. Fine coal fitted between the ribs where a row of low-pressure steam jets distributed it over the fire. Coarse coal ran across the tops of the ribs to be distributed by two rows of high-pressure steam jets. All steam jets were controllable by the fireman. In theory, the upper rows of steam jets made a fence, preventing fine coal from being caught by the draft before it could fall into the fire.

The Standard Type BT stoker, of similar arrangement to the earlier BK and also brought out in 1930, had the same objective, being designed to deliver lump coal with minimal size reduction.[13] Recognizing the pressures toward power stoking, in 1932 the Standard Stoker Co. brought out a variant of their Type BK, designed for smaller locomotives than would normally be stoker fired.[14] This device had a maximum capacity close to 7,000 pounds of coal per hour. By the 1930s, the main types and principles of stoker design and operation had become well established. Current research has not revealed the details of stoker development during the 1930s or the differences, for example, between the Standard Types B, BK, HT and MB which were current at the time.

Stoker firing may have eased the fireman's physical exertions but, in mainline service, demands on the fireman still intensified.[15]

> In full justice to the fireman, we must recognize that with the introduction of the very exacting service during recent years, his job has not been made easier. It takes full steam pressure right from the start and to the finish of the run to maintain the fast schedules of today and the fireman does not have the same opportunity that he used to have, when schedules were slower, to build up his fire after he gets outside the smoke ordinance zone. Incidentally we have found that on locomotives carrying 200 lb. steam pressure, the lack of 5 lb. causes two minutes to be lost on the running time on the trains running on an 80-minute schedule between Milwaukee and Chicago…. Today he must have his fire ready from the moment he gets the go-ahead signal as otherwise the locomotive will not meet the demands placed on it.

The enginemen's unions increased their efforts to enforce the wider use of power stokers. In 1930, the Brotherhood of Locomotive Firemen and Enginemen and the Brotherhood of Locomotive Engineers tried to get the ICC to enforce the use of power stokers on all locomotives.[16] This complaint, and the hearings that followed, point to the ICC's all-pervading regulatory powers. The ICC held hearings in 1931, but then suspended the case until 1936 due to economic conditions, completing the renewed hearings in 1937.[17]

Safety was the major issue. When shoveling coal, the fireman could not keep a lookout on his side of the engine. Exposure of the fireman's eyes to the glare through the open firebox door blinded his night vision; the unions also asserted long-term ill effects on eyesight. In winter, the fireman was exposed to extremes of temperature between the hot cab and the cold outside air, damaging his health. A power stoker avoided the danger of a blow-back through an open fire door. The other major issue was sheer physical exhaustion and uselessness for any other aspect of life. One witness said that he shoveled 20 to 26 tons of coal on a 140-mile run lasting the full 16 hours permitted by law and was too exhausted to attend to his family's needs afterwards. Some witnesses said that shoveling 2,000 pounds per hour was all that could be reasonably expected.

The ICC sided with management in rejecting some of these assertions but nevertheless issued an order on December 30, 1937, requiring stokers on all passenger locomotives of 160,000 pounds or greater adhesion weight and all freight locomotives of 175,000 pounds or greater adhesion weight, built after July 1, 1938. Each railroad operating locomotives of these weights, built before July 1, 1938, in fast or heavy service was to retrofit 20% of them with stokers each year with retrofitting to be complete by July 1, 1943. This requirement would entail retrofitting an estimated 3,500 locomotives at a cost of about $3,000 each.

The hearings disclosed the numbers of engines equipped with stokers by 1936, showing that retrofitting had gone on steadily over the years, as well as new construction. The ICC issued a questionnaire to all railroads, covering 47,393 locomotives. Of 8,154 passenger locomotives, 6,831 were coal-fired, of which 1,347 were stoker-fired. The breakdown by passenger locomotive weight was: more than 250,000 pounds, 100%; 200,000 to 250,000, about 50%; 170,000 to 200,000 pounds, about 35%; less than 170,000 pounds, less than 5%. Of 26,000 freight locomotives, 21,000 burned coal, of which 10,160 were stoker-fired.

In March 1939, following protests from industry, the ICC postponed the two milestone dates to April 15, 1939, and April 15, 1944.[18] Including time extensions, 3,893 stokers were retrofitted by the end of 1944. These big, old engines could not be hand-fired at full power for any length of time, so retrofitting wrung additional power out of the locomotive fleet. In the ICC's opinion, this materially affected the war effort by reducing absenteeism and labor turnover caused by sheer physical exhaustion and making men available who were not strong enough to hand-fire big engines.

The locomotive power stoker was an American triumph; although its acceptance by the industry was slow and late, it was the key—more than any other device—to the enormous power output of the giant locomotives of the twentieth century.

15.1.4 Fuel Economy

The prolonged efforts to improve the appalling thermal inefficiency of the steam locomotive bore no very encouraging results. At the end of the road, after a century of improvements, the heat content of the coal was consumed as follows:

Stack gases	14%
Cinders blown out of the stack	8%
Unburned gases	4%
To ash pan	4%
Making steam	70%

Disposed of as follows:	
Exhaust steam creating draft	52%
Radiation	5%
Operating air pump, blower, injector, generator	7%
Useful work at the drawbar	6%
Sub-total	70%

For comparison, a coal-fired electric powerhouse, using condensing steam turbines, reached a thermal efficiency of about 13%—1.6 pounds of coal per horsepower-hour.

Innovations between 1900 and 1920 produced fuel savings that were significant in themselves: brick arches 9%, superheaters 20%, feedwater heaters 10%. While these were substantial in themselves, the depressing truth remained[19]:

> The thermal efficiency of locomotives built in 1900 was approximately five per cent, while locomotives are being built today that have a thermal efficiency of eight per cent. These per cents were secured from test plant results and show an increase in efficiency of 60 per cent in 25 years.

Test plant results were from perfectly maintained locomotives in the most favorable operating conditions. (As little as 1/16 inch of scale on fire tubes could increase fuel consumption by 10%.) These, moreover, were gross savings; when interest, maintenance and depreciation were taken into account, net cost savings were only 17% for superheaters and 6% for feedwater heaters.

Between 1930 and 1950 most of the countries with any significant locomotive-building capacity experimented with locomotives intended to improve on the conventional steam locomotive's poor efficiency. By 1946, the Swiss were able to summarize the results, expressed as thermal efficiency at the rail[20]:

Saturated steam, single-expansion	5.0%
Superheated steam single-expansion	7.0%
Superheated steam, compound	8.0%
Condensing steam turbine, electric transmission	8.5%
High-pressure steam, single expansion	10.0%
Condensing steam turbine, geared transmission	10.2%
High-pressure, condensing steam	12.0%
Oil-burning gas turbine, electric transmission	16.0%
Diesel-electric	30.0%

Widening diesel experience led to direct comparisons with oil-burning steam locomotives. American experience in the mid–1950s showed that each dollar spent on fuel produced 5,496 gross ton-miles of freight haulage in a diesel-electric locomotive, 3,310 gross ton-miles in a coal-burning steam locomotive, 2,038 in an oil-burner and 2,969 in an electric locomotive.[21] In spite of its operating benefits, the electric locomotive turned out poorly in this regard.

In the early 2000s the Ffestiniog Railway in the UK published the fuel consumption of oil-fired steam locomotives and diesels, hauling the same trains over the same route. The steam locomotives burned 4.0 U.S. gallons of oil per mile, compared to 0.5 U.S. gallons per mile for the diesels. Although these were small locomotives, running on 2-foot gauge track, the comparison remains valid: oil-burning steam locomotives burned eight times the amount of oil burned by diesel-electrics to do the same work.

From 1930 onward, the efficiency issue boiled down to a contest between conventional steam and diesel-electric locomotives. Electric power was too limited in its application to figure in this contest. In spite of the progress in locomotive design achieved in the early twentieth century, the inefficiency of the reciprocating steam locomotive was irredeemable.

Section 15.2. Boilers and Steam Generation

During the 1920s and 1930s, mechanical engineers showed that the fire-tube boiler was still capable of refinement. Until the mid–1920s, maximum obtainable evaporation rates were 15 to 17 pounds of steam per square foot of heating surface per hour; by 1940, this had increased to 21 to 22 pounds.[22] This increase does not distinguish between firebox and fire tube evaporation; it resulted from several refinements: bigger fireboxes, combustion chambers, siphons, circulating plates and arch tubes. Power stoking produced higher and more uniform fire temperatures. In the American steam locomotive of the 1940s, 45% of total evaporation was from the firebox, combustion chamber, siphons and arch tubes; 55% was from the fire tubes.[23]

Conventionally, the firebox was the heat source for the fire-tube boiler. American locomotive design of the 1930s and 1940s inverted this relationship; the fire-tube boiler became little more than a feed water heater for the firebox and combustion chamber and a superheater for the steam that they generated. This perception seems to have been uniquely American in both origin and outcome.

15.2.1 Boiler Pressures in Fire-Tube Boilers

Improvements in steel metallurgy during the 1920s made boiler pressures of 250 pounds per square inch and higher achievable at acceptable weight and cost.[24] The Canadian Pacific was the first to use nickel steel for locomotive boilers, while the Canadian National was the first to use high-silicon steel in an order for 4-8-4s built in 1927. Steam pressures of 225 to 250 pounds per square inch were characteristic of the new superpower locomotives of the late 1920s but only a few major railroads ventured beyond those limits until the late 1930s. Those that did so discovered a number of benefits.[25]

Always bold in its locomotive procurement, the Santa Fe bought fifteen 2-8-4s with 275-pound working pressure in 1927. Only six were run at full pressure—the others being run at 220 pounds—until 1937, when the company cleared all to run at 275 pounds per square inch. They then ordered six 4-6-4s and eleven 4-8-4s with 300 pounds per square inch boiler pressure and ten 2-10-4s with 310 pounds per square inch. (Reconciliation of referenced source with Drury, 27) Between 1929 and 1931, the Delaware & Hudson built three 4-6-2s, of which the first had a boiler pressure of 275 pounds per square inch and the third 325 pounds per square inch.[26]

The Boston & Albany's early superpower 2-8-4, No. 1400, at Boston in 1939, illustrates the enormous size of the firebox relative to the rest of the boiler. The column of black smoke with the locomotive standing still results from use of the blower, suggesting the locomotive is being prepared for its next assignment. The black smoke is either unburnt coal dust or partly burnt soot. The pressure-washing hose seems to go to a standpipe beside the front of the engine; the pressure-washing medium looks like water, rather than steam or compressed air (courtesy California State Railroad Museum, Railway & Locomotive Historical Society Collection, Negative 39072cn).

In early 1937, the Canadian National had eighty engines carrying 250 pounds per square inch, six engines carrying 265 pounds and twenty-eight with 275 pounds. The increased work performed and higher efficiency offset the higher maintenance costs. At the same time, the Chicago & North Western was running 4-8-2s with 275 pounds per square inch boiler pressure. Higher pressures made higher superheat temperatures possible. These resulted in problems with lubrication, sealing and packing but the CNW reckoned that pressures as high as 300 pounds per square inch would pay for themselves in increased performance. The Lehigh Valley found no increase in costs for steam pressure of 275 pounds per square inch. The New Haven bought ten 4-6-4s in 1937 with 285 pounds per square inch; the higher pressure permitted smaller cylinders and lighter reciprocating parts. The Southern Pacific put fourteen 4-8-4s into service with 280-pound boiler pressure, while the Norfolk & Western increased the boiler pressure on a large number of compound Mallets from 240 pounds per square inch to 270 pounds with gratifying results.

By the late 1930s, power density—power output per unit weight and/or volume—was a key issue; the steam locomotive had encountered one more of its ultimate limitations—axle loading. Massive programs of railroad reconstruction, characteristic of the early twentieth century and permitting a rapid increase in axle loading, had run their course, not least because the economic disaster of the early 1930s precluded their continuance. To obtain more power, only increased boiler pressure remained as an option. Improvements in metallurgy, design and manufacturing during the 1920s had raised the pressure limit of the conventional, staybolted boiler/firebox combination to 300 pounds per square inch, and had brought increasing success to water-tube boilers capable of still higher pressures.

The effective application of steam at these pressures to reciprocating, single-expansion, non-condensing engines with restricted cylinder dimensions, supplied through piston valves, raised several problems. About 15 pounds per square inch back pressure in the exhaust nozzle sufficed to draft the fire; if steam was released at a higher pressure, the difference was wasted energy. To expand steam entering the cylinders at 350 pounds per square inch required only a 6% cut-off. Piston valves were increasingly ineffective at cut-offs shorter than 25%; shorter cut-offs needed poppet valves for best efficiency.

Gone were the days when locomotive manufacturers restricted boiler pressure and superheat temperature; they realized that the highest power output would come from the hottest possible steam at the highest possible pressure, limited only by materials and the built-in limitations of the steam locomotive. At that time, typical steam temperatures in American locomotives were 625°F to 650°F, as high as 725°F in some locomotives. The Europeans were obtaining steam temperatures up to 850°F. American engineers reckoned that[27]:

any superheat in the exhaust is … evidence of too much initial superheat and the conclusion is drawn that no economy can be obtained by increasing the initial temperature still further.

H. B. Oatley, Vice-President of The Superheater Company, broke free from this constraint by pointing out that:

This, however, is incorrect as the real measure of cylinder performance is the amount of heat converted into work in relation to the total heat supplied to the cylinder.

Even though the total heat rejected increased with increasing initial temperature, the heat rejection per unit of work done decreased, justifying higher pressures and temperatures.

Ignoring the effects of friction, radiation, wiredrawing, compression in the cylinders and incomplete expansion, saturated steam at 225 pounds per square inch and 397°F consumed 16 pounds of steam per indicated horsepower-hour, declining to only 10 pounds at 350 pounds per square inch and 800°F. Savings therefore awaited those able and willing to use steam at these high pressures and temperatures. Oatley reached these conclusions by considering the heat content of steam expanded from an initial pressure to a back pressure of 15 pounds per square inch. His projections were borne out in practice. The Cole ratios of 1914 estimated steam consumption at 20.8 pounds per indicated horsepower-hour; by 1938, Alco knew that engines working on 275 to 300 pounds per square inch were reducing this figure to only 16 pounds, reliably enough for this figure to be used for design. Tests were achieving still lower steam consumptions.[28]

There was never any mention of shockwave effects on steam moving in pipes at trans-sonic and supersonic velocities. This area of gas dynamics remained unsuspected until the advent of supersonic flight ten years in the future.

15.2.2 Water-Tube Boilers

From the viewpoint of 1932[29]:

> With the present state of the art it is generally considered that the conventional type of locomotive boiler with stayed surfaces is not suitable for pressures above approximately 300 lb. per sq. in. It is essential therefore to utilize some sort of water-tube construction for pressures materially higher than this figure.

In 1929, both the Canadian Pacific and the New York Central started the design of compound locomotives using the Schmidt-Henschel, multi-pressure, water-tube boiler, originating in Germany in 1925 and known as the Elesco type in North America. Current research has not discovered the differences between the German and North American versions of this boiler, nor what patent rights may have existed or been transferred.

Both locomotives resulted from cooperation between Alco, The Superheater Co., and the mechanical departments of the two railroads. Construction of the Canadian Pacific locomotive—an oil-burning 2-10-4, No. 8000, built for the most direct possible comparison with the company's existing class T-1 2-10-4s—began at the CPR's Angus shops in Montreal in November 1930; the locomotive went into service in July 1931.

The New York Central received its locomotive—a coal-burning 4-8-4, No. 800—from Alco Schenectady in late 1931.

By 1932, five such locomotives existed in the world, on the Canadian Pacific, the New York Central, the Paris-Lyon-Méditerranée in

A Canadian Pacific class T-1a 2-10-4, No. 5919, last of a batch of twenty built by the Montreal Locomotive Works in 1929, photographed with its crew in British Columbia in 1939. The T-1's were the most powerful steam locomotives ever built in Canada (Revelstoke Museum and Archives, photo #1508 Engine 5919).

The Canadian Pacific high-pressure 2-10-4, No. 8000, built in company shops, 1931 (courtesy California State Railroad Museum, Railway & Locomotive Historical Society Collection, Negative 39075cn).

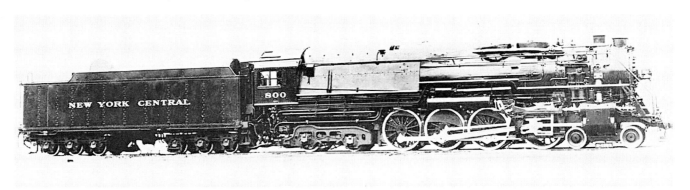

The New York Central high-pressure 4-8-4, No. 800, built by Alco in 1931 (courtesy California State Railroad Museum).

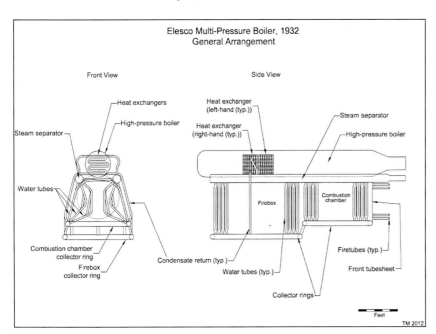

France, the London, Midland & Scottish in Britain and the German State Railways.[30]

The Elesco system comprised three separate elements: the closed circuit, the high-pressure boiler and the low-pressure boiler; each contained steam at a different pressure.

The closed circuit departed from all previous locomotive practice. A 7¼-inch tube, called the collector ring, surrounded the bottom corners of the firebox. A second collector ring surrounded the bottom of the combustion chamber. Riser tubes, 2 and 2½ inches in diameter, formed the walls of the firebox and combustion chamber and connected the collector rings with a 12-inch steam separator drum, positioned at each shoulder of the firebox, running the length of the firebox and combustion chamber. In the firebox, a straight riser alternated with a riser arching across the firebox to the opposite separator drum. The sources

Elesco multi-pressure boiler (redrawn from *RA*, August 27, 1932, 290-4 (best possible interpretation of ambiguous drawings and text).

consulted are unclear whether the firebox contained a brick arch. In the combustion chamber, every alternate riser was bifurcated, with limbs projecting into the combustion chamber. Riser tubes also formed the backhead.

Steam was generated in the riser tubes and collected in the steam space at pressures of 1,300 to 1,700 pounds per square inch and temperatures of the order of 600°F. This steam flowed through heat exchanger coils in the high-pressure boiler, which was a 39-inch drum mounted above the center of the firebox. Steam condensed in the heat exchanger coils, giving up its latent heat; the condensate flowed by gravity through tubes running down to the collector ring outside the firebox. When heated, the system set up a positive water circulation without the flow reversals that had proved dangerous in some types of water-tube boiler. The steam generated in the closed circuit was not for propulsion purposes, but was solely a means of heat transfer. The closed circuit contained distilled water with no make-up or exhaust. Cleaning was a major problem of water-tube boilers; the closed circuit could be sealed, for practical purposes permanently, and was therefore free of this problem.

The high-pressure boiler was a 39-inch drum, mounted above the center of the firebox, generating steam at 850 pounds per square inch.

The low-pressure boiler was a conventional fire-tube boiler placed ahead of the firebox and combustion chamber, generating steam at 250 pounds per square inch. Steel sheets and lagging surrounded the firebox and combustion chamber.

The Canadian Pacific 2-10-4 had a 77-square foot (65 square feet in the NYC 4-8-4—NYC 4-8-4 dimensions in brackets) grate. The closed circuit tubes provided 520 (430) square feet of heating surface. The heat transfer coils inside the high-pressure boiler totaled 750 (660) square feet. The low-pressure boiler measured just over 19 feet (18 feet) over tube sheets and contained 214 (194) 3½-inch flues. These provided 3,745 (3,230) square feet of heating surface and contained Type E superheater elements. The three European locomotives were of somewhat smaller dimensions.

A pump in the tender tank forced water through a feed water heater into the low-pressure boiler at 200°F to 220°F. A second pump took water from the low-pressure boiler at 250 pounds per square inch and 400°F and forced it into the high-pressure boiler. The low-pressure boiler doubled as a feed water heater for the high-pressure

boiler and as a steam generator. Steam from the high-pressure boiler went through a 49-element (44) superheater with 1,100 (1,070) square feet of superheating surface. Steam from the low-pressure boiler went through a separate 65-element (51) superheater with 2,045 (1,905) square feet of superheating surface. High- and low-pressure superheated steam temperatures were expected to be 600°F to 800°F and 550°F to 725°F, respectively. Total maximum steam generation was predicted at 63,000 pounds per hour.

The CPR decided that the high-pressure steam needed compound expansion for maximum efficiency. A two-cylinder cross-compound was impractical because clearance dimensions did not permit an adequately sized low-pressure cylinder. Tandem cylinders would place high- and low-pressure cylinders outside the frames, avoiding crank axles, but the reciprocating parts would be heavy, piston rod packings between the cylinders would be inaccessible and the front part of the locomotive would be undesirably long and heavy. Four cylinders, two inside the frames, two outside, would require an axle with two cranks, which would have to be so massive that they would not fit between the frames. The resulting configuration was a single 15½-inch × 28-inch high-pressure cylinder between the frames, supplied with steam from the high-pressure boiler. Exhaust from this cylinder mixed with steam from the low-pressure boiler and went to two outside 24-inch × 30-inch low-pressure cylinders.

At 370,000 (348,000) pounds engine weight and 77,000 (78,000) pounds of tractive effort without the booster, the 2-10-4 was the most powerful locomotive on the CPR. Numerous adjustments and high maintenance costs marked its first year in service, although in the heavily graded division between Field and Revelstoke, British Columbia, for which it was intended, it saved 15% in fuel, compared to the T-1's.

These two locomotives were bold feats of engineering; current research has not discovered test results from either. They were, however, ultimately unsuccessful. The New York Central scrapped theirs in 1939, followed by the Canadian Pacific locomotive in 1940. Availability and maintenance costs were probably the cause.

In the 1920s, the Delaware & Hudson built a two-cylinder compound 2-8-0 called the *Horatio Allen*, using steam at 350 pounds per square inch, generated in a water-tube boiler. They followed this with a successor built for 400 pounds per square inch, called the *John B.*

The Delaware & Hudson class E-7 high-pressure 4-8-0, No. 1402, *L. F. Loree*, built by Alco in 1933 (courtesy California State Railroad Museum, Paul Darrell Collection, Negative 39086cn).

Jervis, and a third with a boiler pressure of 500 pounds per square inch, called the *James Archbald.*[31]

The Delaware & Hudson persevered in further experiments with a 4-8-0 high-pressure, four-cylinder, triple-expansion compound, built by Alco Schenectady in 1933, called the *L. F. Loree.*[32] In 1932, Alco was building a 500-pounds per square inch locomotive for the Delaware & Hudson, to be called the *Charles P. Wurts.* Either this locomotive was not completed or, more likely, it was renamed the *L. F. Loree.*[33] A 76-square foot grate fired a water-tube firebox and fire-tube boiler of similar configuration to that of the *James Archbald,* generating steam at 500 pounds per square inch. Forging, rather than riveting the boiler drums saved 2½ tons in boiler weight. The water-tube firebox provided 965 square feet of heating surface, with another 2,385 square feet in arch tubes, fire tubes and flues, and 1,075 square feet in the Type A superheater. The 20-inch × 32-inch high-pressure cylinder and the 27½-inch × 32-inch intermediate-pressure cylinder were formed as a single steel casting and placed at the back of the locomotive, behind the firebox, the high-pressure cylinder on the right-hand side of the engine. Both cylinders were outside the frames, each driving a connecting rod to the second from front driving axle. The two 33-inch × 32-inch low-pressure cylinders, also a single casting, were mounted in the conventional position outside the frames beneath the smokebox, also driving on the second axle. Dabeg rotary cam poppet valves, driven by rotating shafts from the second driving axle, controlled steam flow through the cylinders with a single cut-off control for all four cylinders. The arrangement of the cams allowed six cut-off settings in forward gear and three in reverse. High-pressure steam from the boiler passed through the high-pressure cylinder into a receiver formed in the cylinder casting, thence to the intermediate-pressure cylinder. Exhaust from the intermediate-pressure cylinder went through a receiver pipe and chamber to the low-pressure cylinders. An intercepting valve, capable of manual and automatic operation, supplied high-pressure steam to the low-pressure cylinders for starting. Another valve supplied high-pressure steam automatically to the receiver between the high- and intermediate-pressure cylinders, closing when pressure in the receiver reached 170 pounds per square inch. When working in triple-expansion at short cut-off, a manual valve in the cab allowed the engineer to feed high-pressure steam to the low-pressure cylinders. An auxiliary locomotive replaced the rear tender truck. The engine weighed 382,000 pounds, the tender another 275,000 pounds, containing 17½ tons of coal and 14,000 gallons of water.

The Delaware & Hudson displayed the new locomotive at the Century of Progress Exposition in Chicago before testing was completed. In initial tests the engine hauled a 92-car train weighing 6,100 tons up a 0.5% grade, topping the grade at 4 miles per hour. Maximum tractive efforts were 90,000 pounds single-expansion, 75,000 pounds triple-expansion, with the auxiliary locomotive contributing another 18,000 pounds. The company claimed drawbar thermal efficiencies of 8.7% for the *Horatio Allen,* 9.3% for the *John B. Jervis,* 10.4% for the *James Archbald* and anticipated 12% to 13% for the *L. F. Loree.*

The company's experimental program with high-pressure, water-tube boilers, dating back to 1922, ended with the *L. F. Loree.* When a technical representative from Franklin visited the Colonie shops in 1944, he[34]:

> inquired where the four high-pressure water-tube firebox locomotives were (the three 2-8-0s and the 4-8-0). The foreman took me outside of the erecting shop under the crane gantry and pointed out the long tender which belonged to No. 1403. "That is all that remains," he said.

Between 1933 and 1936, the Baltimore & Ohio equipped one 4-4-4 and four 4-6-4s with Emerson water-tube fireboxes in boilers gener-

ating steam at 350 pounds per square inch. The company found that increased boiler maintenance problems resulted, caused by insufficient circulation, remediable by installing a circulation plate. Higher pressures shortened the life of several boiler components. However, as of 1935, the Baltimore & Ohio's view of the Emerson firebox was as follows[35]:

> Since the first Emerson water-tube firebox was applied on a B. & O. locomotive in 1927 a number have been applied, both to new and existing locomotive boiler shells. Throughout the wide experience of the B. & O. with this type of firebox, in service on all parts of the railroad, they have proved more satisfactory than the conventional type. Their first cost is no greater than that of staybolt fireboxes of similar size and they eliminate crown- and side-sheet staybolts.

Even so, water-tube fireboxes never gained widespread acceptance. In 1948, the Steam Locomotive Research Institute produced a design for a water-tube boiler, although this design closely resembled the Elesco high-pressure boiler built twenty years previously.[36]

15.2.3 Boiler Maintenance and Water Quality

By 1920, U.S. railroads were using 900 billion gallons of water each year, three-quarters by steam locomotives.[37] The cost of water supply averaged 7 cents per thousand gallons, or $63 million per year. Rising costs of boiler maintenance forced railroad managements to look at water treatment, yet there were still only 600 treatment plants in the whole country and only 3% of the water used by steam locomotives was treated. Companies found that water treatment plants paid for themselves quickly in reduced boiler maintenance and fuel consumption; water treatment spread during the 1920s.

Railroads could suffer from too much water and too little at the same time. Floods and washouts caused millions of dollars' worth of damage every year, yet the Southern Pacific had serious problems with the quantity and quality of water for its locomotives crossing the deserts of New Mexico and Arizona, between El Paso and Yuma, right from when the line was built in 1879–80.[38] The shallow wells supplying communities along the route would run dry or the pumps would fail; sometimes the company had to haul water 400 miles in tank cars. With increasing traffic, whole divisions became blocked by trains stranded by lack of water. In 1917, the company began an aggressive program of deep well drilling. At Gila, Arizona, they tapped a productive aquifer at 1,746 feet, but the water, though plentiful, reached surface at 110°F, so hot that locomotive injectors would not work, with little chance to cool in the summer weather and so saline that fire tubes would last only four months.

By 1933, the major railroads were making thorough investigations of their water sources, building reservoirs to impound supplies of water that they found suitable. They had installed more than 1,500 treatment plants since 1920; 40% of the 350 billion gallons supplied to locomotives each year was treated, with a further percentage treated by chemicals placed in tender tanks.[39] The payback was enormous. On one railroad, engine failures caused by bad water dropped from 245 a month to five. On another railroad, leaking flues due to bad water dropped from one failure per 100,000 locomotive miles in 1911 to one per 4.34 million locomotive miles in 1929. Others found that the mileage run between boiler washouts increased from 500 to 600 miles to 2,000 to 3,000. Firebox life was doubled in some cases.

Tannin was the miracle feed water treatment of the 1930s.[40] Its benefits became apparent from tests conducted by the Illinois Central in 1930, augmented by tests by the U.S. Bureau of Mines and the Association of American Railroads, seeking the causes and cures of inter-crystalline steel corrosion. Tannins deposited scale-forming chemicals in the bottoms of boilers as soft sludge that could be removed by blowing down, instead of forming hard scale on the steaming surfaces. Tannins prevented corrosion by absorbing oxygen from the water and prevented corrosion and also retarded chemical reactions until feed water had entered the boiler, preventing the incrustation of feed lines, injectors and check valves. Engine crews could dose their tender tanks with suitable tannin compositions.

Many improvements in total locomotive efficiency were obscure and resulted more from operating procedures than from design or fabrication. Operators discovered that systematic blowing down could reduce the necessary frequency of boiler washing; in 1934, this was hailed as: "One of the outstanding achievements in the economic operation of steam locomotives during the past three or four years…."[41]

By 1943, the railroads were handling 55% more freight than during World War I with only two-thirds the number of locomotives.[42] The treatment of boiler water made an obscure but significant contribution to this performance; half the 37,000 steam locomotives on Class I railroads were running on treated water. Comprehensive water treatment and regular blowing down produced enormous reductions in engine failures due to bad water, boiler wash-out labor and damaged boiler parts, and doubled to quadrupled firebox life. One editor commented, extravagantly:

> Probably no other single factor has contributed more to the unprecedented performance of the railways during the last year than the treatment of boiler water.

Bigger engines, higher boiler pressures, longer engine runs and more intensive use of motive power brought on a random cracking of boiler shells, with the cracks starting at rivet holes; this was alarming because it had no known cause.[43] Fourteen years of studies by the American Railway Engineering Association between 1923 and 1938 concluded that the cause was inter-crystalline corrosion of the steel, when under tension, because of excessive concentrations of sodium hydroxide and sodium silicate (both having to be present) in the boiler water. The Chicago & North Western had 221 locomotives affected by this type of cracking between 1912 and 1926; when the company started adding lignin compounds during anti-foaming experiments, it found that cracking almost ceased, with only eight cases between 1926 and 1938. Quebracho was also effective in preventing cracking, with the added benefits that it removed oxygen from the boiler water and dispersed solids; although used in stationary boilers, its high cost was a disincentive to use in locomotives. Further studies between 1938 and 1940 found that the stresses implanted by cold rolling and riveting could start inter-crystalline corrosion. The engineering community hoped that the welded boiler on trial with the Delaware & Hudson from 1937 to 1942 would prevent embrittlement by eliminating riveted joints and their associated stress concentrations.[44]

15.2.4 Superheat

By the early 1930s[45]:

> The practice of superheating steam locomotives has become so well established that no new locomotives have been built for years without superheaters and the majority of existing locomotives in road service have either had superheaters applied when they were built or added later.

In 1930, The Superheater Company started developing new designs that could be retrofitted in place of Type A superheaters, providing higher superheat without retubing the boilers, as was necessary to install a Type E. Designing these was not simple; like many aspects of the steam locomotive, the superheater turned out to be remarkably complicated when examined in detail. Although it was possible to calculate a heat transfer rate per square foot of heating surface per hour per degree of temperature difference, not only did the gas temperature vary along the flue, but heat was being transferred through four surfaces at the same time, all at different temperatures.

Any improvement on an existing superheater had to offer similar resistance to flue gases so that no changes would be necessary to drafting arrangements after retrofitting, equal or lower friction loss to the steam passing through the elements, higher superheat and no additional maintenance problems. Installing each experimental design in a locomotive and road testing it was impractical, so the company built their own test rig in 1930. Over the next ten years, the company tested forty-three different modifications of the Type A superheater.

Two cunning new designs were under road test in 1934. In the first, the saturated steam inlet was a round pipe formed progressively into an annular space with flue gases passing both sides of it. The steam passed rearward through this space, thence into a round pipe with three reverse bends at the back end of the flue. The superheated steam then passed forward through a central pipe to the high-temperature side of the header. This was called the Type H-A and was found to deliver 50°F higher superheat than the Type A. The company convinced one railroad to install a unit and road test it. The road tests validated the results from the Elesco rig and, by 1940, two hundred Type H-A superheaters were installed or on order.

The second survivor provided similar characteristics to the Type A, but with wavy pipes. The pipes slightly increased the surface area and provided a more flexible structure better able to absorb differential expansion without warping or leaking at the header joints. This

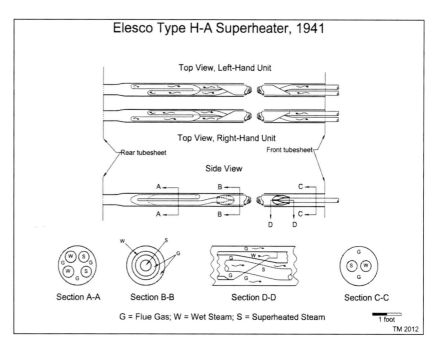

Elesco Type H-A superheater (redrawn from *RA*, June 14, 1941, 1081).

was called the Type ASW ('SW' for "sine wave") and was installed on the Pennsylvania's poppet-valve-equipped K-4s.

The steam temperature produced in a fire-tube superheater was limited by the temperature of the flue gases. The only way to obtain still higher superheat would have been to place the superheater in the firebox. This was never done, probably because of the limited superheating surface obtainable although, considering the gigantic fireboxes of later American locomotives, it is surprising that this was never considered.

15.2.5 Injectors and Feed Water Heaters

By 1935, feed water heaters were standard equipment on the very few new locomotives being built, and were being retrofitted as circumstances and money permitted.[46]

A defect of feed water heaters was that they would deliver cold water to the boiler if they were run when the engine was not working steam, drastically lowering the boiler water temperature and thermally shocking the boiler. In 1935, Wilson Engineering, Chicago, brought out a device to inject live steam into the boiler supply pipe, raising the temperature of the water from the feed water heater by about 100°F.[47]

In 1936, Consolidated Ashcroft Hancock brought out the Hancock Turbo-Injector.[48] A steam turbine drove a four-stage centrifugal pump. The first stage took water from the tender and forced it through nozzles in a "condensing chamber," supplied with exhaust steam. The water entrained the steam and the hot mixture went to the second, third and fourth stages of the pump which raised its pressure progressively to open the boiler check valve and force it into the boiler. The hot water from the condensing chamber passed through a pressure-loaded check valve; this "by-pass valve" could divert some of the flow back to the pump first stage inlet, maintaining a constant delivery temperature, regardless of the flow rate through the pump. A valve in the cab controlled the turbine speed between 30% and 100% of maximum flow. When the locomotive was not working steam, an automatic valve supplied live steam to the condensing chamber. The product of several years of development, this device offered a high degree of flexibility, supplying hot water to the boiler at a controllable flow rate, whether the engine was working steam or not.

Slight improvement in the demand for new locomotives encouraged a flurry of new inventions in 1937. Williams Sellers & Co., Philadelphia, brought out the Type S injector, operated by a single lever, by contrast with all previous injectors in which the steam and water valves were separate.[49] Movement of this lever opened, first, the water valve then the steam valve. As soon as the injector was working, it forced open a check valve which then bled pressure to a valve closing off the water overflow, saving water from being wasted onto the track. Reverse movement of the lever throttled the water flow to match the rate of steam consumption and finally closed the injector altogether. This injector also eliminated the distinction between lifting and non-lifting injectors, placing the injector high enough to avoid damage by material thrown up from the track while still being able to draw from the lowest point of the tender tank. Sellers manufactured three models: the SL for flow rates of 4,900 to 5,800 gallons per hour; the SR for 6,500 to 7,500 gallons per hour and the SW for 8,000 to 12,000 gallons per hour. They also manufactured the Type X for boiler pressures up to 350 pounds per square inch.

The same year, the J. S. Coffin, Jr., Co., Englewood, New Jersey, brought out a new version of their feedwater heater designed for installation inside the smokebox, eliminating the previously distinctive heater over the smokebox brow. As a further refinement, this device incorporated a preheater which sprayed hot condensate from the main heater into the feed water as it left the tender tank.

Also new in 1937 was the Wilson feed water heater, fitted to thirty 4-8-4s supplied by Baldwin to the Milwaukee.[50] The referenced source, however, offers no details of its design.

The Superheater Co. brought out an improved exhaust steam injector with a feedback loop balancing the supply of exhaust steam to the feed water injection rate.[51]

Exhaust-steam injectors at first made only slow inroads into the American locomotive fleet. Sixteen years after the first introduction in the U.S., only fifty-nine were retrofitted in 1937 and only twenty-five new locomotives were ordered with them in 1938.[52] As locomotive building resumed, however, exhaust-steam injectors gained in popularity against feed water heaters, with 1,200 in service in the U.S. and Canada by 1940.[53]

With retrofitting and new construction, feed water heaters in service in the U.S. and Canada totaled 9,050 in 1940, divided between 5,160 closed-type and 3,890 open-type, nearly one-quarter of the fleet.

15.2.6 Welded Boilers

Welding crept onto the locomotive scene between 1910 and 1920, more as a repair tool than for primary fabrication.[54] James Partington, Manager of Engineering with Alco, commented in 1945 that arc, gas and forge welding were used in some locomotive construction and repair work after 1910.

Some new fireboxes were butt welded, first with oxy-acetylene and later with arc welding; the same was true of welded patches in fireboxes already in service. These were always in the staybolted areas of the firebox and usually gave satisfactory results. Some railroad shops repaired the boiler shell by arc welding from the outside only. These welds were not stress-relieved and—obviously—were not carried out according to the codes that were later developed. They were generally unsatisfactory and new cracks soon developed when the locomotives were put back into service.

Partington remarked—guardedly:

> This method was used extensively as a repair tool, sometimes with undesirable results. The use of this welding on boiler shells gave results which were not what might have been hoped for.

The ASME and AWS issued a code for power boilers in 1931, but no code for locomotive boilers until 1942.

In 1932, the Delaware & Hudson began investigating an all-welded boiler in cooperation with Alco. A welded boiler could be 3,000 to 6,000 pounds lighter than an equivalent riveted boiler; the welded seams should be entirely leak-proof, resulting in lower maintenance costs. Four and one-half years of research and experimentation followed. The regulatory environment was now such that the Delaware & Hudson had to make a formal request to the ICC for permission to construct this boiler. The ICC granted permission, provided that the design, specifications and materials were approved by the American Association of Railroads Committee on Locomotive Construction and the General Committee.

Alco built this first all-welded boiler at its Dunkirk, New York, plant. After carefully supervised initial fabrication, with X-ray quality control, Alco sent the boiler to Nashville, Tennessee, for stress-relieving before being returned for installation of the firebox and completion. After hydrostatic and hammer tests at Schenectady, Alco delivered it to the Delaware & Hudson in March 1937.[55]

The D. & H. installed the new boiler on a 2-8-0, but tested it statically for a month before releasing it for road service, in which it was to run a five-year trial.[56] The boiler was thoroughly cleaned, inspected and hydrostatically tested every six months. After two years in service, during which time the locomotive ran 134,000 miles, the inspectors found nothing wrong with the boiler; after 6½ years in service, the boiler still needed no repairs. By late 1941, the Delaware & Hudson boiler was nearing the end of its five-year trial and, when Baldwin built eight 4-6-4s for the Chesapeake & Ohio, delivered in December 1941, and January 1942, the boilers were extensively—but not entirely—welded.[57]

Improved welding aroused new interest in combustion chambers.[58] The first combustion chambers had riveted joints; leakage at the joints caused a reaction against them. In the late 1930s, welding technology and quality control had so improved that pressure vessels resisting high pressures could be safely welded with butt joints and the combustion chamber once more came into its own.

When rising traffic demand prompted the building of new locomotives in the late 1930s and early 1940s, manufacturers used a combination of welding and riveting for boiler and firebox construction. Welding was limited to firebox joints loaded in compression; riveting was retained for boiler joints loaded in tension. Non-structural seal welding was applied to some riveted joints to prevent leakage. In 1945, Alco built more than 200 boilers with the longitudinal seams of each course welded, although the joints between each course were still riveted.

The ICC Bureau of Locomotive Inspection was in no hurry to approve welded locomotive boilers. In 1946[59]:

> No property loss or personal injury or death has occurred in many years because of failures of riveted joints in locomotive boiler shells, some of which have been in service for periods of time exceeding the average life range of human beings. Therefore, it is not apparent that safety would be increased by the use of fusion welded joints in these boiler shells.

The ICC pointed out that, while several railroad shops were equipped to build riveted boilers, none were equipped for all the operations required for welded boilers, including radiography and stress-relieving. Consequently, the ICC was willing to qualify individual railroads only, case by case, after submission of detailed drawings, specifications and procedures.

By mid–1947, twenty-five all-welded boilers were in service or on order, the largest being for a 4-6-6-4, saving 7,000 pounds' weight. Some welded boilers of carbon steel replaced riveted high-tensile steel boilers for no saving in weight but, presumably, savings in cost.[60]

The slow progress toward all-welded boilers in America was cut off by the abandonment of the steam locomotive. Progress continued in other countries that built steam locomotives; by the 1990s, the Chinese were building all-welded boilers for their QJ 2-10-2s with no riveted joints.[61]

15.2.7 Boiler Explosions

The year ending June 30, 1930, was the safest on record in terms of accidents attributable to the steam locomotive itself.[62] Even so, thirteen people were killed and 320 injured; eleven of the thirteen fatalities were caused by boiler explosions. Great progress had been made since 1912, when 856 boiler-related accidents killed ninety-one people and injured 1,005 but, throughout the 1930s, explosions continued at seven to fifteen each year.

In one boiler explosion in 1931[63]:

> The force of the explosion tore the boiler from the frame and hurled it forward 429 ft. The boiler alighted on the track and then slid forward for some distance, where the locomotive running gear and train collided with it, resulting in the derailment of the running gear, tender and 14 freight-train cars, 8 of which caught fire and were destroyed.

When the boiler of a 2-8-4 exploded in 1940, three people were killed and the boiler was torn from its mountings and thrown 495 feet.[64] The train piled up behind the wrecked engine.

The new engines, with huge, high-pressure boilers, were still vulnerable to uncovering of the crown sheet, with devastating results. Even with a modest length over tube sheets, a long, stoker-fired grate and a combustion chamber resulted in a long continuous water space, increasing the fluctuations in water level over the crown sheet caused by changes in grade. This was especially true of the enormously long Mallet boilers. Evidence suggested that enginemen were unaware of the very short time left to them after the water had disappeared below the bottom of the gauge glass until the crown sheet was uncovered. Typically, the bottom of the water glass was 4½ inches above the crown sheet; the evaporation of 6,000 pounds of water, with no injection of feed water, would uncover the crown sheet; at a steaming rate of 70,000 pounds per hour, this would occur in five minutes. An ascending grade easing, or going to level or downgrade, reduced this margin still farther.

Disturbingly, two investigations in 1940–1 showed that the injectors and feed water heaters on the investigated locomotives had been defective for a long time and that reported repair work had not been done.[65] Inspectors also noted serious inattention to maintenance of the gauge glasses and their lamps.

The 1942 report of the Bureau of Locomotive Inspection remarked, cautiously[66]:

> Many locomotives are equipped with protective devices such as syphons, multiple drop or fusible plugs, and low-water alarms, all of which have prevented boiler explosions or minimized the severity thereof.

The comment indicates that such devices were far from universal. Noteworthy is that syphons, introduced for their effect on steaming, were additionally regarded as protective devices.

A crown sheet would fail when the temperature of the steel reached 1,350°F to 1,400°F. Carbon-molybdenum steel offered double the strength at those temperatures; the railroads began to consider this material for fireboxes in 1943.[67]

Boiler explosions continued, often involving well-constructed and well-maintained boilers, discoloration of the crown sheet due to overheating being the only clue to the crown sheet failure that caused the accident. Since the engine crews were usually killed, explanations for the events leading up to these disasters were seldom forthcoming. In 1943, J. E. Bjorkholm, Superintendent of Motive Power on the Milwaukee, examined this question in an article a century overdue.[68] He commented:

> The human element entering into the question, however, has, in my opinion, not been given the consideration it deserves. …
>
> I think it is generally recognized that few other types of boilers are subject to the abuse and difficulties surrounding the operation of locomotive boilers. It is to the everlasting credit of the men who design and build them, to the men who maintain them and to the men who operate them, that with few exceptions they function remarkably well.

Enginemen with decades of experience, getting away with low water levels without mishap, would be inclined to take a chance one more time but the Milwaukee urged them in the strongest possible terms to douse the fire rather than risk a boiler explosion.

> There is only one thing to do when the water begins to play "peek-a-boo" in the basement instead of being in the second or third story of the waterglass and that is to pay strict attention to the lower gauge cock and, when the water is no longer in evidence, to extinguish the fire with the first means at hand: if the water bucket or hose is not available the fire can always be dumped into the ash pan or whatever means must be

resorted to. The result may be a temporary tie up of the railroad but it is far better for the engineman to say good morning to his superintendent or master mechanic and explain what occurred than be called upon to render an account of his earthly doings to St. Peter.

Investigations of several incidents revealed that the crews had averted crown sheet failure by *seconds*. Why then, did conscientious and experienced enginemen, running properly maintained locomotives, take these risks with their lives? The events leading to a crown sheet failure could be complex.

Bjorkholm explained one near-occurrence. The engineer on a freight train was running late ahead of a passenger train, and also running low on water. He believed that he had enough water to reach a passing loop with a water plug where he was due to meet another train. With a short distance remaining, an air hose broke, causing the brakes to apply and stalling the train. This occurred at a low point on the route with adverse grades in both directions. The crew's attempts to repair the air hose left them so short of water that, when the fireman looked into the tender tank, there was no water to be seen. They cut the locomotive loose from the train and tried to reach the next water plug but, when only dry steam came out of the bottom try cock, they killed the fire, resulting in delays for other traffic. Inspection revealed that staybolts had already begun to pull out and a small area of the crown sheet was burnt. Considering the time it would have taken for the firebox to cool, even after dropping the fire, their luck was nearly miraculous.

Lack of awareness was to blame in many cases, whether from inexperience, defective training, boredom or exhaustion.

In another accident, streaks melted in snow by discharged water showed that the injector had not picked up. A working injector typically makes a distinctive noise, usually audible through the noises of the engine, and causes a slow drop in boiler pressure as cool feed water enters the boiler; the absence of these cues is noticeable in less than thirty seconds. Working at night, the crew failed to notice these cues as well as failing to notice low water level in the gauge glasses.

Fortunately, some staybolts pulled out without the whole boiler exploding; the crew survived their resulting injuries.

Under the stress of wartime conditions, the rising accident rate of 1942 peaked at twenty-five boiler explosions in 1943 (fiscal years) killing twenty-four people and injuring fifty-six more, followed by nineteen in 1944, killing twelve and injuring sixty-two.[69]

One of these, on July 7, 1942, a Norfolk & Western Class A, followed a collision and derailment that left the boiler tilted sharply downward, baring the crown sheet.[70] The crew escaped with minor injuries but, ten minutes after the derailment, the engineer went back to the engine to try to douse the fire and was killed when the boiler exploded. Flying wreckage killed a bystander and destroyed a house. The boiler was thrown 177 feet, landing on a car and destroying it. The locomotive was rebuilt and returned to service.

One September day in 1943, the New York Central's *Twentieth Century Limited* left Chicago behind a J-3a with crew changes at Elkhart, Toledo, Collinwood, Buffalo and Syracuse. The Buffalo crew found that the feed water pump throttle control rod became disconnected; they kept the boiler full with the help of the injector. They reconnected the control rod while standing at signals at Rochester but it became disconnected again; the pump throttle was open enough to supply the boiler without using the injector. The crew reconnected the rod while coaling at Waynesport, but it became disconnected again. The fireman managed to open the pump throttle enough that it was over-supplying the boiler and turned it on and off by means of the pump overspeed trip mechanism. Meanwhile, the crew had called ahead to Syracuse to arrange a relief engine. Arriving at Syracuse in the early hours of the morning, the Buffalo crew explained the problem to their relief crew, who decided to press on, rather than take the relief locomotive that had been prepared for them. That decision cost them their lives. They left Syracuse at full throttle at 4.13 a.m., 18 minutes late, making 22 miles in the next 22 minutes. The engine was traveling at 70 miles per hour when the boiler exploded.[71] The boiler came to rest 900 feet ahead of the point

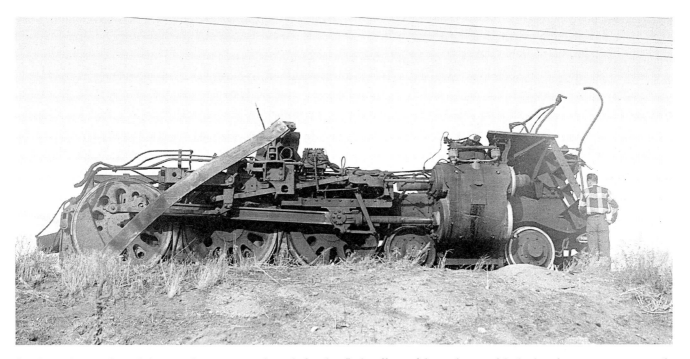

"Boiler explosions dogged the steam locomotive to the end of its days." The effects of the explosion of the boiler of a Denver & Rio Grande Western class L-105 4-6-6-4, No. 3703, built by Baldwin in 1938. The explosion took place near Sedalia, Colorado, on October 19, 1952 (Denver Public Library, Otto C. Perry collection, OP-11104).

of the explosion and 35 feet to the side of the track; the firebox turned inside out and landed 400 feet ahead and 100 feet to the side of the point of the explosion. Other wreckage was scattered over a 500-foot radius. The remains of the locomotive stopped 1,300 feet from the point of the explosion, with all wheels of the locomotive and the first ten cars derailed and the train piled up behind the locomotive. The three men on the footplate—engineer, fireman and a traveling engineer—were killed.

Boiler explosions dogged the steam locomotive to the end of its days.

Section 15.3. Steam Application, Valves and Valve Gear

15.3.1 Reversing Gear

Power reversing went political in 1930, when the Brotherhood of Locomotive Engineers and the Brotherhood of Locomotive Firemen and Enginemen filed a complaint with the ICC, trying to force the railroads to install power reversing gear on all locomotives.[72] The ICC investigated the complaint and issued a ruling in January 1933, requiring all steam locomotives built after April 1, 1933—regardless of size—to be equipped with power reversing gear. Additionally the ICC required that all road engines built before that date with an adhesion weight more than 150,000 pounds, and all switch engines built before that date with an adhesion weight more than 130,000 pounds, be retrofitted with power reversing gear at their next major overhaul and, in any event, before January 1, 1937. The ICC also required that locomotives with air-operated power reversing gear be fitted with a steam connection enabling the power reverser in the event of a failure of the compressed air supply. The railroads blustered, but to no effect. The ICC referred to its accident records and found that, of 232 injuries involving reversing gear in 1929–30, 216 occurred on engines with hand reversing gear and only sixteen on engines with a power reverser. The ICC also pointed out that the railroads were already operating 29,000 locomotives with power reversers and contemplated building most new engines with this equipment. Due to the economic climate, 9,840 locomotives were stored in serviceable condition; many of these were old engines with hand reversers and would probably be scrapped anyway. A federal district court in Cleveland blocked the enforcement of this order on the grounds that it was arbitrary and had not fully examined all the relevant facts; the U.S. Supreme Court supported this ruling. In March 1935, the unions petitioned successfully for the issue to be reopened; the ICC concluded its hearings in March 1936. The railroads protested that the order would entail the installation of power reversing gear on 18,000 locomotives at a cost of $7 million but later downgraded these figures to 11,247 locomotives and $4 million, based on the August 1935, fleet, at which time the railroads were operating 27,587 locomotives (58% of the fleet) with power reversers. In November 1936, the railroads and the unions reached an agreement and asked the ICC to dismiss the original complaint. In January 1937, the ICC refused, asserting its function as the rule-making authority. Instead, it proposed an order of the same substance as its order of January 1933, and the agreement between the railroads and the unions, namely that road engines with an adhesion weight of 150,000 pounds or greater and switch engines of an adhesion weight of 130,000 pounds or greater were to be retrofitted at their next major overhaul and, in any event, not later than January 1, 1942.

This boded well for companies such as Franklin. The Franklin Type G Precision Power Reverse Gear appeared in 1928.[73] Franklin became a major supplier of locomotive appliances during the 1930s.

Power reversers proliferated in the shape of the Alco Types E, G, G1, H, H-12 and K, the Franklin Precision Type F2, the Baldwin Type C, the Barco Types M-1 and M-13, the Lewis Type A and others. Current research has not revealed their construction or the differences between them but all had the objectives of quick, precise action, reliability, ease of maintenance and freedom from creep.

15.3.2 Boosters

The railroads had accepted the booster with alacrity; in the search for ever higher power at ever higher speeds, it was natural that they should seek to increase the maximum speed at which the booster could contribute useful tractive force.

The Bethlehem Auxiliary Locomotive, dating back to 1927, has already been mentioned; the company produced two models, the Series A and S. In 1934, the company brought out the Bethlehem High-Speed Auxiliary Locomotive,[74] Series H, a six-wheel booster intended for installation as one of the six-wheel trucks under a massive tender. One of the first installations was on ten 1932-built Lehigh Valley 4-8-4s as the rear truck of a tender holding 20,000 gallons of water and 30 tons of coal for a gross weight of 398,000 pounds. The 4-8-4's boiler supplied steam at 250 pounds per square inch to two 12¼-inch × 11-inch cylinders, working at a fixed cut-off of 70% and driving 42-inch wheels on roller bearings through 1:2.24 reduction gearing, automatically clutched so that the engine engaged only when the engineer applied steam to it. The unit was balanced and sprung so that it could run at speeds up to 100 miles per hour without damaging either itself or the track. A lever, controlling the booster, was connected to the reversing lever of the main engine so that the booster could be cut in only when the main reversing lever was in forward gear. The 4-8-4 developed 66,000 pounds of tractive effort; the booster added 18,000 pounds on starting, still 6,700 pounds at 20 miles per hour, limited only by the speed above which the booster no longer produced any useful incremental tractive effort. First run in March 1934, behind a succession of engines, the booster showed no undue wear eighteen months later, after running 75,000 miles.[75]

In 1937, Franklin brought out the Type E booster, capable of being cut in at speeds up to 21 miles per hour and continuing to operate at speeds up to 35 miles per hour.[76] The booster was designed to be customized, with cylinders of 10½-inch to 11-inch bore × 12-inch stroke, three optional gear ratios and any fixed cut-off 35% or longer. If the main engine slipped, starving the booster of steam, an automatic device increased the steam supply to the booster. Dynamometer tests with steam at 205 pounds per square inch and 600°F demonstrated a maximum power output of 450 indicated horsepower, 390 brake horsepower, at a crankshaft speed of 508 revolutions per minute (25 to 35 miles per hour wheel speed, depending on gear ratio). In these conditions, the booster consumed 9,000 pounds of steam per hour, 20 pounds per indicated horsepower-hour, 23 pounds per brake horsepower-hour.[77]

Although the booster contributed markedly to motive power development in the 1920s, its popularity did not last and, when locomotive building resumed in the late 1930s, diminishing numbers of new locomotives had boosters. It added significant weight, complexity, initial cost and maintenance expense. It added to the crew's tasks. Its clutch could fail destructively.[78] The railroads favored the simpler solution of higher boiler pressures and long cut-off in full gear.

15.3.3 Poppet Valves

Slide valves and piston valves suffered from the abiding deficiency that a single valve body made both the inlet and exhaust valve events, which could not therefore be separated from each other.[79] Poppet valves overcame this disadvantage, providing separate inlet and exhaust ports, rapid and complete port opening and cut-offs as short as 10%. Separating the inlet and exhaust ports avoided the temperature cycling in conventional steam ports. Although steam locomotives were reaching speeds as high as 80 to 100 miles per hour, given suitable infrastructure, extremely short valve events and steam viscosity limited their power output at such speeds. Poppet valves promised to remove this limitation or, at least, postpone its effect. Increasing steam temperature and pressure made piston valves more difficult to lubricate; poppet valves offered a solution to this problem also. When the engine was not working steam, drifting downgrade, the poppet valves at each end of the cylinder could be held open, connecting both ends of the cylinder in a way that was impossible with a piston valve. Equally important, the cyclic reversal of large, heavy piston valves consumed significant power; the moving parts of a pair of poppet valves weighed only 7 to 8 pounds, compared to 120 pounds for a 12-inch piston valve.

The Germans installed Lentz poppet valves in a locomotive in 1905; the Italians followed with Caprotti valves in 1921.[80] Poppet valves in locomotives made rapid progress in Austria, where more than 400 locomotives were so equipped by 1930–395 Lentz, five Caprotti—indeed, by that date the Austrian Federal Railways had "definitely abandoned the piston valve."[81] Apparently, "several hundred" locomotives were equipped with poppet valves in the British Empire during the 1920s and 1930s. In the late 1920s, Baldwin obtained the U.S. rights to the Caprotti system.

In May 1926, the Delaware & Hudson applied poppet valves, driven by Walschaert valve gear, to a 2-8-0 freight engine with satisfactory results over the next four years.[82] The following year, G. S. Edmonds, Superintendent of Motive Power, visited Arturo Caprotti in Italy and the Lentz representatives in Austria, finding that Italian locomotives with Caprotti poppet valves turned in a 9% better fuel economy than similar engines with piston valves, running at cut-offs as short as 5%. Between 1929 and 1931 the D&H built three 4-6-2s in its Colonie shops, equipping two with poppet valves, driven by Walschaert valve gear.

This sparked considerable enthusiasm; between 1927 and 1930, seven railroads installed poppet valves on twelve locomotives—the Delaware & Hudson (4), the Baltimore & Ohio (3), the Santa Fe, the Southern Pacific, the Union Pacific, the Pennsylvania and the Reading (1 each).[83]

In the late 1920s, the Philadelphia & Reading started rebuilding thirty-one Baldwin 2-8-8-2 compound Mallets, dating from 1917 to 1919, into 2-10-2s.[84] By mid–1930, the company had converted ten, one with Caprotti poppet valves.

Even so, poppet valves for locomotives had little impact in America.[85] As late as 1937:

> Foreign designers have not been slow in attempting to improve steam distribution in the cylinders with the result that poppet valves are in service on many locomotives. Trial applications have been made to locomotives in the United States and the latest development seems to indicate that poppet valves can be successfully adapted to operating conditions in this country.

As the demand for speed grew in the late 1930s, the inertia of the piston valve body began to cause maintenance problems, leading to a tendency to shorten the valve travel, whereas effective steam admission demanded the opposite.[86] The valve body could be made of stronger and lighter materials, providing some relief, and the valve diameter could be increased at the expense of a new cylinder casting—impractical if the cylinder casting was part of an engine bed—but these were palliatives rather than solutions.[87]

Until the late 1930s, poppet valves could be driven in two ways[88]:

an oscillating cam shaft driven by conventional valve gear (e.g. Lentz), or a rotating cam shaft driven from the main axle (e.g. Caprotti). Dabeg produced both types. The oscillating cam shaft had the advantage of using conventional valve gear and cut-off control, but did not allow the inlet and exhaust valves to operate separately. The rotating cam shaft allowed the inlet and exhaust valves to be controlled separately but each cut-off needed a different cam profile, limiting control to a number of discrete cut-offs.

By 1938, poppet-valves had still been applied to only thirteen locomotives on seven U.S. railroads—one Lentz, four Dabeg and eight Caprotti.[89] (Delaware & Hudson: one 2-8-0, Lentz, 1926; two 4-6-2, Dabeg, 1930, 1934; one 4-8-0, Dabeg, 1933. Baltimore & Ohio: one 2-8-0, Caprotti, 1927; one 4-6-2, Caprotti, 1928; one 4-6-4, Dabeg, 1935. Santa Fe: one 4-8-4, Caprotti, 1929. Southern Pacific: one 2-10-2, Caprotti, 1929. Union Pacific: one 4-8-2, Caprotti, 1929. Pennsylvania: one 4-6-2, Caprotti, 1929. Reading: one 4-6-0, Caprotti, 1930; one 2-10-2, Caprotti, 1930. As far as is known, all were retrofits; the year is the date of installation, not that of original locomotive construction.) By that date, however, only the two Dabeg-valve locomotives on the Delaware & Hudson remained in use. The rest had been reconverted back to piston valves or had been withdrawn from traffic; the Caprotti valves were not strong enough for the service to which they were subjected.

Allured by the benefits of poppet valves and inspired by the failure of European imports, Franklin began to develop a poppet valve gear suited to American service in 1937, comprising two oscillating cam shafts, controlling inlet and exhaust valves separately with a single reversing mechanism. The valve gear comprised the French Dabeg valves and cam box with an innovative gear box and driving motion developed by Franklin and Lima. Each cylinder had two inlet and two exhaust valves, weighing about 14 pounds in total, compared to 130 pounds for a 12-inch piston valve, greatly reducing the power needed to operate the valve gear, estimated at 50 horsepower for conventional valve gear and less than 5 horsepower for the poppet valve gear. The penalty was the gear box which weighed 3,600 pounds and a much more complicated mechanism.

In 1939, the Pennsylvania installed Franklin poppet valves on a K-4s 4-6-2, the modification being done by Lima.[90] The locomotive went into service on the Pennsylvania's Fort Wayne division, noted for its fast, heavy passenger traffic. After a one-month running-in period, the company ran dynamometer tests with passenger trains weighing almost exactly 1,000 tons. In one test, the engine developed 2,885 indicated horsepower, running at 30% cut-off at 92 miles per hour. The modified engine developed 54% more power at 90 miles per hour than an unmodified K-4s, reaching 95 miles per hour with the 1,000-ton train.[91] After running the engine for 57,000 miles in this service, the company tested it at Altoona. Performance began to exceed that of a conventional piston-valve engine at speeds above 50 miles per hour, providing faster acceleration and higher top speeds.

Before putting the engine on the test plant, the Pennsylvania made several modifications, replacing the Type A superheater with a Type ASW with longer superheater tubes, so that the Type ASW, as installed, provided 6% more superheating surface than the Type A. Each flue contained two loops in parallel, increasing the cross-section area for steam passage. They enlarged most of the steam pipes to reduce friction losses and installed a front-end throttle, completing the modifications in the summer of 1940. True to Pennsylvania tradition, the test program was immensely thorough, comprising fifty-six test runs with three different sizes of exhaust nozzle.

The result was a dream come true. Maximum indicated horsepower was 4,270 at 75 miles per hour, while at 100 miles per hour—the highest speed tested, the engine was still developing 4,100 indicated horsepower. The company compared the results with those of another K-4s tested in 1937, standardizing the steaming rate to 70,000 pounds per hour. Even at 40 miles per hour the modified K-4s developed 16% more power and consumed 14% less steam than the unmodified engine, but this improved to 47% more power and 32% less steam consumption at 100 miles per hour.

Late in 1940, the Pennsylvania installed poppet valves on a second K-4s, but with less success for reasons that are obscure. Even so, west of Crestline, Ohio, all passenger trains of more than twelve cars needed two K-4s's; the first K-4s with poppet valves handled trains of up to fourteen cars unassisted.[92] In 1942, the Pennsylvania added a Franklin high-speed booster to the K-4s, further adding to its performance.

The poppet valve came too late to penetrate American locomotive construction. By mid–1947, only seventy locomotives on seven railroads were so equipped (Atchison, Topeka & Santa Fe (1), Chesapeake & Ohio (10), Chicago, Burlington & Quincy (1), Delaware & Hudson (2), Missouri Pacific (1), New York Central (1), Pennsylvania (54)). Of the fifty-four on the Pennsylvania, fifty-two were fitted to the class T-1 4-4-4-4s. In 1947, the Chesapeake & Ohio rebuilt five 1926-built 4-6-2s as 4-6-4s with streamlining, roller bearings and poppet valves; only the tender and some boiler parts were used in the rebuilds.[93] The following year, the company bought five 4-6-4s from Baldwin with poppet valves.[94] The same year, the Santa Fe put a 1928-built Baldwin 4-8-4 through a major overhaul and installed rotary cam poppet valves and valve gear.[95] The result was a 17% increase in power; the engine achieved a steam consumption of 13.5 pounds per indicated horsepower-hour at a wide range of speeds from 25 to 55 miles per hour. A recommendation to refit the company's 2-10-4s came to nothing, due to the onset of dieselization. Probably the last poppet valve application in North America was to a Canadian National 4-8-4 in 1950; Dominion Engineering, Montreal, supplied the valves, designed for retrofitting to piston valve steam chests without substantial modification.[96]

As early as 1933, the Delaware & Hudson reported[97]: "A higher rate of craftsmanship is necessary with the poppet valve." American experience indicated that design improvements for maintainability were needed if the valve was to succeed in American conditions. Of the substantial numbers of steam locomotives built elsewhere in the world from 1950 onward, only a small minority ever had poppet valves.

15.3.4 Steam-Turbine Locomotives

An altogether different approach to the steam locomotive was the steam turbine. In theory, a steam turbine offered higher thermal efficiency than a reciprocating engine, typically exhausting into a condenser. The condenser vacuum slightly increased the pressure drop across the turbine but also recovered water and the latent heat of evaporation which were lost to exhaust in a conventional steam engine. In practice, an intermediate drive was needed to match the speed:torque characteristics of the turbine with that of the locomotive; space limited the size of the condenser. Turbine locomotives were especially suited to oil and pulverized coal firing.[98] The steam turbine was well suited to stationary plant but ill-suited to the stops, starts and speed variations of a locomotive. The turbine could not be reversed, necessitating a reversible drive or a second turbine, with a significant penalty in cost, bulk and weight.

The first such locomotive was designed by Professor Belluzzo of Milan, Italy, in 1907.[99] Several European designs reached the experimental stage in the 1920s. The Maffei-Benson design generated steam at 3,200 pounds per square inch and developed 2,000 horsepower. The Krupp type used a water-tube boiler generating steam at

850 pounds per square inch. The Henschel design used exhaust steam from a conventional engine to power a turbine that turned the tender into a separate drive unit.

The Ljungstrom brothers, turbine manufacturers of Stockholm, Sweden, designed and built a steam-turbine locomotive that went into service on the Swedish state railways in 1921.[100] The boiler generated steam at 285 pounds per square inch, applying it to a turbine which drove the wheels through direct gearing. The turbine exhausted into an air-cooled condenser. Waste gas preheated the combustion air; exhaust steam from the auxiliaries heated the feedwater; a turbine-driven fan drafted the furnace. The engine developed 1,800 horsepower with no immediate prospect of obtaining greater power output within the constraints of size and weight.

In 1921–2 the firm of Escher Wyss, of Zurich, built a gear-drive, steam-turbine locomotive known as the Zoelly type while, in Britain, Armstrong Whitworth built a locomotive in which a Ramsay-type steam turbine drove a generator which powered four 275-horsepower electric drive motors, developing 22,000 pounds of tractive effort and 1,100 horsepower. The engine was tested on the London & North Western Railway.

In 1923–4, the Germans built a Zoelly-type locomotive that developed 2,000 horsepower. That power output gained the attention of American railroadmen but high initial cost and maintenance difficulties put them off.

By 1927, several steam turbine locomotives were in experimental service or under construction in Germany; two were in service in Sweden.[101] J. G. Maffei of Munich, Germany, had a 2,500-horsepower turbine locomotive in service. A conventional boiler with a fandrafted furnace supplied steam at 324 pounds per square inch to a condensing turbine driving a geared transmission. Krupp had more than one turbine locomotive under test, using low-pressure steam, but had another under construction to use 854-pound steam pressure from a water-tube boiler, designed to develop 2,500 horsepower.

The Ljungstroms built one locomotive themselves and had a second built in England. In service they achieved coal consumptions of 39 to 46 pounds per thousand ton-miles, compared to 83 to 130 pounds for reciprocating power. Meanwhile, they had designs on the drawing board for an 830,000-pound locomotive developing 8,000 horsepower. Three Ljungstrom engines were in service in Sweden in 1936.[102]

In spite of the fuel savings achieved by the Ljungstrom locomotives, their complexity and high construction cost left the Americans unimpressed. The Armstrong Whitworth locomotive weighed 243 pounds per horsepower, twice that of an American reciprocating locomotive. Turbine locomotives had not exceeded 2,500 horsepower; conventional American locomotives were developing 3,000 horsepower for a much lower first cost. A steam-turbine locomotive lacked the pull-out force of a conventional steam locomotive. High thermal efficiency was achieved by means of a condenser; power output was limited by the space available for the condenser.[103]

In 1933, the London, Midland & Scottish Railway in England started construction of three four-cylinder 4-6-2 express passenger locomotives.[104] Two were completed as planned, numbered 6210 and 6212; the third was completed as a non-condensing, geared turbine locomotive, numbered 6202. The main dimensions of all three locomotives were identical, offering an unparalleled opportunity to compare the performance of reciprocating and turbine locomotives. Extensive dynamometer car tests between London and Glasgow showed that the reciprocating No. 6210 was 8% more economical in fuel and water consumption per drawbar horsepower-hour than the other, identical, reciprocating engine, No. 6212. The fuel and water consumption of No. 6202 was indistinguishable from that of No.

6210 at 3.0 pounds of coal and 24 pounds of water per drawbar horsepower-hour. These results discouraged further development. No. 6202 continued in service during World War II, but was rebuilt as a reciprocating engine in 1952.

In the 1920s, General Electric considered a high-pressure, steam-turbine electric locomotive of small size, light weight and high efficiency, although possibly developing up to 10,000 horsepower, capable of responding quickly to changes in power demand with automatic control of steam generation.[105] GE commissioned Babcock & Wilcox to design and build the steam plant and the Bailey Meter Co. to develop the control system. Locomotives were only one application for this project, called the "Steamotive."

GE built a prototype at its Schenectady works in 1934 and put it through 950 hours of tests. The prototype went into "commercial service" at the GE Lynn Works, although the referenced source does not say what this service was. An oil-fired, water-tube boiler was capable of generating 21,000 pounds of steam per hour. Normal full-load steam output was 16,000 pounds per hour at 870°F. The furnace measured only 3½ feet wide, 3½ feet high and 7½ feet long. Hot gas from the burner gave up its heat at progressively lower temperatures as it went through the furnace, superheater, feed water heater and combustion air heater, then out through the stack. The feed water pump forced water through the feed water heater, thence through floor, wall and roof tubes surrounding the furnace, becoming steam in the process, to a steam separator, thence through a superheater to the steam turbine. The feed water pump had to develop 1,610 pounds per square inch for a steam pressure at the superheater outlet of 1,390 pounds per square inch, friction losses through the water tubes accounting for 220 pounds per square inch. A variable-speed steam turbine, separate from the drive turbine, drove the blower and pumps supplying feed water, fuel oil and lubricants. A centrifugal blower,

capable of 60 inches of water gauge, forced outside air through the air heater, past the burner, through the furnace and out through the stack. Furnace and boiler functions were highly automated. The boiler was capable of producing full power ten minutes after a cold start.

In the summer of 1936, the Union Pacific announced plans to build two 2,500-horsepower, steam-turbine-electric power units in cooperation with General Electric.[106] In each unit a Babcock & Wilcox oil-fired, water-tube boiler with automatic controls generated steam at 1,500 pounds per square inch and 950°F, supplying a two-stage steam turbine and using distilled water in a closed condensing system. A small, propane-fired, fire-tube boiler was included for warming and atomizing the fuel to start the main boiler. The turbine drove a generator, supplying an electric motor for each of the six driving axles. Reversing was by reversing the electric motors; speed control was by changing the generator output voltage. The locomotive was completed in 1938. Both power units were combined as a double-ended 4-6-6-4+4-6-6-4 locomotive, developing 4,000 horsepower at the rail, intended to haul 1,000-ton passenger trains at speeds up to 110 miles per hour and handle 2.2% grades unassisted.[107] With tender half full, the all-up weight was 500 tons. Electric regenerative braking reduced tire and brake wear. Unbalanced reciprocating parts were eliminated. High adhesion weight and multiple driving wheels within a restricted axle loading provided fast acceleration to line speed. The Union Pacific anticipated twice the thermal efficiency of a conventional steam locomotive but the locomotive's service record later politely remarked that: "availability was too low to permit its continued operation."[108] The locomotive was probably a victim of its own complexity, placing heavy demands on as yet immature control technology. The Union Pacific soon returned it to General Electric.[109] The Great Northern used it briefly in 1943 but then returned it to General Electric, where it was scrapped.

The Pennsylvania's class S-2 steam-turbine 6-8-6, No. 6200, built by Baldwin in 1944. Other photographs show that this locomotive was at one time fitted with smoke deflectors (Pennsylvania Historical and Museum Commission and Railroad Museum of Pennsylvania, General Photograph 227-6-4).

The Pennsylvania became interested in a steam-turbine locomotive in 1937; two years of studies by the company and Westinghouse followed. Westinghouse expected that this type of engine would burn coal or oil, would eliminate reciprocating parts and would be 20% to 25% more thermally efficient at high speed than existing steam locomotives.[110] The Pennsylvania considered rebuilding existing locomotives, but decided to engage Baldwin to build a completely new non-condensing, geared, steam-turbine 4-8-4. Work began in 1941 but U.S. entry into the war halted construction and required design modifications to use non-critical materials, resulting in a change to a 6-8-6 wheel arrangement. Baldwin resumed construction in 1943 and delivered the engine in September 1944.

A 120-square foot grate fired a boiler supplying steam at 310 pounds per square inch and 750°F at steaming rates up to 95,000 pounds per hour. A 3-foot-9-inch diameter turbine developed 6,900 shaft horsepower—6,550 horsepower at the rail at 70 miles per hour, the maximum speed being 100 miles per hour at which the turbine turned at 9,000 revolutions per minute. The gearing drove the second and third driving axles; side rods transmitted power to the first and fourth axles. A second, 1,500-horsepower, turbine was installed for reversing, automatically declutched when the locomotive was moving forward and allowing the locomotive to reverse at speeds up to 22 miles per hour. Total engine weight was 583,000 pounds; the axle loading was 65,000 pounds.

The manufacturers claimed that turbine drive would produce 20% more power from a given boiler size than a reciprocating engine. Pis-ton speeds, valve events and rotating and reciprocating masses limited the cycling rate of a reciprocating engine so that engines for high speed needed large driving wheels. The turbine locomotive suffered from no such restrictions; the driving wheels could be smaller and the center of gravity lower. The side rods had only a fraction of the mass of the rotating and reciprocating parts of a conventional engine, greatly reducing dynamic augment and counterbalancing problems. Although starting tractive effort was adequate at 71,000 pounds, the geared transmission meant that the turbine turned slowly at speeds below 30 miles per hour and, as Baldwin predicted, steam consumption was very high at less than 30 miles per hour, only reaching a maximum economy of 15 pounds of steam per wheel-rim horsepower-hour at 70 miles per hour.

By 1946, the engine had run 50,000 miles in revenue service—not a high total. The following year it was "reported to be turning in a good performance in both high-speed passenger and freight service." It remained one of a kind and was scrapped in 1952.[111]

In 1947, Baldwin-Westinghouse delivered a steam turbine-electric locomotive to the Chesapeake & Ohio, a year behind schedule. A conventional boiler with a maximum evaporation rate of 85,000 pounds per hour supplied steam at 290 pounds per square inch and 750°F to a 6,000-horsepower, 6,000-revolutions per minute non-condensing turbine.[112] The turbine was geared to two two-unit 580-volt DC generators supplying power to eight 620-horsepower traction motors, each driving an axle. Starting tractive effort was 98,000 pounds with a maximum continuous rating of 48,000 pounds at 40

One of the Chesapeake & Ohio's steam-turbine locomotives, built by Baldwin in 1947–48. The location and date of the photograph are unknown (courtesy California State Railroad Museum, James E. Boynton Collection, Negative 39082cn).

The Norfolk & Western's steam-turbine locomotive, *Jawn Henry,* built by Baldwin-Lima-Hamilton in 1954. The location and date of this photograph are unknown (courtesy Norfolk Southern Corporation, ns1266).

miles per hour and a maximum speed of 100 miles per hour. The electric drive allowed the turbine to run up to a thermally efficient rotation rate while the locomotive was moving slowly. The locomotive was configured with the coal bunker ahead of the cab, the firebox behind the cab and the boiler behind the firebox. Water was carried in a tender. As early as the end of 1948, Westinghouse was admitting that thermal efficiency was not much higher than that of a conventional steam locomotive. Although the Chesapeake & Ohio bought two more in 1948, they proved uneconomical in fuel and excessively difficult to maintain; all were scrapped in 1950.

In spite of its successful reciprocating steam operations, the Norfolk & Western was not immune to the lure of new forms of power. In 1952, Babcock & Wilcox, Westinghouse and Baldwin-Lima-Hamilton were assembling a 4,500-horsepower steam-turbine electric locomotive for the N&W, following design work going back to 1949.[113] Babcock & Wilcox built a forced-draft, water-tube boiler, fired by coal on a chain grate, supplying steam at 600 pounds per square inch and 900°F to a non-condensing turbine. Westinghouse built the turbine and electrical equipment. Baldwin-Lima-Hamilton built the mechanical parts.

Delivery, scheduled for November 1952, did not take place until May 1954. The locomotive weighed 1,172,000 pounds, including tender, coal and water, with a rated tractive effort of 175,000 pounds and was designed for speeds up to 60 miles per hour. The tender had

a capacity for 22,000 gallons of water; a bunker on the engine held 20 tons of coal. The first six months of road tests, 19,000 miles in direct competition with Y-6b's and A's, were encouraging, demonstrating 30% fuel savings and hauling 13% more tons.[114] In the longer term, maintenance costs were prohibitive. Named *Jawn Henry,* the locomotive was never duplicated and was scrapped in 1958, along with all other Norfolk & Western steam power.

The verdict on *Jawn Henry* was[115]:

Norfolk & Western Experimental Locomotive 2300 "Jawn Henry" was permanently retired December 31st (1957), its mission accomplished. Maintenance cost of the huge coal-fired, steam turbine electric drive engine had become prohibitive, even though it burned some 30 per cent less coal than conventional locomotives. "Jawn Henry" proved the principle of using coal as a fuel in such an engine regardless of deficiencies in various components.

N&W's experience indicates that a more economical and dependable coal-burning steam turbine locomotive could be designed and built. "Jawn Henry" was a prototype, expensive to build and, as time went on, increasingly difficult to maintain.

Various difficulties were encountered in the electrical, feed-water and turbine components. The complexity of the control system and of the locomotive generally combined to cause an excessive number of failures which often took it out of service.

The American steam-turbine locomotives were all of monstrous size and must have consumed enormous capital investments, driven by the pursuit of thermal efficiency, high power at high speed and a desperate desire to retain coal-burning locomotives. They were prototypes and their failings could probably have been rectified. The diesel-electric locomotive swept them away.

15.3.5 Duplex Drive

Duplex drive was an innovation of the 1930s; four single-expansion cylinders were mounted on the outside of a rigid frame, each pair of cylinders powering a separate drive unit. This arrangement aimed to divide the piston thrust, so reducing the reciprocating weights and making it possible to counterbalance the locomotive for very high speeds. The benefits of duplex drive were many and subtle.[116]

In spite of the successes achieved with counterbalancing during the 1930s, a two-cylinder 4-8-4 with 300 pounds per square inch boiler pressure still exerted a piston thrust of up to 185,000 pounds, necessitating massively strong, heavy reciprocating parts. By dividing the piston thrust between two pairs of cylinders, the duplex-drive locomotives that Baldwin built for the Pennsylvania produced higher total piston thrust and lower total reciprocating mass than an equivalent 4-8-4. Dividing four driving axles between two power units reduced the size and weight of the connecting rods. Duplex drive halved the load on driving axles and crank pins, so that they could be less strong and hence of smaller diameter than those on a conventional locomotive. Consequently, the crank pin could be placed closer to the axle, resulting in a shorter piston stroke and lower piston speed with less dissipation of energy each time the piston reversed its direction.

Even the 4-8-4s of the late 1930s were crippled at high speeds by the limited steam flow area available through 12-inch piston valves. A bigger piston valve offered a higher steam flow area but added to the reciprocating mass. The American locomotive industry settled on 12-inch diameter as the biggest practical piston valve for high speeds. When Baldwin started working on duplex drive in the early 1930s, before effective poppet valves were available, steam distribution through four 12-inch piston valves instead of two doubled the steam flow area while limiting the reciprocating mass of each piston valve. In a 4-8-4 with 27-inch cylinders and 12-inch piston valves the ratio of valve area to cylinder area was 20%; in a duplex-drive locomotive with 20-inch cylinders, 12-inch piston valves nearly doubled this ratio to 36%, offering freer steam flow. The poppet valve in a form suited to American locomotive practice was a fortunate development, well suited to the duplex-drive locomotive.

According to Ralph Johnson, Baldwin's Chief Engineer, Baldwin originated this idea with proposals to the Baltimore & Ohio in March 1932, to the Florida East Coast in December 1935, and to the New Haven in January 1936. These proposals were rejected because the second pair of cylinders resulted in an excessively long rigid wheelbase. Such was Baldwin's faith in the 4-4-4-4 as a fast, powerful passenger locomotive that in October 1939, they decided to build a 4-4-4-4 demonstrator; they were forestalled in doing so by an order from the Pennsylvania for two locomotives of this type.

George Emerson, Superintendent of Motive Power with the Baltimore & Ohio, tried to overcome the wheelbase problem by placing the cylinders for the rear drive unit behind the rear driving wheels. In June 1937, the company unveiled a new 4-4-4-4 locomotive, built at its Mount Clare shops and named *George H. Emerson*. The firebox, with an 81-square foot grate, was Emerson's water-tube design, firing a 350-pounds per square inch boiler. The rigid frame carried four 18-inch × 26½-inch cylinders, each driving two axles and developing 65,000 pounds of tractive effort in total. Unfortunately, the rear cylin-

ders, guides and crossheads were in a cramped, inaccessible location, difficult for locating steam pipes, where they were showered with dirt and limited the space available for the grate and ash pan.[117] The Baltimore & Ohio never duplicated this engine.

In 1937, the Pennsylvania invited the chief engineers of Baldwin, Alco and Lima to form a committee to advise them on improved steam locomotive designs. The result was a 6-4-4-6 (class S-1), built at Altoona in 1939, designed to haul a 1,200-ton train at 100 miles per hour on straight, level track.[118] After exhibiting this locomotive at the World's Fair in New York, the Pennsylvania put it into service on its Fort Wayne, Indiana, division, where it was still in service in 1947. The engine was "generally satisfactory," enough for the company to build a 4-6-4-4 for fast freight service in 1942.

The S-1's size restricted the routes over which it could travel but operating results were generally favorable, nonetheless. At the same time, the Pennsylvania's passenger traffic was so heavy that the company had to resort to double heading. The company was therefore responsive to Baldwin's proposal to build a 4-4-4-4 duplex, smaller than the S-1 but more powerful than any passenger locomotive yet built. In July 1940, the Pennsylvania ordered two of these with 300-pounds per square inch boilers and 80-inch driving wheels. The Pennsylvania's poppet valve tests on a K-4s were so successful that Baldwin recommended equipping the new engines with this type of valve, to which the Pennsylvania agreed. Designed to haul an 880-ton train at 100 miles per hour, these engines were delivered in 1942 and "exceeded expectations as to power and economy," with the result that Altoona and Baldwin built a further fifty between January 1945, and August 1946.

V. L. Smith, who was closely involved with the construction and testing of the 4-4-4-4s pointed out[119] that No. 6110, with a train of fourteen cars weighing 1,000 tons, bettered the schedule by 20 minutes over the 132 miles between Crestline and Fort Wayne. No. 6111 with sixteen cars averaged 102 mph over 69 miles on the Fort Wayne Division.

He commented:

> In my opinion, the T1s were the swiftest locomotives ever built. They could go like the wind when under way. What do you think of a locomotive against which a complaint was registered on an engineman's work report that "the spring rigging does not respond well at 125 mph"? Here is a single unit of over 6,550 indicated horsepower. It is irksome to me to read about the claims of LNER 4-6-2 locomotive *Mallard* setting a world's record for steam at 126 mph, and this for a distance of only 300 yards before complete failure occurred. I am certain that the T1s reached that speed on numerous occasions in the daily performance of their regular assignments and without fanfare.

With America involved in the biggest war in history, no time or effort was available to verify such speeds.

The Pennsylvania modified the Altoona test plant for the T-1 and tested No. 6110 in 1944.[120] The maximum recorded indicated horsepower was 6,552 at 85 miles per hour, 295 pounds per square inch boiler pressure, steam at 757°F and 25% cutoff. The boiler produced steam at 101,220 pounds per hour; the cylinders consumed it at 15.4 pounds per indicated horsepower-hour. The maximum firing rate was 250 pounds per square foot of grate per hour; the maximum steaming rate was 105,000 pounds per hour, all of which occurred in the 75- to 100-mile per hour speed range. Design engineers had finally triumphed in producing high efficiency and high power at very high speed—all the things of which the reciprocating steam locomotive was supposed to be incapable.

Meanwhile, the Pennsylvania designed a bigger version of the Q-1 4-6-4-4 freight engine (class Q-2), reversing the wheel arrangement to 4-4-6-4, with a 300-pounds per square inch boiler and 69-inch driving wheels, and built twenty-six of them between August 1944 and June 1945. The designers had placed the Q-1's cylinders ahead of the front driving wheels and behind the rear set; they placed the Q-2's rear cylinders ahead of the rear driving wheels. A Q-2 developed 8,000 indicated horsepower on the Altoona test plant at 57 miles per hour, probably the highest power output ever developed by a reciprocating steam locomotive, generating 137,500 pounds of steam per hour—17.2 pounds per indicated horsepower-hour.

The Pennsylvania was the only significant user of duplex drive, procuring eighty such engines. Some of the T-1's and Q-2's survived until 1956. Although the Pennsylvania experienced problems with its duplex-drive locomotives, these were not insoluble and duplex drive remains one of the unpursued avenues of steam locomotive development. All development of this concept was swept away by the diesel-electric locomotive.

V. L. Smith comments[121]:

> I was with these engines from their inception on the drawing board, and witnessed their operation on the railroad when it was at the very best and the very worst. There are a few writers who have stated that it was a disaster that the PRR built the T1 and Q2 series of duplex locomotives. I think not.

15.3.6 High-Pressure Reciprocating Engines

Reciprocating steam engines, designed from the outset to work at very high pressures, are a little-known facet of 1930s steam power development.

The Buchli engine, originating in Switzerland in the late 1920s, was among the first of these.[122] The Swiss Locomotive Works, Winterthur, built the first Buchli locomotive. A water-tube boiler with feed water heater, superheater and air preheater supplied steam at 800 pounds per square inch to a three-cylinder, uniflow engine with poppet valves, driving the wheels through gearing. The engine could be removed from the locomotive as a unit.

In 1927, the Berlin Machine Builders of Berlin, Germany, were building two 2,500-horsepower locomotives based on the Loeffler system.[123] A water-tube boiler generated steam at 1,420 pounds per square inch. Saturated steam was generated by injecting superheated steam into the boiler water. A pump forced the saturated steam through the superheater; 25% of the superheated steam went to the cylinders, exhausting into a condenser; the balance was injected into the boiler water to make steam. The hot combustion gases came into contact only with the superheater elements.

In 1936, the New Haven put a two-car unit passenger train into service, powered by a Besler high-pressure, compound steam engine, developed by George D. and William J. Besler.[124] The company refurbished two old passenger cars, building a cab on the front of one. The Besler engine used superheated steam, produced at 1,500 pounds per square inch in an oil-fired, vertical, flash boiler with cold water entering at the top and emerging as steam at the bottom. The steam powered a pair of two-cylinder compound condensing engines with 6½-inch and 9-inch × 11-inch cylinders, driving a four-wheel truck directly. The valve gear was compressed-air-controlled Stephenson link motion with two fixed cut-off positions in the forward and reverse directions. The flash boiler allowed working pressure to be attained in four minutes, with a further twelve minutes to pressurize the other train systems. The engine was mounted inside the front of the front car with the condenser in the roof. In service, this train reached 80 miles per hour. At the time, the Besler engine was lighter and cheaper than a diesel-electric engine of similar power.

In 1937, the Baltimore & Ohio completed the design for a 400,000-pound, streamlined locomotive powered by four four-cylinder Besler engines with 9½-inch × 7-inch cylinders, each engine geared directly to one of four driving axles at a 19:55 gear ratio.[125] Four-wheel leading and trailing trucks completed the wheel arrangement. An Emerson water-tube boiler generated steam at 350 pounds per square inch, fired by an 81-square foot grate. Of the 5,800 square feet of heating surface, the firebox water tubes contributed 775 square feet. Rated tractive effort was expected to be 72,500 pounds at a low adhesion ratio of 3.6, permitted by the torque characteristics of the Besler engines. The locomotive was expected to haul fourteen-car express passenger trains at 100 miles per hour on straight, level track, developing 5,000 horsepower. Apparently, the Baltimore & Ohio built one of these engines at its Mount Clare shops and tested it; this study has not revealed any results.

Developing diesel-electric technology made all these engines obsolete.

Section 15.4. Front Ends

The smokebox, with its innumerable possible combinations of dimensions and its complete absence of moving parts, remained one of the most tantalizing, frustrating and baffling components of the steam locomotive. Some of the last work on steam locomotive design—after commercial and operational interest in the steam locomotive had ceased—focused on this area with startling results. Nowhere else in the locomotive could so little cost yield such great dividends—if only inventive minds could hit upon the right shapes and dimensions. New devices came apace in the 1930s.

The Northern Pacific started burning lignite from eastern Montana in the 1920s and adapted—indeed designed—its locomotives to use this fuel. This light, friable material produced voluminous sparks with the consequent danger of lineside fires. In about 1929, M. F. Brown, the Northern Pacific's general fuel supervisor, invented a device that he called the Cyclone spark arrester.[126] A drum, formed of baffles, surrounded the space between the exhaust nozzle and the stack, producing a swirling motion in the gases and causing them to shed their load of cinders without the need for perforated plates or netting. The absence of netting reduced the interference with gas flow, which permitted a slightly larger nozzle to achieve the same furnace draft, reducing back pressure. One night in March 1930, Northern Pacific, U.S. Forest Service and University of Montana staff watched two locomotives working hard on the same train, one with the Cyclone spark arrester and one with the previously standard Master Mechanics' front end. The engine with the new device emitted almost no sparks, an observation confirmed by other tests. The Locomotive Firebox Co., Chicago, built the device and acquired the manufacturing rights in 1931, naming the original version the Type A.[127] They then introduced the Type B, removing the top of the drum and providing a greater intake area, following with the Type C. In the Type A, the intake was at the front of the smokebox, requiring the flue gases to reverse direction before entering the cyclone arrangement; the Type C placed the intake directly ahead of the front tube sheet. By early 1931, three hundred Northern Pacific locomotives had been retrofitted, with other railroads expressing interest.

In 1929, F. R. Mays, General Superintendent of Motive Power on the Illinois Central, developed an innovative front end arrangement, comprising an exhaust nozzle with both a Goodfellow nozzle and a splitter bridge consisting of two bars at right angles to each other, discharging into the bottom end of a petticoat pipe 10 inches above the nozzle, continuous with the stack.[128] The Illinois Central standard front end included a splitter bridge over the nozzle and a petticoat

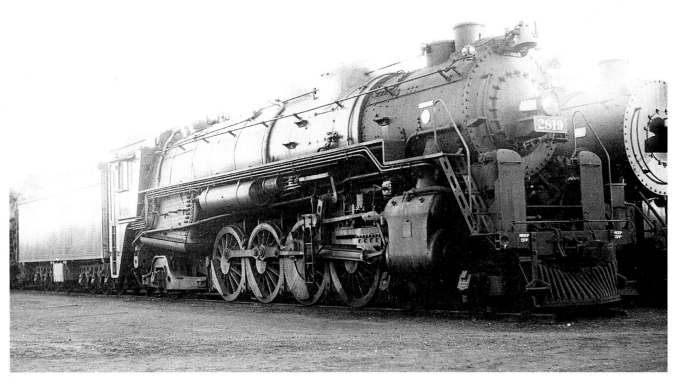

The Wabash increased the power output of these class M-1 4-8-2s by means of front-end modifications. No. 2819 came from Baldwin in 1930; Otto Perry photographed it at Decatur, Illinois, on September 19, 1930 (Denver Public Library, Otto C. Perry collection, OP-19751).

pipe separate from the stack, so that gases were entrained both above and below the petticoat pipe. This older arrangement required a 6⅜-inch diameter nozzle, developing up to 18 pounds per square inch back pressure to obtain the necessary draft. Tests and a series of adjustments to the dimensions showed that the new arrangement obtained the same steaming rate with a 7⅜-inch diameter nozzle, lowering the maximum back pressure to only 8 pounds per square inch. This apparently insignificant change saved 12% in fuel and 5% in water and enabled the company to use retrofitted 4-6-2s on schedules that had previously needed 4-8-2s. By late 1931, the company had made 937 retrofits and reckoned that, by installing this device on 1,761 locomotives at a cost of $25 each, it could save $1.5 million in fuel each year.

Trial and error, devoid of theoretical basis or results predicted by calculation, produced astonishing results, leaving locomotive mechanical engineers with a profound unease.

In 1930, the Wabash took delivery of twenty-five 4-8-2s and twenty-five 4-8-4s from Baldwin.[129] The 4-8-2s had some superpower design features: 85-square foot grates, 245 pounds per square inch boiler pressure, Type E superheaters, Worthington Type S feed water heaters and siphons. They weighed 406,000 pounds with a nominal tractive effort of 69,000 pounds. Some were used in Missouri, running 3,000-ton freight trains over the 125 miles between Kansas City and Moberly at average speeds of more than 30 miles per hour. Even though the terrain was flat, load and schedule demanded the full power of the locomotive, at times reaching 50 to 55 miles per hour at full throttle and 40% to 50% cut-off.

Design calculations predicted a power output of 3,215 indicated horsepower, yet tests on this route showed them developing as much as 3,650 indicated horsepower. Even so, the company felt that the front end design—the Master Mechanics' standard type—could be

improved upon. First, the company made slight changes to the diaphragm plate and spark arrester netting to reduce the resistance to gas flow in the smokebox. Based on research results from the University of Illinois, they increased the stack diameter from 19 inches to 23 inches, and later to 25½ inches. They then changed the round, 6½-inch diameter nozzle, first to a 7½-inch Goodfellow nozzle, then to a Kiesel star-shaped nozzle first used on the Timken demonstrator (see Chapter 15, Section 5.2).[130] At the same time, the company changed the grates from Hulson finger grates with 43% air opening to Hulson tuyere grates with 15% air opening.

The company modified two engines, so that three were available for comparison, all with Hulson tuyere grates. They were:

No. 2800: unmodified, 6½-inch plain nozzle, 19-inch stack
No. 2804: 7½-inch Goodfellow nozzle, 23-inch stack
No. 2818: 16-inch Kiesel nozzle, 25½-inch stack.

These modifications did not save fuel consumption per gross ton-mile but they did produce a startling improvement in smokebox vacuum, combustion rate and, hence, power output. The Master Mechanics' standard front end in No. 2800 developed a smokebox vacuum of 7.3 inches of water gauge, supporting a firing rate of 7,900 pounds per hour (93 pounds of coal per square foot of grate per hour), producing up to 3,650 indicated horsepower.

The Goodfellow nozzle increased smokebox vacuum by 54% to 11.3 inches of water gauge, supporting 23% higher firing rates of 9,750 pounds per hour (still an economical 116 pounds per square foot per hour), increasing power output to 4,235 indicated horsepower.

The Kiesel nozzle more than doubled the smokebox vacuum, compared to the plain nozzle, to 16.1 inches of water gauge, supporting a firing rate of 11,100 pounds of coal per hour (132 pounds per square foot of grate per hour), with power outputs up to 4,930 indicated

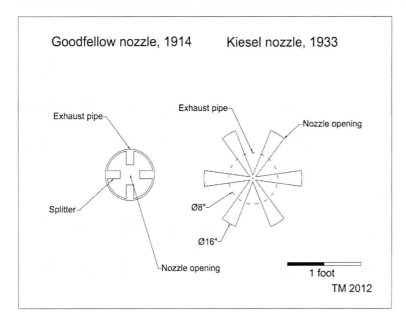

Goodfellow and Kiesel exhaust nozzles (redrawn from *RA*, July 8, 1933, 85).

horsepower—a full 35% higher than the unmodified engine and astonishing for a 4-8-2. Slightly higher superheat temperatures (up to 720°F with the Kiesel nozzle) contributed to this higher power output.

At high speeds, operation at full throttle and long cut-off exacted a penalty in high back pressures of 16 to 18 pounds per square inch, with power loss from this cause in excess of 700 horsepower. Even so, the Kiesel nozzle and 25½-inch stack averaged 16 pounds per square inch back pressure, compared to 18 pounds for the Goodfellow nozzle and 23-inch stack, wasting 10% less power (715 vs. 793 horsepower). The 7½-inch Goodfellow exhaust nozzle had an area of 28 square inches, whereas the 16-inch diameter Kiesel nozzle had an effective area of 53 square inches. The Kiesel nozzle therefore offered more efficient gas entrainment—hence, more efficient vacuum production—than the Goodfellow nozzle, while offering less resistance to steam leaving the cylinders.

Many hoped that the Master Mechanics' front end would be the final answer to the problem of designing an efficient smokebox. So many designs had superseded the Master Mechanics' design that, by the early 1930s, the industry had come to realize that the variables in front end performance were so numerous that no amount of testing with a full-sized locomotive would ever discover their effects. The Railway Engineering Department of the University of Illinois built a quarter-scale model of the smokebox of a USRA heavy Mikado.[131] The university power plant boilers supplied steam, either steady flow or pulsating, at controllable pressure, quality and superheat. Air was drawn into the smokebox through fire tubes and a firebox with a gas burner capable of simulating a controllable mixture of combustion products. The model was supplied with forty different nozzles and ten stacks of varying diameter and taper which could be modified with various flares and extensions. The university ran four thousand tests with 350 different combinations, publishing the results in 1934.

The university took care to check for scale effect and concluded that, while the model could not produce quantitatively accurate results, model testing would still demonstrate the laws applying to various arrangements, using appropriate scale factors. They found that there was no difference in the air flow produced by steady or pulsating steam flow, when the pulsations exceeded one hundred per

minute, corresponding to 25 driving wheel revolutions per minute in a two-cylinder engine. They also found that flue gas temperature had no effect; tests could therefore dispense with air heating.

The researchers reached several significant conclusions. Varying the shape of the nozzle from its plain, round form or varying its taper produced no significant improvement in its performance. An outward flare to the nozzle was detrimental. The tests confirmed that the Goodfellow nozzle performed better than plain, round nozzles but better still were nozzles that split the steam into separate jets, foreshadowing the Kylchap and Lempor nozzles still decades in the future. For a constant distance between the nozzle and the base of the stack, the larger stack diameters, flaring upward at 1 inch in 12, gave the best results. Long stacks performed better than short ones although, by the 1930s, clearance dimensions meant that a longer stack necessitated a nozzle set lower in the smokebox, which affected the way gases were drawn from the front tube sheet. The distance between the nozzle and the base of the stack apparently made little difference, provided the sum of the stack height and the distance between nozzle and base of stack remained constant. Experiments within this test series showed that the steam jet lost only 20% of its kinetic energy due to the desired interaction with the smokebox gases; only one-fifth of this 20% was used in ejecting gases from the stack; most of the steam went from nozzle to atmosphere with no loss of energy.

In late 1937, the Union Pacific took delivery of twenty 4-8-4s from Alco.[132] The engines came with 15% grate air opening, an annular ported exhaust nozzle, Master Mechanics' front end and a 24-inch minimum stack diameter. The following year, the Union Pacific road-tested twenty-seven different drafting arrangements on these engines. The best arrangement resulting from the tests increased the grate air opening to 20%, added secondary air admission, lengthened the brick arch, lowered the ash pan, changed the exhaust nozzle to four jets, replaced the Master Mechanics' front end with a baffle type of spark arrester from the Locomotive Economizer Corp., and increased the minimum stack diameter by one inch. The four-jet nozzle consisted of 3¾-inch and 3⅞-inch jets arranged on a 12-inch circle, similar to the Lempor nozzle of the 1950s. These changes increased the maximum evaporation rate by 24% from 66,000 to 78,000 pounds per hour, increased the maximum power output by 35% from 3,600 to 4,870 indicated horsepower, saving 22% on coal at 3,600 indicated horsepower, bringing steam consumption down to a minimum of 14 pounds per indicated horsepower-hour at 3,000 horsepower, compared to 15.5 for the factory engine.

The New York Central was able to improve the boiler capacity of a class J-1b 4-6-4 by 15% to 20%, merely by changing the dimensions of the front end, following standing tests at Selkirk, New York, in 1939–40.[133]

In spite of the formidable design capability and experience base of these companies, no one had optimized the design before the locomotives were built and, probably, few railroads had the Union Pacific's inclination and ability to carry out tests after manufacture. It is hard to escape the conclusion that most locomotives were built with sub-optimal performance and remained in that condition throughout their working lives.

In 1938, James Partington, engineering manager with Alco, put this subject into perspective.[134] He pointed out that the problem of front end design was supposed to have been solved forty years previously with the Master Mechanics' Front End, developed from tests at Purdue directed by the ARMMA. This arrangement "seemed to work about 30 per cent of the time, but almost every other man you met had different ideas on the subject and none agreed to any great extent."

Further research at the University of Illinois resulted in "much valuable information for the student but mighty little help to the road foreman who had to go out on the road and make the engines steam." Partington did not even mention the massive research program conducted by the Germans in 1892–94.

> The next episode was an epidemic of nozzles; square nozzles, oblong nozzles, stars, waffle irons, radial ported, annular ported and pepperboxes of every imaginable size and shape. Most of them did very well near their place of birth, but few survived transplanting. Then the netting displayed varying phases. Starting with a straight sheet across the front end, it became vertical cylinders, horizontal cylinders, cubical boxes, rhomboidal boxes, and baskets of various shapes. Most of these got by in some sort of fashion, but the most vigorous survivor seems to be the plain barrel type on account of the ease with which the front tube sheet can be inspected. But again we have examples of the extreme delicacy of these devices when removed from their native habitat; a front end that had become practically standard on a large trunk line was installed under expert supervision on another road in the same region, and failed to make a successful trip.

The Milwaukee developed their own Anderson spark eliminator; by the end of 1938, after several years of experiments, 150 of their locomotives were fitted with it.[135] Vertical vanes, mounted between horizontal plates, surrounded the nozzle and petticoat pipe. The vanes were angled to the gas flow so that cinders struck them and were broken up. One division with 535 miles of main line, using friable and spark-producing semi-lignite as fuel, was costing the company $22,000 a year in compensation claims for fires started by locomotives; the Anderson spark arrester reduced the cost of fire claims on this division to nothing in the four years following its introduction.

The Milwaukee found that, although netting had been eliminated, the tortuous gas path around the baffles and table plate added resistance and reduced draft.[136] In 1941, the Locomotive Fire Box Co., which had obtained the manufacturing rights, simplified the arrangement, lowering the exhaust nozzle, lengthening the petticoat pipe and reducing the number of baffle plates. These changes increased the draft, distributed it more evenly across the tube sheet and made it easier to access the superheater header for inspection and maintenance.

The Chicago & North Western's Class H 4-8-4s, built as state-of-the-art engines in 1930, proved disappointing in many ways. The company put up with their defects for fifteen years, but in 1946 began a program of rebuilding them. The whole drafting system came under scrutiny.[137] The company found that back pressures higher than 14 pounds per square inch produced diminishing returns in increasing the gas flow through the boiler, to the extent that pressures higher than 20 pounds per square inch actually diminished the steaming rate. At the higher back pressures, gas flow was concentrated in the upper part of the tube sheet, cinder-cutting the superheater elements, while so little gas went through the tubes and flues at the periphery and lower part of the tube sheet that they plugged with cinders. At the same time, air flow through the grate was concentrated at the back of the grate, where the fierce draft chilled the fire, producing clinker and smoke, and drew fine coal over the brick arch and through the tubes before it could be burned.

To solve these problems, the company replaced the 2-inch fire tubes with 2¼-inch and replaced the 3½-inch flues with 4-inch, thereby increasing the gas area and reducing the friction loss. They installed Hulson tuyere grates with 22% air opening under the brick arch and 18% air opening at the back of the grate. They raised the table plate in the smokebox by 11 inches, increased the stack diameter by 1 inch and installed an annular-ported exhaust nozzle. The result of these changes was that drafting in the rebuilt H-1's was stronger at all back pressures than the original engines, with a continual increase up to 34 pounds per square inch back pressure, resulting in more power and better fuel economy. The Class H was supposedly state-of-the-art in 1930, yet the Chicago & North Western was still making discoveries about their drafting and combustion fifteen years later.

In 1947, faced by rising fuel oil costs, the Southern Pacific built a standing test plant at its Sacramento shops, obtaining permission from Walter F. Collins, Engineer of Tests on the New York Central, to use his patented method of spraying measured amounts of water into the cylinders to cool the steam, thereby simulating the energy used in the cylinders, extracting the same mass of water as steam from the exhaust passage ways.[138] The water nozzles could reduce the steam temperature to any desired level, down to saturation. Gate valves controlled the steam pressure in the cylinders. By this means a complete range of firing and evaporation rates could be tested and boiler efficiencies evaluated and compared. At the same time, the Southern Pacific commissioned experiments on a quarter-scale model of a complete firebox, boiler and front end at the Battelle Memorial Institute and ran dynamometer tests with thirteen combinations of nozzle diameter, splitter type and dimensions, and distance from nozzle to base of stack.

As late as 1948[139]:

> In this country, as well as abroad, the amount of thought and experimental work which has been devoted to this subject (front ends) is almost alarming in view of the relatively meager and conflicting results obtained. The records of the U.S. Patent Office alone reveal close to a thousand inventions relating to locomotive exhaust and smokebox arrangements.

Supposedly, a front end could be designed by calculation from first principles but the calculations were complicated; they depended on information that was difficult to obtain and they did not necessarily produce better results than rule of thumb or trial and error.[140] The necessary theory of gas dynamics developed only gradually during the twentieth century, accelerating at mid-century with increasing experience from the aviation and automotive industries and with the coming of user-friendly electronic computers from the 1970s onward. By then the steam locomotive was as good as extinct.

The sophisticated exhaust systems developed by Giesl-Gieslingen, Chapelon, Lemaitre, Kylala and Porta were products of the 1950s and still more recent times, when American interest in the steam locomotive had ceased. As late as the mid–1980s[141]:

> Despite the comprehensiveness of the Lempor exhaust theory for calculating the optimum areas of the blast nozzle tip and chimney mixing chamber … there were still several parameters of importance to the exhaust system for which there was inadequate data on which to base the design. Given that the exhaust system was thermodynamically the very heart of the locomotive this state of affairs was unfortunate.

In 1987, Wardale built a test rig in China to develop a Lempor exhaust system for a modified class QJ 2-10-2 locomotive, reaching a set of conclusions in early 1988. The modified locomotive was never built and Chinese steam locomotive development ceased at that time.

It is difficult to escape the frightening conclusion that, for more than a century, the performance and efficiency of the steam locomotive depended most heavily on the one component of its functioning that was least well understood, indeed was never understood until after the locomotive itself had been discarded—if then.

Section 15.5 Frames and Running Gear

15.5.1 Engine Beds

Cast-steel engine beds continued to increase in size and complexity. In 1930, General Steel Castings produced engine beds nearly 37 feet long, weighing 52,550 pounds, for retrofitting to Union Pacific 2-10-2s during heavy overhaul.[142] Each casting incorporated not only the cylinders, valve chests, smokebox saddle and exhaust pipe but, for the first time, two compressed air reservoirs between the main frame members; the reservoirs acted as spacers and stiffeners, replacing the reservoirs usually placed under the running board. When Alco Schenectady built twenty-five 4-12-2s for the Union Pacific in 1930, the engine beds incorporated all three cylinders and valve chests. For each raw casting, General Steel Castings poured 100,000 pounds of steel and then machined off 18,000 pounds for a finished product weighing 82,000 pounds, just over 60 feet long.

Engine beds played an obscure but essential role in improving locomotive availability and ease of maintenance.[143] In 1930-1, the Norfolk & Western built twenty Y-5 2-8-8-2 Mallets with built-up frames and plain bearings. In 1936, they built ten Y-6's that closely resembled the Y-5's, but for roller bearings and engine beds. Because of their better maintainability, the Y-6's turned in 42% better utilization than the Y-5's. In December 1937, a Santa Fe 4-6-4 made a through run from Los Angeles to Chicago, which would have been inconceivable only a few years before; locomotives with built-up frames averaged 20,000 to 50,000 miles per year; by the end of the 1930s, locomotives with engine beds were making 100,000 to 150,000 miles per year.

The trend was toward ever-more complicated castings, incorporating more and more components in a single casting. The engine beds for a class of Union Pacific 4-8-4s, built in 1937, incorporated cylinders, valve chests, piston rod guide brackets, air-pump brackets, air reservoirs, supports for boiler expansion slide bearings, a high smokebox saddle with internal steam pipes, the pilot beam and a rear frame extension to support the firebox and trailing truck. This structure took 55% more machining time after casting than a Lackawanna engine bed, hailed as the latest of its type in 1930, but the long-term maintenance benefits far offset the extra manufacturing cost. By 1936 a Mallet could be built with two engine beds, eliminating 700 parts.[144]

At the end of the 1930s, engine beds were not merely a luxury; they were a necessity[145]:

> The use of the one-piece steam-locomotive bed, which now embodies integrally the component parts of the frame and cylinder structure, has since its introduction on the New York Central in 1924 been so extended that with very few exceptions it is now being applied on nearly all modern locomotives built not only in the United States and Canada but also in Australia. The almost impossible task of permanently holding together with bolts the parts of the built-up locomotive frame, especially in high-speed service, has been responsible for this transition.

15.5.2 Roller Bearings

Henry Timken's tapered roller bearing was a sufficient advance over previous anti-friction bearings to be awarded a U.S. patent in 1898. Sven Wingquist patented his self-aligning SKF roller bearing in Sweden in 1907. Tapered roller bearings were used in the center plates of car and locomotive tender trucks at least as early as 1908, when the Santa Fe had 9,000 freight cars, 100 passenger cars and fifty locomotives equipped with various forms of the Barber center plate.[146] Thirty years elapsed before roller bearings were first applied to locomotive axle journals in 1929.[147]

The Timken Roller Bearing Co. had done well enough in the interim to order a new 4-8-4 locomotive from Alco in July of that

Otto Perry photographed the Timken demonstrator 4-8-4, No. 1111, built by Alco in 1930, Seattle, Washington, on July 23, 1939, when it was owned by the Northern Pacific as Class A-1, No. 2626 (Denver Public Library, Otto C. Perry collection, OP-14010).

year, with roller bearings on all axles. After much difficulty obtaining a locomotive for retrofitting, Timken decided to build a completely new locomotive which could be tested on the widest possible range of railroads with no restrictions arising from prior ownership, and compared with the newest power. Timken was also experimenting with roller bearing applications to passenger and freight cars, but the American fleet of those vehicles was so vast that market penetration was necessarily slow, especially in post–1929 economic conditions.

Besides roller bearings, this locomotive had other interesting features. It was designed to be tested on many different railroads; accordingly, the suspension equalizing system was capable of adjusting the weight distribution between the driving wheels and the trucks. Total engine weight was 417,500 pounds. For railroads with track permitting an axle loading in excess of 62,000 pounds, the engine weight was distributed as 264,000 pounds on the driving wheels (axle loading 66,000 pounds), the balance on the trucks. With a boiler pressure of 250 pounds per square inch, the 27-inch × 30-inch cylinders and 73-inch driving wheels provided 63,700 pounds of tractive effort. For railroads with permitted axle loadings less than 62,000 pounds, the adhesion weight could be reduced to 246,000 pounds (axle loading 61,500 pounds), the balance on the trucks; a lower boiler pressure of 235 pounds per square inch was used, resulting in a tractive effort of 59,900 pounds; the adhesion factor would be 4.1 in both cases. The booster contributed an additional 12,000 pounds of tractive effort. Other features and dimensions were normal for a locomotive of that type, including a power stoker, thermic siphons, Type E superheater and Worthington feed water heater. Fifty-three specialty manufacturers supplied components. Heat-treated nickel and vanadium steels allowed the reciprocating parts to be 920 pounds lighter than would otherwise be the case, while carefully designed counterbalancing allowed the engine to reach 85 miles per hour with no more than 10,000 pounds of dynamic augment. The designers took every opportunity to use nickel-steel alloys; a quarter of the engine weight was manufactured from these alloys.

The starting resistance of roller bearings was only 5% of that of similar-sized plain bearings. In a well-known publicity stunt, four young women were able to move the locomotive by pulling on ropes. Timken theorized that the reduction in the starting resistance of the locomotive itself would enable it to start a train 450 tons heavier than a locomotive of similar tractive effort fitted with plain bearings—borne out when the Timken locomotive started a train of 134 loaded coal cars, weighing 9,865 tons. Timken also hoped for lower maintenance costs and reduced demand on shop time and labor.

The engine went into service in April 1930, numbered 1111—*Four Aces.* That year it was tested on the New York Central, the Pennsylvania, the Chesapeake & Ohio and the New Haven. The absence of the pounding associated with plain bearings was a major success. Timken asserted that a power saving of 10% to 20% resulted from reduced bearing friction. In spite of the 4.1 adhesion factor, the Timken locomotive proved to be slippery, both on starting and at speeds above 50 miles per hour; Timken attributed this to reduced bearing friction allowing more power to reach the rail. Peak recorded power output was 3,900 drawbar horsepower at 37 miles per hour. Coal and water consumption averaged 2.6 to 3.3 pounds and 18.8 to 22.1 pounds per drawbar horsepower hour respectively.

The Pennsylvania found that the engine consumed 50 pounds of coal per thousand gross ton-miles—less than half the national average at the time. This figure would vary locally with terrain, but the Pennsylvania had its fair share of gradients and curves; this figure is therefore highly significant. The New Haven was always associated with fast passenger service; on December 24, 1930, the engine hauled the first train fitted entirely with roller bearings—a fourteen-car passenger train between New Haven and Boston.

Roller bearings were not used in the crank pins or side rod bearings, although this was being investigated in 1932. Observers noted that these plain bearings ran at 200°F to 400°F above ambient temperatures, while the roller bearings ran only 15°F to 30°F above ambient. This temperature cycling, present in all plain axle bearings, was bad for the axle metal, a problem that the railroads accepted as unavoidable. Roller bearings now solved this problem, offering the possibility of significant advances in axle design.

In two years, besides the four railroads mentioned above, it was tried on the Erie, the Lackawanna, the Lehigh Valley, the Missouri Pacific, the Burlington, the Boston & Maine, the Nickel Plate, the Chicago & Alton and the Northern Pacific, where it went into service in October 1931. Timken planned to use the engine for only two years; this period expired while it was with the Northern Pacific, during which time it suffered crown sheet damage. Although the Northern Pacific considered it ill-suited to burn low-grade western coal, they bought it in 1933. Its last run was at the head of a railfan special on August 4, 1957. It was scrapped in 1958, after running more than 2.2 million miles.[148]

The railroads had been experimenting with roller bearings for several years. The Michigan Central used them in at least one engine truck and found no signs of wear after 304,000 miles. The Milwaukee had installed roller bearings in 127 passenger cars in 1927. By 1932, these cars averaged more than a million miles in service. The same year, the Pennsylvania installed roller bearings in 304 passenger cars, including electric and gasoline-powered self-propelled multiple units, with no bearing failures in five years. Users found that, if a train had roller bearings throughout, the surging of slack was eliminated, with great benefits to maintenance and safety.

The Delaware & Hudson rebuilt a 2-8-0 with roller bearings on its driving axles at its Colonie, New York, shops in 1930 with satisfactory results.[149]

SKF entered the locomotive game in October 1931, when the New York Central put an Alco 4-6-4 into service with SKF bearings on all engine and tender axles.[150] SKF bearings had been in use in passenger cars since the early 1920s; the first application to a locomotive was to the truck of a New York Central 4-6-2 in about 1927.

Roller bearings were heavier and more costly than plain bearings; SKF bearings added 2,000 pounds to the weight of each driving axle. The railroads were cautious about using roller bearings in locomotives, where the conditions were more demanding than in passenger cars and where the consequences of failure could be more severe. These issues explain the slow penetration of these bearings into the railroad market.

Timken went on to design connecting and side rods with roller bearings; the necessary redesign was extensive, including rods, crank pins, cross heads, piston rods and piston heads.[151] Timken's redesigned rods were made of chrome-nickel-molybdenum high-tensile steel. The first installation was on a Pennsylvania K-4s 4-6-2, already fully equipped with roller-bearing axles, in July 1934. The Timken-designed reciprocating parts were 35% lighter than the assembly they replaced; the new rods gave no trouble in more than a year and nearly 100,000 miles in service.

SKF was neck-and-neck with Timken. In February 1934, the Delaware & Hudson installed SKF bearings on the rods and main driving axle of a 1914-built 4-6-2 in for overhaul, applying a tandem main rod at the same time.[152] This application carried a weight penalty of 2,300 pounds.

Roller bearings were not always the miracle that their promoters would have their customers believe[153]:

While it appears probable that roller bearings will be the answer to the problem of satisfactorily lubricating driving- and truck-axle bearings on long-distance high-speed runs without intermediate attention, we must not overlook the fact that roller bearings are very expensive and, in comparison with plain bearings, add a great deal of weight to the locomotive or tender. Moreover, roller-bearing trouble, when it occurs, practically always results in a complete engine failure and an excessive repair bill, whereas plain bearings can generally be cooled down, repacked, and made safe to proceed with only loss of time and a relatively moderate expense for repairs at the end of the run.

Further, from the New York Central[154]:

> The most serious problem with which our railroad has had to contend in connection with roller-bearing applications is that of axle life. Few axles have failed on the road but an exceptional degree of vigilance has been required to avoid such failures and the number of cracked axles found upon inspection and removal has been too large to be viewed with satisfaction.

Innovations had a way of producing unforeseeable side effects; the solution of one problem could produce others, possibly more costly than the problem solved.

By the end of 1936, penetration of roller bearings into the heavy service of locomotive driving axles amounted to 234 locomotives.[155] Leading and tender trucks equipped with roller bearings were more common, with 626 and 577 locomotives so equipped, respectively. Although these numbers were minute, compared to the total U.S. locomotive fleet, the railroad industry was voting with its pocket book; by early 1937, three quarters of all new locomotive orders specified roller bearings on some or all axles. Even so, only 280 locomotives of the whole vast fleet had driving axles fitted with roller bearings by the end of the year.[156]

Like the state-of-the-art locomotives to which they were increasingly applied, the effect of roller bearings was out of proportion to their numbers. In 1943[157]:

> The chief executive officer of a railroad recently stated that the handling of an increase in traffic would not have been possible if the road had not converted a considerable number of its locomotives and applied roller bearings in the years immediately preceding the present war.

Users reported that roller-bearing equipped freight cars needed 88% less starting effort than cars with plain bearings while locomotives fully equipped with roller bearings exerted 13% more starting tractive effort. A roller-bearing equipped locomotive could move on only 10 to 12 pounds per square inch steam pressure, compared to 40 to 50 pounds in an engine with conventional bearings. The 7% of the Burlington's locomotives that had roller bearings made 23% of the company's 3 million monthly locomotive miles. The reliability of roller bearings had improved since their first introduction into railroad service, to the point that the New York Central reported vanishingly small numbers of delays caused by roller bearing failure while overheated plain bearings continued.

The Mechanical Engineer of the New Haven made the sweeping, but nonetheless revealing, statement that:

> The development and application of roller bearings has undoubtedly had more effect in increasing the availability of the locomotive than anything else that has occurred in the last decade.

15.5.3 Disc Driving Wheels

New in 1932 was the Scullin double-disc driving wheel, developed by the Scullin Steel Co. and tested on the St. Louis & San Francisco, the Missouri Pacific, the Denver & Salt Lake and the New York Central.[158] The new wheel consisted of two cast steel discs, offering a wheel that was stronger, lighter and more easily counterbalanced than the conventional spoked wheel.

In 1934, General Steel Castings brought out a cast-steel wheel center, complete with counterweight, that they called the Boxpok—short for "box spoke."[159] The rim and spokes were not, in fact, solid, as they appear from the outside, but of hollow box section, fabricated from two matching cast-steel plates. This design was stiffer, stronger and lighter than conventional wheel centers; the crank pin was not a part of this casting. In developing this design, General Steel Castings had the cooperation of Alco and American Steel Foundries. Current research has not revealed what, if any, technical or commercial connection there was with the earlier Scullin wheel. The result was stronger, lighter and less likely to deform in service than the conventional spoked design and also—an entirely new consideration in locomotive design—"presents a pleasing appearance."

In 1937, Baldwin brought out a new one-piece, cast steel, disc driving wheel center.[160] The rim was a hollow triangular section, while another hollow triangular section surrounded the hub. The plate was dished and ribbed for added strength. The first user was the Central of Georgia with a retrofit to a 1918-built 2-10-2, followed by five engines on the Union Pacific and ten on the Bessemer & Lake Erie. (It is not clear from the referenced source whether these were new-builds or retrofits.) A Seaboard Airline 2-10-2 was another retrofit, while a single engine for the Alton & Southern and five 4-8-4s for the Richmond, Fredericksburg & Potomac were the first engines known to have been built new with the Baldwin wheel centers.

By March 1937, Boxpok was the leader, with 519 locomotives equipped, followed by Scullin with 207 and the still new Baldwin wheel center with seventy-eight installations.[161] There were other, less well-known new-design driving wheel centers: Birdsboro (11 locomotives), Univan (1), Duquesne (6) and L. F. M. (12). Current

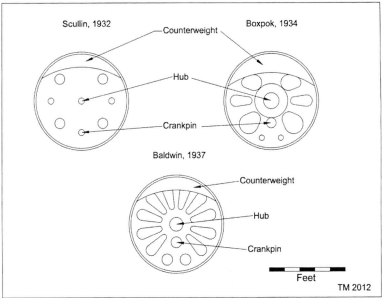

Disc driving wheels (redrawn from *RA*, December 17, 1932, 902; June 30, 1934, 983; June 16, 1937, 1004D39).

research has not uncovered details. All disc- and box-type wheel centers offered lighter weight and greater strength, better counterbalance and better support for tires than conventional spoked wheel centers.

15.5.4 Tenders

Over the years, locomotive tenders developed from the simple vehicles of the 1890s, carrying 4,000 to 5,000 gallons of water and 6 tons of coal, to the massive structures of the 1930s, carrying up to 25,000 gallons of water and 36 tons of coal.[162]

The early tenders were built on timber frames and ran on two four-wheel trucks. Built-up steel frames replaced the timber frames, but corroded quickly due to coal spillage and water leakage. The early years of the twentieth century were plagued by tender derailments which were traced to an absence of any lateral motion in the tender trucks. A self-centering truck allowing lateral motion, with equalized suspension, solved this problem.

The year 1907 saw the first one-piece, cast steel tender frames; their use spread rapidly and was made standard in the USRA engines, by which time capacities had increased to 12,000 gallons of water and 16 tons of coal. The trend toward longer locomotive runs between servicing that followed World War I demanded higher tender capacities, resulting in six-, and even eight-wheel, trucks. Unfortunately, the bigger tank would break loose from the frame in a collision, crushing the cab. The solution to this hazard was the water-bottom tender, in which a single steel casting formed both the frame and the floor of the water tank. This innovation permitted a large increase in capacity, eliminated the telescoping hazard and lowered the center of gravity.

As tenders were built to their clearance limits of height and width, increased capacity could only come from greater length. By the 1920s, a loaded tender could weigh as much as the locomotive itself. At the high speeds demanded by railroad operations, any tendency to pitching, rolling or yawing was dangerous, especially if some resonant frequency was reached, as well as damaging the track and giving a rough ride to the front cars of passenger trains. The tender, with particular regard to its support, braking, suspension and maintenance, therefore demanded careful attention from the manufacturer's design engineers.

The Union Pacific departed from conventional tender designs with a new 14-wheel tender behind fifteen 4-8-4s built by Alco and delivered in 1939.[163] The Union Pacific's Research and Mechanical Standards department designed this tender in cooperation with General Steel Castings which provided the cast-steel bed. Supporting the front of the tender was a four-wheel truck, followed by five axles with axle boxes running in pedestals in the bed. The suspension of the five axles was equalized so that they and the leading truck provided three-point suspension. The design of the axle boxes and pedestals allowed a lateral movement of 1¼ inches on the front four of the five independent axles and ¾ inch on the trailing axle, to accommodate curvature. These enormous tenders weighed 160,000 pounds empty, 445,000 pounds full, carrying 23,500 gallons of water and 25 tons of coal. In their first year of service, the new tenders showed better riding qualities and lower maintenance than the Union Pacific's existing tenders with two six-wheel trucks.

Some railroads, such as the Missouri Pacific, began adding a water car behind the tender to extend the range of the locomotive before taking on water.[164]

Track pans enabled a railroad to sacrifice water capacity for coal capacity in a tender because of the ability to take water without stopping. Tender scoops, however, would function only within a certain speed range. At too low a speed, the scoop would not pick up water; too high a speed risked damage to the scoop and introduced venting problems. The New York Central took this upper limit to extremes with a five-year development program, begun in 1939, aimed at taking water at speeds up to 80 miles per hour.[165] The existing scoop was at its most efficient at 45 miles per hour; the new scoop, derived from studies of the interaction between the scoop and the water in the pan, functioned best at 75 miles per hour, taking up 7,100 gallons during a scoop extension over 1,700 feet. Scoops were extended and retracted by compressed-air power. The company tested the new scoop at speeds up to 80 miles per hour; at such speeds, however, damage to passing trains caused the company to review the whole design of the tank and its venting in a degree of detail that cannot be discussed here. The company applied the results to the tenders of the L-4b 4-8-2s, built by Lima in late 1943, holding 15,200 gallons of water and 42 tons of coal and to sixty new high-capacity tenders.

15.5.5 Counterbalancing and Effects on Track

The obsessive demand for speed in both passenger and freight service of the 1930s gave new emphasis to one of the abiding problems of the steam locomotive—counterbalance. Bigger and more powerful locomotives necessarily had heavier rotating and reciprocating parts; the problem of counterbalance was compounded when these parts were required to move faster than before. Designers, however, solved the counterbalancing problem so effectively that engines of unprecedented size and power were able to move at speeds only attained previously by the nimble 4-4-0s of the 1890s, with acceptable wear and tear on both track and locomotives. Solution of the counterbalancing problem was one of the obscure but essential triumphs of locomotive engineering in the 1930s and 1940s.

Higher speeds demanded heavier counterweights in driving wheels. Counterweights were limited in their radial and circumferential extent; by the early 1930s, their thickness was reaching the clearance limits between the driving boxes and the rods. Lima developed an improved design of driving box, moving the spring rigging to the inside of the box, making possible thicker counterweights and better counterbalancing of the locomotives to which they were applied. At the same time, new, high-tensile steels promised reductions of 40% to 60% in reciprocating weights. Many such obscure developments lay behind the increasing high-speed performance of the American steam locomotive.[166]

Freight locomotives of the early 1900s were designed to exert high tractive effort at low speeds.[167] This emphasized adhesion weight, with the highest possible proportion of engine weight loaded onto the driving wheels which were of small diameter. The heavily loaded driving wheels depressed and released the rails abruptly with a sharp curve of depression ahead of the front driving wheels and behind the rear driving wheels. Customary practice was to add one-half the weight of the reciprocating parts to the counterweights in the driving wheels to combat yawing of the locomotive, but this added to dynamic augment. The greatest demand for counterbalance was on the main driving wheel, where the rotating masses of main rods, side rods, eccentric cranks and crank pins had to be counterbalanced; with a small driving wheel, there was insufficient space to install all the necessary counterweight. Some of the counterweight for the reciprocating parts had, therefore, to be distributed to the front and rear driving wheels, adding to the static weight of these wheels and sharpening the curve of depression in the rail. Driving these older engines faster to meet 1930s demand for higher freight train speeds produced disproportionately greater wear and tear on track, as well as on the engines themselves.

By the 1930s, the locomotive industry had found out how to provide high power at high speed with big boilers and big fireboxes, which had to be supported on leading and trailing trucks. Compared to the 2-8-0s of earlier years, the 2-8-2s and, later, the 4-8-4s loaded decreasing proportions of engine weight onto the driving wheels. This meant that the curve of depression in front of and behind the locomotive was less abrupt than with older power. Bigger driving wheels caused less dynamic augment and provided more space for counterweights, allowing the counterweight for reciprocating parts to be concentrated on the main driving wheel, while the reciprocating parts, themselves, were lighter than in older engines due to design refinements and better metallurgy. Bigger driving wheels meant more space between axles, resulting in the static load on the driving wheels being distributed over a greater length of track. As a result the new engines were easier on the track than the older ones, even though their static weight was vastly greater.

Cross-counterbalancing was an innovation of the late 1930s.[168] The counterweights in the driving wheels did not act in the same plane as the weights they were supposed to balance. At high speeds, this set up a significant rolling couple counteracting the effect of the weights. Cross-counterbalancing took this into account by placing calculated balance weights in each main driving wheel at 180° and 90° to the crankpin. Typically, the main driving wheels were cross-counterbalanced; the other driving wheels were statically balanced as before. Tests showed that a cross-counterbalanced 4-8-4 with an axle loading of 74,000 pounds produced less track stress at 60 miles per hour than a conventionally balanced 2-8-2 with a 60,000-pound axle loading at 40 miles per hour. The benefits of the newer engines in terms of track damage were enormous.

With this in mind, the Kansas City Southern cross-counterbalanced some of its 2-8-0s and substituted 63-inch Boxpok driving wheels for conventional, spoked 57-inch wheels; the original axle spacing sufficed to permit this change. The modified engines produced no more rail stress at 60 miles per hour than the originals did at 40 miles per hour and rode more smoothly.

The higher speeds of the late 1930s, sometimes with equipment not designed for such speeds, brought increased wear and tear on the track and also outright damage.[169] This took the form of kinks punched into the rail both downward and—curiously—inward toward the center of the track. Regularly spaced kinks could be traced to locomotives of particular driving wheel diameters and were an old and well-known problem.

Driving wheels worn out of round became a problem at high speeds; the dimensions of this problem were remarkable:

A locomotive driver tire that is worn $\frac{1}{16}$-in. out-of-round in a length of 24-in. to 40-in. will cause damage and where these tires are continued in service until they are worn to a depth of $\frac{3}{16}$-in. or less they will cause very serious kinks, both inward and downward.

Out-of-round drivers cause us a lot of trouble during winter months when temperatures fall to zero or below. They cause excessive breakage in rails; the breaks start in the base…. We have from 5,000 to 7,000 failures annually in our main line tracks. We removed 8,928 surface bends in 6,898 rails in a distance of about 200 miles in 1936. Some of the rails were on eastbound and others on westbound tracks. Some were north rails and others south rails.

And:

last year we had to straighten about 22,000 rails, practically all of which were engine bent, and to climax the year, one engine on one trip, in a distance of 55 miles damaged 3 miles of 90-lb. rail, a little over 3 track miles of 110-lb. rail, and nearly 4 track miles of 112-lb. rail.

That problem was at least identifiable. More perplexing:

For the past three or four years … we have been experiencing trouble with surface-bent rails. We have not been able to connect these bends with any defect in counterbalance or driver tires. Neither have we been able to attribute it definitely to track conditions, soft ties, etc. There was no uniformity in the location of these bends or in the distance they were apart. They were permanent sets in the rail and produced very bad riding conditions until removed.

The Association of American Railroads issued recommendations for counterbalancing in 1931, amended in 1934.[170] When the new 4-6-4s and 4-8-4s started kinking rails, it became clear that these recommendations were inadequate. A landmark in this situation was the introduction into service of ten new roller-bearing 4-6-4s on the New Haven in 1937.[171] The new engines caused rail damage; the New Haven blamed the roller bearings. In response, Timken challenged the New Haven to carry out slipping tests to high driving wheel speeds on greased track, comparing a new I-5 with roller bearings and a 1916-built I-4 4-6-2 with plain bearings. As a result, the I-5 was cross-counterbalanced, 100 pounds of balance weights were removed, riding qualities improved and track damage disappeared.

In April 1938, the New York Central ran slipping tests with a J-3a 4-6-4.[172] To resolve a slight ambiguity in the referenced sources, the following is quoted in full:

As an illustration of the fact that with good designing the effects of reciprocating overbalance can be well controlled, it may be said that in 1938 a series of slipping tests were conducted on the New York Central over a short stretch of main-line track with 127-lb. rail section on rock ballast. Test runs were made at train speeds varying from 61 to 82 m.p.h. and with maximum slipping speeds of 123 to 164 m.p.h. while working steam. In the tests at the lower speeds no wheel lifting occurred, but in the final run at a revolving speed of 164 m.p.h. the main drivers only lifted slightly, and later examination disclosed a number of very slight markings on the rails which, however, were without significance and had no effect on the rails or track structure requiring attention by maintenance forces. No damage to the locomotive occurred in any of these tests.

It is a tribute to the courage and dedication of the enginemen that they were willing deliberately to slip a large locomotive to wheel speeds at which the rods and motion could disintegrate, potentially derailing the engine. As these enormous wheel speeds caused damage neither to the rail nor to the rods and motion of the engines; the New York Central left the counterbalancing unchanged. It is also interesting that the steam passages and valve events allowed the engine to reach those wheel speeds, although no determination of power output at those speeds was made at the time.

The Santa Fe made a similar test with a 4-8-4, resulting in track damage at a wheel speed of 97 miles per hour.

The Burlington made a much more thorough-going set of tests, using three 4-6-4s, two 4-8-4s and a 2-10-4, a dynamometer car and high-speed cameras capable of up to 400 frames per second. The highest slipping wheel speed was 128 miles per hour by one of the 4-6-4s at a train speed of 80 miles per hour; the 4-8-4s reached wheel speeds of 90 to 115 miles per hour and the 2-10-4 wheels reached 80 miles per hour, hauling a train at just over 50 miles per hour. The 4-8-4 tests showed the main driving wheel lifting off the rail slightly as the counterweight passed through its top quadrant at slipping wheel speeds above 100 miles per hour, but no track damage. The 2-10-4 tests showed slight lifting at 80 miles per hour slipping speed, and also no track damage. Of the 4-6-4s, two had 4,220 pounds of reciprocating parts; the highest slipping wheel speed reached by either of these was 108 miles per hour, at which speed the main driving wheel lifted off the rail by $\frac{7}{8}$ inch and the resulting hammer blow damaged the track. The third had light-weight reciprocating parts, weighing only 2,050 pounds; the main driving wheel lifted only slightly at a slipping speed of 128 miles per hour and caused no track

A Chicago Great Western class T-2 2-10-4, No. 871, built by Baldwin in 1930 and photographed at Des Moines, Iowa, on September 15, 1931 (Denver Public Library, Otto C. Perry collection, OP-4902).

damage. No differences appeared between engines fitted with roller or plain bearings. Careful structural and metallurgical design could halve the reciprocating weights, reducing dynamic augment by two-thirds at 80 miles per hour. The test engineers suspected that elasticity in the track and resonance in the track and locomotive springing could influence the speed at which the driving wheels lifted off the rail but could not pursue this matter for lack of information.

As a result of these tests the Burlington was able to establish maximum line speeds to avoid track damage at 60 miles per hour for the 2-10-4s, 75 miles per hour for the 4-6-4s and 4-8-4s with conventional reciprocating parts and no speed limit for the 4-6-4s and 4-8-4s with light-weight reciprocating parts.

Railroads continued to rebuild their locomotives as innovations and refinements capable of retrofitting became available. The Chicago Great Western bought thirty-six 2-10-4s in 1930, twenty-nine built by Lima, fifteen by Baldwin.[173] In accordance with current practice at the time of manufacture, the wheels were statically balanced and 50% of the reciprocating mass was added to the counterweights. The reciprocating counterbalance was distributed among the first, second, fourth and fifth driving wheels, with none in the main driving wheel. The relatively small driving wheels balanced in this way became a problem at higher speeds, causing rough riding and track damage. At 60 miles per hour, dynamic augment equaled the static load and threatened to lift the wheel from the rail. In 1937, the company replaced the main driving wheels with cross-balanced Baldwin disc wheels. In 1939, they replaced the rods with light-weight, tandem rods, reducing the total revolving weight of the rods by 22% from 1,385 pounds to 1,075. These modifications reduced dynamic augment at 60 miles per hour from 34,200 pounds per main wheel to 2,700. Track damage ceased and wear and tear on the locomotives was much reduced.

When the U.S. entered World War II, counterbalancing became

so important to the rapid movement of traffic without damaging track and locomotives and, hence, to the war effort itself, that the American Association of Railroads was able to organize a test program culminating in a 300-page report issued in March 1944.[174]

After a comprehensive analysis of the theory of locomotive counterbalancing, the Committee on Locomotive Counterbalance Standards organized comprehensive field tests to address six issues: the permissible relationship between reciprocating weight and locomotive weight; the amount of reciprocating weight that could be left unbalanced; the method of balancing the main rod, which was both a reciprocating and a rotating mass; the degree to which cross-balancing was necessary or desirable; the necessity of counterbalancing the valve gear eccentrics and; the maximum permissible dynamic augment.

The Illinois Central provided a 4-8-2; the Soo Line provided a 4-6-2; the Santa Fe provided a 4-6-4; the 4-8-4s were so valuable that none could be released from traffic.

The Chicago & North Western provided a stretch of track between Harvard, Illinois, and Janesville, Wisconsin, as a test site and ran tests in 1940–1, comparing as-built and rebalanced 2-8-2s and a rebalanced 4-6-2.[175] The locomotives were instrumented with accelerometers to record vertical, lateral and longitudinal disturbances; the track was fitted with strain gauges. Each locomotive was tested at several different speeds. Between 1913 and 1923 the CNW bought 310 2-8-2s from Alco, class J-S. Between 1936 and 1941 the company rebuilt thirty-eight of these with higher steam pressure, Boxpok driving wheels of 3 inches larger diameter than the original wheels and cross-counterbalanced main driving wheels, renaming them class J-A. In 1940, the company rebalanced at least one J-S according to up-to-date calculations and found that they could still improve on the counterbalancing of the J-A's. The original class J-S was limited to speeds below 50 miles per hour; the modifications allowed the

The Chicago & North Western obtained more speed from their Class J-S 2-8-2s by means of counterbalancing. Alco built this class over a period of ten years, 1913–23. Otto Perry photographed No. 2530 at Carroll, Iowa, on July 18, 1953 (Denver Public Library, Otto C. Perry collection, OP-3252).

2-8-2s to run at the highest speeds of which they were capable without damaging track or locomotives. The rebalanced 4-6-2 was tested at speeds up to 90 miles per hour with acceptable track stress.

The AAR committee ran 495 tests on these four railroads, totaling 6,300 train miles.

As with so many features of the steam locomotive, the more the matter was studied, the more it retreated into ever more baffling complexity. The intensive instrumentation of the tests revealed previously unsuspected effects, only a few of which can be sketched in here. The elasticity of draw gear between engine and tender and between tender and train, and the lateral resistance of trucks, could affect locomotive stability as much as counterbalancing. In addition to the vertical motion of the frame caused by dynamic augment, at least one of the locomotives set up a rolling motion on its springs every four or five driving wheel revolutions for reasons unknown. Drawbar pull varied markedly during each driving wheel revolution, but not as expected from theory. In addition to the dynamic augment caused by the counterweight once per driving wheel revolution, the main driving wheel was also subject to the out-of-plane vertical component of the main rod thrust twice per revolution; there was no means of counterbalancing this effect. "Quarter slip" was another obscure issue; it is not clear when it was first recognized, but engineers were aware of it by 1946.[176] Due to the cyclic application of piston thrust during each wheel revolution, a driving wheel could slip during part of its revolution while maintaining its overall grip on the track, producing out-of-round tire wear.

Even so, the industry was so successful in counterbalancing that the Norfolk & Western class A 2-6-6-4s ran at speeds up to 65 miles per hour, while the Southern Pacific 4-8-8-2s were reportedly capable of 80 miles per hour. By the 1940s, distinctions between passenger and freight locomotives had vanished.[177]

15.5.6 Streamlining and Decoration

The 1930s were the decade of the streamlined steam locomotive, noteworthy examples appearing in the U.S., Britain and Germany. The Americans applied their first streamlined casings to improve the locomotive's appearance as the railroads pursued their dwindling passenger traffic.[178]

Improbably, the Georgia Northern bought a beautified 2-8-2 from Baldwin in 1929.[179] Even though intended for freight service, the engine was painted blue and tricked out with bare monel metal boiler jacket bands and cylinder casings. The tall smokestack had a chromium-nickel top; the engine was lettered and numbered in the same material. The rods were polished. At 189,500 pounds engine weight and 33,000 pounds of tractive effort, this locomotive was from a bygone day.

Wind tunnel tests on a ⅕₅-scale model by O. G. Tietjens at the Westinghouse Pittsburgh laboratories in 1929–30 suggested that streamlining could reduce the power required by a six-car passenger train by 35% at 80 miles per hour, and was therefore worthy of experimentation on full-sized trains.[180] The study, however, was based on an electric locomotive whose shape lent itself naturally to streamlining.

A growing body of test results from Britain, Germany, Canada and the U.S. suggested that streamlining express passenger locomotives could save 200 to 300 horsepower at 80 miles per hour. In 1931, the Canadian National asked the National Research Council, Ottawa, to investigate the external shape of steam locomotives with a view to reducing both air resistance at high speeds and the tendency of smoke to obscure the crew's forward vision.[181] Wind tunnel tests with ½₂ scale models of the company's class U-2 4-8-4s showed how the shape of the boiler induced downward flows of air in front of the cab

Canadian National class U-2 4-8-4, No. 6131, in as-built condition at Montreal, Quebec, on August 16, 1937. The Canadian Locomotive Co. and the Montreal Locomotive Works built this class between 1927 and 1940 (Denver Public Library, Otto C. Perry collection, OP-20203).

Canadian National class U-2 4-8-4, No. 6148, near St. Anne's, Quebec, on August 13, 1932. Smoke obscuring crew vision was evidently a serious problem with these locomotives, witness this apparently successful deflector which did not become widespread (Denver Public Library, Otto C. Perry collection, OP-20284).

Canadian National class U-2 4-8-4, No. 6162, near Chaudriere, Quebec, on August 14, 1937, with conventional smoke deflectors (Denver Public Library, Otto C. Perry collection, OP-20290).

This Canadian National class U-4a 4-8-4, No. 6162, was fully streamlined. The Canadian Locomotive Co. and Montreal Locomotive Works built the class between 1927 and 1940. Otto Perry photographed No. 6162 at Toronto, Ontario, on August 11, 1937 (Denver Public Library, Otto C. Perry collection, OP-20293).

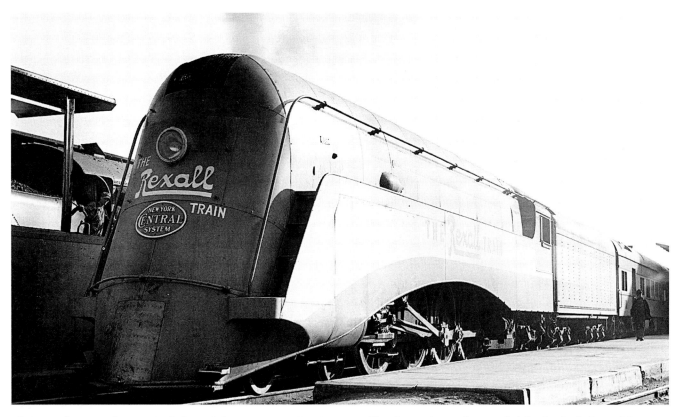

The streamlining on this New York Central class L-2 4-8-2, No. 2873, resembles that on *Commodore Vanderbilt.* Alco built the L-2's between 1925 and 1929. Otto Perry photographed No. 2873 at Denver, Colorado, on June 14, 1936 (Denver Public Library, Otto C. Perry collection, OP-13361).

The four Chicago, Milwaukee & St. Paul Class A's, built by Alco in 1935–37, were probably the last 4-4-2s ever built. Otto Perry photographed No. 2 at Chicago, Illinois, on September 25, 1935 (Denver Public Library, Otto C. Perry collection, OP-4953).

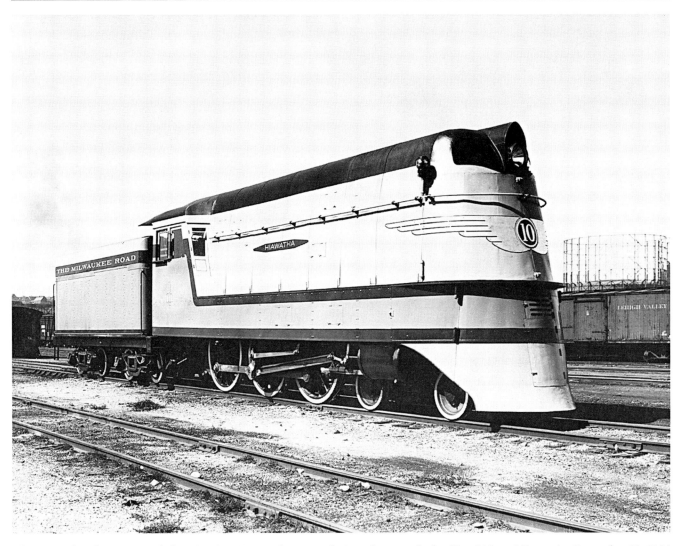

Chicago, Milwaukee & St. Paul class G 4-6-0, No. 10, after streamlining, photographed at New Lisbon, Wisconsin, September 18, 1936 (courtesy *Classic Trains* magazine collection, 20130708, MILW photo).

windows. The enginemen knew the effect of these flows which obscured forward vision with steam and smoke and deposited piles of cinders on the running board in front of the cab; silk thread streamers on the wind tunnel models showed how and why they occurred. Two years of studies developed a streamlined cowling that deflected smoke away from the cab windows and reduced locomotive air resistance by 35%. No existing locomotives were retrofitted with streamlining, but this work provided the basis for streamlining five class U-4a 4-8-4s built by the Montreal Locomotive Works in 1936, six class U-4b's built by Lima for CN subsidiary Grand Trunk Western in 1938 and twenty class U-1f 4-8-2s built by Montreal in 1944. Alco, American Car and Foundry and J. G. Brill also studied streamlining in 1934.[182]

The diesel-powered unit passenger train, first introduced in 1934, found an echo in several steam locomotive designs. That year, the New York Central added a streamlined shroud to a three-year old class J-1 4-6-4 and named it *Commodore Vanderbilt*.[183] The shroud was designed from wind tunnel tests at the Case School of Applied Science at Cleveland, Ohio; engineers predicted a 30% reduction in air resistance, translating into a 2½–12% increase in drawbar pull at 60 to 80 miles per hour, depending on wind conditions.

The Milwaukee's four new 4-4-2 "Hiawathas," built by Alco in

1935–7, were the first American steam locomotives built streamlined from the outset.[184] In addition, they were highly decorated:

> Among the numerous interesting features of these locomotives none is more striking than their exterior appearance. This arises not alone from the complete shrouding of the boiler and skirting which partially conceals the running gear and motion work, but from the bold use of color and skillful ornamentation. The finish includes black, gray, orange yellow, maroon and brown with lettering in gold leaf and the conventionalized Indian headdress on the shrouding front in polished chromium.

Bizarrely, the Milwaukee also streamlined two ancient 4-6-0s.[185] First built by Baldwin in 1900 as Class B-3 of twenty-five 4-6-0 Vauclain compounds, twenty-three were rebuilt between 1915 and 1927 as Class G-6. Two of these were streamlined in 1936–7. The streamlining was removed in 1945; they were scrapped in 1951.

In 1935, the Baltimore & Ohio introduced named, streamlined unit passenger trains, the *Royal Blue* and the *Abraham Lincoln* respectively, propelled by two steam locomotives, purpose-built by the Baltimore & Ohio: one 4-4-4, *Lady Baltimore*, and one 4-6-4, *Lord Baltimore*.

With the beginnings of economic recovery, 1936 brought forth a plethora of streamlined and decorated express passenger engines.

The Southern Pacific bought this air-smoothed class GS-3 4-8-4, No. 4428, from Lima in 1937, photographed at Los Angeles, California, on August 1, 1940. The Southern Pacific bought sixty 4-8-4s from Lima between 1936 and 1943 in seven progressively improved classes (Denver Public Library, Otto C. Perry collection, OP-16068).

The Union Pacific streamlined this class MT-1 4-8-2, No. 7002, built by Alco in 1922, sometime in the 1930s, photographed at Cheyenne, Wyoming, on July 18, 1937 (Denver Public Library, Otto C. Perry collection, OP-17216).

The Chicago, Milwaukee & St. Paul bought six streamlined class F-7 4-6-4s from Alco in 1938. Otto Perry photographed No. 100 at Portage, Wisconsin, on August 9, 1939. Diesel-electrics ended any hopes that locomotives such as this might be the passenger power of the future. The F-7's were scrapped in 1949–51 (Denver Public Library, Otto C. Perry collection, OP-4958).

The Pennsylvania put a streamlined casing on a K-4s at Altoona, developed by the company's engineering staff in consultation with the well-known expert, Raymond Loewy, after testing twenty-four models in the New York University aerodynamic laboratory wind tunnel.[186] They estimated that the casing would reduce the air resistance to a locomotive, hauling one passenger car at 100 miles per hour, from 896 horsepower to 600. The design included paint and striping, with an eye to public appeal as well as reducing air resistance.

The Delaware, Lackawanna & Western remodeled a 4-6-2 entirely for decorative effect, adding a skirt below the running board shaped to resemble a stylized eagle's wing and smoothing and rounding the smokebox front, painted black gloss with chromium striping, trim and skirting and silver-leaf lettering and striping on the tender.[187]

The New York Central brought out a unit express passenger train for service between Cleveland and Detroit.[188] The locomotive was a new K-5 4-6-2 which the company refitted at its West Albany shops with a streamlined shroud to match the train. Bizarrely, the company installed lighting to illuminate the running gear at night.

The well-known Southern Pacific Daylighter 4-8-4s, air-smoothed, painted in red, orange and silver and with polished rodwork were among the most handsome locomotive products of 1936.[189]

By 1941, more than twenty-five railroads were running streamlined, styled and decoratively painted steam locomotives.[190] These ranged from locomotives built new with streamlining to a surprisingly diverse range of retrofits, some of which are shown here.

In 1946–7, the Chesapeake & Ohio rebuilt five 4-6-2s in its own shops at Huntington, West Virginia, as 4-6-4s with roller bearings, poppet valves, high-speed boosters and streamlined shrouds.[191] The rebuild was so extensive that only the tender and part of the boiler were re-used. The new engines were intended to supplement the three steam-turbine electric locomotives also being built at the time in hauling new high-speed passenger trains running to daylight schedules.

Streamlining and decorating steam locomotives lasted just half a dozen years between 1934 and 1940 as the railroads struggled to reverse the decline in passenger traffic. In this they were remarkably successful. World War II put at end to it. The streamlined and decorated locomotives hauling the named trains of the late 1940s were diesel-electrics.

16

Locomotive Construction, 1930–1950

The financial disaster of 1929 and the depression that followed brought locomotive construction almost to a standstill. Nevertheless, refinements continued and manufacture resumed with improving economic conditions in the late 1930s, followed by heavy demand for new locomotives for World War II traffic. These later engines were visually indistinguishable from the superpower designs of the late 1920s but included refinements resulting in markedly better performance. Longer passenger trains of heavier stock and the demand for ever faster freight movement blurred the distinction between passenger and freight traffic.

The railroads could not believe that the contraction in trade in 1930 was more than a temporary aberration; they ordered 440 new locomotives that year.[1] Continued failure of trade led to locomotive orders for domestic service in 1931—at 235 locomotives of all kinds—being the lowest in living memory with the exception of 1919.[2] One hundred fifty of these were electrics bought by the Pennsylvania for its electrification program. The manufacturers completed orders placed in 1929–30; then there was nothing. In 1932, U.S. railroads ordered just five new steam locomotives.[3] The Great Northern bought three 2-8-2s; Hill & Suender, Inc., bought a Heisler; the U.S. Veterans Bureau (!) bought a 2-6-0. That was all. Total orders placed in America for locomotives of all kinds, including export, totaled thirteen. Matters were no better in 1933; the seventeen steam locomotives ordered were outnumbered by twenty diesel-electric, two gasoline-electric and three gasoline direct drive locomotives. The Northern Pacific, with a substantial order for ten 4-8-4s, was one of only three common carrier railroads to order steam locomotives, the others being the Durham & Southern which ordered a single 2-10-0 from Baldwin and the Okmulgee & Northern which gave Alco the only domestic order it received all year. The ruinous effect on the vast locomotive plants can be imagined.

In six depression years, 1931–5, only 531 locomotives were ordered: 186 steam, 150 diesel-electric and 195 electric.[4] Thus had locomotive procurement shrunk from 1,000 to 2,000 locomotives each year during the 1920s. An optimistic spurt of orders for 536 locomotives in 1936 was cause for elation, equaling the total of the previous five years.[5] The steam locomotive made a come-back, with 434 ordered—100 for the New York Central, forty-six for the Southern Pacific, thirty-eight for the Union Pacific, thirty-two for the Milwaukee, twenty-eight for the Santa Fe and twenty-seven for the Bessemer & Lake Erie.

Economic recovery continued weak; the 1936 orders remained unequaled for several years. Steam comprised only one fifth of the new orders placed in 1938–9; the balance included sixty-one electrics and 411 diesel-electrics.[6] Forty of the ninety-five steam locomotives ordered in 1939, and well over half the total value of orders, went to a single buyer, the Southern Pacific: twenty-eight 4-8-8-2s and twelve 2-8-8-4s.

By the end of 1940, faced with rising traffic demand and the threat of another war, the U.S. railroads were becoming worried that they did not have enough locomotives and the ones they had were mostly more than ten years old.[7] Seen from that date:

> Ten years ago the railways of this country were facing two conditions—a major depression and the rising tide of competition—the gravity of neither of which was realized at that time. As the depression progressed toward the low points of 1933–34 the influence of this combination of circumstances with respect to motive power took the form of an almost complete cessation of buying and the apparent decision that the constant falling off in rail traffic warranted the retirement of a substantial portion of the locomotive inventory with the result that there are about 15,000 fewer locomotives now than there were 10 years ago.
>
> While this was going on the encroachment of obsolescence, if not largely ignored, was not given the consideration that its importance justified, for in this period installations of new power fell to such small proportions that less than 2,600 locomotives now in service were built since 1929—only 1,800 of which are steam.

This threat doubled locomotive orders in 1940; the 219 steam locomotives were again in the minority compared to 462 diesel-electric and 13 electric locomotives.[8] Locomotive orders totaling 1,436 in 1941 were the biggest since 1923; for the first time, orders for diesel-electric locomotives exceeded one thousand.[9] Of the 302 steam locomotives, fifty—worth $11 million—went to the Southern Pacific. The New York Central followed in 1942 with a $14 million order for twenty-five 4-8-2s, thirty-two diesel-electrics and 2,500 freight cars, the Santa Fe with a $10 million order for twenty 4-8-4s and ten 5,400-horsepower diesels.[10] These orders fell on a manufacturing industry so weakened by the depression that locomotives ordered in early 1942, might not be delivered until 1943; railroads were doubling their orders even before construction had begun. Baldwin's locomotive capacity was a shadow of its former self; although the company contributed a wide variety of products to the war effort, it delivered only 466 locomotives in 1942, of 727 ordered.

The War Department jumped the line in 1941, ordering 370 2-8-2s—140 from Baldwin, 60 from Alco and 70 from Lima—giving itself high priority.[11] The railroads objected because their own equipment deliveries were "dangerously behind schedule" and the 2-8-2s seemed unsuited for U.S. service. The War Department wanted them for overseas service.[12] It is noteworthy that these engines, with 47-square foot grates, 200 pounds per square inch boiler pressure and 35,000 pounds of tractive effort, were regarded as obsolete in American railroading. Later government orders were secret.[13]

In the first four months of 1942, alone, the railroads ordered 344 locomotives, but these orders were suddenly choked when the War Production Board took control of railroad procurement and froze deliveries on April 4, 1942,[14] putting new pressure on the repair of more than 2,000 locomotives still stored unserviceable. Railroads and industrial concerns ordered 1,255 locomotives in 1942: 368 steam, 875 diesel and twelve electric.[15]

By year-end, the War Production Board had authorized construction of only 216 steam locomotives and 347 diesels. Recognizing the Southern Pacific's role in connecting California with the rest of the U.S., the Board authorized construction of thirty 4-8-8-2s and ten 4-8-4s for the company, adding to the forty 4-8-8-2s and ten 4-8-4s that it ordered in 1941—a massive accumulation of heavy power in two years. The Pennsylvania, suddenly short of freight power, tried to order sixty 2-10-4s. The Board allowed the company to build thirty-five in its own shops, but rejected the twenty-five that it sought to contract out. Besides these, the relationship between requests and authorizations was:

Company	Requested	Type	Authorized
Santa Fe	20	4-8-4	0
Chesapeake & Ohio	15	0-8-0	5
Delaware & Hudson	15	4-8-4	15
Missouri Pacific	15	4-8-4	0
New York Central	25	4-8-2	25
Norfolk & Western	15	2-6-6-4	10
Northern Pacific	12	4-6-6-4	12
Northern Pacific	10	4-8-4	0
Union Pacific	25	4-6-6-4	25

In 1943, the railroads received 434 new steam locomotives (286 from manufacturers, 148 from railroad shops), 556 diesels and twenty-two electrics.[16] Most of these had been ordered in 1942, a pale shadow of the days when the builders could turn out locomotives within two months of receiving an order. Such a backlog built up that only sixty-seven steam locomotives were ordered in the last half of 1943. By the end of 1943, locomotives were still on back order from 1942; there was no certainty that they would be authorized or built in 1944. The WPB let the Pennsylvania build what it wanted at Altoona; in 1943, the company undertook a massive program to build eighty-five 2-10-4s—the biggest single order of the year. The Missouri Pacific's fifteen 4-8-4s were authorized and built by Baldwin in 1943.[17]

The War Production Board did not prolong the life of the steam locomotive by refusing to authorize diesel construction, as is sometimes supposed. In 1942–5, the Board approved the construction of 1,082 steam locomotives, 1,741 diesel-electrics and thirty-eight electrics.[18] The famous designs, such as the Union Pacific Challengers and Big Boys and the Norfolk & Western A's and J's, all predated Board control. The Big Boys were the last of these, built in 1941 and based on design and policy decisions dating back to 1939–40. During 1943–4, the WPB, far from refusing permission to build diesel locomotives, granted blanket authorizations to the manufacturers to build them for stock in anticipation of orders. It did, however, restrict Alco and Baldwin to locomotives of 600 and 1,000 horsepower, while assigning 5,400-horsepower diesel freight engines to the Electro-Motive Division of General Motors; Alco and Baldwin were thus disadvantaged in their post-war efforts. Construction of passenger diesels ceased for the duration of the war. The referenced sources give the impression that the railroads ordered what they wanted and that the WPB approved orders on merit, considering strategic need and manufacturing capacity.

In February 1944, Baldwin built its 70,000th locomotive, a 2-8-0 for the U.S. Army—an average of one locomotive every 14 hours for the 112 years since Matthias Baldwin built his first one.[19] Locomotive orders shrank during the year, only seventy-four steam locomotives

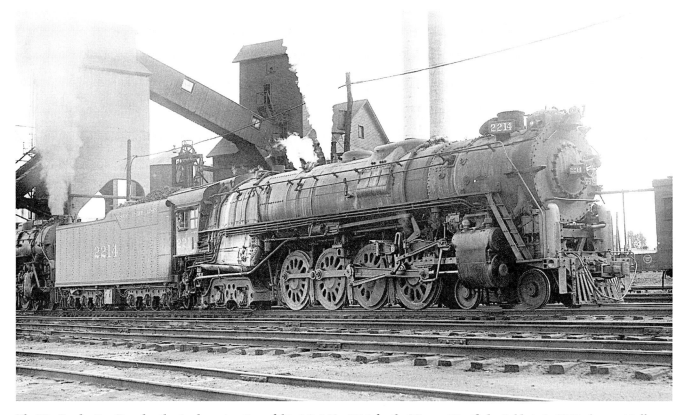

The War Production Board authorized construction of this 4-8-4, No. 2214, for the Missouri Pacific by Baldwin in 1943, shown at Jefferson City, Missouri, on June 30, 1951. Note the huge mechanized coaling plant and the locomotive blowing off vigorously, wasting steam (Denver Public Library, Otto C. Perry collection, OP-12968).

being ordered—down from 413 in 1943, compared to 670 diesel-electrics—up from 635 in 1943. Between 1940 and 1945 inclusive, railroads and industrial plants in the U.S. received 5,536 new locomotives of all kinds.[20]

Orders favored diesels again in 1945 with 826 built for domestic service and only 109 steam.[21] North American builders did well in 1945 with huge orders from overseas for post-war reconstruction, totaling 1,895 steam locomotives from the U.S. and a further 318 from Canada, destined to fourteen different countries—and only ninety-three diesels. The veil of secrecy was lifted to reveal that construction of Russian decapods still went on; the U.S. Government ordered 197 for Russia in 1945, another 13 in 1946. The biggest order was for 699 2-8-2s for France, divided between Alco, Baldwin and Lima.

In 1946, the domestic market ordered only fifty-five steam locomotives, compared to 856 diesels.[22] The only major railroads to order new steam locomotives were the Chesapeake & Ohio (forty 2-8-4s) and the Clinchfield (four 2-6-6-4s). The Chesapeake & Ohio clung to steam power, ordering fifty-eight of the seventy-nine steam locomotives ordered in 1947 (five 4-8-4s, five 4-6-4s, thirty 0-8-0 switchers, fifteen 2-6-6-6s and three fireless 0-6-0 switchers), while Norfolk & Western shops accounted for another ten (2-8-8-2s).[23]

The "diesel buying spree" that erupted in 1947–8 left Alco, Baldwin and Lima stunned.[24] In those two years, American railroads ordered 4,827 diesels and only 148 steam. Export orders totaled 1,090 steam locomotives but, barely able to maintain their huge plants, they asked the Secretary of Defense and the Association of American Railroads for a policy declaration on the future of steam power. Alco built its last steam locomotive for domestic service in 1948, Baldwin and Lima in 1949. Export orders faded as other countries rebuilt their own locomotive plants or dieselized/electrified, or both.

Only thirteen steam locomotives were ordered for domestic service in 1949—all by the Norfolk & Western from its own shops. The Norfolk & Western built another fifty-two steam locomotives in its shops between then and 1952. In 1953, for the first time in more than a century, not one steam locomotive was ordered for U.S. domestic service.[25]

Section 16.1. Multi-Purpose 4-8-4s

The 4-8-4 emerged as the all-purpose locomotive capable of high power at high speed but also high tractive effort on grades.[26] It was no longer necessary to change locomotives for different terrain and by 1945 some 4-8-4s were running 1,800 miles in a single run. Design for maintainability and improved manufacturing techniques resulted in utilization as high as 20,000 miles a month, almost as much as would have been expected in a year forty years previously. The all-purpose capability of the 4-8-4 was unequaled since the 4-4-0 was pushed out of that role in the 1890s, yet only 950 were ever built.

In October 1929, Baldwin delivered the first of thirty-five 4-8-4s to the Chicago & North Western, called the class H, for heavy passenger trains and fast freights, designed in collaboration between Baldwin and the railroad's mechanical department.[27] Winter weather on the prairies could be so severe as to require double-heading some passenger trains; the new 4-8-4s were to eliminate this.

The new locomotives incorporated the latest features. Centerpiece of the structure was an engine bed, including the cylinders, weighing 72,500 pounds, the biggest of its kind cast to date. A power stoker fed a 100-square foot grate; the firebox had three siphons, two in the firebox, one in the 5-foot-long combustion chamber. Fifty-one 2-inch fire tubes and 214 3½-inch flues, 21 feet over tube sheets, pro-

vided 5,215 square feet of evaporative heating surface, with another 2,360 square feet in the Type E superheater. A Worthington Type S feed water heater supplied the 275-pounds per square inch boiler. The crew could direct exhaust from the booster either to atmosphere or through the tender tank, providing extra feed water heating. Five engines had Baker valve gear, the remainder Walschaert; all had Alco power reverse and tandem main rods. The company ran the locomotives in at 250 pounds per square inch boiler pressure; at full design pressure of 275 pounds, they would develop 70,000 pounds of tractive effort with the Franklin booster contributing another 12,400 pounds.

Weighing 498,000 pounds, with a tender on two six-wheel trucks weighing another 320,000 pounds when fully loaded with 20 tons of coal and 18,000 gallons of water, the class H were immense, nearly twice as heavy as the 2-8-2s they were designed to replace and substantially heavier than previous 4-8-4s. The company had to restrict them to the main line between Chicago and Omaha until bridges could be strengthened elsewhere. The engine bed proved overly ambitious for the design and casting capabilities of 1929 and breakages were undesirably frequent.[28] This and other design weaknesses required excessive maintenance. The North Western put up with these problems for seventeen years. In 1945, when the American railroads were dieselizing as fast as they could, the North Western decided to rebuild all thirty-five at its Chicago shops, rather than scrapping them and replacing them with diesels or continuing to repair them piecemeal. This decision implied that the company intended to use steam for at least another 5 to 10 years.

The main dimensions remained unchanged. All the rebuilds received new, redesigned nickel-steel engine beds from General Steel Castings. The steam passages were rebuilt with more generous dimensions to allow a freer flow of steam. All axle bearings were replaced with Timken roller bearings. Boxpok driving wheels were substituted for the original wheels, cross-balanced for 90 miles per hour on 110-pound rail. Rods, pistons and crossheads were replaced with improved designs and metallurgy. All-welded fireboxes replaced the originals, with a second siphon added to the combustion chamber and Hulson tuyere grates. The fire tubes were replaced and increased in diameter from 2 inches to 2¼ inches; flues were replaced and enlarged from 3½ inches to 4 inches; new superheater elements were installed, increased in diameter from 1 inch to 1⅜ inches. Hulson annular-ported exhaust nozzles replaced the original five-splitter circular nozzles. The table plate was raised by 22 inches and the stack choke diameter was increased from 19 inches to 20½ inches, both of these changes allowing freer passage of gases. Numerous other modifications, small in themselves, made for smoother riding and more efficient and maintenance-free operation. Low availability had previously been a problem; these modifications improved availability to 90%. The rebuilds evaporated 25% more water per pound of coal than the originals (7.9 pounds vs. 6.3 pounds) and reduced coal consumption by 26% from 102 pounds per thousand gross ton-miles to 76. After rebuilding twenty-three locomotives between April 1946, and June 1949, the company decided to dieselize and the program was canceled.[29] The last were scrapped in 1956.[30]

Following a take-over by new investors in 1929, the St. Louis Southwestern went straight from seventy-eight 2-8-0s, built mostly by Baldwin between 1909 and 1923, to ten oil-burning 4-8-4s, built by Baldwin and delivered in September 1930, at a cost of $111,000 each.[31] The 423,000-pound 4-8-4s developed only 18% more tractive effort than the older 2-8-0s (62,000 pounds) but hauled 30% more tonnage at higher speeds. Two hundred fifty-pound boiler pressure (up from 200 pounds in the 2-8-0s), Worthington feed water heaters, Type E superheaters, thermic syphons, 87% maximum cut-off and

Otto Perry photographed Chicago & North Western class H 4-8-4, No. 3021, built by Baldwin in 1929, at Omaha, Nebraska, on February 22, 1932. Note the tandem side rods and the enormous counterweight on the main driving wheel (Denver Public Library, Otto C. Perry collection, OP-3280).

roller-bearing engine trucks were among the "modern" features of the new engines that had also to fit the existing infrastructure. High-tensile steel for the boiler shell and outside firebox wrapper sheets contributed to this requirement. Crew comfort was taken care of by seats with arm rests, lockers for clothing and tools, first aid kits, windows, curtains and ventilators to deal with various weather conditions, heating radiators, electric lighting and ice-water containers to an extent that may surprise us at this distance in time. Dark green boiler and cylinder casings, chromium-plated cylinder and steam chest end casings and polished rods were a product of the company's belief in a smart locomotive. Typical of new locomotives at this time was a general cleaning up of the outlines, with much pipework being concealed or placed within the boiler outer casing. The company built two more batches of these engines at its Pine Bluff, Arkansas, shops, five in 1937 and another five in 1942.

In 1930, the Burlington bought eight 4-8-4s and twelve 4-6-4s from Baldwin.[32] The two types were closely similar in design and equipment, differing mainly in weight, tractive effort and function. The 4-8-4s had 74-inch driving wheels and, developing 68,000 pounds of tractive effort, were for fast freight service between Chicago and Nebraska; the 4-6-4s had 78-inch driving wheels, developed 48,000 pounds of tractive effort and were for fast passenger service on the same routes. The similarity between the two classes illustrates the fading distinction between freight and passenger traffic. Both types had engine beds incorporating the cylinders, 250-pounds per square inch boilers, large stoker-fired grates, Type E superheaters, Elesco feed water heaters and power-operated Baker valve gear. Only one 4-8-4 was fitted with a Franklin booster, adding 13,000 pounds to its tractive effort, while all of the 4-6-4s were so equipped, allowing them to start heavy passenger trains without taking up slack and, in

some cases, to dispense with double-heading on grades. The 4-8-4s were notable for their large, 107-square foot grates while, at 326,000 pounds, the 4-6-4s were the biggest of their type built up to that time. High-capacity tenders holding 24 tons of coal were provided with a view to long engine runs for both classes. The Burlington built another twenty-eight 4-8-4s to the same design at its West Burlington shops in 1936–40 and two more 4-6-4s in 1935 and 1938.

The Lehigh Valley made a careful study of its motive power needs with particular reference to hauling 3,000-ton trains to a fast schedule in a loop: Sayre-Buffalo-Jersey City-Sayre with a minimum of helper service.[33] The company was then using 312,000-pound Baldwin 4-6-2s of 49,000 pounds tractive effort, built in 1918–19, and 325,000-pound Alco 2-8-2s of 63,000 pounds tractive effort (without booster), built in 1923–4, in the attempt to meet their tonnage schedules. Even with local helper service, these engines could handle no more than 2,000 to 2,500 tons.

The company asked both Baldwin and Alco to design and build a locomotive that would meet their requirements. Lima were curiously absent from this competition. Baldwin (T-1) and Alco (T-2) each delivered one 4-8-4 in 1931; considering that the engines were independently designed, their similarities are remarkable. They differed in detail, weighing 408,000 and 422,000 pounds, one with Walschaert gear, one with Baker, but not in their modern features that became conventional in new construction in 1930–1: engine beds, extensive welding, 88-square foot stoker-fired grates, combustion chambers, siphons, 250-pound boiler pressures, Type E superheaters, Elesco feed water heaters, power reversers, partial use of roller bearings and high-capacity tenders. Both had 5,400 square feet of primary heating surface with a further 2,250 square feet of superheating surface. Both had 70-inch driving wheels and developed 66,000 pounds

The St. Louis Southwestern modernized its motive power with ten class L-1 4-8-4s, delivered by Baldwin in 1930. No. 802 is seen at East St. Louis, Missouri, in 1956 (courtesy California State Railroad Museum, Negative 900_35208).

of tractive effort with another 18,000 pounds provided by a tender booster. The Lehigh Valley tested both locomotives with a dynamometer car with results closely similar between the two engines, both superior in all respects to the older power and both handling slightly more than the specified tonnage in slightly less than the specified time. Maximum recorded power output was 4,100 indicated and 3,865 drawbar horsepower. So successful were these tests that the company put both into scheduled passenger and fast freight service and at once ordered ten more from each builder that went into service in 1931–2.

The 4-8-4 wheel arrangement attracted several different names; the Lehigh Valley called them *Wyomings*. The company exhibited both locomotives at towns and cities along the route, estimating that ten thousand visitors inspected them at Wilkes-Barre and rarely less than two thousand at other locations. What new device could excite such interest today?

Immense tenders, carrying 30 tons of coal and 20,000 gallons of water, eliminated several water stops. In fast freight service between Jersey City and the Canadian border, the twenty new engines replaced forty 4-6-2s and 2-8-2s. On the 20 miles of 1.2% grade eastbound from Coxton, Pennsylvania, the older engines hauled trains of 2,200 to 2,500 tons, sometimes requiring two helpers; the new engines hauled 3,000 to 3,500 tons on this grade with one helper and eliminated helper service altogether between Easton, Pennsylvania, and West Portal, New Jersey. The new engines hauled 25% more cars in each train 15% faster. In spite of grim economic conditions, the company was able to spend $2.34 million on the twenty new locomotives and reckoned that they returned 38% a year on this investment.

In spite of the depression, the Lehigh Valley ordered another five of these engines from Baldwin, class T-3, delivered in early 1935 with

grate area increased from 88 to 97 square feet and boiler pressure increased from 250 pounds per square inch (T-1) and 255 (T-2) to 275 pounds. A 48-inch combustion chamber projected ahead of the firebox with three siphons in the firebox and one in the combustion chamber. The firebox sheets were all joined by welding. Bigger driving wheels and higher boiler pressure tended toward higher power at speed. The concept of three-point suspension, quite simple in a 4-4-0, became more and more complicated, and the solutions more varied, as the number of wheels increased. In the T-3's, the suspension of all driving wheels was equalized, while a transverse lever behind the rear drivers was connected to the trailing truck equalizers. The front truck was sprung separately. Total engine weight was 435,000 pounds, developing 67,000 pounds of tractive effort.

In 1934, the Northern Pacific, first user of the 4-8-4 in 1926, took delivery of ten more from Baldwin, displaying the first at the Century of Progress Exposition at Chicago.[34] The company needed them for express passenger and silk trains crossing its territory over the 906 miles between Jamestown, North Dakota, and Missoula, Montana. The design included a 115-square foot grate for burning lignite, with a combustion chamber extending 90 inches forward of the firebox, firing a 260-pounds per square inch boiler with a Type E superheater and a total heating surface of just over 7,100 square feet. Five engines had Elesco feed water heaters; five had the Worthington type. An engine bed incorporated the cylinders and air reservoirs. The front-end throttle was power-operated. Walschaert valve gear, controlled by Alco power reverse and limited to 70% cut-off, drove 14-inch piston valves. Boxpok driving wheels, 77 inches in diameter, were the biggest applied to a 4-8-4 to date; roller bearings were fitted to all axles. Total engine weight was 489,000 pounds, approaching that of the Chicago & North Western class H. The Northern Pacific locomotives had no boosters, but developed 70,000 pounds of tractive

Baldwin built eight class O-5 4-8-4s for the Chicago, Burlington & Quincy in 1930, followed by another twenty-eight (O-5A) in 1936–40 when economic conditions improved. O-5A No. 5622 is shown at Denver, Colorado, on May 12, 1940 (Denver Public Library, Otto C. Perry collection, OP-3964).

No. 5101, one of eleven class T-1 4-8-4s built by Baldwin for the Lehigh Valley in 1931–32. The location and date of the photograph are unknown (courtesy California State Railroad Museum, Negative 900_25024).

Otto Perry photographed Northern Pacific class A-2 4-8-4, No. 2656, built by Baldwin in 1934–35, at Livingston, Montana, on August 8, 1938. Note the Boxpok driving wheels (Denver Public Library, Otto C. Perry collection, OP-14013).

effort. The modified Vanderbilt tender carried 27 tons of coal, 20,000 gallons of water and weighed 388,000 pounds when full. The Northern Pacific bought eight more in 1938, another eight in 1941 and ten in 1943, all from Baldwin.

The Delaware, Lackawanna & Western bought its fourth batch of 4-8-4s from Alco in 1934.[35] The Lackawanna was noteworthy in adding substantial new power in the worst of the depression, totaling fifty-five 4-8-4s, most delivered after 1929. Alco Brooks built the first five in 1927. Twenty more followed from Alco Schenectady in 1929 and another ten in 1932. The batch of twenty added in 1934 was built around General Steel Castings engine beds, weighing 68,900 pounds each and incorporating the smokebox saddle, cylinders, valve chests, compressed air reservoir and mounting brackets for the compressor, power reverser and crosshead guides. They carried 250 pounds per square inch boiler pressure and ran on 74-inch Boxpok driving wheels for either passenger or fast freight service. All four batches had 88-square foot grates; the boilers of the new batch contained 5,490 square feet of primary heating surface, including firebox, combustion chamber, arch tubes and siphons, while the superheater added a further 2,180 square feet. Eighteen of the twenty had Worthington feed water heaters, the remaining two had Elesco exhaust steam injectors. Tractive effort remained at 72,000 pounds, higher boiler pressure offsetting the bigger driving wheel diameter. The trailing truck was designed for future installation of a booster. All axles had roller bearings. Walschaert valve gear, controlled by Alco power reverse, drove 12-inch piston valves. Axle loading had to be kept within 68,500 pounds. Total engine weight was 447,000 pounds with another 313,000 pounds in the tender when full with 16,000 gallons of water and 26 tons of coal.

The railroads showed no appetite for emulating or surpassing the size of the Chicago & North Western class H, but the Chesapeake &

Ohio's five new 4-8-4s, built by Lima in 1935, moved in that direction from the more modestly sized engines built in the intervening years.[36]

The Chesapeake & Ohio pioneered the 4-8-2 wheel arrangement in 1911 to haul heavy passenger trains to fast schedules through the Appalachians; demand for this service continued, with an ever-increasing tonnage of accommodation per passenger. The bottleneck was the 175 miles between Hinton, West Virginia, and Charlottesville, Virginia, across the Allegheny and Blue Ridge Mountains with ruling grades up to eight miles of 1.5%. In the early 1930s, the seven class J-2 4-8-2s, built by Alco and Baldwin between 1918 and 1923, handled this service, but they were not only aging but were also outclassed by "such trains as the George Washington, the Sportsman and the F. F. V., all of which are composed of modern, all-steel, air-conditioned Pullman and day coach equipment, and the so-called tavern type diners in which is reproduced the charm of several famous southern colonial taverns." By the 1940s, an all-steel passenger car, fully supplied with heat, light, ventilation, air conditioning and luxurious furniture, weighed as much as 80 tons.

Encouraged by the success of its Lima 2-10-4s, the company contracted with Lima for five large and powerful 4-8-4s to supplement and ultimately replace the 4-8-2s on the Blue Ridge. The Chesapeake & Ohio was proud enough of these engines, when Lima delivered them in 1935, to name them *Thomas Jefferson, Patrick Henry, Benjamin Harrison, James Madison* and *Edward Randolph,* and to name the type *Greenbriar.* Considering their origins and the service for which they were required, they give a good summary of the possibilities of the 4-8-4 at that time.

Surprisingly, each locomotive was still built around a bar frame bolted up from steel castings. The firebox contained 100 square feet of stoker-fired Firebar grates, above which a brick arch was supported on two siphons and two arch tubes. The boiler contained more heat-

The Delaware, Lackawanna & Western bought this 4-8-4, No. 1631, from Alco in 1934, photographed at Buffalo, New York, on August 10, 1937. Note Baldwin cast driving wheels (Denver Public Library, Otto C. Perry collection, OP-7341).

This Chesapeake & Ohio class J-3 4-8-4, No. 601, came from Lima in 1935, photographed at Charlottesville, Virginia, on August 5, 1936 (Denver Public Library, Otto C. Perry collection, OP-2886).

Otto Perry photographed Southern Pacific class GS-2 4-8-4, No. 4410, built by Lima in 1936, at San Luis Obispo, California, on July 26, 1937 (Denver Public Library, Otto C. Perry collection, OP-15724).

Baldwin built this 4-8-4, No. 551, for the Richmond, Fredericksburg & Potomac in 1937, with Baldwin disc driving wheels, photographed at Richmond, Virginia, on August 2, 1939 (Denver Public Library, Otto C. Perry collection, OP-14560).

ing surface than any 4-8-4 built to date with 525 square feet in the firebox, 5,015 square feet in sixty-five 2¼-inch tubes and 220 3½-inch flues, 21 feet over tube sheets, and a further 2,340 square feet in the Type E superheater, generating steam at 250 pounds per square inch. A Worthington feed water heater supplied water to the boiler. An Alco power reverser controlled Walschaert valve gear driving 14-inch piston valves. The two 27½-inch × 30-inch cylinders were expected to develop more than 5,000 horsepower, driving 72-inch wheels through tandem main rods and developing 67,000 pounds of tractive effort; a booster provided another 14,000 pounds. Total

engine weight was 477,000 pounds with an axle loading of 68,000 pounds. The tender, running on two six-wheel trucks, had a capacity for 25 tons of coal and 22,000 gallons of water with a loaded weight of 382,000 pounds. They were hailed as "the most powerful passenger motive-power units in America with the exception of the new electric passenger locomotives built this year for the New York–Washington electrified service of the Pennsylvania Railroad."[37] Lima built two more in 1942 and five more with minor modifications in 1948.

Not only did the 4-8-4 become the standard heavy passenger and

Otto Perry photographed Union Pacific class FEF-1 4-8-4, No. 815, built by Alco in 1937, at North Platte, Nebraska, on November 18, 1939 (Denver Public Library, Otto C. Perry collection, OP-16534).

Union Pacific class FEF-1 4-8-4, No. 817, built by Alco in 1937, had had smoke deflectors added by the time Otto Perry photographed it at Grand Island, Nebraska, on October 14, 1958 (Denver Public Library, Otto C. Perry collection, OP-16536).

Baldwin built forty class S-2 4-8-4s for the Chicago, Milwaukee & St. Paul between 1937 and 1940. No. 228 is shown at Mobridge, South Dakota, on August 13, 1938 (Denver Public Library, Otto C. Perry collection, OP-4963).

fast freight locomotive, but its dimensions came to vary within a narrow range. Thus, when Lima delivered six to the Southern Pacific in 1936, their appearance was more remarkable than their dimensions or design.[38] The company had already bought fourteen 4-8-4s from Baldwin in 1930; they wanted the new engines for the 600-ton Daylight express unit passenger trains between San Francisco and Los Angeles, demanding a fast schedule against extensive 1% grades, locally as steep as 2.2%. The engines were air-smoothed, with a cowling along the top of the boiler, concealed pipework and a smooth boiler casing, rather than fully streamlined, and painted to match the train color scheme. Their dimensions were practically the same as the earlier Baldwins, developing 75,000 pounds of tractive force, including the booster with an engine weight of 448,000 pounds. Lima built another fourteen in 1937 with 280-pound boiler pressure and 80-inch driving wheels, followed by thirty more in 1941–2 with 300-pound boiler pressure.

This increase in boiler pressure was paralleled in other locomotives of the time, such as the five 4-8-4s built by Baldwin, delivered to the Richmond, Fredericksburg & Potomac in 1937 and named after Confederate generals, carrying 275 pounds per square inch boiler pressure.[39] These were potent locomotives, with 96-square foot, stoker-fired Firebar grates, a brick arch supported by two siphons and arch tubes, 5,375 square feet of primary heating surface, 2,090 square feet in the Type E superheater and 77-inch Baldwin disc driving wheels powered by 27-inch × 30-inch cylinders for 67,000 pounds of tractive effort, plus another 16,000 pounds from the booster. Engine weight was 466,000 pounds—mid-range for a 4-8-4 of that day. These engines were limited to clearance dimensions of 15 feet 6 inches height, 11 feet 1 inch width and an axle loading of 69,000 pounds.

The twenty 4-8-4s that Alco built for the Union Pacific in 1937 were not especially large, at 465,000 pounds engine weight and

64,000 pounds of tractive effort, although they did use the high steam pressure of 300 pounds per square inch with huge 100-square foot grates. They were, however, built to run at 90 miles per hour and exceeded 100 miles per hour under test. In 1938, each one averaged 15,000 miles per month with an availability of 93%—spectacular by comparison with other heavy, mobile machinery, even today. The company's 1922-built 4-8-2s by then offered only 65% availability. Handling 20- to 22-car passenger trains between Omaha, Cheyenne, Ogden, Salt Lake City, Green River and Huntington, the new 4-8-4s paid for themselves in reduced train-miles as well as reduced maintenance costs. Heavier trains and faster speeds paid for the higher fuel costs per locomotive-mile than the 4-8-2s. After they had been in service for eighteen months, the company reckoned that they would pay for themselves in two years.[40]

In late 1939, the company took delivery of another fifteen 4-8-4s from Alco, optimized following road tests on the FEF-1's.

The Milwaukee acquired its first 4-8-4 from Baldwin in 1930 but the depression put an end to procurement. With accelerating economic recovery, the company went to Baldwin for thirty 4-8-4s, delivered in 1937–8, that approached the size of the Chicago & North Western H.[41] The Milwaukee also built a single 4-8-4 in its own shops in 1938. The Milwaukee wanted to divide them between freight service from Chicago to Council Bluffs and Minneapolis and passenger service from Minneapolis to Harlowton, Montana. On this latter route they expected the 4-8-4s to increase maximum train length from the twelve cars handled by the 4-6-4s to eighteen cars. In freight service, they would displace fifty-five 2-8-2s to other districts, where the 2-8-2s would displace seventeen still older engines to the scrapyard and fifty-four to storage. The company attached such importance to the 4-8-4s that they strengthened bridges, built longer turntables and enginehouse stalls and improved maintenance facilities to accom-

Baldwin built eleven of these 3765 class 4-8-4s for the Atchison, Topeka & Santa Fe in 1938. Otto Perry photographed No. 3772 at Raton, New Mexico, on March 26, 1939. Note the size of the counterweight in the main driving wheel (Denver Public Library, Otto C. Perry collection, OP-972).

modate them. Even including these costs, the company expected a 12% rate of return on investment.

Each locomotive was built around an engine bed. A 106-square foot Firebar grate, enormous for a 4-8-4, fired a boiler generating steam at 285 pounds per square inch. Two 3-inch arch tubes and two siphons supported the brick arch, with a third siphon in the 72-inch combustion chamber. The boiler, 21 feet over tube sheets, contained sixty-six 2¼-inch fire tubes and 201 3¾-inch flues for the Type E superheater, providing 5,510 square feet of evaporation surface and another 2,335 square feet of superheating surface, this being about the maximum that could be accommodated by a 4-8-4 wheel arrangement within vertical and lateral clearance dimensions. Cylinders measuring 26 inches × 32 inches drove 74-inch Boxpok driving wheels, developing 71,000 pounds of tractive effort with no booster. All axles were fitted with roller bearings. Total engine weight was 490,000 pounds. The company bought ten more in 1940, followed by another ten of an improved design from Alco in 1944. The last was scrapped in 1956.

Renewed traffic demand was such that in 1938 the Santa Fe bought six 4-6-4s, ten 2-10-4s and eleven 4-8-4s, all from Baldwin.[42] Santa Fe mechanical engineers designed the 4-6-4s and 4-8-4s. Although the company bought the 4-8-4s for fast passenger service over the 1,237 miles between La Junta, Colorado, and Los Angeles to tackle grades of up to 3½% that were beyond 4-6-4 capability, the company also had the possible failure of its diesel-powered *Superchief* in mind.[43] The 108-square foot grate was large for a 4-8-4, firing a 300-pounds per square inch boiler, 21 feet over tube sheets. A combustion chamber extended 64 inches ahead of the throat sheet. Two siphons were built into the firebox and one into the combustion chamber. Boiler and firebox joints were partly riveted and partly welded. The engines

were built as oil burners, but were equipped for conversion to coal firing. One live-steam injector and a Worthington feed water heater supplied the boiler. Fifty-two 2¼-inch fire tubes and 220 3½-inch flues for the Type E superheater provided 4,850 square feet of evaporative heating surface, with the firebox, arch tubes and siphons providing another 550 square feet, and a further 2,365 square feet of superheating surface. Abnormally large 15-inch piston valves, driven by Walschaert valve gear with a Baldwin Type C power reverser, controlled steam flow to the 28-inch × 32-inch cylinders, while limiting cut-off to 60%—steadily fewer engines were being built in America with this restriction. There was no booster; popularity of the booster was fading in the late 1930s; 300-pound boiler pressures and 73,000-pound axle loadings replaced the cost and maintenance requirements of the booster. With 80-inch Baldwin disc-type driving wheels on roller bearings, rated tractive effort was 66,000 pounds. Total engine weight was almost exactly 500,000 pounds with an axle loading of 72,000 pounds. The tenders carried 7,000 gallons of oil and 20,000 gallons of water for a total loaded engine weight of 896,000 pounds.

The Santa Fe 4-8-4s probably represented the limits of that wheel arrangement. Other railroads filled their needs with 4-8-4s of more modest dimensions; Alco, Baldwin and Lima built many such locomotives between 1938 and 1945. A typical 4-8-4 of that time weighed 430,000 to 500,000 pounds and developed 60,000 to 70,000 pounds of tractive effort with 65,000 to 70,000-pound axle loadings.[44] The engines were built around engine beds, incorporating smokebox saddles, cylinders, steam chests, air tanks and brackets for crosshead guides, valve gear and power reversers. A 90- to 100-square foot stoker-fired grate, with 15% to 25% air openings, a brick arch supported on arch tubes and siphons, and a combustion chamber, fired a boiler generating steam at 250 to 300 pounds per square inch, 19

The Norfolk & Western built this class J 4-8-4, No. 601, in company shops in 1941–42, shown at Bluefield, West Virginia, on June 29, 1956 (Denver Public Library, Otto C. Perry collection, OP-13778).

to 21 feet over tube sheets. Feed water heaters were universal, exhaust-steam injectors gaining in popularity against the earlier Worthington, Elesco and Coffin types. One or two live-steam injectors and one feed water heater supplied boiler feed water at 10,000 to 12,000 gallons per hour each. Type E superheaters were common, but not universal. Boiler and firebox joints were extensively welded. Front-end throttles were universal, but there was no standardization of front-end drafting and spark arrestor arrangements. Walschaert valve gear, controlled by a power reverser, predominated over Baker gear to drive piston valves 12 to 14 inches in diameter, controlling steam flow to 27 to 29-inch cylinders. An earlier enthusiasm for Baker valve gear faded during the late 1930s. Opinions had always differed on Baker gear; in 1919, the USRA assigned six light Pacifics with Baker gear to the Louisville & Nashville. As early as 1923–4, when the company bought eight more engines of the same design from Baldwin and twelve more from Alco, they not only specified Walschaert gear, but replaced the Baker gear on the original six engines.[45] The Worthington Type 6Sa feed water heater displaced the Elesco and Coffin types. Exhaust-steam injectors made slow headway in America but during the 1940s came to rival the feed water heaters in new construction. The diameters of Boxpok, or other disc-type driving wheels, driven by tandem side rods, ranged from 73 to 80 inches. One or more driving axles were fitted with lateral-motion devices. Reciprocating parts were designed for lightness; running gear was cross-counterbalanced. Roller bearings were used extensively but not exclusively. Boosters had fallen from favor. Cabs were designed with every consideration for crew ergonomics. Tenders typically carried 15 to 25 tons of coal and 15,000 to 25,000 gallons of water. The result was a standardization of motive power unknown since the days of the 4-4-0.

Among the last and finest products of the Norfolk & Western shops at Roanoke were the class J 4-8-4s.[46] When the wartime surge in passenger traffic began, the Norfolk & Western's newest passenger

engines were ten 4-8-2s built in 1926. The company needed locomotives to haul 14- and 15-car passenger trains between Cincinnati and Norfolk and between Monroe, Virginia, and Bristol to fast schedules against ruling grades of 1% to 2%, minimizing servicing, repair time and maintenance costs. At 73,000 pounds of tractive effort for a 72,000-pound axle load and a total engine weight of 494,000 pounds, the J's were among the heaviest and most powerful 4-8-4s ever built. The boiler was shrouded in an air-smoothed casing. Only fourteen were ever built, the first in 1941, the last in 1950.

The boilers were built for 300 pounds per square inch, but the safety valves were initially set at 275 pounds. The rated tractive effort of 73,000 pounds was achieved at a low adhesion factor of 3.9. During dynamometer tests in 1945, the company raised the pressure on the test locomotive to the full working pressure of 300 pounds per square inch, raising the tractive effort to 80,000 pounds—the highest of any 4-8-4—while lowering the adhesion factor to only 3.6. As this did not produce any excessive tendency to slip, the company raised the boiler pressure on all eleven engines. With 275-pound boiler pressure, the maximum power output recorded during the tests was 4,600 drawbar horsepower at 40 miles per hour; 300-pound boiler pressure increased this by 500 horsepower. One of the J's was clocked at 110 miles per hour, hauling a 15-car train weighing 1,025 tons on straight, level track. That this speed was reached, entailing a cycling rate of 540 revolutions per minute, with piston valves, is a tribute to the design of the steam passages, suspension and counterbalancing. On one of the dynamometer runs, with a 1,065-ton train, the firing rate was 13,050 pounds of coal per hour—120 pounds per square foot of grate per hour—evaporating 100,000 pounds of water per hour at 7.6 pounds of water per pound of coal. At this firing rate, at 60% cut-off and moving at 41 miles per hour, the locomotive developed 5,025 drawbar horsepower.

Surprisingly, in view of its immense traffic, the New York Central

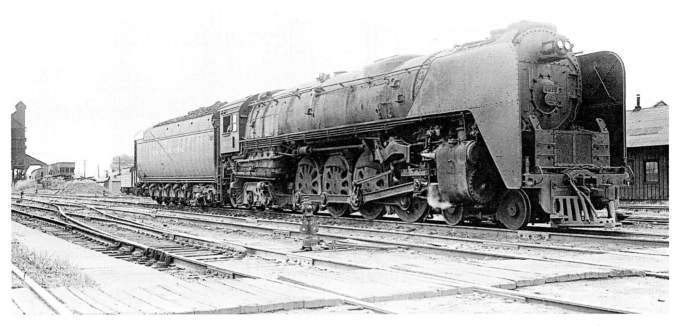

Alco built this New York Central class S-1b 4-8-4, No. 6015, in 1945–46, shown at Indianapolis, Indiana, on June 30, 1956 (Denver Public Library, Otto C. Perry collection, OP-13427).

came late to the 4-8-4.[47] The company did so well with its 4-6-4s and upgraded 4-8-2s that its initial intention in the early 1940s was only to bring out an improved L-class 4-8-2. It became apparent, however, that a four-wheel trailing truck would be needed to carry a firebox big enough to fulfill the company's intentions.

The result was a thorough revision of the L-4 design. The engine was built around an engine bed. The Firebar grate area was increased from 75 square feet to 100; the combustion chamber was increased from 63 to 94 inches with a slight shortening of the boiler from 20½ feet over tube sheets to 19 feet. Five 4-inch arch tubes—but no siphons—carried the brick arch. The boiler length and diameter were both increased, the diameter to the point where no steam dome would fit inside the clearance height, replaced by an 11-inch slotted dry pipe, with baffles to minimize moisture carry-over, leading to a front-end throttle. Boiler pressure was 290 pounds per square inch. A live-steam injector and a Worthington feed water heater supplied the boiler. The ash pan was increased in size to 86 cubic feet, from 50 cubic feet on the L-4, providing increased range between ashing out. All axles ran in Timken roller bearings. Baker valve gear and 14-inch piston valves controlled the steam flow to two 25-inch × 32-inch cylinders, driving 79-inch driving wheels for a tractive effort of 62,000 pounds. Maximum power output was just over 5,000 drawbar horsepower at 60 miles per hour. Total engine weight was 471,000 pounds with an axle loading of 69,000 pounds. The tender ran on a four-wheel leading truck and five axles rigidly mounted in the tender bed casting, instead of the two six-wheel trucks used for the L-4 tenders to provide the same tender capacity as the L-4's but still enabling the 4-8-4s to be turned on the 100-foot turntables between New York and Chicago. Tender capacity was 46 tons of coal and 18,000 gallons of water. The tenders were fitted with the company's improved water scoop design.

Alco delivered a prototype, class S-1a, in early 1945. Even before Alco completed construction the New York Central ordered another twenty-five engines, class S-1b, slightly modified, with delivery beginning the same year. At the same time, the company ordered a twenty-seventh engine, class S-2a, with Franklin poppet valves. The S-1's were deliberately overdesigned, to achieve the fewest possible delays and the lowest possible maintenance cost. As an example, an abnormally high adhesion factor of 4.4 reduced the tendency to slip; as a result, the average mileage between tire turnings was 190,000, with some engines reaching 235,000 miles, whereas 100,000 miles was typical of pre-existing locomotives with a lower adhesion factor. The performance of the S-1's was extraordinary; with 290 pounds per square inch boiler pressure, the New York Central reported a maximum power output of 6,900 indicated horsepower at 85 miles per hour—even more than the Pennsylvania T-1.[48] Good as they were, the last one was scrapped in 1956, concurrent with dieselization.

It is difficult to imagine how the performance and efficiency of these last 4-8-4s could have been improved. With them, the rigid-frame steam locomotive must surely have reached the limits of its box; to break out of the box would have been impractical or excessively costly. But this was not so. It was on just such a locomotive that Wardale's work culminated in 1981 after seven years of studies, testing and development.[49] The locomotive was a metre-gauge 4-8-4, one of 140 built for South African Railways by the North British Locomotive Co. and Henschel in 1953–5, complete with power stokers, security circulators, front-end throttles, feed water heaters and the like. As a result of Wardale's work, drawbar horsepower increased by 37%, with 60% coal savings and 45% water savings, compared to an unmodified locomotive of the same class. The 4-8-4 never reached its full potential; it probably never will.

Section 16.2. Passenger Locomotives

16.2.1 Last of the Pacifics

Not all Americans were equally affected by the depression; the Boston & Maine still needed more potent 4-6-2s than it already possessed to handle its 1934 summer tourist traffic.[50] The company

Lima built two batches—total ten—of class P-4 4-6-2s for the Boston & Maine in 1934 and 1937. No. 3719 is shown at Brunswick, Maine, on August 16, 1937 (Denver Public Library, Otto C. Perry collection, OP-2735).

bought its first twelve 4-6-2s from Alco in 1910, class P-1, followed by seventy P-2's in 1911–16 and ten P-3a's in 1923. The earliest 4-6-2s developed 32,000 pounds of tractive effort, increasing to 47,000 pounds in the booster-equipped P-3a's. By the early 1930s, these engines were aging and undersized for traffic requirements. The five new engines, class P-4a, delivered from Lima in late 1934, were bigger and faster than their predecessors. The stoker-fired firebox contained 67 square feet of Firebar grates, a combustion chamber and three siphons. The 260-pounds per square inch boiler and firebox contained 3,850 square feet of primary heating surface with a Type A superheater adding 965 square feet; water was supplied by a Coffin feed water heater. The company used its own annular ported exhaust nozzle. Cylinders measuring 23 inches × 28 inches drove 80-inch driving wheels, developing 41,000 pounds of tractive effort, with a booster adding 12,000 pounds. Stoker firing and power reversing gear were by now standard on any high-performance engine. The engine weighed 339,000 pounds with an axle loading of 70,000 pounds.

Borrowing a dynamometer car from Westinghouse, the company road-tested one of the new engines in 1935 with thirteen-car, 900-ton trains in midwinter weather over the 143 miles between Boston and White River Junction, Vermont, at start-to-stop speeds of 43 miles per hour.[51] Drawbar horsepower averaged 1,170, peaking at 1,910. Including condensate from the feed water heater, evaporation averaged 8.2 pounds of water per pound of coal, the feed water heater making a difference of 0.8 pounds. Water consumption was 24.6 pounds per drawbar horsepower-hour, including condensate, the feed water heater effecting an economy of 3 pounds. Coal consumption was 3.7 pounds per drawbar horsepower-hour.

With firing rates averaging a modest 65 pounds of coal per square foot of grate per hour, this was not the maximum power output. The company also tested the engine more heavily loaded in fast freight

service with 2,750-ton trains between Boston and Portland. This upped the firing rate to 72 pounds of coal per square foot of grate per hour and maximum sustained power output to 2,740 drawbar horsepower; evaporation decreased to 8.0 pounds of water per pound of coal, water consumption to 20.1 pounds per drawbar horsepower-hour, both figures including feed water heater condensate. Coal consumption dropped to 3.1 pounds per drawbar horsepower-hour. While this performance evidently sufficed for the company's needs higher, but still economical firing rates were possible, suggesting that the locomotive's ultimate power capacity was probably over 3,000 horsepower.

Five more P-4a's followed in 1937; additionally, the company bought four 4-6-2s from the Lackawanna in 1943. Apart from eighteen 4-8-2s supplied by Baldwin in 1935–41, these were the last steam locomotives ordered by the Boston & Maine. They survived into the mid–1950s.

At the New York World's Fair in March 1939, the British exhibited their ultimate passenger power, a four-cylinder, single-expansion 4-6-2, built by the London, Midland & Scottish Railway in 1937–8. The locomotive was built around frames cut from 1⅝-inch plate. A 50-square foot hand-fired grate fired a boiler generating steam at 250 pounds per square inch with no combustion chamber or siphons. Because of smaller clearance dimensions, the permissible boiler diameter limited the heating surface to 2,810 square feet of evaporating surface and 855 square feet of superheating surface in 129 2⅜-inch fire tubes and forty 5⅛-inch flues, 19 feet over tube sheets. One live-steam and one exhaust-steam injector supplied feed water. Power stokers, feed water heaters, power reversers, Baker valve gear and boosters were not used in Britain. (As an exception, the North Eastern Railway slide-valve Q-6 0-8-0 freight engine, currently preserved on the North Yorkshire Moors Railway, has a power reverser.) The outside Walschaert valve gear driving the piston valves on the two outside cylinders drove the piston valves on the two inside cylinders through rocking levers. The four cylinders exhausted through two exhaust nozzles. The outside cylinders drove the middle driving wheels; the inside cylinders drove the cranked front driving axle. Plain bearings housed all axles. The tender, running on six rigidly mounted wheels, carried 11 tons of coal and 4,800 gallons of water. The four 16½-inch × 28-inch cylinders drove 81-inch driving wheels to develop 40,000 pounds of tractive effort. Engine weight was 242,000 pounds. A locomotive of this class developed 3,300 indicated horsepower, the highest recorded power output of a British steam locomotive.

The last Pacifics built in Britain in the 1950s retreated from the LMS design for the sake of easier maintenance and better route availability, being slightly smaller with two outside cylinders. The last North American Pacifics were built in Canada in 1948 after about 6,800 had been built.

16.2.2 Triumph of the Hudsons

As the Rutland replaced 4-6-0s with 4-6-2s, so the Milwaukee replaced 1910-built 4-6-2s with fourteen Baldwin 4-6-4s, delivered in 1930.[52] With 225-pounds per square inch boilers stoker-fired on 80-square foot grates, 26-inch × 28-inch cylinders and 79-inch driving wheels, these 376,000-pound engines developed 46,000 pounds of tractive force. Even though the boilers were only 19 feet over tube sheets, they accommodated 4,205 square feet of primary heating surface, including a combustion chamber, arch tubes and siphons, with Type E superheaters adding 1,815 square feet of superheating surface. Tenders running on two six-wheel trucks held 20 tons of coal and 15,000 gallons of water to increase range between replenishments.

Engine beds incorporated the cylinders. High availability and ease of maintenance were becoming major objectives in locomotive design; by the end of 1933, these engines were an acknowledged success, averaging 10,000 miles per month since being put into service, one running 18,390 miles in one 30-day period. In July 1934, a Milwaukee F-6 hauled five passenger cars, weighing 408 tons, from Chicago to Milwaukee at a start-to-stop average speed of 76 miles per hour, including 90 miles per hour over the 69 miles between city outskirts.[53] The F-6's were so successful that the Milwaukee ordered another eight, class F-6a, with some improvements, delivered in 1931.

In 1931, the Burlington took delivery of twelve 4-6-4s from Baldwin of a size and power output that remained unsurpassed for that wheel arrangement for nearly ten years.[54] An 88-square foot grate fired a 250-pounds per square inch boiler containing 4,250 square feet of primary heating surface and another 1,830 square feet of superheating surface. Cylinders measuring 25 inches × 28 inches drove 78-inch driving wheels, developing 59,000 pounds of tractive effort, including 12,000 pounds from a booster. The engine weighed 392,000 pounds.

In 1937, the New Haven took delivery of ten air-smoothed 4-6-4s from Baldwin, the company's first and only purchase of this type.[55] Baldwin delivered the first with much ceremony; Baldwin Vice-President R. S. Binkerd made an almost pathetic attempt to regain the steam locomotive's position as a wonder of modern science—a position that it had lost two to three decades previously:

> In the locomotive now before you the liners on the pedestals fit in grooves on the roller-bearing boxes with a tolerance of only 15 thousandths of an inch. Modern alloys are used to lighten the rods and motion work. With a steam pressure of 285 lb. it has double the horsepower per ton of dead weight of most of the locomotives of yesterday.

The Chicago, Milwaukee & St. Paul bought fourteen class F-6 4-6-4s from Baldwin in 1930. No. 6410 is shown at St. Paul, Minnesota, on September 20, 1931 (Denver Public Library, Otto C. Perry collection, OP-5071).

Otto Perry photographed this Chicago, Burlington & Quincy class S-4 4-6-4, No. 3009, built by Baldwin in 1930, at Lincoln, Nebraska, on February 21, 1932 (Denver Public Library, Otto C. Perry collection, OP-3788).

Baldwin built ten Class I-5 4-6-4s for the New York, New Haven & Hartford in 1937. No. 1400 is shown at New Haven, Connecticut, on August 18, 1937. Note the overhead wires for electric locomotives (Denver Public Library, Otto C. Perry collection, OP-13701).

Even the tender weighs about 6,000 lb. less than normal through the use of Cor-Ten sheets in the tank. Dollar for dollar, in first cost or in operating expenses, this modern steam locomotive of yours can show her heels to her counterpart in any other form of power.

These were the first engines supplied to an eastern railroad built air-smoothed or streamlined from the outset.

The company intended the locomotives to haul fifteen-car trains to fast schedules between Boston and New Haven. The locomotive was built around an engine bed. A stoker-fired 77-square foot grate fired a 285-pounds per square inch boiler containing 3,815 square feet of evaporative heating surface and 1,040 square feet of superheating surface in a Type A superheater, supplied by a Hancock Turbo Injector. Cylinders measuring 22 inches × 30 inches drove 80-inch Boxpok driving wheels for a tractive force of 44,000 pounds. All axles had roller-bearings: five locomotives with Timken, five with SKF. The engine weighed 365,000 pounds, the tender, carrying 16 tons of coal and 18,000 gallons of water, weighed another 332,000 pounds.

A trend developed for the locomotive builders to outsource an increasing number of components, so that locomotive manufacturing supported a substantial secondary industry of supply companies. For these New Haven engines Baldwin contracted eighty-one components and materials to an only slightly smaller number of suppliers, ranging in size from the engine beds—from General Steel Castings, Eddystone, Pennsylvania—down to the washout plugs—from Huron Manufacturing, Detroit. They bought flexible staybolts, springs and driving wheel tires from their competitor, Alco. The primary manufacturer had to coordinate the procurement and quality control of all these components so that building a new locomotive in the 1930s was a formidable undertaking, making the fast delivery times achieved by the big three all the more remarkable.

Always bold in its procurement, the Santa Fe advanced the 4-6-4 to new heights of size and power when it bought six from Baldwin in 1938 for fast passenger service between Chicago and La Junta, Colorado.[56] Designed by Santa Fe engineers, these engines were intended to pinch-hit for the diesel-powered *Superchief*.[57] All were oil-burners, but with provision for conversion to burn coal; one was streamlined. A 99-square foot grate—vast for a six-coupled engine—fired a 300-pounds per square inch boiler, 21 feet over tube sheets with no combustion chamber, containing 4,770 square feet of evaporative surface, with a further 2,080 square feet of superheating surface in the Type E superheater, producing 49,000 pounds of tractive effort through 84-inch Baldwin disc driving wheels. All axles had SKF roller bearings. The moving parts were so carefully designed for lightness and were so carefully counterbalanced that at the "diametral speed" of 84 miles per hour, dynamic augment was estimated to be only 14,200 pounds per main driving wheel and 9,500 pounds per secondary driving wheel. The resulting engine was the heaviest 4-6-4 built to date, at 412,000 pounds. The Santa Fe bought no more 4-6-4s, acquiring only 4-8-4s and 2-10-4s to meet wartime traffic demand in the 1940s.

The New York Central ran more 4-6-4s than any other American railroad, taking more than half the total production of this type. The fifty class J-3a's that Alco Schenectady built for the company in 1937–8 used the experience from 225 predecessors built since 1927.[58] The last ten were air-smoothed, the others were of conventional exterior.

The locomotive was built around an engine bed. The grate area was the same as the J-1: 82 square feet of Firebar grates, but the design engineers juggled the available boiler length, shortening the smokebox, reducing the length over tube sheets from 21½ feet to 19 feet and inserting a 43-inch combustion chamber, while increasing boiler pressure from 225 to 275 pounds per square inch. Compared to the J-1, the boiler provided 7% less evaporative surface and 10% less superheating surface but, even so, produced 30°F to 40°F higher superheat at medium and high steaming rates. No siphons were used, the brick arch being supported on four 3½-inch arch tubes. Four "combustion tubes" provided secondary air through each side of the firebox. An Elesco feed water heater was mounted inside the smoke-

The Atchison, Topeka & Santa Fe bought six 3460 class 4-6-4s from Baldwin in 1938. No. 3463 is shown at La Junta, Colorado, on January 23, 1938 (Denver Public Library, Otto C. Perry collection, OP-843).

No. 3460 was the one air-smoothed member of the Atchison, Topeka & Santa Fe 3460 class 4-6-4s, built by Baldwin in 1938, photographed near La Junta, Colorado, on June 4, 1939 (Denver Public Library, Otto C. Perry collection, OP-1604).

box. All axles had Timken roller bearings. The 79-inch driving wheels were of the Boxpok type on twenty-five engines, Scullin disc type on the other twenty-five. Baker valve gear, controlled by a Franklin Precision power reverser drove 14-inch piston valves. The reversing gear was innovatively mounted on the engine bed on the centerline of the engine, thereby equalizing any effect on valve events caused by torsion of the reversing shaft. Careful design of moving parts and counterbalancing kept estimated dynamic augment to 6,020 pounds per wheel for the main driving wheels and 8,100 pounds per wheel for the other driving wheels at 90 miles per hour. Tractive effort was 43,000 pounds, with the trailing truck booster adding 12,000 pounds. The tender carried 30 tons of coal and 14,000 gallons of water, biased in favor of coal because the New York Central had track pans. Total engine weight was 360,000 pounds.

Eighty-five suppliers contributed to the construction of the J-3a's, with products ranging in size from the Franklin C-2 booster from Franklin or the Baker valve gear, still manufactured by The Pilliod Co., down to the water tank filling hole latch from the Ramapo Ajax Corporation.

The New York Central's strong engineering group was well able to compare the results of rigorous testing between the J-1's and the J-3a's. The new engines evaporated 63,000 pounds of water per hour at a firing rate of 5,500 pounds per hour (a remarkably high 11.5 pounds of water per pound of coal, probably including the effect of the feed water heater). Increasing the firing rate by 50% to 8,250 pounds of coal per hour increased the steaming rate by 40% to 89,000 pounds per hour (10.8 pounds of water per pound of coal). Considering that, in 1898, the Purdue laboratory locomotive evaporated 5.1 to 6.4 pounds of water per pound of coal and that the absolute limit attainable by burning coal in a calorimeter is 13.5–14.5 pounds of water per pound of coal, American locomotive engineering had made remarkable advances in forty years.

Dynamometer tests showed the new engines developing a maximum of 4,700 indicated horsepower at 80 miles per hour, 3,880 drawbar horsepower at 65 miles per hour. Whereas the J-1's flatlined specific coal consumption at 4 pounds per drawbar horsepower-hour at 2,000 to 2,300 drawbar horsepower, the J-3a's brought this down to 3.25 pounds at 2,300 drawbar horsepower. Even though only a skilled eye could distinguish between a J-1 and a J-3a, better boiler design during the 1930s improved on the J-1's evaporative efficiency by 9%; the new engines produced 21% more power than the original J-1's for only 5% more engine weight. These were the last 4-6-4s bought by the New York Central; 1940s procurement comprised 4-8-2s and 4-8-4s.

Only 500 4-6-4's were ever built in North America.

16.2.3 The Last Mountains

By the late 1930s, the New York Central's 275 4-6-4s still could not handle peak vacation traffic, the shortfall being made up by an aging, shrinking and insufficiently powerful fleet of K-3 4-6-2s. The company pressed L-2 4-8-2 freight engines, built in 1926–30, into this service but riding qualities and plain bearings limited their speed to 60 miles per hour. The company had been an early user of the 4-8-2, with 485 bought from Alco and Lima between 1916 and 1930, and continued to favor this wheel arrangement.

In 1939, the company modified two L-2's to provide satisfactory passenger haulage at speeds up to 80 miles per hour, without losing their freight haulage capability, increasing boiler pressure from 225 to 250 pounds per square inch, reducing cylinder diameter from 27 inches to 25½ inches, substituting new, 43%-lighter reciprocating parts, dynamically counterbalancing all driving wheels—reducing dynamic augment by 61%, installing roller bearings, adding a coal pusher to the tender and a lateral-motion device to the front driving wheels and improving the drawgear between engine and tender. They

The fifty class J-3a 4-6-4s were one of the New York Central's success stories, built by Alco in 1937–38. No. 5414 is shown at Buffalo, New York, on August 7, 1939 (Denver Public Library, Otto C. Perry collection, OP-13420).

Otto Perry photographed New York Central class J-3a 4-6-4, No. 5450, one of ten air-smoothed members of this class, built by Alco in 1937–38, at Buffalo, New York, on August 7, 1939. Note the Scullin disc driving wheels (Denver Public Library, Otto C. Perry collection, OP-13421).

New York Central class L-2 4-8-2, No. 2813, one of 300 built by Alco in 1925–29, hauling 122 cars over the track pans near Silver Creek, New York, on August 10, 1937 (Denver Public Library, Otto C. Perry collection, OP-13538).

ran one of the rebuilds on instrumented track at speeds up to 87 miles per hour with no greater track stress than a J-1, demonstrating the possibilities of careful counterbalancing and light-weight reciprocating parts.

As a result of the success of these tests, the New York Central bought fifty improved 4-8-2s, class L-3, thirty-five from Alco and fifteen from Lima, delivered in 1940–2.[59] Twenty-five of the Alco engines were equipped for passenger and freight service without boosters but with provision for retrofitting; the remainder were for freight only with boosters. General Steel Castings supplied the engine beds to both manufacturers. The company accepted the limitations of a 75-square foot grate in exchange for the benefits of retaining the 4-8-2 wheel arrangement, although the boiler contained a large heating area—4,660 square feet of evaporative surface, 2,080 square feet in the Type E superheater, 20½ feet over tube sheets. Both batches had Baker valve gear. Cylinders measuring 25½ inches × 30 inches and 69-inch driving wheels provided 60,000 pounds of tractive effort, the same as the L-2's, with another 14,000 from the booster.

The company retained the 4-8-2 wheel arrangement because it provided the required weight distribution without a four-wheel truck and allowed an enormous tender, holding 43 tons of coal and 15,000 gallons of water, while being still able to turn the engine on a 100-foot turntable. The New York Central was well provided with track pans and could afford to trade water capacity for a very high coal capacity; the L-3's incorporated an improved, quick-acting water scoop. Even though the new engines had 69-inch driving wheels, the frames were built for retrofitting with 72-inch wheels. The company wanted a 275-pound boiler pressure, but limited wartime availability of high-tensile steel enforced the retention of 250-pound pressure. The Alcos came with Worthington feed water heaters, the Limas with Elesco heaters.

The original L-2's developed 3,800 indicated horsepower at 50 miles per hour. The modified L-2's increased this to 4,200; the L-3's developed 4,400 indicated horsepower at 55 miles per hour, although, during a road test, one of them developed 5,260 indicated horsepower, 4,120 drawbar horsepower, at 58 miles per hour.[60] Fifteen more L-3's followed from Lima in 1942 and fifty further modified L-4's from Lima in 1942–4. The L-4's differed from the L-3's only in an increased driving wheel diameter—72 inches instead of 69 inches—and an increase in cylinder bore from 25½ inches to 26 inches. They were expected to develop up to 5,400 indicated horsepower, 4,300 drawbar horsepower, at 60 miles per hour.

Mountains built for the Baltimore & Ohio in 1948 were among the last steam locomotives built in the U.S. for domestic service.

16.2.4 Oddities

In 1934, the Baltimore & Ohio decided to buy two unit passenger trains of light-weight cars and built two locomotives in their Mount Clare shops to power them.[61] First was the 4-4-4 *Lady Baltimore*, completed in 1934, followed by the 4-6-4 *Lord Baltimore*, completed early the following year. These locomotives were preceded by an experimental modification of a 4-6-2 to a 4-6-4 with a water-tube firebox at Mount Clare in 1933. The two locomotives were given British styling and were designed for rapid acceleration at medium and high speeds in order to make fast schedules without excessively high top speeds.

Both locomotives had Emerson water-tube fireboxes and conventional boilers, generating steam at 350 pounds per square inch. A Gaines wall divided the firebox into a stoker-fired 62-square foot table grate beneath a brick arch supported on arch tubes and a 36-inch combustion chamber. The boilers measured 17¾ feet (4-4-4) and 25 feet (4-6-4) over tube sheets and contained 1,780 and 3,340

Baltimore & Ohio class J-1 4-4-4, No.1, *Lady Baltimore*, built in company shops in 1934, shown at St. Louis, Missouri, on September 24, 1935. The box at the front of the locomotive is a temporary shelter for instrument technicians (Denver Public Library, Otto C. Perry collection, OP-2551).

Baltimore & Ohio class V-2 4-6-4, No.2, *Lord Baltimore*, built in company shops in 1935, shown at Washington, D.C., on August 5, 1936 (Denver Public Library, Otto C. Perry collection, OP-2552).

square feet of primary heating surface respectively with Type A super-heaters in both cases.

Cut-off in full gear was limited to 75%. Cylinders measuring 17½ inches × 28 inches (4-4-4) and 19 inches × 28 inches (4-6-4) drove 84-inch driving wheels, producing 28,000 pounds of tractive effort (4-4-4) and 34,000 pounds (4-6-4), augmented by 7,000 pounds from a high-speed booster. The 4-4-4 was designed for a cylinder horsepower of 1,800; in tests with a 250-ton train, it developed 1,570 horsepower at 95 miles per hour. The 4-6-4 was designed for 2,200 cylinder horsepower. Engine weights were 218,000 pounds and 294,000 pounds respectively. The 4-4-4 had a very low adhesion ratio of only 3.6, accounting for its reputation for slipperiness, while that of the 4-6-4 was 4.6. The engines remained sole examples and were scrapped in 1949.

The 4-4-2 wheel arrangement came alive once more with the Milwaukee's *Hiawathas*. If a train could be scheduled for daylight hours only, the heavy and costly sleeping car service could be eliminated. *Lord Baltimore* and *Lady Baltimore* were built with this in mind. In 1935, the Milwaukee inaugurated a train to cover the 410 miles between Chicago and Minneapolis in 6½ daylight hours—the *Hiawatha*—and bought two oil-burning 4-4-2s from Alco to haul them.[62] With 300-pounds per square inch boiler pressure and weighing 280,000 pounds with a 70,000-pound axle loading and 31,000 pounds of tractive effort, these were a significant advance over previous 4-4-2s, including the Pennsylvania's E-6s.

The engines were built around an engine bed incorporating cylinders, valve chests, smokebox saddle and compressed air reservoir with brackets for attachments. The firebox was welded. The 84-inch Boxpok driving wheels and the free axles were fitted with roller bearings. The 4-4-2 wheel arrangement lent itself naturally to light-weight rods and motion; as well, all moving parts were carefully designed as to both shape and metallurgy for lightness. Tandem main rods and counterbalancing reduced dynamic augment to 11,000 pounds at 100 miles per hour. The heating surface was similar to that of the E-6s at 3,245 square feet, still with a Type A superheater, but with 50% higher boiler pressure.

Careful attention was given to braking in view of the anticipated high speeds. All locomotive wheels were air-braked. Two cylinders powered the brakes on the leading truck, one cylinder applying the brake shoes to the front side of all four wheels, the second applying the brake shoes to the rear side. One cylinder applied the brake shoes to the front sides of all four driving wheels, mechanically equalized. One cylinder applied the brake shoes to the rear sides of the driving wheels, pneumatically equalized. A fifth cylinder applied all four brake shoes to the trailing truck wheels. The system, designed by the American Brake Co., used compressed air at 50 pounds per square inch.

The most distinctive feature of the two new engines was a complete streamline shroud, embellished by paintwork and chromium plate. Alco built two more of these engines in 1937. The *Hiawatha* made 115 miles per hour under test between Milwaukee and New Lisbon in 1935.[63]

16.2.5 Duplex Drive Locomotives

The new streamlined locomotive that the Pennsylvania unveiled at the New York World's Fair in March 1939, was of spectacular design and promised performance to match.[64] Designed by the mechanical engineers of Alco, Baldwin, Lima and the Pennsylvania, it was a tribute to the manufacturing capability of the Altoona shops that built it. The S-1 had a 6-4-4-6 wheel arrangement with a six-wheel leading truck, two four-wheel drive units powered by single-expansion cylinders and a six-wheel trailing truck under the firebox. Two eight-wheel

trucks carried the tender. The locomotive was built around a Commonwealth engine bed, 77 feet long, weighing 97,620 pounds, the heaviest cast to date. The grate was enormous at 132 square feet with a 10-foot combustion chamber. Symbolizing the importance that the design engineers gave to the firebox as the source of power, the firebox and combustion chamber totaled 27 feet in length, while the boiler measured only 22 feet over tube sheets. Otherwise, the 300-pounds per square inch boiler, with 7,750 square feet of total heating surface and, curiously, a Type A superheater, resembled that of a contemporary 4-8-4, although the smokebox was nearly 13 feet long. Inside the firebox were seven security circulators. For clearance reasons, there was no steam dome; steam went through a slotted dry pipe to the front-end throttle. The four cylinders, supplied through 12-inch piston valves, measured 22 × 26 inches; the very short stroke minimized counterbalancing problems. A single Alco power reverser controlled all four sets of Walschaert valve gear. Each pair of cylinders exhausted through its own nozzle and stack. All axles had roller bearings. The front truck was independently sprung, equalized to provide its own three-point suspension. The four 84-inch Baldwin disc driving wheels and the three trailing truck wheels on each side were continuously equalized. The engine was expected to develop 76,000 pounds of starting tractive effort and 6,500 indicated horsepower, hauling 1,200 tons at 100 miles per hour. The last experimental American steam locomotives were all monsters. The locomotive weighed 608,200 pounds; the tender carried 26 tons of coal and 24,200 gallons of water for an all-up weight of 452,000 pounds.

At the World's Fair, the engine was mounted on an extravagant demonstration stand designed so that, not only could the locomotive be run under its own steam, but the idling wheels of the engine trucks and tender would run at the same speed as the driving wheels. It continued on display into 1940. In service, the Pennsylvania found that its 26½-foot rigid wheelbase and 124-foot total wheelbase limited its route availability. They therefore assigned it to the route between Chicago and Crestline, Ohio, a stretch of straight, level track long noted for high-speed passenger runs.

This engine was the first of the famous Pennsylvania duplexes. Although the engine, itself, was not repeated, it was the forerunner of three classes of duplex locomotives built at Altoona and by Baldwin between 1942 and 1946, totaling seventy-nine. The company took the S-1 out of service in 1944 and scrapped it in 1949.

The Pennsylvania put the first two of a new class of 4-4-4-4s, built by Baldwin, into service in 1942, class T-1.[65] Fifty more would follow from Baldwin and Altoona in 1945–6, making them the most numerous of the Pennsylvania duplexes. These engines "marked the culmination of almost four years of engineering effort directed toward the ultimate objective of the development of a steam locomotive having service characteristics similar to the Pennsylvania GG-1 electrics." The Pennsylvania wanted electric locomotive performance in areas where traffic density did not justify electrification; it is interesting that the company took on this objective with steam power in 1938 when the performance of diesel-electric locomotives was making rapid progress. It took Baldwin nearly two years to build the T-1s, the order being placed in July 1940, and completed in April–May 1942. The two engines went into service between Harrisburg, Pennsylvania, and Chicago, covering the 713 miles with only one fuel stop and handling 880-ton trains at 100 miles per hour on straight, level track. Like the New York Central, the Pennsylvania could rely on track pans to replenish water, so the tender carried 41 tons of coal but only 19,500 gallons of water.

Ninety-two square feet of table grates with 16% air opening, a brick arch supported on five circulators and a 96-inch combustion chamber fired a 300-pounds per square inch boiler containing 184 2¼-inch

The Pennsylvania's class S-1 6-4-4-6, No. 6100, built in company shops in 1939, hauling *The Trail Blazer* from Chicago to New York (courtesy California State Railroad Museum, Negative 20550, Kaufmann and Farber photograph).

Shown is Pennsylvania class T-1 4-4-4-4, No. 5549, photographed about 1946. Altoona and Baldwin built the T-1's in 1945–47 (Pennsylvania Historical and Museum Commission and Railroad Museum of Pennsylvania, Photograph 227-7-7).

fire tubes, 18 feet over tube sheets. The Type AS superheater comprised 138 sine-waved elements in 69 5½-inch flues. Total evaporative surface was 4,220 square feet with a further 1,680 square feet in the superheater. A live-steam injector and a Hancock Turbo-Injector taking exhaust steam from the rear drive unit, each with a capacity of 13,000 gallons per hour, forced feed water into the boiler. The Walschaert valve gear differed from normal in that the expansion link was driven from the crosshead, instead of from an eccentric crank.

Franklin poppet valves supplied 19¾-inch × 26-inch cylinders. Eighty-inch Baldwin disc driving wheels contributed to 65,000 pounds of tractive effort, with a further 13,500 pounds available from a trailing truck booster. Total engine weight was 508,000 pounds, with an axle loading of 67,000 pounds.

The first two locomotives were an immediate success. No. 6110 made its first through run from Harrisburg to Chicago with fourteen cars, weighing 1,000 tons, bettering the normal schedule and reaching

100 miles per hour between Crestline and Chicago. No. 6111, hauling sixteen cars, ran for 69 miles on the Fort Wayne division at an average speed of 102 miles per hour. The two engines were so powerful that the Pennsylvania reserved them for trains usually needing double heading. By April 1944, No. 6110 had run 120,000 miles and was sent to Altoona for thorough testing. The Pennsylvania rebuilt the test plant to accommodate it.

The coal used in the static tests was better than most locomotive coal—14,000 BTU per pound, high in volatiles, only 7.6% ash, ¾-inch minus screened out; this may have favorably influenced the test results. Even so, the figures emerging from Altoona were cause for jubilation.

The absolute maximum steaming rate obtained was 105,500 pounds per hour, at 420 revolutions per minute (100 miles per hour), full throttle, 20% cut-off and a firing rate of 252 pounds of coal per square foot of grate per hour (11½ tons per hour). (Specified here as dry coal. Most sources do not distinguish between dry coal, coal as fired or combustibles, notwithstanding the significant differences between them.) Baldwin considered 150 pounds per square foot per hour "normal" suggesting that older ideas, that 120 pounds per square foot per hour was the maximum rate for acceptable efficiency, had been discarded. Most of the Altoona tests on the T-1 went up to 240 pounds per square foot per hour, with a smokebox vacuum of 23 inches of water gauge. This firing rate did carry a penalty; 25% of the heat energy was lost in coal blown out through the stack or as carbon monoxide due to imperfect combustion. Earlier experience indicated that combustion stonewalled at 200 pounds per square foot per hour; current research has not revealed how or why higher rates now achieved a useful result.

Boiler pressure was maintained at 295 pounds per square inch, losing only 9 pounds in dry pipe, superheater, steam pipes and valves. This resulted from high boiler pressure, generously dimensioned steam pipes, ranging from the 10½-inch dry pipe down to the 7-inch steam pipes to the cylinders, and good valve design.

Even with the single-loop Type AS superheater, steam temperatures approached 800°F at high firing rates—770°F at a firing rate of 150 pounds per square foot per hour. At a firing rate of 240 pounds per square foot per hour, smokebox and steam temperatures were the same, suggesting an ultimate heat transfer barrier governed by the fire temperature.

Feed water heating results were gratifying. As the steaming rate increased, so did the water saved by the Turbo-Injector, from 5% at 30,000 pounds per hour to 11½% at 100,000 pounds per hour.

The lowest specific steam consumption was 13.6 pounds per indicated horsepower-hour while developing 5,000 indicated horsepower at 76 miles per hour and 20% cut-off—14.0 to 15.5 pounds being typical. These were the lowest specific steam consumptions recorded at Altoona in forty years. The power output of the T-1 was 40% higher than any locomotive previously tested at Altoona, although this omits to mention that locomotive developments outran the capacity of the plant twenty years previously.

The maximum recorded power output was 6,550 indicated horsepower at 86 miles per hour and 25% cut-off. At very high speed, the T-1 produced nearly maximum power at 15% cut-off, needing throttling to control power output. At low and moderate power output, coal consumption per drawbar horsepower-hour was below 2.5 pounds, rising from 2.5 pounds at 5,500 horsepower to 3.5 pounds at 6,000 horsepower. The T-1 developed 46% more power than a Pennsylvania M-1a 4-8-2 for a steaming rate only 11% higher. Poppet valves and roller bearings resulted in mechanical efficiencies above 90%; overall thermal efficiency was still only 6.5% to 7.5%.

The T-1 was designed to haul 880 tons at 100 miles per hour on straight, level track. The Davis formula for train resistance indicated that this required a drawbar pull of 11,200 pounds. The Davis formula was: $R = 1.3 + (29/w) + (0.03V) + (0.014V^2/wn)$, where R = resistance in pounds per ton of train weight; n = number of axles per car; w = weight per axle in tons; V = speed in miles per hour. The AAR road tests of 1938 validated this formula. On the test plant, the T-1 developed 25,000 pounds of drawbar pull at 100 miles per hour.

In 1945, when the tests were complete, Ralph Johnson declaimed, with justification:

> It is believed that the foregoing attainments stamp this locomotive as one of the outstanding designs of this day. To develop over 6,550 i.h.p., evaporate over 100,000 lb. of water per hour, attain steam temperatures of 800 deg. F., at steam rates around 15, and to ride comfortably at speeds up to 100 m.p.h. while hauling 16 cars, is so outstanding a performance as to warrant the interest of all railroad men.
>
> These locomotives will out-perform a 5,400-h.p. Diesel locomotive at all speeds above 26 m.p.h. ... and, if given comparable facilities for servicing and maintenance will do the work more cheaply.

The rub was the facilities needed for handling coal, water and ash. Even so, the most up-to-date coaling plants could dump 43 tons of coal in 75 seconds; some water towers could dispense 5,000 gallons per minute.

Based on this success, the Pennsylvania and Baldwin built another fifty T-1's in 1945–6; the Pennsylvania scrapped them in 1952–6, along with most other steam power. Apparently,[66] the T-1's were slippery although, at an adhesion factor of 4.1, it is not clear why this should have been so. They also suffered from trouble with the poppet valves and their long rigid wheelbase. Streamlining was insufficiently developed, causing smoke and cinders to swirl around the engine and train. Duplex drive brought with it the problem of drive units moving in and out of synchronization with each other. None of these problems were insoluble and duplex-drive, swept away by the diesel, remains one of the undeveloped opportunities of steam locomotive development.

Section 16.3. Freight Locomotives

16.3.1 Eight-Coupled Locomotives

The coming of the 4-8-4 rendered other eight-coupled freight power obsolete; procurement of these types practically ended with the cessation of locomotive building in the early 1930s.

The Wabash bought twenty-five 4-8-2s from Baldwin in 1930 to replace 2-8-2s, the newest of which had been built only five years before.[67] Two thirds of the 2-8-2s had boosters, providing a maximum of 77,000 pounds of tractive effort; the new engines developed only 67,000 pounds, designed for future installation of a booster but initially supplied without. The main reason for this substantial new purchase was to accelerate freight trains over the 272 miles of flat terrain between Decatur, Illinois, and Montpelier, Ohio. In particular, the new engines were cross-counterbalanced. A stoker-fired 84-square foot Hulson tuyere grate fired a 235-pounds per square inch boiler with a Type E superheater. The firebox, combustion chamber, arch tubes, siphons, tubes and flues provided 4,620 square feet of primary heating surface, with the Type E superheater providing an additional 2,000 square feet. Twenty engines had Worthington feed water heaters, while the remaining five had Sellers exhaust-steam injectors. The 2-8-2s had no feed water heaters. Engine weight was 406,000 pounds for an axle loading of 67,500 pounds, up from 64,400 pounds in the heaviest of the three preceding classes of 2-8-2. The tender had a capacity for 18 tons of coal and 15,000 gallons of water.

The new engines fully bore out the intentions of their designers; dynamometer tests showed 22% more ton-miles per train hour than the 2-8-2s and 20% better fuel efficiency. The company also took the opportunity to test the tuyere grate against the standard Hulson finger grate and three different exhaust nozzles. The difference in performance between the two grate types was not significant. Two of the nozzle types were the so-called "hook-type," where the edge of the nozzle was formed into a small downward-projecting lip, while the "open-type" had no lip. Neither nozzle included any form of splitter. The open type provided a slightly better fuel efficiency—4.1 pounds of coal per drawbar horsepower-hour, compared to 4.3 for the hook-type. Fuel efficiency for the 2-8-2s, by contrast, was 5.0 to 5.3 pounds per drawbar horsepower-hour. The new engines also showed improved evaporation per pound of coal—6.1 pounds of water compared to 5.5 to 5.8 in the 2-8-2s. The 1912-built Alco K-1 2-8-2s developed 900 drawbar horsepower. The 1918-built Baldwin K-2's increased this to 1,060, and the 1925-built Alco K-4b's further to 1,285. The new 4-8-2s turned in 1,725 drawbar horsepower, almost double that of the engines built in 1912. The power output of some other 4-8-2s suggests that these were not tested to their maximum capacity.

At the same time, the company bought twenty-five 4-8-4s of similar design, using a four-wheel trailing truck to support a 96-square foot grate.[68]

The 2-8-4 was so successful that companies continued to order them with only minor refinements. By 1934, 298 were in service on nine railroads: the Boston & Albany (55, Lima, 1925), the Illinois Central (50, Lima, 1926), the Chicago & North Western (12, Alco, 1927), the Erie (25, Alco, 1927; 45, Lima, 1927; 35, Baldwin, 1928), the Boston & Maine (25, Lima, 1928–9), the Toronto, Hamilton & Buffalo (2, Montreal, 1928), the Missouri Pacific (5, Alco, 1928; 25,

Lima, 1929), the Santa Fe (4, Baldwin, 1927) and the Nickel Plate (15, Alco, 1934).[69] Of these, Lima built 200; Alco 57; Baldwin 39; Montreal Locomotive Works 2. At a time when most railroads had stopped buying new engines, the aggressive new management of the Nickel Plate, which took over in 1933, tried to overcome the depression by buying new power. With 245-pound boiler pressure, 416,000-pound engine weight and 64,000-pound tractive effort, the Nickel Plate 2-8-4s were of conservative, mid-range design.

With an eye to interchangeability between fast freight and passenger service, the Boston & Maine ordered five 4-8-2s from Baldwin in 1935.[70] These engines were designed to provide higher speed than the company's existing 2-10-2s, bought in 1920–3, and 2-8-4s, bought in 1928–9, while remaining within weight limits imposed by track and substructures.

Each locomotive was built around an engine bed with an integral air reservoir. The firebox contained 79 square feet of stoker-fired Firebar grates, three siphons in the firebox and one in the 66-inch combustion chamber. The boiler, 19 feet over tube sheets, provided 4,540 square feet of primary heating surface, generating steam at 240 pounds per square inch, while the Type E superheater added another 1,925 square feet. A Coffin feed water heater was concealed inside the smokebox. Roller bearings were applied to the leading truck axles only. Cylinders measuring 28 inches × 31 inches and 73-inch driving wheels produced 67,000 pounds of tractive effort. Weight restrictions precluded the use of a bigger firebox or a booster.

To obtain tonnage ratings, the company borrowed a dynamometer car from Westinghouse and ran two tests from East Deerfield, Massachusetts, through the Hoosac tunnel to Mechanicville, New York, a distance of 84 miles. The first trailing load comprised sixty-three cars, weighing 2,060 tons, simulating fast freight service; the second comprised ninety cars, weighing 2,310 tons, simulating a maximum-

Wabash Class M-1 4-8-2, No. 2805, built by Baldwin in 1930, photographed at Decatur, Illinois, on September 19, 1930 (Denver Public Library, Otto C. Perry collection, OP-19750).

The Chesapeake & Ohio bought ninety of these class K-4 2-8-4s from Alco and Lima between 1943 and 1947. No. 2708 is shown at Handley, West Virginia, on July 10, 1953 (Denver Public Library, Otto C. Perry collection, OP-2933).

tonnage train. The first test resulted in 20.5 pounds of water, 2.7 pounds of coal per drawbar horsepower-hour and 123 pounds of coal per thousand gross ton-miles; the second came in at 20.9 pounds of water and 2.9 pounds of coal per drawbar horsepower-hour and 114 pounds of coal per thousand gross ton-miles. The highest recorded drawbar horsepower, sustained over two miles, was 3,670.

The Chesapeake & Ohio returned to the 2-8-4 when they needed new medium-sized freight engines in the early 1940s. As the War Production Board limited them to existing designs, they bought forty 2-8-4s from Alco in 1944,[71] basing the design on the ninety-four such engines built by Alco and Lima for Chesapeake & Ohio subsidiaries, the Nickel Plate and Pere Marquette. At 460,000 pounds engine weight, they were toward the upper end of the 2-8-4 size range. Engine beds and roller bearings were design improvements over the Nickel Plate and Pere Marquette engines. The boiler was conservatively designed with a 90-square foot Firebar grate, a 42-inch combustion chamber, 245 pounds per square inch boiler pressure, 19 feet length over tube sheets, a Type E superheater and a Worthington feed water heater. Baker valve gear drove 14-inch piston valves, supplying 26-inch × 34-inch cylinders, powering 69-inch driving wheels. The 73,000-pound axle loading permitted 69,000 pounds of tractive effort. Although boosters were becoming less common in new construction, they were still being improved. These engines were fitted with boosters developing 14,000 pounds of tractive effort, making a remarkable total of 83,000 pounds from an eight-coupled engine. Tender capacity was increased to 30 tons of coal at the expense of water capacity reduced to 21,000 gallons.

A 2-8-4 for the Pittsburgh & Lake Erie marked the end of steam locomotive production at Alco Schenectady in June 1948.[72] Production of 2-8-4s totaled 750 since their introduction in 1925.

16.3.2 Ten-Coupled Locomotives

By 1930, the heyday of the 2-10-2 was long gone, outclassed by the new types of the 1920s. A few railroads continued to buy them for reasons of their own. Lima supplied four to the Chicago & Illinois Midland in 1931.[73] They developed 88,000 pounds of tractive effort, with the booster cut in, from a boiler pressure of 200 pounds per square inch. One hauled a 109-car train, weighing 10,829 tons, over the 17 miles from Cimic to Springfield in 52 minutes, including stopping and restarting the train once on the way. The last and biggest was supplied by Baldwin to the Reading the same year.[74] Total 2-10-2 procurement by U.S. Class I railroads was about 2,300.

The ultimate rigid-frame American freight locomotive was the 2-10-4. In the fall of 1930, the Chesapeake & Ohio began to take delivery of forty from Lima. Weighing 566,000 pounds with a 75,000-pound axle loading and developing 92,000 pounds of tractive effort (106,000 pounds with booster), they were the biggest and most powerful two-cylinder engines in the world at that time.[75]

Designed jointly by the company and Lima, they were built to haul 11,000-ton coal trains between Russell, Kentucky, and Toledo, Ohio. Hitherto, an H-7a single-expansion 2-8-8-2 hauled the trains from Russell to Columbus at which point they were broken up and hauled to Toledo by compound Mallets and 2-10-2s. In 1929, the company began to look for ways to haul a complete train over the whole 236 miles, running road tests with its own H-7a's and a 2-8-4 borrowed from the Erie. The 57-inch driving wheels on the 2-8-8-2s were too small, yet bigger driving wheels on the articulated design would not allow sufficient boiler capacity; the 2-8-4 was not powerful enough. The company therefore turned to the 2-10-4 wheel arrangement. Additionally, they wanted a tender tank big enough for the 110 miles between Russell and Columbus with only one water stop. The design investigations began in August 1929. The company placed an order

Otto Perry photographed this Chesapeake & Ohio Class T-1 2-10-4, No. 3025, built by Lima in 1930, near Chillicothe, Ohio, on August 16, 1933 (Denver Public Library, Otto C. Perry collection, OP-2972).

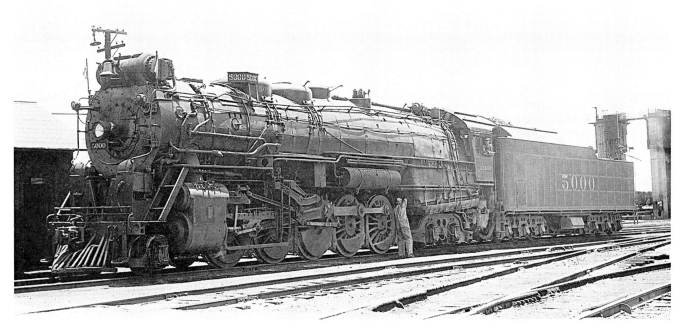

Baldwin built the Atchison, Topeka & Santa Fe's prototype 2-10-4, No. 5000, in 1930. Otto Perry photographed it at Raton, New Mexico, on June 29, 1935 (Denver Public Library, Otto C. Perry collection, OP-1067).

with Lima in January 1930; the first engine went into service that September.

The design called for a stoker-fired 122-square foot Firebar grate in a firebox with a combustion chamber and three siphons. This fired a 260-pounds per square inch boiler through 6,635 square feet of primary heating surface with a Type E superheater adding a further 3,030 square feet. The 2¼-inch fire tubes numbered only 59, most of the tube space being occupied by 275 3½-inch superheater flues. Steam went to the 29-inch × 34-inch cylinders through 14-inch piston valves driven by Baker valve gear with a Precision Type F power reverser and maximum 80% cut-off. Other up-to-date features were a Worthington feed water heater and tandem side rods. Driving wheels 69 inches in diameter provided the required speed. The tender held 30 tons of coal and 23,500 gallons of water, weighing 415,000 pounds when full. The cab was designed with an attention to crew comfort ("large and roomy cabs in which large, comfortable seats with flexible back rests are provided for the engineman and fireman. A comfortably cushioned seat is also provided for the head-end brakeman") that would astonish British enginemen when the first American 2-8-0s appeared in that country during World War II.

The Chesapeake & Ohio ran four dynamometer tests with the first new 2-10-4 as soon as they could, hauling 141 cars, weighing just under 11,000 tons, over the full route between Russell and Toledo. The 2-10-4 completed the run in about 13 hours at an average speed of 22 miles per hour, including eleven stops. The locomotive itself might be capable of sustained running but the enormous trains still had to be stopped and restarted numerous times due to other traffic. During the run, the engine burned 38 tons of coal; the enormous grate permitted an efficient firing rate of 71 pounds per square foot of grate per hour, resulting in a fuel efficiency of 3.8 pounds of coal per drawbar horsepower-hour. Fuel efficiency was less than startling, although the effectiveness of the new engines was beyond doubt. The boiler evaporated 6.8 pounds of water per pound of coal on average for a water efficiency of 23 pounds per drawbar horsepower-hour. While a large grate could bring the firing rate down to a level where combustion was efficient, it could not prevent a loss of evaporative efficiency with increasing firing rate. At 55 pounds of coal per square foot of grate per hour, evaporative efficiency was 7.8 pounds of water per pound of coal, declining to 6.5 pounds at 90 pounds per square foot per hour. The Type E superheater delivered steam at 765°F. Peak recorded power output was 4,775 indicated horsepower at 30 miles per hour and 50% cut-off. At that cut-off, back pressure was 12 to 14 pounds per square inch; the company expected to optimize the nozzle diameter by further testing. Total thermal efficiency at the drawbar was 6%. The new 2-10-4 saved 10% to 15% on all efficiency parameters, compared to an H-7a hauling the same tonnage over the same route.

While the 2-10-4 that the Santa Fe bought from Baldwin in December 1930, was slightly smaller than the Chesapeake & Ohio monsters, it still turned in economies of 15–17% over the 2-10-2s that it was intended to replace.[76]

The new locomotive featured a 121-square foot, stoker-fired, coal-burning table grate firing a 300-pounds per square inch boiler, 21 feet over tube sheets, with 6,150 square feet of primary heating surface, the Type E superheater providing a further 2,550 square feet. Two siphons were fitted to the firebox, one to the combustion chamber. Cylinders measuring 30 inches × 34 inches, limited to 60% cut-off (allowing the adhesion factor to be reduced to only 3.75), drove 69-inch driving wheels through tandem main rods, this combination producing 93,000 pounds of starting tractive effort. (The dimensions quoted in *Railway Age*, September 4, 1937, p. 312, and the standard tractive effort formula, $T = (0.85pD^2S)/W$, suggest a tractive effort of 113,000 pounds. The referenced source, however, gives 93,000 pounds, both for these engines and for the 1937-built Kansas City Southern engines, and cites the KCS engines as having the highest tractive force of any 2-10-4 built to date. This apparent discrepancy may result from differing factors used to calculate mean effective pressure). The company evidently felt that this was enough, as no booster was provided or contemplated. Power output peaked at 5,250 indicated horsepower at 40 miles per hour; drawbar horsepower peaked at 4,300 horsepower and 30 miles per hour. Total engine weight was 503,000 pounds with an axle loading of 70,000 pounds.

In one test eastbound over the 109 miles from Belen to Vaughn, this engine moved 6,000 tons, comprising the locomotive and 130 cars, at an average speed of 19.5 miles per hour. A helper was provided for the 40 miles of 1.25% grade from Belen to Mountainair but, otherwise, the locomotive handled the train alone against 0.6% grades. In a total running time just under 9 hours, it burned 28 tons of coal and evaporated 38,000 gallons of water.

In twelve tests in both directions between Clovis and Belen, the engine averaged an evaporation rate of 6.4 pounds of water per pound of coal. Even though 6,100 pounds of coal were burned per total hour

The Atchison, Topeka & Santa Fe bought ten of these 5001 class 2-10-4s from Baldwin when the economy improved in 1938. No. 5010 is shown at Trinidad, Colorado, on March 26, 1950 (Denver Public Library, Otto C. Perry collection, OP-1075).

Lima built this Kansas City Southern class J 2-10-4, No. 903, in 1937, shown at Pittsburg, Kansas, on September 5, 1937 (Denver Public Library, Otto C. Perry collection, OP-12393).

The Bessemer & Lake Erie acquired forty-seven class H-1 2-10-4s from Baldwin in seven batches between 1929 and 1944. No. 605 is shown at Shenango, Pennsylvania, on September 30, 1930. The photograph date indicates that this locomotive is from the first batch; current research has not revealed what changes in dimensions or appearance took place in later batches (Denver Public Library, Otto C. Perry collection, OP-2638).

Otto Perry photographed this Bessemer & Lake Erie class H-1 2-10-4, No. 623, near Hewitts, Pennsylvania, on August 9, 1937, at the head of a 115-car train (Denver Public Library, Otto C. Perry collection, OP-2639).

Otto Perry stayed to photograph these two Bessemer & Lake Erie class D1A 2-10-2s, Nos. 520 and 514, built by Baldwin in 1916, pushing on the same 115-car train shown in the previous photograph. Both locomotives have water tank cars to extend range. The caboose comes last of all to avoid the risk of being crushed by the pushers in the event of a derailment or sudden stop (Denver Public Library, Otto C. Perry collection, OP-2640).

en route, the enormous grate kept firing rates down to 58 pounds per square foot of grate per hour and cinder losses to 14% of coal fired. As a result, the boiler, Type E superheater and Elesco feed water heater evaporated 8.6 pounds of water per square foot of heating surface per hour, while specific consumptions were 24.3 pounds of water and 3.8 pounds of coal per drawbar horsepower-hour. The final consumption was only 66 pounds of coal per 1,000 gross ton-miles. Total thermal efficiency at the drawbar was still only 5%.

No. 5000 remained the only one of its class until the company dusted off the design when economic conditions improved in the late 1930s, receiving ten more even bigger 2-10-4s from Baldwin in 1938.[77] Of these, five were coal-burners, five were oil-burners with 310-pound steam pressure, 74-inch driving wheels and 42,000 pounds more engine weight, followed by twenty-five more—all oil-burners—in 1944. The engines built in 1938 featured an engine bed weighing 84,520 pounds from General Steel Castings, the heaviest yet produced. They remained in service until 1959.

In spite of the colossal effort devoted to improving the efficiency of the steam locomotive, the figures for evaporation per pound of coal and square foot of heating surface and coal and water consumption per horsepower-hour show a depressing similarity to those obtained forty years previously. In that time the steam locomotive improved enormously in effectiveness, but little in efficiency. The real advances were in coal consumption per ton-mile and ton-miles per train hour; the steam locomotive had gained vastly in transportation effectiveness, but little in either mechanical or thermal efficiency.

Already the heaviest and most powerful rigid-frame locomotives in the world, the 2-10-4 type continued to develop during the 1930s. Given that there were practical limits to the useful length of firebox, combustion chamber, tubes and smokebox, some of the Mallet wheel arrangements must have left their designers wondering how best to occupy the available length above a long total wheelbase. The 2-10-4 wheel arrangement allowed a generous, but not excessive, total length for the various boiler components.

The Kansas City Southern used 310 pounds per square inch boiler pressure in the ten—five oil-burners, five coal-burners—that it bought from Lima in 1937.[78] These engines were built around cast steel engine beds and fitted with Boxpok driving wheels and tandem main rods. To provide the necessary three-point suspension, the suspension of the first three pairs of driving wheels was cross-equalized and linked to that of the leading truck. The suspension of the last two pairs was equalized separately on each side with the trailing truck. Braking for these massive engines was provided by five 12-inch × 10-inch compressed-air cylinders, two side by side operating the brakes on the first and second driving wheel pairs, while single cylinders applied the brakes to the third, fourth and fifth driving wheel pairs. The trucks were also fully braked.

Although the Bessemer & Lake Erie with its iron ore traffic was an obvious potential Mallet user, the company chose the relative simplicity of rigid-frame engines running on some of the heaviest track in America—130-pound rail being introduced in 1917, 152-pound in 1939 and 155-pound in 1948—receiving its first 2-10-4s in 1927, followed by forty-seven more between then and 1944.

The ten that Alco built in 1937 were of conservative design, with 73,000-pound axle loading to run on 130-pound rail.[79] Unusually for North America, the locomotives were built around plate frames, flame-cut from rolled steel and supplied by Carnegie-Illinois Steel. The firebox contained a 107-square foot grate, a brick arch supported on two siphons and three arch tubes and a 50-inch combustion chamber. An Elesco exhaust-steam injector supplied feed water to the

The Pennsylvania built this class J-1 2-10-4, No. 6160, at Altoona in 1943–4. The location and date of this photograph are unknown (courtesy California State Railroad Museum, Sacramento, California, Negative 900_28295).

boiler, 21½ feet over tube sheets, containing 5,900 square feet of evaporative surface and 2,400 square feet of superheating surface in the Type E superheater, producing steam at 250 pounds per square inch. Two 31-inch × 32-inch cylinders, supplied with steam through 15-inch piston valves, driven by Walschaert valve gear with power reverse, drove 64-inch driving wheels to produce 97,000 pounds of tractive effort which the trailing truck booster increased to 110,000 pounds. The main driving wheels, only, were of the Baldwin disc type, the others being of conventional, spoked design. The tender carried 26 tons of coal and 23,000 gallons of water.

The last 2-10-4s to be built were also the most numerous—the 125 built by the Pennsylvania in 1942–4, based on a Chicago, Burlington & Quincy design. Procurement of 2-10-4s by U.S. Class I railroads totaled 450 between 1925 and 1945.

16.3.3 Mallets

By 1930, the Baltimore & Ohio was running heavy freight tonnage over several districts where bridges limited the size of locomotive to heavy 2-8-0s and light 2-8-2s, often double-heading.[80] The company had plenty of Mallets, heavy 2-8-2s, 4-8-2s and 2-10-2s, but could not use them on these routes. Rebuilding bridges to accept heavier power was costly in time and money; accordingly the company looked for new types of locomotive. In 1930–1, they took delivery of four experimental engines from Baldwin: two 4-8-2s and two 2-6-6-2s, all single-expansion. Of each type, one had an Emerson water-tube firebox; one had a conventional firebox with siphons; the Emerson firebox provided 82% more heating surface than the conventional fireboxes. Boiler pressures were 250 pounds per square inch in all four engines. The company intended the 4-8-2s for passenger service, the 2-6-6-2s for fast freight, expecting that the 2-6-6-2s would provide better performance and economy than the heavy 2-8-2s and 2-10-2s on routes where these could be used. In spite of favorable results from the first road tests, further orders did not follow, probably because of the deteriorating economy. The conventional-firebox 4-8-2 was refitted with an Emerson firebox in 1931. The Emerson-firebox 2-6-6-2 was rebuilt as a 4-4-6-2 that same year, but was rebuilt back to its original wheel arrangement in 1933.

New construction continued into 1931 as railroads refused to believe in the permanency of the depression. That summer the Western Pacific put six single-expansion 2-8-8-2s into service, built by Baldwin.[81] Although the Western Pacific's competitive advantage over the Southern Pacific between San Francisco and Salt Lake City lay in its highest elevation being 2,000 feet lower than the Southern Pacific, this was achieved at a cost of 150 more route miles with steep grades and incessant sharp curves for 116 miles through the Feather River Canyon between Oroville, California, and Portola. Until 1931, company strategy was to run heavy freight trains through the canyon, accepting the cost of double-heading with two 2-6-6-2s, built by Alco in 1917–24, one 2-6-6-2 and one 2-8-2 (Alco and Baldwin, 1919–29), or a combination of 2-6-6-2s and ancient 2-8-0s, the most recent of which were built in 1909. The new engines were to replace these combinations with a single locomotive.

The result was gigantic. With 235 pounds per square inch boiler pressure and Type A superheaters, the new engines were of conservative design in everything except size. The oil-burning grate measured 145 square feet with 6 feet of combustion chamber ahead of the firebox. The boiler measured 23 feet over tube sheets; its 102-inch diameter made space for 272 2½-inch fire tubes and 75 5½-inch flues for 6,140 square feet of primary heating surface with another 740 square feet provided by the firebox, combustion chamber and siphons and 2,150 square feet of superheating surface, a total of 9,030 square feet. This enormous heating surface enabled the boiler to supply steam to four 26-inch × 32-inch cylinders, limited to 85% maximum cut-off. Driving wheels 63 inches in diameter and careful counterbalancing made it possible for the engine to equal the speeds of the 2-8-2s and outpace the 2-6-6-2s. Even though the engines were articulated, their four-axle rigid wheelbases were still long for the curves they were required to negotiate; Franklin lateral-motion driving boxes were fitted on the rear driving wheels of the front unit and the front driving wheels of the rear unit. This combination, plus axle loadings of 69,000 pounds and an engine weight of 665,000 pounds, produced 137,000 pounds of starting tractive effort, augmented by 14,000 pounds from a Franklin trailing truck booster that cut out automatically as soon as the engineer shortened the cut-off. This tractive effort equaled that of any two of the engines that the 2-8-8-2s were intended to replace. When the U.S. economy began

The Baltimore & Ohio's experimental class KK-1 2-6-6-2, No. 7400, while temporarily rebuilt to a 4-4-6-2 wheel arrangement. The photograph must date from 1931–32 (courtesy California State Railroad Museum, Railway & Locomotive Historical Society Collection, Negative 39071cn).

Baldwin built this Western Pacific class M-137-151 2-8-8-2 in 1931. No. 256 is shown at Oroville, California, on August 2, 1935 (Denver Public Library, Otto C. Perry collection, OP-20016).

The Norfolk & Western built this class A 2-6-6-4, No. 1201, in company shops in 1936, shown at Roanoke, Virginia, on August 4, 1936 (Denver Public Library, Otto C. Perry collection, OP-13799).

to recover, the Western Pacific bought four more from Baldwin in 1938.

One of the more obscure American railroads was the 138-mile Pittsburgh & West Virginia, hauling coal from mines in Pennsylvania and West Virginia to Pittsburgh and the west. The Pittsburgh & West Virginia faced the usual Appalachian coalfield operating conditions, hauling heavy coal trains over steep grades and sharp curves. In the early 1930s, twenty-two 2-8-0s and three 2-8-2s handled this traffic. The 2-8-0s dated from 1907 and 1921, the three 2-8-2s from 1918. Both types developed 54,000 to 59,000 pounds of tractive effort. In 1934, the company bought three single-expansion locomotives with Mallet-type articulation from Baldwin of a new, 2-6-6-4, wheel arrangement, mainly to tackle the 111 miles between Connellsville, Pennsylvania, and Pittsburgh.[82]

Though large, the design was conservative. Baldwin used a four-wheel truck to support a 102-square foot grate inside a Belpaire firebox with a 72-inch combustion chamber and a brick arch supported on five arch tubes, but no siphons. The boiler contained 5,915 square feet of primary heating surface and 1,875 square feet of superheating surface in a Type A superheater, generating steam at 225 pounds per square inch and powering four 23-inch × 32-inch cylinders driving 63-inch wheels. No feed water heater was applied. Baldwin Type C power reversing gear controlled Walschaert valve gear, driving 12-inch piston valves. This combination produced 98,000 pounds of tractive effort, augmented by 16,000 pounds from a six-wheel auxiliary locomotive in place of the rear tender truck. Total engine weight was 528,000 pounds, designed with an axle loading limited to 66,000 pounds. Clearances were generous at 16 feet 2 inches over stack and 11 feet 4 inches extreme width. By 1934, a 2-10-4 could have provided the same tractive effort, but the 2-6-6-4 wheel arrangement provided one extra driving axle, better weight distribution and greater flexibility on curves with a maximum rigid wheel base of only 11 feet.

The Pittsburgh & West Virginia order for 2-6-6-4s was soon followed by another, for five locomotives, from the Seaboard Air Line.[83] Lighter than the Pittsburgh & West Virginia engines at 480,000

pounds and developing 82,000 pounds of tractive effort with no booster, these engines were intended initially for fast freight service with the possibility of fast passenger service as well.

The welded firebox contained 96 square feet of Firebar grates, two siphons and two arch tubes supporting the brick arch, and a 72-inch combustion chamber with a third siphon. The boiler, 24 feet over tube sheets, contained forty-four 2¼-inch tubes and two hundred 3½-inch flues for the Type E superheater, providing 5,515 square feet of primary heating surface (including 515 square feet for the firebox) and 2,400 square feet of superheating surface, generating steam at 230 pounds per square inch. Four locomotives had Elesco feed water heaters; one had a Worthington type. An Alco power reverser controlled Baker valve gear driving 12-inch piston valves. Four single-expansion cylinders, 22 inches × 30 inches, powered 69-inch driving wheels with an axle loading of 55,000 pounds. Baldwin supplied five more of these engines in 1937, all with Worthington feed water heaters and Walschaert valve gear.

The new locomotives went into fast freight service between Richmond, Virginia, and Raleigh, North Carolina, hauling 50% more tonnage than the 4-8-2s that they replaced. These engines were:

> unusual in that they are designed for high-speed handling of heavy freight trains, a class of service for which the articulated type has not heretofore been considered suitable in this country.

The company sold them to the Baltimore & Ohio when it dieselized in 1947.

In May 1936, one of the ultimate developments of American steam power rolled out of the Norfolk & Western shops at Roanoke.[84] This was the first class A 2-6-6-4; forty-two more would follow between then and 1950, all from the Roanoke shops. Everything about these engines was gigantic. The electrically welded firebox contained a 122-square foot grate with a combustion chamber extending 9¾ feet ahead of the throat sheet, providing 587 square feet of heating surface, including five 3½-inch arch tubes, and secured by 4,925 staybolts; no siphons were installed. The boiler was the longest and heaviest

The Norfolk & Western built this class Y-6 2-8-8-2. Thirty-five Y-6's came from the company's shops between 1936 and 1940. Otto Perry photographed No. 2128 at Hagerstown, Maryland, on August 24, 1938 (Denver Public Library, Otto C. Perry collection, OP-13823).

ever applied to a Norfolk & Western locomotive, 148,500 pounds empty, containing 8,100 gallons of water. Clearance limits restricted the maximum diameter to just under 9 feet; the available length between combustion chamber and smokebox was 24 feet over tube sheets. Fifty-seven 2¼-inch fire tubes and 239 3½-inch flues for the Type E superheater provided 6,065 square feet of primary heating surface with an additional 2,700 square feet of superheating surface. The boiler was built for 300 pounds per square inch pressure, but the four safety valves were set to open at 275 pounds. A 12,000-gallon per hour Worthington feed water heater and a 10,000-gallon per hour injector supplied water to the boiler. Four 24-inch × 30-inch single-expansion cylinders, supplied with steam through 12-inch piston valves driven by Baker valve gear, limited to 75% cut-off, drove 70-inch wheels for a rated tractive effort of 105,000 pounds. No booster was installed. All wheels had Timken roller bearings. The drive units were built around two engine beds with a combined weight of 141,000 pounds, replacing more than seven hundred parts in a conventional pair of engine frames. Total engine weight was 570,000 pounds. The tender held 26 tons of coal and 22,000 gallons of water with a loaded weight of 379,000 pounds.

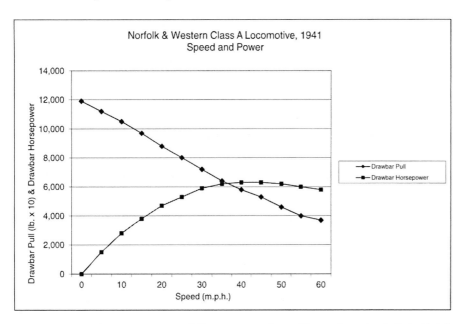

Speed and power characteristics, Norfolk & Western Class A (figures from Pond, C. E., *Freight Motive Power on the Norfolk & Western, RA*, July 5, 1941, 26).

Road tests included handling 4,800 tons at 25 miles per hour against a 0.5% grade and 7,500 tons at 64 miles per hour on straight, level track. Drawbar power output peaked at 6,300 horsepower at 40 to 45 miles per hour, developing more than 6,000 horsepower between 30 and 60 miles per hour. At this power output the stoker threw coal into the firebox at the rate of 7 tons an hour, 115 pounds per square foot of grate per hour, resulting in an evaporation rate of 116,000 pounds of water per hour. By 1941, the class A's were averaging 8,540 miles per month.

The same year as the first class A, Roanoke shops built their first class Y-6 2-8-8-2. Whereas the class A was a single-expansion locomotive with Mallet-type articulation, intended for speed in both passenger and freight service, the Y-6 was a traditional compound Mallet. Although heavier than the A at 583,000 pounds engine weight, the grate area and heating surface were smaller—106 square feet of grate, 5,655 square feet of primary heating surface and 1,775 square feet

superheating surface—as were the 57-inch driving wheels. Boiler pressure at 300 pounds per square inch supplied 39-inch and 25-inch × 32-inch cylinders to produce 152,000 pounds of tractive effort single-expansion, 127,000 pounds compound. (These figures are from the quoted reference. The ARMMA 1923 formula gives 179,000 pounds single-expansion, 127,000 pounds compound, from these dimensions.) The ultimate Y-6 development—the Y-6b of 1950–2—would produce 170,000 pounds of tractive effort single-expansion, 132,000 pounds compound with a maximum power output of 5,600 drawbar horsepower at 25 miles per hour. The last ran in 1960.

The A's and the Y-6's were so successful that the Norfolk & Western upgraded nineteen of their twenty Y-5 2-8-8-2s, built in 1930–2, in 1940–1 (one having been wrecked) with engine beds, roller bearings and mechanical lubrication.

The Norfolk & Western moved 45 million tons of coal in 1940—excluding coal hauled for its own use. In 1925, 653 Norfolk & Western road engines handled 27 billion freight ton-miles. In 1940, 347 road engines handled 30 billion ton-miles, an increase of 80% in ton-miles per train-hour. Behind this improvement were ten Y-3b/Y-4 2-8-8-2s built by Alco Richmond in 1927, twenty Y-4a/Y-5 2-8-8-2s built at Roanoke in 1930–2, thirty-five Y-6 2-8-8-2s built at Roanoke in 1936–40 and ten A 2-6-6-4s, built at Roanoke in 1936–7—in all, seventy-five new engines. The backbone of Norfolk & Western motive power, however, remained the 190 Z-1 and Z-1a 2-6-6-2 compound Mallets built between 1912 and 1918; although scrapping of these engines began in 1934, the last survived until 1958. The even older 212 2-8-0s, built between 1901 and 1905, still played their part, although scrapping began in 1926; the last survived until 1952.

The new engines had an effect on operating economics out of proportion to their numbers. Norfolk & Western coal consumption per thousand gross ton-miles decreased 39% from 147 pounds in 1925 to 89 in 1940. Design for reliability, and improved maintenance practices, resulted in an 80% decrease in freight engine failures on the road. At the same time the cost of repairs declined by 32%.

The Union Pacific main line between Cheyenne, Wyoming, and Ogden, Utah, was always a focal point of the company's motive power development. By the mid–1930s, the company wanted more power at higher speeds on this route than the existing 2-10-2s, 2-8-8-0s, 2-8-8-2s and 4-12-2s could produce. Some of these engines dated back to 1917; the 4-12-2s built in 1930 were the newest.[85]

Consultation between Union Pacific and Alco staff produced a locomotive with a 4-6-6-4 wheel arrangement, Mallet-type articulation and four equally-sized, single-expansion cylinders. The new design was conservative in many respects. The drive units were built on conventional bar frames, although the front frame was built around a "backbone casting," providing superior rigidity against loosening of the bolted joints. The firebox comprised 108 square feet of Firebar grates with a Gaines wall, a brick arch supported on five 4-inch arch tubes and no siphons. The throat sheet was 5¾ feet ahead of the Gaines wall, with an 86-inch combustion chamber ahead of the throat sheet. The boiler contained 5,380 square feet of primary evaporating surface with 1,650 square feet of superheating surface in

Union Pacific class CSA-1 4-6-6-4, No. 3900, built by Alco in 1936, was the first Challenger, shown at Green River, Wyoming, on November 15, 1936 (Denver Public Library, Otto C. Perry collection, OP-17010).

This class C-2 2-8-0, No. 619, built by Alco in 1908, was one of the Union Pacific's huge fleet of Consolidations, still in service when photographed at Banks, Idaho, on September 20, 1941 (courtesy *Classic Trains* magazine collection, 20120907).

This Northern Pacific class Z-6 4-6-6-4, No. 5102, was one of twenty-one built by Alco in 1936–37, shown at Livingston, Montana, on June 26, 1937 (Denver Public Library, Otto C. Perry collection, OP-14042).

This Denver & Rio Grande Western class L-105 4-6-6-4, No. 3700, was Baldwin's first Challenger, built in 1938, shown at Denver, Colorado, on April 2, 1938 (Denver Public Library, Otto C. Perry collection, OP-9930).

the Type A superheater. Ten engines were equipped with Worthington feed water heaters, the remainder with Sellers exhaust-steam injectors. A boiler pressure of 255 pounds per square inch, working through four 22-inch × 32-inch cylinders on 69-inch Boxpok driving wheels, produced 97,000 pounds of tractive effort with no booster for an engine weight of 566,000 pounds.

The 4-6-6-4 design sprang from the strengths and weaknesses of the 4-12-2s. The grate area was the same, although the bigger, and extensively welded, firebox provided more combustion volume and was supported on a four-wheel truck. Compared to the 4-12-2s, the boiler carried 15% higher pressure but contained 17% less total heating surface and supplied an 11% smaller cylinder volume, producing the same tractive effort through bigger driving wheels, which allowed higher speeds. Dividing the weight of the 4-12-2s' reciprocating parts between two drive units made for more effective counterbalancing and lower dynamic augment. The 4-12-2s' rigid wheel base was already excessive and would have been made even more so by bigger driving wheels, hence the division of the six driving axles into two units. The four outside cylinders eliminated the 4-12-2s' crank axle and the conjugate valve gear. Smooth riding reduced track damage and wear and tear to frames and running gear—a subtle benefit of the Mallet configuration that Anatole Mallet probably never foresaw. The 4-12-2s used the low adhesion factor of 3.5 with a 59,000-pound axle loading; the 4-6-6-4s reverted to the conventional adhesion factor of 4.0 while accepting a 64,000-pound axle loading. Counterbalancing and oscillation damping gave the new engines stability at high speeds.

Impressive though they were, the fifteen Challengers—as the new locomotives were called—were but a tiny fraction of the freight locomotives at work on the vast Union Pacific system. The company's heaviest freight power still consisted of seventy 2-8-8-0 Mallets, built between 1918 and 1923, forty-four 2-8-8-2s, built between 1909 and 1926, 185 2-10-2s, built between 1917 and 1924 and the eighty-nine 4-12-2s, built between 1926 and 1930. Even these were greatly outnumbered by 482 2-8-0s, built between 1900 and 1909, mostly by Baldwin, and 397 2-8-2s, built by Baldwin, Alco and Lima between 1910 and 1921; many of these were still active at the end of Union Pacific steam operations in the early 1960s.

The Challengers were a landmark in American motive power development, offering high power at high speed.[86] The original fifteen were so successful that the company bought another twenty-five in 1937, followed by a further sixty-five in 1942–4, all from Alco, some continuing in service until 1961. Several other railroads took up this design: the Northern Pacific (27), the Denver & Rio Grande Western (10) and the Western Pacific (7). The Union Pacific has preserved one in working order.

The Northern Pacific followed the Union Pacific to the Alco order desk with an order for twelve 4-6-6-4s, delivered at the end of 1936.[87] As the Union Pacific sought to overcome the limitations of the 4-12-2s, the Northern Pacific intended its engines to overcome the speed and power deficiencies of its disappointing 2-8-8-4s. At an engine weight of 625,000 pounds, the new engines were bigger than the Union Pacific engines, but smaller than the 2-8-8-4s. Although the area of the lignite-burning grate was still huge, at 152 square feet, it was a retreat from the 182 square feet of the Yellowstones. The Northern Pacific specified its own design of table grate for burning lignite. A Gaines wall was built at the front of the grate; the firebox extended a further 54 inches to the throat sheet with an 89-inch combustion chamber ahead of that, providing 625 square feet of firebox heating surface. Three siphons supported the brick arch. Boiler pressure was the same at 250 pounds per square inch but with 24% less heating surface; curiously, the new engines had Type A superheaters

Southern Pacific class AC-6 4-8-8-2, No. 4144, built by Baldwin in 1930 and photographed at Dunsmuir, California, on July 25, 1938 (Denver Public Library, Otto C. Perry collection, OP-15678).

Southern Pacific class AC-8 4-8-8-2, No. 4190, built by Baldwin in 1939, is shown at Los Angeles, California, on August 2, 1940 (Denver Public Library, Otto C. Perry collection, OP-15936).

rather than the Type E applied to the Yellowstones. Even so, the heating surface was still enormous, at 5,830 square feet of primary evaporating surface and a further 2,110 square feet of superheating surface. Cylinder bore was reduced from 26 inches to 23 inches for 22% less cylinder volume, while the driving wheel diameter was increased from 63 inches to 69. Rated tractive effort was 105,000 pounds with no booster. The drive units were built around bar frames but Alco produced a front frame design differing from that used in the Union Pacific engines. Instead of a single backbone casting, the front frame was stiffened by three box castings bolted to each other and to the frames. Tender capacity was 27 tons of coal and 20,000 gallons of water. The first batch of twelve was followed by another nine in 1937 and a further twenty-six, all from Alco, the last being built in 1944.

Baldwin produced their first 4-6-6-4s with an order for ten from the Denver & Rio Grande Western, delivered in 1938.[88] That company's operations in the mountains of Colorado are a saga in themselves, moving a heavy freight traffic over sharp curves and grades as steep as 3%, not to mention the difficulties and hazards of winter snow. The company wanted these engines to speed up freight service between Grand Junction, Colorado, and Salt Lake City.

The locomotive was built around two engine beds, the rear engine bed accommodating the main and auxiliary compressed-air reservoirs. Le Chatelier brakes augmented the engine air brakes. A 137-square foot Rosebud pinhole table grate fired a boiler, 22 feet over tube sheets, generating steam at 255 pounds per square inch from 6,340 square feet of evaporative surface and 2,625 square feet of superheating surface in the Type E superheater. A Gaines wall was built 42 inches behind the throat sheet, with a 110-inch combustion chamber ahead of the throat sheet. Nine locomotives had Elesco feed water heaters; one had a Worthington heater. Additionally, feed water was supplied by a Hancock injector at up to 12,000 gallons per hour.

The sixty-one 2¼-inch fire tubes and 238 3½-inch flue tubes were the most that could be accommodated within the permissible boiler diameter. Four 23-inch × 32-inch cylinders drove 70-inch wheels for 105,000 pounds of tractive effort with an axle loading of 73,000 pounds. Total engine weight was 642,000 pounds with another 394,000 pounds in the tender which carried the—by then—normal load of 26 tons of coal and 20,000 gallons of water for a combined weight of engine and tender just over 500 tons.

Each drive unit had its own Baldwin Type C power reverser controlling the Walschaert valve gear, driving 14-inch piston valves. The reversing gear shaft also drove a reach rod connected to a bell crank, which raised and lowered a block fixed to the front end of the radius rod. This block moved up and down in a slide in the upper end of the combination lever, thereby varying its effective length. This had the effect of automatically increasing lead from zero in full gear to ⅜ inch at 25% cut off. This device had been applied to fourteen 4-8-4s built by Baldwin for the company in 1929 and must have worked well enough to be built into the new 4-6-6-4s. The company bought five more of these engines from Baldwin in 1942. They continued in service until 1956.

As befitted its territory, the Southern Pacific had a long history of operating Mallet-type articulated locomotives.[89] First was a succession of oil-burning 2-8-8-2 compounds built by Baldwin between 1909 and 1913, totaling forty-nine; all except the first two were cab-forwards. The Southern Pacific converted many of these to single expansion between 1928 and 1931. A class of twelve 2-6-6-2s, built in 1911, was likewise converted to single expansion in the late 1920s and 1930s as well as being fitted with four-wheel leading trucks. The next batch of articulated locomotives was ordered from the outset with four-wheel leading trucks and single expansion, a batch of ten 4-8-8-2s bought from Baldwin in 1928, followed by another forty-

The Southern Pacific bought these class AC-9 coal-burning 2-8-8-4s from Lima in 1939. No. 3809 is shown at Tucumcari, New Mexico, on February 25, 1940 (Denver Public Library, Otto C. Perry collection, OP-15647).

one in 1929–30, fifty-four in 1937–9 as traffic resumed and a further ninety under wartime pressure between 1942 and 1944, all from Baldwin. The cab-forward arrangement made it necessary that these were oil-burners.

The Southern Pacific's Shasta division offered grades, curvature and adverse weather as severe as any on the continent.[90] This route took on a strategic importance during the war. While an unaided 4-8-8-2 could handle 7,000 tons between Grass Lake and Klamath Falls, the grades were so severe between Dunsmuir and Black Butte that it could handle only 1,500 tons. The company stationed a fleet of 2-10-2 helpers so that trains of 4,000 to 5,000 tons could be worked through the division. Between Dunsmuir and Black Butte four or five locomotives were needed on each train.

In 1939, the company bought twelve single-expansion 2-8-8-4s of conventional layout from Lima, designed to burn low-grade bituminous coal mined in New Mexico.[91] The company put them to haul fast, heavy passenger and freight trains over the 332 miles between El Paso and Tucumcari, New Mexico, with sharp curves and long grades up to 1%. Designed for speeds up to 75 miles per hour, the AC-9's were air-smoothed, with pipework concealed and a cowling along the top of the boiler. Each drive unit was built around an engine bed incorporating the cylinders. The firebox contained seven Security circulators. A combustion chamber extended 59 inches ahead of the throat sheet with six drop plugs in its crown sheet—but apparently none in the crown sheet of the firebox itself. A monstrous 139-square foot Firebar grate fired a boiler 22 feet over tube sheets containing 6,920 square feet of evaporative surface and another 2,830 square feet of superheating surface in the Type E superheater, generating steam at 250 pounds per square inch. An injector and a Hancock Turbo-Injector with a capacity of 13,000 gallons per hour supplied water to the boiler. The exhaust-steam injector was gradually

gaining in popularity against Elesco and Worthington feed water heaters at this time.

The steam piping in a single-expansion, Mallet-articulated locomotive was marginally simpler than in a compound Mallet, but the problem of articulating the steam pipes remained and all had to carry high-pressure steam. In the AC-9's, two insulated 9-inch pipes conveyed steam from the superheater header along each side of the locomotive to a slip-joint at the front of the rear cylinders; thence, a single insulated 8-inch pipe with ball- and slip-joints conveyed steam to the front cylinders. Twin 8-inch slip-jointed pipes conveyed exhaust steam from the rear cylinders to the smokebox with a bleed to the exhaust-steam injector; ball- and slip-jointed pipes conveyed exhaust steam from the front cylinders to the smokebox. Walschaert valve gear drove 11-inch piston valves with the very short travel of 6½ inches. Four 24-inch × 32-inch cylinders and 64-inch Boxpok driving wheels produced 124,000 pounds of tractive effort, while power output reached 6,000 indicated horsepower at 40 miles per hour. Braking downgrade was as important as power upgrade; Lima fitted a Southern Pacific-designed system to spray cooling water onto the driving and tender wheels when the brakes were applied. Total engine weight was 690,000 pounds with another 401,000 pounds in a tender holding 28 tons of coal and 22,000 gallons of water. These twelve locomotives apparently occupied a niche in Southern Pacific requirements; no further orders followed. The SP converted them to burn oil in 1950 and scrapped them between 1953 and 1956.

The Delaware & Hudson had a curious history of locomotive procurement. A small railroad in Pennsylvania, it was symbiotic with the mining and sale of anthracite.[92] Heavy coal traffic over steep grades and sharp curves made it an obvious Mallet user, but such was not the case. Core of its locomotive fleet were 282 2-8-0s built by Dickson, Alco Schenectady and company shops in progressively more

Alco built forty of these Class J 4-6-6-4s for the Delaware & Hudson between 1940 and 1946. The location and date of this photograph are unknown (courtesy California State Railroad Museum, Negative 900_36670).

powerful batches between 1900 and 1930, and possibly others built before 1900. Seen in this light, the three high-pressure 2-8-0 compounds, *Horatio Allen, John B. Jervis* and *James Archbald* were logical attempts to develop the company's favorite wheel arrangement. Sixty 4-6-0s and ten 4-6-2s handled the company's limited passenger traffic. Mallets, 2-8-2s, 2-10-2s and superpower passed the company by, except for thirteen 0-8-8-0 pushers, bought in 1910. The company bought exclusively from Alco, except for the few engines that it built in its own shops.

During the 1930s, the company handled an increasing tonnage of freight as a connector between Wilkes-Barre, Pennsylvania, and Binghamton and Mechanicsville, New York. The 2-8-0s were completely unsatisfactory for this service in the conditions of the late 1930s and early 1940s; the trains needed two and sometimes three locomotives which, even so, were speed-limited by their counterbalancing and small driving wheels. In hindsight, the substantial effort that the Delaware & Hudson devoted to high-pressure, eight-coupled engines was misdirected. In 1940, the company suddenly bought twenty single-expansion 4-6-6-4s from Alco, followed by twenty more over the next six years. Boiler pressures of 285 pounds per square inch, applied to quite small 20½-inch cylinders and 69-inch Boxpok driving wheels, produced 94,000 pounds of tractive effort. Axle loading was limited to 68,000 pounds.

Even though the railroad ran through the heart of the anthracite country, the 108-square foot Firebar grate was designed to burn bituminous coal; slow-burning anthracite would have required an impractical grate area to generate adequate power. Five 4-inch arch tubes supported the brick arch with a Gaines wall at its front end. A Hancock 10,000-gallon per hour injector and an Elesco 12,000-gallon per hour exhaust-steam injector supplied water to the boiler. The company chose a Type A superheater.

Even though the Americans had been building Mallets for thirty-

five years, the design was still being refined. Two problems, accentuated by high speed and power output, were a pitching oscillation of the front drive unit and a loss of adhesion weight at the front drive unit when the locomotive was climbing a grade stack-first, due to lowering of the water level in the front of the boiler. To solve these problems, for the D & H order, Alco supported the front of the boiler on the articulation hinge as well as on the usual boiler support bearing. They also transferred 2½ tons of engine weight from the rear to the front drive unit. Both drive units were built around engine beds incorporating the cylinders and steam chests.

In 1941, the Western Maryland bought twelve 4-6-6-4s from Baldwin to replace twenty Baldwin 2-10-0s, built in 1927, on the 171 miles between Hagerstown, Maryland, and Connellsville, Pennsylvania, including 23 miles of 1.75% grade west of Cumberland.[93] The 2-10-0s, with 240 pounds per square inch boiler pressure, developed 96,000 pounds of tractive effort at the expense of heavy axle loading and low maximum speeds. Although the new 4-6-6-4s developed the same tractive effort, they were capable of hauling greater tonnage at higher speeds and were intended to operate straight through from Hagerstown to Connellsville, whereas the 2-10-0s had to split the division at Cumberland.

The firebox was gigantic, 17¾ feet long inside the foundation ring; a Gaines wall was built 4¼ feet behind the throat sheet, providing a grate 13½ feet long with 119 square feet of Hulson tuyere grates. A combustion chamber extended 8 feet ahead of the throat sheet, for a total length of 25¾ feet behind the back tube sheet, longer than the fire tubes which measured 23 feet over tube sheets. Five siphons were built into the firebox, three in the firebox itself, two in the combustion chamber. Each firebox siphon had two inlets; the two outer siphons connected through the throat and side sheets; the middle siphon connected through the throat sheet and the bottom of the combustion chamber. The firebox and combustion chamber were of

Western Maryland class M-2 4-6-6-4, No. 1203, built by Baldwin in 1941–22. The location and date of the photograph are unknown (courtesy *Classic Trains* magazine collection, 20110816).

Union Pacific class 4884-1 4-8-8-4, No. 4008, built by Alco in 1941, at Green River, Wyoming, on November 30, 1941 (Denver Public Library, Otto C. Perry collection, OP-17070).

welded construction. A 14,000-gallon per hour Worthington feed water heater and an 11,000-gallon per hour injector supplied boiler feed water. Two hundred twenty-two 2¼-inch fire tubes and sixty 5½-inch flues provided 5,770 square feet of evaporative surface with another 1,735 square feet in the Type A superheater. A boiler pressure of 250 pounds per square inch, four 22-inch × 32-inch cylinders and 69-inch driving wheels provided 96,000 pounds of tractive effort for an axle loading of 67,000 pounds and a total engine weight of 601,000 pounds.

The Union Pacific needed a still more powerful locomotive than the Challengers, specifically to maintain fast schedules with heavy tonnage and no helper service against a ruling grade of 1.14% between Ogden, Utah, and Green River, Wyoming. Accordingly, the company developed a design in cooperation with Alco that would become the legendary 4-8-8-4 *Big Boy*—at 762,000 pounds the heaviest single-expansion steam locomotive ever built. The first of twenty-five came out of Alco's shops in 1941.[94]

The heaviest steam locomotives ever built were the last two Erie 2-8-8-8-2 triplex Mallets of 1916 at 860,000 pounds. This, however, included weight that would have been a separate tender in other locomotives, leaving the Big Boy as the heaviest reciprocating steam locomotive ever built. The highest-ever tractive effort from a reciprocating steam locomotive was the 177,000 pounds exerted by the Virginian 2-10-10-2 Mallets working single-expansion. They weighed 684,000 pounds, engine only. The Norfolk & Western 1954 steam-turbine *Jawn Henry* weighed 818,000 pounds—including an on-board coal bunker—and developed 199,000 pounds of tractive effort.

The design of this enormous and complicated machine for smooth running at high speeds was a major exercise in itself. All locomotives tended to slam from side to side within the track gauge, following curves by a series of impacts between the flanges and the outer rail; Mallet-articulated locomotives were additionally liable to pitching and yawing oscillations of the front drive unit. The Big Boy drive units were built around engine beds derived from the Challengers. The pocket in the front of the rear casting placed a load of 7 tons on the tongue at the back of the front casting, so that the locomotive was rigid in the vertical plane to eliminate oscillation, all accommodation to vertical curvature being taken up by the suspension. Locomotives of very long wheelbase tended to overload the driving wheel springs when passing over a hump, overloading the truck springs at the expense of adhesion weight when passing over a dip. Alco met this problem by installing cushioning coil springs wherever the spring rigging was anchored to the trucks and engine beds. Further, the locomotive was designed to be laterally rigid on straight track to minimize sidewise oscillation, while offering the easiest possible accommodation to curves. The back pair of driving wheels on the front drive unit was selected as the pivot point, about which the locomotive would swivel on curves, having no freedom of lateral movement relative to the engine bed. The driving and truck wheels in front of and behind these wheels were built with varying lateral movement against progressive lateral resistance. This massive locomotive retained the three-point suspension dating back to the 4-4-0s of the previous century. The driving wheels of the front drive unit were equalized on each side, cross-equalized at the front to the back of an equalizer beam, the front end of which bore on the center pin of the leading truck. The back drive unit and trailing truck were equalized along each side. Further yet, the designers kept the weight of reciprocating parts down to 2,106 pounds each side on the front drive unit and 1,912 pounds each side on the back drive unit. Light-weight reciprocating parts and counterbalancing kept dynamic augment to only 7,590 pounds at the diametral speed—68 miles per hour, much less than many smaller and less powerful engines. The Big Boys were built for continuous maximum power at 70 miles per hour and speeds up to 80 miles per hour on any part of the Union Pacific permitting such speeds. The necessary propulsive power was only one issue; producing an engine that would run at such speeds without derailing itself or destroying the track was a major, if obscure, engineering triumph.

That propulsive power came from an immense, 150-square foot grate and a boiler generating steam at 300 pounds per square inch with a Type E superheater. The all-welded firebox was 19½ feet long with Firebar grates, having 15% air opening, seven Security circulators, a Gaines wall at the throat and 9⅓ feet of combustion chamber.

Twenty tubes supplied secondary air through the firebox sidewalls above the firebed. Seventy-five 2¼-inch fire tubes and 184 4-inch flues, 22 feet over tube sheets, provided 5,890 square feet of evaporative surface and 2,465 square feet of superheating surface. The boiler was equipped with a foam-collapsing trough and an automatic blowdown system with air-operated valves, manufactured by the Electro-Chemical Engineering Co., the details of which current research has not revealed. The boiler could also be blown down by valves hand-operated from the ground. One live- and one exhaust-steam injector supplied feed water to the boiler. The exhaust-steam injector was a newly developed Elesco Type TP unit with simplified and semi-automated controls. The throttle arrangement included an auxiliary throttle, drawing saturated steam from the dome for use by hostlers and when drifting downgrade.

Immense and unprecedented care was taken to guard against uncovering the crown sheet. Two water columns were installed in the backhead; each contained two gauge glasses, offset vertically by 5½ inches, one to read the boiler water level on level or ascending grades, one to read the boiler water level on descending track. The right-hand water column had three try-cocks; the bottom try-cock was 10½ inches above the highest point of the crown sheet.

The steam pipes were designed from data supplied by the Union Pacific Research and Mechanical Standards Department and were of larger diameter than any previously applied to single-expansion articulated locomotives. Locomotive design engineers were still discovering new truths about steam distribution:

> Test data developed by the Research and Mechanical Standards Department of the Union Pacific conclusively demonstrated that, to utilize full boiler capacity and develop maximum power output, past practices could not be followed.

An innovative design of steam piping substituted rotating connections for slip joints and simplified the ball-joint design.

Walschaert valve gear and 12-inch piston valves controlled the steam supply to the four 23¾-inch × 32-inch cylinders and 68-inch Boxpok driving wheels, developing 135,000 pounds of tractive effort. Each drive unit exhausted through its own four-jet nozzle; each jet exhausted through a separate petticoat pipe, thence into two stacks mounted one behind the other. In the smokebox, longitudinal plates directed the gases around the sides of the exhaust nozzles, meeting in the front of the smokebox, passing thence over the top of a vertical plate and through a labyrinth, developed and patented by the Union Pacific, to the stacks. The gas area within the smokebox exceeded the gas area of the tubes and flues.

The Big Boy was comprehensively redesigned from first principles. The proliferation of valves and gauges on the backhead shows that running a Big Boy was an altogether more complicated and demanding task for the crew than running previously existing locomotives. Design engineers had clearly abandoned the simplicity of earlier years, accepting whatever degree of complexity was needed to achieve their goals. Even so, the design was simplified, there being no compounding, booster, or feed water heater; Baker valve gear and limited cut-off were likewise ideas that had run their course. The result was one of the ultimate developments of American steam power. The Big Boys were among the last Union Pacific steam locomotives in operation, continuing in service until 1962.

Lima had built almost no articulated locomotives since its disastrous foray into that market in 1915—only the twelve enormous AC-9's for the Southern Pacific in 1939. It was therefore something of a bold new venture for the company when it built twenty articulated, single-expansion locomotives for the Chesapeake & Ohio in 1942 with a two-wheel leading truck, two six-wheel drive units and an unprecedented 6-wheel trailing truck, called the *Alleghany* type.[95] The design originated with the Chesapeake & Ohio's mechanical department—not with Lima as might be supposed—specifically for operation over the Allegheny mountains and to supplement the 2-10-4s running between Russell, Kentucky, and Toledo, Ohio, developing maximum continuous power at 30 to 35 miles per hour. Drury (p. 83) is at variance with the referenced source in stating that Lima proposed the design, based on an earlier proposal for a 2-12-6 and that the first Alleghanies weighed 771,300 pounds.

The trailing truck supported a partly welded firebox containing 135 square feet of Firebar grates with 25% air opening and three siphons with a combustion chamber extending 9 feet 10 inches ahead of the throat sheet. The 6–wheel trailing truck alone, with cast-steel frame and brakes, weighed 43,000 pounds.[96] The water legs were generously sized at 7 inches. A 14,500-gallon per hour injector and a 14,000-gallon per hour Worthington feed water heater supplied the boiler. The total crown sheet length of 27 feet exceeded the 23-foot length of the tubes, providing 7,240 square feet of evaporative surface and 3,185 square feet in the Type E superheater (probably the biggest heating surface ever built into a steam locomotive) and generating steam at 260 pounds per square inch. Baker valve gear and 12-inch piston valves supplied steam to four 22½-inch × 33-inch cylinders driving 67-inch Boxpok driving wheels for a tractive effort of 110,000 pounds. There was no booster. The tender, supported on a six-wheel leading truck and an eight-wheel trailing truck, carried 25 tons of coal and 25,000 gallons of water, these capacities being common for engines built at that time. The engine weighed 725,000 pounds with a very high axle loading of 79,000 pounds. Forty more followed from Lima, the last being delivered in 1948, remaining in service until the Chesapeake & Ohio dieselized in the 1950s.

The power of these engines was phenomenal.[97] Tests showed a sustained power output of 6,700 to 6,900 drawbar horsepower at 42 to 46 miles per hour with an instantaneous reading as high as 7,500 drawbar horsepower at 46 miles per hour—97 pounds of engine weight per horsepower. One of them accelerated 160 loaded cars, weighing 14,100 tons, from a standstill to 19 miles per hour in one mile and reached 29 miles per hour in 11 minutes.

In spite of having commissioned the Big Boys, the Union Pacific still needed more Challengers and bought another twenty in 1942.[98] As these engines were a new batch of an existing design, built six years after the originals, the modifications highlight certain trends in locomotive design. The drive units were built around engine beds. The boiler was modified to increase the size of the firebox, shorten the tubes and increase the superheating surface. Security circulators replaced the arch tubes and Gaines wall, enlarging the grate area from 108 square feet to 132 square feet. The combustion chamber was lengthened from 86 to 106 inches. The tubes were shortened from 22 to 20 feet. These changes reduced evaporative heating surface by 11%. A Type E superheater replaced the Type A, providing 30% more superheating surface; total heating surface was practically the same. The boiler was fed by one live-steam injector and one Elesco exhaust-steam injector. Boiler pressure was increased from 255 to 280 pounds per square inch, driving 21-inch pistons, reduced from 22 inches. The front end incorporated the Union Pacific's proprietary four-jet nozzles—one nozzle and stack for each drive unit—and labyrinth spark arrestor. Rated tractive effort remained the same at 97,000 pounds. The new engines were significantly heavier than the originals at 627,000 pounds, compared to 566,000. Axle loading was up from 64,000 pounds to a specified maximum of 67,500 pounds. Tender capacity was increased from 22 tons of coal to 28 and from 18,350

Otto Perry photographed this Chesapeake & Ohio class H-8 2-6-6-6, No. 1628, at Handley, West Virginia, on July 9, 1953. Lima built sixty between 1941 and 1948 (Denver Public Library, Otto C. Perry collection, OP-2925).

Alco built this Union Pacific class 4664-3 4-6-6-4, No. 3955, in 1942, shown at Cheyenne, Wyoming, on October 31, 1954 (Denver Public Library, Otto C. Perry collection, OP-17052).

gallons of water to 25,000. These engines were designed for continuous maximum power at speeds up to 70 miles per hour and the ability to climb 3% grades; they were followed by twenty-five more in 1943 and twenty more in 1944 for a total of 105.

The Alco 4-6-6-4 design was so successful that, by late 1942, the company had built or received orders for 155 on six different railroads.

In spite of great advances in designing Mallet articulation for high speeds, by 1945 the verdict was still[99]:

> Such engines, while powerful, were not suited to high speeds, since the front unit is not sufficiently stable; spring-centering devices are not effective against slight lateral displacements. In addition, the hinged connection between front and rear units has always been a high maintenance item.

After the lack of success of the Northern Pacific's Yellowstones, the 2-8-8-4 came into its own to meet the traffic demand of World War II. By 1940, the Duluth, Missabe & Iron Range was facing increasing demand for iron ore traffic from the mines on the Missabe and Vermilion ranges to the docks at Duluth with an aging and undersized locomotive fleet.[100] Most powerful were twelve 2-8-8-2 Mallets, built as compounds between 1910 and 1917 and later converted to single-expansion, but they were too slow. Next came sixteen 2-10-2s, built in 1916 and 1919—and no new power in twenty years. In 1941, the company bought eight 2-8-8-4s from Baldwin, followed by another ten in 1943, capable of hauling 6,000-ton ore trains against adverse grades up to 0.6%. The company limited its trains to 35 miles per hour, so pulling power was more important than speed.

The new engines were built around engine beds. A 125-square foot Firebar grate fired a 240-pounds per square inch boiler, 21 feet over tube sheets. The firebox was 17½ feet long, with a Gaines wall

and a combustion chamber extending 7 feet ahead of the throat sheet. Three siphons and two arch tubes supported the brick arch, while a fourth siphon was installed in the combustion chamber. The firebox, siphons, arch tubes and combustion chamber provided 725 square feet of evaporative heating surface, while the tubes and flues provided another 5,025 square feet. The Type E superheater provided 2,770 square feet of superheating surface. Boiler water was supplied by a 12,000-gallon per hour live-steam injector and a 14,400-gallon per hour Worthington (five engines) or 12,000-gallon per hour Elesco (five engines) feed water heater. Baker valve gear with a Baldwin power reverser controlled steam flow through 12-inch piston valves to four 26-inch × 32-inch cylinders, providing a rated tractive effort of 140,000 pounds through 63-inch driving wheels. Total engine weight was 700,000 pounds for an axle loading of 71,000 pounds. The last of them was scrapped in 1963.

Having had no new freight engines since 1926 and being unable to buy diesels due to wartime restrictions, the Baltimore & Ohio bought twenty 2-8-8-4s from Baldwin in 1944 for the 17-mile Altamont grade, west of Cumberland, Maryland, with westbound grades up to 2.2%.[101] These engines were modestly dimensioned for their type, being restricted to a 61,000-pound axle loading. Even so, a 118-square foot Hulson grate fired a 235-pounds per square inch boiler, 20½ feet over tube sheets with a 90-inch combustion chamber and a Type E superheater, supplied by an injector and a Worthington feed water heater. The firebox, 26½ feet long, contained five siphons— three in the firebox, two in the combustion chamber and a Gaines wall 50 inches behind the throat sheet. Walschaert valve gear drove 12-inch piston valves, supplying four 24-inch × 32-inch cylinders. Boxpok driving wheels, 64 inches in diameter, produced 115,000 pounds of tractive effort with no booster. Counterbalancing produced no more than 7,800 pounds of dynamic augment at diametral

Duluth, Missabe & Iron Range class M-3 2-8-8-4, No. 225, built by Baldwin in 1941, leased to the Denver & Rio Grande Western, at Denver, Colorado, on December 13, 1942 (Denver Public Library, Otto C. Perry collection, OP-11471).

The Baltimore & Ohio was another user of 2-8-8-4s. Baldwin built this class EM-1, No. 669, in 1944–45, shown at Fairmont, West Virginia, in May 1957 (Denver Public Library, Otto C. Perry collection, OP-2409).

speed—64 miles per hour. Engine weight was 629,000 pounds. These engines illustrate the compromises reached in the 1940s—a very large firebox, a boiler of modest pressure no longer than 20½ feet over tube sheets, Type E superheater, Worthington feed water heater, Walschaert valve gear and the absence of a booster.

The gigantic locomotives just described were among the culminating achievements of American steam power. Nothing comparable was ever built anywhere else in the world. These were not just isolated, freakish experiments; the single-expansion Mallets were a definite phase in American locomotive construction, made possible by a hundred years of development and, at the same time, demanded by the war effort. It is appropriate that some of the last of them were built for the railroad that introduced the Mallet to America. Following their introduction to the United States in 1904, the Americans built about 3,065 locomotives with Mallet articulation for U.S. domestic service.

16.3.4 Duplex Drive Locomotives

The Pennsylvania's first duplex-drive locomotives were intended for fast passenger service. In 1942, the Pennsylvania produced a prototype 4-6-4-4 duplex freight engine, the Q-1, with the rear cylinders behind the rear driving wheels. This locomotive suffered from the same problem as George Emerson's engine on the Baltimore & Ohio, that the rear cylinders were showered with dirt, both picked up by the wheels and coming from the ash pan; cylinders, guides, crossheads and ash pan interfered with each other.

Having faith in the promise of duplex drive, the Pennsylvania followed through with the class Q-2 freight engine in 1944, which had a 4-4-6-4 wheel arrangement, with the rear cylinders mounted ahead of the rear drive unit.[102]

The Pennsylvania's design engineers spared nothing to achieve all-out, raw power. Altoona built a prototype in 1944, followed by twenty-five engines in 1945. At 619,000 pounds, these were the heaviest and most powerful rigid-frame reciprocating steam locomotives ever built. The long rigid wheelbase supported a Mallet-sized boiler, capable of steaming at 137,500 pounds per hour. A 122-square foot grate with a 124-inch combustion chamber fired a 300-pounds per square inch boiler. Nine circulators supported the brick arch, this combination providing 725 square feet of evaporative surface. Fifty-one 2½-inch tubes and 277 3½-inch flues, 21 feet over tube sheets, provided a further 6,000 square feet, while the Type E superheater added 2,930 square feet of heating surface. Walschaert valve gear drove 12-inch piston valves on the front cylinders, 14-inch on the rear cylinders—a significant choice in view of the Pennsylvania's several years of experience with poppet valves. Two 19¾-inch × 28-inch cylinders drove the front four driving wheels; two 23¾-inch × 29-inch cylinders drove the rear six driving wheels. All driving wheels had Boxpok centers, 69 inches diameter; the axles ran in Timken roller bearings. A booster was built into the rear truck. This combination produced 101,000 pounds of tractive effort with another 15,000 from the booster. The tender had a capacity for 40 tons of coal and 19,000 gallons of water. At 79,000 pounds axle loading, the engine needed the Pennsylvania's heaviest track to run on.

New designs brought new problems: one drive unit could slip independently of the other and then regain its grip, tearing holes in the fire and causing rough running. This was enough of a problem for the Pennsylvania to design a preventive for the Q-2's. A differential electric switch detected any difference in the speed of two small wheels, one running on the rear wheel of each drive unit, and controlled a compressed-air-driven butterfly valve in each of the four steam pipes. The system cut off steam to the overspeeding drive unit until the slipping stopped, when steam was restored.

The Pennsylvania rebuilt the Altoona test plant for its duplex engines. One of the Q-2's developed 7,987 indicated horsepower at 57 miles per hour, probably the highest power output ever recorded for a steam locomotive. The Q-2's peak evaporation rate was 39%

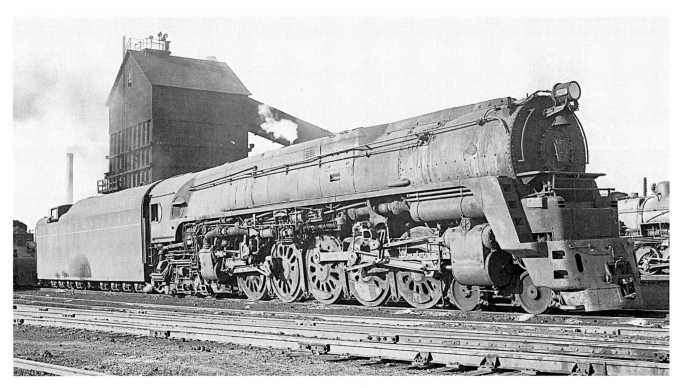

The Pennsylvania built this class Q-1 4-6-4-4, No. 6130, at Altoona in 1942 (Pennsylvania Historical and Museum Commission and Railroad Museum of Pennsylvania, Negative 10469).

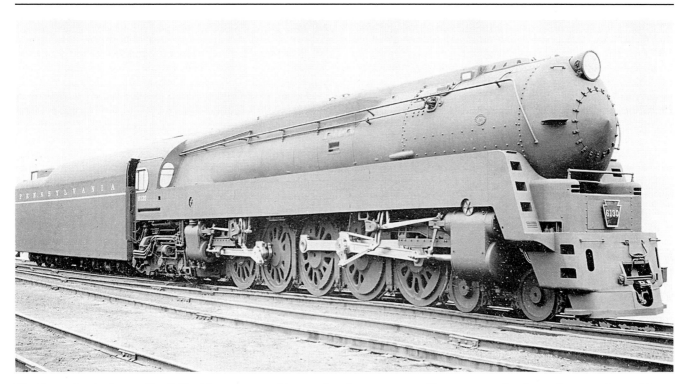

The Pennsylvania also ran No. 6130 with an air-smoothing cowling. It seems reasonable to suppose that the cowling was a later addition (Pennsylvania Historical and Museum Commission and Railroad Museum of Pennsylvania, General Negative 25538).

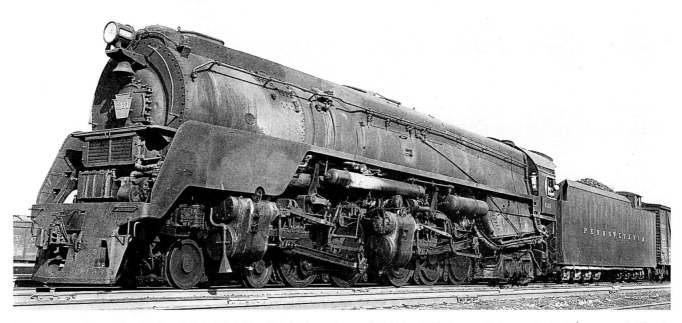

The prototype Pennsylvania class Q-2 4-4-6-4, No. 6131, built at Altoona in 1944, at Wilmington, Delaware, in 1947 (courtesy California State Railroad Museum, Negative 39088cn).

higher than that of the M-1a 4-8-2s; thermal efficiency at the drawbar was 25% higher. Coal consumption ranged from 2.8 pounds per drawbar horsepower-hour up to 3.6, depending on speed and cut-off.

Although the Pennsylvania was an acknowledged leader in steam locomotive engineering throughout the first half of the twentieth century, its procurement policies were enigmatic. While most other heavy-haul railroads embraced the Mallet with enthusiasm, the Pennsylvania eschewed them; its whole locomotive fleet contained only nineteen. Superpower passed the Pennsylvania by and, while the rest of the railroad industry accepted the 4-8-4 as the new multi-purpose locomotive, the Pennsylvania never used them. When Altoona built the J-1's, it used a Chesapeake & Ohio design under stress of wartime conditions. Now the Pennsylvania, alone except for the Baltimore & Ohio's experiments, pioneered the duplex-drive locomotive. Intermediate in weight and tractive effort between a 2-10-4 and a single-expansion Mallet, duplex drive avoided many of the problems of articulation, but introduced others of its own. Described by one authority (Drury, p.326) as "an expensive blunder" that "may well have sparked PRR's decision to dieselize," the duplex-drive locomotive was the last significant innovation in steam locomotive design before the diesel-electric locomotive swept it from the rails. Was the duplex locomotive a failure? If so, were its deficiencies irremediable, or were they merely the teething troubles of a prototype? Was its demise merely part of a wider initiative to do away with steam locomotives altogether? By 1945, the Pennsylvania had a ragbag of locomotives dating back to the early 1900s. Was the duplex really so disappointing that it induced the Pennsylvania to dieselize? Or did the company decide to scrap this mass of aging power and start afresh with new diesels?

Mark Reutter[103] points out that the October 1946, promotion of James M. Symes to the position of Deputy Vice-President, Operations, brought the steam vs. diesel issue to a head. Since 1940, the Pennsylvania had spent more than $35 million on advanced steam locomotives which were still problematical, with still more investment required. This contrasted with fully developed, off-the-shelf, diesel-electric locomotives that were making ever-wider inroads into American railroad motive power. Symes had diesel experience and no faith in further steam developments; H. T. Cover, Superintendent of Motive Power, agreed with him and admitted that the steam development program had been a failure. Symes spearheaded the dieselization of the Pennsylvania.

Section 16.4 Switchers

Switching and short-distance transfer service was a significant industry sector in major urban areas, using purpose-built engines; these typically did not have leading or trailing trucks, maximizing the adhesion weight, but used modern design features as they became available.

In 1931, Baldwin delivered an 0-10-0 to the Alton & Southern, a subsidiary of the Aluminum Co. of America, for transfer service over the East St. Louis Outer Belt Line.[104] Typical work schedules did not demand continuous high power and so the 80-square foot grate was hand-fired; two siphons were fitted to the firebox. The 230-pounds per square inch boiler contained a Type A superheater for 4,000 square feet of primary and 1,110 square feet of superheating surface. Cylinders 28 inches × 30 inches drove small, 57-inch diameter driving wheels for a rated tractive effort of 81,000 pounds, augmented by 16,000 pounds from the tender booster. The engine weighed 320,000 pounds; a tender holding 18 tons of coal and 12,000 gallons of water not only provided for long runs between fuel and water stops but provided up to 239,000 pounds of adhesion weight for the booster. This engine was characterized by the extensive use of aluminum and aluminum alloys for rods and numerous other small parts for an estimated weight saving of 10%.

In 1934, the Nickel Plate bought five 0-8-0 switchers from Lima which may be taken as typical of that time.[105] They closely resembled the sixty-five switchers that Alco built for the Chesapeake & Ohio in 1930 and were an upgrade from the twenty 0-8-0s that the Nickel Plate had bought from Lima in 1924 and 1925. Boiler pressure was 200 pounds per square inch—up from 175—fired by a 47-square foot Firebar grate. Two siphons replaced the arch tubes of the earlier design. Firebox, siphons, tubes and flues provided 2,600 square feet

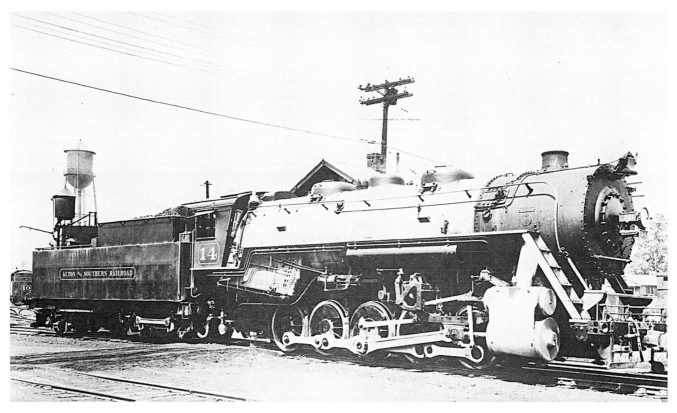

Baldwin built this 0-10-0, No. 14, for the Alton & Southern in 1931, shown probably at St. Louis, Missouri, date unknown (Pennsylvania Historical and Museum Commission and the Railroad Museum of Pennsylvania, General Negative 00139).

The Chesapeake & Ohio bought eighty of these class C-16 0-8-0s from Alco in 1930. No. 179 is shown at Handley, West Virginia, on June 27, 1950 (Denver Public Library, Otto C. Perry collection, OP-2861).

The Norfolk & Western rebuilt this class M-2 4-8-0, No. 1112, as a switcher with automated accessories, in its own shops, 1947–8. This photograph was taken in September 1948, location unknown (courtesy Norfolk Southern Corporation, ns788).

of heating surface, with another 640 square feet in the Type A super-heater. Baker valve gear with Alco power reverse drove the piston valves. The engines weighed 239,000 pounds and developed 58,000 pounds of tractive effort through 25-inch × 28-inch cylinders and 51-inch driving wheels. They had no stokers, feed water heaters or boosters.

The transfer locomotive was developed to an extreme degree in the five 0-10-2s built by Baldwin in 1936 for the Union Railroad, which operated 45 miles of connecting line around Pittsburgh.[106] These locomotives were intermediate between switchers that moved only very short distances and road engines. They were built around conventional bar frames. The firebox contained an 85-square foot stoker-fired Firebar grate, three siphons supporting the brick arch, and a 36-inch combustion chamber with one siphon. The boiler generated steam at 260 pounds per square inch from 4,810 square feet of primary heating surface and 1,390 square feet of superheating surface in the Type A superheater. A Hancock Turbo-Injector acted as an exhaust-steam feed water heater, assisted by an Ohio injector. Cylinders measuring 28 inches × 32 inches and 61-inch driving wheels developed 91,000 pounds of tractive effort, with another 17,000 pounds from a reversible Franklin booster replacing the front tender truck. The tender carried up to 14 tons of coal and 14,000 gallons of water.

In 1947, the Norfolk & Western unveiled a prototype switcher with fan drafting and a control system to automate firing in response to boiler pressure, using a rebuilt class M-2 4-8-0.[107] World War II fan developments made it possible to reconsider locomotive fan drafting which had previously failed because of inadequate fan capacity and cinder abrasion. The input to the control system was boiler pressure. A fall in boiler pressure below a set pressure would activate, first, the steam-turbine-driven fan, then the power stoker, as well as controlling the dampers. Cylinder exhaust went out through the stack with no drafting function. A 28-pounds per square inch compressed air system, supplied by the engine's air compressor, actuated the controls. An automatic boiler feed pump allowed the engine to be left unattended. An ejector blew cinders from the smokebox back to the fire. Over-fire air jets and a combustion chamber were added to the firebox. The enginemen could override the system manually. The purpose was 24-hour operation, lower back pressure, reduced emission of noise, smoke and cinders and stand-by without crew attention. The company built another prototype of this interesting automation concept in 1948, but no others followed.

17

Traction Other Than Steam, 1930–1950

Section 17.1 Internal-Combustion Power

The diesel-electric locomotive made its debut into the American railroad industry at two points: switching and passenger service. Switching and transfer service were particularly inefficient uses of steam power; diesel locomotives could be built, offering high tractive effort at low speeds, that were powerful enough for these duties, if not for road service.[1] After the switchers, the next area penetrated by diesel-electric traction was the light-weight unit passenger train, requiring high speed but relatively low power.[2]

The 1930s opened with ninety-eight diesel locomotives in railroad (74) and industrial (24) service in the U.S. and Canada.[3] All but three were 900-horsepower or less.

In May 1929, Baldwin built a diesel-electric locomotive around a 1,000-horsepower Krupp diesel engine. This engine had no lack of pull-out tractive force—68,000 pounds with a total engine weight of 270,000 pounds—but the problem was the maximum power output from the diesel engine which, like most diesels of the day, was limited by the rate of drive shaft rotation and cooling capacity. The Pennsylvania, Illinois Central, Rock Island, Santa Fe, Nickel Plate and Northern Pacific all tested it in yard service where it demon-

strated a 45% fuel saving compared to steam switchers.[4] The Oliver Iron Mining Co. tested it on ore trains in Minnesota.

A few years later, Baldwin speculatively designed a diesel-electric locomotive with two 1,975-horsepower diesel engines.[5] Because the engines were not directly connected to the driving wheels, they could be run at their speed for maximum power output when the locomotive was moving slowly or not at all. Baldwin predicted that this locomotive would have a higher starting tractive effort than an equivalent steam locomotive, hence the successful early use of diesel-electrics as switchers, but that the steam locomotive would produce more power than the diesel at speeds higher than 15 to 20 miles per hour. On the other hand: "We designed it, but nobody has yet come forward to pay the four hundred or five hundred thousand dollars which it would cost to build."

Seen from 1934[6]:

There is a very definite place for the Diesel locomotive in the railroad field. That place is primarily in switching and transfer service. The time may come, however, when it will replace the steam locomotive to a greater extent than now seems probable. There are close to 1,000 gasoline rail cars and over 100 Diesel locomotives in service in this country today.

Otto Perry photographed anything that moved on rails, such as this Chicago, Burlington & Quincy diesel-electric unit passenger train at Denver, Colorado, on October 24, 1936 (Denver Public Library, Otto C. Perry collection, OP-4065).

543

The high-speed, streamlined, diesel-powered passenger unit train took root in the vast distances of the American west, where travelers crossed the mountains and deserts between the Midwest and the Pacific coast as quickly as they could. A significant development took place in 1934 when both the Union Pacific and the Chicago, Burlington & Quincy took delivery of light-weight, streamlined, self-propelled, unit passenger trains.[7] Pullman built the Union Pacific train; Edward G. Budd built the train for the Burlington.

Ralph Budd, president of the Burlington, provided an interesting insight into the motivation behind the company's decision in 1933 to construct this train.[8] Current researches have not revealed the relationship, if any, between Edward G. and Ralph Budd.

> So far as Burlington is concerned, the original concept was primarily to provide an economical unit in a situation where some train had to be operated but earnings were insufficient for any profit. It was also hoped that the new unit would be more popular than the small steam trains or the gas-electric cars, of which many were and are in use. Under these circumstances, since a train had to be provided to accommodate the communities along the route, the new train would be successful if it did no more than reduce the cost of operation. If it should also stimulate travel, it would be doubly successful. Only after the economy had been shown to meet expectations, and the increase in patronage to be even more important, was the streamlined Diesel-powered type of train assigned to longer and more important schedules.

Freed from the counterbalance problems of the steam locomotive and with a lower center of gravity, the diesel unit trains were a spectacular success. In 1934, the Burlington *Zephyr* covered the 1,015 miles between Chicago and Denver non-stop in 13 hours 5 minutes at speeds up to 112 miles per hour—making a long day but eliminating sleeping car service; the Union Pacific unit train ran from Los Angeles to New York, 3,258 miles, in just under 57 hours—a tribute both to the design and construction of the trains and to the condition of the track.[9] A diesel unit train weighed half as much as a steam-hauled train of the same capacity. This type of train could therefore spend more of its time at line speed with quicker deceleration to stops and speed restrictions and faster acceleration from such delays.[10]

For the Santa Fe speed, alone, was the issue.[11] To compete with speeds which "carriers other than railroads" had established, the Santa

Fe looked for the fastest possible locomotive—of whatever kind—capable of hauling passengers between Chicago and Los Angeles. To this end, they placed an order with Electro-Motive in September 1934, for a 3,600-horsepower diesel-electric locomotive—the most powerful built to date—having a top speed of 98 miles per hour. When E-M delivered the locomotive a year later, the Santa Fe realized that maximizing its potential entailed substantial refettling of track and installation of fuel and water stations at appropriate intervals. Axle loads and the heat generated by heavy braking challenged the metallurgy of the locomotive's four-wheel trucks, with the result that a second locomotive of the same power output, and rated for speeds up to 118 miles per hour, ran on six-wheel trucks with wheels of improved metallurgy. The new locomotive hauled a nine-car train from Los Angeles to Chicago in 39½ hours.[12]

The Santa Fe's mechanical engineers were far from idle, developing conventional 4-6-4s and 4-8-4s, described earlier in this book. They designed the 4-6-4 for 100 miles per hour top speed and a maximum power output of 4,300 indicated horsepower and the 4-8-4 for 90 miles per hour and 5,750 indicated horsepower. The 4-6-4s were for use on flat country, the 4-8-4s through the mountains and:

> While these steam locomotives were not designed specifically for handling trains on a 39¾-hour schedule (between Chicago and Los Angeles), they were so designed that, in case it was necessary for them to handle these trains, the speed and horsepower which they developed would allow them to make such a schedule.

The first cost of the Santa Fe diesels per horsepower was three times that of the steam locomotives; the weight per horsepower of the diesels was midway between the two steam designs. Early operating results showed the diesels averaging 18,500 miles per month, compared to 12,400 miles for the steam locomotives. The steam locomotives burned Bunker C oil, while the diesels needed more highly refined oil costing 1.8 times as much per gallon; the diesels burned only 30% as much as the steam locomotives, offsetting the higher price. As cost data came in, the diesel unit trains all cost less per passenger seat-mile than steam-hauled trains.[13] An explosive labor issue lurked in the background; a diesel locomotive engineer had an unobstructed view of the track ahead and needed no fireman.

At that time, passenger cars were massive objects, weighing 60 to

An early high-power diesel-electric locomotive belonging to the Chicago, Burlington & Quincy at Denver, Colorado, on March 17, 1940 (Denver Public Library, Otto C. Perry collection, OP-4069).

80 tons; sleeping cars weighed nearly 90 tons. Air-conditioning—introduced in the early1930s—added still further to weight and cost. Passenger trains of 1,000 to 1,200 tons were common, requiring locomotives of 3,000 to 4,000 horsepower to make the ever-faster schedules with which the railroads tried to retain their dwindling passenger traffic. The Burlington and Union Pacific unit trains weighed only 100 tons, powered by diesel engines of only 600 horsepower and designed from first principles, using the latest construction materials, smaller cross-sections than existing passenger cars and streamlining designed with the aid of wind tunnels. The Union Pacific train comprised three car bodies carried on four trucks.

Named unit trains followed; the Union Pacific's *City of Portland*, which went into service in late 1934, consisted of six car bodies and a 1,200-horsepower locomotive. The *City of San Francisco* of 1936 was driven by two 1,200-horsepower diesel power units. The same year the Santa Fe's *Super Chief* comprised nine cars, powered by a two-unit diesel locomotive, each unit driven by two 900-horsepower diesel engines. At the end of 1937, the Union Pacific took delivery of a 5,400-horsepower diesel locomotive from Electro-Motive, comprising three power units, each with two 900-horsepower diesel engines, to power the new *City of Los Angeles* and *City of San Francisco* fourteen-car unit trains between Chicago and the Pacific coast over Chicago & North Western, Union Pacific and Southern Pacific track. An additional 1,200-horsepower generator was provided for train auxiliaries. After only eight years, the *City of Salina* was declared too small and obsolete and was scrapped for its aluminum in 1942.[14]

By 1937, diesel power had reduced passenger schedules between Chicago and the Pacific coast by one-third from 56 hours to 39¾ and from Denver to Chicago by 40% from 26 hours to 16.[15] The light construction of the new rail cars could, however, be a liability. A Pennsylvania gasoline-engined rail car collided with a freight train at Cuyahoga Falls, Ohio, in July 1940.[16] Forty-one of the forty-four people aboard the rail car were killed.

In the mid–1930s the American traveling public became obsessed with speed, offered to them by the aircraft and the automobile—with comfort and convenience—as never before. The railroad companies had no option but to run this race, competing both with each other and with these other modes of transport. Into this arena stepped the diesel-electric locomotive—quiet, fast and clean, competing head-to-head with the slow, dirty, noisy steam locomotive. Streamlined cowlings over steam locomotives, imitating the new diesels, barely even postponed their doom.

Doubts, bickering and prejudices in favor of the steam locomotive notwithstanding, the American railroads welcomed the diesel locomotive with alacrity. Its full economy lay not only in its higher thermal efficiency and availability but also in the elimination of facilities for handling coal, ash and water. In 1937 one (unidentified) railroad dieselized a complete branch line, replacing five steam locomotives with two diesels and eliminating the steam infrastructure.[17]

The graph of the number of diesel power units in U.S. domestic service—locomotives and self-propelled rail cars—went exponential from 1925 onward, flattened only by the depression years, 1930–1933.[18] Between 1925 and 1937, 234 diesel locomotives were placed in service on U.S. railroads,[19] comprising ninety-six 300-horsepower units, eighty-four 600-horsepower and fifty-four of various sizes. The first three months of 1937 saw a major upswing in both quantity and power, with sixty-five engines ordered or built, averaging 1,046 horsepower. This resulted both from a gradual revival of the economy and from increasing interest in the diesel locomotive. These were still very small numbers, compared to the 50,000-strong steam locomotive fleet.

Electro-Motive was quick to ram the message home[20]:

Check Your Operating Costs (with a sketch of a depressed railroad officer, in shirtsleeves and tie, burning the midnight oil over his account books) A comparison of costs reveals that non–Diesel users are paying a terrific premium for switching service. They are carrying a 400 per cent extra burden in hourly fuel costs—200 per cent higher roundhouse costs—100 per cent extra for maintenance.

If operating costs are out of line, surely a 50 per cent reduction in such a magnitudinous [*sic*] expense as yard switching should interest you. This service cost the Class I railroads $328,000,000 in 1936. The major items included $35,403,983 for coal (exclusive of transportation costs); $39,676,146 for repairs; $16,539,115 for roundhouse expenses and $326,531 for water.

Actual records show that EMC Diesel operation reduces fuel cost by 80 per cent, maintenance by 50 per cent, engine-house expenses by 66 per cent and water costs are eliminated entirely.

In March 1939[21]:

Seventeen barrels of oil in a Diesel-electric locomotive will haul a high-speed, de luxe train at 80 m.p.h., non-stop, from New York to Boston, Mass. Seventeen barrels of fuel oil, fed into the firebox of the steam locomotive scarcely will move the same 12 heavy cars as far as Bridgeport, Conn., eastbound. There is a 4.5 to 1 advantage shown in favor of the Diesel. It represents the improvement in overall thermal efficiency secured by the direct combustion of oil above the piston of the Diesel as compared with its atomization within a locomotive furnace, the evaporation of boiler feedwater, and subsequent expansion of steam in two simple cylinders of large dimensions.

To the well-known catalog of thermal losses of the steam locomotive was now compared the losses of the diesel-electric locomotive[22]:

Item	% of total heat in fuel lost	
	Steam	Diesel
Radiation	3.3	
Unburned coal	16.3	
Carbon Monoxide	0.6	
Smokebox gases	11.1	
Subtotal, boiler	31.3	Nil
Auxiliaries	3.3	2.5
Cylinder radiation, throttling, etc.	5.8	1.6
Jacket cooling water	Nil	33.2
Heat in exhaust	51.7	24.2
Machine friction	1.2	10.6
Useful work	6.7	27.9

On the other hand:

Locomotives are not selected on the basis of thermal performance alone…. The Diesel is not adapted to burn coal, and there are pronounced territorial influences on the relative fuel costs. The personnel and facilities for the maintenance of steam locomotives, highly proficient in all familiar operations, often prove most awkward and incompetent when called upon to transfer their skill and adapt their physical routines from boilers, grates, 1,500-lb. rods, and 80-in. wheels, to crankshafts, fuel-injection systems, timing mechanisms, electric generators, and traction motors. Despite the fact that thermal efficiency is not the only advantage of the Diesel, the simplicity of the steam engine is preventing any early supersession of the type.

This state of affairs would not long continue.

By the end of the 1930s, the diesel-electric locomotive was well established in switching service; some users had cost information going back nearly ten years. One eastern railroad, operating six 300-horsepower switchers, broke out their costs as follows:

Item	Steam	Diesel
Service hours per year	4,500	6,500
Availability	53%	74%
Coal, per ton, on tender	$1.63	
Oil, per gallon, on engine		$0.042
Costs per operating hour:		
Fuel	$0.820	$0.296
Water	$0.036	$0
Lubrication	$0.020	$0.044
Repairs	$0.725	$0.535
Enginehouse expense	$0.505	$0.016
Other supplies	$0.024	$0.024
Wages, 2 men	$1.490	$1.490
Ownership cost, based on capital costs estimated for 1939, 5% interest, 4% depreciation, 2% insurance & taxes	$0.971	$1.542
Total cost per operating hour	$4.591	$3.947
Saving by diesel: 14%		

By 1939, the Burlington, the Chicago & North Western, the Santa Fe and the Baltimore & Ohio were all reporting good results from their diesel-electric locomotives.[23] Besides its eleven switchers, the Burlington had two 1,800-horsepower and two 3,000-horsepower road locomotives in service. The Baltimore & Ohio had been running six 3,600-horsepower diesel-electrics since 1937–8. The Santa Fe bought a 3,600-horsepower locomotive in 1935, but split it into two 1,800-horsepower units. One-third of the 749 diesel locomotives in service by the end of 1939 were commissioned during that year. This was repeated the following year; by the end of 1940, 1,300 diesel-electric locomotives were in service on U.S. railroads, one-third of which went into service in that year.[24]

In early 1940, the Electro-Motive Division of General Motors brought out a diesel-electric locomotive, comprising four drive units, each powered by a 1,350-horsepower diesel engine for a total of 5,400 horsepower. The complete locomotive weighed 924,000 pounds—similar to the total weight of a large steam locomotive including tender—but as all the wheels of the diesel-electric locomotive were powered, it could exert up to 220,000 pounds of tractive force. This meant that it could start a train unassisted that existing steam locomotives could not while its high power development at low speed enabled it to accelerate the train faster than a steam locomotive, even though maximum speeds were similar for both types. Dynamic braking, that reduced brake wear and thermal stress in wheels, was an innovation possible with diesel-electric locomotives but impossible for steam. The nearest steam locomotive equivalent was the rarely used Le Chatelier brake. The Santa Fe later proved that dynamic braking saved nearly a ton of brake shoe metal on a single trip between Chicago and Los Angeles.[25]

Several railroads tested this locomotive and recognized that here was a diesel-electric that could outperform any steam locomotive, in addition to its other benefits, which were enormous. In 1940, EMD loaned this locomotive to the Santa Fe with such successful results that the Santa Fe ordered five such locomotives in 1940–1, then another eighty between 1942 and 1944.[26]

Orders for diesel-electric and electric locomotives outnumbered steam every year after 1934. Although 382 switchers made up the majority of the 462 diesel-electrics ordered in 1940, the high-power diesels were becoming available in quantity.[27] The Union Pacific ordered two of 6,000 horsepower; five other railroads ordered thirteen 4,000-horsepower locomotives and thirty-two of 2,000 horsepower. The railroads hungered for diesel-electrics, even though they cost more than twice as much as steam locomotives. The new 5,400-horsepower diesels cost $480,000-$505,000 each, compared to $215,000-$230,000 for a Mallet.[28] A rigid-frame locomotive cost $140,000-$200,000. Mass production and increasing experience would bring down the price of diesel-electric locomotives.

The diesel-electric's drawbar thermal efficiency of 26% to 28%, compared to 6% to 8% for a steam locomotive, meant that less fuel had to be carried and refueling stops were less frequent. Diesel fuel was more expensive per pound than coal but the higher thermal efficiency resulted in fuel costs per unit of power only 50% to 65% of those of a steam locomotive. Additionally, the diesels needed practically no water. Refueling was quicker than for a steam locomotive, with no ash handling. Diesel locomotives were running 250,000 miles a year, compared to 180,000 for a modern steam locomotive, recording availabilities of 95% to 99%, even though diesel power was more complicated than steam, requiring different maintenance skills and more rigorous maintenance. Diesel locomotives were hauling trains over grades that needed double-heading or helper service with steam. Their unvarying wheel torque and multiplicity of driving wheels gave them better traction on wet, snowy or icy track. Counterbalance problems and track damage vanished.

The new, high-power diesels enabled direct comparison with equivalent steam locomotives. Now the diesel-electric competed head-to-head in the steam locomotive's traditional realm—high pull-out torque—because the diesel engine was not directly connected to the driving wheels. Worse, yet, for the steam locomotive, it was more powerful than an equivalent diesel in its optimum speed range, but the diesel-electric developed higher power at both lower and higher speeds, as can be seen from the accompanying graphs. The diesels were fully competitive with all modern, rigid-frame steam locomotive types.

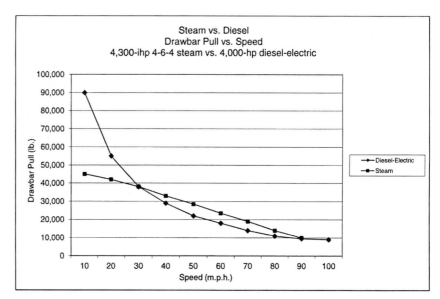

Speed:drawbar pull curves for steam and diesel locomotives, 1940s (figures from Sillcox, L. K., *Will Railroad Traffic of the Future Require Steam or Diesel? RA*, December 5, 1942, 913).

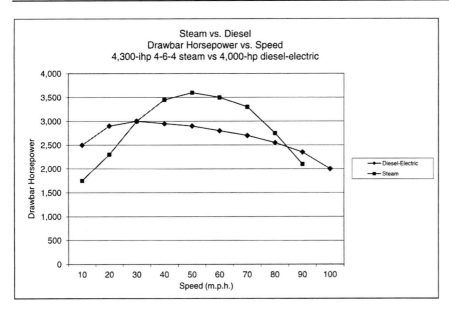

Speed:power curves for steam and diesel locomotives, 1940s (figures from Sillcox, L. K., *Will Railroad Traffic of the Future Require Steam or Diesel? RA*, December 5, 1942, 913).

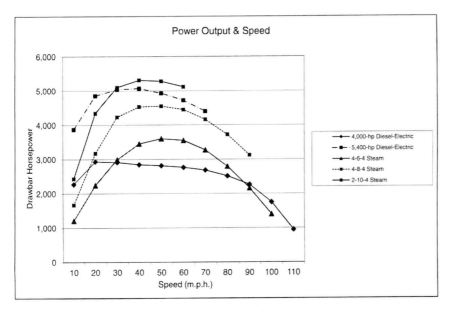

Speed:power characteristics of various types of motive power, c. 1940 (figures from Chapman, E. E. *Steam vs. Diesel-Electric Power, RA*, July 26, 1941, 149).

In spite of the immense and increasingly proven benefits of diesel operation, from the viewpoint of 1941: "it would be farfetched to intimate that the Diesel locomotives will displace steam locomotives altogether in railroad service." Yet that state of affairs was only ten years away in the future.

Steam locomotive enginemen had to learn how to handle the new diesels, in particular their enormous power[29]:

In freight service, with the Diesel-electric locomotive of 5,400 hp. capacity, care should be taken that the brakes are fully released before starting. Caution should also be used in opening the throttle, as it has been proved that these locomotives will start whether the train does or not. Trains can be broken in two unless instructions are adhered to.

In 1939, diesel-electric switchers comprised 4% of the 12,770 switching locomotives in U.S. railroad service, but worked 7% of the total hours with a utilization of 19 hours per day, compared to only 9 for a steam switcher. The new diesel switchers were more flexible than steam switchers and would go anywhere a freight car would go with less regard to track conditions than a steam locomotive. Yard crews found that visibility was no longer obscured by drifting smoke and steam and, in winter, there was no ice buildup on the ground from injector overflow. In fact: "The Diesel locomotive is ideal yard power."[30]

As diesel-electrics became more numerous, they became more reliable and information about them accumulated. In 1940, the Railway Fuel and Traveling Engineers' Association asked thirty-five railroads to pick out groups of 5 to 10 locomotives of various types and report their average mileage for the month of May.[31] The highest-performing group of diesel-electrics averaged 24,500 miles, while the highest figure for any group of steam locomotives was only 17,500 miles; the diesels ran 41% more miles than their best steam competitors. In switching service the difference was less, but still noticeable—3,850 miles for coal-burning steam locomotives, 4,000 miles for oil-burners and 4,250 miles for diesels.

The Santa Fe was never bolder in its locomotive procurement than in buying eighty-five 5,400-horsepower freight diesels from EMD between 1940 and 1944.[32] The Santa Fe experience was among the pivotal factors in the dieselization of the American railroads. By 1943, diesel power was handling 13% of the company's passenger traffic and 7% of its freight.[33] Small though this percentage may have been, it is difficult to imagine a higher-profile application of diesel power:

The eighty 5,400-hp. freight locomotives acquired in 1942 to 1944 comprised the largest fleet of (diesel) locomotives in service at that time and was the first real test of the diesel-electric locomotive in mass quantity eliminating steam operation in heavy mountain service, and proved conclusively the availability and economy inherent in this type of locomotive. These locomotives were a major factor in handling war materials to the Pacific Coast and played their part in winning World War II.

Astonishingly, the new diesels encountered fewer and slighter teething problems than some designs of steam locomotive. The problems were extraordinarily few.[34] Cast iron pistons replaced aluminum. Crankshafts, crankshaft bearings, valves, cylinder heads and radiators were improved and made more reliable. Lubrication systems leaked. Snow and rain got into sensitive parts of the engines. Radiator covers had to be made strong enough for a man to walk on. Intensive maintenance played a part in this success; the Santa Fe employed 158 mechanics to ride on its diesels until they found that this was unnecessary.

New in 1941—and a further nail in the coffin being built for the steam locomotive—was the "road-switcher," first built by an Alco-General Electric joint venture for the Atlanta & St. Andrews Bay, a short line connecting Panama City, Florida, and Dothan, Alabama.[35] The railroad bought three, specifying them to be capable of hauling 3,200-ton freight trains over the route but also to be capable of speeds up to 70 miles per hour in passenger service. Although each locomotive was rated at 1,000 horsepower, control technology allowed one engineer to control more than one locomotive. The railroad used them individually for switching by day, two coupled together for a freight run during the night. The diesels ran 58% cheaper in direct operating expenses than steam locomotives, although this margin shrank to only 7% when interest, depreciation, insurance and taxes were taken into account.

In 1941, an Alco-General Electric joint venture built a class of two-unit, 4,000-horsepower diesels for the New Haven to haul passengers by day and freight by night, such was the availability of that type of locomotive. Indeed, the majority of diesel switchers was working 6⅔ days per week (95% availability), needing only eight hours a week for servicing, compared to 73% availability for the Norfolk & Western's 2-8-8-2s, which was considered exceptional. By 1944, 224 diesel locomotives of 1,000 to 6,000 horsepower were in service on twenty-two U.S. railroads, of which 136 were rated at 2,000 horsepower. The total number of diesel engines of all power classes was more than 4,000.[36] Even so, American railroad freight was still 97% steam-hauled.

Switchers had been in service for long enough to build up a substantial database. During its first year of service, a 600-horsepower diesel switcher cost only 44% of the maintenance cost of a 200,000-pound steam switcher; when both were eight years old, the diesel's maintenance cost was 65% of that of the steam switcher. The diesel's total thermal efficiency of about 23%, compared to 6% for a steam locomotive, still resulted in a similar fuel cost per horsepower-hour, due to the higher cost of oil. At that time, American petroleum reserves were thought to be limited, compared to coal reserves which were practically unlimited; the ability to run on locally mined coal was still a compelling advantage of the steam locomotive.

The 1,000- and 2,000-horsepower road switcher proved highly versatile, especially as more than one could be ganged together under the control of one engineer. Manufacturers offered standard models, accelerating delivery.[37]

> [O]ne railroad president not long ago said he was buying some Diesel locomotives. He didn't want to buy Diesels, but he needed locomotives and he could get delivery of Diesels in three months and he couldn't even get the specifications for steam locomotives through his own mechanical department in three months, let alone getting them built. The Diesel locomotive is much like the automobile. You go into a showroom, select your paint job and either buy it or not. If you say, "Please change this and this and that," they say, "We don't want your business; thank you. This is our standard product."

Wherever diesels were installed, they were an outstanding success, whether it was switching, passenger service or—last hold-out of the steam locomotive—heavy freight. Between 1942 and 1944, the Denver & Rio Grande Western bought twelve, four-unit, 5,400-horsepower diesels and successfully put them into the most arduous service over the 570 miles through the mountains between Denver and Salt Lake City.[38] The diesels handled 2,100 tons against a 2% grade, compared to 1,750 tons for the biggest Mallets.

The Erie's wartime surge in traffic bottlenecked due to grade and curvature between Meadville, Pennsylvania, and Marion, Ohio, requiring trains approaching this area from east or west to be split in two for passage through it.[39] In April 1943, the company ordered six 5,400-horsepower diesels from EMD to solve this problem. Manufacture of the locomotives took eighteen months but, when they arrived, they hauled 4,800 tons over the district in question, compared to 2,550 tons for a 2-8-4 steam locomotive.

The Pittsburgh & West Virginia connected the Wheeling & Lake Erie at Pittsburgh with the Western Maryland at Connellsville with 111 miles of track through rough terrain with ruling grades of 1.3% westbound, 1.5% eastbound.[40] This was where the Baldwin 2-6-6-4s applied their 98,000 pounds of tractive effort. In 1947, the company installed two Fairbanks-Morse 2,000-horsepower diesels. Although each was a self-sufficient locomotive, the company used them as a double unit with a starting tractive effort of 150,000 pounds which handled one-fifth more tonnage than a 2-6-6-4 with savings in time and cost.

By the late 1940s, most railroad executives would probably have dieselized overnight, could they have done so. Three main factors retarded the process.[41] There were physical and financial limitations on the numbers of diesels that could be built. Not only the steam locomotives themselves but their supporting infrastructure had to be written off and new servicing and maintenance facilities built for the diesels. Hundreds of thousands of employees had to be trained to operate and maintain the new power. These factors preserved steam into the late 1950s.

As diesel experience grew during the war, with labor in short supply, the railroads came to realize that the fireman had very little to do. J. P. Morris, Assistant Chief of Motive Power with the Santa Fe, testified before the Railway Labor Board in 1943[42]:

> A fireman on a Diesel yard locomotive has less work to do than any other man employed by the American railroads.

And:

> Next to the fireman on a Diesel switcher, an engineer on a Diesel locomotive has the easiest job on the railroad. The engineer and fireman on Diesel power ride in a comfortable enclosed cab. They do not have to contend with the heat of the boiler. The hazards of their employment are considerably less than the hazards of running a steam locomotive. Both the engineer and the fireman have a better view of the right-of-way. The riding qualities of the Diesel locomotives are much better than those of the steam locomotives, and the Diesel locomotive is much easier to operate.

The possibility of eliminating the fireman's position altogether seems not to have figured in the railroads' assessment of the diesel locomotive, but the issue began to arise. The position was eventually eliminated but only after years of wrangling with the unions.

The short lines were the first to dieselize completely; for bigger railroads with bigger investment in steam power, the process had to be more gradual.[43] The Southern Pacific's view in 1951 typified this state of affairs[44]:

> Ultimately Southern Pacific is aiming at complete dieselization. That is still some years in the future, because our many modern steam locomotives are still giving economical, efficient service. Our program is to retire the older and smaller steam engines first, retaining the larger and more modern ones or sending them to other territories to replace less efficient engines. This process is in progress all over our railroad, but until dieselization is complete there must necessarily be maintained facilities for servicing the two types of locomotives—steam and diesel. Gradually some of our steam facilities are being reduced and those for diesels increased.

From 691 in 1945, diesel orders exploded in the late 1940s, reaching 2,661 in 1948, falling back to 1,782 in the weak economy of 1949,

An Atchison, Topeka & Santa Fe diesel-electric road switcher at Waynoka, Oklahoma, on August 6, 1940 (Denver Public Library, Otto C. Perry collection, OP-1109).

breaking all records in 1950 with 4,393 ordered.[45] (1948, 1949 and 1950 quantities were "units," some of which were self-sufficient locomotives, some were not. As at April 1, 1951, orders for 1,883 locomotives comprised 2,420 power units.[46]) U.S. domestic orders in 1950 were the highest since 1918, all diesel but for fifteen switchers that the Norfolk & Western built in its own shops.

In 1946, Alco-GE brought out a three-unit, 6,000-horsepower locomotive for the Santa Fe.[47] While a market existed for diesel locomotives of 4,000 horsepower and greater, the possibility of operating smaller locomotives, of 1,000 to 2,000 horsepower, as multiple units under the control of a single throttle offered greater flexibility and served a wide variety of traffic needs. Nothing like this was ever possible with steam locomotives.

General Motors outmaneuvered Baldwin, Alco and Lima in all possible ways.[48] In 1935, when recovery from the depression was barely perceptible and the diesel-electric locomotive was still new and unproven, the company built a plant at La Grange, Illinois, specifically to build diesel-electric locomotives, with an initial workforce of four hundred people; by 1947, two locomotive plants, totaling 2.5 million square feet of floor space with 12,000 employees, were building five locomotives a day. That year, GM celebrated the 25th anniversary of the founding of Electro-Motive with a dinner for 750 railroad executives and industry leaders and a convention of laudatory speeches, exhibiting triumphs of the new technology and unveiling a new 114,000-square foot locomotive development center.

The new GM diesels were superbly manufactured and fully supported after sale. The Southern Railway reported 100% availability on one locomotive that ran a million miles between 1941 and 1946, while a second locomotive reported 99.6% availability over five years of operation.[49]

Between 1946 and 1951, the Santa Fe put 23,000 men through its own diesel instruction course and made it clear that the diesel locomotive was the way onward and upward for ambitious young men.[50]

> The Santa Fe diesel organization has proved to be a training field for young men desirous of gaining knowledge with respect to the maintenance and operation of this type of motive power, and presents unlimited opportunities for those who merit further promotion. As a testimonial to this vast organization, those who started in the diesel organization early are now holding positions of responsibility and trust including roundhouse foremen, supervisors of diesels, master mechanics, superintendents of shops, and mechanical superintendents.

The halfway point to the full dieselization of the American railroads came in 1950, when diesels handled 40% of total train miles and 60% of switching service.[51] Leaders, with 90% or more of gross ton-miles handled by diesel power were the Delaware, Lackawanna & Western, the Boston & Maine, the Lehigh Valley, the Elgin, Joliet & Eastern (100%), the Seaboard Air Line, the Gulf, Mobile & Ohio (100%), the St. Louis & San Francisco, the Missouri-Kansas-Texas and the Western Pacific. The Norfolk & Western was the only major railroad to have no diesel power at all. The Nickel Plate and the Illinois Central had very little.[52]

The new technology resulted in a realignment of the locomotive manufacturers so that, in 1951, the New York Central split a $64-million order for 387 diesel locomotives between EMD, Baldwin-Lima-Hamilton, Alco-General Electric and Fairbanks-Morse.[53] Demand kept the former big three locomotive builders in business.

The Union Pacific was one of the earlier diesel users, but one of the latest to dieselize completely. It bought its first passenger diesel in 1934 but, because of its relatively up-to-date steam fleet and abundant coal supply from a wholly-owned subsidiary in Wyoming, delayed buying its first diesel freight locomotive until 1947. By the mid–1950s, the cost of coal, the cost of spare parts for steam locomotives and traffic demands were all rising. In 1954, the company took the plunge with $53 million worth of orders for 244 freight diesels, fifteen passenger diesels and fifteen gas-turbine locomotives.[54]

By 1955 dieselization was practically complete; orders for new locomotives were the lowest in ten years.[55] Even the Norfolk & Western started to buy diesels in that year, with an initial order of twenty-five 1,600-horsepower locomotives, followed by fifty more in 1956.[56] In the summer of 1958, the N&W finally gave way, ordering 268 diesel locomotives for $50 million.[57] Of 262 steam locomotives on the company's roster, it planned to dispose of 202 by the end of 1960, retaining only sixty for peak demand.

In ten years, the American railroads shucked more than a century of steam locomotive operation, including the men, skills, attitudes and plant that went with it.

Section 17.2 Gas-Turbine Locomotives

In 1939, Allis-Chalmers unveiled the possibility of an entirely new locomotive engine, the gas turbine, then known as a "combustion turbine," burning low-grade fuel oil in the turbine itself.[58]

The gas turbine was the descendant of the reciprocating internal combustion engine in the same way that the steam turbine was the descendant of the reciprocating steam engine, using heated air instead of steam as the working fluid. The idea dated back certainly as far as 1791, when John Barber was granted a patent describing such a device. Its realization, however, depended on efficient compressors and metals capable of withstanding very high stresses and temperatures, neither of which was available to the necessary degree before 1930.[59] New metal alloys and wartime research into aircraft jet engines advanced this technology rapidly. The idea was attractive for a locomotive engine, offering higher thermal efficiency than a reciprocating steam locomotive and freedom from problems with boilers, feed water and reciprocating parts.

The first gas-turbine locomotive went into service in Switzerland in 1941, built by Brown Boveri, burning oil. By 1947, twelve gas-turbine locomotives were being designed in Britain, Switzerland, France and the U.S.

Allis-Chalmers was involved in this technology at an early date, applying for patent protection in 1944 (U.S. Patent 2,575,242), proposing to apply a 1,500-horsepower gas turbine to each of four driving axles through hydraulic transmissions. In a diesel-electric locomotive a 500-horsepower electric motor was the biggest that would fit into the space available on the truck. The gas turbine locomotive thus offered the possibility of a 6,000-horsepower single locomotive, weighing 500,000 pounds, instead of the three units, weighing 950,000 pounds, required by a diesel-electric locomotive of the same power—an astonishing power density, especially compared to steam locomotives. Allis-Chalmers admitted that the fuel efficiency was only half that of diesel-electric power, but the low-grade fuel oil cost half as much as diesel fuel.

By 1944, the threat posed by the diesel locomotive to the symbiosis between the coal-carrying railroads and the coal producers caused eight railroads (the Baltimore & Ohio, Chesapeake & Ohio, Illinois Central, Louisville & Nashville, New York Central, Norfolk & Western, Pennsylvania and Virginian) and four coal producers (M. A. Hanna, Island Creek Coal, Pocahontas Fuel and Sinclair Coal) to affiliate a Locomotive Development Committee with Bituminous Coal Research Inc. to develop a coal-burning locomotive of superior economy and operating characteristics. The New York, Chicago &

St. Louis and the Union Pacific joined later. R. B. White, president of the Baltimore & Ohio and chairman of the committee, was already attracted by the gas turbine, especially if it could be adapted to burn coal. In 1945, the committee's Mechanical Advisory Group recommended that the committee develop a coal-burning gas-turbine locomotive, ideally one that could burn coal or oil interchangeably.

The problems were substantial.[60] The fuel would have to be pulverized coal, produced by an on-board pulverizer. Coal firing posed the unacceptable problem that turbine blades would be abraded by fly ash or unbalanced by slag formation; efficient fly ash separation was therefore essential to the functioning of the turbine. The resulting research effort was enormous, involving more than twenty research organizations and potential suppliers, including such names as General Electric, Westinghouse, Alco, Allis-Chalmers, Dow Chemical, the Battelle Memorial Institute and Johns Hopkins and Purdue Universities. Alco built a test rig in 1946 at Dunkirk, New York, using an Allis-Chalmers turbine designed for a Russian oil refinery, but diverted to Alco by the U.S. Bureau of Mines; Westinghouse built a second rig in 1947.[61] The Locomotive Development Committee planned to build and road-test two locomotives in 1948; such were the problems that had to be solved that this objective was still unrealized ten years later.

No one ever pretended that the gas-turbine would reach the thermal efficiency of the diesel engine. Preliminary studies suggested a machine thermal efficiency of 20%, compared to 26% for a diesel-electric locomotive and 7% for a steam locomotive. On the other hand, coal energy at that time cost only 15 cents per million BTU, compared to 52 to 59 cents for diesel fuel. Adding to the advantages of the gas turbine was the very large amount of waste heat readily recoverable for the substantial energy needs of passenger trains. In the northern winter, a long-distance passenger train could consume as much energy for heat, light, cooking and other services as the locomotive put into the rail to haul the train.

In early 1948, Gwilym A. Price, President of Westinghouse Electric, had this to say about the history and current status of the gas-turbine locomotive[62]:

> A still newer locomotive, built around the gas-turbine, has exciting possibilities. Westinghouse believes very firmly in its future. In fact, we have under construction a 4,000-horsepower gas turbine locomotive. Because we cannot anticipate all the problems that may arise, it is impossible to name a completion date, but we expect to have it running in 1949. This is a logical step in our work with the gas-turbine, which began on December 8, 1941, when at the Navy's request we undertook the development of a jet-propulsion power plant for high-speed military aircraft. Under great wartime pressure, we accumulated in short order a vast body of experience with axial-flow compressors, combustors, and gas-turbines.

While the war was still in progress, Westinghouse was determined to transfer their jet propulsion experience to the development of a gas-turbine power plant for industrial and railroad use; a prototype went on test late in 1946, burning liquid fuel. Since then, the prototype had run successfully for more than a thousand hours, including extended periods at temperatures between 1,300° and 1,400° F., temperatures at which ordinary steel would soften. This is made possible by special alloys, some of which had been developed in Westinghouse laboratories. Much of the testing had simulated railroad service. No fundamental weakness in any part of the compressor, combustor, or turbine design had appeared thus far.

Even so, Westinghouse was uncertain about the coal-burning gas-turbine locomotive:

> While our first gas-turbine locomotive will burn liquid fuel, we are not overlooking the possibility of making a coal-burning gas-turbine loco-

motive. For years we have been conducting experiments with powdered coal combustors and are continuing the research aggressively this year in a new direction. While we cannot say we are yet ready to throw our hats in the air over what we have found, we are going to prove to our satisfaction that a gas turbine either can or cannot burn coal.

A year later[63]: "The burning of coal satisfactorily in a gas turbine is no easy problem and the solution is somewhere in the future. In the meantime oil will be used as fuel." This fuel could, however, be heavy fuel oil, rather than the distillate required for diesel engines.[64] In 1949, Alco was still experimenting at Dunkirk, but was not optimistic.[65]

On the other hand, that same year, the Union Pacific put an Alco-GE 4,500-horsepower oil-burning gas-turbine locomotive into service with enough success that they owned twenty-five by 1955.[66] After GE got the unit power up to 8,500 horsepower, the Union Pacific bought another fifteen in 1956, planning to order thirty more to haul a 5,000-ton train at 17 miles per hour up a 1.14% grade.[67] The Union Pacific ran more gas-turbine locomotives than any other American railroad. In the end, however, the oil-burning gas turbine was less efficient than the diesel engine.

The Baldwin-Westinghouse experimental, oil-burning, gas-turbine locomotive went into trial service in 1950; operations were intermittent as the locomotive had to be taken out of service for frequent modifications and repairs.[68] In 1952, it went into trial service on the Pennsylvania with at least initial success.

Gas-turbine locomotive research continued into the 1950s.[69] Alco erected an Allis-Chalmers turbine, configured for locomotive application, at Dunkirk in 1951.[70] Progress was slow and difficult; by 1954, when the railroads had already converted to diesel power, Alco and the Locomotive Development Committee of Bituminous Coal Research were still hoping for success with a new ash separator. At this point the LDC comprised representatives from Alco Products, the Baltimore & Ohio, the Chesapeake & Ohio, the Louisville & Nashville, the Illinois Central, the Norfolk & Western, the Virginian, the Nickel Plate, M. A. Hanna, Pocahontas Fuel, Island Creek Coal, Pittsburgh Consolidation Coal and Sinclair Coal. The Jersey Central released their mechanical engineer, P. R. Broadley, to manage research. By 1955, work was far enough advanced for tests to include actual load cycles taken from the Union Pacific and the Norfolk & Western and typical load cycles from the New York Central.[71]

The 1955 test results were intensely alluring. Fuel consumption averaged 0.96 pounds of coal per horsepower-hour with a power output of 3,300 horsepower, including runs up to 53 hours with the new ash separation system.[72] Based on New York Central fuel costs and typical operating cycles, the coal-burning, gas-turbine locomotive offered 20% thermal efficiency and 64% lower fuel cost than a diesel-electric.

The Union Pacific became interested in the program in 1955. One of the tests that year simulated 8,290 miles of operation with a 2,080-ton freight train between Ogden and Cheyenne, burning Wyoming coal. The tests consumed 370 tons of this coal in 243 hours, resulting in an average 16% thermal efficiency at a power output of 2,250 horsepower. Fuel consumption was 43 pounds per thousand gross ton-miles, half that of a steam locomotive.

The LDC hoped to build a coal-fired gas-turbine locomotive in 1957; the Union Pacific entered into a development agreement with Alco that year.[73] Over the twelve years of its existence, the LDC had made great progress in the key issues of pulverized coal handling and ash separation. Now, however, the gas-turbine locomotive had to

A Union Pacific gas-turbine locomotive near Dale, Wyoming, on September 18, 1958 (Denver Public Library, Otto C. Perry collection, OP-19453).

compete, not against the reciprocating steam locomotive, but against the diesel-electric. By 1959, the LDC considered that they had proven the feasibility of a coal-burning, gas-turbine locomotive but no locomotive construction followed. In that year, the LDC transferred the test plant to the U.S. Bureau of Mines which moved it to Morgantown, West Virginia, and continued research for stationary power plants.[74] Some of the LDC's discoveries found applications in other industries.

By the end of 1960, forty-eight oil-burning, gas-turbine electric locomotives were in U.S. service, most if not all on the Union Pacific.[75] This type of locomotive never made significant inroads into railroad service.

Section 17.3 Electric Power

Electric traction reached a plateau in the 1930s; by 1941, the 900 electric locomotives in service on U.S. railroads were outnumbered by diesel-electrics.[76] The railroads' economic and financial condition did not encourage the heavy capital investment required by electrification. "Locomotives" cannot have included the numerous self-propelled passenger cars of the interurban lines and the suburban lines of the Class I railroads. By 1941 more than one half the suburban car-miles were electrically powered.[77]

The Pennsylvania soldiered on, in spite of the depression, with an electrification plan begun in 1927 and completed in 1938, encompassing 675 route miles between New York, Philadelphia, Washington and Harrisburg.[78] Single-phase, 25-cycle AC power was supplied at 11,000 volts through catenary wires. On completion, the system operated 118 electric locomotives for passenger service and ninety-three for freight. The biggest of these were capable of 4,620 continuous horsepower and up to 8,520 horsepower for short periods. This enabled them to handle acceleration and short adverse grades with 18- to 20-car passenger trains and 12,000-ton freight trains that matched passenger schedules. Even then, Westinghouse was working on electric locomotives capable of 7,500 horsepower continuous, 12,000 maximum.

In 1950, the Norfolk & Western astonished the railroad world by decommissioning its electric system between Bluefield and Iaeger on completion of the new double-track Elkhorn tunnel, reverting entirely to steam.[79]

Electrification found its niche early on and never broke out of it. By 1955, electric locomotives comprised only 2% of the locomotive fleet; 85% had been built before 1940.[80] The economic imperative of very high traffic density never changed in a hundred years and persists to this day.

Conclusion

The American giant steam locomotive flourished and became extinct in fifty years. It would be easy to suppose that these gigantic engines were nothing more than vastly bigger versions of the Stephensonian locomotive of 1830 and that attempts to break away from that configuration failed, implying a barrenness of endeavor. But was this the whole story?

A locomotive is a set of wheels, running on rails and driven by an on-board power unit. During the 1800s the American railroads sought after more powerful locomotives to haul the increasing volumes of freight and passengers that were offered to them. In the 1890s and early 1900s competition, rising costs and an increasingly hostile political environment forced them to look for locomotives of greater efficiency as well as greater power. Management science and increasingly sophisticated testing methods enabled them to measure locomotive performance and to gauge the effect of innovations. At that time their quest focused on more powerful and more efficient steam locomotives because no other possibilities existed. From about 1910 onward, however, this quest for greater power and efficiency branched into three parallel paths which railroad managers and mechanical engineers pursued with open minds, with a capacity for the most rigorous economic analysis and with no particular attachment to the steam locomotive. They looked for: (a) better locomotives, regardless of the type of power unit; (b) better coal-burning locomotives, regardless of the type of power unit; (c) better reciprocating steam locomotives.

The first path produced the electric locomotive with lineside or overhead power pickup and the self-contained diesel-electric locomotive and was thus ultimately successful.

The second path produced the monstrous experimental steam- and gas-turbine locomotives of the late 1940s. It is arguable whether these failed irredeemably or whether they failed only as prototypes in competition with mature electric and diesel-electric locomotives, but fail they did.

The third path is the main subject of this book. Four major lines of advance in steam locomotive technology failed in America without question: compounding, water-tube boilers, the use of extremely high steam pressure and the use of small, high-speed reciprocating engines with indirect drive to the driving wheels. Several other lines of advance succeeded, however. Steam locomotives could not have been built to the size, power and reliability that they were without the enabling improvements in steel metallurgy, design engineering and manufacturing techniques. The new, enhanced steam locomotives of the twentieth century could not have been designed without the benefit of a database accumulated from decades of dynamometer car and static plant testing. Stoker firing and very large grates broke through the power limitations imposed by the strength of a human fireman, at the same time bringing the firing rate per square foot of grate down to a level that permitted efficient combustion. Improved heat recovery by superheating, feed water heaters and exhaust-steam injectors added to both power and thermal efficiency. Power-operated reversing gear was essential to very large locomotives. Articulation and duplex drive were not features of the original Stephensonian locomotive. Opinions differ as to the success of duplex drive, but Mallet-type articulation played a major role in American locomotive development. Although boosters came and went from American locomotive construction, their role was significant while it lasted. Improved counterbalancing and light-weight reciprocating parts made higher speeds possible while reducing wear and tear on both track and locomotives. These developments roughly doubled the thermal efficiency of the American steam locomotive, tripled its tractive effort and quadrupled its power output in fifty years. Even so, more than 90% of the fuel energy still went to waste and the steam locomotive remained grossly and irredeemably inefficient in many other ways discussed in this book.

Let us suppose that the builders and operators of the first American steam locomotives were shown an American locomotive of 1950—such as a Norfolk & Western A, a J or a Y-6b. Once they had comprehended its enormous size and power, and the massive track and sub-structures on which it ran, they would have found the machine and its operating techniques to be instantly familiar. Being men of active intelligence, they would never have contented themselves with the dismissive comment that nothing had changed in a century. They would want to delve into the detailed developments that had gone into the design and construction of this monster. When these developments, and the engineering effort that went into them, were explained—not to mention the countless innovations, large and small, that had been tried and rejected over the decades, they would regard this ultimate development of American steam power with fascination and astonishment. So may we.

Appendix A: Thermodynamics and Dimensions

This book describes the twentieth-century development of the American steam locomotive in two ways: its physical structure and the subtle and violent thermodynamic processes that made it move. The steam engine existed before the science of thermodynamics, in other words, before any theory existed as to why it worked. It was later studied by means of the science that it nurtured.

A steam engine is a heat engine, a device that converts the energy contained in a fuel into mechanical energy. In 1824, the French engineer Carnot published a paper, *Reflections on the Motive Power of Heat*, which remained unnoticed for another twenty-five years, theorizing that a heat engine—they were few at that time—entailed the input of heat, the conversion of heat into work and the disposal of unused heat. He postulated a perfect process cycle that has remained the theoretical ideal against which real heat engines have been compared ever since.

In the 1840s and 1850s, Joule, Thomson, Clausius, Rankine and others established the science of thermodynamics. By that time the steam engine had been in existence for 130 years and steam locomotives had been at work for nearly half a century.

The first law of thermodynamics states that energy can neither be created nor destroyed; an exact energy accounting balance is possible—it all has to go somewhere, somehow. The second law of thermodynamics states that the thermal efficiency of any thermodynamic cycle has an upper limit that is proportional to the temperature difference across the heat engine. The maximum theoretical thermal efficiency of a Carnot-cycle engine, working between 380°F (the temperature of saturated steam at a boiler pressure of 180 psi) and atmosphere at 60°F, is 40%. For comparison, the efficiency of the human body as a heat engine converting fat (a stored fuel) into work is 24%, the balance being given off as heat.[1] (The maximum sustainable power output of a trained athlete is about 0.24 horsepower.)

In a steam locomotive, work output can be measured as "indicated" or "cylinder" horsepower, or as "drawbar" horsepower. "Indicated horsepower" refers to an indicator diagram, plotting piston displacement against pressure, a device invented by James Watt early in the history of the steam engine. "Drawbar horsepower" is the power that the locomotive applies to its trailing load, in other words, indicated horsepower minus the internal friction and rolling resistance of the locomotive. The thermal efficiency of the locomotive is the work output, specified as drawbar horsepower or indicated horsepower, divided by the calorific value of the fuel.

The actual thermal efficiency of steam locomotives was low, even when considering that their (unreachable) Carnot efficiency was no higher than 40%. The Carnot efficiency applied only to the engine, i.e., the cylinders. The boiler was only 80% efficient at best, declining to as low as 50%, depending on how strongly it was drafted. Lawford H. Fry in 1928 calculated a theoretical cylinder efficiency of 15%, based on expanding steam from 220 pounds per square inch down to 25 pounds; tests showed actual cylinder efficiencies of 10% to 12%;

the difference resulted from friction.[2] Of the power developed in the cylinders, only 75% reached the drawbar, the rest being consumed in friction of moving parts and rolling resistance. It is easy to see how the total thermal efficiency of a steam locomotive was 4% to 8% at best. Typical coal consumption was 4.5 pounds per drawbar horsepower-hour, burning bituminous coal with a calorific value of 13,000 BTU (13,700,000 joules) per pound. A horsepower-hour is 2,685,600 joules. Therefore the thermal efficiency of a typical steam locomotive was no more than 3% to 4%, calculated as $(2,685,600/(4.5 \times 13,700,000))$ × 100%.

This book uses dimensions and ratios that need to be explained here, divided into those inherent in the locomotive itself, as when it is motionless, and those which describe its power and efficiency when it is working.

Weight: The weight of a steam locomotive can be measured as engine with or without tender, full of fuel and water, or empty. As these weights could differ by 100 tons, these are significant distinctions. The most common measure was "engine only, in full working order." This was measured with the boiler full of water, a fire burning, steam raised to maximum working pressure and the two-man crew on board.[3]

Another common weight was "weight on driving wheels" or "adhesion weight." For an engine, such as an 0–6–0 with no leading or trailing truck, adhesion weight and engine weight are the same. For a 2–8–0, adhesion weight was about 90% of engine weight. The maximum possible tractive effort was typically 25% of the adhesion weight due to the friction coefficient between driving wheel and rail.

"Axle loading" was the adhesion weight divided by the number of driving axles. Axle loading was limited by the strength of track and substructures.

Tender weights and capacities for fuel and water are sometimes given, but one engine could haul several different tenders without affecting the characteristics of the engine itself.

Cylinder Bore and Stroke: Cylinder bore and piston stroke are given as "bore × stroke" in inches. The bigger the bore and stroke of the cylinders and pistons, the higher the possible tractive effort and power output.

In compound engines the high-pressure cylinder was of smaller bore than the low-pressure cylinder. The cylinder dimensions of compound engines are therefore given as "high-pressure cylinder bore & low-pressure cylinder bore × stroke."

Driving Wheel Diameter: A steam locomotive driving wheel acts as a lever. The distance from the crank pin to the wheel hub is the short arm of the lever; the wheel hub is the fulcrum; the distance from the hub to the point of contact of the tire with the rail is the long arm of the lever. The shorter this long arm, in other words, the smaller the driving wheel diameter, the greater the tractive effort that the pistons could exert. The number of revolutions per minute made by the driving wheels was the cycling rate of the engine.

Counterbalancing difficulties, valve events in the cylinders and steam flow rates limited the speed that engines with small driving wheels could achieve. Engines for passenger service were therefore built with large driving wheels, typically more than 60 inches in diameter, to achieve high speeds at some sacrifice of pulling power. Engines for freight service were built with small driving wheels, typically less than 60 inches in diameter, for maximum pulling power at low speeds.

Grate Area and Heating Surface: Grate area—length × width of the fire grate—is a measure of the likely coal combustion rate and, hence, power output. Heating surface is the surface area of the firebox and firetubes, sometimes distinguished between "fire side" and "water side," which would give slightly different dimensions, differing in proportion to the thickness of the firebox sheets and firetubes. In superheated locomotives, the superheater surface area may be given separately. Heating surface is a measure of the likely rate of steam generation.

Combustion Rate/Firing Rate: The rate of firing and combustion was given as pounds of coal per square foot of grate per hour. Evaporation increased as this figure increased, but at the expense of evaporative efficiency per pound of coal.

Steam Pressure: A gauge in the cab measured boiler steam pressure in pounds per square inch above atmospheric pressure.

The figure given as "boiler pressure" was the maximum safe working pressure for which a boiler was designed and at which the safety valves were set to open. By 1900, this included a factor of safety of 4 to 5 so that a 200-pounds per square inch boiler would burst from overpressure at 800 to 1,000 pounds per square inch. The actual pressure in the boiler at any one time depended on the strength of the fire and the steam demand. Typically, a locomotive with a 180 pounds per square inch boiler will move itself, without a load, at steam pressures of 80 to 100 pounds per square inch. To haul a load, such a locomotive would need a steam pressure of at least 160 pounds per square inch, preferably close to 180 pounds.

Steam entered the cylinders at an "initial pressure" lower than the boiler pressure due to friction losses in the throttle valve, dry pipe and steam valves. Each return stroke of the pistons forced exhaust steam through the exhaust nozzle, creating a "back pressure." The exhaust nozzle traded pressure for the velocity of the exhaust steam jet which entrained air in the smokebox and ejected it through the stack, causing a vacuum in the smokebox which drafted the fire. Some degree of back pressure was therefore necessary. The average of the difference between initial pressure and back pressure, in other words, the average pressure inside the cylinder as the steam expanded in the course of a stroke, was the "mean effective pressure." Mean effective pressure dropped when the cut-off was shortened and when speed increased, due to friction losses in the increasing steam flow.

Boiler pressure was continuously displayed on a gauge in the cab. Initial pressure, back pressure and mean effective pressure were measured only when a locomotive was instrumented and under test.

Evaporation Rate and Steaming Rate: Two measures of evaporative efficiency were pounds of water evaporated per pound of coal and per square foot of heating surface. The boiling point of water varies with pressure; for uniformity, evaporation rates were corrected to "evaporation from and at 212°F." The steam generating capacity of the boiler (steaming rate) was measured in pounds per hour. These statistics can be ambiguous. Even when evaporation was adjusted to "from and at 212°F," evaporation per pound of coal as fired, per pound of dry coal and per pound of combustible (coal less ash and water) differed significantly; one series of tests produced the following results:

Pounds of water per pound of coal	
Actual evaporation, coal as fired (incl. ash and moisture)	5.39
Equivalent evaporation, as fired, from and at 212°F	6.54
Equivalent evaporation per pound of dry coal (incl. ash, excl. moisture)	7.28
Equivalent evaporation per pound of combustible (excl. ash & moisture)	8.37

The difference between the highest and lowest figures is almost 65%, the difference being the calculation method. In the sources consulted, it is often unclear which measure is being used. These parameters could not be continuously instrumented, but were measured only when a locomotive was under test.

Temperatures and Smokebox Vacuum: The relative temperatures of the fire and of the gases passing through the smokebox provided a useful measure of heat absorption by the boiler. The smokebox vacuum, in inches of water gage, was a measure of the strength of draft being applied to the fire. These parameters were not continuously instrumented, but were measured only when a locomotive was under test.

Cut-Off: "Cut-off," controlled by the engineer in the cab through the reversing lever, was the length in percentage of the piston strokes during which steam was admitted to the cylinders. Thus, "long cut-off" meant that steam was being admitted for a long portion, or high percentage, of the piston stroke. "Shortening the cut-off," "notching up" or "hooking up" meant reducing the portion of the stroke during which steam was admitted to the cylinders, allowing the steam to work by expansion. Practical cut-offs ranged between 90% in full gear and 15% at short cut-off.

The engineer distinguished between long and short cut-off by the position of the reversing lever. Controls graduated in percent cut-off came only with precision controls in the 1930s.

Train Weights: Several measures of train weights were used, including or excluding the locomotive and dead weight of cars. The sources consulted are often unclear as to what is included.

In this book, "trailing load" means the total dead weight of cars and their loads behind the engine.

Tractive Effort: Measurement of the power output of a steam locomotive is still more complicated than the dimensions given. The most commonly given, and easily calculated, measure and, hence, the most useful benchmark, is called "tractive effort," "tractive force" or "tractive power," best described as "calculated drawbar pull on starting." Tractive effort was measured only when a locomotive was under test; most commonly, it was calculated from dimensions. In one dynamometer test in 1898, a 2–8–0 with a tractive effort calculated at 22,848 pounds stalled at a measured drawbar pull of 24,000 pounds.[4] The commonly used coefficient of friction between driving wheel rim and rail was 0.25. Locomotives were not designed with tractive efforts much greater than 0.25 of the adhesion weight; if they were, they tended to slip.

For a two-cylinder engine the formula is:

$$T = (pD^2S)/W$$

T is the tractive effort in pounds;
p is the mean effective pressure in pounds per square inch (boiler pressure × one of the factors given below);
D is the cylinder diameter in inches;
S is the piston stroke in inches;
W is the driving wheel diameter in inches.

The factor used to calculate mean effective pressure is almost never quoted when tractive effort figures are published. The most commonly used factor—and that used in this book—was 0.85. The American steam locomotive authority of the early 1900s, G. R. Henderson, used 0.80, as did the British, although the British firm, Beyer Peacock, used 0.75. The French and the Belgians used 0.65. The Germans used 0.75 for locomotives with a Schmidt superheater. Baldwin used 0.90; Alco used 0.85; the Interstate Commerce Commission used 0.94.[5] When locomotives with limited cut-off were introduced in the 1920s, design engineers used 0.75 for an engine limited to 50% cut-off.[6]

The formula is often quoted in publications, but rarely derived. The derivation[7] states that the work done at the driving wheel rim during one complete revolution equals the work done in the cylinders during one complete cycle (one full stroke in each direction), ignoring friction in the cylinders, valves and rods. Work is force multiplied by distance. At the wheel rim this is equal to $T\pi W$ (the tractive force exerted on the rail multiplied by the wheel circumference). In the cylinders this is equal to $(4p\pi D^2 S)/4$, (two strokes in each of the two cylinders × the mean effective pressure × the piston area × the stroke). Therefore, $T\pi W = (4p\pi D^2 S)/4$ or $T = (pD^2 S)/W$.

For a three-cylinder single-expansion locomotive, the tractive effort resulting from the standard formula was multiplied by 1.5, for a four-cylinder single-expansion engine, such as a simple Mallet, by 2.

Over the years, manufacturers developed many variants on this formula to calculate the tractive force of compound engines. Space does not permit their enumeration or derivation. The 1923 ARMMA convention arrived at the following[8]:

For a two-cylinder compound, working compound:

$$T = (p\, D_L^2\, S)/((R + 1)W)$$

Where p is the mean effective pressure in pounds per square inch;
D_L is the diameter of the low-pressure cylinder in inches;
D_H is the diameter of the high-pressure cylinder in inches;
S is the piston stroke in inches;
R is the ratio of the volumes of the high- and low-pressure
   cylinders, where $R = D_L^2/D_H^2$;
W is the driving wheel diameter in inches.

For a two-cylinder compound, working single-expansion:

$$T = (pD_H^2 S)/W$$

For a four-cylinder compound, such as a Vauclain, tandem, balanced or Mallet type, working compound:

$$T = (2p\, D_L^2\, S)/((R + 1)W)$$

Lima developed a formula for calculating the tractive effort of a Shay:

$$T = (pD^2\, S\, 1.5\, G)/(W\, P)$$

where
p is the mean effective pressure in pounds per square inch;
D is the cylinder diameter in inches;
S is the piston stroke in inches;
G is the number of teeth in the main gear;
W is the diameter of the driving wheels in inches;
P is the number of teeth in the pinion gear.

Power Output: Electric motors, turbines and internal combustion engines are described in terms of their maximum power output in horsepower or kilowatts. Because of their speed:torque characteristics, these engines are typically arranged so that they can run up to efficient drive shaft rotation rates before the load is connected. Because a steam locomotive drove its wheels directly, no simple "nameplate" power could be applied to it. Different factors determined tractive effort and power output at different speeds. The graph on page 251 shows the relationship between speed, power and tractive effort for a typical steam locomotive.

At speeds up to 10 to 15 miles per hour, tractive effort was at a maximum, limited only by boiler pressure and cylinder size; power

output was zero on pull-out, increasing with increasing speed. Until the 1930s, freight locomotives spent much of their time in this regime.

As speed increased through 10 to 15 miles per hour (depending on design) the boiler could no longer supply the steam demand of the cylinders in full gear; the engineer had to shorten the cut-off.

At speeds of 15 to 60 miles per hour, power output reached its maximum, limited by the steaming rate of the boiler. Tractive effort declined with increasing speed. Counterbalancing the moving parts and the risk of track damage imposed a speed limit for many locomotives in this range.

At speeds higher than 60 miles per hour, friction losses choked off the steam flow to and through the cylinders, reducing power output. Counterbalancing was also a speed limiting factor. Raising this limiting speed was a major achievement of the 1920s and 1930s.

Steam locomotive power output was measured in two ways. An "indicator" could be applied to the cylinders, producing a trace of cylinder pressure versus piston displacement. The resulting loop had the dimensions of force and distance; multiplying in the piston area gave the work done per piston cycle. The number of cycles per minute, calculated from the engine's speed and driving wheel diameter, multiplied by the work done in each cycle, gave an "indicated horsepower."

A more direct measurement was obtained from a dynamometer car, coupled between the engine and its train, measuring speed and drawbar pull. Multiplying the two together gave "drawbar horsepower." The difference between "indicated" and "drawbar" horsepower was a measure of the locomotive's internal friction and rolling resistance.

Neither dynamometers nor indicators were permanent fixtures. Road tests, using either or both, were time-consuming and had to be carefully prepared and meticulously executed. Even so, the results were sometimes ambiguous.

Accuracy and Tolerances: A word of caution is warranted for all parameters and dimensions quoted in this book. Mechanical engineers were in the habit of quoting figures to an unwarranted—even absurd—precision.

In 1930[9]:

The water evaporated per lb. of coal as fired was 6.00 lb. for the Tuyere-type grates, as compared with 5.92 lb. for the standard Hulson grates, the relative boiler efficiencies being 63.51 per cent and 63.28 per cent, respectively. The Tuyere–type grates, therefore, gave a slightly better performance.

The difference in calculated efficiency amounts to 0.3%, well within testing error and therefore yielding no significant result. The authors of this and innumerable other articles show no awareness of testing error which, in a machine with as many independent variables as a steam locomotive, would have been large.

As late as 1946[10]:

The report of the Chicago Association of Commerce Committee of Investigation on Smoke Abatement and Electrification of Railroad Terminals, made under the direction of the late Dr. W. F. M. Goss in 1915, showed, for instance, that the visible smoke from locomotives at that time accounted for 22.06 per cent of the total smoke in Chicago.

This parameter is quoted to one hundredth of one percent when rational consideration would suggest that an accuracy as fine as ± twenty-five per cent would be suspect.

This book rounds parameters and dimensions to a degree of accuracy that the author believes to be both reasonable and useful to the reader. Thus the author has no compunction in rounding a dimension given as "12 feet 7¹⁵⁄₁₆ inches" to "12½ feet."

Appendix B: *Railroad Gazette/Railroad Age Gazette/Railway Age* Locomotive Type Articles

Railroad	Type	Title	Issue Date	Pages
Alabama Great Southern	4-4-0, 4-6-0	*Two Pittsburgh Compound Locomotives*	14-June-1895	379–80
(Alco demonstrator)	4-6-2	*Experimental Pacific Type Locomotive*	29-Dec-1911	1322–7
Alton & Southern	0-10-0	*Ten-Wheel Switcher with Aluminum Rods*	18-Apr-1931	759–60
Atchison, Topeka & Santa Fe	4-6-0	*Ten-Wheel Passenger Locomotive—Atchison, Topeka & Santa Fe*	22-Oct-1897	740–2
Atchison, Topeka & Santa Fe	2-8-0	*The Simple and Compound Consolidation Locomotives of the Atchison, Topeka and Santa Fe*	16-Jun-1899	422–5
Atchison, Topeka & Santa Fe	4-6-0	*Some Ten-Wheel Passenger Locomotives—Atchison, Topeka & Santa Fe*	18-Jan-1901	38–9
Atchison, Topeka & Santa Fe	4-6-0	*Ten-Wheel Passenger Locomotives—Atchison, Topeka & Santa Fe Class B-15*	25-Jan-1901	54–5
Atchison, Topeka & Santa Fe	4-6-0	*Baldwin-Vanderbilt Ten-Wheel Passenger Locomotive—Atchison, Topeka & Santa Fe*	04-Oct-1901	677
Atchison, Topeka & Santa Fe	2-6-2	*Prairies Type Passenger Locomotives—Atchison, Topeka & Santa Fe*	22-Nov-1901	800–1
Atchison, Topeka & Santa Fe	4-6-0	*Heavy Passenger Locomotives of the Atchison, Topeka & Santa Fe*	22-Nov-1901	808–9
Atchison, Topeka & Santa Fe	4-6-0	*Baldwin-Vanderbilt Ten-Wheel Passenger Locomotives—Atchison, Topeka & Santa Fe*	29-Nov-1901	823
Atchison, Topeka & Santa Fe	2-8-0	*Heavy Freight Locomotives of the Atchison, Topeka & Santa Fe*	20-Dec-1901	878
Atchison, Topeka & Santa Fe	2-6-2	*Prairie Type Passenger Locomotive with Traction Increaser—Atchison, Topeka & Santa Fe*	17-Jan-1902	41
Atchison, Topeka & Santa Fe	2-10-0	*The A., T. & S. F. Tandem Compound Decapod—Heaviest and Most Powerful*	31-Jan-1902	75
Atchison, Topeka & Santa Fe	2-6-2	*Prairie Type Freight Locomotives with Traction Increasers—Atchison, Topeka & Santa Fe*	16-May-1902	358
Atchison, Topeka & Santa Fe	2-10-0	*Tandem Compound for the Atchison, Topeka & Santa Fe*	30-May-1902	392–4
Atchison, Topeka & Santa Fe	2-8-0	*Tandem Compounds on the Atchison, Topeka & Santa Fe Railway*	06-Jun-1902	410
Atchison, Topeka & Santa Fe	2-8-2	*Mikado (2-8-2) Compounds for the Atchison*	03-Apr-1903	242–3
Atchison, Topeka & Santa Fe	2-10-2	*Tandem-Compound "Santa Fe" Type (2-10-2) Locomotive for the Santa Fe.*	09-Oct-1903	720
Atchison, Topeka & Santa Fe	2-6-2	*Balanced Compound Prairie Type Locomotives for the Atchison, Topeka & Santa Fe*	09-Nov-1906	414
Atchison, Topeka & Santa Fe	2-8-0, 4-6-2	*New Locomotives for the Atchison, Topeka & Santa Fe*	27-Mar-1908	453–4
Atchison, Topeka & Santa Fe	4-4-6-2, 2-8-8-2	*Mallet Locomotives for the Atchison*	26-Nov-1909	1018–24
Atchison, Topeka & Santa Fe	Tender	*Tender of 12,000 Gallons Capacity for Mallet Locomotives, Atchison, Topeka & Santa Fe*	21-Jan-1910	131–4
Atchison, Topeka & Santa Fe	4-4-2	*Balanced Compound Atlantic Type Locomotives; Atchison, Topeka & Santa Fe*	23-Dec-1910	1189–92
Atchison, Topeka & Santa Fe	2-6-6-2	*Mallet Locomotive with Articulated Boiler Rebuilt from Old Power*	10-Feb-1911	278–81
Atchison, Topeka & Santa Fe	2-6-6-2	*Mallet Locomotives on the Santa Fe*	24-Feb-1911	351–4
Atchison, Topeka & Santa Fe	2-6-6-2	*Locomotive Building During 1910; Baldwin Locomotive Works*	28-Apr-1911	993–7
Atchison, Topeka & Santa Fe	2-10-10-2	*The Largest Locomotive*	14-Apr-1911	906
Atchison, Topeka & Santa Fe	2-10-10-2	*Mallet Locomotive with 20 Drivers for the Santa Fe*	25-Aug-1911	379–81
Atchison, Topeka & Santa Fe	4-6-2	*Santa Fe Balanced Compound Pacific Type Locomotive*	19-Jun-1914	1519–20
Atchison, Topeka & Santa Fe	4-6-2	*Simple Pacific Type Locomotive for the Santa Fe*	09-Apr-1915	793–5
Atchison, Topeka & Santa Fe	2-8-2	*Mikado Type Locomotive for the Santa Fe System*	25-Jan-1918	209–11
Atchison, Topeka & Santa Fe	4-8-2	*First Mounain Type Locomotives for the Santa Fe*	29-Nov-1918	957–9
Atchison, Topeka & Santa Fe	4-8-4	*Santa Fe 4-8-4 Type Meets Expectations*	02-Jun-1928	1279–85
Atchison, Topeka & Santa Fe	2-10-4	*Santa Fe Locomotive 5000 Tested*	28-Nov-1931	829–32
Atchison, Topeka & Santa Fe	4-6-4	*Santa Fe Installs High-Speed Passenger Locomotives*	12-Mar-1938	450–2

Railroad	Type	Title	Issue Date	Pages
Atchison, Topeka & Santa Fe	4-8-4, 2-10-4	*New Passenger and Freight Power for the Santa Fe*	03-Dec-1938	803–9
Atlanta & West Point	4-6-2	*Pacific Locomotive for the Atlanta & West Point*	07-Jun-1907	784–5
Atlanta & West Point	4-6-2	*Pacific Type Locomotives for the A. & W. P. and W. of A.*	02-Oct-1926	641–2
Atlanta, Birmingham & Atlantic	2-8-2	*Mikado Locomotive for the Atlanta, Birmingham & Atlantic*	12-Aug-1910	282–3
Atlantic Coast Line	4-6-2	*Pacific Type for Passenger and Fast Freight*	18-Nov-1922	947–8
Atlantic Coast Line	2-10-2	*Santa Fe Type Locomotives for Atlantic Coast Line*	28-Nov-1925	1001–2
Atlantic Coast Line	4-8-4	*Passenger Locomotives for the Atlantic Coast Line*	24-Dec-1938	908–10
(Baldwin demonstrator)	2-4-2	*The Baldwin Locomotive "Columbia."*	26-May-1893	387
(Baldwin demonstrator)	2-4-2	*Performance of Baldwin Locomotive "Columbia."*	11-May-1894	333
(Baldwin)	2-8-8-8-2	*Triplex Compound Locomotive*	12-Apr-1912	851–2
Baltimore & Ohio	4-4-0	*Eight-Wheel Express Locomotive, Class I-6—Baltimore & Ohio*	14-Jul-1893	516–7
Baltimore & Ohio	2-8-0	*Cooke Consolidation Locomotive for the Baltimore & Ohio*	16-Oct-1896	717
Baltimore & Ohio	2-8-0	*Pittsburgh Consolidation Locomotive for the Baltimore & Ohio*	06-Nov-1896	770–1
Baltimore & Ohio	4-6-0	*Baldwin 10-Wheel Locomotive for the Baltimore & Ohio*	18-Dec-1896	877
Baltimore & Ohio	2-8-0	*Compound Consolidation Locomotives for the Baltimore & Ohio*	15-Jun-1900	385
Baltimore & Ohio	4-4-2	*Wide Fire-Box, Atlantic Type Locomotive—Baltimore & Ohio Railroad*	11-Jan-1901	22
Baltimore & Ohio	2-8-0	*Consolidation Locomotive for the Baltimore & Ohio*	05-Dec-1902	928–9
Baltimore & Ohio	4-4-2	*Atlantic Type (4-4-2) Locomotive for the Baltimore & Ohio*	31-Jul-1903	552–3
Baltimore & Ohio	0-6-6-0	*Heavy Mallet-Type Locomotive for the B. & O.*	04-Sep-1903	636–7
Baltimore & Ohio	0-6-6-0	*Mallet Articulated Compound for the Baltimore & Ohio*	27-May-1904	401
Baltimore & Ohio	2-8-0	*Heavy Consolidation Locomotives for the B. & O.*	08-Dec-1905	508
Baltimore & Ohio	2-8-0	*Consolidation Locomotive for the Baltimore & Ohio Railroad*	15-Dec-1905	563–4
Baltimore & Ohio	Various	*Baltimore & Ohio Railroad Motive Power*	15-Jun-1906	616–9
Baltimore & Ohio	4-4-2	*Atlantic Type Locomotives for the Baltimore & Ohio*	20-May-1910	1255–6
Baltimore & Ohio	0-8-8-0	*Heavy Mallet Locomotives; Baltimore & Ohio*	14-Jun-1911	1346–8
Baltimore & Ohio	2-8-2, 4-6-2	*Mikado and Pacific Type Locomotives; Baltimore & Ohio*	16-Jun-1911	1411–3
Baltimore & Ohio	2-10-2	*Baltimore & Ohio 2-10-2 Type Locomotive*	07-Aug-1914	242–4
Baltimore & Ohio	2-8-8-0	*Mallet Locomotives for Use in Road Service*	28-Jul-1916	145–7
Baltimore & Ohio	2-10-2	*Heavy Santa Fe Locomotives for B. & O.*	16-Feb-1924	413–4
Baltimore & Ohio	2-10-2, 4-8-2	*Santa Fe Type Locomotive Converted to 4-8-2*	01-Aug-1925	239–40
Baltimore & Ohio	4-6-2	*The Baltimore & Ohio's "President" Class Locomotives*	09-Apr-1927	1121–2
Baltimore & Ohio	4-8-2, 2-6-6-2	*Test Locomotives of 4-8-2 and 2-6-6-2 Types on the B. & O.*	11-Jul-1931	46–49, 55
Baltimore & Ohio	4-4-4, 4-6-4	*Baltimore & Ohio Builds Steam Power for High Speed*	04-May-1935	681–5
Baltimore & Ohio	2-8-8-4	*The B. & O. 2-8-8-4 Locomotives*	27-May-1944	1014–6
Bangor & Aroostook	4-6-2	*Bangor & Aroostook Purchases 4-6-2 Locomotives*	26-May-1928	1207–8
Bangor & Aroostook	4-8-2	*Freight Locomotives for the Bangor & Aroostook*	15-Mar-1930	635–6
Bessemer & Lake Erie	2-10-4	*B. & L. E. Receives Ten 2-10-4 Locomotives*	04-Sep-1937	312–3
Bismarck, Washburn & Great Falls	2-8-2	*Test of Bismarck, Washburn & Great Falls Lignite-Burning Locomotive, No. 3*	28-Mar-1902	223
Booth-Kelly Lumber Co.	2-6-6-2	*Locomotive Building During 1910; Baldwin Locomotive Works*	28-Apr-1911	993–7
Boston & Albany	4-4-0, 4-6-0	*New Boston & Albany Locomotives*	03-Feb-1893	90
Boston & Albany	4-4-0	*Schenectady Locomotives for the Boston & Albany*	02-Nov-1894	750–1
Boston & Albany	0-8-0	*Conversion of Consolidation Type Locomotives to Eight-Wheel Switchers*	10-Aug-1917	235–6
Boston & Albany	2-8-4	*Lima Builds 2-8-4 Type Locomotive*	02-May-1925	1077–82
Boston & Albany	2-8-4	*Tests of 2-8-4 Locomotive on B. & A.*	12-Sep-1925	467–71
Boston & Maine	4-6-0	*Schenectady Compound Ten-Wheelers for the Boston & Maine*	25-Mar-1898	217
Boston & Maine	4-6-0	*Ten-Wheel Engines for the Boston & Maine*	21-Oct-1898	754–5
Boston & Maine	2-8-0	*Some Schenectady Consolidation Locomotives*	05-Apr-1901	233–4
Boston & Maine	0-8-0	*Eight-Wheel switchers for B. & M.*	04-Feb-1928	325–6
Boston & Maine	2-8-4	*Boston & Maine Acquires Twenty 2-8-4 Type Locomotives*	28-Jul-1928	144–6
Boston & Maine	4-6-2	*High Speed Pacific Type Locomotives Received by Boston & Maine*	29-Dec-1934	851–2
Boston & Maine	4-6-2	*B. & M. Tests New Pacific Type Locomotives*	28-Dec-1935	849–50
Boston & Maine	4-8-2	*Boston & Maine 4-8-2 Locomotives for Fast Freight*	17-Aug-1935	213–4
Boston & Maine	4-8-2	*Dynamometer Tests of B. & M. 4-8-2 Type Locomotives*	25-Jan-1936	171–2
Brooklyn Bridge Terminals	2-4-2T	*Switching Locomotive for the Brooklyn Bridge Terminals*	16-Mar-1894	192
Buffalo & Susquehanna	Shay	*The Shay Locomotive*	09-Aug-1895	514
Buffalo & Susquehanna	2-8-0	*Buffalo & Susquehanna Consolidation Locomotive*	01-Nov-1895	717
Buffalo, Rochester & Pittsburgh	4-8-0	*Brooks Twelve-Wheelers for the Buffalo, Rochester & Pittsburgh*	24-Sep-1897	662–3
Buffalo, Rochester & Pittsburgh	4-6-0	*Ten-Wheel Passenger Locomotive for the B. R. & P. R.*	31-Mar-1899	224–5
Buffalo, Rochester & Pittsburgh	4-8-0	*Twelve-Wheel Wide Fire-Box Freight Locomotive—Buffalo, Rochester & Pittsburgh Ry.*	12-Oct-1900	666–7
Buffalo, Rochester & Pittsburgh	2-8-0	*Vanderbilt-Baldwin Consolidation Locomotive—Buffalo, Rochester & Pittsburgh Railway*	13-Sep-1901	631

Railroad	Type	Title	Issue Date	Pages
Buffalo, Rochester & Pittsburgh	4-4-2	Brooks Chautauqua Type Passenger Locomotives—Buffalo, Rochester & Pittsburgh	13-Dec-1901	853
Buffalo, Rochester & Pittsburgh	2-10-0	Decapod Locomotive for the Buffalo, Rochester & Pittsburgh	09-Aug-1907	151–2
Burlington & Missouri River	2-8-0	Pittsburgh Consolidation Locomotives for the Burlington & Missouri River	26-Aug-1898	607
Burlington, Cedar Rapids & Northern	4-4-2	Brooks "Chautauqua" Type Passenger Locomotives—Burlington, Cedar Rapids & Northern	30-Nov-1900	792–3
Butte, Anaconda & Pacific	4-8-0	Schenectady Twelve-Wheelers for the Butte, Anaconda & Pacific	05-Nov-1897	780–1
Calumet Terminal	2-8-2	Double-Ender Freight Transfer Locomotive—Calumet Terminal Railway	23-Jun-1893	458–9
Cambria Steel Co.	0-8-0	Heavy Power for Industrial Switching Service	05-Nov-1920	797–9
Canadian Pacific	0-6-6-0	Experimental Mallet Articulated Locomotive	05-Aug-1910	246–54
Canadian Pacific	0-6-6-0	Simple High-Speed Articulated Locomotive	12-Jul-1912	50–3
Carolina, Clinchfield & Ohio	2-8-0, 4-6-0	?	19-Mar-1909	560–1
Carolina, Clinchfield & Ohio	2-6-6-2, 4-6-2	Mallet and Pacific type Locomotives; Carolina, Clinchfield & Ohio	09-Sep-1910	469–70
Carolina, Clinchfield & Ohio	4-6-2	Pacific Type Locomotives for the Clinchfield	27-Nov-1914	1005–6
Carolina, Clinchfield & Ohio	2-8-8-2, 2-8-2	Carolina, Clinchfield & Ohio Freight Locomotives	15-Aug-1919	317–9
Central of Georgia	2-10-2	Central of Georgia 2-10-2 Locomotives	20-Mar-1926	869–70
Central of Georgia	4-8-4	Central of Georgia Locomotives	12-Feb-1944	344–6
Central of New Jersey	4-4-2	A New Baldwin Locomotive for the Central of New Jersey	12-June-1896	407
Central of New Jersey	4-4-2	A Brooks "Chautauqua" Type Locomotive—Central Railroad of New Jersey	03-Jan-1902	4–5
Central of New Jersey	2-6-2T	New Suburban Engines of the Central Railroad of New Jersey	20-Jun-1902	462–3
Central of New Jersey	4-4-0	Heavy, Eight-Wheeled Passenger Locomotive for the Central R. R. of New Jersey	19-Jan-1906	56–8
Central of New Jersey	4-6-2	Pacific Type Locomotives for the Central of New Jersey	01-Nov-1918	760–70
Central of New Jersey	4-6-2, 0-8-0	Passenger and Switching Locomotives for the C. R. R. of N. J.	03-Mar-1928	540–2
Central of New Jersey	4-6-2	Pacific 4-6-2 Types on the New Jersey Central	21-Feb-1931	413–4
Central Vermont	4-8-2	4-8-2 Type Locomotive for the Central Vermont	10-Sep-1927	478
Central Vermont	2-10-4	Central Vermont Receives Ten 2-10-4 Type Locomotivs	26-Jan-1929	242–3
Chicago & North Western	4-6-0	Schenectady Passenger Engine "Columbus."	16-Jun-1893	429
Chesapeake & Ohio	4-6-0	The Richmond Compound Locomotive on the Chesapeake & Ohio	21-Apr-1893	294–6
Chesapeake & Ohio	4-6-0	A Richmond Ten-Wheel Compound for the Chesapeake & Ohio	08-Nov-1895	736–7
Chesapeake & Ohio	2-8-0	Class G-6 Consolidation Locomotive for the Chesapeake & Ohio	19-Aug-1898	558
Chesapeake & Ohio	2-8-0	Two Recent Locomotives from the Richmond Works	16-Mar-1900	165
Chesapeake & Ohio	4-6-2	Passenger Engines for the Chesapeake & Ohio and the Missouri Pacific	01-Aug-1902	603–5
Chesapeake & Ohio	4-4-2	Atlantic Type Passenger Engines for the Chesapeake & Ohio	12-Sep-1902	699
Chesapeake & Ohio	0-6-0	Switch Engines for Bridge Service at Cincinnati	11-Aug-1905	129
Chesapeake & Ohio	2-8-0	Consolidation Locomotive; Chesapeake & Ohio	31-Jul-1908	627
Chesapeake & Ohio	2-6-6-2	Recent Mallet Articulated Locomotives	16-Dec-1910	1144–7
Chesapeake & Ohio	4-8-2	Mountain Type Locomotives for Heavy Passenger Service	22-Sep-1911	555–7
Chesapeake & Ohio	2-8-2	Mikado Locomotives for Heavy Freight Service	02-Feb-1912	201–4
Chesapeake & Ohio	4-6-2	Large Passenger Locomotives for the C. & O.	26-Sep-1913	571–2
Chesapeake & Ohio	4-6-2	Two Pacific Type Locomotives of High Power	25-Dec-1914	1185–9
Chesapeake & Ohio	0-10-0	Heavy Ten-Wheel Locomotives for Switching Service	30-Jan-1920	359–63
Chesapeake & Ohio	2-8-8-2	Simple Mallets for the Chesapeake & Ohio	12-Apr-1924	927–9
Chesapeake & Ohio	2-10-4	C. & O. Runs Road Tests on 2-10-4 Locomotives	17-Jan-1931	182–6
Chesapeake & Ohio	2-10-4	Chesapeake & Ohio Receives Large Two-Cylinder Locomotives	15-Nov-1930	1025–7
Chesapeake & Ohio	4-8-4	Chesapeake & Ohio Receives High-Power Passenger Locomotives	11-Jan-1936	111–2
Chesapeake & Ohio	2-6-6-6	C. & O. "Allegheny" Locomotives First of 2-6-6-6 Type	07-Mar-1942	478–83
Chesapeake & Ohio	4-6-4	Welding Assists in the Building of C. & O. Locomotives	29-Aug-1942	333–6
Chesapeake & Ohio	2-8-4	2-8-4 Type Freight Locomotives for the C.& O.	29-Jul-1944	200–3
Chesapeake & Ohio	Turbine	C. & O. Turbine-Electric Locomotives	20-Sep-1947	472–5
Chicago & Alton	4-6-0	Chicago & Alton Eight-Wheel Passenger Locomotive	05-Jan-1900	8–9
Chicago & Alton	4-6-2	Heavy Pacific Type Locomotive for the Chicago & Alton	07-Nov-1902	855
Chicago & Alton	4-6-2	Pacific Locomotives for the Chicago & Alton	02-Oct-1908	1041–4
Chicago & Eastern Illinois	4-8-0	Twelve-Wheel Locomotive for the Chicago & Eastern Illinois	24-Dec-1897	907
Chicago & Eastern Illinois	4-8-0	Twelve-Wheel Compound Chicago & Eastern Illinois Railroad	23-Feb-1900	117
Chicago & Eastern Illinois	4-8-0	Wide Fire-Box Freight Locomotive for the Chicago & Eastern Illinois	16-Nov-1900	755
Chicago & Eastern Illinois	2-8-0, 0-6-0	Conversion of Freight to Switch Locomotives	02-Nov-1917	799–800
Chicago & Grand Trunk	4-4-0	Passenger Locomotives,Chicago & Grand Trunk Railway	30-Oct-1896	751
Chicago & North Western	4-4-0	Schenectady Eight-Wheel Locomotives for the Chicago & Northwestern	11-Oct-1895	667–8
Chicago & North Western	4-4-0	Fast Passenger Locomotive of the Chicago & Northwestern Railway	26-May-1899	369

Railroad	Type	Title	Issue Date	Pages
Chicago & North Western	4-4-2	*New Class "D" Passenger Locomoties of the Chicago & Northwestern*	03-Aug-1900	520–1
Chicago & North Western	4-6-0	*Ten-Wheel Locomotive for the Chicago & Northwestern*	05-Jul-1907	6–8
Chicago & North Western	4-6-2	*Pacific Type Superheater Locomotive; Chicago & North Western*	17-Feb-1911	325–6
Chicago & North Western	4-4-2	*North Western Pulverized Coal Locomotive*	11-Aug-1916	227–30
Chicago & North Western	0-6-0	*Chicago & North Western Transfer Engines*	30-Mar-1917	698
Chicago & North Western	2-8-4	*2-8-4 Type Locomotives for the Chicago & North Western*	19-Nov-1927	988–90
Chicago & North Western	4-8-4	*North Western Gets Heavier Power*	11-Jan-1930	144–6
Chicago & North Western	4-8-4	*North Western Class-H Locomotives Are Being Modernized*	27-Apr-1946	860–2
Chicago & North Western	4-8-4	*Improvement of Power, Modernization of Repair Methods Save Money on C. & N. W.*	12-Nov-1949	834–7
Chicago Great Western	2-6-0	*New Mogul Locomotives of the Chicago Great Western Railway*	23-Sep-1898	686–7
Chicago Great Western	4-6-0	*Heavy Freight Locomotives of the Chicago Great Western Railway*	22-Sep-1899	657
Chicago Great Western	2-8-0, 4-6-0	*New Locomotives for the Chicago Great Western*	11-Feb-1910	313
Chicago Great Western	2-6-6-2	*Converted Mallet Locomotives for the Chicago Great Western*	04-Nov-1910	867–9
Chicago Great Western	2-6-6-2	*Mallet Articulated Locomotive; Chicago Great Western*	17-Mar-1911	495–7
Chicago Great Western	4-6-2	*Chicago Great Western "English Type" Locomotive*	02-Oct-1926	643
Chicago Union Transfer	2-8-0	*Consolidation Switching Locomotives for the Chicago Union Transfer Railway*	25-Apr-1902	307
Chicago, Burlington & Quincy	4-4-0	*C., B. & Q. Class "M" Locomotive*	16-Jun-1893	428
Chicago, Burlington & Quincy	2-4-2	*The Chicago, Burlington & Quincy Fast Passenger Locomotive—Class N.*	06-Dec-1895	798–800
Chicago, Burlington & Quincy	2-6-2, 0-6-0	*New Locomotives for the Chicago, Burlington & Quincy*	30-Mar-1900	195–6
Chicago, Burlington & Quincy	2-6-2	*New Class R "Prairie Type" Locomotive—Chicago, Burlington & Quincy R. R.*	22-Jun-1900	417
Chicago, Burlington & Quincy	2-6-2	*Prairie Type Engine for the Chicago, Burlington & Quincy*	20-Oct-1905	362–3
Chicago, Burlington & Quincy	2-6-6-2	*Mallet Locomotive for the Burlington*	13-May-1910	1213–6
Chicago, Burlington & Quincy	2-6-6-2	*Locomotive Building During 1910; Baldwin Locomotive Works*	28-Apr-1911	993–7
Chicago, Burlington & Quincy	2-10-2	*Largest Non-Articulated Locomotive*	03-May-1912	1006–10
Chicago, Burlington & Quincy	2-8-2	*Mikado Locomotives for the Burlington*	1912	?
Chicago, Burlington & Quincy	2-10-2	*Chicago, Burlington & Quincy 2-10-2 Freight Locomotive*	28-Aug-1914	387–8
Chicago, Burlington & Quincy	4-6-2	*Pacific Type Locomotives for the Burlington*	13-Aug-1915	275–8
Chicago, Burlington & Quincy	4-6-2, 2-8-2	*Pacific and Mikado Type Locomotives for C. B. & Q.*	02-Aug-1918	224–5
Chicago, Burlington & Quincy	2-10-4	*Burlington Freight Engine Shows Marked Economies*	23-Jun-1928	1425–8
Chicago, Burlington & Quincy	4-6-4, 4-8-4	*4-6-4 and 4-8-4 Type Power for the C. B. & Q.*	07-Mar-1931	499–500
Chicago, Indianapolis & Louisville	4-4-0	*New Passenger Engines of the Chicago, Indianapolis & Louisville*	30-Jul-1897	534–6
Chicago, Milwaukee & St. Paul	4-6-2	*Rhode Island Compoud Locomotive for the Chicago, Milwaukee & St. Paul*	09-Jun-1893	412–3
Chicago, Milwaukee & St. Paul	4-6-2	*Compound Passenger Locomotive for the Chicago, Milwaukee & St. Paul*	29-Sep-1893	715
Chicago, Milwaukee & St. Paul	4-4-2	*Compound Passenger Locomotives for the St. Paul*	24-Jul-1896	517
Chicago, Milwaukee & St. Paul	4-4-2	*Atlantic Type Passenger Locomotives—Chicago, Milwaukee & St. Paul Ry.*	20-Sep-1901	646–7
Chicago, Milwaukee & St. Paul	4-4-2	*The Atlantic Tyoe Locomotives of the Chicago, Milwaukee & St. Paul*	31-Jan-1902	71
Chicago, Milwaukee & St. Paul	4-4-2	*Atlantic (4-4-2) Type Locomotive for the Chicago, Milwaukee & St. Paul*	17-Jul-1903	526–7
Chicago, Milwaukee & St. Paul	4-6-2	*Heavy Passenger Locomotives for the C., M. & St. P.*	09-Jun-1905	654–6
Chicago, Milwaukee & St. Paul	4-4-2	*Balanced Compound Atlantic Locomotive for the Chicago, Milwaukee & St. Paul*	15-Nov-1907	596–7
Chicago, Milwaukee & St. Paul	2-8-2	*Mikado Locomotives for the Chicago, Milwaukee & Puget Sound*	16-Jul-1909	95–7
Chicago, Milwaukee & St. Paul	2-8-0	*Consolidation Locomotive, Chicago, Milwaukee & St. Paul*	06-May-1910	1157–9
Chicago, Milwaukee & St. Paul	4-6-2	*Pacific Locomotives for the St. Paul*	18-Jun-1910	1639
Chicago, Milwaukee & St. Paul	2-6-6-2	*Mallet Locomotives for the Chicago, Milwaukee & St. Paul*	21-Apr-1911	942–3
Chicago, Milwaukee & St. Paul	4-6-4	*Fourteen 4-6-4 Type Locomotives for the Milwaukee*	01-Mar-1930	559–60
Chicago, Milwaukee & St. Paul	4-6-4	*Milwaukee Motive Power Makes High Mileage*	23-Dec-1933	875–6
Chicago, Milwaukee & St. Paul	4-6-4	*New Milwaukee Locomotives Notable for Refinements in Design 166*	23-Jan-1932	154–5,
Chicago, Milwaukee & St. Paul	4-4-2	*Milwaukee Buys Steam Locomotives for Fast Schedules*	11-May-1935	719–25
Chicago, Milwaukee & St. Paul	4-8-4	*Freight and Passenger Power for the Milwaukee*	30-Apr-1938	761–3
Chicago, Milwaukee & St. Paul	4-8-4	*Milwaukee Buys 4-8-4 Type Freight Locomotives*	01-Jun-1940	967–8
Chicago, Rock Island & Pacific	4-4-0	*Chicago, Rock Island & Pacific Fast Passenger Locomotive, Class 22-A*	16-Jul-1896	488
Chicago, Rock Island & Pacific	4-4-2	*Wide Fire-Box Passenger Locomotives for the Chicago, Rock Island & Pacific Railway*	26-Apr-1901	278–9
Chicago, Rock Island & Pacific	2-8-0	*Rock Island Consolidation (2-8-0) Locomotive*	17-Apr-1903	276–7

Railroad	Type	Title	Issue Date	Pages
Chicago, Rock Island & Pacific	4-4-2, 4-6-2	Two Baldwin Four-Cylinder Balanced Compound Locomotives	17-Nov-1905	440
Chicago, Rock Island & Pacific	4-4-2	Four-Cylinder Balanced Simple Locomotives, Chicago, Rock Island and Pacific	06-Jan-1911	41–5
Chicago, Rock Island & Pacific	Various	Recent Power for the Rock Island Lines	09-Jan-1914	86–8
Chicago, Rock Island & Pacific	2-10-2	2-10-2 Type Locomotive for the Rock Island Lines	06-Dec-1918	992–4
Chicago, Rock Island & Pacific	2-8-2	Powerful Mikado Locomotives	23-Aug-1912	352
Chicago, Rock Island & Pacific	4-8-2	Mountain Type Features New Rock Island Power	25-Feb-1921	447–50
Chicago, Rock Island & Pacific	4-8-4	Rock Island Buys 4-8-4 Type Locomotives	07-Dec-1929	1325–6
Chicago, Rock Island & Pacific	4-8-4	Rock Island 4-8-4 Locomotives	26-Aug-1944	334–5, 337
Chicago, West Pullman & Southern	0-6-0	Heavy Power for Industrial Switching Service	05-Nov-1920	797–9
Cincinnati, Hamilton & Dayton	4-6-0	Ten-Wheel Freighter for the C. H. & D.	01-Aug-1902	612
Cleveland, Cincinnati, Chicago & St. Louis	4-4-0	Passenger Locomotive—Class "Y."	14-Apr-1893	274
Cleveland, Cincinnati, Chicago & St. Louis	4-6-0	Richmond Two-Cylinder Compound Freight Locomotive	09-Mar-1894	169–70
Cleveland, Cincinnati, Chicago & St. Louis	4-4-0	The New Schenectady Eight-Wheelers of the "Big Four"	18-Oct-1895	686–8
Cleveland, Cincinnati, Chicago & St. Louis	2-8-0	Consolidation Locomotive—Cleveland, Cincinnati, Chicago & St. Louis	15-Apr-1898	274–5
Cleveland, Cincinnati, Chicago & St. Louis	4-4-0	Eight-Wheel Passenger Locomotives—Cleveland, Cincinnati, Chicago & St. Louis Railway	15-Jul-1898	505–6
Cleveland, Cincinnati, Chicago & St. Louis	2-8-0	Heavy Consolidation Locomotive for the Cleveland, Cincinnati, Chicago & St. Louis Railway	28-Apr-1899	296–7
Cleveland, Cincinnati, Chicago & St. Louis	4-6-0	Heavy Ten-Wheel Passenger Locomotives of the Cleveland, Cincinnati, Chicago & St. Louis	24-May-1901	344–5
Cleveland, Cincinnati, Chicago & St. Louis	4-4-2	Atlantic Type Locomotive for the Big Four	31-Oct-1902	832–3
Colorado & Northern	Climax	A 50-ton Geared Locomotive	26-Nov-1897	838
Colorado & Southern	2-8-0	Tandem-Compound Consolidations for the Colorado & Southern	13-Nov-1903	808
Colorado Springs & Cripple Creek	2-8-0, 0-6-0	Locomotives for the Colorado Springs & Cripple Creek District Railroad	01-Mar-1901	138
Cross Creek Coal Co.	0-4-0	A Rogers Switcher	02-Aug-1895	511
Delaware & Hudson	4-4-0	A New Schenectady Locomotive	17-May-1895	309
Delaware & Hudson	2-8-0	Consolidated Locomotive for the Delaware & Hudson	18-Nov-1898	827
Delaware & Hudson	2-8-0	Schenectady Consolidation Locomotives for the D. & H.	28-Jul-1899	539
Delaware & Hudson	2-8-0	Consolidation (2-8-0) Locomotive for the Delaware & Hudson	08-Apr-1904	266–7
Delaware & Hudson	4-6-0	Delaware & Hudson Locomotives With Young Valves and Gear	02-Feb-1906	102–3
Delaware & Hudson	0-8-8-0	Mallet Articulated Compound Locomotive for the Delaware & Hudson Co.	27-May-1910	1303–10
Delaware & Hudson	0-8-8-0	Mallet Superheater Locomotives; Delaware & Hudson	11-Aug-1911	291–2
Delaware & Hudson	4-6-2	Two Pacific Type Locomotives of High Power	25-Dec-1914	1185–9
Delaware & Hudson	2-8-0	The D. & H. Pulverized Fuel Consolidation	16-Jun-1916	1384
Delaware & Hudson	2-8-0	A High-Capacity Consolidation	19-Jun-1916	1425
Delaware & Hudson	2-8-0	D. & H. Christens New Locomotive	13-Dec-1924	1071–2
Delaware & Hudson	4-6-2	D. & H.Pacific Type Locomotive	20-Jul-1929	201–2
Delaware & Hudson	4-6-2	Pacific Type Locomotive Equipped with Poppet Valves	29-Mar-1930	767–8
Delaware & Hudson	2-8-0	Third High-Pressure Locomotive on the D. & H.	26-Jul-1930	143–7
Delaware & Hudson	4-8-0	Delaware & Hudson Develops Fourth High-Pressure Locomotive	17-Jun-1933	854–7
Delaware & Hudson	4-6-2	Locomotive with Roller Bearings on Main and Side Rods	07-Jul-1934	4–6
Delaware & Hudson	4-6-6-4	D. & H. Installs Articulated Freight Locomotives	10-Aug-40	207–13, 219
Delaware & Hudson	4-8-4	D. & H. 4-8-4 Type Freight Power	17-Jul-1943	93–6
Delaware, Lackawanna & Western	4-6-0	Ten-Wheel Passenger Locomotive—Delaware, Lackawanna & Western	08-Sep-1893	667
Delaware, Lackawanna & Western	4-4-0	New Locomotives for the Delaware, Lackawanna & Western	28-Aug-1896	601
Delaware, Lackawanna & Western	2-6-0	Mogul Locomotive for the Delaware, Lackawanna & Western	02-Dec-1898	859
Delaware, Lackawanna & Western	2-8-0	New Consolidation Engine of the Delaware, Lackawanna & Western	25-Aug-1899	592
Delaware, Lackawanna & Western	4-8-0	Brooks 12-Wheel Engines for the Lackawanna Railroad	20-Oct-1899	724–5

Railroad	Type	Title	Issue Date	Pages
Delaware, Lackawanna & Western	4-6-0	*Heavy Ten-Wheel Passenger Locomotive—Delaware, Lackawanna & Western*	22-Jun-1900	427–8
Delaware, Lackawanna & Western	4-4-0	*Heavy Eight-Wheel Passenger Locomotive—Delaware, Lackawanna & Western*	03-May-1901	299
Delaware, Lackawanna & Western	4-4-2	*Lackawanna Locomotive with Schenectady Superheater*	13-Oct-1905	342–3
Delaware, Lackawanna & Western	4-6-0	*Heavy Ten-Wheel Passenger Locomotive for the Delaware, Lackawanna & Western R. R.*	24-Nov-1905	474
Delaware, Lackawanna & Western	2-8-0	*Walschaerts Valve Gear on Lackawanna Consolidation Locomotives*	15-Oct-1909	708–11
Delaware, Lackawanna & Western	4-6-2	*Anthracite Burning Pacific Type Locomotives*	19-Jul-1912	88–91
Delaware, Lackawanna & Western	2-8-2	*Powerful Mikados for the Lackawanna*	30-Aug-1912	377–9
Delaware, Lackawanna & Western	4-6-2	*4-6-2 Type Freight Locomotive*	14-Jun-1913	1390–1
Delaware, Lackawanna & Western	4-6-2	*Lackawanna Pacific Type Freight Locomotive*	09-Oct-1914	657–9
Delaware, Lackawanna & Western	4-6-2	*Heavy Pacific Type Locomotive for the Lackawanna*	24-Dec-1915	1185–7
Delaware, Lackawanna & Western	2-8-2	*Heavy Mikado Type Locomotives for D. L. & W.*	03-Mar-1923	510–3
Delaware, Lackawanna & Western	4-8-2	*Lackawanna Buys Twenty-Five Three-Cylinder Locomotives*	15-Jan-1927	251–2
Delaware, Lackawanna & Western	4-8-4	*Lackawanna Buys Five 4-8-4 Type Locomotives*	03-Dec-1927	1120–2
Delaware, Lackawanna & Western	4-8-4	*Lackawanna Rceives Twenty More 4-8-4 Type Locomotives*	16-Feb-1935	267–9
Delaware, Lackawanna & Western	4-6-4	*Lackawanna Receives High-Speed Passenger Locomotives*	19-Feb-1938	345–6
Denver & Rio Grande	4-6-0	*Ten-Wheel Passenger Locomotives for the Denver & Rio Grande*	28-Jul-1899	537
Denver & Rio Grande	2-10-2	*The Heaviest Santa Fe Type Locomotives*	03-Aug-1917	189–192
Denver & Rio Grande Western	4-8-2	*Three-Cylinder Mountain Type Locomotive*	04-Sep-1926	431–4
Denver & Rio Grande Western	4-8-4	*D. & R. G. W. Buys Ten 4-8-4 Type Locomotives*	24-Aug-1929	456–8
Denver & Rio Grande Western	2-8-8-2	*Ten 2-8-8-2 Type Locomotives for the D. & R. G. W.*	03-Sep-1927	434–8
Denver & Rio Grande Western	4-6-6-4	*Ten Articulated Locomotives for the D. & R. G. W.*	09-Jul-1938	42–4, 70
Detroit, Toledo & Ironton	2-8-4	*Detroit, Toledo & Ironton Receives 2-8-4 Type Locomotives*	01-Feb-1936	213–4
Duluth, Missabe & Iron Range	2-8-8-4	*D. M. & I. R. Freight Power*	05-Jun-1943,	1135–9
Duluth, Missabe & Northern	2-8-8-2	*Mallet Locomotives; Duluth, Missabe & Northern*	18-Aug-1911	312–4
Duluth, Missabe & Northern	2-8-8-2, 2-10-2	*Heavy Freight Locomotives for the D. M. & N.*	22-Dec-1916	1125–7
El Paso & Southwestern	4-6-2	*Heavy Pacific-Type Locomotives for the El Paso & Southwestern*	06-Nov-1903	793
El Paso Rock Island Route	Shay	*The Largest Shay Locomotive Ever Built*	20-Jun-1902	466
Erie	4-6-0	*New Brooks Locomotives for the Erie*	09-Oct-1896	701
Erie	4-4-2	*Atlantic Type Locomotives for the Erie*	21-Jul-1899	519
Erie	0-6-0	*The Erie's Six-Wheel Switching Locomotives—Wide Fire-Box*	21-Dec-1900	836
Erie	2-8-0	*Erie Class H-12 Consolidation Locomotive*	14-Jun-1901	398–9
Erie	2-8-0	*Tandem Compound Consolidation for the Erie*	05-Sep-1902	685
Erie	4-6-2	*Pacific Locomotive with Superheater for the Erie Railroad*	09-Jun-1905	620–2
Erie	4-4-2	*Cole Balanced Compound for the Erie*	14-Jul-1905	37
Erie	0-8-8-0	*Mallet Compounds for the Erie*	02-Nov-1906	389
Erie	0-8-8-0	*Mallet Compound Locomotive for the Erie Railroad*	16-Aug-07	170–5
Erie	0-8-8-0	*Details of Mallet Articulated Compound Locomotive*	04-Oct-1907	384–8
Erie	2-8-2	*Mikado Locomoties for the Erie*	09-Feb-1912	241–4
Erie	4-6-2	*Powerful Pacifics for the Erie*	14-Jun-1913	1392–3
Erie	2-8-8-8-2	*Articulated Locomotive With One Engine on the Tender*	08-May-1914	1027–31
Erie	2-10-2	*Erie 2-10-2 Type Locomotive*	26-Mar-1915	706–8
Erie	2-10-2	*Recent Examples of 2-10-2 Type Locomotives*	21-Apr-1916	887–891
Erie	2-8-8-8-2	*Triplex Articulated Locomotives of the Erie*	14-Jul-1916	74–5
Erie	2-8-4	*Erie Acquires 2-8-4 Freight Locomotives*	08-Oct-1927	668–71
Erie	2-8-4	*Erie Places 2-8-4 Type Locomotives in Freight Service*	22-Oct-1927	776–8
Erie & Wyoming Valley	2-6-0	*Smith's Three-Cylinder Locomotive*	15-Mar-1895	164–5
Erie & Wyoming Valley	4-2-2	*Steam Motor Car for the Erie & Wyoming Valley*	03-Feb-1899	83
Fitchburg	4-6-0	*Ten-Wheel Passenger Locomotives for the Fitchburg*	21-Oct-1898	757
Florida Central & Peninsular	4-4-0	*?*	15-Nov-1895	752–3
Florida Central & Peninsular	4-4-0	*Long Stroke Locomotive on the Florida Central*	24-Feb-1899	139

Railroad	Type	Title	Issue Date	Pages
Georgia Northern	2-8-2	Mikado Type Locomotive for the Georgia Northern	29-Jun-1929	1552–4
Grand Trunk	4-6-0	Two New Grand Trunk Locomotives	11-Feb-1898	92
Grand Trunk	2-8-2	Grand Trunk Mikados	13-Jun-1913	1359
Grand Trunk	4-6-4T	Grand Trunk Locomotives for Suburban Service	12-Mar-1915	628–9
Grand Trunk	0-6-0	Grand Trunk 0-6-0 Type Switching Locomotives	04-Jul-1919	7–8
Great Northern	2-6-0	Brooks Freight Locomotives for the Great Northern	23-Oct-1896	737
Great Northern	4-8-0	Heavy 12-Wheel Locomotive for the Great Northern	07-Jan-1898	3–5
Great Northern	4-6-0	Ten-Wheel Passenger Locomotives for the Great Northern Railway	07-Oct-1898	719–20
Great Northern	2-6-6-2	Mallet Compound Locomotive for the Great Northern	17-Aug-1906	148
Great Northern	2-6-6-2	Mallet Compound Locomotive for the Great Northern	12-Oct-1906	315–21
Great Northern	Various	New Locomotives for the Great Northern	26-Oct-1906	371–2
Great Northern	2-6-8-0	Locomotive Building During 1910; Baldwin Locomotive Works	28-Apr-1911	993–7
Great Northern	2-8-2	Mikado Locomotives for the Great Northern	15-Dec-1911	1214–6
Great Northern	2-6-8-0	Mallet Locomotives for the Great Northern	27-Sep-1912	572–5
Great Northern	4-6-2	Passenger Locomotives for the Great Northern	04-Dec-1914	1047–50
Great Northern	4-8-2	Mountain Type Locomotive for Great Northern	08-Dec-1923	1065–6
Great Northern	2-10-2	2-10-2 Type Replace Mallets on Great Northern	23-Feb-1924	459–60
Great Northern	2-8-8-2	Great Northern Acquires Mallet Locomotives	22-Aug-1925	359–61
Great Northern	4-8-4	Great Northern Buys Six 4-8-4 Type Passenger Locomotives	09-Nov-1929	1097–8
Great Northern	2-8-8-2	Great Northern Adds to 2-8-8-2 Type Motive Power	28-Dec-1929	1477–8
Great Northern	4-8-4	4-8-4 Type Locomotives for Passenger Service	26-Apr-1930	965–6
Gulf, Colorado & Santa Fe	4-4-0	Oil Burning Locomotives on the Gulf, Colorado & Santa Fe	22-Nov-1901	804
Harriman Lines	4-4-2, 2-6-0	Standard Atlantic and Mogul Locomotives for the Harriman Lines	01-Jan-1909	26–8
Illinois Central	2-6-0	The Rogers Compound Locomotive on the Illinois Central	17-Mar-1893	200–1
Illinois Central	4-4-0	New Eight-Wheel Passenger Locomotives—Illinois Central Railroad	05-Feb-1897	92–4
Illinois Central	4-6-0	New Ten-Wheel Passenger Locomotive—Louisville Division, Illinois Central	02-Jul-1897	474–5
Illinois Central	2-6-0	Mogul Locomotives for the Illinois Central	20-Aug-1897	585
Illinois Central	4-6-0	Some Recent Rogers Locomotives	02-Dec-1898	857
Illinois Central	4-8-0	The 116-Ton Illinois Central Twelve Wheel Locomotive	29-Sep-1899	670–1
Illinois Central	2-8-0	A Very Heavy Consolidation Engine for the Illinois Central	15-Dec-1899	858–9
Illinois Central	4-6-0	Vanderbilt Locomotive and Tender—Illinois Central Railroad	31-May-1901	366–7
Illinois Central	2-6-2	Competitive Locomotive Types for the Illinois Central	20-Jun-1902	458–9
Illinois Central	2-8-2	Heavy Mikado Locomotives for the Illinois Central	29-Sep-1911	585–6
Illinois Central	0-6-0	Superheater Switch Engines with Gaines Combustion Chamber	14-Feb-1913	289
Illinois Central	2-10-2	Illinois Central 2-10-2 Type Locomotives	20-Jul-1917	107–8
Illinois Central	2-8-4	2-8-4 Locomotives for the Illinois Central	11-Dec-1926	1161–2
Illinois Central	0-8-0	Illinois Central Buys Eight-Wheel Switchers	14-Dec-1929	1367–8
Indiana Harbor Belt	2-8-2	Two Light Mikado Locomotives Built at Lima	01-Mar-1924	505–6
Indiana Harbor Belt	0-8-0	Eight-Wheel Switch Engine with Large Boiler Capacity	06-Aug-1927	265–6
Intercolonial	4-6-0	Intercolonial Locomotives with Cleveland Cylinders	14-Jun-1901	395–6
Iowa Central	2-6-0	Mogul Engines for the Iowa Central	02-Oct-1908	1058–9
Kansas City Southern	2-10-4	Heavy Freight Power for K.C.S.	08-Jan-1938	113–6
Kentucky & Tennessee	2-8-2	Mikado Locomotive for the Kentucky & Tennessee Railway	29-May-1908	731–3
Lake Shore & Michigan Southern	4-4-0	Brooks Passenger Engine for the Lake Shore & Michigan Southern	02-Jun-1893	409
Lake Shore & Michigan Southern	4-4-0	The "Exposition Flyer" Locomotive of the Lake Shore	09-Jun-1893	410–1
Lake Shore & Michigan Southern	4-6-0	Lake Shore Ten-Wheel Passenger Engine	01-Nov-1895	719–20
Lake Shore & Michigan Southern	4-6-0	Ten-Wheel Passenger Locomotives for the Lake Shore & Michigan Southern	01-Jan-1897	5
Lake Shore & Michigan Southern	4-6-0	Freight Locomotives for the Lake Shore & Michigan Southern	19-May-1899	348–9
Lake Shore & Michigan Southern	4-6-0	Brooks Ten-Wheelers for the Michigan Southern	10-Nov-1899	778–9
Lake Shore & Michigan Southern	2-8-0	New Consolidation Locomotives for the Lake Shore & Michigan Southern	02-Mar-1900	133
Lake Shore & Michigan Southern	2-6-2	New Passenger Locomotives for the Lake Shore & Michigan Southern	29-Mar-1901	220–1
Lake Shore & Michigan Southern	0-6-0	Six-Wheel Switcher—Lake Shore & Michigan Southern	19-Sep-1902	728
Lake Shore & Michigan Southern	4-4-0	New Inspection Locomotive on the Lake Shore	19-Jun-1903	444

Railroad	Type	Title	Issue Date	Pages
Lake Shore & Michigan Southern	2-6-2	*New Passenger Locomotives for the Lake Shore*	02-Dec-1904	600–2
Lake Shore & Michigan Southern	0-10-0	*Powerful Switching Locomotives for the Lake Shore*	21-Jul-1905	64–5
Lake Shore & Michigan Southern	4-4-0	*The Lake Shore Four-Cylinder Simple Inspection Locomotive*	07-Sep-1906	198–9
Lake Shore & Michigan Southern	4-6-2	*Pacific Locomotive for the Lake Shore & Michigan Southern*	06-Sep-1907	258–9
Lake Shore & Michigan Southern	2-8-2	*Powerful Mikados for the Lake Shore*	02-May-1913	987–90
Lake Shore & Michigan Southern	0-8-8-0	*Mallet Compounds for Hump Yard Service*	12-Jun-1914	1335–7
Lake Superior & Ishpeming	2-8-0	*Pittsburgh Compound Locomotives for the Lake Superior & Ishpeming*	04-Sep-1896	617
Lake Superior & Ishpeming	2-8-0	*Large Locomotives of the Consolidation Type*	16-Jun-1916	1327–9
Lehigh & Hudson River	2-8-0	*Consolidation Type Locomotives for Lehigh & Hudson River*	05-Sep-1925	439–40
Lehigh & Hudson River	4-8-2	*L. & H. R. 4-8-2 Type Locomotives*	12-Aug-1944	260–1
Lehigh Valley	4-6-0	*Lehigh Valley Tenwheeler*	14-June-1895	381
Lehigh Valley	4-4-0	*Lehigh Valley Wide-Firebox Express Locomotive*	25-Oct-1895	698–700
Lehigh Valley	4-4-2	*A New Baldwin Locomotive for the Lehigh Valley Railroad*	09-Oct-1896	696–7
Lehigh Valley	2-8-0	*A Heavy Consolidation for the Lehigh Valley*	13-Jan-1899	20–1
Lehigh Valley	2-8-0	*Consolidation Locomotive with Large Drivers for the Lehigh Valley Railroad*	10-Mar-1899	171
Lehigh Valley	4-6-0	*Heavy Ten-Wheel Compound Passenger Locomotives with Wide Fire-Box—Lehigh Valley Railroad*	28-Dec-1900	854
Lehigh Valley	2-6-2	*Prairie Type (2-6-2) Locomotive for the Lehigh Valley*	29-May-1903	375
Lehigh Valley	4-6-0	*Heavy Ten-Wheel Locomotives for the Lehigh Valley*	27-Oct-1905	399
Lehigh Valley	2-8-2	*Mikados for the Lehigh Valley*	16-Jun-1913	1408–9
Lehigh Valley	4-6-2	*Anthracite Burning Pacific Type Locomotive*	06-Mar-1914	473–5
Lehigh Valley	4-6-2, 2-10-2	*Heavy Locomotives for the Lehigh Valley*	27-Apr-1917	897–900
Lehigh Valley	2-8-2	*Mikado Locomotives for the Lehigh Valley*	24-Nov-1923	959–60
Lehigh Valley	4-8-2	*Lehigh Valley Three-Cylinder Locomotive Tests*	15-Mar-1924	755–7
Lehigh Valley	4-8-2	*Lehigh Valley Three-Cylinder Locomotive*	14-Jun-1924	1585–7
Lehigh Valley	4-8-4	*Lehigh Valley Buys Two 4-8-4 Locomotives*	04-Apr-1931	669–70
Lehigh Valley	4-8-4	*Lehigh Valley Tests 4-8-4 Type Locomotives*	19-Mar-1932	469–72
Lehigh Valley	4-8-4	*Lehigh Valley Acquires Five More 4-8-4 Type Locomotives*	23-Feb-1935	293–5
Lehigh Valley	4-8-4	*Lehigh Valley 4-8-4 Freight Power*	29-Apr-1944	816–8
Lehigh& New England	2-8-0	*Powerful Consolidation for the L. & N. E.*	23-Dec-1922	1197–8
Long Island	2-8-0	*Consolidation Locomotives for the Long Island Railroad*	24-Feb-1899	137
Long Island	4-4-2	*Atlantic Type Locomotives for the Long Island*	05-Jul-1901	483
Louisville & Nashville	2-8-0	*Cooke Consolidation for the Louisville & Nashville*	26-Jan-1900	55
Louisville & Nashville	4-6-2	*Pacific Type Locomotive, Louisville & Nashville*	17-Jun-1912	1446–7
Louisville & Nashville	2-8-2, 4-6-2	*New Power for the Louisville & Nashville*	17-Jun-1914	1471–2
Louisville & Nashville	0-8-0	*Switch Engines for the Louisville & Nashville*	01-Dec-1916	998–9
Maine Central	2-6-0	*?*	14-Aug-1896	567
Maine Central	4-6-0	*Maine Central Purchases Ten-Wheel Locomotives*	08-Mar-1924	555–6
Mesabi Iron Co.	0-6-0T	*Heavy Power for Industrial Switching Service*	05-Nov-1920	797–9
Michigan Central	4-6-0	*Some Michigan Central Locomotives*	11-Jun-1897	411–12
Michigan Central	2-8-2	*A Remarkable Mikado on the Michigan Central*	22-Jul-1922	171–2
Michigan Central	2-8-2	*Michigan Central Mikado Has Many Special Features*	02-Sep-1922	411–5
Michigan Central	2-8-2	*Performance of Lima Locomotive No.8000*	07-Feb-1925	373–4
Midland Terminal	2-8-0	*A Recent Schenectady Consolidation Locomotive*	06-Mar-1896	159
Minneapolis, St. Paul & Sault Ste. Marie	2-10-0	*Compound Decapod—Minneapolis, St. Paul & Sault St. Marie Railway*	22-Jun-1900	429
Minneapolis, St. Paul & Sault Ste. Marie	2-10-0	*The Soo Line Compound Decapod*	17-Aug-1900	551
Minneapolis, St. Paul & Sault Ste. Marie	2-8-0	*Schenectady Two-Cylinder Compound Locomotive—Soo Line*	21-Feb-1902	124
Minneapolis, St. Paul & Sault Ste. Marie	2-6-0	*Class D2 Mogul (2-6-0) Locomotive for the "Soo Line."*	23-Oct-1903	757
Minneapolis, St. Paul & Sault Ste. Marie	2-8-0	*Cross-Compound Consolidation for the "Soo" Line*	09-Jun-1905	658
Minneapolis, St. Paul & Sault Ste. Marie	4-8-4	*Soo Line Locomotives Built by Lima*	01-Oct-1938	483–4
Missouri Pacific	4-6-0	*?*	14-Oct-1898	736–7

Railroad	Type	Title	Issue Date	Pages
Missouri Pacific	4-6-0	*Rogers Locomotives for the Missouri Pacific*	21-Oct-1898	761
Missouri Pacific	4-6-2	*Passenger Engines for the Chesapeake & Ohio and the Missouri Pacific*	01-Aug-1902	603–5
Missouri Pacific	2-8-2	*Mikado Superheater Locomotives for the Missouri Pacific*	12-Jan-1912	55–7
Missouri Pacific	2-8-2, 4-8-2	*New Locomotives for the Missouri Pacific*	10-Sep-1921	495–7
Missouri Pacific	4-8-2	*4-8-2 Type Locomotives for the Missouri Pacific*	05-Nov-1927	891
Missouri Pacific	0-8-0	*Eight-Wheel Switchers for the Missouri Pacific*	16-Nov-1929	1139–41
Missouri Pacific	4-8-4	*Missouri Pacific Freight Power*	25-Mar-1944	603–4
Missouri, Kansas & Texas	2-6-0	*Compound Mogul Locomotive—Missouri, Kansas & Texas Railway*	31-Jan-1896	71
Mobile & Ohio	4-6-0	*Rogers Locomotives for the Mobile & Ohio*	30-Dec-1898	931
Nashville, Chattanooga & St. Louis	2-8-2, 4-6-2	*Mikado and Pacific Type Locomotives of Moderate Size*	07-May-1915	976–7
Nashville, Chattanooga & St. Louis	2-8-8-2	*Mallet Locomotives for the N. C. & St. L.*	05-May-1916	985–8
Nashville, Chattanooga & St. Louis	2-8-2	*Locomotive Service Tests on the N. C. & St. L.*	16-Jun-1923	1425–6
New Orleans & Northeastern	2-8-2, 4-6-2	*Pacific and Mikado Type Locomotives for the New Orleans & Northeastern*	22-Jan-1915	134–5
New York & Brooklyn Bridge	2-4-2T	*Porter Locomotive, New York & Brooklyn Bridge*	24-May-1895	327
New York Central	4-4-0	*New York Central Fast Express Locomotive*	07-Apr-1893	262–3
New York Central	4-4-0	*New York Central Engine for the World's Fair*	28-Apr-1893	312–4
New York Central	0-6-0	*Compound Switching Locomotive*	24-Apr-1896	284–5
New York Central	4-4-0	*New Passenger Locomotives for the New York Central & Hudson River Railroad*	15-Jan-1897	43
New York Central	4-4-0	*New Suburban Locomotives for the New York Central*	1897	702
New York Central	2-6-0	*A Schenectady Mogul for the New York Central*	28-Oct-1898	776–7
New York Central	2-6-0	*New York Central Moguls in 1889 and 1899*	30-Jun-1899	470–1
New York Central	2-6-0	*The New York Central Class P Mogul Freight Locomotive*	29-Sep-1899	673
New York Central	2-6-0	*A Mogul Engine for the New York Central*	30-Mar-1900	197
New York Central	4-4-0	*Development of New York Central Locomotive, Class I-3*	26-Oct-1900	701
New York Central	4-4-2	*The New Class I Central-Atlantic Type Locomotives—New York Central Railroad*	01-Feb-1901	72–3
New York Central	2-8-0	*Two-Cylinder Compound Consolidation Locomotives, Class G-1—New York Central Railroad*	01-Mar-1901	140
New York Central	4-4-0	*Performance of Class I and Class C Locomotives—New York Central Railroad*	01-Nov-1901	751
New York Central	2-6-4T	*Heavy Double-End Suburban Locomotive for the New York Central*	28-Mar-1902	224–5
New York Central	4-4-2	*Cole's Four-Cylinder Balanced Compound Locomotive for the New York Central*	13-May-1904	360–2
New York Central	2-8-0	*Consolidation Locomotive for the N. Y. Central, with Walschaert Gear*	09-Jun-1905	636
New York Central	2-8-0	*Consolidation Locomotive for the New York Central Lines*	15-Jun-1906	613–5
New York Central	4-6-2	*Pacific Locomotive for the New York Central*	03-Apr-1908	468–9
New York Central	2-6-6-2	*Mallet Articulated Compound Locomotive, New York Central Lines*	01-Apr-1910	888–90
New York Central	4-6-2	*Heavy Pacific Type Locomotives; New York Central Lines*	31-Mar-1911	785–9
New York Central	4-8-2	*New York Central 4-8-2 Type Locomotives*	28-Dec-1917	1167–70
New York Central	4-8-2	*Three-Cylinder Locomotive on New York Central*	03-Nov-1923	821–2
New York Central	4-6-4	*First Hudson Type Locomotive*	19-Feb-1927	523–6
New York Central	4-8-4	*Multi-Pressure 3-Cylinder Locomotive for N. Y. C.*	03-Oct-1931	521
New York Central	4-6-4	*New York Central "Streamlines" Passenger Locomotive*	22-Dec-1934	825–6
New York Central	4-6-2	*New York Central Builds Distinctive Streamline Train*	11-Jul-1936	50–62
New York Central	4-6-4	*New N. Y. C. Locomotives Show High Power Concentration*	02-Apr-1938	506–605
New York Central	4-6-2, 4-6-4	*High-Capacity Steam Passenger Locomotives, Part 1*	16-Aug-1941	273–7
New York Central	4-6-2, 4-6-4	*High-Capacity Steam Passenger Locomotives, Part 2*	06-Sep-1941	376–80
New York Central	4-8-2	*New York Central Buys All-round Road Locomotives*	07-Dec-1940	856–61, 864
New York Central	4-8-2	*Versatile Road Motive Power for the New York Central*	26-Jun-1943	1250–4
New York Central	4-8-2	*N. Y. C. Locomotives Scoop Water Without Reducing Speed*	22-Jul-1944	149–51
New York Central	4-8-4	*First 4-8-4 on the New York Central*	22-Sep-1945	480–4
New York Central	4-8-4	*An Evaluation of Railroad Motive Power, Part I*	23-Aug-1947	323–7
New York, Chicago & St. Louis	2-8-0	*Consolidation Locomotive for the New York, Chicago & St. Louis*	08-Aug-1902	622
New York, Chicago & St. Louis	2-8-2	*2-8-2 Type Locomotives for the Nickel Plate*	19-Nov-1921	1002–4
New York, Chicago & St. Louis	2-8-2	*Two Light Mikado Locomotives Built at Lima*	01-Mar-1924	505–6
New York, Chicago & St. Louis	2-8-4	*Nickel Plate Buys 2-8-4 Type Locomotives*	17-Nov-1934	609–11
New York, Chicago & St. Louis	0-8-0	*Nickel Plate Receives Five Heavy Switching Locomotives*	19-Jan-1935	79–80
New York, New Haven & Hartford	4-4-0	*Express Locomotive, New York, New Haven & Hartford Railroad*	23-Jun-1893	447

Railroad	Type	Title	Issue Date	Pages
New York, New Haven & Hartford	2-8-0	Consolidation Locomotive, N. Y., N. H. & H. R. R.	26-Apr-1895	263
New York, New Haven & Hartford	2-6-0	Mogul Freight Locomotive	02-Oct-1896	681
New York, New Haven & Hartford	4-4-0	Eight-Wheel Passenger Locomotive—New York, New Haven & Hartford Railroad	23-Oct-1896	733
New York, New Haven & Hartford	0-6-0	Compound Six-Wheel Switching Engine	24-Oct-1902	813
New York, New Haven & Hartford	4-6-0	Ten-Wheel Locomotives for the New Haven	25-Nov-1904	582
New York, New Haven & Hartford	4-6-0	Four-Cylinder Balanced Compounds for the New Haven	17-Feb-1905	151
New York, New Haven & Hartford	4-6-0, 4-6-2	Pacific Locomotives for the New York, New Haven & Hartford	08-Nov-1907	554–6
New York, New Haven & Hartford	4-6-2	4-6-2 Type Locomotive for the New Haven	12-Jun-1913	1293–4
New York, New Haven & Hartford	4-8-2	New Mountain Type Locomotives for Fast Freight	08-Oct-1920	608–11
New York, New Haven & Hartford	4-8-2	New Haven Acquires Ten Three-Cylinder Locomotives	25-Feb-1928	452–4
New York, New Haven & Hartford	4-6-4	New Haven Installs Streamline Passenger Locomotives	27-Mar-1937	540–4
New York, Ontario & Western	2-8-0	A Consolidation Locomotive for the New York, Ontario & Western	23-Mar-1900	185
New York, Ontario & Western	4-4-0	Eight-Wheel Passenger Locomotive for the New York, Ontario & Western Railway	20-Apr-1900	253
New York, Ontario & Western	2-6-0	A New Mogul for the New York, Ontario & Western	26-Jul-1901	531
New York, Ontario & Western	2-10-2	Recent Examples of 2-10-2 Type Locomotives	21-Apr-1916	887–891
New York, Ontario & Western	4-8-2	Ten 4-8-2 Type Locomotives for the N. Y. O. & W.	30-Nov-1929	1281–2
Norfolk & Western	2-8-0	Consolidation Freight Locomotive—Norfolk & Western Railway	25-Apr-1902	302–3
Norfolk & Western	4-4-2	Atlantic-Type Locomotive for the Norfolk & Western	06-Feb-1903	97
Norfolk & Western	4-6-2, 4-8-0	Locomotives for Heavy Service on the Norfolk & Western	19-Jun-1908	170–1
Norfolk & Western	4-8-2	Norfolk & Western Mountain Type Locomotives	07-Apr-1916	799–801
Norfolk & Western	4-8-2	Norfolk & Western Mountain Type Locomotives	25-Aug-1916	362
Norfolk & Western	2-8-8-2	Norfolk & Western 267-Ton Mallet Locomotive	12-Jul-1918	59–63
Norfolk & Western	2-8-8-2	Freight Motive Power on the Norfolk & Western	05-Jul-1941	26–8
Norfolk & Western	2-6-6-4	Norfolk & Western Locomotives Equipped with Roller Bearings	26-Sep-1936	435–7
Norfolk & Western	4-8-4	Norfolk & Western Class J Locomotives	02-Jun-1945	971–5
Norfolk & Western	Various	Modern Power on the Norfolk & Western	24-Aug-1946	335–8
Norfolk & Western	4-8-0	Norfolk & Western Steam Switcher Has Automatic Controls	19-Jul-1947	105–8
Northern Pacific	4-8-0	Schenectady 12-Wheelers for the Northern Pacific	26-Feb-1897	145
Northern Pacific	4-6-0	Heavy Compound Freight Locomotive for the Northern Pacific	26-Mar-1897	217
Northern Pacific	4-6-0	Schenectady Locomotives for the Northern Pacific	11-May-1897	335–6
Northern Pacific	4-6-0	New Locomotives for the Northern Pacific	14-Jan-1898	24
Northern Pacific	2-8-0	A Northern Pacific Compound Consolidation Engine	27-Jan-1899	59
Northern Pacific	4-6-0	Schenectady Ten-Wheelers for the Northern Pacific	01-Dec-1899	825
Northern Pacific	2-8-0	Schenectady Four-Cylinder Tandem Compound Locomotives—Classes Y-2 and Y-3, Northern Pacific Railway	30-Aug-1901	598–9
Northern Pacific	2-8-2	Mikado (2-8-2) Locomotive for the Northern Pacific	20-Jan-1905	50–1
Northern Pacific	4-6-2	Heavy Pacific Type Locomotive for the Northern Pacific	09-Nov-1906	406–9
Northern Pacific	2-8-8-2, 2-8-2	Heavy Power for the Northern Pacific	29-Aug-1913	377–8
Northern Pacific	2-6-2, 2-8-2	Northern Pacific Converts Prairie Type to Mikado	14-Nov-1919	960–2
Northern Pacific	4-6-2, 2-8-8-2	New Locomotives for the Northern Pacific	22-Oct-1921	767–9
Northern Pacific	4-8-4	The Northern Pacific 4-8-4 Type Locomotives	23-Apr-1927	1239–42
Northern Pacific	2-8-8-4	World's Largest Locomotive Built for the Northern Pacific	29-Dec-1928	1295–1301
Northern Pacific	4-8-4	Northern Pacific Receives Heavy Passenger Power	03-Nov-1934	537–9
Northern Pacific	4-6-6-4	Northern Pacific High-Speed Freight Locomotives	06-Mar-1937	389–91
Ogdensburg & Lake Champlain	2-8-0	Compound Consolidation Locomotives for the Ogdensburg & Lake Champlain	11-Feb-1898	93
Oliver Iron Mining Co.	0-6-0	Lima Locomotives for the Oliver Iron Mining Company	20-Jun-1910	1679
Oliver Iron Mining Co.	0-8-0	A New Switching Locomotive	23-Jul-1927	153–4
Oregon Railroad & Navigation	2-8-0	Consolidation Locomotives for the Oregon Railroad & Navigation Co.	03-Feb-1899	78–9
Oregon Railroad & Navigation	2-8-2	Mikado Locomotive for Burning Lignite; Oregon Railroad & Navigation Company	27-Jan-1911	167–9

Railroad	Type	Title	Issue Date	Pages
Oregon Short Line	2-8-0	*A Cooke Consolidation for the Oregon Short Line*	24-Dec-1897	905
Oregon Short Line	4-8-0	*Twelve-Wheel Locomotive for the Oregon Short Line Railroad*	09-Mar-1900	149
Oregon Short Line	2-8-0	*Consolidation Locomotives for the Oregon Short Line*	20-Apr-1900	251
Oregon Short Line	0-6-0	*Cooke Six-Wheel Switching Locomotives—Oregon Short Line*	08-Feb-1901	94
Pennsylvania	4-4-0	*The Class "P" Locomotive and the Pennsylvania Railroad*	22-Feb-1895	116-7
Pennsylvania	4-4-0	*The Class "P" Locomotive of the Pennsylvania*	22-Feb-1895	122-3
Pennsylvania	2-6-0	*Pennsylvania Compound Locomotive*	20-Dec-1895	835
Pennsylvania	4-4-0	*The Pennsylvania Class "L" Locomotive*	27-Dec-1895	852
Pennsylvania	2-6-0	*The New Freight Locomotives of the Pennsylvania Railroad*	18-Sep-1896	651
Pennsylvania	0-8-0T	*A Tank Locomotive on the Pennsylvania Lines*	27-Nov-1896	823
Pennsylvania	2-8-0	*The New Consolidation Locomotive of the Pennsylvania*	10-Dec-1897	864
Pennsylvania	2-8-0	*The Class H-5 Consolidation of the Pennsylvania*	10-Jun-1898	401
Pennsylvania	4-4-2	*Atlantic Type Locomotive—Class E-1 No. 698*	07-Jul-1899	487
Pennsylvania	2-8-0	*Pennsylvania Railroad Class H6 Locomotives*	14-Jul-1899	503
Pennsylvania	2-6-0	*Pennsylvania Class F 1-A Freight Locomotives*	22-Sep-1899	653
Pennsylvania	4-4-2	*The Pennsylvania's Class E-2 Experimental Locomotive*	20-Jul-1900	492
Pennsylvania	4-6-0, 4-4-0	*Some of the Recent Passenger Locomotives of the Pennsylvania*	10-Aug-1900	535
Pennsylvania	4-4-2	*The Pennsylvania Class E-2 Locomotive*	14-Sep-1900	605
Pennsylvania	4-4-2	*New Class E-2 Locomotive—Pennsylvania Railroad*	14-Jun-1901	409
Pennsylvania	2-6-0	*Pennsylvania Moguls—Classes F-3 and F-3-b*	01-Nov-1901	753
Pennsylvania	2-8-0	*New Consolidation Locomotives for the Pennsylvania*	24-Jan-1902	58
Pennsylvania	2-8-0	*The Class H-6-a Consolidation Locomotive of the Pennsylvania*	04-Apr-1902	241-2
Pennsylvania	0-6-0	*Class B6 Six-Wheel Switcher for the Pennsylvania Lines West of Pittsburgh*	23-Jan-1903	60
Pennsylvania	Various	*Experimental Locomotives for the Pennsylvania Railroad*	05-Jan-1906	16-21
Pennsylvania	4-6-2	*Pacific Locomotives for the Pennsylvania Lines West*	30-Aug-1907	238-40
Pennsylvania	2-8-0	*Consolidation Locomotives for the Pennsylvania*	02-Jul-1909	9-14
Pennsylvania	4-4-2	*Atlantic Type Class E 6 Locomotive; Pennsylvania Railroad*	07-Apr-1911	854-60
Pennsylvania	2-8-8-2	*Experimental Mallet Locomotive for the Pennsylvania*	01-Mar-1912	377-8
Pennsylvania	4-4-2	*Atlantic Type Locomotives on the Pennsylvania*	20-Feb-1914	356-9
Pennsylvania	2-8-2, 4-6-2	*Pennsylvania Mikado and Pacific Type Locomotives*	03-Jul-1913	12-16
Pennsylvania	2-10-0	*Pennsylvania Locomotive of the Decapod Type*	15-Jun-1917	1241-3
Pennsylvania	2-10-2	*Heaviest 2-10-2 Type Built for Pennsylvania Lines*	24-Jan-1919	249-51
Pennsylvania	2-8-8-0	*Simple Mallet Locomotive with Short Maximum Cut-off*	23-Jun-1919	1675-81
Pennsylvania	2-10-0	*Pennsylvania Decapod Develops 3,500 Horsepower*	02-Apr-1920	1097-1103
Pennsylvania	2-10-0	*Tests of Decapod Show 14 Per Cent Fuel Saving*	11-Oct-1924	635-9
Pennsylvania	4-6-0	*Pennsylvania Ten-Wheel Passenger Locomotive*	10-Nov-1923	859-60
Pennsylvania	0-8-8	*Pennsylvania Builds Eight-wheel Switching Locomotive*	25-Jul-1925	195-6
Pennsylvania	4-8-2	*Mountain Type Locomotives for the Pennsylvania*	20-Nov-1926	989-92
Pennsylvania	6-4-4-6	*High-Capacity Locomotive for Fast Service*	24-Jun-1939	1067-75
Pennsylvania	4-4-4-4	*Pennsylvania 4-4-4-4 Locomotives*	12-Dec-1942	956-62
Pennsylvania	4-4-4-4	*Pennsylvania Tests Duplex Locomotive*	26-May-1945	925-9
Pennsylvania	6-8-6	*A Geared Steam-Turbine Locomotive*	12-Feb-1945	337-40, 349
Pennsylvania	4-4-6-4	*Pennsylvania Q-2 Freight Locomotives*	22-Dec-1945	1014-6
Pere Marquette	2-8-0	*Brooks Locomotives for the Pere Marquette*	03-May-1901	296-7
Philadelphia & Reading	4-2-2	*The Reading's Single-Driver Express Locomotive*	09-Aug-1895	526-8
Philadelphia & Reading	4-2-2		13-Mar-1896	180
Philadelphia & Reading	2-6-4T	*Heavy Suburban Locomotives for the Philadelphia & Reading*	25-Sep-1903	682-3
Philadelphia & Reading	Various	*Rebuilding Locomotives—Philadelphia & Reading*	24-Jun-1904	46-8
Philadelphia & Reading	4-4-2	*The Reading Three Cylinder Locomotive*	2-Jun-1909	1434
Philadelphia & Reading	4-4-2	*Atlantic Type Inspection Locomotive*	05-Sep-1913	404-5
Philadelphia & Reading	4-4-0	*Philadelphia & Reading 4-4-0 Type Locomotive*	17-Apr-1914	872-5
Philadelphia & Reading	4-4-4	*The Reading Type Locomotive*	09-Jun-1915	1184
Philadelphia & Reading	4-4-4	*A Passenger Locomotive of Unusual Interest*	09-Jun-1915	1193-7
Philadelphia & Reading	4-6-2	*Pacific Type Locomotives for the Reading*	21-Jul-1916	107-9
Philadelphia & Reading	2-8-0	*Large Consolidation Type Locomotive for the P. & R.*	21-Mar-1919	760-2
Philadelphia & Reading	2-8-0	*Reading Consolidation Type Locomotive*	05-Jul-1924	19-20
Philadelphia & Reading	4-6-2	*Pacific Type Locomotives for the Reading*	11-Sep-1926	461-2
(Pittsburgh demonstrator)	2-6-0	*Pittsburgh Compound Mogul Locomotive*	02-Feb-1894	80
Pittsburgh & Lake Erie	2-8-0	*Consolidation Locomotive for the Pittsburgh & Lake Erie Railroad*	17-Sep-1902	796
Pittsburgh & Lake Erie	0-6-0	*Heavy Switching Locomotive for the Pittsburgh & Lake Erie*	03-Aug-1906	98-9
Pittsburgh & West Virginia	2-6-6-4	*P. & W. V. Articulated Locomotive Replaces Two Consolidations*	09-Mar-1935	361-2
Pittsburgh & Western	4-6-0	*Ten-Wheel Passenger Locomotive for the Pittsburgh & Western*	05-Nov-1897	779-80

Railroad	Type	Title	Issue Date	Pages
Pittsburgh & Western	4-4-0, 4-6-0	*New Passenger Locomotives of the Pittsburgh & Western Railway*	04-Aug-1899	551–2
Pittsburgh Junction	2-8-0	*A New Pittsburgh Consolidation Locomotive*	03-May-1895	276–7
Pittsburgh, Bessemer & Lake Erie	2-6-0	*Freight Locomotives for the Pittsburgh, Bessemer & Lake Erie*	30-Jul-1897	537
Pittsburgh, Bessemer & Lake Erie	2-8-0	*Great Consolidation Locomotives for the Pittsburgh, Bessemer & Lake Erie Railroad*	29-Jun-1900	447
Pittsburgh, Cincinnati, Chicago & St. Louis	2-8-0	*Consolidation Locomotive for the P. C. C. & St. L.*	06-Jun-1902	496
Plant System	4-6-0	*Some New Locomotives of the Plant System*	02-Nov-1900	722–3
Plant System	4-6-0	*A Baldwin Four-Cylinder Balanced Compound for the Plant System*	28-Feb-1902	139–40
(Purdue University)	4-4-0	*New Experimental Locomotive "Schenectady No 2," Purdue University*	17-Dec-1897	883–5
Richmond, Fredericksburg & Potomac	4-6-2	*Powerful Pacific Type Locomotive for the R., F. & P.*	17-Dec-1915	1129–31
Richmond, Fredericksburg & Potomac	4-8-4	*R. F. & P. 4-8-4 Type Freight and Passenger Locomotives*	19-Jun-1937	1013–4
Rio Grande Western	2-8-0	*Richmond Consolidation for the Rio Grande Western*	07-Sep-1900	594
Rio Grande Western	2-8-0	*Richmond Compound Locomotives for the Rio Grande Western*	28-Jun-1901	451
(Russian Decapods)	2-10-0	*Locomotives for the Russian State Railways*	10-Sep-1915	474–6
(Russian Decapods)	2-10-0	*Decapod Locomotives for Russian Government*	12-Oct-1917	637–40
Rutland	4-6-2	*Pacific Type Locomotives for the Rutland*	15-Feb-1930	437–8
Seaboard Air Line	4-8-2	*Seaboard Air Line Mountain Type Locomotives*	16-Jul-1915	87–9
Seaboard Air Line	2-6-6-4	*Seaboard Air Line Locomotives*	01-Jun-1935	849–50
(Siemens & Halske demonstrator)	4-6-0	*A Siemens & Halske Steam Locomotive*	30-Aug-1895	571–2
South Buffalo	2-8-0	*Consolidation (2-8-0) Locomotives for the South Buffalo Railway*	08-May-1903	329
South Carolina & Georgia	2-8-0	*Compound Consolidation Locomotives for the South Carolina & Georgia Railroad*	22-Apr-1898	290–1
Southern	4-6-0, 2-8-0	*New Locomotives for the Southern Railway*	04-Mar-1898	159–61
Southern	2-8-2	*Duplex Locomotives for the Southern Railway*	16-Feb-1917	267–9
Southern Pacific	4-6-0	*Cooke Locomotives for the Southern Pacific*	05-Apr-1895	215
Southern Pacific	4-8-0	*A Schenectady 12-Wheeler for the Southern Pacific*	06-Jan-1899	3
Southern Pacific	2-6-0	*Schenectady Moguls for the Southern Pacific*	31-Mar-1899	222–3
Southern Pacific	2-6-0	*A Cooke Locomotive for the Southern Pacific*	14-Apr-1899	261
Southern Pacific	2-8-0	*Compound Consolidation Locomotives for the Southern Pacific*	05-May-1899	315
Southern Pacific	4-6-0	*Cooke Ten-Wheel Locomotive—Southern Pacific Company*	22-Mar-1901	199
Southern Pacific	2-8-0	*Some Schenectady Consolidation Locomotives*	05-Apr-1901	233–4
Southern Pacific	2-6-0	*Mogul Freight Locomotives for the Southern Pacific*	29-Nov-1901	821
Southern Pacific	2-8-0	*Consolidation Locomotives for the Southern Pacific*	07-Mar-1902	160–1
Southern Pacific	4-4-2	*Oil Burning Atlantic (4-4-2) Type Locomotive for the Southern Pacific*	12-Jun-1903	402
Southern Pacific	4-6-0	*Ten-Wheel Locomotives for the Southern Pacific*	18-Sep-1908	944–6
Southern Pacific	2-6-6-2	*Details of Articulated Mallet Compound Locomotive for the Southern Pacific*	04-Jun-1909	1168–70
Southern Pacific	2-8-8-2	*Mallet Articulated Compound for the Southern Pacific*	30-Apr-1909	933–8
Southern Pacific	2-8-8-2	*Mallet Locomotives for the Southern Pacific*	22-Apr-1910	1034–5
Southern Pacific	2-8-8-2	*Oil Burning Mallets; Southern Pacific*	16-Jun-1911	1476
Southern Pacific	2-8-8-2	*Mallet Locomotives for the Southern Pacific*	10-Nov-1911	952–4
Southern Pacific	4-8-2	*Heavy 4-8-2 Type Southern Pacific Locomotives*	09-Feb-1924	375–7
Southern Pacific	4-8-8-2	*Southern Pacific Simple Articulated Locomotive*	15-Dec-1928	1181–5
Southern Pacific	4-8-4	*Largest Streamline Locomotives*	20-Feb-1937	319–21
Southern Pacific	2-8-8-4	*Southern Pacific Buys Articulated Coal-Burning Locomotives*	16-Dec-1939	918–22
Southern Pacific	4-8-8-2	*Southern Pacific 4-8-8-2 Cab-Ahead Locomotives*	03-Feb-1940	239–40, 248
Southern Utah	2-8-0	*Consolidation Locomotive for the Southern Utah Railroad*	10-Dec-1909	1142
St. Louis & Adirondack	4-4-0	*Eight-Wheel Passenger Locomotive—St. Louis & Adirondack Railroad*	27-Aug-1897	598–9
St. Louis & San Francisco	2-8-0	*Consolidation Locomotive—St. Louis & San Francisco*	06-Jun-1902	413
St. Louis & San Francisco	4-6-0	*?*	26-Apr-1907	572–3
St. Louis & San Francisco	4-6-0	*Ten-Wheel Passenger Locomotives for the 'Frisco*	08-May-1908	647–8
St. Louis & San Francisco	2-8-82	*Recent Mallet Articulated Locomotives*	16-Dec-1910	1144–7
St. Louis & San Francisco	4-8-2, 2-8-2	*Mountain and Mikado Types for the Frisco*	19-May-1923	1207–8
St. Louis & San Francisco	4-8-4	*Baldwin Builds 4-8-4 Locomotives For Service on Frisco*	27-Feb-1943	424–7
St. Louis Southwestern	4-8-4	*Cotton Belt Replaces Consolidation Type Motive Power*	27-Dec-1930	1363–5
Terre Haute & Indianapolis	4-6-0	*Pittsburgh Ten-Wheel Passenger Engine*	13-Apr-1894	264–5
Texas & Pacific	4-6-0	*Some Recent Rogers Locomotives*	02-Dec-1898	857
Texas & Pacific	2-10-4	*First Texas Type Locomotives for T. & P.*	19-Dec-1925	1142–8

Railroad	Type	Title	Issue Date	Pages
Texas & Pacific	2-10-4	*Texas Type Locomotives Show Marked Fuel Economy*	17-Jul-1926	101–2
Texas & Pacific	0-8-0	*Eight-Wheel Switchers for the T. & P.*	27-Mar-1926	901–3
(Timken demonstrator)	4-8-4	*A 4-8-4 Type Demonstration Locomotive for Timken*	24-May-1930	1225–9
Union Pacific	4-4-0	*Union Pacific Fast Mail Locomotive*	12-May-1893	349–51
Union Pacific	2-8-0	*Consolidation Locomotives for the Union Pacific*	18-Nov-1898	829
Union Pacific	4-6-0	*Heavy Ten-Wheel Freight Locomotives for the Union Pacific*	25-Aug-1899	593
Union Pacific	4-6-2	*Pacific Type Locomotives for the Union Pacific*	09-Apr-1915	781–2
Union Pacific	4-8-2	*A Mountain Type Locomotive of High Capacity*	10-Jun-1922	1324–9
Union Pacific	4-8-2	*Service Records of U. P. Mountain Type Locomotives*	14-Oct-1922	687–9
Union Pacific	4-12-2	*Union Pacific Type Locomotive*	15-May-1926	1295–1300
Union Pacific	4-12-2	*Union Pacific Type Locomotive Performance*	25-Dec-1926	1265–7
Union Pacific	4-6-6-4	*A Powerful High-Speed Freight Locomotive*	19-Dec-1936	900–3
Union Pacific	4-8-4	*U. P. Adds to High-Capacity Motive-Power Fleet*	07-Oct-1939	515–18, 531
Union Pacific	4-8-4	*Intensive Locomotive Use Pays Union Pacific Big Dividends*	11-Mar-1939	415–18, 420
Union Pacific	4-8-8-4	*Union Pacific Gets Heaviest Articulated Locomotives*	04-Oct-1941	519–26
Union Pacific	4-6-6-4	*20 More Articulated Locomotives for the Union Pacific*	03-Oct-1942	516–9
Union Railroad	0-10-2	*Union Railroad Receives Transfer Locomotives from Baldwin*	18-Jul-1936	105–6
USRA	2-8-2	*First of the U. S. Standard Locomotives Completed*	19-Jul-1918	131–3
USRA	2-8-2	*The U. S. Standard Heavy Mikado Type Locomotive*	30-Aug-1918	374–6
USRA	0-8-0	*The First Standard 0-8-0 Type Switching Locomotive*	20-Sep-1918	542–4
USRA	0-6-0	*U. S. R. A. Standard Six-Wheel Switching Locomotive*	11-Oct-1918	654–7
USRA	4-8-2, 2-10-2	*Standard Heavy 4-8-2 and Light 2-10-2 Locomotives*	13-Dec-1918	1066–73
USRA	2-6-6-2	*The U. S. Standard Light Mallet Type Locomotive*	31-Jan-1919	290–2
USRA	2-10-2	*The Standard Heavy Santa Fe Type Locomotive*	14-Feb-1919	388–92
USRA	2-8-8-2	*Heavy Standard Mallet Type Locomotive*	14-Mar-1919	575–8
USRA	4-6-2	*Light and Heavy Standard Pacific Type Locomotives*	11-Apr-1919	950–4
USRA	4-8-2	*The Administration Standard Light Mountain Type*	16-May-1919	1193–6
Vandalia	4-4-2	*Atlantic Type Locomotive for the Vandalia*	19-Dec-1902	957
Vandalia	2-6-0	*Mogul Locomotive for the Vandalia*	04-Jan-1907	10–12
Vandalia	4-6-2	*Heavy Pacific Type for the Vandalia*	23-Sep-1910	539–40
Virginian	2-8-2	*Mikado Locomotive for the Virginian Railway*	03-Jul-1908	420–6
Virginian	2-6-6-0	*Mallet Articulated Compound for the Virginian Railway*	18-Jun-1909	1316–8
Virginian	2-8-8-2	*Locomotive Building During 1910; Baldwin Locomotive Works*	28-Apr-1911	993–7
Virginian	2-8-2	*Locomotive Building During 1910; Baldwin Locomotive Works*	28-Apr-1911	993–7
Virginian	2-8-8-2	*Most Powerful Locomotive in the World*	13-Jun-1912	1321–3
Virginian	2-8-2	*Simple Freight Locomotives for the Virginian*	05-Jul-1912	20–1
Virginian	2-8-8-8-4	*Virginian Triplex Type Pusher Locomotive*	26-Jan-1917	141–3
Virginian	2-10-10-2	*Heavy Mallet Locomotives for the Virginian*	18-Oct-1918	688–91
Wabash	4-4-2	*New Class "G" Locomotives for the Wabash*	01-Apr-1898	232–3
Wabash	4-6-0	*A Pittsburgh Ten-Wheeler for the Wabash*	29-Apr-1898	305
Wabash	4-4-0	*Eight-Wheel, Class H, Passenger Locomotive—Wabash Railroad*	24-Mar-1899	206
Wabash	4-4-2	*Wabash Atlantic-Type Locomotives*	25-Dec-1903	923
Wabash	2-6-2	*Prairie Locomotive for the Wabash*	17-Jul-1908	536–8
Wabash	2-10-2	*Locomotives of the 2-10-2 Type for the Wabash*	07-Dec-1917	1025–8
Wabash	4-8-2	*Mountain Type Locomotives for the Wabash*	01-Apr-1930	821–2
Wabash	4-8-2	*New Wabash Locomotives Make Good in Service Tests*	27-Sep-1930	616–8
Wabash	4-8-4	*Wabash Operates 4-8-4 Types in Freight Service*	14-Feb-1931	374
Wabash-Pittsburgh Terminal	2-8-0	*Consolidation Locomotive for the Wabash-Pittsburgh Terminal with Cole Superheater*	16-Jun-1909	1237–8
Western Maryland	2-8-0	*Western Maryland Consolidation Locomotive*	17-Jul-1914	101–2
Western Maryland	2-8-0	*Consolidation Locomotives for the Western Maryland*	13-May-1920	1117–20
Western Maryland	2-10-0	*Decapod Locomotives for the Western Maryland*	25-Jun-1927	2007–8
Western Maryland	4-6-6-4	*High-Capacity Freight Locomotives for Western Maryland*	25-Jan-1941	209–15
Western Maryland	Shay	*Western Maryland Uses Shay Locomotive On Heavy Grades in Mining District*	06-Oct-1945	549–52
Western of Alabama	4-6-2	*Pacific Type Locomotives for the A. & W. P. and W. of A.*	02-Oct-1926	641–2
Western Pacific	2-8-8-2	*Western Pacific Operating 2-8-8-2 Types in Fast-Freght Service*	26-Dec-1931	975–6
Wheeling & Lake Erie	2-8-0	*Compound Consolidation for the Wheeling & Lake Erie*	11-Jul-1902	557
Wisconsin Central	4-6-0	*Ten-Wheel Locomotives for the Wisconsin Central Lines*	03-Jun-1898	387–9
Wisconsin Central	4-6-0	*Ten-Wheel Wide Fire-Box Locomotive for the Wisconsin Central Railway*	10-May-1901	312–3

Appendix C. The Cole Ratios

The work of F. J. Cole at Alco was so important to locomotive design that his words, spoken in 1914, are here quoted at length[1]:

In recent years, locomotives have increased so much in dimensions, weight and power that methods employed in the past are no longer adequate in proportioning the grate, heating surface, length and diameter of tubes, etc., or to predetermine how best a locomotive boiler may be designed to suit certain requirements, the type, tractive effort and limitations of weight being known.

The size of cylinders is usually fixed by the permissible axle load allowed upon the track or bridges, in connection with the type, the diameter of the driving wheels, the boiler pressure and the factor of adhesion. After these fundamental features are decided upon, the boiler proportions must be outlined to see whether the required amount of heating surface can be obtained without exceeding the limits of weight.

There are two general questions involved in the consideration of this subject, namely, how many pounds of steam per hour are required to supply the cylinders in order to develop the maximum horsepower; and what proportion of grate, firebox and tube heating surface will best produce this amount of steam.

The locomotive, unlike most steam plants, varies in the speed and power developed. It must be able to run at any intermediate speed between starting and its full velocity and at the same time develop all degrees of tractive effort within its capacity. At slow speeds the maximum pull must be exerted in order to start the trains easily, and for this reason the live steam is admitted to the cylinders during 80 to 87 per cent of the stroke. As the speed increases it is necessary to reduce the admission period, thereby increasing the expansion of the steam; therefore for any speed there is some point for the valves to cut off the live steam, at which the engine will develop its maximum power.[2] There is also some minimum velocity at which the full horsepower of the locomotive is attained; after this velocity is reached the horsepower remains constant or slowly decreases. This critical point may be taken at 700 ft. to 1,000 ft. per minute piston speed.

It has been customary to use certain ratios, based on cylinder volume, for locomotive proportions. These ratios left to individual preference such matters as rate of combustion per square foot of grate, length of flues, evaporative value of firebox heating surface or value of tube or flue heating surface in relation to the length, making it desirable to proportion boilers upon more uniform methods in which these variable factors are given due consideration.

Four or five years ago the writer collected a considerable amount of data on this subject and drew up a report with the object of reducing this matter to a more uniform basis, substituting for the ratios hitherto employed, cylinder horsepower requirements.[3] Suitable values were assigned to grate surface, firebox heating surface, tube heating surface, etc., with corresponding evaporative values, so that the balance between the amount of steam required by the cylinders and the amount of steam which the boiler was capable of generating could be expressed in percentage of cylinder horsepower. The tests made on sectional boilers on the Northern Railway and the Paris, Lyons & Mediterranean Railway of France, those of Dr. Goss on a Jacobs-Shupert boiler, and tests by the Pennsylvania Railroad on the Altoona testing plant were examined in order to obtain data on which to base the evaporative values of different points of the boiler. It is obvious that the evaporative value of a boiler tube of given diameter varies greatly with its length. The temperature of the firebox is fairly constant under similar conditions of draft and rate of combustion, therefore the temperature of the smokebox will be reduced with an increase in tube length. While some additional draft will be required to draw the gases through the tubes, yet the net result is a greater heat absorption between the firebox and the smokebox. The thermal efficiency of the engine is increased within certain limitations by the use of long tubes. Of course there is a certain economical length of tube which is determined mostly by the number and arrangement of wheels or the type of the engine which the service requires and only partly by thermal conditions.

About 1899 the wide firebox Atlantic (4–4–2) type locomotive was introduced. Because the firebox was placed behind the driving wheels the grate area could be made to suit to power of the locomotive; therefore it was no longer necessary to force the combustion to 180 lb. and 200 lb. of coal per square foot of grate area per hour. Very poor results were obtained when high rates of combustion were necessary, because much unburned coal was drawn through the tubes into the smokebox and thrown out through the stack by the violent draft. With the Atlantic type locomotive, tubes 15 ft. and 16 ft. long, and sometimes longer, were necessary. While at first there was some apprehension as to leakage with tubes of these lengths, it was soon found that no more difficulty was experienced in maintenance than with short tubes. With the introduction of the Pacific (4–6–2) type and Mikado (2–8–2) type, and other locomotives using trailing trucks, still longer tubes were required. Tests made on long tube engines, compared with older locomotives with shorter tubes, showed a noticeable reduction in smokebox temperatures.

Instead of the old arbitrary method of designing locomotive heating surface by cylinder ratios, the idea of using the cylinder horsepower suggested itself as forming a very desirable basis for the heating surface, grate area and tube area. Curves were prepared from the most recent available data showing speed factors or drop in M. E. P. in relation to velocity.[4] With saturated steam the average maximum horsepower is reached at about 700 ft. piston speed per minute, speed factor .412; constant horsepower is obtained at 700 to 1,000 ft. piston speed, speed factor .445, and the horsepower decreases slightly at higher velocities for average conditions when engines are especially constructed for the highest speeds. For superheated steam the average maximum horsepower is reached at 1,000 ft. piston speed, speed factor .445 and constant horsepower at higher speeds. Because the horsepower is based on piston speeds, the stroke and diameter of wheels is omitted in the following figures, the calculation becoming by cancellation:

$$\frac{.85P \times .412 \times 1,000 \times 2A}{33,000} = \frac{1.7P \times .412 \times A}{33} = .0212 \times P \times A$$

$$HP = .0212 \times P \times A$$

In which   A = area of one cylinder in square inches
             P = the boiler pressure
             .412 = speed factor

In a similar manner the horsepower calculation for superheated steam becomes:

$$HP = .0229 \times P \times A$$
Using .445 as the speed factor

The maximum horsepower can sometimes be increased when the locomotive is operated under the most favorable conditions. It is considered safer and better practice, however, to take figures which represent average conditions rather than the abnormal and unusual figures obtained when all conditions are most favorable.

The horsepower basis affords many additional advantages in designing locomotives. For instance, in determining the maximum amount of water and coal required per hour, the size of the grate is found to be proportional to the amount of coal that can be burned to the best advantage, to be varied according to the quality. Knowing the amount of coal required per hour directs attention to the question of hand firing or the use of a mechanical stoker. Knowing the amount of water evaporated per hour determines the location of water stations, size of tender tank, the size of injectors and safety valve capacity, also the size of steam pipes and other features of the boiler. Through the stack a mixture of gas and exhaust steam is ejected at substantially the same velocity for all locomotives in similar service, and proportional to the amount of coal burned. For this reason, the area of the stack may be taken as proportional to the maximum amount of coal burned per hour in the firebox.

From the reports of the Pennsylvania Railroad testing plant at St. Louis and Altoona, and from road tests, the conclusion is reached that with saturated steam a horsepower can be obtained from 25 to 29 lb., of saturated steam in simple cylinders with piston speeds of 700 to 1,000 ft. per minute; 27 lb. has been taken as a fair average value, and in a corresponding was 23 ½ lb. for compound engines, 20.8 lb. for steam superheated 200 deg. and over, and 19.7 lb. for superheated steam used in compound cylinders. These figures provide for steam for auxiliaries. While careful tests show that the evaporation can be increased under the most advantageous conditions, such as best quality of picked coal, clean fire, high degrees of smokebox vacuum, etc., it is considered better practice to take the lower figure in order to provide a margin or average conditions.

The great increase in the length of tubes which took place with the building of trailing truck locomotives, naturally directed attention to the values of heating surface of different lengths of tubes and emphasized the fact that a square foot of heating surface in tubes 10 ft. or 11 ft. long had a much greater evaporative value than in tubes 18 ft., 20 ft. or 22 ft. long. In the absence of definite temperature tests of different parts of a tube, it was thought that the evaporative value varies inversely as the square root of its length. Pyrometer tests recently made by the Pennsylvania Railroad at Altoona with various locomotives on the testing plant showed that the temperature curve of tubes of various lengths and diameters follows somewhat different laws. From the many observations of pyrometer readings taken at various portions of the boiler tube, curves have been drawn which show the decrease in temperature from the firebox to the smoekbox. From these curves the increase or decrease of tube evaporation may be calculated.

Short tubes have much greater evaporative value per square foot of heating surface than long tubes, but they discharge the gases into the smokebox at much higher temperatures. Therefore, while the heat absorbed per foot of length is much greater for short than long tubes, it

is not so economical. The short tube boiler, other things being equal, requires more coal for a given evaporation than a boiler having long tubes. Where tube lengths of 12 or 14 ft. were common 14 or 15 years ago, lengths of 20, 22 and even 24 ft. are used in the modern locomotive. The result is that the smokebox temperatures have decreased from between 750 and 800 deg. to 550 or 600 deg., the only increase in energy required being the slightly greater draft in the smokebox to pull the gases through the long tubes. This is not intended as a defense of the long tube in modern engines, especially of the 4-6-2, 2-8-2, Mallet and other types, because in most cases their construction requires long boilers. Tests show that economy results from the better utilization of heat in the modern engine than in older types because the range of temperatures between the furnace and the stack is greater with the long tube locomotive.

As a result of the investigations previously outlined, conclusions have been arrived at as follows:

Firebox Evaporation.—An evaporation of 55 lb. per square foot of firebox heating surface, combustion chamber and arch tubes has been adopted. The greater absorption of heat by the firebox than by the rear portion of tubes per unit of area is largely due to radiant heat. This varies as the square of the distance from the surface of the fire to the sheets separating the gases from the water. Again, it is probable that within certain limitations the amount of heat absorbed is independent of heating surface and is a function of the grate area or the area of the bed of live coals. Assuming that there is sufficient heating surface to absorb the radiant heat, it is probable that very little additional heat will be absorbed by increasing the firebox heating surface. It therefore follows that the relatively greater area of the fire in wide firebox locomotives is more efficient than in the old narrow firebox.

Diameter, Length and Spacing of Tubes.—The evaporative value in pounds of water per square foot of outside heating surface has been approximately calculated for 2 in. and 2¼ in. tubes, and for superheater flues 5⅜ in. and 5½ in. The range of length is 10 to 25 ft., and the spacing ⁹⁄₁₆ in. to 1 in. The best data available shows that the evaporative value of a tube or flue varies considerably with differences in length, diameter and spacing. The curves of temperature compared with length have been used as a basis for determining the evaporation for different lengths of tubes and flues. The rate of evaporation on this basis will vary directly as the difference of temperature of the tube or flue gases and that of the steam contained in the boiler.

Tubes and flues from 10 to 24 ft. long, spaced ⁹⁄₁₆ and 1 in. apart, outside diameter 2 in., 2¼ in. and 5½ in. will evaporate from 7.50 to 14 lb. of water per square foot per hour.

Grate Area.—The grate area required for bituminous coal is based on the assumption that 120 lb. of coal per square foot of grate per hour is a maximum figure for economical evaporation. While 200 and 225 lb. have at times been burnt in small, deep fireboxes and the engines made to produce sufficient steam, it is wasteful of fuel and it has been found after numerous and careful tests that the evaporation per pound of fuel is very low. If, on the other hand, the rate of combustion is too slow, economical results will not be produced owing to the fact that at least 20 per cent of the coal burned produces no useful work in hauling trains, but is consumed in firing up, waiting at roundhouses or terminals, on sidetracks, or to the fact that the greater portion of the time locomotives are used at considerably less than their maximum power.

For hard coal the grates should be proportioned for a range of from 55 to 70 lb. of coal per square foot per hour, according to the grade of the fuel.

Complete tables of horsepower for saturated and superheated steam, evaporation of tubes and flues of various lengths, diameters and spacing, as well as diagrams of temperature for different flue lengths, have all been prepared to facilitate the calculations in determining the proportions of grate, firebox, tube and flue heating surface.

It must be remembered, however, that the boiler capacity for a locomotive when other things are in proportion cannot usually be made too large within the permissible limits of weight, and it can be shown by numerous tests that such increase in boiler capacity makes for considerable economy in the use of fuel and steam. For passenger service the boiler may often be made with advantage over 100 percent.

In a general way, a boiler will have ample steam making capacity if proportioned by this method for 100 per cent, provided the grate is sufficiently large and deep so that the rate of combustion at maximum horsepower does not exceed 120 lb. of coal per square foot of grate per hour for bituminous coal of average quality. For gas coal a smaller grate may be used, but it is better practice to use the larger grate and brick off a portion at the front end in order to obtain sufficient volume of firebox for proper combustion, because nearly all modern locomotives are deficient in firebox volume.

Chapter Notes

Abbreviations

AARMD: Association of American Railroads, Mechanical Division (formerly ARMMA)
AIEE: American Institute of Electrical Engineers.
AREA: American Railroad Engineering Association.
ARMMA: American Railway Master Mechanics' Association.
ASME: American Society of Mechanical Engineers.
ICC: Interstate Commerce Commission.
RA: *Railway Age.*
RAG: *Railroad Age Gazette.*
R&HLS: Railway & Locomotive Historical Society.
RRG: *Railroad Gazette.*

Where a railroad company is named in these notes with initial capital letters, the distinction between "Railroad" and "Railway" is in accordance with Drury, *Guide to North American Steam Locomotives.* Where a railroad company is named in *italics*, as in the title of an article, the distinction is in accordance with the title of the article.

Introduction

1. Sinclair, A., *Development of the Locomotive Engine,* New York: Angus Sinclair, 1907, 262; see also Davies, H., *George Stephenson: The Remarkable Life of the Founder of the Railways,* Stroud, UK: Sutton, 2004, 67.
2. Storer, J. D., *A Simple History of the Steam Engine,* London, UK: John Baker, 1969.
3. Rolt, L.T.C., Allen, J.S., *The Steam Engine of Thomas Newcomen,* Hartington, UK: Moorland, 1977; Barton, D.B., *The Cornish Beam Engine,* Truro, UK: D.B. Barton, 1969; Barton, D.B., *A History of Tin Mining and Smelting in Cornwall,* Truro, UK: D.B.Barton, 1967; Pursell, C.W. *Early Stationary Steam Engines in America,* Washington: Smithsonian Institution, 1969.
4. *Locomotive Classification,* RRG, April 3, 1903, 253
5. *Locomotive Classification on the Pennsylvania,* RRG, February 1, 1901, 74; *New Classification of Locomotives—New York Central & Hudson River Railroad,* RRG, April 5, 1901, 232.
6. Exhaustively cataloged in Wiener, L., *Articulated Locomotives,* New York: Richard R. Smith, 1930; repub. Milwaukee: Kalmbach, 1970.
7. Le Massena, R.A., *Articulated Steam Locomotives of North America,* Silverton, CO: Sundance, 1979; Durrant, A.E., *The Mallet Locomotive,* New York: Arco, 1975.

8. Dickerman, W. C., President, Alco, *Possibilities of the Modern Steam Locomotive,* Western Railway Club, Chicago, April, 1938, abstracted RA, May 7, 1938, 796.
9. Park, D. K. *U.S. Steam Locomotive Builders,* R&LHS Bulletin #132, Spring 1975, 47.
10. RAG, December 30, 1910, 1262.
11. Bruce, A. W., *The Steam Locomotive in America: Its Development in the Twentieth Century,* New York: Bonanza, 1952, 47.
12. *Our Locomotives and the Englishman,* RRG, November 16, 1900, 758.
13. RRG, January 8, 1904, 32.
14. *Steam Locomotive Firebox Explosion on the Gettysburg Railroad Near Gardners, Pennsylvania, June 16, 1995.* National Transportation Safety Board, Special Investigation Report, Notation 6768, November 15, 1996.

Chapter 1

SECTION 1.1

1. Pack, A. G., Chief Inspector, Bureau of Locomotive Inspection in address to AREA convention, 1928, reported RA, June 23, 1928, 1490D6.
2. *The Movement in Receiverships During 1898,* RRG, January 6, 1899, 8–9.
3. Foster, T. R. *Pooling Locomotives,* RRG, June 14, 1895, 380.
4. RRG, October 5, 1900, 650.
5. RA July 20, 1929, 207.
6. If 1 ton is hauled 10 miles, the result is $1 \times 10 = 10$ ton-miles.
7. Morris, W. S., Superintendent of Motive Power, Chesapeake & Ohio Railway, presidential address, American Railroad Master Mechanics' Association convention, 1901, reproduced RRG, June 28, 1901, 451.
8. The Master Car Builders coupler replaced the dangerous link and pin and continues in use to the present time.
9. RRG, October 9, 1896, 704; Hines, W. D., Assistant Chief Attorney, Louisville & Nashville Railroad, *The Extraordinary Demands of the Interstate Commerce Commission,* pamphlet abstracted RRG, March 11, 1898, 175.
10. *Mr. Hines on Government Regulations of Railroad Rates,* RRG, January 9, 1903, 28.
11. McConnell, J.H., Superintendent of Motive Power, Union Pacific Railroad, *Locomotive Service,* Western Railway Club, December 1895, discussion reproduced RRG, February 21, 1896, 126.

12. *Car Famines and the Pittsburgh District,* RRG, November 22, 1901, 799.
13. Acworth, W. M., *The Recent History of Federal Control of Railroads in the United States,* lecture to School of Economics, London University, October 25, 1905, reproduced RRG, November 17, 1905, 153.
14. Henderson, G. R., *The Cost of Locomotive Operation,* RRG, September 8, 1905, 220.
15. RRG, March 17, 1905, 81.
16. RRG, August 17, 1906, 42.
17. RRG, January 13, 1905, 40.
18. *The Dangers of Speed,* RRG, March 1, 1907, 263.
19. *The Efficiency of Railway Equipment,* RAG, April 24, 1911, 953.
20. Huebner, G. G., *Five Years of Railroad Legislation by the States* in Annals of the American Academy of Political and Social Science, extracted RRG, August 7, 1908, 665.
21. *Increases in Motive Power Expenses Due to Severe Weather,* RRG, May 13, 1910, 1206.
22. Delano, F. A. President, Wabash Railway, *What Is the Matter With the Railways?* convention of Commercial Associations of the State of Michigan, Detroit, April 17, 1912, reproduced RAG, April 19, 1912, 884.
23. Martin, A., *Enterprise Denied: Origins of the Decline of American Railroads, 1897–1917,* New York: Columbia University Press, 1971, 182.
24. *United We Stand; Divided We Fall,* RAG, January 27, 1911, 151.
25. Potter, M. W., President, Carolina, Clinchfield & Ohio Railroad, *Limiting Length of Trains by Law,* letter to Spartanburg *Herald,* abstracted RAG, February 12, 1915, 268.
26. *An Analysis of Train-Crew Legislation,* Bureau of Railway Economics, Bulletin # 53, abstracted RAG, October 24, 1913, 750.
27. *The Seecurities Commission Report,* RAG, December 15, 1912, 1204.
28. *One More to Come,* RAG, February 13, 1914, 333.
29. *The Truth About Railway Accidents,* RAG, December 8, 1911, 166.
30. *Objectionable Public Legislation,* RAG, June 12, 1913, 1278.
31. Traveling Engineers' Association convention, 1914, presidential address, reported RAG, September 25, 1914, 559.
32. *Bureau of Locomotive Inspection,* RAG, December 5, 1919, 883.
33. *Railway Results in 1912 Compared With 1902,* RAG, August 22, 1913, 345.

34. Hill, J. J., *The Country's Need of Greater Railroad Facilities,* Railway Business Association, December 19, 1912, reproduced RAG, December 20, 1912.

35. *Some Reasons For Optimism,* RAG, January 1, 1915, 2.

36. Elliott, H., Chairman and President, New York, New Haven & Hartford Railroad, *The Malady of the Railways of the United States,* Chamber of Commerce of the United States, Washington, DC, February 8, 1916, abstracted RAG, February 11, 1916, 237.

37. *An Analysis of Train-Crew Legislation,* Bureau of Railway Economics, Bulletin # 53, abstracted RAG, October 24, 1913, 750.

38. *Arbitration of Engineers' and Firemen's Demands,* RAG, February 19, 1915, 308.

39. *Arbitration of Engineers' and Firemen's Demands,* RAG, January 22, 1915, 125.

40. *Increasing Efficiency as Indicated by Larger Train Loads,* RAG, December 3, 1915, 1041.

41. La Bach, P. M., Assistant Engineer, Chicago, Rock Island & Pacific, *Superheater Locomotives and Grade Revision,* RAG, September 10, 1915, 469.

42. *Freight Congestion in the West Still Acute,* RAG, January 5, 1917, 29.

43. *I.C.C. Modifies Headlight Order,* RAG, January 5, 1917, 29.

44. RAG, January 4, 1918, 49.

45. *Immediate Relief Recommended for the Railroads,* RAG, December 7, 1917, 1045.

46. *The Pennsylvania's Fight with Jack Frost and the Snow Banks,* RAG, March 1, 1918, 447.

47. Lemmerich, G. E., Layout Engineer, The Austin Co., Cleveland, Ohio, *An Analysis of the Locomotive Terminal Problem,* RA, March 7, 1919, 538.

48. *Firemen Given Hearing Before Wage Board,* RA, October 3, 1919, 695.

49. RAG, March 29, 1918, 809.

50. RAG, April 5, 1918, 863.

51. RAG, February 21, 1919, 426, 436.

52. Herr, E. M., *Prospect of Increased Electrification of Railroads,* RA, January 3, 1925, 25.

53. *War-Time Government and Transportation,* RA, May 2, 1942, 851.

54. Basford, G. M., President, Locomotive Feed Water Heater Co., *The Locomotive as an Investment,* ARMMA convention, 1920, reported RA, June 12, 1920, 1743.

55. RA January 7, 1921, 3.

56. RA January 7, 1922, 15.

57. RA October 22, 1921, 790; July 15, 1922, 98; August 22, 1922, 370, 392; September 9, 1922, 473, 475.

58. *Locomotive Market in Quiescent State During 1921,* RA, January 7, 1922, 124.

59. McManamy, F., Commissioner, ICC, *The Development of Railroad Regulation,* American Railway Association 1924 convention, reproduced RA, June 17, 1924, 1623.

60. RA June 24, 1921, 1461.

61. *I.C.C. Inquires Into Salary Increases,* RA, July 17, 1925, 92.

62. Duff, R. C., President, Waco, Beaumont, Trinity & Sabine Railroad, *Are the Short Lines Mistreated?* RA, February 15, 1936, 283.

63. *More About the Decline of Railroad Mileage,* RA, September 27, 1924, 529.

64. Dunn, S. O., *Progress of Missouri, Kansas & Texas Since 1913,* RA, June 10, 1921, 1321; June 17, 1921, 1385.

65. *Changing a Road From a Liability to an Asset,* RA, October 7, 1922, 666.

66. Parmelee, J. H., Director, Bureau of Railway Economics, *A Review of Railway Operations in 1925,* RA, January 2, 1926, 30.

67. *The Chesapeake & Ohio Railway Company—Forty-sixth Annual Report,* abstracted RA, May 10, 1924, 1177.

68. RA January 1, 1927, 1.

69. *Pennsylvania Reports Best Year,* 1926 annual report, abstracted RA, April 16, 1927, 1199.

70. Parmelee, J. H., Director, Bureau of Railway Economics, *A Statistical Review of the Railroad Year 1924,* RA, January 3, 1925, 53.

71. Parmelee, J. H., Director, Bureau of Railway Economics, *A Review of Railway Operations in 1927,* RA, January 7, 1928, 23; *A Review of Railway Operations in 1928,* RA, January 5, 1929, 22.

72. Basford, G. M., Consulting Engineer, Lima Locomotive Works, *As To the Locomotive—What Next?* Pacific Railway Club, March, 1923, reported RA, March 10, 1923, 553.

73. *Train-Miles and Train-Hours Decrease,* RA, February 25, 1928, 449.

74. Dunn, S. O., Editor, *Railway Age, Tax Increase Offsets Saving in Fuel,* 1930 International Railway Fuel Association convention, reported RA, May 10, 1930, 1132.

75. Parmelee, J. H., Director, Bureau of Railway Economics, *A Review of Railway Operations in 1929,* RA, January 4, 1930, 23.

76. RA November 2, 1929, 1040; RA, January 4, 1930, 1.

77. *Railway Employment Further Reduced in December,* RA, February 20, 1932, 341.

78. *Freight Car Loading,* RA, May 30, 1931, 1081.

79. *Locomotive Prices in 1930,* RA, January 3, 1931, 104; *Roads Doing Much to Improve Passenger Service,* RA, December 3, 1932, 831; *Improvement Work Must Go On,* RA, December 3, 1932, 835.

80. Parmelee, J. H., Director, Bureau of Railway Economics, *A Review of Railway Operations in 1932,* RA, February 4, 1933, 134.

81. *Motive Power Obsolescence High,* RA, October 28, 1933, 593.

82. *Prospective Expenditures on Rolling Stock and Shops,* RA, December 1, 1934, 718; RA, August 4, 1934, 133; Parmelee, J. H., Director, Bureau of Railway Economics, *A Review of Railway Operations in 1934,* RA, January 26, 1935, 101.

83. Parmelee, J. H., Director, Bureau of Railway Economics, *A Review of Railway Operations in 1936,* RA, January 2, 1937, 4.

84. Parmelee, J. H., Director, Bureau of Railway Economics, *A Review of Railway Operations in 1935,* RA, January 4, 1936, 6.

85. Lyne, J. G., *Bankruptcies Break Record in 1935,* RA, January 4, 1936, 41.

86. Lyne, J. G, *Financial Outlook Is Improving,* RA, January 2, 1937, 38.

87. RA January 4, 1941, 1.

88. RA April 16, 1938, 716.

89. Duff, R. C., President, Waco, Beaumont, Trinity & Sabine Railroad, *Are the Short Lines Mistreated?* RA, February 15, 1936, 283.

90. For insight into the nascent airline industry, the reader is referred to Gann, E. K., *Fate Is the Hunter* (New York: Simon & Schuster, 1961) and to the present author's *Quest For All-Weather Flight,* Shrewsbury, UK: Airlife, 2002.

91. Parmelee, J. H., Director, Bureau of Railway Economics, *A Review of Railway Operations in 1946,* RA, January 4, 1947, 58.

92. Parmelee, J. H., Director, Bureau of Railway Economics, *A Review of Railway Operations in 1936,* RA, January 2, 1937, 4.

93. RA August 11, 1928, 249; RA, September 21, 1929, 671.

94. *Leading the Passenger Progress Parade,* RA, October 14, 1939, 554.

95. Wallace, L. W., Director, Equipment Research Division, Association of American Railroads, *Research Results in Steam Railway Transport,* RA, February 20, 1937, 325.

96. RA September 16, 1957, 33.

97. Peck, C. B., *Reserves of Equipment Approach Vanishing Point,* RA, January 2, 1937, 25.

98. RA January 1, 1938, 25.

99. *More for the Transportation Dollar,* RA, May 25, 1940, 885.

100. Parmelee, J. H., Director, Bureau of Railway Economics, *A Review of Railway Operations in 1940,* RA, January 4, 1941, 34.

101. *Proposed Train Limit Legislation,* RA, May 8, 1937, 781.

102. Parmelee, J. H., Director, Bureau of Railway Economics, *A Review of Railway Operations in 1937,* RA, January 1, 1938, 30.

103. Parmelee, J. H., Director, Bureau of Railway Economics, *A Review of Railway Operations in 1938,* RA, January 7, 1939, 33.

104. *The Significant Railway Results of 1938,* RA, January 7, 1938, 1.

105. RA July 20, 1940, 97; September 4, 1940, 358; October 18, 1940, 537.

106. Parmelee, J. H., Director, Bureau of Railway Economics, *a Review of Railway Operations in 1939,* RA, January 6, 1940, 29.

107. Parmelee, J. H., Director, Bureau of Railway Economics, *a Review of Railway Operations in 1939,* RA, January 6, 1940, 29; *Are the Railroads Prepared?* RA, June 22, 1940, 1090.

108. Parmelee, J. H., Director, Bureau of Railway Economics, *A Review of Railway Operations in 1940,* RA, January 4, 1941, 34; RA, July 5, 1941, 9 August 9, 1941, 244.

109. *1941—Railway Review and Outlook—1942,* RA, January 3, 1942, 1.

110. *Locomotive Inspection Report,* RA, February 7, 1948, 56 (302.)

111. Wilcox, H. C., *Locomotive Utilization Continues At Traffic Peak Rates,* RA, January 1, 1944, 36.

112. Parmelee, J. H., Director, Bureau of Railway Economics, *1942 Railway Operations Reviewed,* RA, January 3, 1943, 59.

113. RA January 2, 1943, 40, 107; February 20, 1943, 398.

114. *Greatest Year in Railroad History,* RA, January 1, 1944, 1.

115. McGinnis, A. J., *Locomotive Orders Were Limited by W. P. B. Control of Deliveries,* RA, January 1, 1944, 88.

116. Parmelee, J. H., Director, Bureau of Rail-

way Economics, *Railway Operations in 1945,* RA, January 5, 1946, 69.

117. Yellott, J. I., Kottcamp, C. F., Bituminous Coal Research Inc., *Coal and the Gas-Turbine Locomotive,* RA, June 25, 1947, 1294D122.

118. Ennis, J. B., Senior Vice-President, Alco, *The Last Fifty Years—and the Next,* RA, December 15, 1945, 970.

119. Parmelee, J. H., Director, Bureau of Railway Economics, *A Review of Railway Operations in 1946,* RA, January 4, 1947, 58.

120. RA October 19, 1946, 653.

121. RA November 15, 1947, 817.

122. Miles, F. C., *Locomotives Ordered in 1947,* RA, January 3, 1948, 209.

SECTION 1.2

123. Track length, including parallel tracks, passing loops and yard tracks, was greater. This figure refers to common-carrier, steam-hauled railroads, including narrow-gauge. It does not include city tramlines, inter-urban electric railways and track laid by mining, logging and manufacturing companies for their own use.

124. RRG, December 8, 1893, 890; December 31, 1897, 924.

125. Swartz, W. *The Wabash Railroad,* R&LHS Bulletin #133, Fall 1975, 5.

126. *Train Accidents in the United States in February (1897),* RRG, March 26, 1897, 222.

127. *Railroad Construction in the United States,* RAG, May 7, 1909, 1008.

128. RAG, February 21, 1913, 1245.

129. Myrick, D. F., *Railroads of Nevada and Eastern California,* Berkeley, CA: Howell-North, 1963, vol. 2, 835.

130. *Results of Railroad Operations in 1892,* RRG, March 31, 1893, 240. Southern Pacific; Northern Pacific; New York Central & Hudson River; Pennsylvania; Chicago, Milwaukee & St. Paul; Chicago & Northwestern; New York, Lake Erie & Western; Chicago, Burlington & Quincy; Lake Shore & Michigan Southern; Delaware Lackawanna & Western.

131. Delaware, Lackawanna & Western; Pittsburgh & Lake Erie; Pennsylvania; Boston & Albany; New York, Providence & Boston; New York, New Haven & Hartford; Central of New Jersey; New York Central & Hudson River.

132. Morris, R., *An American View of British Railways,* Atlantic Monthly, excerpted RRG, July 20, 1907, 60.

133. Adams, R. B., *The High-Speed Mania,* Scribner's Magazine, excerpted RRG, April 26, 1907, 586.

134. *Annual report, Atchison, Topeka & Santa Fe, year ending June 30, 1905,* abstracted RRG, September 29, 1905, 289; see also *Nineteen Years' Development Work on the Santa Fe,* RAG, June 18, 1915, 1404; June 25, 1915, 1465.

135. *Annual report, Pennsylvania Railroad, 1905,* abstracted RRG, March 9, 1906, 219.

136. *Annual report, New York Central & Hudson River, 1909,* abstracted RAG, March 18, 1910, 719, 757.

137. *Annual report, Atchison, Topeka & Santa Fe, 1918,* abstracted RAG, July 11, 1919, 48.

138. *The Operation of the Norfolk & Western,* RAG, March 31, 1916, 739.

139. Fowler, G. L., *Development of the Western*

Maryland, RAG, February 3, 1911, 195; Fowler, G. L., *Traffic and Operation of the Virginian Railway,* RAG, March 31, 1911, 783; *Comparative Study in Operation—Virginian and C. C. & O.* RAG, April 24, 1914, 935.

140. *The Denver, Northwestern & Pacific Road,* RRG, March 17, 1905, 234; *Railroading Two Miles Above Sea Level,* RAG, December 27, 1918, 1157.

141. RAG, April 11, 1919, 931.

142. RA April 26, 1924, 1055; RA, June 28, 1924, 1134–1140.

143. *Annual Report: The New York Central Railroad Company,* abstracted RA, May 31, 1924, 1342.

144. *How Large Systems Are Formed,* RA, June 27, 1925, 1653.

145. *The Atchison, Topeka & Santa Fe Railway Co.,* abstracted RA, April 18, 1925, 1009; *Union Pacific Railroad Company Annual Report,* abstracted RA, May 2, 1925, 1115.

146. *Pennsylvania Reports Best Year,* RA, April 26, 1927, 1199.

147. RA October 8, 1921, 690; Young, C. D., General Purchasing Agent, Pennsylvania Railroad, *Pennsylvania Country's Largest Buyer of Coal,* RA, August 4, 1928, 232.

148. Pack, A. G., Chief Inspector, Bureau of Locomotive Inspection, ICC, *The Railroads' Interest in Safe Locomotives,* Western Railway Club, Chicago, April, 1925, abstracted RA, April 25, 1925, 1027.

149. Comparison of statistics printed in *Railroad Age Gazette* and *Railway Age* with figures produced by Aldrich, M., R&LHS Bulletin #171, 38.

150. RA July 24, 1948, 204.

151. *Locomotive Builders' Consolidation,* RRG, May 17, 1901, 338.

152. Park, D. K., *U.S. Steam Locomotive Builders,* R&LHS Bulletin #132, Spring 1975, 47.

153. Swengel, F. M., *The American Steam Locomotive,* Davenport, IA: Midwest Rail, 1967, 77.

154. Park, D. K., *U.S. Steam Locomotive Builders,* R&LHS Bulletin #132, Spring 1975, 47.

SECTION 1.3

155. American Society of Mechanical Engineers, Chicago, 1886.

156. Bartol, K.M., Martin, D.C., *Management,* New York: McGraw Hill, 2nd ed., 1994, 39–43.

157. Eaton, J. Shirley, *Making Railroad Statistics* in *The Station Agent,* abstracted RRG, April 7, 1899, 248.

158. Mahl, W., *The Beginnings of Unit Statistics,* RRG, November 16, 1906, 438.

159. Stanier, W. A., *The Position of the Locomotive in Mechanical Engineering,* presidential address to Institution of Mechanical Engineers, London, UK, October, 1941, reported as *Status of the Steam Locomotive in Great Britain,* RA, February 21, 1942, 415, February 28, 1942, 445.

160. RRG, August 2, 1900, 138; Quereau, C. H., *Ton-Mileage for Motive Power Statistics,* RRG, August 31, 1900, 575; *The Engine-Mile and the Ton-Mile,* RRG, August 1, 1902, 601.

161. Brandt, C. A., The Superheater Co., *The Design and Proportion of Locomotive Boilers,* Canadian Railway Club, February, 1928, reported RA, March 10, 1928, 575.

162. Cooley, T. M., *American Railway,* New York, 1892, quoted in White, 1997, 81.

163. Quayle, Robert, Superintendent of Motive Power, Chicago & North Western Railway, *Business Problems of the Motive Power Depot,* lecture at Purdue University, abstracted RRG, February 18, 1898, 120.

164. *Studies in Operation—St. Louis & San Francisco,* RAG, March 13, 1914, 501.

165. For comparison, the heaviest known trailing load ever hauled by a single steam locomotive in Britain was 2,178 tons in 1982. The engine was a preserved 1950s 2-10-0—weighing 194,000 pounds with 2,014 square feet of primary heating surface, 250-pounds per square inch boiler pressure, 20-inch × 28-inch cylinders, and 60-inch driving wheels. (Steam Railway, March 1–28, 2002, 61.)

166. Dudley, P. *Wear of Tires on the Passenger Engines of the New York Central & Hudson River Railroad for the Past Twenty Years,* RRG, March 13, 1896, 174.

167. Gaines, F. F., Mechanical Engineer, Lehigh Valley Railroad, *Helper Engines,* ARMMA convention, 1902, reproduced RRG, June 27, 1902, 494.

168. Orr, John W. *Set Up Running: The Life of a Pennsylvania Railroad Engineman, 1904–1949,* University Park: Pennsylvania State University Press, 2001, 301.

169. Speare, C. F., *The Possibility of Future Increases in Train Loads,* RAG, April 10, 1914, 828.

170. McConnell, J. H., Superintendent of Motive Power, Union Pacific Railroad, *Locomotive Service,* Western Railway Club, December 1895, abstracted RRG, January 10, 1896, 18.

171. *Car Clearances,* RAG, June 12, 1908, 50.

172. British Railways (amalgamated and nationalized in 1948) were still using four-wheeled freight cars, without power brakes, with a capacity of 20,000 to 30,000 pounds, as late as the 1960s.

173. Waitt, A. M., *The Era of Steel and the Passing of Wood in Car Construction,* New York Railroad Club, January, 1908, abstracted RRG, January 24, 1908, 127.

174. *Evolution of the Lehigh Valley Coal Car,* RRG, May 2, 1902, 326.

175. RRG, February 20, 1897, 143.

176. Townsend, J. F., Traffic Manager, National Tube Co., *Increasing the Car Load,* American Iron & Steel Institute, New York, May, 1914, abstracted RAG, September 25, 1914, 574.

177. Burgess, G. H., Kennedy, M. C., *Centennial History of the Pennsylvania Railroad Company, 1846–1896,* Philadelphia, PA: Pennsylvania Railroad, 1949, 771.

178. Hitt, R., Editor RRG, *High Capacity Cars,* International Railway Congress, 1905, reproduced RRG, May 19, 1905, 551.

179. *Train Accidents in the Unites States in February (1897),* RRG, March 26, 1897, 222.

180. *Injuries to Employees,* RRG, February 23, 1906, 187; *The Disposition of Light Freight Cars,* RAG, June 12, 1908, 50.

181. *The Interstate Commerce Commission Car-Inspection,* RRG, May 2, 1902, 327.

182. RRG, February 9, 1900, 81.

183. Burgess, G. H., Kennedy, M. C., *Centennial History of the Pennsylvania Railroad Company 1846–1946,* Philadelphia: Pennsylvania Railroad, 1949, 717.

184. *Handling Long Trains with Modern Air Brake Equipment,* committee report to Traveling Engineers' Association convention, 1912, abstracted RAG, September 6,1912, 426.

185. Bailey Thomas, W., *Why Long Trains Are Hard to Start,* letter published RAG, July 7, 1916, 4.

186. *An Analysis of Train-Crew Legislation,* Bureau of Railway Economics, Bulletin # 53, abstracted RAG, October 24, 1913, 750.

187. RRG, March 3, 1893, 170.

188. *A 100-Car Test of the Automatic Straight Air Brake,* RAG, July 26, 1918, 173.

189. Blyth, W. S., Traveling Engineer, Canada Atlantic Railroad, *Locomotive and Train Handling,* Canadian Railway Club, Montreal, February 7, 1905, abstracted RRG, April 7, 1905, 338; *Handling Long Trains With Modern Air Brake Equipment,* Traveling Engineers' Association convention, 1912, report of committee on air brakes, abstracted RAG, September 6, 1912, 426.

190. RAG, January 3, 1913, 16.

191. RAG, February 8, 1918, 313.

192. RAG, June 18, 1919, 1461.

193. *Operating Economies Effected by Using 120-Ton Cars,* RA, February 18, 1921, 401; *Record Train Loading Features Virginian Operation,* RA, May 27, 1921, 1203; *Virginian Demonstration of Double-Capacity Brake,* RA, June 17, 1921, 1407.

194. Quereau, C. H., Engineer of Tests, Chicago, Burlington & Quincy Railroad, *Steam Distribution for High Speed Locomotives,* Western Railway Club, February 1894, abstracted RRG, March 9, 1894, 174.

195. *Handling Fast Freight on the Santa Fe,* RRG, August 25, 1905, 184; *Time Freight on the Boston & Maine,* RRG, August 25, 1905, 186.

196. RAG, October 27, 1911, 848.

197. *A Very Fast Run,* RRG, November 17, 1905, 456.

198. *Records of Fast Runs,* RRG, November 2, 1906, 394.

199. Fisher, C. E., *The Steam Locomotives of the Pennsylvania Railroad System,* R&LHS Bulletin #91, October, 1954, 130.

200. Ross, H. H., Assistant Engineer, Lake Shore & Michigan Southern Railroad, *Railroad Track Tanks,* RRG, March 13, 1908, 337.

201. *Water Stations for Track Pans,* report of Committee on Water Service, American Railway Engineering and Maintenance of Way Association, 1911 annual meeting, reproduced RAG, March 24, 1911, 762.

202. *Firemen's Arbitration Award,* RAG, April 25, 1913, 961.

203. Basford, G. M., President, Locomotive Feed Water Heater Co., *The Locomotive as an Investment,* ARMMA convention, 1920, reported RA, June 12, 1920, 1743.

204. *Speeding Up Train Movement,* RA, September 30, 1922, 597.

205. Basford, G. M., *Locomotives for Business Purposes,* RA, January 3, 1925, 25.

206. Gurley, F. G., Vice-President, Atchison, Topeka & Santa Fe Railway, *New Technologies in Transport,* excerpted RA, January 27, 1940, 208.

207. Peterson, R. A., *Hogger: From Fantasy to Fulfillment, a Locomotive Engineer Remembers,* Lincoln, NE: iUniverse, 2003, 123.

208. The Milwaukee called its 4-6-4s "Baltics."

209. RA October 11, 1941, 590.

210. *Faster Trains Give Shippers "Streamlined" Service,* RA, May 25, 1940, 910.

211. *January (1894) Accidents,* RRG, February 23, 1894, 139, 143.

212. RRG, May 12, 1893, 357; October 13, 1893, 744.

213. Dudley, P. H., Inspecting Engineer, New York Central System, *Rails For Lines With Fast Trains,* International Railway Congress, May, 1905, abstracted RRG, January 6, 1905, 9.

214. *The Rail Situation,* RAG, January 12, 1912, 42.

215. *Weight of Rails in Track,* RAG, September 27, 1912, 584; *Many Roads Considering the Use of Heavier Rail,* RA, August 27, 1921, 413.

216. *Rail Sections and Wheel Loads,* RAG, July 16, 1915, 108.

217. *Stronger Track Will Cost Less,* RA, August 22, 1931, 276.

218. *Annual Reports: Delaware, Lackawanna & Western Railway Company,* 1932 annual report, abstracted RA, April 8, 1933, 530.

219. *Annual Reports: Atchison, Topeka & Santa Fe Railway System,* 1930 annual report, abstracted RA, April 25, 1931, 839; *Thirty-fourth Annual Report of the Northern Pacific Railway Company,* abstracted RA, May 9, 1931, 945.

220. Basford, G. M., Consulting Engineer, Lima Locomotive Works, *As to the Locomotive—What Next?* Pacific Railway Club, March, 1923, reported RA, March 10, 1923, 553.

221. *P. R. R. to Use 152-lb. Rail,* RA, April 18, 1931, 783; Skilliman, T. J., Chief Engineer, Pennsylvania System, *Pennsylvania Adopts 152-lb. Rail,* RA, August 8, 1931, 205.

222. Dilts, J. H., *The Great Road: The Building of the Baltimore & Ohio, the Nation's First Railroad, 1828–1853,* Stanford, CA: Stanford University Press, 1993, 295.

223. Reinhard, R. *Workin' on the Railroad: Reminiscences From the Age of Steam,* New York: Weathervane Books, 1970, 198ff.

224. *Hall Signals on the Philadelphia & Reading,* RRG, November 9, 1894, 771.

225. *Automatic Train Control Demonstrated on B., R. & P.,* RA, October 29, 1921, 817; *The Webb Automatic Train Stop Tested on the Erie,* RA, January 14, 1922, 175; *G. R. S. Company's Auto-Manual Train Control,* RA, March 4, 1922, 521; *The Sprague System of Auxiliary Train Control,* RA, April 22, 1922, 963; *Big Four Tests I. E. C. Train Control Device,* RA, July 21, 1923, 103.

226. *Automatic Train Stops,* RAG, September 20, 1912, 506.

227. *I.C.C. Proposes to Order Automatic Train Control,* RA, January 14, 1922, 189.

228. *Signaling Developments Have Improved the Operation of Trains,* RA, July 1, 1933, 51.

229. RRG, October 6, 1898, 691–2.

230. *Nineteen Years' Development Work on the Santa Fe,* RAG, June 18, 1915, 1404; June 25, 1915, 1465.

231. *Studies in Operation—The Erie Railroad,* RAG, April 28, 1916, 939.

232. *Studies of Operation—The C. B & Q.* RAG, July 18, 1913, 85; Drury, G. H. (ed.). *Guide to North American Steam Locomotives: History and Development of Steam Power Since 1900.* Waukesha, WI: Kalmbach, 1993, 106.

233. *Running Time Reduced 1 Hour 44 Minutes on Single-Track Division,* RA, August 4, 1928, 213.

234. *Ironing Out a Mountain Railway,* RA, September 1, 1928, 403.

235. Teal, J. E., Chesapeake & Ohio Railway, *How the C. & O. Has Increased Its Operating Efficiency,* New England Railroad Club, Boston, February, 1932, abstracted RA, June 4, 1932, 936.

236. *Gulf, Mobile & Northern,* 1926 annual report, abstracted RA, March 25, 1927, 991.

237. *The Causes of High Wages,* RA, July 10, 1926, 42; RA, February 23, 1929, 460; *Utilization of Locomotives and Conservation of Fuel,* report to 1929 AARMD convention, reported RA, July 6, 1929, 114; RA, January 4, 1930, 1; Parmelee, J. H., Director, Bureau of Railway Economics, *A Review of Railway Operations in 1929,* RA, January 4, 1930, 23.

238. Sillcox, L. K., First Vice-President, New York Air Brake Co., *Will Railroad Traffic of the Future Require Steam or Diesel?* Institution of Locomotive Engineers, London, UK, abstracted RA, December 5, 1942, 913.

239. *The Norfolk & Western Is Ready,* RA, December 6, 1941, 941.

240. *How to Increase Terminal Locomotive Efficiency,* report to American Association of Railroad Superintendents, January, 1940, abstracted RA, February 3, 1940, 249; Stewart, C. D., Chief Engineer, Westinghouse Air Brake Co., *Advancements in the Braking of High-Speed Trains,* New York Railroad Club, April, 1940, abstracted RA, May 18, 1940, 861; *Eliminating Bottleneck Terminal Delay,* RA, May 25, 1940, 904; *Faster Trains Give Shippers "Streamlined" Service,* RA, May 25, 1940, 910; *Big Possibilities of Freight Car Weight Reduction,* RA, May 25, 1940, 945; *Freight Car Trucks for Speed,* RA, May 25, 1940, 921; *Freight Car Specialties for Speed,* RA, May 25, 1940, 924; Stewart, C. D., Chief Engineer Westinghouse Air Brake Co., *Load-Compensating Freight Brakes,* ASME Railroad Division, New York, November, 1944, abstracted RA, December 30, 1944, 985.

241. *S. P. Handles a Staggering Load, Part I,* RA, April 10, 1943, 706.

242. *Utilization of Locomotives and Conservation of Fuel,* report to AARMD 1937 convention. Reported RA, June 21, 1937, 1040D22.

243. *Utilization of Locomotives and Conservation of Fuel,* AARMD 1938 annual meeting. Reported RA, July 1, 1938, 34; Yellott, J. I., Kottcamp, C. F., Bituminous Coal Research Inc., *Coal and the Gas-Turbine Locomotive,* RA, June 25, 1947, 1294D122.

244. Oehler, A. G., Wilcox, H. C., *Electric, or Diesel, or Both?* RA, January 9, 1956, 140.

245. Blyth, W. S., Traveling Engineer, Canada Atlantic Railroad, *Locomotive and Train Handling,* Canadian Railway Club, Montreal, February 7, 1905, abstracted RRG, April 7, 1905, 338.

246. Harris, D. B., *Reflections of a Civil War Locomotive Engineer: A Ghost-Written Memoir,* CreateSpace, 2011, 202.

247. *Firemen's Arbitration Award,* RAG, April 25, 1913, 961.

248. *Assignment of Power,* report of committee to Traveling Engineers' Association convention, 1916, reported RAG, November 3, 1916, 799.

249. Dunham, W. E., Mechanical Engineer, Chicago & North Western Railway, *American Roundhouses and Their Operation*, International Railway Congress, 1905, reproduced RRG, May 19, 1905, 519.

250. Haas, E. M., Railroad Specialist, The Austin Co., Cleveland, Ohio, *Some Modern Tendencies in Roundhouse Design*, Western Society of Engineers, Chicago, May 1919, abstracted RA, May 16, 1919, 1199.

251. Goodwin, G. S. Mechanical Engineer, Chicago, Rock Island & Pacific Railway, *Value of a Locomotive in Terms of Earning Capacity*, Western Railway Club, February 1915, abstracted RAG, February 19, 1915, 305.

252. *The Largest Coaling Station*, RAG, August 3, 1917, 188.

253. Pickard, F. C., Master Mechanic, Delaware, Lackawanna & Western Railroad, *Handling Locomotives at Railway Terminals*, Central Railway Club, March, 1918, abstracted RAG, March 22, 1918, 713; Lemmerich, G. E., Layout Engineer, The Austin Co., Cleveland, Ohio, *An Analysis of the Locomotive Terminal Problem*, RA, March 7, 1919, 538.

254. RA July 14, 1923, 68.

255. British steam locomotive enginemen typically did not (and do not) wear gloves, taking the utmost pride in the cleanliness of the cab and using only a rag to protect their hands when grasping hot objects. When this writer was training as an oil-burner fireman in the UK in 2011, one instructor told him to take his gloves off so as to be more sensitive in handling the controls.

256. Sheafe, J. S., Engineer of Tests, Illinois Central, *Overloading Freight Locomotives Not Economical*, RAG, November 14, 1913, 915.

257. Ballantine, N. D., Assistant to Second Vice-President, Rock Island Lines, *The Real Value of a Freight Locomotive*, Western Railway Club, April, 1915, abstracted RAG, April 23, 1915, 885.

258. Williams, T. H., Assistant General Manager, Southern Pacific Lines, *Securing the Maximum Efficiency in Train Loading*, Pacific Railway Club, February, 1919, abstracted RA, April 25, 1919, 1051; Lemmerich, G. E., Layout Engineer, The Austin Co., Cleveland, Ohio, *The Design of Modern Locomotive Repair Shops*, RA, August 8, 1919, 261.

259. *Equipment Prices*, RA, January 2, 1937, 44.

260. Sheafe, J. S., Engineer of Tests, Illinois Central Railroad, *Overloading Freight Locomotives Not Economical*, RAG, November 14, 1913, 915.

261. *Repairs to Locomotives by Contract Shops*, RAG, September 3, 1909, 399.

262. *Locomotive Repair Facilities*, RAG, July 28, 1916, 137.

263. Damon, G. A., Managing Engineer, The Arnold Co., Chicago, *Arrangement of Railroad Shops*, Canadian Railway Club, January 1908, abstracted RRG, January 10, 1908, 59.

264. *Studies of Operation—The Pittsburgh and Lake Erie*, RAG, February 13, 1914, 308.

265. *Locomotive Maintenance*, RAG, September 10, 1915, 452.

266. *Locomotive Repairs Without Removing Drivers*, RAG, May 6, 1910, 1134.

267. *Large Locomotive Mileage*, RAG, February 3, 1911, 216.

268. *Pooling Locomotives*, RAG, Juny 29, 1910, 183.

269. *Are Modern Locomotives Efficiently Used?* RA, February 11, 1921, 359.

270. *The Union Pacific Overhauls Its Engine Terminals*, RA, October 1, 1920, 557; *Large Shop Marks Development of Western Road*, RA, October 22, 1920, 687; Plant, L. G. *The Locomotive Terminal as an Operating Factor*, RA, November 19, 1920, 877; November 26, 1920, 929; December 3, 1920, 985.

271. *Motive Power Effectively Maintained on the Union Pacific*, RA, June 20, 1931, 1181.

272. *Reducing Expenses at the Enginehouse*, RA, September 5, 1931, 350.

273. *Long Engine Runs on the Burlington*, RA, April 18, 1925, 971.

274. Basford, G. M., Consulting Engineer, Lima Locomotive Works, *As to the Locomotive—What Next?* Pacific Railway Club, March, 1923, reported RA, March 10, 1923, 553.

275. Kruttschnitt, J., Chairman, Executive Committee, Southern Pacific Lines, *Fuel—A Reducible 13 Per Cent of Expense*, RA, May 26, 1923, 1277.

276. *Long Engine Runs*, RA, June 24, 1933, 890.

277. *The Longest Locomotive Run*, RA, March 8, 1924, 556.

278. Jackson, O.S., Superintendent Motive Power and Machinery, Union Pacific Railroad, discussion to Giles, C. F., Superintendent of Machinery, Louisville & Nashville, *Increasing the Average Mileage of Locomotives*, American Railway Association, June, 1923, reported RA, June 23, 1923, 1601; *Union Pacific Water Work Proves Profitable*, RA, October 4, 1924, 585.

279. *Missouri Pacific Finds Extended Engine Runs Profitable*, RA, October 6, 1928, 650.

280. Report on Locomotive Fuel, RA, October 8, 1929, 819.

281. Pyeatt, J. S., President, Denver & Rio Grande Western Railroad, *Further Fuel Economies*, International Railway Fuel Association 1930 convention, reported RA, May 10, 1930, 1131.

282. *Santa Fe Locomotive Makes Record Run*, RA, December 25, 1937, 907.

283. Fry, L. H., *Motive Power—Wartime and After*, Engineering Institute of Canada, Toronto, Ontario, September, 1943, abstracted RA, October 9, 1943, 559; Morris, J. P. General Manager, Mechanical, Atchison, Topeka & Santa Fe Railway, *How the Santa Fe Got Results with Diesels*, St. Louis Railroad Diesel Club, St. Louis, June, 1951, abstracted RA, July 30, 1951, 37.

284. *The Proper Utilization of Motive Power*, RRG, January 10, 1902, 17.

285. Brunner, H. E., Taylor, B. W., SKF Industries, New York, *New York Central Locomotive No. 5343 Makes Over 130,000 Miles*, RA, September 24, 1932, 421.

286. Macken, J. R., Canadian Pacific Railway, *Economic Life of Locomotives*, RA, September 7, 1940, 334.

287. Orr, John W. *Set Up Running: The Life of a Pennsylvania Railroad Engineman 1904–1949*, University Park, PA: Pennsylvania State University Press, 2001, 19.

288. Grant, H. R. (ed.) *Brownie the Boomer: The Life of Chas. P. Brown, an American Railroader*, De Kalb, IL: Northern Illinois University Press, 1991, 172–3.

289. Orr, John W. *Set Up Running: The Life of a Pennsylvania Railroad Engineman 1904–1949*, University Park, PA: Pennsylvania State University Press, 2001, 6.

290. RAG, February 26, 1909, 425.

291. RAG, November 13, 1914, 914.

292. *Studies in Operation—The M. K. & T.,* RAG, May 30, 1913, 1167.

293. Myrick, David F. *Railroads of Nevada and Eastern California*, Vol. 2 Berkeley, CA: Howell-North, 1963, 559.

294. Kesler, D. D., Chairman, Traveling Engineers' Association, *Lightening the Work of Enginemen and Firemen*, Traveling Engineers' Association convention, 1905, abstracted RRG, September 22, 1905, 276.

295. *Headlight Rule Slightly Modified*, RAG, January 5, 1917.

296. Personal communication from Arnold Menke, kindly transmitted by Robert Church.

297. Coel, Margaret, *Goin' Railroading*, Niwot, CO: University Press of Colorado, 1998, 109. 1st ed. Boulder, CO: Pruett, 1991.

298. Cooper E. C., *Cotton Belt Engineer: The Life and Times of C. W. "Red" Standefer 1898–1981*, Bloomington, IN: AuthorHouse, 2011, 93, 110.

299. Steffes, C. F., *The Life and Times of a Locomotive Engineer*, Bakersfield, CA: Old World Publishers, 1992, 29, 129, 131.

300. Dougherty, S. M., *Call The Big Hook*, San Marino, CA: Golden West, 1984, 123.

301. Essery, T., *Saltley Firing Days*, Kettering, UK: Silver Link, collector's edition, 2010, 279.

302. Dougherty, S. M., *Call The Big Hook*, San Marino, CA: Golden West, 1984.

303. *Percentages of Casualties in Dangerous Occupations*, RRG, July 20, 1900, 50; the books by Alan Villiers on the sailing ships of this time make it clear why this was so.

304. *Train Accidents in 1899*, RRG, February 23, 1900, 120.

305. *Train Accidents in 1898*, RRG, March 10, 1899, 173.

306. *While Other Accidents Decline Trespassing Accidents Still Increase*, RAG, September 10, 1915, 452.

307. *Train Accidents in the United States in March (1893)*, RRG, April 28, 1893, 318.

308. *A Study of Derailment Statistics*, RAG, April 17, 1914, 890.

309. *Government Investigation of the Terra Cotta Collision*, RRG, January 18, 1907, 76, and numerous other references.

310. *December (1892) Accidents*, RRG, January 20, 1893, 53.

311. *Train Accidents in the United States in April (1905)*, RRG, May 26, 1905, 590.

312. *Discipline of Enginemen*, RAG, August 18, 1911, 310.

313. *The Reduction in Railway Accidents in 1915*, RAG, January 21, 1916, 88.

314. RAG, April 7, 1916, 805.

315. *Government Accident Bulletin No. 60*, RAG, February 16, 1917, 272.

316. McKenzie, E. F., Engineman, Pennsylvania Railroad, *Rules for Keeping a Lookout on a*

Busy Road, prize-winning article submitted to RAG, published November 7, 1913, 902.

317. Hamilton, F., Engineer, Chicago, Burlington & Quincy Railroad, *Advantage of Being Always Alert,* essay published RAG, November 28, 1913, 1009.

318. Bruce, J., Engineer, Pennsylvania Railroad, *Experiences and Philosophies of a Panhandle Engineman,* essay published RAG, November 28, 1913, 1010.

319. *Safety on the Santa Fe,* RA, February 28, 1931, 470.

320. RA July 8, 1933, 78.

321. *Some Current Lessons from the Railway Safety Record,* RA, July 20, 1935, 65.

322. *Accidents in 1936,* RA, October 23, 1937, 567.

323. *Increase of Train Accidents,* RA, September 26, 1942, 474.

324. RA June 15, 1940, 1071.

325. *Central's "Lake Shore" Piles Up at Little Falls Curve,* RA, April 27, 1940, 741.

326. *P. R. R. Express Derailed By Saboteurs; Five Killed,* RA, March 22, 1941, 537.

327. *Accident on D. L. at Wayland, N. Y.* RA, September 4, 1943, 388.

328. *Crew at Fault in Accident on A. C. L.,* RA, January 22, 1944, 253.

329. *Finds Excessive Speed Caused July 3 Derailment of "Chief,"* RA, September 2, 1944, 383.

330. Winterrowd, W. H., Vice-President, Franklin Railway Supply Co., *Importance of Modern Locomotives to Railroad Income Account,* Toronto Railway Club, May, 1934, abstracted RA, June 2, 1934, 802.

331. Kerr, C., *Motive Power for High-Speed Operation,* New York Railroad Club, February, 1936, abstracted RA, February 22, 1936, 312.

332. Fiscal year.

333. *Locomotive Accidents Show Decline,* RA, January 21, 1950 (179) 37.

334. *A Target to Aim At,* RA, May 7, 1949, 36 (904.)

335. RA March 8, 1954, 16.

336. RA May 9, 1955, 8.

337. *Steam Vanishes From N&W Passenger Runs,* RA, July 28, 1958, 30.

338. *Locomotive Accidents Continue Decline,* RA, February 5, 1951, 52.

339. *Locomotive Service Becoming Safer,* RA, February 23, 1953, 55.

340. *ICC Bureau Reports on the Condition of Locomotives,* RA, February 7, 1955, 36.

341. *Freight Motive Power Establishes a Peak Operating Record,* RA, May 22, 1944, 992; *Obsolete Locomotives—Why Keep Them Alive?* RA, June 12, 1944, 1159.

342. *Freight Motive Power Establishes a Peak Operating Record,* RA, May 22, 1944, 992; *Obsolete Locomotives—Why Keep Them Alive?* RA, June 12, 1944, 1159.

343. Wilcox, H. C., Miles, F. C., *Motive Power Orders in 1952,* RA, January 12, 1953, 226; RA, January 12, 1953, 154; RA, January 10, 1955, 151.

344. *Diesel-Electrics Handling Nearly Two-Thirds of Road Freight Service,* RA, September 22, 1952, 11.

345. *War's Lessons Shape Motive Power Future,* RA, May 19, 1945, 886.

346. Letter from R. W. Morrison, President,

Texas Mexican Railway, RA, August 25, 1945, 339.

347. *Susquehanna Abandons Steam Power,* RA, June 30, 1945, 1132.

348. *Freight Service Survey Shows Many Improvements by Individual Roads,* RA, May 15, 1948 (941) 143.

349. Bangor & Aroostook; Boston & Maine; Central of New Jersey; Chicago, Burlington & Quincy; Chicago Great Western; Chicago, Indianapolis & Louisville; Milwaukee; Elgin, Joliet & Eastern; Erie; Great Northern; Green Bay & Western; Kansas City Southern; Soo Line; Missouri-Kansas-Texas; Nashville, Chattanooga & St. Louis; New York Central; Norfolk Southern; Pittsburgh & West Virginia; Reading; Union Pacific.

350. Oehler, A. G., Wilcox, H. C., *Electric, Diesel or Both?* RA, January 9, 1956, 140.

351. *Here's the Story of the Iron Horse in the Diesel Age,* RA, February 3, 1958, 22.

352. *New Look At Fuel, Power Trends,* RA, January 20, 1958, 37.

353. *The Last of Steam,* RA, February 3, 1958, 21; www.steamlocomotive.com.

Chapter 2

1. Cornwell, E. L. (ed.), *History of Railways,* Secaucus, NJ: Chartwell, 1976, 67.

2. Sinclair, A., *Development of the Locomotive Engine,* New York: Angus Sinclair, 1907, 647.

3. White, J. H. *American Locomotives: An Engineering History, 1830–1880.* Baltimore, MD: Johns Hopkins University Press, 1997, 76.

4. White, 62.

5. White, 427.

6. Drury, 34.

7. Sinclair, A. *Development of the Locomotive Engine,* New York: Angus Sinclair, 1907, 322.

8. *Ibid.*

9. Drury, 311.

10. Drury, 320.

11. Goss, W. F. M. *Possibilities in American Locomotive Design,* Baltimore & Ohio Officers' convention, September, 1902, reproduced RRG, October 17, 1902, 787.

12. *Ibid.*

13. Goss, W. F. M. *The Modern Steam Locomotive,* American Society of Mechanical Engineers, April, 1904, abstracted RRG, April 29, 1904, 323.

14. White, 1997, 57.

15. RRG, April 7, 1893, 262.

16. *The Speed of the Locomotive,* RRG, January 18, 1895, 39.

17. RRG, April 28, 1893, 312.

18. RRG, May 12, 1893, 358.

19. Barnes, D. L., *Differences Between American and Foreign Locomotives,* International Engineering Congress of the Columbian Exposition, 1893, reproduced RRG, December 29, 1893, 940.

20. *Comparative Tests of English and American Railroad Trains,* RRG, March 30, 1894, 225.

21. Reder, G., *The World of Steam Locomotives,* New York: Putnam's, 1974, 322.

22. Caruthers, C. H., *The Norris Locomotive Works,* RAG, August 20, 1909, 313; Harwood, H. H. *Corporate History of the Lehigh Valley R. R.,* R&LHS Bulletin #126, April, 1972, 5.

23. Church, R. J., *Southern Pacific Ten-*

Coupled Locomotives, Berkeley, CA: Signature Press, 2013, 15.

24. Brown, J. K., Vauclain, S. M., *Comments on the System and Shop Practices of the Baldwin Locomotive Works,* Journal R&LHS, Bulletin #173, Autumn, 1995, 103; Reder, G., *The World of Steam Locomotives,* New York: Putnam's, 1974, 142–3.

25. *Baldwin and Schenectady Locomotives at the World's Fair,* RRG, June 16, 1893; *Table No. 1.—Comparative Dimensions of Locomotives at the World's Fair,* RRG, November 17, 1893, 834; Best, G. M., *All Time Erie Locomotive Roster,* Journal R&LHS, Autumn, 1974, 20.

26. RRG, September 7, 1894, 605.

27. *An Important Experiment in Locomotive Counterbalancing at Purdue University,* RRG, December 15, 1893, 906.

28. *Russian Method of Testing Locomotives,* RA, May 30, 1919, 1311.

29. Goss, W. F. M., Professor of Mechanical Engineering, Purdue University, *Locomotive Performance: The Result of a Series of Researches Conducted by the Engineering Laboratory of Purdue University,* New York: John Wiley, 1911.

30. Nock, O. S., *The British Steam Railway Locomotive from 1925 to 1965.* London, UK: Ian Allen, 1966, 147.

31. Streeter, T., *A New "P2"—Feasible or Fantasy? 'Steam Railway,'* #382, November 12–December 9, 2010, 91.

32. Stanier, W. A., *The Position of the Locomotive in Mechanical Engineering,* presidential address to Institution of Mechanical Engineers, London, UK, October, 194, reported as *Status of the Steam Locomotive in Great Britain,* RA, February 21, 1942, 415, February 28, 1942, 445.

33. RRG, August 7, 1903, 569.

34. Whitney, C. W. *Increased Heating Surface in Locomotives,* letter published RRG, January 31, 1896, 69.

35. Demoulin, M. *The Future Development of the Locomotive,* Bulletin of International Railway Congress, reproduced RRG, August 12, 1898, 573.

36. *Large Freight Engines,* RRG, June 17, 1898, 436.

37. *The Two Heaviest Locomotives,* RRG, November 25, 1898, 846.

38. *Large Freight Engines,* RRG, June 17, 1898, 436.

39. *Tank Capacity of Large Freight Locomotives,* RRG, August 12, 1898, 580.

40. *Locomotives At the World's Fair,* RRG, October 28, 1904, 481.

41. *Tendencies in Locomotive Design,* RRG, June 19, 1903, 426.

42. Wardale, D., *The Red Devil and Other Tales From the Age of Steam,* privately published, 1998, 105–6.

Chapter 3

SECTION 3.1

1. RRG, August 28, 1904, 281.

2. Forsyth, W., Mechanical Engineer, Chicago, Burlington & Quincy Railroad, *The Heat Value of Western Coals,* Western Railway Club, December 1894, abstracted RRG, December 28, 1894, 887; February 1, 1895, 66.

3. Fowler, George L., *Coke for Locomotive Fuel*, RRG, June 22, 1900, 422.

4. *Fuel Oil for Locomotives*, RRG, April 24, 1903, 298.

5. White, 1997, 90; *Oil Fuel for Locomotives*, RRG, October 31, 1902, 834.

6. *Fuel Oil for Locomotives*, RRG, April 24, 1903, 298.

7. *Operating and Maintaining Oil Burning Locomotives*, Traveling Engineers' Asociation, Chicago, September 1922, abstracted RA, May 20, 1922, 1187.

8. McDonough, J., *Oil Fuel for Locomotives*, Traveling Engineers' Association, Chicago, September 9, 1902, abstracted RRG, October 10, 1902, 771.

9. *Recent Experiments with Oil Fuel*, RRG, February 8, 1895, 82.

10. Vauclain, S. M., *The Locomotive of the Future*, RRG, April 5, 1901, 235.

11. Best, W. N., Superintendent of Motive Power and Machinery, Los Angeles Terminal Railway, *Burning Crude Oil in Locomotives*, Pacific Coast Railway Club, June, 1901, abstracted RRG, June 21, 1901, 431.

12. *Smoke Preventing Device Used on the Chicago & Northwestern Railway*, RRG, July 14, 1893, 519.

13. Nock, O. S. *Locomotion: A World Survey of Railway Traction*, New York: Scribners, 1975, 68.

14. Lyon, T., Master Mechanic, Chicago Great Western Railway, *Locomotive Rating and Fuel*, Western Railway Club, April, 1896, reproduced RRG, July 16, 1896, 488.

15. "H. D. L.," *How to Fire a Locomotive*, RRG, September 22, 1893, 699; circular issued by the Office of the Fuel Agent, Wabash Railway, February, 1898, abstracted RRG, March 11, 1898, 185; British Transport Commission, *Handbook for Railway Steam Locomotive Enginemen*, 1957, reprint Ian Allan, UK, 1977, 30; Porta, L. D., quoted in Wardale, D., *The Red Devil and Other Tales from the Age of Steam*, privately published, Inverness, UK, 1998, 515; various firemen, Welsh Highland Railway, UK, 2011.

16. *Thick and Thin Firing of Locomotives*, RAG, December 15, 1911, 1204.

17. RRG, July 8, 1904, 136.

18. Nelson, E. D., Engineer of Tests, Pennsylvania Railroad, *Bank Versus Level Firing*, ARMMA convention 1909, reproduced RAG, June 18, 1909, 1340.

19. Bush, S. P., Superintendent of Motive Power, Pennsylvania Railroad, *The Economy in the Use of Coal by the Railroads*, Western Railway Club, January, 1895, abstracted RRG, February 1, 1895, 66.

20. Grant, H. R. (ed.) *Brownie the Boomer: The Life of Charles P. Brown, an American Railroader*, Dekalb, IL: Northern Illinois University Press, 1991.

21. RRG, July 20, 1900, 499.

22. Goss, W. F. M., *The Modern Steam Locomotive*, American Society of Mechanical Engineers, April, 1902, reproduced RRG, April 29, 1904, 323; May 6, 1904, 348.

23. RRG, May 29, 1896, 381.

24. *The Kincaid Locomotive Stoker*, RRG, May 17, 1901, 348.

25. RRG, July 1, 1904, 109.

26. Discussion on automatic stokers, ARMMA,

1904, reproduced RRG, July 8, 1904, 133.

27. Goss, W. F. M., *Locomotive Sparks*, New York: John Wiley, 1902, abstracted RRG, February 28, 1902, 139.

28. Goss, W. F. M., *Locomotive Performance: The Result of a Series of Researches Conducted by the Engineering Laboratory of Purdue University*, New York: John Wiley & Sons, 1907, 50.

29. Gardner, W. J., *Cleaner to Controller, Volume 2: Further Reminiscences of the GWR at Taunton*, Usk, UK: Oakwood, 2000, 105.

30. Coel, M. *Goin' Railroading*, Niwot, CO: University Press of Colorado, 2d ed. 1998, 111.

31. *Exhaust and Draft in Locomotives*, RRG, January 19, 1900, 32.

32. *Tests of Coal for Locomotives*, RRG, January 1, 1899, 40.

33. RRG, July 8, 1904, 136.

34. Emery, C. E., *The Cost of Steam Power With Engines of Different Types*, American Institute of Electrical Engineers, New York, March 21, 1893, abstracted RRG, March 24, 1893, 226.

35. Letter Ira C. Hubbell to Editor, RRG, New York, September 9, 1900; RRG, October 5, 1900, 645.

36. *Fuel Performance of a Heavy Locomotive*, RRG, September 14, 1900, 609.

37. RRG, January 1, 1893.

38. Report to the Master Mechanics' Association, June, 1904, abstracted RRG, July 8, 1904, 136.

39. *Ibid.*

40. Henderson, G. R., *Fuel Consumption of Locomotives*, American Society of Mechanical Engineers, December, 1904, reproduced RRG, December 9, 1904, 624.

41. Shurtleff, A. K., Chicago, Rock Island & Pacific Railway, *Locomotive Fuel Consumption and the Speed Diagram*, American Railway Engineering Association Bulletin #148, abstracted RRG, September 20, 1912, 513.

42. *Efficiency of Locomotive Fuels*, RRG, February 28, 1894, 887.

SECTION 3.2

43. Sanderson, R.P.C. *Locomotive Firebox Design*, RRG, June 11, 1897, 412.

44. *Construction and Inspection of Locomotive Boilers to Prevent Explosions*, RRG, December 22, 1893, 925.

45. Holton, J. L., *Wootten and the Reading Shops*, R&LHS Bulletin #141, Fall 1979, 61.

46. Best, G. M., *Erie Locomotive Notes*, R&LHS Bulletin #131, Fall 1974, 12.

47. Kraft, E., *The Mightiest of Them All: The Pennsylvania Railroad*, Orange Park, FL: Neighborhood Press, 2002, 18.

48. Best, G. M., *Erie Locomotive Notes*, R&LHS Bulletin #131, Fall 1974, 12.

49. RRG, July 23, 1897, 521.

50. RRG, February 15, 1895, 108.

51. *Staybolt Breakage*, RRG, June 13, 1902, 425.

52. *New Eight-Wheeled Locomotive of the Boston & Maine*, RRG, June 19, 1896, 425.

53. Seley, C. A., President, American Flexible Bolt Co., *Locomotive Staybolts*, New York Railroad Club, April, 1914, abstracted RAG, August 21, 1914, 333.

54. *The Tate Flexible Staybolt*, RRG, April 29, 1904, 323.

55. Bruce, A. W., *The Steam Locomotive in

America: Its Development in the Twentieth Century*, New York: Bonanza, 1952, 138.

56. *Brick Lined or Water Lined Fireboxes*, RRG, September 8, 1893, 672.

57. Goss, W. F. M., *The Effect of High Rates of Combustion upon the Efficiency of Locomotive Boilers*, New York Railroad Club, September, 1896, abstracted RRG, September 18, 1896, 651.

58. Barnes, D. L., *Distinctive Features and Advantages of American Locomotive Practice*, Civil Engineering Section, World's Engineering Congress, August, 1893, abstracted RRG, March 2, 1894, 157.

59. Goss, W. F. M., *The Effect of High Rates of Combustion on the Efficiency of Locomotive Boilers*, New York Railroad Club, September 1896, abstracted RRG, October 16, 1896, 722; October 23, 1896, 734, 741.

60. *Recent Improvements in the Design and Construction of Locomotives*, RRG, February 7, 1896, 93.

61. *Wider Fireboxes* RRG, January 11, 1901, 26.

62. RRG, June 25, 1897, 459.

63. *The Vanderbilt Locomotive Boiler with Corrugated Firebox*, RRG, September 1, 1899, 612.

64. *The Vanderbilt Locomotive Boiler*, RRG, May 10, 1901, 316.

65. *Another Watertube Locomotive Boiler*, letter from J. Christianson to RRG, Hartford, Connecticut, December 20, 1895, printed RRG, January 10, 1896, 17.

66. *Perkins Water-Tube Locomotive Boiler*, RRG, October 16, 1896, 720.

67. Riegel, S. S., *A Water-Tube Locomotive Boiler*, RRG, May 9, 1902, 340; *Lackawanna Pacific Type Freight Locomotive*, RAG, October 9, 1914, 657.

68. *Heavy Pacific Type Locomotive for the Lackawanna*, RAG, December 24, 1915, 1183.

69. *The Brotan Water Tube Fire-Box*, RRG, September 18, 1903, 676.

70. White, 1997, 108.

71. *Locomotive Grates for Anthracite Coal*, Report of Committee of ARMMA, 1897, abstracted RRG, July 23, 1897, 520; *The Weaver Grate*, RRG, March 3, 1895, 146.

72. *The Hancock Shaking Grate*, RRG, February 23, 1900, 116.

73. Carney, J. A., *Grates for Bituminous Coal*, ARMMA convention, 1904, abstracted RRG, July 1, 1904, 114.

74. White, 1997, 108; Nock, O. S., *Locomotion: A World Survey of Railway Traction*, New York: Scribners, 1975, 68; Ringel, C., *History, Development and Function of the Locomotive Brick Arch*, R&LHS Journal, October, 1956, 79.

75. *The Boiler of the New York Central Locomotive No. 999*, RRG, May 19, 1894, 368.

76. *A Water Arch for a Locomotive Fire-box*, RRG, September 26, 1902, 746.

77. *A Fire Brick Arch for Locomotive Fire-Boxes*, RRG, July 27, 1894, 521.

78. Bruce, 150, gives an earliest date of 1900 but see *Union Pacific Fast Mail Locomotive*, RRG, May 12, 1894, 349.

79. *A Richmond Ten-Wheel Compound for the Chesapeake & Ohio*, RRG, November 8, 1895, 736.

80. Ringel, C., *History, Development and Function of the Locomotive Brick Arch*, R&LHS, New

York, NY, January, 1948, printed Journal R&LHS, October, 1956, 79.

81. *A Locomotive Boiler Explosion,* RRG, November 4, 1898, 795.

82. *Concerning a Recent Boiler Explosion,* RRG, December 21, 1894, 870.

83. *Construction and Inspection of Locomotive Boilers to Prevent Explosions,* RRG, December 22, 1893, 925.

84. Sanderson, R. P. C., *Locomotive Firebox Design,* RRG, June 11, 1897, 412.

85. Burt, J. C., *The Savor of Old-Time Southern Railroading,* R&LHS Bulletin #84, October, 1951, 36.

86. *Fusible Plugs in Crownsheets,* RRG, October 5, 1900, 651.

87. Florida Department of State, Division of Library and Information Services, comment on Image # N038697 (www.floridamemory.com.)

88. *Train Accidents in the United States in January (1903),* RRG, February 27, 1903, 150.

89. *Train Accidents in the United States in January (1896),* RRG, February 28, 1896, 148–9.

90. *Boiler Explosion at Bridgeport, Ala.* RRG, April 24, 1896, 291.

91. *Train Accidents in the United States in March (1896),* RRG, April 24, 1896, 292.

92. *Train Accidents in the United States in May (1895),* RRG, June 28, 1895, 437.

93. *Train Accidents in the United States in April (1897),* RRG, May 28, 1897, 367.

94. *Train Accidents in the United States in June (1897),* RRG, August 13, 1897, 569.

SECTION 3.3

95. Carruthers, C. H., *Early Experiments with Smoke-Consuming Fire-boxes on American Locomotives,* RRG, December 1, 1905, 514.

96. Dickerman, W. C., Chairman of the Board, American Locomotive Co., *Awful Immediacy of the Present!,* Newcomen Society, Schenectady, New York, reported RA, December 4, 1943, 901.

97. *The Boiler of the New York Central Locomotive No. 999,* RRG, May 19, 1893, 368; *Seventy-Two Inch Crown Bar Boiler—Schenectady Locomotive Works,* RRG, March 29, 1895, 194.

98. Koyl, C. Herschel, *The Work of Railroad Men on the Problem of Pure Water for Steam Boilers,* RRG, March 23, 1900, 180.

99. Stillman, H., Engineer of Tests, Southern Pacific Lines, *The Treatment of Water for Boilers,* Pacific Coast Railway Club, September 1900, abstracted RRG, October 12, 1900, 675.

100. Breckenridge, L. P., Head of Mechanical Engineering, University of Illinois, *The Effect of Scale on the Evaporation of a Locomotive Boiler,* RRG, January 27, 1899, 60.

101. *Effect of Boiler Scale,* RRG, April 5, 1901, 232.

102. Desgeans, Engineer, Eastern Railway of France in *Revue Generale des Chemins de Fer, Boiler Defects and Failure,* abstracted RRG, November 3, 1899, 756.

103. Stillman, H., Engineer of Tests, Southern Pacific Lines, *The Treatment of Water for Boilers,* Pacific Coast Railway Club, September 1900, abstracted RRG, October 12, 1900, 675.

104. *Effect of Boiler Scale,* RRG, April 5, 1901, 232.

105. Knowles, C. R., Superintendent, Water Service, Illinois Central, *What Tannins Do in the Treatment of Locomotive Boiler Water,* RA, December 18, 1943, 971.

106. Aspinall, J. A. F., General Manager, Lancashire & Yorkshire Railway, *Report on the Purification of Feed-Water of Locomotives and the Use of Disincrustants,* International Railway Congress, 1900, abstracted RRG, August 24, 1900, 569.

107. Fowler, G. L., *Long Tubes for Locomotive Boilers,* letter to RRG, September 12, 1900, printed RRG, September 21, 1900, 615.

108. Fry, L. H., *Locomotive Boiler Tubes,* RRG, September 11, 1903, 648.

109. *Relative Steam-Making Capacity of Firebox and Tube Surface,* RRG, December 4, 1896, 847.

110. *The Steaming Capacity of Locomotives,* RRG, June 19, 1903, 440.

111. *Railway Review,* May 9, 1891, quoted R&LHS Bulletin #141, Fall 1979, 4.

112. RRG, June 30, 1898, 478.

113. Conger, C. B., *Water Glasses for Locomotive Boilers,* Traveling Engineers' Association abstracted RRG, September 18, 1903, 676.

114. Harding, J. W., series of home study guides published by International Text Book Co., Scranton, PA, 1923–1946, republished as *Steam Locomotive Home Study Course,* Townsend, TN: Little River Locomotive Co., 2000, Vol. I, 458.

115. *Comparative Tests of Steam Injectors,* RRG, December 31, 1897, 922.

116. *Test of the Performance of a Locomotive Injector,* RRG, December 11, 1896, 855.

117. *Self-Acting Injectors with Adjustable Cones,* RRG, June 2, 1896, 408.

118. *The Ohio Locomotive Injector,* RRG, June 7, 1895, 364.

119. *The Hancock Inspirator,* RRG, June 24, 1904, 84.

120. Steingress, F. M., Frost, A. J., *Stationary Engineering,* Homewood, Illinois: American Technical Press, 1991, Fig. 3–31.

121. White, 1997, 137–142.

122. *The Barnes Feed-Water Heater,* RRG, March 19, 1897, 208.

123. *Exhaust and Draft in Locomotives,* International Railroad Congress, 1900, reported RRG, June 29, 1900, 448.

124. *M. N. Forney's Feed-Water Heater for Locomotives,* RRG, June 27, 1902, 496.

125. *McBride's Locomotive Feed Water Heater,* RRG, July 17, 1903, 523.

126. Vaughan, H. H., Superintendent of Motive Power, Canadian Pacific Railway, *The Use of Superheated Steam on Locomotives,* ARMMA, June 1905, abstracted RRG, June 23, 1905, 719. This paper offers considerable detail on nineteenth-century superheating work.

127. *Ibid.*

128. *Superheated Steam in Locomotive Service,* RRG, June 12, 1903, 402.

129. Schubert, K., *Wilhelm Schmidt—bedeutender Erfinder aus dem Harzvorland,* Allgemeiner Harz-Berg-Kalender für das Jahr 2014, Clausthal-Zellerfeld, Germany: Papierflieger Verlag, 2014, 160.

130. *The Use of Superheated Steam in Locomotives,* RRG, October 10, 1902, 775.

131. *A 6,000 Horse Power Westinghouse Engine,* RRG, May 24, 1901, 345.

132. Otis, S., *The Future Simple Locomotive,* Northwest Railway Club, March, 1901, abstracted RRG, April 26, 1901, 284.

133. Bruce, 1952, 154.

134. Drury, 1993, 380; Vaughan, H. H., Superintendent of Motive Power, Canadian Pacific Railway, *The Use of Superheated Steam on Locomotives,* ARMMA, June 1905, abstracted RRG, June 23, 1905, 719.

135. Vaughan, H. H., Assistant to the Vice-President, Canadian Pacific Railway, *Superheated Steam on Locomotives,* American Society of Mechanical Engineers, May, 1907, abstracted RRG, June 7, 1907, 792.

136. *The Schenectady Locomotive Superheater,* RRG, September 2, 1904, 292.

SECTION 3.4

137. Reder, G., 1974, 17.

138. Discussion on Squire, W. C., *Draft Appliances on Locomotives Exhibited at the World's Fair,* Western Railway Club, November, 1893, abstracted RRG, December 29, 1893, 944.

139. White, J. H. *American Locomotives: An Engineering History 1830–1880,* Baltimore: Johns Hopkins University Press, 1997, 112.

140. Discussion on blast nozzles, New York Railroad Club, February, 1893. Abstracted RRG, February 24, 1893, 150.

141. *Plain and Vortex Blast Pipes,* RRG, December 8, 1893, 886.

142. *Draft Appliances on Locomotives Exhibited at the World's Fair,* RRG, December 29, 1893, 944.

143. Quereau, C. H., Engineer of Tests, Chicago, Burlington & Quincy Railroad, in discussion of Squire, W. C., *Draft Appliances on Locomotives Exhibited at the World's Fair,* Western Railway Club, November, 1893, abstracted RRG, January 12, 1894, 24.

144. von Borries, A., Director, Prussian State Railway, *Experiments With Locomotive Exhaust Pipes and Smokestacks,* original in *Organ für Fortschritte des Eisenbahnwesens,* translated and condensed RRG, March 20, 1896, 196.

145. *Locomotive Smokestacks,* RRG, April 20, 1894, 281.

146. *Long or Short Smokeboxes,* RRG, May 4, 1894, 322.

147. Deems, J. F., Division Master Mechanic, Chicago, Burlington & Quincy Railroad, *The Form of the Exhaust Jet,* Western Railway Club, April, 1896, reproduced RRG, June 5, 1896, 398; Goss, W. F. M., *A Glimpse of the Exhaust Jet,* Western Railway Club, October, 1895, reproduced RRG, November 8, 1895, 737.

148. *The Continuation of the Exhaust Nozzle Tests,* RRG, September 7, 1894, 616.

149. ARMMA convention, 1897, discussion of report of committee on exhaust nozzles and steam passages, abstracted RRG, June 25, 1897, 457.

150. *A New Locomotive Exhaust Nozzle,* RRG, June 16, 1899, 426.

151. *Exhaust and Draft in Locomotives,* RRG, January 19, 1900, 32.

152. *Exhaust and Draft in Locomotives,* RRG, June 29, 1900, 448.

153. *Locomotive Draft and Exhaust*, RRG, June 26, 1900, 453.

154. Gardner, W. J., *Cleaner to Controller. Vol. 2. Further Reminiscences of the GWR at Taunton*, Usk, UK: Oakwood, 2000, 29.

155. *Locomotive Draft and Exhaust*, RRG, June 26, 1900, 453.

156. *Exhaust and Draft in Locomotives*, RRG, May 23, 1902, 374.

157. Slater, F. Master Mechanic, Chicago & North Western Railway, *Self-Cleaning Locomotive Front Ends*, Western Railway Club, November, 1902, abstracted RRG, November 21, 1902, 889.

158. Symington, T. H., *Experiments With Stacks and Exhaust Pipes*, Richmond Railroad Club, October, 1903, abstracted RRG, October 30, 1903, 774.

159. Goss, W. F. M., *Recent Progress in the Design of Locomotive Front-Ends*, Central Railway Club, November, 1903, abstracted RRG, November 13, 1903, 810.

Section 3.5

160. Dean, F. W., *Inside Cylinder Locomotives*, RRG, July 29, 1904, 204.

161. *Long Stroke Locomotives*, RRG, April 21, 1899, 282.

162. Sinclair, A., 1907.

163. Snowden Bell, J., *Three-Cylinder Locomotives*, paper at 1913 ARMMA convention, reproduced RAG, June 14, 1913, 1374.

164. *The Smith Three-Cylinder Engine*, RRG, July 20, 1894, 511; Warner, P. T., *Mogul Type Locomotives*, R&LHS Bulletin #100, April, 1959, 7.

165. Warner, P. T., *Mogul Type Locomotives*, R&LHS Bulletin #100, April, 1959, 7.

166. *Smith's Three-Cylinder Locomotive*, RRG, March 15, 1895, 164.

167. King, C. R., *The Origin of Four-Cylinder Balanced Locomotives*, RRG, December 8, 1905, 543.

168. Cole, F. J., Mechanical Engineer, American Locomotive Company, *Four-Cylinder Compound Locomotives in America*, International Railway Congress, 1905, reproduced RRG, May 19, 1905, 524.

169. *A New Locomotive Cylinder*, RRG, August 19, 1898, 558.

170. *Intercolonial Locomotives With Cleveland Cylinders*, RRG, June 14, 1901, 395.

171. *Variation in Temperature in Locomotive Cylinders*, RRG, November 2, 1894, 759.

172. Discussion on compound locomotives, ARMMA convention, 1895, abstracted RRG, June 28, 1895, 430.

173. Barton, D. B., *The Cornish Beam Engine*, Truro, UK: D. Bradford Barton, 1969, 25.

174. *The Chicago Discussion on Compound Locomotives*, RRG, May 5, 1893, 338.

175. Weinstein, E. G., *André Chapelon and French Locomotives in the Twentieth Century*, R&LHS Bulletin, Spring 1997, 7.

176. Vauclain, S. M., *The Locomotive of the Future*, New England Railroad Club, February, 1901, abstracted RRG, April 5, 1901, 235.

177. King, C. R., *The Origin of Four-Cylinder Balanced Compound Locomotives*, RRG, December 8, 1905, 543.

178. Reder, G., 1974, 205; Best, G. M., *Erie Locomotive Notes*, R&LHS Journal, Fall 1974; White, J. H., 1997, 210.

179. Marshall, W. P., *The Evolution of the Locomotive Engine*, RRG, December 2, 1898, 855; February 24, 1899, 142.

180. Durrant, A. E., *The Mallet Locomotive*, New York: Arco, 1975.

181. Demoulin, M., Engineer, Western Railway of France, *The Present Status of the Compound Locomotive in France*, RRG, October 2, 1896, 683.

182. Reder, G., 1974, 204.

183. *Four-Cylinder Tandem Compound Locomotives*, RRG, August 30, 1901, 606.

184. Dean, F. W., *The Efficiency of Compound Locomotives*, ASME, May, 1895, reproduced RRG, May 17, 1895, 310.

185. Vauclain, S. M., President, Baldwin Locomotive Works, *The History of Locomotive Development*, RA, June 23, 1923, 1573.

186. Sinclair, A., 1907, 651, 653.

187. Muhlfeld, J. E., President, Locomotive Pulverized Fuel Co., Oatley, H. B., Chief Engineer, Locomotive Superheater Co., *What Is the Relative Economy of the Locomotive of 1900 and Today?* ASME, Worcester, MA, June 1918, reported RA, August 16, 1918, 305; *Baldwin Celebrates Its Hundredth Birthday*, RA, May 16, 1931, 964.

188. *Pulling and Starting Power of Electric and Steam Locomotives*, RRG, October 6, 1893, 734.

189. Caruthers, C. H., *Locomotive Development on the Pennsylvania Railroad 1849–1905*, RRG, April 28, 1905, 396.

190. *Two Pittsburgh Compound Locomotives*, RRG, June 14, 1895, 379.

191. *Two Pittsburgh Compound Locomotives*, RRG, June 14, 1895, 379.

192. *The Richmond Compound Locomotive on the Chesapeake & Ohio Railroad*, RRG, April 21, 1893, 294.

193. *The Rogers Compound Locomotive on the Illinois Central*, RRG, March 17, 1893, 200.

194. Forsyth, W., Western Railway Club, February, 1893, quoted in Report on Compound Locomotives, ARMMA convention, 1893, abstracted RRG, June 23, 1893, 466.

195. *The Chicago Discussion on Compound Locomotives*, RRG, May 5, 1893, 338.

196. ARMMA convention, 1893, reported RRG, June 23, 1893, 466.

197. Letter published RRG, December 1, 1893, 863.

198. *Recent Improvements in the Design and Construction of Locomotives*, RRG, February 14, 1896, 111.

199. *The Rhode Island System of Compounding*, RRG, September 15, 1893, 686.

200. *Starting Valves of the Baldwin Locomotive Works*, RRG, August 18, 1893, 620.

201. *The Pittsburgh Compound Mogul Locomotive*, RRG, February 2, 1894, 80.

202. White, J. H., *Richmond Locomotive Builders*, Journal R&LHS, Spring, 1974, 68.

203. *Gölsdorf Compound Locomotives*, RRG, January 16, 1903, 41.

204. Best, G. M., *Erie Locomotive Notes*, R&LHS Bulletin #131, Fall 1974, 12.

205. Report on compound locomotives, ARMMA convention, 1900, abstracted RRG, June 26, 1900, 443. Unfortunately, this source does not identify the railroads concerned.

206. Gaines, F. F., Mechanical Engineer, Lehigh Valley Railroad, *A Review of Different Types of Compounding*, RRG, September 27, 1901, 661.

207. McCarroll, W. J., *The Proper Handling of Compound Locomotives*, Traveling Engineers' Association, September, 1902, abstracted RRG, September 26, 1902, 738.

208. *Tests of Compound and Simple Locomotives*, RRG, March 3, 1893, 162.

209. Report of Committee on Compound Locomotives, ARMMA convention, 1893, reported RRG, June 28, 1893, 466.

210. *High Speed Compounds*, RRG, January 3, 1896, 9.

211. *Compound Locomotives in Actual Service*, RRG, September 22, 1893, 706.

212. Quereau, C. H., Engineer of Tests, Chicago, Burlington & Quincy Railroad, *Steam Distribution for High-Speed Locomotives*, Western Railway Club, February, 1894, abstracted RRG, March 9, 1894, 174.

213. Dean, F. W., *The Efficiency of Compound Locomotives*, ASME, May, 1895, reproduced RRG, May 17, 1895, 310.

214. *Performance of Compound Locomotives*, RRG, December 13, 1895, 821.

215. Jukes, F., *Early Northern Pacific Consolidations*, R&LHS Bulletin #102, April, 1960, 35.

216. *A Ride on a Richmond Freight Compound*, RRG, August 14, 1896, 565; *The Compound on the Chesapeake & Ohio*, RRG, July 16, 1897, 511.

217. *Class G-6 Consolidation Locomotive for the Chesapeake & Ohio*, RRG, August 19, 1898, 558.

218. *Compound Locomotives on the Wabash*, RRG, November 8, 1899, 763.

219. Custer, E. A., *No Royal Road*, New York: H. C. Kinsey, 1937, quoted in Reinhardt, R., *Workin' on the Railroad: Reminiscences from the Age of Steam*, New York: Weathervane Books, 1970, 151.

220. Beardsley, A. L., Atchison, Topeka & Santa Fe Railway, *Care and Handling of the Compound Locomotive*, Traveling Engineers' Association convention, 1903, abstracted RRG, September 18, 1903, 664.

221. Herr, E. M., Northern Pacific Railway, *Compound Locomotives on the Northern Pacific*, Western Railway Club, March, 1899, abstracted RRG, April 28, 1899, 293.

222. *Early Player Tandem Compounds*, RRG, August 4, 1899, 550.

223. Reder, G., 1974, 207.

224. *Four-Cylinder Tandem Compound Locomotives*, RRG, August 30, 1901, 606.

225. *Cylinders and Valves of the Vauclain Tandem Compound*, RRG, May 27, 1904, 395.

226. *A New Type of Locomotive*, RRG, June 14, 1895, 379.

227. King, C. R., *The Origin of Four-Cylinder Balanced Compound Locomotives*, RRG, December 8, 1895, 543.

228. *French Four-Cylinder Compounds*, RRG, September 28, 1900, 638.

229. Gaines, F. F., Mechanical Engineer, Lehigh Valley Railroad, *A Review of the Different Systems of Compounding*, RRG, September 27, 1901, 661.

230. Goss, W. F. M. *Four-Cylinder Balanced Compound Locomotives,* letter to RRG, December 1, 1902, reproduced RRG, January 2, 1903, 1.

231. Cole, F. J., Mechanical Engineer, American Locomotive Company, *Four-Cylinder Compound Locomotives In America,* International Railway Congress, 1905, reproduced RRG, May 19, 1905, 524; Morison, G. S., *Report on a Balanced Locomotive,* RRG, February 22, 1895, 117.

232. Prince, S. F., *A New Design for a Four-Cylinder Balanced Compound Locomotive,* RRG, June 9, 1916, 637.

233. Cole, F. J., Mechanical Engineer, American Locomotive Company, *Four-Cylinder Compound Locomotives In America,* International Railway Congress, 1905, reproduced RRG, May 19, 1905, 524.

234. Sinclair, A., 1907, 655.

235. Cole, F. J., Mechanical Engineer, American Locomotive Company, *Four-Cylinder Compound Locomotives In America,* International Railway Congress, 1905, reproduced RRG, May 19, 1905, 524.

236. Fisher, C. E., *The Steam Locomotives of the Pennsylvania Railroad System,* R&LHS Bulletin #91, October, 1954, 130.

237. *Baldwin Four-Cylinder Balanced Compound Locomotives for the Santa Fe,* RRG, January 22, 1904, 57; Drury, 27.

238. *Valve Gear of the Symons Four-Cylinder Balanced Compound Locomotive,* RRG, November 10, 1905, 451.

239. *The Limits of Size of a Locomotive,* RRG, October 27, 1899, 746.

240. Mallet, A., *Locomotive Compound Articulée, Systeme Mallet,* Revue Generale des Chemins de Fer, May, 1900, abstracted RRG, September 14, 1900, 603.

241. RRG, September 14, 1900, 610.

242. Harding, J. W., 2002, Vol. I, 50.

SECTION 3.6

243. Sinclair, A., 1907, 8; Rolt, L. T. C., Allen, J. S., *The Steam Engine of Thomas Newcomen,* Hartington, UK: Moorland, 1977, 89.

244. Goss, W. F. M., *Locomotive Valves and Valve-Gears,* Southern and Southwestern Railway Club, June, 1905, reported RRG, July 7, 1905, 6.

245. Storer, J. D., *A Simple History of the Steam Engine,* London, UK: John Baker, 1969, 66.

246. Church, R. J., *Southern Pacific Ten-Coupled Locomotives,* Berkeley, CA: Signature Press, 2013, 15.

247. Harding, J. W., 2000, Vol. I, 209–30.

248. Dean, F. W., *The Efficiency of Compound Locomotives,* American Institute of Mechanical Engineers, May, 1895, reproduced RRG, May 17, 1895, 310.

249. *Locomotive Road Tests—Illinois Central Railroad,* RRG, June 17, 1898, 432.

250. Symons, W. E., *Fuel Economy Resulting from a Study of Indicator Cards,* Southern and Southwestern Railway Club, November 9, 1899, abstracted RRG, December 29, 1899, 893.

251. *Modern Appliances on Large Locomotives,* Traveling Engineers' Association convention, 1915, reported RAG, September 17, 1915, 505.

252. Quereau, C. H., General Foreman of Motive Power, Burlington & Missouri River Railroad, *Lead for Locomotives,* Western Railway Club, January, 1897, abstracted RRG, March 19, 1897, 199; Quereau, C. H., *Lead for Locomotives,* RRG, August 9, 1895, 525.

253. Quereau, C. H., *Lead for Locomotives,* RRG, August 9, 1895, 525.

254. Quereau, C. H., General Foreman of Motive Power, Burlington & Missouri River Railroad, *Lead for Locomotives,* Western Railway Club, January, 1897, abstracted RRG, March 19, 1897, 199.

255. *Lead and Steam Distribution,* RRG, June 8, 1900, 368.

256. Quereau, C. H., Engineer of Tests, Chicago, Burlington & Quincy Railroad, *Steam Distribution for High Speed Locomotives,* Western Railway Club, February, 1894, abstracted RRG, March 9, 1894, 174.

257. Pomeroy, L. R., *Balanced Slide Valves,* New York Railroad Club, December, 1895, abstracted RRG, February 7, 1896, 88.

258. Discussion on balanced slide valves, New York Railroad Club, December, 1895, abstracted RRG, February 7, 1896, 88.

259. Sanderson, R. P., Divisional Superintendent of Motive Power, Norfolk & Western Railway, *Balancing of Slide Valves,* Southern and Southwestern Railway Club, November, 1893, quoted RRG, November 17, 1893, 836.

260. Edmonds, G. S., Superintendent Motive Power, Delaware & Hudson Railroad, *Locomotive Valves and Valve Gears,* RA, July 1, 1933, 27.

261. White, J. H., 1997, 148, 203.

262. Report of Committee on Slide Valves, ARMMA convention, 1896, abstracted RRG, July 3, 1896, 468.

263. Goss, W. F. M., Professor of Mechanical Engineering, Purdue University, *Performance of the Purdue Locomotive "Schenectady,"* reproduced RRG, June 5, 1896, 396.

264. Report of Committee on Slide Valves, ARMMA convention, 1896, abstracted RRG, July 3, 1896, 468; Quereau, C. H., *The Allen Valve for Locomotives,* American Society of Mechanical Engineers, 1899, abstracted RRG, June 30, 1899, 470.

265. Edmonds, G. S., Superintendent Motive Power, Delaware & Hudson Railroad, *Locomotive Valves and Valve Gears,* RA, July 1, 1933, 27.

266. Player, J., Mechanical Engineer, Brooks Locomotive Works, *Locomotive Piston Valves,* Central Railway Club, November 1901, abstracted RRG, December 27, 1901, 887.

267. Vauclain, S. M., *The Locomotive of the Future,* New England Railroad Club, February, 1901, abstracted RRG, April 5, 1901, 235.

268. *A Plea for the Piston Valve,* RRG, July 29, 1898, 549.

269. *Balanced Piston Valves—Inside Admission,* RRG, July 6, 1900, 462.

270. ARMMA convention, 1900, reported RRG, June 29, 1900, 445.

271. *Piston Valves,* ARMMA convention, 1904, reported RRG, July 1, 1904, 112.

272. Sanderson, R. P., Divisional Superintendent of Motive Power, Norfolk & Western Railway, *Balancing of Slide Valves,* Southern and Southwestern Railway Club, November, 1893, quoted RRG, November 17, 1893, 836.

273. Henderson, G. R., *Fuel Consumption of Locomotives,* ASME, December, 1904, reproduced RRG, December 9, 1904, 624.

274. Cheney, J. V. N., *Proposed Design of Locomotive Valves for High Speeds,* RRG, April 10, 1903, 264.

275. Forsyth, W., *American Locomotives,* International Engineering Congress, St. Louis, October, 1904, reproduced RRG, October 14, 1904, 434.

276. Quereau, C. H., General Foreman of Motive Power, Burlington & Missouri River Railroad, *Lead for Locomotives,* Western Railway Club, January, 1897, abstracted RRG, March 19, 1897, 199; Quereau, C. H., *Lead for Locomotives,* RRG, August 9, 1895, 525; *Locomotive Road Tests—Illinois Central Railroad,* RRG, June 17, 1898, 433.

277. *The Lewis Locomotive Valve Gear,* RRG, April 27, 1894, 296; McShane, C., *Classic American Locomotives: The 1909 Classic on Steam Locomotive Technology,* Guilford, CT: Globe Pequot, 2003, 196.

278. *Lamplough's Valve Gear,* RRG, June 15, 1894, 419.

279. *The Haberkorn Valve Mechanism for Locomotives,* RRG, October 28, 1904, 493.

280. *The Young Valve and Gear for Locomotives,* RRG, November 4, 1904, 516; Young, O. W., *Cylinder Clearance and Valve Events,* Western Railway Club, December, 1904, abstracted RRG, December 23, 1904, 666.

281. www.steamlocomotive.com.

282. *Locomotive Valve Gears,* RRG, November 4, 1904, 505.

283. Boulvin, M. J., Professor, University of Ghent, *History of the Walschaerts Valve Motion,* RRG, November 24, 1905, 492.

284. Frey, B., *Walschaert Valve Gear,* RAG, September 2, 1910, 417.

285. *Early Locomotive Works,* RAG, September 11, 1908, 914; Fisher, C. E., *Walschaert Valve Gear Used in This Country in the Seventies,* letter, RA, January 23, 1920, 286.

SECTION 3.7

286. White, J. H., 1997, 158ff.

287. Sague, J. E., Mechanical Engineer, Schenectady Locomotive Works, *Cast Steel in Locomotive Building,* New England Railroad Club, November, 1896, reproduced RRG, December 18, 1896, 873.

288. Barba, Midvale Steel Works, *Cast Steel in Locomotive Building,* New England Railroad Club, November, 1896, abstracted RRG, December 18, 1896, 874.

289. Quoted in Galbraith, R. M., *An Improved Cast Steel Locomotive Frame,* RRG, June 14, 1901, 401.

290. *Cast Steel Locomotive Frames,* RRG, January 6, 1899, 10.

291. *Cast Steel Locomotive Frames,* RRG, September 20, 1901, 654.

292. *Locomotive Frames,* report to ARMMA convention, 1904, abstracted RRG, July 1, 1904, 113.

293. Bruce, A. W., 1952, 242.

294. Bullock, S. A., Baldwin Locomotive Works, *Evolution of the Locomotive Truck,* RAG, July 24, 1908, 574.

295. Harding, J. W., 2002, Vol. I, 65.

296. Bruce, A. W., 1952, 238.

297. White, J. H., 1997, 174.

298. Bruce, A. W., 1952, 246 and Fig. 49.

299. Bruce, A. W., 1952, 250 and Fig. 51. Drawings and text are contradictory as to when these devices first appeared. *Cole's Radial Locomotive Trailing Truck*, RRG, January 20, 1905, 64; Bullock, S. A., Baldwin Locomotive Works, *Evolution of the Locomotive Truck*, RAG, July 24, 1908, 574; *Improved Designs of Engine and Tender Trucks*, RAG, October 23, 1914, 741.

300. *Heavy Passenger Locomotives for the C., M. & St. P.*, RRG, June 9, 1905, 654.

301. Bruce, A. W., 1952, 254 and Fig. 53.

302. *The Distribution of Weight on Driving Wheels*, RRG, March 9, 1894, 178; Harding, J. W., 2002, Vol. I, 170.

303. Grafstrom, H., *Helical versus Elliptical Driving Springs*, RRG, October 1, 1897, 685.

304. *The Probable Place of the Traction Increaser for Locomotives*, RRG, November 8, 1901, 774.

305. Harding, J. W., 2002, Vol. I, 161.

306. Walker, H. T., *Compensated Locomotives*, RAG, August 14, 108, 708; August 21, 1908, 768; August 28, 1908, 815.

307. *Ibid.*

308. Walker, H. T., *Compensated Locomotives*, RAG, August 14, 108, 708; August 21, 1908, 768; August 28, 1908, 814; *The Earliest Balanced Locomotives*, RAG, July 23, 1909, 141; August 6, 1909, 231.

309. *An Important Experiment in Locomotive Counterbalancing at Purdue University*, RRG, December 15, 1893, 906.

310. *Effects of Driving Wheel Blows*, letter from A. J. Lowe, Lexington, Kentucky, and letter signed "Headlight," RRG, August 24, 1894, 573.

311. *Locomotive Blows and Bridges*, letter signed "Bridge Engineer" in RRG, July 27, 1894, 515.

312. Anonymous letter quoted in *Counterbalancing in the Laboratory and on the Track*, RRG, March 29, 1894, 214.

313. *More Experience With the Locomotive Hammer Blow*, letter signed "Headlight" RRG, August 10, 1894, 543.

314. Barnes, D. L., *Rail Pressures of Locomotive Driving Wheels*, abstracted RRG, December 21, 1894, 869.

315. *Counterbalance Tests of the Strong Engine at Purdue University*, RRG, August 6, 1897, 552.

316. Parke, R. A. *The Vertical Influence of the Counterbalance*, New York Railroad Club, February, 1894, abstracted RRG, February 23, 1894, 136.

317. Henderson, G. R., Mechanical Engineer, Norfolk & Western Railway, *Locomotive Counterbalancing*, Association of Engineers of Virginia, June, 1896, reproduced RRG, September 4, 1896, 621.

318. von Borries, A. *Disturbing Influences of a Locomotive's Reciprocating Parts*, Verein für Eisenbahnkunde, October, 1903, abstracted RRG, November 27, 1903, 845.

319. Parke, R. A., Westinghouse Air-Brake Co., *Locomotive Counterbalancing*, New England Railroad Club, December, 1903, abstracted RRG, December 11, 1903, 879.

320. *Internal Friction of Locomotives*, RRG, June 15, 1894, 426.

321. Goss, W. F. M., *The Determination of the Friction Losses of Locomotives*, Purdue University Exponent, 1899, reproduced RRG, June 9, 1899, 404.

322. *Internal Friction of Locomotives*, RRG, August 3, 1894, 536.

323. *Internal Friction in Locomotives*, RRG, May 12, 1901, 254.

Section 3.8

324. *Vauclain Speaks at Fifth Session of Mechanical Division*, proceedings of 1930 ARA convention, Mechanical Division, formerly ARMMA, reported RA, June 25, 1930, 1548D140.

325. *A New Dynamometer Car*, RRG, November 25, 1898, 843.

326. Forsyth, W., Mechanical Engineer, Chicago, Burlington & Quincy Railroad, *Tests of Locomotives in Heavy Express Service*, Western Railway Club, February, 1893, reproduced RRG, March 17, 1893, 202.

327. *Locomotive Tests on the Chicago, Burlington & Quincy Railroad*, RRG, March 17, 1893, 211.

328. Ahrons, E. L., *The British Steam Railway Locomotive 1825–1925*, London, UK: Ian Allan, 1927, 356; Nock, O. S., *The British Steam Railway Locomotive from 1925 to 1965*, London, UK: Ian Allan, 1966, 20, 30.

329. ARMMA 1894 convention, report of Committee on Conducting Locomotive Tests, abstracted RRG, June 29, 1894, 460.

330. *Traction Tests on the Northern Pacific*, RRG, October 18, 1895, 684.

331. *Tests of a Baldwin Locomotive on the Louisville & Nashville*, RRG, August 12, 1898, 576.

332. *Test of the New 10-Wheel Locomotives of the Great Northern*, RRG, October 14, 1898, 735.

333. McHenry, E. H., Chief Engineer, Northern Pacific Railway, *Locomotive Design*, RRG, April 13, 1900, 229.

334. *Test of the New 10-Wheel Locomotives of the Great Northern*, RRG, October 14, 1898, 735.

335. Hitchcock, E. A., *Road Tests of Brooks Passenger Locomotives*, ASME, December, 1904, abstracted RRG, December 9, 1904, 620.

336. Forsyth, W., *American Locomotives*, International Engineering Congress, St. Louis, October, 1904, reproduced RRG, October 14, 1904, 434.

337. *Compound Locomotive Tests on the Long Island Railroad*, RRG, February 9, 1894, 106.

338. *Locomotive Testing at Purdue University*, RRG, December 17, 1897, 890; Young, G. A., Purdue University, *Forty Years of Railway Research at Purdue*, RA, July 1, 1933, 12.

339. Kunz, A. H., *Did You Know?: Purdue Locomotive Testing Plant*, Purdue Today, January 23, 2015.

340. *New Experimental Locomotive "Schenectady No.2*," Purdue University, RRG, December 17, 1897, 883.

341. Goss, W. F. M., Professor of Mechanical Engineering, Purdue University, *Performance of the Purdue Locomotive "Schenectady*," reproduced RRG, June 5, 1896, 396.

342. *Locomotive Testing Plants*, RRG, May 17, 1901, 336.

343. Herr, E. M., *Notes From Work Done on the Chicago & Northwestern Locomotive Testing Plant*, Western Railway Club, January, 1897, abstracted RRG, February 19, 1897, 129.

344. *Locomotive Testing Plants*, RRG, May 17, 1901, 336.

345. *Locomotive Testing Plant of the Pennsylvania at St. Louis*, Pennsylvania Railroad Company Bulletin #2, abstracted in RRG, May 13, 1904, 356; Fry, L. H., *Influence of the Testing Plant on Locomotive Designs*, ASME regional meeting, Altoona, October, 1925, reported RA, October 24, 1925, 752.

346. *Purdue University and Its Work in Railroad Engineering*, RRG, June 14, 1901, 415.

347. *An Early Tonnage Rating Sheet*, RAG, December 22, 1911, 1285.

348. Eaton, J. S., *The Basis of Engine Rating*, RRG, June 14, 1901, 397; Henderson, G. R., *Practical Tonnage Rating*, ARMMA convention, 1901, reproduced RRG, June 21, 1901, 423.

349. Lyon, T., Master Mechanic, Chicago Great Western Railroad, *Locomotive Rating and Fuel*, Western Railway Club, April, 1896, reproduced RRG, July 16, 1896, 488.

350. *Train Resistance and Express Locomotives*, RRG, July 12, 1895, 466.

351. Raymond, W. G., *Some Questions in Locomotive Design*, RRG, March 30, 1900, 198.

352. *Tonnage Rating for Locomotives*, report to committee at ARMMA convention, 1898, abstracted RRG, June 24, 1898, 453.

353. Eaton, J. S., *The Basis of Engine Rating*, RRG, June 14, 1901, 397; Henderson, G. R., *Practical Tonnage Rating*, ARMMA convention, 1901, reproduced RRG, June 21, 1901, 423.

354. *Concerning the Present Status of Steam Engineering*, article in *The Engineer*, London, UK, abstracted RRG, April 19, 1901, 263.

355. Letter signed "M.E.," RRG, October 19, 1900, 681.

356. McHenry, E. H., Chief Engineer, Northern Pacific Railway, *Locomotive Design*, RRG, April 13, 1900, 229.

357. Goss, W. F. M., *The Modern Steam Locomotive*, ASME, April, 1902, reproduced RRG, April 29, 1904, 323; May 6, 1904, 348.

358. *Tendencies in Locomotive Design*, RRG, June 19, 1903, 426.

359. *What Is the Most Promising Direction in Which to Effect a Reduction in Locomotive Fuel Consumption?* report to ARMMA convention, 1901, abstracted in RRG, June 1, 1901, 426.

360. *Tendencies in Locomotive Design*, RRG, June 19, 1903, 426.

Chapter 4

Section 4.1

1. *The Class P Locomotive and the Pennsylvania Railroad*, RRG, February 22, 1895, 116; *The "Class P" Locomotive of the Pennsylvania*, RRG, February 22, 1895, 122.

2. *New York Central Fast Express Locomotive*, RRG, April 7, 1893, 262.

3. *Eight-Wheel Express Locomotive, Class I-6—Baltimore & Ohio*, RRG, July 14, 1893, 516.

4. *Schenectady Locomotives for the Boston & Albany*, RRG, November 2, 1894, 751.

5. *Schenectady Eight-Wheel Locomotives for the Chicago & Northwestern,* RRG, October 11, 1895, 667.

6. *The New Schenectady Eight-Wheelers of the "Big Four,"* RRG, October 18, 1895, 687.

7. *Lehigh Valley Wide-Firebox Express Locomotive,* RRG, October 25, 1895, 698.

8. *New Eight-Wheel Passenger Locomotive—Illinois Central Railroad,* RRG, February 5, 1897, 92.

9. *Two Pittsburgh Compound Locomotives,* RRG, June 14, 1895, 379.

10. *A Schenectady 8-Wheeler for the Vandalia Line,* RRG, April 28, 1899, 297.

11. *Fast Passenger Locomotives of the Chicago and Northwestern Railway,* RRG, May 26, 1899, 369.

12. *Chicago & Alton Eight-Wheel Passenger Locomotive,* RRG, January 5, 1900, 3.

13. *Some of the Recent Passenger Locomotives of the Pennsylvania Railroad,* RRG, August 10, 1900, 535.

14. Drury, 58, 90.

SECTION 4.2

15. Reder, G, 1974.

16. *The Reading's Single-Driver Express Locomotive,* RRG, August 9, 1895, 526.

17. R&LHS, Bulletin #96, May, 1957, 62; *Rebuilding Locomotives—Philadelphia & Reading,* RRG, June 24, 1904, 46.

18. *Practical Reconstruction of Old Locomotives,* RA, January 21, 1921, 237, including photograph on p. 240.

19. *The Baldwin Locomotive "Columbia,"* RRG, May 26, 1893, 387.

20. *Performance of the Baldwin Locomotive "Columbia,"* RRG, May 11, 1894, 333.

21. *Baldwin and Schenectady Locomotives at the World's Fair,* RRG, June 16, 1893, 434.

22. Holton, J. L., *Wootten and the Reading Shops,* R&LHS Bulletin #141, Fall, 1979, 61.

23. *Rebuilding Locomotives—Philadelphia & Reading,* RRG, June 24, 1904, 46; Warner, P. T., *Mogul Type Locomotives,* R&LHS Bulletin #100, April, 1959, 7.

24. *The Chicago, Burlington & Quincy Fast Passenger Locomotive, Class N,* RRG, December 6, 1895, 798.

25. R&LHS, Bulletin #96, May, 1957, 62.

26. Vauclain, S. M. in discussion on Cole, F. J., Assistant Mechanical Engineer, American Locomotive Co., *Recent Locomotive Construction and Performance,* New York Railroad Club, November, 1901, abstracted RRG, November 22, 1901, 817.

27. Drury, 32.

28. *A New Baldwin Locomotive for the Central of New Jersey,* RRG, June 12, 1896, 407.

29. Holton, J. L., *Wootten and the Reading Shops,* R&LHS Journal, Fall 1979, 61; *The New Atlantic City Engine of the Philadelphia & Reading,* RRG, June 19, 1896, 429.

30. *Compound Passenger Locomotives for the St. Paul,* RRG, July 24, 1896, 517.

31. *A New Baldwin Locomotive for the Lehigh Valley Railroad,* RRG, October 9, 1896, 696.

32. *New Class "G" Locomotives for the Wabash,* RRG, April 1, 1898, 232.

33. *The New Passenger Engines of the Burlington,* RRG, May 5, 1899, 312.

34. *Atlantic Type Locomotive—Class E-1 No. 698,* RRG, July 7, 1899, 487.

35. *The Pennsylvania's Class E-2 Experimental Locomotive,* RRG, July 20, 1900, 492.

36. Fisher, C. E., *The Steam Locomotives of the Pennsylvania Railroad System,* R&LHS Bulletin #91, October, 1954, 154.

37. *The New Class E-2 Locomotive—Pennsylvania Railroad,* RRG, June 14, 1901, 409; Drury, 328.

38. *New Class "D" Passenger Locomotives of the Chicago & Northwestern,* RRG, August 3, 1900, 520.

39. Drury, 97.

40. *Brooks "Chautauqua" Type Passenger Locomotive—Burlington, Cedar Rapids & Northern,* RRG, November 30, 1900, 792.

41. *The New Class I Central-Atlantic Type Locomotives—New York Central Railroad,* RRG, February 4, 1901, 73.

42. Drury, 279.

43. *Performance of Class I and Class C Locomotives—New York Central Railroad,* RRG, November 1, 1901, 751.

44. *Atlantic Type Passenger Locomotives—Chicago, Milwaukee & St. Paul Railway,* RRG, September 20, 1901, 646.

45. *The Atlantic Type Locomotive of the Chicago, Milwaukee & St. Paul,* RRG, January 31, 1902, 71.

46. *Brooks Chautauqua Type Passenger Locomotives—Buffalo, Rochester & Pittsburgh,* RRG, December 13, 1901, 853.

47. *A Brooks "Chautauqua" Type Locomotive—Central Railroad of New Jersey,* RRG, January 3, 1902, 4; Drury, 76.

48. *Atlantic Type Passenger Engines for the Chesapeake & Ohio,* RRG, September 12, 1902, 699; Drury, 88.

49. *Atlantic Type Locomotive for the Big Four,* RRG, October 31, 1902, 832; Drury, 279.

50. *Oil Burning Atlantic (4-4-2) Type Locomotive for the Southern Pacific,* RRG, June 12, 1903, 402; Drury, 365.

51. *Atlantic Type (4-4-2) Locomotive for the Baltimore & Ohio,* RRG, July 31, 1903, 553; Drury, 47.

52. *Cole's Four-Cylinder Balanced Compound Locomotive for the New York Central,* RRG, May 13, 1904, 360; Drury, 279.

53. *Baldwin Four-Cylinder Balanced Compound for the Burlington,* RRG, June 3, 1904, 412; Drury, 27, 106.

54. Sinclair, A., 1907, 320.

55. *Rhode Island Compound Locomotive for the Chicago, Milwaukee & St. Paul,* RRG, June 9, 1893, 412; *Compound Passenger Locomotive for the Chicago, Milwaukee & St. Paul,* RRG, September 29, 1893, 715; Drury, 34; *More About the Rhode Island 4-6-2's for the C. M. & St. P.,* R&LHS Bulletin #89, November, 1953, 163.

56. Compilation and reconciliation of information provided by H. M. Ghormley, Oakdale, Tennessee, to editor of R&LHS Journal and published therein as *More About the Rhode Island 4-6-2's for the C. M. & St. P.,* R&LHS Journal, November, 1953, 163.

57. *Passenger Engines for the Chesapeake & Ohio and Missouri Pacific,* RRG, August 1, 1902, 603.

58. Drury, 88.

59. Drury, 254.

60. *Heavy Pacific Type Locomotives for the Chicago & Alton,* RRG, November 7, 1902, 855.

61. Drury, 438.

62. *Heavy Pacific Type Locomotives for the El Paso & Southwestern,* RRG, November 6, 1903, 793.

63. *Pacific Type (4-6-2) Locomotive for the Michigan Central,* RRG, April 29, 1904, 320.

SECTION 4.3

64. *Schenectady Passenger Locomotive "Columbus,"* RRG, June 16, 1893, 429.

65. *Ten-Wheel Passenger Locomotive—Delaware, Lackawanna & Western,* RRG, September 8, 1893, 667.

66. *Pittsburgh Ten-Wheel Passenger Engine,* RRG, April 13, 1894, 264.

67. *Cooke Locomotives for the Southern Pacific,* RRG, April 5, 1895, 215.

68. *The Siemens & Halske Steam Locomotive,* RRG, August 30, 1895, 571.

69. *A Richmond Ten-Wheel Compound for the Chesapeake & Ohio,* RRG, November 8, 1895, 736.

70. *Ten-Wheel Passenger Locomotives for the Lake Shore & Michigan Southern,* RRG, January 1, 1897, 5.

71. *Heavy Compound Freight Locomotive for the Northern Pacific,* RRG, March 26, 1897, 217.

72. *Schenectady Locomotives for the Northern Pacific,* RRG, May 11, 1897, 335.

73. *Ten-Wheel Passenger Locomotive—Atchison, Topeka & Santa Fe,* RRG, October 22, 1897, 741.

74. *Ten-Wheel Freight Engine, Chicago & Northwestern Railway,* RRG, October 29, 1897, 762.

75. *Ten-Wheel Passenger Locomotives for the Great Northern Railway,* RRG, October 7, 1898, 719.

76. *Ten-Wheel Passenger Locomotives for the Fitchburg,* RRG, October 21, 1898, 757.

77. *Schenectady Ten-Wheelers for the Northern Pacific,* RRG, December 1, 1899, 825.

78. *Some of the Recent Passenger Locomotives of the Pennsylvania Railroad,* RRG, August 10, 1900, 535.

79. *Heavy Ten-Wheel Compound Passenger Locomotives With Wide Fire-Boxes—Lehigh Valley Railroad,* RRG, December 28, 1900, 854.

80. *Some Ten-Wheel Passenger Locomotives—Atchison, Topeka & Santa Fe,* RRG, January 18, 1901, 38.

81. *120 Miles an Hour,* RRG, March 22, 1901, 199.

82. Drury, 279; *Heavy Ten-Wheel Passenger Locomotives of the Cleveland, Cincinnati, Chicago & St. Louis Railway,* RRG, May 24, 1901, 344.

83. *Baldwin-Vanderbilt Ten-Wheel Passenger Locomotive—Atchison, Topeka & Santa Fe,* RRG, October 4, 1901, 677; November 29, 1901, 823; Drury, 27.

84. *A Baldwin Four-Cylinder Balanced Compound for the Plant System,* RRG, February 28, 1902, 139.

85. *Ten-Wheel Locomotives for the New Haven,* RRG, November 25, 1904, 582; Drury, 294.

86. *Pittsburgh Compound Mogul Locomotive,* RRG, February 2, 1894, 80.

87. *The New Freight Locomotives of the Pennsylvania Railroad,* RRG, September 18, 1896, 651.

88. Warner, P. T., *Mogul Type Locomotives*, R&LHS Bulletin #100, April, 1959, 7.

89. Adams, R. D., *2000 Plus; The Pennsy's H-6*, R&LHS Bulletin #124, April, 1971, 51.

90. *Mogul Freight Locomotive*, RRG, October 2, 1896, 681.

91. *A Schenectady Mogul for the New York Central*, RRG, October 28, 1898, 776; *New York Central Moguls in 1889 and 1899*, RRG, June 30, 1899, 470.

92. Warner, P. T., *The Mogul Type Locomotive*, R&LHS Bulletin #100, April, 1959, 7.

93. Caruthers, C. H., *Locomotive Development on the Pennsylvania Railroad 1849–1905*, RRG, April 28, 1905, 396.

94. *Pennsylvania Moguls—Classes F-3 and F-3-b*, RRG, November 1, 1901, 753.

95. *Mogul Freight Locomotives for the Southern Pacific*, RRG, November 29, 1901, 821; Drury, 364.

96. Durocher, A. A., *The Lake Superior & Ishpeming Railroad Company*, R&LHS Bulletin #98, April, 1958, 7.

97. *New Locomotives of the Chicago, Burlington & Quincy*, RRG, March 30, 1900, 195.

98. *Prairie Type Freight Locomotives of the Chicago, Burlington & Quincy*, RRG, June 22, 1900, 417.

99. *New Passenger Locomotives for the Lake Shore & Michigan Southern*, RRG, March 29, 1901, 220; Drury, 277.

100. *Locomotives for the Colorado Springs & Cripple Creek District Railroad*, RRG, March 1, 1901, 138.

101. *Prairie Type Passenger Locomotives—Atchison, Topeka & Santa Fe*, RRG, November 22, 1901, 800; Drury, 27; *Heavy Passenger Locomotives of the Atchison, Topeka & Santa Fe*, RRG, November 22, 1901, 808.

102. *Prairie Type Passenger Locomotive With Traction Increaser—Atchison, Topeka & Santa Fe*, RRG, January 17, 1902, 41; *Prairie Type Freight Locomotives With Traction Increasers—Atchison, Topeka & Santa Fe*, RRG, May 16, 1902, 358.

103. *Competitive Locomotive Types for the Illinois Central*, RRG, June 20, 1902, 458; Drury, 26.

104. Drury, 207.

105. *New Passenger Locomotives for the Lake Shore*, RRG, December 2, 1904, 600; Drury, 277.

106. Warner, P. T., *Mogul Type Locomotives*, R&LHS Bulletin #100, April, 1959, 7.

107. Warner, P. T., *Mogul Type Locomotives*, R&LHS Bulletin #100, April, 1959, 7; Drury, 358, 364.

108. *Steam Locomotive Firebox Explosion on the Gettysburg Railroad Near Gardners, Pennsylvania, June 16, 1995*. National Transportation Safety Board, Special Investigation Report, Notation 6768, November 15, 1996.

Section 4.4

109. Carter, C. F., *The Passing of the Pay Car*, American Magazine, July, 1907, reprinted RRG, July 26, 1907, 91.

110. *Comparative Dimensions of Locomotives at the World's Fair*, RRG, November 17, 1893, 834.

111. *Train Accidents in the United States in August (1899)*, RRG, October 20, 1899, 726.

112. *Consolidation Locomotive, N.Y.N.H. & H. R. R.*, RRG, April 26, 1895, 263.

113. *Pittsburgh Compound Locomotives for the Lake Superior & Ishpeming*, RRG, September 4, 1896, 617.

114. Durocher, A. A., *The Lake Superior & Ishpeming Railroad Company*, R&LHS Bulletin #98, April, 1958, 7.

115. *The New Consolidation Locomotive of the Pennsylvania*, RRG, December 10, 1897, 864.

116. Adams, in *2000 Plus; The Pennsy's H-6* (R&LHS Bulletin #124, April, 1971, 51) writes that the H-4's were the Pennsylvania's first engines with 205-pounds per square inch boiler pressure. Possibly the prototype was built with a 185-pounds per square inch boiler, while production engines had the pressure raised to 205 pounds per square inch.

117. Adams, R. D., *2000 Plus; The Pennsy's H-6*, R&LHS Bulletin #124, April, 1971, 51.

118. *The Class H-5 Consolidation of the Pennsylvania*, RRG, June 10, 1898, 401; RRG, July 8, 1898, 491.

119. Adams, R. D., *2000 Plus; The Pennsy's H-6*, R&LHS Bulletin #124, April, 1971, 51.

120. Fisher, C. E., *The Steam Locomotives of the Pennsylvania Railroad System, Part III*, R&LHS Journal, October, 1954, 130.

121. *Consolidation Locomotives for the Union Pacific*, RRG, November 18, 1898, 829.

122. *A Heavy Consolidation for the Lehigh Valley*, RRG, January 13, 1899, 20.

123. *A Northern Pacific Compound Consolidation Engine*, RRG, January 27, 1899, 59.

124. *Compound Consolidation Locomotives for the Southern Pacific*, RRG, May 5, 1899, 315.

125. *Simple and Compound Consolidation Locomotives of the Atchison, Topeka & Santa Fe*, RRG, June 16, 1899, 422.

126. *A Very Heavy Consolidation for the Illinois Central*, RRG, December 15, 1899, 858.

127. Drury, 207.

128. *New Consolidation Locomotives for the Lake Shore & Michigan Southern*, RRG, March 2, 1900, 135.

129. RRG, September, 2, 1904, 313.

130. *A Consolidation Locomotive for the New York, Ontario & Western*, RRG, March 23, 1900, 185.

131. *New Consolidation Locomotives or the Oregon Short Line*, RRG, April 20, 1900, 251.

132. *Compound Consolidation Locomotives for the Baltimore & Ohio*, RRG, June 15, 1900, 385.

133. *Great Consolidation Locomotives for the Pittsburgh, Bessemer & Lake Erie*, RRG, June 29, 1900, 447; Drury, 52.

134. *The New Class I Central-Atlantic Type Locomotives—New York Central Railroad*, RRG, February 1, 1901, 72; *Two-Cylinder Compound Locomotives, Class G-1—New York Central Railroad*, RRG, March 1, 1901, 140; Drury, 277.

135. *Some Heavy Freight Trains*, RRG, October 4, 1902, 815.

136. *Some Schenectady Consolidation Locomotives*, RRG, April 5, 1901, 233; Drury, 365.

137. *Schenectady Four-Cylinder Tandem Compound Locomotives—Classes Y-2 and Y-3, Northern Pacific Railway*, RRG, August 30, 1901, 598.

138. Drury, 317.

139. *Tandem Compounds on the Atchison, Topeka & Santa Fe*, RRG, June 6, 1902, 410; Drury, 27.

140. *Schenectady Two-Cylinder Compound Locomotive—Soo Line*, RRG, February 22, 1902, 124; Drury, 240, 242.

141. *Consolidation Locomotives for the Southern Pacific*, RRG, March 7, 1902, 160; Drury, 364.

142. *Consolidation Freight Locomotives—Norfolk & Western Railway*, RRG, April 25, 1902, 302; Drury, 308.

143. *Rock Island Consolidation (2-8-0) Locomotive*, RRG, April 17, 1903, 277; Drury, 129.

144. *Consolidation (2-8-0) Locomotive for the Great Western of England*, RRG, October 23, 1903, 755.

145. Church, R. J., *Southern Pacific Ten-Coupled Locomotives*, Berkeley and Wilton, California: Signature Press, 2013, 15.

146. RRG, March 17, 1893, 214.

147. *Schenectady 12-Wheelers for the Northern Pacific*, RRG, February 26, 1897, 145.

148. *Heavy 12-Wheel Locomotives for the Great Northern*, RRG, January 7, 1898, 3.

149. *The Class H-5 Consolidation of the Pennsylvania*, RRG, June 10, 1898, 401.

150. Drury, 196.

151. *A Schenectady 12-Wheeler for the Southern Pacific*, RRG, January 6, 1899, 3.

152. *The 116-Ton Illinois Central Twelve Wheel Locomotive*, RRG, September 29, 1899, 670.

153. *Twelve-Wheel Wide Fire-Box Locomotive—Buffalo, Rochester & Pittsburgh Railway*, RRG, October 12, 1900, 666; Drury, 434.

154. Drury, 434.

155. Fisher, C. E., *Locomotives of the Buffalo, Rochester & Pittsburgh Ry.* R&LHS, October 1951, 46.

156. *Wide Fire-Box Freight Locomotive for the Chicago & Eastern Illinois*, RRG, November 16, 1900, 755; Drury, 441.

157. *Performance of Heavy Freight Locomotives on the Union Pacific*, RRG, May 11, 1900, 300.

158. *Twelve-Wheel Compound Chicago & Eastern Illinois Railroad*, RRG, February 23, 1900, 117; Drury, 442; *Twelve-Wheel Freight Locomotive for the Oregon Short Line Railroad*, RRG, March 9, 1900, 149; Drury, 404.

159. Harwood, H. H., *Corporate History of the Lehigh Valley R. R.* R&LHS Bulletin #126, April, 1972, 5.

160. *Double-Ender Freight Transfer Locomotive for the Chicago & Calumet Terminal Railway*, RRG, June 23, 1893, 458; Drury, 311; Fowler, G. L., *The Development of American Freight Locomotives*, RRG, October 19, 1906, 344.

161. McLeod, R., *History of the Wisconsin & Michigan Railway*, R&LHS Bulletin #118, April, 1968, 7.

162. *Locomotive Building During 1910; Baldwin Locomotive Works*, RAG, April 28, 1911, 993.

163. *Special Mountain Locomotive for the Mexican Central*, RRG, October 29, 1897, 757.

164. *Test of Bismarck, Washburn & Great Falls Lignite-Burning Locomotive, No. 3*, RRG, March 28, 1902, 223; Drury, 311.

165. *Mikado (2-8-2) Compounds for the Atchison*, RRG, April 3, 1903, 242; Drury, 16, 27.

166. *Mikados for the Lehigh Valley*, RAG, June 16, 1913, 1408; Drury 222; Harwood, H. H., *Corporate History of the Lehigh Valley R. R.*, R&LHS Bulletin #126, April, 1972, 5.

167. *Compound Decapod—Minneapolis, St. Paul & Sault Ste. Marie Railway*, RRG, June 22, 1900, 429; Drury, 239; *The Soo Line Compound Decapod*, RRG, August 17, 190, 551.

168. *Heavy Freight Locomotives of the Atchison, Topeka & Santa Fe*, RRG, December 20, 1901, 878.

169. *Tandem Compound for the Atchison, Topeka & Santa Fe*, RRG, May 30, 1902, 392.

170. *The A. T. & S. F. Tandem Compound Decapod—Heaviest and Most Powerful*, RRG, January 31, 1902, 75.

171. Swengel, F. M., *The American Steam Locomotive*, Davenport, Iowa: Midwest Rail Publications, 1967, 92.

172. *Tandem-Compound "Santa Fe" Type (2-10-2) Locomotive for the Santa Fe*, RRG, October 9, 1903, 720; Drury, 19, 27.

SECTION 4.5

173. White, J. H., 494.

174. *New Locomotives for the Southern Pacific*, RRG, September 30, 1904, 386; Drury, 364.

175. Bruce, A. W., 1952, 47.

176. *Suburban Locomotive Development*, RRG, May 15, 1903, 338.

177. Caruthers, C. H., *Successive Experiments and Improvements on Locomotives of the Pennsylvania Railroad*, RRG, February 22, 1907, 235.

178. Durocher, A. A., *The Lake Superior & Ishpeming Railroad Company*, R&LHS Bulletin #98, April, 1958, 7.

179. Bruce, A. W., 46.

180. *Double-End Suburban Locomotive for the New York Central*, RRG, March 28, 1902, 224; Drury, 277.

181. *Heavy Suburban Locomotives for the Philadelphia & Reading*, RRG, September 25, 1903, 683; Drury, 333.

182. Langsdale, F. J., *The Story of a Mountain Railroad*, R&LHS Bulletin #96, May, 1957, 63.

183. Bruce, A. W., 59–60.

184. *The Shay Locomotive*, RRG, August 2, 1895, 514.

185. *The Largest Shay Locomotive Ever Built*, RRG, June 26, 1902, 466.

186. *Tests of a Heavy Shay Locomotive*, RAG, June 9, 1905, 647.

187. *Coal for the Country's Furnaces*, RA, May 16, 1942, 948.

188. *Western Maryland Uses Shay Locomotive On Heavy Grades in Mining District*, RA, October 6, 1945, 549; Drury, 427.

189. Edson, W. D., White, J. H., *Lima Locomotive Works*, Journal R&LHS, October, 1970, 81; Hirsimaki, E., *Lima: The History*, Edmonds, WA: Hundman, 1986.

190. Bruce, A. W., 46.

191. *A 50-Ton Geared Locomotive*, RRG, November 26, 1897, 838.

192. *The Heisler Geared Locomotive*, RRG, February 11, 1898, 93.

193. Bruce, A. W., 46.

194. *Steam Motor Car for the Erie & Wyoming Valley*, RRG, February 3, 1899, 83; *New Inspection Locomotive on the Lake Shore & Michigan Southern*, RRG, June 19, 1903, 444.

195. *Tank Engines*, RA, July 26, 1918, 158.

Chapter 5

SECTION 5.1

1. Sprague, F. J., *The Development of Electric Traction*, American Institute of Electrical Engineers, February 8, 1905, reproduced RRG, February 24, 1905, 166.

2. Cornwell, E. L. (ed.) *History of Railways*, Secaucus, NJ: Chartwell, 1976, 129.

3. *Development of Electric Traction during 15 Years—1899 to 1914*, report to 1914 ARMMA convention, RAG, 1914, 594.

4. Baldwin centennial feature, RA, May 16, 1931, 11.

5. Short, S. H., *Electricity as a Motive Power on Elevated Railroads*, RRG, August 6, 1897, 552.

6. *The Heilmann Electric Locomotive*, RRG, May 5, 1893, 337; *The Heilmann Locomotive*, RRG, August 21, 1896, 589.

7. *Electric Motors for Steam Roads—A Step in Progress*, RRG, July 14, 1893, 527; *Approaching Trials of Electric Locomotives*, RRG, September 14, 1894, 634; *Testing the B & O Electric Locomotive*, RRG, March 6, 1896, 161, from Parker, L. H., engineer in charge of electric installation, B. & O. Belt Line tunnel, Baltimore, *Experience With the Electric Locomotive in Baltimore*.

8. *Electrical Equipment of the Burlington & Mount Holly Branch of the Pennsylvania Railroad*, RRG, April 24, 1896, 282.

9. *Classic Trains*, Interurban special edition, Vol. 14, No. 2, June, 2013.

10. Gibson, G. H., *High Speed Electric Interurban Roads*, excerpted from 'Engineering Magazine,' RRG, September 5, 1902, 686.

11. *The Status of Electric Railroading*, RRG, July 9, 1897, 492.

12. Burch, E. P., *Electric Traction for Heavy Railroad Service*, Northwest Railway Club, discussion, March, 1901, abstracted RRG, April 9, 1901, 268.

13. *The Status of Electric Railroading*, RRG, July 9, 1897, 492.

14. Arnold, R. J., *A Comparative Study of Steam and Electric Power in Heavy Railroad Service*, American Institute of Electrical Engineers convention, 1902, reproduced RRG, June 27, 1902, 498.

15. *Electric Locomotives for the New York Central*, RRG, June 3, 1904, 418; *Test of New York Central Electric Locomotive*, RRG, November 18, 1904, 552.

SECTION 5.2

16. *A Gasoline Motor Inspection Car*, RRG, May 17, 1895, 312.

17. *A Gasoline Motor Car*, RRG, May 5, 1899, 313.

Chapter 6

1. *Heavy Locomotives and the Railroads of the Future*, RRG, November 16, 1906, 422.

2. Demoulin, M., *National Characteristics of Locomotive Building, La Locomotive Actuelle.* Translated and abstracted RRG, January 26, 1907, 116.

3. Beyer, O. S., Rock Island Lines, *Factors in the Selection of Locomotives in Relation to the Economics of Railway Operation*, ASME, December, 1912, abstract and discussion RAG, December 13, 1912, 1145.

4. Oudet, M. J., *A Study of American Locomotives*, 'Revue Mechanique,' February, 1902, translated RRG, October 20, 1905, 365.

5. Bloch, M., *Comparison of Locomotive Building in the United States, Germany and France*, 'Revue Generale des Chemins de Fer,' translated RAG, June 11, 1909, 1202.

6. Basford, G. M., American Locomotive Co., *The Motive Power Officer*, address to Mechanical Engineering Society, Purdue University, reproduced RRG, June 8, 1906, 581; *Excessive Weights of Locomotive Machinery*, RAG, March 3, 1911, 389.

7. *Single Expansion and Lower Pressures*, RRG, December 21, 1906, 543.

8. Basford, G. M., American Locomotive Co., *The Motive Power Officer*, address to Mechanical Engineering Society, Purdue University, reproduced RRG, June 8, 1906, 581; *Excessive Weights of Locomotive Machinery*, RAG, March 3, 1911, 389.

9. *Comparative Service Tests of Locomotives*, RAG, September 13, 1912, 470.

10. *Motive Power on the Chesapeake & Ohio*, RAG, February 23, 1912, 352; Drury, 87–8.

11. *A Record Locomotive Performance*, RAG, June 18, 1912, 1472.

12. 'Steam Railway,' November 13–December 10, 2009, 66.

13. Beyer, O. S., Rock Island Lines, *Factors in the Selection of Locomotives in Relation to the Economics of Railway Operation*, ASME, December, 1912, abstract and discussion RAG, December 13, 1912, 1145.

14. *Recent Locomotive Development*, RAG, June 15, 1914, 140.

15. Cole, F. J., consulting engineer, American Locomotive Co., Young, C. D., engineer of tests, Pennsylvania Railroad, *Boiler Design in Respect to Heating Surface*, discussion on paper *Steam Locomotives of Today*, ASME, New York, December, 1914, RAG, December 11, 1914, 1079.

16. Ibid.

17. *A Year's Progress in Locomotive Building*, RAG, December 29, 1916, 1169.

18. Basford, G. M., President, Locomotive Feed Water Heater Co., Railway Club of Pittsburgh, September 1916, reproduced RAG, September 29, 1916, 539.

19. Bixby, A. M., *How a New Haven I-4 Pacific Became One of a Kind*, R&LHS Bulletin, Spring 1985, 105.

20. Pomeroy, L. R., *Alloy Steel in Locomotive Design*, 1916 ARMMA convention, reproduced RAG, June 21, 1916, 1499.

21. *The Mechanical Department and Locomotive Development*, RAG, July 21, 1916, 92.

22. *Modernizing of Existing Locomotives*, report of committee to 1916 ARMMA convention, reported RAG, June 22, 1916, 1519.

23. *The Increase in Locomotive Efficiency*, RAG, November 2, 1917.

24. Winterrowd, W. H., *Locomotive Design*

from a Maintenance Standpoint, Canadian Railway Club, reported RAG, October 19, 1917, 683.

25. *The Locomotive Situation,* RA, January 4, 1918, 11.

26. *Increase the Service of Available Power,* RAG, June 22, 1917, 1343.

27. *Should Standard Locomotives Be Considered as a War Measure?* RA, February 22, 1918, 436.

28. Wikipedia entry: William Gibbs McAdoo.

29. *What Does Standardization of Locomotives Mean?* RA, March 22, 1918, 692; Edson, W. D., *The U. S. R. A. Locomotives,* Journal R&LHS, October, 1955, 73.

30. Muhlfeld, J. E., *Modern Versus Standardized Railway Equipment,* RA, April 26, 1918, 1066.

31. Givin, E. F., *Consolidation vs. Mikado Locomotives,* RA, May 3, 1918, 1110.

32. *Tentative Specifications for Standard Locomotives,* RA, April 19, 1918, 1039.

33. *Has Locomotive Standardization Been Justified?* RA, January 3, 1919, 50.

34. Drury, 405; Edson, W. D., *The U.S.R.A. Locomotives,* Journal R&LHS, October, 1955, 73.

35. Edson, W. D., *The U.S.R.A. Locomotives,* Journal R&LHS, October, 1955, 73.

36. Winterrowd, W. H., Assistant to the President, Lima Locomotive Works, *Engineering and Business Considerations of the Steam Locomotive,* ?ARMMA convention, 1924, reported RA, June 13, 1924, 1468.

37. *Locomotive Feed Water Heating,* Railway Fuel Association Convention report, 1917, reported RAG, May 25, 1917, 1101.

Chapter 7

SECTION 7.1

1. Emerson, R., *Relation of the Fuel Problem to Railway Operation,* International Railway Fuel Association convention, 1911, abstracted RAG, May 26, 1911, 1209.

2. McManamy, F., Manager Locomotive Section, USRA, *The Relation of Locomotive Maintenance to Fuel* Economy; Quayle, R., General Superintendent Motive Power, Chicago & North Western Railway, *The Motive Power Department and Fuel Economy,* International Railway Fuel Association convention, 1918, reported RA, May 24, 1918, 1289.

3. Kinyon, A.G., Locomotive Fuel Engineer, Clinchfield Fuel Co., *Sizing Coal for Locomotive Use,* International Railway Fuel Association convention, 1914, reported RAG, May 22, 1914, 1153.

4. *Wheeling & Lake Erie Coal Tests,* RAG, April 22, 1910, 1049.

5. *Purchasing Coal on a Mine-Run Basis,* International Railway Fuel Association convention, 1911, reported RAG, May 19, 1911, 1149.

6. Wood, W. D., *Powdered Fuel For Locomotives,* RAG, July 4, 1913, 13.

7. Wadleigh, F. R., *Coal Briquettes and Their Use in Railroad, Marine and Domestic Service,* RRG, June 19, 1908, 184.

8. Wadleigh, F. R., *Coal Briquettes and Their Use in Railroad, Marine and Domestic Service,* RAG, June 26, 1908, 379.

9. Gibbs, A. W., General Superintendent of Motive Power, Pennsylvania Railroad, *Result of*

Tests with Briquetted Coal Made on the Locomotive Testing Plant of the Pennsylvania Railroad at Altoona, Pa., ARMMA convention, 1908, reproduced RAG, June 24, 1908, 323.

10. *Briquets For Locomotive Fuel,* RAG, June 25, 1908, 341.

11. International Railway Fuel Association convention, 1911, reported RAG, May 19, 1911, 1149.

12. Muhlfeld, J. E., President, Locomotive Pulverized Fuel Co., *Pulverized Fuel for Locomotive Service,* New York Railroad Club, February, 1916, reported RAG, February 25, 1916, 349.

13. *The Use of Pulverized Fuel for Locomotives,* RAG, April 30, 1915, 951; Robinson, W. L., Supervisor of Coal Consumption, Baltimore & Ohio Railroad, *Powdered Coal,* RAG, May 21, 1915, 1055.

14. Wood, W.D., *Pulverized Fuel for Locomotives,* letter to RAG, published August 1, 1913, 174.

15. *Powdered Coal,* report of committee to International Railway Fuel Association convention, 1917, abstracted RAG, June 15, 1917, 1230.

16. *The D & H Pulverized Fuel Consolidation,* RAG, June 19, 1916, 1424.

17. *Powdered Fuel,* report to committee of International Railway Fuel Association, presented at 1916 convention, reported RAG, May 19, 1916, 1081; *Pulverized Fuel For Locomotives,* RAG, June 22, 1916, 1508; *North Western Pulverized Coal Locomotive,* RAG, August 11, 1916, 27.

18. *A Pulverized Fuel Equipment for Locomotives,* RA, September 12, 1919, 519.

19. Report on pulverized fuel, International Railway Fuel Association convention, 1919, reported RA, May 23, 1919, 1249.

20. *Lignite Fuel for Locomotives,* RAG, January 27, 1911, 150; Flagg, S. B., Engineer, U.S. Bureau of Mines, *Sub-bituminous and Lignitic Coals,* International Railway Fuel Association convention, 1913, abstracted RAG, May 30, 1913, 1178.

21. *Lignite Fuel for Locomotives,* RAG, January 19, 1912, 89.

22. *Anthracite Burning Pacific Type Locomotives,* RAG, July 19, 1912, 88; *Anthracite Burning Pacific Type Locomotive,* RAG, March 6, 1914, 473; *Heavy Pacific Type Locomotive for the Lackawanna,* December 24, 1915, 1185.

23. Stillman, H., Engineer of Tests, Southern Pacific Lines, *Oil Fuel for Locomotives,* International Railroad Congress, 1905, reproduced RRG, May 19, 1905, 555.

24. *Oil Fuel for Locomotives,* RAG, June 16, 1911, 1451.

25. Emerson, H., *A Solution of the Oil-Burning Locomotive Problem,* RRG, June 7, 1907, 764.

26. *Economical Oil Burning on Locomotives,* RAG, February 2, 1912, 188.

27. Stillman, H., Mechanical Engineer, Southern Pacific Lines, ASME, 1911, abstracted RAG, March 15, 1912, 482.

28. Bean, G. M., American Arch Co., Los Angeles, *Fuel Oil for Locomotive Use,* RAG, May 28, 1915, 1115.

29. Davidson, J. H., Water Engineer, Missouri-Kansas-Texas Railroad, *Benefits of Better Water on M-K-T,* RA, September 5, 1925, 445; *100,772 Miles Per Engine Failure on the Katy,* RA, September 5, 1925, 448.

30. Muhlfeld, J. E., President Locomotive

Pulverized Fuel Co., Oatley, H. B., Chief Engineer, Locomotive Superheater Co., *What Is the Relative Economy of the Locomotive of 1900 and Today?* ASME, Worcester, MA, June 1918, reported RA, August 16, 1918, 305.

31. *Use of Powdered Fuel in Locomotives,* report of committee to ARMMA convention, 1916, reported RAG, June 22, 1916, 1511.

32. RRG, June 21, 1907, 906.

33. Wadleigh, F. R., Fuel Engineer and Assistant General Manager, Chesapeake & Ohio Coal & Coke Co., *Notes For the Engineman and Fireman,* RAG, October 6, 1911, 661.

34. *Production of Smoke by the Railways of Chicago,* report on smoke abatement and the electrification of railway terminals at Chicago to Chicago Association of Commerce, abstracted RAG, December 24, 1915, 1193.

35. Bradley, R., Inspector of Fuel Service, Boston & Maine, *The Human Fireman,* International Railway Fuel Association convention, 1916, reported RAG, May 26, 1916, 1126.

36. Randolph, V. C., Supervisor of Locomotive Operation, Erie Railroad, *Practical Instruction in Fuel Economy,* Traveling Engineers' Association convention, 1911, abstracted RAG, September 8, 1911, 467.

37. Pyle, L. R., Traveling Fireman, Minneapolis, St. Paul & Sault Ste. Marie Railway, *Coal Space and the Adjuncts of Tenders,* International Railway Fuel Association convention, 1914, reported RAG, May 22, 1914, 1155.

38. *Duties and Responsibilities of Engineers and Firemen,* RA, February 15, 1918, 373.

39. Street, C. F., Locomotive Stoker Co., New York, *Mechanical Stokers for Locomotives,* Western Railway Club, October, 1914, abstracted RAG, October 23, 1914, 739.

40. *The Mechanical Stoker,* RRG, June 9, 1905, 616.

41. RRG, May 12, 1905, 448.

42. Street, C. F., Locomotive Stoker Co., New York, *Mechanical Stokers for Locomotives,* Western Railway Club, October, 1914, abstracted RAG, October 23, 1914, 739.

43. *The Victor Stoker,* RRG, June 9, 1905, 643.

44. *A New Mechanical Stoker,* RRG, January 6, 1905, 3.

45. *The Hayden Mechanical Stoker,* RRG, March 2, 1906, 210.

46. *Mechanical Stokers,* RAG, June 23, 1908, 276.

47. Discussion on mechanical stokers, ARMMA convention, 1908, reproduced RAG, June 23, 1908, 282.

48. *Strouse Patent Locomotive Stoker,* RAG, February 5, 1909, 255.

49. *Mechanical Stokers,* report of committee to ARMMA convention, 1913, reported RAG, June 12, 1913, 1285.

50. Report of committee on mechanical stokers and discussion, ARMMA convention, 1909, reported RAG, June 17, 1909, 1275, 1280.

51. *Mechanical Stokers,* report by committee to ARMMA convention, 1912, reported RAG, June 18, 1912, 1463.

52. *Marshall Locomotive Stoker,* RAG, June 18, 1909, 1319.

53. *Mechanical Stokers,* RAG, September 3, 1909, 393.

54. *Mechanical Stokers,* committee report to ARMMA convention, 1910, reproduced RAG, June 21, 1910, 1695; *The Street Locomotive Stoker,* RAG, May 26, 1911, 1196; *Street Mechanical Stoker,* RAG, January 5, 1912, 25.

55. *The Street Locomotive Stoker,* RAG, May 26, 1911, 1196.

56. Westing, F., *"Fat Annie"—Pioneer "Pennsy" Pacific,* Journal R&LHS, April, 1959, 44; Bennett, T. W., Bennett, H. T., *The Broom Handle That Made Stoker History,* Journal R&LHS, Spring 1973, 50.

57. Luckey, J. R., *Automatic Stokers,* report to Traveling Engineers' Association convention, 1911, reported RAG, September 8, 1911, 477.

58. *Mechanical Stokers,* committee report to ARMMA convention, 1911, reproduced RAG, June 15, 1911, 1372.

59. *Improved Hanna Locomotive Stoker,* RAG, April 3, 1913, 792.

60. Bartholomew, W. S., President, Locomotive Stoker Co., *Mechanical Stoking of Locomotive an Economy,* Western Railway Club, July, 1919, abstracted RA, July 25, 1919, 163.

61. *Mechanical Stokers,* committee report to ARMMA convention, 1911, reproduced RAG, June 15, 1911, 1372.

62. *Giving Mechanical Stokers a Fair Chance,* RAG, June 15, 1911, 1367.

63. *Mechanical Stokers,* committee report to ARMMA convention, 1912, reported RAG, June 18, 1912, 1463.

64. *Mechanical Stokers,* committee report to ARMMA convention, 1911, reproduced RAG, June 15, 1911, 1372.

65. *Mechanical Stokers,* committee report to ARMMA convention, 1912, reported RAG, June 18, 1912, 1463.

66. *Mechanical Stokers,* committee report to ARMMA convention, 1913, reported RAG, June 12, 1913, 1285.

67. *Mechanical Stokers,* committee report to ARMMA convention, 1910, reproduced RAG, June 21, 1910, 1695.

68. *Locomotive Stokers,* RAG, June 18, 1912, 1456.

69. *Mechanical Stokers,* committee report to ARMMA convention, 1912, reported RAG, June 18, 1912, 1463.

70. *Mechanical Stokers,* committee report to ARMMA convention, 1913, reported RAG, June 12, 1913, 1285.

71. *Ibid.*

72. Bartholomew, W. S., President, Locomotive Stoker Co., *Mechanical Stoking of Locomotive an Economy,* Western Railway Club, July, 1919, abstracted RA, July 25, 1919, 163.

73. *The Mechanical Stoker,* RAG, June 16, 1914, 1428.

74. *The Gee Locomotive Stoker,* RAG, March 14, 1913, 486.

75. *The "Standard" Mechanical Stoker,* RAG, June 14, 1913, 1399.

76. *The Standard Locomotive Stoker,* RAG, October 10, 1913, 647.

77. *Hervey Locomotive Stoker,* RAG, August 29, 1913, 385.

78. *Locomotive Stokers,* committee report to ARMMA convention, 1914, reported RAG, June 16, 1914, 1434.

79. Discussion on committee report to ARMMA convention, 1914, reported RAG, June 16, 1914, 1437.

80. Traveling Engineers' Association convention, 1914, presidential address, reported RAG, September 25, 1914, 559.

81. Henderson, G. R., Consulting Engineer, Baldwin Locomotive Works, *Recent Developments in Steam Locomotives,* New York Railroad Club, April, 1915, abstracted RAG, April 23, 1915, 897.

82. Street, C. F., Locomotive Stoker Co., New York, *Mechanical Stokers for Locomotives,* Western Railway Club, October, 1914, abstracted RAG, October 23, 1914, 739.

83. Report of Committee on Mechanical Stokers, ARMMA convention, 1916, reported RAG, June 20, 1916, 1451.

84. Fisher, C. E., *The Steam Locomotives of the New Haven R. R.,* Journal R&LHS, April, 1959, 67.

85. *Advantages of Mechanical Stoking,* report of committee to Traveling Engineers' Association convention, 1916, reported RAG, November 3, 1916, 795.

86. Bennett, T. W., Bennett, H. T., *The Broom Handle That Made Stoker History,* Journal R&LHS, Spring 1973, 50.

87. *Duplex Locomotive Stoker,* RAG, July 13, 1917, 72; Bennett, T. W., Bennett, H. T., *The Broom Handle That Made Stoker History,* Journal R&LHS, Spring 1973, 50.

88. Bartholomew, W. S., President, Locomotive Stoker Co., *Mechanical Stoking of Locomotive an Economy,* Western Railway Club, July, 1919, abstracted RA, July 25, 1919, 163.

89. *New Locomotive Stoker Tested Out on Erie,* RA, January 17, 1919, 203.

90. Report of committee on mechanical stokers, ARMMA convention, 1919, reported RA, June 24, 1919, 1705.

91. Mayer, J., *Steam Locomotive and Electric Locomotive Power,* letter RRG, November 16, 1906, 428.

92. Buell, D. C., *Wastes of Fuel, Power and Time in Railroad Operation,* Traveling Engineers' Association convention, 1907, abstracted RRG, December 6, 1907, 692.

93. Collett, R., Superintendent of Locomotive Fuel Services, Frisco Lines, *Locomotive Fuel Economy on the Frisco,* St. Louis Railway Club, May, 1913, abstracted RAG, November 7, 1913, 874.

94. Muhlfeld, J. E., President, Locomotive Pulverized Fuel Co., *Pulverized Fuel for Locomotive Service,* RAG, December 15, 1916, 1097.

95. *Pennsylvania Locomotive Brick Arch Tests,* RAG, May 4, 1917, 933.

96. Pomeroy, L. R., *The Electrification of Trunk Lines,* RRG, May 19, 1905, 531.

97. Plant, L. G., Fuel Engineer, Seaboard Air Line, *Fuel and Tonnage Performance on the Seaboard,* RAG, March 5, 1915, 405.

Section 7.2

98. Anthony, J. T., *Combustion in Locomotive Practice,* RAG, June 6, 1913, 1220.

99. *Locomotive Grate Area,* RAG, September 18, 1908, 936.

100. *Locomotive Grate Area,* RAG, September 18, 1908, 936; *Locomotive Grate Area,* RAG, November 20, 1908, 1384.

101. *Tests in Smoke Abatement on Santa Fe Switching Locomotives,* Bulletin 6, Committee on Investigation on Smoke Abatement and Electrification of Railway Terminals, Chicago, Chicago Association of Commerce, reported RAG, February 23, 1912, 343; *Production of Smoke by the Railways of Chicago,* report on smoke abatement and the electrification of railway terminals at Chicago to Chicago Association of Commerce, abstracted RAG, December 24, 1915, 1193.

102. MacBain, D. R., Superintendent of Motive Power, Lake Shore & Michigan Southern Railroad, *Elimination of Smoke From Locomotives,* International Association for the Prevention of Smoke, Indianapolis, September 25, 1912, reported RAG, October 11, 1912, 669; *Bituminous Coal Research Develops Locomotive Smoke Consumer,* RA, September 29, 1945, 518.

103. *Smoke Prevention,* committee report to 1913 ARMMA convention, reported RAG, June 14, 1913, 1377.

104. *Superheater Locomotives,* report of committee to 1912 ARMMA convention, reported RAG, June 14, 1913, 1373.

105. Crawford, D. F., General Superintendent of Motive Power, Pennsylvania Lines West of Pittsburgh, *The Abatement of Locomotive Smoke,* International Society for the Prevention of Smoke, abstracted RAG, October 24, 1913, 762.

106. Hatch, M. C. M., Superintendent Fuel Service, Delaware, Lackawanna & Western Railroad, *Front End Design and Air Openings of Grates and Ash-Pans,* International Railway Fuel Association convention, 1914, reported RAG, May 22, 1914, 1149.

107. *Front Ends, Grates and Ash Pans,* committee report to International Railway Fuel Association 1915 convention, reported RAG, May 28, 1915, 1119.

108. Anthony, J. T., American Arch Co., *Firebox Design,* ASME annual meeting, 1914, abstracted RAG, January 8, 1915, 55.

109. *Fuel Economy,* report to 1915 ARMMA convention, reported RAG, June 11, 1915, 1275.

110. Anthony, J. T., American Arch Co., *Firebox Design,* ASME annual meeting, 1914, abstracted RAG, January 8, 1915, 55.

111. *Production of Smoke by the Railways of Chicago,* report on smoke abatement and the electrification of railway terminals at Chicago to Chicago Association of Commerce, abstracted RAG, December 24, 1915, 1193; Anthony, J. T., American Arch Co., *Locomotive Fuel Economy and Boiler Design,* New England Railroad Club, October 1916, abstracted RAG, October 20, 1916, 695.

112. *The Locomotive Ashpan Situation,* RAG, August 27, 1909, 349.

113. *Self Dumping Ash Pans,* Traveling Engineers' Association convention, 1910, reported RAG, June 21, 1910, 1707.

114. Address to Master Boilermakers' Convention, 1914, reported RAG, May 29, 1914, 1187.

115. *Design of Ash Pan and Draft Appliances,* Master Boiler Makers' Association annual convention, 1919, reported RA, May 30, 1919, 1329.

116. Anthony, J. T., *Factors in Locomotive*

Smoke Abatement, Smoke Prevention Association annual convention, 1917, reported RAG, September 28, 1917, 557.

117. Wagstaff, G., *The Brick Arch,* Central Railway Club, November, 1909, abstracted RAG, January 15, 1909, 109.

118. *Smoke Prevention,* committee report to 1913 ARMMA convention, reported RAG, June 14, 1913, 1377; *Production of Smoke by the Railways of Chicago,* report on smoke abatement and the electrification of railway terminals at Chicago to Chicago Association of Commerce, abstracted RAG, December 24, 1915, 1193.

119. Neff, J. P., Vice-President, American Arch Co., *The Brick Arch and Circulating Arch Tubes,* ASME annual meeting, 1914, abstracted RAG, January 8, 1915, 55.

120. Bond, J. E., *The Use and Abuse of Fire Brick for Locomotive Fire-boxes,* RRG, June 7, 1907, 808.

121. Henderson, G. R., Consulting Engineer, Baldwin Locomotive Works, *Recent Developments in Steam Locomotives,* New York Railway Club, April, 1915, abstracted RAG, April 23, 1915, 897.

122. Ringel, C., *History, Development and Function of the Locomotive Brick Arch,* New York, January, 1948, printed Journal R&LHS, October, 1956, 79.

123. *Fuel Economy,* report of committee to 1910 Traveling Engineers' Association convention, reported RAG, August 26, 1910, 353.

124. *The Brick Arch,* report of committee to Traveling Engineers' Association convention, 1911, reported RAG, September 8, 1911, 475.

125. *Modern Appliances on Large Locomotives,* in report to Traveling Engineers' Association convention, 1915, reported in RAG, September 17, 1915, 505.

126. Anthony, J. T., American Arch Co., *Locomotive Fuel Economy and Boiler Design,* New England Railroad Club, October 1916, abstracted RAG, October 20, 1916, 695.

127. *Pennsylvania Locomotive Brick Arch Tests,* Pennsylvania Railroad Bulletin #30, 1917, abstracted RAG, May 4, 1917, 933.

128. Basford, G. M., *Vitalizing Locomotives to Improve Operation,* New York Railroad Club, May, 1921, reported RA, May 27, 1921, 1227.

129. Wardale, D., *The Red Devil and Other Tales From the Age of Steam,* Inverness, UK: private publication, 1998, 9.

130. Ringel, C., *History, Development and Function of the Locomotive Brick Arch,* Journal R&LHS, October, 1956, 79.

131. *Combustion Chamber and Hollow Brick Wall,* RAG, November 10, 1911, 963.

132. Gaines, F. F., Superintendent of Motive Power, Central of Georgia Railway, *Improved Firebox with Hollow Arch and Combustion Chamber,* RAG, August 5, 1910, 225.

133. White, J. H., 1997, 107.

134. Church, R. J., *Southern Pacific Ten-Coupled Locomotives,* Berkeley, CA: Signature Press, 2013, 24.

135. *Heavy Pacific Type Locomotive for the Northern Pacific,* RRG, November 9, 1906, 406.

136. *Decapod Locomotive for the Buffalo, Rochester & Pittsburg,* RRG, August 9, 1907, 151.

137. *Combustion Chambers in Large Locomotives,* report to Master Boilermakers' convention, 1914, reported RAG, May 29, 1914, 1191.

138. Anthony, J. T., *Combustion in Locomotive Practice,* RAG, June 6, 1913, 1220.

139. Anthony, J. T., American Arch Co., *Locomotive Fuel Economy and Boiler Design,* New England Railroad Club, October 1916, abstracted RAG, October 20, 1916, 695.

140. Gaines, F. F., Chairman, Board of Railway Wages and Working Conditions, USRA, *Combustion Chambers,* RA, June 26, 1919, 1797.

141. Anthony, J. T., *Factors in Locomotive Smoke Abatement,* Smoke Prevention Association annual convention, 1917, reported RAG, September 28, 1917, 557.

142. *Boiler Efficiency Increased by New Type of Firebox,* RA, January 10, 1919, 151.

143. Warnock, H. R. in discussion on Report of Committee on Superheater Locomotives, report to ARMMA convention, 1919, reported RA, June 25, 1919, 1761.

144. Seley, C. A., President, American Flexible Bolt Co., *Locomotive Staybolts,* New York Railroad Club, April, 1914, abstracted RAG, August 21, 1914, 332.

145. Wells, M. E., Traveling Master Mechanic, Wabash Railway, *The Care of Boilers,* Western Railway Club, November 1905, reported RRG, January 19, 1906, 62.

146. Crowther, D., *Firebox Failures,* letter published RAG, December 3, 1909, 1051.

147. Vaughan, H. H., Assistant to the Vice-President, Canadian Pacific Railway, *Life of Fireboxes and Tubes.* Report to International Railway Congress, 1910, reported RAG, September 16, 1910, 497.

148. Wells, M. E., traveling master mechanic, Wabash Railway, *The Care of Boilers,* Western Railway Club, November 1905, reported RRG, January 19, 1906, 62; Bowersox, C., General Foreman, Toledo, St. Louis & Western Railroad, Voges, C. H., General Foreman, Cleveland, Cincinnati, Chicago & St. Louis Railroad, Olson, H. O., Foreman, Machine Shop, Duluth & Iron Range Railroad, ARMMA convention, 1910, *The Wide Fire Box,* reported RAG, May 6, 1910, 1167.

149. Fowler, G. L., *Deflections of Staybolts in Locomotive Boilers,* RA, December 15, 1919, 1088, in *Design, Construction and Inspection of Locomotive Boilers,* discussion of report to ARMMA convention, 1915, reported RAG, June 11, 1915, 1273.

150. *Wm. H. Wood's Corrugated Firebox and Flexible Tube Plates for Locomotive Boilers,* RAG, October 23, 1908, 1204.

151. *The Jacobs-Shupert Locomotive Firebox,* RAG, May 28, 1909, 1107.

152. *Test of Jacobs-Shupert Firebox,* RAG, November 18, 1910, 965.

153. Whiteford, A. W., mechanical manager, Jacobs-Shupert Firebox Co., *Jacobs-Shupert Firebox,* ARMMA convention, 1911, reported RAG, June 2, 1911, 1263; McFarland, H. B., Engineer of Tests, Atchison, Topeka & Santa Fe Railway, *Water Circulation in Locomotive Fireboxes,* RAG, September 15 1911, 505.

154. Drury, 341.

155. *Tests of Jacobs-Shupert Firebox,* RAG, May 24, 1912, 1159; *Results of Comparative Firebox Tests,* RAG, February 7, 1913, 252.

156. *Low Water Locomotive Boiler Tests,* RAG, June 28, 1912, 1595.

157. *Oil Burning Locomotive Firebox Temperatures,* RAG, September 21, 1917, 515.

158. Gaines, F. F., Chairman, Board of Railway Wages and Working Conditions, USRA, *Combustion Chambers,* RA, June 26, 1919, 1797.

159. *Lackawanna Locomotive With Water Tube Firebox,* RAG, March 12, 1915, 445.

160. *McClellon Water-Tube Firebox,* RAG, April 13, 1917, 781.

161. *Locomotive Boiler Explosions,* RAG, May 29, 1912, 1146.

162. *The Failure of Locomotive Crown Sheets,* RAG, March 3, 1911, 388.

163. ICC, Accident Bulletin No. 18, abstracted RAG, May 11, 1906, 478.

164. Thurston's Manual on Steam Boilers, quoted RAG, May 29, 1912, 1146.

165. Mohun, J. L., Assistant to Consulting Engineer, Union Pacific System, *Personal Injuries Due to Locomotive Failures,* RAG, July 18, 1919, 113.

166. *State Inspection Of Locomotive Boilers,* RRG, June 30, 1905, 748.

167. *Locomotive Boiler Inspections in New York State,* RRG, September 13, 1907, 295.

168. *Report of the Federal Boiler Inspector,* RAG, January 24, 1913, 135.

169. *Report of Chief Inspector of Locomotive Boilers,* RAG, December 26, 1913, 1233.

170. *Federal Government Boiler Inspection Report,* RAG, December 25, 1914, 1196; McManamy, F., Chief Inspector, Locomotive Boilers, ICC, *Results of the Locomotive Boiler Inspection Law,* Western Railway Club, March, 1915, reported RAG, March 19, 1915, 621.

171. *Annual Report of the Chief Inspector of Locomotive Boilers,* RAG, January 7, 1916, 24.

172. Wescott family archive.

Section 7.3

173. Goss, W. F. M., *High Steam Pressures in Locomotive Service,* Western Railway Club, November, 1906, abstracted RRG, November 30, 1906, 489.

174. Goss, W. F. M., Dean of College of Engineering, University of Illinois, *High Steam-Pressures in Locomotive Service,* RAG, February 12, 1909, 310, February 19, 1909, 357, February 26, 1909, 403, March 5, 1909, 449, March 12, 1909, 502.

175. *Modern Locomotive Boilers,* RAG, June 7, 1912, 1224.

176. Van Alstyne, D., Mechanical Superintendent, Northern Pacific Railway, *Some Essentials in Boiler Design,* North West Railway Club, July, 1906, reported RRG, July 20, 1906, 66.

177. Churchward, G. J., *Large Locomotive Boilers,* Institution of Mechanical Engineers, UK, 1906, reported RRG, May 18, 1906, 508.

178. *Leakage of Locomotive Boiler Tubes,* RAG, November 5, 1909, 863.

179. *Jacobs-Shupert Firebox,* report of committee to 1911 Master Boiler Makers' convention, reported RAG, June 2, 1911, 1263.

180. McFarland, H. B., Engineer of Tests, Atchison, Topeka & Santa Fe Railway, *Water Circulation in Locomotive Fireboxes,* RAG, September 15 1911, 505; *Boiler Circulation,* RAG, September 15, 1911, 496.

181. Austin, G., Malone, J., *Care, Use and Design of Locomotive Boilers,* Pacific Railroad Club, November, 1905, abstracted RRG, December 29, 1905, 616.

182. *Washing Out Locomotive Boilers,* report to ARMMA convention, 1908, abstracted RAG, June 23, 1908, 296, discussion reported RAG, June 23, 1908, 290.

183. Pownall, W. A., Water Engineer, Chicago, Burlington & Quincy Railroad, *Water Treatment and Boiler Troubles,* Western Railway Club, April, 1912, abstracted RAG, August 16, 1912, 288.

184. *Washing Out Locomotive Boilers,* report to ARMMA convention, 1908, abstracted RAG, June 23, 1908, 296.

185. *Washing Out and Filling Boilers with Hot Water,* committee report to Traveling Engineers' Association convention, 1907, abstracted RRG, September 6, 1907, 265; Harris, E. J., Chicago, Rock Island & Pacific Railway, *A Modern Method of Locomotive Boiler Washing,* Iowa Railway Club, September, 1907, reproduced RRG, October 11, 1907, 421.

186. *Washing and Filling Locomotive Boilers With Hot Water,* committee report to ARMMA convention, 1908, reported RAG, October 16, 1908, 1133.

187. McManamy, F., Manager Locomotive Section, USRA, *Relation of Locomotive Maintenance to Fuel Economy,* reported RAG, May 24, 1918, 1289.

188. *The Chemical Treating of Feed Water,* report to Master Boilermakers' Convention, 1914, reported RAG, May 29, 1914, 1190.

189. Koyl, C. H., Engineer of Water Service, Great Northern Railway, *Treating Water Reduces Boiler Troubles,* RA, April 25, 1919, 1053.

190. Bardwell, R. C., Chief Chemist, Missouri Pacific Railroad, *Missouri Pacific Saves $279,843 By Water Treatment,* RA, May 30, 1919, 1321.

191. *Boiler Washing,* committee report to ARMMA convention, 1915, reported RAG, June 12, 1915, 1296.

192. Dunning, F. W., *Operating Locomotive Boilers Using Treated Water,* RA, December 5, 1919, 1116.

193. *The Superheater on American Locomotives,* RRG, April 27, 1906, 418.

194. Basford, G. M., American Locomotive Co., *The Motive Power Officer,* address to Mechanical Engineering Society, Purdue University, reproduced RRG, June 8, 1906, 581.

195. *The Superheater on American Locomotives,* RRG, April 27, 1906, 418.

196. Vaughan, H. H., Assistant to the Vice-President, Canadian Pacific Railway, *Superheated Steam on Locomotives,* ASME, May, 1907, abstracted RRG, June 7, 1907, 792.

197. *Superheated Steam in Locomotive Service,* RRG, June 9, 1905, 616.

198. *Superheating,* committee report to ARMMA convention, 1908, abstracted RAG, June 24, 1908, 321.

199. Discussion of committee report on superheating to ARMMA convention, 1908, reported RAG, June 24, 1908, 315.

200. *The Baldwin Superheater,* RRG, June 7, 1907, 780.

201. Vaughan, H. H., Superintendent of Mo-

tive Power, Canadian Pacific Railway, *The Use of Superheated Steam on Locomotives,* ARMMA, June, 1905, abstracted RAG, June 23, 1905, 719.

202. Goss, W. F. M., *Locomotive Performance Under Saturated and Superheated Steam,* ARMMA convention, 1909, abstracted RAG, June 18, 1909, 1342; Endsley, L. E., Professor, University of Pittsburgh, in discussion on *Report of Committee on Superheater Locomotives,* report to ARMMA convention, 1919, reported RA, June 25, 1919, 1759.

203. Schmidt, W., *The Use of Superheated Steam in Locomotives,* RAG, July 17, 1908, 515, July 24, 1908, 566, July 31, 1908, 617.

204. *Superheat,* report to Traveling Engineers' Association convention, 1910, reported RAG, August 26, 1910, 351.

205. *Mallet Locomotive for the Burlington,* RAG, May 13, 1910, 1213.

206. *Superheaters,* committee report to ARMMA convention, 1910, reported RAG, June 22, 1910, 1734.

207. *Improved Cole Superheater,* RAG, May 7, 1909, 992.

208. *Tests of Pacific Type Superheater Locomotive,* RAG, March 31, 1911, 790.

209. Schmidt, W., *The Use of Superheated Steam in Locomotives,* RAG, July 17, 1908, 515, July 24, 1908, 566, July 31, 1908, 617; Ball, A. L., General Foreman, Chicago & Illinois Southern Railroad, *Superheaters,* RAG, May 6, 1910, 1166.

210. *Superheater Locomotives,* discussion at Traveling Engineers' Association convention, 1916, reported RAG, November 3, 1916, 798.

211. *Discussion of Paper on Locomotive Performance Under Saturated and Superheated Steam,* ARMMA convention, June 1909, reported RAG, June 18, 1909, 1350; *Test of the Jacobs Superheater on the Santa Fe,* RAG, October 29, 1909, 814.

212. *Tests of Pacific Type Superheater Locomotive,* RAG, March 31, 1911, 790.

213. *The Baldwin Smokebox Superheater,* RAG, November 20, 1908, 1401.

214. *The Use of Superheated Steam in Locomotives,* RAG, June 22, 1910, 1730.

215. *Locomotive Performance Under Different Degrees of Superheated Steam.* Committee report to ARMMA convention, 1910, reported RAG, June 22, 1910, 1737.

216. Benjamin, C. H., Dean, School of Engineering, Endsley, L. E., Associate Professor of Railway Mechanical Engineering, Purdue University, Lafayette, Indiana, *Locomotive Performance Under Different Degrees of Superheat,* ARMMA convention, 1910, reported RAG, June 22, 1910, 1734.

217. *Superheated Steam in Locomotive Service,* RAG, February 24, 1911, 357.

218. *Superheated Steam on Passenger Locomotives,* RAG, June 10, 1911, 1386.

219. Morris, W. S., comment to discussion, report to ARMMA convention, 1912, reported RAG, June 29, 1912, 1523.

220. *Different Degrees of Superheated Steam,* RAG, June 16, 1911, 1468.

221. *Lubrication of Locomotives Using Superheated Steam,* report of committee to Traveling Engineers' Association convention, 1911, reported RAG, September 8, 1911, 472.

222. Ryder G. E., *Highly Superheated Steam*

for *Locomotives,* Southern and Southwestern Railway Club, January, 1912, reported RAG, January 26, 1912, 156.

223. *Automatic Drifting Valve,* RAG, June 24, 1919, 1725; *Ripken Automatic Drifting Valve for Locomotives,* RA, November 28, 1919, 1079.

224. *Superheaters Applied to Old Engines,* RAG, June 18, 1911, 1536; Ryder G. E., *Highly Superheated Steam for Locomotives,* Southern and Southwestern Railway Club, January, 1912, reported RAG, January 26, 1912, 156.

225. *Maintenance of Superheater Locomotives,* report to committee, ARMMA convention, 1912, reported RAG, June 29, 1912, 1518.

226. *S. Hoffman on the Superheater,* Railway Session, ASME convention, 1912, reported RAG, December 13, 1912, 1147; *Superheater Locomotives,* committee report to ARMMA convention, 1913, reported RAG, June 14, 1913, 1373.

227. *C. D. Young on Advantages of Superheat as Shown by the Indicator Cards,* Railway Session, ASME convention, 1912, reported RAG, December 13, 1912, 1149.

228. *S. Hoffman on the Superheater,* Railway Session, ASME convention, 1912, reported RAG, December 13, 1912, 1147.

229. Coddington, H. W., Engineer of Tests, Norfolk & Western Railway, *Road Tests of Schmidt Superheater and Brick Arch,* ARMMA convention, 1914, reported RAG, June 18, 1914, 1497.

230. *Superheaters on Small Locomotives,* RAG, October 20, 1914, 936.

231. La Bach, P. M., Assistant Engineer, Chicago, Rock Island & Pacific Railway, *Superheater Locomotives and Grade Revision,* RAG, September 10, 1915, 469; *Report on Superheater Locomotives,* report to committee, ARMMA convention, 1916, reported RAG, June 21, 1916, 1483; Riegel, S. S., Mechanical Engineer, Delaware, Lackawanna & Western Railroad, *Modern Superheater and Its Performance,* Central Railway Club, May, 1916, reported RAG, June 30, 1916, 1581.

232. *Superheater Locomotives and Grade Revision,* anonymous letter, RAG, October 8, 1915, 637.

233. Riegel, S. S., Mechanical Engineer, Delaware, Lackawanna & Western Railroad, *Modern Superheater and Its Performance,* Central Railway Club, May, 1916, reported RAG, June 30, 1916, 1581.

234. *Modern Appliances on Large Locomotives,* in report to Traveling Engineers' Association convention, 1915, reported RAG, September 17, 1915, 505.

235. *Report on Superheater Locomotives,* report to committee, ARMMA convention, 1916, reported RAG, June 21, 1916, 1483.

236. Harding, J. W., 2002. Vol. I, 498.

237. Oatley, H. B., Locomotive Superheater Co., comment on Riegel, S. S., Mechanical Engineer, Delaware, Lackawanna & Western Railroad, *Modern Superheater and Its Performance,* Central Railway Club, May, 1916, reported RAG, June 30, 1916, 1586.

238. Harding, J. W., Vol. 1, Fig. 28, p.511.

239. *Superheater Locomotive Performance,* committee report to Railway Fuel Association convention, 1918, reported RA, September 13, 1918, 498; *Report of Committee on Superheater*

Locomotives, report to ARMMA convention, 1919, reported RA, June 25, 1919, 1759; Discussion on superheating at ARMMA convention, 1919, reported RA, June 25, 1919, 1759.

240. Holley, A. L., *American and European Railway Practice in the Economical Generation of Steam,* 1861; Lanier, M. B., Vice-President, Norton Coal Mining Co., *Pre-Heating Locomotive Boiler Feed Water,* International Railway Fuel Association convention, 1914, reported RAG, May 22, 1914, 1156; Snowden Bell, J., *Development of Locomotive Feed Water Heaters,* committee report to ARMMA convention, 1918, reported RA, June 21, 1918, 1531.

241. McBride, T.C., *Development of Locomotive Feed Water Heating,* ASME, St. Louis, Missouri, May, 1920, abstracted RA, July 9, 1920, 59.

242. *Brown Feed Water Heater for Locomotives,* RAG, December 25, 1908, 1655.

243. *G. R. Henderson on Feed Water Heaters,* Railway Session, ASME convention, 1912, reported RAG, December 13, 1912, 1147.

244. Lanier, M. B., Vice-President, Norton Coal Mining Co. *Pre-Heating Locomotive Boiler Feed Water,* International Railway Fuel Association convention, 1914, reported RAG, May 22, 1914, 1156.

245. Brown, H. M., Assistant Master Mechanic, Chesapeake & Ohio Railroad, paper contributed to *Location of Point of Water Delivery to Locomotives,* ARMMA convention, 1910, reported RAG, May 6, 1910, 1168.

246. Vaughan, H. H., Assistant to Vice-President, Canadian Pacific Railway, Gaines, F. F., Superintendent of Motive Power, Central of Georgia Railway, discussion on report, *Steam Locomotives of Today,* ASME, December, 1914, reported RAG, February 12, 1915, 270.

247. *Locomotive Feed Water Heating,* RAG, May 25, 1917, 1080.

248. *Locomotive Feedwater Heating,* RA, January 18, 1918, 177; *Type E Locomotive Feedwater Heater,* RA, June 24, 1919, 1731.

249. *Locomotive Feed Water Heating,* Railway Fuel Association Convention report, 1917, reported RAG, May 25, 1917, 1101.

Section 7.4

250. *Valve Gear of the Symons Four-Cylinder Balanced Compound Locomotive,* RRG, November 10, 1905, 451.

251. *Advantages of Four-Cylinder Balanced Compounds,* Baldwin Record of Recent Construction, Bulletin #49, 1905, quoted RRG, February 10, 1905, 120.

252. *Four-Cylinder Balanced Compound Locomotives,* RRG, February 10, 1905, 114.

253. Drury, 104.

254. Wille, H. V., Assistant to the Superintendent, Baldwin Locomotive Works, *Balanced Compound Locomotives,* RRG, June 15, 1906, 644.

255. *Ibid.*

256. *Discussion on 4-Cylinder Compound Locomotives,* ARMMA convention, 1908, reported RRG, June 25, 1908, 344.

257. *Various Designs of Four-Cylinder Compound Locomotives in Service,* committee report to ARMMA convention, 1908, reported RAG, June 25, 1908, 349.

258. *A Revived Compound,* RAG, November 6, 1908, 1278.

259. *Compounding and Superheating in Locomotives,* RAG, June 8, 1910, 1403.

260. Fry, L. H., Baldwin Locomotive Works, *Compounding Superheater Locomotives,* ARMMA convention, 1915, reported RAG, June 10, 1915, 1220.

261. Muhlfeld, J. E., President, Locomotive Pulverized Fuel Co., Oatley, H. B., Chief Engineer, Locomotive Superheater Co., *What Is the Relative Economy of the Locomotive of 1900 and Today?* ASME, Worcester, MA, June, 1918, reported RA, August 16, 1918, 305.

262. *Some Advantages of Heavy Compound Freight Locomotives,* RRG, March 9, 1900, 154.

263. Basford, G. M., American Locomotive Co., *The Motive Power Officer,* Mechanical Engineering Society, Purdue University, 1906, reproduced RRG, June 8, 1906, 581.

264. Warner, P. T., *Mogul Type Locomotives,* R&LHS Bulletin #100, April, 1959, 7.

265. White, J. H., *Richmond Locomotive Builders,* Journal R&LHS, Spring, 1974, 68.

266. Fisher, C. E., *The Wabash,* Journal R&LHS, October, 1955, 116; Drury 419, 422.

267. Drury, 242.

268. Fisher, C. E., *The Steam Locomotives of the New Haven R.R.,* Journal R&LHS, April, 1959, 67.

269. Durocher, A., *The Lake Superior and Ishpeming Railroad Company,* Journal R&LHS, April, 1958, 7.

270. Edson, W. D., *Locomotives of the Chicago Great Western,* R&LHS Bulletin, Spring 1986, 86.

271. Best, G. M., *Erie Locomotive Notes; All Time Erie Locomotive Roster,* Journal R&LHS, Fall 1974.

272. Keyes, N. C., Middleton, K. R., *The Great Northern Railway Company: All-Time Locomotive Roster, 1861–1970,* R&LHS Bulletin, Fall 1980, 20.

273. Hirsimaki, E., *Lima: The History,* Edmonds, WA: Hundman, 1986, 73.

274. Morris, W. S., Superintendent of Motive Power, Chesapeake & Ohio Railroad, President's address to ARMMA convention, 1901, reproduced RRG, June 28, 1901, 451.

275. *Results of Use of Different Valve Gears on Locomotives,* committee report to ARMMA convention, 1907, reported in RRG, June 14, 1907, 857.

276. Quereau, C. H., General Foreman of Motive Power, Burlington & Missouri River Railroad, *Lead for Locomotives,* Western Railway Club, January, 1897, abstracted RRG, March 19, 1897, 199; Quereau, C. H. *Lead for Locomotives,* RRG, August 9, 1895, 525; *Locomotive Road Tests—Illinois Central Railroad,* RRG, June 17, 1898, 433; Frey, B., Apprentice Instructor, Michigan Central Railroad, *Walschaerts Valve Gear,* course introduction for machinist apprentices, New York Central System, reproduced RAG, September 2, 1910, 417.

277. Crawford, T. F., *Walschaerts Valve Gear in Service,* letter to RRG, published January 12, 1906, 32.

278. *Results of Use of Different Valve Gears on Locomotives,* committee report to ARMMA convention, 1907, reported RRG, June 14, 1907, 857.

279. Crawford, T. F., *Walschaerts Valve Gear in Service,* letter to RRG, published January 12, 1906, 32.

280. *Performance of an Allfree-Hubbell Locomotive on the Pittsburgh & Lake Erie,* RRG, September 1, 1905, 200; *Results of Use of Different Valve Gears on Locomotives,* committee report to ARMMA convention, 1907, reported RRG, June 14, 1907, 857.

281. Higgins, J. W., *The Orient Road: A History of the Kansas City, Mexico & Orient Railroad,* Journal R&LHS, October, 1946, 10.

282. *The Hobart Allfree Valve Gear,* RAG, June 17, 1910, 1575.

283. *Progress in Locomotive Design,* RAG, December 26, 1913, 1215.

284. Rink, G. W., Mechanical Engineer, Central Railroad of New Jersey, *Cylinders and Valve Gears,* discussion at ASME annual meeting, December, 1914, reported RAG, April 2, 1915, 750.

285. *Baker-Pilliod Valve Gear,* RRG, June 23, 1908, 302.

286. *The Baker-Pilliod Valve Gear,* RAG, January 15, 1909, 102.

287. *The Improved Baker-Pilliod Valve Gear,* RAG, December 23, 1910, 1210.

288. *Pilliod Locomotive Valve Gear,* RAG, December 22, 1911, 1285.

289. *Baker Valve Gear on Old Power,* RAG, June 18, 1912, 1481.

290. Edmonds, G. S., Superintendent Motive Power, Delaware & Hudson Railroad, *Locomotive Valves and Valve Gears,* RA, July 1, 1933, 27.

291. *Young Rotary Valve and Gear for Locomotives,* RAG, November 13, 1908, 1342.

292. *Delaware & Hudson Locomotives With Young Valves and Gear,* RRG, February 2, 1906, 102.

293. *Test of the Young Valve and Valve Gear,* RAG, April 7, 1916, 802.

294. *The Screw Reverse Gear,* RAG, January 6, 1911, 72.

295. *Details of Articulated Mallet Compound Locomotive for the Southern Pacific,* RAG, June 4, 1909, 1168.

296. Proceedings of Traveling Engineers' Association convention, Chicago, September, 1921, reported RA, September 17, 1921, 533.

297. *New Power Reverse Gear,* RAG, October 17, 1913, 713.

298. *Snyder Reverse Gear; Brown Power Reverse Gear,* RAG, June 19, 1916, 1440, 1441.

299. *Locomotive Power Reverse Gear,* RAG, November 10, 1916, 840.

300. *Type "B" Ragonnet Reverse Gear,* RAG, November 16, 1917, 900.

301. *Lewis Power Reverse Gear,* RAG, December 28, 1917, 1184.

302. Harding, J. W., 2000, Vol. 2, 57.

303. Harding, J. W., 2002, Vol. 2, 57–80.

304. Harding, J. W., 2002, Vol. 2, 65–9.

Section 7.5

305. *The Netting and Diaphragm in Locomotive Front-Ends,* RRG, November 9, 1906, 398.

306. *Tests of Self-Cleaning Front Ends,* Pennsylvania Railroad, RAG, July 15, 1910, 124; *The Survival of the Exhaust Bridge,* RAG, November 25, 1910, 993.

307. *Front Ends, Grates and Ash Pans,* report of committee to 1919 International Railway Fuel Association convention, reported RA, May 30, 1919, 1315.

308. *The Survival of the Exhaust Bridge,* RAG, November 25, 1910, 993.

309. Young, C. D., Engineer of Tests, Pennsylvania Railroad, in discussion on *Locomotive Front Ends and Draft Appliances,* ASME, New York, December, 1914, reported RAG, February 12, 1915, 273.

310. *Exhaust Nozzle With Internal Projections,* RAG, April 9, 1915, 799.

311. Snowden Bell, J., *Variable Exhausts,* ARMMA convention, 1915, reported RAG, June 12, 1915, 1290.

312. *Van Horn-Endsley Spark Arrester,* RAG, December 23, 1910, 1181.

313. *Slater Front End,* RAG, November 1, 1912, 846.

314. *Brooks Spark Arrester,* RAG, February 24, 1911, 349.

315. *Locomotive Front End Spark Arrester,* RA, February 15, 1918, 372.

316. Hatch, M. C. M., Superintendent of Fuel Service, Delaware, Lackawanna & Western Railroad, *Front End Design and Air Openings of Grates and Ash-Pans,* International Railway Fuel Association convention, 1914, reported RAG, May 22, 1914, 1149.

317. *Little Improvement in 116 Years,* RA, August 6, 1920, 212.

318. MacFarland, H. B., Engineer of Tests, Atchison, Topeka & Santa Fe Railway, *Locomotive Drafting and Its Relation to Fuel Consumption,* International Railway Fuel Association convention, 1912, reported RAG, May 31, 1912, 1201; *Fan Drafting as Applied to Locomotives,* contribution to report on Steam Locomotives of Today, ASME, New York, December, 1914, reported RAG, December 18, 1914, 1118.

319. Roesch, F. P., Fuel Conservation Section, USRA, *The Effect of Reducing Exhaust Nozzles to Overcome Front End Air Leaks,* International Railway Fuel Association convention, 1919, reported RA, May 30, 1919, 1316.

SECTION 7.6

320. *Cast Steel Locomotive Frames,* RRG, March 3, 1905, 180.

321. *Cast Steel Locomotive Frames,* RAG, June 18, 1912, 1457.

322. *Best Construction of Locomotive Frames,* report of committee to ARMMA convention, 1911, reported RAG, June 14, 1911, 1378.

323. *One-Piece Cast Steel Frames for Electric Locomotives,* RA, September 26, 1919, 643.

324. *Driving Wheel Impact and Light Reciprocating Parts,* RAG, May 12, 1916, 1020.

325. Strong, E. W., *Reduce Dynamic Augment for Heavy Locomotives,* New York Railroad Club, February 1918, reported RAG, February 22, 1918.

SECTION 7.7

326. *Disturbing Factors in Locomotive Capacity and Train Resistance,* RAG, March 16, 1910, 596.

327. *Improved Locomotive Efficiency,* RAG, August 30, 1912, 372.

328. *Locomotive Performance Data Developed at Purdue,* RRG, May 3, 1907, 603.

329. Schmidt, E. C., Professor of Railway Engineering, University of Illinois, *Locomotive Laboratory at the University of Illinois,* Western Railway Club, March 1913, abstracted RAG, March 28, 1913, 752; *Locomotive Testing Plants,* RAG, March 23, 1917, 612.

330. Asakura, K., Japanese Government Railways, *Locomotive Resistance and Mechanical Efficiency,* RA, July 30, 1921, 211.

331. Vauclain, S. M., President, Baldwin Locomotive Works, *Vauclain Discusses Outlook for Diesel Locomotive,* Midwest Power Conference, Chicago, January, 1926, reported RA, February 6, 1926, 388.

332. Pennsylvania Railroad Co., Bulletin #4, abstracted as *Locomotive Tests at St. Louis,* RRG, April 7, 1905, 322.

333. *Record of the Pennsylvania Locomotive Tests,* RRG, February 9, 1906, 122.

334. Drury, 328.

335. Loudon, A. C., *Pennsylvania Atlantic Type Locomotive Tests,* RAG, March 23, 1917, 636; Pennsylvania Railroad Testing Plant Bulletin No. 27, 1915.

336. 'Steam Railway,' May, 2009, 95.

337. Drury, 328; *Mikado and Consolidation Types Compared,* RAG, June 8, 1917, 1187; Pennsylvania Railroad Testing Plant Bulletin No. 28, 1915.

338. Henderson, G. R., *The Cost of Locomotive Operation,* RRG, March 31, 1905, 311; Goss, W. F. M., *Locomotive Performance Under a Steam Pressure of 250 Pounds,* RRG, June 9, 1905, 651; Raymond, W. G., *Acceleration and Some Locomotive Problems,* reprinted from "The Transit," RRG, September 14, 1906, 217; *Limited Speed of Passenger Locomotives,* RAG, December 24, 1909, 1225; Allman, W. L., *Tractive Power of Locomotives,* RAG, February 11, 1910, 310; *A Record Locomotive Performance,* RAG, June 18, 1912, 1472; *Disturbing Factors in Locomotive Capacity and Train Resistance,* RAG, March 16, 1910, 596; *Economics of Railway Location,* excerpted from a report to American Railway Engineering & Maintenance of Way Association annual meeting, 1910, RAG, March 17, 1910, 662; Van Zandt, J. G., *Tonnage Rating for Fast Freight Trains,* RAG, June 17, 1910, 1547, June 24, 1910, 1788; Wickhorst, M. R., *Tonnage Rating of Locomotives on the Burlington,* Bulletin No.138, AREA, August 1911, excerpted RAG, September 29, 1911, 592; Webb, W. L., *Economical Limits of Grade Reduction,* RAG, March 28, 1913, 750; Houston, H. A., Rock Island Lines, *Locomotive Tractive Effort,* RAG, September 12, 1913, 455; *Superheater Locomotives and Grade Revision,* anonymous letter, RAG, October 8, 1915, 637; Goodwin, G. S., Chicago, Rock Island & Pacific Railway, *Value of a Locomotive in Terms of Earning Capacity,* Western Railway Club, February, 1915, abstracted RAG, February 19, 1915, 306; Tollerton, W. J., General Mechanical Superintendent, Rock Island Lines, *Tests of a Mountain Type Locomotive on the Rock Island,* RAG, April 16, 1915, 829; Ballantine, N. D., Assistant to 2nd Vice-President, Rock Island Lines, *The Real Value of a Freight Locomotive,* Western Railway Club, April, 1915, abstracted RAG, April 23, 1915, 886; Beyer O. S.,

Chicago, Rock Island & Pacific Railway, *Scientific Train Loading, Tonnage Rating,* Traveling Engineers' Association convention, 1915, reported RAG, September 17, 1915, 507; *Tests with 2-10-2 Locomotive on the Union Pacific,* June 28, 1918, 1572; *Standard Heavy 4-8-2 and Light 2-10-2 Locomotives,* RA, December 13, 1918, 1067; Milner, B. B., Engineer of Motive Power, New York Central System, *Drawbar Pull-Speed-Cut-off Calibration as an Adjunct to Efficient Locomotive and Train Operation,* ARMMA convention, 1919, reproduced RA, June 25, 1919, 1766.

339. Houston, H. A., Rock Island Lines, *Analysis of Steam Train Resistance,* RAG, March 27, 1914, 741.

340. Milner, B. B., Engineer of Motive Power, New York Central System, *Drawbar Pull-Speed-Cut-off Calibration as an Adjunct to Efficient Locomotive and Train Operation,* ARMMA convention, 1919, reproduced RA, June 25, 1919, 1766.

341. Henderson, G. R., *The Cost of Locomotive Operation,* RRG, April 28, 1905, 386; Raymond, W. G., *Acceleration and Some Locomotive Problems,* reprinted from "The Transit," RRG, September 14, 1906, 217; Thomas, F. W., Engineer of Tests, Atchison, Topeka & Santa Fe Railway, *Tonnage Rating for Locomotives,* Traveling Engineers' Association convention, 1906, excerpted RRG, September 21, 1906, 237; Stucki, A, *Train Resistance,* RAG, May 7, 1909, 982; Cole, F. J., *Train Resistance,* RAG, August 27, 1909, 361, September 10, 1909, 451; Schmidt, E. C., Assistant Professor of Railway Engineering, University of Illinois, *Freight Train Resistance,* ARMMA convention, 1910, reported RAG, June 23, 1910, 1763; Daly, J. M., General Superintendent of Transportation, Illinois Central Railroad, *Train Tonnage,* Traveling Engineers' Association convention, 1912, abstracted RAG, September 6, 1912, 428; Begien, R. N., Assistant General Superintendent, Baltimore & Ohio Railroad, *Application of Baltimore & Ohio Dynamometer Tests to Tonnage Rating,* AREA convention, 1913, Report to the Committee on the Economics of Railway Location, abstracted RAG, March 20, 1913, 642; Houston, H. A., Rock Island Lines, *Analysis of Steam Train Resistance,* RAG, March 27, 1914, 741; *Train Resistance and Tonnage Rating,* report to ARMMA convention, 1916, reported RAG, June 22, 1916, 1523; Vincent, H. S., *Tonnage Rating of the Standard Locomotives,* RA, October 4, 1918, 627.

342. Schmidt, E. C., Assistant Professor of Railway Engineering, University of Illinois, *Freight Train Resistance,* ARMMA convention, 1910, reported RAG, June 23, 1910, 1763.

Chapter 8

SECTION 8.1

1. Edson, W. D., White, J. H. *Lima Locomotive Works,* Journal R&LHS, October 1970, 81.

2. *Consolidation Locomotive for the Southern Utah Railroad,* RAG, December 10, 1909, 1142.

3. Hirsimaki, E. *Lima: The History,* Edmonds, WA: Hundman, 1986.

4. Drury, 319, 328.

5. *Locomotive Building*, RAG, April 1, 1910, 923; *Consolidation Locomotive, Chicago, Milwaukee & St. Paul*, RAG, May 6, 1910, 1157.

6. *Pacific Type Locomotive, Louisville & Nashville*, RAG, June 17, 1912, 1446; Drury, 226; *New Power for the Louisville & Nashville*, RAG, June 17, 1914, 1471.

7. *Locomotive Equipment Ordered in 1910*, RAG, December 30, 1910, 1262.

8. Brown, A. E., *The Louisiana & Arkansas Railway: Structure and Operation in the Age of Steam*, Journal R&LHS, Spring, 1981, 51.

9. McLeod, R., *History of the Wisconsin & Michigan Railway*, Journal R&LHS, April, 1968, 7; Webber, J. F., *The Goldfield Railroads*, Journal R&LHS, April, 1959, 23.

10. *Northern Pacific Railway Company—Fourteenth Annual Report*, abstracted RAG, October 28, 1910, 822.

11. *Northern Pacific Railway Company—Sixteenth Annual Report*, abstracted RAG, November 22, 1912, 1016.

12. *Northern Pacific Railway Company –Eighteenth Annual Report*, abstracted RAG, March 19, 1915, 650.

13. New York, New Haven & Hartford annual report, 1915, abstracted RAG, October 27, 1916, 776.

14. Northern Pacific Railway annual report, 1916, abstracted RAG, December 1, 1916, 1019.

15. *Missouri, Kansas & Texas*, 1916 annual report, abstracted RAG, January 12, 1917, 45.

16. RRG, May 5, 1905, 149.

17. *Lackawanna Locomotive with Schenectady Superheater*, RRG, October 13, 1905, 342; Drury, 153.

18. Drury, 291.

19. *Heavy Ten Wheel Passenger Locomotive for the Delaware, Lackawanna & Western R. R.*, RRG, November 24, 1905, 474.

20. *Heavy Ten-Wheel Locomotives for the Lehigh Valley*, RRG, October 27, 1905, 399.

21. *Heavy, Eight-Wheeled Passenger Locomotive for the Central R. R. of New Jersey*, RRG, January 19, 1906, 56.

22. *Prairie Type Engine for the Chicago, Burlington & Quincy*, RRG, October 20, 1905, 363.

23. *Ten-Wheeled (4-6-0) Locomotive for the New York Central & Hudson River*, RRG, December 15, 1905, 556.

24. RRG, February 9, 1906, 44; *New Locomotives for the Great Northern*, RRG, October 26, 1906, 371.

25. *Mogul Locomotives for the Vandalia*, RRG, January 4, 1907, 9.

26. *Balanced Compound Prairie Type Locomotives for the Atchison, Topeka & Santa Fe*, RRG, November 9, 1906, 414; Drury, 15, 26.

27. RRG, April 5, 1907, 498.

28. *Four-Cylinder Simple Express Locomotives; Great Western Railway*, RRG, 1907, 390.

29. RAG, December 10, 1909, 1172.

30. *New Locomotives for the Chicago Great Western*, RAG, February 11, 1910, 313; *Locomotive Building*, RAG, February 18, 1910, 384.

31. *Philadelphia & Reading 4-4-0 Type Locomotives*, RAG, April 17, 1914, 872.

32. Drury, 55, 91, 100.

33. *Cole Balanced Compound for the Erie*, RRG, July 14, 1905, 37.

34. *The Reading Three-Cylinder Locomotive*, RAG, June 22, 1909, 1434.

35. *Four-Cylinder Balanced Simple Locomotives, Chicago, Rock Island and Pacific*, reprinted from Alco Bulletin 1007, RAG, January 6, 1911, 41.

36. Drury, 129.

37. *Atlantic Type Locomotives for the Baltimore & Ohio*, RAG, May 20, 1910, 1255.

38. *Balanced Compound Atlantic Type Locomotives; Atchison, Topeka & Santa Fe*, RAG, December 23, 1910, 1189.

39. *Atlantic Type Class E 6 Locomotive; Pennsylvania Railroad*, RAG, April 7, 1911, 854.

40. Fisher, C. E., *The Steam Locomotives of the Pennsylvania Railroad System, Part III*, Journal R&LHS, October, 1954, 130.

41. *Atlantic Type Locomotives on the Pennsylvania*, RAG, February 20, 1914, 356.

42. *The Reading Type Locomotive*, RAG, June 9, 1915, 1184; *A Passenger Locomotive of Unusual Interest*, RAG, June 9, 1915, 1193; Drury, 333.

43. *Heavy Consolidation Locomotives for the B. & O.*, RRG, December 8, 1905, 508; *Consolidation Locomotive for the Baltimore & Ohio Railroad*, RRG, December 15, 1905, 563; *Baltimore & Ohio Railroad Motive Power*, RRG, June 15, 1906, 616.

44. Morgan, D. P., *Louisville & Nashville's Pacifics and Mountains*, Journal R&LHS, October, 1952, 36.

45. *Heavy Passenger Locomotives for the C., M. & St. P.*, RRG, June 9, 1905, 654.

46. *Pacific Locomotive with Superheater for the Erie Railroad*, RRG, June 9, 1905, 620.

47. *Two Baldwin Four-Cylinder Balanced Compound Locomotives*, RRG, November 17, 1905, 440; Drury, 27.

48. *Heavy Pacific Type Locomotive for the Northern Pacific*, RRG, November 9, 1906, 406.

49. *Pacific Locomotive for the Pennsylvania Lines West*, RRG, August 30, 1907, 238.

50. Fisher, C. E., *The Steam Locomotives of the Pennsylvania Railroad System*, Journal R&LHS, October, 1954, 130; Drury, 328.

51. Drury, 328; *Pennsylvania Mikado and Pacific Type Locomotives*, RAG, July 3, 1914, 12.

52. Fisher, C. E., *The Steam Locomotives of the Pensylvania Railroad System*, Journal R&LHS, October, 1954, 130.

53. *Pacific Locomotive for the Lake Shore & Michigan Southern*, RRG, September 6, 1907, 259.

54. *Pacific Locomotive for the New York Central*, RRG, April 3, 1908, 468.

55. *Pacific Type Superheater Locomotive; Chicago & North Western*, RAG, February 17, 1911, 325.

56. *Heavy Pacific Type Locomotives; New York Central Lines*, RAG, March 31, 1911, 785.

57. Drury, 279.

58. *Experimental Pacific Type Locomotive*, RAG, December 29, 1911, 1322.

59. RAG, October 4, 1912, 645; Weatherwax, D. S., *Hail and Farewell: Erie 2509 ex, A. L. Co. 50000, 1910–1950*, Journal R&LHS, March, 1952, 28.

60. *Powerful Pacifics for the Erie*, RAG, June 14, 1913, 1392.

61. *Anthracite Burning Pacific Type Locomotives*, RAG, July 19, 1912, 88; Drury, 153.

62. Drury, 85, 88; *Large Passenger Locomotives for the C & O*, RAG, September 26, 1913, 571.

63. *Anthracite Burning Pacific Type Locomotive*, RAG, March 6, 1914, 473; Drury, 222.

64. *Santa Fe Balanced Compound Pacific Type Locomotive*, RAG, June 19, 1914, 1519.

65. *4-6-2 Type Freight Locomotive*, RAG, June 14, 1913, 1390.

66. *Lackawanna Pacific Type Freight Locomotive*, RAG, October 9, 1914, 657.

67. *Two Pacific Type Locomotives of High Power*, RAG, December 25, 1914, 1185.

68. *Pacific Type Locomotives for the Union Pacific*, RAG, April 9, 1915, 781.

69. *Simple Pacific Locomotive for the Santa Fe*, RAG, April 9, 1915, 793; Drury, 27.

70. *Powerful Pacific Type Locomotive for the R., F. & P.*, RAG, December 17, 1915, 1179.

71. *Heavy Pacific Type Locomotive for the Lackawanna*, RAG, December 24, 1915, 185.

72. *Pacific Type Locomotives for the Reading*, RAG, July 21, 1916, 107; Drury, 331.

73. *Heavy Locomotives for the Lehigh Valley*, RAG, April 27, 1917, 897.

74. *Light and Heavy Standard Pacific Type Locomotives*, RA, April 11, 1919, 951.

75. Drury, 230; Morgan, D. P., *Louisville & Nashville's Pacifics and Mountains*, Journal R&LHS, October, 1952, 36.

76. *Mountain Type Locomotives for Heavy Passenger Service*, RAG, September 22, 1911, 555; Drury, 85.

77. "Steam Railway," No. 378, July 23–August 19, 2010, 21.

78. Tollerton, W. J., General Mechanical Superintendent, Chicago, Rock Island & Pacific Railway, *Recent Power for the Rock Island Lines*, RAG, January 9, 1914, 86.

79. Drury, 252.

80. *Passenger Locomotives for the Great Northern*, RAG, December 4, 1914, 1047.

81. *Norfolk & Western Mountain Type Locomotives*, RAG, April 7, 1916, 799; *Norfolk & Western Mountain Type Locomotives*, RAG, August 25, 1916, 362.

82. *Seaboard Air Line Mountain Type Locomotives*, RAG, July 16, 1915, 87.

83. Freeman, L. D., Assistant Superintendent of Motive Power, Seaboard Air Line in discussion of Partington, J., *Modern Tendencies in Locomotive Design*, ASME, Newport News, Virginia, April, 1922, abstracted RA, April 15, 1922, 909.

84. Drury, 279; RAG, December 28, 1917, 1167.

85. *Standard Heavy 4-8-2 and Light 2-10-2 Locomotives*, RA, December 13, 1918, 1067.

86. *The Administration Standard Light Mountain Type*, RA, May 16, 1919, 1193; Drury, 290, 294.

Section 8.2

87. *Baltimore & Ohio Railroad Motive Power*, RRG, June 15, 1905, 616.

88. *Consolidation Locomotive for the New York Central Lines*, RRG, June 15, 1906, 613.

89. *Consolidation Locomotive for the N. Y. Central with Walschaert Gear*, RRG, June 9, 1905, 636.

90. *Consolidation Locomotive for the New York Central Lines*, RRG, June 15, 1906, 613.

91. *Cross-Compound Consolidation for the "Soo" Line*, RRG, June 9, 1905, 658.

92. *Consolidation Locomotives for the Pennsylvania*, RAG, July 2, 1909, 9.

93. *Record Freight Train Haul on the Pennsylvania*, RAG, June 22, 1909, 1420.

94. Fisher, C. E., *The Steam Locomotives of the Pennsylvania Railroad System, Part III*, Journal R&LHS, October, 1954, 130; Drury, 328.

95. *Consolidation Locomotive for the Wabash-Pittsburgh Terminal with Cole Superheater*, RAG, June 16, 1909, 1237.

96. *Western Maryland Consolidation Locomotive*, RAG, July 17, 1914, 101.

97. *U. S. A. War Locomotive Completed in 20 Days*, RAG, 1917; *Decapod Locomotives for Russian Government*, RAG, October 12, 1917, 637.

98. Edson, W. D., *The U.S.R.A. Locomotives*, Journal R&LHS, October, 1955, 73.

99. Church, R. J., *Southern Pacific Ten-Coupled Locomotives*, Berkeley and Wilton, CA: Signature Press, 2013, 52–3.

100. *Large Consolidation Type Locomotive for the P & R*, RA, March 21, 1919, 761; Drury, 333.

101. *Mikado (2-8-2) Locomotive for the Northern Pacific*, RRG, January 20, 1905, 50; *Heavy Power for the Northern Pacific*, RAG, August 29, 1913, 377.

102. *Mikado Locomotive for the Virginian Railway*, RAG, July 3, 1908, 420.

103. Sanderson, R. P. C., Superintendent of Motive Power, Virginian Railway, *Big Trains on the Virginian*, letter to RAG, published October 22, 1909, 744.

104. *Mikado Locomotives for the Chicago, Milwaukee & Puget Sound*, RAG, July 16, 1909, 95.

105. *Locomotive Building*, RAG, July 29, 1910, 209; *Mikado and Pacific Type Locomotives; Baltimore & Ohio*, RAG, June 16, 1911, 1411.

106. *Mikado Locomotive for the Atlanta, Birmingham & Atlantic*, August 12, 1910, 282.

107. *Mikado Locomotive for Burning Lignite; Oregon Railroad & Navigation Company*, RAG, January 27, 1911, 167.

108. RAG, February 10, 1911, 306.

109. *Heavy Mikado Locomotives for the Illinois Central*, RAG, September 29, 1911, 585.

110. Drury, 207.

111. *Mikado Locomotives for the Great Northern*, RAG, December 15, 1911, 1214; Drury 196.

112. *Mikado Superheater Locomotives for the Missouri Pacific*, RAG, January 12, 1912, 55; *Mikado Locomotives for Heavy Freight Service*, RAG, February 2, 1912, 201.

113. *Mikado Locomotives for the Erie*, RAG, February 9, 1912, 241.

114. Tollerton, W. J., General Mechanical Superintendent, Chicago, Rock Island & Pacific Railway, *Recent Power for the Rock Island Lines*, RAG, January 9, 1914, 86; *Powerful Mikado Locomotives*, RAG, August 23, 1912, 352.

115. *Train of 99 Cars Hauled 111 Miles by One Locomotive*, RAG, August 15, 1913, 270.

116. *Powerful Mikados for the Lake Shore*, RAG, May 2, 1913, 987.

117. Drury, 328; *Pennsylvania Mikado and Pacific Type Locomotives*, RAG, July 3, 1914, 12.

118. *Duplex Locomotives for the Southern Railway*, RAG, February 16, 1917, 267.

119. 'Steam Railway', No. 395, 6; No. 396, 60.

120. *Northern Pacific Converts Prairie Type to Mikado*, RA, November 14, 1919, 961.

121. *First of the U.S. Standard Locomotives Completed*, RA, July 19, 1918, 131.

122. *T. & P. Is Geared for High Speed*, RA, August 5, 1944, 236.

123. *The U.S. Standard Heavy Mikado Type Locomotive*, RA, August 30, 1918, 374.

124. *Decapod Locomotive for the Buffalo, Rochester & Pittsburg*, RRG, August 9, 1907, 151.

125. RAG, May 28, 1909, 1146.

126. *Locomotives for the Russian State Railways*, RAG, September 10, 1915, 474; *Decapod Locomotives for Russian Government*, RAG, October 12, 1917, 637.

127. Edson, W. D., *The Russian Decapods*, Journal R&LHS Journal, April 1971, 64.

128. *Pennsylvania Locomotive of the Decapod Type*, RAG, June 15, 1917, 1242; Drury, 328; *Moving 6,700 Cars Daily Over the Alleghenies*, RA, May 5, 1923, 1089.

129. *Report on Locomotive Construction*, ARMMA convention, 1923, reported RA, June 23, 1923, 1591.

130. Pennsylvania Railroad Technical Bulletin #31, 1919, quoted in Partington, J., American Locomotive Co., *Designing Locomotives for Economical Operation*, ASME, New York, December, 1921, reported RA, November 5, 1921, 899; *Pennsylvania Decapod Develops 3,500 Horsepower*, RA, April 2, 1920, 1097.

131. *Largest Non-Articulated Locomotive*, RAG, May 3, 1912, 1006.

132. Drury, 47; *Baltimore & Ohio 2-10-2 Type Locomotive*, RAG, August 7, 1914, 242.

133. *Erie 2-10-2 Type Locomotive*, RAG, March 26, 1915, 706; Drury, 173, 180.

134. *Recent Examples of 2-10-2 Type Locomotives*, RAG, April 21, 1916, 887.

135. *Heavy Freight Locomotives for the D. M. & N.*, RAG, December 22, 1916, 1125.

136. *Heavy Locomotives for the Lehigh Valley*, RAG, April 27, 1917, 897.

137. Harwood, H. H., *Corporate History of the Lehigh Valley R. R.*, Journal R&LHS April, 1972, 5.

138. *The Heaviest Santa Fe Type Locomotives*, RAG, August 3, 1917, 189.

139. *Tests with 2-10-2 Locomotive on the Union Pacific*, June 28, 1918, 1572.

140. *Locomotives of the 2-10-2 Type for the Wabash*, RAG, December 7, 1917, 1025; Drury, 422.

141. *Heaviest 2-10-2 Type Built for Pennsylvania Lines*, RA, January 24, 1919, 249.

142. *Standard Heavy 4-8-2 and Light 2-10-2 Locomotives*, RA, December 13, 1918, 1067.

143. *The Standard Heavy Santa Fe Type Locomotive*, RA, February 14, 1919, 389.

144. Edson, W. D., *The U. S. R. A. Locomotives*, Journal R&LHS, October, 195, 73.

SECTION 8.3

145. *Heavy Mallet-Type Locomotive for the B. & O.*, RRG, September 4, 1903, 636; *Mallet Articulated Compound for the Baltimore & Ohio*, RRG, May 27, 1904, 401.

146. Mellin, C. J., American Locomotive Company, *Articulated Compound Locomotives*, ASME, New York, December, 1908, reported RAG, December 11, 1908, 1529; RAG, December 18, 1908, 1583.

147. *Road Tests of the B & O Mallet Compound*, RRG, July 14, 1905, 42.

148. Drury, 41.

149. Mellin, C. J., American Locomotive Company, *Articulated Compound Locomotives*, ASME, New York, December, 1908, reported RAG, December 11, 1908, 1529; RAG, December 18, 1908, 1583.

150. Sinclair, A., 1907, 195–6.

151. Loggingmallets.railfan.net website.

152. *Mallet Compound Locomotive for the Great Northern*, RRG, August 17, 1906, 148.

153. Drury, 192; *The Converted Mallet Locomotive*, RAG, December 3, 1909, 1046.

154. *The Mallet Compound Locomotives on the Great Northern*, RRG, May 17, 1907, 684.

155. *Mallet Compounds for the Erie*, RRG, November 2, 1906, 389; *Mallet Compound Locomotive for the Erie Railroad*, RRG, August 16, 1907, 170; *Details of Mallet Articulated Compound Locomotive*, RRG, October 4, 1907, 384.

156. *Mallet Articulated Compound Steam Locomotives*, committee report to ARMMA convention, 1908, reported RRG, June 24, 1908, 316, 324.

157. Drury, 172.

158. Drury, 317.

159. *Mallet Articulated Compound Locomotive for the Southern Pacific*, RAG, April 30, 1909, 933.

160. *Southern Pacific Orange Train*, RAG, July 10, 1908, 490.

161. *Mallet Locomotives for the Southern Pacific*, RAG, April 22, 1910, 1034.

162. Bruce, A. W., 1952, 103.

163. Drury, 27.

164. *The Converted Mallet Locomotive*, RAG, December 3, 1909, 1046.

165. *Converted Mallet Locomotive for the Great Northern*, RAG, December 17, 1909, 1185.

166. Drury, 193, 196; *Locomotive Building During 1910; Baldwin Locomotive Works*, RAG, April 28, 1911, 993.

167. RAG, November 5, 1909, 899.

168. *Mallet Articulated Compound Locomotives for the Eastern Railway of France*, RAG, November 19, 1909, 969.

169. Drury, 27; *Mallet Locomotives for the Atchison*, RAG, November 26, 1909, 1018; *The Mallet Articulated Locomotive*, RAG, December 3, 1909, 1002.

170. *Mallet Articulated Compound Locomotive for the Virginian Railway*, RAG, June 18, 1909, 1316.

171. Evans, G. I., Canadian Pacific Railway, *Experimental Mallet Articulated Locomotive*, Canadian Railway Club, 1910, reproduced RAG, August 5, 1910, 246.

172. Drury, 69; Turner, R. D., *West of the Great Divide: An Illustrated History of the Canadian Pacific Railway in British Columbia, 1880–1986*, Victoria, BC, Canada: Sono Nis Press, 1987, 78.

173. *Simple High Speed Articulated Locomotive*, RAG, July 12, 1912, 50.

174. *The Mallet Locomotive in Service*, RAG, March 11, 1910, 513.

175. *The Speed Limits of Mallet Locomotives,* RAG, April 1, 1910, 870.

176. Prescott, C. F., *The Speed Limits of Mallet Locomotives,* letter published RAG, April 29, 1910, 1077.

177. *Performance of Mallet Engines on the Great Northern,* RAG, April 15, 1910, 980.

178. Drury, 27; *The Mallet Compound Locomotive and Its Limitations,* RAG, April 22, 1910, 1027; McFarland, H. B., *Speed Limits of Mallet Compounds,* letter published RAG, May 20, 1910, 1249.

179. *Locomotive Building During 1910; Baldwin Locomotive Works,* RAG, April 28, 1911, 993;

180. *Comparative Study in Operation—Virginian and C. C. & O.* RAG, April 24, 1914, 935.

181. *Mallet Articulated Compound Locomotive for the Delaware & Hudson Co.,* RAG, May 27, 1910, 1303.

182. *Mallet Superheater Locomotives; Delaware & Hudson,* RAG, August 11, 1911, 291.

183. *Mallet Locomotive for the Burlington,* RAG, May 13, 1910, 1213; *Locomotive Building During 1910; Baldwin Locomotive Works,* RAG, April 28, 1911, 993.

184. *Recent Mallet Articulated Locomotives,* RAG, December 16, 1910, 1144; *Mallet Results in Road Service,* RAG, April 5, 1912, 797.

185. Drury, 88.

186. Drury, 417.

187. Drury, 170, 419.

188. *Converted Mallet Locomotives for the Chicago Great Western,* RAG, November 4, 1910, 867.

189. Haig, M. H., Mechanical Engineer, Atchison, Topeka & Santa Fe Railway, *Mallet Locomotive With Articulated Boiler Built From Old Power,* RAG, February 10, 1911, 278; *Mallet Locomotives for the Santa Fe,* RAG, February 24, 1911, 351.

190. *Locomotive Building During 1910; Baldwin Locomotive Works,* RAG, April 28, 1911, 993; Drury, 27; *Mallet Locomotive with 20 Drivers for the Santa Fe,* RAG, August 25, 1911, 379; *The Largest Locomotive,* RAG, April 14, 1911, 906.

191. Drury, 27.

192. Drury, 172.

193. *Comparative Tests of Mallet Locomotives; Norfolk & Western,* RAG, May 19,1911, 1153.

194. *Superheated Steam on Mallet Locomotives,* RAG, June 16, 1911, 1477.

195. Daugherty, J. B., Baltimore & Ohio Railroad, *Mallet Compound in Road Service,* Traveling Engineers' Association convention, 1911, abstracted RAG, September 8, 1911, 471.

196. *Economies Effected by Mallet Locomotives on the New York Central & Hudson River,* RAG, November 24, 1911, 1054.

197. RAG, July 12, 1912, 39; *Simple High Speed Articulated Locomotive,* RAG, July 12, 1912, 50.

198. Turner, R. D., 1987, 78.

199. Drury, 41.

200. *Heavy Mallet Locomotives; Baltimore & Ohio,* RAG, June 14, 1911, 1346.

201. *Mallets on the Norfolk & Western,* RAG, May 9, 1913, 1025.

202. Drury, 419; *Most Powerful Locomotive in the World,* RAG, June 13, 1912, 1321; *Large Steam Locomotives, Present and Future,* discussion on paper *Steam Locomotives of Today,* ASME, New York, December, 1914, reported RAG, January 22, 1915, 123.

203. *Starting Heavy Trains on the Norfolk & Western Electrified Line,* RAG, January 27, 1916, 170.

204. *Mallet Locomotives for the Great Northern,* RAG, September 29, 1912, 572.

205. RA July 21, 1923, 130.

206. *Handling Fourteen Thousand Ton Trains,* RA, September 27, 1930, 609.

207. *Triplex Compound Locomotive,* RAG, April 12, 1912, 851; Drury, 174; Mounce, R. S., *Articulated Locomotive With One Engine on the Tender,* RAG, May 8, 1914, 1027.

208. Mounce, R. S., *New High Record Train Load,* RAG, July 31, 1914, 208.

209. *Triplex Articulated Locomotives for the Erie,* RAG, July 14, 1916, 74.

210. *Virginian Triplex Type Pusher Locomotive,* RAG, January 26, 1917, 141.

211. Drury, 174.

212. *Heavy Standard Mallet Type Locomotive,* RA, March 14, 1919, 575; Drury, 426–7.

213. *Mallet Locomotives for Use in Road Service,* RAG, July 28, 1916, 145; Drury, 47.

214. Drury, 41, 47; Edson, W. D., *The U.S.R.A. Locomotives,* Journal R&LHS, October, 1955, 73.

215. Drury, 308; *Norfolk & Western 267-Ton Mallet Locomotive,* RA, July 12, 1918, 59.

216. *The Virginian Mallet Locomotives,* RA, October 4, 1918, 623; *Heavy Mallet Locomotives for the Virginian,* RA, October 18, 1918, 688; Drury, 413–19; Partington, J., American Locomotive Co., *Designing Locomotives for Economical Operation,* ASME, New York, December, 1921, reported RA, November 5, 1921, 899.

217. *One Locomotive Moves 189 Cars Over Division,* RA, July 7, 1928, 39.

218. *The Longest Train?* RA, July 21, 1928, 122.

219. *The U.S. Standard Light Mallet Type Locomotive,* RA, January 31, 1919, 291.

220. *Heavy Standard Mallet Type Locomotive,* RA, March 14, 1919, 575.

221. Fisher, C. E., *Locomotives of the Buffalo, Rochester & Pittsburgh Ry.,* Journal R&LHS, October, 1951, 48; *Experimental Mallet Locomotive for the Pennsylvania,* RAG, March 1, 1912, 377.

222. *Simple Mallet Locomotive with Short Maximum Cut-off,* RA, June 23, 1919, 1675.

223. Orr, J. W., *Set Up Running: The Life of a Pennsylvania Railroad Engineman 1904–1949,* University Park, PA: Pennsylvania State University Press, 2001.

SECTION 8.4

224. *Powerful Switching Locomotives for the Lake Shore,* RRG, July 21, 1905, 64.

225. *Superheater Switch Engines With Gaines Combustion Chamber,* RAG, February 14, 1913, 289.

226. *Mallet Compounds for Hump Yard Service,* RAG, June 12, 1914, 1335; Kiracofe, J. H., *100 Years of Railroad Progress 1851–1951,* Journal R&LHS, October, 1952, 60.

227. *Switch Engines for the Louisville & Nashville,* RAG, December 1, 1916, 998.

228. Carty, F. J., Mechanical Engineer, Boston & Albany Railroad, *Conversion of Consolidation Type Locomotives to Eight-Wheel Switchers,* RAG, August 10, 1917, 235.

229. Hauser, W. H., Mechanical Engineer, Chicago & Eastern Illinois Railway, *Conversion of Freight to Switch Locomotives,* RAG, November 2, 1917, 799.

230. *The First Standard 0-8-0 Type Switching Locomotive,* RA, September 20, 1918, 542; U.S. R. A. Standard Six-Wheel Switching Locomotive, RA, October 11, 1918, 654.

Chapter 9

1. Crawford, D. F., General Superintendent of Motive Power, Pennsylvania Lines West of Pittsburgh, *The Abatement of Locomotive Smoke,* International Society for the Prevention of Smoke, abstracted RAG, October 24, 1913, 762.

SECTION 9.1

2. Pomeroy, L. R., *The Electrification of Trunk Lines,* RRG, May 19, 1905, 531; Street, C. F., *Electricity on Steam Railroads,* Western Railway Club, May 1905, reproduced RRG, April 28, 1905, 390; Morris, R., *Electric Railway Competition,* ARRMA convention, 1905; reproduced RRG, May 12, 1905, 473.

3. *Acceleration Tests of Steam and Electric Locomotives,* RRG, May 26, 1905, 584.

4. Murray, W. S., *The Success of Main Line Electrification,* RAG, April 30, 1915, 923.

5. *The New Haven's Electric Expansion,* RRG, December 21, 1906, 543.

6. Murray, W. S., *The Advance of Electrification,* Western Society of Engineers, March, 1915, reproduced RAG, March 17, 1915, 549.

7. Murray, W. S., *The Success of Main Line Electrification,* RAG, April 30, 1915, 923.

8. *Design, Maintenance and Operation of Electric Rolling Stock,* committee report to ARA convention, 1920, reported RA, June 11, 1920, 1711.

9. RA April 4, 1931, 676.

10. *Design, Maintenance and Operation of Electric Rolling Stock,* committee report to ARA convention, 1920, reported RA, June 11, 1920, 1711.

11. Griffith, H. C., *Electric Locomotive Operation,* ASME, Kansas City, Missouri, June, 1941, reported RA, August 9, 1941, 230.

12. RAG, February 10, 1911, 306.

13. De Muralt, C. L., Professor, University of Michigan, *Aspects of Steam Railway Electrification,* RAG, October 4, 1912, 623.

14. Bellinger, F. W., Electrical Superintendent, Butte, Anaconda & Pacific Railroad, *Electric Operations—Butte, Anaconda & Pacific,* National Electric Light Association, Pasadena, California, May, 1920, reported RA, June 5, 1920, 1657.

15. *Thirty Mile Electrification on Norfolk & Western,* RAG, June 13, 1913, 1319; Gibbs, G., *Electrification Work on the Norfolk & Western and Pennsylvania Railroads,* Western Society of Engineers, March, 1915, reproduced RAG, March 17, 1915, 551; *Norfolk & Western Elkhorn Grade Electrification,* RAG, June 4, 1915, 1153.

16. *Development of Electric Traction During 15 Years—1899 to 1914,* RAG, 1914, 594.

17. Goodnow, C. A., Assistant to the Pres-

ident, Chicago, Milwaukee & St. Paul Railroad, *Electrification Work on the Milwaukee*, Western Society of Engineers, March, 1915, reproduced RAG, March 17, 1915, 551; *Electrification of 440.5 Miles of the St. Paul*, RAG, October 15, 1915, 683; *St. Paul to Electrify Over Cascade Mountains*, RAG, February 2, 1917, 175.

18. *St. Paul to Electrify Over Cascade Mountains*, RAG, February 2, 1917, 175.

19. Katte, E. B., Chief Engineer, Electric Traction, New York Central System, *Operating Results of Steam Railroad Electrification*, Western Society of Engineers, March 1915, reproduced RAG, March 17, 1915, 548.

SECTION 9.2

20. *The Passing (?) of the Steam Locomotive*, RRG, June 8, 1906, 563.

21. *Motor Cars*, report to ARMMA convention, 1909, abstracted RAG, June 17, 1909, 1281.

22. *The Self-Propelled Motor Car*, RRG, June 23, 1908, 279.

23. Diesel, R., *The Diesel Locomotive*, excerpted RAG, August 9, 1912, 241.

24. Dodd, S. T., Arnold, B. H., Engineering Department, General Electric, *Self-Propelled Cars*, International Railway Fuel Association convention, 1913, abstracted RAG, May 30, 1913, 1180.

25. *Gas-Electric Locomotive*, RAG, November 14, 1913, 916; *60-Ton Gas-Electric Locomotive*, RAG, October 8, 1915, 658.

26. *Gasolene Switching Locomotive*, RAG, January 15, 1915, 101.

27. *Gasolene Switching Locomotive for the Erie*, RAG, 1916, Vol. 61, No. 6, p. 232.

28. Coleman, L. G., Manager, Locomotive Dept., Ingersoll-Rand Co., *Automotive Engines and Cars*, RA, July 1, 1933, 21.

Part Four

1. Basford, G. M., President, Locomotive Feed Water Heater Co., *The Locomotive as an Investment*, ARMMA convention, 1920, reported RA, June 12, 1920, 1743.

Chapter 10

1. Stuebing, A. F., *A Year of Innovations in Locomotive Design*, RA, January 6, 1923, 41.

2. Stuebing, A. F., *The Next Step in Locomotive Construction*, from *Are We Due for a Radical Change in Locomotive Construction?*, New York Railroad Club, January, 1923, abstracted RA, February 3, 1923, 323.

3. *Five-Coupled vs. Mallet Locomotives*, RA, November 26, 1920, 908.

4. Bruce, A. W., Design Engineer, Alco, *The Locomotive Yardstick*, Western Railway Club, Chicago, November, 1927, reported RA, November 26, 1927, 1025. A. W. Bruce would later write one of the major histories of the American steam locomotive, *The Steam Locomotive in America: Its Development in the Twentieth Century*, New York, W. W. Norton, 1952.

5. *Tendencies in Equipment Design*, RA, January 3, 1925, 40.

6. Lipetz, A. I. discussion on Report on Utilization of Locomotives, AARMD convention, 1926, reported RA, June 17, 1926, 1882.

7. Vauclain, S., discussion on Report on Utilization of Locomotives, AARMD convention, 1926, reported RA, June 17, 1926, 1882.

8. Campbell, H. A. F., Assistant to the Consulting Vice-President, Baldwin Locomotive Works, *Suggested Design for a 4,000 h. p. Passenger Locomotive*, RA, October 20, 1923, 707; Basford, G. M., *As to the Locomotive—What Next?* Pacific Railway Club, March, 1923, reported RA, March 10, 1923, 553.

9. Peck, C. B., *Three New Locomotive Types in '25*, RA, January 2, 1926, 47.

10. *The Modern Locomotive—What and Why*, RA, November 21, 1931, 776.

11. Woodard, W. E., Vice-President, Lima Locomotive Works, *Modern Locomotives for Secondary Service*, New England Railroad Club, Boston, April, 1929, abstracted RA, April 20, 1929, 909.

12. *Operation of 2-10-4 Locomotives on T. & P; Lima 2-8-4 Type Locomotive*, report to AARMD convention, 1926, reported RA, June 15, 1926, 1828; Winterrowd, W. H., Vice-President, Lima, *Relation of Locomotive Development to the Cost of Operation*, AARMD convention, 1927, reported RA, June 11, 1927, 1877.

13. *The Modern Locomotive—What and Why*, RA, November 21, 1931, 776.

14. Peck, C. B., *An Era of Intensive Locomotive Development*, RA, January 1, 1927, 49.

15. Vincent, H. S., Franklin Railway Supply Co., *Locomotive Design for Switching and Yard Service*, Central Railway Club, Buffalo, NY, May, 1929, reported RA, May 25, 1929, 1197.

16. J. T. Anthony, Vice-President, American Arch Co., in discussion of Smith, C. B., Mechanical Engineer, Boston & Maine Railroad, *Increasing the Capacity of Old Locomotives*, ASME, December, 1920, abstracted RA, December, 24, 1920, 1115.

17. Foss, C. W., Lyne, J. G., *Lackawanna Success the Result of Supervision*, RA, November 26, 1921, 1027; December 3, 1921, 1097.

18. Basford, G. M., *Vitalizing Locomotives to Improve Operation*, New York Railroad Club, May, 1921, reported RA, May 27, 1921, 1227; Smith, C. B., Mechanical Engineer, Boston & Maine Railroad, *Increasing the Capacity of Old Locomotives*, ASME, December, 1920, abstracted RA, December, 24, 1920, 1115; *Improved Versus Unimproved Locomotives*, RA, December 31, 1920, 1139.

19. *How the Need for More Motive Power Will Be Met*, RA, January 7, 1921, 43; *Practical Reconstruction of Old Locomotives*, RA, January 21, 1921, 237.

20. *Santa Fe Type Locomotive Converted to 4-8-2*, RA, August 1, 1925, 239.

21. Drury, 333; *Track Exhibits of Steam Locomotives at Two Points*, AARMD convention, 1930, reported RA, June 23, 1930, 1548D68.

22. Drury, 196.

23. Elmer, W., Superintendent Middle Division, Pennsylvania Railroad, *Avoiding Waste in the Operation of Locomotives*, ASME, New York, December, 1921, abstracted RA, December 3, 1921, 1081.

24. *Utilization of Locomotives and Conservation of Fuel*, report to AARMD convention, 1929, reported RA, July 6, 1929, 114, contributed discussion by Demarest.

25. *Erie in Promising Position*, RA, October 22, 1927, 768.

26. *Rock Island Has Good Year*, RA, July 7, 1928, 25.

27. *Northern Pacific Earnings Improve*, RA, August 18, 1928, 305.

28. Parmelee, J. H., Director, Bureau of Railway Economics, *A Review of Railway Operations in 1927*, RA, January 7, 1928, 23.

29. Parmelee, J. H., Director, Bureau of Railway Economics, *A Review of Railway Operations in 1927*, RA, January 7, 1928, 23.

30. Peck, C. B., Mechanical Department Editor, "Railway Age," *Progress in Locomotive Design Ahead of Utilization*, RA, January 3, 1931, 31.

Chapter 11

SECTION 11.1

1. Presidential address, International Railway Fuel Association convention, 1924, reported RA, May 31, 1924, 1319.

2. Darling, S. M., *Possibility of Lignite Coals*, Railway Fuel Association convention, 1920, abstracted RA, May 28, 1920, 1509.

3. *Operating and Maintaining Oil Burning Locomotives*, Traveling Engineers' Association, Chicago, September, 1921, abstracted RA, May 20, 1922, 1187.

4. *How to Improve Oil Burning on Locomotives*, report to Traveling Engineers' Association convention, 1924, abstracted RA, September 27, 1924, 555.

5. *Ibid.*

6. Bohnstengel, W., *Santa Fe Locomotive Oil Burning Practice and Fuel Performance*, Railway Fuel Association convention, 1920, abstracted RA, May 28, 1920, 1510.

7. *How to Improve Oil Burning on Locomotives*, report to Traveling Engineers' Association convention, 1924, abstracted RA, September 27, 1924, 555.

8. *Operating and Maintaining Oil-Burning Locomotives*, report to Traveling Engineers' Association convention, 1922, abstracted RA, November 18, 1922, 949.

9. *T. & P. Tests Special Firebox for Oil-Burning Lcomotives*, RA, June 9, 1928, 1324.

10. *Tests of the Martin Circulator*, RA, January 25, 1930, 255.

11. Vincent, H. J., Franklin Railway Supply Co., *Full Gear Versus Limited Cut-Off*, Central Railway Club, Buffalo, NY, May, 1927, abstracted RA, July 30, 1927, 219.

12. Basford, G. M., Lima Locomotive Works, *As to the Locomotive—What Next?*, Pacific Railway Club, March, 1923, reported RA, March 10, 1923, 553.

13. *The Hulson Shaking Dump Grate*, RA, February 4, 1921, 339.

14. *Report on Grates with Restricted Air Openings*, International Railway Fuel Association convention, 1925, abstracted RA, June 6, 1925, 1390.

15. *Hulson Locomotive Tuyere-Type Grate Surface*, RA, June 20, 1923, 1420D35.

16. *Report on Grates with Restricted Air Openings*, International Railway Fuel Association con-

vention, 1925, abstracted RA, June 6, 1925, 1391; *Report on Front Ends, Grates and Ash Pans*, AARMD convention, 1926, abstracted RA, May 22, 1926, 1380.

17. Bjorkholm, J. F., Assistant Superintendent of Motive Power, Chicago, Milwaukee & St. Paul Railroad, *Important Factors in Obtaining Fuel Economy*, RA, August 3, 1929, 345.

18. *T. E. A. Displays Keen Interest in Long Engine Runs*, Traveling Engineers' Association convention, 1922, abstracted RA, November 11, 1922, 901; *Ten Years of Progress in Locomotive Stokers*, RA, March 24, 1923, 797.

19. *Report of Committee on Mechanical Stokers*, RA, June 10, 1920, 1633.

20. Crawford, D. F., Vice-President, Locomotive Stoker Co., *Operating Economy of Stoker Fired Locomotives*, Railway Club of Pittsburgh, abstracted RA, March 5, 1920, 701.

21. RA January 12, 1924, 216.

22. *Stoker Fired Locomotives and the Future Engineman*, Traveling Engineers' Association convention, 1924, reported RA, September 27, 1924, 554.

23. *Ibid.*

24. *Improved Hanna Locomotive Stoker, Type H-2*, RA, February 18, 1922, 431.

25. *The du Pont-Simplex Type Locomotive Stoker*, RA, October 10, 1922, 809.

26. *Du Pont Simplex Type B Stoker*, RA, May 31, 1924, 1327.

27. *Report on Locomotive Construction*, AARMD convention, 1923, reported RA, June 23, 1923, 1591.

28. *The D-4 and D-1-A Duplex Locomotive Stokers*, RA, June 14, 1926, 1791; *Type D-3 Duplex Locomotive Stoker*, RA, June 15, 1926, 1840.

29. *Standard Stoker Engine Placed on the Tender*, RA, July 10, 1926, 64.

30. *Stoker for Installation on Hand-Fired Locomotives*, RA, June 30, 1928, 1420D33.

31. Roesch, F., Sales Manager, Standard Stoker Co., *Locomotive Stoker Development*, RA, October 8 1929, 820.

32. Railway Fuel Association convention, 1924, abstracted RA, May 31, 1924, 1319.

33. Bruce, A. W., Design Engineer, American Locomotive Co., *The Locomotive as a Factor in Fuel Economy*, International Railway Fuel Association convention, 1928, abstracted RA, May 19, 1928, 1153.

34. *Locomotive Condition and Its Effect on Fuel Economy*, RA, June 8, 1929, 1315.

35. Bjorkholm, J. E., Assistant Superintendent of Motive Power, Chicago, Milwaukee, St. Paul & Pacific Railroad, *Important Factors in Obtaining Fuel Economy*, RA, August 3, 1929, 345.

36. Brandt, C. A., The Superheater Co., *The Design and Proportion of Locomotive Boilers*, Canadian Railway Club, February, 1928, reported RA, March 10, 1928, 575.

37. *Report of Committee on Utilization of Locomotives*, AARMD convention, 1928, reported RA, June 23, 1928, 1490D7.

Section 11.2

38. Seley, C. A., Locomotive Firebox Co., *The Paying Weight in Locomotive Boilers*, RA, May 17, 1924, 1216.

39. 'Scientific American,' vol. 248, 139.

40. *Mountain Type Features New Rock Island Power*, RA, February 25, 1921, 447.

41. *Locomotive Service Tests on the N. C. & St. L.*, RA, June 16, 1923, 1425.

42. *Thermic Syphons Used in Combustion Chambers*, RA, March 16, 1926, 819.

43. *A Crown Sheet Failure Without an Explosion*, RA, April 8, 1921, 885.

44. Ringel, C., *History, Development and Function of the Locomotive Brick Arch*, R&LHS, New York, January, 1948, printed Journal R&LHS, October, 1956, 79.

45. Basford, G. M., *Vitalizing Locomotives to Improve Operation*, New York Railroad Club, May, 1921, reported RA, May 27, 1921, 1227.

46. Presidential address, International Railway Fuel Association convention, 1924, reported RA, May 31, 1924, 1319.

47. Plant, L. G., National Boiler Washing Co., *Locomotive Feedwater Heating*, Central Railway Club, Buffalo, NY, February, 1925, abstracted RA, February 21, 1925, 468; *Front Ends, Grates and Ash Pans*, committee report to International Railway Fuel Association convention, 1930, reported RA, May 17, 1930, 1180.

48. Harding, J. W., 2002, vol. 1, 469.

49. Williams, A., *Superheater-Unit Research*, ASME, February, 1941, reported RA, March 29, 1941, 570.

50. *Michigan Central Mikado Has Many Special Features*, RA, September 2, 1922, 411; Sinclair, A.,1907, 208.

51. *Front End Locomotive Throttle Valve*, RA, February 10, 1923, 384.

52. *Report on Locomotive Economy Devices*, International Railway Fuel Association convention, 1927, reported RA, May 21, 1927, 1512.

53. *Front-End Locomotive Throttle Valve*, RA, February 10, 1923, 384; White, J. H., 1997, 145–6.

54. *Multiple Throttle Located in Superheater Header*, RA, June 14, 1926, 1793.

55. Oatley, H. B., Vice-President, The Superheater Company, *The Locomotive Boiler*, RA, July 1, 1933, 25.

56. *The Master Boiler Makers' Convention*, proceedings of annual convention, 1920, reported RA, June 4, 1920, 1579.

57. Peck, C. B., *An Era of Intensive Locomotive Development*, RA, January 1, 1927, 49.

58. *Ibid.*

59. Fry, L. H., ASME, Spring meeting, 1927, reported in *Locomotive Efficiencies*, RA, August 11, 1928, 250.

60. Bruce, A. W., American Locomotive Co., *The Locomotive as a Factor in Fuel Economy*, International Railway Fuel Association convention, 1928, abstracted RA, May 19, 1928, 1153.

61. Smith, V. L., *One Man's Locomotives:50 Years Experience with Railway Motive Power*, Glendale, CA: Trans-Anglo Books, 1987, 82.

62. *Ibid.*

63. *McClellon Water-Tube Boiler Tests*, RA, March 6, 1926, 575.

64. Drury, 290.

65. Stuebing, A. F., *A Year of Innovations in Locomotive Design*, RA, January 6, 1923, 41; *D. & H. Christens New Locomotive*, RA, December

13, 1924, 1071; *What the "Horatio Allen" Is Doing in Service*, RA, January 24, 1925, 279; *D. & H. Christens New Locomotive*, RA, December 13, 1924, 1071.

66. AREA annual general meeting, 1926, report on Locomotive Design and Construction, reported RA, June 15, 1926, 1819.

67. RA March 12, 1927, 893.

68. *Third High-Pressure Locomotive on the D. & H.*, RA, July 26, 1930, 143.

69. *Use of High Steam Pressure in Locomotives*, discussion at ASME annual meeting, 1926, reported RA, January 8, 1927, 196; Fry, L. H., Standard Steel Works Co., *Locomotive 60,000 Test Results*, Western Railway Club, March, 1927, reported RA, March 26, 1927, 975.

70. *French Records for Weight Per Locomotive Horsepower*, RA, September 30, 1922, 617.

71. *Will Compound Locomotives Come Back?* RA, February 23, 1924, 443.

72. *Track Exhibits of Locomotives Shown at Two Points*, RA, June 20, 1928, 1420D12.

73. Drury, 362.

74. Taft, W. J., *Locomotives Ordered in 1935*, RA, January 4, 1936, 71.

75. Drury,45; *Test Locomotives of 4-8-2 and 2-6-6-2 Types on the B. & O.*, RA, July 11, 1931, 46; *Baltimore & Ohio Builds Steam Power for High Speed*, RA, May 4, 1935, 681.

76. *Baltimore & Ohio Builds Steam Power for High Speed*, RA, May 4, 1935, 681.

77. Plant, L. G., National Boiler Washing Co., *Locomotive Feedwater Heating*, Central Railway Club, Buffalo, NY, February, 1925, abstracted RA, February 21, 1925, 468.

78. *Ibid.*

79. Report of Committee on Feed Water Heating, International Railway Fuel Association convention, 1920, reported RA, May 28, 1920, 1508.

80. Harding, J. W., 2002, Vol. 1, 520.

81. Report on Feed-Water Heaters for Locomotives, ARMMA convention, 1920, reported RA, June 12, 1920, 1739.

82. *Ibid.*

83. *Locomotive Feed Water Heating*, Railway Fuel Association convention, 1921, reported RA, May 27, 1921, 235; proceedings of Traveling Engineers' Association convention, Chicago, September, 1921, reported RA, September 17, 1921, 533.

84. *Locomotive Feed Water Heaters*, Railway Fuel Association convention, 1922, reported RA, May 27, 1922, 1235.

85. Stuebing, A. F., *A Year of Innovations in Locomotive Design*, RA, January 6, 1923, 41.

86. *Report on Locomotive Construction*, AARMD convention, 1923, reported RA, June 23, 1923, 1591.

87. Report to International Railway Fuel Association convention, 1924, reported RA, May 31, 1924, 1320.

88. *Report on Boiler Feed Water Heaters*, report to International Railway Fuel Association convention, 1925, reported RA, June 6, 1925, 1391.

89. *Report on Locomotive Economy Devices*, International Railway Fuel Association convention, 1927, reported RA, May 21, 1927, 1512.

90. *Circulating System in the Coffin Feed-Water*

Heater, RA, June 20, 1923, 1420D40; Harding, J. W., 2002, Vol. 1, 557.

91. *Report on Locomotive Design and Construction,* report to AARMD convention, 1929, reported RA, July 6, 1929, 104; compiled statistics.

92. *Locomotive Feed Water Heaters,* report to Traveling Engineers' Association convention, 1923, reported RA, September 22, 1923, 523; Harding, J. W., 2002, Vol. 1, 567.

93. *Report on Locomotive Construction,* discussion on report to AARMD convention, 1923, reported RA, June 23, 1923, 1591.

94. Harding, J. W., 2002, Vol. 1, 567; Topping, B., *The Engine Driver's Manual,* Yeovil, UK: Oxford Co., 1998, 101.

95. *Report on Boiler Feed Water Heaters,* report to International Railway Fuel Association convention, 1925, reported RA, June 6, 1925, 1391.

96. *Sellers Exhaust Feedwater Heater Injector,* RA, June 4, 1927, 1744; Harding, J. W., 2002, Vol. 1, 572.

97. *New Locomotive Economy Devices,* report to International Fuel Association convention, 1929, abstracted RA, May 18, 1929, 1163; *Report on Locomotive Design and Construction,* report to AARMD convention, 1929, reported RA, July 6, 1929, 104.

98. *Report on Locomotive Design and Construction,* report to AARMD convention, 1929, contributed discussion by Demarest, reported RA, July 6, 1929, 104.

99. Davidson, J. H., Water Engineer, Missouri-Kansas-Texas Railroad, *Benefits of Better Water on M-K-T,* RA, September 5, 1925, 445.

100. *Co-operation in the Cab,* RA, February 26, 1927, 553.

101. Pownall, W. A., Mechanical Engineer, Wabash Railway, *Treated Water Improves Locomotive Performance,* RA, March 25, 1922, 794.

102. Koyl, C. H., Chicago, Milwaukee, St. Paul & Pacific Railroad, *Feedwater Heaters Reduce Pitting,* RA, March 17, 1928, 629; Koyl, C. H., Chicago, Milwaukee, St. Paul & Pacific Railroad, *Causes of Boiler Pitting and Means of Prevention in Neutral and Alkaline Waters,* and *The Prevention of Boiler Pitting in Neutral and Alkaline Waters by the Exclusion of Dissolved Oxygen from the Feedwater,* Master Boilermakers' Association convention, 1928, abstracted RA, March 7, 1928, 560-D63.

103. Gunderson, L. O., Chicago & Alton, *The Prevention of Pitting and Corrosion by Electro-Chemical Polarization,* Master Boilermakers' Association convention, 1928, abstracted RA, March 7, 1928, 560-D3; *Chicago & Alton Checks Corrosion in Locomotive Boilers,* RA, April 13, 1929, 828.

104. Plant, L. G., National Boiler Washing Co., *Locomotive Feedwater Heating,* Central Railway Club, Boston, February, 1925, abstracted RA, February 21, 1925, 468; *The Fireless Steaming System at Locomotive Terminals,* RA, July 18, 1925, 146.

105. *Report on Boiler Feed Water Heaters,* report to International Railway Fuel Association convention, 1925, reported RA, June 6, 1925, 1391.

106. *Grand Trunk Western Equips Fireless Enginehouse at Chicago,* RA, April 14, 1928, 861.

107. *Big Four Completes New Terminal at Cincinnati,* RA, October 20, 1928, 749.

108. *Design and Maintenance of Boilers,* report of committee to ARMMA convention, 1920, reported RA, June 12, 1920, 1748; Pack, A. G., Chief Inspector, Bureau of Locomotive Inspection, ICC, *Improved Water Indicating Devices Necessary,* abstracted RA, August 27, 1920, 359.

109. *Report of the Bureau of Locomotive Inspection,* RA, February 24, 1923, 473.

110. *Changes in Nathan Low Water Alarm,* RA, June 15, 1926, 1843; *Annual Report of the Bureau of Locomotive Inspection,* RA, January 14, 1928, 144.

111. *The Master Boiler Makers' Convention,* proceedings of annual convention, 1920, reported RA, June 4, 1920, 1579.

112. *Report of the Bureau of Locomotive Inspection,* RA, February 4, 1922, 331.

113. Partington, J., Manager, Engineering Department, American Locomotive Co., *Welded Locomotive Boiler Construction,* Northwest Locomotive Association, St. Paul, Minnesota, March, 1945, abstracted RA, April 28, 1945, 752.

114. *Bureau of Locomotive Inspection Report,* RA, January 26, 1924, 285.

115. *Annual Report of the Bureau of Locomotive Inspection,* RA, January 17, 1925, 225.

116. *Fusible Plugs Not Essential in Crown Sheets Under Boiler Inspection Act,* RA, January 31, 1925, 337.

117. Wisconsin Boiler Inspectors' Association website, July, 2012.

118. Dougherty, S. A., *Call the Big Hook,* San Marino, CA: Golden West Books, 1984, 37.

119. *Annual Report of Bureau of Locomotive Inspection,* RA, December 14, 1929, 1385.

120. Vauclain, S. M., President, Baldwin Locomotive Works, *Vauclain Discusses Outlook for Diesel Locomotive,* Midwest Power Conference, Chicago January, 1926, abstracted RA, February 6, 1926, 388.

Section 11.3

121. *Three-Cylinder Locomotives on American Railroads,* RA, May 16, 1925, 1197; ASME, Chicago, February, 1926, meeting on three-cylinder locomotives, papers by Pownall, W. A., Wabash Railway, Blunt, J. G., American Locomotive Co., Woodward, E. L., 'Railway Age,' reported RA, February 27, 1926, 527, March 20, 1926, 849.

122. Church, R. J., *Southern Pacific Ten-Coupled Locomotives,* Berkeley, CA: Signature Press, 2013, 164; Drury, 332.

123. Partington, J., *Some Notable Locomotives of Recent Design,* Canadian Railway Club, Montreal, January, 1924, abstracted RA, January 12, 1924, 193; Blunt, J. G., American Locomotive Co., *The Three-Cylinder Locomotive,* AARMD convention, 1924, reported RA, June 13, 1924, 1473.

124. *Three-Cylinder Locomotive on New York Central,* RA, November 3, 1923, 821.

125. *Lehigh Valley Three-Cylinder Locomotive Tests,* RA, March 15, 1924, 755; *Lehigh Valley Three-Cylinder Locomotive,* RA, June 14, 1924, 1585.

126. *Lackawanna Buys Twenty-Five Three-Cylinder Locomotives,* RA, January 15, 1927, 251.

127. *Three-Cylinder Locomotives versus Two-Cylinder Type* in *Report on Locomotive Design and Construction,* AARMD convention, 1927, reported RA, June 11, 1927, 1884.

128. Morgan, D. P., *Louisville & Nashville's Pacifics and Mountains,* Journal R&LHS, October, 1952, 36.

129. Smith, V. L., *One Man's Locomotives: 50 Years Experience with Railway Motive Power,* Glendale, CA: Trans-Anglo Books, 1987, 81.

130. *New Haven Acquires Ten Three-Cylinder Locomotives,* RA, February 26, 1928, 452.

131. *Three-Cylinder Mountain Type Locomotive,* RA, September 4, 1926, 431.

132. *Three Cylinder Locomotives on the Southern Pacific,* RA, January 23, 1925, 283.

133. Fetters, A. H., Chief Engineer, Union Pacific Railroad, in discussion to Blunt, J. G., American Locomotive Co., *The Three-Cylinder Locomotive,* AARMD convention, 1924, reported RA, June 13, 1924, 1473.

134. *Four-Cylinder Locomotive for Express Service in England,* RA, May 7, 1927, 1403; *A New English Express Locomotive,* RA, August 6, 1927, 253.

135. RA June 12, 1924, 1429.

136. *D. M. & I. R. Freight Power,* RA, June 5, 1943, 1135; *The B. & O. 2-8-8-4 Locomotives,* RA, May 27, 1944, 1014.

137. Campbell, H. A. F., *Notes on the Steam Locomotive,* RA, November 5, 1927, 900.

138. Drury, 83.

139. *Operating Tests of a Pacific Type Booster Locomotive,* RA, October 22, 1920, 699; proceedings of Traveling Engineers' Association convention, Chicago, September, 1921, reported RA, September 17, 1921, 533; *Locomotive Boosters—Effect on Design and Train Operations,* Traveling Engineers' Association convention, 1924, reported RA, September 27, 1924, 553.

140. *Dynamometer Tests of the Locomotive Booster,* RA, September 16, 1922, 511.

141. *Booster for Tender Trucks Developed on D. & H.,* RA, July 22, 1922, 145; *Tender Booster Increases Tonnage 31 Per Cent,* RA, June 16, 1923, 1433.

142. Shaughnessy, J., *Delaware & Hudson,* Syracuse, NY: Syracuse University Press, 1997, 324.

143. *Mo. Pac. Tests Power Tender Trucks,* RA, December 17, 1927, 1221; *Franklin Reversible Locomotive Booster,* International Railway Fuel Association convention, 1928, reported RA, May 12, 1928, 1109; *N.& W. Applies Power Tender Trucks for Hump Yard Service,* RA, July 14, 1928, 59.

144. Vincent, H. S., Franklin Railway Supply Co., *Locomotive Design for Switching and Yard Service,* Central Railway Club, Buffalo, NY, May, 1929, reported RA, May 25, 1929, 1197.

145. *Auxiliary Locomotive Tested on the Plant at Altoona,* RA, September 29, 1928, 603.

146. Armstrong, G. W., Bethlehem Steel Co., *Locomotive Auxiliary Power Mediums,* ASME annual meeting, New York, 1929, reported RA, December 21, 1929, 1419.

147. Kiesel, W. F. jr., Mechanical Engineer, Pennsylvania Railroad, *Possibilities of Half Stroke Cut-Off Locomotive,* New York Railroad Club, November, 1923, reported RA, November 17, 1923, 903; Pennsylvania Test Department Bulletin #31; Vincent, H. J., Franklin Railway Supply

Co., *Full Gear Versus Limited Cut-Off*, Central Railway Club, Buffalo, NY, May, 1927, abstracted RA, July 30, 1927, 219.

148. Bruce, A. W., 1952, 98.

149. *Engine Operation Standardized by Pressure Gages*, RA, June 19, 1926, 1903.

150. *Report on Locomotive Design and Construction*, report to AARMD convention, 1929, reported RA, July 6, 1929, 104.

151. Davidson, J. L., *Scientific Cut-Off Control Improves Locomotive Performance*, RA, July 15, 1933, 111; Harding, J. W., 2002, Vol. 2, 92.

152. Peterson, R. A., *Hogger: From Fantasy to Fulfillment, a Locomotive Engineer Remembers*, Lincoln, NE: iUniverse, 2003, 55.

153. Pearce, E. S., Cleveland, Cincinnati, Chicago & St. Louis Railroad, *The Automatic Control of Locomotive Cutoff*, RA, June 24, 1921, 1451.

154. *Automatic Cut-Off Control Tested in Service*, RA, April 26, 1924, 1033.

SECTION 11.4

155. *What Are the Most Suitable Draft Appliances?*, report to Traveling Engineers' Association convention, 1920, reported RA, September 24, 1920, 521.

156. Report on Front Ends, Grates and Ash Pans to International Railway Fuel Association annual convention, 1922, abstracted RA, May 27, 1922, 1237.

157. Pilcher, J. A., Norfolk & Western Railway, discussion of committee report to ARA convention, 1920, reported RA, June 11, 1920, 1705; *What Are the Most Suitable Draft Appliances?* report to Traveling Engineers' Association convention, 1920, reported RA, September 24, 1920, 521.

158. Milner, B. B., New York Central System, discussion of committee report to ARA convention, 1920, reported RA, June 11, 1920, 1705; *What Are the Most Suitable Draft Appliances?*, report to Traveling Engineers' Association convention, 1920, reported RA, September 24, 1920, 521.

159. Report on Front Ends, Grates and Ash Pans to International Railway Fuel Association annual convention, 1920, abstracted RA, May 28, 1920, 1511.

160. *Ibid.*

161. Report on Front Ends, Grates and Ash Pans to International Railway Fuel Association annual convention, 1920, abstracted RA, May 28, 1920, 1511; *The Lewis Draft Appliance*, RA, June 4, 1920, 1582.

162. *Southern Pacific Oil-Burning Drafting Apparatus*, report to International Railway Fuel Association convention, 1924, reported RA, June 14, 1924, 1514.

163. Committee report to ARA convention, 1920, reported RA, June 11, 1920, 1705.

164. *Locomotive Drafting Tests*, RA, September 1, 1928, 399; *Front Ends, Grates and Ash Pans*, report to International Railway Fuel Association convention, 1929, reported RA, May 18, 1929, 1163.

165. *Missouri-Pacific Tests Three-Cylinder Locomotive*, RA, June 27, 1925, 1624.

166. *Further Proceedings of the Fuel Association*, International Railway Fuel Association annual convention, 1924, reported RA, June 14, 1924, 1513.

167. *Mechanical Draft*, papers read at International Railway Fuel Association convention, 1924, reported RA, June 14, 1924, 1513.

168. Coppus, F. H. C., Coppus Engineering Corp., *The Mechanical Drafting of Locomotives*, ASME annual meeting, 1922, reported RA, December 9, 1922, 1099.

169. *Forced Draft Through Closed Ash Pans in Locomotives*, RA, July 9, 1927, 63.

170. Goss, W. F. M., *The Next Step in the Development of Locomotive Drafting*, RA, June 11, 1927, 1900.

SECTION 11.5

171. Basford, G. M., President, Locomotive Feed Water Heater Co., *The Locomotive as an Investment*, RA, June 12, 1920, 1743.

172. *Effect of Locomotive Counterbalancing on Stresses in Rails*, RA, April 2, 1920, 1084; *A Scientific Study of Railway Track Under Load*, RA, March 5, 1920, 670.

173. Campbell, H. A. F.., Assistant to the Consulting Vice-President, Baldwin Locomotive Works, *Modern Counterbalance Conditions*, RA, November 3, 1928, 881.

174. Campbell, H. A. F., Assistant to the Consulting Vice-President, Baldwin Locomotive Works, *Counterbalancing Heavy Locomotives*, letter published RA, April 10, 1926, 1000; *Modern Counterbalance Conditions*, RA, November 3, 1928, 881.

175. Ripley, C. T., Chief Mechanical Engineer, Atchison, Topeka & Santa Fe Railway, *Some Important Details* in *The Locomotive of Today—a Symposium Conducted by Samuel O. Dunn*, reported RA, September 18, 1926, 492.

176. *High-Test Vanadium Steel Locomotive Frames*, RA, June 16, 1923, 1477.

177. Sheehan, W. H., General Steel Castings Corp., Eddystone, Pennsylvania, *Steel Castings and the Railroad*, New York Railroad Club, January, 1938, abstracted RA, February 5, 1938, 267.

178. *One-Piece Engine Bed*, RA, September 4, 1926, 422; *Integral Cylinder and Frame Casting, Rivetless Tank*, RA, October 30, 1926, 848; RA, November 26, 1956, 12.

179. Harding, J. W., 2002, Part 1, 75–91.

180. Woodard, W. E., Vice-President, Lima Locomotive Works, *Locomotive Designs to Reduce Maintenance*, International Railway Fuel Association convention, May, 1928, reported RA, June 16, 1928, 1375.

Chapter 12

1. *Adequate Motive Power for Railroads a Necessity*, RA, January 2, 1920, 33; *Few Railroad Orders for Locomotives in 1919*, RA, January 2, 1920, 125.

2. RA February 27, 1920, 652.

3. *How the Need for More Motive Power Will Be Met*, RA, January 7, 1921, 48.

4. *Locomotive Orders Show Increase in 1920*, RA, January 7, 1921, 135.

5. *Locomotives Ordered in 1929*, RA, January 4, 1930, 78.

SECTION 12.1

6. *Pennsylvania Ten-Wheel Passenger Locomotive*, RA, November 10, 1923, 859; Drury, 328.

7. *Maine Central Purchases Ten-Wheel Locomotives*, RA, March 8, 1924, 555.

8. *New Locomotives for the Northern Pacific*, RA, October 22, 1921, 767.

9. *Chicago Great Western "English Type" Locomotive*, RA, October 2, 1926, 643; Drury, 109.

10. *The Baltimore & Ohio's "President" Class Locomotives*, RA, April 9, 1927, 1121.

11. Drury, 47.

12. *D. & H. Pacific Type Locomotive*, RA, July 20, 1929, 201.

13. *Fast Running on the Great Western in England*, RA, July 23, 1932, 111.

14. Peck, C. B., *An Era of Intensive Locomotive Development*, RA, January 1, 1927, 49.

15. *Passenger and Switching Locomotives for the C. R. R. of N. J.*, RA, March 3, 1928, 540.

16. *Pacific 4-6-2 Types on the New Jersey Central*, RA, February 21, 1931, 413; Drury, 76.

17. *Pacific Type Locomotives for the Rutland*, RA, February 15, 1930, 437; Drury, 336.

18. *New Mountain Type Locomotives for Fast Freight*, RA, October 8, 1920, 609; Drury, 290.

19. *Mountain Type Features New Rock Island Power*, RA, February 25, 1921, 447.

20. Drury, 130.

21. *New Locomotives for the Missouri Pacific*, RA, September 10, 1921, 495.

22. Drury, 252.

23. *A Mountain Type Locomotive for High Capacity*, RA, June 10, 1922, 1325; *Service Records of U. P. Mountain Type Locomotives*, RA, October 14, 1922, 687; Stuebing, A. F., *A Year of Innovations in Locomotive Design*, RA, January 6, 1923, 41.

24. *Mountain Type Locomotive for Great Northern*, RA, December 8, 1923, 1065.

25. *Heavy 4-8-2 Type Southern Pacific Locomotives*, RA, February 9, 1924, 375.

26. *Mountain Type Locomotives for the Pennsylvania*, RA, November 20, 1926, 989.

27. Drury, 328.

28. RA October 12, 1929, 880; Drury, 328; *Track Exhibits of Steam Locomotives at Two Points*, AARMD convention, 1930, reported RA, June 23, 1930, 1548D68.

29. *4-8-2 Type Locomotives for the Missouri Pacific*, RA, November 5, 1927, 891.

30. *Ten 4-8-2 Type Locomotives for the N. Y. O. & W.*, RA, November 30, 1929, 1281.

31. *Freight Locomotives for the Bangor & Aroostook*, RA, March 15, 1930, 635; Drury, 48.

32. *First Hudson Type Locomotive*, RA, February 19, 1927, 523; Kiefer, P. W., Chief Engineer Motive Power and Rolling Stock, New York Central System, *High-Capacity Steam Passenger Locomotives*, ASME semi-annual meeting, June 1941, Kansas City, Missouri, abstracted RA, August 16, 1941, 273, September 6, 1941, 376; Drury, 278–9.

33. *Track Exhibits of Locomotives Shown at Two Points*, RA, June 20, 1928, 1420D12.

34. *New N.Y.C. Locomotives Show High Power Concentration*, RA, April 2, 1938, 597.

35. Drury, 279.

36. *The Northern Pacific 4-8-4 Type Locomotives*, RA, April 23, 1927, 1239.

37. Drury, 318.

38. *Santa Fe 4-8-4 Type Meets Expectations*, RA, June 2, 1928, 1279; Drury, 27.

39. *Lackawanna Buys Five 4-8-4 Type Locomotives*, RA, December 3, 1927, 1121.

40. Drury, 153.

41. *Rock Island Buys 4-8-4 Type Locomotives*, RA, December 7, 1929, 1325.

42. Drury, 126, 130.

43. *D. & R. G. W. Buys Ten 4-8-4 Type Locomotives*, RA, August 24, 1929, 457.

44. *Great Northern Buys Six 4-8-4 Type Passenger Locomotives*, RA, November 9, 1929, 1097.

45. Drury, 195–6; *4-8-4 Type Locomotives for Passenger Service*, RA, April 26, 1930, 965.

SECTION 12.2

46. *Consolidation Locomotives for the Western Maryland*, RA, May 13, 1920, 1117.

47. *Powerful Consolidation Locomotive for the L. & N. E.*, RA, December 23, 1922, 1197.

48. Drury, 146.

49. *Reading Consolidation Type Locomotive*, RA, July 5, 1924, 19; Drury, 330.

50. *Decapod Locomotives for the Western Maryland*, RA, June 25, 1927, 2007.

51. *Heavy Santa Fe Locomotives for B. & O.*, RA, February 16, 1924, 413.

52. Drury, 47.

53. *2-10-2 Type Replace Mallets on Great Northern*, RA, February 23, 1924, 459.

54. Drury, 19.

55. *Union Pacific Type Locomotive*, RA, May 15, 1926, 1295; *Union Pacific Type Locomotive Performance*, RA, December 25, 1926, 1265; Brandt, C. A., *The Design and Proportion of Locomotive Boilers*, Canadian Railway Club, February, 1928, reported RA, March 10, 1928, 575.

56. Swengel, F. M., *The American Steam Locomotive*, Davenport, IA: Midwest Rail Publications, 1967, 223.

57. *New Locomotives for the Missouri Pacific*, RA, September 10, 1921, 495.

58. *2-8-2 Type Locomotives for the Nickel Plate*, RA, November 19, 1921, 1002.

59. *A Remarkable Mikado on the Michigan Central*, RA, July 22, 1922, 171; *Michigan Central Mikado Has Many Special Features*, RA, September 2, 1922, 411; *Performance of Lima Locomotive No. 8000*, RA, February 7, 1925, 373.

60. *Lima Builds 2-8-4 Type Locomotive*, RA, May 2, 1925, 1077; Butler, F. A., Superintendent Motive Power and Rolling Stock, Boston & Albany Railroad, *Tests of 2-8-4 Locomotive on B. & A.*, RA, September 12, 1925, 467.

61. Woodard, W. E., Vice-President, Lima Locomotive Works, *Research Related to Locomotive Development*, RA, July 1, 1933, 24.

62. Woodard, W. E., Vice-President, Lima Locomotive Works, *Recent Locomotive Developments*, Western Railway Club, Chicago, December, 1926, reported RA, December 25, 1926, 1268.

63. *2-8-4 Locomotives for the Illinois Central*, RA, December 11, 1926, 1161.

64. *Erie Places 2-8-4 Type Locomotives in Freight Service*, RA, October 22, 1927, 777; *2-8-4 Type Locomotives for the Chicago & North Western*, RA, November 19, 1927, 989.

65. Drury, 27.

66. Harwood, H. H., *Corporate History of the Lehigh Valley R. R.*, Journal R&LHS, April, 1972, 5.

67. *Erie Acquires 2-8-4 Locomotives for Freight Service*, RA, October 8, 1927, 669.

68. *Boston & Maine Acquires Twenty 2-8-4 Type Locomotives*, RA, July 28, 1928, 144.

69. *First Texas Type Locomotives for T. & P.*, RA, December 19, 1925, 1143; *Texas Type Locomotives Show Marked Fuel Economy*, RA, July 17, 1926, 101; *Report on Locomotive Economy Devices*, report to International Railway Fuel Association convention, 1927, reported RA, May 21, 1927, 1511; *Performance of Texas Type Locomotives*, RA, June 27, 1928, 1490D128.

70. Lanning, H. H., Atchison, Topeka & Santa Fe Railway, discussion of Winterrowd, W. H., Assistant to President, Lima Locomotive Works, *Engineering and Business Considerations of the Steam Locomotive*, ARMMA convention, 1924, reported RA, June 13, 1924, 1468; Drury, 19.

71. *Burlington Freight Engine Shows Marked Economies*, RA, June 23, 1928, 1425.

72. *Simple Mallets for the Chesapeake & Ohio*, RA, April 12, 1924, 927.

73. Drury, 88.

74. *Great Northern Acquires Mallet Locomotives*, RA, August 22, 1925, 359; Blanchard, H., Manager, Baldwin Locomotive Works, *Service of Simple Mallets*, "Baldwin Locomotives," July, 1926, reproduced RA, June 12, 1926, 1673.

75. *Handling Fourteen Thousand Ton Trains*, RA, September 27, 1930, 609.

76. *Ten 2-8-8-2 Type Locomotives for the D. & R. G. W.*, RA, September 3, 1927, 435.

77. Ahern, T., Division Superintendent, Southern Pacific Lines, *The Problems of Winter Operation In the Sierra Nevadas*, Pacific Railway Club, February 1925, abstracted RA, February 14, 1925, 425.

78. *Southern Pacific Simple Articulated Locomotive*, RA, December 15, 1928, 1181.

79. *World's Largest Locomotive Built for the Northern Pacific*, RA, December 29, 1928, 1295; Drury, 312.

80. *Great Northern Adds to 2-8-8-2 Type Motive Power*, RA, December 28, 1929, 1477.

SECTION 12.3

81. *Heavy Ten-Wheel Locomotives for Switching Service*, RA, January 30, 1920, 359.

82. *Pennsylvania Builds Eight-wheel Switching Locomotive*, RA, July 25, 1925, 195.

83. *A New Switching Locomotive*, RA, July 23, 1927, 153.

84. *Eight-Wheel Switch Engine with Large Boiler Capacity*, RA, August 6, 1927, 265.

85. *Eight-Wheel Switchers for B. & M.*, RA, February 4, 1928, 325.

86. Swengel, F. M., *The American Steam Locomotive*, Davenport, IA: Midwest Rail Publications, 1967, 185.

Chapter 13

1. Coleman, L. G., Assistant General Manager, Boston & Maine Railroad, *Advantages of Diesel Electric Locomotives*, New England Railway Club, January, 1923, abstracted RA, January 20, 1923, 241.

2. RA February 27, 1926, 538.

SECTION 13.1

3. Armstrong, A. H., Railway and Traction Engineering Dept., General Electric Co., *A Comparison of Electric and Steam Motive Power: From Which It Would Appear That the Steam Locomotive Has About Outlived Its Usefulness*, AIEE, Schenectady, NY, February, 1920, reported RA, February 20, 1920, 521.

4. Muhlfeld, J. E., *Advantages of Electric Locomotives Have Been Greatly Overstated*, AIEE/ASME joint meeting, New York, October, 1920, reported RA, October 29, 1920, 739.

5. Smith, H. K., Westinghouse Electric & Manufacturing Co., *The Virginian Railway Electrification*, RA, June 7, 1924, 1353.

6. *Track Exhibits of Locomotives Shown at Two Points*, RA, June 20, 1928, 1420D12; Barriger, J. W., President, Chicago, Indianapolis & Louisville Railway, *Super-Power for Super-Railroads*, Railway Fuel and Traveling Engineers' Association, Car Department Officers' Association, Master Boiler Makers' Association, Locomotive Maintenance Officers' Association, Air Brake Association joint annual meeting, 1947, reported RA, September 20, 1947 (476) 52.

7. RA November 3, 1928, 870.

SECTION 13.2

8. Partington, J., Estimating Engineer, American Locomotive Co., *Modern Tendencies in Locomotive Design*, ASME, Newport News, Virginia, April, 1922, abstracted RA, April 15, 1922, 909.

9. Stuebing, A. F., *A Year of Innovations in Locomotive Design*, RA, January 6, 1923, 41.

10. *Burlington Gas-Electrics Cut Operating Costs*, RA, February 28, 1931, 439.

11. *Tendencies in Equipment Design*, RA, January 3, 1925, 40.

12. Stuebing, A. F., *The Next Step in Locomotive Construction*, from *Are We Due for a Radical Change in Locomotive Construction?*, New York Railroad Club, January, 1923, abstracted RA, February 3, 1923, 323; *The Diesel-Electric Locomotive*, joint meeting of engineering societies, New York, February, 1926, reported RA, March 13, 1926, 809.

13. *Tendencies in Equipment Design*, RA, January 3, 1925, 40.

14. Reck, F. M., *On Time*, Electro-Motive Division, General Motors Co., 1949, reviewed RA, April 23, 1949 (835) 45.

15. *Electro-Motive Silver Anniversary*, RA, November 1, 1947, 26 (726.)

16. Katte, E. B., New York Central System, *Characteristics of the Oil Engine Locomotive*, ASME, New York, April, 1925, reported RA, July 11, 1925, 88.

17. *Motive Power 1900–1950*, RA, October 28, 1950, 154.

18. *Locomotive Exhibit Shows Development*, RA, June 14, 1926, 1773; Peck, C. B., *An Era of Intensive Locomotive Development*, RA, January 1, 1927, 49.

19. Bentley, H. T., in discussion of Report on Utilization of Locomotives, ARMMA convention, 1926, reported RA, June 17, 1926, 1882; *Erie Cuts Tops Off Hills with Diesels*, RA, August 16, 147, 62 (286.)

20. *Tabulation and Specifications of Oil-Electric Locomotives*, ARMMA convention, 1927, reported RA, June 11, 1927, 1890.

21. *Track Exhibits of Locomotives Shown at Two Points*, RA, June 20, 1928, 1420D12.

22. Peck, C. B., Mechanical Department Editor, "Railway Age," *The Year's Trend in Equipment Development*, RA, January 4, 1930, 39; *Canadian National Demonstrates High-Power Oil Locomotive*, RA, September 27, 1929, 585.

23. RA August 29, 1931, 327.

24. Candee, A. H., Westinghouse Electric & Manufacturing Co., *Why the Diesel Engine Is a Good Railroad Tool*, New York Railroad Club, October 1935, abstracted RA, October 26, 1925, 522.

25. *Electro-Motive Silver Anniversary*, RA, November 1, 1947, 26 (726.)

Chapter 14

1. *The Locomotive of Tomorrow*, Traveling Engineers' Association convention, 1930, reported RA, October 4, 1930, 685.

2. Black, R. A., Engineer of Transportation, Canadian National Railway, *Operating Methods Affect Fuel*, RA, August 22, 1931, 280.

3. Peck, C. B., Mechanical Department Editor, 'Railway Age,' *Progress in Locomotive Design Ahead of Utilization*, RA, January 3, 1931, 31.

4. Dickerman, W. C., President, American Locomotive Co., *Modern Trends in Motive Power*, New York Railroad Club, April, 1933, abstracted RA, April 29, 1933, 620; Winterrowd, W. H., Vice-President, Franklin Railway Supply Co., *Research and Steam Locomotive Development*, AARMD convention, 1937, reported RA, June 18, 1937, 1004D82.

5. *High-Pressure Condensing Steam Locomotive Design*, report of Committee on Steam-Turbine and Condensing Locomotives to International Railway Fuel Association 1933 yearbook, reported RA, September 30, 1933, 465.

6. Winterrowd, W. H., Vice-President, Franklin Railway Supply Co., *Importance of Modern Locomotives to Railroad Income Account*, Toronto Railway Club, May, 1934, abstracted RA, June 2, 1934, 802.

7. *Research Has Contributed to Locomotive Fuel Economy*, International Railway Fuel Association, Chicago, September, 1934, abstracted RA, October 6, 1934, 399.

8. *The Future of the Steam Locomotive*, RA, October 6, 1934, 393.

9. Woodard, W. E., Vice-President, Lima Locomotive Works, *Steam Locomotive for Light, High-Speed Passenger Trains*, RA, September 29, 1934, 370.

10. Drury, 68, 70.

11. Quoted in Davenport, J. E., Vice-President of Engineering, Development and Research, American Locomotive Co., *A Look at Tomorrow's Power*, Western Railway Club, April, 1944, reported RA, May 6, 1944, 851.

12. *Steam Turbine and Condensing Locomotive*, RA, September 28, 1935, 403.

13. Lipetz, A., Chief Consulting Engineer, American Locomotive Co., *Power Plant on Wheels*, Metropolitan Power Plants Committee,

New York, March, 1936, abstracted RA, June 6, 1936, 910.

14. *Motive Power—Now and Post-War*, RA, November 20, 1943, 826.

15. Kiefer, P. W., Chief Engineer Motive Power and Rolling Stock, New York Central System, *High-Capacity Steam Passenger Locomotives*, ASME semi-annual meeting, June 1941, Kansas City, Missouri, abstracted RA, August 16, 1941, 273, September 6, 1941, 376; Chapman, E. E., Atchison, Topeka & Santa Fe Railway, *Steam vs. Diesel-Electric Power*, ASME, Kansas City, Missouri, June, 1941, reported RA, July 26, 1941, 149.

16. Johnson, R. P., Chief Engineer, Baldwin Locomotive Works, *Pennsylvania Tests Duplex Locomotive*, RA, May 26, 1945, 925, abstracted from paper to New York Railway Club, May, 1945.

17. Stanier, W. A., Chief Mechanical Engineer, London, Midland & Scottish Railway, *Status of the Steam Locomotive in Great Britain*, Institution of Mechanical Engineers, October, 1941, reported RA, February 21, 1942, 415, February 28, 1942, 445.

18. Johnson, R. P., Chief Engineer, Baldwin Locomotive Works, ASME, 1945, quoted in Wilcox, H. C., *Variety in Motive Power Promised by Developments of the Future*, RA, January 5, 1946, 28.

19. Ryan, J. L., Mechanical Engineer, St. Louis-San Francisco Railway, *Suggestions for the Improvement of Steam Locomotives*, Railroad Division, ASME, Milwaukee, Wisconsin, June, 1940, abstracted RA, July 20, 1940, 106.

20. *The "Doctors" Were Wrong*, RA, June 8, 1940, 1000.

21. Peck, C. B., Mechanical Department Editor, 'Railway Age,' *The Year's Trend in Equipment Development*, RA, January 4, 1930, 39; Dickerman, W. C., President, American Locomotive Co., *Possibilities of the Modern Steam Locomotive*, Western Railway Club, Chicago, April, 1938, abstracted RA, May 7, 1938, 796.

22. RA January 20, 1934, 12.

23. *Large Motive Power Units Feature Track Exhibit*, RA, June 16, 1937, 1004D15.

24. *Turbine Locomotive Design Proposed*, report of Committee on Steam Turbine and Steam Condensing Locomotives to Railway Fuel and Traveling Engineers' Association convention, 1937, abstracted RA, November 13, 1937, 677.

25. Sillcox, L. K., First Vice-President, The New York Air Brake Co., *Steam or Diesel-Electrics?* paper for transportation engineering students, Yale University, March, 1939, abstracted RA, March 18, 1939, 459.

26. *What Will the Atomic Locomotive Be Like?* RA, June 14, 1954, 58.

27. Winterrowd, W. H., Vice-President, Franklin Railway Supply Co., *Research and Steam Locomotive Development*, AARMD convention, 1937, reported RA, June 18, 1937, 1004D82.

28. *Mechanical Division Reports Presented at General Committee Meeting*, RA, July 9, 1938, 45.

29. Davenport, J. E., Vice-President of Engineering, Development and Research, American Locomotive Co., *A Look at Tomorrow's Power*, Western Railway Club, April, 1944, reported RA, May 6, 1944, 851; Drury, 324, 328.

30. *What Horsepower for 1,000-Ton Passenger Trains?* report on AAR passenger locomotive tests, October, 1938, issued by AARMD, February, 1939, abstracted RA, April 22, 1939, 699.

31. *Report on Further Development of Reciprocating Steam Locomotive*, AARMD annual meeting, 1939, reported RA, July 1, 1939, 34.

32. Bjorkholm, J., Assistant Superintendent of Motive Power, Chicago, Milwaukee, St. Paul & Pacific Railroad, *What the Railroads Are Doing to Prevent Smoke*, Smoke Prevention Association, Milwaukee, Wisconsin, June, 1939, abstracted RA, August 5, 1939, 213.

33. *What Motive Power for Modern Freight Trains?* RA, May 24, 1941, 926; *Motive Power for Higher Speeds*, RA, November 22, 1941, 858.

34. *"Victory" Locomotive is Christened*, RA, September 5, 1942, 366.

35. *New Life for the War Emergency*, RA, March 13, 1943, 510; Drury, 47.

36. Morgan, D. P., *Louisville & Nashville's Pacifics and Mountains*, Journal R&LHS, October, 1952, 36.

37. *C. R. I. & P. Steam Power Breaks Records*, RA, May 12, 1945, 830; Drury, 130.

38. *Motive Power—Now and Post-War*, RA, November 20, 1943, 826; *Passenger Power for the Future*, RA, November 18, 1944, 767.

39. Buckwalter, T. V., Vice-President, Timken Roller Bearing Co., *Steam Locomotive Has Important Advantages*, letter printed RA, April 24, 1943, 833.

40. *Equipment and Supplies: Post-War Locomotive Demand Seen by Duncan W. Fraser*, RA, February 12, 1944, 369.

41. Ireland, R. L., President, Hanna Coal Co., *Competition and the Coal Situation*, Railway Fuel and Traveling Engineers' Association, Chicago, September, 1946, reported RA, September 38, 1946, 508.

42. Young, C. D., Deputy Director, Office of Defense Transportation, *Factors in Motive Power Selection*, ASME, New York, December, 1943, abstracted RA, December 11, 1943, 930.

43. *War's Lessons Shape Motive Power Future*, RA, May 19, 1945, 886.

44. *Passenger Power for the Future*, RA, November 18, 1944, 767.

45. Petersen, R. A., *Hogger. From Fantasy to Fulfillment: A Locomotive Engineer Remembers*, New York: iUniverse, 2003, 54.

46. *Reliable Motive Power*, RA, October 26, 1946, 672.

47. Johnson, R. P., Chief Engineer, Baldwin Locomotive Works, *A Look at the Coming Locomotive*, Pittsburgh Railway Club, November, 1944, abstracted RA, November 25, 1944, 810.

48. *War's Lessons Shape Motive Power Future*, RA, May 19, 1945, 886.

49. *Checking Up Locomotive Efficiency*, RA, November 5, 1920, 779.

50. Wilcox, H. C., Associate Editor, 'Railway Age,' *Variety in Motive Power Promised by Developments of the Future*, RA, January 5, 1946, 28, quoting Johnson, R. P., Chief Engineer, Baldwin Locomotive Works, paper presented to ASME, December, 1945.

51. *Heavy or Light?* RA, May 18, 1946, 986.

52. *What Is LDC?* RA, March 5, 1956, 39.

53. Barriger, J. W., President, Chicago, Indi-

anapolis & Louisville Railway, *Super-Power for Super-Railroads,* Railway Fuel and Traveling Engineers' Association, Car Department Officers' Association, Master Boiler Makers' Association, Locomotive Maintenance Officers' Association, Air Brake Association joint annual meeting, 1947, reported RA, September 20, 1947 (476) 52.

54. *Refinement of Existing Designs Will Produce Tomorrow's Power,* RA, November 17, 1945, 802.

55. Pond, C. E., Assistant Superintendent Motive Power, Norfolk & Western Railway, *Modern Power on the Norfolk & Western,* Southern & Southwestern Railway Club, Atlanta, May, 1946, abstracted RA, August 24, 1946, 335.

56. *L. & N. Steam-Diesel Team Cuts Costs,* RA, September 10, 1949, 58 (458.)

57. *The Western Maryland Joins The "Century Club,"* RA, May 12, 1952, 53.

58. RA April 2, 1949, 708; RA, March 18, 1950, 566.

59. Kiefer, P. W., Chief Engineer Motive Power and Rolling Stock, New York Central System, *An Evaluation of Railroad Motive Power,* RA, August 23, 1947 (323) 43, August 30, 1947 (359) 41.

60. *Locomotive Construction Report,* RA, June 25, 1947, 1294D130.

61. Barriger, J. W., President, Chicago, Indianapolis & Louisville Railway, *Super-Power for Super-Railroads,* Railway Fuel and Traveling Engineers' Association, Car Department Officers' Association, Master Boiler Makers' Association, Locomotive Maintenance Officers' Association, Air Brake Association joint annual meeting, 1947, reported RA, September 20, 1947 (476) 52.

62. Parmelee, J. H., Director, Bureau of Railway Economics, *A Review of Railway Operations in 1949,* RA, January 7, 1950, 200 (46.)

63. RA September 10, 1951, 57.

64. RA February 18, 1952, 12.

65. RA April 28, 1952, 13.

66. RA September 8, 1952, 12.

67. RA September 17, 1951, 70.

68. RA December 14, 1953, 13.

69. RA May 9, 1955, 8.

70. RA October 20, 1958, 33.

71. *No Gain in Storing Locomotives For War, Says Alco President,* RA, May 7, 1949, 62 (930.)

72. *French Roads Consider Construction of Three-Cylinder Compounds,* RA, September 27, 1947 (535) 57.

73. *Alco Production Now 100 Per Cent Diesel-Electric,* RA, June 19, 1948, 1225.

74. Bruce, A. W., 1952, 94.

75. Wardale, D., *The Red Devil and Other Tales From the Age of Steam,* privately published, Inverness, UK, 1998, 418.

76. Wardale, D., 1998.

Chapter 15

SECTION 15.1

1. Yellott, J. I., Kottcamp, C. F., Bituminous Coal Research Inc., *Coal and the Gas-Turbine Locomotive,* RA, June 25, 1947, 1294D122.

2. Ireland, R. L., President, Hanna Coal Co., *Competition and the Coal Situation,* Railway Fuel and Traveling Engineers' Association, Chicago, September, 1946, reported RA, September 38, 1946, 508.

3. Quoted in Weihofen, G. J., *Fuel and Future Motive-Power Selection,* RA, January 8, 1949, 180 (84.)

4. *Union Pacific Makes Service Tests of Firebar Grates,* RA, November 18, 1933, 719.

5. *Welding Assists in the Building of C. & O. Locomotives,* RA, August 29, 1942, 333.

6. Pownall, W. A., *Wabash Tests Effect of Front-End and Grate Design,* RA, July 8, 1933, 84.

7. Partington, J., Manager, Engineering Department, American Locomotive Co., *Modern Locomotive Design and Smoke Prevention,* Central Railway Club, Buffalo, NY, March, 1938, reported RA, March 19, 1938, 488.

8. Roesch, F. P., Vice-President, Standard Stoker Co, *Conditions Required to Burn Screenings Successfully,* Western Society of Engineers, November, 1941, reported RA, December 6, 1941, 950.

9. *Air Preheater for Locomotive Fireboxes,* RA, June 29, 1935, 1041.

10. *Bituminous Coal Research Develops Locomotive Smoke Consumer,* RA, September 29, 1945, 518.

11. Matzke, W. W., Assistant to Vice-President, Mechanical, Chicago & North Western Railway, *Smoke Abatement on the North Western,* Union League Club of Chicago, April, 1948, reported RA, May 29, 1948 (1071) 33.

12. *Lower Class Four Locomotive Stoker,* RA, June 23, 1930, 1548D84.

13. *Standard Type B-T Stoker,* RA, June 23, 1930, 1548D86.

14. *Locomotive Stoker Of Small Capacity,* RA, June 18, 1932, 1029.

15. Bjorkholm, J., Assistant Superintendent of Motive Power, Chicago, Milwaukee, St. Paul & Pacific Railroad, *What the Railroads Are Doing to Prevent Smoke,* Smoke Prevention Association, Milwaukee, June, 1939, abstracted RA, August 5, 1939, 213.

16. *Enginemen Ask I.C.C.to Require Mechanical Stokers,* RA, March 28, 1931, 651.

17. *I. C. C. Would Require Stokers on Big Locomotives,* September 25, 1937, 415; *I. C. C. Issues Stoker Order,* RA, January 8, 1938, 115.

18. *The 1944 Locomotive Inspection Report,* RA, January 27, 1945, 227.

19. Purcell, J., Assistant to Vice-President, Atchison, Topeka & Santa Fe Railway, *How Can a Mechanical Officer Effect Fuel Economy?* Railway Fuel Association convention, 1925, abstracted RA, June 6, 1925, 1389.

20. Giger, W., Chief Engineer, Traction Engineering Department, Brown, Boveri & Co., *Proposed Gas Turbine Locomotives,* ASME, New York, May, 1946, reported RA, June 8, 1946, 1135.

21. *Diesel Fuel-Cost Showing Dropped,* RA, April 23, 1956, 13.

SECTION 15.2

22. *What Motive Power for Modern Freight Trains?* RA, May 24, 1941, 926.

23. *Why Locomotive Boilers Foam,* RA, August 12, 1944, 268.

24. Peck, C.B., Mechanical Department Editor, 'Railway Age,' *The Year's Trend in Equipment Development,* RA, January 4, 1930, 39.

25. *Report of Committee on Locomotive Construction,* AARMD convention, 1937, reported RA, June 18, 1937, 1004D90.

26. *Pacific Type Locomotive Equipped with Poppet Valves,* RA, March 29, 1930, 767.

27. Oatley, H. B., Vice-President, The Superheater Company, *Superheat Versus Steam Pressure,* RA, October 16, 1937, 531

28. Partington, J., Manager, Engineering Department, American Locomotive Co., *Modern Locomotive Design and Smoke Prevention,* Central Railway Club, Buffalo, New York, March, 1938, reported RA, March 19, 1938, 488.

29. *Development of the Multi-Pressure Locomotive,* RA, August 27, 1932, 290.

30. *Development of the Multi-Pressure Locomotive,* RA, August 27, 1932, 290; RA, September 3, 1932, 328.

31. Peck, C.B., Mechanical Department Editor, 'Railway Age,' *The Year's Trend in Equipment Development,* RA, January 4, 1930, 39; Drury, 143; *Third High-Pressure Locomotive on the D. & H.,* RA, July 26, 1930, 143.

32. *Delaware & Hudson Develops Fourth High-Pressure Locomotive,* RA, June 17, 1933, 854.

33. Edmonds, G. S., Superintendent Motive Power, Delaware & Hudson Railroad, *D & H Locomotive Records,* letter published RA, January 16, 1932, 135.

34. Smith, V. L., 1987, 85.

35. *Baltimore & Ohio Builds Steam Power for High Speed,* RA, May 4, 1935, 681.

36. *A High-Pressure Locomotive Boiler,* RA, March 27, 1948, 48 (620.)

37. Knowles, C. R., Illinois Central Railroad, *Modern Tendencies in Railway Water Supply,* RA, April 30, 1920, 1301.

38. *Traffic Troubles Reduced by Enlarging Water Supply,* RA, June 10 1921, 1339.

39. *Railroad Water Problems Yield to Technical Advances,* RA, July 1, 1933, 44.

40. Knowles, C. R., Superintendent, Water Service, Illinois Central Railroad, *What Tannins Do in the Treatment of Locomotive Boiler Water,* RA, December 18, 1943, 971.

41. *Research Has Contributed to Locomotive Fuel Economy,* International Railway Fuel Association, Chicago, September, 1934, abstracted RA, October 6, 1934, 399.

42. Knowles, C. R., Superintendent of Water Service, Illinois Central Railroad, *Save Critical Materials by Softening Water,* RA, April 24, 1943, 820.

43. *Pitting and Corrosion in Locomotive Boilers,* RA, September 3, 1938, 345, abstract of *Cause of and Remedy for Pitting and Corrosion of Locomotive Boiler Tubes and Sheets, with Special Reference to Status of Embrittlement Investigation,* AREA Bulletin 404, June-July, 1938, 73–96; *Inter-crystalline Corrosion: How Can It Be Eliminated?* RA, May 18, 1940, 855, abstract of report presented to AREA, March, 1940.

44. *Motive Power for Higher Speeds,* RA, November 22, 1941, 858.

45. *Research Has Contributed to Locomotive Fuel Economy,* International Railway Fuel Association, Chicago, September, 1934, abstracted RA, October 6, 1934, 399.

46. *New Locomotive Fuel Economy Devices,*

RA, September 28, 1935, 402; *Elesco H-A Super-heater Units,* RA, June 14, 1941, 1080.

47. *Feedwater Heat Booster,* RA, October 19, 1935, 492.

48. *The Hancock Turbo-Injector,* RA, January 30, 1937, 232.

49. *Sellers Type S Injector Operated by Single Control,* RA, April 10, 1937, 638.

50. *Freight and Passenger Power for the Milwaukee,* RA, April 30, 1938, 761.

51. *Exhaust-Steam Injector Improved,* RA, June 17, 1937, 1004D61.

52. *Mechanical Division Reports Presented at General Committee Meeting,* RA, July 9, 1938, 45.

53. *Locomotive Construction,* report to AARMD annual meeting, 1940, reported RA, July 6, 1940, 33.

54. Partington, J., Manager, Engineering Department, American Locomotive Co., *Welded Locomotive Boiler Construction,* Northwest Locomotive Association, St. Paul, Minnesota, March, 1945, abstracted RA, April 28, 1945, 752.

55. *Report of Committee on Locomotive Construction,* AARMD convention, 1937, reported RA, June 18, 1937, 1004D90.

56. *Motive Power for Higher Speeds,* RA, November 22, 1941, 858.

57. *Welding Assists in the Building of C. & O. Locomotives,* RA, August 29, 1942, 333.

58. Partington, J., Manager, Engineering Department, American Locomotive Co., *Modern Locomotive Design and Smoke Prevention,* Central Railway Club, Buffalo, New York, March, 1938, reported RA, March 19, 1938, 488.

59. Hall, J. M., Director, Bureau of Locomotive Inspection, ICC, *Fusion-Welded Locomotive Boilers,* contribution to ASME spring meeting, April, 1946, reported RA, April 20, 1946, 816.

60. *Steam Locomotive Development,* report from Committee on Further Development of the Steam Locomotive, AARMD convention, 1947, reported RA, June 26, 1947, 1294D173.

61. Wardale, D., 1998, 418.

62. *Annual Report of Bureau of Locomotive Inspection,* RA, December 20, 1930, 1329.

63. *What Price Boiler Explosions?* RA, February 6, 1932, 231.

64. *Locomotive Inspection Report Shows Casualty Increase,* RA, February 22, 1941, 349.

65. *Casualties Decrease—Locomotive Defects Increase,* RA, January 17, 1942, 208.

66. *Locomotive Defects and Casualties Show Decided Increase,* RA, January 30, 1943, 279.

67. McBrian, R., Engineer Standards & Research, Denver & Rio Grande Western Railroad, *Lessons from Boiler Explosions,* Association of Railway Claim Agents, Chicago, June, 1943, abstracted RA, July 10, 1943, 47; *Locomotive Boiler Explosions,* RA, October 16, 1943, 595; *Locomotive Boiler Explosions,* RA, October 23, 1943, 630.

68. Bjorkholm, J. E., Superintendent Motive Power, Chicago, Milwaukee, St. Paul & Pacific Railroad, *If There's No Water, Kill the Fire,* RA, December 18, 1943, 978.

69. *Locomotive Casualties and Defects Continue to Increase,* RA, January 29, 1944, 281; *The 1944 Locomotive Inspection Report,* RA, January 27, 1945, 227.

70. King, E., *The A: Norfolk & Western's Mercedes of Steam,* Glendale, CA: Trans-Anglo Books, 1989, 87.

71. *"Century" Derailed,* RA, September 11, 1943, 429; *Low Water Cause of "Century" Accident,* RA, October 9, 1943, 575.

SECTION 15.3

72. *Power Reverse Gear Required by I.C.C.,* RA, January 21, 1933, 83; *Railroads Ask I. C. C. to Dismiss Power Reverse Gear Case,* RA, June 18, 1936, 125; *Reverse Gear Order Proposed to I. C. C.,* RA, February 20, 1937, 331.

73. *Franklin Type G Precision Power Reverse Gear,* RA, June 20, 1928, 1420D37.

74. *New Appliances for Locomotives and Cars,* RA, June 30, 1934, 975.

75. *High-speed Auxiliary Locomotive Tested on Lehigh Valley,* RA, September 21, 1935, 361.

76. *Franklin Type E High-Speed Booster,* RA, June 17, 1937, 1004D63.

77. *Dynamometer Test Plant Results on the Type E Booster,* RA, August 19, 1944, 309.

78. Wardale, D., 1998, 392.

79. Freeman, L. D., Assistant Superintendent of Motive Power, Seaboard Air Line in discussion of Partington, J. *Modern Tendencies in Locomotive Design,* ASME, Newport News, Virginia, April, 1922, abstracted RA, April 15, 1922, 909.

80. Smith, V. L., 1987, 62.

81. Giesl-Gieslingen, A., *Austrian 2-8-4 Locomotive of Unique Design,* RA, March 22, 1930, 685.

82. *Pacific Type Locomotive Equipped with Poppet Valves,* RA, March 29, 1930, 767; Drury, 145; Edmonds, G. S., Superintendent Motive Power, Delaware & Hudson Railroad, *Locomotive Valves and Valve Gears,* RA, July 1, 1933, 27.

83. Smith, V. L., 1987, 62.

84. Drury, 333; *Track Exhibits of Steam Locomotives at Two Points,* AARMD convention, 1930, reported RA, June 23, 1930, 1548D68.

85. Winterrowd, W. H., Vice-President, Franklin Railway Supply Co., *Research and Steam Locomotive Development,* AARMD convention, 1937, reported RA, June 18, 1937, 1004D82.

86. Ryan, J. L., St. Louis-San Francisco Railway, *Locomotive Performance As Affected by Steam Distribution,* Railway Fuel and Traveling Engineers' Association annual meeting, 1941, reported RA, October 4, 1941, 527.

87. *Steam Locomotive Development,* report from Committee on Further Development of the Steam Locomotive, AARMD convention, 1947, reported RA, June 26, 1947, 1294D173.

88. *Poppet Valve Gear for Steam Locomotives in America,* RA, June17, 1939, 1019.

89. Smith, V. L., 1987, 62.

90. *Poppet Valves Tested on the Pennsylvania Railroad,* RA, March 1, 1941, 375; *Poppet Valves Prove Capacity on P.R.R. Test Plant at Altoona,* RA, March 8, 1941, 405.

91. Smith, V. L., 1987, 65.

92. Smith, V. L., 1987, 71.

93. *C. & O. Shows First of Five Streamlined Locomotives,* RA, February 1, 1947, 284.

94. RA September 25, 1948, 67.

95. Smith, V. L., 1987, 104.

96. Smith, V. L., 1987, 84.

97. Edmonds, G. S., Superintendent Motive Power, Delaware & Hudson Railroad, *Locomotive Valves and Valve Gears,* RA, July 1, 1933, 27.

98. *Report on Steam Turbine Locomotives,* International Railway Fuel Association convention, 1928, reported RA, May 12, 1928, 1106.

99. *Ibid.*

100. *Mechanical Draft,* report to International Railway Fuel Association convention, 1924, reported RA, June 14, 1924, 1513; Stuebing, A. F., *A Year of Innovations in Locomotive Design,* RA, January 6, 1923, 41.

101. *Boiler Pressures Higher Than 200 lb.* in *Report on Locomotive Design and Construction,* ARMMA convention, 1927, reported RA, June 11, 1927, 1889.

102. RA April 17, 1936, 682.

103. Bruce, A. W., American Locomotive Co., *The Locomotive as a Factor in Fuel Economy,* International Railway Fuel Association convention, 1928, abstracted RA, May 19, 1928, 1153.

104. Poultney, E. C., *Tests of L.M.S. Turbine Locomotive,* RA, June 15, 1946, 1178.

105. Bailey, E. G., Smith, A. R., Dickey, P. S., *Steamotive Unit for Turbo-Electric U. P. Locomotive,* ASME, December, 1936, abstracted RA, March 20, 1937, 468.

106. RA August 1, 1936, 178.

107. Dickerman, W. C., President, American Locomotive Co., *Possibilities of the Modern Steam Locomotive,* Western Railway Club, Chicago, April, 1938, abstracted RA, May 7, 1938, 796; Davenport, J. E., Vice-President of Engineering, Development and Research, American Locomotive Co., *A Look at Tomorrow's Power,* Western Railway Club, April, 1944, reported RA, May 6, 1944, 851; *Union Pacific's Steam-Electric Locomotive,* RA, December 24, 1938, 916.

108. Ennis, J. B., Senior Vice-President, American Locomotive Co., *The Last Fifty Years—and the Next,* RA, December 15, 1945, 970.

109. Drury, 394.

110. Powers, F. B., Manager Engineering, Transportation & Generator Division, Westinghouse Electric & Manufacturing Co., *Railroad Motive Power of the Future,* New York Railroad Club, March, 1942, abstracted RA, April 4, 1942, 702.

111. *Pennsylvania Announces Steam Turbine Locomotive,* RA, December 2, 1944, 861; Newton, J. S., Brecht, W. A., Westinghouse Electric Co., *A Geared Steam-Turbine Locomotive,* RA, February 17, 1945, 337; Kerr, C., Westinghouse Electric Co., *Locomotives for Today and Tomorrow,* New York Railroad Club, March, 1946, reported RA, April 13, 1946,765; Drury, 328; *Steam Locomotive Development,* report from Committee on Further Development of the Steam Locomotive, AARMD convention, 1947, reported RA, June 26, 1947, 1294D173.

112. *Chesapeake & Ohio Proposes to Buy Steam-Turbine Locomotives,* RA, March 31, 1945, 599; Putz, T. J., Baston, C. E., Westinghouse Electric Co., *C. & O. Turbine-Electric Locomotives,* RA, September 20, 1947, 48 (472); Dralle, H. E., Manager, Transportation Application Engineering, Westinghouse Electric Co., *What Type Motive Power?* RA, January 1, 1949, 14 (4.)

113. *New Locomotive Types,* RA, April 7, 1952, 125; Drury, 307, 393; *Turbine Locomotive Shipped to N&W,* RA, May 31, 1954, 9.

114. *N&W Turbine Locomotive Tests,* RA, January 17, 1955, 19.

115. *Coal Fires Go Out—"Jawn Henry" Dies,* RA, February 3, 1958, 23.

116. Johnson, R. P., Chief Engineer, Baldwin Locomotive Works, *Pennsylvania Tests Duplex Locomotive,* RA, May 26, 1945, 925, abstracted from paper to New York Railway Club, May, 1945.

117. *Ibid.*

118. *Steam Locomotive Development,* report from Committee on Further Development of the Steam Locomotive, AARMD convention, 1947, reported RA, June 26, 1947, 1294D173; Drury, 324, 328.

119. Smith, V. L., 1987, 75.

120. Smith, V. L., *One Man's Locomotives: 50 Years Experience with Railway Motive Power,* Glendale, California: Trans-Anglo Books, 1987, 77.

121. *Ibid.*

122. *Boiler Pressures Higher Than 200 lb.* in *Report on Locomotive Design and Construction* AARMD convention, 1927, reported RA, June 11, 1927, 1889; *Advantages and Disadvantages of Boiler Pressure Higher Than 200 lb.,* discussion at AREA convention, 1928, reported RA, June 23, 1928, 1490D9.

123. *Boiler Pressures Higher Than 200 lb.* in *Report on Locomotive Design and Construction* AARMD convention, 1927, reported RA, June 11, 1927, 1889.

124. *New Haven Two-Car Train With Besler Steam Power Plant,* New York Railroad Club, October, 1936, abstracted RA, October 24, 1936, 581.

125. *B. & O. to Build 16-Cylinder Loco.,* RA, September 25, 1937, 428; Drury, 45.

SECTION 15.4

126. *Improved Spark Arrester Developed on the Northern Pacific,* RA, April 25, 1931, 813.

127. *Soo Line Tests Cyclone Front End,* RA, May 20, 1933, 723.

128. *Illinois Central Effects Economies With Improved Front End,* RA, October 3, 1931, 513.

129. Pownall, W. A., Wabash Railway, *Wabash Tests Effect of Front End and Grate Design,* RA, July 8, 1933, 84; Drury, 422.

130. Buckwalter, T. V., Vice-President, Timken Roller Bearing Co., *Operating Results with the Timken Locomotive,* Central Railway Club, Buffalo, NY, November, 1930, abstracted RA, November 29, 1930, 1177.

131. Young, E. G., *A Study of the Locomotive Front End, Including Tests of a Front End Model,* University of Illinois, Engineering Experiment Station, Bulletin 256, abstracted as *A Study of the Locomotive Front End by Means of Tests on a Model,* RA, March 10, 1934, 345.

132. *Intensive Locomotive Use Pays Union Pacific Big Returns,* RA, March 11, 1939, 415; *U. P. Adds to High-Capacity Motive-Power Fleet,* RA, October 7, 1939, 515.

133. Collins, W. F., Engineer of Tests, New York Central System, *Standing Locomotive Tests of the New York Central,* Railway Fuel and Traveling Engineers' Association annual meeting, 1940, reported RA, January 18, 1941, 177.

134. Partington, J., Manager, Engineering Department, American Locomotive Co., *Modern Locomotive Design and Smoke Prevention,* Central Railway Club, Buffalo, NY, March, 1938, reported RA, March 19, 1938, 488.

135. *Anderson Spark Eliminator Shows Good Results,* RA, December 10, 1938, 844.

136. *Further Development of Anderson Front End,* RA, April 26, 1941, 719.

137. *Improving Steam Locomotive Performance,* RA, December 2, 1950, 64.

138. Collins, W. F., Engineer of Tests, New York Central System, *How Locomotive Boiler Performance Is Related to Boiler Proportions,* RA, January 19, 1946, 186; Drury, 279; *Improving Steam Locomotive Performance,* RA, November 25, 1950, 23; December 2, 1950, 64.

139. Giesl-Gieslingen, A., *Tendencies in Front-End Design,* RA, March 13, 1948, 82 (530.)

140. Wardale, D., 1998, 92–98.

141. Wardale, D., 1998, 474.

SECTION 15.5

142. *Main Reservoirs in Engine Bed Casting,* RA, March 15, 1930, 654; Drury, 403.

143. Sheehan, W. H., General Steel Castings Corp., Eddystone, Pennsylvania, *Steel Castings and the Railroad,* New York Railroad Club, January, 1938, abstracted RA, February 5, 1938, 267.

144. Henley, R. G., Norfolk & Western Railway, in discussion on Winterrowd, W. H., Vice-President, Franklin Railway Supply Co., *Research and Steam Locomotive Development,* AARMD convention, 1937, reported RA, June 18, 1937, 1004D82.

145. Sheehan, W. M., Manager, Eastern District Sales, General Steels Castings Corp., *Steel Castings for High-Speed Railroad Service,* Central Railway Club, Buffalo, March, 1937, abstracted RA, April 3, 1937, 603.

146. *Roller Bearing Center Plates,* RAG, June 19, 1908, 171.

147. Peck, C.B., Mechanical Department Editor, 'Railway Age,' *The Year's Trend in Equipment Development,* RA, January 4, 1930, 39; *A 4-8-4 Type Demonstration Locomotive for Timken,* RA, May 24, 1930, 1225; Buckwalter, T. V., Vice-President, Timken Roller Bearing Co., *Operating Results with the Timken Locomotive,* Central Railway Club, Buffalo, NY, November, 1930, abstracted RA, November 29, 1930, 1177; *Timken Locomotive Completes First 100,000 Miles of Service,* RA, February 13, 1932, 274; Buckwalter, T. V., Vice-President, Timken Roller Bearing Co., *Roller-Bearing Service in Locomotive, Passenger and Freight Equipment,* Railroad Division, ASME, Bigwin, Ontario, Canada, June, 1932, abstracted RA, August 20, 1932, 255; Drury, 316.

148. *NP Scraps Timken's 'Four Aces,'* RA, October 20, 1958, 33.

149. Edmonds, G. S., Superintendent Motive Power, Delaware & Hudson Railroad, *D & H Locomotive Records,* letter published RA, January 16, 1932, 135.

150. Brunner, H. E., Taylor, B. W., SKF Industries, New York, *New York Central Locomotive No. 5343 Makes Over 130,000 Miles,* RA, September 24, 1932, 421.

151. *Roller-Bearing Rods Pass Test Service,* RA, November 2, 1935, 566.

152. Taylor, B. W., SKF Industries, *Locomotive with Roller Bearings on Main and Side Rods,* RA, July 7, 1934, 4.

153. *Report on Lubrication of Locomotives,* AARMD convention, 1937, reported RA, June 17, 1937, 1004D53.

154. *Report of Committee on Locomotive Construction,* AARMD convention, 1937, reported RA, June 18, 1937, 1004D90.

155. *Ibid.*

156. *Mechanical Division Reports Presented at General Committee Meeting,* RA, July 9, 1938, 45.

157. Sanders, W. C., General Manager, Railway Division, Timken Roller Bearing Co., *Railroading on Roller Bearings,* Pacific Railway Club, Los Angeles, August, 1943, condensed RA, September 4, 1943, 379.

158. *Double-Disc Driving Wheel,* RA, December 17, 1932, 902.

159. *Boxpok Locomotive Driving-Wheel Center,* RA, June 30, 1934, 983.

160. *Disc Centers For Driving Wheels,* RA, June 16, 1937, 1004D39; Drury, 73.

161. *Report of Committee on Locomotive Construction,* AARMD convention, 1937, reported RA, June 18, 1937, 1004D90.

162. Sheehan, W. H., General Steel Castings Corp., Eddystone, Pennsylvania, *Steel Castings and the Railroad,* New York Railroad Club, January, 1938, abstracted RA, February 5, 1938, 267.

163. *Union Pacific Tenders Embody Many Improved Features,* RA, August 17, 1940, 246.

164. Weeks, T. O., Missouri Pacific Railroad, *What a Chief Dispatcher Thinks of Fuel Economy,* Railway Fuel and Traveling Engineers' Association annual meeting, 1940, reported RA, November 2, 1940, 616.

165. *N. Y. C. Locomotives Scoop Water Without Reducing Speed,* RA, July 22, 1944, 149.

166. Trumbull, A. G., Chief Mechanical Engineer, Advisory Mechanical Committee, Chesapeake & Ohio, Pere Marquette, Erie, New York, Chicago & St. Louis Railroads, *Locomotive Running Gear and Counterbalancing* RA, July 1, 1933, 26.

167. Magee, G. M., Assistant Engineer, Kansas City Southern Railway, *Locomotive Design and Rail Stresses,* RA, May 15, 1937, 825.

168. Cartwright, K., New York, New Haven & Hartford Railroad, *Relation of Locomotive Design to Rail Maintenance: As the Mechanical Man Faces It,* RA, March 25, 1939, 517.

169. Miller, A. A., Engineer Maintenance of Way, Missouri Pacific Railroad, Ellis, D. S., Chief Mechanical Officer, Chesapeake & Ohio Railroad, *Rail Damage and the Relation of Locomotives Thereto,* Western Railway Club of Chicago, March, 1938, reported RA, April 9, 1938, 653.

170. *Counterbalancing for High Speeds,* RA, March 31, 1945, 579, digest of report on counterbalance tests for high-speed locomotives issued by Association of American Railroads, March, 1944.

171. Buckwalter, T. V., Vice-President, Horger, O. J., Research Engineer, Timken Roller Bearing Co., *Steam Locomotive Slipping Tests,* New York Railroad Club, February, 1939, reported RA, March 4, 1939, 377; Cartwright, K., New York, New Haven & Hartford Railroad, *Relation of Locomotive Design to Rail Maintenance: As the Mechanical Man Faces It,* RA, March 25, 1939, 517.

172. Kiefer, P. W., Chief Engineer Motive Power and Rolling Stock, New York Central System, *High-Capacity Steam Passenger Locomotives*, ASME semi-annual meeting, June 1941, Kansas City, Missouri, abstracted RA, August 16, 1941, 273, September 6, 1941, 376; Kiefer, P. W., *An Evaluation of Railroad Motive Power*, RA, August 23, 1947 (323) 43, August 30, 1947 (359) 41.

173. *C. G. W. Freight Power Improved*, RA, April 5, 1941, 601.

174. *Counterbalancing for High Speeds*, RA, March 31, 1945, 579, digest of report on counterbalance tests for high-speed locomotives issued by Association of American Railroads, March, 1944.

175. *Rail Stress Measurements of Counterbalancing Effects*, Mechanical Division AAR, abstracted RA, June 14, 1941, 1049.

176. Converse, J. O., Minneapolis & St. Louis Railroad, *Availability of Steam Locomotives*, Northwest Locomotive Association, St. Paul, Minnesota, March, 1946, abstracted RA, May 4, 1946, 904.

177. Fry, L. H., *Motive Power—Wartime and After*, Engineering Institute of Canada, Toronto, Ontario, September, 1943, abstracted RA, October 9, 1943, 559.

178. Kuhler, O., *Making Steam Locomotives Beautiful*, RA, July 25, 1931, 129.

179. *Mikado Type Locomotive for the Georgia Northern*, RA, June 29, 1929, 1553.

180. Tietjens, O. G., Ripley, K. C., *A Study of Air Resistance at High Speeds*, ASME annual meeting, New York, December, 1931, abstracted RA, February 6, 1932, 241; Drury, 62, 64.

181. *Locomotive Streamlining Developed by Wind Tunnel Test*, RA, May 13, 1933, 695, abstract of paper by J. J. Green, National Research Council, Ottawa, published 'Canadian Journal of Research,' January, 1933.

182. *What the Streamliners Have Done for Passenger Motive Power*, RA, April 22, 1944, 776.

183. *New York Central "Streamlines" Passenger Locomotive*, RA, December 22, 1934, 825; *N. Y. C. Locomotive of Streamline Design*, RA, December 1, 1934, 751.

184. *What the Streamliners Have Done for Passenger Motive Power*, RA, April 22, 1944, 776; Drury, 123, 378; *Milwaukee Buys Steam Locomotives for Fast Schedules*, RA, May 11, 1935, 719.

185. Drury, 123.

186. *Pennsylvania "Streamlines" a Steam Passenger Locomotive*, RA, March 7, 1936, 391.

187. RA October 3, 1936, 496.

188. *New York Central Builds Distinctive Streamline Train*, RA, July 11, 1936, 50.

189. *Largest Streamline Steam Locomotives*, RA, February 20, 1938, 319.

190. *Motive Power for Higher Speeds*, RA, November 22, 1941, 858.

191. *C. & O. Shows First of Five Streamlined Locomotives*, RA, February 1, 1947, 284.

Chapter 16

SECTION 16.1

1. Taft, W. J., *Locomotives Ordered in 1930*, RA, January 3, 1931, 82.

2. Taft, W. J., *Locomotives Ordered in 1931*, RA, January 2, 1932, 43.

3. Taft, W. J., *Locomotives Ordered in 1932*, RA, February 4, 1933, 171.

4. Lipetz, A., Chief Consulting Engineer, American Locomotive Co., *Power Plant on Wheels*, Metropolitan Power Plants Committee, New York, March, 1936, abstracted RA, June 6, 1936, 910.

5. Taft, W. J., *Locomotives Ordered in 1936*, RA, January 2, 1937, 70.

6. Schmidt, W. H., *Locomotives Ordered in 1939*, RA, January 6, 1940, 78.

7. Wilcox, H. C., *Reduced Locomotive Inventory Is Affecting Capacity*, RA, January 4, 1941.

8. McGinnis, A. J., *Locomotives Ordered in 1940*, RA, January 4, 1941, 95.

9. *1941—Railway Review and Outlook—1942*, RA, January 3, 1942, 1; McGinnis, A. J., *Locomotive Orders in 1941 Greatest Since 1923*, RA, January 3, 1942, 113.

10. *Equipment and Supplies: Heavy Equipment Buying Once More*, RA, March 7, 1942, 512.

11. RA September 27, 1941, 23.

12. RA March 7, 1942, 509, November 29, 1941, 932, December 13, 1941, 1014, August 15, 1942.

13. McGinnis, A. J., *Locomotive Backlog Reduced*, RA, January 6, 1945, 90.

14. *Equipment and Supplies: Equipment Orders Dwindle*, RA, May 9, 1942, 922.

15. McGinnis, A. J., *Many Locomotives Ordered Were Unauthorized by WPB*, RA, January 2, 1943, 117.

16. McGinnis, A. J., *Locomotive Orders Were Limited by W. P. B. Control of Deliveries*, RA, January 1, 1944, 88; McGinnis, A. J., *Locomotive Backlog Reduced*, RA, January 6, 1945, 90.

17. Drury, 254.

18. McGinnis, A. J., *Locomotive Orders Were Limited by W. P. B. Control of Deliveries*, RA, January 1, 1944, 88; Parmelee, J. H., Director, Bureau of Railway Economics, *Railway Operations in 1945*, RA, January 5, 1946, 69.

19. RA March 4, 1944, 472.

20. Miles, F. C., *Locomotives Ordered and Built in 1946*, RA, January 4, 1947, 110.

21. McGinnis, A. J., *Locomotives Ordered and Built in 1945*, RA, January 5, 1946, 88.

22. Miles, F. C., *Locomotives Ordered and Built in 1946*, RA, January 4, 1947, 110.

23. Miles, F. C., *Locomotives Ordered in 1947*, RA, January 3, 1948, 209.

24. Payne, E. C., Pittsburgh Consolidated Coal Co., *The Outlook for Coal as Railroad Fuel*, New York Railroad Club, April, 1948, abstracted RA, May 22, 1948 (1025) 37.

25. Wilcox, H. C., Miles, F. C., *Motive Power Ordered in 1953*, RA, January 11, 1954, 189.

26. Johnson, R. P., Chief Engineer, Baldwin Locomotive Works, *Pennsylvania Tests Duplex Locomotive*, RA, May 26, 1945, 925, abstracted from paper to New York Railway Club, May, 1945.

27. *North Western Gets Heavier Power*, RA, January 11, 1930, 144; Drury, 96.

28. *North Western Class-H Locomotives Are Being Modernized*, RA, April 27, 1946, 860.

29. *Improvement of Power—Modernization of Repair Methods Save Money on C. & N. W.*, RA, November 12, 1949, 38 (834.)

30. Drury, 97.

31. *Cotton Belt Replaces Consolidation Type Motive Power*, RA, December 27, 1930, 1363; Drury, 348.

32. *4-6-4 and 4-8-4 Type Power for the C. B. & Q.*, RA, March 7, 1931, 499.

33. *Lehigh Valley Buys Two 4-8-4 Locomotives*, RA, April 4, 1931, 669; Lyford, F. E., Lehigh Valley Railroad, *Lehigh Valley Tests 4-8-4 Type Locomotives*, RA, March 19, 1932, 469; *Lehigh Valley Locomotives Return 38 Per Cent on Investment*, RA, October 15, 1932, 537; *Lehigh Valley Acquires Five More 4-8-4 Type Locomotives*, RA, February 23, 1935; Drury, 222–3.

34. *Northern Pacific Receives Heavy Passenger Power*, RA, November 3, 1934, 537; Drury, 318.

35. *Lackawanna Received Twenty More 4-8-4 Type Locomotives*, RA, February 16, 1935, 267.

36. *Chesapeake & Ohio Receives High-Power Passenger Locomotives*, RA, January 11, 1936, 111; Drury, 88.

37. RA January 4, 1936, 26, 87.

38. *Largest Streamline Steam Locomotives*, RA, February 20, 1937, 319; Drury, 363.

39. *R. F. & P. 4-8-4 Type Freight and Passenger Locomotives*, RA, June 19, 1937, 1013.

40. *Intensive Locomotive Use Pays Union Pacific Big Returns*, RA, March 11, 1939, 415; *U. P. Adds to High-Capacity Motive-Power Fleet*, RA, October 7, 1939, 515.

41. *Freight and Passenger Power for the Milwaukee*, RA, April 30, 1938, 761; Drury, 117, 123.

42. *New Passenger and Freight Power for the Santa Fe*, RA, December 3, 1938, 803.

43. Chapman, E. E., Atchison, Topeka & Santa Fe Railway, *Diesel and Steam Locomotives in High-Speed Service*, Society of Automotive Engineers, New York, October, 1938, reported RA, November 19, 1938, 733.

44. *Baldwin Builds 4-8-4 Locomotives For Service on Frisco*, RA, February 27, 1943, 424; *D. & H. 4-8-4 Type Freight Power*, RA, July 17, 1943, 93; *Central of Georgia Locomotives*, RA, February 12, 1944, 344; *Missouri Pacific Freight Power*, RA, March 25, 1944, 603; *Lehigh Valley 4-8-4 Freight Power*, RA, April 29, 1944, 816; *Rock Island 4-8-4 Locomotives*, RA, August 26, 1944, 334.

45. Morgan, D. P., *Louisville & Nashville's Pacifics and Mountains*, Journal R&LHS, October, 1952, 36.

46. *Norfolk & Western Class J Locomotives*, RA, June 2, 1945, 971; Pond, C. E., Assistant Superintendent Motive Power, Norfolk & Western Railway, *Modern Power on the Norfolk & Western*, Southern & Southwestern Railway Club, Atlanta, Georgia, May, 1946, abstracted RA, August 24, 1946, 335; Drury, 304.

47. *First 4-8-4 on the New York Central*, RA, September 22, 1945, 480.

48. Kiefer, P. W., Chief Engineer Motive Power and Rolling Stock, New York Central System, *An Evaluation of Railroad Motive Power*, RA, August 23, 1947 (323) 43, August 30, 1947 (359) 41.

49. Wardale, D., 1998.

SECTION 16.2

50. *High Speed Pacific Type Locomotives Received by Boston & Maine*, RA, December 29, 1934, 851; Drury, 58.

51. *B. & M. Tests New Pacific Type Locomotives*, RA, December 28, 1935, 849; Drury, 123.

52. *Fourteen 4-6-4 Type Locomotives for the Milwaukee*, RA, March 1, 1930, 559; *Milwaukee Motive Power Makes High Mileage*, RA, December 23, 1933, 875; *New Milwaukee Locomotives Notable for Refinements in Design*, RA, January 23, 1932, 154; Drury, 120.

53. Baldwin advertisement, RA, August 18, 1934, 2.

54. *4-6-4 and 4-8-4 Type Power for the C. B. & Q.*, RA, March 7, 1931, 499.

55. *New Haven's First Streamline Engine*, RA, March 6, 1937, 402; *New Haven Installs Streamline Passenger Locomotives*, RA, March 27, 1937, 540; Drury, 294.

56. *Santa Fe Installs High-Speed Passenger Locomotives*, RA, March 12, 1938, 450; Drury, 27.

57. Chapman, E. E., Atchison, Topeka & Santa Fe Railway, *Diesel and Steam Locomotives in High-Speed Service*, Society of Automotive Engineers, New York, October, 1938, reported RA, November 19, 1938, 733.

58. *New N. Y. C. Locomotives Show High Power Concentration*, RA, April 2, 1938, 597; Kiefer, P. W., Chief Engineer Motive Power and Rolling Stock, New York Central System, *High-Capacity Steam Passenger Locomotives*, ASME semi-annual meeting, June, 1941, Kansas City, Missouri, abstracted RA, August 16, 1941, 273, September 6, 1941, 376; Drury, 271ff.

59. *New York Central Buys All-round Locomotives*, RA, December 7, 1940, 856.

60. *Versatile Road Motive Power for the New York Central*, RA, June 26, 1943, 1250.

61. *Baltimore & Ohio Builds Steam Power for High Speed*, RA, May 4, 1935, 681; Drury, 44.

62. *Milwaukee Buys Steam Locomotives for Fast Schedules*, RA, May 11, 1935, 719.

63. RA May 18, 1935, 778.

64. *New Four-Cylinder Locomotive Settled at N. Y. World's Fair*, RA, March 18, 1938, 502; *High-Capacity Locomotive for Fast Service*, RA, June 24, 1938, 1067; Drury, 324.

65. *Pennsylvania 4-4-4-4 Locomotives*, RA, December 12, 1942, 956; Drury, 328; Johnson, R. P., Chief Engineer, Baldwin Locomotive Works, *Pennsylvania Tests Duplex Locomotive*, RA, May 26, 1945, 925, abstracted from paper to New York Railway Club, May, 1945.

66. Drury, 326.

SECTION 16.3

67. *Mountain Type Locomotives for the Wabash*, RA, April 5, 1930, 821; *New Wabash Locomotives Make Good in Service Tests*, RA, September 27, 1930, 616; Drury, 422.

68. *Wabash Operates 4-8-4 Types in Freight Service*, RA, February 14, 1931, 374.

69. *Nickel Plate Buys 2-8-4 Type Locomotives*, RA, November 17, 1934, 609; Drury, 280.

70. *Boston & Maine 4-8-2 Locomotives for Fast Freight*, RA, August 17, 1935, 213; *Dynamometer Tests of B. & M. 4-8-2 Type Locomotives*, RA, January 25, 1936, 171.

71. *2-8-4 Type Freight Locomotives for the C. & O.*, RA, July 29, 1944, 200; Drury, 81.

72. RA June 19, 1948, 1225.

73. *A Record Haul for Chicago & Illinois Mid-*

land (advertisement) RA, August 6, 1932, 16; Drury. 89.

74. Drury, 18.

75. *Chesapeake & Ohio Receives Large Two-Cylinder Locomotives*, RA, November 15, 1930, 1025; *C. & O. Runs Road Tests on 2-10-4 Locomotives*, RA, January 17, 1931, 182.

76. *Santa Fe Locomotive 5000 Tested*, RA, November 28, 1931, 829.

77. *New Passenger and Freight Power for the Santa Fe*, RA, December 3, 1938, 803; Drury, 27.

78. *Heavy Freight Power for K. C. S.*, RA, January 8, 1938, 113; Drury, 88.

79. *B. & L. E. Receives Ten 2-10-4 Locomotives*, RA, September 4, 1937, 312; Drury, 20, 50.

80. *Test Locomotives of 4-8-2 and 2-6-6-2 Types on the B. & O.*, RA, July 11, 1931, 46; Drury, 45.

81. *Western Pacific Operating 2-8-8-2 Types in Fast Freight Service*, RA, December 26, 1931, 975; Drury, 431.

82. Baldwin advertisement, RA, December 8, 1934, 2; *P. & W. V. Articulated Locomotive Replaces Two Consolidations*, RA, March 9, 1935, 361; Drury, 300.

83. *Seaboard Air Line Locomotives*, RA, June 1, 1935, 849.

84. *Norfolk & Western Locomotives Equipped with Roller Bearings*, RA, September 29, 1936, 435; Pond, C. E., Assistant to Superintendent of Motive Power, Norfolk & Western Railway, *Freight Motive Power on the Norfolk & Western*, ASME semi-annual meeting, Kansas City, Missouri, June, 1941, abstracted RA, July 5, 1941, 26; Drury 299.

85. *A Powerful High-Speed Freight Locomotive*, RA, December 19, 1936, 900; Drury, 399.

86. Partington, J., Manager, Engineering Department, American Locomotive Co., *Modern Locomotive Design and Smoke Prevention*, Central Railway Club, Buffalo, New York, March, 1938, reported RA, March 19, 1938, 488.

87. *Northern Pacific High-Speed Freight Locomotives*, RA, March 6, 1937, 389; Drury, 312.

88. *Ten Articulated Locomotives for the D. & R. G. W.*, RA, July 9, 1938, 43.

89. Drury, 359ff.

90. *Operating a "Hot-Shot" Division*, RA, February 19, 1944, 382.

91. *Southern Pacific Buys Articulated Coal-Burning Locomotives*, RA, December 16, 1939, 918.

92. *D. & H. Installs Articulated Freight Locomotives*, RA, August 10, 1940, 207; Drury, 143ff.

93. *High-Capacity Freight Locomotives For Western Maryland*, RA, January 25, 1941, 209.

94. *Union Pacific Gets Heaviest Articulated Locomotives*, RA, October 4, 1941, 519; Drury, 404.

95. *C. & O. "Allegheny" Locomotives First of 2-6-6-6 Type*, RA, March 7, 1942, 478; Drury, 84.

96. Bruce, A. W., 1952, 240.

97. RA, December 27, 1947, 61.

98. *20 More Articulated Locomotives for the Union Pacific*, RA, October 3, 1942, 516.

99. Johnson, R. P., Chief Engineer, Baldwin Locomotive Works, *Pennsylvania Tests Duplex Locomotive*, RA, May 26, 1945, 925, abstracted from paper to New York Railway Club, May, 1945.

100. *D. M. & I. R. Freight Power*, RA, June 5, 1943, 1135; Drury, 168.

101. *The B. & O. 2-8-8-4 Locomotives*, RA, May 27, 1944, 1014; Drury, 41.

102. *Pennsylvania Q-2 Freight Locomotives*, RA, December 22, 1945, 1014; Drury, 324.

103. Reutter, M., *The Great (Motive) Power Struggle: The Pennsylvania Railroad v. General Motors, 1935–1949*, Journal R&LHS, Bulletin #170, Spring, 1994, 15.

SECTION 16.4

104. *Ten-Wheel Switcher with Aluminum Rods*, RA, April 18, 1931, 759

105. *Nickel Plate Received Five Heavy Switching Locomotives*, RA, January 19, 1935, 79.

106. *Union Railroad Receives Transfer Locomotives from Baldwin*, RA, July 18, 1936, 105.

107. *Norfolk & Western Steam Switcher Has Automatic Controls*, RA, July 19, 1947 (105) 49; Drury, 306.

Chapter 17

SECTION 17.1

1. Walker, E. B., General Superintendent, Montreal & Southern Counties Railroad, *Steam, Electric, and Internal Combustion Locomotives*, RA, October 17, 1931, 593.

2. *New Locomotive Fuel Economy Devices*, RA, September 28, 1935, 402.

3. *Diesel Locomotives*, committee report to International Railway Fuel Association convention, 1930, reported RA, May 10, 1930, 1134.

4. RA, July 4, 1931, 4.

5. Binkerd, R. S., Vice-President, Baldwin Locomotive Works, *What About the Steam Locomotive?* New York Railroad Club, April, 1935, reported RA, May 25, 1935, 800.

6. Sawyer, R. T., American Locomotive Co., *The Future Possibilities of Diesel Motive Power*, Western Railway Club, Chicago, April, 1934, abstracted RA, May 12, 1934, 685.

7. *What the Streamliners Have Done for Passenger Motive Power*, RA, April 22, 1944, 776.

8. Gurley, F. G., Assistant Vice-President, Chicago, Burlington & Quincy Railroad, *Diesel Engines in Railway Service*, conference on 'Diesel Engines and Transportation,' Purdue University, March, 1936, abstracted RA, May 9, 1936, 763; Budd, R., President, Chicago, Burlington & Quincy Railroad, address to luncheon celebrating 40th anniversary of completion of first successful oil-burning Diesel engine, New York, October, 1937, reported RA, November 6, 1937, 636.

9. RA, May 19, 1934, 747, June 2, 1934, 819; Doster, R. A., Layng, C., *Speed an Outstanding Development in 1934*, RA, January 26, 1935, 108.

10. Candee, A. H., Westinghouse Electric & Manufacturing Co., *Why the Diesel Engine Is a Good Railroad Tool*, New York Railroad Club, October, 1935, abstracted RA, October 26, 1935, 522.

11. Chapman, E. E., Atchison, Topeka & Santa Fe Railway, *Diesel and Steam Locomotives in High-Speed Service*, Society of Automotive Engineers, New York, October, 1938, reported RA, November 19, 1938, 733.

12. RA, November 9, 1935, 595.

13. Sillcox, L. K., First Vice-President, The New York Air Brake Co., *Steam or Diesel-Electrics?* paper for transportation engineering students, Yale University, March, 1939, abstracted RA, March 18, 1939, 459.

14. RA, April 25, 1942, 832.

15. Hamilton, H. L., President, Electro-Motive Corporation, address to luncheon celebrating 40th anniversary of completion of first successful oil-burning Diesel engine, New York, October, 1937, reported RA, November 6, 1937, 636.

16. RA, August 3, 1940, 193.

17. Hamilton, H. L., President, Electro-Motive Corporation, address to luncheon celebrating 40th anniversary of completion of first successful oil-burning Diesel engine, New York, October, 1937, reported RA, November 6, 1937, 636.

18. RA, April 16, 1938, 715.

19. *Report of Committee on Locomotive Construction,* AARMD convention, 1937, reported RA, June 18, 1937, 1004D90.

20. RA, October 17, 1938.

21. Sillcox, L. K., First Vice-President, The New York Air Brake Co., *Steam or Diesel-Electrics?* paper for transportation engineering students, Yale University, March, 1939, abstracted RA, March 18, 1939, 459.

22. *Ibid.*

23. Urbach, H. H., Mechanical Assistant to Executive Vice-President, Chicago, Burlington & Quincy Railroad, *Diesel-Locomotive Operation,* AARMD annual meeting, 1939, abstracted RA, July 15, 1939, 108.

24. Chapman, E. E., Atchison, Topeka & Santa Fe Railway, *Steam vs. Diesel-Electric Power,* ASME, Kansas City, Missouri, June, 1941, reported RA, July 26, 1941, 149.

25. Morris, J. P. General Manager, Mechanical, Atchison, Topeka & Santa Fe Railway, *How the Santa Fe Got Results with Diesels,* St. Louis Railroad Diesel Club, St. Louis, June, 1951, abstracted RA, July 30, 1951, 37.

26. Morris, J. P. General Manager, Mechanical, Atchison, Topeka & Santa Fe Railway, *How the Santa Fe Got Results with Diesels,* St. Louis Railroad Diesel Club, St. Louis, June, 1951, abstracted RA, July 30, 1951, 37.

27. McGinnis, A. J., *Locomotives Ordered in 1940,* RA, January 4, 1941, 95.

28. *Equipment Prices,* RA, January 3, 1942, 124.

29. Powell, L. W., Road Foreman of Engines, Atchison, Topeka & Santa Fe Railway, *Operating Diesel-Electric Locomotives,* Railway Fuel and Traveling Engineers' Association annual meeting, 1940, reported RA, November 2, 1940, 620; Chapman, E. E., Atchison, Topeka & Santa Fe Railway, *Steam vs. Diesel-Electric Power,* ASME, Kansas City, Missouri, June, 1941, reported RA, July 26, 1941, 149.

30. Powell, L. W., Road Foreman of Engines, Atchison, Topeka & Santa Fe Railway, *Operating Diesel-Electric Locomotives,* Railway Fuel and Traveling Engineers' Association annual meeting, 1940, reported RA, November 2, 1940, 620.

31. Railway Fuel and Traveling Engineers' Association annual meeting, 1940, reported RA, November 2, 1940, 618.

32. Morris, J. P., General Manager, Mechan-ical, Atchison, Topeka & Santa Fe Railway, *How the Santa Fe Got Results with Diesels,* St. Louis Railroad Diesel Club, St. Louis, June, 1951, abstracted RA, July 30, 1951, 37.

33. Fry, L. H., *Motive Power—Wartime and After,* Engineering Institute of Canada, Toronto, Ontario, September, 1943, abstracted RA, October 9, 1943, 559.

34. Morris, J. P., General Manager, Mechanical, Atchison, Topeka & Santa Fe Railway, *How the Santa Fe Got Results with Diesels,* St. Louis Railroad Diesel Club, St. Louis, June, 1951, abstracted RA, July 30, 1951, 37; Bloss, E. K., Mechanical Superintendent, Boston & Maine Railroad, *Diesel Locomotive Progress—And Some Problems It Entails,* SAE, Chicago, October, 1951, adapted RA, November 19, 1951, 53.

35. *Road-Switcher Diesel-Electrics In Short-Line Service,* RA, May 1, 1943, 852.

36. Davenport, J. E., Vice-President of Engineering, Development and Research, American Locomotive Co., *A Look at Tomorrow's Power,* Western Railway Club, April, 1944, reported RA, May 6, 1944, 851.

37. Ireland, R. L., President, Hanna Coal Co., *Competition and the Coal Situation,* Railway Fuel and Traveling Engineers' Association, Chicago, September, 1946, reported RA, September 38, 1946, 508.

38. *Freight Diesels on Heavy Grades,* RA, October 20, 1945, 639; *Diesels Aid the Rio Grande,* RA, August 31, 1946, 367.

39. *Erie Cuts Tops Off Hills with Diesels,* RA, August 16, 1947, 62 (286.)

40. *Road Diesel is Economical in Short-Run Service,* RA, January 24, 1948, 204.

41. Akers, J. B., Southern Railway, *Effect of Diesels on Obsolescence,* AREA, Chicago, adapted RA, April 9, 1951, 45.

42. *More Evidence on Engine Pay Basis,* RA, April 17, 1943, 775.

43. *Diesel Road-Switchers Trim Short Line's Costs,* RA, April 9, 1951, 50; *All-Diesel Operation Exceeds G. M. & O.'s Expectations,* RA, April 30, 1951, 25.

44. Corbett, J. W., Vice-President Operation, Southern Pacific Lines, *Moving Transcontinental Trains With Diesel Power,* Pacific Railway Club, November, 1950, abstracted RA, March 5, 1951, 51.

45. Miles, F. C., Wilcox, H. C., *Motive Power in 1950,* RA, January 15, 1951, 216.

46. *Record Total of Motive Power on Order,* RA, April 23, 1951, 51.

47. *Passenger Power Is Undergoing Peacetime Road Tests,* RA, November 16, 1946, 818.

48. *Electro-Motive Silver Anniversary,* RA, November 1, 1947, 26 (726.)

49. RA November 16, 1946.

50. Morris, J. P., General Manager, Mechanical, Atchison, Topeka & Santa Fe Railway, *How the Santa Fe Got Results with Diesels,* St. Louis Railroad Diesel Club, St. Louis, June, 1951, abstracted RA, July 30, 1951, 37.

51. Bloss, E. K., Mechanical Superintendent, Boston & Maine Railroad, *Diesel Locomotive Progress—And Some Problems It Entails,* Society of Automotive Engineers, Chicago, October, 1951, adapted RA, November 19, 1951, 53.

52. *Increased Use of Diesel Power,* RA, September 1, 1952, 76.

53. RA March 19, 1951, 86.

54. RA May 16, 1955, 100.

55. Oehler, A. G., Wilcox, H. C., *Electric, Diesel or Both?* RA, January 9, 1956, 140.

56. *N&W to Buy 2,050 Freight Cars and 25 Diesels,* RA, November 7, 1955, 13; RA, February 6, 1956, 9.

57. *N&W to Buy 268 Diesels for $50 Million,* RA, June 30, 1958, 31.

SECTION 17.2

58. *Turbine and Condensing Locomotives,* report of committee to Railway Fuel and Traveling Engineers' Association annual meeting, 1940, reported RA, November 2, 1940, 619.

59. Yellott, J. I., Kottcamp, C. F., Bituminous Coal Research Inc., *Coal and the Gas-Turbine Locomotive,* RA, June 25, 1947, 1294D122; Steins, C. K., Pennsylvania Railroad, *The Coal-Burning Gas Turbine Locomotive,* National Coal Association, New York, October, 1948, reported RA, November 27, 1948, 26 (1020.)

60. Yellott, J. I., Kottcamp, C. F., Bituminous Coal Research Inc., *The Coal-Fired Gas Turbine Locomotive,* Railway Fuel & Traveling Engineers' Association, Chicago, September, 1946, abstracted RA, October 5, 1946, 551.

61. Putz, T. J., Westinghouse Electric Corp., *Gas-Turbine Operating Experience,* RA, April 10, 1948, 47 (713); Yellott, J. I., *The Experimental Coal-Burning Gas Turbine,* Midwest Power Conference, Chicago, April, 1950, abstracted RA, April 15, 1950 (745) 59.

62. Price, G. A., President, Westinghouse Electric Corp., *Looking Ahead With the Railroads,* New York Railroad Club, New York, March, 1948. Reported RA, March 20, 1948 (581) 87.

63. Dralle, H. E., Manager, Transportation Application Engineering, Westinghouse Electric Corp., *What Type Motive Power?* RA, January 1, 1949, 14 (4.)

64. Weihofen, G. J., *Fuel and Future Motive Power Selection,* RA, January 8, 1949, 180 (84.)

65. *No Gain in Storing Locomotives For War, Says Alco President,* RA, May 7, 1949, 62 (930.)

66. *Performance of Turbine Locomotives,* RA, July 4, 1955, 29.

67. RA, December 5, 1955, 64; Oehler, A. G., Wilcox, H. C., *Electric, Diesel or Both?* RA, January 9, 1956, 140; RA, January 27, 1958, 25.

68. *New Locomotive Types,* RA, April 7, 1952, 125.

69. Yellott, J. I., Kottcamp, C. F., Bituminous Coal Research Inc., *Coal and the Gas-Turbine Locomotive,* RA, June 25, 1947, 1294D122; Yellott, J. I., Broadley, P. R., Kottcamp, C. F., Bituminous Coal Research Inc., *Coal-Burning Gas-Turbine Locomotive,* ASME, Atlantic City, December, 1947, reported RA, January 31, 1948, 46 (254); Putz, T. J., Westinghouse Electric, *Gas-Turbine Operating Experience,* RA, April 10, 1948, 47 (713); Steins, C. K., Pennsylvania Railroad, *The Coal-Burning Gas Turbine Locomotive,* National Coal Association, New York, October, 1948, reported RA, November 27, 1948, 26 (1020); Yellott, J. I., *The Experimental Coal-Burning Gas Turbine,* Midwest Power Conference, Chicago, April, 1950, abstracted RA, April 15, 1950 (745) 59; Yellott, J. I., Broadley, P. R., Locomotive Development Committee, Buckley, F. D., American

Locomotive Co., *Coal-Burning Gas-Turbine Moves Ahead*, Midwest Power Conference, Chicago, April, 1951, abstracted RA, June 18, 1951, 39; *Coal-Burning Turbine Progress*, RA, April 19, 1954, 44.

70. Yellott, J. I., Broadley, P. R., Locomotive Development Committee, Buckley, F. D., American Locomotive Co., *Coal-Burning Gas-Turbine Moves Ahead*, Midwest Power Conference, Chicago, April, 1951, abstracted RA, June 18, 1951, 39.

71. *Gas Turbines Can Burn Coal*, RA, March 5, 1956, 36.

72. *Performance of Turbine Locomotives*, RA, July 4, 1955, 29.

73. *New Developments in Coal Are Leading to New Developments in Coal-Fired Gas Turbine*, RA, August 5, 1957, 20.

74. McGee, J. P., Smith, J., Cargill, R. W., Strimbeck, D. C., *Bureau of Mines Coal-Fired Gas Turbine Research Project*, U.S. Bureau of Mines, 1961.

75. *New Equipment*, RA, March 5, 1962, 51.

Section 17.3

76. Chapman, E. E., Atchison, Topeka & Santa Fe Railway, *Steam vs. Diesel-Electric Power*, ASME, Kansas City, Missouri, June, 1941, reported RA, July 26, 1941, 149.

77. Powers, F. B., Manager Engineering, Transportation & Generator Division, Westinghouse Electric & Manufacturing Co., *Railroad Motive Power of the Future*, New York Railroad Club, March, 1942, abstracted RA, April 4, 1942, 702.

78. Griffith, H. C., *Electric Locomotive Operation*, ASME, Kansas City, Missouri, June, 1941, reported RA, August 9, 1941, 230.

79. *N.&W. to Abandon Electric Operation*, RA, July 1, 1950, 77.

80. *All But 2% of Diesels Were Built Since 1940*, RA, September 5, 1955, 10.

Appendix A

1. Dorsey, Gary, *The Fullness of Wings: The Making of a New Daedalus*, New York: Viking Penguin, 1990, 111.

2. Fry, L. H., referred to in *Locomotive Efficiencies*, RA, August 11, 1928, 250.

3. Smith, Vernon L., *One Man's Locomotives: 50 Years Experience With Railway Motive Power*, Glendale, California: Trans-Anglo, 1987.

4. RRG, February 17, 1899, 122.

5. Wiener, L. *Articulated Locomotives*, New York: Richard R. Smith, 1930 and Milwaukee, Wisconsin: Kalmbach, 1970, 9 (although p. 343 states that Baldwin used 0.85.)

6. *Report on Locomotive Construction*, 1923 ARMMA convention. Reported RA, June 23, 1923, 1591.

7. Hay, W. H., *Railroad Engineering*, New York: John Wiley, 1953, 86.

8. *Report on Locomotive Construction*, 1923 ARMMA convention. Reported RA, June 23, 1923, 1591.

9. *New Wabash Locomotives Make Good in Service Tests*, RA, September 27, 1930, 616.

10. *Elimination of Locomotive Smoke*, RA, July 13, 1946, 51.

Appendix C

1. Cole, F. J., consulting engineer, American Locomotive Co., *Boiler Design in Respect to Heating Surface*, discussion on paper *Steam Locomotives of Today*, American Society of Mechanical Engineers, New York, December, 1914. RAG, December 11, 1914, 1079.

2. Continual setting of optimum cutoff was never achieved in the life of the steam locomotive.

3. For the first time the importance of power output is noticed, rather than tractive effort.

4. Due to friction losses in the steam flow.

Bibliography

The literature on railroading in general and steam locomotives in particular is immense; only the merest indication of some works that may be of particular interest, or that may not occur to the reader, can be given here.

Ahrons, E. L. *The British Steam Railway Locomotive, 1825–1925.* London: Ian Allen, 1927. (History of the British steam locomotive.)

Barfield, T. *When There Was Steam.* Newton Abbot, UK: D. Bradford Barton, 1976. (British memoir.)

Barlow, B. *Didcot Engineman.* Didcot, UK: Wild Swan, 1994. (British memoir.)

Barton, D. B. *The Cornish Beam Engine.* Newton Abbot, UK: D. Bradford Barton, 1969. (History of the stationary precursor to the steam locomotive.)

British Transport Commission. *Handbook for Railway Steam Locomotive Enginemen.* 1957, reprint Hersham, UK: Ian Allan, 2009. (Steam locomotive operation.)

Bromley, J. *Clear the Tracks: The Story of an Old-Time Locomotive Engineer.* New York: Whittlesey House, 1943. (Memoir.)

Bruce, A. W. *The Steam Locomotive in America: Its Development in the Twentieth Century.* New York: W. W. Norton, 1952. (History of the American steam locomotive.)

Church, R. J. *Southern Pacific Ten-Coupled Locomotives.* Berkeley and Wilton, CA: Signature, 2013. (Detailed and comprehensive history of stated subject and related matter.)

Coel, M. *Goin' Railroading.* Niwot: University Press of Colorado, 1998, originally published Boulder, CO: Pruett, 1991. (Ghost-written memoir.)

Cooper, E. C. *Cotton Belt Engineer: The Life and Times of C. W. "Red" Standefer, 1898–1981.* Bloomington, IN: AuthorHouse, 2011. (Ghost-written memoir.)

Cornwell, E.L. (ed.). *History of Railways.* Secaucus, NJ: Chartwell, 1976. (General history of railways and the steam locomotive.)

Del French, C. *Railroadman.* New York: Macmillan, 1938. (Memoir.)

Dougherty, S. M. *Call the Big Hook.* San Merino, CA: Golden West, 1984. (Memoir.)

Drury, G. H. (ed.). *Guide to North American Steam Locomotives: History and Development of Steam Power Since 1900.* Waukesha, WI: Kalmbach, 1993. (History of the American steam locomotive.)

Essery, T. *Saltley Firing Days.* Kettering, UK: Silver Link, 2010. (British memoir.)

Gardner, W. J. *Cleaner to Controller: Reminiscences of the G W R at Taunton.* Oxford, UK: Oakwood, 1994. (British memoir.)

Gardner, W. J. *Cleaner to Controller, Volume 2: Further Reminiscences of the G W R at Taunton.* Oxford, UK: Oakwood, 2000. (British memoir.)

Gasson, H. *Firing Days: Reminiscences of a Great Western Fireman.* Oxford, UK: Oxford Publishing, 1973. (British memoir.)

Grant, H. R. (ed.). *Brownie the Boomer: The Life of Charles P. Brown, an American Railroader.* Dekalb: Northern Illinois University Press, 1991. (Memoir. The original is out of print and rare; this edited version is faithful to the original.)

Hamblen, H. E. *The General Manager's Story.* New York: Macmillan, 1898. (Memoir.)

Harding, J. W. *Steam Locomotive Home Study Course.* Scranton, PA: 1923–46, International Text Book Co., reprint, Townsend, TN: Little River Locomotive, 2002. (Functioning of the steam locomotive.)

Harris, D. B. *Reflections of a Civil War Locomotive Engineer: A Ghost-Written Memoir.* CreateSpace, 2011.

Hilton, G. W. *American Narrow-Gauge Railroads.* Stanford, CA: Stanford University Press, 1990. (Narrow-gauge railroads of America.)

Hooker, A. E. *Bert Hooker: Legendary Railwayman.* Oxford, UK: Oxford Publishing, 1994. (British memoir.)

Klein, M. *Union Pacific. Volume I, Birth of a Railroad, 1862–1893.* New York: Doubleday, 1987. (General insight into U.S. railroad history as well as specific history of the Union Pacific.)

Klein, M. *Union Pacific. Volume II, The Rebirth, 1894–1969.* New York: Doubleday, 1989.

Kraft, E. *The Mightiest of Them All: The Pennsylvania Railroad.* Orange Park, FL: Neighborhood, 2001. (Memoir.)

Martin, A. *Enterprise Denied: Origins of the Decline of American Railroads, 1897–1917.* New York: Columbia University Press, 1971. (History of the American railroad industry.)

Martin, A. *Railroads Triumphant: The Growth, Rejection and Rebirth of a Vital American Force.* New York: Oxford University Press, 1992. (History of the American railroad industry.)

Murdock, R. *Smoke in the Canyon: My Steam Days in Dunsmuir.* Ross, CA: May-Murdock, 1986. (Memoir.)

Neason, J. *Tom Keenan Locomotive Engineer.* Ann Arbor: University of Michigan Library, 2009. (Memoir.)

Noble, J. A. *From Cab to Caboose: Fifty Years of Railroading.* Norman: University of Oklahoma Press, 1964. (Memoir.)

Nock, O. S. *British Steam Railways.* London, UK: Adam & Charles Black, 1961. (History of the British steam locomotive.)

Nock, O. S. *The British Steam Railway Locomotive from 1925 to 1965.* London, UK: Ian Allen, 1966. (History of the British steam locomotive.)

Nock, O. S. *Steam Locomotive: The Unfinished Story of Steam Locomotives and Steam Locomotive Men on the Railways of Great Britain,* 2nd ed. London, UK: George Allen & Unwin, 1968. (History of the British steam locomotive.)

Orr, J. W. *Set Up Running: The Life of a Pennsylvania Railroad Engineman, 1904–1949.* University Park: Pennsylvania State University Press, 2001. (Ghost-written memoir.)

Petersen, R. A. *Hogger: From Fantasy to Fulfillment: A Locomotive Engineer Remembers.* Bloomington, IN: iUniverse.com, 2003. (Memoir.)

Pursell, C. W. *Early Stationary Steam Engines in America.* Washington: Smithsonian Institution, 1969. (History of the stationary precursor to the steam locomotive.)

Reder, G. *The World of Steam Locomotives.* New York: Putnam, 1974. (General history of the steam locomotive.)

Reed, J. H. *Forty Years a Locomotive Engineer: Thrilling Tales of the Rail.* Whitefish, MT: Kessinger, 2007. (Memoir.)

Robertson, R. *Steaming Through the War Years: Reminiscences on the Ex-GER Lines in London.* Oxford, UK: Oakwood, 1996. (British memoir.)

Rolt, L. T. C., and J.S. Allen. *The Steam Engine of Thomas Newcomen.* Buxton, UK: Moorland, 1977. (History of the stationary precursor to the steam locomotive.)

Ross, D. *The Willing Servant: A History of the Steam Locomotive.* Stroud, UK: Tempus, 2004. (General history of the steam locomotive.)

Semmens, P. W. B., and A.J. Goldfinch. *How Steam Locomotives Really Work.* Oxford: Oxford University Press, 2000. (Functioning of the steam locomotive.)

Sinclair, A. *Development of the Locomotive Engine.* New York: Angus Sinclair, 1907. (History of the American steam locomotive.)

Smith, V. L. *One Man's Locomotives: 50 Years Experience With Railway Motive Power.* Glendale, CA: Trans-Anglo, 1987. (Memoir.)

Solomon, B. *American Steam Locomotive.* Osceola, WI: MBI, 1998. (History of the American steam locomotive.)

Steffes, C. F. *The Life and Times of a Locomotive Engineer.* Bakersfield, CA: Old World, 1992. (Memoir.)

Story, D. A. *Daily Except Sundays: The Diaries of a Nineteenth Century Locomotive Engineer.* St. Paul, MN: Edinborough, 2005. (Memoir.)

Swengel, F. M. *The Evolution of the Steam Locomotive.* Davenport, IA: Midwest Rail, 1967. (History of the American steam locomotive.)

Symes, S. *55 Years on the Footplate: Reminiscences of the Southern at Bournemouth.* Oxford, UK: Oakwood, 1995 (British memoir.)

Terry, K. *On the Footplate at Bushbury, 1947–1962.* Oxford, UK: Oakwood, 2006. (British memoir.)

Topping, B. *The Engine Driver's Manual: How to Prepare, Fire and Drive a Steam Locomotive.* Oxford, UK: Oxford Publishing, 1998. (Steam locomotive operation.)

White, J. H. *American Locomotives: An Engineering History, 1830–1880.* Baltimore, MD: Johns Hopkins University Press, 1997. (History of the American steam locomotive.)

Young, J. O. *The Life of a Locomotive Engineer: From Steam to Diesel.* Bloomington, IN: Trafford, 2007. (Memoir.)

Ziel, R. *Mainline Steam Revival.* Mattituck, NY: Amereon House, 1990. (Steam preservation.)

Index